The Practical Imagination

Northrop Frye

MASSEY COLLEGE, UNIVERSITY OF TORONTO

Sheridan Baker

THE UNIVERSITY OF MICHIGAN

George Perkins

EASTERN MICHIGAN UNIVERSITY

The Practical Imagination

STORIES,

POEMS,

PLAYS

1817

HARPER & ROW, PUBLISHERS, New York
Cambridge, Hagerstown, Philadelphia, San Francisco,
London, Mexico City, São Paulo, Sydney

Acknowledgments

Conrad Aiken. "Tetélestai" from *Collected Poems* by Conrad Aiken. Copyright© 1953, 1970 by Conrad Aiken. Reprinted by permission of Oxford University Press, Inc.

Vasily Aksenov. "Halfway to the Moon" from *The New Writing in Russia* by Thomas Whitney. Copyright© by The University of Michigan 1964. Reprinted by permission.

Edward Albee. *The American Dream*. Reprinted by permission of Coward, McCann & Geoghegan, Inc. Copyright© 1960, 1961 by Edward Albee. *The American Dream* is the sole property of the author and is fully protected by copyright. It may not be acted either by professionals or amateurs without written consent. Public readings, radio and television broadcasts likewise are forbidden. All inquiries concerning these rights should be addressed to the William Morris Agency, 1350 Avenue of the Americas, New York City, 10019.

A. R. Ammons. "Kind" is reprinted from *Collected Poems, 1951–1971*, by A. R. Ammons, with the permission of W. W. Norton & Company, Inc. Copyright© 1972 by A. R. Ammons.

Sherwood Anderson. "I'm a Fool." Copyright© 1922 by Dial Publishing Company, Inc., renewed 1949 by Eleanor Copenhaver Anderson. Reprinted by permission of Harold Ober Associates Incorporated.

Anonymous. "Barbry Ellen" from *The Ballad Tree* by Evelyn Kendrick Wells. Copyright© renewed 1978. Reprinted by permission of John Wiley & Sons, Inc.

(*Acknowledgments are continued on page 1483*)

Sponsoring Editor: Phillip Leininger
Project Editor: Robert Ginsberg
Designer: Robert Sugar
Production Manager: Marion A. Palen
Compositor: TriStar Graphics
Printer and Binder: Halliday Lithograph Corporation
Art Studio: Vantage Art Inc.
Cover Painting: Helen Iranyi (Photo: Michel Craig)

The Practical Imagination: Stories, Poems, Plays
Copyright © 1980 by Northrop Frye, Sheridan Baker, and George Perkins

Library of Congress Cataloging in Publication Data
Frye, Northrop.
　The practical imagination.

　Includes indexes.
　1. Literature—History and criticism.
2. Rhetoric.　3. Literature—Collections.
I. Baker, Sheridan Warner, 1918–　joint author.
II. Perkins, George B., 1930–　joint author.
III. Title.
PN524.F76　　808　　79-18314
ISBN 0-06-040455-8

Contents

POETRY

CHAPTER 6
Traditional Forms   655

DRAMA

Preface

The Practical Imagination introduces students to the view that literature is both enjoyable and practically useful as it awakens our consciousness of how and where we live: in our imaginations, really—in our perceptions of ourselves as we face the world. Indeed, literature is perhaps our most immediately practical educator, from fairy tale and nursery rhyme onward, engaging our responses as it widens our vision and clarifies our perspectives.

This book is an anthology. It covers the forms and varieties of fiction, poetry, and drama, moving from the simple elements to the more subtle and complex, with introductory principles and questions to guide the student's progress. Each section begins with an introduction to the genre and concludes with a chapter on how to write about it. Some works are given full discussion, with questions; others not. We have been liberal with footnotes to help the student. We have closed few doors. The aim is to acquaint students with good literature in its various modes, to familiarize them with the questions to ask and the principles to support their judgments, and to show them how discussion and writing can deepen their appreciation and understanding, not only of the literary work, but of themselves.

Our generic survey introducing fiction emphasizes the relationship between oral and written traditions. In Chapter 1, "The Narrative Impulse," we begin with the oral tale—"Rumpelstiltskin" and "Stone Soup"—and examine the ways the ancient theme of wish-fulfillment has been shaped by three sophisticated modern storytellers, ending with the narrative complexities of Kipling's "The Man Who Would Be King." In the next four chapters, we explore narrative point of view, stressing at first the "I" narrator in stories as varied as Poe's "The Tell-Tale Heart" and Lessing's "The Old Chief Mshlanga," before moving on to omniscient narration in Fitzgerald, Lawrence, and Chopin. Chapters 5 and 6 shift the emphasis back from point of view to content, as we illustrate realism and then show metaphor, symbol, and allegory at work: writers range from Dreiser and Langston Hughes through Joyce and Dylan Thomas. Chapter 7 invites students to put their knowledge together in a consideration of meaning, not only in established and realistic writers such as Porter, London, and Dostoevsky, but in newer, experimental, and "absurd" authors such as Le Guin, Lem, Borges, and Pynchon. Chapter 8 presents for extended study two outstanding longer fictions, "The Death of Ivan Ilych" and "The Secret Sharer." Throughout, we attempt to increase the joy of reading by the pleasure of improved understanding, so that discussion and writing can be attractive challenges, successfully met.

Poetry follows fiction because beginning students generally do best when armed with a confidence, a vocabulary, and a strategy of criticism won through successful study of short stories. Nevertheless, because poetry still strikes some as an alien form, we begin slowly, with additional assistance in definition, discussion, and footnotes. After the introductory overview, we divide the field into "lyric" and "narrative," before considering the elements of dramatic situation and character fundamental to poetry. Then comes a chapter on language, followed by a chapter to show the beginner how poets often turn anew to timeless human themes. Next come images and metaphors, then sound and meter, after which we turn to traditional forms, free forms, consideration of poems in specific times and places, and a small gathering of popular poems. "Poems for Study" presents, chronologically, some valuable poems not otherwise represented. All told, we have printed almost 350 poems, a sampling rich enough for all approaches.

Our plays represent the Western tradition, from the Greeks to the present. We begin with tragedy and comedy, with Sophocles, Shakespeare, Aristophanes, and Molière as examples against which students may measure the plays from later times. A chapter on "Social Drama" directs attention to theme; we pursue the question into "Farce, Fantasy, and the Absurd," with Pirandello, Ionesco, and Albee. In "Writing About Drama," we print and discuss Beckett's "Not I" as a paradigm of how difficulties in interpretation may be met and surmounted. Because many of the plays have been translated, we have taken particular pains to ensure authoritative texts that are also accessible to students, beginning with the Dudley Fitts and Robert Fitzgerald *Oedipus Rex* and the Donald Sutherland *Lysistrata*. Shakespeare's *Macbeth* is presented as edited by Alfred Harbage, with his notes, and *The Tempest* as edited, with notes, by Northrop Frye.

Northrop Frye has written the three generic introductions. Sheridan Baker has written the three "Writing Abouts" and the framework for the fiction section. George Perkins has written the framework for poetry and drama and supplied most of the questions, headnotes, and footnotes. The three of us have put our heads together to pool our concepts and to organize and select the best stories, poems, and plays to illustrate them. We have shared our literary and editorial perceptions as we have revised and aligned our individual contributions into what we feel is a unified and effective whole to bring students the joys and practical understanding of literature.

Of our many debts to innumerable teachers, students, and colleagues, we would like to express particular gratitude to Jane Widdicombe, Robert Elias, and Louis Budd, who gave valuable assistance in the final stages.

NORTHROP FRYE

SHERIDAN BAKER

GEORGE PERKINS

Fiction

On Fiction

The Oral Tradition

Stories were told orally long before they came to depend on reading
and writing. Many such stories have survived as folk tales preserved in
a community's memory, and a few examples of such tales are given
here. As a rule folk tales have simple characterization, seldom going
beyond, say, a contrast between a clever and a stupid person. The story
line is what is important, and it usually drives straight to the end,
with few if any surprises. As there is little dependence on local or specific allusion, folk tales can travel through the world past all barriers
of language and culture. In *The Pardoner's Tale* Chaucer tells a story
that had probably reached him from a French source, but the story itself can be traced to India, where, five centuries later, Rudyard Kipling
heard it and put it into his *Second Jungle Book*. Kipling's story is recog-
nizably the "same" story as Chaucer's, even though all the details are
different.

Similarly, the motif of the impossible task that is somehow accomplished, in "Rumpelstiltskin," can be found in a famous Classical
myth, the story of Cupid and Psyche, and the story of the soup made
of stones forms the subject of a play by W. B. Yeats. In W. W. Jacobs'
"The Monkey's Paw," the three wishes remind us of folk tale again, as
does the sardonic treatment of the love potion in John Collier's "The
Chaser." Even Kipling's "The Man Who Would Be King," for all the
realism of detail, turns on the theme of the hero betrayed through a
woman that we find in the stories of Samson and Hercules.

The oral story with its linear drive can be, like many simple structures,
a very powerful one, and we can see its influence in, for example, Jack
London's "To Build a Fire." Here there is only one character (except
for the dog), and the only suspense is that of inevitability. We know
what will happen: the story seems to exist in only one dimension, that
of time, and we are anxious to reach the end, not because we are
bored, but because the end gives us the sense of resolution, of a pattern completing itself. The man in the story is not a sympathetic character, and the workings of his imagination are kept to a minimum. No

identification with him is wanted: our attention is wholly absorbed in
the sequence of movements he makes to keep alive. The smallest details become gigantic: the spark of life in his body depends on the tiny
flame of his match, and as some snow slides off a branch it carries his
death sentence with it. Such urgency of narrative movement, even in a
story written to be read, still derives from the sense of listening to a
speaking voice. Even a story as long and complex as Tolstoy's "The
Death of Ivan Ilych" preserves the same feeling of inexorable advance.
The emphasis on narrative pacing reaches an extreme in Poe's "The
Tell-Tale Heart," where the movement of time, represented by the
ticking of a watch and the heartbeat associated with it, enters the story
as, in a way, its chief character.

The Written Tradition

Most stories now, however, are written to be read, and a printed page
gives a second dimension, a sense of space as well as time. When the
whole story is visually before us, a number of things can go on simultaneously, and the plot may twist unexpectedly. If we read Ambrose
Bierce's "The Boarded Window" or Faulkner's "A Rose for Emily"
quickly, concentrating on the narrative movement, the last sentence
may come as a puzzling surprise, but we can always look back to see
what clues the author gave us that we missed. The nightmarish experiences of the young man in Hawthorne's "My Kinsman, Major Molineux" may also impel us to see whether the opening paragraph, about
political upsets in pre-Revolutionary America, was really as irrelevant
as it may have seemed on first reading. In a written story a sense of
the difference between appearance and reality makes itself felt, so that
we feel that we are discovering something behind the narrative movement.

Narrative Techniques

Naturally, most writers will look for some way of preserving both the
driving energy of the oral tale and the sense of discovery in the written one. The most common way of doing this is to tell the story
through one of the main characters, in contrast to the so-called "omniscient" narrator who is not tied to a single point of view. The urgency of a speaking voice still dominates our attention, but the speaking
character is not the whole story, and the interactions with the other
characters provide the second or spatial dimension. The narrator is of-

ten not aware of all the implications in the story he is telling. When the narrator of Ring Lardner's "Haircut" says at the end, "it probably served Jim right, what he got," the reader agrees verbally, but the agreement is on different levels of comprehension. In John Updike's "A & P" the narrator tells us his side of a confrontation of two attitudes which are both quixotic, though for different reasons. The narrator, however, has enough self-knowledge to say "it seems to me that once you begin a gesture it's fatal not to go through with it," so he also understands that he is only part of the story.

There are two limitations, not necessarily hampering ones, in telling a story through a major character. One is that the author is restricted to that character's speech, and in modern times standard literary English and colloquial speech are often almost different languages. In Faulkner's "A Rose for Emily" the story is told by a minor character whom we never really see, hence a full vocabulary can be used, with such phrases as "stubborn and coquettish decay" in describing Emily's house. But in Sherwood Anderson's "I'm a Fool" the inarticulateness of the boy narrator is part of the point of the story: he knows what has happened to him, but cannot break out of his immature framework of language with its recurrent "gee whiz." The reader has to supply an understanding that makes up for this. On the other hand inarticulateness has its own eloquence, as a failure of expression increases pathos. A more precise vocabulary would not give the concentrated desolation of the last sentence of Hemingway's "My Old Man": "Seems like when they get started they don't leave a guy nothing." Elsewhere we can see reasons for not using a narrator. Fitzgerald's "Babylon Revisited," though focused on Charles Wales, is not told by him, and the different technique makes it easier for the author to present the two points of view about the custody of Honoria as equally strong, and, for those who hold them, equally justifiable.

The other limitation is one of positive sympathy: we do not need to "identify" with, or even like, the teller of a story, but we have to accept him sufficiently to be willing to see the story through his eyes. The narrator in Charlotte Perkins Gilman's "The Yellow Wall-Paper" is mad, but madness is not alienating: we have reservations about the reality of what she sees, but a mad world can have both a logic of its own and a logical reason for deviating from the "normal," besides being related to our own phobias. But in Flannery O'Connor's "Good

Country People," where the Bible salesman first appears to us as naive and innocent, we realize, as he gradually turns nastier with every paragraph, how difficult, perhaps impossible, it would be to make him a narrator. We prefer to look at such people objectively: there is something about real evil that has to remain inscrutable.

There is a corresponding limitation in the "omniscient" technique. In D. H. Lawrence's "Mother and Daughter" the author tells us a good deal about the motivation of his characters, and he has opinions about many other subjects as well, such as the difference between male and female attitudes to holding jobs. We may feel that we are free to disagree with Lawrence, if we like: he gives the impression of "omniscience" only to the extent that he is telling his story. Once he starts commenting on it, he has no more authority than we have. A good story, apparently, has a life of its own, and its author does not so much make it up as release it. Lawrence himself remarked, in fact, that we are not to trust an author, only the story he tells.

Meaning

If these observations have any validity, we seem to be led to some such principle as this: story writers do not moralize, or if they do they are apt to weaken their creative authority, but they keep us in touch with moral realities. What we get from the story, therefore, is not a "message" or any concept to be inferred from the story, but the vision presented by the story itself. In modern stories this vision is normally ironic, in a special sense of seeing more of the whole situation than the characters in the story do. Irony does not, in this context, mean any lack of sympathy, but it excludes the sentimental sympathy that refuses to see the whole picture. Thus in Katherine Anne Porter's "He" we can understand Mrs. Whipple's love for her retarded son, but we can also see an obsessive element in it that is bound to lead to trouble. In James Joyce's "A Little Cloud" we can understand Little Chandler's provincial wistfulness and his envy for the glamorous life of Gallaher, but we can also see that Gallaher's real life is not likely to be glamorous at all.

Even here, however, we are still in a moral and human area, and irony is not confined to that. In Katherine Mansfield's "Bliss" the long dammed-up sexual feelings of the heroine are suddenly released in an enveloping sense of euphoria. The euphoria enables her, while feeling complacent about the rather foolish babble of her guests, to find her real affinity with a blossoming pear tree. This latter is what T. S. Eliot calls an objective correlative, a natural image symbolizing, and corresponding to, a human emotion. But it appears that while pear trees usually blossom on schedule, human emotions often do not. There is no moral factor directly involved here: only the irony of a humanity imprisoned in a world that it so often feels it does not belong to. There is a similar irony in Dreiser's "The Lost Phoebe," where the pastoral opening, with its leisurely evocation of the routines of life on a farm, is followed by the account of the shattered life of Reifsneider, which fits no cycle of seasons.

Such a perspective, in which we struggle to see the whole story, as the characters in it ordinarily cannot, brings us closer to the universality of what is presented. The story expands from being that particular story to being a story about human life as a whole. The characters at the opening of "The Death of Ivan Ilych" are very unsure of their most trivial actions and gestures, because they are trying to pretend that they are not thinking only of their own lives and of the fact that at least they are not dead. As the story goes on, we see how utterly unique every man's death is for him, and thus how even the unique can be the universal. When the pilot in Ralph Ellison's "Flying Home" remarks that "jimcrows" is an appropriate name for buzzards, hardly knowing at that moment what he is saying, we begin to see that Ellison's story is not simply a story about an injured pilot, but about the outlook of black people in a society dominated by hostile whites. Literature, then, may be among other things a technique for training us to look at life with an enlarged vision.

But we can hardly stop here, enlarging our vision at the expense of the illusions and frustrations of imaginary characters. In Eudora Welty's "A Memory" a vision from waking life moves across the dream-world of a young woman, threatening her emotional security with a reality that she struggles to keep within her picture-frame of reverie. But we suspect that she has really grown beyond that point, and is now ready to deal with reality on its own terms. Similarly, at any moment our ironic perspective may go into reverse, and show us that we have illusions too that protect us from reality, and that the story we are reading may be part of that reality. Thus as we read Doris Lessing's account of how a shy white child fails to make any human contact with Africans, the appalling callousness of the white attitude to the blacks looms out of the background of the story and confronts us directly.

But it is not only social and outward realities that literature presents: the conflict of reality and illusion goes on inside our minds too. In John Barth's "Lost in the Funhouse" we eavesdrop on the inner debate in an author's mind about how he is to write his story. The uncertainty in the "funhouse" itself about what is real is a projection of that inner debate. In Conrad's "The Secret Sharer" the story of how an inexperienced sea captain tries to get rid of a stowaway is given a new dimension by the unexplained mystery of the stowaway's resemblance to the captain, "my double," as the captain calls him. The story is told with a psychological resonance that gives to it the universal theme of separating from a self that we do not want and yet is a part of ourselves.

This twofold focus of reality, inside and outside the mind at once, is particularly important when we are reading what is called fantasy. Stanislaus Lem's story of a kingdom created from robots, "The Seventh Sally," raises questions that have tormented us for centuries, about the relation of God or the gods to man, about the distinction between an organism and a mechanism, about the difference between what is created and what has come into existence by itself. Pynchon's story of Byron the Bulb turns on a similar paradox. If people can behave mechanically, why cannot mechanisms represent human life? And in Ursula Le Guin's story, "The Ones Who Walk Away from Omelas," the science-fiction setting does not make the central situation less relevant to our own lives: we have all asked ourselves how far it is possible to be happy in a society based on making other people miserable. It is these fantastic stories in particular that lead us to another critical principle. A story presents us with what is technically an illusion, something that did not happen or could not happen. But whatever reality may be, one of the most direct and intense ways that we can grasp it is through the deliberate illusions of literature.

We began with the folk tales that can travel through the world past all social and linguistic barriers, and we end with the suggestion that when a story presents a form of universal experience, there are no limits to its communicating power. In Borges' little story, "The Gospel According to Mark," we are in a remote part of South America, as far as we can get from all our normal cultural habits and references. Yet the story which is familiar to us in the Gospels makes its way there, too, in a most disconcerting form. The narrator in Dostoevsky's "Dream of a Ridiculous Man" is also remote from us in culture and attitude, and keeps excluding himself from our understanding, so far as he can, by dwelling on his own "ridiculous" qualities. Yet he has a dream of a kind that was described by an English Romantic essayist, Thomas De Quincey, writing many years before Dostoevsky's time. De Quincey says: "Perhaps not one of us escapes that dream . . . every one of us . . . has a bait offered to the infirm places of his own individual will; once again a snare is presented for tempting him into captivity to a luxury of ruin; once again, as in aboriginal Paradise, the man falls by his own choice." In other words, the vision described in the Biblical story of the fall of man has a permanent place in our own minds. This is not a religious doctrine: it is a statement about the intelligibility of great stories, which may come to us from immense distances of time and space, and yet are stories that we recognize because we have lived through them.

CHAPTER 1

The Narrative Impulse

"Once upon a time, long long ago." We are already flying on the story-teller's carpet to some magical otherwhere and otherwhen, eager to find out what happened. In an instant, we are in another reality that yet seems intensely real, no matter how indistinct its historical and geographical setting. We follow the happenstances of some character as if they were our own, no matter how different from us and how thinly outlined. *Mutato nomine, de te fabula narratur*—with name changed, the story tells of you—as Horace observed some years before psychologists invented "identification."

This is the story's essential way and magical appeal, even when realism focuses on the here and now and the love next door. We observe people other than ourselves. We experience their fears and triumphs, because they tell us something about ourselves, about how we are all alike, and they do this at the very time we are feeling how it is in another apartment, in another sex or age, in another country. The story has a lesson, because it illustrates something about this life we share. Something in us craves and enjoys this vicarious excursion, unscathed, into another reality that yet reflects and illuminates our own.

All stories are really wish-fulfilling, some more obviously than others. We wish we may; we wish we might. And for a few minutes or hours our wishes come true. We adventure on the Malayan archipelago; we sigh on the Left Bank of Paris. Even the most squalid realism satisfies our wish to know, and rewards us in safety. The fairy tale dreams our wishes more directly into being. We start with the simple narrative urge to find out what happened. We soon discover that we are involved, satisfying that even deeper psychological urge to come out on top. We identify our interests with those of the central character. We want the miller's innocent daughter to be queen and stay happy. We want the old soldier to win his feast. We are responding to the child's essential need to believe that he can overcome the adversities and giants surrounding him and that, in the big world, he "will make a significant contribution," as Bruno Bettelheim has pointed out[1]—the deep wish-fulfillment we seem never to outgrow. We need to believe, at least while the enchantment lasts, that life has a moral order rewarding the good and tri-

---

[1] Bruno Bettelheim, *The Uses of Enchantment: The Meaning and Importance of Fairy Tales* (New York: Alfred A. Knopf, 1976), p.4.

umphing over evil. We secretly believe ourselves to be, like those in the story, the best of the good, no matter how unlucky and misunderstood. Our noble unselfishness rises resplendent from the cinders as the cruel and selfish stepsisters get their due.

All the stories in this section reveal the two basic narrative impulses: the first and most simple, to find out what happened; the second and deeper, to hope for the best for our secret selves—even when the realities turn against our unrealistic hopes. All illustrate the moral dimension. In "Rumpelstiltskin" and "Stone Soup," the impossible task is finally accomplished. In all, greediness, the wish to outwit fate and our natural doom is punished, or at least twitted. The appeal of magic, with its magical three wishes, tempts us always, because we always know it cannot really be.

That magical three suggests how deeply these narratives are rooted in our psychological being. Throughout our imaginative fairyland, the bell rings thrice—three wishes, three sons, three daughters. Three is a part of our narrative expectation and satisfaction, a basic fact of our psychology. Three dots, psychologists tell us, are the largest number everyone automatically sees as a unit. Add another dot, and many see two units of two. Three is built into our perceptions and our thinking. Our ideal family is just Mother, Father, and us. All life has a beginning, middle, and end. The world we live in has three dimensions.

So these simple narratives meet basic psychological needs. Above all, we need to see ourselves in the world outside ourselves, to expand our sense of what life means, to confirm that we are not alone, that we share the hopes and frustrations of our human lot.

"Rumpelstiltskin" starts with what is wrong. It begins with the miller's unseemly ostentation and thrives on the king's greed. Both impose on the innocent girl. Rumpelstiltskin, the diabolically attractive imp, apparently embodies these vices, and the gruesome ending has delighted generations of listeners.

RUMPELSTILTSKIN

*Anonymous**

There was once upon a time a poor miller who had a very beautiful daughter. Now it happened one day that he had an audience with the King, and in order to appear a person of some importance he told him that he had a daughter who could spin straw into gold.

'Now that's a talent worth having,' said the King to the miller. 'If your daughter is as clever as you say, bring her to my palace tomorrow, and I'll put her to the test.'

When the girl was brought to him he led her into a room full of straw, gave

---

*One of the many fairy tales collected by the brothers Jacob (1785-1863) and Wilhelm (1786-1859) Grimm. The version presented here was first printed by Andrew Lang in *The Blue Fairy Book* (1889).

her a spinning-wheel and spindle, and said, 'Now set to work and spin all night till early dawn, and if by that time you haven't spun the straw into gold you shall die.' Then he closed the door behind him and left her alone inside.

So the poor miller's daughter sat down, and didn't know what in the world she was to do. She hadn't the least idea of how to spin straw into gold, and became at last so miserable that she began to cry.

Suddenly the door opened, and in stepped a tiny little man and said, 'Good-evening, Miss Miller-maid; why are you crying so bitterly?'

'Oh!' answered the girl, 'I have to spin straw into gold, and haven't a notion how it's done.'

'What will you give me if I spin it for you?' asked the manikin.

'My necklace,' replied the girl.

The little man took the necklace, sat himself down at the wheel, and whir, whir, whir, the wheel went round three times, and the bobbin was full. Then he put on another, and whir, whir, whir, the wheel went round three times, and the second too was full; and so it went on till the morning, when all the straw was spun away, and all the bobbins were full of gold.

As soon as the sun rose the King came, and when he perceived the gold he was astonished and delighted, but his heart was only the more filled with greed. He had the miller's daughter put into another room, much bigger than the first, and full of straw. He bade her, if she valued her life, spin it all into gold before the following morning.

The girl didn't know what to do, and began to cry; then the door opened as before, and the tiny little man appeared and said, 'What'll you give me if I spin the straw into gold for you?'

'The ring from my finger,' answered the girl.

The manikin took the ring, and whir! round went the spinning wheel again, and when morning broke he had spun all the straw into glittering gold.

The King was pleased beyond measure at the sight, but his greed for gold was still not satisfied, and he had the miller's daughter brought into a yet bigger room full of straw, and said, 'You must spin all this away in the night; but if you succeed this time you shall become my wife.'

'She's only a miller's daughter, it's true,' he thought; 'but I couldn't find a richer wife if I were to search the whole world over.'

When the girl was alone the little man appeared for the third time, and said, 'What'll you give me if I spin the straw for you once again?'

'I've nothing more to give,' answered the girl.

'Then promise me when you are Queen to give me your first child.'

'Who knows what mayn't happen before that?' thought the miller's daughter; and besides, she saw no other way out of it, so she promised the manikin what he demanded, and he set to work once more and spun the straw into gold. When the King came in the morning, and found everything as he had desired, he straightaway made her his wife, and the miller's daughter became a Queen.

When a year had passed a beautiful little son was born to her, and she thought no more of the little man, till all of a sudden one day he stepped into her room and said, 'Now give me what you promised.'

The Queen was in a great state, and offered the little man all the riches in her kingdom if he would only leave her the child. But the manikin said, 'No, a living creature is dearer to me than all the treasures in the world.'

Then the Queen began to cry and sob so bitterly that the little man was sorry for her, and said, 'I'll give you three days to guess my name, and if you find out in that time you may keep your child.'

Then the Queen pondered the whole night over all the names she had ever heard, and sent a messenger to scour the land, and to pick up far and near all the names he should come across. When the little man arrived on the following day she began with Kasper, Melchior, Belshazzar, and all the other names she knew, in a string, but at each one the manikin called out, 'That's not my name.'

The next day she sent to inquire of all the names of all the people in the neighborhood, and had a long list of the most uncommon and extraordinary for the little man when he made his appearance. 'Is your name, perhaps Sheep-shanks, Cruickshanks, Spindleshanks?' but he always replied, 'That's not my name.'

On the third day the messenger returned and announced, 'I have not been able to find any new names, but as I came upon a high hill round the corner of the wood, where the foxes and hares bid each other good night, I saw a little house, and in front of the house burned a fire, and round the fire danced the most grotesque little man, hopping on one leg and crying:

> "Tomorrow I brew, today I bake,
> And then the child away I'll take;
> For little deems my royal dame
> That Rumpelstiltskin is my name!"'

You may imagine the Queen's delight at hearing the name, and when the little man stepped in shortly afterwards and asked, 'Now my lady Queen, what's my name?' she asked first, 'Is your name Conrad?'

'No.'

'Is your name Harry?'

'No.'

'Is your name, perhaps, Rumpelstiltskin?'

'Some demon has told you that, some demon has told you that,' screamed the little man, and in his rage drove his right foot so far into the ground that it sank in up to his waist; then in a passion he seized the left foot with both hands and tore himself in two.

The next sophisticated little tale is one of many in which we enjoy seeing the deceivers deceived. We enjoy, too, its dramatic irony in our knowing, with the author and the old soldier, what the villagers do not know and never understand.

STONE SOUP
A FOLK TALE
*Anonymous**

Once three soldiers were coming home from the wars. They had eaten nothing since early morning when they had brushed themselves free from a haystack and

---

* Retold by Sheridan Baker.

finished the last crusts of their rations. Suddenly, the youngest soldier said, "Ah, at last, a village. Now for a good hot meal and a bed."

"Something to eat and a haystack will do for me," said the second soldier.

"We'll see," said the old soldier.

In the village, a boy ran into the marketplace. "The soldiers are coming," he shouted.

"Quick," said the elder, "hide everything. They'll clean us out of house and home."

When the soldiers came into the village square, they marched in good order up to the little group of men sitting in the shade by the well.

"Good evening," said the old soldier, saluting, "We are three weary soldiers coming home from the wars. We would be most grateful for a bite to eat and a place to rest for the night."

"I am sorry," said the elder, "but there is nothing to eat in this village. You soldiers have gone back and forth over us all year, first one side then the other, picking our bones clean every time. We ourselves have nothing to eat. You had better go on to the next village."

"Nothing to eat at all?" said the old soldier.

"Nothing at all," said the elder.

"Well," said the old soldier, "in that case we must make some stone soup."

"Stone soup!" the villagers exclaimed.

"Yes," said the old soldier, "it's a trick we learned in the wars, when everything else ran out. I suppose you have a big iron kettle."

"Oh, yes," said the villagers.

"Well," said the old soldier, "bring it here to the marketplace, and fill it full of good clear water, and get a good fire going under it, and in the meantime find me three big round stones, all of a size."

The village began to hum with life. Four came up with the village's biggest kettle. They set up a tripod and filled the kettle with buckets from the well as others brought armloads of wood and started the fire. Still others came carrying stones from the fields, each wanting his to be chosen. The soldier examined them all carefully, finding one, matching another, carefully matching a third, three big oval stones as smooth as ostrich eggs or loaves of bread. He dropped these carefully into the water, which soon began to simmer.

The soldier took out his sword, nudged the stones a little, and stirred the water as the boiling increased. The villagers watched him breathlessly.

He nodded in satisfaction. "These are some of the finest soup stones I have ever seen," he said. "Your village is very fortunate. This will be a fine stone soup, though it will take a while. Too bad we don't have some salt and pepper, and perhaps a cup of barley.

"Well," said one of the women, "I think I could find some salt and pepper the last troops overlooked." And another ran off and came back redfaced with a bag of barley.

"Ah," said the soldier as he sprinkled and stirred. "I can smell the stones already, and now we will really have a soup. Too bad we don't have a few carrots, or an onion, or perhaps a small cabbage."

"Well," said the women, "perhaps . . . ," and soon came back with aprons filled, some with carrots, some with onions, some with cabbage.

"Now," said the soldier, lopping the vegetables in with his sword, lopping and stirring, "this will be a stone soup fit for a general. A little more water to give it time. With a soup like this, it's a shame we don't have some bacon for a finishing touch.

"Well," said an old villager, "I might just possibly. . . . ," and soon the soldier was chopping a side of bacon into the soup. "More pepper," he cried, "more water, the stones are just beginning to work." And the rich aroma and the soldier's own pleasure as he stirred with his sword made everyone happy. "Now we'll have a stone soup fit for the king himself," the soldier cried. "A soup like this calls for a feast and a festival and a roasted ox and plenty of wine. Ah, well. Too bad. But it would be fine.

"Well," said the elder himself, "I think perhaps I have a small side of beef under my bed which the last troops may have overlooked."

And soon a whole ox was spitted and turning over a new blazing fire, and as the soldier hummed, and stirred in new loppings of this and that, the women set tables in the square, and brought out flowers and bunting and jugs of wine, and the whole village feasted on the most delicious soup and roast they had ever tasted, and the three soldiers enjoyed it most of all. And then they all danced in the square to the accordian and violin.

Then the elder said to the three soldiers, "This has been a day and a night to remember. You, sir, shall sleep in my own bed itself, the best in the village, and the middle soldier shall sleep in the miller's bed, and the young one in the priest's. And the villagers all escorted the soldiers to their beds, where they sank to sleep between clean sheets smelling of fresh air and sun.

In the morning, after baths and breakfast, when the soldiers were ready to leave, all the village gathered to see them off.

"We want to thank you for your splendid hospitality," said the old soldier. "Of all the villages we have ever seen, yours is the best. You have treated us like kings."

"You well deserve it," said the elder, "for you have taught us a priceless secret, how to make soup from stones."

"Yes," said the old soldier, "it's all in knowing how."

The villagers waved as the three soldiers marched bravely off. They shook their heads and sighed. "Such men don't grow on every bush," they said.

"The Monkey's Paw" rationalizes the magical three as coming from India, the mysterious East colonized by practical whisky-drinking Britishers. Modern skepticism ends in horror to suggest the impossibility in man's persistent wish to outwit the natural order.

THE MONKEY'S PAW
W. W. Jacobs (1863–1943)

I

Without, the night was cold and wet, but in the small parlour of Laburnam Villa the blinds were drawn and the fire burned brightly. Father and son were at chess, the former, who possessed ideas about the game involving radical changes, putting his king into such sharp and unnecessary perils that it even provoked comment from the white-haired lady knitting placidly by the fire.

"Hark at the wind," said Mr. White, who, having seen a fatal mistake after it was too late, was amiably desirous of preventing his son from seeing it.

"I'm listening," said the latter, grimly surveying the board as he stretched out his hand. "Check."

"I should hardly think that he'd come tonight," said his father, with his hand poised over the board.

"Mate," replied the son.

"That's the worst of living so far out," bawled Mr. White, with sudden and unlooked-for violence; "of all the beastly, slushy, out-of-the-way places to live in, this is the worst. Pathway's a bog, and the road's a torrent. I don't know what people are thinking about. I suppose because only two houses in the road are let, they think it doesn't matter."

"Never mind, dear," said his wife, soothingly; "perhaps you'll win the next one."

Mr. White looked up sharply, just in time to intercept a knowing glance between mother and son. The words died away on his lips, and he hid a guilty grin in his thin grey beard.

"There he is," said Herbert White, as the gate banged to loudly and heavy footsteps came toward the door.

The old man rose with hospitable haste, and opening the door, was heard condoling with the new arrival. The new arrival also condoled with himself, so that Mrs. White said, "Tut, tut!" and coughed gently as her husband entered the room, followed by a tall, burly man, beady of eye and rubicund of visage.

"Sergeant-Major Morris," he said, introducing him.

The sergeant-major shook hands, and taking the proffered seat by the fire, watched contentedly while his host got out whiskey and tumblers and stood a small copper kettle on the fire.

At the third glass his eyes got brighter, and he began to talk, the little family circle regarding with eager interest this visitor from distant parts, as he squared his broad shoulders in the chair and spoke of wild scenes and doughty deeds; of wars and plagues and strange peoples.

"Twenty-one years of it," said Mr. White, nodding at his wife and son. "When he went away he was a slip of a youth in the warehouse. Now look at him."

"He don't look to have taken much harm," said Mrs. White, politely.

"I'd like to go to India myself," said the old man, "just to look round a bit, you know."

"Better where you are," said the sergeant-major, shaking his head. He put down the empty glass, and sighing softly, shook it again.

"I should like to see those old temples and fakirs and jugglers," said the old man. "What was that you started telling me the other day about a monkey's paw or something, Morris?"

"Nothing," said the soldier, hastily. "Leastways nothing worth hearing."

"Monkey's paw?" said Mrs. White, curiously.

"Well, it's just a bit of what you might call magic, perhaps," said the sergeant-major, off-handedly.

His three listeners leaned forward eagerly. The visitor absent-mindedly put his empty glass to his lips and then set it down again. His host filled it for him.

"To look at," said the sergeant-major, fumbling in his pocket, "it's just an ordinary little paw, dried like a mummy."

He took something out of his pocket and proffered it. Mrs. White drew back with a grimace, but her son, taking it, examined it curiously.

"And what is there special about it?" inquired Mr. White as he took it from his son, and having examined it, placed it upon the table.

"It had a spell put on it by an old fakir," said the sergeant-major, "a very holy man. He wanted to show that fate ruled people's lives, and that those who interfered with it did so to their sorrow. He put a spell on it so that three separate men could each have three wishes from it."

His manner was so impressive that his hearers were conscious that their light laughter jarred somewhat.

"Well, why don't you have three, sir?" said Herbert White, cleverly.

The soldier regarded him in the way that middle age is wont to regard presumptuous youth. "I have," he said, quietly, and his blotchy face whitened.

"And did you really have the three wishes granted?" asked Mrs. White.

"I did," said the sergeant-major, and his glass tapped against his strong teeth.

"And has anybody else wished?" persisted the old lady.

"The first man had his three wishes. Yes," was the reply; "I don't know what the first two were, but the third was for death. That's how I got the paw."

His tones were so grave that a hush fell upon the group.

"If you've had your three wishes, it's no good to you now, then, Morris," said the old man at last. "What do you keep it for?"

The soldier shook his head. "Fancy, I suppose," he said slowly. "I did have some idea of selling it, but I don't think I will. It has caused enough mischief already. Besides, people won't buy. They think it's a fairy tale; some of them, and those who do think anything of it want to try it first and pay me afterward."

"If you could have another three wishes," said the old man, eyeing him keenly, "would you have them?"

"I don't know," said the other. "I don't know."

He took the paw, and dangling it between his forefinger and thumb, suddenly threw it upon the fire. White, with a slight cry, stooped down and snatched it off.

"Better let it burn," said the soldier, solemnly.

"If you don't want it, Morris," said the other, "give it to me."

"I won't," said his friend, doggedly. "I threw it on the fire. If you keep it, don't blame me for what happens. Pitch it on the fire again like a sensible man."

The other shook his head and examined his new possession closely. "How do you do it?" he inquired.

"Hold it up in your right hand and wish aloud," said the sergeant-major, "but I warn you of the consequences."

"Sounds like the *Arabian Nights*," said Mrs. White, as she rose and began to set the supper. "Don't you think you might wish for four pairs of hands for me?"

Her husband drew the talisman from pocket, and then all three burst into laughter as the sergeant-major, with a look of alarm on his face, caught him by the arm.

"If you must wish," he said, gruffly, "wish for something sensible."

Mr. White dropped it back in his pocket, and placing chairs, motioned his friend to the table. In the business of supper the talisman was partly forgotten, and afterward the three sat listening in an enthralled fashion to a second instalment of the soldier's adventures in India.

"If the tale about the monkey's paw is not more truthful than those he has been telling us," said Herbert, as the door closed behind their guest, just in time for him to catch the last train, "we sha'nt make much out of it."

"Did you give him anything for it, father?" inquired Mrs. White, regarding her husband closely.

"A trifle," said he, colouring slightly. "He didn't want it, but I made him take it. And he pressed me again to throw it away."

"Likely," said Herbert, with pretended horror. "Why, we're going to be rich, and famous and happy. Wish to be an emperor, father, to begin with; then you can't be henpecked."

He darted round the table, pursued by the maligned Mrs. White armed with an antimacassar.

Mr. White took the paw from his pocket and eyed it dubiously. "I don't know what to wish for, and that's a fact," he said, slowly. "It seems to me I've got all I want."

"If you only cleared the house, you'd be quite happy, wouldn't you?" said Herbert, with his hand on his shoulder. "Well, wish for two hundred pounds, then; that'll just do it."

His father, smiling shamefacedly at his own credulity, held up the talisman, as his son, with a solemn face, somewhat marred by a wink at his mother, sat down at the piano and struck a few impressive chords.

"I wish for two hundred pounds," said the old man distinctly.

A fine crash from the piano greeted the words, interrupted by a shuddering cry from the old man. His wife and son ran toward him.

"It moved," he cried, with a glance of disgust at the object as it lay on the floor.

"As I wished, it twisted in my hand like a snake."

"Well, I don't see the money," said his son as he picked it up and placed it on the table, "and I bet I never shall."

"It must have been your fancy, father," said his wife, regarding him anxiously.

He shook his head. "Never mind, though; there's no harm done, but it gave me a shock all the same."

They sat down by the fire again while the two men finished their pipes. Outside, the wind was higher than ever, and the old man started nervously at the sound of a door banging upstairs. A silence unusual and depressing settled upon all three, which lasted until the old couple rose to retire for the night.

"I expect you'll find the cash tied up in a big bag in the middle of your bed," said Herbert, as he bade them good-night, "and something horrible squatting up on top of the wardrobe watching you as you pocket your ill-gotten gains."

He sat alone in the darkness, gazing at the dying fire, and seeing faces in it. The last face was so horrible and so simian that he gazed at it in amazement. It got so vivid that, with a little uneasy laugh, he felt on the table for a glass containing a little water to throw over it. His hand grasped the monkey's paw, and with a little shiver he wiped his hand on his coat and went up to bed.

II

In the brightness of the wintry sun next morning as it streamed over the breakfast table he laughed at his fears. There was an air of prosaic wholesomeness about the room which it had lacked on the previous night, and the dirty, shrivelled little paw was pitched on the sideboard with a carelessness which betokened no great belief in its virtues.

"I suppose all old soldiers are the same," said Mrs. White. "The idea of our listening to such nonsense! How could wishes be granted in these days? And if they could, how could two hundred pounds hurt you, father?"

"Might drop on his head from the sky," said the frivolous Herbert.

"Morris said the things happened so naturally," said his father, "that you might if you so wished attribute it to coincidence."

"Well, don't break into the money before I come back," said Herbert as he rose from the table. "I'm afraid it'll turn you into a mean, avaricious man, and we shall have to disown you."

His mother laughed, and followed him to the door, watched him down the road; and returning to the breakfast table, was very happy at the expense of her husband's credulity. All of which did not prevent her from scurrying to the door at the postman's knock, nor prevent her from referring somewhat shortly to retired sergeant-majors of bibulous habits when she found that the post brought a tailor's bill.

"Herbert will have some more of his funny remarks, I expect, when he comes home," she said, as they sat at dinner.

"I dare say," said Mr. White, pouring himself out some beer; "but for all that, the thing moved in my hand; that I'll swear to."

"You thought it did," said the old lady soothingly.

"I say it did," replied the other. "There was no thought about it; I had just— What's the matter?"

His wife made no reply. She was watching the mysterious movements of a man outside, who, peering in an undecided fashion at the house, appeared to be trying to make up his mind to enter. In mental connection with the two hundred pounds, she noticed that the stranger was well dressed, and wore a silk hat of glossy newness. Three times he paused at the gate, and then walked on again. The fourth time he stood with his hand upon it, and then with sudden resolution flung it open and walked up the path. Mrs. White at the same moment placed her hands behind her, and hurriedly unfastening the strings of her apron, put that useful article of apparel beneath the cushion of her chair.

She brought the stranger, who seemed ill at ease, into the room. He gazed at her furtively, and listened in a preoccupied fashion as the old lady apologized for the appearance of the room, and her husband's coat, a garment which he usually reserved for the garden. She then waited as patiently as her sex would permit, for him to broach his business, but he was at first strangely silent.

"I—was asked to call," he said at last, and stooped and picked a piece of cotton from his trousers. "I come from 'Maw and Meggins.'"

The old lady started. "Is anything the matter?" she asked, breathlessly. "Has anything happened to Herbert? What is it? What is it?"

Her husband interposed. "There, there, mother," he said, hastily. "Sit down, and don't jump to conclusions. You've not brought bad news, I'm sure, sir;" and he eyed the other wistfully.

"I'm sorry—" began the visitor.

"Is he hurt?" demanded the mother, wildly.

"The visitor bowed in assent. "Badly hurt," he said, quietly, "but he is not in any pain."

"Oh, thank God!" said the old woman, clasping her hands. "Thank God for that! Thank—"

She broke off suddenly as the sinister meaning of the assurance dawned upon her and she saw the awful confirmation of her fears in the other's perverted face. She caught her breath, and turning to her slower-witted husband, laid her trembling old hand upon his. There was a long silence.

"He was caught in the machinery," said the visitor at length in a low voice.

"Caught in the machinery," repeated Mr. White, in a dazed fashion, "yes."

He sat staring blankly out the window, and taking his wife's hand between his own, pressed it as he had been wont to do in their old courting-days nearly forty years before.

"He was the only one left to us," he said, turning gently to the visitor. "It is hard."

The other coughed, and rising, walked slowly to the window. "The firm wished me to convey their sincere sympathy with you in your great loss," he said, without looking around. "I beg that you will understand I am only their servant and merely obeying orders."

There was no reply; the old woman's face was white, her eyes staring, and her breath inaudible; on the husband's face was a look such as his friend the sergeant might have carried into his first action.

"I was to say that Maw and Meggins disclaim all responsibility," continued the other. "They admit no liability at all, but in consideration of your son's services, they wish to present you with a certain sum as compensation."

Mr. White dropped his wife's hand, and rising to his feet, gazed with a look of horror at his visitor. His dry lips shaped the words, "How much?"

"Two hundred pounds," was the answer.

Unconscious of his wife's shriek, the old man smiled faintly, put out his hands like a sightless man, and dropped, a senseless heap, to the floor.

III

In the huge new cemetery, some two miles distant, the old people buried their dead, and came back to a house steeped in shadow and silence. It was all over so quickly that at first they could hardly realize it, and remained in a state of expectation as though of something else to happen—something else which was to lighten this load, too heavy for their old hearts to bear.

But the days passed, and expectation gave place to resignation—the hopeless resignation of the old, sometimes miscalled, apathy. Sometimes they hardly exchanged a word, for now they had nothing to talk about, and their days were long to weariness.

It was about a week after that the old man, waking suddenly in the night, stretched out his hand and found himself alone. The room was in darkness, and the sound of subdued weeping came from the window. He raised himself in bed and listened.

"Come back," he said, tenderly. "You will be cold."

"It is colder for my son," said the old woman, and wept afresh.

The sound of her sobs died away on his ears. The bed was warm, and his eyes heavy with sleep. He dozed fitfully, and then slept until a sudden wild cry from his wife awoke him with a start.

"*The paw!*" she cried wildly. "The monkey's paw!"

He started up in alarm. "Where? Where is it? What's the matter?"

She came stumbling across the room toward him. "I want it," she said, quietly. "You've not destroyed it?"

"It's in the parlour, on the bracket," he replied, marvelling. "Why?"

She cried and laughed together, and bending over, kissed his cheek.

"I only just thought of it," she said, hysterically. "Why didn't I think of it before? Why didn't *you* think of it?"

"Think of what?" he questioned.

"The other two wishes," she replied, rapidly. "We've only had one."

"Was not that enough?" he demanded, fiercely.

"No," she cried triumphantly; "we'll have one more. Go down and get it quickly, and wish our boy alive again."

The man sat up in bed and flung the bedclothes from his quaking limbs. "Good God, you are mad!" he cried, aghast.

"Get it," she panted; "get it quickly, and wish—Oh, my boy, my boy!"

Her husband struck a match and lit the candle. "Get back to bed," he said, unsteadily. "You don't know what you are saying."

"We had the first wish granted," said the old woman, feverishly; "why not the second?"

"A coincidence," stammered the old man.

"Go and get it and wish," cried his wife, quivering with excitement.

The old man turned and regarded her, and his voice shook. "He has been dead ten days, and besides he—I would not tell you else, but—I could only recognize him by his clothing. If he was too terrible for you to see then, how now?"

"Bring him back," cried the old woman, and dragged him toward the door. "Do you think I fear the child I have nursed."

He went down in the darkness, and felt his way to the parlour, and then to the mantelpiece. The talisman was in its place, and a horrible fear that the unspoken wish might bring his mutilated son before him ere he could escape from the room seized upon him, and he caught his breath as he found that he had lost the direction of the door. His brow cold with sweat, he felt his way round the table, and groped along the wall until he found himself in the small passage with the unwholesome thing in his hand.

Even his wife's face seemed changed as he entered the room. It was white and expectant, and to his fears seemed to have an unnatural look upon it. He was afraid of her.

"*Wish!*" she cried, in a strong voice.

"It is foolish and wicked," he faltered.

"*Wish!*" repeated his wife.

He raised his hand. "I wish my son alive again."

The talisman fell to the floor, and he regarded it fearfully. Then he sank trembling into a chair as the old woman, with burning eyes, walked to the window and raised the blind.

He sat until he was chilled with the cold, glancing occasionally at the figure of the old woman peering through the window. The candle-end, which had burned below the rim of the china candlestick, was throwing pulsating shadows on the ceiling and walls, until, with a flicker larger than the rest, it expired. The old man, with an unspeakable sense of relief at the failure of the talisman, crept back to his bed, and a minute or two afterward the old woman came silently and apathetically beside him.

Neither spoke, but lay silently listening to the ticking of the clock. A stair creaked, and the squeaky mouse scurried noisily through the wall. The darkness was oppressive, and after lying for some time screwing up his courage, he took the box of matches, and striking one, went downstairs for a candle.

At the foot of the stairs the match went out, and he paused to strike another; and at the same moment a knock, so quiet and stealthy as to be scarcely audible, sounded on the front door.

The matches fell from his hand and spilled in the passage. He stood motionless, his breath suspended until the knock was repeated. Then he turned and fled swiftly back to his room, and closed the door behind him. A third knock sounded through the house. .

"What's that?" cried the old woman, starting up.

"A rat," said the old man in shaking tones—"a rat. It passed me on the stairs."

His wife sat up in bed listening. A loud knock resounded through the house.

"It's Herbert!" she screamed. "It's Herbert!"

She ran to the door, but her husband was before her, and catching her by the arm, held her tightly.

"What are you going to do?" he whispered hoarsely.

"It's my boy; it's Herbert!" she cried, struggling mechanically. "I forgot it was two miles away. What are you holding me for? Let me go. I must open the door."

"For God's sake don't let it in," cried the old man, trembling.

"You're afraid of your own son," she cried, struggling. "Let me go. I'm coming, Herbert; I'm coming."

There was another knock, and another. The old woman with a sudden wrench broke free and ran from the room. Her husband followed to the landing, and called after her appealingly as she hurried downstairs. He heard the chain rattle back and the bottom bolt drawn slowly and stiffly from the socket. Then the old woman's voice, strained and panting.

"The bolt," she cried, loudly. "Come down. I can't reach it."

But her husband was on his hands and knees groping wildly on the floor in search of the paw. If he could only find it before the thing outside got in. A perfect fusillade of knocks reverberated through the house, and he heard the scraping of a chair as his wife put it down in the passage against the door. He heard the creaking of the bolt as it came slowly back, and at the same moment he found the monkey's paw, and frantically breathed his third and last wish.

The knocking ceased suddenly, although the echoes of it were still in the house. He heard the chair drawn back, and the door opened. A cold wind rushed up the staircase, and a long loud wail of disappointment and misery from his wife gave him courage to run down to her side, and then to the gate beyond. The street lamp flickering opposite shone on a quiet and deserted road.

In "The Chaser" the magical wish to conquer nature moves into a modern fairyland—on Pell Street, two blocks in New York City's Chinatown, lower Manhattan. The reader must deduce what a "chaser" is, and the difference between "Good-bye" and *Au revoir.*

THE CHASER

John Collier   (1901–   )

Alan Austen, as nervous as a kitten, went up certain dark and creaky stairs in the neighborhood of Pell Street, and peered about for a long time on the dim landing before he found the name he wanted written obscurely on one of the doors.

He pushed open this door, as he had been told to do, and found himself in a tiny room, which contained no furniture but a plain kitchen table, a rocking chair, and an ordinary chair. On one of the dirty buff-colored walls were a couple of shelves, containing in all perhaps a dozen bottles and jars.

An old man sat in the rocking chair, reading a newspaper. Alan, without a word, handed him the card he had been given. "Sit down, Mr. Austen," said the old man very politely. "I am glad to make your acquaintance."

"Is it true," asked Alan, "that you have a certain mixture that has—er—quite extraordinary effects?"

"My dear sir," replied the old man, "my stock in trade is not very large—I don't deal in laxatives and teething mixtures—but, such as it is, it is varied. I think nothing I sell has effects which could be precisely described as ordinary."

"Well, the fact is—" began Alan.

"Here, for example," interrupted the old man, reaching for a bottle from the shelf. "Here is a liquid as colorless as water, almost tasteless, quite imperceptible in coffee, milk, wine, or any other beverage. It is also quite imperceptible to any known method of autopsy."

"Do you mean it is a poison?" cried Alan, very much horrified.

"Call it cleaning fluid if you like," said the old man indifferently. "Lives need cleaning. Call it a spot-remover. 'Out, damned spot!' Eh? 'Out, brief candle!' "

"I want nothing of that sort," said Alan.

"Probably it is just as well," said the old man. "Do you know the price of this? For one teaspoonful, which is sufficient, I ask five thousand dollars. Never less. Not a penny less."

"I hope all your mixtures are not as expensive," said Alan apprehensively.

"Oh, dear, no," said the old man. "It would be no good charging that sort of price for a love-potion, for example. Young people who need a love-potion very seldom have five thousand dollars. If they had they would not need a love-potion."

"I'm glad to hear you say so," said Alan.

"I look at it like this," said the old man. "Please a customer with one article, and he will come back when he needs another. Even if it *is* more costly. He will save up for it, if necessary."

"So," said Alan, "you really do sell love-potions?"

"If I did not sell love-potions," said the old man, reaching for another bottle,

"I should not have mentioned the other matter to you. It is only when one is in a position to oblige that one can afford to be so confidential."

"And these potions," said Alan. "They are not just—just—er—"

"Oh, no," said the old man. "Their effects are permanent and extend far beyond the mere carnal impulse. But they include it. Oh, yes, they include it. Bountifully. Insistently. Everlastingly."

"Dear me!" said Alan, attempting a look of scientific detachment. "How very interesting!"

"But consider the spiritual side," said the old man.

"I do, indeed," said Alan.

"For indifference," said the old man, "they substitute devotion. For scorn, adoration. Give one tiny measure of this to the young lady—its flavor is imperceptible in orange juice, soup, or cocktails—and however gay and giddy she is, she will change altogether. She'll want nothing but solitude, and you."

"I can hardly believe it," said Alan. "She is so fond of parties."

"She will not like them anymore," said the old man. "She'll be afraid of the pretty girls you may meet."

"She'll actually be jealous?" cried Alan in a rapture. "Of me?"

"Yes, she will want to be everything to you."

"She is, already. Only she doesn't care about it."

"She will, when she has taken this. She will care intensely. You'll be her sole interest in life."

"Wonderful!" cried Alan.

"She'll want to know all you do," said the old man. "All that has happened to you during the day. Every word of it. She'll want to know what you are thinking about, why you smile suddenly, why you are looking sad."

"That is love!" cried Alan.

"Yes," said the old man. "How carefully she'll look after you! She'll never allow you to be tired, to sit in a draft, to neglect your food. If you are an hour late, she'll be terrified. She'll think you are killed, or that some siren has caught you."

"I can hardly imagine Diana like that!" cried Alan, overwhelmed with joy.

"You will not have to use your imagination," said the old man. "And by the way, since there are always sirens, if by any chance you *should*, later on, slip a little, you need not worry. She will forgive you, in the end. She'll be terribly hurt, of course, but she'll forgive you—in the end."

"That will not happen," said Alan fervently.

"Of course not," said the old man. "But, if it does, you need not worry. She'll never divorce you. Oh, no! And, of course, she herself will never give you the least, the very least, grounds for—not divorce, of course—but even uneasiness."

"And how much," said Alan, "how much is this wonderful mixture?"

"It is not so dear," said the old man, "as the spot-remover, as I think we agreed to call it. No. That is five thousand dollars; never a penny less. One has to be older than you are to indulge in that sort of thing. One has to save up for it."

"But the love-potion?" said Alan.

"Oh, that," said the old man, opening the drawer in the kitchen table and taking out a tiny, rather dirty-looking phial. "That is just a dollar."

"I can't tell you how grateful I am," said Alan, watching him fill it.

"I like to oblige," said the old man. "Then customers come back, later in life, when they are rather better-off, and want more expensive things. Here you are. You will find it very effective."

"Thank you again," said Alan. "Good-bye."

"*Au revoir*," said the old man.

Again British India rationalizes the fairy tale, as Kipling puts the realities of geography and social history up against the most basic impulse in fairyland—that we, who are poor and unknown, will be recognized and crowned at last. Notice the difference in the way this story is told.

THE MAN WHO WOULD BE KING

Rudyard Kipling   (1865–1936)

Brother to a Prince and fellow to a beggar if he be found worthy.

The law, as quoted, lays down a fair conduct of life, and one not easy to follow. I have been fellow to a beggar again and again under circumstances which prevented either of us finding out whether the other was worthy. I have still to be brother to a Prince, though I once came near to kinship with what might have been a veritable King and was promised the reversion of a Kingdom—army, law-courts, revenue and policy all complete. But, to-day, I greatly fear that my King is dead, and if I want a crown I must go hunt it for myself.

The beginning of everything was in a railway train upon the road to Mhow from Ajmir. There had been a Deficit in the Budget, which necessitated traveling, not Second-class, which is only half as dear as First-class, but by Intermediate, which is very awful indeed. There are no cushions in the Intermediate class, and the population are either Intermediate, which is Eurasian, or native, which for a long night journey is nasty, or Loafer, which is amusing though intoxicated. Intermediates do not buy from refreshment-rooms. They carry their food in bundles and pots, and buy sweets from the native sweetmeat-sellers, and drink the roadside water. That is why in hot weather Intermediates are taken out of the carriages dead, and in all weathers are most properly looked down upon.

My particular Intermediate happened to be empty till I reached Nasirabad, when a big black-browed gentleman in shirt-sleeves entered, and, following the custom of Intermediates, passed the time of day. He was a wanderer and a vagabond like myself, but with an educated taste for whiskey. He told tales of things he had seen and done, of out-of-the-way corners of the Empire into which he had penetrated, and of adventures in which he risked his life for a few days' food.

"If India was filled with men like you and me, not knowing more than the crows where they'd get their next day's rations, it isn't seventy millions of revenue the land would be paying—it's seven hundred millions," said he; and as I looked at his mouth and chin I was disposed to agree with him.

We talked politics—the politics of Loaferdom that sees things from the underside where the lath and plaster is not smoothed off—and we talked postal arrangements because my friend wanted to send a telegram back from the next station to Ajmir, the turning-off place from the Bombay to the Mhow line as you travel westward. My friend had no money beyond eight annas which he wanted for dinner, and I had no money at all, owing to the hitch in the Budget before mentioned. Further, I was going into a wilderness where, though I should resume touch with the Treasury, there were no telegraph offices. I was, therefore, unable to help him in any way.

"We might threaten a Station-master, and make him send a wire on tick," said my friend, "but that'd mean inquiries for you and for me, and I've got my hands full these days. Did you say you were traveling back along this line within any days?"

"Within ten," I said.

"Can't you make it eight?" said he. "Mine is rather urgent business."

"I can send your telegram within ten days if that will serve you," I said.

"I couldn't trust the wire to fetch him now I think of it. It's this way. He leaves Delhi on the 23rd for Bombay. That means he'll be running through Ajmir about the night of the 23rd."

"But I'm going into the Indian Desert," I explained.

"Well *and* good," said he. "You'll be changing at Marwar Junction to get into Jodhpore territory—you must do that—and he'll be coming through Marwar Junction in the early morning of the 24th by the Bombay Mail. Can you be at Marwar Junction on that time? 'Twon't be inconveniencing you because I know that there's precious few pickings to be got out of these Central India States—even though you pretend to be correspondent of the *Backwoodsman*."

"Have you ever tried that trick?" I asked.

"Again and again, but the Residents find out and then you get escorted to the Border before you've time to get your knife into them. But about my friend here. I *must* give him a word o' mouth to tell him what's come to me or else he won't know where to go. I would take it more than kind of you if you was to come out of Central India in time to catch him at Marwar Junction, and say to him: 'He was gone South for the week.' He'll know what that means. He's a big man with a red beard, and a great swell he is. You'll find him sleeping like a gentleman with all his luggage round him in a Second-class apartment. But don't you be afraid. Slip down the window and say: 'He has gone South for the week,' and he'll tumble. It's only cutting your time of stay in those parts by two days. I ask you as a stranger—going to the West," he said with emphasis.

"Where have *you* come from?" said I.

"From the East," said he, "and I am hoping that you will give him the message on the Square—for the sake of my Mother as well as your own."

Englishmen are not usually softened by appeals to the memory of their mothers; but for certain reasons, which will be fully apparent, I saw fit to agree.

"It's more than a little matter," said he, "and that's why I asked you to do it—and now I know that I can depend on you doing it. A Second-class carriage at Marwar Junction, and a red-haired man asleep in it. You'll be sure to remember. I get out at the next station, and I must hold on there till he comes or sends me what I want."

"I'll give the message if I catch him," I said, "and for the sake of your Mother as well as mine I'll give you a word of advice. Don't try to run the Central India

States just now as the correspondent of the *Backwoodsman*. There's a real one knocking about here, and it might lead to trouble.

"Thank you," said he simply, "and when will the swine be gone? I can't starve because he's ruining my work. I wanted to get hold of the Degumber Rajah down here about his father's widow, and give him a jump."

"What did he do to his father's widow, then?"

"Filled her up with red pepper and slippered her to death as she hung from a beam. I found that out myself and I'm the only man that would dare going into the State to get hush-money for it. They'll try to poison me, same as they did in Chortumna when I went on the loot there. But you'll give the man at Marwar Junction my message?"

He got out at a little roadside station, and I reflected. I had heard, more than once, of men personating correspondents of newspapers and bleeding small Native States with threats of exposure, but I had never met any of the caste before. They lead a hard life, and generally die with great suddenness. The Native States have a wholesome horror of English newspapers, which may throw light on their peculiar methods of government, and do their best to choke correspondents with champagne, or drive them out of their mind with four-in-hand barouches.[1] They do not understand that nobody cares a straw for the internal administration of Native States, so long as oppression and crime and kept within decent limits, and the ruler is not drugged, drunk, or diseased from one end of the year to the other. They are the dark places of the earth, full of unimaginable cruelty, touching the Railway and Telegraph on one side, and, on the other, the days of Harunal-Raschid.[2] When I left the train I did business with divers Kings, and in eight days passed through many changes of life. Sometimes I wore dress-clothes and consorted with Princes and Politicals, drinking from crystal and eating from silver. Sometimes I lay out upon the ground and devoured what I could get, from a plate made of leaves, and drank the running water, and slept under the same rug as my servant. It was all in the day's work.

Then I headed for the Great Indian Desert upon the proper date, as I had promised, and the night Mail set me down at Marwar Junction, where a funny little, happy-go-lucky, native-managed railway runs to Jodhpore. The Bombay Mail from Delhi makes a short halt at Marwar. She arrived as I got in, and I had just time to hurry to her platform and go down the carriages. There was only one Second-class on the train. I slipped the window and looked down upon a flaming red beard, half covered by a railway rug. That was my man, fast asleep, and I dug him gently in the ribs. He woke with a grunt and I saw his face in the light of the lamps. It was a great and shining face.

"Tickets again?" said he.

"No," said I. "I am to tell you that he is gone South for the week. He has gone South for the week!"

The train had begun to move out. The red man rubbed his eyes. "He has gone South for the week," he repeated. "Now that's just like his impidence. Did he say that I was to give you anything? 'Cause I won't."

"He didn't," I said and dropped away, and watched the red lights die out in

[1] A carriage with collapsible top, pulled by four horses.
[2] The legendary sultan in *Arabian Nights*.

the dark. It was horribly cold because the wind was blowing off the sands. I climbed into my own train—not an Intermediate carriage this time—and went to sleep.

If the man with the beard had given me a rupee I should have kept it as a memento of a rather curious affair. But the consciousness of having done my duty was my only reward.

Later on I reflected that two gentlemen like my friends could not do any good if they foregathered and personated correspondents of newspapers, and might, if they blackmailed one of the little rat-trap states of Central India or Southern Rajputana, get themselves into serious difficulties. I therefore took some trouble to describe them as accurately as I could remember to people who would be interested in deporting them: and succeeded, so I was later informed, in having them headed back from the Degumber borders.

Then I became respectable, and returned to an Office where there were no Kings and no incidents outside the daily manufacture of a newspaper. A newspaper office seems to attract every conceivable sort of person, to the prejudice of discipline. Zenana-mission ladies arrive, and beg that the Editor will instantly abandon all his duties to describe a Christian prize-giving in a back-slum of a perfectly inaccessible village; Colonels who have been over-passed for command sit down and sketch the outline of a series of ten, twelve, or twenty-four leading articles on Seniority *versus* Selection; missionaries wish to know why they have not been permitted to escape from their regular vehicles of abuse and swear at a brother-missionary under special patronage of the editorial We; stranded theatrical companies troop up to explain that they cannot pay for their advertisements, but on their return from New Zealand or Tahiti will do so with interest; inventors of patent punkah-pulling machines, carriage couplings, and unbreakable swords and axle-trees call with specifications in their pockets and hours at their disposal; tea-companies enter and elaborate their prospectuses with the office pens; secretaries of ball-committees clamor to have the glories of their last dance more fully described; strange ladies rustle in and say: "I want a hundred lady's cards printed *at once,* please," which is manifestly part of an Editor's duty; and every dissolute ruffian that ever tramped the Grand Trunk Road makes it his business to ask for employment as a proof-reader. And all the time, the telephone-bell is ringing madly, and Kings are being killed on the Continent, and Empires are saying—"You're another," and Mister Gladstone is calling down brimstone upon the British Dominions, and the little black copy-boys are whining, *"kaa-pi chay-ha-yeh"* (copy wanted) like tired bees, and most of the paper is as blank as Modred's shield.[3]

But that is the amusing part of the year. There are six other months when none ever come to call, and the thermometer walks inch by inch up to the top of the glass, and the office is darkened to just above reading-light, and the press-machines are red-hot to touch, and nobody writes anything but accounts of amusements in the Hill-stations or obituary notices. Then the telephone becomes a tinkling terror, because it tells you of the sudden deaths of men and women that you know intimately, and the prickly heat covers you with a garment, and

---

[3] The treacherous nephew—son in some versions—of King Arthur, whom Arthur mortally wounds in the last battle. His shield was plain.

you sit down and write: "A slight increase of sickness is reported from the Khuda Janta Khan District. The outbreak is purely sporadic in its nature, and, thanks to the energetic efforts of the District authorities, is now almost at an end. It is, however, with deep regret that we record the death," etc.

Then the sickness really breaks out, and the less recording and reporting the better for the peace of the subscribers. But the Empires and the Kings continue to divert themselves as selfishly as before, and the Foreman thinks that a daily paper really ought to come out once in twenty-four hours, and all the people at the Hill-stations in the middle of their amusements say: "Good gracious! Why can't the paper be sparkling? I'm sure there's plenty going on up here."

That is the dark half of the moon, and, as the advertisements say, "Must be experienced to be appreciated."

It was in that season, and a remarkably evil season, that the paper began running the last issue of the week on Saturday night, which is to say Sunday morning, after the custom of a London paper. This was a great convenience, for immediately after the paper was put to bed, the dawn would lower the thermometer from 96° to almost 84° for half an hour, and in that chill—you have no idea how cold is 84° on the grass until you begin to pray for it—a very tired man could get off to sleep ere the heat roused him.

One Saturday night it was my pleasant duty to put the paper to bed alone. A King or courtier or a courtesan or a Community was going to die or get a new Constitution, or do something that was important on the other side of the world, and the paper was to be held open till the latest possible minute in order to catch the telegram.

It was pitchy black night, as stifling as a June night can be, and the *loo*, the red-hot wind from the westward, was booming among the tinder-dry trees and pretending that the rain was on its heels. Now and again a spot of almost boiling water would fall on the dust with a flop of a frog, but all our weary world knew that was only pretence. It was a shade cooler in the press-room than the office, so I sat there, while the type ticked and clicked, and the night-jars hooted at the windows, and the all but naked compositors wiped the sweat from their foreheads, and called for water. The thing that was keeping us back, whatever it was, would not come off, though the *loo* dropped and the last type was set, and the whole round earth stood still in the choking heat, with its finger on its lip, to wait the event. I drowsed, and wondered whether the telegraph was a blessing, and whether this dying man, or struggling people, might be aware of the inconvenience the delay was causing. There was no special reason beyond the heat and worry to make tension, but, as the clock-hands crept up to three o'clock and the machines spun their fly-wheels two and three times to see that all was in order, before I said the word that would set them off, I could have shrieked aloud.

Then the roar and rattle of the wheels shivered the quiet into little bits. I rose to go away, but two men in white clothes stood in front of me. The first one said: "It's him!" The second said: "So it is!" And they both laughed almost as loudly as the machinery roared, and mopped their foreheads. "We seed there was a light burning across the road and we were sleeping in that ditch there for coolness, and I said to my friend here, The office is open. Let's come along and speak to him as turned us back from the Degumber State," said the smaller of the two. He was the man I had met in the Mhow train, and his fellow was the red-bearded man of Marwar Junction. There was no mistaking the eyebrows of the one or the beard of the other.

I was not pleased, because I wished to go to sleep, not to squabble with loafers. "What do you want?" I asked.

"Half an hour's talk with you, cool and comfortable, in the office," said the red-bearded man. "We'd *like* some drink—the Contrack doesn't begin yet, Peachey, so you needn't look—but what we really want is advice. We don't want money. We ask you as a favor, because we found out you did us a bad turn about Degumber State."

I led from the press-room to the stifling office with the maps on the walls, and the red-haired man rubbed his hands. "That's something like," said he. "This was the proper shop to come to. Now, Sir, let me introduce to you Brother Peachey Carnehan, that's him, and Brother Daniel Dravot, that is *me*, and the less said about our professions the better, for we have been most things in our time. Soldier, sailor, compositor, photographer, proof-reader, street-preacher, and correspondent of the *Backwoodsman* when we thought the paper wanted one. Carnehan is sober, and so am I. Look at us first, and see that's sure. We'll take one of your cigars apiece, and you shall see us light up."

I watched the test. The men were absolutely sober, so I gave them each a tepid whiskey and soda.

"Well *and* good," said Carnehan of the eyebrows, wiping the froth from his moustache. "Let me talk now, Dan. We have been all over India, mostly on foot. We have been boiler-fitters, engine-drivers, petty contractors, and all that, and we have decided that India isn't big enough for such as us."

They certainly were too big for the office. Dravot's beard seemed to fill half the room and Carnehan's shoulders the other half, as they sat on the big table. Carnehan continued: "The country isn't half worked out because they that governs it won't let you touch it. They spend all their blessed time in governing it, and you can't lift a spade, nor chip a rock, nor look for oil, nor anything like that without all the Government saying—'Leave it alone, and let us govern.' Therefore, such as it is, we will let it alone, and go away to some other place where a man isn't crowded and can come to his own. We are not little men, and there is nothing that we are afraid of except Drink, and we have signed a Contrack on that. *Therefore,* we are going away to be Kings."

"Kings in own right," muttered Dravot.

"Yes, of course," I said. "You've been tramping in the sun, and it's a very warm night, and hadn't you better sleep over the notion? Come to-morrow."

"Neither drunk nor sunstruck," said Dravot. "We have slept over the notion half a year, and require to see Books and Atlases, and we have decided that there is only one place now in the world that two strong men can Sar-a-*whack*. They call it Kafiristan.[4] By my reckoning it's the top right-hand corner of Afghanistan, not more than three hundred miles from Peshawar. They have two-and-thirty heathen idols there, and we'll be the thirty-third and fourth. It's a mountaineous country, and the women of those parts are very beautiful."

[4] A mountainous region in central Afghanistan, now called Nuristan ("land of light"). Dravot's "Sar-a-*whack*" is a pun on Sarawak, Borneo, of which the British soldier of fortune, Sir James Brooke, became ruler. (See note 10.)

"But that is provided against in the Contrack," said Carnehan. "Neither Woman nor Liqu-or, Daniel."

"And that's all we know, except that no one has gone there, and they fight, and in any place where they fight a man who knows how to drill men can always be a King. We shall go to those parts and say to any King we find—'D'you want to vanquish your foes?' and we will show him how to drill men; for that we know better than anything else. Then we will subvert that King and seize his Throne and establish a Dy-nasty."

"You'll be cut to pieces before you're fifty miles across the Border," I said. "You have to travel through Afghanistan to get to that country. It's one mass of mountains and peaks and glaciers, and no Englishman has been through it. The people are utter brutes, and even if you reached them you couldn't do anything."

"That's more like," said Carnehan. "If you could think us a little more mad we would be more pleased. We have come to you to know about this country, to read a book about it, and to be shown maps. We want you to tell us that we are fools and to show us your books." He turned to the book-cases.

"Are you at all in earnest?" I said.

"A little," said Dravot sweetly. "As big a map as you have got, even if it's all blank where Kafiristan is, and any books you've got. We can read, though we aren't very educated."

I uncased the big thirty-two-miles-to-the-inch map of India, and two smaller Frontier maps, hauled down volume INF-KAN of the *Encyclopaedia Britannica*, and the men consulted them.

"See here!" said Dravot, his thumb on the map. "Up to Jagdallak, Peachey and me know the road. We was there with Roberts' Army. We'll have to turn off to the right at Jagdallak through Laghmann territory. Then we get among the hills—fourteen thousand feet—fifteen thousand—it will be cold work there, but it don't look very far on the map."

I handed him Wood on the *Sources of the Oxus*.⁵ Carnehan was deep in the *Encyclopaedia*.

"They're a mixed lot," said Dravot reflectively; "and it won't help us to know the names of their tribes. The more tribes the more they'll fight, and the better for us. From Jagdallak to Ashang. H'mm!"

"But all the information about the country is as sketchy and inaccurate as can be," I protested. "No one knows anything about it really. Here's the file of the *United Services' Institute*. Read what Bellew says."

"Blow Bellew!" said Carnehan. "Dan, they're a stinkin' lot of heathens, but this book here says they think they're related to us English."

⁵ Captain John Wood, *A Journey to the Source of the Oxus* (London, 1872). Other references are to Henry Walter Bellew, "Record of Seistan Mission," *Journal of the Royal Geographical Society*, 43 (1873), and Major H[enry] G[eorge] Raverty, *The Mihrân of Sind and its Tributaries: A Geographical and Historical Study* (Calcutta, 1893). Bellew reported the claims, still considered valid, of Hebrew descent by a people of western Afghanistan (from the tribes captured by Nebuchadnezzar) and of Greek lineage by others, particularly the Tajiks in Kafiristan, where some claim direct descent from Alexander the Great. Pre-Alexandrian Greek colonies probably account for the remnants of Greek mythology and Greek hymns in Kafir culture, as well as for the Tajik's light complexion (10% blond, 15% blue eyed). Greeks and British are both members of the Indo-European family of races and languages. The Kafirs were conquered and forcibly converted to Mohammedanism in 1895.

I smoked while the men pored over *Raverty, Wood,* the maps, and the *Encyclopaedia.*

"There is no use your waiting," said Dravot politely. "It's about four o'clock now. We'll go before six o'clock if you want to sleep, and we won't steal any of the papers. Don't you sit up. We're two harmless lunatics, and if you come tomorrow evening down to the Serai we'll say good-bye to you."

"You *are* two fools," I answered. "You'll be turned back at the Frontier or cut up the minute you set foot in Afghanistan. Do you want any money or a recommendation down-country? I can help you to the chance of work next week."

"Next week we shall be hard at work ourselves, thank you," said Dravot. "It isn't so easy being a King as it looks. When we've got our Kingdom in going order we'll let you know, and you can come up and help us to govern it."

"Would two lunatics make a Contrack like that?" said Carnehan, with subdued pride, showing me a greasy half-sheet of notepaper on which was written the following. I copied it, then and there, as a curiosity—

This Contract between me and you persuing witnesseth in the name of God—Amen and so forth.

(One)   *That me and you will settle this matter together; i.e., to be Kings of Kafiristan.*

(Two)   *That you and me will not, while this matter is being settled, look at any Liquor, nor any Woman black, white or brown, so as to get mixed up with one or the other harmful.*

(Three)   *That we conduct ourselves with Dignity and Discretion, and if one of us gets into trouble the other will stay by him.*

                                  Signed by you and me this day.
                                  Peachey Taliaferro Carnehan.
                                  Daniel Dravot.
                                  Both Gentlemen at Large.

"There was no need for the last article," said Carnehan, blushing modestly; "but it looks regular. Now you know the sort of men that loafers are—we *are* loafers, Dan, until we get out of India—and *do* you think that we would sign a Contrack like that unless we was in earnest? We have kept away from the two things that make life worth having."

"You won't enjoy your lives much longer if you are going to try this idiotic adventure. Don't set the office on fire," I said, "and go away before nine o'clock."

I left them still poring over the maps and making notes on the back of the "Contrack." "Be sure to come down to the Serai to-morrow," were their parting words.

The Kumharsen Serai is the great four-square sink of humanity where the strings of camels and horses from the North load and unload. All the nationalities of Central Asia may be found there, and most of the folk of India proper. Balkh and Bokhara there meet Bengal and Bombay, and try to draw eye-teeth. You can buy ponies, turquoises, Persian pussy-cats, saddle-bags, fat-tailed sheep and musk in the Kumharsen Serai, and get many strange things for nothing. In the afternoon I went down to see whether my friends intended to keep their word or were lying there drunk.

A priest attired in fragments of ribbons and rags stalked up to me, gravely twisting a child's paper whirligig. Behind him was his servant bending under the load of a crate of mud toys. The two were loading up two camels, and the inhabitants of the Serai watched them with shrieks of laughter.

"The priest is mad," said a horse-dealer to me. "He is going up to Kabul to sell toys to the Amir. He will either be raised to honor or have his head cut off. He came in here this morning and has been behaving madly ever since."

"The witless are under the protection of God," stammered a flat-cheeked Usbeg in broken Hindi. "They foretell future events."

"Would they could have foretold that my caravan would have been cut up by the Shinwaris almost within shadow of the Pass!" grunted the Eusufzai agent of a Rajputana trading-house whose goods had been diverted into the hands of other robbers just across the Border, and whose misfortunes were the laughing-stock of the bazaar. "Ohé, priest, whence come you and whither do you go?"

"From Roum have I come," shouted the priest, waving his whirligig; "from Roum, blown by the breath of a hundred devils across the sea! O thieves, robbers, liars, the blessing of Pir Khan on pigs, dogs, and perjurers! Who will take the Protected of God to the North to sell charms that are never still to the Amir? The camels shall not gall, the sons shall not fall sick, and the wives shall remain faithful while they are away, of the men who give me place in their caravan. Who will assist me to slipper the King of the Roos with a golden slipper with a silver heel? The protection of Pir Khan be upon his labors!" He spread out the skirts of his gaberdine and pirouetted between the lines of tethered horses.

"There starts a caravan from Peshawar to Kabul in twenty days, *Huzrut*," said the Eusufzai trader. "My camels go therewith. Do thou also go and bring us good-luck."

"I will go even now!" shouted the priest. "I will depart upon my winged camels, and be at Peshawar in a day! Ho! Hazar Mir Khan," he yelled to his servant, "drive out the camels, but let me first mount my own."

He leaped on the back of his beast as it knelt, and, turning round to me, cried: "Come thou also, Sahib, a little along the road, and I will sell thee a charm—an amulet that shall make thee King of Kafiristan."

Then the light broke upon me, and I followed the two camels out of their Serai till we reached open road and the priest halted.

"What d'you think o' that?" said he in English. "Carnehan can't talk their patter, so I've made him my servant. He makes a handsome servant. 'Tisn't for nothing that I've been knocking about the country for fourteen years. Didn't I do that talk neat? We'll hitch on to a caravan at Peshawar till we get to Jagdallak, and then we'll see if we can get donkeys for our camels, and strike into Kafiristan. Whirligigs for the Amir, O Lor! Put your hand under the camel-bags and tell me what you feel."

I felt the butt of a Martini,[6] and another and another.

"Twenty of 'em," said Dravot placidly. "Twenty of 'em and ammunition to

---

[6] The Martini-Henry rifle, adopted by the British in 1871. This was their first complete breech-loading rifle, replacing the Snider rifle (see p.41), which had been converted to breech loading, by Jacob Snider's device, from the Enfield muzzle-loader.

correspond, under the whirligigs and the mud dolls."

"Heaven help you if you are caught with those things!" I said. "A Martini is worth her weight in silver among the Pathans."

"Fifteen hundred rupees of capital—every rupee we could beg, borrow, or steal—are invested on these two camels," said Dravot. "We won't get caught. We're going through the Khaiber with a regular caravan. Who'd touch a poor mad priest?"

"Have you got everything you want?" I asked, overcome with astonishment.

"Not yet, but we shall soon. Give us a memento of your kindness, *Brother*. You did me a service, yesterday, and that time in Marwar. Half my Kingdom shall you have, as the saying is." I slipped a small charm compass from my watch chain and handed it up to the priest.

"Good-bye," said Dravot, giving me hand cautiously. "It's the last time we'll shake hands with an Englishman these many days. Shake hands with him, Carnehan," he cried, as the second camel passed me.

Carnehan leaned down and shook hands. Then the camels passed away along the dusty road, and I was left alone to wonder. My eye could detect no failure in the disguises. The scene in the Serai proved that they were complete to the native mind. There was just the chance, therefore, that Carnehan and Dravot would be able to wander through Afghanistan without detection. But, beyond, they would find death—certain and awful death.

Ten days later a native correspondent giving me the news of the day from Peshawar, wound up his letter with: "There has been much laughter here on account of a certain mad priest who is going in his estimation to sell petty gauds and insignificant trinkets which he ascribes as great charms to H. H. the Amir of Bokhara. He passed through Peshawar and associated himself to the Second Summer caravan that goes to Kabul. The merchants are pleased because through superstition, they imagine that such mad fellows bring good-fortune."

The two, then, were beyond the Border. I would have prayed for them, but, that night, a real King died in Europe, and demanded an obituary notice.

● ● ●

The wheel of the world swings through the same phases again and again. Summer passed and winter thereafter, and came and passed again. The daily paper continued and I with it, and upon the third summer there fell a hot night, a night-issue, and a strained waiting for something to be telegraphed from the other side of the world, exactly as had happened before. A few great men had died in the past two years, the machines worked with more clatter, and some of the trees in the Office garden were a few feet taller. But that was all the difference.

I passed over to the press-room, and went through just such a scene as I have already described. The nervous tension was stronger than it had been two years before, and I felt the heat more acutely. At three o'clock I cried, "Print off," and turned to go, when there crept to my chair what was left of a man. He was bent into a circle, his head was sunk between his shoulders, and he moved his feet one over the other like a bear. I could hardly see whether he walked or crawled—this rag-wrapped, whining cripple who addressed me by name, crying that he was come back. "Can you give me a drink?" he whimpered. "For the Lord's sake, give me a drink!"

I went back to the office, the man following with groans of pain, and I turned up the lamp.

"Don't you know me?" he gasped, dropping into a chair, and he turned his drawn face, surmounted by a shock of gray hair, to the light.

I looked at him intently. Once before had I seen eyebrows that met over the nose in an inch-broad black band, but for the life of me I could not tell where.

"I don't know you," I said, handing him the whiskey. "What can I do for you?"

He took a gulp of the spirit raw, and shivered in spite of the suffocating heat.

"I've come back," he repeated; "and I was the King of Kafiristan—me and Dravot—crowned Kings we was! In this office we settled it—you setting there and giving us the books. I am Peachey—Peachey Taliaferro Carnehan, and you've been setting here ever since—O Lord!"

I was more than a little astonished, and expressed my feelings accordingly.

"It's true," said Carnehan, with a dry cackle, nursing his feet, which were wrapped in rags. "True as gospel. Kings we were, with crowns upon our heads—me and Dravot—poor Dan—oh, poor, poor Dan, that would never take advice, not though I begged of him!"

"Take the whiskey," I said, "and take your own time. Tell me all you can recollect of everything from beginning to end. You got across the border on your camels, Dravot dressed as a mad priest and you his servant. Do you remember that?"

"I ain't mad—yet, but I shall be that way soon. Of course I remember. Keep looking at me, or maybe my words will go all to pieces. Keep looking at me in my eyes and don't say anything."

I leaned forward and looked into his face as steadily as I could. He dropped one hand upon the table and I grasped it by the wrist. It was twisted like a bird's claw, and upon the back was a ragged, red, diamond-shaped scar.

"No, don't look there. Look at *me*," said Carnehan. "That comes afterwards, but for the Lord's sake don't distrack me. We left with that caravan, me and Dravot playing all sorts of antics to amuse the people we were with. Dravot used to make us laugh in the evenings when all the people was cooking their dinners—cooking their dinners, and . . . what did they do then? They lit little fires with sparks that went into Dravot's beard, and we all laughed—fit to die. Little red fires they was, going into Dravot's big red beard—so funny." His eyes left mine and he smiled foolishly.

"You went as far as Jagdallak with that caravan," I said at a venture, "after you had lit those fires. To Jagdallak, where you turned off to try to get into Kafiristan."

"No, we didn't neither. What are you talking about? We turned off before Jagdallak, because we heard the roads was good. But they wasn't good enough for our two camels—mine and Dravot's. When we left the caravan, Dravot took off all his clothes and mine too, and said we would be heathen, because the Kafirs didn't allow Mohammedans to talk to them.[7] So we dressed betwixt and between,

---

[7] The Kafirs, the only non-Mohammedans in Afghanistan, allowed no contact or trade with the surrounding Mohammedans. They were idol worshipers whose religion combined elements of Greek mythology, Zoroastrianism, and Buddhism. *Kafir* means "nonbeliever" in Arabic.

and such a sight as Daniel Dravot I never saw yet nor expect to see again. He burned half his beard, and slung a sheep-skin over his shoulder, and shaved his head into patterns. He shaved mine, too, and made me wear outrageous things to look like a heathen. That was in a most mountaineous country, and our camels couldn't go along any more because of the mountains. They were tall and black, and coming home I saw them fight like wild goats—there are lots of goats in Kafiristan. And these mountains, they never keep still, no more than the goats. Always fighting they are, and don't let you sleep at night."

"Take some more whiskey," I said very slowly. "What did you and Daniel Dravot do when the camels could go no further because of the rough roads that led into Kafiristan?"

"What did which do? There was a party called Peachey Taliaferro Carnehan that was with Dravot. Shall I tell you about him? He died out there in the cold. Slap from the bridge fell old Peachey, turning and twisting in the air like a penny whirligig that you can sell to the Amir.—

No; they was two for three ha'pence, those whirligigs, or I am much mistaken and woeful sore. . . . And then these camels were no use, and Peachey said to Dravot—'For the Lord's sake, let's get out of this before our heads are chopped off,' and with that they killed the camels all among the mountains, not having anything in particular to eat, but first they took off the boxes with the guns and the ammunition, till two men came along driving four mules. Dravot up and dances in front of them, singing—'Sell me four mules.' Says the first man—'If you are rich enough to buy, you are rich enough to rob;' but before ever he could put his hand to his knife, Dravot breaks his neck over his knee, and the other party runs away. So Carnehan loaded the mules with the rifles that was taken off the camels, and together we starts forward into those bitter cold mountaineous parts, and never a road broader than the back of your hand."

He paused for a moment, while I asked him if he could remember the nature of the country through which he had journeyed.

"I am telling you as straight as I can, but my head isn't as good as it might be. They drove nails through it to make me hear better how Dravot died. The country was mountaineous and the mules were most contrary, and the inhabitants was dispersed and solitary. They went up and up, and down and down, and that other party, Carnehan, was imploring of Dravot not to sing and whistle so loud, for fear of bringing down the tremenjus avalanches. But Dravot says that if a King couldn't sing it wasn't worth being King, and whacked the mules over the rump, and never took no heed for ten cold days. We came to a big level valley all among the mountains, and the mules were near dead, so we killed them, not having anything in special for them or us to eat. We sat upon the boxes, and played odd and even with the cartridges that was jolted out.

"Then ten men with bows and arrows ran down that valley, chasing twenty men with bows and arrows, and the row was tremenjus. They was fair men— fairer than you or me—with yellow hair and remarkable well built. Says Dravot, unpacking the guns—'This is the beginning of the business. We'll fight for the ten men,' and with that he fires two rifles at the twenty men, and drops one of them at two hundred yards from the rock where he was sitting. The other men began to run, but Carnehan and Dravot sits on the boxes picking them off at all ranges, up and down the valley. Then he goes up to the ten men that had run across the snow too, and they fires a footy little arrow at us. Dravot he shoots above their heads and they all falls down flat. Then he walks over them and kicks them, and then he lifts them up and shakes hands all round to make them friendly like. He calls them and gives them the boxes to carry, and waves his hand for all the world as though he was King already. They take the boxes and him across the valley and up the hill into a pine wood on the top, where there was half a dozen big stone idols. Dravot he goes to the biggest—a fellow they call Imbra—and lays a rifle and a cartridge at his feet, rubbing his nose respectful with his own nose, patting him on the head, and saluting in front of it. He turns round to the men and nods his head, and says—'That's all right. I'm in the know too, and all these old jim-jams are my friends.' Then he opens his mouth and points down it, and when the first man brings him food, he says—'No;' and when the second man brings him food he says—'No;' but when one of the old priests and the boss of the village brings him food, he says—'Yes;' very haughty, and eats it slow. That was how we came to our first village, without any trouble, just as though we had tumbled from the skies. But we tumbled from one of those damned rope-bridges, you see and—you couldn't expect a man to laugh much after that?''

"Take some more whiskey and go on," I said. "That was the first village you came into. How did you get to be King?"

"I wasn't King," said Carnehan. "Dravot he was the King, and a handsome man he looked with the gold crown on his head and all. Him and the other party stayed in that village, and every morning Dravot sat by the side of old Imbra, and the people came and worshipped. That was Dravot's order. Then a lot of men came into the valley, and Carnehan and Dravot picks them off with the rifles before they knew where they was, and runs down into the valley and up again the other side and finds another village, same as the first one, and the people all falls down flat on their faces, and Dravot says—'Now what is the trouble between you two villages?' and the people points to a woman, as fair as you or me, that was carried off, and Dravot takes her back to the first village and counts up the dead—eight there was. For each dead man Dravot pours a little milk on the ground and waves his arms like a whirlagig and 'That's all right,' says he. Then he and Carnehan takes the big boss of each village by the arm and walks them down into the valley, and shows them how to scratch a line with a spear right down the valley, and gives each a sod of turf from both sides of the line. Then all the people comes down and shouts like the devil and all, and Dravot says—'Go and dig the land, and be fruitful and multiply,' which they did, though they didn't understand. Then we asks the names of things in their lingo—bread and water and fire and idols and such, and Dravot leads the priest of each village up to the idol, and says he must sit there and judge the people, and if anything goes wrong he is to be shot.

"Next week they was all turning up the land in the valley as quiet as bees and much prettier, and the priests heard all the complaints and told Dravot in dumb show what it was about. 'That's just the beginning,' says Dravot. 'They think we're Gods.' He and Carnehan picks out twenty good men and shows them how to click off a rifle, and form fours, and advance in line, and they was very pleased to do so, and clever to see the hang of it. Then he takes out his pipe and his baccy-pouch and leaves one at one village, and one at the other, and off we two goes to see what was to be done in the next valley. That was all rock, and there was a little village there, and Carnehan says—'send 'em to the old valley to plant,' and takes 'em there and gives 'em some land that wasn't took before. They were a poor lot, and we blooded 'em with a kid before letting 'em into the new Kingdom. That was to impress the people, and then they settled down quiet, and Carnehan went back to Dravot who had got into another valley, all snow and ice and most mountaineous. There was no people there and the Army got afraid, so Dravot shoots one of them, and goes on till he finds some people in a village, and the Army explains that unless the people wants to be killed they had better not shoot their little matchlocks; for they had matchlocks. We makes friends with the priest and I stays there alone with two of the Army, teaching the men how to drill and a thundering big Chief comes across the snow with kettle-drums and horns twanging, because he heard there was a new God kicking about. Carnehan sights for the brown of the men half a mile across the snow and wings one of them. Then he sends a message to the Chief that, unless he wished to be killed, he must come and shake hands with me and leave his arms behind. The Chief comes alone first, and Carnehan shakes hands with him and whirls his arms about, same as Dravot used, and very much surprised that Chief was, and strokes my eyebrows. Then Carnehan goes alone to the Chief, and asks him in dumb show if he had an enemy he hated. 'I have,' says the Chief. So Carnehan weeds out the pick of his men, and sets the two of the Army to show them drill and at the end of two weeks the men can maneuvre about as well as Volunteers. So he marches with the Chief to a great big plain on the top of a mountain, and the Chief's men rushes into a village and takes it; we three Martinis firing into the brown of the enemy. So we took that village too, and I gives the chief a rag from my coat and says, 'Occupy till I come;' which was scriptural. By way of a remind-er, when me and the Army was eighteen hundred yards away, I drops a bullet near him standing on the snow, and all the people falls flat on their faces. Then I sends a letter to Dravot wherever he be by land or by sea."

At the risk of throwing the creature out of train, I interrupted—"How could you write a letter up yonder?"

"The letter?—Oh!—The letter! Keep looking at me between the eyes, please. It was a string-talk letter, that we'd learned the way of it from a blind beggar in the Punjab.

I remember that there had once come to the office a blind man with a knotted twig and a piece of string which he wound round the twig according to some ci-pher of his own. He could, after the lapse of days or hours, repeat the sentence which he had reeled up. He had reduced the alphabet to eleven primitive sounds; and tried to teach me his method, but I could not understand.

"I sent that letter to Dravot," said Carnehan; "and told him to come back be-cause this Kingdom was growing too big for me to handle, and then I struck for the first valley, to see how the priests were working. They called the village we took along with the Chief, Bashkai, and the first village we took, Er-Heb. The priests at Er-Heb was doing all right, but they had a lot of pending cases about land to show me, and some men from another village had been firing arrows at night. I went out and looked for that village, and fired four rounds at it from a thousand yards. That used all the cartridges I cared to spend, and I waited for Dravot, who had been away two or three months, and I kept my people quiet.

"One morning I heard the devil's own noise of drums and horns, and Dan

Dravot marches down the hill with his Army and a tail of hundreds of men, and which was the most amazing, a great gold crown on his head. 'My Gord, Carnehan,' said Daniel, 'this is a tremenjus business, and we've got the whole country as far as it's worth having. I am the son of Alexander by Queen Semiramis, and you're my younger brother and a God too! It's the biggest thing we've ever seen. I've been marching and fighting for six weeks with the Army, and every footy little village for fifty miles has come in rejoiceful; and more than that, I've got the key of the whole show, as you'll see, and I've got a crown for you! I told 'em to make two of 'em at a place called Shu, where the gold lies in the rock like suet in mutton. Gold I've seen, and turquoise I've kicked out of the cliffs, and there's garnets in the sands of the river, and there's a chunk of amber that a man brought me. Call up all the priests and here, take your crown.'

"One of the men opens a black hair bag, and I slips the crown on. It was too small and too heavy, but I wore it for the glory. Hammered gold it was—five pound weight, like a hoop of a barrel.

" 'Peachey,' says Dravot, 'we don't want to fight no more. The Craft's the trick so help me!' and he brings forward that same Chief that I left at Bashkai—Billy Fish we called him afterwards, because he was so like Billy Fish that drove the big tank-engine at Mach on the Bolan[8] in the old days. 'Shake hands with him' says Dravot, and I shook hands and nearly dropped, for Billy Fish gave me the Grip. I said nothing, but tried him with the Fellow Craft Grip. He answers, all right, and I tried the Master's Grip, but that was a slip. 'A Fellow Craft[9] he is!' I says to Dan. 'Does he know the word?'—'He does,' says Dan, 'and all the priests know. It's a miracle. The Chiefs and the priests can work a Fellow Craft Lodge in a way that's very like ours, and they've cut the marks on the rocks, but they don't know the Third Degree, and they've come to find out. It's Gord's Truth. I've known these long years that the Afghans knew up to the Fellow Craft Degree, but this a miracle. A God and a Grand-Master of the Craft am I, and a Lodge in the Third Degree I will open, and we'll raise the head priests and the Chiefs of the villages.'

" 'It's against all the law,' I says, 'holding a Lodge without warrant from any one; and you know we never held office in any Lodge.'

" 'It's a master-stroke o' policy,' says Dravot. 'It means running the country as easy as a four-wheeled bogie on a down grade. We can't stop to inquire now, or they'll turn against us. I've forty Chiefs at my heel, and passed and raised according to their merit they shall be. Billet these men on the villages, and see that we run up a Lodge of some kind. The temple of Imbra will do for the Lodge-room. The women must make aprons as you show them. I'll hold a levee of Chiefs to-night and Lodge to-morrow.

"I was fair run off my legs, but I wasn't such a fool as not to see what a pull this Craft business gave us. I showed the priests' families how to make aprons of the degrees, but for Dravot's apron the blue border and marks was made of turquoise lumps on white hide, not cloth. We took a great square stone in the temple for the Master's chair, and little stones for the officers' chairs, and painted the

---

[8] Mach is a town on the Bolan River in the Bolan Pass, important in Britain's Afghan wars in the 1860s and 1870s.

[9] Freemason.

black pavement with white squares, and did what we could to make things regular.

"At the levee which was held that night on the hillside with big bonfires, Dravot gives out that him and me were Gods and sons of Alexander, and Past Grand-Masters in the Craft, and was come to make Kafiristan a country where every man should eat in peace and drink in quiet, and specially obey us. Then the Chiefs came round to shake hands, and they were so hairy and white and fair it was just shaking hands with old friends. We gave them names according as they was like men we had known in India—Billy Fish, Holly Dilworth, Pikky Kergan, that was Bazar-master when I was at Mhow, and so on, and so on.

"The most amazing miracles was at Lodge next night. One of the old priests was watching us continuous, and I felt uneasy, for I knew we'd have to fudge the Ritual, and I didn't know what the men knew. The old priest was a stranger come in from beyond the village of Bashkai. The minute Dravot puts on the Master's apron and that the girls had made for him, the priest fetches a whoop and a howl, and tries to overturn the stone that Dravot was sitting on. 'It's all up now,' I says. 'That comes of meddling with the Craft without warrant!' Dravot never winked an eye, not when ten priests took and tilted over the Grand-Master's chair—which was to say the stone of Imbra. The priest begins rubbing the bottom end of it to clear away the black dirt, and presently he shows all the other priests the Master's Mark, same as was on Dravot's apron, cut into the stone. Not even the priests of the temple of Imbra knew it was there. The old chap falls flat on his face at Dravot's feet and kisses 'em. 'Luck again,' says Dravot, across the Lodge to me, 'they say it's the missing Mark that no one could understand the why of. We're more than safe now.' Then he bangs the butt of his gun for a gavel and says: 'By virtue of the authority vested in me by my own right hand and the help of Peachey, I declare myself Grand-Master of all Free-masonry in Kafiristan in this the Mother Lodge o' the country, and King of Kafiristan equally with Peachey!' At that he puts on his crown and I puts on mine—I was doing Senior Warden—and we opens the Lodge in most ample form. It was a amazing miracle! The priests moved in Lodge through the first two degrees almost without telling, as if the memory was coming back to them. After that, Peachey and Dravot raised such as was worthy—high priests and Chiefs of far-off villages. Billy Fish was the first, and I can tell you we scared the soul out of him. It was not in any way according to Ritual, but it served our turn. We didn't raise more than ten of the biggest men, because we didn't want to make the Degree common. And they was clamoring to be raised.

" 'In another six months,' says Dravot; 'we'll hold another Communication, and see how you are working.' Then he asks them about their villages, and learns that they was fighting one against the other, and were sick and tired of it. And when they wasn't doing that they was fighting with the Mohammedans. 'You can fight those when they come into our country,' says Dravot. 'Tell off every tenth man of your tribes for a Frontier guard, and send two hundred at a time to this valley to be drilled. Nobody is going to be shot or speared any more so long as he does well, and I know that you won't cheat me, because you're white people—sons of Alexander—and not like common, black Mohammedans. You are *my* people, and by God,' says he, running off into English at the end— 'I'll make a damned fine Nation of you, or I'll die in the making!'

"I can't tell all we did for the next six months, because Dravot did a lot I couldn't see the hang of, and he learned their lingo in a way I never could. My work was to help the people plow, and now and again go out with some of the Army and see what the other villages were doing, and make 'em throw rope-bridges across the ravines which cut up the country horrid. Dravot was very kind to me, but when he walked up and down in the pine wood pulling that bloody red beard of his with both fists I knew he was thinking plans I could not advise about, and I just waited for orders.

"But Dravot never showed me disrespect before the people. They were afraid of me and the Army, but they loved Dan. He was the best of friends with the priests and the Chiefs; but any one could come across the hills with a complaint, and Dravot would hear him out fair, and call four priests together and say what was to be done. He used to call in Billy Fish from Bashkai, and Pikky Kergan from Shu, and an old Chief we called Kafuzelum—it was like enough to his real name—and hold councils with 'em when there was any fighting to be done in small villages. That was his Council of War, and the four priests of Bashkai, Shu, Khawak, and Madora was his Privy Council. Between the lot of 'em they sent me, with forty men and twenty rifles, and sixty men carrying turquoises, into the Ghorband country to buy those hand-made Martini rifles, that come out of the Amir's workshops at Kabul, from one of the Amir's Herati regiments that would have sold the very teeth out of their mouths for turquoises.

"I stayed in Ghorband a month, and gave the Governor there the pick of my baskets for hush-money, and bribed the Colonel of the regiment some more, and between the two and the tribes-people, we got more than a hundred hand-made Martinis, a hundred good Kohat Jezails that'll throw to six hundred yards, and forty manloads of very bad ammunition for the rifles. I came back with what I had, and distributed 'em among the men that the Chiefs sent in to me to drill. Dravot was too busy to attend to those things, but the old Army that we first made helped me, and we turned out five hundred men that could drill, and two hundred that knew how to hold arms pretty straight. Even those cork-screwed, hand-made guns was a miracle to them. Dravot talked big about powder-shops and factories, walking up and down in the pine wood when the winter was coming on.

" 'I won't make a Nation,' says he. 'I'll made an Empire! These men aren't niggers; they're English! Look at their eyes—look at their mouths. Look at the way they stand up. They sit on chairs in their own houses. They're the Lost Tribes, or something like it, and they've grown to be English. I'll take a census in the spring if the priests don't get frightened. There must be a fair two million of 'em in these hills. The villages are full o' little children. Two million people—two hundred and fifty thousand fighting men—and all English! They only want the rifles and a little drilling. Two hundred and fifty thousand men, ready to cut in on Russia's right flank when she tries for India! Peachey, man.' he says, chewing his beard in great hunks, 'we shall be Emperors—Emperors of the Earth! Rajah Brooke[10] will be suckling to us. I'll treat with the Viceroy on equal terms. I'll ask

[10] Sir James Brooke (1803–1868), former soldier for the East India Company, financed and led an expedition of twenty men to Borneo to suppress piracy in 1838. He joined in suppressing a rebellion in the province of Sarawak, for which he was made Rajah. For continuing to fight piracy in the Malay Archepelago, with British support, he was knighted by Queen Victoria in 1847.

him to send me twelve picked English—twelve that I know of—to help us govern a bit. There's Mackray, Sergeant-pensioner at Segowli—many's the good dinner he's given me, and his wife a pair of trousers. There's Donkin, the Warder of Tounghoo Jail; there's hundreds that I could lay my hand on if I was in India. The Viceroy shall do it for me, I'll send a man through in the spring for those men, and I'll write for a dispensation from the Grand Lodge for what I've done as Grand-Master. That—and all the Sniders that'll be thrown out when the native troops in India take up the Martini.[11] They'll be worn smooth, but they'll do for fighting in these hills. Twelve English, a hundred thousand Sniders run through the Amir's country in driblets—I'd be content with twenty thousand in one year—and we'd be an Empire. When everything was shipshape, I'd hand over the crown—this crown I'm wearing now—to Queen Victoria on my knees, and she'd say: "Rise up, Sir Daniel Dravot." Oh, it's big! It's big, I tell you! But there's so much to be done in every place—Bashkai, Khawak, Shu, and everywhere else.'

" 'What is it?' I says. 'There are no more men coming to be drilled this autumn. Look at those fat, black clouds. They're bringing the snow.'

" 'It isn't that,' says Daniel, putting his hand very hard on my shoulder: 'and I don't wish to say anything that's against you, for no other living man would have followed me and made me what I am as you have done. You're a first-class Commander-in-Chief, and the people know you: but—it's a big country, and somehow you can't help me, Peachey, in the way I want to be helped.'

" 'Go to your blasted priests, then!' I said, and I was sorry when I made that remark, but it did hurt me sore to find Daniel talking so superior when I'd drilled all the men, and done all he told me.

" 'Don't let's quarrel, Peachey,' says Daniel, without cursing. 'You're a King too, and the half of this Kingdom is yours; but can't you see, Peachey, we want cleverer men than us now—three or four of 'em, that we can scatter about for our Deputies. It's a hugeous great State, and I can't always tell the right thing to do, and I haven't time for all I want to do, and here's the winter coming on and all.' He put half his beard into his mouth, all red like the gold of his crown.

" 'I'm sorry, Daniel,' says I. 'I've done all I could. I've drilled the men and shown the people how to stack their oats better; and I've brought in those tinware rifles from Ghorband—but I know what you're driving at. I take it Kings always feel oppressed that way.'

" 'There's another thing too,' says Dravot, walking up and down. 'The winter's coming and these people won't be giving much trouble, and if they do we can't move about. I want a wife.'

" 'For Gord's sake leave the women alone!' I says. 'We've both got all the work we can, though I *am* a fool. Remember the Contrack, and keep clear o' women.'

" 'The Contrack only lasted till such time as we was Kings; and Kings we have been these months past,' says Dravot, weighing his crown upon his hand. 'You go get a wife too, Peachey—a nice, strappin', plump girl that'll keep you warm in the winter. They're prettier than English girls, and we can take the pick of 'em. Boil 'em once or twice in hot water, and they'll come out like chicken and ham.'

" 'Don't tempt me!' I says. 'I will not have any dealings with a woman not till we are a dam' side more settled than we are now. I've been doing the work o'

[11] See note 6.

two men, and you've been doing the work o' three. Let's lie off a bit, and see if we can get some better tobacco from Afghan country and run in some good liquor; but no women.'

" 'Who's talking o' *women?*' says Dravot. 'I said *wife*—a queen to breed a King's son for the King. A Queen out of the strongest tribe, that'll make them your blood-brothers and that'll lie by your side and tell you all the people thinks about you and their own affairs. That's what I want.'

" 'Do you remember that Bengali woman I kept at Mogul Serai when I was a plate-layer?' says I. 'A fat lot o' good she was to me. She taught me the lingo and one or two other things; but what happened? She ran away with the Station Master's servant and half my month's pay. Then she turned up at Dadur Junction in tow of a half-caste, and had the impidence to say I was her husband—all among the drivers in the running-shed too!'

" 'We've done with that,' says Dravot. 'these women are whiter than you or me, and a Queen I will have for the winter months.'

" 'For the last time o' asking, Dan, do *not*,' I says. 'It'll only bring us harm. The Bible says that Kings ain't to waste their strength on women, 'specially when they've got a new raw Kingdom to work over.'

" 'For the last time of answering I will,' said Dravot, and he went away through the pine-trees looking like a big red devil, the sun being on his crown and beard and all.

"But getting a wife was not as easy as Dan thought. He put it before the Council, and there was no answer till Billy Fish said he'd better ask the girls. Dravot damned them all round. 'What's wrong with me?' he shouts, standing by the idol Imbra. 'Am I a dog or am I not enough of a man for your wenches? Haven't I put the shadow of my hand over this country? Who stopped the last Afghan raid?' It was me really, but Dravot was too angry to remember. 'Who bought your guns? Who repaired the bridges? Who's the Grand-Master of the sign cut in the stone?' says he, and he thumped his hand on the block that he used to sit on in Lodge, and at Council, which opened like Lodge always. Billy Fish said nothing and no more did the others. 'Keep your hair on, Dan,' said I; 'and ask the girls. That's how it's done at Home, and these people are quite English.'

" 'The marriage of the King is a matter of State,' says Dan, in a white-hot rage, for he could feel, I hope, that he was going against his better mind. He walked out of the Councilroom, and the others sat still, looking at the ground.

" 'Billy Fish,' says I to the Chief of Bashkai, 'what's the difficulty here? A straight answer to a true friend.'

" 'You know,' says Billy Fish. 'How should a man tell you who knows everything? How can daughters of men marry Gods or Devils? It's not proper.'

"I remembered something like that in the Bible; but if, after seeing us as long as they had, they still believed we were Gods, it wasn't for me to undeceive them.

" 'A God can do anything,' says I. 'If the King is fond of a girl he'll not let her die.'—'She'll have to,' said Billy Fish. 'There are all sorts of Gods and Devils in these mountains, and now and again a girl marries one of them and isn't seen any more. Besides, you two know the Mark cut in the stone. Only the Gods know that. We thought you were men till you showed the sign of the Master.'

"I wished then that we had explained about the loss of the genuine secrets of a Master-Mason at the first go-off; but I said nothing. All that night there was a blowing of horns in a little dark temple half-way down the hill, and I heard a girl crying fit to die. One of the priests told us that she was being prepared to marry the King.

" 'I'll have no nonsense of that kind.' says Dan. 'I don't want to interfere with your customs, but I'll take my own wife.'—'The girl's a little bit afraid,' says the priest. 'She thinks she's going to die, and they are aheartening of her up down in the temple.'

" 'Hearten her very tender, then,' says Dravot, 'or I'll hearten you with the butt of a gun so you'll never want to be heartened again.' He licked his lips, did Dan, and stayed up walking about more than half the night, thinking of the wife that he was going to get in the morning. I wasn't by any means comfortable, for I knew that dealings with a woman in foreign parts, though you was a crowned King twenty times over, could not but be risky. I got up very early in the morning while Dravot was asleep, and I saw the priests talking together in whispers, and the Chiefs talking together too, and they looked at me out of the corners of their eyes.

" 'What is up, Fish?' I say to the Bashkai man, who was wrapped up in his furs and looking splendid to behold.

" 'I can't rightly say,' says he; 'but if you can make the King drop all this nonsense about marriage, you'll be doing him and me and yourself a great service.'

" 'That I do believe,' says I. 'But sure, you know, Billy, as well as me, having fought against and for us, that the King and me are nothing more than two of the finest men that God Almighty ever made. Nothing more, I do assure you.'

" 'That may be,' says Billy Fish, 'and yet I should be sorry if it was.' He sinks his head upon his great fur cloak for a minute and thinks. 'King,' says he, 'be you man or God or Devil, I'll stick by you to-day.' I have twenty of my men with me, and they will follow me. We'll go to Bashkai until the storm blows over.'

"A little snow had fallen in the night, and everything was white except the greasy fat clouds that blew down and down from the north. Dravot came out with his crown on his head, swinging his arms and stamping his feet, and looking more pleased than Punch.

" 'For the last time, drop it, Dan,' says I in a whisper, 'Billy Fish here says that there will be a row.'

" 'A row among my people!' says Dravot. 'Not much. Peachey, you're a fool not to get a wife, too. Where's the girl?' says he with a voice as loud as the braying of a jackass. 'Call up the Chiefs and priests, and let the Emperor see if his wife suits him.'

"There was no need to call any one. They were all there leaning on their guns and spears round the clearing in the center of the pine wood. A lot of priests went down to the little temple to bring up the girl, and the horns blew fit to wake the dead. Billy Fish saunters round and gets as close to Daniel as he could, and behind him stood his twenty men with matchlocks. Not a man of them under six feet. I was next to Dravot, and behind me was twenty men of the regular Army. Up comes the girl, and a strapping wench she was, covered with silver and turquoises but white as death, and looking back every minute at the priests.

" 'She'll do,' said Dan, looking her over. 'What's to be afraid of, lass? Come and kiss me.' He puts his arm round her. She shuts her eyes, gives a bit of a squeak, and down goes her face in the side of Dan's flaming red beard.

" 'That slut's bitten me!' says he, clapping his hand to his neck, and, sure enough, his hand was red with blood. Billy Fish and two of his matchlock-men catches hold of Dan by the shoulders and drags him into the Bashkai lot, while the priests howls in their lingo.—'Neither God nor Devil but a man!' I was all taken aback, for a priest cut at me in front, and the Army began firing into the Bashkai men.

" 'God A'mighty!' says Dan. 'What is the meaning o' this?'

" 'Come back! Come away!' says Billy Fish. 'Ruin and Mutiny is the matter. We'll break for Bashkai if we can.'

"I tried to give some sort of orders to my men—the men of the regular Army—but it was no use, so I fired into the brown of 'em with an English Marti-ni and drilled three beggars in a line. The valley was full of shouting, howling creatures, and every soul was shrieking, 'Not a God nor a Devil but only a man!' The Bashkai troops stuck to Billy Fish all they were worth, but their matchlocks wasn't half as good as the Kabul breech-loaders, and four of them dropped. Dan was bellowing like a bull, for he was very wrathy; and Billy Fish had a hard job to prevent him running out at the crowd.

" 'We can't stand,' says Billy Fish. 'Make a run for it down the valley! The whole place is against us.' The matchlock-men ran, and we went down the valley in spite of Dravot. He was swearing horrible and crying out he was a King. The priests rolled great stones on us, and the regular Army fired hard, and there wasn't more than six men, not counting Dan, Billy Fish, and Me, that came down to the bottom of the valley alive.

"Then they stopped firing and the horns in the temple blew again. 'Come away—for Gord's sake come away!' says Billy Fish. 'They'll send runners out to all the villages before ever we get to Bashkai. I can protect you there, but I can't do anything now.'

"My own notion is that Dan began to go mad in his head from that hour. He stared up and down like a stuck pig. Then he was all for walking back alone and killing the priests with his bare hands; which he could have done. 'An Emperor I am,' says Daniel, 'and next year I shall be a Knight of the Queen.'

" 'All right, Dan.' says I; 'but come along now while there's time.'

" 'It's your fault,' says he, 'for not looking after your Army better. There was mutiny in the midst, and you didn't know—you damned engine-driving, plate-laying, missionary's-pass-hunting-hound!' He sat upon a rock and called me every foul name he could lay tongue to. I was too heart-sick to care, though it was all his foolishness that brought the smash.

" 'I'm sorry, Dan,' says I, 'but there's no accounting for natives. This business is our Fifty-seven.[12] Maybe we'll make something out of it yet, when we've got to Bashkai.'

" 'Let's get to Bashkai, then,' says Dan, 'and, by God, when I come back here again I'll sweep the valley so there isn't a bug in a blanket left.'

"We walked all that day, and all that night Dan was stumping up and down on the snow, chewing his beard and muttering to himself.

[12] The mutiny of the native Indian army in 1857, after which the British Crown took over rule of India from the East India Company.

" 'There's no hope o' getting clear,' said Billy Fish. 'The priests will have sent runners to the villages to say that you are only men. Why didn't you stick on as Gods till things was more settled? I'm a dead man,' says Billy Fish, and he throws himself down on the snow and begins to pray to his Gods.

"Next morning we was in a cruel bad country—all up and down, no level ground at all, and no food either. The six Bashkai men looked at Billy Fish hungry-way as if they wanted to ask something, but they said never a word. At noon we came to the top of a flat mountain all covered with snow, and when we climbed up into it, behold, there was an Army in position waiting in the middle!

" 'The runners have been very quick,' says Billy Fish, with a little bit of a laugh. 'They are waiting for us.'

"Three or four men began to fire from the enemy's side, and a chance shot took Daniel in the calf of the leg. That brought him to his senses. He looks across the snow at the Army, and sees the rifles that we had brought into the country.

" 'We're done for,' says he. 'They are Englishmen, these people:—and it's my blasted nonsense that has brought you to this. Get back, Billy Fish, and take your men away; you've done what you could, and now cut for it. Carnehan,' says he, 'shake hands with me and go along with Billy. Maybe they won't kill you. I'll go and meet 'em alone. It's me that did it. Me, the King!'

" 'Go!' says I. 'Go to Hell, Dan. I'm with you here, Billy Fish, you clear out, and we two will meet those folk.'

" 'I'm a Chief,' says Billy Fish, quite quiet. 'I stay with you. My men can go.'

"The Bashkai fellows didn't wait for a second word but ran off, and Dan and Me and Billy Fish walked across to where the drums were drumming and the horns were horning. It was cold—awful cold. I've got that cold in the back of my head now. There's a lump of it there."

The punkah-coolies had gone to sleep. Two kerosene lamps were blazing in the office, and the perspiration poured down my face and splashed on the blotter as I leaned forward. Carnehan was shivering, and I feared that his mind might go. I wiped my face, took a fresh grip of the piteously mangled hands, and said, "What happened after that?"

The momentary shift of my eyes had broken the clear current.

"What was you pleased to say?" whined Carnehan. "They took them without any sound. Not a little whisper all along the snow, not though the King knocked down the first man that set hand on him—not though old Peachey fired his last cartridge into the brown of 'em. Not a single solitary sound did those swines make. They just closed up tight, and I tell you their furs stunk. There was a man called Billy Fish, a good friend of us all, and they cut his throat, Sir, then and there, like a pig; and the King kicks up the bloody snow and says: 'We've had a dashed fine run for our money. What's coming next?' But Peachey, Peachey Taliaferro, I tell you, Sir, in confidence as betwixt two friends, he lost his head, Sir. No, he didn't neither. The King lost his head, so he did all along o' one of those cunning rope-bridges. Kindly let me have the paper-cutter, Sir. It tilted this way. They marched him a mile across that snow to a rope-bridge over a ravine with a river at the bottom. You may have seen such. They prodded him behind like an ox. 'Damn your eyes!' says the King. 'D'you suppose I can't die like a gentleman?' He turns to Peachey—Peachey that was crying like a child. 'I've brought you to this, Peachey,' says he. 'Brought you out of your happy life to be killed in Kafiristan where you was late Commander-in-Chief of the Emperor's forces. Say you forgive me, Peachey.'—'I do,' says Peachey. 'Fully and freely do I forgive you, Dan.'—'Shake hands, Peachey,' says he. 'I'm going now.' Out he goes, looking neither right nor left, and when he was plumb in the middle of those dizzy dancing ropes,—'Cut, you beggars,' he shouts, and they cut, and old Dan fell, turning round and round and round, twenty thousand miles, for he took half an hour to fall till he struck the water, and I could see his body caught on a rock with the gold crown close beside.

"But do you know what they did to Peachey between two pine-trees? They crucified him, Sir, as Peachey's hands will show. They used wooden pegs for his hands and feet; and he didn't die. He hung there and screamed, and they took him down next day, and said it was a miracle that he wasn't dead. They took him down—poor old Peachey that hadn't done them any harm—that hadn't done them any—"

He rocked to and fro and wept bitterly, wiping his eyes with the back of his scarred hands and moaning like a child for some ten minutes.

"They was cruel enough to feed him up in the temple, because they said he was more of a God than old Daniel that was a man. Then they turned him out on the snow, and told him to go home, and Peachey came home in about a year, begging along the roads quite safe; for Daniel Dravot he walked before and said: 'Come along, Peachey. It's a big thing we're doing.' The mountains they danced at night, and the mountains they tried to fall on Peachey's head, but Dan he held up his hand, and Peachey came along bent double. He never let go of Dan's hand, and he never let go of Dan's head. They gave it to him as a present in the temple, to remind him not to come again, and though the crown was pure gold, and Peachey was starving, never could Peachey sell the same. You knew Dravot, Sir! You knew Right Worshipful Brother Dravot! Look at him now!"

He fumbled in the mass of rags round his bent waist; brought out a black horsehair bag embroidered with silver thread; and shook therefrom on to my table—the dried, withered head of Daniel Dravot! The morning sun that had long been paling the lamps struck the red beard and blind sunken eyes; struck, too, a heavy circlet of gold studded with raw turquoises, that Carnehan placed tenderly on the battered temples.

"You be'old now," said Carnehan, "the Emperor in his 'abit as he lived—the King of Kafiristan with his crown upon his head. Poor old Daniel that was a monarch once!"

I shuddered, for, in spite of defacements manifold, I recognized the head of the man of Marwar Junction. Carnehan rose to go. I attempted to stop him. He was not fit to walk abroad. "Let me take away the whiskey, and give me a little money," he gasped. "I was a King once. I'll go to the Deputy Commissioner and ask to set in the Poorhouse till I get my health. No, thank you, I can't wait till you get a carriage for me. I've urgent private affairs—in the south—at Marwar."

He shambled out of the office and departed in the direction of the Deputy Commissioner's house. That day at noon I had occasion to go down the blinding hot Mall, and I saw a crooked man crawling along the white dust of the roadside, his hat in his hand, quavering dolorously after the fashion of street-singers at Home. There was not a soul in sight, and he was out of all possible earshot of the houses. And he sang through his nose, turning his head from right to left:—

"The Son of Man goes forth to war,
A golden crown to gain;
His blood-red banner streams afar—
Who follows in his train?"

I waited to hear no more, but put the poor wretch into my carriage and drove him off to the nearest missionary for eventual transfer to the Asylum. He repeated the hymn twice while he was with me whom he did not in the least recognize, and I left him singing it to the missionary.

Two days later I inquired after his welfare of the Superintendent of the Asylum.

"He was admitted suffering from sun-stroke. He died early yesterday morning," said the Superintendent. "Is it true that he was half an hour bare-headed in the sun at midday?"

"Yes," said I, "but do you happen to know if he had anything upon him by any chance when he died?"

"Not to my knowledge," said the Superintendent.

And there the matter rests.

CHAPTER 2

The Narrator as Participant

Narrating a personal experience, you adopt the grammatical first person, using the pronoun "I" as focal point. "I came, I saw, I conquered," wrote Julius Caesar to begin the history of his *Gallic War*. Creating fiction, a writer sometimes invents an "I" to narrate, appropriating for the world of make-believe the authority you command when you narrate your true experience, or Caesar commanded when he narrated his. "I was there, I saw it happen": the first-person perspective helps the fiction work its magic. The "I" thus created may serve as *protagonist*, the hero or main character of the story, or as *participant*, filling a smaller role. Sometimes he is merely an *observer*. Whatever his position, the narrator's invented personality has sometimes a crucial effect.

A first-person narration limits the reader's understanding of the story. We know only what the narrator knows, or has chosen to tell. Caesar's report may not be in all respects as the Gauls would have it. A fictional narrator, too, shapes and interprets according to the dictates of his personality; the story might be different from another viewpoint. Often, the time between the event and the narration is important: a report long after leaves time for reflection that perhaps changes attitudes or understanding.

In "The Tell-Tale Heart," Poe's narrator is the protagonist of his story. The *antagonist*, or opposing character, is an old man with an evil eye and a loud-beating heart. But is the old man's eye truly evil? Does his heart really beat so loudly? We have only the word of the narrator.

THE TELL-TALE HEART
Edgar Allan Poe   (1809–1849)

True!—nervous—very, very dreadfully nervous I had been and am; but why *will* you say that I am mad? The disease had sharpened my senses—not destroyed—not dulled them. Above all was the sense of hearing acute. I heard all things in the heaven and in the earth. I heard many things in hell. How, then, am I mad? Hearken! and observe how healthily—how calmly I can tell you the whole story.

It is impossible to say how first the idea entered my brain; but once conceived, it haunted me day and night. Object there was none. Passion there was none. I loved the old man. He had never wronged me. He had never given me insult. For his gold I had no desire. I think it was his eye! yes, it was this! He had the eye of a vulture—a pale blue eye, with a film over it. Whenever it fell upon me, my blood ran cold; and so by degrees—very gradually—I made up my mind to take the life of the old man, and thus rid myself of the eye forever.

Now this is the point. You fancy me mad. Madmen know nothing. But you should have seen *me*. You should have seen how wisely I proceeded—with what caution—with what foresight—with what dissimulation I went to work! I was never kinder to the old man than during the whole week before I killed him. And every night, about midnight, I turned the latch of his door and opened it— oh so gently! And then, when I had made an opening sufficient for my head, I put in a dark lantern, all closed, closed, so that no light shone out, and then I thrust in my head. Oh, you would have laughed to see how cunningly I thrust it in! I moved it slowly—very, very slowly, so that I might not disturb the old man's sleep. It took me an hour to place my whole head within the opening so far that I could see him as he lay upon his bed. Ha!—would a madman have been so wise as this? And then, when my head was well within the room, I undid the lantern cautiously—oh, so cautiously—cautiously (for the hinges creaked)—I un- did it just so much that a single thin ray fell upon the vulture eye. And this I did for seven long nights—every night just at midnight—but I found the eye always closed; and so it was impossible to do the work; for it was not the old man who vexed me, but his Evil Eye. And every morning, when the day broke, I went boldly into the chamber, and spoke courageously to him, calling him by name in a hearty tone, and inquiring how he had passed the night. So you see he would have been a very profound old man indeed, to suspect that every night, just at twelve, I looked in upon him while he slept.

Upon the eighth night I was more than usually cautious in opening the door. A watch's minute hand moves more quickly than did mine. Never before that night, had I *felt* the extent of my own powers—of my sagacity. I could scarcely contain my feelings of triumph. To think that there I was, opening the door, lit- tle by little, and he not even to dream of my secret deeds or thoughts. I fairly chuckled at the idea; and perhaps he heard me; for he moved on the bed sudden- ly, as if startled. Now you may think that I drew back—but no. His room was black as pitch with the thick darkness, (for the shutters were close fastened, through fear of robbers,) and so I knew that he could not see the opening of the door, and I kept pushing it on steadily, steadily.

I had my head in, and was about to open the lantern, when my thumb slipped upon the tin fastening, and the old man sprang up in bed, crying out—"Who's there?"

I kept quite still and said nothing. For a whole hour I did not move a muscle, and in the meantime I did not hear him lie down. He was still sitting up in the bed listening;—just as I have done, night after night, hearkening to the death watches in the wall.

Presently I heard a slight groan, and I knew it was the groan of mortal terror. It was not a groan of pain or of grief—oh, no!—it was the low stifled sound that arises from the bottom of the soul when overcharged with awe. I knew the sound well. Many a night, just at midnight, when all the world slept, it has welled up from my own bosom, deepening, with its dreadful echo, the terrors that distracted me. I say I knew it well. I knew what the old man felt, and pitied him, although I chuckled at heart. I knew that he had been lying awake ever since the first slight noise, when he had turned in the bed. His fears had been ever since growing upon him. He had been trying to fancy them causeless, but could not. He had been saying to himself—"It is nothing but the wind in the chimney—it is only a mouse crossing the floor," or "it is merely a cricket which has made a single chirp." Yes, he had been trying to comfort himself with these suppositions: but he had found all in vain. *All in vain;* because Death, in approaching him had stalked with his black shadow before him, and enveloped the victim. And it was the mournful influence of the unperceived shadow that caused him to feel—although he neither saw nor heard—to *feel* the presence of my head within the room.

When I had waited a long time, very patiently, without hearing him lie down, I resolved to open a little—a very, very little crevice in the lantern. So I opened it—you cannot imagine how stealthily, stealthily—until, at length, a simple dim ray, like the thread of the spider, shot from out the crevice and fell full upon the vulture eye.

It was open—wide, wide open—and I grew furious as I gazed upon it. I saw it with perfect distinctness—all dull blue, with a hideous veil over it that chilled the very marrow in my bones; but I could see nothing else of the old man's face or person: for I had directed the ray as if by instinct, precisely upon the damned spot.

And have I not told you that what you mistake for madness is but over acuteness of the senses?—now, I say, there came to my ears a low, dull, quick sound, such as a watch makes when enveloped in cotton. I knew *that* sound well, too. It was ths beating of the old man's heart. It increased my fury, as the beating of a drum stimulates the soldier into courage.

But even yet I refrained and kept still. I scarcely breathed. I held the lantern motionless. I tried how steadily I could maintain the ray upon the eye. Meantime the hellish tatoo of the heart increased. It grew quicker and quicker, and louder and louder every instant. The old man's terror *must* have been extreme! It grew louder, I say, louder every moment!—do you mark me well? I have told you that I am nervous: so I am. And now at the dead hour of the night, amid the dreadful silence of that old house, so strange a noise as this excited me to uncontrollable terror. Yet, for some minutes longer I refrained and stood still. But the beating grew louder, louder! I thought the heart must burst. And now a new anxiety seized me—the sound would be heard by a neighbour! The old man's hour had come! With a loud yell, I threw open the lantern and leaped into the room. He shrieked once—once only. In an instant I dragged him to the floor, and pulled the heavy bed over him. I then smiled gaily, to find the deed so far done. But, for many minutes, the heart beat on with a muffled sound. This, however, did not vex me; it would not be heard through the wall. At length it ceased. The old man was dead. I removed the bed and examined the corpse. Yes, he was stone, stone dead. I placed my hand upon the heart and held it there many minutes. There was no pulsation. He was stone dead. His eye would trouble me no more.

If still you think me mad, you will think so no longer when I describe the wise precautions I took for the concealment of the body. The night waned, and I worked hastily, but in silence. First of all I dismembered the corpse. I cut off the head and the arms and the legs.

I then took up three planks from the flooring of the chamber, and deposited all between the scantlings. I then replaced the boards so cleverly, so cunningly, that no human eye—not even *his*—could have detected any thing wrong. There was nothing to wash out—no stain of any kind—no blood-spot whatever. I had been too wary for that. A tub had caught all—ha! ha!

When I had made an end of these labors, it was four o'clock—still dark as midnight. As the bell sounded the hour, there came a knocking at the street door. I went down to open it with a light heart,—for what had I *now* to fear? There entered three men, who introduced themselves, with perfect suavity, as officers of the police. A shriek had been heard by a neighbor during the night; suspicion of foul play had been aroused; information had been lodged at the police office, and they (the officers) had been deputed to search the premises.

I smiled,—for *what* had I to fear? I bade the gentlemen welcome. The shriek, I said, was my own in a dream. The old man, I mentioned, was absent in the country. I took my visitors all over the house. I bade them search—search *well*. I led them, at length, to *his* chamber. I showed them his treasures, secure, undisturbed. In the enthusiasm of my confidence, I brought chairs into the room, and desired them *here* to rest from their fatigues, while I myself, in the wild audacity of my perfect triumph, placed my own seat upon the very spot beneath which reposed the corpse of the victim.

The officers were satisfied. My *manner* had convinced them. I was singularly at ease. They sat, and while I answered cheerily, they chatted of familiar things. But, ere long, I felt myself getting pale and wished them gone. My head ached, and I fancied a ringing in my ears: but still they sat and still chatted. The ringing became more distinct:—it continued and became more distinct: I talked more freely to get rid of the feeling: but it continued and gained definiteness—until, at length, I found that the noise was *not* within my ears.

No doubt I now grew *very* pale;—but I talked more fluently, and with a heightened voice. Yet the sound increased—and what could I do? It was *a low, dull, quick sound—much such a sound as a watch makes when enveloped in cotton.* I gasped for breath—and yet the officers heard it not. I talked more quickly—more vehemently; but the noise steadily increased. I arose and argued about trifles, in a high key and with violent gesticulations; but the noise steadily increased. Why *would* they not be gone? I paced the floor to and fro with heavy strides, as if excited to fury by the observations of the men—but the noise steadily increased. Oh God! what *could* I do? I foamed—I raved—I swore! I swung the chair upon which I had been sitting, and grated it upon the boards, but the noise arose over all and continually increased. It grew louder—louder—*louder!* And still the men chatted pleasantly, and smiled. Was it possible they heard not? Almighty God!— no, no! They heard!—they suspected!—they *knew!*—they were making a mockery out of my horror—this I thought, and this I think. But anything was better than this agony! Anything was more tolerable than this derision! I could bear those hypocritical smiles no longer! I felt that I must scream or die! and now—again!— hark! louder! louder! louder! *louder!*

"Villains!" I shrieked, "dissemble no more. I admit the deed!—tear up the planks! here, here!—it is the beating of his hideous heart!"

In "The Yellow Wall-Paper" we again have a protagonist as narrator, but there is no antagonist, unless it is the husband, John.

THE YELLOW WALL-PAPER
Charlotte Perkins Gilman   (1860–1935)

It is very seldom that mere ordinary people like John and myself secure ancestral halls for the summer.

A colonial mansion, a hereditary estate, I would say a haunted house, and reach the height of romantic felicity—but that would be asking too much of fate!

Still I will proudly declare that there is something queer about it.

Else, why should it be let so cheaply? And why have stood so long untenanted?

John laughs at me, of course, but one expects that in marriage.

John is practical in the extreme. He has no patience with faith, an intense horror of superstition, and he scoffs openly at any talk of things not to be felt and seen and put down in figures.

John is a physician, and *perhaps*—(I would not say it to a living soul, of course, but this is dead paper and a great relief to my mind)—*perhaps* that is one reason I do not get well faster.

You see he does not believe I am sick! And what can one do?

If a physician of high standing, and one's own husband, assures friends and relatives that there is really nothing the matter with one but temporary nervous depression—a slight hysterical tendency—what is one to do?

My brother is also a physician, and also of high standing, and he says the same thing.

So I take phosphates or phosphites—whichever it is—and tonics, and journeys, and air, and exercise, and am absolutely forbidden to "work" until I am well again.

Personally, I disagree with their ideas.

Personally, I believe that congenial work, with excitement and change, would do me good.

But what is one to do?

I did write for a while in spite of them; but it *does* exhaust me a good deal—having to play so sly about it, or else meet with heavy opposition.

I sometimes fancy that in my condition if I had less opposition and more society and stimulus—but John says the very worst thing I can do is to think about my condition, and I confess it always makes me feel bad.

So I will let it alone and talk about the house.

The most beautiful place! It is quite alone, standing well back from the road, quite three miles from the village. It makes me think of English places that you read about, for there are hedges and walls and gates that lock, and lots of separate little houses for the gardeners and people.

There is a *delicious* garden! I never saw such a garden—large and shady, full of box-bordered paths, and lined with long grape-covered arbors with seats under them.

There were greenhouses, too, but they are all broken now.

There was some legal trouble, I believe, something about the heirs and co-heirs; anyhow, the place has been empty for years.

That spoils my ghostliness, I am afraid, but I don't care—there is something strange about the house—I can feel it.

I even said so to John one moonlight evening, but he said what I felt was a draught, and shut the window.

I get unreasonably angry with John sometimes. I'm sure I never used to be so sensitive. I think it is due to this nervous condition.

But John says if I feel so I shall neglect proper self-control; so I take pains to control myself—before him, at least, and that makes me very tired.

I don't like our room a bit. I wanted one downstairs that opened on the piazza and had roses all over the window, and such pretty old-fashioned chintz hangings! But John would not hear of it.

He said there was only one window and not room for two beds, and no near room for him if he took another.

He is very careful and loving, and hardly lets me stir without special direction.

I have a schedule prescription for each hour in the day; he takes all care from me, and so I feel basely ungrateful not to value it more.

He said we came here solely on my account, that I was to have perfect rest and all the air I could get. "Your exercise depends on your strength, my dear," said he, "and your food somewhat on your appetite; but air you can absorb all the time." So we took the nursery at the top of the house.

It is a big, airy room, the whole floor nearly, with windows that look all ways, and air and sunshine galore. It was nursery first and then playroom and gymnasium, I should judge; for the windows are barred for little children, and there are rings and things in the walls.

The paint and paper look as if a boys' school had used it. It is stripped off—the paper—in great patches all around the head of my bed, about as far as I can reach, and in a great place on the other side of the room low down. I never saw a worse paper in my life.

One of those sprawling flamboyant patterns committing every artistic sin.

It is dull enough to confuse the eye in following, pronounced enough constantly to irritate and provoke study, and when you follow the lame certain curves for a little distance they suddenly commit suicide—plunge off at outrageous angles, destroy themselves in unheard of contradictions.

The color is repellant, almost revolting; a smouldering unclean yellow, strangely faded by the slow-turning sunlight.

It is a dull yet lurid orange in some places, a sickly sulphur tint in others.

No wonder the children hated it! I should hate it myself if I had to live in this room long.

There comes John, and I must put this away—he hates to have me write a word.

• • •

We have been here two weeks, and I haven't felt like writing before, since that first day.

I am sitting by the window now, up in this atrocious nursery, and there is nothing to hinder my writing as much as I please, save lack of strength.

John is away all day, and even some nights when his cases are serious.

I am glad my case is not serious!

But these nervous troubles are dreadfully depressing.

John does not know how much I really suffer. He knows there is no *reason* to suffer, and that satisfies him.

Of course it is only nervousness. It does weigh on me so not to do my duty in any way!

I meant to be such a help to John, such a real rest and comfort, and here I am a comparative burden already!

Nobody would believe what an effort it is to do what little I am able—to dress and entertain, and order things.

It is fortunate that Mary is so good with the baby. Such a dear baby!

And yet I *cannot* be with him, it makes me so nervous.

I suppose John never was nervous in his life. He laughs at me so about this wall-paper!

At first he meant to repaper the room, but afterwards he said that I was letting it get the better of me, and that nothing was worse for a nervous patient than to give way to such fancies.

He said that after the wall-paper was changed it would be the heavy bedstead, and then the barred windows, and then the gate at the head of the stairs, and so on.

"You know the place is doing you good," he said, "and really, dear, I don't care to renovate the house just for a three months' rental."

"Then do let me go downstairs," I said, "there are such pretty rooms there."

Then he took me in his arms and called me a blessed little goose, and said he would go down cellar, if I wished, and have it whitewashed into the bargain.

But he is right enough about the beds and windows and things.

It is an airy and comfortable room as any one need wish, and, of course, I would not be so silly as to make him uncomfortable just for a whim.

I'm really getting quite fond of the big room, all but that horrid paper.

Out of one window I can see the garden, those mysterious deep-shaded arbors, the riotous old-fashioned flowers, and bushes and gnarly trees.

Out of another I get a lovely view of the bay and a little private wharf belonging to the estate. There is a beautiful shaded lane that runs down there from the house. I always fancy I see people walking these numerous paths and arbors, but John has cautioned me not to give way to fancy in the least. He says that with my imaginative power and habit of story-making, a nervous weakness like mine is sure to lead to all manner of excited fancies, and that I ought to try to use my will and good sense to check the tendency. So I try.

I think sometimes that if I were only well enough to write a little it would relieve the press of ideas and rest me.

But I find I get pretty tired when I try.

It is so discouraging not to have any advice and companionship about my work. When I get really well, John says, we will ask Cousin Henry and Julia down for a long visit; but he says he would as soon put fireworks in my pillow-case as to let me have those stimulating people about now.

I wish I could get well faster.

But I must not think about that. This paper looks to me as if it *knew* what a vicious influence it had!

There is a recurrent spot where the pattern lolls like a broken neck and two bulbous eyes stare at you upside down.

I get positively angry with the impertinence of it and the everlastingness. Up and down and sideways they crawl, and those absurd, unblinking eyes are everywhere. There is one place where two breadths didn't match, and the eyes go all up and down the line, one a little higher than the other.

I never saw so much expression in an inanimate thing before, and we all know how much expression they have! I used to lie awake as a child and get more entertainment and terror out of blank walls and plain furniture than most children could find in a toy-store.

I remember what a kindly wink the knobs of our big, old bureau used to have, and there was one chair that always seemed like a strong friend.

I used to feel that if any of the other things looked too fierce I could always hop into that chair and be safe.

The furniture in this room is no worse than unharmonious, however, for we had to bring it all from downstairs. I suppose when this was used as a playroom they had to take the nursery things out, and no wonder! I never saw such ravages as the children have made here.

The wall-paper, as I said before, is torn off in spots, and it sticketh closer than a brother—they must have had perseverance as well as hatred.

Then the floor is scratched and gouged and splintered, the plaster itself is dug out here and there, and this great heavy bed which is all we found in the room, looks as if it had been through the wars.

But I don't mind it a bit—only the paper.

There comes John's sister. Such a dear girl she is, and so careful of me! I must not let her find me writing.

She is a perfect and enthusiastic housekeeper, and hopes for no better profession. I verily believe she thinks it is the writing which made me sick!

But I can write when she is out, and see her a long way off from these windows.

There is one that commands the road, a lovely shaded winding road, and one that just looks off over the country. A lovely country, too, full of great elms and velvet meadows.

This wall-paper has a kind of sub-pattern in a different shade, a particularly irritating one, for you can only see it in certain lights, and not clearly then.

But in the places where it isn't faded and where the sun is just so—I can see a strange, provoking, formless sort of figure, that seems to skulk about behind that silly and conspicuous front design.

There's sister on the stairs!

• • •

Well, the Fourth of July is over! The people are all gone and I am tired out. John thought it might do me good to see a little company, so we just had mother and Nellie and the children down for a week.

Of course I didn't do a thing. Jennie sees to everything now.

But it tired me all the same.

John says if I don't pick up faster he shall send me to Weir Mitchell[1] in the fall.

But I don't want to go there at all. I had a friend who was in his hands once, and she says he is just like John and my brother, only more so!

Besides, it is such an undertaking to go so far.

I don't feel as if it was worth while to turn my hand over for anything, and I'm getting dreadfully fretful and querulous.

I cry at nothing, and cry most of the time.

Of course I don't when John is here, or anybody else, but when I am alone.

And I am alone a good deal now. John is kept in town very often by serious cases, and Jennie is good and lets me alone when I want her to.

So I walk a little in the garden or down that lovely lane, sit on the porch under the roses, and lie down up here a good deal.

I'm getting really fond of the room in spite of the wallpaper. Perhaps *because* of the wallpaper.

It dwells in my mind so!

I lie here on this great immovable bed—it is nailed down, I believe—and follow that pattern about by the hour. It is as good as gymnastics, I assure you. I start, we'll say, at the bottom, down in the corner over there where it has not been touched, and I determine for the thousandth time that I *will* follow that pointless pattern to some sort of a conclusion.

I know a little of the princple of design, and I know this thing is not arranged on any laws of radiation, or alternation, or repetition, or symmetry, or anything else that I ever heard of.

It is repeated, of course, by the breadths, but not otherwise.

Looked at in one way each breadth stands alone, the bloated curves and flourishes—a kind of "debased Romanesque" with delirium tremens—go waddling up and down in isolated columns of fatuity.

But, on the other hand, they connect diagonally, and the sprawling outlines run off in great slanting waves of optic horror, like a lot of wallowing sea-weeds in full chase.

The whole thing goes horizontally, too, at least it seems so, and I exhaust myself trying to distinguish the order of its going in that direction.

They have used a horizontal breadth for a frieze, and that adds wonderfully to the confusion.

There is one end of the room where it is almost intact, and there, when the crosslights fade and the low sun shines directly upon it, I can almost fancy radiation after all,—the interminable grotesques seem to form around a common centre and rush off in headlong plunges of equal distraction.

It makes me tired to follow it. I will take a nap I guess.

● ● ●

I don't know why I should write this.

I don't want to.

I don't feel able.

---

[1] Silas Weir Mitchell (1829-1914), an internationally known neurologist who was also a well-known novelist.

And I know John would think it absurd. But I *must* say what I feel and think in some way—it is such a relief!

But the effort is getting to be greater than the relief.

Half the time now I am awfully lazy, and lie down ever so much.

John says I mustn't lose my strength, and has me take cod liver oil and lots of tonics and things, to say nothing of ale and wine and rare meat.

Dear John! He loves me very dearly, and hates to have me sick. I tried to have a real earnest reasonable talk with him the other day, and tell him how I wish he would let me go and make a visit to Cousin Henry and Julia.

But he said I wasn't able to go, nor able to stand it after I got there; and I did not make out a very good case for myself, for I was crying before I had finished.

It is getting to be a great effort for me to think straight. Just this nervous weakness I suppose.

And dear John gathered me up in his arms, and just carried me upstairs and laid me on the bed, and sat by me and read to me till it tired my head.

He said I was his darling and his comfort and all he had, and that I must take care of myself for his sake, and keep well.

He says no one but myself can help me out of it, that I must use my will and self-control and not let any silly fancies run away with me.

There's one comfort, the baby is well and happy, and does not have to occupy this nursery with the horrid wallpaper.

If we had not used it, that blessed child would have! What a fortunate escape! Why, I wouldn't have a child of mine, an impressionable little thing, live in such a room for worlds.

I never thought of it before, but it is lucky that John kept me here after all, I can stand it so much easier than a baby, you see.

Of course I never mention it to them any more—I am too wise—but I keep watch for it all the same.

There are things in that paper that nobody knows but me, or ever will.

Behind that outside pattern the dim shapes get clearer every day.

It is always the same shape, only very numerous.

And it is like a woman stooping down and creeping about behind that pattern. I don't like it a bit. I wonder—I begin to think—I wish John would take me away from here!

● ● ●

It is so hard to talk with John about my case, because he is so wise, and because he loves me so.

But I tried it last night.

It was moonlight. The moon shines in all around just as the sun does.

I hate to see it sometimes, it creeps so slowly, and always comes in by one window or another.

John was asleep and I hated to waken him, so I kept still and watched the moonlight on that undulating wallpaper till I felt creepy.

The faint figure behind seemed to shake the pattern, just as if she wanted to get out.

I got up softly and went to feel and see if the paper *did* move, and when I came back John was awake.

"What is it, little girl?" he said. "Don't go walking about like that—you'll get cold."

I thought it was a good time to talk so I told him that I really was not gaining here, and that I wished he would take me away.

"Why darling!" said he, "our lease will be up in three weeks, and I can't see how to leave before.

"The repairs are not done at home, and I cannot possibly leave town just now. Of course if you were in any danger, I could and would, but you really are better, dear, whether you can see it or not. I am a doctor, dear, and I know. You are gaining flesh and color, your appetite is better, I feel really much easier about you."

"I don't weigh a bit more," said I, "nor as much; and my appetite may be better in the evening when you are here, but it is worse in the morning when you are away!"

"Bless her little heart!" said he with a big hug, "she shall be as sick as she pleases! But now let's improve the shining hours by going to sleep, and talk about it in the morning!"

"And you won't go away?" I asked gloomily.

"Why, how can I, dear? It is only three weeks more and then we will take a nice little trip of a few days while Jennie is getting the house ready. Really, dear, you are better!"

"Better in body perhaps—" I began, and stopped short, for he sat up straight and looked at me with such a stern, reproachful look that I could not say another word.

"My darling," said he, "I beg of you, for my sake and for our child's sake, as well as for your own, that you will never for one instant let that idea enter your mind! There is nothing so dangerous, so fascinating, to a temperament like yours. It is a false and foolish fancy. Can you not trust me as a physician when I tell you so?"

So of course I said no more on that score, and we went to sleep before long. He thought I was asleep first, but I wasn't, and lay there for hours trying to decide whether that front pattern and the back pattern really did move together or separately.

• • •

On a pattern like this, by daylight, there is a lack of sequence, a defiance of law, that is a constant irritant to a normal mind.

The color is hideous enough, and unreliable enough, and infuriating enough, but the pattern is torturing.

You think you have mastered it, but just as you get well underway in following, it turns a back-somersault and there you are. It slaps you in the face, knocks you down, and tramples upon you. It is like a bad dream.

The outside pattern is a florid arabesque, reminding one of a fungus. If you can imagine a toadstool in joints, an interminable string of toadstools, budding and sprouting in endless convolutions—why, that is something like it.

That is, sometimes!

There is one marked peculiarity about this paper, a thing nobody seems to notice but myself, and that is that it changes as the light changes.

When the sun shoots in through the east window—I always watch for that first, long, straight ray—it changes so quickly that I never can quite believe it.

That is why I watch it always.

By moonlight—the moon shines in all night when there is a moon—I wouldn't know it was the same paper.

At night in any kind of light, in twilight, candlelight, lamplight, and worst of all by moonlight, it becomes bars! The outside pattern I mean, and the woman behind it is as plain as can be.

I didn't realize for a long time what the thing was that showed behind, that dim sub-pattern, but now I am quite sure it is a woman.

By daylight she is subdued, quiet. I fancy it is the pattern that keeps her so still. It is so puzzling. It keeps me quiet by the hour.

I lie down ever so much now. John says it is good for me, and to sleep all I can.

Indeed he started the habit by making me lie down for an hour after each meal.

It is a very bad habit I am convinced, for you see I don't sleep.

And that cultivates deceit, for I don't tell them I'm awake—O, no!

The fact is I am getting a little afraid of John.

He seems very queer sometimes, and even Jennie has an inexplicable look.

It strikes me occasionally, just as a scientific hypothesis, that perhaps it is the paper!

I have watched John when he did not know I was looking, and come into the room suddenly on the most innocent excuses, and I've caught him several times *looking at the paper!* And Jennie too. I caught Jennie with her hand on it once.

She didn't know I was in the room, and when I asked her in a quiet, a very quiet voice, with the most restrained manner possible, what she was doing with the paper—she turned around as if she had been caught stealing, and looked quite angry—asked me why I should frighten her so!

Then she said that the paper stained everything it touched, that she had found yellow smooches on all my clothes and John's, and she wished we would be more careful!

Did not that sound innocent? But I know she was studying that pattern, and I am determined that nobody shall find it out but myself!

•   •   •

Life is very much more exciting now than it used to be. You see I have something more to expect, to look forward to, to watch. I really do eat better, and am more quiet than I was.

John is so pleased to see me improve! He laughed a little the other day, and said I seemed to be flourishing in spite of my wallpaper.

I turned it off with a laugh. I had no intention of telling him it was *because* of the wallpaper—he would make fun of me. He might even want to take me away.

I don't want to leave now until I have found it out. There is a week more, and I think that will be enough.

•   •   •

I'm feeling ever so much better! I don't sleep much at night, for it is so interesting to watch developments; but I sleep a good deal in the daytime.

In the daytime it is tiresome and perplexing.

There are always new shoots on the fungus, and new shades of yellow all over it. I cannot keep count of them, though I have tried conscientiously.

It is the strangest yellow, that wallpaper! It makes me think of all the yellow things I ever saw—not beautiful ones like buttercups, but old foul, bad yellow things.

But there is something else about that paper—the smell! I noticed it the moment we came into the room, but with so much air and sun it was not bad. Now we have had a week of fog and rain, and whether the windows are open or not, the smell is here.

It creeps all over the house.

I find it hovering in the dining-room, skulking in the parlor, hiding in the hall, lying in wait for me on the stairs.

It gets into my hair.

Even when I go to ride, if I turn my head suddenly and surprise it—there is that smell!

Such a peculiar odor, too! I have spent hours in trying to analyze it, to find what it smelled like.

It is not bad—at first, and very gentle, but quite the subtlest, most enduring odor I ever met.

In this damp weather it is awful, I wake up in the night and find it hanging over me.

It used to disturb me at first. I thought seriously of burning the house—to reach the smell.

But now I am used to it. The only thing I can think of that it is like is the *color* of the paper! A yellow smell.

There is a very funny mark on this wall, low down, near the mopboard. A streak that runs round the room. It goes behind every piece of furniture, except the bed, a long, straight, even *smooch*, as if it had been rubbed over and over.

I wonder how it was done and who did it, and what they did it for. Round and round and round—round and round and round—it makes me dizzy!

• • •

I really have discovered something at last.

Through watching so much at night, when it changes so, I have finally found out.

The front pattern *does* move—and no wonder! The woman behind it shakes it!

Sometimes I think there are a great many women behind, and sometimes only one, and she crawls around fast, and her crawling shakes it all over.

Then in the very bright spots she keeps still, and in the very shady spots she just takes hold of the bars and shakes them hard.

And she is all the time trying to climb through. But nobody could climb through that pattern—it strangles so; I think that is why it has so many heads.

They get through, and then the pattern strangles them off and turns them upside down, and makes their eyes white!

If those heads were covered or taken off it would not be half so bad.

• • •

I think that woman gets out in the daytime!

And I'll tell you why—privately—I've seen her!

I can see her out of every one of my windows!

It is the same woman, I know, for she is always creeping, and most women do not creep by daylight.

I see her in that long shaded lane, creeping up and down. I see her in those dark grape arbors, creeping all around the garden.

I see her on that long road under the trees, creeping along, and when a carriage comes she hides under the blackberry vines.

I don't blame her a bit. It must be very humiliating to be caught creeping by daylight!

I always lock the door when I creep by daylight. I can't do it at night, for I know John would suspect something at once.

And John is so queer now, that I don't want to irritate him. I wish he would take another room! Besides, I don't want anybody to get that woman out at night but myself.

I often wonder if I could see her out of all the windows at once.

But, turn as fast as I can, I can only see out of one at one time.

And though I always see her, she *may* be able to creep faster than I can turn!

I have watched her sometimes away off in the open country, creeping as fast as a cloud shadow in a high wind.

•   •   •

If only that top pattern could be gotton off from the under one! I mean to try it, little by little.

I have found out another funny thing, but I shan't tell it this time! It does not do to trust people too much.

There are only two more days to get this paper off, and I believe John is beginning to notice. I don't like the look in his eyes.

And I heard him ask Jennie a lot of professional questions about me. She had a very good report to give.

She said I slept a good deal in the daytime.

John knows I don't sleep very well at night, for all I'm so quiet!

He asked me all sorts of questions, too, and pretended to be very loving and kind.

As if I couldn't see through him!

Still, I don't wonder he acts so, sleeping under this paper for three months.

It only interests me, but I feel sure John and Jennie are secretly affected by it.

•   •   •

Hurrah! This is the last day, but it is enough. John to stay in town over night, and won't be out this evening.

Jennie wanted to sleep with me—the sly thing! but I told her I should undoubtedly rest better for a night alone.

That was clever, for really I wasn't alone a bit! As soon as it was moonlight and that poor thing began to crawl and shake the pattern, I got up and ran to help her.

I pulled and she shook, I shook and she pulled, and before morning we had peeled off yards of that paper.

A strip about as high as my head and half around the room.

And then when the sun came and that awful pattern began to laugh at me, I declared I would finish it to-day!

We go away to-morrow, and they are moving all my furniture down again to leave things as they were before.

Jennie looked at the wall in amazement, but I told her merrily that I did it out of pure spite at the vicious thing.

She laughed and said she wouldn't mind doing it herself, but I must not get tired.

How she betrayed herself that time!

But I am here, and no person touches this paper but Me—not *alive!*

She tried to get me out of the room—it was too patent! But I said it was so quiet and empty and clean now that I believed I would lie down again and sleep all I could; and not to wake me even for dinner—I would call when I woke.

So now she is gone, and the servants are gone, and the things are gone, and there is nothing left but that great bedstead nailed down, with the canvas mattress we found on it.

We shall sleep downstairs to-night, and take the boat home to-morrow.

I quite enjoy the room, now it is bare again.

How those children did tear about here!

This bedstead is fairly gnawed!

But I must get to work.

I have locked the door and thrown the key down into the front path.

I don't want to go out, and I don't want to have anybody come in, till John comes.

I want to astonish him.

I've got a rope up here that even Jennie did not find. If that woman does get out, and tries to get away, I can tie her.

But I forgot I could not reach far without anything to stand on!

This bed will *not* move!

I tried to lift and push it until I was lame, and then I got so angry I bit off a little piece at one corner—but it hurt my teeth.

Then I peeled off all the paper I could reach standing on the floor. It sticks horribly and the pattern just enjoys it! All those strangled heads and bulbous eyes and waddling fungus growths just shriek with derision!

I am getting angry enough to do something desperate. To jump out of the window would be admirable exercise, but the bars are too strong even to try.

Besides I wouldn't do it. Of course not. I know well enough that a step like that is improper and might be misconstrued.

I don't like to *look* out of the windows even—there are so many of those creeping women, and they creep so fast.

I wonder if they all come out of that wallpaper as I did?

But I am securely fastened now by my well-hidden rope—you don't get *me* out in the road there!

I suppose I shall have to get back behind the pattern when it comes night, and that is hard!

It is so pleasant to be out in this great room and creep around as I please!

I don't want to go outside. I won't, even if Jennie asks me to.

For outside you have to creep on the ground, and everything is green instead of yellow.

But here I can creep smoothly on the floor, and my shoulder just fits in that long smooch around the wall, so I cannot lose my way.

Why there's John at the door!

It is no use, young man, you can't open it!

How he does call and pound!

Now he's crying for an axe.

It would be a shame to break down that beautiful door!

"John dear!" said I in the gentlest voice, "the key is down by the front steps, under a plantain leaf!"

That silenced him for a few moments.

Then he said, very quietly indeed, "Open the door, my darling!"

"I can't," said I. "The key is down by the front door under a plantain leaf!"

And then I said it again, several times, very gently and slowly, and said it so often that he had to go and see, and he got it of course, and came in. He stopped short by the door.

"What is the matter?" he cried. "For God's sake, what are you doing!"

I kept on creeping just the same, but I looked at him over my shoulder.

"I've got out at last," said I, "in spite of you and Jane. And I've pulled off most of the paper, so you can't put me back!"

Now why should that man have fainted? But he did, and right across my path by the wall, so that I had to creep over him every time!

QUESTIONS

1. "John is a physician," the narrator tells us, "and *perhaps*—(I would not say it to a living soul, of course, but this is dead paper and a great relief to my mind)—*perhaps* that is one reason I do not get well faster." What is meant here? Is there any evidence that the comment is accurate?

2. Characterize John as he is seen by the narrator. Does her attitude toward him change? Can we tell whether her characterization of him is fair?

3. Some of what the narrator reports is fantasy (the women behind the wallpaper, for instance). Has the author so controlled the point of view that we can always tell which details possess objective reality and which do not?

4. The subject of the story is madness. Is there an underlying *thematic idea* (central thought) about madness? Perhaps about madness in women?

The "I" narrator tells the truth, as best he can. If he is insane, like the narrator of "The Tell-Tale Heart" or "The Yellow Wall-Paper," his truth is distorted by his perceptions. In "I'm a Fool" the narrator is sane but has acted foolishly. He tells the story as honestly as he knows how.

I'M A FOOL

Sherwood Anderson (1876-1941)

It was a hard jolt for me, one of the most bitterest I ever had to face. And it all came about through my own foolishness, too. Even yet sometimes, when I think of it, I want to cry or swear or kick myself. Perhaps, even now, after all this time, there will be a kind of satisfaction in making myself look cheap by telling of it.

It began at three o'clock one October afternoon as I sat in the grandstand at the fall trotting and pacing meet at Sandusky, Ohio.

To tell the truth, I felt a little foolish that I should be sitting in the grandstand at all. During the summer before I had left my home town with Harry White-head and, with a nigger named Burt, had taken a job as swipe with one of the two horses Harry was campaigning through the fall race meets that year. Mother cried and my sister Mildred, who wanted to get a job as a school teacher in our town that fall, stormed and scolded about the house all during the week before I left. They both thought it something disgraceful that one of our family should take a place as a swipe with race horses. I've an idea Mildred thought my taking the place would stand in the way of her getting the job she'd been working so long for.

But after all I had to work, and there was no other work to be got. A big lum-bering fellow of nineteen couldn't just hang around the house and I had got too big to mow people's lawns and sell newspapers. Little chaps who could get next to people's sympathies by their sizes were always getting jobs away from me. There was one fellow who kept saying to everyone who wanted a lawn mowed or a cistern cleaned, that he was saving money to work his way through college, and I used to lay awake nights thinking up ways to injure him without being found out. I kept thinking of wagons running over him and bricks falling on his head as he walked along the street. But never mind him.

I got the place with Harry and I liked Burt fine. We got along splendid togeth-er. He was a big nigger with a lazy sprawling body and soft, kind eyes, and when it came to a fight he could hit like Jack Johnson. He had Bucephalus, a big black pacing stallion that could do 2.09 or 2.10, if he had to, and I had a little gelding named Doctor Fritz that never lost a race all fall when Harry wanted him to win.

We set out from home late in July in a box car with the two horses and after that, until late November, we kept moving along to the race meets and the fairs. It was a peachy time for me, I'll say that. Sometimes now I think that boys who are raised regular in houses, and never have a fine nigger like Burt for a best friend, and go to high schools and college, and never steal anything, or get drunk a little, or learn to swear from fellows who know how, or come walking up in front of a grandstand in their shirt sleeves and with dirty horsey pants on when the races are going on and the grandstand is full of people all dressed up— What's the use of talking about it? Such fellows don't know nothing at all. They've never had the opportunity.

But I did. Burt taught me how to rub down a horse and put the bandages on after a race and steam a horse out and a lot of valuable things for any man to know. He could wrap a bandage on a horse's leg so smooth that if it had been the same color you would think it was his skin, and I guess he's have been a big driver, too, and got to the top like Murphy and Walter Cox and the others if he hadn't been black.

Gee whizz, it was fun. You got to a county seat town, maybe say on a Saturday or Sunday, and the fair began the next Tuesday and lasted until Friday afternoon. Doctor Fritz would be, say in the 2.25 trot on Tuesday afternoon and on Thursday afternoon Bucephalus would knock 'em cold in the "free-for-all" pace. It left you a lot of time to hang around and listen to horse talk, and see Burt knock some yap cold that got too gay, and you'd find out about horses and men and pick up a lot of stuff you could use all the rest of your life, if you had some sense and salted down what you heard and felt and saw.

And then at the end of the week when the race meet was over, and Harry had run home to tend up to his livery stable business, you and Burt hitched the two horses to carts and drove slow and steady across country, to the place for the next meeting, so as to not overheat the horses, etc., etc., you know.

Gee whizz, Gosh amighty, the nice hickorynut and beechnut and oaks and other kinds of trees along the roads, all brown and red, and the good smells, and Burt singing a song that was called Deep River, and the country girls at the windows of houses and everything. You can stick your colleges up your nose for all me. I guess I know where I got my education.

Why, one of those little burgs of towns you come to on the way, say now on a Saturday afternoon, and Burt says, "let's lay up here." And you did.

And you took the horses to a livery stable and fed them, and you got your good clothes out of a box and put them on.

And the town was full of farmers gaping, because they could see you were race-horse people, and the kids maybe never see a nigger before and was afraid and run away when the two of us walked down their main street.

And that was before prohibition and all that foolishness, and so you went into a saloon, the two of you, and all the yaps came and stood around, and there was always someone pretended he was horsey and knew things and spoke up and began asking questions, and all you did was to lie and lie all you could about what horses you had, and I said I owned them, and then some fellow said, "will you have a drink of whisky" and Burt knocked his eye out the way he could say, off-handlike, "Oh well, all right, I'm agreeable to a little nip. I'll split a quart with you." Gee whizz.

But that isn't what I want to tell my story about. We got home late in November and I promised mother I'd quit the race horses for good. There's a lot of things you've got to promise a mother because she don't know any better.

And so, there not being any work in our town any more than when I left there to go to the races, I went off to Sandusky and got a pretty good place taking care of horses for a man who owned a teaming and delivery and storage and coal and real estate business there. It was a pretty good place with good eats, and a day off each week, and sleeping on a cot in a big barn, and mostly just shoveling in hay and oats to a lot of big good-enough skates of horses, that couldn't have trotted a race with a toad. I wasn't dissatisfied and I could send money home.

And then, as I started to tell you, the fall races came to Sandusky and I got the day off and I went. I left the job at noon and had on my good clothes and my new brown derby hat, I'd just bought the Saturday before, and a stand-up collar.

First of all I went downtown and walked about with the dudes. I've always thought to myself, "put up a good front" and so I did it. I had forty dollars in my pocket and so I went into the West House, a big hotel, and walked up to the cigar stand. "Give me three twenty-five cent cigars," I said. There was a lot of horsemen and strangers and dressed-up people from other towns standing around in the lobby and in the bar, and I mingled amongst them. In the bar there was a fellow with a cane and a Windsor tie on, that it made me sick to look at him. I like a man to be a man and dress up, but not to go put on that kind of airs. So I pushed him aside, kind of rough, and had me a drink of whisky. And then he looked at me, as though he thought maybe he'd get gay, but he changed his mind and didn't say anything. And then I had another drink of whisky, just to show him something, and went out and had a hack out to the races, all to myself, and when I got there I bought myself the best seat I could get up in the grandstand, but didn't go in for any of these boxes. That's putting on too many airs.

And so there I was, sitting up in the grandstand as gay as you please and looking down on the swipes coming out with their horses, and with their dirty horsey pants on and the horse blankets swung over their shoulders, same as I had been doing all the year before. I liked one thing about the same as the other, sitting up there and feeling grand and being down there and looking up at the yaps and feeling grander and more important, too. One thing's about as good as another, if you take it just right. I've often said that.

Well, right in front of me, in the grandstand that day, there was a fellow with a couple of girls and they was about my age. The young fellow was a nice guy all right. He was the kind maybe that goes to college and then comes to be a lawyer or maybe a newspaper editor or something like that, but he wasn't stuck on himself. There are some of that kind all right and he was one of the ones.

He had his sister with him and another girl and the sister looked around over his shoulder, accidental at first, not intending to start anything—she wasn't that kind—and her eyes and mine happened to meet.

You know how it is. Gee, she was a peach! She had on a soft dress, kind of a blue stuff and it looked carelessly made, but was well sewed and made and everything. I knew that much. I blushed when she looked right at me and so did she. She was the nicest girl I've ever seen in my life. She wasn't stuck on herself and she could talk proper grammar without being like a school teacher or something like that. What I mean is, she was O.K. I think maybe her father was well-to-do, but not rich to make her chesty because she was his daughter, as some are. Maybe he owned a drugstore or a drygoods store in their home town, or something like that. She never told me and I never asked.

My own people are all O.K. too, when you come to that. My grandfather was Welsh and over in the old country, in Wales he was—But never mind that.

The first heat of the first race come off and the young fellow setting there with the two girls left them and went down to make a bet. I knew what he was up to, but he didn't talk big and noisy and let everyone around know he was a sport, as some do. He wasn't that kind. Well, he come back and I heard him tell the two girls what horse he'd bet on, and when the heat was trotted they all half got to their feet and acted in the excited, sweaty way people do when they've got money down on a race, and the horse they bet on is up there pretty close at the end, and they think maybe he'll come on with a rush, but he never does because he hasn't got the old juice in him, come right down to it.

And then, pretty soon, the horses came out for the 2.18 pace and there was a horse in it I knew. He was a horse Bob French had in his string but Bob didn't own him. He was a horse owned by a Mr. Mathers down at Marietta, Ohio.

This Mr. Mathers had a lot of money and owned some coal mines or something, and he had a swell place out in the country, and he was stuck on race horses, but was a Presbyterian or something, and I think more than likely his wife was one, too, maybe a stiffer one than himself. So he never raced his horses hisself, and the story round the Ohio race tracks was that when one of his horses got ready to go to the races he turned him over to Bob French and pretended to his wife he was sold.

So Bob had the horses and he did pretty much as he pleased and you can't blame Bob, at least, I never did. Sometimes he was out to win and sometimes he wasn't. I never cared much about that when I was swiping a horse. What I did want to know was that my horse had the speed and could go out in front, if you wanted him to.

And, as I'm telling you, there was Bob in this race with one of Mr. Mather's horses, was named "About Ben Ahem" or something like that, and was fast as a streak. He was a gelding and had a mark of 2.21, but could step in .08 or .09.

Because when Burt and I were out, as I've told you, the year before, there was a nigger, Burt knew, worked for Mr. Mathers and we went out there one day when we didn't have no race on at the Marietta Fair and our boss Harry was gone home.

And so everyone was gone to the fair but just this one nigger and he took us all through Mr. Mather's swell house and he and Burt tapped a bottle of wine Mr. Mathers had hid in his bedroom, back in a closet, without his wife knowing, and he showed us this Ahem horse. Burt was always stuck on being a driver but didn't have much chance to get to the top, being a nigger, and he and the other nigger gulped that whole bottle of wine and Burt got a little lit up.

So the nigger let Burt take this About Ben Ahem and step him a mile in a track Mr. Mathers had all to himself, right there on the farm. And Mr. Mathers had one child, a daughter, kinda sick and not very good-looking, and she came home and we had to hustle and get About Ben Ahem stuck back in the barn.

I'm only telling you to get everything straight. At Sandusky, that afternoon I was at the fair, this young fellow with the two girls was fussed, being with the girls and losing his bet. You know how a fellow is that way. One of them was his girl and the other his sister. I had figured that out.

"Gee whizz," I says to myself, "I'm going to give him the dope."

He was mighty nice when I touched him on the shoulder. He and the girls were nice to me right from the start and clear to the end. I'm not blaming them.

And so he leaned back and I give him the dope on About Ben Ahem. "Don't bet a cent on this first heat because he'll go like an oxen hitched to a plow, but when the first heat is over go right down and lay on your pile." That's what I told him.

Well, I never saw a fellow treat anyone sweller. There was a fat man sitting beside the little girl, that had looked at me twice by this time, and I at her, and both blushing, and what did he do but have the nerve to turn and ask the fat man to get up and change places with me so I could set with his crowd.

Gee whizz, craps amighty. There I was. What a chump I was to go and get gay up there in the West House bar, and just becuase that dude was standing there with a cane and that kind of a necktie on, to go and get all balled up and drink that whisky, just to show off.

Of course she would know, me setting right beside her and letting her smell of my breath. I could have kicked myself right down out of that grandstand and all around that race track and made a faster record than most of the skates of horses they had there that year.

Because that girl wasn't any mutt of a girl. What wouldn't I have give right then for a stick of chewing gum to chew, or a lozenger, or some liquorice, or most anything. I was glad I had those twenty-five cent cigars in my pocket and right away I give that fellow one and lit one myself. Then that fat man got up and we changed places and there I was, plunked right down beside her.

They introduced themselves and the fellow's best girl, he had with him, was named Miss Elinor Woodbury, and her father was a manufacturer of barrels from a place called Tiffin, Ohio. And the fellow himself was named Wilbur Wessen and his sister was Miss Lucy Wessen.

I suppose it was their having such swell names got me off my trolley. A fellow, just because he has been a swipe with a race horse, and works taking care of horses for a man in the teaming, delivery, and storage business, isn't any better or worse than anyone else. I've often thought that, and said it too.

But you know how a fellow is. There's something in that kind of nice clothes, and the kind of nice eyes she had, and the way she had looked at me, awhile before, over her brother's shoulder, and me looking back at her, and both of us blushing.

I couldn't show her up for a boob, could I?

I made a fool of myself, that's what I did. I said my name was Walter Mathers from Marietta, Ohio, and then I told all three of them the smashingest lie you ever heard. What I said was that my father owned the horse About Ben Ahem and that he had let him out to this Bob French for racing purposes, because our family was proud and had never gone into racing that way, in our own name, I mean. Then I had got started and they were all leaning over and listening, and Miss Lucy Wessen's eyes were shining, and I went the whole hog.

I told about our place down at Marietta, and about the big stables and the grand brick house we had on a hill, up above the Ohio River, but I knew enough not to do it in no bragging way. What I did was to start things and then let them drag the rest out of me. I acted just as reluctant to tell as I could. Our family hasn't got any barrel factory, and, since I've known us, we've always been pretty poor, but not asking anything of anyone at that, and my grandfather, over in Wales—But never mind that.

We sat there talking like we had known each other for years and years, and I went and told them that my father had been expecting maybe this Bob French wasn't on the square, and had sent me up to Sandusky on the sly to find out what I could.

And I bluffed it through I had found out all about the 2.18 pace, in which About Ben Ahem was to start.

I said he would lose the first heat by pacing like a lame cow and then he would come back and skin 'em alive after that. And to back up what I said I took thirty dollars out of my pocket and handed it to Mr. Wilbur Wessen and asked him, would he mind, after the first heat, to go down and place it on About Ben Ahem for whatever odds he could get. What I said was that I didn't want Bob French to see me and none of the swipes.

Sure enough the first heat come off and About Ben Ahem went off his stride, up the back stretch, and looked like a wooden horse or a sick one, and come in to be last. Then this Wilbur Wessen went down to the betting place under the grandstand and there I was with the two girls, and when that Miss Woodbury was looking the other way once, Lucy Wessen kinda, with her shoulder you know, kinda touched me. Not just tucking down, I don't mean. You know how a woman can do. They get close, but not getting gay either. You know what they do. Gee whizz.

And then they give me a jolt. What they had done, when I didn't know, was to get together, and they had decided Wilbur Wessen would bet fifty dollars, and the two girls had gone and put in ten dollars each, of their own money, too. I was sick then, but I was sicker later.

About the gelding, About Ben Ahem, and their winning their money, I wasn't worried a lot about that. It come out O.K. Ahem stepped the next three heats like a bushel of spoiled eggs going to market before they could be found out, and Wilbur Wessen had got nine to two for the money. There was something else eating at me.

Because Wilbur come back, after he had bet the money, and after that he spent most of his time talking to that Miss Woodbury, and Lucy Wessen and I was left alone together like on a desert island. Gee, if I'd only been on the square or if there had been any way of getting myself on the square. There ain't any Walter Mathers, like I said to her and them, and there hasn't ever been one, but if there was, I bet I'd go to Marietta, Ohio, and shoot him tomorrow.

There I was, big boob that I am. Pretty soon the race was over, and Wilbur had gone down and collected our money, and we had a hack downtown, and he stood us a swell supper at the West House, and a bottle of champagne beside.

And I was with that girl and she wasn't saying much, and I wasn't saying much either. One thing I know. She wasn't stuck on me because of the lie about my father being rich and all that. There's a way you know. . . . Craps amighty. There's a kind of girl, you see just once in your life, and if you don't get busy and make hay, then you're gone for good and all, and might as well go jump off a bridge. They give you a look from inside of them somewhere, and it ain't no vamping, and what it means is—you want that girl to be your wife, and you want nice things around her like flowers and swell clothes, and you want her to have the kids you're going to have, and you want good music played and no ragtime. Gee whizz.

There's a place over near Sandusky, across a kind of bay, and it's called Cedar Point. And after we had supper we went over to it in a launch, all by ourselves. Wilbur and Miss Lucy and that Miss Woodbury had to catch a ten o'clock train back to Tiffin, Ohio, because when you're out with girls like that you can't get careless with some kinds of Janes.

And Wilbur blowed himself to the launch and it cost him fifteen cold plunks, but I wouldn't never have knew if I hadn't listened. He wasn't no tin horn kind of a sport.

Over at the Cedar Point place, we didn't stay around where there was a gang of common kind of cattle at all.

There was big dance halls and dining places for yaps, and there was a beach you could walk along and get where it was dark, and we went there.

She didn't talk hardly at all and neither did I, and I was thinking how glad I was my mother was all right, and always made us kids learn to eat with a fork at table, and not swill soup, and not be noisy and rough like a gang you see around a race track that way.

Then Wilbur and his girl went away up the beach and Lucy and I sat down in a dark place, where there was some roots of old trees, the water had washed up, and after that the time, till we had to go back in the launch and they had to catch their trains, wasn't nothing at all. It went like winking your eye.

Here's how it was. The place we were setting in was dark, like I said, and there was the roots from that old stump sticking up like arms, and there was a watery smell, and the night was like—as if you could put your hand out and feel it—so warm and soft and dark and sweet like an orange.

I most cried and I most swore and I most jumped up and danced, I was so mad and happy and sad.

When Wilbur come back from being alone with his girl, and she saw him coming, Lucy she says, "we got to go to the train now", and she was most crying too, but she never knew nothing I knew, and she couldn't be so all busted up. And then, before Wilbur and Miss Woodbury got up to where we was, she put her face up and kissed me quick and put her head up against me and she was all quivering and—Gee whizz.

Sometimes I hope I have cancer and die. I guess you know what I mean. We went in the launch across the bay to the train like that, and it was dark, too. She whispered and said it was like she and I could get out of the boat and walk on the water, and it sounded foolish, but I knew what she meant.

And then quick we were right at the depot, and there was a big gang of yaps, the kind that goes to the fairs, and crowded and milling around like cattle, and how could I tell her? "It won't be long because you'll write and I'll write to you." That's all she said.

I got a chance like a hay barn afire. A swell chance I got.

And maybe she would write me, down at Marietta that way, and the letter would come back, and stamped on the front of it by the U.S.A. "there ain't any such guy," or something like that, whatever they stamp on a letter that way.

And me trying to pass myself off for a bigbug and a swell—to her, as decent a little body as God ever made. Craps amighty—a swell chance I got!

And then the train come in, and she got on it, and Wilbur Wessen he come and shook hands with me, and that Miss Woodbury was nice too and bowed to me, and I at her, and the train went and I busted out and cried like a kid.

Gee, I could have run after that train and made Dan Patch look like a freight train after a wreck but, socks amighty, what was the use? Did you ever see such a fool?

I'll bet you what—if I had an arm broke right now or a train had run over my foot—I wouldn't go to no doctor at all. I'd go set down and let her hurt and hurt—that's what I'd do.

I'll bet you what—if I hadn't a drunk that booze I'd a never been such a boob as to go tell such a lie—that couldn't never be made straight to a lady like her.

I wish I had that fellow right here that had on a Windsor tie and carried a cane. I'd smash him for fair. Gosh darn his eyes. He's a big fool—that's what he is.

And if I'm not another you just go find me one and I'll quit working and be a bum and give him my job. I don't care nothing for working, and earning money, and saving it for no such boob as myself.

QUESTIONS

1. What has Anderson gained by adopting the point of view of the boy?
2. Characterize the narrator. He has been foolish, but is he a fool?
3. Why does he make so much of the man with the cane and the Windsor tie?
4. The narrator says of "boys who are raised regular in houses" that they "don't know nothing at all. They've never had no opportunity." Later he says: "You can stick your colleges up your nose for all me. I guess I know where I got my education." Sharing the narrator's perspective on the story, do we also share his opinions?

A MEMORY

Eudora Welty (1909–)

One summer morning when I was a child I lay on the sand after swimming in the small lake in the park. The sun beat down—it was almost noon. The water shone like steel, motionless except for the feathery curl behind a distant swimmer. From my position I was looking at a rectangle brightly lit, actually glaring at me, with sun, sand, water, a little pavilion, a few solitary people in fixed attitudes, and around it all a border of dark rounded oak trees, like the engraved thunderclouds surrounding illustrations in the Bible. Ever since I had begun taking painting lessons, I had made small frames with my fingers, to look out at everything.

Since this was a weekday morning, the only persons who were at liberty to be in the park were either children, who had nothing to occupy them, or those older people whose lives are obscure, irregular, and consciously of no worth to anything: this I put down as my observation at that time. I was at an age when I formed a judgment upon every person and every event which came under my eye, although I was easily frightened. When a person, or a happening, seemed to me not in keeping with my opinion, or even my hope or expectation, I was terrified by a vision of abandonment and wildness which tore my heart with a kind of sorrow. My father and mother, who believed that I saw nothing in the world which was not strictly coaxed into place like a vine on our garden trellis to be presented to my eyes, would have been badly concerned if they had guessed how frequently the weak and inferior and strangely turned examples of what was to come showed themselves to me.

I do not know even now what it was that I was waiting to see; but in those days I was convinced that I almost saw it at every turn. To watch everything about me I regarded grimly and possessively as a *need*. All through this summer I had lain on the sand beside the small lake, with my hands squared over my eyes, finger tips touching, looking out by this device to see everything: which appeared as a kind of projection. It did not matter to me what I looked at; from any observation I would conclude that a secret of life had been nearly revealed to me—for I was obsessed with notions about concealment, and from the smallest gesture of a stranger I would wrest what was to me a communication or a presentiment.

This state of exaltation was heightened, or even brought about, by the fact that I was in love then for the first time: I had indentified love at once. The truth is that never since has any passion I have felt remained so hopelessly unexpressed within me or appeared so grotesquely altered in the outward world. It is strange that sometimes, even now, I remember unadulteratedly a certain morning when I touched my friend's wrist (as if by accident, and he pretended not to notice) as we passed on the stairs in school. I must add, and this is not so strange, that the child was not actually my friend. We had never exchanged a word or even a nod of recognition; but it was possible during the entire year for me to think endlessly on this minute and brief encounter which we endured on the stairs, until it would swell with a sudden and overwhelming beauty, like a rose forced into premature bloom for a great occasion.

My love had somehow made me doubly austere in my observations of what went on about me. Through some intensity I had come almost into a dual life, as observer and dreamer. I felt a necessity for absolute conformity to my ideas in any happening I witnessed. As a result, all day long in school I sat perpetually alert, fearing for the untoward to happen. The dreariness and regularity of the school day were a protection for me, but I remember with exact clarity the day in Latin class when the boy I loved (whom I watch constantly) bent suddenly over and brought his handkerchief to his face. I saw red—vermilion—blood flow over the handkerchief and his square-shaped hand; his nose had begun to bleed. I remember the very moment: several of the older girls laughed at the confusion and distraction; the boy rushed from the room; the teacher spoke sharply in warning. But this small happening which had closed in upon my friend was a tremendous shock to me; it was unforeseen, but at the same time dreaded; I recognized it, and suddenly I leaned heavily on my arm and fainted. Does this explain why, ever since that day, I have been unable to bear the sight of blood?

I never knew where this boy lived, or who his parents were. This occasioned during the year of my love a constant uneasiness in me. It was unbearable to think that his house might be slovenly and unpainted, hidden by tall trees, that his mother and father might be shabby—dishonest—crippled—dead. I speculated endlessly on the dangers of his home. Sometimes I imagined that his house might catch on fire in the night and that he might die. When he would walk into the schoolroom the next morning, a look of unconcern and even stupidity on his face would dissipate my dream; but my fears were increased through his unconsciousness of them, for I felt a mystery deeper than danger which hung about him. I watched everything he did, trying to learn and translate and verify. I could reproduce for you now the clumsy weave, the exact shade of faded blue in his sweater. I remember how he used to swing his foot as he sat at his desk—softly, barely not touching the floor. Even now it does not seem trivial.

As I lay on the beach that sunny morning, I was thinking of my friend and remembering in a retarded, dilated, timeless fashion the incident of my hand brushing his wrist. It made a very long story. But like a needle going in and out among my thoughts were the children running on the sand, the upthrust oak trees growing over the clean pointed roof of the white pavilion, and the slowly changing attitudes of the grown-up people who had avoided the city and were lying prone and laughing on the water's edge. I still would not care to say which was more real—the dream I could make blossom at will, or the sight of the bathers. I am presenting them, you see, only as simultaneous.

I did not notice how the bathers got there, so close to me. Perhaps I actually fell asleep, and they came out then. Sprawled close to where I was lying, at any rate, appeared a group of loud, squirming, ill-assorted people who seemed thrown together only by the most confused accident, and who seemed driven by foolish intent to insult each other, all of which they enjoyed with a hilarity which astonished my heart. There were a man, two women, two young boys. They were brown and roughened, but not foreigners; when I was a child such people were called "common." They wore old and faded bathing suits which did not hide either the energy or the fatigue of their bodies, but showed it exactly.

The boys must have been brothers, because they both had very white straight hair, which shone like thistles in the red sunlight. The older boy was greatly overgrown—he protruded from his costume at every turn. His cheeks were ballooned outward and hid his eyes, but it was easy for me to follow his darting sly glances as he ran clumsily around the others, inflicting pinches, kicks, and idiotic sounds upon them. The smaller boy was thin and defiant; his white bangs were plastered down where he had thrown himself time after time headfirst into the lake when the older child chased him to persecute him.

Lying in leglike confusion together were the rest of the group, the man and the two women. The man seemed competely given over to the heat and glare of the sun; his relaxed eyes sometimes squinted with faint amusement over the brilliant water and the hot sand. His arms were flabby and at rest. He lay turned on his side, now and then scooping sand in a loose pile about the legs of the older woman.

She herself stared fixedly at his slow, undeliberate movements, and held her body perfectly still. She was unnaturally white and fatly aware, in a bathing suit which had no relation to the shape of her body. Fat hung upon her upper arms like an arrested earthslide on a hill. With the first motion she might make, I was afraid that she would slide down upon herself into a terrifying heap. Her breasts hung heavy and widening like pears into her bathing suit. Her legs lay prone one on the other like shadowed bulwarks, uneven and deserted, upon which, from the man's hand, the sand piled higher like the teasing threat of oblivion. A slow, repetitious sound I had been hearing for a long time unconsciously, I identified as a continuous laugh which came through the motionless open pouched mouth of the woman.

The younger girl, who was lying at the man's feet, was curled tensely upon herself. She wore a bright green bathing suit like a bottle from which she might, I felt, burst in a rage of churning smoke. I could feel the genie-like rage in her narrowed figure as she seemed both to crawl and to lie still, watching the man heap the sand in his careless way about the larger legs of the older woman. The two little boys were running in wobbly ellipses about the others, pinching them indiscriminately and pitching sand into the man's roughened hair as though they were not afraid of him. The woman continued to laugh, almost as she would hum an annoying song. I saw that they were all resigned to each other's daring and ugliness.

There had been no words spoken among these people, but I began to comprehend a progression, a circle of answers, which they were flinging toward one another in their own way, in the confusion of vulgarity and hatred which twined among them all like a wreath of steam rising from the wet sand. I saw the man lift his hand filled with crumbling sand, shaking it as the woman laughed, and pour it down inside her bathing suit between her bulbous descending breasts. There it hung, brown and shapeless, making them all laugh. Even the angry girl laughed, with an insistent hilarity which flung her to her feet and tossed her about the beach, her stiff, cramped legs jumping and tottering. The little boys pointed and howled. The man smiled, the way panting dogs seem to be smiling, and gazed about carelessly at them all and out over the water. He even looked at me, and included me. Looking back, stunned, I wished that they all were dead.

But at that moment the girl in the green bathing suit suddenly whirled all the way around. She reached rigid arms toward the screaming children and joined them in a senseless chase. The small boy dashed headfirst into the water, and the larger boy churned his overgrown body through the blue air onto a little bench, which I had not even known was there! Jeeringly he called to the others, who laughed as he jumped, heavy and ridiculous, over the back of the bench and tumbled exaggeratedly in the sand below. The fat woman leaned over the man to smirk, and the child pointed at her, screaming. The girl in green then came running toward the bench as though she would destroy it, and with a fierceness which took my breath away, she dragged herself through the air and jumped over the bench. But no one seemed to notice, except the smaller boy, who flew out of the water to dig his fingers into her side, in mixed congratulation and derision; she pushed him angrily down into the sand.

I closed my eyes upon them and their struggles but I could see them still, large and almost metallic, with painted smiles, in the sun. I lay there with my eyes pressed shut, listening to their moans and their frantic squeals. It seemed to me that I could hear also the thud and the fat impact of all their ugly bodies upon one another. I tried to withdraw to my most inner dream, that of touching the wrist of the boy I loved on the stair; I felt the shudder of my wish shaking the darkness like leaves where I had closed my eyes; I felt the heavy weight of sweetness which always accompanied this memory; but the memory itself did not come to me.

I lay there, opening and closing my eyes. The brilliance and then the blackness were like some alternate experiences of night and day. The sweetness of my love seemed to bring the dark and to swing me gently in its suspended wind; I sank into familiarity; but the story of my love, the long narrative of the incident on the stairs, had vanished. I did not know, any longer, the meaning of my happiness; it held me unexplained.

Once when I looked up, the fat woman was standing opposite the smiling man. She bent over and in a condescending way pulled down the front of her bathing suit, turning it outward, so that the lumps of mashed and folded sand came emptying out. I felt a peak of horror, as though her breasts themselves had turned to sand, as though they were of no importance at all and she did not care.

When finally I emerged again from the protection of my dream, the undefined austerity of my love, I opened my eyes onto the blur of an empty beach. The group of strangers had gone. Still I lay there, feeling victimized by the sight of the unfinished bulwark where they had piled and shaped the wet sand around their bodies, which changed the appearance of the beach like the ravages of a storm. I looked away, and for the object which met my eye, the small worn white pavilion, I felt pity suddenly overtake me, and I burst into tears.

That was my last morning on the beach. I remember continuing to lie there, squaring my vision with my hands, trying to think ahead to the time of my return to school in winter. I could imagine the boy I loved walking into a classroom, where I would watch him with this hour on the beach accompanying my recovered dream and added to my love. I could even foresee the way he would stare back, speechless and innocent, a medium-sized boy with blond hair, his unconscious eyes looking beyond me and out the window, solitary and unprotected.

QUESTIONS
1. The title places the story in the past. How much time do you think has passed between the events and the telling? Where is the evidence?
2. Characterize the girl as she appears in the story. Can we tell whether she is different now from what she was? What is the significance of the line: "Even now it does not seem trivial"? (end of paragraph six).
3. Why does the girl make frames with her fingers, "to look out at everything"? Does the habit suggest anything about her attitude toward life?
4. Why is she so upset by the "common" people?
5. How important is imagery to the effect? How does the choice of imagery help to characterize the narrator?

More bathing suits, but this time in an A&P. Updike's narrator is a boy, but like the girl of "A Memory" he is a keen observer.

A&P
John Updike (1932–)

In walks these three girls in nothing but bathing suits. I'm in the third checkout slot, with my back to the door, so I don't see them until they're over by the bread. The one that caught my eye first was the one in the plaid green two-piece. She was a chunky kid, with a good tan and a sweet broad soft-looking can with those two crescents of white just under it, where the sun never seems to hit, at the top of the backs of her legs. I stood there with my hand on a box of HiHo crackers trying to remember if I rang it up or not. I ring it up again and the customer starts giving me hell. She's one of these cash-register-watchers, a witch about fifty with rouge on her cheekbones and no eyebrows, and I know it made her day to trip me up. She'd been watching cash registers for fifty years and probably never seen a mistake before.

By the time I got her feathers smoothed and her goodies into a bag—she gives me a little snort in passing, if she'd been born at the right time they would have burned her over in Salem—by the time I get her on her way the girls had circled around the bread and were coming back, without a pushcart, back my way along the counters, in the aisle between the checkouts and the Special bins. They didn't even have shoes on. There was this chunky one, with the two-piece—it was bright green and the seams on the bra were still sharp and her belly was still pretty pale so I guessed she just got it (the suit)—there was this one, with one of those chubby berry-faces, the lips all bunched together under her nose, this one, and a tall one, with black hair that hadn't quite frizzed right, and one of these sunburns right across under the eyes, and a chin that was too long—you know, the kind of girl other girls think is very "striking" and "attractive" but never quite makes it, as they very well know, which is why they like her so much—and then the third one, that wasn't quite so tall. She was the queen. She kind of led them, the other two peeking around and making their shoulders round. She didn't look around, not this queen, she just walked straight on slowly, on these long white prima-donna legs. She came down a little hard on her heels, as if she didn't walk in her bare feet that much, putting down her heels and then letting the weight move along to her toes as if she was testing the floor with every step, putting a little deliberate extra action into it. You never know for sure how girls' minds work (do you really think it's a mind in there or just a little buzz like a bee in a glass jar?) but you got the idea she had talked the other two into coming in here with her, and now she was showing them how to do it, walk slow and hold yourself straight.

She had on a kind of dirty-pink—beige maybe, I don't know—bathing suit with a little nubble all over it and, what got me, the straps were down. They were off her shoulders looped loose around the cool tops of her arms, and I guess as a result the suit had slipped a little on her, so all around the top of the cloth there was this shining rim. If it hadn't been there you wouldn't have known there could have been anything whiter than those shoulders. With the straps pushed off, there was nothing between the top of the suit and top of her head except just *her*, this clean bare plane of the top of her chest down from the shoulder bones like a dented sheet of metal tilted in the light. I mean, it was more than pretty.

She had sort of oaky hair that the sun and salt had bleached, done up in a bun that was unravelling, and a kind of prim face. Walking into the A&P with your straps down, I suppose it's the only kind of face you *can* have. She held her head so high her neck, coming up out of those white shoulders, looked kind of stretched, but I didn't mind. The longer her neck was, the more of her there was.

She must have felt in the corner of her eye me and over my shoulder Stokesie in the second slot watching, but she didn't tip. Not this queen. She kept her eyes moving across the racks, and stopped, and turned so slow it made my stomach rub the inside of my apron, and buzzed to the other two, who kind of huddled against her for relief, and then they all three of them went up the cat-and-dog-food - breakfast - cereal - macaroni-rice-raisins-seasonings-spreads-spaghetti-soft-drinks-crackers-and-cookies aisle. From the third slot I look straight up this aisle to the meat counter, and I watched them all the way. The fat one with the tan sort of fumbled with the cookies, but on second thought she put the package back. The sheep pushing their carts down the aisle—the girls were walking against the usual traffic (not that we have one-way signs or anything)—were pretty hilarious. You could see them, when Queenie's white shoulders dawned on them, kind of jerk, or hop, or hiccup, but their eyes snapped back to their own baskets and on they pushed. I bet you could set off dynamite in an A&P and the people would by and large keep reaching and checking oatmeal off their lists and muttering "Let me see, there was a third thing, began with A, asparagus, no, ah, yes, applesauce!" or whatever it is they do mutter. But there was no doubt, this jiggled them. A few houseslaves in pin curlers even looked around after pushing their carts past to make sure what they had seen was correct.

You know, it's one thing to have a girl in a bathing suit down on the beach, where what with the glare nobody can look at each other much anyway, and another thing in the cool of the A&P, under the fluorescent lights, against all those stacked packages, with her feet paddling along naked over our checkerboard green-and-cream rubber-tile floor.

"Oh Daddy," Stokesie said beside me. "I feel so faint."

"Darling," I said. "Hold me tight." Stokesie's married, with two babies chalked up on his fuselage already, but as far as I can tell that's the only difference. He's twenty-two, and I was nineteen this April.

"Is it done?" he asks, the responsible married man finding his voice. I forgot to say he thinks he's going to be manager some sunny day, maybe in 1990 when it's called the Great Alexandrov and Petrooshki Tea Company or something.

What he meant was, our town is five miles from a beach, with a big summer colony out on the Point, but we're right in the middle of town, and the women generally put on a shirt or shorts or something before they get out of the car into the street. And anyway these are usually women with six children and varicose veins mapping their legs and nobody, including them, could care less. As I say, we're right in the middle of town, and if you stand at our front doors you can see two banks and the Congregational church and the newspaper store and three real-estate offices and about twenty-seven old freeloaders tearing up Central Street because the sewer broke again. It's not as if we're on the Cape; we're north of Boston and there's people in this town haven't seen the ocean for twenty years.

The girls had reached the meat counter and were asking McMahon something. He pointed, they pointed, and they shuffled out of sight behind a pyramid of Diet Delight peaches. All that was left for us to see was old McMahon patting his mouth and looking after them sizing up their joints. Poor kids, I began to feel sorry for them, they couldn't help it.

Now here comes the sad part of the story, at least my family says it's sad, but I don't think it's so sad myself. The store's pretty empty, it being Thursday afternoon, so there was nothing much to do except lean on the register and wait for the girls to show up again. The whole store was like a pinball machine and I

didn't know which tunnel they'd come out of. After a while they come around
out of the far aisle, around the light bulbs, records at discount of the Caribbean
Six or Tony Martin Sings or some such gunk you wonder they waste the wax on,
sixpacks of candy bars, and plastic toys done up in cellophane that fall apart
when a kid looks at them anyway. Around they come, Queenie still leading the
,way, and holding a little gray jar in her hand. Slots Three through Seven are unmanned and I could see her wondering between Stokes and me, but Stokesie
with his usual luck draws an old party in baggy gray pants who stumbles up
with four giant cans of pineapple juice (what do these bums *do* with all that pineapple juice? I've often asked myself) so the girls come to me. Queenie puts down
the jar and I take it into my fingers icy cold. Kingfish Fancy Herring Snacks in
Pure Sour Cream: 49¢. Now her hands are empty, not a ring or a bracelet, bare as
God made them, and I wonder where the money's coming from. Still with that
prim look she lifts a folded dollar bill out of the hollow at the center of her nub-
bled pink top. The jar went heavy in my hand. Really, I thought that was so cute.

Then everybody's luck begins to run out. Lengel comes in from haggling with
a truck full of cabbages on the lot and is about to scuttle into that door marked
MANAGER behind which he hides all day when the girls touch his eye. Lengel's
pretty dreary, teaches Sunday school and the rest, but he doesn't miss that much.
He comes over and says, "Girls, this isn't the beach."

Queenie blushes, though maybe it's just a brush of sunburn I was noticing for
the first time, now that she was so close. "My mother asked me to pick up a jar of
herring snacks." Her voice kind of startled me, the way voices do when you see
the people first, coming out so flat and dumb yet kind of tony, too, the way it
ticked over "pick up" and "snacks." All of a sudden I slid right down her voice
into her living room. Her father and the other men were standing around in ice-
cream coats and bow ties and the women were in sandals picking up herring
snacks on toothpicks off a big glass plate and they were all holding drinks the
color of water with olives and sprigs of mint in them. When my parents have
somebody over they get lemonade and if it's a real racy affair Schlitz in tall glasses with "They'll Do It Every Time" cartoons stencilled on.

"That's all right," Lengel said. "But this isn't the beach." His repeating this
struck me as funny, as if it had just occurred to him, and he had been thinking all
these years the A&P was a great big dune and he was the head lifeguard. He
didn't like my smiling—as I say he doesn't miss much—but he concentrates on
giving the girls that sad Sunday-school-superintendent stare.

Queenie's blush is no sunburn now, and the plump one in plaid, that I liked
better from the back—a really sweet can—pipes up. "We weren't doing any
shopping. We just came in for the one thing."

"That makes no difference," Lengel tells her, and I could see from the way his
eyes went that he hadn't noticed she was wearing a two-piece before. "We want
you decently dressed when you come in here."

"We *are* decent," Queenie says suddenly, her lower lip pushing, getting sore
now that she remembers her place, a place from which the crowd that runs the A
& P must look pretty crummy. Fancy Herring Snacks flashed in her very blue
eyes.

"Girls, I don't want to argue with you. After this come in here with your
shoulders covered. It's our policy." He turns his back. That's policy for you. Poli-

cy is what the kingpins want. What the others want is juvenile delinquency.

All this while, the customers had been showing up with their carts but, you know, sheep, seeing a scene, they had all bunched up on Stokesie, who shook open a paper bag as gently as peeling a peach, not wanting to miss a word. I could feel in the silence everybody getting nervous, most of all Lengel, who asks me, "Sammy, have you rung up their purchase?"

I thought and said "No" but it wasn't about that I was thinking. I go through the punches, 4, 9. GROC, TOT—it's more complicated than you think, and after you do it often enough, it begins to make a little song, that you hear words to, in my case "Hello (*bing*) there, you (*gung*) hap-py *pee*-pul (*splat*)!"—the *splat* being the drawer flying out. I uncrease the bill, tenderly as you may imagine, it just having come from between the two smoothest scoops of vanilla I had even known were there, and pass a half and a penny into her narrow pink palm, and nestle the herrings in a bag and twist its neck and hand it over, all the time thinking.

The girls, and who'd blame them, are in a hurry to get out, so I say "I quit" to Lengel quick enough for them to hear, hoping they'll stop and watch me, their unsuspected hero. They keep right on going, into the electric eye; the door flies open and they flicker across the lot to their car, Queenie and Plaid and Big Tall Goony-Goony (not that as raw material she was so bad), leaving me with Lengel and a kink in his eyebrow.

"Did you say something, Sammy?"

"I said I quit."

"I thought you did."

"You didn't have to embarrass them."

"It was they who were embarrassing us."

I started to say something that came out "Fiddle-de-doo." It's a saying of my grandmother's, and I know she would have been pleased.

"I don't think you know what you're saying," Lengel said.

"I know you don't," I said, "But I do." I pull the bow at the back of my apron and start shrugging it off my shoulders. A couple customers that had been heading for my slot begin to knock against each other, like scared pigs in a chute. Lengel sighs and begins to look very patient and old and gray. He's been a friend of my parents for years. "Sammy, you don't want to do this to your Mom and Dad," he tells me. It's true, I don't. But it seems to me that once you begin a gesture it's fatal not to go through with it. I fold the apron, "Sammy" stitched in red on the pocket, and put it on the counter, and drop the bow tie on top of it. The bow tie is theirs, if you've ever wondered. "You'll feel this for the rest of your life," Lengel says, and I know that's true, too, but remembering how he made that pretty girl blush makes me so scrunchy inside I punch the No Sale tab and the machine whirs "pee-pul" and the drawer splats out. One advantage to this scene taking place in summer, I can follow this up with a clean exit, there's no fumbling around getting your coat and galoshes, I just saunter into the electric eye in my white shirt that my mother ironed the night before, and the door heaves itself open, and outside the sunshine is skating around on the asphalt.

I look around for my girls, but they're gone, of course. There wasn't anybody but some young married screaming with her children about some candy they didn't get by the door of a powder-blue Falcon station wagon. Looking back in the big windows, over the bags of peat moss and aluminum lawn furniture stacked on the pavement, I could see Lengel in my place in the slot, checking the sheep through. His face was dark gray and his back stiff, as if he'd just had an injection of iron, and my stomach kind of fell as I felt how hard the world was going to be to me hereafter.

CHAPTER 3

The Narrator as Observer

Sometimes the first-person narrator is less participant than observer. The line is hard to draw, however, because the inevitable shaping and filtering of the story by the narrator's personality tends to make him an important part of its final effect. As readers, when we focus on plot we are likely to play down the importance of the narrator, but when we focus on interpretation we come back to this crucial point: from all of the narrative perspectives the author might have selected, why did he choose this one?

MY OLD MAN
Ernest Hemingway (1899–1961)

I guess looking at it, now, my old man was cut out for a fat guy, one of those regular little roly fat guys you see around, but he sure never got that way, except a little toward the last, and then it wasn't his fault, he was riding over the jumps only and he could afford to carry plenty of weight then. I remember the way he'd pull on a rubber shirt over a couple of jerseys and a big sweat shirt over that, and get me to run with him in the forenoon in the hot sun. He'd have, maybe, taken a trial trip with one of Razzo's skins early in the morning after just getting in from Torino at four o'clock in the morning and beating it out to the stables in a cab and then with the dew all over everything and the sun just starting to get going, I'd help him pull off his boots and he'd get into a pair of sneakers and all these sweaters and we'd start out.

"Come on, kid," he'd say, stepping up and down on his toes in front of the jock's dressing room, "let's get moving."

Then we'd start off jogging around the infield once, maybe, with him ahead, running nice, and then turn out the gate and along one of those roads with all the trees along both sides of them that run out from San Siro. I'd go ahead of him when we hit the road and I could run pretty good and I'd look around and he'd be jogging easy just behind me and after a little while I'd look around again and he'd begun to sweat. Sweating heavy and he'd just be dogging it along with his eyes on my back, but when he'd catch me looking at him he'd grin and say, "Sweating plenty?" When my old man grinned, nobody could help but grin too. We'd keep right on running out toward the mountains and then my old man would yell, "Hey, Joe!" and I'd look back and he'd be sitting under a tree with a towel he'd had around his waist wrapped around his neck.

I'd come back and sit down beside him and he'd pull a rope out of his pocket and start skipping rope out in the sun with the sweat pouring off his face and him skipping rope out in the white dust with the rope going cloppetty, cloppetty, clop, clop, clop, and the sun hotter, and him working harder up and down a patch of the road. Say, it was a treat to see my old man skip rope, too. He could whirr it fast or lop it slow and fancy. Say, you ought to have seen wops look at us sometimes, when they'd come by, going into town walking along with big steers hauling the cart. They sure looked as though they thought the old man was nuts. He'd start the rope whirring till they'd stop dead still and watch him, then give the steers a cluck and a poke with the goad and get going again.

When I'd sit watching him working out in the hot sun I sure felt fond of him. He sure was fun and he done his work so hard and he'd finish up with a regular whirring that'd drive the sweat out on his face like water and then sling the rope at the tree and come over and sit down with me and lean back against the tree with the towel and a sweater wrapped around his neck.

"Sure is hell keeping it down, Joe," he'd say and lean back and shut his eyes and breathe long and deep, "it ain't like when you're a kid." Then he'd get up and before he started to cool we'd jog along back to the stables. That's the way it was keeping down to weight. He was worried all the time. Most jocks can just about ride off all they want to. A jock loses about a kilo every time he rides, but my old man was sort of dried out and he couldn't keep down his kilos without all that running.

I remember once at San Siro, Regoli, a little wop, that was riding for Buzoni, came out across the paddock going to the bar for something cool; and flicking his boots with his whip, after he'd just weighed in and my old man had just weighed in too, and came out with the saddle under his arm looking red-faced and tired and too big for his silks and he stood there looking at young Regoli standing up to the outdoors bar, cool and kid-looking, and I said, "What's the matter, Dad?" cause I thought maybe Regoli had bumped him or something and he just looked at Regoli and said, "Oh, to hell with it," and went on to the dressing room.

Well, it would have been all right, maybe, if we'd stayed in Milan and ridden at Milan and Torino, 'cause if there ever were any easy courses, it's those two. "Pianola, Joe," my old man said when he dismounted in the winning stall after what the wops thought was a hell of steeplechase. I asked him once. "This course rides itself. It's the pace you're going at, that makes riding the jumps dangerous, Joe. We ain't going any pace here, and they ain't really bad jumps either. But it's the pace always—not the jumps—that makes the trouble."

San Siro was the swellest course I'd ever seen but the old man said it was a dog's life. Going back and forth between Mirafiore and San Siro and riding just about every day in the week with a train ride every other night.

I was nuts about the horses, too. There's something about it, when they come out and go up the track to the post. Sort of dancy and tight looking with the jock keeping a tight hold on them and maybe easing off a little and letting them run a little going up. Then once they were at the barrier it got me worse than anything. Especially at San Siro with that big green infield and the mountains way off and the fat wop starter with his big whip and the jocks fiddling them around and then the barrier snapping up and that bell going off and them all getting off in a bunch and then commencing to string out. You know the way a bunch of skins gets off. If you're up in the stand with a pair of glasses all you see is them plunging off and then that bell goes off and it seems like it rings for a thousand years and then they come sweeping round the turn. There wasn't ever anything like it for me.

But my old man said one day, in the dressing room, when he was getting into his street clothes, "None of these things are horses, Joe. They'd kill that bunch of skates for their hides and hoofs up at Paris." That was the day he'd won the Premio Commercio with Lantorna shooting her out of the field the last hundred meters like pulling a cork out of a bottle.

It was right after the Premio Commercio that we pulled out and left Italy. My old man and Holbrook and a fat wop in a straw hat that kept wiping his face with a handkerchief were having an argument at a table in the Galleria. They were all talking French and the two of them was after my old man about something. Finally he didn't say anything any more but just sat there and looked at Holbrook, and the two of them kept after him, first one talking and then the other, and the fat wop always butting in on Holbrook.

"You go out and buy me a *Sportsman,* will you Joe?" my old man said, and handed me a couple of soldi without looking away from Holbrook.

So I went out of the Galleria and walked over to in front of the Scala and bought a paper, and came back and stood a little way away because I didn't want to butt in and my old man was sitting back in his chair looking down at his coffee and fooling with a spoon and Holbrook and the big wop were standing and the big wop was wiping his face and shaking his head. And I came up and my old man acted just as though the two of them weren't standing there and said, "Want an ice, Joe?" Holbrook looked down at my old man and said slow and careful, "You son of a bitch," and he and the fat wop went out through the tables.

My old man sat there and sort of smiled at me, but his face was white and he looked sick as hell and I was scared and felt sick inside because I knew something had happened and I didn't see how anybody could call my old man a son of a bitch, and get away with it. My old man opened up the *Sportsman* and studied the handicaps for a while and then he said, "You got to take a lot of things in this world, Joe." And three days later we left Milan for good on the Turin train for Paris, after an auction sale out in front of Turner's stables of everything we couldn't get into a trunk and a suit case.

We got into Paris early in the morning in a long, dirty station the old man told me was the Gare de Lyon. Paris was an awful big town after Milan. Seems like in Milan everybody is going somewhere and all the trams run somewhere and there ain't any sort of a mix-up, but Paris is all balled up and they never do straighten it out. I got to like it, though, part of it, anyway, and say, it's got the best race courses in the world. Seems as though that were the thing that keeps it all going and about the only thing you can figure on is that every day the buses will be going out to whatever track they're running at, going right out through everything to the track. I never really got to know Paris well, because I just came in about once or twice a week with the old man from Maisons and he always sat at the Café de la Paix on the Opera side with the rest of the gang from Maisons and I guess that's one of the busiest parts of the town. But, say, it is funny that a big town like Paris wouldn't have a Galleria, isn't it?

Well, we went out to live at Maisons-Lafitte, where just about everybody lives except the gang at Chantilly, with a Mrs. Meyers that runs a boarding house. Maisons is about the swellest place to live I've ever seen in all my life. The town ain't so much, but there's a lake and a swell forest that we used to go off bumming in all day, a couple of us kids, and my old man made me a sling shot and we got a lot of things with it but the best one was a magpie. Young Dick Atkinson shot a rabbit with it one day and we put it under a tree and were all sitting around and Dick had some cigarettes and all of a sudden the rabbit jumped up and beat it into the brush and we chased it but we couldn't find it. Gee, we had fun at Maisons. Mrs. Meyers used to give me lunch in the morning and I'd be gone all day. I learned to talk French quick. It's an easy language.

As soon as we got to Maisons, my old man wrote to Milan for his license and he was pretty worried till it came. He used to sit around the Café de Paris in Maisons with the gang, there were lots of guys he'd known when he rode up at Paris, before the war, lived at Maisons, and there's a lot of time to sit around because the work around a racing stable, for the jocks, that is, is all cleaned up by nine o'clock in the morning. They take the first bunch of skins out to gallop them at 5:30 in the morning and they work the second lot at 8 o'clock. That means getting up early all right and going to bed early, too. If a jock's riding for somebody too, he can't go boozing around because the trainer always has an eye on him if he's a kid and if he ain't a kid he's always got an eye on himself. So mostly if a jock ain't working he sits around the Café de Paris with the gang and they can all sit around about two or three hours in front of some drink like a vermouth and seltz and they talk and tell stories and shoot pool and it's sort of like a club or the Galleria in Milan. Only it ain't really like the Galleria because there everybody is going by all the time and there's everybody around at the tables.

Well, my old man got his license all right. They sent it through to him without a word and he rode a couple of times. Amiens, up country and that sort of thing, but he didn't seem to get any engagement. Everybody liked him and whenever I'd come into the Café in the forenoon I'd find somebody drinking with him because my old man wasn't tight like most of these jockies that have got the first dollar they made riding at the World's Fair in St. Louis in nineteen ought four. That's what my old man would say when he'd kid George Burns. But it seemed like everybody steered clear of giving my old man any mounts.

We went out to wherever they were running every day with the car from Maisons and that was the most fun of all. I was glad when the horses came back from Deauville and the summer. Even though it meant no more bumming in the woods, 'cause then we'd ride to Enghien or Tremblay or St. Cloud and watch them from the trainers' and jockeys' stand. I sure learned about racing from going out with that gang and the fun of it was going every day.

I remember once out at St. Cloud. It was a big two hundred thousand franc race with seven entries and Kzar a big favorite. I went around to the paddock to see the horses with my old man and you never saw such horses. This Kzar is a great big yellow horse that looks like just nothing but run. I never saw such a horse. He was being led around the paddocks with his head down and when he went by me I felt all hollow inside he was so beautiful. There never was such a wonderful, lean, running built horse. And he went around the paddock putting his feet just so and quiet and careful and moving easy like he knew just what he had to do and not jerking and standing up on his legs and getting wild eyed like you see these selling platers with a shot of dope in them. The crowd was so thick I couldn't see him again except just his legs going by and some yellow and my old man started out through the crowd and I followed him over to the jock's dressing room back in the trees and there was a big crowd around there, too, but the man at the door in a derby nodded to my old man and we got in and everybody was sitting around and getting dressed and pulling shirts over their heads and pulling boots on and it all smelled hot and sweaty and linimenty and outside was the crowd looking in.

The old man went over and sat down beside George Gardner that was getting into his pants and said, "What's the dope, George?" just in an ordinary tone of voice 'cause there ain't any use him feeling around because George either can tell him or he can't tell him.

"He won't win," George says very low, leaning over and buttoning the bottoms of his breeches.

"Who will?" my old man says, leaning over close so nobody can hear.

"Kircubbin," George says, "and if he does, save me a couple of tickets."

My old man says something in a regular voice to George and George says, "Don't ever bet on anything I tell you," kidding like, and we beat it out and through all the crowd that was looking in, over to the 100 franc mutuel machine. But I knew something big was up because George is Kzar's jockey. On the way he gets one of the yellow odds-sheets with the starting prices on and Kzar is only paying 5 for 10, Cefisidote is next at 3 to 1 and fifth down the list this Kircubbin at 8 to 1. My old man bets five thousand on Kircubbin to win and puts a thousand to place and we went around back of the grandstand to go up the stairs and get a place to watch the race.

We were jammed in tight and first a man in a long coat with a gray tall hat and a whip folded up in his hand came out and then one after another the horses, with the jocks up and a stable boy holding the bridle on each side and walking along, followed the old guy. That big yellow horse Kzar came first. He didn't look so big when you first looked at him until you saw the length of his legs and the whole way he's built and the way he moves. Gosh, I never saw such a horse. George Gardner was riding him and they moved along slow, back of the old guy in the gray tall hat that walked along like he was a ring master in a circus. Back of Kzar, moving along smooth and yellow in the sun, was a good looking black with a nice head with Tommy Archibald riding him; and after the black was a string of five more horses all moving along slow in a procession past the grandstand and the pesage.[1] My old man said the black was Kircubbin and I took a good look at him and he was a nice-looking horse, all right, but nothing like Kzar.

Everybody cheered Kzar when he went by and he sure was one swell-looking horse. The procession of them went around on the other side past the pelouse[2] and then back up to the near end of the course and the circus master had the stable boys turn them loose one after another so they could gallop by the stands on their way up to the post and let everybody have a good look at them. They weren't at the post hardly any time at all when the gong started and you could

---

[1] Paddock (French).
[2] Lawn, grassy plot (French).

see them way off across the infield all in a bunch starting on the first swing like a lot of little toy horses. I was watching them through the glasses and Kzar was running well back, with one of the bays making the pace. They swept down and around and came pounding past and Kzar was way back when they passed us and this Kircubbin horse in front and going smooth. Gee, it's awful when they go by you and then you have to watch them go farther away and get smaller and smaller and then all bunched up on the turns and then come around towards into the stretch and you feel like swearing and goddamming worse and worse. Finally they made the last turn and came into the straightaway with this Kircubbin horse way out in front. Everybody was looking funny and saying "Kzar" in sort of a sick way and them pounding nearer down the stretch, and then something came out of the pack right into my glasses like a horse-headed yellow streak and everybody began to yell "Kzar" as though they were crazy. Kzar came on faster than I'd ever seen anything in my life and pulled up on Kircubbin that was going fast as any black horse could go with the jock flogging hell out of him with the gad and they were right dead neck and neck for a second but Kzar seemed going about twice as fast with those great jumps and that head out—but it was while they were neck and neck that they passed the winning post and when the numbers went up in the slots the first one was 2 and that meant that Kircubbin had won.

I felt all trembly and funny inside, and then we were all jammed in with the people going downstairs to stand in front of the board where they'd post what Kircubbin paid. Honest, watching the race I'd forgot how much my old man had bet on Kircubbin. I'd wanted Kzar to win so damned bad. But now it was all over it was swell to know we had the winner.

"Wasn't it a swell race, Dad?" I said to him.

He looked at me sort of funny with his derby on the back of his head. "George Gardner's a swell jockey, all right," he said. "It sure took a great jock to keep that Kzar horse from winning."

Of course I knew it was funny all the time. But my old man saying that right out like that sure took the kick all out of it for me and I didn't get the real kick back again ever, even when they posted the numbers upon the board and the bell rang to pay off and we saw that Kircubbin paid 67.50 for 10. All round people were saying, "Poor Kzar! Poor Kzar!" And I thought, I wish I were a jockey and could have rode him instead of that son of a bitch. And that was funny, thinking of George Gardner as a son of a bitch because I'd always liked him and besides he'd given us the winner, but I guess that's what he is, all right.

My old man had a big lot of money after that race and he took to coming into Paris oftener. If they raced at Tremblay he'd have them drop him in town on their way back to Maisons and he and I'd sit out in front of the Café de la Paix and watch the people go by. It's funny sitting there. There's streams of people going by and all sorts of guys come up and want to sell you things, and I loved to sit there with my old man. That was when we'd have the most fun. Guys would come by selling funny rabbits that jumped if you squeezed a bulb and they'd come up to us and my old man would kid with them. He could talk French just like English and all those kind of guys knew him 'cause you can always tell a jockey—and then we always sat at the same table and they got used to seeing us there. There were guys selling matrimonial papers and girls selling rubber eggs that when you squeezed them a rooster came out of them and one old wormy-looking guy that went by with post-cards of Paris, showing them to everybody, and, of course, nobody ever bought any, and then he would come back and show the under side of the pack and they would all be smutty post-cards and lots of people would dig down and buy them.

Gee, I remember the funny people that used to go by. Girls around supper time looking for somebody to take them out to eat and they'd speak to my old man and he'd make some joke at them in French and they'd pat me on the head and go on. Once there was an American woman sitting with her kid daughter at the next table to us and they were both eating ices and I kept looking at the girl and she was awfully good looking and I smiled at her and she smiled at me but that was all that ever came of it because I looked for her mother and her every day and I made up ways that I was going to speak to her and I wondered if I got to know her if her mother would let me take her out to Auteuil or Tremblay but I never saw either of them again. Anyway, I guess it wouldn't have been any good, anyway, because looking back on it I remember the way I thought out would be best to speak to her was to say, "Pardon me, but perhaps I can give you a winner at Enghien today?" and, after all, maybe she would have thought I was a tout instead of really trying to give her a winner.

We'd sit at the Café de la Paix, my old man and me, and we had a big drag with the waiter because my old man drank whisky and it cost five francs, and that meant a good tip when the saucers were counted up. My old man was drinking more than I'd ever seen him, but he wasn't riding at all now and besides he said that whisky kept his weight down. But I noticed he was putting it on, all right, just the same. He'd busted away from his old gang out at Maisons and seemed to like just sitting around on the boulevard with me. But he was dropping money every day at the track. He'd feel sort of doleful after the last race, if he'd lost on the day, until we'd get to our table and he'd have his first whisky and then he'd be fine.

He'd be reading the *Paris-Sport* and he'd look over at me and say, "Where's your girl, Joe?" to kid me on account I had told him about the girl that day at the next table. And I'd get red, but I liked being kidded about her. It gave me a good feeling. "Keep your eye peeled for her, Joe," he'd say, "she'll be back."

He'd ask me questions about things and some of the things I'd say he'd laugh. And then he'd get started talking about things. About riding down in Egypt, or at St. Moritz on the ice before my mother died, and about during the war when they had regular races down in the south of France without any purses, or betting or crowd or anything just to keep the breed up. Regular races with the jocks riding hell out of the horses. Gee, I could listen to my old man talk by the hour, especially when he'd had a couple or so of drinks. He'd tell me about when he was a boy in Kentucky and going coon hunting, and the old days in the States before everything went on the bum there. And he'd say, "Joe, when we've got a decent stake, you're going back there to the States and go to school."

"What've I got to go back there to go to school for when everything's on the bum there?" I'd ask him.

"That's different," he'd say and get the waiter over and pay the pile of saucers and we'd get a taxi to the Gare St. Lazare and get on the train out to Maisons.

One day at Auteuil, after a selling steeplechase, my old man bought in the winner for 30,000 francs. He had to bid a little to get him but the stable let the horse go finally and my old man had his permit and his colors in a week. Gee, I felt proud when my old man was an owner. He fixed it up for stable space with Charles Drake and cut out coming in to Paris, and started his running and sweating out again, and him and I were the whole stable gang. Our horse's name was Gilford, he was Irish bred and a nice, sweet jumper. My old man figured that training him and riding him, himself, he was a good investment. I was proud of everything and I thought Gilford was as good a horse as Kzar. He was a good, solid jumper, a bay, with plenty of speed on the flat, if you asked him for it, and he was a nice-looking horse, too.

Gee, I was fond of him. The first time he started with my old man up, he finished third in a 2500 meter hurdle race and when my old man got off him, all sweating and happy in the place stall, and went in to weigh, I felt as proud of him as though it was the first race he'd ever placed in. You see, when a guy ain't been riding for a long time, you can't make yourself really believe that he has ever rode. The whole thing was different now, 'cause down in Milan, even big races never seemed to make any difference to my old man, if he won he wasn't ever excited or anything, and now it was so I couldn't hardly sleep the night before a race and I knew my old man was excited, too, even if he didn't show it. Riding for yourself makes an awful difference.

Second time Gilford and my old man started, was a rainy Sunday at Auteuil, in the Prix du Marat, a 4500 meter steeplechase. As soon as he'd gone out I beat it up in the stand with the new glasses my old man had bought for me to watch them. They started way over at the far end of the course and there was some trouble at the barrier. Something with goggle blinders on was making a great fuss and rearing around and busted the barrier once, but I could see my old man in our black jacket, with a white cross and a black cap, sitting up on Gilford, and patting him with his hand. Then they were off in a jump and out of sight behind the trees and the gong going for dear life and the pari-mutuel wickets rattling down. Gosh, I was so excited, I was afraid to look at them, but I fixed the glasses on the place where they would come out back of the trees and then out they came with the old black jacket going third and they all sailing over the jump like birds. Then they went out of sight again and then they came pounding out and down the hill and all going nice and sweet and easy and taking the fence smooth in a bunch, and moving away from us all solid. Looked as though you could walk across on their backs they were all so bunched and going so smooth. Then they bellied over the big double Bullfinch[3] and something came down. I couldn't see who it was, but in a minute the horse was up and galloping free and the field, all bunched still, sweeping around the long left turn into the straightaway. They jumped the stone wall and came jammed down the stretch toward the big water-jump right in front of the stands. I saw them coming and hollered at my old man as he went by, and he was leading by about a length and riding way out, and light as a monkey, and they were racing for the water-jump. They took off over the big hedge of the water-jump in a pack and then there was a crash, and two horses pulled sideways out off it, and kept on going, and three others were piled up. I couldn't see my old man anywhere. One horse kneed himself up and the

---

[3] A hedge with a ditch on one side.

jock had hold of the bridle and mounted and went slamming on after the place money. The other horse was up and away by himself, jerking his head and galloping with the bridle rein hanging and the jock staggered over to one side of the track against the fence. Then Gilford rolled over to one side off my old man and got up and started to run on three legs with his front off hoof dangling and there was my old man laying there on the grass flat out with his face up and blood all over the side of his head. I ran down the stand and bumped into a jam of people and got to the rail and a cop grabbed me and held me and two big stretcher-bearers were going out after my old man and around on the other side of the course I saw three horses, strung way out, coming out of the trees and taking the jump.

My old man was dead when they brought him in and while a doctor was listening to his heart with a thing plugged in his ears, I heard a shot up the track that meant they'd killed Gilford. I lay down beside my old man, when they carried the stretcher into the hospital room, and hung onto the stretcher and cried and cried, and he looked so white and gone and so awfully dead, and I couldn't help feeling that if my old man was dead maybe they didn't need to have shot Gilford, his hoof might have got well. I don't know. I loved my old man so much.

Then a couple of guys came in and one of them patted me on the back and then went over and looked at my old man and then pulled a sheet off the cot and spread it over him; and the other was telephoning in French for them to send the ambulance to take him out to Maisons. And I couldn't stop crying, crying and choking, sort of, and George Gardner came in and sat down beside me on the floor and put his arm around me and says, "Come on, Joe, old boy. Get up and we'll go out and wait for the ambulance."

George and I went out to the gate and I was trying to stop bawling and George wiped off my face with his handkerchief and we were standing back a little ways while the crowd was going out of the gate and a couple of guys stopped near us while we were waiting for the crowd to get through the gate and one of them was counting a bunch of mutuel tickets and he said, "Well, Butler got his, all right."

The other guy said, "I don't give a good goddam if he did, the crook. He had it coming to him on the stuff he's pulled."

"I'll say he had," said the other guy, and tore the bunch of tickets in two.

And George Gardner looked at me to see if I'd heard and I had all right and he said, "Don't you listen to what those bums said, Joe. Your old man was one swell guy."

But I don't know. Seems like when they get started they don't leave a guy nothing.

QUESTIONS

1. The young narrator of Anderson's "I'm a Fool" stands in the center of plot. This narrator, little involved in the action, reports his father's racing activities in Italy and France. What is his attitude toward his father? What does he mean by "they don't leave a guy nothing"?

2. Are there things about the father that the boy doesn't know?

3. Reporting the race lost by the horse Kzar, the boy says of the jockey "that was funny, thinking of George Gardner as a son of a bitch because I'd always liked him and besides he'd given us the winner, but I guess that's what he is, all right." Earlier he had heard some men in Milan refer to his father in the same way. What is the connection? Does the boy see it?
4. Could the story have been told from another narrative perspective?

"The Old Chief Mshlanga" begins in the third person. The narrator, like the omniscient teller of a fairy tale, describes a land distant in time and space. But suddenly the viewpoint shifts. We are in that land, observing it through the eyes of a girl who is growing up as a stranger to its ancient ways.

THE OLD CHIEF MSHLANGA
Doris Lessing   (1919–   )

They were good, the years of ranging the bush over her father's farm which, like every white farm, was largely unused, broken only occasionally by small patches of cultivation. In between, nothing but trees, the long sparse grass, thorn and cactus and gully, grass and outcrop and thorn. And a jutting piece of rock which had been thrust up from the warm soil of Africa unimaginable eras of time ago, washed into hollows and whorls by sun and wind that had travelled so many thousands of miles of space and bush, would hold the weight of a small girl whose eyes were sightless for anything but a pale willowed river, a pale gleaming castle—a small girl singing: "Out flew the web and floated wide, the mirror cracked from side to side . . ."

Pushing her way through the green aisles of the mealie stalks, the leaves arching like cathedrals veined with sunlight far overhead, with the packed red earth underfoot, a fine lace of red starred witchweed would summon up a black bent figure croaking premonitions: the Northern witch, bred of cold Northern forests, would stand before her among the mealie fields, and it was the mealie fields that faded and fled, leaving her among the gnarled roots of an oak, snow falling thick and soft and white, the woodcutter's fire glowing red welcome through crowding tree trunks.

A white child, opening its eyes curiously on a sun-suffused landscape, a gaunt and violent landscape, might be supposed to accept it as her own, to take the msasa trees and the thorn trees as familiars, to feel her blood running free and responsive to the swing of the seasons.

This child could not see a msasa tree, or the thorn, for what they were. Her books held tales of alien fairies, her rivers ran slow and peaceful, and she knew the shape of the leaves of an ash or an oak, the names of the little creatures that lived in English streams, when the words "the veld"[1] meant strangeness, though she could remember nothing else.

---

[1] Open pasture land in South Africa (from Dutch).

Because of this, for many years, it was the veld that seemed unreal; the sun was a foreign sun, and the wind spoke a strange language.

The black people on the farm were as remote as the trees and the rocks. They were an amorphous black mass, mingling and thinning and massing like tadpoles, faceless, who existed merely to serve, to say "Yes, Baas," take their money and go. They changed season by season, moving from one farm to the next, according to their outlandish needs, which one did not have to understand, coming from perhaps hundreds of miles North or East, passing on after a few months—where? Perhaps even as far away as the fabled gold mines of Johannesburg, where the pay was so much better than the few shillings a month and the double handful of mealie meal twice a day which they earned in that part of Africa.

The child was taught to take them for granted: the servants in the house would come running a hundred yards to pick up a book if she dropped it. She was called "Nkosikaas"—Chieftainess, even by the black children her own age.

Later, when the farm grew too small to hold her curiosity, she carried a gun in the crook of her arm and wandered miles a day, from vlei[2] to vlei, from *kopje*[3] *to kopje*, accompanied by two dogs: the dogs and the gun were an armour against fear. Because of them she never felt fear.

If a native came into sight along the kaffir[4] paths half a mile away, the dogs would flush him up a tree as if he were a bird. If he expostulated (in his uncouth language which was by itself ridiculous) that was cheek. If one was in a good mood, it could be a matter for laughter. Otherwise one passed on, hardly glancing at the angry man in the tree.

On the rare occasions when white children met together they could amuse themselves by hailing a passing native in order to make a buffoon of him; they could set the dogs on him and watch him run; they could tease a small black child as if he were a puppy—save that they would not throw stones and sticks at a dog without a sense of guilt.

Later still, certain questions presented themselves in the child's mind; and because the answers were not easy to accept, they were silenced by an even greater arrogance of manner.

It was even impossible to think of the black people who worked about the house as friends, for if she talked to one of them, her mother would come running anxiously: "Come away; you mustn't talk to natives."

It was this instilled consciousness of danger, of something unpleasant, that made it easy to laugh out loud, crudely, if a servant made a mistake in his English or if he failed to understand an order—there is a certain kind of laughter that is fear, afraid of itself.

One evening, when I was about fourteen, I was walking down the side of a mealie field that had been newly ploughed, so that the great red clods showed fresh and tumbling to the vlei beyond, like a choppy red sea; it was that hushed and listening hour, when the birds send long sad calls from tree to tree, and all the colours of earth and sky and leaf are deep and golden. I had my rifle in the curve of my arm, and the dogs were at my heels.

[2] Small valley.
[3] Small hill.
[4] The white South African term for Zulus and related blacks, borrowed from the Arabic slavers' word meaning "nonbeliever."

In front of me, perhaps a couple of hundred yards away, a group of three Africans came into sight around the side of a big antheap. I whistled the dogs close in to my skirts and let the gun swing in my hand, and advanced, waiting for them to move aside, off the path, in respect for my passing. But they came on steadily, and the dogs looked up at me for the command to chase. I was angry. It was "cheek" for a native not to stand off a path, the moment he caught sight of you.

In front walked an old man, stooping his weight on to a stick, his hair grizzled white, a dark red blanket slung over his shoulders like a cloak. Behind him came two young men, carrying bundles of pots, assegais,[5] hatchets.

The group was not a usual one. They were not natives seeking work. These had an air of dignity, of quietly following their own purpose. It was the dignity that checked my tongue. I walked quietly on, talking softly to the growling dogs, till I was ten paces away. Then the old man stopped, drawing his blanket close.

"Morning, Nkosikaas," he said, using the customary greeting for any time of the day.

"Good morning," I said, "Where are you going?" My voice was a little truculent.

The old man spoke in his own language, then one of the young men stepped forward politely and said in careful English: "My Chief travels to see his brothers beyond the river."

A Chief! I thought, understanding the pride that made the old man stand before me like an equal—more than an equal, for he showed courtesy, and I showed none.

The old man spoke again, wearing dignity like an inherited garment, still standing ten paces off, flanked by his entourage, not looking at me (that would have been rude) but directing his eyes somewhere over my head at the trees.

"You are the little Nkosikaas from the farm of Baas Jordan?"

"That's right," I said.

"Perhaps your father does not remember," said the interpreter for the old man, "but there was an affair with some goats. I remember seeing you when you were . . ." The young man held his hand at knee level and smiled.

We all smiled.

"What is your name?" I asked.

"This is Chief Mshlanga," said the young man.

"I will tell my father that I met you," I said.

The old man said: "My greetings to your father, little Nkosikaas."

"Good morning," I said politely, finding the politeness difficult, from lack of use.

"Morning, little Nkosikaas," said the old man, and stood aside to let me pass.

I went by, my gun hanging awkwardly, the dogs sniffing and growling, cheated of their favourite game of chasing natives like animals.

Not long afterwards I read in an old explorer's book the phrase: "Chief Mshlanga's country." It went like this: "Our destination was Chief Mshlanga's country, to the north of the river; and it was our desire to ask his permission to prospect for gold in his territory."

[5] Spears.

The phrase "ask his permission" was so extraordinary to a white child, brought up to consider all natives as things to use, that it revived those questions, which could not be suppressed: they fermented slowly in my mind.

On another occasion one of those old prospectors who still move over Africa looking for neglected reefs, with their hammers and tents, and pans for sifting gold from crushed rock, came to the farm and, in talking of the old days, used that phrase again: "This was the Old Chief's country," he said. "It stretched from those mountains over there way back to the river, hundreds of miles of country." That was his name for our district: "The Old Chief's Country"; he did not use our name for it—a new phrase which held no implication of usurped ownership.

As I read more books about the time when this part of Africa was opened up, not much more than fifty years before, I found Old Chief Mshlanga had been a famous man, known to all the explorers and prospectors. But then he had been young; or maybe it was his father or uncle they spoke of—I never found out.

During that year I met him several times in the part of the farm that was traversed by natives moving over the country. I learned that the path up the side of the big red field where the birds sang was the recognized highway for migrants. Perhaps I even haunted it in the hope of meeting him: being greeted by him, the exchange of courtesies, seemed to answer the questions that troubled me.

Soon I carried a gun in a different spirit; I used it for shooting food and not to give me confidence. And now the dogs learned better manners. When I saw a native approaching, we offered and took greetings; and slowly that other landscape in my mind faded, and my feet struck directly on the African soil, and I saw the shapes of tree and hill clearly, and the black people moved back, as it were, out of my life: it was as if I stood aside to watch a slow intimate dance of landscape and men, a very old dance, whose steps I could not learn.

But I thought: this is my heritage, too; I was bred here; it is my country as well as the black man's country; and there is plenty of room for all of us, without elbowing each other off the pavements and roads.

It seemed it was only necessary to let free that respect I felt when I was talking with old Chief Mshlanga, to let both black and white people meet gently, with tolerance for each other's differences: it seemed quite easy.

Then, one day, something new happened. Working in our house as servants were always three natives: cook, houseboy, garden boy. They used to change as the farm natives changed: staying for a few months, then moving on to a new job, or back home to their kraals. They were thought of as "good" or "bad" natives; which meant: how did they behave as servants? Were they lazy, efficient, obedient, or disrespectful? If the family felt good-humoured, the phrase was. "What can you expect from raw black savages?" If we were angry, we said: "These damned niggers, we would be much better off with out them."

One day, a white policeman was on his rounds of the district, and he said laughingly: "Did you know you have an important man in your kitchen?"

"What!" exclaimed my mother sharply. "What do you mean?"

"A Chief's son." The policeman seemed amused. "He'll boss the tribe when the old man dies."

"He'd better not put on a Chief's son act with me," said my mother.

When the policeman left, we looked with different eyes at our cook: he was a good worker, but he drank too much at week-ends—that was how we knew him.

He was a tall youth, with very black skin, like black polished metal, his tight-ly-growing black hair parted white man's fashion at one side, with a metal comb from the store stuck into it; very polite, very distant, very quick to obey an order. Now that it had been pointed out, we said: "Of course, you can see. Blood always tells."

My mother became strict with him now she knew about his birth and pros-pects. Sometimes, when she lost her temper, she would say: "You aren't the Chief yet, you know." And he would answer her very quietly, his eyes on the ground: "Yes, Nkosikaas."

One afternoon he asked for a whole day off, instead of the customary half-day, to go home next Sunday.

"How can you go home in one day?"

"It will take me half an hour on my bicycle," he explained.

I watched the direction he took; and the next day I went off to look for this kraal[6]; I understood he must be Chief Mshlanga's successor: there was no other kraal near enough our farm.

Beyond our boundaries on that side the country was new to me. I followed unfamiliar paths past *kopjes* that till now had been part of the jagged horizon, hazed with distance. This was Government land, which had never been cultivat-ed by white men; at first I could not understand why it was that it appeared, in merely crossing the boundary, I had entered a completely fresh type of land-scape. It was a wide green valley, where a small river sparkled, and vivid water-birds darted over the rushes. The grass was thick and soft to my calves, the trees stood tall and shapely.

I was used to our farm, whose hundreds of acres of harsh eroded soil bore trees that had been cut for the mine furnaces and had grown thin and twisted, where the cattle had dragged the grass flat, leaving innumerable criss-crossing trails that deepened each season into gullies, under the force of the rains.

This country had been left untouched, save for prospectors whose picks had struck a few sparks from the surface of the rocks as they wandered by; and for migrant natives whose passing had left, perhaps, a charred patch on the trunk of a tree where their evening fire had nestled.

It was very silent; a hot morning with pigeons cooing throatily, the midday shadows lying dense and thick with clear yellow spaces of sunlight between and in all that wide green park-like valley, not a human soul but myself.

I was listening to the quick regular tapping of a woodpecker when slowly a chill feeling seemed to grow up from the small of my back to my shoulders, in a constricting spasm like a shudder, and at the roots of my hair a tingling sensa-tion began and ran down over the surface of my flesh, leaving me goosefleshed and cold, though I was damp with sweat. Fever? I thought; then uneasily, turned to look over my shoulder; and realized suddenly that this was fear. It was ex-traordinary, even humiliating. It was a new fear. For all the years I had walked by myself over this country I had never known a moment's uneasiness; in the be-ginning because I had been supported by a gun and the dogs, then because I had learnt an easy friendliness for the Africans I might encounter.

I had read of this feeling, how the bigness and silence of Africa, under the an-

[6] Native village.

cient sun, grows dense and takes shape in the mind, till even the birds seem to call menacingly, and a deadly spirit comes out of the trees and the rocks. You move warily, as if your very passing disturbs something old and evil, something dark and big and angry that might suddenly rear and strike from behind. You look at groves of entwined trees, and picture the animals that might be lurking there; you look at the river running slowly, dropping from level to level through the vlei, spreading into pools where at night the bucks come to drink, and the crocodiles rise and drag them by their soft noses into underwater caves. Fear possessed me. I found I was turning round and round, because of that shapeless menace behind me that might reach out and take me; I kept glancing at the files of *kopjes* which, seen from a different angle, seemed to change with every step so that even known landmarks, like a big mountain that had sentinelled my world since I first became conscious of it, showed an unfamiliar sunlit valley among its foothills. I did not know where I was. I was lost. Panic seized me. I found I was spinning round and round, staring anxiously at this tree and that, peering up at the sun which appeared to have moved into an eastern slant, shedding the sad yellow light of sunset. Hours must have passed! I looked at my watch and found that this state of meaningless terror had lasted perhaps ten minutes.

The point was that it was meaningless. I was not ten miles from home: I had only to take my way back along the valley to find myself at the fence; away among the foothills of the *kopjes* gleamed the roof of a neighbour's house, and a couple of hours' walking would reach it. This was the sort of fear that contracts the flesh of a dog at night and sets him howling at the full moon. It had nothing to do with what I thought or felt; and I was more disturbed by the fact that I could become its victim than of the physical sensation itself: I walked steadily on, quietened, in a divided mind, watching my own pricking nerves and apprehensive glances from side to side with a disgusted amusement. Deliberately I set myself to think of this village I was seeking, and what I should do when I entered it—if I could find it, which was doubtful, since I walking aimlessly and it might be anywhere in the hundreds of thousands of acres of bush that stretched about me. With my mind on that village, I realized that a new sensation was added to the fear: loneliness. Now such a terror of isolation invaded me that I could hardly walk; and if it were not that I came over the crest of a small rise and saw a village below me, I should have turned and gone home. It was a cluster of thatched huts in a clearing among trees. There were neat patches of mealies and pumpkins and millet, and cattle grazed under some trees at a distance. Fowls scratched among the huts, dogs lay sleeping on the grass, and goats friezed a *kopje* that jutted up beyond a tributary of the river lying like an enclosing arm round the village.

As I came close I saw the huts were lovingly decorated with patterns of yellow and red and ochre mud on the walls; and the thatch was tied in place with plaits of straw.

This was not at all like our farm compound, a dirty and neglected place, a temporary home for migrants who had no roots in it.

And now I did not know what to do next. I called a small black boy, who was sitting on a lot playing a stringed gourd, quite naked except for the strings of blue beads round his neck, and said: "Tell the Chief I am here." The child stuck his thumb in his mouth and stared shyly back at me.

For minutes I shifted my feet on the edge of what seemed a deserted village, till at last the child scuttled off, and then some women came. They were draped in bright cloths, with brass glinting in their ears and on their arms. They also stared, silently; then turned to chatter among themselves.

I said again: "Can I see Chief Mshlanga?" I saw they caught the name; they did not understand what I wanted. I did not understand myself.

At last I walked through them and came past the huts and saw a clearing under a big shady tree, where a dozen old men sat crosslegged on the ground, talking. Chief Mshlanga was leaning back against the tree, holding a gourd in his hand, from which he had been drinking. When he saw me, not a muscle of his face moved, and I could see he was not pleased: perhaps he was afflicted with my own shyness, due to being unable to find the right forms of courtesy for the occasion. To meet me, on our own farm, was one thing; but I should not have come here. What had I expected? I could not join them socially; the thing was unheard of. Bad enough that I, a white girl, should be walking the veld alone as a white man might: and in this part of the bush where only Government officials had the right to move.

Again I stood, smiling foolishly, while behind me stood the groups of brightly-clad, chattering women, their faces alert with curiosity and interest, and in front of me sat the old men, with old lined faces, their eyes guarded, aloof. It was a village of ancients and children and women. Even the two young men who kneeled beside the Chief were not those I had seen with him previously: the young men were all away working on the white men's farms and mines, and the Chief must depend on relatives who were temporarily on holiday for his attendants.

"The small white Nkosikaas is far from home," remarked the old man at last.

"Yes," I agreed, "it is far." I wanted to say: "I have come to pay you a friendly visit, Chief Mshlanga." I could not say it. I might now be feeling an urgent helpless desire to get to know these men and women as people, to be accepted by them as a friend, but the truth was I had set out in a spirit of curiosity: I had wanted to see the village that one day our cook, the reserved and obedient young man who got drunk on Sundays, would one day rule over.

"The child of Nkosi Jordan is welcome," said Chief Mshlanga.

"Thank you," I said, and could think of nothing more to say. There was a silence, while the flies rose and began to buzz around my head; and the wind shook a little in the thick green tree that spread its branches over the old men.

"Good morning," I said at last. "I have to return now to my home."

"Morning, little Nkosikaas," said Chief Mshlanga.

I walked away from the indifferent village, over the rise past the staring amber-eyed goats, down through the tall stately trees into the great rich green valley where the river meandered and the pigeons cooed tales of plenty and the woodpecker tapped softly.

The fear had gone; the loneliness had set into stiff-necked stoicism; there was now a queer hostility in the landscape, a cold, hard, sullen indomitability that walked with me, as strong as a wall, as intangible as smoke; it seemed to say to me: you walk here as a destroyer. I went slowly homewards, with an empty heart: I had learned that if one cannot call a country to heel like a dog, neither can one dismiss the past with a smile in an easy gush of feeling, saying: I could not help it, I am also a victim.

I only saw Chief Mshlanga once again.

One night my father's big red land was trampled down by small sharp hooves, and it was discovered that the culprits were goats from Chief Mshlanga's kraal. This had happened once before, years ago.

My father confiscated all the goats. Then he sent a message to the old Chief that if he wanted them he would have to pay for the damage.

He arrived at our house at the time of sunset one evening, looking very old and bent now, walking stiffly under his regally-draped blanket, leaning on a big stick. My father sat himself down in his big chair below the steps of the house; the old man squatted carefully on the ground before him, flanked by his two young men.

The palaver was long and painful, because of the bad English of the young man who interpreted, and because my father could not speak dialect, but only kitchen kaffir.

From my father's point of view, at least two hundred pounds' worth of damage had been done to the crop. He knew he could not get the money from the old man. He felt he was entitled to keep the goats. As for the old Chief, he kept repeating angrily: "Twenty goats! My people cannot lose twenty goats! We are not rich, like the Nkosi Jordan, to lose twenty goats at once."

My father did not think of himself as rich, but rather as very poor. He spoke quickly and angrily in return, saying that the damage done meant a great deal to him, and that he was entitled to the goats.

At last it grew so heated that the cook, the Chief's son, was called from the kitchen to be interpreter, and now my father spoke fluently in English, and our cook translated rapidly so that the old man could understand how very angry my father was. The young man spoke without emotion, in a mechanical way, his eyes lowered, but showing how he felt his position by a hostile uncomfortable set of the shoulders.

It was now in the late sunset, the sky a welter of colours, the birds singing their last songs, and the cattle, lowing peacefully, moving past us towards their sheds for the night. It was the hour when Africa is most beautiful; and here was this pathetic, ugly scene, doing no one any good.

At last my father stated finally: "I'm not going to argue about it. I am keeping the goats."

The old Chief flashed back in his own language: "That means that my people will go hungry when the dry season comes."

"Go to the police, then," said my father, and looked triumphant.

There was, of course, no more to be said.

The old man sat silent, his head bent, his hands dangling helplessly over his withered knees. Then he rose, the young men helping him, and he stood facing my father. He spoke once again, very stiffly; and turned away and went home to his village.

"What did he say?" asked my father of the young man, who laughed uncomfortably and would not meet his eyes.

"What did he say?" insisted my father.

Our cook stood straight and silent, his brows knotted together. Then he spoke. "My father says: All this land, this land you call yours, is his land, and belongs to our people."

Having made this statement, he walked off into the bush after his father, and we did not see him again.

Our next cook was a migrant from Nyasaland, with no expectations of greatness.

Next time the policeman came on his rounds he was told this story. He remarked: "That kraal has no right to be there; it should have been moved long ago. I don't know why no one has done anything about it. I'll have a chat with the Native Commissioner next week. I'm going over for tennis on Sunday, anyway."

Some time later we heard that Chief Mshlanga and his people had been moved two hundred miles east, to a proper Native Reserve; the Government land was going to be opened up for white settlement soon.

I went to see the village again, about a year afterwards. There was nothing there. Mounds of red mud, where the huts had been, had long swathes of rotting thatch over them, veined with the red galleries of the white ants. The pumpkin vines rioted everywhere, over the bushes, up the lower branches of trees so that the great golden balls rolled underfoot and dangled overhead: it was a festival of pumpkins. The bushes were crowding up, the new grass sprang vivid green.

The settler lucky enough to be allotted the lush warm valley (if he chose to cultivate this particular section) would find, suddenly, in the middle of a mealie field, the plants were growing fifteen feet tall, the weight of the cobs dragging at the stalks, and wonder what unsuspected vein of richness he had struck.

QUESTIONS
1. What purpose is served by beginning in the third person?
2. Read again the last two paragraphs. What point is made through reporting this last visit to the village? Is there an irony in the "vein of richness" of the last sentence?
3. Summarize the narrator's attitude toward the old Chief.
4. Do the observations of a girl of fourteen provide an edge to the story that would be missing in the observations of an adult?
5. At the time she writes, the narrator has become an adult. How has that affected the story? Compare, for instance, Hemingway's "My Old Man."
6. At one point the narrator writes, "I had learned that if one cannot call a country to heel like a dog, neither can one dismiss the past with a smile in an easy gush of feeling, saying: I could not help it, I am also a victim." What does she mean?

Occasionally the teller does not react to his story the way most people would. Reading "Haircut," we do not see Jim Kendall the way the narrator does. In characterizing Jim, he reveals much about himself.

HAIRCUT

Ring Lardner   (1885–1933)

I got another barber that comes over from Carterville and helps me out Saturdays, but the rest of the time I can get along all right alone. You can see for yourself that this ain't no New York City and besides that, the most of the boys works all day and don't have no leisure to drop in here and get themselves prettied up.

You're a newcomer, ain't you? I thought I hadn't seen you round before. I hope you like it good enough to stay. As I say, we ain't no New York City or Chicago, but we have pretty good times. Not as good, though, since Jim Kendall got killed. When he was alive, him and Hod Meyers used to keep this town in an uproar. I bet they was more laughin' done here than any town its size in America.

Jim was comical, and Hod was pretty near a match for him. Since Jim's gone, Hod tries to hold his end up just the same as ever, but it's tough goin' when you ain't got nobody to kind of work with.

They used to be plenty fun in here Saturdays. This place is jam-packed Saturdays, from four o'clock on. Jim and Hod would show up right after their supper, round six o'clock. Jim would set himself down in that big chair, nearest the blue spittoon. Whoever had been settin' in that chair, why they'd get up when Jim come in and give it to him.

You'd of thought it was a reserved seat like they have sometimes in a theayter. Hod would generally always stand or walk up and down, or some Saturdays, of course, he'd be settin' in this chair part of the time, gettin' a haircut.

Well, Jim would set there a w'ile without openin' his mouth only to spit, and then finally he'd say to me, "Whitey,"—my right name, that is, my right first name, is Dick, but everybody round here calls me Whitey—Jim would say, "Whitey, your nose looks like a rosebud tonight. You must of been drinkin' some of your aw de cologne."

So I'd say, "No, Jim, but you look like you'd been drinkin' somethin' of that kind or somethin' worse."

Jim would have to laugh at that, but then he'd speak up and say, "No, I ain't had nothin' to drink, but that ain't sayin' I wouldn't like somethin'. I wouldn't even mind if it was wood alcohol."

Then Hod Meyers would say, "Neither would your wife." That would set everybody to laughin' because Jim and his wife wasn't on very good terms. She'd of divorced him only they wasn't no chance to get alimony and she didn't have no way to take care of herself and the kids. She couldn't never understand Jim. He *was* kind of rough, but a good fella at heart.

Him and Hod had all kinds of sport with Milt Sheppard. I don't suppose you've seen Milt. Well, he's got an Adam's apple that looks more like a mushmelon. So I'd be shavin' Milt and when I'd start to shave down here on his neck, Hod would holler, "Hey, Whitey, wait a minute! Before you cut into it, let's make up a pool and see who can guess closest to the number of seeds."

And Jim would say, "If Milt hadn't of been so hoggish, he'd of ordered a half a cantaloupe instead of a whole one and it might not of stuck in his throat."

All the boys would roar at this and Milt himself would force a smile, though the joke was on him. Jim certainly was a card!

There's his shavin' mug, settin' on the shelf, right next to Charley Vail's.

"Charles M. Vail." That's the druggist. He comes in regular for his shave, three times a week. And Jim's is the cup next to Charley's. "James H. Kendall." Jim won't need no shavin' mug no more, but I'll leave it there just the same for old time's sake. Jim certainly was a character!

Years ago, Jim used to travel for a canned goods concern over in Carterville. They sold canned goods. Jim had the whole northern half of the State and was on the road five days out of every week. He'd drop in here Saturdays and tell his experiences for that week. It was rich.

I guess he paid more attention to playin' jokes than makin' sales. Finally the concern let him out and he come right home here and told everybody he'd been fired instead of sayin' he'd resigned like most fellas would of.

It was a Saturday and the shop was full and Jim got up out of that chair and says, "Gentlemen, I got an important announcement to make. I been fired from my job."

Well, they asked him if he was in earnest and he said he was and nobody could think of nothin' to say till Jim finally broke the ice himself. He says, "I been sellin' canned goods and now I'm canned goods myself."

You see, the concern he'd been workin' for was a factory that made canned goods. Over in Carterville. And now Jim said he was canned himself. He was certainly a card!

Jim had a great trick that he used to play w'ile he was travelin'. For instance, he'd be ridin' on a train and they'd come to some little town like, well, like, we'll say, like Benton. Jim would look out the train window and read the signs on the stores.

For instance, they'd be a sign, "Henry Smith, Dry Goods." Well, Jim would write down the name and the name of the town and when he got to wherever he was goin' he'd mail back a postal card to Henry Smith at Benton and not sign no name to it, but he'd write on the card, well, somethin' like "Ask your wife about that book agent that spent the afternoon last week," or "Ask your Missus who kept her from gettin' lonesome the last time you was in Carterville." And he'd sign the card, "A Friend."

Of course, he never knew what really come of none of these jokes, but he could picture what *probably* happened and that was enough.

Jim didn't work very steady after he lost his position with the Carterville people. What he did earn, doin' odd jobs round town, why he spent pretty near all of it on gin and his family might of starved if the stores hadn't of carried them along. Jim's wife tried her hand at dressmakin', but they ain't nobody goin' to get rich makin' dresses in this town.

As I say, she'd of divorced Jim, only she seen that she couldn't support herself and the kids and she was always hopin' that some day Jim would cut out his habits and give her more than two or three dollars a week.

They was a time when she would go to whoever he was workin' for and ask them to give her his wages, but after she done this once or twice, he beat her to it by borrowin' most of his pay in advance. He told it all round town, how he had outfoxed his Missus. He certainly was a caution!

But he wasn't satisfied with just outwittin' her. He was sore the way she had acted, tryin' to grab off his pay. And he made up his mind he'd get even. Well, he waited till Evans's Circus was advertised to come to town. Then he told his wife and two kiddies that he was goin' to take them to the circus. The day of the circus, he told them he would get the tickets and meet them outside the entrance to the tent.

Well, he didn't have no intentions of bein' there or buyin' tickets or nothin'. He got full of gin and laid round Wright's poolroom all day. His wife and the kids waited and waited and of course he didn't show up. His wife didn't have a dime with her, or nowhere else, I guess. So she finally had to tell the kids it was all off and they cried like they wasn't never goin' to stop.

Well, it seems, w'ile they was cryin', Doc Stair came along and he asked what was the matter, but Mrs. Kendall was stubborn and wouldn't tell him, but the kids told him and he insisted on takin' them and their mother in the show. Jim found this out afterwards and it was one reason why he had it in for Doc Stair.

Doc Stair come here about a year and a half ago. He's a mighty handsome young fella and his clothes always look like he has them made to order. He goes to Detroit two or three times a year and w'ile he's there he must have a tailor take his measure and then make him a suit to order. They cost pretty near twice as much, but they fit a whole lot better than if you just bought them in a store.

For a w'ile everybody was wonderin' why a young doctor like Doc Stair should come to a town like this where we already got old Doc Gamble and Doc Foote that's both been here for years and all the practice in town was always divided between the two of them.

Then they was a story got round that Doc Stair's gal had throwed him over, a gal up in the Northern Peninsula somewheres, and the reason he come here was to hide himself away and forget it. He said himself that he thought they wasn't nothin' like general practice in a place like ours to fit a man to be a good all round doctor. And that's why he'd came.

Anyways, it wasn't long before he was makin' enough to live on, though they tell me that he never dunned nobody for what they owed him, and the folks here certainly has got the owin' habit, even in my business. If I had all that was comin' to me for just shaves alone, I could go to Carterville and put up at the Mercer for a week and see a different picture every night. For instance, they's old George Purdy—but I guess I shouldn't ought to be gossipin'.

Well, last year, our coroner died, died of the flu. Ken Beatty, that was his name. He was the coroner. So they had to choose another man to be coroner in his place and they picked Doc Stair. He laughed at first and said he didn't want it, but they made him take it. It ain't no job that anybody would fight for and what a man makes out of it in a year would just about buy seeds for their garden. Doc's the kind, though, that can't say no to nothin' if you keep at him long enough.

But I was goin' to tell you about a poor boy we got here in town—Paul Dickson. He fell out of a tree when he was about ten years old. Lit on his head and it done somethin' to him and he ain't never been right. No harm in him, but just silly. Jim Kendall used to call him cuckoo; that's a name Jim had for anybody that was off their head, only he called people's head their bean. That was another of his gags, callin' head bean and callin' crazy people cuckoo. Only poor Paul ain't crazy, but just silly.

You can imagine that Jim used to have all kinds of fun with Paul. He'd send him to the White Front Garage for a left-handed monkey wrench. Of course they ain't no such a thing as a left-handed monkey wrench.

And once we had a kind of a fair here and they was a baseball game between the fats and the leans and before the game started Jim called Paul over and sent him way down to Schrader's hardware store to get a key for the pitcher's box.

They wasn't nothin' in the way of gags that Jim couldn't think up, when he put his mind to it.

Poor Paul was always kind of suspicious of people, maybe on account of how Jim had kept foolin' him. Paul wouldn't have much to do with anybody only his own mother and Doc Stair and a girl here in town named Julie Gregg. That is, she ain't a girl no more, but pretty near thirty or over.

When Doc first come to town, Paul seemed to feel like here was a real friend and he hung round Doc's office most of the w'ile; the only time he wasn't there was when he'd go home to eat or sleep or when he seen Julie Gregg doin' her shoppin'.

When he looked out Doc's window and seen her, he'd run downstairs and join her and tag along with her to the different stores. The poor boy was crazy about Julie and she always treated him mighty nice and made him feel like he was welcome, though of course it wasn't nothin' but pity on her side.

Doc done all he could to improve Paul's mind and he told me once that he really thought the boy was gettin' better, that they was times when he was as bright and sensible as anybody else.

But I was goin' to tell you about Julie Gregg. Old Man Gregg was in the lumber business, but got to drinkin' and lost the most of his money and when he died, he didn't leave nothin' but the house and just enough insurance for the girl to skimp along on.

Her mother was a kind of a half invalid and didn't hardly ever leave the house. Julie wanted to sell the place and move somewheres else after the old man died, but the mother said she was born here and would die here. It was tough on Julie, as the young people round this town—well, she's too good for them.

She's been away to school and Chicago and New York and different places and they ain't no subject she can't talk on, where you take the rest of the young folks here and you mention anything to them outside of Gloria Swanson or Tommy Meighan and they think you're delirious. Did you see Gloria in Wages of Virtue? You missed somethin'!

Well, Doc Stair hadn't been here more than a week when he come in one day to get shaved and I recognized who he was as he had been pointed out to me, so I told him about my old lady. She's been ailin' for a couple years and either Doc Gamble or Doc Foote, neither one, seemed to be helpin' her. So he said he would come out and see her, but if she was able to get out herself, it would be better to bring her to his office where he could make a completer examination.

So I took her to his office and w'ile I was waitin' for her in the reception room, in come Julie Gregg. When somebody comes in Doc Stair's office, they's a bell that rings in his inside office so as he can tell they's somebody to see him.

So he left my old lady inside and come out to the front office and that's the first time him and Julie met and I guess it was what they call love at first sight. But it wasn't fifty-fifty. This young fella was the slickest lookin' fella she'd ever seen in this town and she went wild over him. To him she was just a young lady that wanted to see the doctor.

She'd came on about the same business I had. Her mother had been doctorin' for years with Doc Gamble and Doc Foote and without no results. So she'd heard they was a new doc in town and decided to give him a try. He promised to call and see her mother that same day.

I said a minute ago that it was love at first sight on her part. I'm not only judgin' by how she acted afterwards but how she looked at him that first day in his office. I ain't no mind reader, but it was wrote all over her face that she was gone.

Now Jim Kendall, besides bein' a jokesmith and a pretty good drinker, well, Jim was quite a lady-killer. I guess he run pretty wild durin' the time he was on the road for them Carterville people, and besides that, he'd had a couple little affairs of the heart right here in town. As I say, his wife could of divorced him, only she couldn't.

But Jim was like the majority of men, and women, too, I guess. He wanted what he couldn't get. He wanted Julie Gregg and worked his head off tryin' to land her. Only he'd of said bean instead of head.

Well, Jim's habits and his jokes didn't appeal to Julie and of course he was a married man, so he didn't have no more chance than, well, than a rabbit. That's an expression of Jim's himself. When somebody didn't have no chance to get elected or somethin', Jim would always say they didn't have no more chance than a rabbit.

He didn't make no bones about how he felt. Right in here, more than once, in front of the whole crowd, he said he was stuck on Julie and anybody that could get her for him was welcome to his house and his wife and kids included. But she wouldn't have nothin' to do with him; wouldn't even speak to him on the street. He finally seen he wasn't gettin' nowheres with his usual line so he decided to try the rough stuff. He went right up to her house one evenin' and when she opened the door he forced his way in and grabbed her. But she broke loose and before he could stop her, she run in the next room and locked the door and phoned to Joe Barnes. Joe's the marshal. Jim could hear who she was phonin' to and he beat it before Joe got there.

Joe was an old friend of Julie's pa. Joe went to Jim the next day and told him what would happen if he ever done it again.

I don't know how the news of this little affair leaked out. Chances is that Joe Barnes told his wife and she told somebody else's wife and they told their husband. Anyways, it did leak out and Hod Meyers had the nerve to kid Jim about it, right here in this shop. Jim didn't deny nothin' and kind of laughed it off and said for us all to wait, that lots of people had tried to make a monkey out of him, but he always got even.

Meanw'ile everybody in town was wise to Julie's bein' wild mad over the Doc. I don't suppose she had any idear how her face changed when him and her was together; of course she couldn't of, or she'd of kept away from him. And she didn't know that we was all noticin' how many times she made excuses to go up to his office or pass it on the other side of the street and look up in his window to see if he was there. I felt sorry for her and so did most other people.

Hod Meyers kept rubbin' it into Jim about how the Doc had cut him out. Jim didn't pay no attention to the kiddin' and you could see he was plannin' one of his jokes.

One trick Jim had was the knack of changin' his voice. He could make you think he was a girl talkin' and he could mimic any man's voice. To show you how good he was along this line, I'll tell you the joke he played on me once.

You know, in most towns of any size, when a man is dead and needs a shave, why the barber that shaves him soaks him five dollars for the job; that is, he don't soak *him*, but whoever ordered the shave. I just charge three dollars because personally I don't mind much shavin' a dead person. They lay a whole lot stiller than live customers. The only thing is that you don't feel like talkin' to them and you get kind of lonesome.

Well, about the coldest day we ever had here, two years ago last winter, the phone rung at the house w'ile I was home to dinner and I answered the phone and it was a woman's voice and she said she was Mrs. John Scott and her husband was dead and would I come out and shave him.

Old John had always been a good customer of mine. But they live seven miles out in the country, on the Streeter road. Still I didn't see how I could say no.

So I said I would be there, but would have to come in a jitney and it might cost three or four dollars besides the price of the shave. So she, or the voice, it said that was all right, so I got Frank Abbott to drive me out to the place and when I got there, who should open the door but old John himself! He wasn't no more dead than, well, than a rabbit.

It didn't take no private detective to figure out who had played me this little joke. Nobody could of thought it up but Jim Kendall. He certainly was a card!

I tell you this incident just to show you how he could disguise his voice and make you believe it was somebody else talkin'. I'd of swore it was Mrs. Scott had called me. Anyways, some woman.

Well, Jim waited till he had Doc Stair's voice down pat; then he went after revenge.

He called Julie up on a night when he knew Doc was over in Carterville. She never questioned but what it was Doc's voice. Jim said he must see her that night; he couldn't wait no longer to tell her somethin'. She was all excited and told him to come to the house. But he said he was expectin' an important long distance call and wouldn't she please forget her manners for once and come to his office. He said they couldn't nothin' hurt her and nobody would see her and he just *must* talk to her a little w'ile. Well, poor Julie fell for it.

Doc always keeps a night light in his office, so it looked to Julie like they was somebody there.

Meanw'ile Jim Kendall had went to Wright's poolroom, where they was a whole gang amusin' themselves. The most of them had drank plenty of gin, and they was a rough bunch even when sober. They was always strong for Jim's jokes and when he told them to come with him and see some fun they give up their card games and pool games and followed along.

Doc's office is on the second floor. Right outside his door they's a flight of stairs leadin' to the floor above. Jim and his gang hid in the dark behind these stairs.

Well, Julie come up to Doc's door and rung the bell and they was nothin' doin'. She rung it again and she rung it seven or eight times. Then she tried the door and found it locked. Then Jim made some kind of a noise and she heard it and waited a minute, and then she says, "Is that you, Ralph?" Ralph is Doc's first name.

They was no answer and it must of came to her all of a sudden that she'd been bunked. She pretty near fell downstairs and the whole gang after her. They chased her all the way home, hollerin', "Is that you, Ralph?" and "Oh, Ralphie, dear, is that you?" Jim says he couldn't holler it himself, as he was laughin' too hard.

Poor Julie! She didn't show up here on Main Street for a long, long time afterward.

And of course Jim and his gang told everybody in town, everybody but Doc Stair. They was scared to tell him, and he might of never knowed only for Paul Dickson. The poor cuckoo, as Jim called him, he was here in the shop one night when Jim was still gloatin' yet over what he'd done to Julie. And Paul took in as much of it as he could understand and he run to Doc with the story.

It's a cinch Doc went up in the air and swore he'd make Jim suffer. But it was a kind of a delicate thing, because if it got out that he had beat Jim up, Julie was bound to hear of it and then she'd know that Doc knew and of course knowin' that he knew would make it worse for her than ever. He was goin' to do somethin', but it took a lot of figurin'.

Well, it was a couple days later when Jim was here in the shop again, and so was the cuckoo. Jim was goin' duck-shootin' the next day and had came in lookin' for Hod Meyers to go with him. I happened to know that Hod had went over to Carterville and wouldn't be home till the end of the week. So Jim said he hated to go alone and he guessed he would call it off. Then poor Paul spoke up and said if Jim would take him he would go along. Jim thought a w'ile and then he said, well, he guessed a half-wit was better than nothin'.

I suppose he was plottin' to get Paul out in the boat and play some joke on him, like pushin' him in the water. Anyways, he said Paul could go. He asked him had he ever shot a duck and Paul said no, he'd never even had a gun in his hands. So Jim said he could set in the boat and watch him and if he behaved himself, he might lend him his gun for a couple of shots. They made a date to meet in the mornin' and that's the last I seen of Jim alive.

Next mornin', I hadn't been open more than ten minutes when Doc Stair come in. He looked kind of nervous. He asked me had I seen Paul Dickson. I said no, but I knew where he was, out duck-shootin' with Jim Kendall. So Doc says that's what he had heard, and he couldn't understand it because Paul had told him he wouldn't never have no more to do with Jim as long as he lived.

He said Paul had told him about the joke Jim had played on Julie. He said Paul had asked him what he thought of the joke and the Doc had told him that anybody that would do a thing like that ought not to be let live.

I said it had been a kind of a raw thing, but Jim just couldn't resist no kind of a joke, no matter how raw. I said I thought he was all right at heart, but just bubblin' over with mischief. Doc turned and walked out.

At noon he got a phone call from old John Scott. The lake where Jim and Paul had went shootin' is on John's place. Paul had came runnin' up to the house a few minutes before and said they'd been an accident. Jim had shot a few ducks and then give the gun to Paul and told him to try his luck. Paul hadn't never handled a gun and he was nervous. He was shakin' so hard that he couldn't control the gun. He let fire and Jim sunk back in the boat, dead.

Doc Stair, bein' the coroner, jumped in Frank Abbott's flivver and rushed out to Scott's farm. Paul and old John was down on the shore of the lake. Paul had rowed the boat to shore, but they'd left the body in it, waitin' for Doc to come.

Doc examined the body and said they might as well fetch it back to town. They was no use leavin' it there or callin' a jury, as it was a plain case of accidental shootin'.

Personally I wouldn't never leave a person shoot a gun in the same boat I was in unless I was sure they knew somethin' about guns. Jim was a sucker to leave a new beginner have his gun, let alone a half-wit. It probably served Jim right, what he got. But still we miss him round here. He certainly was a card!

Comb it wet or dry?

QUESTIONS
1. What is the narrator's attitude toward Jim Kendall?
2. How is the reader's attitude different?
3. What is the attitude of the author, Ring Lardner? How do we know?

The events in Miss Emily's story take place at different times over many years. Indeed, because of the manner of telling, we may experience difficulty relating the events to one another in their proper chronological order.

A ROSE FOR EMILY

William Faulkner (1897–1962)

I

When Miss Emily Grierson died, our whole town went to her funeral: the men through a sort of respectful affection for a fallen monument, the women mostly out of curiosity to see the inside of her house, which no one save an old manservant—a combined gardener and cook—had seen in at least ten years.

It was a big, squarish frame house that had once been white, decorated with cupolas and spires and scrolled balconies in the heavily lightsome style of the seventies, set on what had once been our most select street. But garages and cotton gins had encroached and obliterated even the august names of that neighborhood; only Miss Emily's house was left, lifting its stubborn and coquettish decay above the cotton wagons and the gasoline pumps—an eyesore among eyesores. And now Miss Emily had gone to join the representatives of those august names where they lay in the cedar-bemused cemetery among the ranked and anonymous graves of Union and Confederate soldiers who fell at the battle of Jefferson.

Alive, Miss Emily had been a tradition, a duty, and a care; a sort of hereditary obligation upon the town, dating from that day in 1894 when Colonel Sartoris, the mayor—he who fathered the edict that no Negro woman should appear on the streets without an apron—remitted her taxes, the dispensation dating from the death of her father on into perpetuity. Not that Miss Emily would have accepted charity. Colonel Sartoris invented an involved tale to the effect that Miss Emily's father had loaned money to the town, which the town, as a matter of business, preferred this way of repaying. Only a man of Colonel Sartoris' generation and thought could have invented it, and only a woman could have believed it.

When the next generation, with its more modern ideas, became mayors and aldermen, this arrangement created some little dissatisfaction. On the first of the year they mailed her a tax notice. February came, and there was no reply. They wrote her a formal letter, asking her to call at the sheriff's office at her convenience. A week later the mayor wrote her himself, offering to call or to send his car for her, and received in reply a note on paper of an archaic shape, in a thin, flowing calligraphy in faded ink, to the effect that she no longer went out at all. The tax notice was also enclosed, without comment.

They called a special meeting of the Board of Aldermen. A deputation waited upon her, knocked at the door through which no visitor had passed since she ceased giving china-painting lessons eight or ten years earlier. They were admitted by the old Negro into a dim hall from which a stairway mounted into still more shadow. It smelled of dust and disuse—a close, dank smell. The Negro led them into the parlor. It was furnished in heavy, leather-covered furniture. When the Negro opened the blinds of one window, they could see that the leather was cracked; and when they sat down, a faint dust rose sluggishly about their thighs, spinning with slow motes in the single sun-ray. On a tarnished gilt easel before the fireplace stood a crayon portrait of Miss Emily's father.

They rose when she entered—a small, fat woman in black, with a thin gold chain descending to her waist and vanishing into her belt, leaning on an ebony cane with a tarnished gold head. Her skeleton was small and spare; perhaps that was why what would have been merely plumpness in another was obesity in her. She looked bloated, like a body long submerged in motionless water, and of that pallid hue. Her eyes, lost in the fatty ridges of her face, looked like two small pieces of coal pressed into a lump of dough as they moved from one face to another while the visitors stated their errand.

She did not ask them to sit. She just stood in the door and listened quietly until the spokesman came to a stumbling halt. Then they could hear the invisible watch ticking at the end of the gold chain.

Her voice was dry and cold. "I have no taxes in Jefferson. Colonel Sartoris explained it to me. Perhaps one of you can gain access to the city records and satisfy yourselves."

"But we have. We are the city authorities, Miss Emily. Didn't you get a notice from the sheriff, signed by him?"

"I received a paper, yes," Miss Emily said. "Perhaps he considers himself the sheriff . . . I have no taxes in Jefferson."

"But there is nothing on the books to show that, you see. We must go by the—"

"See Colonel Sartoris. I have no taxes in Jefferson."

"But, Miss Emily—"

"See Colonel Sartoris." (Colonel Sartoris had been dead almost ten years.) "I have no taxes in Jefferson. Tobe!" The Negro appeared. "Show these gentlemen out."

II

So she vanquished them, horse and foot, just as she had vanquished their fathers thirty years before about the smell. That was two years after her father's death and a short time after her sweetheart—the one we believed would marry her—

had deserted her. After her father's death she went out very little; after her sweetheart went away, people hardly saw her at all. A few of the ladies had the temerity to call, but were not received, and the only sign of life about the place was the Negro man—a young man then—going in and out with a market basket.

"Just as if a man—any man—could keep a kitchen properly," the ladies said; so they were not surprised when the smell developed. It was another link between the gross, teeming world and the high and mighty Griersons.

A neighbor, a woman, complained to the mayor, Judge Stevens, eighty years old.

"But what will you have me do about it, madam?" he said.

"Why, send her word to stop it," the woman said. "Isn't there a law?"

"I'm sure that won't be necessary," Judge Stevens said. "It's probably just a snake or a rat that nigger of hers killed in the yard. I'll speak to him about it."

The next day he received two more complaints, one from a man who came in diffident deprecation. "We really must do something about it, Judge. I'd be the last one in the world to bother Miss Emily, but we've got to do something." That night the Board of Aldermen met—three graybeards and one younger man, a member of the rising generation.

"It's simple enough," he said. "Send her word to have her place cleaned up. Give her a certain time to do it in, and if she don't . . ."

"Dammit, sir," Judge Stevens said, "will you accuse a lady to her face of smelling bad?"

So the next night, after midnight, four men crossed Miss Emily's lawn and slunk about the house like burglars, sniffing along the base of the brickwork and at the cellar openings while one of them performed a regular sowing motion with his hand out of a sack slung from his shoulder. They broke open the cellar door and sprinkled lime there, and in all the outbuildings. As they recrossed the lawn, a window that had been dark was lighted and Miss Emily sat in it, the light behind her, and her upright torso motionless as that of an idol. They crept quietly across the lawn and into the shadow of the locusts that lined the street. After a week or two the smell went away.

That was when people had begun to feel really sorry for her. People in our town, remembering how old lady Wyatt, her great-aunt, had gone completely crazy at last, believed that the Griersons held themselves a little too high for what they really were. None of the young men were quite good enough for Miss Emily and such. We had long thought of them as a tableau, Miss Emily a slender figure in white in the background, her father a spraddled silhouette in the foreground, his back to her and clutching a horsewhip, the two of them framed by the back-flung front door. So when she got to be thirty and was still single, we were not pleased exactly, but vindicated; even with insanity in the family she wouldn't have turned down all of her chances if they had really materialized.

When her father died, it got about that the house was all that was left to her; and in a way, people were glad. At last they could pity Miss Emily. Being left alone, and a pauper, she had become humanized. Now she too would know the old thrill and the old despair of a penny more or less.

The day after his death all the ladies prepared to call at the house and offer condolence and aid, as is our custom. Miss Emily met them at the door, dressed as usual and with no trace of grief on her face. She told them that her father was not dead. She did that for three days, with the ministers calling on her, and the doctors, trying to persuade her to let them dispose of the body. Just as they were about to resort to law and force, she broke down, and they buried her father quickly.

We did not say she was crazy then. We believed she had to do that. We remembered all the young men her father had driven away, and we knew that with nothing left, she would have to cling to that which had robbed her, as people will.

III

She was sick for a long time. When we saw her again, her hair was cut short, making her look like a girl, with a vague resemblance to those angels in colored church windows—sort of tragic and serene.

The town had just let the contracts for paving the sidewalks, and in the summer after her father's death they began the work. The construction company came with niggers and mules and machinery, and a foreman named Homer Barron, a Yankee—a big, dark, ready man, with a big voice and eyes lighter than his face. The little boys would follow in groups to hear him cuss the niggers, and the niggers singing in time to the rise and fall of picks. Pretty soon he knew everybody in town. Whenever you heard a lot of laughing anywhere about the square, Homer Barron would be in the center of the group. Presently we began to see him and Miss Emily on Sunday afternoons driving in the yellow-wheeled buggy and the matched team of bays from the livery stable.

At first we were glad that Miss Emily would have an interest, because the ladies all said, "Of course a Grierson would not think seriously of a Northerner, a day laborer." But there were still others, older people, who said that even grief could not cause a real lady to forget *noblesse oblige*—without calling it *noblesse oblige*. They just said, "Poor Emily. Her kinsfolk should come to her." She had some kin in Alabama; but years ago her father had fallen out with them over the estate of old lady Wyatt, the crazy woman, and there was no communication between the two families. They had not even been represented at the funeral.

And as soon as the old people said, "Poor Emily," the whispering began. "Do you suppose it's really so?" they said to one another. "Of course it is. What else could . . ." This behind their hands; rustling of craned silk and satin behind jalousies closed upon the sun of Sunday afternoon as the thin, swift clop-clop-clop of the matched team passed: "Poor Emily."

She carried her head high enough—even when we believed that she was fallen. It was as if she demanded more than ever the recognition of her dignity as the last Grierson; as if it had wanted that touch of earthiness to reaffirm her imperviousness. Like when she bought the rat poison, the arsenic. That was over a year after they had begun to say "Poor Emily," and while the two female cousins were visiting her.

"I want some poison," she said to the druggist. She was over thirty then, still a slight woman, though thinner than usual, with cold, haughty black eyes in a face the flesh of which was strained across the temples and about the eyesockets as you imagine a lighthouse-keeper's face ought to look. "I want some poison," she said.

"Yes, Miss Emily. What kind? For rats and such? I'd recom—"

"I want the best you have. I don't care what kind."

The druggist named several. "They'll kill anything up to an elephant. But what you want is—"

"Arsenic," Miss Emily said. "Is that a good one?"

"Is . . . arsenic? Yes, ma'am. But what you want—"

"I want arsenic."

The druggist looked down at her. She looked back at him, erect, her face like a strained flag. "Why, of course," the druggist said. "If that's what you want. But the law requires you to tell what you are going to use it for."

Miss Emily just stared at him, her head tilted back in order to look him eye for eye, until he looked away and went and got the arsenic and wrapped it up. The Negro delivery boy brought her the package; the druggist didn't come back. When she opened the package at home there was written on the box, under the skull and bones: "For rats."

IV

So the next day we all said, "She will kill herself"; and we said it would be the best thing. When she had first begun to be seen with Homer Barron, we had said, "She will marry him." Then we said, "She will persuade him yet," because Homer himself had remarked—he liked men, and it was known that he drank with the younger men in the Elks' Club—that he was not a marrying man. Later we said, "Poor Emily" behind the jalousies as they passed on Sunday afternoon in the glittering buggy, Miss Emily with her head high and Homer Barron with his hat cocked and a cigar in his teeth, reins and whip in a yellow glove.

Then some of the ladies began to say that it was a disgrace to the town and a bad example to the young people. The men did not want to interfere, but at last the ladies forced the Baptist minister—Miss Emily's people were Episcopal—to call upon her. He would never divulge what happened during that interview, but he refused to go back again. The next Sunday they again drove about the streets, and the following day the minister's wife wrote to Miss Emily's relations in Alabama.

So she had blood-kin under her roof again and we sat back to watch developments. At first nothing happened. Then we were sure that they were to be married. We learned that Miss Emily had been to the jeweler's and ordered a man's toilet set in silver, with the letters H. B. on each piece. Two days later we learned that she had bought a complete outfit of men's clothing, including a nightshirt, and we said, "They are married." We were really glad. We were glad because the two female cousins were even more Grierson than Miss Emily had ever been.

So we were not surprised when Homer Barron—the streets had been finished some time since—was gone. We were a little disappointed that there was not a public blowing-off, but we believed that he had gone on to prepare for Miss Emily's coming, or to give her a chance to get rid of the cousins. (By that time it was a cabal, and we were all Miss Emily's allies to help circumvent the cousins.) Sure enough, after another week they departed. And, as we had expected all along, within three days Homer Barron was back in town. A neighbor saw the Negro man admit him at the kitchen door at dusk one evening.

And that was the last we saw of Homer Barron. And of Miss Emily for some time. The Negro man went in and out with the market basket, but the front door remained closed. Now and then we would see her at a window for a moment, as the men did that night when they sprinkled the lime, but for almost six months she did not appear on the streets. Then we knew that this was to be expected too; as if that quality of her father which had thwarted her woman's life so many times had been too virulent and too furious to die.

When we next saw Miss Emily, she had grown fat and her hair was turning gray. During the next few years it grew grayer and grayer until it attained an even pepper-and-salt iron-gray, when it ceased turning. Up to the day of her death at seventy-four it was still that vigorous iron-gray, like the hair of an active man.

From that time on her front door remained closed, save for a period of six or seven years, when she was about forty, during which she gave lessons in china-painting. She fitted up a studio in one of the downstairs rooms, where the daughters and granddaughters of Colonel Sartoris' contemporaries were sent to her with the same regularity and in the same spirit that they were sent to church on Sundays with a twenty-five-cent piece for the collection plate. Meanwhile her taxes had been remitted.

Then the newer generation became the backbone and the spirit of the town, and the painting pupils grew up and fell away and did not send their children to her with boxes of color and tedious brushes and pictures cut from the ladies' magazines. The front door closed upon the last one and remained closed for good. When the town got free postal delivery, Miss Emily alone refused to let them fasten the metal numbers above her door and attach a mailbox to it. She would not listen to them.

Daily, monthly, yearly we watched the Negro grow grayer and more stooped, going in and out with the market basket. Each December we sent her a tax notice, which would be returned by the post office a week later, unclaimed. Now and then we would see her in one of the downstairs windows—she had evidently shut up the top floor of the house—like the carven torso of an idol in a niche, looking or not looking at us, we could never tell which. Thus she passed from generation to generation—dear, inescapable, impervious, tranquil, and perverse.

And so she died. Fell ill in the house filled with dust and shadows, with only a doddering Negro man to wait on her. We did not even know she was sick; we had long since given up trying to get any information from the Negro. He talked to no one, probably not even to her, for his voice had grown harsh and rusty, as if from disuse.

She died in one of the downstairs rooms, in a heavy walnut bed with a curtain, her gray head propped on a pillow yellow and moldy with age and lack of sunlight.

V

The Negro met the first of the ladies at the front door and let them in, with their hushed, sibilant voices and their quick, curious glances, and then he disappeared. He walked right through the house and out the back and was not seen again.

The two female cousins came at once. They held the funeral on the second day, with the town coming to look at Miss Emily beneath a mass of bought flowers, with the crayon face of her father musing profoundly above the bier and the ladies sibilant and macabre; and the very old men—some in their brushed Confederate uniforms—on the porch and the lawn, talking of Miss Emily as if she had been a contemporary of theirs, believing that they had danced with her and courted her perhaps, confusing time with its mathematical progression, as the old do, to whom all the past is not a diminishing road but, instead, a huge meadow which no winter ever quite touches, divided from them now by the narrow bottle-neck of the most recent decade of years.

Already we knew that there was one room in that region above stairs which no one had seen in forty years, and which would have to be forced. They waited until Miss Emily was decently in the ground before they opened it.

The violence of breaking down the door seemed to fill this room with pervading dust. A thin, acrid pall as of the tomb seemed to lie everywhere upon this room decked and furnished as for a bridal: upon the valance curtains of faded rose color, upon the rose-shaded lights, upon the dressing table, upon the delicate array of crystal and the man's toilet things backed with tarnished silver, silver so tarnished that the monogram was obscured. Among them lay a collar and tie, as if they had just been removed, which, lifted, left upon the surface a pale crescent in the dust. Upon a chair hung the suit, carefully folded; beneath it the two mute shoes and the discarded socks.

The man himself lay in the bed.

For a long while we just stood there, looking down at the profound and fleshless grin. The body had apparently once lain in the attitude of an embrace, but now the long sleep that outlasts love, that conquers even the grimace of love, had cuckolded him. What was left of him, rotted beneath what was left of the nightshirt, had become inextricable from the bed in which he lay; and upon him and upon the pillow beside him lay that even coating of the patient and biding dust.

Then we noticed that in the second pillow was the indentation of a head. One of us lifted something from it, and leaning forward, that faint and invisible dust dry and acrid in the nostrils, we saw a long strand of iron-gray hair.

QUESTIONS

1. Who is the narrator? Do we know as much about him as we need to?
2. Since the teller is indistinct as a character, why did Faulkner choose not to tell the story simply in the third person? Why bring the "we" into it?
3. In some ways the story is a puzzle, at least at first. Does it become fully clear upon reflection?

The narrator of "The Boarded Window" tells a story heard from his grandfather, rather than one observed at first hand, but he has been close enough to the events to have thrown a stone at the cabin where they occurred. He fills out the details with an imaginative grasp akin to that of the omniscient storyteller.

THE BOARDED WINDOW
Ambrose Bierce   (1842–1914?)

In 1830, only a few miles away from what is now the great city of Cincinnati, lay an immense and almost unbroken forest. The whole region was sparsely settled by people of the frontier—restless souls who no sooner had hewn fairly habitable homes out of the wilderness and attained to that degree of prosperity which today we should call indigence than impelled by some mysterious impulse of their nature they abandoned all and pushed farther westward, to encounter new perils and privations in the effort to regain the meagre comforts which they had voluntarily renounced. Many of them had already forsaken that region for the remoter settlements, but among those remaining was one who had been of those first arriving. He lived alone in a house of logs surrounded on all sides by the great forest, of whose gloom and silence he seemed a part, for no one had ever known him to smile nor speak a needless word. His simple wants were supplied by the sale or barter of skins of wild animals in the river town, for not a thing did he grow upon the land which, if needful, he might have claimed by right of undisturbed possession. There were evidences of "improvement"—a few acres of ground immediately about the house had once been cleared of its trees, the decayed stumps of which were half concealed by the new growth that had been suffered to repair the ravage wrought by the ax. Apparently the man's zeal for agriculture had burned with a failing flame, expiring in penitential ashes.

The little log house, with its chimney of sticks, its roof of warping clapboards weighted with traversing poles and its "chinking" of clay, had a single door and, directly opposite, a window. The latter, however, was boarded up—nobody could remember a time when it was not. And none knew why it was so closed; certainly not because of the occupant's dislike of light and air, for on those rare occasions when a hunter had passed that lonely spot the recluse had commonly been seen sunning himself on his doorstep if heaven had provided sunshine for his need. I fancy there are few persons living today who ever knew the secret of that window, but I am one, as you shall see.

The man's name was said to be Murlock. He was apparently seventy years old, actually about fifty. Something besides years had had a hand in his aging. His hair and long, full beard were white, his gray, lustreless eyes sunken, his face singularly seamed with wrinkles which appeared to belong to two intersecting systems. In figure he was tall and spare, with a stoop of the shoulders—a burden bearer. I never saw him; these particulars I learned from my grandfather, from whom also I got the man's story when I was a lad. He had known him when living near by in that early day.

One day Murlock was found in his cabin, dead. It was not a time and place for coroners and newspapers, and I suppose it was agreed that he had died from natural causes or I should have been told, and should remember. I know only that with what was probably a sense of the fitness of things the body was buried near the cabin, alongside the grave of his wife, who had preceded him by so many years that local tradition had retained hardly a hint of her existence. That closes the final chapter of this true story—excepting, indeed, the circumstances that many years afterward, in company with an equally intrepid spirit, I penetrated to the place and ventured near enough to the ruined cabin to throw a stone against it, and ran away to avoid the ghost which every well-informed boy thereabout knew haunted the spot. But there is an earlier chapter—that supplied by my grandfather.

When Murlock built his cabin and began laying sturdily about with his ax to hew out a farm—the rifle, meanwhile, his means of support—he was young, strong and full of hope. In that eastern country whence he came he had married, as was the fashion, a young woman in all ways worthy of his honest devotion, who shared the dangers and privations of his lot with a willing spirit and light heart. There is no known record of her name; of her charms of mind and person tradition is silent and the doubter is at liberty to entertain his doubt; but God forbid that I should share it! Of their affection and happiness there is abundant assurance in every added day of the man's widowed life; for what but the magnetism of a blessed memory could have chained that venturesome spirit to a lot like that?

One day Murlock returned from gunning in a distant part of the forest to find his wife prostrate with fever, and delirious. There was no physician within miles, no neighbor; nor was she in a condition to be left, to summon help. So he set about the task of nursing her back to health, but at the end of the third day she fell into unconsciousness and so passed away, apparently, with never a gleam of returning reason.

From what we know of a nature like his we may venture to sketch in some of the details of the outline picture drawn by my grandfather. When convinced that she was dead, Murlock had sense enough to remember that the dead must be prepared for burial. In performance of this sacred duty he blundered now and again, did certain things incorrectly, and others which he did correctly were done over and over. His occasional failures to accomplish some simple and ordinary act filled him with astonishment, like that of a drunken man who wonders at the suspension of familiar natural laws. He was surprised, too, that he did not weep—surprised and a little ashamed; surely it is unkind not to weep for the dead. "Tomorrow," he said aloud, "I shall have to make the coffin and dig the grave; and then I shall miss her, when she is no longer in sight; but now—she is dead, of course, but it is all right—it *must* be all right, somehow. Things cannot be so bad as they seem."

He stood over the body in the fading light, adjusting the hair and putting the finishing touches to the simple toilet, doing all mechanically, with soulless care. And still through his consciousness ran an undersense of conviction that all was right—that he should have her again as before, and everything explained. He had had no experience in grief; his capacity had not been enlarged by use. His heart could not contain it all, nor his imagination rightly conceive it. He did not know he was so hard struck; *that* knowledge would come later, and never go. Grief is an artist of powers as various as the instruments upon which he plays his dirges for the dead, evoking from some the sharpest, shrillest notes, from others the low, grave chords that throb recurrent like the slow beating of a distant drum. Some natures it startles; some it stupefies. To one it comes like the stroke of an arrow, stinging all the sensibilities to a keener life; to another as the blow of a bludgeon, which in crushing benumbs. We may conceive Murlock to have been that way affected, for (and here we are upon surer ground than that of conjecture) no sooner had he finished his pious work than, sinking into a chair by the side of the table upon which the body lay, and noting how white the profile showed in the deepening gloom, he laid his arms upon the table's edge, and dropped his face into them, tearless yet and unutterably weary. At that moment came in through the open window a long, wailing sound like the cry of a lost child in the far deeps of the darkening wood! But the man did not move. Again, and nearer than before, sounded that unearthly cry upon his failing sense. Perhaps it was a wild beast; perhaps it was a dream. For Murlock was asleep.

Some hours later, as it afterward appeared, this unfaithful watcher awoke and lifting his head from his arms intently listened—he knew not why. There in the black darkness by the side of the dead, recalling all without a shock, he strained his eyes to see—he knew not what. His senses were all alert, his breath was suspended, his blood had stilled its tides as if to assist the silence. Who—what had waked him, and where was it?

Suddenly the table shook beneath his arms, and at the same moment he heard, or fancied that he heard, a light, soft step—sounds as of bare feet upon the floor!

He was terrified beyond the power to cry out or move. Perforce he waited—waited there in the darkness through seeming centuries of such dread as one may know, yet live to tell. He tried vainly to speak the dead woman's name, vainly to stretch forth his hand across the table to learn if she were there. His throat was powerless, his arms and hands were like lead. Then occurred something most frightful. Some heavy body seemed hurled against the table with an impetus that pushed it against his breast so sharply as nearly to overthrow him, and at the same instant he heard and felt the fall of something upon the floor with so violent a thump that the whole house was shaken by the impact. A scuffling ensued, and a confusion of sounds impossible to describe. Murlock had risen to his feet. Fear had by excess forfeited control of his faculties. He flung his hands upon the table. Nothing was there!

There is a point at which terror may turn to madness; and madness incites to action. With no definite intent, from no motive but the wayward impulse of a madman, Murlock sprang to the wall, with a little groping seized his loaded rifle, and without aim discharged it. By the flash which lit up the room with a vivid illumination, he saw an enormous panther dragging the dead woman toward the window, its teeth fixed in her throat! Then there were darkness blacker than before, and silence; and when he returned to consciousness the sun was high and the wood vocal with songs of birds.

The body lay near the window, where the beast had left it when frightened away by the flash and report of the rifle. The clothing was deranged, the long hair in disorder, the limbs lay anyhow. From the throat, dreadfully lacerated, had issued a pool of blood not yet entirely coagulated. The ribbon with which he had bound the wrists was broken; the hands were tightly clenched. Between the teeth was a fragment of the animal's ear.

CHAPTER 4

The Omniscient Narrator

The *omniscient narrator* stands outside the story. He pretends no immediate relationship to it as protagonist, participant, or observer. He is the traditional storyteller, all-knowing, all-powerful, and—when he chooses to be—ever present. He takes us into the minds of protagonist and antagonist alike, exposing their most secret desires and hidden motives. He transcends time and crosses seas, unhindered by the pretense that his is a personal involvement or observation. Although he tells us of the miller's daughter and the king and Rumpelstiltskin, we have no illusion he was there: instead we move easily and invisibly with him from hut to palace to forest as no single participant or observer can do.

But though he is in name "all-knowing," the omniscient narrator is first of all a storyteller. He tells not what he knows, in the order that he knows it, but what makes a good story, in the order that makes it effective. Sometimes, as readers, we want to distinguish a *limited omniscient* narrative perspective: A point of view that follows the actions of one character only, or enters into the thoughts of only one, or in some other respect important to the story withholds knowledge that a truly omniscient narrator might have presented.

BABYLON REVISITED
F. Scott Fitzgerald (1896–1940)

I

"And where's Mr. Campbell?" Charlie asked.

"Gone to Switzerland. Mr. Campbell's a pretty sick man, Mr. Wales."

"I'm sorry to hear that. And George Hardt?" Charlie inquired.

"Back in America, gone to work."

"And where is the Snow Bird?" .

"He was in here last week. Anyway, his friend, Mr. Schaeffer, is in Paris."

Two familiar names from the long list of a year and a half ago. Charlie scribbled an address in his notebook and tore out the page.

"If you see Mr. Schaeffer, give him this," he said. "It's my brother-in-law's address. I haven't settled on a hotel yet."

He was not really disappointed to find Paris was so empty. But the stillness in the Ritz bar was strange and portentous. It was not an American bar any more—he felt polite in it, and not as if he owned it. It had gone back into France. He felt the stillness from the moment he got out of the taxi and saw the doorman, usually in a frenzy of activity at this hour, gossiping with a *chasseur*[1] by the servants' entrance.

Passing through the corridor, he heard only a single, bored voice in the once-clamorous women's room. When he turned into the bar he traveled the twenty feet of green carpet with his eyes fixed straight ahead by old habit; and then, with his foot firmly on the rail, he turned and surveyed the room, encountering only a single pair of eyes that fluttered up from a newspaper in the corner. Charlie asked for the head barman, Paul, who in the latter days of the bull market had come to work in his own custom-built car—disembarking, however, with due nicety at the nearest corner. But Paul was at his country house today and Alix giving him information.

"No, no more," Charlie said, "I'm going slow these days."

Alix congratulated him: "You were going pretty strong a couple of years ago."

"I'll stick to it all right," Charlie assured him. "I've stuck to it for over a year and a half now."

"How do you find conditions in America?"

"I haven't been to America for months. I'm in business in Prague, representing a couple of concerns there. They don't know about me down there."

Alix smiled.

"Remember the night of George Hardt's bachelor dinner here?" said Charlie. "By the way, what's become of Claude Fessenden?"

Alix lowered his voice confidentially: "He's in Paris, but he doesn't come here any more. Paul doesn't allow it. He ran up a bill of thirty thousand francs, charging all his drinks and his lunches, and usually his dinner, for more than a year. And when Paul finally told him he had to pay, he gave him a bad check."

Alix shook his head sadly.

"I don't understand it, such a dandy fellow. Now he's all bloated up—" He made a plump apple of his hands.

Charlie watched a group of strident queens installing themselves in a corner.

"Nothing affects them," he thought. "Stocks rise and fall, people loaf or work, but they go on forever." The place oppressed him. He called for the dice and shook with Alix for the drink.

"Here for long, Mr. Wales?"

"I'm here for four or five days to see my little girl."

"Oh-h! You have a little girl?"

Outside, the fire-red, gas-blue, ghost-green signs shone smokily through the tranquil rain. It was late afternoon and the streets were in movement; the *bistros* gleamed. At the corner of the Boulevard des Capucines he took a taxi. The Place de la Concorde moved by in pink majesty; they crossed the logical Seine, and Charlie felt the sudden provincial quality of the left bank.

Charlie directed his taxi to the Avenue de l'Opera, which was out of his way. But he wanted to see the blue hour spread over the magnificent façade, and imagine that the cab horns, playing endlessly the first few bars of *Le Plus que Lent*, were the trumpets of the Second Empire. They were closing the iron grill in front of Brentano's Book-store, and people were already at dinner behind the

[1] Footman.

trim little bourgeois hedge of Duval's. He had never eaten at a really cheap restaurant in Paris. Five-course dinner, four francs fifty, eighteen cents, wine included. For some odd reason he wished that he had.

As they rolled on to the Left Bank and he felt its sudden provincialism, he thought, "I spoiled this city for myself. I didn't realize it, but the days came along one after another, and then two years were gone, and everything was gone, and I was gone."

He was thirty-five, and good to look at. The Irish mobility of his face was sobered by a deep wrinkle between his eyes. As he rang his brother-in-law's bell in the Rue Palatine, the wrinkle deepened till it pulled down his brows; he felt a cramping sensation in his belly. From behind the maid who opened the door darted a lovely little girl of nine who shrieked "Daddy!" and flew up, struggling like a fish, into his arms. She pulled his head around by one ear and set her cheek against his.

"My old pie," he said.

"Oh, daddy, daddy, daddy, daddy, dads, dads, dads!"

She drew him into the salon, where the family waited, a boy and a girl his daughter's age, his sister-in-law and her husband. He greeted Marion with his voice pitched carefully to avoid either feigned enthusiasm or dislike, but her response was more frankly tepid, though she minimized her expression of unalterable distrust by directing her regard toward his child. The two men clasped hands in a friendly way and Lincoln Peters rested his for a moment on Charlie's shoulder.

The room was warm and comfortably American. The three children moved intimately about, playing through the yellow oblongs that led to other rooms; the cheer of six o'clock spoke in the eager smacks of the fire and the sounds of French activity in the kitchen. But Charlie did not relax; his heart sat up rigidly in his body and he drew confidence from his daughter, who from time to time came close to him, holding in her arms the doll he had brought.

"Really extremely well," he declared in answer to Lincoln's question. "There's a lot of business there that isn't moving at all, but we're doing even better than ever. In fact, damn well. I'm bringing my sister over from America next month to keep house for me. My income last year was bigger than it was when I had money. You see, the Czechs——"

His boasting was for a specific purpose; but after a moment, seeing a faint restiveness in Lincoln's eye, he changed the subject:

"Those are fine children of yours, well brought up, good manners."

"We think Honoria's a great little girl too."

Marion Peters came back from the kitchen. She was a tall woman with worried eyes, who had once possessed a fresh American loveliness. Charlie had never been sensitive to it and was always surprised when people spoke of how pretty she had been. From the first there had been an instinctive antipathy between them.

"Well, how do you find Honoria?" she asked.

"Wonderful, I was astonished how much she's grown in ten months. All the children are looking well."

"We haven't had a doctor for a year. How do you like being back in Paris?"

"It seems very funny to see so few Americans around."

"I'm delighted," Marion said vehemently. "Now at least you can go into a store without their assuming you're a millionaire. We've suffered like everybody, but on the whole it's a good deal pleasanter."

"But it was nice while it lasted," Charlie said. "We were a sort of royalty, almost infallible, with a sort of magic around us. In the bar this afternoon"—he stumbled, seeing his mistake—"there wasn't a man I knew."

She looked at him keenly. "I should think you'd have had enough of bars."

"I only stayed a minute. I take one drink every afternoon, and no more."

"Don't you want a cocktail before dinner?" Lincoln asked.

"I take only one drink every afternoon, and I've had that."

"I hope you keep to it," said Marion.

Her dislike was evident in the coldness with which she spoke, but Charlie only smiled; he had larger plans. Her very aggressiveness gave him an advantage, and he knew enough to wait. He wanted them to initiate the discussion of what they knew had brought him to Paris.

At dinner he couldn't decide whether Honoria was most like him or her mother. Fortunate if she didn't combine the traits of both that had brought them to disaster. A great wave of protectiveness went over him. He thought he knew what to do for her. He believed in character; he wanted to jump back a whole generation and trust in character again as the eternally valuable element. Everything else wore out.

He left soon after dinner, but not to go home. He was curious to see Paris by night with clearer and more judicious eyes than those of other days. He bought a *strapontin*[2] for the Casino and watched Josephine Baker[3] go through her chocolate arabesques.

After an hour he left and strolled toward Montmartre, up the Rue Pigalle into the Place Blanche. The rain had stopped and there were a few people in evening clothes disembarking from taxis in front of cabarets, and *cocottes*[4] prowling singly or in pairs, and many Negroes. He passed a lighted door from which issued music, and stopped with the sense of familiarity; it was Bricktop's, where he had parted with so many hours and so much money. A few doors farther on he found another ancient rendezvous and incautiously put his head inside. Immediately an eager orchestra burst into sound, a pair of professional dancers leaped to their feet and a maître d'hôtel swooped toward him, crying, "Crowd just arriving, sir!" But he withdrew quickly.

"You have to be damn drunk," he thought.

Zelli's was closed, the bleak and sinister cheap hotels surrounding it were dark; up in the Rue Blanche there was more light and a local, colloquial French crowd. The Poet's Cave had disappeared, but the two great mouths of the Café of Heaven and the Café of Hell still yawned—even devoured, as he watched, the meager contents of a tourist bus—a German, a Japanese, and an American couple who glanced at him with frightened eyes.

So much for the effort and ingenuity of Montmartre. All the catering to vice and waste was on an utterly childish scale, and he suddenly realized the meaning of the word "dissipate"—to dissipate into thin air; to make nothing out of

[2] A type of theater seat.
[3] American entertainer.
[4] Prostitutes.

something. In the little hours of the night every move from place to place was an enormous human jump, an increase of paying for the privilege of slower and slower motion.

He remembered thousand-franc notes given to an orchestra for playing a single number, hundred-franc notes tossed to a doorman for calling a cab.

But it hadn't been given for nothing.

It had been given, even the most wildly squandered sum, as an offering to destiny that he might not remember the things most worth remembering, the things that now he would always remember—his child taken from his control, his wife escaped to a grave in Vermont.

In the glare of a *brasserie*[5] a woman spoke to him. He bought her some eggs and coffee, and then, eluding her encouraging stare, gave her a twenty-franc note and took a taxi to his hotel.

II

He woke upon a fine fall day—football weather. The depression of yesterday was gone and he liked the people on the streets. At noon he sat opposite Honoria at Le Grand Vatel, the only restaurant he could think of not reminiscent of champagne dinners and long luncheons that began at two and ended in a blurred and vague twilight.

"Now, how about vegetables? Oughtn't you to have some vegetables?"

"Well, yes."

"Here's *épinards* and *chou-fleur* and carrots and *haricots*."[6]

"I'd like *chou-fleur*."

"Wouldn't you like to have two vegetables?"

"I usually only have one at lunch."

The waiter was pretending to be inordinately fond of children. *"Qu'elle est mignonne la petite! Elle parle exactement comme une Francqise."*[7]

"How about dessert? Shall we wait and see?"

The waiter disappeared. Honoria looked at her father expectantly.

"What are we going to do?"

"First, we're going to that toy store in the Rue Saint-Honoré and buy you anything you like. And then, we're going to the vaudeville at the Empire."

She hesitated. "I like it about the vaudeville, but not the toy store."

"Why not?"

"Well, you brought me this doll." She had it with her. "And I've got lots of things. And we're not rich any more, are we?"

"We never were. But today you are to have anything you want."

"All right," she agreed resignedly.

When there had been her mother and a French nurse he had been inclined to be strict; now he extended himself, reached out for a new tolerance; he must be both parents to her and not shut any of her out of communication.

"I want to get to know you," he said gravely. "First let me introduce myself. My name is Charles J. Wales, of Prague."

---

[5] Tavern.
[6] Spinach, cauliflower, beans.
[7] "What a darling little girl! She speaks exactly like a French girl."

"Oh, daddy!" her voice cracked with laughter.

"And who are you, please?" he persisted, and she accepted a role immediately: "Honoria Wales, Rue Palatine, Paris."

"Married or single?"

"No, not married. Single."

He indicated the doll. "But I see you have a child, madame."

Unwillingly to disinherit it, she took it to her heart and thought quickly: "Yes, I've been married, but I'm not married now. My husband is dead."

He went on quickly, "And the child's name?"

"Simone. That's after my best friend at school."

"I'm very pleased that you're doing so well at school."

"I'm third this month," she boasted. "Elsie"—that was her cousin—"is only about eighteenth, and Richard is about at the bottom."

"You like Richard and Elsie, don't you?"

"Oh, yes. I like Richard quite well and I like her all right."

Cautiously and casually he asked: "And Aunt Marion and Uncle Lincoln—which do you like best?"

"Oh, Uncle Lincoln, I guess."

He was increasingly aware of her presence. As they came in, a murmur of " . . . adorable" followed them, and now the people at the next table bent all their silences upon her, staring as if she were something no more conscious than a flower.

"Why don't I live with you?" she asked suddenly. "Because mamma's dead?"

"You must stay here and learn more French. It would have been hard for daddy to take care of you so well."

"I don't really need much taking care of any more. I do everything for myself."

Going out of the restaurant, a man and a woman unexpectedly hailed him.

"Well, the old Wales!"

"Hello there, Lorraine. . . . Dunc."

Sudden ghosts out of the past: Duncan Schaeffer, a friend from college. Lorraine Quarrles, a lovely, pale blonde of thirty; one of a crowd who had helped them make months into days in the lavish times of three years ago.

"My husband couldn't come this year," she said, in answer to his question. "We're poor as hell. So he gave me two hundred a month and told me I could do my worst on that. . . . This your little girl?"

"What about coming back and sitting down?" Duncan asked.

"Can't do it." He was glad for an excuse. As always, he felt Lorraine's passionate, provocative attraction, but his own rhythm was different now.

"Well, how about dinner?" she asked.

"I'm not free. Give me your address and let me call you."

"Charlie, I believe you're sober," she said judicially. "I honestly believe he's sober, Dunc. Pinch him and see if he's sober."

Charlie indicated Honoria with his head. They both laughed.

"What's your address?" said Duncan skeptically.

He hesitated, unwilling to give the name of his hotel.

"I'm not settled yet. I'd better call you. We're going to see the vaudeville at the Empire."

"There! That's what I want to do," Lorraine said. "I want to see some clowns and acrobats and jugglers. That's just what we'll do, Dunc."

"We've got to do an errand first," said Charlie. "Perhaps we'll see you there."

"All right, you snob. . . . Good-by beautiful little girl."

"Good-by."

Honoria bobbed politely.

Somehow, an unwelcome encounter. They liked him because he was functioning, because he was serious; they wanted to see him, because he was stronger than they were now, because they wanted to draw a certain sustenance from his strength.

At the Empire, Honoria proudly refused to sit upon her father's folded coat. She was already an individual with a code of her own, and Charlie was more and more absorbed by the desire of putting a little of himself into her before she crystallized utterly. It was hopeless to try to know her in so short a time.

Between the acts they came upon Duncan and Lorraine in the lobby where the band was playing.

"Have a drink?"

"All right, but not up at the bar. We'll take a table."

"The perfect father."

Listening abstractedly to Lorraine, Charlie watched Honoria's eyes leave their table, and he followed them wistfully about the room, wondering what they saw. He met her glance and she smiled.

"I liked that lemonade," she said.

What had she said? What had he expected? Going home in a taxi afterward, he pulled her over until her head rested against his chest.

"Darling, do you ever think about your mother?"

"Yes, sometimes," she answered vaguely.

"I don't want you to forget her. Have you got a picture of her?"

"Yes, I think so. Anyhow, Aunt Marion has. Why don't you want me to forget her?"

"She loved you very much."

"I loved her too."

They were silent for a moment.

"Daddy, I want to come and live with you," she said suddenly.

His heart leaped; he had wanted it to come like this.

"Aren't you perfectly happy?"

"Yes, but I love you better than anybody. And you love me better than anybody, don't you, now that mummy's dead?"

"Of course I do. But you won't always like me best, honey. You'll grow up and meet somebody your own age and go marry him and forget you ever had a daddy."

"Yes, that's true," she agreed tranquilly.

He didn't go in. He was coming back at nine o'clock and he wanted to keep himself fresh and new for the thing he must say then.

"When you're safe inside, just show yourself in that window."

"All right. Good-by, dads, dads, dads, dads."

He waited in the dark street until she appeared, all warm and glowing, in the window above and kissed her fingers out into the night.

III

They were waiting. Marion sat behind the coffee service in a dignified black dinner dress that just faintly suggested mourning. Lincoln was walking up and down with the animation of one who had already been talking. They were as anxious as he was to get into the question. He opened it almost immediately:

"I suppose you know what I want to see you about—why I really came to Paris."

Marion played with the black stars on her necklace and frowned.

"I'm awfully anxious to have a home," he continued. "And I'm awfully anxious to have Honoria in it. I appreciate your taking in Honoria for her mother's sake, but things have changed now"—he hesitated and then continued more forcibly—"changed radically with me, and I want to ask you to reconsider the matter. It would be silly for me to deny that about three years ago I was acting badly—"

Marion looked up at him with hard eyes.

"—but all that's over. As I told you, I haven't had more than a drink a day for over a year, and I take that drink deliberately, so that the idea of alcohol won't get too big in my imagination. You see the idea?"

"No," said Marion succinctly.

"It's a sort of stunt I set myself. It keeps the matter in proportion."

"I get you," said Lincoln. "You don't want to admit it's got any attraction for you."

"Something like that. Sometimes I forget and don't take it. But I try to take it. Anyhow, I couldn't afford to drink in my position. The people I represent are more than satisfied with what I've done, and I'm bringing my sister over from Burlington to keep house for me, and I want awfully to have Honoria too. You know that even when her mother and I weren't getting along well we never let anything that happened touch Honoria. I know she's fond of me and I know I'm able to take care of her and—well, there you are. How do you feel about it?"

He knew that now he would have to take a beating. It would last an hour or two hours, and it would be difficult, but if he modulated his inevitable resentment to the chastened attitude of the reformed sinner, he might win his point in the end.

Keep your temper, he told himself. You don't want to be justified. You want Honoria.

Lincoln spoke first: "We've been talking it over ever since we got your letter last month. We're happy to have Honoria here. She's a dear little thing, and we're glad to be able to help her, but of course that isn't the question—"

Marion interrupted suddenly. "How long are you going to stay sober, Charlie?" she asked.

"Permanently, I hope."

"How can anybody count on that?"

"You know I never did drink heavily until I gave up business and came over here with nothing to do. Then Helen and I began to run around with—"

"Please leave Helen out of it. I can't bear to hear you talk about her like that."

He stared at her grimly; he had never been certain how fond of each other the sisters were in life.

"My drinking only lasted about a year and a half—from the time we came over until I—collapsed."

"It was time enough."

"It was time enough," he agreed.

"My duty is entirely to Helen," she said. "I try to think what she would have wanted me to do. Frankly, from the night you did that terrible thing you haven't really existed for me. I can't help that. She was my sister."

"Yes."

"When she was dying she asked me to look out for Honoria. If you hadn't been in a sanitarium then, it might have helped matters."

He had no answer.

"I'll never in my life be able to forget the morning when Helen knocked at my door, soaked to the skin and shivering and said you'd locked her out."

Charlie gripped the sides of the chair. This was more difficult than he expected; he wanted to launch out into a long expostulation and explanation, but he only said: "The night I locked her out—" and she interrupted, "I don't feel up to going over that again."

After a moment's silence Lincoln said: "We're getting off the subject. You want Marion to set aside her legal guardianship and give you Honoria. I think the main point for her is whether she has confidence in you or not."

"I don't blame Marion," Charlie said slowly, "but I think she can have entire confidence in me. I had a good record up to three years ago. Of course, it's within human possibilities I might go wrong any time. But if we wait much longer I'll lose Honoria's childhood and my chance for a home." He shook his head. "I'll simply lose her, don't you see?"

"Yes, I see," said Lincoln.

"Why didn't you think of all this before?" Marion asked.

"I suppose I did, from time to time, but Helen and I were getting along badly. When I consented to the guardianship, I was flat on my back in a sanitarium and the market had cleaned me out. I knew I'd acted badly, and I thought if it would bring any peace to Helen, I'd agree to anything. But now it's different. I'm functioning, I'm behaving damn well, so far as—"

"Please don't swear at me," Marion said.

He looked at her, startled. With each remark the force of her dislike became more and more apparent. She had built up all her fear of life into one wall and faced it toward him. This trivial reproof was possibly the result of some trouble with the cook several hours before. Charlie became increasingly alarmed at leaving Honoria in this atmosphere of hostility against himself; sooner or later it would come out, in a word here, a shake of the head there, and some of that distrust would be irrevocably implanted in Honoria. But he pulled his temper down out of his face and shut it up inside him; he had won a point, for Lincoln realized the absurdity of Marion's remark and asked her lightly since when she had objected to the word "damn."

"Another thing," Charlie said: "I'm able to give her certain advantages now. I'm going to take a French governess to Prague with me. I've got a lease on a new apartment—"

He stopped, realizing that he was blundering. They couldn't be expected to accept with equanimity the fact that his income was again twice as large as their own.

"I suppose you can give her more luxuries than we can," said Marion. "When you were throwing away money we were living along watching every ten francs. . . . I suppose you'll start doing it again."

"Oh, no," he said. "I've learned. I worked hard for ten years, you know—until I got lucky in the market, like so many people. Terribly lucky. It won't happen again."

There was a long silence. All of them felt their nerves straining, and for the first time in a year Charlie wanted a drink. He was sure now that Lincoln Peters wanted him to have his child.

Marion shuddered suddenly; part of her saw that Charlie's feet were planted on the earth now, and her own maternal feeling recognized the naturalness of his desire; but she had lived for a long time with a prejudice—a prejudice founded on a disbelief in her sister's happiness, and which, in the shock of one terrible night, had turned to hatred for him. It had all happened at a point in her life where the discouragement of ill health and adverse circumstances made it necessary for her to believe in tangible villainy and a tangible villain.

"I can't help what I think!" she cried out suddenly. "How much you were responsible for Helen's death, I don't know. It's something you'll have to square with your own conscience."

An electric current of agony surged through him; for a moment he was almost on his feet, an unuttered sound echoing in his throat. He hung on to himself for a moment, another moment.

"Hold on there," said Lincoln uncomfortably. "I never thought you were responsible for that."

"Helen died of heart trouble," Charlie said dully.

"Yes, heart trouble." Marion spoke as if the phrase had another meaning for her.

Then, in the flatness that followed her outburst, she saw him plainly and she knew he had somehow arrived at control over the situation. Glancing at her husband, she found no help from him, and as abruptly as if it were a matter of no importance, she threw up the sponge.

"Do what you like!" she cried, springing up from her chair. "She's your child. I'm not the person to stand in your way. I think if it were my child I'd rather see her—" She managed to check herself. "You two decide it. I can't stand this. I'm sick. I'm going to bed."

She hurried from the room; after a moment Lincoln said:

"This has been a hard day for her. You know how strongly she feels—" His voice was almost apologetic: "Where a woman gets an idea in her head."

"Of course."

"It's going to be all right. I think she sees now that you—can provide for the child, and so we can't very well stand in your way or Honoria's way."

"Thank you, Lincoln."

"I'd better go along and see how she is."

"I'm going."

He was still trembling when he reached the street, but a walk down the Rue Bonaparte to the *quais*[8] set him up, and as he crossed the Seine, fresh and new by the *quai* lamps, he felt exultant. But back in his room he couldn't sleep. The im-

[8] Wharfs.

age of Helen haunted him. Helen whom he had loved so until they had senselessly begun to abuse each other's love, tear it into shreds. On that terrible February night that Marion remembered so vividly, a slow quarrel had gone on for
hours. There was a scene at the Florida, and then he attempted to take her home,
and then she kissed young Webb at a table; after that there was what she had
hysterically said. When he arrived home alone he turned the key in the lock in
wild anger. How could he know she would arrive an hour later alone, that there
would be a snowstorm in which she wandered about in slippers, too confused to
find a taxi? Then the aftermath, her escaping pneumonia by a miracle, and all the
attendant horror. They were "reconciled," but that was the beginning of the end,
and Marion, who had seen with her own eyes and who imagined it to be one of
many scenes from her sister's martyrdom, never forgot.

Going over it again brought Helen nearer, and in the white, soft light that
steals upon half sleep near morning he found himself talking to her again. She
said that he was perfectly right about Honoria and that she wanted Honoria to be
with him. She said she was glad he was being good and doing better. She said a
lot of other things—very friendly things—but she was in a swing in a white
dress, and swinging faster and faster all the time, so that at the end he could not
hear clearly all that she said.

IV

He woke up feeling happy. The door of the world was open again. He made
plans, vistas, futures for Honoria and himself, but suddenly he grew sad, remembering all the plans he and Helen had made. She had not planned to die. The
present was the thing—work to do and someone to love. But not to love too
much, for he knew the injury that a father can do to a daughter or a mother to a
son by attaching them too closely: afterward, out in the world, the child would
seek in the marriage partner the same blind tenderness and, failing probably to
find it, turn against love and life.

It was another bright, crisp day. He called Lincoln Peters at the bank where
he worked and asked if he could count on taking Honoria when he left for
Prague. Lincoln agreed that there was no reason for delay. One thing—the legal
guardianship. Marion wanted to retain that a while longer. She was upset by the
whole matter, and it would oil things if she felt that the situation was still in her
control for another year. Charlie agreed, wanting only the tangible, visible child.

Then the question of a governess. Charles sat in a gloomy agency and talked
to a cross Béarnaise and to a buxom Breton peasant, neither of whom he could
have endured. There were others whom he would see tomorrow.

He lunched with Lincoln Peters at Griffons, trying to keep down his exultation.

"There's nothing quite like your own child," Lincoln said. "But you understand how Marion feels too."

"She's forgotten how hard I worked for seven years there," Charlie said. "She
just remembers one night."

"There's another thing." Lincoln hesitated. "While you and Helen were tearing around Europe throwing money away, we were just getting along. I didn't
touch any of the prosperity because I never got ahead enough to carry anything
but my insurance. I think Marion felt there was some kind of injustice in it—you

not even working toward the end, and getting richer and richer."

"It went just as quick as it came," said Charlie.

"Yes, a lot of it stayed in the hands of *chasseurs* and saxophone players and maitres d'hôtel—well, the big party's over now. I just said that to explain Marion's feeling about those crazy years. If you drop in about six o'clock tonight before Marion's too tired, we'll settle the details on the spot."

Back at his hotel, Charlie found a *pneumatique*⁹ that had been redirected from the Ritz bar where Charlie had left his address for the purpose of finding a certain man.

> DEAR CHARLIE: You were so strange when we saw you the other day that I wondered if I did something to offend you. If so, I'm not conscious of it. In fact, I have thought about you too much for the last year, and it's always been in the back of my mind that I might see you if I came over here. We *did* have such good times that crazy spring, like the night you and I stole the butcher's tricycle, and the time we tried to call on the president and you had the old derby rim and the wire cane. Everybody seems so old lately, but I don't feel old a bit. Couldn't we get together some time today for old time's sake? I've got a vile hang-over for the moment, but will be feeling better this afternoon and will look for you about five in the sweat-shop at the Ritz.
>
> "Always devotedly,
>
> "LORRAINE."

His first feeling was one of awe that he had actually, in his mature years, stolen a tricycle and pedaled Lorraine all over the Etoile between the small hours and dawn. In retrospect it was a nightmare. Locking out Helen didn't fit in with any other act of his life, but the tricycle incident did—it was one of many. How many weeks or months of dissipation to arrive at that condition of utter irresponsibility?

He tried to picture how Lorraine had appeared to him then—very attractive; Helen was unhappy about it, though she said nothing. Yesterday, in the restaurant, Lorraine had seemed trite, blurred, worn away. He emphatically did not want to see her, and he was glad Alix had not given away his hotel address. It was a relief to think, instead, of Honoria, to think of Sundays spent with her and of saying good morning to her and of knowing she was there in his house at night, drawing her breath in the darkness.

At five he took a taxi and bought presents for all the Peters—a piquant cloth doll, a box of Roman soldiers, flowers for Marion, big linen handkerchiefs for Lincoln.

He saw, when he arrived in the apartment, that Marion had accepted the inevitable. She greeted him now as though he were a recalcitrant member of the family, rather than a menacing outsider. Honoria had been told she was going; Charlie was glad to see that her tact made her conceal her excessive happiness. Only on his lap did she whisper her delight and the question "When?" before she slipped away with the other children.

He and Marion were alone for a minute in the room, and on an impulse he spoke out boldly:

"Family quarrels are bitter things. They don't go according to any rules.

⁹ Special-delivery letter.

They're not like aches or wounds; they're more like splits in the skin that won't heal because there's not enough material. I wish you and I could be on better terms."

"Some things are hard to forget," she answered. "It's a question of confidence." There was no answer to this and presently she asked, "When do you propose to take her?"

"As soon as I can get a governess. I hoped the day after tomorrow."

"That's impossible. I've got to get her things in shape. Not before Saturday."

He yielded. Coming back into the room, Lincoln offered him a drink.

"I'll take my daily whisky," he said.

It was warm here, it was a home, people together by a fire. The children felt very safe and important; the mother and father were serious, watchful. They had things to do for the children more important than his visit here. A spoonful of medicine was, after all, more important than the strained relations between Marion and himself. They were not dull people, but they were very much in the grip of life and circumstances. He wondered if he couldn't do something to get Lincoln out of his rut at the bank.

A long peal at the door-bell; the *bonne à tout faire*[10] passed through and went down the corridor. The door opened upon another long ring, and then voices, and the three in the salon looked up expectantly; Richard moved to bring the corridor within his range of vision, and Marion rose. Then the maid came back along the corridor, closely followed by the voices, which developed under the light into Duncan Schaeffer and Lorraine Quarrles.

They were gay, they were hilarious, they were roaring with laughter. For a moment Charlie was astounded; unable to understand how they ferreted out the Peters' address.

"Ah-h-h!" Duncan wagged his finger roguishly at Charlie. "Ah-h-h!"

They both slid down another cascade of laughter. Anxious and at a loss, Charlie shook hands with them quickly and presented them to Lincoln and Marion. Marion nodded, scarcely speaking. She had drawn back a step toward the fire; her little girl stood beside her, and Marion put an arm about her shoulder.

With growing annoyance at the intrusion, Charlie waited for them to explain themselves. After some concentration Duncan said:

"We came to invite you out to dinner. Lorraine and I insist that all this shishi, cagy business 'bout your address got to stop."

Charlie came closer to them, as if to force them backward down the corridor.

"Sorry, but I can't. Tell me where you'll be and I'll phone you in half an hour."

This made no impression. Lorraine sat down suddenly on the side of a chair, and focusing her eyes on Richard, cried, "Oh, what a nice little boy! Come here, little boy." Richard glanced at his mother, but did not move. With a perceptible shrug of her shoulders, Lorraine turned back to Charlie:

"Come and dine. Sure your cousins won' mine. See you so sel'om. Or solemn."

"I can't," said Charlie sharply. "You two have dinner and I'll phone you."

Her voice became suddenly unpleasant. "All right, we'll go. But I remember

---

[10] Maid of all work.

once when you hammered on my door at four A.M. I was enough of a good sport to give you a drink. Come on, Dunc."

Still in slow motion, with blurred, angry faces, with uncertain feet, they retired along the corridor.

"Good night," Charlie said.

"Good night!" responded Lorraine emphatically.

When he went back into the salon Marion had not moved, only now her son was standing in the circle of her other arm. Lincoln was still swinging Honoria back and forth like a pendulum from side to side.

"What an outrage!" Charlie broke out. "What an absolute outrage!"

Neither of them answered. Charlie dropped into an armchair, picked up his drink, set it down again and said:

"People I haven't seen for two years having the colossal nerve—"

He broke off. Marion had made the sound "Oh!" in one swift, furious breath, turned her body from him with a jerk and left the room.

Lincoln set down Honoria carefully.

"You children go in and start your soup," he said, and when they obeyed, he said to Charlie:

"Marion's not well and she can't stand shocks. That kind of people make her really physically sick."

"I didn't tell them to come here. They wormed your name out of somebody. They deliberately—"

"Well, it's too bad. It doesn't help matters. Excuse me a minute."

Left alone, Charlie sat tense in his chair. In the next room he could hear the children eating, talking in monosyllables, already oblivious to the scene between their elders. He heard a murmur of conversation from a farther room and then the ticking bell of a telephone receiver picked up, and in a panic he moved to the other side of the room and out of earshot.

In a minute Lincoln came back. "Look here, Charlie, I think we'd better call off dinner for tonight. Marion's in bad shape."

"Is she angry with me?"

"Sort of," he said, almost roughly. "She's not strong and—"

"You mean she's changed her mind about Honoria?"

"She's pretty bitter right now. I don't know. You phone me at the bank tomorrow."

"I wish you'd explain to her I never dreamed these people would come here. I'm just as sore as you are."

"I couldn't explain anything to her now."

Charlie got up. He took his coat and hat and started down the corridor. Then he opened the door of the dining room and said in a strange voice, "Good night, children."

Honoria rose and ran around the table to hug him.

"Good night, sweetheart," he said vaguely, and then trying to make his voice more tender, trying to conciliate something, "Good night, dear children."

V

Charlie went directly to the Ritz bar with the furious idea of finding Lorraine and Duncan, but they were not there, and he realized that in any case there was nothing he could do. He had not touched his drink at the Peters, and now he ordered a whisky-and-soda. Paul came over to say hello.

"It's a great change," he said sadly. "We do about half the business we did. So many fellows I hear about back in the States lost everything, maybe not in the first crash, but then in the second. Your friend George Hardt lost every cent, I hear. Are you back in the States?"

"No, I'm in business in Prague."

"I heard that you lost a lot in the crash."

"I did," and he added grimly, "but I lost everything I wanted in the boom."

"Selling short."

"Something like that."

Again the memory of those days swept over him like a nightmare—the people they had met travelling; then people who couldn't add a row of figures or speak a coherent sentence. The little man Helen had consented to dance with at the ship's party, who had insulted her ten feet from the table; the women and girls carried screaming with drink or drugs out of public places——

—The men who locked their wives out in the snow, because the snow of twenty-nine wasn't real snow. If you didn't want it to be snow, you just paid some money.

He went to the phone and called the Peters' apartment; Lincoln answered.

"I called up because this thing is on my mind. Has Marion said anything definite?"

"Marion's sick," Lincoln answered shortly. "I know this thing isn't altogether your fault, but I can't have her go to pieces about it. I'm afraid we'll have to let it slide for six months; I can't take the chance of working her up to this state again."

"I see."

"I'm sorry, Charlie." .

He went back to his table. His whisky glass was empty, but he shook his head when Alix looked at it questioningly. There wasn't much he could do now except send Honoria some things; he would send her a lot of things tomorrow. He thought rather angrily that this was just money—he had given so many people money. . . .

"No, no more," he said to another waiter. "What do I owe you?"

He would come back some day; they couldn't make him pay forever. But he wanted his child, and nothing was much good now, beside that fact. He wasn't young any more, with a lot of nice thoughts and dreams to have by himself. He was absolutely sure Helen wouldn't have wanted him to be so alone.

QUESTIONS

1. Fitzgerald adopted a limited omniscience for this story. What are the limitations?
2. Do we sympathize fully with Charlie Wales? Does the author expect us to? How do we know?
3. What should be our attitude toward Marion and Lincoln? Is it the same as Charlie's?

4. In the Ritz bar, in the last scene, Charlie says: "I lost everything I wanted in the boom." What does he mean?
5. Why is the story called "Babylon Revisited"?

MOTHER AND DAUGHTER

D. H. Lawrence (1885–1930)

Virginia Bodoin had a good job: she was head of a department in a certain government office, held a responsible position, and earned, to imitate Balzac[1] and be precise about it, seven hundred and fifty pounds a year. That is already something. Rachel Bodoin, her mother, had an income of about six hundred a year, on which she had lived in the capitals of Europe since the effacement of a never very important husband.

Now, after some years of virtual separation and 'freedom', mother and daughter once more thought of settling down. They had become, in course of time, more like a married couple than mother and daughter. They knew one another very well indeed, and each was a little 'nervous' of the other. They had lived together and parted several times. Virginia was now thirty, and she didn't look like marrying. For four years she had been as good as married to Henry Lubbock, a rather spoilt young man who was musical. Then Henry let her down: for two reasons. He couldn't stand her mother. Her mother couldn't stand him. And anybody whom Mrs. Bodoin could not stand she managed to sit on, disastrously. So Henry had writhed horribly, feeling his mother-in-law sitting on him tight, and Virginia after all, in a helpless sort of family loyalty, sitting alongside her mother. Virginia didn't really want to sit on Henry. But when her mother egged her on, she couldn't help it. For ultimately her mother had power over her; a strange *female* power, nothing to do with parental authority. Virginia had long thrown parental authority to the winds. But her mother had another, much subtler form of domination, female and thrilling, so that when Rachel said: "Let's squash him!" Virginia had to rush wickedly and gleefully to the sport. And Henry knew quite well when he was being squashed. So that was one of his reasons for going back on Vinny. He called her Vinny, to the superlative disgust of Mrs. Bodoin, who always corrected him: "My daughter *Virginia—*"

The second reason was, again to be Balzacian, that Virginia hadn't a sou of her own. Henry had a sorry two hundred and fifty. Virginia, at the age of twenty-four, was already earning four hundred and fifty. But she was earning them. Whereas Henry managed to earn about twelve pounds per annum, by his precious music. He had realised that he would find it hard to earn more. So that marrying, except with a wife who could keep him, was rather out of the question. Vinny would inherit her mother's money. But then Mrs. Bodoin had the health and muscular equipment of the Sphinx. She would live for ever, seeking whom she might devour, and devouring him. Henry lived with Vinny for two years, in the married sense of the words: and Vinny felt they were married, mi-

[1] Honoré de Balzac (1799–1850), a French novelist noted for generous and precise detail.

nus a mere ceremony. But Vinny had her mother always in the background; often as far back as Paris or Biarritz, but still, within letter reach. And she never realised the funny little grin that came on her own elvish face when her mother, even in a letter, spread her skirts and calmly sat on Henry. She never realised that in spirit she promptly and mischievously sat on him too: she could no more have helped it than the tide can help turning to the moon. And she did not dream that he felt it, and was utterly mortified in his masculine vanity. Women, very often, hypnotise one another, and then, hypnotised, they proceed gently to wring the neck of the man they think they are loving with all their hearts. Then they call it utter perversity on his part, that he doesn't like having his neck wrung. They think he is repudiating a heart-felt love. For they are hypnotised. Women hypnotise one another, without knowing it.

In the end, Henry backed out. He saw himself being simply reduced to nothingness by two women, an old witch with muscles like the Sphinx, and a young, spell-bound witch, lavish, elvish and weak, who utterly spoilt him but who ate his marrow.

Rachel would write from Paris: "My Dear Virginia, as I had a windfall in the way of an investment, I am sharing it with you. You will find enclosed my cheque for twenty pounds. No doubt you will be needing it to buy Henry a suit of clothes, since the spring is apparently come, and the sunlight may be tempted to show him up for what he is worth. I don't want my daughter going around with what is presumably a street-corner musician, but please pay the tailor's bill yourself, or you may have to do it over again later." Henry got a suit of clothes, but it was as good as a shirt of Nessus,[2] eating him away with subtle poison.

So he backed out. He didn't jump out, or bolt, or carve his way out at the sword's point. He sort of faded out, distributing his departure over a year or more. He was fond of Vinny, and he could hardly do without her, and he was sorry for her. But at length he couldn't see her apart from her mother. She was a young, weak, spendthrift witch, accomplice of her tough-clawed witch of a mother.

Henry made other alliances, got a good hold on elsewhere, and gradually extricated himself. He saved his life, but he had lost, he felt, a good deal of his youth and marrow. He tended now to go fat, a little puffy, somewhat insignificant. And he had been handsome and striking-looking.

The two witches howled when he was lost to them. Poor Virginia was really half-crazy, she didn't know what to do with herself. She had a violent recoil from her mother. Mrs. Bodoin was filled with furious contempt for her daughter: that she should let such a hooked fish slip out of her hands! That she should allow such a person to turn her down! "I don't quite see my daughter seduced and thrown over by a sponging individual such as Henry Lubbock," she wrote. "But if it has happened, I suppose it is somebody's fault—"

There was a mutual recoil, which lasted nearly five years. But the spell was not broken. Mrs. Bodoin's mind never left her daughter, and Virginia was ceaselessly aware of her mother, somewhere in the universe. They wrote, and met at intervals, but they kept apart in recoil.

[2] Heracles died as a result of contact with the poisoned blood of Nessus on a shirt given to him by his wife.

The spell, however, was between them, and gradually it worked. They felt more friendly. Mrs. Bodoin came to London. She stayed in the same quiet hotel with her daughter: Virginia had had two rooms in an hotel for the past three years. And, at last, they thought of taking an apartment together.

Virginia was now over thirty. She was still thin and odd and elvish, with a very slight and piquant cast in one of her brown eyes, and she still had her odd, twisted smile, and her slow, rather deep-toned voice, that caressed a man like the stroking of subtle fingertips. Her hair was still a natural tangle of curls, a bit dishevelled. She still dressed with a natural elegance which tended to go wrong and a tiny bit sluttish. She still might have a hole in her expensive and perfectly new stockings, and still she might have to take off her shoes in the drawing-room, if she came to tea, and sit there in her stockinged-feet. True, she had elegant feet: she was altogether elegantly shaped. But it wasn't that. It was neither coquetry nor vanity. It was simply that, after having gone to a good shoemaker and paid five guineas for a pair of perfectly simple and natural shoes, made to her feet, the said shoes would hurt her excruciatingly, when she had walked half a mile in them, and she would simply have to take them off, even if she sat on the kerb to do it. It was a fatality. There was a touch of the *gamin* in her very feet, a certain sluttishness that wouldn't let them stay properly in nice proper shoes. She practically always wore her mother's old shoes. "Of course, I go through life in mother's old shoes. If she died and left me without a supply, I suppose I should have to go in a bath-chair," she would say, with her odd twisted little grin. She was so elegant, and yet a slut. It was her charm, really.

Just the opposite of her mother. They would wear each other's shoes and each other's clothes, which seemed remarkable, for Mrs. Bodoin seemed so much the bigger of the two. But Virginia's shoulders were broad; if she was thin, she had a strong frame, even when she looked a frail rag.

Mrs. Bodoin was one of those women of sixty or so, with a terrible inward energy and a violent sort of vitality. But she managed to hide it. She sat with perfect repose, and folded hands. One thought: What a calm woman! Just as one may look at the snowy summit of a quiescent volcano, in the evening light, and think: What peace!

It was strange *muscular* energy which possessed Mrs. Bodoin, as it possesses, curiously enough, many women over fifty, and is usually distasteful in its manifestations. Perhaps it accounts for the lassitude of the young.

But Mrs. Bodoin recognised the bad taste in her energetic coevals, so she cultivated repose. Her very way of pronouncing the word, in two syllables: re-pòse, making the second syllable run on into the twilight, showed how much suppressed energy she had. Faced with the problem of iron-grey hair and black eyebrows, she was too clever to try dyeing herself back into youth. She studied her face, her whole figure, and decided that it was *positive*. There was no denying it. There was no wispiness, no hollowness, no limp frail blossom-on-a-bending-stalk about her. Her figure, though not stout, was full, strange, and *cambré*.[3] Her face had an aristocratic arched nose, aristocratic, who-the-devil-are-you grey eyes, and cheeks rather long but also rather full. Nothing appealing or youthfully skittish here.

[3] Well set.

Like an independent woman, she used her wits, and decided most emphatically not to be youthful or skittish or appealing. She would keep her dignity, for she was fond of it. She was positive. She liked to be positive. She was used to her positivity. So she would just *be* positive.

She turned to the positive period; to the eighteenth century, to Voltaire, to Ninon de l'Enclos and the Pompadour, to Madame la Duchesse and Monsieur le Marquis. She decided that she was not much in the line of la Pompadour or la Duchesse, but almost exactly in the line of Monsieur le Marquis. And she was right. With hair silvering to white, brushed back clean from her positive brow and temples, cut short, but sticking out a little behind, with her rather full, pink face and thin black eyebrows plucked to two fine, superficial crescents, her arching nose and her rather full insolent eyes she was perfectly eighteenth century, the early half. That she was Monsieur le Marquis rather than Madame la Marquise made her really modern.

Her appearance was perfect. She wore delicate combinations of grey and pink, maybe with a darkening iron-grey touch, and her jewels were of soft old coloured paste. Her bearing was a sort of alert repose, very calm, but very assured. There was, to use a vulgarism, no getting past her.

She had a couple of thousand pounds she could lay hands on. Virginia, of course, was always in debt. But, after all, Virginia was not to be sniffed at. She made seven hundred and fifty a year.

Virginia was oddly clever, and not clever. She didn't *really* know anything, because anything and everything was interesting to her for the moment, and she picked it up at once. She picked up languages with extraordinary ease, she was fluent in a fortnight. This helped her enormously with her job. She could prattle away with heads of industry, let them come from where they liked. But she didn't *know* any language, not even her own. She picked things up in her sleep, so to speak, without knowing anything about them.

And this made her popular with men. With all her curious facility, they didn't feel small in front of her, because she was like an instrument. She had to be prompted. Some man had to set her in motion, and then she worked, really cleverly. She could collect the most valuable information. She was very useful. She worked with men, spent most of her time with men, her friends were practically all men. She didn't feel easy with women.

Yet she had no lover, nobody seemed eager to marry her, nobody seemed eager to come close to her at all. Mrs. Bodoin said: "I'm afraid Virginia is a one-man woman. I am a one-man woman. So was my mother, and so was my grandmother. Virginia's father was the only man in my life, the only one. And I'm afraid Virginia is the same, tenacious. Unfortunately, the man was what he was, and her life is just left there."

Henry had said, in the past, that Mrs. Bodoin wasn't a one-man woman, she was a no-man woman, and that if she could have had her way, everything male would have been wiped off the face of the earth, and only the female element left.

However, Mrs. Bodoin thought that it was now time to make a move. So she and Virginia took a quite handsome apartment in one of the old Bloomsbury squares, fitted it up and furnished it with extreme care, and with some quite lovely things, got in a very good man, an Austrian, to cook, and they set up married life together, mother and daughter.

At first it was rather thrilling. The two reception-rooms, looking down on the dirty old trees of the Square gardens, were of splendid proportions, and each with three great windows coming down low, almost to the level of the knees. The chimney-piece was late eighteenth century. Mrs. Bodoin furnished the rooms with a gentle suggestion of Louis-Seize merged with Empire, without keeping to any particular style. But she had, saved from her own home, a really remarkable Aubusson carpet. It looked almost new, as if it had been woven two years ago, and was startling, Yet somehow rather splendid, as it spread its rose-red borders and wonderful florid array of silver-grey and gold-grey roses, lilies and gorgeous swans and trumpeting volutes away over the floor. Very aesthetic people found it rather loud, they preferred the worn, dim yellowish Aubusson in the big bedroom. But Mrs. Bodoin loved her drawing-room carpet. It was positive, but it was not vulgar. It had a certain grand air in its floridity. She felt it gave her a proper footing. And it behaved very well with her painted cabinets and grey-and-gold brocade chairs and big Chinese vases, which she liked to fill with big flowers: single Chinese peonies, big roses, great tulips, orange lilies. The dim room of London, with all its atmospheric colour, would stand the big, free, fisticuffing flowers.

Virginia, for the first time in her life, had the pleasure of making a home. She was again entirely under her mother's spell, and swept away, thrilled to her marrow. She had had no idea that her mother had got such treasures as the carpets and painted cabinets and brocade chairs up her sleeve: many of them the débris of the Fitzpatrick home in Ireland, Mrs. Bodoin being a Fitzpatrick. Almost like a child, like a bride, Virginia threw herself into the business of fixing up the rooms. "Of course, Virginia, I consider this is your apartment," said Mrs. Bodoin. "I am nothing but your *dame de compagnie*,[4] and shall carry out your wishes entirely, if you will only express them."

Of course Virginia expressed a few, but not many. She introduced some wild pictures bought from impecunious artists whom she patronised. Mrs. Bodoin thought the pictures positive about the wrong things, but as far as possible, she let them stay: looking on them as the necessary element of modern ugliness. But by that element of modern ugliness, wilfully so, it was easy to see the things that Virginia had introduced into the apartment.

Perhaps nothing goes to the head like setting up house. You can get drunk on it. You feel you are creating something. Nowadays it is no longer the 'home', the domestic nest. It is 'my rooms', or 'my house', the great garment which reveals and clothes 'my personality'. Mrs. Bodoin, deliberately scheming for Virginia, kept moderately cool over it, but even she was thrilled to the marrow, and of an intensity and ferocity with the decorators and furnishers, astonishing. But Virginia was just all the time tipsy with it, as if she had touched some magic button on the grey wall of life, and with an Open Sesame![5] her lovely and coloured rooms had begun to assemble out of fairyland. It was far more vivid and wonder-

[4] Female companion.
[5] The magic words that opened the cave of jewels in "Ali Baba and the Forty Thieves."

ful to her than if she had inherited a duchy.

The mother and daughter, the mother in a sort of faded russet crimson and the daughter in silver, began to entertain. They had, of course, mostly men. It filled Mrs. Bodoin with a sort of savage impatience to entertain women. Besides, most of Virginia's acquaintances were men. So there were dinners and well-arranged evenings.

It went well, but something was missing. Mrs. Bodoin wanted to be gracious, so she held herself rather back. She stayed a little distant, was calm, reposed, eighteenth-century, and determined to be a foil to the clever and slightly-elvish Virginia. It was a pose, and alas, it stopped something. She was very nice with the men, no matter what her contempt of them. But the men were uneasy with her: afraid.

What they all felt, all the men guests, was that *for them*, nothing really happened. Everything that happened was between mother and daughter. All the flow was between mother and daughter. A subtle, hypnotic spell encompassed the two women, and, try as they might, the men were shut out. More than one young man, a little dazzled, *began* to fall in love with Virginia. But it was impossible. Not only was he shut out, he was, in some way, annihilated. The spontaneity was killed in his bosom. While the two women sat, brilliant and rather wonderful, in magnetic connection at opposite ends of the table, like two witches, a double Circe[6] turning the men not into swine—the men would have liked that well enough—but into lumps.

It was tragic. Because Mrs. Bodoin wanted Virginia to fall in love and marry. She really wanted it, and she attributed Virginia's lack of forthcoming to the delinquent Henry. She never realised the hypnotic spell, which of course encompassed her as well as Virginia, and made men just an impossibility to both women, mother and daughter alike.

At this time, Mrs. Bodoin hid her humour. She had a really marvellous faculty of humorous imitation. She could imitate the Irish servants from her old home, or the American women who called on her, or the modern ladylike young men, the asphodels, as she called them: "Of course, you know the asphodel is a kind of onion! Oh yes, just an over-bred onion": who wanted, with their murmuring voices and peeping under their brows, to make her feel very small and very bourgeois. She could imitate them all with a humour that was really touched with genius. But it was devastating. It demolished the objects of her humour so absolutely, smashed them to bits with a ruthless hammer, pounded them to nothing so terribly, that it frightened people, particularly men. It frightened men off.

So she hid it. She hid it. But there it was, up her sleeve, her merciless, hammer-like humour, which just smashed its object on the head and left him brained. She tried to disown it. She tried to pretend, even to Virginia, that she had the gift no more. But in vain the hammer hidden up her sleeve hovered over the head of every guest, and every guest felt his scalp creep, and Virginia felt her inside creep with a little, mischievous, slightly idiotic grin, as still another fool male was mystically knocked on the head. It was a sort of uncanny sport.

No, the plan was not going to work: the plan of having Virginia fall in love and marry. Of course, the men *were* such lumps, such *oeufs farcies*.[7] There was

---

[6] The enchantress who turns men to swine in Homer's *Odyssey*, Book X.
[7] Stuffed eggs.

one, at least, that Mrs. Bodoin had real hopes of. He was a healthy and normal and very good-looking boy of good family, with no money, alas, but clerking to the House of Lords and very hopeful, and not very clever, but simply in love with Virginia's cleverness. He was just the one Mrs. Bodoin would have married for herself. True, he was only twenty-six, to Virginia's thirty-one. But he had rowed in the Oxford eight, and adored horses, talked horses adorably, and was simply infatuated by Virginia's cleverness. To him Virginia had the finest mind on earth. She was as wonderful as Plato, but infinitely more attractive because she was a woman, and winsome with it. Imagine a winsome Plato with untidy curls and the tiniest little brown-eyed squint and just a hint of woman's pathetic need for a protector, and you may imagine Adrian's feeling for Virginia. He adored her on his knees, but he felt he could protect her.

"Of course, he's just a very nice *boy*!" said Mrs. Bodoin. "He's a boy, and that's all you can say. And he always will be a boy. But that's the very nicest kind of man, the only kind you can live with: the eternal boy. Virginia, aren't you attracted to him?"

"Yes, mother! I think he's an awfully nice *boy*, as you say," replied Virginia, in her rather low, musical, whimsical voice. But the mocking little curl in the intonation put the lid on Adrian. Virginia was not marrying a nice *boy*! She could be malicious too, against her mother's taste. And Mrs. Bodoin let escape her a faint gesture of impatience.

For she had been planning her own retreat, planning to give Virginia the apartment outright, and half of her own income, if she would marry Adrian. Yes, the mother was already scheming how best she could live with dignity on three hundred a year, once Virginia was happily married to that most attractive if slightly brainless *boy*.

A year later, when Virginia was thirty-two, Adrian, who had married a wealthy American girl and been transferred to a job in the legation at Washington in the meantime, faithfully came to see Virginia as soon as he was in London, faithfully kneeled at her feet, faithfully thought her the most wonderful spiritual being, and faithfully felt that she, Virginia, could have done wonders with him, which wonders would now never be done, for he had married in the meantime.

Virginia was looking haggard and worn. The scheme of a *ménage à deux*[8] with her mother had not succeeded. And now, work was telling on the younger woman. It is true, she was amazingly facile. But facility wouldn't get her all the way. She had to earn her money, and earn it hard. She had to slog, and she had to concentrate. While she could work by quick intuition and without much responsibility, work thrilled her. But as soon as she had to get down to it, as they say, grip and slog and concentrate, in a really responsible position, it wore her out terribly. She had to do it all off her nerves. She hadn't the same sort of fighting power as a man. Where a man can summon his old Adam in him to fight through his work, a woman has to draw on her nerves, and on her nerves alone. For the old Eve in her will have nothing to do with such work. So that mental responsibility, mental concentration, mental slogging wear out a woman terribly, especially if she is head of a department, and not working *for* somebody.

---

[8] Housekeeping for two.

So poor Virginia was worn out. She was thin as a rail. Her nerves were frayed to bits. And she could never forget her beastly work. She would come home at tea-time speechless and done for. Her mother, tortured by the sight of her, longed to say: "Has anything gone wrong, Virginia? Have you had anything particularly trying at the office to-day?" But she learned to hold her tongue, and say nothing. The question would be the last straw to Virginia's poor overwrought nerves, and there would be a little scene which, despite Mrs. Bodoin's calm and forbearance, offended the elder woman to the quick. She had learned, by bitter experience, to leave her child alone, as one would leave a frail tube of vitriol alone. But, of course, she could not keep her *mind* off Virginia. That was impossible. And poor Virginia, under the strain of work and the strain of her mother's awful ceaseless mind, was at the very end of her strength and resources.

Mrs. Bodoin had always disliked the fact of Virginia's doing a job. But now she hated it. She hated the whole government office with violent and virulent hate. Not only was it undignified for Virginia to be tied up there, but it was turning her, Mrs. Bodoin's daughter, into a thin, nagging, fearsome old maid. Could anything be more utterly English and humiliating to a well-born Irishwoman?

After a long day attending to the apartment, skilfully darning one of the brocade chairs, polishing the Venetian mirrors to her satisfaction, selecting flowers, doing certain shopping and housekeeping, attending perfectly to everything, then receiving callers in the afternoon, with never-ending energy, Mrs. Bodoin would go up from the drawing-room after tea and write a few letters, take her bath, dress with great care—she enjoyed attending to her person—and come down to dinner as fresh as a daisy, but far more energetic than that quiet flower. She was ready now for a full evening.

She was conscious, with gnawing anxiety, of Virginia's presence in the house, but she did not see her daughter till dinner was announced. Virginia slipped in, and away to her room unseen, never going into the drawing-room to tea. If Mrs. Bodoin heard her daughter's key in the latch, she quickly retired into one of the rooms till Virginia was safely through. It was too much for poor Virginia's nerves even to catch sight of anybody in the house, when she came in from the office. Bad enough to hear the murmur of visitors' voices behind the drawing-room door.

And Mrs. Bodoin would wonder: How is she? How is she to-night? I wonder what sort of a day she's had? And this thought would roam prowling through the house, to where Virginia was lying on her back in her room. But the mother would have to consume her anxiety till dinner-time. And then Virginia would appear, with black lines under her eyes, thin, tense, a young woman out of an office, the stigma upon her: badly dressed, a little acid in humour, with an impaired digestion, not interested in anything, blighted by her work. And Mrs. Bodoin, humiliated at the very sight of her, would control herself perfectly, say nothing but the mere smooth nothings of casual speech, and sit in perfect form presiding at a carefully-cooked dinner thought out entirely to please Virginia. Then Virginia hardly noticed what she ate.

Mrs. Bodoin was pining for an evening with life in it. But Virginia would lie on the couch and put on the loud-speaker. Or she would put a humorous record on the gramophone, and be amused, and hear it again, and be amused, and hear it again, six times, and six times be amused by a mildly funny record that Mrs.

Bodoin now knew off by heart. "Why, Virginia, I could repeat that record over to you, if you wished it, without your troubling to wind up that gramophone." And Virginia, after a pause in which she seemed not to have heard what her mother said, would reply: "I'm sure you could, mother." And that simple speech would convey such volumes of contempt for all that Rachel Bodoin was or ever could be or ever had been, contempt for her energy, her vitality, her mind, her body, her very existence, that the elder woman would curl. It seemed as if the ghost of Robert Bodoin spoke out of the mouth of the daughter, in deadly venom. Then Virginia would put on the record for the seventh time.

During the second ghastly year, Mrs. Bodoin realised that the game was up. She was a beaten woman, a woman without object or meaning any more. The hammer of her awful female humour, which had knocked so many people on the head, all the people, in fact, that she had come into contact with, had at last flown backwards and hit herself on the head. For her daughter was her other self, her *alter ego*. The secret and the meaning and the power of Mrs. Bodoin's whole life lay in the hammer, that hammer of her living humour which knocked everything on the head. That had been her lust and her passion, knocking everybody and everything humorously on the head. She had felt inspired in it: it was a sort of mission. And she had hoped to hand on the hammer to Virginia, her clever, unsolid but still actual daughter, Virginia. Virginia was the continuation of Rachel's own self. Virginia was Rachel's *alter ego*, her other self.

But, alas, it was a half-truth. Virginia had had a father. The fact, which had been utterly ignored by the mother, was gradually brought home to her by the curious recoil of the hammer. Virginia was her father's daughter. Could anything be more unseemly, horrid, more perverse in the natural scheme of things? For Robert Bodoin had been fully and deservedly knocked on the head by Rachel's hammer. Could anything, then, be more disgusting than that he should resurrect again in the person of Mrs. Bodoin's own daughter, her own *alter ego* Virginia, and start hitting back with a little spiteful hammer that was David's pebble against Goliath's battle-axe!

But the little pebble was mortal. Mrs. Bodoin felt it sink into her brow, her temple, and she was finished. The hammer fell nerveless from her hand.

The two women were now mostly alone. Virginia was too tired to have company in the evening. So there was the gramophone or loud-speaker, or else silence. Both women had come to loathe the apartment. Virginia felt it was the last grand act of bullying on her mother's part, she felt bullied by the assertive Aubusson carpet, by the beastly Venetian mirrors, by the big over-cultured flowers. She even felt bullied by the excellent food, and longed again for a Soho restaurant and her two poky, shabby rooms in the hotel. She loathed the apartment: she loathed everything. But she had not the energy to move. She had not the energy to do anything. She crawled to her work, and for the rest, she lay flat, gone.

It was Virginia's worn-out inertia that really finished Mrs. Bodoin. That was the pebble that broke the bone of her temple: "To have to attend my daughter's funeral, and accept the sympathy of all her fellow-clerks in her office, no, that is a final humiliation which I must spare myself. No! If Virginia must be a lady-clerk, she must be it henceforth on her own responsibility. I will retire from her existence."

Mrs. Bodoin had tried hard to persuade Virginia to give up her work and

come and live with her. She had offered her half her income. In vain. Virginia
stuck to her office.

Very well! So be it! The apartment was a fiasco, Mrs. Bodoin was longing,
longing to tear it to pieces again. One last and final blow of the hammer! "Virginia, don't you think we'd better get rid of this apartment, and live around as
we used to do? Don't you think we'll do that?"—"But all the money you've put
into it? and the lease for ten years!" cried Virginia, in a kind of inertia.—"Never
mind! We had the pleasure of making it. And we've had as much pleasure out of
living in it as we shall ever have. Now we'd better get rid of it—quickly—don't
you think?"

Mrs. Bodoin's arms were twitching to snatch the pictures off the walls, roll up
the Aubusson carpet, take the china out of the ivory-inlaid cabinet there and
then, at that very moment.

"Let us wait till Sunday before we decide," said Virginia.

"Till Sunday! Four days! As long as that? Haven't we already decided in our
own minds?" said Mrs. Bodoin.

"We'll wait till Sunday, anyhow," said Virginia.

The next evening, the Armenian came to dinner. Virginia called him Arnold,
with the French pronunciation, Arnault. Mrs. Bodoin, who barely tolerated him,
and could never get his name, which seemed to have a lot of bouyoums in it,
called him either the Armenian or the Rahat Lakoum, after the name of the
sweetmeat, or simply the Turkish Delight.

"Arnault is coming to dinner to-night, mother."

"Really! The Turkish Delight is coming here to dinner? Shall I provide anything special?" Her voice sounded as if she would suggest snails in aspic.

"I don't think so."

Virginia had seen a good deal of the Armenian at the office when she had to
negotiate with him on behalf of the Board of Trade. He was a man of about sixty,
a merchant, had been a millionaire, was ruined during the war, but was now
coming on again, and represented trade in Bulgaria. He wanted to negotiate with
the British Government, and the British Government sensibly negotiated with
him: at first through the medium of Virginia. Now things were going satisfactorily between Monsieur Arnault, as Virginia called him, and the Board of Trade,
so that a sort of friendship had followed the official relations.

The Turkish Delight was sixty, grey-haired and fat. He had numerous grandchildren growing up in Bulgaria, but he was a widower. He had a grey moustache cut like a brush, and glazed brown eyes over which hung heavy lids with
white lashes. His manner was humble, but in his bearing there was a certain dogged conceit. One notices the combination sometimes in Jews. He had been very
wealthy and kow-towed to, he had been ruined and humiliated, terribly humiliated, and now, doggedly, he was rising up again, his sons backing him, away in
Bulgaria. One felt he was not alone. He had his sons, his family, his tribe behind
him, away in the Near East.

He spoke bad English, but fairly fluent guttural French. He did not speak
much, but he sat. He sat, with his short, fat thighs, as if for eternity, *there*. There
was a strange potency in his fat immobile sitting, as if his posterior were connected with the very centre of the earth. And his brain, spinning away at the one
point in question, business, was very agile. Business absorbed him. But not in a

nervous, personal way. Somehow the family, the tribe was always felt behind him. It was business for the family, the tribe.

With the English he was humble, for the English like such aliens to be humble, and he had had a long schooling from the Turks. And he was always an outsider. Nobody would ever take any notice of him in society. He would just be an outsider, *sitting*.

"I hope, Virginia, you won't ask that Turkish-carpet gentleman when we have other people. I can bear it," said Mrs. Bodoin. "Some people might mind."

"Isn't it hard when you can't choose your own company in your own house," mocked Virginia.

"No! I don't care. I can meet anything and I'm sure, in the way of selling Turkish carpets, your acquaintance is very good. But I don't suppose you look on him as a personal friend—?"

"I do. I like him quite a lot."

"Well—! As you will. But consider your *other* friends."

Mrs. Bodoin was really mortified this time. She looked on the Armenian as one looks on the fat Levantine in a fez who tries to sell one hideous tapestries at Port Said, or on the seafront at Nice, as being outside the class of human beings, and in the class of insects. That he had been a millionaire, and might be a millionaire again, only added venom to her feeling of disgust at being forced into contact with such scum. She could not even squash him, or annihilate him. In scum there is nothing to squash, for scum is only the unpleasant residue of that which was never anything but squashed.

However, she was not quite just. True, he was fat, and he sat, with short thighs, like a toad, as if seated for a toad's eternity. His colour was of a dirty sort of paste, his brown eyes were glazed under heavy lids. And he never spoke until spoken to, waiting in his toad's silence, like a slave.

But his thick, fine white hair, which stood up on his head like a soft brush, was curiously virile. And his curious small hands, of the same soft dull paste, had a peculiar, fat, soft masculine breeding of their own. And his dull brown eye could glint with the subtlety of serpents, under the white brush of eyelash. He was tired, but he was not defeated. He had fought, and won, and lost, and was fighting again, always at a disadvantage. He belonged to a defeated race which accepts defeat, but which gets its own back by cunning. He was the father of sons, the head of a family, one of the heads of a defeated but indestructible tribe. He was not alone, and so you could not lay your finger on him. His whole consciousness was patriarchal and tribal. And somehow, he was humble, but he was indestructible.

At dinner he sat half-effaced, humble, yet with the conceit of the humble. His manners were perfectly good, rather French. Virginia chattered to him in French, and he replied with that peculiar nonchalance of the boulevards, which was the only manner he could command when speaking French. Mrs. Bodoin understood, but she was what one would call a heavy-footed linguist, so when she said anything, it was intensely in English. And the Turkish Delight replied in his clumsy English, hastily. It was not his fault that French was being spoken. It was Virginia's.

He was very humble, conciliatory, with Mrs. Bodoin. But he cast at her sometimes that rapid glint of a reptilian glance as if to say: "Yes! I see you! You are a handsome figure. As an *objet de vertu*[9] you are almost perfect." Thus his connoisseur's, antique-dealer's eye would appraise her. But then his thick white eyebrows would seem to add: "But what, under holy Heaven, are you as a woman? You are neither wife nor mother nor mistress, you have no perfume of sex, you are more dreadful than a Turkish soldier or an English official. No man on earth could embrace you. You are a ghoul, you are a strange genie from the underworld!" And he would secretly invoke the holy names to shield him.

Yet he was in love with Virginia. He saw, first and foremost, the child in her, as if she were a lost child in the gutter, a waif with a faint, fascinating cast in her brown eyes, waiting till someone would pick her up. A fatherless waif! And he was tribal father, father through all the ages.

Then, on the other hand, he knew her peculiar disinterested cleverness in affairs. That, too, fascinated him: that odd, almost second-sight cleverness about business, and entirely impersonal, entirely in the air. It seemed to him very strange. But it would be an immense help to him in his schemes. He did not really understand the English. He was at sea with them. But with her, he would have a clue to everything. For she was, finally, quite a somebody among these English, these English officials.

He was about sixty. His family was established in the East, his grandsons were growing up. It was necessary for him to live in London for some years. This girl would be useful. She had no money, save what she would inherit from her mother. But he would risk that: she would be an investment in his business. And then the apartment. He liked the apartment extremely. He recognised the *cachet*,[10] and the lilies and swans of the Aubusson carpet really did something to him. Virginia said to him: "Mother gave me the apartment." So he looked on that as safe. And finally, Virginia was almost a virgin, probably quite a virgin, and, as far as the paternal Oriental male like himself was concerned, entirely virgin. He had a very small idea of the silly puppy-sexuality of the English, so different from the prolonged male voluptuousness of his own pleasures. And last of all, he was physically lonely, getting old and tired.

Virginia, of course, did not know why she liked being with Arnault. Her cleverness was amazingly stupid when it came to life, to living. She said he was 'quaint'. She said his nonchalant French of the boulevards was 'amusing'. She found his business cunning 'intriguing', and the glint in his dark glazed eyes, under the white, thick lashes, 'shieky'. She saw him quite often, had tea with him in his hotel, and motored with him one day down to the sea.

When he took her hand in his own soft still hands, there was something so caressing, so possessive in his touch, so strange and positive in his leaning towards her, that though she trembled with fear, she was helpless.—"But you are so thin, dear little thin thing, you need repose, repose, for the blossom to open, poor little blossom, to become a little fat!" he said in his French.

She quivered, and was helpless. It certainly was quaint! He was so strange and positive, he seemed to have all the power. The moment he realised that she would succumb into his power, he took full charge of the situation, he lost all his

[9] Object of quality.
[10] Style.

hesitation and his humility. He did not want just to make love to her: he wanted to marry her, for all his multifarious reasons. And he must make himself master of her.

He put her hand to his lips, and seemed to draw her life to his in kissing her thin hand. "The poor child is tired, she needs repose, she needs to be caressed and cared for," he said in his French. And he drew nearer to her.

She looked up in dread at his glinting, tired dark eyes under the white lashes. But he used all his will, looking back at her heavily and calculating that she must submit. And he brought his body quite near to her, and put his hand softly on her face, and made her lay her face against his breast, as he soothingly stroked her arm with his other hand. "Dear little thing! Dear little thing! Arnault loves her so dearly! Arnault loves her! Perhaps she will marry her Arnault. Dear little girl, Arnault will put flowers in her life, and make her life perfumed with sweetness and content."

She leaned against his breast and let him caress her. She gave a fleeting, half poignant, half vindictive thought to her mother. Then she felt in the air the sense of destiny, destiny. Oh, so nice, not to have to struggle. To give way to destiny.

"Will she marry her old Arnault? Eh? Will she marry him?" he asked in a soothing, caressing voice, at the same time compulsive.

She lifted her head and looked at him: the thick white brows, the glinting, tired dark eyes. How queer and comic! How comic to be in his power! And he was looking a little baffled.

"Shall I?" she said, with her mischievous twist of a grin.

"*Mais oui!*" he said, with all the sang-foid of his old eyes. "*Mais oui! Je te contenterai, tu le verras.*"[11]

"*Tu me contenteras!*"[12] she said, with a flickering smile of real amusement at his assurance. "Will you really content me?"

"But surely! I assure it you. And you will marry me?"

"You must tell mother," she said, and hid wickedly against his waistcoat again, while the male pride triumphed in him.

Mrs. Bodoin had no idea that Virginia was intimate with the Turkish Delight: she did not inquire into her daughter's movements. During the famous dinner, she was calm and a little aloof, but entirely self-possessed. When, after coffee, Virginia left her alone with the Turkish Delight, she made no effort at conversation, only glanced at the rather short, stout man in correct dinner-jacket, and thought how his sort of fatness called for a fez and the full muslin breeches of a bazaar merchant in *The Thief of Baghdad*.

"Do you really prefer to smoke a hookah?" she asked him, with a slow drawl.

"What is a hookah, please?"

"One of those water-pipes. Don't you all smoke them in the East?"

He only looked mystified and humble, and silence resumed. She little knew what was simmering inside his stillness.

"Madame," he said, "I want to ask you something."

[11] "Yes, indeed! I will content you, you will see."
[12] "You will content me?"

"You do? Then why not ask it?" came her slightly melancholy drawl.

"Yes! It is this. I wish I may have the honour to marry your daughter. She is willing."

There was a moment's blank pause. Then Mrs. Bodoin leaned towards him from her distance with curious portentousness.

"What was that you said?" she asked. "Repeat it!"

"I wish I may have the honour to marry your daughter. She is willing to take me."

His dark, glazed eyes looked at her, then glanced away again. Still leaning forward, she gazed fixedly on him, as if spellbound, turned to stone. She was wearing pink topaz ornaments, but he judged they were paste, moderately good.

"Did I hear you say she is willing to take you?" came the slow, melancholy, remote voice.

"Madame, I think so," he said, with a bow.

"I think we'll wait till she comes," she said, leaning back.

There was silence. She stared at the ceiling. He looked closely round the room, at the furniture, at the china in the ivory-inlaid cabinet.

"I can settle five thousand pounds on Mademoiselle Virginia, madame," came his voice. "Am I correct to assume that she will bring this apartment and its appointments into the marriage settlement?"

Absolute silence. He might as well have been on the moon. But he was a good sitter. He just sat until Virginia came in.

Mrs. Bodoin was still staring at the ceiling. The iron had entered her soul finally and fully. Virginia glanced at her, but said:

"Have a whisky-and-soda, Arnault?"

He rose and came towards the decanters, and stood beside her: a rather squat, stout man with white head, silent with misgiving. There was the fizz of the syphon: then they came to their chairs.

"Arnault has spoken to you, mother?" said Virginia.

Mrs. Bodoin sat up straight and gazed at Virginia with big, owlish eyes, haggard. Virginia was terrified, yet a little thrilled. Her mother was beaten.

"Is it true, Virginia, that you are *willing* to marry this—Oriental gentlemen?" asked Mrs. Bodoin slowly.

"Yes, mother, quite true," said Virginia, in her teasing soft voice.

Mrs. Bodoin looked owlish and dazed.

"May I be excused from having any part in it, or from having anything to do with your future *husband*—I mean having any business to transact with him?" she asked dazedly, in her slow, distinct voice.

"Why, of course!" said Virginia, frightened, smiling oddly.

There was a pause. Then Mrs. Bodoin, feeling old and haggard, pulled herself together again.

"Am I to understand that your future husband would like to possess this apartment?" came her voice.

Virginia smiled quickly and crookedly. Arnault just sat, planted on his posterior, and heard. She reposed on him.

"Well—perhaps!" said Virginia. "Perhaps he would like to know that I possessed it." She looked at him.

Arnault nodded gravely.

"And do you *wish* to possess it?" came Mrs. Bodoin's slow voice. "Is it your intention to *inhabit* it, with your *husband*?" She put eternities into her long, stressed words.

"Yes, I think it is," said Virginia. "You know you *said* the apartment was mine, mother."

"Very well! It shall be so. I shall send my lawyer to this—Oriental gentleman, if you will leave written instructions on my writing-table. May I ask when you think of getting—*married*?"

"When do you think, Arnault?" said Virginia.

"Shall it be in two weeks?" he said, sitting erect, with his fists on his knees.

"In about a fortnight, mother," said Virginia.

"I have heard? In two weeks! Very well! In two weeks everything shall be at your disposal. And now, please excuse me." She rose, made a slight general bow, and moved calmly and dimly from the room. It was killing her, that she could not shriek aloud and beat that Levantine out of the house. But she couldn't. She had imposed the restraint on herself.

Arnault stood and looked with glistening eyes round the room. It would be his. When his sons came to England, here he would receive them.

He looked at Virginia. She, too, was white and haggard now. And she flung away from him, as if in resentment. She resented the defeat of her mother. She was still capable of dismissing him for ever, and going back to her mother.

"Your mother is a wonderful lady," he said, going to Virginia and taking her hand. "But she has no husband to shelter her, she is unfortunate. I am sorry she will be alone. I should be happy if she would like to stay here with us."

The sly old fox knew what he was about.

"I'm afraid there's no hope of that," said Virginia, with a return of her old irony.

She sat on the couch, and he caressed her softly and paternally, and the very incongruity of it, there in her mother's drawing-room, amused her. And because he saw that the things in the drawing-room were handsome and valuable, and now they were his, his blood flushed and he caressed the thin girl at his side with passion, because she represented these valuable surroundings, and brought them to his possession. And he said: "And with me you will be very comfortable, very content, oh, I shall make you content, not like madame your mother. And you will get fatter, and bloom like the rose. I shall make you bloom like the rose. And shall we say next week, hein? Shall it be next week, next Wednesday, that we marry? Wednesday is a good day. Shall it be then?"

"Very well!" said Virginia, caressed again into a luxurious sense of destiny, reposing on fate, having to make no effort, no more effort, all her life.

Mrs. Bodoin moved into an hotel next day, and came into the apartment to pack up and extricate herself and her immediate personal belongings only when Virginia was necessarily absent. She and her daughter communicated by letter, as far as was necessary.

And in five days' time Mrs. Bodoin was clear. All business that could be settled was settled, all her trunks were removed. She had five trunks, and that was all. Denuded and outcast, she would depart to Paris, to live out the rest of her days.

The last day she waited in the drawing-room till Virginia should come home.

She sat there in her hat and street things, like a stranger.

"I just waited to say good-bye" she said. "I leave in the morning for Paris. This is my address. I think everything is settled; if not, let me know and I'll attend to it. Well, good-bye!—and I hope you'll be *very happy!*"

She dragged out the last words sinisterly; which restored Virginia, who was beginning to lose her head.

"Why, I think I may be," said Virginia, with the twist of a smile.

"I shouldn't wonder," said Mrs. Bodoin pointedly and grimly. "I think the Armenian grandpapa knows very well what he's about. You're just the harem type, after all." The words came slowly, dropping, each with a plop! of deep contempt.

"I suppose I am! Rather fun!" said Virginia. "But I wonder where I got it? Not from you, mother—" she drawled mischievously.

"I should say *not.*"

"Perhaps daughters go by contraries, like dreams'" mused Virginia wickedly. "All the harem was left out of you, so perhaps it all had to be put back into me."

Mrs. Bodoin flashed a look at her.

"You have *all* my *pity!*" she said.

"Thank you, dear. You have just a bit of mine."

QUESTIONS

1. Lawrence's omniscience is much less limited than Fitzgerald's. Is the omniscience limited in any significant way? Does the narrator focus on any character more than on others?
2. What are the differences between Virginia's first suitor and her last? Why is the last more successful?
3. Summarize the relationship between mother and daughter. Does it remain the same throughout the story? Does the narrator approve of one more than the other? Should we?
4. Is it true that "Women hypnotise one another, without knowing it"? Are other observations of the narrator true, or matters of opinion?
5. Can we use the narrator's many opinions and attitudes to draw a character study of him?
6. Explain the meaning of the last two lines of the story.

We present one last example of the omniscient narrator. Observe the cumulative effect here of the storyteller's sweeping presence and all-encompassing knowledge. Note how different the technique is from the far more limited omniscience of "Babylon Revisited."

THE STORM

Kate Chopin   (1851–1904)

I

The leaves were so still that even Bibi thought it was going to rain. Bobinôt, who was accustomed to converse on terms of perfect equality with his little son, called the child's attention to certain sombre clouds that were rolling with sinister intention from the west, accompanied by a sullen, threatening roar. They were at Friedheimer's store and decided to remain there till the storm had passed. They sat within the door on two empty kegs. Bibi was four years old and looked very wise.

"Mama'll be 'fraid, yes," he suggested with blinking eyes.

"She'll shut the house. Maybe she got Sylvie helpin' her this evenin'," Bobinôt responded reassuringly.

"No; she ent got Sylvie. Sylvie was helpin' her yistiday," piped Bibi.

Bobinôt arose and going across to the counter purchased a can of shrimps, of which Calixta was very fond. Then he returned to his perch on the keg and sat stolidly holding the can of shrimps while the storm burst. It shook the wooden store and seemed to be ripping great furrows in the distant field. Bibi laid his little hand on his father's knee and was not afraid.

II

Calixta, at home, felt no uneasiness for their safety. She sat at a side window sewing furiously on a sewing machine. She was greatly occupied and did not notice the approaching storm. But she felt very warm and often stopped to mop her face on which the perspiration gathered in beads. She unfastened her white sacque at the throat. It began to grow dark, and suddenly realizing the situation she got up hurriedly and went about closing windows and doors.

Out on the small front gallery she had hung Bobinôt's Sunday clothes to air and she hastened out to gather them before the rain fell. As she stepped outside, Alcée Laballière rode in at the gate. She had not seen him very often since her marriage, and never alone. She stood there with Bobinôt's coat in her hands, and the big rain drops began to fall. Alcée rode his horse under the shelter of a side projection where the chickens had huddled and there were plows and a harrow piled up in the corner.

"May I come and wait on your gallery till the storm is over, Calixta?" he asked.

"Come 'long in, M'sieur Alcée."

His voice and her own startled her as if from a trance, and she seized Bobinôt's vest. Alcée, mounting to the porch, grabbed the trousers and snatched Bibi's braided jacket that was about to be carried away by a sudden gust of wind. He expressed an intention to remain outside, but it was soon apparent that he might as well have been out in the open: the water beat in upon the boards in driving sheets, and he went inside, closing the door after him. It was even necessary to put something beneath the door to keep the water out.

"My! what a rain! It's good two years since it rain' like that," exclaimed Calixta as she rolled up a piece of bagging and Alcée helped her to thrust it beneath the crack.

She was a little fuller of figure than five years before when she married; but she had lost nothing of her vivacity. Her blue eyes still retained their melting quality; and her yellow hair, dishevelled by the wind and rain, kinked more stubbornly than ever about her ears and temples.

The rain beat upon the low, shingled roof with a force and clatter that threatened to break an entrance and deluge them there. They were in the dining room—the sitting room—the general utility room. Adjoining was her bed room, with Bibi's couch along side her own. The door stood open, and the room with its white, monumental bed, its closed shutters, looked dim and mysterious.

Alcée flung himself into a rocker and Calixta nervously began to gather up from the floor the lengths of a cotton sheet which she had been sewing.

"If this keeps up, *Dieu sait*[1] if the levees goin' to stan' it!" she exclaimed.

"What have you got to do with the levees?"

"I got enough to do! An' there's Bobinôt with Bibi out in that storm—if he only didn' left Friedheimer's!"

"Let us hope, Calixta, that Bobinôt's got sense enough to come in out of a cyclone."

She went and stood at the window with a greatly disturbed look on her face. She wiped the frame that was clouded with moisture. It was stiflingly hot. Alcée got up and joined her at the window, looking over her shoulder. The rain was coming down in sheets obscuring the view of far-off cabins and enveloping the distant wood in a gray mist. The playing of the lightning was incessant. A bolt struck a tall chinaberry tree at the edge of the field. It filled all visible space with a blinding glare and the crash seemed to invade the very boards they stood upon.

Calixta put her hands to her eyes, and with a cry, staggered backward. Alcée's arm encircled her, and for an instant he drew her close and spasmodically to him.

"*Bonté!*"[2] she cried, releasing herself from his encircling arm and retreating from the window, "the house'll go next! If I only knew w'ere Bibi was!" She would not compose herself; she would not be seated. Alcée clasped her shoulders and looked into her face. The contact of her warm, palpitating body when he had unthinkingly drawn her into his arms, had aroused all the old-time infatuation and desire for her flesh.

"Calixta," he said, "don't be frightened. Nothing can happen. The house is too low to be struck, with so many tall trees standing about. There! aren't you going to be quiet? say, aren't you?" He pushed her hair back from her face that was warm and steaming. Her lips were as red and moist as pomegranate seed. Her white neck and a glimpse of her full, firm bosom disturbed him powerfully. As she glanced up at him the fear in her liquid blue eyes had given place to a drowsy gleam that unconsciously betrayed a sensuous desire. He looked down into her eyes and there was nothing for him to do but to gather her lips in a kiss. It reminded him of Assumption.

"Do you remember—in Assumption, Calixta?" he asked in a low voice broken by passion. Oh! she remembered; for in Assumption he had kissed her and kissed and kissed her; until his senses would well nigh fail, and to save her he would resort to a desperate flight. If she was not an immaculate dove in those days, she was still inviolate; a passionate creature whose very defenselessness had made her defense, against which his honor forbade him to prevail. Now—well, now—her lips seemed in a manner free to be tasted, as well as her round, white throat and her whiter breasts.

They did not heed the crashing torrents, and the roar of the elements made her laugh as she lay in his arms. She was a revelation in that dim, mysterious

[1] "God knows."
[2] "Goodness!"

chamber; as white as the couch she lay upon. Her firm, elastic flesh that was knowing for the first time its birthright, was like a creamy lily that the sun invites to contribute its breath and perfume to the undying life of the world.

The generous abundance of her passion, without guile or trickery, was like a white flame which penetrated and found response in depths of his own sensuous nature that had never yet been reached.

When he touched her breasts they gave themselves up in quivering ecstasy, inviting his lips. Her mouth was a fountain of delight. And when he possessed her, they seemed to swoon together at the very borderland of life's mystery.

He stayed cushioned upon her, breathless, dazed, enervated, with his heart beating like a hammer upon her. With one hand she clasped his head, her lips lightly touching his forehead. The other hand stroked with a soothing rhythm his muscular shoulders.

The growl of the thunder was distant and passing away. The rain beat softly upon the shingles, inviting them to drowsiness and sleep. But they dared not yield.

The rain was over; and the sun was turning the glistening green world into a palace of gems. Calixta, on the gallery, watched Alcée ride away. He turned and smiled at her with a beaming face; and she lifted her pretty chin in the air and laughed aloud.

III

Bobinôt and Bibi, trudging home, stopped without at the cistern to make themselves presentable.

"My! Bibi, w'at will yo' mama say! You ought to be ashame'. You oughtn' put on those good pants. Look at 'em! An' that mud on yo' collar! How you got that mud on yo' collar, Bibi? I never saw such a boy!" Bibi was the picture of pathetic resignation. Bobinôt was the embodiment of serious solicitude as he strove to remove from his own person and his son's the signs of their tramp over heavy roads and through wet fields. He scraped the mud off Bibi's bare legs and feet with a stick and carefully removed all traces from his heavy brogans. Then, prepared for the worst—the meeting with an over-scrupulous housewife, they entered cautiously at the back door.

Calixta was preparing supper. She had set the table and was dripping coffee at the hearth. She sprang up as they came in.

"Oh, Bobinôt! You back! My! but I was uneasy. W'ere you been during the rain? An' Bibi? he ain't wet? he ain't hurt?" She had clasped Bibi and was kissing him effusively. Bobinôt's explanations and apologies which he had been composing all along the way, died on his lips as Calixta felt him to see if he were dry, and seemed to express nothing but satisfaction at their safe return.

"I brought you some shrimps, Calixta," offered Bobinôt, hauling the can from his ample side pocket and laying it on the table.

"Shrimps! Oh, Bobinôt! you too good fo' anything!" and she gave him a smacking kiss on the cheek that resounded. "*J'vous réponds*,[3] we'll have a feas' to night! umph-umph!"

Bobinôt and Bibi began to relax and enjoy themselves, and when the three

[3] "I tell you."

seated themselves at table they laughed much and so loud that anyone might have heard them as far away as Laballière's.

IV

Alcée Laballière wrote to his wife, Clarisse, that night. It was a loving letter, full of tender solicitude. He told her not to hurry back, but if she and the babies liked it at Biloxi, to stay a month longer. He was getting on nicely; and though he missed them, he was willing to bear the separation a while longer—realizing that their health and pleasure were the first things to be considered.

V

As for Clarisse, she was charmed upon receiving her husband's letter. She and the babies were doing well. The society was agreeable; many of her old friends and acquaintances were at the bay. And the first free breath since her marriage seemed to restore the pleasant liberty of her maiden days. Devoted as she was to her husband, their intimate conjugal life was something which she was more than willing to forego for a while.

So the storm passed and every one was happy.

CHAPTER 5

Realism

The story of wish fulfillment carries us frequently to a never-never land, unlike the world we live in. Romance lingers abroad, scudding through southern seas or treading the corridors of ancient castles. In contrast, *realism* stresses the ordinary in subject matter and technique. Although wish fulfillment and romance sometimes remain, they are hidden under a concern for everyday realities: the colors, shapes, and sounds of our daily lives. The author strives for *verisimilitude* (the appearance of reality) through an accumulation of minutely observed details: menus, railroad timetables, fashions in clothes, speech patterns, table manners. Wish fulfillment at home and romance in the drugstore on Main Street seem realistic to us only if the author places them convincingly in the context of ordinary surroundings.

Because writers write most convincingly of what they know from their personal experience and observation, realistic stories take us sometimes to a time and place far from our own experience, but close to the author's. Ringing with the truth of precise observation, the details framing such stories carry conviction to the invented characters and plots.

THE LOST PHOEBE
Theodore Dreiser (1871–1945)

They lived together in a part of the country which was not so prosperous as it had once been, about three miles from one of those small towns that, instead of increasing in population, is steadily decreasing. The territory was not very thickly settled; perhaps a house every other mile or so, with large areas of corn- and wheat-land and fallow fields that at odd seasons had been sown to timothy and clover. Their particular house was part log and part frame, the log portion being the old original home of Henry's grandfather. The new portion, of now rain-beaten, time-worn slabs, through which the wind squeaked in the chinks at times, and which several overshadowing elms and a butternut-tree made picturesque and reminiscently pathetic, but a little damp, was erected by Henry when he was twenty-one and just married.

That was forty-eight years before. The furniture inside, like the house outside, was old and mildewy and reminiscent of an earlier day. You have seen the whatnot of cherry wood, perhaps, with spiral legs and fluted top. It was there. The old-fashioned four poster bed, with its ball-like protuberances and deep curving

incision, was there also, a sadly alienated descendant of an early Jacobean ancestor. The bureau of cherry was also high and wide and solidly built, but faded-
looking, and with a musty odor. The rag carpet that underlay all these sturdy examples of enduring furniture was a weak, faded, lead-and-pink-colored affair
woven by Phoebe Ann's own hands, when she was fifteen years younger than
she was when she died. The creaky wooden loom on which it had been done
now stood like a dusty, bony skeleton, along with a broken rocking-chair, a
worm-eaten clothes-press—Heavens knows how old—a lime-stained bench that
had once been used to keep flowers on outside the door, and other decrepit factors of household utility, in an east room that was a lean-to against this so-called
main portion. All sorts of other broken-down furniture were about this place; an
antiquated clothes-horse, cracked in two of its ribs; a broken mirror in an old
cherry frame, which had fallen from a nail and cracked itself three days before
their youngest son, Jerry, died; an extension hat-rack, which once had had porcelain knobs on the ends of its pegs; and a sewing-machine, long since outdone in
its clumsy mechanism by rivals of a newer generation.

The orchard to the east of the house was full of gnarled old apple-trees,
worm-eaten as to trunks and branches, and fully ornamented with green and
white lichens, so that it had a sad, greenish-white, silvery effect in moonlight.
The low outhouses, which had once housed chickens, a horse or two, a cow, and
several pigs, were covered with patches of moss as to their roof, and the sides
had been free of paint for so long that they were blackish gray as to color, and a
little spongy. The picket-fence in front, with its gate squeaky and askew, and the
side fences of the stake-and-rider type were in an equally run-down condition.
As a matter of fact, they had aged synchronously with the persons who lived
here, old Henry Reifsneider and his wife Phoebe Ann.

They had lived here, these two, ever since their marriage, forty-eight years
before, and Henry had lived here before that from his childhood up. His father
and mother, well along in years when he was a boy, had invited him to bring his
wife here when he had first fallen in love and decided to marry; and he had
done so. His father and mother were the companions of himself and his wife for
ten years after they were married, when both died; and then Henry and Phoebe
were left with their five children growing lustily apace. But all sorts of things
had happened since then. Of the seven children, all told, that had been born to
them, three had died; one girl had gone to Kansas; one boy had gone to Sioux
Falls, never even to be heard of after; another boy had gone to Washington; and
the last girl lived five counties away in the same State, but was so burdened with
cares of her own that she rarely gave them a thought. Time and a commonplace
home life that had never been attractive had weaned them thoroughly, so that,
wherever they were, they gave little thought as to how it might be with their father and mother.

Old Henry Reifsneider and his wife Phoebe were a loving couple. You perhaps know how it is with simple natures that fasten themselves like lichens on
the stones of circumstance and weather their days to a crumbling conclusion.
The great world sounds widely, but it has no call for them. They have no soaring
intellect. The orchard, the meadow, the corn-field, the pig-pen, and the chicken-
lot measure the range of their human activities. When the wheat is headed it is
reaped and threshed; when the corn is browned and frosted it is cut and

shocked; when the timothy is in full head it is cut, and the hay-cock erected. After that comes winter, with the hauling of grain to market, the sawing and splitting of wood, the simple chores of fire-building, meal-getting, occasional re-pairing, and visiting. Beyond these and the changes of weather—the snows, the rains, and the fair days—there are no immediate, significant things. All the rest of life is a far-off, clamorous phantasmagoria, flickering like Northern lights in the night, and sounding as faintly as cow-bells tinkling in the distance.

Old Henry and his wife Phoebe were as fond of each other as it is possible for two old people to be who have nothing else in this life to be fond of. He was a thin old man, seventy when she died, a queer, crotchety person with coarse gray-black hair and beard, quite straggly and unkempt. He looked at you out of dull, fishy, watery eyes that had deep-brown crow's-feet at the sides. His clothes, like the clothes of many farmers, were aged and angular and baggy, standing out at the pockets, not fitting about the neck, protuberant and worn at elbow and knee. Phoebe Ann was thin and shapeless, a very umbrella of a woman, clad in shabby black, and with a black bonnet for her best wear. As time had passed, and they had only themselves to look after, their movements had become slower and slower, their activities fewer and fewer. The annual keep of pigs had been re-duced from five to one grunting porker, and the single horse which Henry now retained was a sleepy animal, not overnourished and not very clean. The chick-ens, of which formerly there was a large flock, had almost disappeared, owing to ferrets, foxes, and the lack of proper care, which produces disease. The former healthy garden was now a straggling memory of itself, and the vines and flower-beds that formerly ornamented the windows and dooryard had now become choking thickets. A will had been made which divided the small tax-eaten prop-erty equally among the remaining four, so that it was really of no interest to any of them. Yet these two lived together in peace and sympathy, only that now and then old Henry would become unduly cranky, complaining almost invariably that something had been neglected or mislaid which was of no importance at all.

"Phoebe, where's my corn-knife? You ain't never minded to let my things alone no more."

"Now you hush, Henry," his wife would caution him in a cracked and squeaky voice. "If you don't, I'll leave yuh. I'll git up and walk out of here some day, and then where would y' be? Y' ain't got anybody but me to look after yuh, so yuh just behave yourself. Your corn-knife's on the mantel where it's allus been unless you've gone an' put it summers else."

Old Henry, who knew his wife would never leave him in any circumstances, used to speculate at times as to what he would do if she were to die. That was the one leaving that he really feared. As he climbed on the chair at night to wind the old, long-pendulumed, double-weighted clock, or went finally to the front and the back door to see that they were safely shut in, it was a comfort to know that Phoebe was there, properly ensconced on her side of the bed, and that if he stirred restlessly in the night, she would be there to ask what he wanted.

"Now, Henry, do lie still! You're as restless as a chicken."

"Well, I can't sleep, Phoebe."

"Well, yuh needn't roll so, anyhow. Yuh kin let me sleep."

This usually reduced him to a state of somnolent ease. If she wanted a pail of water, it was a grumbling pleasure for him to get it; and if she did rise first to build the fires, he saw that the wood was cut and placed within easy reach. They divided this simple world nicely between them.

As the years had gone on, however, fewer and fewer people had called. They were well-known for a distance of as much as ten square miles as old Mr. and Mrs. Reifsneider, honest, moderately Christian, but too old to be really interesting any longer. The writing of letters had become an almost impossible burden too difficult to continue or even negotiate via others, although an occasional letter still did arrive from the daughter in Pemberton County. Now and then some old friend stopped with a pie or cake or a roasted chicken or duck, or merely to see that they were well; but even these kindly minded visits were no longer frequent.

One day in the early spring of her sixty-fourth year Mrs. Reifsneider took sick, and from a low fever passed into some indefinable ailment which, because of her age, was no longer curable. Old Henry drove to Swinnerton, the neighboring town, and procured a doctor. Some friends called, and the immediate care of her was taken off his hands. Then one chill spring night she died, and old Henry, in a fog of sorrow and uncertainty, followed her body to the nearest graveyard, an unattractive space with a few pines growing in it. Although he might have gone to the daughter in Pemberton or sent for her, it was really too much trouble and he was too weary and fixed. It was suggested to him at once by one friend and another that he come to stay with them awhile, but he did not see fit. He was so old and so fixed in his notions and so accustomed to the exact surroundings he had known all his days, that he could not think of leaving. He wanted to remain near where they had put his Phoebe; and the fact that he would have to live alone did not trouble him in the least. The living children were notified and the care of him offered if he would leave, but he would not.

"I kin make a shift for myself," he continually announced to old Dr. Morrow, who had attended his wife in this case. "I kin cook a little, and, besides, it don't take much more'n coffee an' bread in the mornin's to satisfy me. I'll get along now well enough. Yuh just let me be." And after many pleadings and proffers of advice, with supplies of coffee and bacon and baked bread duly offered and accepted, he was left to himself. For a while he sat idly outside his door brooding in the spring sun. He tried to revive his interest in farming, and to keep himself busy and free from thought by looking after the fields, which of late had been much neglected. It was a gloomy thing to come in of an evening, however, or in the afternoon and find no shadow of Phoebe where everything suggested her. By degrees he put a few of her things away. At night he sat beside his lamp and read in the papers that were left him occasionally or in a Bible that he had neglected for years, but he could get little solace from these things. Mostly he held his hand over his mouth and looked at the floor as he sat and thought of what had become of her, and how soon he himself would die. He made a great business of making his coffee in the morning and frying himself a little bacon at night; but his appetite was gone. The shell in which he had been housed so long seemed vacant, and its shadows were suggestive of immediate griefs. So he lived quite dolefully for five long months, and then a change began.

It was one night, after he had looked after the front and the back door, wound the clock, blown out the light, and gone through all the selfsame motions that he had indulged in for years, that he went to bed not so much to sleep as to think. It was a moonlight night. The green-lichen-covered orchard just outside and to be seen from his bed where he now lay was a silvery affair, sweetly spectral. The moon shone through the east windows, throwing the pattern of the panes on the wooden floor, and making the old furniture, to which he was accustomed, stand out dimly in the room. As usual he had been thinking of Phoebe and the years when they had been young together, and of the children who had gone, and the poor shift he was making of his present days. The house was coming to be in a very bad state indeed. The bed-clothes were in disorder and not clean, for he made a wretched shift of washing. It was a terror to him. The roof leaked, causing things, some of them, to remain damp for weeks at a time, but he was getting into that brooding state where he would accept anything rather than exert himself. He preferred to pace slowly to and fro or to sit and think.

By twelve o'clock of this particular night he was asleep, however, and by two had waked again. The moon by this time had shifted to a position on the western side of the house, and it now shone in through the windows of the living-room and those of the kitchen beyond. A certain combination of furniture—a chair near a table, with his coat on it, the half-open kitchen door casting a shadow, and the positon of a lamp near a paper—gave him an exact representation of Phoebe leaning over the table as he had often seen her do in life. It gave him a great start. Could it be she—or her ghost? He had scarcely ever believed in spirits; and still—He looked at her fixedly in the feeble half-light, his old hair tingling oddly at the roots, and then sat up. The figure did not move. He put his thin legs out of the bed and sat looking at her, wondering if this could really be Phoebe. They had talked of ghosts often in their lifetime, of apparitions and omens; but they had never agreed that such things could be. It had never been a part of his wife's creed that she could have a spirit that could return to walk the earth. Her after-world was quite a different affair, a vague heaven, no less, from which the righteous did not trouble to return. Yet here she was now, bending over the table in her black skirt and gray shawl, her pale profile outlined against the moonlight.

"Phoebe," he called, thrilling from head to toe and putting out one bony hand, "have yuh come back?"

The figure did not stir, and he arose and walked uncertainly to the door, looking at it fixedly the while. As he drew near, however, the apparition resolved itself into its primal content—his old coat over the high-backed chair, the lamp by the paper, the half-open door.

"Well," he said to himself, his mouth open, "I thought shore I saw her." And he ran his hand strangely and vaguely through his hair, the while his nervous tension relaxed. Vanished as it had, it gave him the idea that she might return.

Another night, because of this first illusion, and because his mind was now constantly on her and he was old, he looked out of the window that was nearest his bed and commanded a hen-coop and pig-pen and a part of the wagon-shed, and there, a faint mist exuding from the damp of the ground, he thought he saw her again. It was one of those little wisps of mist, one of those faint exhalations of the earth that rise in a cool night after a warm day, and flicker like small white cypresses of fog before they disappear. In life it had been a custom of hers to cross this lot from her kitchen door to the pig-pen to throw in any scrap that was left from her cooking, and here she was again. He sat up and watched it strangely, doubtfully, because of his previous experience, but inclined, because of the nervous titillation that passed over his body, to believe that spirits really were, and that Phoebe, who would be concerned because of his lonely state, must be thinking about him, and hence returning. What other way would she have? How otherwise could she express herself? It would be within the province of her charity so to do, and like her loving interest in him. He quivered and watched it eagerly; but, a faint breath of air stirring, it wound away toward the fence and disappeared.

A third night, as he was actually dreaming, some ten days later, she came to his bedside and put her hand on his head.

"Poor Henry!" she said. "It's too bad."

He roused out of his sleep, actually to see her, he thought, moving from his bed-room into the one living-room, her figure a shadowy mass of black. The weak straining of his eyes caused little points of light to flicker about the outlines of her form. He arose, greatly astonished, walked the floor in the cool room, convinced that Phoebe was coming back to him. If he only thought sufficiently, if he made it perfectly clear by his feeling that he needed her greatly, she would come back, this kindly wife, and tell him what to do. She would perhaps be with him much of the time, in the night, anyhow; and that would make him less lonely, this state more endurable.

In age and with the feeble it is not such a far cry from the subtleties of illusion to actual hallucination, and in due time this transition was made for Henry. Night after night he waited, expecting her return. Once in his weird mood he thought he saw a pale light moving about the room, and another time he thought he saw her walking in the orchard after dark. It was one morning when the details of his lonely state were virtually unendurable that he woke with the thought that she was not dead. How he had arrived at this conclusion it is hard to say. His mind had gone. In its place was a fixed illusion. He and Phoebe had had a senseless quarrel. He had reproached her for not leaving his pipe where he was accustomed to find it, and she had left. It was an aberrated fulfillment of her old jesting threat that if he did not behave himself she would leave him.

"I guess I could find yuh ag'in," he had always said. But her cackling threat had always been.

"Yuh'll not find me if I ever leave yuh. I guess I kin git some place where yuh can't find me."

This morning when he arose he did not think to build the fire in the customary way or to grind his coffee and cut his bread, as was his wont, but solely to meditate as to where he should search for her and how he should induce her to come back. Recently the one horse had been dispensed with because he found it cumbersome and beyond his needs. He took down his soft crush hat after he had dressed himself, a new glint of interest and determination in his eye, and taking his black crook cane from behind the door, where he had always placed it, started out briskly to look for her among the nearest neighbors. His old shoes clumped soundly in the dust as he walked, and his gray-black locks, now grown rather long, straggled out in a dramatic fringe or halo from under his hat. His short coat stirred busily as he walked, and his hands and face were peaked and pale.

"Why, hello, Henry! Where're yuh goin' this mornin'?" inquired Farmer

Dodge, who, hauling a load of wheat to market, encountered him on the public road. He had not seen the aged farmer in months, not since his wife's death, and he wondered now, seeing him looking so spry.

"Yuh ain't seen Phoebe, have yuh?" inquired the old man, looking up quizzically.

"Phoebe who?" inquired Farmer Dodge, not for the moment connecting the name with Henry's dead wife.

"Why, my wife Phoebe, o' course. Who do yuh s'pose I mean?" He stared up with a pathetic sharpness of glance from under his shaggy, gray eyebrows.

"Wall, I'll swan, Henry, yuh ain't jokin', are yuh?" said the solid Dodge, a pursy man, with a smooth, hard, red face. "It can't be your wife yuh're talkin' about. She's dead."

"Dead! Shucks!" retorted the demented Reifsneider. "She left me early this mornin', while I was sleepin'. She allus got up to build the fire, but she's gone now. We had a little spat last night, an' I guess that's the reason. But I guess I kin find her. She's gone over to Matilda Race's; that's where she's gone."

He started briskly up the road, leaving the amazed Dodge to stare in wonder after him.

"Well, I'll be switched!" he said aloud to himself. "He's clean out'n his head. That poor old feller's been livin' down there till he's gone outen his mind. I'll have to notify the authorities." And he flicked his whip with great enthusiasm. "Geddap!" he said, and was off.

Reifsneider met no one else in this poorly populated region until he reached the whitewashed fence of Matilda Race and her husband three miles away. He had passed several other houses en route, but these not being within the range of his illusion were not considered. His wife, who had known Matilda well, must be here. He opened the picket-gate which guarded the walk, and stamped briskly up to the door.

"Why, Mr. Reifsneider," exclaimed old Matilda herself, a stout woman, looking out of the door in answer to his knock, "what brings yuh here this mornin'?"

"Is Phoebe here?" he demanded eagerly.

"Phoebe who? What Phoebe?" replied Mrs. Race, curious as to this sudden development of energy on his part.

"Why, my Phoebe, o' course. My wife Phoebe. Who do yuh s'pose? Ain't she here now?"

"Lawsy me!" exclaimed Mrs. Race, opening her mouth. "Yuh pore man! So you're clean out'n your mind now. Yuh come right in and sit down. I'll git yuh a cup o' coffee. O' course your wife ain't here; but yuh come in an' sit down. I'll find her fer yuh after a while. I know where she is."

The old farmer's eyes softened, and he entered. He was so thin and pale a specimen, pantalooned and patriarchal, that he aroused Mrs. Race's extremest sympathy as he took off his hat and laid it on his knees quite softly and mildly.

"We had a quarrel last night, an' she left me," he volunteered.

"Laws! laws!" sighed Mrs. Race, there being no one present with whom to share her astonishment as she went to her kitchen. "The pore man! Now somebody's just got to look after him. He can't be allowed to run around the country this way lookin' for his dead wife. It's turrible."

She boiled him a pot of coffee and brought in some of her new-baked bread and fresh butter. She set out some of her best jam and put a couple of eggs to boil, lying whole-heartedly the while.

"Now yuh stay right there, Uncle Henry, till Jake comes in, an' I'll send him to look for Phoebe. I think it's more'n likely she's over to Swinnerton with some o' her friends. Anyhow, we'll find out. Now yuh just drink this coffee an' eat this bread. Yuh must be tired. Yuh've had a long walk this mornin'." Her idea was to take counsel with Jake, "her man," and perhaps have him notify the authorities.

She bustled about, meditating on the uncertainties of life, while old Reifs-neider thrummed on the rim of his hat with his pale fingers and later ate ab-stractedly of what she offered. His mind was on his wife, however, and since she was not here, or did not appear, it wandered vaguely away to a family by the name of Murray, miles away in another direction. He decided after a time that he would not wait for Jake Race to hunt his wife but would seek her for himself. He must be on, and urge her to come back.

"Well, I'll be goin'," he said, getting up and looking strangely about him. "I guess she didn't come here after all. She went over to the Murrays', I guess. I'll not wait any longer, Mis' Race. There's a lot to do over to the house to-day." And out he marched in the face of her protests taking to the dusty road again in the warm spring sun, his cane striking the earth as he went.

It was two hours later that this pale figure of a man appeared in the Murrays' doorway, dusty, perspiring, eager. He had tramped all of five miles, and it was noon. An amazed husband and wife of sixty heard his strange query, and real-ized also that he was mad. They begged him to stay to dinner, intending to no-tify the authorities later and see what could be done; but though he stayed to partake of a little something, he did not stay long, and was off again to another distant farmhouse, his idea of many things to do and his need of Phoebe impell-ing him. So it went for that day and the next and the next, the circle of his inqui-ry ever widening.

The process by which a character assumes the significance of being peculiar, his antics weird, yet harmless, in such a community is often involute and pathet-ic. This day, as has been said, saw Reifsneider at other doors, eagerly asking his unnatural question, and leaving a trail of amazement, sympathy, and pity in his wake. Although the authorities were informed—the county sheriff, no less—it was not deemed advisable to take him into custody; for when those who knew old Henry, and had for so long, reflected on the condition of the county insane asylum, a place which, because of the poverty of the district, was of staggering aberration and sickening environment, it was decided to let him remain at large; for, strange to relate, it was found on investigation that at night he returned peaceably enough to his lonesome domicile there to discover whether his wife had returned, and to brood in loneliness until the morning. Who would lock up a thin, eager, seeking old man with iron-gray hair and an attitude of kindly, in-nocent inquiry, particularly when he was well known for a past of only kindly servitude and reliability? Those who had known him best rather agreed that he should be allowed to roam at large. He could do no harm. There were many who were willing to help him as to food, old clothes, the odds and ends of his daily life—at least at first. His figure after a time became not so much a common-place as an accepted curiosity, and the replies, "Why, no, Henry; I ain't see her," or "No, Henry; she ain't been here to-day," more customary.

For several years thereafter then he was an odd figure in the sun and rain, on dusty roads and muddy ones, encountered occasionally in strange and unexpected places, pursuing his endless search. Undernourishment, after a time, although the neighbors and those who knew his history gladly contributed from their store, affected his body; for he walked much and ate little. The longer he roamed the public highway in this manner, the deeper became his strange hallucination; and finding it harder and harder to return from his more and more distant pilgrimages, he finally began taking a few utensils with him from his home, making a small package of them, in order that he might not be compelled to return. In an old tin coffee-pot of large size he placed a small tin cup, a knife, fork, and spoon, some salt and pepper, and to the outside of it, by a string forced through a pierced hole, he fastened a plate, which could be released, and which was his woodland table. It was no trouble for him to secure the little food that he needed, and with a strange, almost religious dignity, he had no hesitation in asking for that much. By degrees his hair became longer and longer, his once black hat became an earthen brown, and his clothes threadbare and dusty.

For all of three years he walked, and none knew how wide were his perambulations, nor how he survived the storms and cold. They could not see him, with homely rural understanding and forethought, sheltering himself in hay-cocks, or by the sides of cattle, whose warm bodies protected him from the cold, and whose dull understandings were not opposed to his harmless presence. Overhanging rocks and trees kept him at times from the rain, and a friendly hay-loft or corn-crib was not above his humble consideration.

The involute progression of hallucination is strange. From asking at doors and being constantly rebuffed or denied, he finally came to the conclusion that although his Phoebe might not be in any of the houses at the doors of which he inquired, she might nevertheless be within the sound of his voice. And so, from patient inquiry, he began to call sad, occasional cries, that ever and anon waked the quiet landscapes and ragged hill regions, and set to echoing his thin "O-o-o Phoebe! O-o-o Phoebe!" It had a pathetic, albeit insane, ring, and many a farmer or plowboy came to know it even from afar and say, "There goes old Reifsneider."

Another thing that puzzled him greatly after a time and after many hundreds of inquiries was, when he no longer had any particular dooryard in view and no special inquiry to make, which way to go. These cross-roads, which occasionally led in four or even six directions, came after a time to puzzle him. But to solve this knotty problem, which became more and more of a puzzle, there came to his aid another hallucination. Phoebe's spirit or some power of the air or wind or nature would tell him. If he stood at the center of the parting of the ways, closed his eyes, turned thrice about, and called "O-o-o Phoebe!" twice, and then threw his cane straight before him, that would surely indicate which way to go for Phoebe, or one of these mystic powers would surely govern its direction and fall! In whichever direction it went, even though, as was not infrequently the case, it took him back along the path he had already come, or across fields, he was not so far gone in his mind but that he gave himself ample time to search before he called again. Also the hallucination seemed to persist that at some time he would surely find her. There were hours when his feet were sore, and his limbs weary, when he would stop in the heat to wipe his seamed brow, or in the cold to beat his arms. Sometimes, after throwing away his cane, and finding it indicating the direction from which he had just come, he would shake his head wearily and philosophically, as if contemplating the unbelievable or an untoward fate, and then start briskly off. His strange figure came finally to be known in the farthest reaches of three or four counties. Old Reifsneider was a pathetic character. His fame was wide.

Near a little town called Watersville, in Green County, perhaps four miles from that minor center of human activity, there was a place or precipice locally known as the Red Cliff, a sheer wall of red sandstone, perhaps a hundred feet high, which raised its sharp face for half a mile or more above the fruitful corn-fields and orchards that lay beneath, and which was surmounted by a thick grove of trees. The slope that slowly led up to it from the opposite side was covered by a rank growth of beech, hickory, and ash, through which threaded a number of wagontracks crossing at various angles. In fair weather it had become old Reifsneider's habit, so inured was he by now to the open, to make his bed in some such patch of trees as this to fry his bacon or boil his eggs at the foot of some tree before laying himself down for the night. Occasionally, so light and inconsequential was his sleep, he would walk at night. More often, the moonlight or some sudden wind stirring in the trees or a reconnoitering animal arousing him, he would sit up and think, or pursue his quest in the moonlight or the dark, a strange, unnatural, half wild, half savage-looking but utterly harmless creature, calling at lonely road crossings, staring at dark and shuttered houses, and wondering where, where Phoebe could really be.

That particular lull that comes in the systole-diastole of this earthly ball at two o'clock in the morning invariably aroused him, and though he might not go any farther he would sit up and contemplate the darkness or the stars, wondering. Sometimes in the strange processes of his mind he would fancy that he saw moving among the trees the figure of his lost wife, and then he would get up to follow, taking his utensils, always on a string, and his cane. If she seemed to evade him too easily he would run, or plead, or, suddenly losing track of the fancied figure, stand awed or disappointed, grieving for the moment over the almost insurmountable difficulties of his search.

It was in the seventh year of these hopeless peregrinations, in the dawn of a similar springtime to that in which his wife had died, that he came at last one night to the vicinity of this self-same patch that crowned the rise to the Red Cliff. His far-flung cane, used as a divining-rod at the last cross-roads, had brought him hither. He had walked many, many miles. It was after ten o'clock at night, and he was very weary. Long wandering and little eating had left him but a shadow of his former self. It was a question now not so much of physical strength but of spiritual endurance which kept him up. He had scarcely eaten this day, and now exhausted he set himself down in the dark to rest and possibly to sleep.

Curiously on this occasion a strange suggestion of the presence of his wife surrounded him. It would not be long now, he counseled with himself, although the long months had brought him nothing, until he should see her, talk to her. He fell asleep after a time, his head on his knees. At midnight the moon began to rise, and at two in the morning, his wakeful hour, was a large silver disk shining through the trees to the east. He opened his eyes when the radiance became strong, making a silver pattern at his feet and lighting the woods with strange lusters and silvery, shadowy forms. As usual, his old notion that his wife must be near occurred to him on this occasion, and he looked about him with a speculative, anticipatory eye. What was it that moved in the distant shadows along the path by which he had entered—a pale, flickering will-o'-the-wisp that bobbed gracefully among the trees and riveted his expectant gaze? Moonlight and shadows combined to give it a strange form and a stranger reality, this fluttering of bogfire or dancing of wandering fireflies. Was it truly his lost Phoebe? By a circuitous route it passed about him, and in his fevered state he fancied that he could see the very eyes of her, not as she was when he last saw her in the black dress and shawl but now a strangely younger Phoebe, gayer, sweeter, the one whom he had known years before as a girl. Old Reifsneider got up. He had been expecting and dreaming of this hour all these years, and now as he saw the feeble light dancing lightly before him he peered at it questioningly, one thin hand in his gray hair.

Of a sudden there came to him now for the first time in many years the full charm of her girlish figure as he had known it in boyhood, the pleasing, sympathetic smile, the brown hair, the blue sash she had once worn about her waist at a picnic, her gay, graceful movements. He walked around the base of the tree, straining with his eyes, forgetting for once his cane and utensils, and following eagerly after. On she moved before him, a will-o'-the-wisp of the spring, a little flame above her head, and it seemed as though among the small saplings of ash and beech and the thick trunks of hickory and elm that she signaled with a young, a lightsome hand.

"O Phoebe! Phoebe!" he called. "Have yuh really come? Have yuh really answered me?" And hurrying faster, he fell once, scrambling lamely to his feet, only to see the light in the distance dancing illusively on. On and on he hurried until he was fairly running, brushing his ragged arms against the trees, striking his hands and face against impeding twigs. His hat was gone, his lungs were breathless, his reason quite astray, when coming to the edge of the cliff he saw her below among a silvery bed of apple-trees now blooming in the spring.

"O Phoebe!" he called. "O Phoebe! Oh, no, don't leave me!" And feeling the lure of a world where love was young and Phoebe as this vision presented her, a delightful epitome of their quondam youth, he gave a gay cry of "Oh, wait, Phoebe!" and leaped.

Some farmer-boys, reconnoitering this region of bounty and prospect some few days afterward, found first the tin utensils tied together under the tree where he had left them, and then later at the foot of the cliff, pale, broken, but elate, a molded smile of peace and delight upon his lips, his body. His old hat was discovered lying under some low-growing saplings the twigs of which had held it back. No one of all the simple population knew how eagerly and joyously he had found his lost mate.

QUESTIONS

1. Phoebe appears to her husband several times after her death. Is she a ghost? Does Dreiser's realistic explanation detract from the effect?
2. What motivates Henry's friends to go along with his belief that his wife is still alive? Is this motivation convincing?

3. What is the light that lures Henry over the cliff? Is this, after all, a ghost story? Explain the last sentence.
4. A man's seven year search for a dead wife is hardly an ordinary experience. Are we sure we want to call this story "realistic"?
5. What is the function of the three descriptive paragraphs at the beginning? Could these details have been deleted?

THE USE OF FORCE

William Carlos Williams (1883–1963)

They were new patients to me, all I had was the name, Olson. Please come down as soon as you can, my daughter is very sick.

When I arrived I was met by the mother, a big startled looking woman, very clean and apologetic who merely said, Is this the doctor? and let me in. In the back, she added. You must excuse us, doctor, we have her in the kitchen where it is warm. It is very damp here sometimes.

The child was fully dressed and sitting on her father's lap near the kitchen table. He tried to get up, but I motioned for him not to bother, took off my overcoat and started to look things over. I could see that they were all very nervous, eyeing me up and down distrustfully. As often, in such cases, they weren't telling me more than they had to, it was up to me to tell them; that's why they were spending three dollars on me.

The child was fairly eating me up with her cold, steady eyes, and no expression to her face whatever. She did not move and seemed, inwardly, quiet; an unusually attractive little thing, and as strong as a heifer in appearance. But her face was flushed, she was breathing rapidly, and I realized that she had a high fever. She had magnificent blonde hair, in profusion. One of those picture children often reproduced in advertising leaflets and the photogravure sections of the Sunday papers.

She's had a fever for three days, began the father and we don't know what it comes from. My wife has given her things, you know, like people do, but it don't do no good. And there's been a lot of sickness around. So we tho't you'd better look her over and tell us what is the matter.

As doctors often do I took a trial shot at it as a point of departure. Has she had a sore throat?

Both parents answered me together, No . . . No, she says her throat don't hurt her.

Does your throat hurt you? added the mother to the child. But the little girl's expression didn't change nor did she move her eyes from my face.

Have you looked?

I tried to, said the mother, but I couldn't see.

As it happens we had been having a number of cases of diphtheria in the school to which this child went during that month and we were all, quite apparently, thinking of that, though no one had as yet spoken of the thing.

Well, I said, suppose we take a look at the throat first. I smiled in my best professional manner and asking for the child's first name I said, come on, Mathilda, open your mouth and let's take a look at your throat.

Nothing doing.

Aw, come on, I coaxed, just open your mouth wide and let me take a look. Look, I said opening both hands wide, I haven't anything in my hands. Just open up and let me see.

Such a nice man, put in the mother. Look how kind he is to you. Come on, do what he tells you to. He won't hurt you.

At that I ground my teeth in disgust. If only they wouldn't use the word "hurt" I might be able to get somewhere. But I did not allow myself to be hurried or disturbed but speaking quietly and slowly I approached the child again.

As I moved my chair a little nearer suddenly with one catlike movement both her hands clawed instinctively for my eyes and she almost reached them too. In fact she knocked my glasses flying and they fell, though unbroken, several feet away from me on the kitchen floor.

Both the mother and father almost turned themselves inside out in embarrassment and apology. You bad girl, said the mother, taking her and shaking her by one arm. Look what you've done. The nice man . . .

For heaven's sake, I broke in. Don't call me a nice man to her. I'm here to look at her throat on the chance that she might have diphtheria and possibly die of it. But that's nothing to her. Look here, I said to the child, we're going to look at your throat. You're old enough to understand what I'm saying. Will you open it now by yourself or shall we have to open it for you?

Not a move. Even her expression hadn't changed. Her breaths however were coming faster and faster. Then the battle began. I had to do it. I had to have a throat culture for her own protection. But first I told the parents that it was entirely up to them. I explained the danger but said that I would not insist on a throat examination so long as they would take the responsibility.

If you don't do what the doctor says you'll have to go to the hospital, the mother admonished her severely.

Oh yeah? I had to smile to myself. After all, I had already fallen in love with the savage brat, the parents were contemptible to me. In the ensuing struggle they grew more and more abject, crushed, exhausted while she surely rose to magnificent heights of insane fury of effort bred of her terror of me.

The father tried his best, and he was a big man but the fact that she was his daughter, his shame at her behavior and his dread of hurting her made him release her just at the critical moment several times when I had almost achieved success, till I wanted to kill him. But his dread also that she might have diphtheria made him tell me to go on, go on though he himself was almost fainting, while the mother moved back and forth behind us raising and lowering her hands in an agony of apprehension.

Put her in front of you on your lap, I ordered, and hold both her wrists.

But as soon as he did the child let out a scream. Don't, you're hurting me. Let go of my hands. Let them go I tell you. Then she shrieked terrifyingly, hysterically. Stop it! Stop it! You're killing me!

Do you think she can stand it, doctor! said the mother.

You get out, said the husband to his wife. Do you want her to die of diphtheria?

Come on now, hold her, I said.

Then I grasped the child's head with my left hand and tried to get the wooden tongue depressor between her teeth. She fought, with clenched teeth, desperately! But now I also had grown furious—at a child. I tried to hold myself down but I couldn't. I know how to expose a throat for inspection. And I did my best. When finally I got the wooden spatula behind the last teeth and just the point of it into the mouth cavity, she opened up for an instant but before I could see anything she came down again and gripping the wooden blade between her molars she reduced it to splinters before I could get it out again.

Aren't you ashamed, the mother yelled at her. Aren't you ashamed to act like that in front of the doctor?

Get me a smooth-handled spoon of some sort, I told the mother. We're going through with this. The child's mouth was already bleeding. Her tongue was cut and she was screaming in wild hysterical shrieks. Perhaps I should have desisted and come back in an hour or more. No doubt it would have been better. But I have seen at least two children lying dead in bed of neglect in such cases, and feeling that I must get a diagnosis now or never I went at it again. But the worst of it was that I too had got beyond reason. I could have torn the child apart in my own fury and enjoyed it. It was a pleasure to attack her. My face was burning with it.

The damned little brat must be protected against her own idiocy, one says to one's self at such times. Others must be protected against her. It is social necessity. And all these things are true. But a blind fury, a feeling of adult shame, bred of a longing for muscular release are the operatives. One goes on to the end.

In a final unreasoning assault I overpowered the child's neck and jaws. I forced the heavy silver spoon back of her teeth and down her throat till she gagged. And there it was—both tonsils covered with membrane. She had fought valiantly to keep me from knowing her secret. She had been hiding that sore throat for three days at least and lying to her parents in order to escape just such an outcome as this.

Now truly she *was* furious. She had been on the defensive before but now she attacked. Tried to get off her father's lap and fly at me while tears of defeat blinded her eyes.

QUESTIONS

1. The author, a doctor, must have experienced scenes similar to the one reported here. Is his report convincing?

2. Which elements of the story are most clearly the result of narrating from the point of view of the doctor? In what ways would the story have been different if the narrator had been one of the parents? The girl herself? You may wish to try narrating it yourself from one of these other viewpoints.

3. How might the story be different if it were narrated omnisciently? If you were to tell it this way, what limitations would you consider placing on the omniscience?

4. Characterize the doctor. Do you know him well enough to understand the reason for each of his actions?

5. Not much happens and little time passes. We see neither doctor nor

patient before or after the few minutes it takes to confirm the diagnosis. Why has Williams concentrated his effort on such a small space? Is the result worth the effort?

FEET LIVE THEIR OWN LIFE
Langston Hughes   (1902–1967)

"If you want to know about my life," said Simple as he blew the foam from the top of the newly filled glass the bartender put before him, "don't look at my face, don't look at my hands. Look at my feet and see if you can tell how long I been standing on them."

"I cannot see your feet through your shoes," I said.

"You do not need to see through my shoes," said Simple. "Can't you tell by the shoes I wear—not pointed, not rocking-chair, not French-toed, not nothing but big, long, broad, and flat—that I been standing on these feet a long time and carrying some heavy burdens? They ain't flat from standing at no bar, neither, because I always sets at a bar. Can't you tell that? You know I do not hang out in a bar unless it has stools, don't you?"

"That I have observed," I said, "but I did not connect it with your past life."

"Everything I do is connected up with my past life," said Simple. "From Virginia to Joyce, from my wife to Zarita, from my mother's milk to this glass of beer, everything is connected up."

"I trust you will connect up with that dollar I just loaned you when you get paid," I said. "And who is Virginia? You never told me about her."

"Virginia is where I was borned," said Simple. "I would be borned in a state named after a woman. From that day on, women never give me no peace."

"You, I fear, are boasting. If the women were running after you as much as you run after them, you would not be able to sit here on this bar stool in peace. I don't see any women coming to call you out to go home, as some of these fellows' wives do around here."

"Joyce better not come in no bar looking for me," said Simple. "That is why me and my wife busted up—one reason. I do not like to be called out of no bar by a female. It's a man's prerogative to just set and drink sometimes."

"How do you connect that prerogative with your past?" I asked.

"When I was a wee small child," said Simple, "I had no place to set and think in, being as how I was raised up with three brothers, two sisters, seven cousins, one married aunt, a common-law uncle, and the minister's grandchild—and the house only had four rooms. I never had a place just to set and think. Neither to set and drink —not even much my milk before some hongry child snatched it out of my hand. I were not the youngest, neither a girl, nor the cutest. I don't know why, but I don't think nobody liked me much. Which is why I was afraid to like anybody for a long time myself. When I did like somebody, I was full-grown and then I picked out the wrong woman because I had no practice in liking anybody before that. We did not get along."

"Is that when you took to drink?"

"Drink took to me," said Simple. "Whiskey just naturally likes me but beer likes me better. By the time I got married I had got to the point where a cold bottle was almost as good as a warm bed, especially when the bottle could not talk and the bed-warmer could. I do not like a woman to talk to me too much—I mean about me. Which is why I like Joyce. Joyce most in generally talks about herself."

"I am still looking at your feet," I said, "and I swear they do not reveal your life to me. Your feet are no open book."

"You have eyes but you see not," said Simple. "These feet have stood on every rock from the Rock of Ages to 135th and Lenox. These feet have supported everything from a cotton bale to a hongry woman. These feet have walked ten thousand miles working for white folks and another ten thousand keeping up with colored. These feet have stood at altars, crap tables, free lunches, bars, graves, kitchen doors, betting windows, hospital clinics, WPA desks, social security railings, and in all kinds of lines from soup lines to the draft. If I just had four feet, I could have stood in more places longer. As it is, I done wore out seven hundred pairs of shoes, eighty-nine tennis shoes, twelve summer sandals, also six loafers. The socks that these feet have bought could build a knitting mill. The corns I've cut away would dull a German razor. The bunions I forgot would make you ache from now till Judgment Day. If anybody was to write the history of my life, they should start with my feet."

"Your feet are not all that extraordinary," I said. "Besides, everything you are saying is general. Tell me specifically some one thing your feet have done that makes them different from any other feet in the world, just one."

"Do you see that window in that white man's store across the street?" asked Simple. "Well, this right foot of mine broke out that window in the Harlem riots right smack in the middle. Didn't no other foot in the world break that window but mine. And this left foot carried me off running as soon as my right foot came down. Nobody else's feet saved me from the cops that night but these *two* feet right here. Don't tell me these feet ain't had a life of their own."

"For shame," I said, "going around kicking out windows. Why?"

"Why?" said Simple. "You have to ask my great-great-grandpa why. He must of been simple—else why did he let them capture him in Africa and sell him for a slave to breed my great-grandpa in slavery to breed my grandpa in slavery to breed my pa to breed me to look at that window and say, 'It ain't mine! Bam-mmm-mm-m!' and kick it out?"

"This bar glass is not yours either," I said. "Why don't you smash it?"

"It's got my beer in it," said Simple.

Just then Zarita came in wearing her Thursday-night rabbitskin coat. She didn't stop at the bar, being dressed up, but went straight back to a booth. Simple's hand went up, his beer went down, and the glass back to its wet spot on the bar.

"Excuse me a minute," he said, sliding off the stool.

Just to give him pause, the dozens, that old verbal game of maligning a friend's female relatives, came to mind. "Wait," I said. "You have told me about what to ask your great-great-grandpa. But I want to know what to ask your great-great-grand*ma*."

"I don't play the dozens that far back," said Simple, following Zarita into the smoky juke-box blue of the back room.

QUESTIONS
1. Although an "I" narrates, Simple does most of the talking. What is the reason for the "I"?
2. Observe the difference between Simple's manner of speaking and the narrator's. Is the difference important?
3. Is there any seriousness behind Simple's fooling?
4. How effective is Hughes's use of dialect in establishing verisimilitude?

GOOD COUNTRY PEOPLE
Flannery O'Connor (1915–1964)

Besides the neutral expression that she wore when she was alone, Mrs. Freeman had two others, forward and reverse, that she used for all her human dealings. Her forward expression was steady and driving like the advance of a heavy truck. Her eyes never swerved to left or right but turned as the story turned as if they followed a yellow line down the center of it. She seldom used the other expression because it was not often necessary for her to retract a statement, but when she did, her face came to a complete stop, there was an almost imperceptible movement of her black eyes, during which they seemed to be receding, and then the observer would see that Mrs. Freeman, though she might stand there as real as several grain sacks thrown on top of each other, was no longer there in spirit. As for getting anything across to her when this was the case, Mrs. Hopewell had given it up. She might talk her head off. Mrs. Freeman could never be brought to admit herself wrong on any point. She would stand there and if she could be brought to say anything, it was something like, "Well, I wouldn't of said it was and I wouldn't of said it wasn't," or letting her gaze range over the top kitchen shelf where there was an assortment of dusty bottles, she might remark, "I see you ain't ate many of them figs you put up last summer."

They carried on their most important business in the kitchen at breakfast. Every morning Mrs. Hopewell got up at seven o'clock and lit her gas heater and Joy's. Joy was her daughter, a large blonde girl who had an artificial leg. Mrs. Hopewell thought of her as a child though she was thirty-two years old and highly educated. Joy would get up while her mother was eating and lumber into the bathroom and slam the door, and before long, Mrs. Freeman would arrive at the back door. Joy would hear her mother call, "Come on in," and then they would talk for a while in low voices that were indistinguishable in the bathroom. By the time Joy came in, they had usually finished the weather report and were on one or the other of Mrs. Freeman's daughters, Glynese or Carramae. Joy called them Glycerin and Caramel. Glynese, a redhead, was eighteen and had many admirers; Carramae, a blond, was only fifteen but already married and pregnant. She could not keep anything on her stomach. Every morning Mrs. Freeman told Mrs. Hopewell how many times she had vomited since the last report.

Mrs. Hopewell liked to tell people that Glynese and Carramae were two of the finest girls she knew and that Mrs. Freeman was a *lady* and that she was never ashamed to take her anywhere or introduce her to anybody they might meet. Then she would tell how she had happened to hire the Freemans in the first place and how they were a godsend to her and how she had had them four years. The reason for her keeping them so long was that they were not trash. They were good country people. She had telephoned the man whose name they had given as a reference and he had told her that Mr. Freeman was a good farmer but that his wife was the nosiest woman ever to walk the earth. "She's got to be into everything," the man said. "If she don't get there before the dust settles, you can bet she's dead, that's all. She'll want to know all your business. I can stand him real good," he had said, "but me nor my wife neither could have stood that woman one more minute on this place." That had put Mrs. Hopewell off for a few days.

She had hired them in the end because there were no other applicants but she had made up her mind beforehand exactly how she would handle the woman. Since she was the type who had to be into everything, then, Mrs. Hopewell had decided, she would not only let her be into everything, she would *see to it* that she was into everything—she would give her the responsibility of everything, she would put her in charge. Mrs. Hopewell had no bad qualities of her own but she was able to use other people's in such a constructive way that she never felt the lack. She had hired the Freemans and she had kept them four years.

Nothing is perfect. This was one of Mrs. Hopewell's favorite sayings. Another was: that is life! And still another, the most important, was: well, other people have their opinions too. She would make these statements, usually at the table, in a tone of gentle insistence as if no one held them but her, and the large hulking Joy, whose constant outrage had obliterated every expression from her face, would stare just a little to the side of her, her eyes icy blue, with the look of someone who has achieved blindness by an act of will and means to keep it.

When Mrs. Hopewell said to Mrs. Freeman that life was like that, Mrs. Freeman would say, "I always said so myself." Nothing had been arrived at by anyone that had not first been arrived at by her. She was quicker than Mr. Freeman. When Mrs. Hopewell said to her after they had been on the place a while, "You know, you're the wheel behind the wheel," and winked, Mrs. Freeman had said, "I know it. I've always been quick. It's some that are quicker than others."

"Everybody is different," Mrs. Hopewell said.

"Yes, most people is," Mrs. Freeman said.

"It takes all kinds to make the world."

"I always said it did myself."

The girl was used to this kind of dialogue for breakfast and more of it for dinner; sometimes they had it for supper too. When they had no guest they ate in the kitchen because that was easier. Mrs. Freeman always managed to arrive at some point during the meal and to watch them finish it. She would stand in the doorway if it were summer but in the winter she would stand with one elbow on top of the refrigerator and look down on them, or she would stand by the gas heater, lifting the back of her skirt slightly. Occassionally she would stand against the wall and roll her head from side to side. At no time was she in any hurry to leave. All this was very trying on Mrs. Hopewell but she was a woman of great patience. She realized that nothing is perfect and that in the Freemans she had good country people and that if, in this day and age, you get good country people, you had better hang onto them.

She had had plenty of experience with trash. Before the Freemans she had averaged one tenant family a year. The wives of these farmers were not the kind you would want to be around you for very long. Mrs. Hopewell, who had divorced her husband long ago, needed someone to walk over the fields with her; and when Joy had to be impressed for these services, her remarks were usually so ugly and her face so glum that Mrs. Hopewell would say, "If you can't come pleasantly, I don't want you at all," to which the girl, standing square and rigid-shouldered with her neck thrust slightly forward, would reply, "If you want me, here I am—LIKE I AM."

Mrs. Hopewell excused this attitude because of the leg (which had been shot off in a hunting accident when Joy was ten). It was hard for Mrs. Hopewell to realize that her child was thirty-two now and that for more than twenty years she had had only one leg. She thought of her still as a child because it tore her heart to think instead of the poor stout girl in her thirties who had never danced a step or had any *normal* good times. Her name was really Joy but as soon as she was twenty-one and away from home, she had had it legally changed. Mrs. Hopewell was certain that she had thought and thought until she had hit upon the ugliest name in any language. Then she had gone and had the beautiful name, Joy, changed without telling her mother until after she had done it. Her legal name was Hulga.

When Mrs. Hopewell thought the name, Hulga, she thought of the broad blank hull of a battleship. She would not use it. She continued to call her Joy to which the girl responded but in a purely mechanical way.

Hulga had learned to tolerate Mrs. Freeman who saved her from taking walks with her mother. Even Glynese and Carramae were useful when they occupied attention that might otherwise have been directed at her. At first she had thought she could not stand Mrs. Freeman for she had found that it was not possible to be rude to her. Mrs. Freeman would take on strange resentments and for days together she would be sullen but the source of her displeasure was always obscure; a direct attack, a positive leer, blatant ugliness to her face—these never touched her. And without warning one day, she began calling her Hulga.

She did not call her that in front of Mrs. Hopewell who would have been incensed but when she and the girl happened to be out of the house together, she would say something and add the name Hulga to the end of it, and the big spectacled Joy-Hulga would scowl and redden as if her privacy had been intruded upon. She considered the name her personal affair. She had arrived at it first purely on the basis of its ugly sound and then the full genius of its fitness had struck her. She had a vision of the name working like the ugly sweating Vulcan[1] who stayed in the furnace and to whom, presumably, the goddess had to come when called. She saw it as the name of her highest creative act. One of her major triumphs was that her mother had not been able to turn her dust into Joy, but the greater one was that she had been able to turn it herself into Hulga. However, Mrs. Freeman's relish for using the name only irritated her. It was as if Mrs. Free-

---

[1] Roman god of fire, lame blacksmith to the gods and husband of Venus, goddess of love.

man's beady steel-pointed eyes had penetrated far enough behind her face to reach some secret fact. Something about her seemed to fascinate Mrs. Freeman and then one day Hulga realized that it was the artificial leg. Mrs. Freeman had a special fondness for the details of secret infections, hidden deformities, assaults upon children. Of diseases, she preferred the lingering or incurable. Hulga had heard Mrs. Hopewell give her the details of the hunting accident, how the leg had been literally blasted off, how she had never lost consciousness. Mrs. Freeman could listen to it any time as if it had happened an hour ago.

When Hulga stumped into the kitchen in the morning (she could walk without making the awful noise but she made it—Mrs. Hopewell was certain—because it was ugly-sounding), she glanced at them and did not speak. Mrs. Hopewell would be in her red kimono with her hair tied around her head in rags. She would be sitting at the table, finishing her breakfast and Mrs. Freeman would be hanging by her elbow outward from the refrigerator, looking down at the table. Hulga always put her eggs on the stove to boil and then stood over them with her arms folded, and Mrs. Hopewell would look at her—a kind of indirect gaze divided between her and Mrs. Freeman—and would think that if she would only keep herself up a little, she wouldn't be so bad looking. There was nothing wrong with her face that a pleasant expression wouldn't help. Mrs. Hopewell said that people who looked on the bright side of things would be beautiful even if they were not.

Whenever she looked at Joy this way, she could not help but feel that it would have been better if the child had not taken the Ph.D. It had certainly not brought her out any and now that she had it, there was no more excuse for her to go to school again. Mrs. Hopewell thought it was nice for girls to go to school to have a good time but Joy had "gone through." Anyhow, she would not have been strong enough to go again. The doctors had told Mrs. Hopewell that with the best of care, Joy might see forty-five. She had a weak heart. Joy made it plain that if it had not been for this condition, she would be far from these red hills and good country people. She would be in a university lecturing to people who knew what she was talking about. And Mrs. Hopewell could very well picture her there, looking like a scarecrow and lecturing to more of the same. Here she went about all day in a six-year-old skirt and a yellow sweat shirt with a faded cowboy on a horse embossed on it. She thought this was funny; Mrs. Hopewell thought it was idiotic and showed simply that she was still a child. She was brilliant but she didn't have a grain of sense. It seemed to Mrs. Hopewell that every year she grew less like other people and more like herself—bloated, rude, and squint-eyed. And she said such strange things! To her own mother she had said—without warning, without excuse, standing up in the middle of a meal with her face purple and her mouth half full—"Woman! do you ever look inside? Do you ever look inside and see what you are *not*? God!" she had cried sinking down again and staring at her plate, "Malebranche was right: we are not our own light. We are not our own light!" Mrs. Hopewell had no idea to this day what brought that on. She had only made the remark, hoping Joy would take it in, that a smile never hurt anyone.

The girl had taken the Ph.D. in philosophy and this left Mrs. Hopewell at a complete loss. You could say, "My daughter is a nurse," or "My daughter is a school teacher," or even, "My daughter is a chemical engineer." You could not say, "My daughter is a philosopher." That was something that had ended with the Greeks and Romans. All day Joy sat on her neck in a deep chair, reading. Sometimes she went for walks but she didn't like dogs or cats or birds or flowers or nature or nice young men. She looked at nice young men as if she could smell their stupidity.

One day Mrs. Hopewell had picked up one of the books the girl had just put down and opening it at random, she read, "Science, on the other hand, has to assert its soberness and seriousness afresh and declare that it is concerned solely with what-is. Nothing—how can it be for science anything but a horror and a phantasm? If science is right, then one thing stands firm: science wishes to know nothing of nothing. Such is after all the strictly scientific approach to Nothing. We know it by wishing to know nothing of Nothing." These words had been underlined with a blue pencil and they worked on Mrs. Hopewell like some evil incantation in gibberish. She shut the book quickly and went out of the room as if she were having a chill.

This morning when the girl came, Mrs. Freeman was on Carramae. "She thrown up four times after supper," she said, "and was up twict in the night after three o'clock. Yesterday she didn't do nothing but ramble in the bureau drawer. All she did. Stand up there and see what she could run up on."

"She's got to eat," Mrs. Hopewell muttered, sipping her coffee, while she watched Joy's back at the stove. She was wondering what the child had said to the Bible salesman. She could not imagine what kind of a conversation she could possibly have had with him.

He was a tall gaunt hatless youth who had called yesterday to sell them a Bible. He had appeared at the door, carrying a large black suitcase that weighted him so heavily on one side that he had to brace himself against the door facing. He seemed on the point of collapse but he said in a cheerful voice, "Good morning, Mrs. Cedars!" and set the suitcase down on the mat. He was not a bad-looking young man though he had on a bright blue suit and yellow socks that were not pulled up far enough. He had prominent face bones and a streak of sticky-looking brown hair falling across his forehead.

"I'm Mrs. Hopewell," she said.

"Oh!" he said, pretending to look puzzled but with his eyes sparkling, "I saw it said 'The Cedars,' on the mailbox so I thought you was Mrs. Cedars!" and he burst out in a pleasant laugh. He picked up the satchel and under cover of a pant, he fell forward into her hall. It was rather as if the suitcase had moved first, jerking him after it. "Mrs. Hopewell!" he said and grabbed her hand. "I hope you are well!" and he laughed again and then all at once his face sobered completely. He paused and gave her a straight earnest look and said, "Lady, I've come to speak of serious things."

"Well, come in," she muttered, none too pleased because her dinner was almost ready. He came into the parlor and sat down on the edge of a straight chair and put the suitcase between his feet and glanced around the room as if he were sizing her up by it. Her silver gleamed on the two sideboards; she decided he had never been in a room as elegant as this.

"Mrs. Hopewell," he began, using her name in a way that sounded almost intimate, "I know you believe in Chrustian service."

"Well yes," she murmured.

"I know," he said and paused, looking. very wise with his head cocked on one side, "that you're a good woman. Friends have told me."

Mrs. Hopewell never liked to be taken for a fool. "What are you selling?" she asked.

"Bibles," the young man said and his eye raced around the room before he added, "I see you have no family Bible in your parlor, I see that is the one lack you got!"

Mrs. Hopewell could not say, "My daughter is an atheist and won't let me keep the Bible in the parlor." She said, stiffening slightly, "I keep my Bible by my bedside." This was not the truth. It was in the attic somewhere.

"Lady," he said, "the word of God ought to be in the parlor."

"Well, I think that's a matter of taste," she began. "I think . . ."

"Lady," he said, "for a Chrustian, the word of God ought to be in every room in the house besides in his heart. I know you're a Chrustian because I can see it in every line of your face."

She stood up and said, "Well, young man, I don't want to buy a Bible and I smell my dinner burning."

He didn't get up. He began to twist his hands and looking down at them, he said softly, "Well lady, I'll tell you the truth—not many people want to buy one nowadays and besides, I know I'm real simple. I don't know how to say a thing but to say it. I'm just a country boy." He glanced up into her unfriendly face. "People like you don't like to fool with country people like me!"

"Why!" she cried, "good country people are the salt of the earth! Besides, we all have different ways of doing, it takes all kinds to make the world go 'round. That's life!"

"You said a mouthful," he said.

"Why, I think there aren't enough good country people in the world!" she said, stirred. "I think that's what's wrong with it!"

His face had brightened. "I didn't inraduce myself," he said. "I'm Manley Pointer from out in the country around Willohobie, not even from a place, just from near a place."

"You wait a minute," she said. "I have to see about my dinner." She went out to the kitchen and found Joy standing near the door where she had been listening.

"Get rid of the salt of the earth," she said, "and let's eat."

Mrs. Hopewell gave her a pained look and turned the heat down under the vegetables. "I can't be rude to anybody," she murmured and went back into the parlor.

He had opened the suitcase and was sitting with a Bible on each knee.

"You might as well put those up," she told him. "I don't want one."

"I appreciate your honesty," he said. "You don't see any more real honest people unless you go way out in the country."

"I know," she said, "real genuine folks!" Through the crack in the door she heard a groan.

"I guess a lot of boys come telling you they're working their way through college," he said, "but I'm not going to tell you that. Somehow," he said, "I don't want to go to college. I want to devote my life to Chrustian service. See," he said, lowering his voice, "I got this heart condition. I may not live long. When you know it's something wrong with you and you may not live long, well then, lady . . ." He paused, with his mouth open, and stared at her.

He and Joy had the same condition! She knew that her eyes were filling with tears but she collected herself quickly and murmured, "Won't you stay for dinner? We'd love to have you!" and was sorry the instant she heard herself say it.

"Yes mam," he said in an abashed voice, "I would sher love to do that!"

Joy had given him one look on being introduced to him and then throughout the meal had not glanced at him again. He had addressed several remarks to her, which she had pretended not to hear. Mrs. Hopewell could not understand deliberate rudeness, although she lived with it, and she felt she had always to overflow with hospitality to make up for Joy's lack of courtesy. She urged him to talk about himself and he did. He said he was the seventh child of twelve and that his father had been crushed under a tree when he himself was eight year old. He had been crushed very badly, in fact, almost cut in two and was practically not recognizable. His mother had got along the best she could by hard working and she had always seen that her children went to Sunday School and that they read the Bible every evening. He was now nineteen year old and he had been selling Bibles for four months. In that time he had sold seventy-seven Bibles and had the promise of two more sales. He wanted to become a missionary because he thought that was the way you could do most for people. "He who losest his life shall find it," he said simply and he was so sincere, so genuine and earnest that Mrs. Hopewell would not for the world have smiled. He prevented his peas from sliding onto the table by blocking them with a piece of bread which he later cleaned his plate with. She could see Joy observing sidewise how he handled his knife and fork and she saw too that every few minutes, the boy would dart a keen appraising glance at the girl as if he were trying to attract her attention.

After dinner Joy cleared the dishes off the table and disappeared and Mrs. Hopewell was left to talk with him. He told her again about his childhood and his father's accident and about various things that had happened to him. Every five minutes or so she would stifle a yawn. He sat for two hours until finally she told him she must go because she had an appointment in town. He packed his Bibles and thanked her and prepared to leave, but in the doorway he stopped and wrung her hand and said that not on any of his trips had he met a lady as nice as her and he asked if he could come again. She had said she would always be happy to see him.

Joy had been standing in the road, apparently looking at something in the distance, when he came down the steps toward her, bent to the side with his heavy valise. He stopped where she was standing and confronted her directly. Mrs. Hopewell could not hear what he said but she trembled to think what Joy would say to him. She could see that after a minute Joy said something and that then the boy began to speak again, making an excited gesture with his free hand. After a minute Joy said something else at which the boy began to speak once more. Then to her amazement, Mrs. Hopewell saw the two of them walk off together, toward the gate. Joy had walked all the way to the gate with him and Mrs. Hopewell could not imagine what they had said to each other, and she had not yet dared to ask.

Mrs. Freeman was insisting upon her attention. She had moved from the refrigerator to the heater so that Mrs. Hopewell had to turn and face her in order to seem to be listening. "Glynese gone out with Harvey Hill again last night," she said. "She had this sty."

"Hill," Mrs. Hopewell said absently, "is that the one who works in the garage?"

"Nome, he's the one that goes to chiropracter school," Mrs. Freeman said. "She had this sty. Been had it two days. So she says when he brought her in the other night he says, 'Lemme get rid of that sty for you,' and she says, 'How?' and he says, 'You just lay yourself down acrost the seat of that car and I'll show you.' So she done it and he popped her neck. Kept on a-popping it several times until she made him quit. This morning," Mrs. Freeman said, "she ain't got no sty. She ain't got no traces of a sty."

"I never heard of that before," Mrs. Hopewell said.

"He ast her to marry him before the Ordinary," Mrs. Freeman went on, "and she told him she wasn't going to be married in no *office*."

"Well, Glynese is a fine girl," Mrs. Hopewell said. "Glynese and Carramae are both fine girls."

"Carramae said when her and Lyman was married Lyman said it sure felt sacred to him. She said he said he wouldn't take five hundred dollars for being married by a preacher."

"How much would he take?" the girl asked from the stove.

"He said he wouldn't take five hundred dollars," Mrs. Freeman repeated.

"Well we all have work to do," Mrs. Hopewell said.

"Lyman said it just felt more sacred to him," Mrs. Freeman said. "The doctor wants Carramae to eat prunes. Says instead of medicine. Says them cramps is coming from pressure. You know where I think it is?"

"She'll be better in a few weeks," Mrs. Hopewell said.

"In the tube," Mrs. Freeman said. "Else she wouldn't be as sick as she is."

Hulga had cracked her two eggs into a saucer and was bringing them to the table along with a cup of coffee that she had filled too full. She sat down carefully and began to eat, meaning to keep Mrs. Freeman there by questions if for any reason she showed an inclination to leave. She could perceive her mother's eye on her. The first round-about question would be about the Bible salesman and she did not wish to bring it on. "How did he pop her neck?" she asked.

Mrs. Freeman went into a description of how he had popped her neck. She said he owned a '55 Mercury but that Glynese said she would rather marry a man with only a '36 Plymouth who would be married by a preacher. The girl asked what if he had a '32 plymouth and Mrs. Freeman said what Glynese had said was a '36 Plymouth.

Mrs. Hopewell said there were not many girls with Glynese's common sense. She said what she admired in those girls was their common sense. She said that reminded her that they had a nice visitor yesterday, a young man selling Bibles. "Lord," she said, "he bored me to death but he was so sincere and genuine I couldn't be rude to him. He was just good country people, you know," she said, "—just the salt of the earth."

"I seen him walk up," Mrs. Freeman said, "and then later—I seen him walk off," and Hulga could feel the slight shift in her voice, the slight insinuation, that he had not walked off alone, had he? Her face remained expressionless but the color rose into her neck and she seemed to swallow it down with the next spoonful of egg. Mrs. Freeman was looking at her as if they had a secret together.

"Well, it takes all kinds of people to make the world go 'round," Mrs. Hopewell said. "It's very good we aren't all alike."

"Some people are more alike than others," Mrs. Freeman said.

Hulga got up and stumped, with about twice the noise that was necessary, into her room and locked the door. She was to meet the Bible salesman at ten o'clock at the gate. She had thought about it half the night. She had started thinking of it as a great joke and then she had begun to see profound implications in it. She had lain in bed imagining dialogues for them that were insane on the surface but that reached below to depths that no Bible salesman would be aware of. Their conversation yesterday had been of this kind.

He had stopped in front of her and had simply stood there. His face was bony and sweaty and bright, with a little pointed nose in the center of it, and his look was different from what it had been at the dinner table. He was gazing at her with open curiosity, with fascination, like a child watching a new fantastic animal at the zoo, and he was breathing as if he had run a great distance to reach her. His gaze seemed somehow familiar but she could not think where she had been regarded with it before. For almost a minute he didn't say anything. Then on what seemed an insuck of breath, he whispered, "You ever ate a chicken that was two days old?"

The girl looked at him stonily. He might have just put this question up for consideration at the meeting of a philosophical association "Yes," she presently replied as if she had considered it from all angles.

"It must have been mighty small!" he said triumphantly and shook all over with little nervous giggles, getting very red in the face, and subsiding finally into his gaze of complete admiration, while the girl's expression remained exactly the same.

"How old are you?" he asked softly.

She waited some time before she answered. Then in a flat voice she said, "Seventeen."

His smiles came in succession like waves breaking on the surface of a little lake. "I see you got a wooden leg," he said. "I think you're real brave. I think you're real sweet."

The girl stood blank and solid and silent.

"Walk to the gate with me," he said. "You're a brave sweet little thing and I liked you the minute I seen you walk in the door."

Hulga began to move forward.

"What's your name?" he asked, smiling down on the top of her head.

"Hulga," she said.

"Hulga," he murmured, "Hulga. Hulga. I never heard of anybody named Hulga before. You're shy, aren't you, Hulga?" he asked.

She nodded, watching his large red hand on the handle of the giant valise.

"I like girls that wear glasses," he said, "I think a lot. I'm not like these people that a serious thought don't ever enter their heads. It's because I may die."

"I may die too," she said suddenly and looked up at him. His eyes were very small and brown, glittering feverishly.

"Listen," he said, "don't you think some people was meant to meet on account of what all they got in common and all? Like they both think serious thoughts and all?" He shifted the valise to his other hand so that the hand nearest her was free. He caught hold of her elbow and shook it a little. "I don't work on Saturday," he said. "I like to walk in the woods and see what Mother Nature is wearing. O'er the hills and far away. Pic-nics and things. Couldn't we go on a pic-nic tomorrow? Say yes, Hulga," he said and gave her a dying look as if he felt his insides about to drop out of him. He had even seemed to sway slightly toward her.

During the night she had imagined that she seduced him. She imagined that the two of them walked on the place until they came to the storage barn beyond the two back fields and there, she imagined, that things came to such a pass that she very easily seduced him and that then, of course, she had to reckon with his remorse. True genius can get an idea across even to an inferior mind. She imagined that she took his remorse in hand and changed it into a deeper understanding of life. She took all his shame away and turned it into something useful.

She set off for the gate at exactly ten o'clock, escaping without drawing Mrs. Hopewell's attention. She didn't take anything to eat, forgetting that food is usually taken on a picnic. She wore a pair of slacks and a dirty white shirt, and as an afterthought, she had put some Vapex on the collar of it since she did not own any perfume. When she reached the gate no one was there.

She looked up and down the empty highway and had the furious feeling that she had been tricked, that he had only meant to make her walk to the gate after the idea of him. Then suddenly he stood up, very tall, from behind a bush on the opposite embankment. Smiling, he lifted his hat which was new and wide-brimmed. He had not worn it yesterday and she wondered if he had bought it for the occasion. It was toast-colored with a red and white band around it and was slightly too large for him. He stepped from behind the bush still carrying the black valise. He had on the same suit and the same yellow socks sucked down in his shoes from walking. He crossed the highway and said, "I knew you'd come!"

The girl wondered acidly how he had known this. She pointed to the valise and asked, "Why did you bring your Bibles?"

He took her elbow, smiling down on her as if he could not stop. "You can never tell when you'll need the word of God, Hulga," he said. She had a moment in which she doubted that this was actually happening and then they began to climb the embankment. They went down into the pasture toward the woods. The boy walked lightly by her side, bouncing on his toes. The valise did not seem to be heavy today; he even swung it. They crossed half the pasture without saying anything and then, putting his hand easily on the small of her back, he asked softly, "Where does your wooden leg join on?"

She turned an ugly red and glared at him and for an instant the boy looked abashed. "I didn't mean you no harm," he said. "I only meant you're so brave and all. I guess God takes care of you."

"No," she said, looking forward and walking fast, "I don't even believe in God."

At this he stopped and whistled. "No!" he exclaimed as if he were too astonished to say anything else.

She walked on and in a second he was bouncing at her side, fanning with his hat. "That's very unusual for a girl," he remarked, watching her out of the corner of his eye. When they reached the edge of the wood, he put his hand on her back again and drew her against him without a word and kissed her heavily.

The kiss, which had more pressure than feeling behind it, produced that extra surge of adrenalin in the girl that enables one to carry a packed trunk out of a burning house, but in her, the power went at once to the brain. Even before he released her, her mind, clear and detached and ironic anyway, was regarding him from a great distance, with amusement but with pity. She had never been kissed before and she was pleased to discover that it was an unexceptional experience and all a matter of the mind's control. Some people might enjoy drain water if they were told it was vodka. When the boy, looking expectant but uncertain, pushed her gently away, she turned and walked on, saying nothing as if such business, for her, were common enough.

He came along panting at her side, trying to help her when he saw a root that she might trip over. He caught and held back the long swaying blades of thorn vine until she had passed beyond them. She led the way and he came breathing heavily behind her. Then they came out on a sunlit hillside, sloping softly into another one a little smaller. Beyond, they could see the rusted top of the old barn where the extra hay was stored.

The hill was sprinkled with small pink weeds. "Then you ain't saved?" he asked suddenly, stopping.

The girl smiled. It was the first time she had smiled at him at all. "In my economy," she said, "I'm saved and you are damned but I told you I didn't believe in God."

Nothing seemed to destroy the boy's look of admiration. He gazed at her now as if the fantastic animal at the zoo had put its paw through the bars and given him a loving poke. She thought he looked as if he wanted to kiss her again and she walked on before he had the chance.

"Ain't there somewheres we can sit down sometime?" he murmured, his voice softening toward the end of the sentence.

"In that barn," she said.

They made for it rapidly as if it might slide away like a train. It was a large two-story barn, cool and dark inside. The boy pointed up the ladder that led into the loft and said, "It's too bad we can't go up there."

"Why can't we?" she asked.

"Yer leg," he said reverently.

The girl gave him a contemptuous look and putting both hands on the ladder, she climbed it while he stood below, apparently awestruck. She pulled herself expertly through the opening and then looked down at him and said, "Well, come on if you're coming," and he began to climb the ladder, awkwardly bringing the suitcase with him.

"We won't need the Bible," she observed.

"You never can tell," he said, panting. After he had got into the loft, he was a few seconds catching his breath. She had sat down in a pile of straw. A wide sheath of sunlight, filled with dust particles, slanted over her. She lay back against a bale, her face turned away, looking out the front opening of the barn where hay was thrown from a wagon into the loft. The two pink-speckled hillsides lay back against a dark ridge of woods. The sky was cloudless and cold blue. The boy dropped down by her side and put one arm under her and the other over her and began methodically kissing her face, making little noises like a fish.

He did not remove his hat but it was pushed far enough back not to interfere. When her glasses got in his way, he took them off of her and slipped them into his pocket.

The girl at first did not return any of the kisses but presently she began to and after she had put several on his cheek, she reached his lips and remained there, kissing him again and again as if she were trying to draw all the breath out of him. His breath was clear and sweet like a child's and the kisses were sticky like a child's. He mumbled about loving her and about knowing when he first seen her that he loved her, but the mumbling was like the sleepy fretting of a child being put to sleep by his mother. Her mind, throughout this, never stopped or lost itself for a second to her feelings. "You ain't said you loved me none," he whispered finally, pulling back from her." You got to say that."

She looked away from him off into the hollow sky and then down at a black ridge and then down father into what appeared to be two green swelling lakes. She didn't realize he had taken her glasses but this landscape could not seem exceptional to her for she seldom paid any close attention to her surroundings.

"You got to say it," he repeated. "You got to say you love me."

She was always careful how she committed herself. "In a sense," she began, "if you use the word loosely, you might say that. But it's not a word I use. I don't have illusions. I'm one of those people who see *through* to nothing."

The boy was frowning. "You got to say it. I said it and you got to say it," he said.

The girl looked at him almost tenderly. "You poor baby," she murmured. "It's just as well you don't understand," and she pulled him by the neck, face-down, against her. "We are all damned," she said, "but some of us have taken off our blindfolds and see that there's nothing to see. It's a kind of salvation."

The boy's astonished eyes looked blankly through the ends of her hair. "Okay," he almost whined, "but do you love me or don'tcher?"

"Yes," she said and added, "in a sense. But I must tell you something. There mustn't be anything dishonest between us." She lifted his head and looked him in the eye. "I am thirty years old," she said. "I have a number of degrees."

The boy's look was irritated but dogged. "I don't care," he said. "I don't care a thing about what all you done. I just want to know if you love me or don'tcher?" and he caught her to him and wildly planted her face with kisses until she said, "Yes, yes."

"Okay then," he said, letting her go. "Prove it."

She smiled, looking dreamily out on the shifty landscape. She had seduced him without even making up her mind to try. "How?" she asked, feeling that he should be delayed a little.

He leaned over and put his lips to her ear. "Show me where your wooden leg joins on," he whispered.

The girl uttered a sharp little cry and her face instantly drained of color. The obscenity of the suggestion was not what shocked her. As a child she had sometimes been subject to feelings of shame but education had removed the last traces of that as a good surgeon scrapes for cancer; she would no more have felt it over what he was asking than she would have believed in his Bible. But she was as sensitive about the artificial leg as a peacock about his tail. No one ever touched it but her. She took care of it as someone else would his soul, in private and almost with her own eyes turned away. "No," she said.

"I known it," he muttered, sitting up. "You're just playing me for a sucker."

"Oh no no!" she cried. "It joins on at the knee. Only at the knee. Why do you want to see it?"

The boy gave her a long penetrating look. "Because," he said, "it's what makes you different. You ain't like anybody else."

She sat staring at him. There was nothing about her face or her round freezing-blue eyes to indicate that this had moved her; but she felt as if her heart had stopped and left her mind to pump her blood. She decided that for the first time in her life she was face to face with real innocence. This boy, with an instinct that came from beyond wisdom, had touched the truth about her. When after a minute, she said in a hoarse high voice, "All right," it was like surrendering to him completely. It was like losing her own life and finding it again, miraculously, in his.

Very gently he began to roll the slack leg up. The artificial limb, in a white sock and brown flat shoe, was bound in a heavy material like canvas and ended in an ugly jointure where it was attached to the stump. The boy's face and his voice were entirely reverent as he uncovered it and said, "Now show me how to take it off and on."

She took it off for him and put it back on again and then he took it off himself, handling it as tenderly as if it were a real one. "See!" he said with a delighted child's face. "Now I can do it myself!"

"Put it back on," she said. She was thinking that she would run away with him and that every night he would take the leg off and every morning put it back on again. "Put it back on," she said.

"Not yet," he murmured, setting it on its foot out of her reach. "Leave it off for a while. You got me instead."

She gave a little cry of alarm but he pushed her down and began to kiss her again. Without the leg she felt entirely dependent on him. Her brain seemed to have stopped thinking altogether and to be about some other function that it was not very good at. Different expressions raced back and forth over her face. Every now and then the boy, his eyes like two steel spikes, would glance behind him where the leg stood. Finally she pushed him off and said, "Put it back on me now."

"Wait," he said. He leaned the other way and pulled the valise toward him and opened it. It had a pale blue spotted lining and there were only two Bibles in it. He took one of these out and opened the cover of it. It was hollow and contained a pocket flask of whiskey, a pack of cards, and a small blue box with printing on it. He laid these out in front of her one at a time in an evenly-spaced row, like one presenting offerings at the shrine of a goddess. He put the blue box in her hand. THIS PRODUCT TO BE USED ONLY FOR THE PREVENTION OF DISEASE, she read, and dropped it. The boy was unscrewing the top of the flask. He stopped and pointed, with a smile, to the deck of cards. It was not an ordinary deck but one with an obscene picture on the back of each card. "Take a swig," he said, offering her the bottle first. He held it in front of her, but like one mesmerized, she did not move.

Her voice when she spoke had an almost pleading sound. "Aren't you," she murmured, "aren't you just good country people?"

The boy cocked his head. He looked as if he were just beginning to understand that she might be trying to insult him. "Yeah," he said, curling his lip slightly, "but it ain't held me back none. I'm as good as you any day in the week."

"Give me my leg," she said.

He pushed it farther away with his foot. "Come on now, let's begin to have us a good time," he said coaxingly. "We ain't got to know one another good yet."

"Give me my leg!" she screamed and tried to lunge for it but he pushed her down easily.

"What's the matter with you all of a sudden?" he asked, frowning as he screwed the top on the flask and put it quickly back inside the Bible. "You just a while ago said you didn't believe in nothing. I thought you was some girl!"

Her face was almost purple. "You're a Christian!" she hissed. "You're a fine Christian! You're just like them all—say one thing and do another. You're a perfect Christian, you're . . ."

The boy's mouth was set angrily. "I hope you don't think," he said in a lofty indignant tone, "that I believe in that crap! I may sell Bibles but I know which end is up and I wasn't born yesterday and I know where I'm going!"

"Give me my leg!" she screeched. He jumped up so quickly that she barely saw him sweep the cards and the blue box back into the Bible and throw the Bible into the valise. She saw him grab the leg and then she saw it for an instant slanted forlornly across the inside of the suitcase with a Bible at either side of its opposite ends. He slammed the lid shut and snatched up the valise and swung it down the hole and then stepped through himself. .

When all of him had passed but his head, he turned and regarded her with a look that no longer had any admiration in it. "I've gotten a lot of interesting things," he said. "One time I got a woman's glass eye this way. And you needn't to think you'll catch me because Pointer ain't really my name. I use a different name at every house I call at and don't stay nowhere long. And I'll tell you another thing, Hulga," he said, using the name as if he didn't think much of it, "you ain't so smart. I been believing in nothing ever since I was born!" and then the toast-colored hat disappeared down the hole and the girl was left, sitting on the straw in the dusty sunlight. When she turned her churning face toward the opening, she saw his blue figure struggling successfully over the green speckled lake.

Mrs. Hopewell and Mrs. Freeman, who were in the back pasture, digging up onions, saw him emerge a little later from the woods and head across the meadow toward the highway. "Why, that looks like that nice dull young man that tried to sell me a Bible yesterday," Mrs. Hopewell said, squinting. "He must have been selling them to the Negroes back in there. He was so simple," she said, "but I guess the world would be better off if we were all that simple."

Mrs. Freeman's gaze drove forward and just touched him before he disappeared under the hill. Then she returned her attention to the evil-smelling onion shoot she was lifting from the ground. "Some can't be that simple," she said. "I know I never could."

QUESTIONS

1. List the unusual elements in plot and character in this story. Has Flannery O'Connor managed to put them together in a believable whole? What devices assist her toward that end?

2. Could Hulga have told her own story effectively or is it better told by the omniscient narrator? Why?
3. In what way is the omniscience limited?
4. Explain the title. To how many people does it apply? Does it apply to all of them in the same way?
5. Explain the significance of the Bible salesman's comment to Hulga, "you ain't so smart. I been believing in nothing ever since I was born!"
6. How many ironies can you detect in this story?

FLYING HOME
Ralph Ellison   (1914–   )

When Todd came to, he saw two faces suspended above him in a sun so hot and blinding that he could not tell if they were black or white. He stirred, feeling pain that burned as though his whole body had been laid open to the sun which glared into his eyes. For a moment an old fear of being touched by white hands seized him. Then the very sharpness of the pain began slowly to clear his head. Sounds came to him dimly. He done come to. Who are they? he thought. Naw he aint, I coulda sworn he was white. Then he heard clearly:

"You hurt bad?"

Something within him uncoiled. It was a Negro sound.

"He's still out," he heard.

"Give 'im time . . . . Say, son, you hurt bad?"

Was he? There was that awful pain. He lay rigid, hearing their breathing and trying to weave a meaning between them and his being stretched painfully upon the ground. He watched them warily, his mind traveling back over a painful distance. Jagged scenes, swiftly unfolding as in a movie trailer, reeled through his mind, and he saw himself piloting a tailspinning plane and landing and landing and falling from the cockpit and trying to stand. Then, as in a great silence, he remembered the sound of crunching bone, and now, looking up into the anxious faces of an old Negro man and a boy from where he lay in the same field, the memory sickened him and he wanted to remember no more.

"How you feel, son?"

Todd hesitated, as though to answer would be to admit an inacceptable weakness. Then, "It's my ankle," he said.

"Which one?"

"The left."

With a sense of remoteness he watched the old man bend and remove his boot, feeling the pressure ease.

"That any better?"

"A lot. Thank you."

He had the sensation of discussing someone else, that his concern was with some far more important thing, which for some reason escaped him.

"You done broke it bad," the old man said. "We have to get you to a doctor."

He felt that he had been thrown into a tailspin. He looked at his watch; how long had he been here? He knew there was but one important thing in the world, to get the plane back to the field before his officers were displeased.

"Help me up," he said. "Into the ship."

"But it's broke too bad . . . ."

"Give me you arm!"

"But, son . . ."

Clutching the old man's arm he pulled himself up, keeping his left leg clear, thinking, "I'd never make him understand," as the leather-smooth face came parallel with his own.

"Now, let's see."

He pushed the old man back, hearing a bird's insistent shrill. He swayed giddily. Blackness washed over him, like infinity.

"You best sit down."

"No, I'm O.K."

"But, son, You jus' gonna make it worse . . . ."

It was a fact that everything in him cried out to deny, even against the flaming pain in his ankle. He would have to try again.

"You mess with that ankle they have to cut your foot off," he heard.

Holding his breath, he started up again. It pained so badly that he had to bite his lips to keep from crying out and he allowed them to help him down with a pang of despair.

"It's best you take it easy. We gon' git you a doctor."

Of all the luck, he thought. Of all the rotten luck, now I have done it. The fumes of high-octane gasoline clung in the heat taunting him.

"We kin ride him into town on old Ned," the boy said.

Ned? He turned, seeing the boy point toward an ox team browsing where the buried blade of a plow marked the end of a furrow. Thoughts of himself riding an ox through the town, past streets full of white faces, down the concrete runways of the airfield made swift images of humiliation in his mind. With a pang he remembered his girl's last letter. "Todd," she had written, "I don't need the papers to tell me you had the intelligence to fly. And I have always known you to be as brave as anyone else. The papers annoy me. Don't you be contented to prove over and over again that you're brave or skillful just because you're black, Todd. I think they keep beating that dead horse because they don't want to say why you boys are not yet fighting. I'm really disappointed, Todd. Anyone with brains can learn to fly, but then what? What about using it, and who will you use it for? I wish, dear, you'd write about this. I sometimes think they're playing a trick on us. It's very humiliating . . . ." He wiped cold sweat from his face, thinking, What does she know of humiliation? She's never been down South. Now the humiliation would come. When you must have them judge you, knowing that they never accept your mistakes as your own, but hold it against your whole race—that was humiliation. Yes and humiliation was when you could never be simply yourself, when you were always a part of this old black ignorant man. Sure, he's all right. Nice and kind and helpful. But he's not you. Well, there's one humiliation I can spare myself.

"No," he said, "I have orders not to leave the ship . . . ."

"Aw," the old man said. Then turning to the boy, "Teddy, then you better hustle down to Mister Graves and get him to come . . . ."

"No, wait!" he protested before he was fully aware. Graves might be white. "Just have him get word to the field, please. They'll take care of the rest."

He saw the boy leave, running.

"How far does he have to go?"

"Might' nigh a mile."

He rested back, looking at the dusty face of his watch. But now they know something has happened, he thought. In the ship there was a perfectly good radio, but it was useless. The old fellow would never operate it. That buzzard knocked me back a hundred years, he thought. Irony danced within him like the gnats circling the old man's head. With all I've learned I'm dependent upon this "peasant's" sense of time and space. His leg throbbed. In the plane, instead of time being measured by the rhythms of pain and a kid's legs, the instruments would have told him at a glance. Twisting upon his elbows he saw where dust had powdered the plane's fuselage, feeling the lump form in his throat that was always there when he thought of flight. It's crouched there, he thought, like the abandoned shell of a locust. I'm naked without it. Not a machine, a suit of clothes you wear. And with a sudden embarrassment and wonder he whispered, "It's the only dignity I have . . . ."

He saw the old man watching, his torn overalls clinging limply to him in the heat. He felt a sharp need to tell the old man what he felt. But that would be meaningless. If I tried to explain why I need to fly back, he'd think I was simply afraid of white officers. But it's more than fear . . . a sense of anguish clung to him like the veil of sweat that hugged his face. He watched the old man, hearing him humming snatches of a tune as he admired the plane. He felt a furtive sense of resentment. Such old men often came to the field to watch the pilots with childish eyes. At first it had made him proud; they had been a meaningful part of a new experience. But soon he realized they did not understand his accomplishments and they came to shame and embarrass him, like the distasteful praise of an idiot. A part of the meaning of flying had gone then, and he had not been able to regain it. If I were a prizefighter I would be more human, he thought. Not a monkey doing tricks, but a man. They were pleased simply that he was a Negro who could fly, and that was not enough. He felt cut off from them by age, by understanding, by sensibility, by technology and by his need to measure himself against the mirror of other men's appreciation. Somehow he felt betrayed, as he had when as a child he grew to discover that his father was dead. Now for him any real appreciation lay with his white officers; and with them he could never be sure. Between ignorant black men and condescending whites, his course of flight seemed mapped by the nature of things sway from all needed and natural landmarks. Under some sealed orders, couched in ever more technical and mysterious terms, his path curved swiftly away from both the shame the old man symbolized and the cloudy terrain of white men's regard. Flying blind, he knew but one point of landing and there he would receive his wings. After that the enemy would appreciate his skill and he would assume his deepest meaning, he thought sadly, neither from those who condescended nor from those who praised without understanding, but from the enemy who would recognize his manhood and skill in terms of hate . . . .

He sighed, seeing the oxen making queer, prehistoric shadows against the dry brown earth.

"You just take it easy, some," the old man soothes. "That boy won't take long. Crazy as he is about airplanes."

"I can wait," he said.

"What kinda airplane you call this here'n?"

"An Advanced Trainer," he said, seeing the old man smile. His fingers were like gnarled dark wood against the metal as he touched the low-slung wing.

"'Bout how fast can she fly?"

"Over two hundred an hour."

"Lawd! That's so fast I bet it don't seem like you moving!"

Holding himself rigid, Todd opened his flying suit. The shade had gone and he lay in a ball of fire.

"You mind if I take a look inside? I was always curious to see . . . ."

"Help yourself. Just don't touch anything."

He heard him climb upon the metal wing, grunting. Now the questions would start. Well, so you don't have to think to answer . . . .

He saw the old man looking over into the cockpit, his eyes bright as a child's.

"You must have to know a lot to work all these here things."

He was silent, seeing him step down and kneel beside him.

"Son, how come you want to fly way up there in the air?"

Because it's the most meaningful act in the world . . . because it makes me less like you, he thought.

But he said: "Because I like it, I guess. It's as good a way to fight and die as I know."

"Yeah? I guess you right," the old man said. "But how long you think before they gonna let you all fight?"

He tensed. This was the question all Negroes asked, put with the same timid hopefulness and longing that always opened a greater void within him than that he had felt beneath the plane the first time he had flown. He felt light-headed. It came to him suddenly that there was something sinister about the conversation, that he was flying unwillingly into unsafe and uncharted regions. If he could only be insulting and tell this old man who was trying to help him to shut up!

"I bet you one thing . . ."

"Yes?"

"That you was plenty scared coming down."

He did not answer. Like a dog on a trail the old man seemed to smell out his fears and he felt anger bubble within him.

"You sho' scared me. When I seen you coming down in that thing with it a-rollin' and a-jumpin' like a pitchin' hoss, I thought sho' you was a goner. I almost had me a stroke!"

He saw the old man grinning, "Ever'thin's been happening round here this morning, come to think of it."

"Like what?" he asked.

"Well, first thing I know, here come two white fellers looking for Mister Rudolph, that's Mister Graves's cousin. That got me worked up right away . . . ."

"Why?"

"Why? 'Cause he done broke outta the crazy house, that's why. He liable to kill somebody," he said. "They oughta have him by now though. Then here you come. First I think it's one of them white boys. Then doggone if you don't fall outta there. Lawd, I'd done heard about you boys but I haven't never seen one o' you-all. Cain't tell you how it felt to see somebody what look like me in a airplane!"

The old man talked on, the sound steaming around Todd's thoughts like air flowing over the fuselage of a flying plane. You were a fool, he thought, remembering how before the spin the sun had blazed bright against the billboard signs beyond the town, and how a boy's blue kite had bloomed beneath him, tugging gently in the wind like a strange, odd-shaped flower. He had once flown such kites himself and tried to find the boy at the end of the invisible cord. But he had been flying too high and too fast. He had climbed steeply away in exultation. Too steeply, he thought. And one of the first rules you learn is that if the angle of thrust is too steep the plane goes into a spin. And then, instead of pulling out of it and going into a dive you let a buzzard panic you. A lousy buzzard!

"Son, what made all that blood on the glass?"

"A buzzard," he said, remembering how the blood and feathers had sprayed back against the hatch. It had been as though he had flown into a storm of blood and blackness.

"Well, I declare! They's lots of 'em around here. They after dead things. Don't eat nothing what's alive."

"A little bit more and he would have made a meal out of me," Todd said grimly.

"They bad luck all right. Teddy's got a name for 'em, calls 'em jimcrows," the old man laughed.

"It's a damned good name."

"They the damnedest birds. Once I seen a hoss all stretched out like he was sick, you know. So I hollers, 'Gid up from there, suh!' Just to make sho! An' doggone, son, if I don't see two ole jimcrows come flying right up outa that hoss's insides! Yessuh! The sun was shinin' on 'em and they couldn't a been no greasier if they'd been eating barbecue."

Todd thought he would vomit, his stomach quivered.

"You made that up," he said.

"Nawsuh! Saw him just like I see you."

"Well, I'm glad it was you."

"You see lots a funny things down here, son."

"No, I'll let you see them," he said.

"By the way, the white folks round here don't like to see you boys up there in the sky. They ever bother you?"

"No."

"Well, they'd like to."

"Someone always wants to bother someone else," Todd said. "How do you know?"

"I just know."

"Well," he said defensively, "no one has bothered us."

Blood pounded in his ears as he looked away into space. He turned, seeing a black spot in the sky, and strained to confirm what he could not clearly see.

"What does that look like to you?" he asked excitedly.

"Just another bad luck, son."

Then he saw the movement of wings with disappointment. It was gliding smoothly down, wings outspread, tail feathers gripping the air, down swiftly— gone behind the green screen of trees. It was like a bird he had imagined there, only the sloping branches of the pines remained, sharp against the pale stretch of sky. He lay barely breathing and stared at the point where it had disappeared, caught in a spell of loathing and admiration. Why did they make them so disgusting and yet teach them to fly so well? It's like when I was up in heaven, he heard, starting.

The old man was chuckling, rubbing his stubbled chin.

"What did you say?"

"Sho', I died and went to heaven . . . maybe by time I tell you about it they be done come after you."

"I hope so," he said wearily.

"You boys ever sit around and swap lies?"

"Not often. Is this going to be one?"

"Well, I ain't so sho', on account of it took place when I was dead."

The old man paused, "That wasn't no lie 'bout the buzzards, though."

"All right," he said.

"Sho' you want to hear 'bout heaven?"

"Please," he answered, resting his head upon his arm.

"Well, I went to heaven and right away started to sproutin' me some wings. Six good ones, they was. Just like them the white angels had. I couldn't hardly believe it. I was so glad that I went off on some clouds by myself and tried 'em out. You know, 'cause I didn't want to make a fool outta myself the first thing. . . ."

It's an old tale, Todd thought. Told me years ago. Had forgotten. But at least it will keep him from talking about buzzards.

He closed his eyes, listening.

". . . First thing I done was to git up on a low cloud and jump off. And doggone, boy, if them wings didn't work! First I tried the right; then I tried the left; then I tried 'em both together. Then Lawd, I started to move on out among the folks. I let 'em see me. . . ."

He saw the old man gesturing flight with his arms, his face full of mock pride as he indicated an imaginary crowd, thinking, It'll be in the newspapers, as he heard, ". . . so I went and found me some colored angels—somehow I didn't believe I was an angel till I seen a real black one, ha, yes! Then I was sho'—but they tole me I better come down 'cause us colored folks had to wear a special kin' a harness when we flew. That was how come they wasn't flyin'. Oh yes, an' you had to be extra strong for a black man even, to fly with one of them harnesses. . . ."

This is a new turn, Todd thought, what's he driving at?

"So I said to myself, I ain't gonna be bothered with no harness! Oh naw! 'Cause if God let you sprout wings you oughta have sense enough not to let nobody make you wear something what gits in the way of flyin'. So I starts to flyin'. Heck, son," he chuckled, his eyes twinkling, "you know I had to let ev'ybody know that old Jefferson could fly good as anybody else. And I could too, fly smooth as a bird! I could even loop-the-loop—only I had to make sho' to keep my long white robe down roun' my ankles. . . ."

Todd felt uneasy. He wanted to laugh at the joke, but his body refused, as of an independent will. He felt as he had as a child when after he had chewed a sugar-coated pill which his mother had given him, she had laughed at his efforts to remove the terrible taste.

". . . Well," he heard, "I was doing all right 'til I got to speeding. Found out I could fan up a right strong breeze, I could fly so fast. I could do all kin'sa stunts too. I started flying up to the stars and divin' down and zooming roun' the moon. Man, I like to scare the devil outa some ole white angels. I was raisin' hell. Not that I meant any harm, son. But I was just feeling good. It was so good to know I was free at last. I accidently knocked the tops offa some stars and they tell me I caused a storm and a coupla lynchings down here in Macon County—though I swear I believe them boys what said that was making up lies on me. . . ."

He's mocking me, Todd thought angrily. He thinks it's a joke. Grinning down at me . . . His throat was dry. He looked at his watch; why the hell didn't they come? Since they had to, why? One day I was flying down one of them heavenly streets. You got yourself into it, Todd thought. Like Jonah in the whale.

"Justa throwin' feathers in everybody's face. An' ole Saint Peter called me in. Said, 'Jefferson, tell me two things, what you doin' flyin' without a harness; an' how come you flyin' so fast?' So I tole him I was flyin' without a harness 'cause it got in my way, but I couldn'ta been flyin' so fast, 'cause I wasn't usin' but one wing. Saint Peter said, 'You wasn't flyin' with but one wing?' 'Yessuh,' I says, scared-like. So he says, 'Well, since you got sucha extra fine pair of wings you can leave off yo' harness awhile. But from now on none of that there one-wing flyin', 'cause you gittin' up too damn much speed!' "

And with one mouth full of bad teeth you're making too damned much talk, thought Todd. Why don't I send him after the boy? His body ached from the hard ground and seeking to shift his position he twisted his ankle and hated himself for crying out.

"It gittin' worse?"

"I . . . I twisted it," he groaned.

"Try not to think about it, son. That's what I do."

He bit his lip, fighting pain with counter-pain as the voice resumed its rhythmical droning. Jefferson seemed caught in his own creation.

". . . After all that trouble I just floated roun' heaven in slow motion. But I forgot, like colored folks will do, and got to flyin' with one wing again. This time I was restin' my old broken arm and got to flyin' fast enough to shame the devil. I was comin' so fast, Lawd, I got myself called befo' ole Saint Peter again. He said, 'Jeff, didn't I warn you 'bout that speedin'?' 'Yessuh,' I says, 'but it was an accident.' He looked at me sad-like and shook his head and I knowed I was gone. He said, 'Jeff, you and that speedin' is a danger to the heavenly community. If I was to let you keep on flyin', heaven wouldn't be nothin' but uproar. Jeff, you got to go!' Son, I argued and pleaded with that old white man, but it didn't do a bit of good. They rushed me straight to them pearly gates and gimme a parachute and a map of the state of Alabama . . ."

Todd heard him laughing so that he could hardly speak, making a screen between them upon which his humiliation glowed like fire.

"Maybe you'd better stop awhile," he said, his voice unreal.

"Ain't much more," Jefferson laughed. "When they gimme the parachute ole Saint Peter ask me if I wanted to say a few words before I went. I felt so bad I couldn't hardly look at him, specially with all them white angels standin' around. Then somebody laughed and made me mad. So I tole him, 'Well, you done took my wings. And you puttin' me out. You got charge of things so's I can't do nothing' about it. But you got to admit just this: While I was up here I was the flyinest sonofabitch what ever hit heaven!' "

At the burst of laughter Todd felt such an intense humiliation that only great violence would wash it away. The laughter which shook the old man like a boiling purge set up vibrations of guilt within him which not even the intricate machinery of the plane would have been adequate to transform and he heard himself screaming, "Why do you laugh at me this way?"

He hated himself at that moment, but he had lost control. He saw Jefferson's mouth fall open, "What—?"

"Answer me!"

His blood pounded as though it would surely burst his temples and he tried to reach the old man and fell, screaming, "Can I help it because they won't let us actually fly? Maybe we are a bunch of buzzards feeding on a dead horse, but we can hope to be eagles, can't we? Can't we?"

He fell back, exhausted, his ankle pounding. The saliva was like straw in his mouth. If he had the strength he would strangle this old man. This grinning, gray-headed clown who made him feel as he felt when watched by the white officers at the field. And yet this old man had neither power, prestige, rank nor technique. Nothing that could rid him of this terrible feeling. He watched him, seeing his face struggle to express a turmoil of feeling.

"What you mean, son? What you talking 'bout . . . ?"

"Go away. Go tell your tales to the white folks."

"But I didn't mean nothing like that. . . . I . . . I wasn't tryin' to hurt your feelings. . . ."

"Please. Get the hell away from me!"

"But I didn't, son. I didn't mean all them things a-tall."

Todd shook as with a chill, searching Jefferson's face for a trace of the mockery he had seen there. But now the face was somber and tired and old. He was confused. He could not be sure that there had ever been laughter there, that Jefferson had ever really laughed in his whole life. He saw Jefferson reach out to touch him and shrank away, wondering if anything except the pain, now causing his vision to waver, was real. Perhaps he had imagined it all.

"Don't let it get you down, son," the voice said pensively.

He heard Jefferson sigh wearily, as though he felt more than he could say. His anger ebbed, leaving only the pain.

"I'm sorry," he mumbled.

"You just wore out with pain, was all . . . ."

He saw him through a blur, smiling. And for a second he felt the embarrassed silence of understanding flutter between them.

"What you was doin' flyin' over this section, son? Wasn't you scared they might shoot you for a cow?"

Todd tensed. Was he being laughed at again. But before he could decide, the pain shook him and a part of him was lying calmly behind the screen of pain that had fallen between them, recalling the first time he had ever seen a plane. It was as though an endless series of hangars had been shaken ajar in the air base of his memory and from each, like a young wasp emerging from its cell, arose the memory of a plane.

The first time I ever saw a plane I was very small and planes were new in the world. I was four-and-a-half and the only plane that I had ever seen was a model suspended from the ceiling of the automobile exhibit at the State Fair. But I did not know that it was only a model. I did not know how large a real plane was, nor how expensive. To me it was a fascinating toy, complete in itself, which my mother said could only be owned by rich little white boys. I stood rigid with admiration, my head straining backwards as I watched the gray little plane describing arcs above the gleaming tops of the automobiles. And I vowed that, rich or poor, someday I would own such a toy. My mother had to drag me out of the exhibit and not even the merry-go-round, the Ferris wheel, or the racing horses could hold my attention for the rest of the Fair. I was too busy imitating the tiny drone of the plane with my lips, and imitating with my hands the motion, swift and circling, that it made in flight.

After that I no longer used the pieces of lumber that lay about our back yard to construct wagons and autos . . . now it was used for airplanes. I built biplanes, using pieces of board for wings, a small box for the fuselage, another piece of wood for the rudder. The trip to the Fair had brought something new into my small world. I asked my mother repeatedly when the Fair would come back again. I'd lie in the grass and watch the sky, and each fighting bird became a soaring plane. I would have been good a year just to have seen a plane again. I became a nuisance to everyone with my questions about airplanes. But planes were new to the old folks, too, and there was little that they could tell me. Only my uncle knew some of the answers. And better still, he could carve propellers from pieces of wood that would whirl rapidly in the wind, wobbling noisily upon oiled nails.

I wanted a plane more than I'd wanted anything, more than I wanted the red wagon with rubber tires, more than the train that ran on a track with its train of cars. I asked my mother over and over again:

"Mamma?"

"What do you want, boy?" she'd say.

"Mamma, will you get mad if I ask you?" I'd say.

"What do you want now? I ain't got time to be answering a lot of fool questions. What you want?"

"Mamma, when you gonna get me one . . . ?" I'd ask.

"Get you one what?" she'd say.

"You know, Mamma; what I been asking you . . . ."

"Boy," she'd say, "if you don't want a spanking you better come on an' tell me what you talking about so I can get on with my work."

"Aw, Mamma, you know . . . ."

"What I just tell you?" she'd say.

"I mean when you gonna buy me a airplane."

"AIRPLANE! Boy, is you crazy? How many times I have to tell you to stop that foolishness. I done told you them things cost too much. I bet I'm gon' wham the living daylight out of you if you don't quit worrying me 'bout them things!"

But this did not stop me, and a few days later I'd try all over again.

Then one day a strange thing happened. It was spring and for some reason I had been hot and irritable all morning. It was a beautiful spring. I could feel it as I played barefoot in the backyard. Blossoms hung from the thorny black locust trees like clusters of fragrant white grapes. Butterflies flickered in the sunlight above the short new dew-wet grass. I had gone in the house for bread and butter and coming out I heard a steady unfamiliar drone. It was unlike anything I had ever heard before. I tried to place the sound. It was no use. It was a sensation like that I had when searching for my father's watch, heard ticking unseen in a room. It made me feel as though I had forgotten to perform some task that my mother had ordered . . . then I located it, overhead. In the sky, flying quite low and about a hundred yards off was a plane! It came so slowly that it seemed barely to move. My mouth hung wide; my bread and butter fell into the dirt. I wanted to jump up and down and cheer. And when the idea struck I trembled with excitement: "Some little white boy's plane's done flew away and all I got to do is stretch out my hands and it'll be mine!" It was a little plane like that at the Fair, flying no higher than the eaves of our roof. Seeing it come steadily forward I felt the world grow warm with promise. I opened the screen and climbed over it and clung there, waiting. I would catch the plane as it came over and swing down fast and run into the house before anyone could see me. Then no one could come to claim the plane. It droned nearer. Then when it hung like a silver cross in the blue directly above me I stretched out my hand and grabbed. It was like sticking my finger through a soap bubble. The plane flew on, as though I had simply blown my breath after it. I grabbed again, frantically, trying to catch the tail. My fingers clutched the air and disappointment surged tight and hard in my throat. Giving one last desperate grasp, I strained forward. My fingers ripped from the screen, I was falling. The ground burst hard against me. I drummed the earth with my heels and when my breath returned, I law there bawling.

My mother rushed through the door.

"What's the matter, chile! What on earth is wrong with you?"

"It's gone! It's gone!"

"What gone?"

"The airplane . . ."

"Airplane?"

"Yessum, jus' like the one at the Fair . . . . I . . . I tried to stop it an' it kep' right on going . . ."

"When, boy?"

"Just now," I cried, through my tears.

"Where it go, boy, what way?"

"Yonder, there . . ."

She scanned the sky, her arms akimbo and her checkered apron flapping in the wind as I pointed to the fading plane. Finally she looked down at me, slowing shaking her head.

"It's gone! It's gone!" I cried.

"Boy, is you a fool?" she said. "Don't you see that there's a real airplane 'stead of one of them toy ones?"

"Real . . . ?" I forgot to cry. "Real?"

"Yass, real. Don't you know that thing you reaching for is bigger'n a auto? You here trying to reach for it and I bet it's flying 'bout two hundred miles high-er'n this roof." She was disgusted with me. "You come on in this house before somebody else sees what a fool you done turned out to be. You must think these here lil ole arms of you'n is mighty long . . . ."

I was carried into the house and undressed for bed and the doctor was called. I cried bitterly, as much from the disappointment of finding the plane so far beyond my reach as from the pain.

When the doctor came I heard my mother telling him about the plane and asking if anything was wrong with my mind. He explained that I had had a fever for several hours. But I was kept in bed for a week and I constantly saw the plane in my sleep, lying just beyond my fingertips, sailing so slowly that it seemed barely to move. And each time I'd reach out to grab it I'd miss and through each dream I'd hear my grandma warning:

> Young man, young man,
> Yo' arms too short
> To box with God . . . .

"Hey, son!"

At first he did not know where he was and looked at the old man pointing, with blurred eyes.

"Ain't that one of you-all's airplanes coming after you?"

As his vision cleared he saw a small black shape above a distant field, soaring through waves of heat. But he could not be sure and with the pain he feared that somehow a horrible recurring fantasy of being split in twain by the whirling blades of a propeller had come true.

"You think he sees us?" he heard.

"See? I hope so."

"He's coming like a bat outa hell!"

Straining, he heard the faint sound of a motor and hoped it would soon be over.

"How you feeling?"

"Like a nightmare," he said.

"Hey, he's done curved back the other way!"

"Maybe he saw us," he said. "Maybe he's gone to send out the ambulance and ground crew." And, he thought with despair, maybe he didn't even see us.

"Where did you send the boy?"

"Down to Mister Graves," Jefferson said. "Man what owns this land."

"Do you think he phoned?"

Jefferson looked at him quickly.

"Aw sho'. Dabney Graves is got a bad name on accounta them killings but he'll call though. . . . "

"What killings?"

"Them five fellers . . . ain't you heard?" he asked with surprise.

"No."

"Everybody knows 'bout Dabney Graves, especially the colored. He done killed enough of us."

Todd had the sensation of being caught in a white neighborhood after dark.

"What did they do?" he asked.

"Thought they was men," Jefferson said. "An' some he owed money, like he do me. . . . "

"But why do you stay here?"

"You black, son."

"I know, but . . . "

"You have to come by the white folks, too."

He turned away from Jefferson's eyes, at once consoled and accused. And I'll have to come by them soon, he thought with despair. Closing his eyes, he heard Jefferson's voice as the sun burned blood-red upon his lips.

"I got nowhere to go," Jefferson said, "an' they'd come after me if I did. But Dabney Graves is a funny fellow. He's all the time making jokes. He can be mean as hell, then he's liable to turn right around and back the colored against the white folks. I seen him do it. But me, I hates him for that more'n anything else. 'Cause just as soon as he gits tired helping a man he don't care what happens to him. He just leaves him stone cold. And then the other white folks is double hard on anybody he done helped. For him it's just a joke. He don't give a hilla beans for nobody—but hisself. . . . "

Todd listened to the thread of detachment in the old man's voice. It was as though he held his words arm's length before him to avoid their destructive meaning.

"He'd just as soon do you a favor and then turn right around and have you strung up. Me, I stays outa his way 'cause down here that's what you gotta do."

If my ankle would only ease for a while, he thought. The closer I spin toward the earth the blacker I become, flashed through his mind. Sweat ran into his eyes and he was sure that he would never see the plane if his head continued whirling. He tried to see Jefferson, what it was that Jefferson held in his hand? It was a little black man, another Jefferson! A little black Jefferson that shook with fits of belly-laughter while the other Jefferson looked on with detachment. Then Jefferson looked up from the thing in his hand and turned to speak, but Todd was far away, searching the sky for a plane in a hot dry land on a day and age he had long forgotten. He was going mysteriously with his mother through empty streets where black faces peered from behind drawn shades and someone was rapping at a window and he was looking back to see a hand and a frightened face frantically beckoning from a cracked door and his mother was looking down the empty perspective of the street and shaking her head and hurrying him along and at first it was only a flash he saw and a motor was droning as through the sun-glare he saw it gleaming silver as it circled and he was seeing a burst like a puff of white smoke and hearing his mother yell, Come along, boy, I got no time for them fool airplanes, I got no time, and he saw it a second time, the plane flying high, and the burst appeared suddenly and fell slowly, billowing out sparkling like fireworks and he was watching and being hurried along as the air filled with a flurry of white pinwheeling cards that caught in the wind and scattered over the rooftops and into the gutters and a woman was running and snatching a card and reading it and screaming and he darted into the shower, grabbing as in winter he grabbed for snowflakes and bounding away at his mother's, Come in here, boy! Come on, I say! and he was watching as she took the card away, seeing her face grow puzzled and turning taut as her voice quavered, "Niggers Stay From The Polls," and died to a moan of terror as he saw the eyeless sockets of a white hood staring at him from the card and above he saw the plane spiraling gracefully, agleam in the sun like a fiery sword. And seeing it soar he was caught, transfixed between a terrible horror and a horrible fascination.

The sun was not so high now, and Jefferson was calling and gradually he saw three figures moving across the curving roll of the field.

"Look like some doctors, all dressed in white," said Jefferson.

They're coming at last, Todd thought. And he felt such a release of tension within him that he thought he would faint. But no sooner did he close his eyes than he was seized and he was struggling with three white men who were forcing his arms into some kind of coat. It was too much for him, his arms were pinned to his sides as the pain blazed in his eyes, he realized that it was a straitjacket. What filthy joke was this?

"That oughta hold him, Mister Graves," he heard.

His total energies seemed focused in his eyes as he searched their faces. That was Graves; the other two wore hospital uniforms. He was poised between two poles of fear and hate as he heard the one called Graves saying, "He looks kinda purty in that there suit, boys. I'm glad you dropped by."

"This boy ain't crazy, Mister Graves," one of the others said. "He needs a doctor, not us. Don't see how you led us way out here anyway. It might be a joke to you, but your cousin Rudolph liable to kill somebody. White folks or niggers, don't make no difference. . . . "

Todd saw the man turn red with anger. Graves looked down upon him, chuckling.

"This nigguh belongs in a straitjacket, too, boys. I knowed that the minit Jeff's kid said something 'bout a nigguh flyer. You all know you cain't let the nigguh git up that high without his going crazy. The nigguh brain ain't built right for high altitudes. . . . "

Todd watched the drawling red face, feeling that all the unnamed horror and obscenities that he had ever imagined stood materialized before him.

"Let's git outta here," one of the attendants said.

Todd saw the other reach toward him, realizing for the first time that he lay upon a stretcher as he yelled.

"Don't put your hands on me!"

They drew back, surprised.

"What's that you say, nigguh?" asked Graves.

He did not answer and thought that Graves's foot was aimed at his head. It landed on his chest and he could hardly breathe. He coughed helplessly, seeing Graves's lips stretch taut over his yellow teeth, and tried to shift his head. It was as though a half-dead fly was dragging slowly across his face and a bomb seemed to burst within him. Blasts of hot, hysterical laughter tore from his chest, causing his eyes to pop and he felt that the veins in his neck would surely burst. And then a part of him stood behind it all, watching the surprise in Graves's red face and his own hysteria. He thought he would never stop, he would laugh himself to death. It rang in his ears like Jefferson's laughter and he looked for him, centering his eyes desperately upon his face, as though somehow he had become his sole salvation in an insane world of outrage and humiliation. It brought a certain relief. He was suddenly aware that although his body was still contorted it was an echo that no longer rang in his ears. He heard Jefferson's voice with gratitude.

"Mister Graves, the Army done tole him not to leave his airplane."

"Nigguh, Army or no, you gittin' off my land! That airplane can stay 'cause it was paid for by taxpayers' money. But you gittin' off. An' dead or alive, it don't make no difference to me."

Todd was beyond it now, lost in a world of anguish.

"Jeff," Graves said, "you and Teddy come and grab holt. I want you to take this here black eagle over to that nigguh airfield and leave him."

Jefferson and the boy approached him silently. He looked away, realizing and doubting at once that only they could release him from his overpowering sense of isolation.

They bent for the stretcher. One of the attendants moved toward Teddy.

"Think you can manage it, boy?"

"I think I can, suh," Teddy said.

"Well, you better go behind then, and let yo' pa go ahead so's to keep that leg elevated."

He saw the white men walking ahead as Jefferson and the boy carried him along in silence. Then they were pausing and he felt a hand wiping his face; then he was moving again. And it was as though he had been lifted out of his isolation, back into the world of men. A new current of communication flowed between the man and boy and himself. They moved him gently. Far away he heard a mockingbird liquidly calling. He raised his eyes, seeing a buzzard poised unmoving in space. For a moment the whole afternoon seemed suspended and he waited for the horror to seize him again. Then like a song within his head he heard the boy's soft humming and saw the dark bird glide into the sun and glow like a bird of flaming gold.

QUESTIONS

1. In what sense (or senses) is Todd "flying home"?
2. Some of this narration is present action, some memory, some dream and delirium. Can you always tell which is which? What are the signs?
3. After the child reaches for and misses the real airplane, he dreams that his grandmother warns "Yo' arms too short / To box with God." What connection does this incident have with the larger story?
4. Why does Todd become angry at the story the old man tells about flying to heaven?
5. Describe the narrative perspective. Is it effective?

HALFWAY TO THE MOON*

Vasily Aksenov (1932–   )

"Would you like some coffee?"

"Why not?"

"Turkish?"

"Huh?"

"Turkish coffee," the waitress sang out triumphantly and sailed past down the aisle.

"Nonsense, just one more skirt!" Kirpichenko consoled himself, chasing her with his eyes.

"Nonsense!" he thought to himself, scowling from his headache. "Only fifty

*Translated by Thomas P. Whitney.

minutes left anyway. They're just about to announce the flight—and you might as well never have seen this city. What a city! Some hick town! Not Moscow! Maybe some people like it, but as for me I couldn't care less. The hell with it! Maybe the next time I'll like it."

The evening before he had lots to drink. Not enough to get really drunk, to pass out, but plenty. Yesterday evening, the evening before too, and the one before that. All because of that snake, Banin, and his darling little sister. They certainly took you for a ride on your own well-earned rubles!

Kirpichenko had run into Banin three days before at the airport in Yuzhny. He hadn't even known their vacations came at the same time. He really didn't have much to do with Banin. At the lumber trust they were always making a big to-do over him, always shouting: "Banin, Banin! Catch up with Banin!" Valery Kirpichenko couldn't care less. Of course, he knew the name and was acquainted with him—the electrician Banin. But in sum total he wasn't much of an impressive personality notwithstanding all the to-do made over him on holidays.

"So that's Banin! There's Banin for you!"

In the lumber camp were fellows who worked no worse than Banin, who could even give him a handicap in all departments. But, after all, with the management it's always the same: it grabs hold of one person and dances around him. There's no cause to envy such chaps. They should be pitied. In Bayukly there was a certain Sinitsyn who also worked on a diesel just as Kirpichenko did. The newspaper reporters discovered him and made a big to-do about him. The fellow at first collected his newspaper clippings but soon couldn't stand it any more and took off for Okha. With Banin it was all right. He took it in his stride. He went about neat and bright. He kept himself in line, that little type, kept himself quiet and inconspicuous. Last spring 200 girls from the mainland, seasonal workers, had been brought to the fish cannery. The boys had gotten together to pay them a visit. They climbed up on the truck, hollered, made a racket. They looked: in the rear corner sat Banin, so quietly, not to be seen or heard.

"That Banin . . ."

At the airdrome in Yuzhny Banin had thrown himself upon Kirpichenko as if they were the best of friends. Literally gasping with gladness, he howled he was terribly glad, that he had a sister in Khabarovsk, that she had girl friends—swell gals. He began to describe the whole thing in detail and Kirpichenko nearly fainted. After the departure of the girls from the fish combine Valery had seen only two women the whole winter, more exactly two elderly crocodiles—the timekeeper and the cook.

"Oh you, Banin, Banin."

In the airplane Banin had kept shouting at the pilots:

"Hey, you pilots, pile on more coal!"

It was impossible to recognize him, he was such a comedian.

"I should have really given you the works, Banin!"

The house in which Banin's sister lived just barely stuck up above the top of a snowdrift. The humped street was evidently cleaned by special machines, and the piles of snow had not been carried off and almost buried the little bits of houses. The houses lay as if in a trench. In the crackling frosty air light blue pillars of smoke rose above the chimneys. Antennae and poles with birdhouses stuck up at all angles. This was really a village street. Even difficult to believe that just beyond on the hill a trolleybus route ran along the avenue.

Kirpichenko had already gone a little bit off his rocker while still at the airport when he saw a long line of automobiles with green lights and the glass wall of a restaurant through whose frosty patterns glimmered a sedate jazz orchestra. In the *gastronome*—the store for fancy foods, drinks, and delicacies—on the main street he let himself go completely. He pulled out of his pockets green fifty-ruble notes. He shouted with laughter and shoveled up armfuls of canned goods. The gay Banin laughed even more than Kirpichenko but also picked up some cheese and canned goods and then got into a conversation with the head of the section and bought a sausage besides. Banin and Kirpichenko rolled up to the little house in a taxi piled high with all kinds of food and bottles of Chechen-Ingush cognac. One might say they did not arrive at his sister's house with empty hands.

Kirpichenko entered the room—his shaggy cap almost at ceiling level—and dropped the foodstuffs onto the bed covered with a white pique bedspread. He straightened up and right away saw his red, lean, unpleasant face in the mirror.

Larisa, Banin's sister, such a plump little nurse to judge from her appearance, was already unbuttoning his coat and repeating:

"My brother's friends are my friends."

Then she put on her own coat and galoshes and went out somewhere.

Banin went to work with the corkscrew and the knife, and Kirpichenko for a time looked around. The room was decently furnished: a chiffonier with a mirror, a chest of drawers, a radio-phonograph. Over the chest of drawers hung a portait of Marshal Voroshilov, a prewar picture, without shoulder boards, with his marshal's stars in tabs, and next to it a certificate in a frame: "To a distinguished marksman of the guards for successes in defense and political preparation. Signed: Administration for Labor Camps of the Northeast."

"My father's," Banin explained.

"And what was he, a camp guard?"

"He was and he went," Banin sighed. "He died."

However he was not sad very long—he began to twirl some records. The records were familiar: "Rio-Rita," "Black Sea Seagull," and one in French—three men singing in different voices so magnificently it seemed as if they had traveled the whole wide world over and seen things no one else would ever see.

Larisa returned with her girl friend called Toma and began to put the table in order. She ran back and forth to the kitchen, brought pickles and mushrooms while Toma sat in the corner as if she were made of stone and kept her hands on her knees. How things would work out with her Kirpichenko didn't know. He tried not to look at her and as soon as he took a glance he began to see spots in his eyes and got faint.

Banin exclaimed with nervous joyfulness:

"Our hands are frozen, our feet are chill. Isn't it time to drink our fill! I beg you to sit down at the table, Mesdames et Messieurs."

Kirpichenko was smoking long *papirosy*—Russian cigarettes with long hollow paper mouthpieces—a brand called "Forty years of the Soviet Ukraine." He was smoking and puffing out smoke rings. Larisa was roaring with laughter, trying to catch them on her little finger. The atmosphere in the low-ceilinged room was stuffy. Kirpichenko's feet grew damp in his felt boots and steam evidently was rising from them. Banin was dancing with Toma. She had not said one word all evening. Banin whispered in her ear and she made a crooked smile with tightly closed mouth. The girl had a well-proportioned figure. From beneath her nylon blouse gleamed rose-colored undergarments. In front of Kirpichenko in dark orange-colored circles, swam walls, the portrait of Voroshilov, the little elephant on the chest of drawers. The smoke rings he was blowing jumped about, and Larisa's finger described signals in the air.

Banin and Toma went into the other room. The lock clicked quietly behind them.

"Ha, ha, ha!" laughed Larisa, "Why didn't you dance, Valery? You should have danced."

The record came to an end and silence fell. Larisa looked at him, squinting her crossed brown eyes. From the neighboring room came the sound of subdued squeals.

"From you, Valery, there's only food and no fun," Larisa giggled, and Kirpichenko suddenly saw she was pushing thirty and that she had been around.

She slipped up to him and whispered:

"Let's dance."

"But I'm wearing felt boots," he said.

"That's all right."

He got up. She put on a record and in the room smelling of tomatoes and Chechen-Ingush cognac the three Frenchmen sang in different voices about the fact they had traveled the wide world over and seen sights such as you would never see.

"Not that one," Kirpichenko said hoarsely.

"Which one?" cried out Larisa. "Just think, he has to have a special record! Putting on airs!"

She was circling around the room. Her skirt was swishing about her legs. Kirpichenko took off the record and put on "Rio-Rita." Then he stepped over to Larisa and seized her by the shoulders.

That's always the way, when fingers slip along your neck in the darkness, it seems as if they are the fingers of the moon, no matter what cheap broad is lying beside you . . . just the same afterwards, when fingers touch your neck—and you should slap her hands—it seems as if . . . Indeed what doesn't it seem, with the moon up high, looking through the frosty glass like a runny egg yolk? But that never ever happens really, and don't you fool yourself into thinking that it ever will. You're already 29, and for all of your disorganized and organized, all of your beautiful, hot, cold life, such as it is, when fingers touch your neck in the darkness, it seems as if . . .

"How old are you?" the woman asked.

"Thirty-two."

"You're a truck driver?"

"Well?"

"Do you make much?"

Valery lit a match and saw her round face with her brown crossed eyes.

"And what's it to you?" He lit up.

The next morning Banin shuffled around the room in warm Chinese-style underwear. He squeezed dill pickles into a glass and threw them, wrinkled and squeezed out, into a saucer. Toma sat in a corner, neat and silent, just as yesterday evening. After breakfast she and Larisa went to work.

"Well, so you had fun? How about it, Valery?" Banin laughed ingratiatingly. "Well all right, so let's go to a movie."

They saw three motion pictures in a row and then went back to the *gastronome* where Kirpichenko really let himself go again: He dragged out of his pocket red ruble notes and piled into Banin's arms cheeses and canned goods.

This went on for three days and three nights in a row and that morning when the girls had left, Banin all of a sudden had put it to him:

"So I guess we're relatives, you and I, Valery?"

Kirpichenko choked on the pickle brine he was drinking.

"Whaatt?"

"What-what!" Banin yelled back. "Are you sleeping with my sister or not? Come on, let's talk about when we're going to have a wedding, or else I'm going to turn you in to the bosses. For immorality, do you understand?"

Kirpichenko hit him on the cheekbone from all the way across the table. Banin flew off into a corner and got up immediately and grabbed hold of a chair.

"You're a bastard!" Kirpichenko growled and renewed his attack. "Marry every cheap broad!"

"Concentration camp scum!" screeched Banin. "Convict!" And he threw the chair at him.

And right then and there Kirpichenko gave it to him. When Banin, grabbing his sheepskin coat, jumped out into the yard, Kirpichenko, his teeth chattering from anger, agitation, and wild loneliness, dragged out his suitcase, threw his duds in it, put on his overcoat and on top of it his sheepskin coat, pulled out of his pocket his photo (dressed in necktie and his very best sports shirt) and quickly wrote: "To Larisa with affectionate memories," put it in Larisa's room on her pillow and left. In the courtyard Banin, spitting and swearing, let loose an angry dog on him. Kirpichenko kicked the dog aside and went on out of the gate.

"Well, how was your coffee?" the waitress asked him.

"Not so bad, it helps," Kirpichenko sighed and stroked her arm.

"Careful there," the waitress smiled.

At that moment they announced his flight.

With lightness in his heart and with strong, long strides Kirpichenko went out onto the airfield to get away farther, farther, farther! There are some years of life one doesn't have a vacation just to hang around in a suffocating hut in the sticks and eat Dutch cheese. There are characters who spend their whole vacation in such shacks, but he was not a fool. He would go to Moscow, would buy three new suits and some shoes in the Central Department Store and then go farther, farther, to the Black Sea. "Seagull, Black Sea seagull, my dream," he hummed to himself. He would eat *chebureki* and wander around in his jacket without an overcoat.

He saw himself at that moment as he looked to others—big, strong, in an overcoat and sheepskin coat over it, in a cap of muskrat fur, in felt boots. Stepping ahead. One broad with whom he had an affair the previous summer told him he had the face of an Indian chief. And she was chief of a geological expedition, what about that! She was a good one, too, Anna Petrovna, even had a degree. She had written him letters and he had answered: "How do you do, respected Anna Petrovna! Valery Kirpichenko is writing you . . ."—and all kinds of other stuff and nonsense.

A large crowd of passengers had already gathered at the turnstile. Not far away Larisa was jumping up and down in her boots. Her face was white and bluish, her lips bright red, her brooch which represented a running deer and which she was wearing on her collar looked terribly stupid.

"Why did you come?" Kirpichenko asked.

Larisa could hardly say it: "To see you off."

"Listen, stop it!" he cut her off with his hand. "So you and your brother worked me over for three days—all right, but don't try to make love out of it . . ."

Larisa wept and Valery got frightened.

"All right, all right . . ."

"Yes we worked you over," Larisa babbled. "So we worked you over . . . Well, all right . . . I know what you think about me . . . That's what I am . . . And so because of that I can't love you, is that it?"

"Cut it out."

"But I will, I will!" Larisa almost shouted. "You, Valya," she moved up close to him, "You're not like the rest . . ."

"I'm just the same as everyone, only I can . . ." And Kirpichenko slowly dragged out his lips into a smile.

Larisa turned away and wept still harder. All her pitiful body shook.

"Well, come on, come on . . ." Kirpichenko was taken aback and stroked her shoulder.

Then the crowd moved out onto the airfield. And Kirpichenko went along, without looking behind, thinking of the fact that he was sorry for Larisa, that she had become no longer a stranger to him but, as a matter of fact, every one of them became no longer a stranger, such was his silly character, but then you forgot them, and everything was normal, normal. Normal—and an end to it.

He stepped along in the crowd of passengers, looking at the enormous airplane waiting for him, gleaming in the sun, and quick, quick he forgot everything—the whole nasty mess of his three-day stay here and those fingers on his neck. He wouldn't fall for that. It was always that way. He would not fall for that. He would not be broken. Some who were not just cheap broads had even come his way. He had had fine women too. Anna Petrovna, the scientist, for example—a really good person. They had all fallen in love with him, and Valery understood this took place not because of his cruelty but for quite a different reason: perhaps, because of his silence, perhaps, because every one of them wanted to become something special for him, because they, evidently, felt in those minutes that he was groping forward like a blind man. But he always said to himself: You can't buy me with those tricks. You can't break me. It's over and that's an end to it. And everything is normal. Normal.

The airplane was frighteningly enormous: It was enormous and heavy like a cruiser. Kirpichenko had not yet flown on such airplanes and at this moment his breath was simply taken away with delight. That's what he loved—technology. He climbed up the high set of steps leading to the plane. The stewardess in a blue suit and cap examined his ticket and told him where his seat was. The seat was in the first salon but there was already some character sitting in it, a bespectacled type in a pie-shaped cap.

"Beat it," Kirpichenko said peacefully and showed the bespectacled character his ticket.

"Couldn't you sit in my seat?" asked the bespectacled character. "I get sick in the rear."

"Beat it, I'm telling you," Kirpichenko barked at him.

"Couldn't you be more polite," the bespectacled type was hurt. For some reason he didn't get up.

Kirpichenko grabbed his cap from off him and threw it into the back of the airplane, in the direction of his rightful seat. In general he showed him where—beat it back there, take your place according to your ticket.

"Citizen, why are you being disorderly?" asked the stewardess.

"Take it easy," said Kirpichenko.

The bespectacled individual in extreme consternation went to look for his cap and Kirpichenko took his rightful seat.

He took off his sheepskin coat and put it at his feet. Consolidated himself, so to speak, in his place.

The passengers came into the airplane one after another. It seemed as if they would never stop. Light music was playing in the plane. Sunny, frosty steam rolled into the hatchway. The stewardesses busily ran up and down the passageway. All of them were in identical dark-blue suits, long-legged, and in high heels. Kirpichenko read the newspaper. About disarmament and about Berlin, about preparation for the championship in Chile, and about the problem of retaining snow on collective farm fields.

An elderly woman, wrapped up in a shawl was sitting by the window, and a rosy-cheeked sailor took the seat next to Kirpichenko. He kept joking:

"Lady, have you made your will?" And he shouted to the stewardess: "Girl, who shall I give my will to?"

It was Kirpichenko's luck to travel with such comedians! Finally, the door of the hatchway was slammed shut and a red sign lit up: "Don't smoke. Fasten your seat belts." And there was something in English, perhaps the same, and perhaps something different. Perhaps, just the opposite: "Please smoke. Don't fasten your seat belts." Kirpichenko did not know English.

A woman's voice came over the loudspeaker system:

"I ask your attention! The commander of the airplane welcomes aboard the passengers of the Soviet liner TU–114. Our airplane-giant is traveling on the route from Knabarovsk to Moscow. The flight will take place at a height of 9,000 meters with a speed of 700 kilometers an hour. The elapsed time will be 8 hours 30 minutes. I thank you for your attention."

And then in English: "Kurly, shurly, lops, drops . . . Senk you."

"That's how it should be done," said Kirpichenko with satisfaction and winked at the sailor. "On the nose."

"And what did you think," said the sailor just as if the airplane were his own personal property, as if he had arranged the whole thing: an announcement in two languages and all kinds of other conveniences.

The airplane was pulled out to the take-off strip. The elderly female sat concentrated. Outside the porthole the airport buildings swam by.

"May I take your overcoat?" asked the stewardess.

It was the same one who had rebuked Kirpichenko. He looked at her and was stupefied. She smiled. Over him hung her smiling face and her dark hair, no, not black, just dark, and it must be, soft, and with a dense exact hairdo just like fur, like mouton, like nylon, like all the treasures of the world. Her fingers touched the fur collar of his sheepskin coat. Such fingers don't exist. No, all of that exists in magazines, and that means not only there, but it just doesn't happen that there is all of that and also such a smile and the voice of the very first woman in the world—that just doesn't happen.

"You understand, she took my sheepskin coat," said Kirpichenko smiling stupidly at the sailor, and the sailor winked at him and said proudly:

"Is the personnel satisfactory? So-so."

She returned and took the woman's sheepskin coat, the sailor's leather coat and Kirpichenko's overcoat. She pressed all the coats at once to her divine body and said:

"Buckle your seat belts, comrades."

The motors roared. The elderly woman at the window shrank in fear and quietly crossed herself. The sailor teased her without mercy, looking all the time out of the corner of his eye to see whether Kirpichenko was laughing. But Kirpichenko was craning his neck, following the girl, that girl, that very girl, as she carried off to somewhere the overcoats and jackets. Then she reappeared with a tray and offered them all candies, and maybe not really candies but gold nuggets, or pills for the heart, and then, with the plane already aloft, she went about to everyone with water, with soft drinks and mineral water, that very same water which flows from the highest and cleanest waterfalls. And then she disappeared.

"Would you like to play cards?" asked the sailor. "We could get a game together."

The red sign went out and Kirpichenko understood he could smoke. He got up and went to the front of the plane, into the small section behind the curtain from which billows of smoke were rolling.

"We are reporting information on the flight," the loud speaker said. "Altitude 9,000 meters, speed 750 kilometers an hour. Temperature of the air outside the ship minus 58 degrees Centigrade. I thank you for your attention."

Below, a long distance away, there flowed past a stony, lifeless country. Kirpichenko shuddered, picturing to himself, how in that icy space over cruel, desert land there floated a metal cigar filled with human warmth, politeness, cigarette smoke, the hollow rumble of conversation and laughter, jokes (tear them off and throw them away) with mineral water, the drops of a waterfall from fertile regions. And he was sitting there and smoking and somewhere in the tail, and maybe in the middle of the plane a woman who does not exist in actual fact, of a kind to whom for you it is a long long ways, as far as to the moon, was walking back and forth.

He began to think about his life and to reminisce. He had never before reminisced. Unless, when he had to say something, he had told some little story or other. But now all of a sudden he thought: "It's the fourth time I have rolled across the whole country and the first time I have paid my own way. What fun!"

Previously all of his trips had been at the expense of the government. In 1939 when Valery was still a very small boy, their whole collective farm—in the Stavropol region—had been resettled in the Far Eastern Maritime Province. It was a long trip. He remembered that trip only a little. Sour milk and sour cabbage

soup. His mother doing the wash in the corner of a heated freight car and hanging the laundry outside. It fluttered outside the window, like flags, and then began to rattle and bang because it had frozen from the cold, and he sang the song:

> "The planes are flying high, high, high,
> The pilots are looking at us from the sky . . ."

His mother had died during the war, and his father had "fallen the death of
the brave"—perished in the last days of the war—in the Kurile Islands in 1945.
In the orphanage Valery finished seven years of school, then went to vocational
training and worked in a mine. As the phrase went: "He gave his country coal,
small coal, but much . . ." In 1950 he went to do his military service. Again he
traveled across the entire country—this time to the Baltic area. In the army he
had become a truck driver and after demobilization he and a friend of his had
settled down in Novorossisk on the Black Sea. A year later he was picked up by
the police. Some scoundrel had stolen spare parts from the garage, but they
hadn't spent long on figuring out on whom to pin the blame. They had sent him
up as "the person, materially to be held responsible for the loss." He got three
years and was sent to a labor camp in Sakhalin. He had spent a year and a half in
the prison camp. He had been freed on points, and later they removed his conviction from his record. From then on he had worked in the lumber camp. He
liked the work. He earned lots of money. His work was to haul trailers loaded
with timber up through the pass and then to come on down on all his brakes. He
drank straight alcohol, saw movies, went to the dances in summer at the fish cannery. He lived in a dormitory. He had always lived in dormitories, barracks,
camps. Cots, cots, simple two-storied bunks, board beds, in bins . . . He had no
friends but many acquaintances. He was feared. He was not one to fool with. He
didn't stop to consider before giving you a black eye. And at work he was a leader. He loved technology. He remembered the machines on which he had worked
as one remembers friends: "Ivan Willys" in the army, and then a tractor, and
then a one-and-a-half-ton GAZ, and a "Tatra," and now his present diesel . . . In
towns, in Yuzhno-Sakhalinsk, in Poronaisk, in Korsakov, he sometimes stopped
at a corner and looked into the windows of new apartment houses, at the stylish
floor lamps and curtains, and this filled him with alarm. He did not count his
years and only recently had come to understand that in a few months he would
pass thirty. Take it easy! In Moscow he would buy himself three suits and a green
hat and would go south, like some engineer or technician. Sewn in his underdrawers were letters of credit, money—a whole carload. It would be gay in the
south. Everything was normal. Normal—and that was all!

He got up and went back to look for her. Where had she gone? Really! The
passengers had dry throats and there she was standing and gossiping in English
with some kind of a capitalist.

She was chattering, squinting her eyes, smiling with her mouth. Evidently
she found it pleasant to chatter in English. The capitalist stood next to her, tall
and thin, with a gray crew cut, young in years. His jacket was unbuttoned. From
his belt hung a thin gold chain which disappeared into his pocket. He spoke
with a roll. His words thundered in his mouth just as if they were knocking
against his teeth. We know that kind of conversation!

He: Let's go to San Francisco, darling, and we'll drink whiskey.

She: You are very presumptuous.

He: In banana-lemon Singapore[1] . . . Do you understand?

She: Do you really mean it? When the banana tree bends beneath the wind?

He: And so we climbed up to the 102nd floor. The jazz orchestra there was knocking out boogie-woogie.

Kirpichenko approached and shouldered the capitalist away. The latter was surprised and said: "Ai em saree," which, of course, meant: "Watch it, boy, you're looking for trouble."

"Take it easy," said Kirpichenko. "Peace—friendship."

He knew politics.

The capitalist said something to her over his head, probably: "You choose, me or him, San Francisco or Bayukly."

And she said to him with a smile: "I know this comrade," and, "Leave me, I am a Soviet person."

"What do you want, comrade?" she asked Kirpichenko.

"That," he pointed. "My throat is dry. Could I wet it with something?"

"Let's go," she said, and went ahead like some kind of a nanny goat, as in the cinema, as in a dream. Ah, how he had longed for her while he was smoking there, up in front.

She went ahead like I don't know who and led him into something like a buffet, and maybe to herself at home where there was nobody and where the high sun with peaceful fury shone through the porthole, and maybe, through a window in a new apartment building on the ninth floor. She took a bottle and poured out bubbling water into a glass cup. She raised this little cup, and it caught fire beneath the high sun. And he looked at the girl and he wanted to have her children, but he didn't even picture to himself that it might be possible to do with her what people do when they want to have children. And that was the first time this had ever happened, and he was all of a sudden burning with the unexpected first feeling of happiness.

"What's your name?" he asked with that feeling which he had every time after he had crossed the pass—it was terrifying and everything was behind him.

"Tatyana Viktorovna," she answered. "Tanya."

"And I am Kirpichenko—Valery," he said and reached out his hand. She gave him her fingers and smiled.

"You're an unrestrained comrade."

"Just a trifle," he said blushingly.

For several seconds they looked at each other in silence. She was seized with laughter. She struggled with herself and he also struggled, but all of a sudden he could no longer restrain himself and smiled in such a way as, in all probability, he had never smiled in all his life.

At that moment she was called and she ran down the stairway to the first floor of the plane.

Kirpichenko turned and saw his smiling face in some sort of a mirror: "Some mug you have, Valery," he thought to himself. "Awful. Like a thug. But it seems

---

[1] "In banana-lemon Singapore" and "When the banana tree bends beneath the wind" come from a popular song, "Tango Magnolia."

as if the girl isn't afraid of you. I'm sure she isn't afraid, not a drop."

He went back along the aisle and saw the bespectacled character who had tried before to take over his rightful seat. The bespectacled type was lying back in his armchair with his eyes shut. He had a handsome face, pure marble.

"Listen, friend," Kirpichenko punched him in the shoulder, "do you want to take my seat?"

The bespectacled character opened his eyes and weakly smiled:

"Thank you, I'm all right . . ."

Maybe it wasn't the first time that he had flown on such airplanes, that bespectacled type, and took the seat in the first salon in order to watch how the door into the pilot's cabin opens, and watch there the pilots, watch them scratch themselves, smoke, joke, and laugh, read the newspapers, and now and again look at the instruments.

Tanya began to distribute the meal. She also gave Valery a tray and looked at him as at an acquaintance.

"And where do you live, Tanya?" he asked.

And he thought to himself: "Tanya, Ta-Nya, T-A-N-Y-A."

"In Moscow," she answered and left.

Kirpichenko ate and it seemed to him that his steak was thicker than for the rest, that his apple was larger, that she had given him more bread. And then she brought tea.

"So that means you are a Muscovite?" again he asked.

"Uh-huh," she answered smartly and went away.

"It's all for nothing that you're trying so hard, fellow countryman," smirked the sailor. "There's probably a well-dressed little character waiting for her in Moscow."

"Take it easy," said Kirpichenko with an even and broad sensation of his well-being and happiness.

But, after all, such flights do not last forever and it is a characteristic of airplanes to descend from up above, from such great altitudes. And work shifts come to an end, official duties are completed, and they give you back your overcoat, and the thin little fingers bring you your sheepskin coat, and eyes wander somewhere already far away, and everything slowly runs down just like the spring in toys, and everything becomes flat like a page from a magazine. "Aeroflot—your representative during trips by air"—how wonderful—all those manicures, high-heeled slippers, and hairdos.

No, no, no, nothing runs down, nothing becomes flat, although already we are rolling along the ground . . .

Such a rush began and the dark blue stewardess's cap was already somewhere distant . . .

"Don't dally, citizen . . ."

"Let's get a move on, fellow countryman . . ."

"Boys, there she is, and Moscow . . ."

"Moscow, that's something . . ."

"Well, move along with you, really . . ."

Still not understanding what was taking place with him, Kirpichenko emerged with the sailor from the airplane, descended the stair, and climbed up into an autobus. The autobus rolled along to the airport building and soon the

"Soviet liner TU–114, the airplane-giant," the flying fortress of his incomprehensible hopes, had disappeared from sight.

The taxi flew along the broad, broad highway. There was traffic in two lanes. Trucks, vans, dump trucks pressed over to the edge, and passenger cars went at high speed and passed them as if they were standing still. And then the forest came to an end and Kirpichenko and the sailor saw the rosy thousand-eyed apartment blocks of the South-West. The sailor began to fidget and put his hand on Valery's shoulder.

"The capital! Well, how about it, Valery!"

"Listen, is our airplane going to fly back now?" Kirpichenko asked.

"Of course. They'll fly tomorrow."

"With the same crew?"

The sailor whistled derisively.

"Stop it. A wonder indeed—a modern skirt. There are a million in Moscow. Don't be crazy."

"I was simply asking." Kirpichenko murmured.

"Where are you going, boys?" asked the chauffeur.

"Let's go to GUM!" Kirpichenko barked and immediately forgot all about the airplane.

The car was already rolling along the streets of Moscow.

In GUM—the Main Department Store—he quickly bought three suits—dark blue, gray, and brown. He kept on the new brown suit and wrapped his old suit made four years before in a tailor shop in Korsakov into a bundle and left it in a booth in the toilet. The sailor picked out a piece of gabardine cloth for a mackintosh for himself and said he would have it made up in Odessa. Then in the *gastronome* they each drank a bottle of champagne and went on an excursion to the Kremlin. Then they went to the Hotel Natsional to have lunch and ate the devil only knew what—julien—and drank a drink called "KS." There were many girls here looking like Tanya, and maybe Tanya herself came here. Maybe she was sitting with them at a table and pouring out "Narzan" mineral water for him, running to the kitchen and seeing how his steak was being cooked. In any case the capitalist was here. Kirpichenko waved his hand to him, and he stood up and bowed. Then they went out onto the street and each drank still another bottle of champagne. Tanya manifested furious activity on Gorky Street. She jumped from out of trolley busses and ran into stores, promenaded with *pijons*[2] on the other side of the street, and even smiled from out of show windows. Kirpichenko and the sailor, firmly arm-in-arm, went along Gorky Street and smiled. The sailor sang:

"Ma-da-gas-car, my country . . ."

This was the hour when twilight was already thickening but when street lights had not yet gone on. Yes, and at the end of the street, at the edge of the earth, spring was burning. Yes, this was the land of hopes come true. They were surprised that the girls shied away from them.

Later, everywhere there were closed doors, queues, and it wasn't possible to get in anywhere. They thought about the question of a place to spend the night, took a taxi, and went to the airport at Vnukovo. They rented a double room in

[2] Young women, prostitutes.

the airport hotel and only on seeing the white sheets did Kirpichenko understand how tired he was. He pulled his new suit off and threw himself onto the
bed.

In an hour the sailor woke him up. He was running about the room, scraping
his cheeks with an electric razor called "Sputnik,"[3] and chirping, crowing, and
gasping:

"Let's go, Valery! I got acquainted with such girls, ah, ah! Get up, let's go and
visit them! They live here in the dormitory. It's a sure thing, brother. No difficulties . . . I have a nose for that . . . Get up, get out of bed! Ma-da-gas-car . . ."

"Stop cackling as if you'd laid an egg!" said Kirpichenko, taking a cigarette off
the bedstand and lighting up.

"Are you coming or not?" the sailor asked, already at the door.

"Turn out the light," Kirpichenko asked him.

The light went out and the moonlit rectangle of the window was immediately
projected onto the wall, intersected by the frames and the rocking shadows of
naked branches. It was silent. Somewhere far off a phonograph was playing.
Through the wall he could hear: "Who has a six?"—and heard a blow on the table. Then an airplane thundered in to land. Kirpichenko smoked and pictured to
himself how she was lying alongside him, how they were lying together, the
two of them, already after everything, and how her fingers were stroking his
neck. No, that is what this world really is, not make-believe, but actually real, because everything incomprehensible that took place with him in childhood when
goose pimples ran along his whole body and in his youth—the Far Eastern rolling knolls imprinted with the rosy fire of the dawn, and the sea in the darkness,
and the melting snow, and fatigue after work, and Saturday and Sunday morning—this is she.

"Well, that's the thing," he thought to himself and again he was overcome
with an even and broad sensation of well-being and happiness. He was happy
that this had happened to him. He feared only one thing, that a century would
go by and that he would forget her face and voice.

The sailor came into the room. He undressed and lay down, took a cigarette
from off the bedstand, lit up and sadly sang:

"Ma-da-gas-car, my country, here like everywhere the spring is in
flower . . . Oh, the devil take it," he said heartily, "Well, what a life! Eternal passage . . ."

"How many years have you been a sailor?" Kirpichenko asked.

"From half a century seven," the sailor answered and again sang:

> "Madagascar across the sea
> Madagascar my own country
> Madagascar of thee I sing
> Madagascar where blooms the spring.
> We're people too
> And we love like you.
> Black is our skin
> But our blood's not thin."

[3] After the first man-made satellite, launched by Russia, October 1957.

"Write me out the words," Kirpichenko asked him.

They lit the light and the sailor dictated to Valery the words of this entrancing song. Kirpichenko loved such songs very much.

The next day they had their tickets stamped: Kirpichenko for Adler on the Black Sea, the sailor for Odessa. They had their breakfast. Kirpichenko bought a book by Chekhov and the magazine *Ogonyek* in a kiosk.

"Listen," said the sailor, "she really does have a good-looking girl friend. Maybe we could go and see them in Moscow?"

Kirpichenko sat down in an armchair and opened the book.

"No," he said. "You go, just the two of you, and I'm going to sit here and read this politics."

The sailor waved out a naval signal: "Your signal read. Wish you success. Continuing on course."

All day long Kirpichenko hung around the airport, but he didn't see Tanya. In the evening he saw the sailor off for Odessa, well, and they each drank a bottle of champagne, and then he saw the sailor's girl friend to her dormitory, and returned to the airport, went to the ticket window and bought a ticket on the airplane-giant TU-114, Flight No. 901, Moscow to Khabarovsk.

In the airplane it was all just as it had been before. The announcements in two languages and other conveniences, but there was no Tanya. There was another crew. There were girls just as young, just as beautiful, just like Tanya, but nevertheless they were not the first one—Tanya was the first one. All the rest of this breed came after her.

In the morning Kirpichenko was in Khabarovsk and one hour later he again flew to Moscow, already on another airplane. But Tanya was not there either.

And so he flew and kept flying on TU-114 airplanes, at a height of 9,000 meters, at a speed of 750 kilometers an hour. The temperature of the air outside hovered between minus 50 to 60 degrees Centigrade. All the apparatus worked normally.

He already knew by face almost all of the stewardesses on this line and even some of the pilots. He was afraid they might remember him.

He was afraid they might even take him for a spy.

He changed his suits. One trip in the dark blue, another in the brown, a third in the gray.

He opened up his underdrawers and took out the letters of credit and put them into his jacket pocket. The letters of credit grew less and less in number.

Still there was no Tanya.

There was a bright high sun, and the sunrises and the sunsets took place above a snowy cloudy waste. There was a moon and it seemed to be close. It in fact was not so far away.

On occasion he got lost in time and space and stopped changing his watch. Khabarovsk seemed to him to be a suburb of Moscow and Moscow a new district of Khabarovsk.

He read very much. He never in his life had read so much. He never in his life had thought so much.

He never in his life had wept.

He never in his life had taken such a first-class restful vacation.

In Moscow spring had begun. Drops from those very same high and pure waterfalls fell down into his collar. He bought himself a gray scarf in large black checks.

In case of a meeting he had prepared a gift for Tanya—a perfume set, "May First," and a piece of material for a dress.

I met him in the building of Khabarovsk Airport. He was sitting in an armchair, one leg crossed over the other and reading a book by Stanyukovich. On the arm of the armchair hung a string bag, full of oranges. On the cover of the book a clipper flew under hurricane sails.

"Are you a sailor?" he asked me, looking over my leather coat.

"No."

I stared at his surprising face which aroused misgiving and he read a few lines more and again asked:

"Are you sorry you're not a sailor?"

"Of course it's too bad," I said.

"I also regret it," he laughed. "I have a friend who is a sailor. Here he sent me a radiogram from the sea."

He showed me the radiogram.

"Uh-huh," I said.

And he asked me, changing over to the intimate personal pronoun:

"What's your year of birth?"

"Nineteen thirty-two," I answered him.

He was all aglow:

"Listen, you and I are the same age!"

The coincidence was really phenomenal and I shook his hand.

"Maybe you live in Moscow?" he asked.

"You guessed it," I answered. "In Moscow."

"Maybe you have an apartment, yes? A wife, a kid, yes? And the other stuff and nonsense?"

"You guessed it. That's just the way things are."

"Let's go and have our breakfast, what?"

I was all ready to go with him but right at that moment they announced my flight. I was flying to Petropavlovsk. We exchanged addresses and I went off to my plane. I went along the airfield, bending beneath the wind, and I thought to myself: "What a strange chap."

And during that time he looked at his watch, took up his string bag, and went out. He took a taxi and went to the city. He and the taxi driver together just barely found that humped-up village street because he had not remembered its name. The houses on that street were all like one another. In all the courtyards enormous dogs were barking, and he was a little at a loss. Finally, he remembered that particular little house. He got out of the car, hung his string bag with its oranges on the fence, covered it with a newspaper so that passers-by or neighbors should not steal this treasure, and returned to the car.

"Come on, chief, speed it up! I don't want to be late for my plane."

"Where are you flying?" asked the driver.

"To Moscow, to the capital."

Tanya he finally saw two days later at the airport in Khabarovsk, when he was already returning home to Sakhalin, when all of his letters of credit had already come to an end and there remained only several red bills in his pocket. She was in a white fur coat, belted about with a leather strap. She was laughing, eating candies, getting them out of her bag, offering them to the other girls who were also laughing. He immediately lost all his strength and sat down on his suitcase. He watched how Tanya was giving away candies, taking off their wrappings, and how all the other girls were doing exactly the same, and he did not understand why they were all standing in one place, laughing and going nowhere. Then he realized spring had come, that it was now a spring night and that the moon over the airdrome was like an orange, that now at this moment it was not cold, and that one could stand just this way and simply look at the light and laugh and take thought for a moment with a candy in one's mouth . . .

"What are you doing, Kirpichenko?" His Sakhalin acquaintance, Manyevich, touched him on the shoulder. Manyevich was also returning from vacation. "Let's go! They've already announced the flight."

"Manyevich, do you know how many kilometers it is to the moon?" Kirpichenko asked.

"Evidently you must have had too much to drink during your vacation," Manyevich said angrily and went away.

Kirpichenko caught him out on the field.

"You're a young specialist, Manyevich," he said beggingly, looking at Tanya. "You ought to know . . ."

"Well 300,000 maybe," said Manyevich, moving back.

"It's not so far," thought Kirpichenko to himself. "A spitting distance." He looked at Tanya and pictured to himself how he would remember her on the road up to the pass, and on the pass all of a sudden he would forget, he would not be up to that up there, and afterward, at the end of the descent, he would remember her again and from then on he would remember her for the entire evening and night and in the morning he would awaken with thoughts of her.

Then he got up from his suitcase.

QUESTIONS

1. Which details best establish verisimilitude? Do any seem pointless or superfluous?
2. Like "Flying Home," this story contains a first-person passage, but the "I" here is not the major character, nor is he in any way closely connected with him. Do you see any point to the passage?
3. Characterize Kirpichenko. Does he seem especially Russian, or could he just as well be an American? Is his experience possible to an American?
4. The story appears to focus on Kirpichenko's infatuation with the stewardess. What purpose is served by the earlier pages?

CHAPTER 6

Metaphor, Symbol, and Allegory

A *metaphor* is an implied comparison between unlike objects, a *symbol*, an object or act made to carry extra meaning that similar things do not carry. An *allegory* is a narrative in which a set of metaphoric or symbolic equivalents work consistently together to suggest interpretation on both a literal and figurative level. Used extensively in poetry (we discuss them more fully in our poetry section, pp. 596–618), metaphor, symbol, and allegory are also important to many prose fictions. In each of the following stories the author forces comparisons upon us. Metaphors are heavy, symbols insistent, or allegories carefully controlled. We may not agree precisely upon interpretation, but we see clearly the direction the author is pointing.

Joyce Cary's "Evangelist" defines nicely the difference between a world perceived objectively and one perceived metaphorically, and at the same time reminds us that metaphoric vision is not reserved for writers alone. His character, John Pratt, sees houses at the beginning as "old kept women on the look out for some city lecher" and at the end as "veteran soldiers in line, meeting with stoic pride the injuries of time." The story makes clear that Pratt's mood affects his vision, as mood does the vision of all of us.

EVANGELIST
Joyce Cary (1888–1957)

John Pratt, fifty-five, on holiday at the sea, gets up one sunny morning, looks from the window, says, 'It won't last,' and picks from his seven suits the only dark one. He dresses himself with care, and eats for breakfast one piece of dry toast.

'A touch of liver,' he says to himself, takes his umbrella and a bowler,[1] and goes for his morning walk along the Parade.[2]

'Why the bowler?' he asks himself. 'I'm not going back to town.' And sudden-

---

[1] Hat.
[2] Public promenade, in this instance at a seaside resort.

ly it strikes him that he is bored. 'Impossible,' he says; 'I've only been here a week and my regular time is always a fortnight.'

He looks about him to discover some usual source of pleasure in this charming old place; and immediately he is seized, possessed, overwhelmed with boredom, with the most malignant and hopeless of all boredoms, holiday boredom. It rises from his stomach, it falls from the lukewarm air. Everything in sight is instantly perceived as squalid, mercenary, debased by mean use and vulgar motives. The Regency façades[3] whose delicate taste he has so much admired, which bring him year after year to a place neither smart nor quiet, seem to leer at him with the sly, false primness of old kept women on the look out for some city lecher, willing to set off cracked plaster against lewd dexterity.

He looks at the sea for freshness. But it appears thick, greasy: he murmurs with horror, 'The cesspool of the whole earth.' He sees the drains discharging from a million towns, the rubbish unbucketed from ten thousand years of ships, wrecks full of corpses; the splash of glitter beyond the pier is like the explosion of some hidden corruption. The ozone comes to his nose like a stench.

He sees from the distance a friend, the Colonel in his light-grey suit, stepping briskly. He is whirling his stick—it is plain that he is in his usual high spirits.

Pratt crosses the road to avoid him. A taxi hoots in an angry and distracted manner, but he does not hurry, he would rather be killed than betray the dignity of his despair. The taxi's brakes squawk like Donald Duck—it comes to a stop at his elbow—a furious young man with upstanding black hair and red-rimmed eyes thrusts out his neck and bawls insults. Bystanders laugh and stare. Pratt does not turn his head or quicken his walk. He accepts these humiliations as appropriate to such a morning in such a world.

The shopping housewives with their predatory eyes and anxious wrinkled foreheads fill him with a lofty and scornful pity, as for insects generated by a conspiracy of gases and instinct to toil in blind necessity for the production of more insects.

Yes, he thinks, humanity is like the maggots on a perishing carcass. Its history is the history of maggots; the fly, the buzz, the coupling of flies, the dropping of their poison on every clean thing, the hunt for some ordure, some corpse, the laying of eggs, and another generation of maggots. Foulness upon foulness. Tides of disgust and scorn rise in his soul; he stalks more grandly; he has become a giant for whom all history is meaner than the dust on his boot soles.

Suddenly he is accosted by a red-faced man, an hotel acquaintance, who starts out of a shop and seizes him by the hand—impossible to avoid this person. The red-faced man is in a fluster. Has Mr. Pratt seen the news? Is there going to be a war, is this it? Should he sell out his investments and pay his debts; should he fetch back his family from abroad?

Pratt draws himself up and out of mere wrath at this intrusion, utters in severe tones such banalities as amaze his own ears. If war comes, he says, it will come, and if not, then not. There are good arguments on both sides of the question. If we believe our freedom is worth defending, then we should be ready to defend it at all costs. For faith is not faith, not what we truly believe, unless we are prepared to die for it. And in a conflict of faith those alone who are prepared

---

[3] Early nineteenth-century house fronts.

to die for what they believe deserve to win. As for bombs, one can die but once. One will die anyhow and possibly much worse than by a bomb.

And all these panic-mongers, are they not more than foolish? Panic is not only useless, it is a treachery—a defeat—an invitation to the enemy within as well as without.

The red-faced man is taken aback by this rigmarole of eloquence. He listens with surprised attention in his green eyes—then with respect. Pratt's unmoved solemnity, his severe tone born of scornful indifference, impress him. He ejaculates murmurs of approval. He says that this is just what he himself has always thought. And this is probably true. He could scarcely have escaped such reflections.

At last he is greatly moved. He turns even redder, his gooseberry eyes shine. He grasps Pratt's hand with fervour and a glance that means, 'This is an important, a solemn occasion. You are a bigger man than I took you for. Men of sense and courage, like ourselves, should be better acquainted.' He departs exalted.

Pratt walks on alone, his step is still majestic but full of spring. He is exhilarated; he looks at the sea and it appears to him noble in its vastness, transcendent in its unconcern, venerable in its intimation of glorious deeds. The houses are like veteran soldiers in line, meeting with stoic pride the injuries of time. The housewives, striving, saving for their families, wear the brows of angels; the battered angels roughly carved on some primitive church. He salutes with heroic elation a world made for heroes. He perceives with joy that it is going to be a fine day, that he is hungry. He whirls his umbrella.

QUESTIONS
1. List the most telling metaphors.
2. Does Cary describe Pratt himself metaphorically, or with complete objectivity?
3. How many ironies are in the story? Which are most important?
4. Is this a realistic story?
5. Is it an allegory?

One message of the following story may be found in its closing words: "You may rise in the world without the help of your kinsman, Major Molineux." It is a complex story, however, rich in metaphor and symbol, and carrying strong allegorical overtones.

MY KINSMAN, MAJOR MOLINEUX
Nathaniel Hawthorne (1804–1864)

After the kings of Great Britain had assumed the right of appointing the colonial governors, the measures of the latter seldom met with the ready and generous approbation which had been paid to those of their predecessors, under the original charters. The people looked with most jealous scrutiny to the exercise of power which did not emanate from themselves, and they usually rewarded their rulers with slender gratitude for the compliances by which, in softening their instructions from beyond the sea, they had incurred the reprehension of those who gave them. The annals of Massachusetts Bay will inform us, that of six governors in the space of about forty years from the surrender of the old charter, under James II, two were imprisoned by a popular insurrection; a third, as Hutchinson[1] inclines to believe, was driven from the province by the whizzing of a musket-ball; a fourth, in the opinion of the same historian, was hastened to his grave by continual bickerings with the House of Representatives; and the remaining two, as well as their successors, till the revolution, were favored with few and brief intervals of peaceful sway. The inferior members of the court party, in times of high political excitement, led scarcely a more desirable life. These remarks may serve as a preface to the following adventures, which chanced upon a summer night, not far from a hundred years ago. The reader, in order to avoid a long and dry detail of colonial affairs, is requested to dispense with an account of the train of circumstances that had caused much temporary inflammation of the popular mind.

It was near nine o'clock of a moonlight evening, when a boat crossed the ferry with a single passenger, who had obtained his conveyance at that unusual hour by the promise of an extra fare. While he stood on the landing-place, searching in either pocket for the means of fulfilling his agreement, the ferryman lifted a lantern, by the aid of which, and the newly risen moon, he took a very accurate survey of the stranger's figure. He was a youth of barely eighteen years, evidently country-bred, and now, as it should seem, upon his first visit to town. He was clad in a coarse gray coat, well worn, but in excellent repair; his under garments were durably constructed of leather, and fitted tight to a pair of serviceable and well-shaped limbs; his stockings of blue yarn were the incontrovertible work of a mother or a sister; and on his head was a three-cornered hat, which in its better days had perhaps sheltered the graver brow of the lad's father. Under his left arm was a heavy cudgel formed of an oak sapling, and retaining a part of the hardened root; and his equipment was completed by a wallet, not so abundantly stocked as to incommode the vigorous shoulders on which it hung. Brown, curly hair, well-shaped features, and bright, cheerful eyes were nature's gifts, and worth all that art could have done for his adornment.

The youth, one of whose names was Robin, finally drew from his pocket the half of a little province bill of five shillings, which, in the depreciation in that sort of currency, did but satisfy the ferryman's demand, with the surplus of a sexangular piece of parchment, valued at three pence. He then walked foward into the town, with as light a step as if his day's journey had not already exceeded thirty miles, and with as eager an eye as if he were entering London city, instead of the little metropolis of a New England colony. Before Robin had proceeded far, however, it occurred to him that he knew not whither to direct his steps; so he paused, and looked up and down the narrow street, scrutinizing the small and mean wooden buildings that were scattered on either side.

"This low hovel cannot be my kinsman's dwelling," thought he, "nor yonder old house, where the moonlight enters at the broken casement; and truly I see none hereabouts that might be worthy of him. It would have been wise to in-

---

[1] Thomas Hutchinson (1711–1780), governor of Massachusetts and Colonial historian.

quire my way of the ferryman, and doubtless he would have gone with me, and earned a shilling from the Major for his pains. But the next man I meet will do as well."

He resumed his walk, and was glad to perceive that the street now became wider, and the houses more respectable in their appearance. He soon discerned a figure moving on moderately in advance, and hastened his steps to overtake it. As Robin drew nigh, he saw that the passenger was a man in years, with a full periwig of gray hair, a wide-skirted coat of dark cloth, and silk stockings rolled above his knees. He carried a long and polished cane, which he struck down perpendicularly before him at every step; and at regular intervals he uttered two successive hems, of a peculiarly solemn and sepulchral intonation. Having made these observations, Robin laid hold of the skirt of the old man's coat, just when the light from the open door and windows of a barber's shop fell upon both their figures.

"Good evening to you, honored sir," said he, making a low bow and still retaining his hold of the skirt. "I pray you tell me whereabouts is the dwelling of my kinsman, Major Molineux."

The youth's question was uttered very loudly; and one of the barbers, whose razor was descending on a well-soaped chin, and another who was dressing a Ramillies wig,[2] left their occupations, and came to the door. The citizen, in the mean time, turned a long-favored countenance upon Robin, and answered him in a tone of excessive anger and annoyance. His two sepulchral hems, however, broke into the very centre of his rebuke, with most singular effect, like a thought of the cold grave obtruding among wrathful passions.

"Let go my garment, fellow! I tell you, I know not the man you speak of. What! I have authority, I have—hem, hem—authority; and if this be the respect you show for your betters, your feet shall be brought acquainted with the stocks by daylight, tomorrow morning!"

Robin released the old man's skirt, and hastened away, pursued by an ill-mannered roar of laughter from the barber's shop. He was at first considerably surprised by the result of his question, but, being a shrewd youth, soon thought himself able to account for the mystery.

"This is some country representative," was his conclusion, "who has never seen the inside of my kinsman's door, and lacks the breeding to answer a stranger civilly. The man is old, or verily—I might be tempted to turn back and smite him on the nose. Ah, *Robin, Robin!* even the barber's boys laugh at you for choosing such a guide! You will be wiser in time, friend Robin."

He now became entangled in a succession of crooked and narrow streets, which crossed each other, and meandered at no great distance from the waterside. The smell of tar was obvious to his nostrils, the masts of vessels pierced the moonlight above the tops of the buildings, and the numerous signs, which Robin paused to read, informed him that he was near the centre of business. But the streets were empty, the shops were closed, and lights were visible only in the second stories of a few dwelling-houses. At length, on the corner of a narrow lane, through which he was passing, he beheld the broad countenance of a Brit-

---

[2] A wig with a long plaited tail and a bow at top and bottom, fashionable after Marlborough's victory at Ramillies, Belgium, in 1706.

ish hero swinging before the door of an inn, whence proceeded the voices of many guests. The casement of one of the lower windows was thrown back, and a very thin curtain permitted Robin to distinguish a party at supper, round a well-furnished table. The fragrance of the good cheer steamed forth into the outer air, and the youth could not fail to recollect that the last remnant of his travelling stock of provision had yielded to his morning appetite, and that noon had found and left him dinnerless.

"Oh, that a parchment three-penny might give me a right to sit down at yonder table!" said Robin, with a sigh. "But the Major will make me welcome to the best of his victuals; so I will even step boldly in, and inquire my way to his dwelling."

He entered the tavern, and was guided by the murmur of voices and the fumes of tobacco to the public-room. It was a long and low apartment, with oaken walls, grown dark in the continual smoke, and a floor which was thickly sanded, but of no immaculate purity. A number of persons—the larger part of whom appeared to be mariners, or in some way connected with the sea—occupied the wooden benches, or leather-bottomed chairs, conversing on various matters, and occasionally lending their attention to some topic of general interest. Three or four little groups were draining as many bowls of punch, which the West India trade had long since made a familiar drink in the colony. Others, who had the appearance of men who lived by regular and laborious handicraft, preferred the insulated bliss of an unshared potation, and became more taciturn under its influence. Nearly all, in short, evinced a predilection for the Good Creature in some of its various shapes, for this is a vice to which, as Fast Day sermons of a hundred years ago will testify, we have a long hereditary claim. The only guests to whom Robin's sympathies inclined him were two or three sheepish countrymen, who were using the inn somewhat after the fashion of a Turkish caravansary; they had gotten themselves into the darkest corner of the room, and heedless of the Nicotian[3] atmosphere, were supping on the bread of their own ovens, and the bacon cured in their own chimney-smoke. But though Robin felt a sort of brotherhood with these strangers, his eyes were attracted from them to a person who stood near the door, holding whispered conversation with a group of ill-dressed associates. His features were separately striking almost to grotesqueness, and the whole face left a deep impression on the memory. The forehead bulged out into a double prominence, with a vale between; the nose came boldly forth in an irregular curve, and its bridge was of more than a finger's breadth; the eyebrows were deep and shaggy, and the eyes glowed beneath them like fire in a cave.

While Robin deliberated of whom to inquire respecting his kinsman's dwelling, he was accosted by the innkeeper, a little man in a stained white apron, who had come to pay his professional welcome to the stranger. Being in a second generation from a French Protestant, he seemed to have inherited the courtesy of his parent nation; but no variety of circumstances was ever known to change his voice from the one shrill note in which he now addressed Robin.

"From the country, I presume, sir?" said he, with a profound bow. "Beg leave to congratulate you on your arrival, and trust you intend a long stay with us.

[3] From nicotine.

Fine town here, sir, beautiful buildings, and much that may interest a stranger. May I hope for the honor of your commands in respect to supper?"

"The man sees a family likeness! The rogue has guessed that I am related to the Major!" thought Robin, who had hitherto experienced little superfluous civility.

All eyes were now turned on the country lad, standing at the door, in his worn three-cornered hat, gray coat, leather breeches, and blue yarn stockings, leaning on an oaken cudgel, and bearing a wallet on his back.

Robin replied to the courteous innkeeper, with such an assumption of confidence as befitted the Major's relative. "My honest friend," he said, "I shall make it a point to patronize your house on some occasion, when"—here he could not help lowering his voice—"when I may have more than a parchment three-pence in my pocket. My present business," continued he, speaking with lofty confidence, "is merely to inquire my way to the dwelling of my kinsman, Major Molineux."

There was a sudden and general movement in the room, which Robin interpreted as expressing the eagerness of each individual to become his guide. But the innkeeper turned his eyes to a written paper on the wall, which he read, or seemed to read, with occasional recurrences to the young man's figure.

"What have we here?" said he, breaking his speech into little dry fragments. " 'Left the house of the subscriber, bounden servant, Hezekiah Mudge,—had on, when he went away, gray coat, leather breeches, master's third-best hat. One pound currency reward to whosoever shall lodge him in any jail in the providence.' Better trudge, boy; better trudge!"

Robin had begun to draw his hand towards the lighter end of the oak cudgel, but a strange hostility in every countenance induced him to relinquish his purpose of breaking the courteous innkeeper's head. As he turned to leave the room, he encountered a sneering glance from the bold-featured personage whom he had before noticed; and no sooner was he beyond the door, than he heard a general laugh, in which the innkeeper's voice might be distinguished, like the dropping of small stones into a kettle.

"Now, is it not strange," thought Robin, with his usual shrewdness,—"is it not strange that the confession of an empty pocket should outweigh the name of my kinsman, Major Molineux? Oh, if I had one of those grinning rascals in the woods, where I and my oak sapling grew up together, I would teach him that my arm is heavy though my purse be light!"

On turning the corner of the narrow lane, Robin found himself in a spacious street, with an unbroken line of lofty houses on each side, and a steepled building at the upper end, whence the ringing of a bell announced the hour of nine. The light of the moon, and the lamps from the numerous shop-windows, discovered people promenading on the pavement, and amongst them Robin had hoped to recognize his hitherto inscrutable relative. The result of his former inquiries made him unwilling to hazard another, in a scene of such publicity, and he determined to walk slowly and silently up the street, thrusting his face close to that of every elderly gentleman, in search of the Major's lineaments. In his progress, Robin encountered many gay and gallant figures. Embroidered garments of showy colors, enormous periwigs, gold-laced hats, and silver-hilted swords glided past him and dazzled his optics. Travelled youths, imitators of the European fine gentlemen of the period, trod jauntily along, half dancing to the fashionable tunes which they hummed, and making poor Robin ashamed of his quiet and natural gait. At length, after many pauses to examine the gorgeous display of goods in the shop-windows, and after suffering some rebukes for the impertinence of his scrutiny into people's faces, the Major's kinsman found himself near the steepled building, still unsuccessful in his search. As yet, however, he had seen only one side of the thronged street; so Robin crossed, and continued the same sort of inquisition down the opposite pavement, with stronger hopes than the philosopher seeking an honest man, but with no better fortune. He had arrived about midway towards the lower end, from which his course began, when he overheard the approach of some one who struck down a cane on the flag-stones at every step, uttering at regular intervals, two sepulchral hems.

"Mercy on us!" quoth Robin, recognizing the sound.

Turning a corner, which chanced to be close at his right hand, he hastened to pursue his researches in some other part of the town. His patience now was wearing low, and he seemed to feel more fatigue from his rambles since he crossed the ferry, than from his journey of several days on the other side. Hunger also pleaded loudly with him, and Robin began to balance the propriety of demanding, violently, and with lifted cudgel, the necessary guidance from the first solitary passenger whom he should meet. While a resolution to this effect was gaining strength, he entered a street of mean appearance, on either side of which a row of ill-built houses was straggling towards the harbor. The moonlight fell upon no passenger along the whole extent, but in the third domicile which Robin passed there was a half-opened door, and his keen glance detected a woman's garment within.

"My luck may be better here," said he to himself.

Accordingly, he approached the door, and beheld it shut closer as he did so; yet an open space remained, sufficing for the fair occupant to observe the stranger, without a corresponding display on her part. All that Robin could discern was a strip of scarlet petticoat, and the occasional sparkle of an eye, as if the moonbeams were trembling on some bright thing.

"Pretty mistress," for I may call her so with a good conscience, thought the shrewd youth, since I know nothing to the contrary,—"my sweet pretty mistress, will you be kind enough to tell me whereabouts I must seek the dwelling of my kinsman, Major Molineux?"

Robin's voice was plaintive and winning, and the female, seeing nothing to be shunned in the handsome country youth, thrust open the door, and came forth into the moonlight. She was a dainty little figure, with a white neck, round arms, and a slender waist, at the extremity of which her scarlet petticoat jutted out over a hoop, as if she were standing in a balloon. Moreover, her face was oval and pretty, her hair dark beneath the little cap, and her bright eyes possessed a sly freedom, which triumphed over those of Robin.

"Major Molineux dwells here," said this fair woman.

Now, her voice was the sweetest Robin had heard that night, yet he could not help doubting whether that sweet voice spoke Gospel truth. He looked up and down the mean street, and then surveyed the house before which they stood. It was a small, dark edifice of two stories, the second of which projected over the lower floor, and the front apartment had the aspect of a shop for petty commodities.

"Now, truly, I am in luck," replied Robin, cunningly, "and so indeed is my kinsman, the Major, in having so pretty a housekeeper. But I prithee trouble him to step to the door; I will deliver him a message from his friends in the country, and then go back to my lodgings at the inn."

"Nay, the Major has been abed this hour or more," said the lady of the scarlet petticoat; "and it would be to little purpose to disturb him to-night, seeing his evening draught was of the strongest. But he is a kind-hearted man, and it would be as much as my life's worth to let a kinsman of his turn away from the door. You are the good old gentleman's very picture, and I could swear that was his rainy-weather hat. Also he has garments very much resembling those leather small-clothes. But come in, I pray, for I bid you hearty welcome in his name."

So saying, the fair and hospitable dame took our hero by the hand; and the touch was light, and the force was gentleness, and though Robin read in her eyes what he did not hear in her words, yet the slender-waisted woman in the scarlet petticoat proved stronger than the athletic country youth. She had drawn his half-willing footsteps nearly to the threshold, when the opening of a door in the neighborhood startled the Major's housekeeper, and, leaving the Major's kinsman, she vanished speedily into her own domicile. A heavy yawn preceded the appearance of a man, who, like the Moonshine of Pyramus and Thisbe,[4] carried a lantern, needlessly aiding his sister luminary in the heavens. As he walked sleepily up the street, he turned his broad, dull face on Robin, and displayed a long staff, spiked at the end.

"Home, vagabond, home!" said the watchman, in accents that seemed to fall asleep as soon as they were uttered. "Home, or we'll set you in the stocks by peep of day!"

"This is the second hint of this kind," thought Robin. "I wish they would end my difficulties, by setting me there to-night."

Nevertheless, the youth felt an instinctive antipathy towards the guardian of midnight order, which at first prevented him from asking his usual question. But just when the man was about to vanish behind the corner, Robin resolved not to lose the opportunity, and shouted lustily after him,—

"I say, friend! will you guide me to the house of my kinsman, Major Molineux?"

The watchman made no reply, but turned the corner and was gone; yet Robin seemed to hear the sound of drowsy laughter stealing along the solitary street. At that moment, also, a pleasant titter saluted him from the open window above his head; he looked up, and caught the sparkle of a saucy eye; a round arm beckoned to him, and next he heard light footsteps descending the staircase within. But Robin, being of the household of a New England clergyman, was a good youth, as well as a shrewd one; so he resisted temptation, and fled away.

He now roamed desperately, and at random, through the town, almost ready to believe that a spell was on him, like that by which a wizard of his country had once kept three pursuers wandering, a whole winter night, within twenty paces of the cottage which they sought. The streets lay before him, strange and desolate, and the lights were extinguished in almost every house. Twice, however, little parties of men, among whom Robin distinguished individuals in outlandish attire, came hurrying along; but, though on both occasions, they paused to address him, such intercourse did not at all enlighten his perplexity. They did

---

[4]In Shakespeare's *A Midsummer Night's Dream*.

but utter a few words in some language of which Robin knew nothing, and perceiving his inability to answer, bestowed a curse upon him in plain English and hastened away. Finally, the lad determined to knock at the door of every mansion that might appear worthy to be occupied by his kinsman, trusting that perseverance would overcome, the fatality that had hitherto thwarted him. Firm in this resolve, he was passing beneath the walls of a church, which formed the corner of two streets, when, as he turned into a shade of its steeple, he encountered a bulky stranger, muffled in a cloak. The man was proceeding with the speed of earnest business, but Robin planted himself full before him, holding the oak cudgel with both hands across his body as a bar to further passage.

"Halt, honest man, and answer me a question," said he, very resolutely. "Tell me, this instant, whereabouts is the dwelling of my kinsman, Major Molineux!"

"Keep your tongue between your teeth, fool, and let me pass!" said a deep, gruff voice, which Robin partly remembered. "Let me pass, or I'll strike you to the earth!"

"No, no, neighbor!" cried Robin, flourishing his cudgel, and then thrusting its larger end close to the man's muffled face. "No, no, I'm not the fool you take me for, nor do you pass till I have an answer to my question. Whereabouts is the dwelling of my kinsman, Major Molineux?"

The stranger, instead of attempting to force his passage, stepped back into the moonlight, unmuffled his face, and stared full into that of Robin.

"Watch here an hour, and Major Molineux will pass by," said he.

Robin gazed with dismay and astonishment on the unprecedented physiognomy of the speaker. The forehead with its double prominence, the broad hooked nose, the shaggy eyebrows, and fiery eyes were those which he had noticed at the inn, but the man's complexion had undergone a singular, or, more properly, a twofold change. One side of the face blazed an intense red, while the other was black as midnight, the division line being in the broad bridge of the nose; and a mouth which seemed to extend from ear to ear was black or red, in contrast to the color of the cheek. The effect was as if two individual devils, a fiend of fire and a fiend of darkness, had united themselves to form this infernal visage. The stranger grinned in Robin's face, muffled his party-colored features, and was out of sight in a moment.

"Strange things we travellers see!" ejaculated Robin.

He seated himself, however, upon the steps of the church-door, resolving to wait the appointed time for his kinsman. A few moments were consumed in philosophical speculations upon the species of man who had just left him; but having settled this point shrewdly, rationally, and satisfactorily, he was compelled to look elsewhere for his amusement. And first he threw his eyes along the street. It was of more respectable appearance than most of those into which he had wandered; and the moon, creating, like the imaginative power, a beautiful strangeness in familiar objects, gave something of romance to a scene that might not have possessed it in the light of day. The irregular and often quaint architecture of the houses, some of whose roofs were broken into numerous little peaks, while others ascended, steep and narrow, into a single point, and others again were square; the pure snow-white of some of their complexions, the aged darkness of others, and the thousand sparklings, reflected from bright substances in the walls of many; these matters engaged Robin's attention for a while, and then began to grow wearisome. Next he endeavored to define the forms of distant objects, starting away, with almost ghostly indistinctness, just as his eye appeared to grasp them; and finally he took a minute survey of an edifice which stood on the opposite side of the street, directly in front of the church-door, where he was stationed. It was a large, square mansion, distinguished from its neighbors by a balcony, which rested on tall pillars, and by an elaborate Gothic window, communicating therewith.

"Perhaps this is the very house I have been seeking," thought Robin.

Then he strove to speed away the time, by listening to a murmur which swept continually along the street, yet was scarcely audible, except to an unaccustomed ear like his; it was a low, dull, dreamy sound, compounded of many noises, each of which was at too great a distance to be separately heard. Robin marvelled at this snore of a sleeping town, and marvelled more whenever its continuity was broken by now and then a distant shout, apparently loud where it originated. But altogether it was a sleep-inspiring sound, and, to shake off its drowsy influence, Robin arose, and climbed a window-frame, that he might view the interior of the church. There the moonbeams came trembling in, and fell down upon the deserted pews, and extended along the quiet aisles. A fainter yet more awful radiance was hovering around the pulpit, and one solitary ray had dared to rest upon the open page of the great Bible. Had nature, in that deep hour, become a worshipper in the house which man had builded? Or was that heavenly light the visible sanctity of the place,—visible because no earthly and impure feet were within the walls? The scene made Robin's heart shiver with a sensation of loneliness stronger than he had ever felt in the remotest depths of his native woods; so he turned away and sat down again before the door. There were graves around the church, and now an uneasy thought obtruded into Robin's breast. What if the object of his search, which had been so often and so strangely thwarted, were all the time mouldering in his shroud? What if his kinsman should glide through yonder gate, and nod and smile to him in dimly passing by?

"Oh that any breathing thing were here with me!" said Robin.

Recalling his thoughts from the uncomfortable track, he sent them over forest, hill, and stream, and attempted to imagine how that evening of ambiguity and weariness had been spent by his father's household. He pictured them assembled at the door, beneath the tree, the great old tree, which had been spared for its huge twisted trunk and venerable shade, when a thousand leafy brethren fell. There, at the going down of the summer sun, it was his father's custom to perform domestic worship, that the neighbors might come and join with him like brothers of the family, and that the wayfaring man might pause to drink at the fountain, and keep his heart pure by freshening the memory of home. Robin distinguished the seat of every individual of the little audience; he saw the good man in the midst, holding the Scriptures in the golden light that fell from the western clouds; he beheld him close the book and all rise up to pray. He heard the old thanksgiving for daily mercies, the old supplications for their continuance, to which he had so often listened in weariness, but which were now among his dear remembrances. He perceived the slight inequality of his father's voice when he came to speak of the absent one; he noted how his mother turned her face to the broad and knotted trunk; how his elder brother scorned, because the beard was rough upon his upper lip, to permit his features to be moved; how the younger sister drew down a low hanging branch before her eyes; and how the little one of all, whose sports had hitherto broken the decorum of the scene, understood the prayer for her playmate, and burst into clamorous grief. Then he saw them go in at the door; and when Robin would have entered also, the latch tinkled into its place, and he was excluded from his home.

"Am I here, or there?" cried Robin, starting; for all at once, when his thoughts had become visible and audible in a dream, the long, wide, solitary street shone out before him.

He aroused himself, and endeavored to fix his attention steadily upon the large edifice which he had surveyed before. But still his mind kept vibrating between fancy and reality; by turns, the pillars of the balcony lengthened into the tall, bare stems of pines, dwindled down to human figures, settled again into their true shape and size, and then commenced a new succession of changes. For a single moment, when he deemed himself awake, he could have sworn that a visage—one which he seemed to remember, yet could not absolutely name as his kinsman's—was looking towards him from the Gothic window. A deeper sleep wrestled with and nearly overcame him, but fled at the sound of footsteps along the opposite pavement. Robin rubbed his eyes, discerned a man passing at the foot of the balcony, and addressed him in a loud, peevish, and lamentable cry.

"Hallo, friend! must I wait here all night for my kinsman, Major Molineux?"

The sleeping echoes awoke, and answered the voice; and the passenger, barely able to discern a figure sitting in the oblique shade of the steeple, traversed the street to obtain a nearer view. He was himself a gentleman in the prime, of open, intelligent, cheerful, and altogether prepossessing countenance. Perceiving a country youth, apparently homeless and without friends, he accosted him in a tone of real kindness, which had become strange to Robin's ears.

"Well, my good lad, why are you sitting here?" inquired he. "Can I be of service to you in any way?"

"I am afraid not, sir," replied Robin, despondingly; "yet I shall take it kindly, if you'll answer me a single question. I've been searching, half the night, for one Major Molineux; now, sir, is there really such a person in these parts, or am I dreaming?"

"Major Molineux! The name is not altogether strange to me," said the gentleman, smiling. "Have you any objection to telling me the nature of your business with him?"

Then Robin briefly related that his father was a clergyman, settled on a small salary, at a long distance back in the country, and that he and Major Molineux were brothers' children. The Major, having inherited riches, and acquired civil and military rank, had visited his cousin, in great pomp, a year or two before; had manifested much interest in Robin and an elder brother, and, being childless himself, had thrown out hints respecting the future establishment of one of them in life. The elder brother was destined to succeed to the farm which his father cultivated in the interval of sacred duties; it was therefore determined that Robin should profit by his kinsman's generous intentions, especially as he seemed to be rather the favorite, and was thought to possess other necessary endowments.

"For I have the name of being a shrewd youth," observed Robin, in this part of his story.

"I doubt not you deserve it," replied his new friend, good-naturedly; "but pray proceed."

"Well, sir, being nearly eighteen years old, and well grown, as you see," continued Robin, drawing himself up to his full height, "I thought it high time to begin in the world. So my mother and sister put me in handsome trim, and my father gave me half the remnant of his last year's salary, and five days ago I started for this place, to pay the Major a visit. But, would you believe it, sir! I crossed the ferry a little after dark, and have yet found nobody that would show me the way to his dwelling; only, an hour or two since, I was told to wait here, and Major Molineux would pass by."

"Can you describe the man who told you this?" inquired the gentleman.

"Oh, he was a very ill-favored fellow, sir," replied Robin, "with two great bumps on his forehead, a hook nose, fiery eyes; and, what struck me as the strangest, his face was of two different colors. Do you happen to know such a man, sir?"

"Not intimately," answered the stranger, "but I chanced to meet him a little time previous to your stopping me. I believe you may trust his word, and that the Major will very shortly pass through this street. In the mean time, as I have a singular curiosity to witness your meeting, I will sit down here upon the steps and bear you company."

He seated himself accordingly, and soon engaged his companion in animated discourse. It was but of brief continuance, however, for a noise of shouting, which had long been remotely audible, drew so much nearer that Robin inquired its cause.

"What may be the meaning of this uproar?" asked he. "Truly, if your town be always as noisy, I shall find little sleep while I am an inhabitant."

"Why, indeed, friend Robin, there do appear to be three or four riotous fellows abroad to-night," replied the gentleman. "You must not expect all the stillness of your native woods here in our street. But the watch will shortly be at the heels of these lads and"—

"Ay, and set them in the stocks by peep of day," interrupted Robin, recollecting his own encounter with the drowsy lantern-bearer, "But, dear sir, if I may trust my ears, an army of watchmen would never make head against such a multitude of rioters. There were at least a thousand voices went up to make that one shout."

"May not a man have several voices, Robin, as well as two complexions?" said his friend.

"Perhaps a man may; but Heaven forbid that a woman should!" responded the shrewd youth, thinking of the seductive tones of the Major's housekeeper.

The sounds of a trumpet in some neighboring street now became so evident and continual, that Robin's curiosity was strongly excited. In addition to the shouts, he heard frequent bursts from many instruments of discord, and a wild and confused laughter filled up the intervals, Robin rose from the steps, and looked wistfully towards a point whither people seemed to be hastening.

"Surely, some prodigious merry-making is going on," exclaimed he. "I have laughed very little since I left home, sir, and should be sorry to lose an opportunity. Shall we step round the corner by that darkish house, and take our share of the fun?"

"Sit down again, sit down, good Robin," replied the gentleman, laying his hand on the skirt of the gray coat. "You forget that we must wait here for your kinsman; and there is reason to believe that he will pass by, in the course of a very few moments."

The near approach of the uproar had now disturbed the neighborhood; windows flew open on all sides; and many heads, in the attire of the pillow, and confused by sleep suddenly broken, were protruded to the gaze of whoever had leisure to observe them. Eager voices hailed each other from house to house, all demanding the explanation, which not a soul could give. Half-dressed men hurried towards the unknown commotion, stumbling as they went over the stone steps that thrust themselves into the narrow footwalk. The shouts, the laughter, and the tuneless bray, the antipodes of music, came onwards with increasing din, till scattered individuals, and then denser bodies, began to appear round a corner at the distance of a hundred yards.

"Will you recognize your kinsman, if he passes in this crowd?" inquired the gentleman.

"Indeed, I can't warrant it, sir; but I'll take my stand here, and keep a bright lookout," answered Robin, descending to the outer edge of the pavement.

A mighty stream of people now emptied into the street, and came rolling slowly towards the church. A single horseman wheeled the corner in the midst of them, and close behind him came a band of fearful wind-instruments, sending forth a fresher discord now that no intervening buildings kept it from the ear. Then a redder light disturbed the moonbeams, and a dense multitude of torches shone along the street, concealing, by their glare, whatever object they illuminated. The single horseman, clad in a military dress, and bearing a drawn sword, rode onward as the leader, and, by his fierce and variegated countenance, appeared like war personified; the red of one cheek was an emblem of fire and sword; the blackness of the other betokened the mourning that attends them. In his train were wild figures in the Indian dress, and many fantastic shapes without a model, giving the whole march a visionary air, as if a dream had broken forth from some feverish brain, and were sweeping visibly through the midnight streets. A mass of people, inactive, except as applauding spectators, hemmed the procession in; and several women ran along the sidewalk, piercing the confusion of heavier sounds with their shrill voices of mirth or terror.

"The double-faced fellow has his eye upon me," muttered Robin, with an indefinite but an uncomfortable idea that he was himself to bear a part in the pageantry.

The leader turned himself in the saddle, and fixed his glance full upon the country youth, as the steed went slowly by. When Robin had freed his eyes from those fiery ones, the musicians were passing before him, and the torches were close at hand but the unsteady brightness of the latter formed a veil which he could not penetrate. The rattling of wheels over the stones sometimes found its way to his ear, and confused traces of a human form appeared at intervals, and then melted into the vivid light. A moment more, and the leader thundered a command to halt: the trumpets vomited a horrid breath, and then held their peace; the shouts and laughter of the people died away, and there remained only a universal hum, allied to silence. Right before Robin's eyes was an uncovered cart. There the torches blazed the brightest, there the moon shouted out like day, and there, in tar-and-feathery dignity, sat his kinsman, Major Molineux!

He was an elderly man, of large and majestic person, and strong, square features, betokening a steady soul; but steady as it was his enemies had found means to shake it. His face was pale as death, and far more ghastly; the broad forehead was contracted in his agony, so that his eyebrows formed one grizzled line; his eyes were red and wild, and the foam hung white upon his quivering lip. His whole frame was agitated by a quick and continual tremor, which his pride strove to quell, even in those circumstances of overwhelming humiliation. But perhaps the bitterest pang of all was when his eyes met those of Robin; for he evidently knew him on the instant, as the youth stood witnessing the foul disgrace of a head grown gray in honor. They stared at each other in silence, and Robin's knees shook, and his hair bristled, with a mixture of pity and terror. Soon, however, a bewildering excitement began to seize upon his mind; the preceding adventures of the night, the unexpected appearance of the crowd, the torches, the confused din and the hush that followed, the spectre of his kinsman reviled by that great multitude,—all this, and, more than all, a perception of tremendous ridicule in the whole scene, affected him with a sort of mental inebriety. At that moment a voice of sluggish merriment saluted Robin's ears, he turned instinctively, and just behind the corner of the church stood the lantern-bearer, rubbing his eyes, and drowsily enjoying the lad's amazement. Then he heard a peal of laugher like the ringing of silvery bells; a woman twitched his arm, a saucy eye met his, and he saw the lady of the scarlet petticoat. A sharp, dry cachinnation appealed to his memory, and standing on tiptoe in the crowd, with his white apron over his head, he beheld the courteous little innkeeper. And lastly, there sailed over the heads of the multitude a great, broad laugh, broken in the midst by two sepulchral hems, thus, "Haw, haw, haw,—hem, hem,—haw, haw, haw, haw!"

The sound proceeded from the balcony of the opposite edifice, and thither Robin turned his eyes. In front of the Gothic window stood the old citizen, wrapped in a wide gown, his gray periwig exchanged for a nightcap, which was thrust back from his forehead, and his silk stockings hanging about his legs. He supported himself on his polished cane in a fit of convulsive merriment, which manifested itself on his solemn old features like a funny inscription on a tombstone. Then Robin seemed to hear the voices of the barbers, of the guests of the inn, and of all who had made sport of him that night. The contagion was spreading among the multitude, when all at once, it seized upon Robin, and he sent forth a shout of laughter that echoed through the street,—every man shook his sides, every man emptied his lungs, but Robin's shout was the loudest there. The cloud-spirits peeped from their silvery islands, as the congregated mirth went roaring up the sky! The Man in the Moon heard the far bellow. "Oho," quoth he, "the old earth is frolicsome to-night!"

When there was a momentary calm in that tempestuous sea of sound, the leader gave the sign, the procession resumed its march. On they went, like fiends that throng in mockery around some dead potentate, mighty no more, but majestic still in his agony. On they went, in counterfeited pomp, in senseless uproar, in frenzied merriment, trampling all on an old man's heart. On swept the tumult, and left a silent street behind.

"Well, Robin, are you dreaming?" inquired the gentleman, laying his hand on the youth's shoulder.

Robin started, and withdrew his arm from the stone post to which he had instinctively clung, as the living stream rolled by him. His cheek was somewhat pale, and his eye not quite as lively as in the earlier part of the evening.

"Will you be kind enough to show me the way to the ferry?" said he, after a moment's pause.

"You have, then, adopted a new subject of inquiry?" observed his companion, with a smile.

"Why, yes, sir," replied Robin, rather dryly. "Thanks to you, and to my other friends, I have at last met my kinsman, and he will scarce desire to see my face again. I begin to grow weary of a town life, sir. Will you show me the way to the ferry?"

"No, my good friend Robin—not to-night, at least," said the gentleman. "Some few days hence, if you wish it, I will speed you on your journey. Or, if you prefer to remain with us, perhaps, as you are a shrewd youth, you may rise in the world without the help of your kinsman, Major Molineux."

QUESTIONS

1. Summarize Robin's adventure on both a literal and an allegorical level. Which details make it most likely that Hawthorne intended an allegorical meaning? Is the allegory detailed and consistent, or more generalized and suggestive than specific?
2. Can all of the actions be understood literally, or do some make sense only as allegory?
3. Which characters seem most realistic? Which seem most clearly to point to allegory?
4. Observe how important the images of darkness and of light are to the story. Do they point to symbolism?
5. What are some of the themes in addition to the one suggested by the last sentence?

In "Bliss" the omniscient narrator focuses our attention upon the perceptions of Bertha Young, so that we see the world metaphorically and symbolically, as she does. "Why be given a body," Bertha asks, "if you have to keep it shut up in a case like a rare, rare fiddle?" Only at the end do we perceive the dramatic irony that undercuts her vision.

BLISS

Katherine Mansfield   (1888–1923)

Although Bertha Young was thirty she still had moments like this when she wanted to run instead of walk, to take dancing steps on and off the pavement, to bowl a hoop, to throw something up in the air and catch it again, or to stand still and laugh at—nothing—at nothing, simply.

What can you do if you are thirty and, turning the corner of your own street, you are overcome, suddenly, by a feeling of bliss—absolute bliss!—as though you'd suddenly swallowed a bright piece of that late afternoon sun and it burned in your bosom, sending out a little shower of sparks into every particle, into every finger and toe? . . .

Oh, is there no way you can express it without being "drunk and disorderly"? How idiotic civilization is! Why be given a body if you have to keep it shut up in a case like a rare, rare fiddle?

"No, that about the fiddle is not quite what I mean," she thought, running up the steps and feeling in her bag for the key—she'd forgotten it, as usual—and rattling the letter-box. "It's not what I mean, because—Thank you, Mary"—she went into the hall. "Is nurse back?"

"Yes, M'm."

"And has the fruit come?"

"Yes, M'm. Everything's come."

"Bring the fruit up to the dining-room, will you? I'll arrange it before I go up-stairs."

It was dusky in the dining-roon and quite chilly. But all the same Bertha threw off her coat; she could not bear the tight clasp of it another moment, and the cold air fell on her arms.

But in her bosom there was still that bright glowing place—that shower of lit-tle sparks coming from it. It was almost unbearable. She hardly dared to breathe for fear of fanning it higher, and yet she breathed deeply, deeply. She hardly dared to look into the cold mirror—but she did look, and it gave her back a wom-an, radiant, with smiling, trembling lips, with big, dark eyes and an air of listen-ing, waiting for something . . . divine to happen . . . that she knew must happen-. . . infallibly.

Mary brought in the fruit on a tray and with it a glass bowl, and a blue dish, very lovely, with a strange sheen on it as though it had been dipped in milk.

"Shall I turn on the light, M'm?"

"No, thank you. I can see quite well."

There were tangerines and apples stained with strawberry pink. Some yellow pears, smooth as silk, some white grapes covered with a silver bloom and a big cluster of purple ones. These last she had bought to tone in with the new dining-room carpet. Yes, that did sound rather far-fetched and absurd, but it was really why she had bought them. She had thought in the shop: "I must have some pur-ples ones to bring the carpet up to the table." And it had seemed quite sense at the time.

When she had finished with them and had made two pyramids of these bright round shapes, she stood away from the table to get the effect—and it real-ly was most curious. For the dark table seemed to melt into the dusky light and the glass dish and the blue bowl to float in the air. This, of course in her present mood, was so incredibly beautiful. . . . She began to laugh.

"No, no. I'm getting hysterical." And she seized her bag and coat and ran up-stairs to the nursery.

Nurse sat at a low table giving Little B her supper after her bath. The baby had on a white flannel gown and a blue woollen jacket, and her dark, fine hair was brushed up into a funny little peak. She looked up when she saw her mother and began to jump.

"Now, my lovey, eat it up like a good girl," said Nurse, setting her lips in a way that Bertha knew, and that meant she had come into the nursery at another wrong moment.

"Has she been good, Nanny?"

"She's been a little sweet all the afternoon," whispered Nanny. "We went to the park and I sat down on a chair and took her out of the pram and a big dog came along and put its head on my knee and she clutched its ear, tugged it. Oh, you should have seen her."

Bertha wanted to ask if it wasn't rather dangerous to let her clutch at a strange dog's ear. But she did not dare to. She stood watching them, her hands by her side, like the poor little girl in front of the rich little girl with the doll.

The baby looked up at her again, stared, and then smiled so charmingly that Bertha couldn't help crying:

"Oh, Nanny, do let me finish giving her her supper while you put the bath things away."

"Well, M'm, she oughtn't to be changed hands while she's eating," said Nanny, still whispering. "It unsettles her; it's very likely to upset her."

How absurd it was. Why have a baby if it has to be kept—not in a case like a rare, rare fiddle—but in another woman's arms?

"Oh, I must!" said she.

Very offended, Nanny handed her over.

"Now, don't excite her after her supper. You know you do, M'm. And I have such a time with her after!"

Thank heaven! Nanny went out of the room with the bath towels.

"Now I've got you to myself, my little precious," said Bertha, as the baby leaned against her.

She ate delightfully, holding up her lips for the spoon and then waving her hands. Sometimes she wouldn't let the spoon go; and sometimes, just as Bertha had filled it, she waved it away to the four winds.

When the soup was finished Bertha turned round to the fire. "You're nice—you're very nice!" said she, kissing her warm baby. "I'm fond of you. I like you."

And, indeed, she loved Little B so much—her neck as she bent forward, her exquisite toes as they shone transparent in the firelight—that all her feeling of bliss came back again, and again she didn't know how to express it—what to do with it.

"You're wanted on the telephone," said Nanny, coming back in triumph and seizing *her* Little B.

Down she flew. It was Harry.

"Oh, is that you, Ber? Look here. I'll be late. I'll take a taxi and come along as quickly as I can, but get dinner put back ten minutes—will you? All right?"

"Yes, perfectly. Oh, Harry!"

"Yes?"

What had she to say? She'd nothing to say. She only wanted to get in touch with him for a moment. She couldn't absurdly cry: "Hasn't it been a divine day!"

"What is it?" rapped out the little voice.

"Nothing. *Entendu*,"[1] said Bertha, and hung up the receiver, thinking how more than idiotic civilization was.

They had people coming to dinner. The Norman Knights—a very sound couple—he was about to start a theatre, and she was awfully keen on interior decoration, a young man, Eddie Warren, who had just published a little book of po-

[1] "Agreed" (French).

ems and whom everybody was asking to dine, and a "find" of Bertha's called Pearl Fulton. What Miss Fulton did, Bertha didn't know. They had met at the club and Bertha had fallen in love with her, as she always did fall in love with beautiful women who had something strange about them.

The provoking thing was that, though they had been about together and met a number of times and really talked, Bertha couldn't yet make her out. Up to a certain point Miss Fulton was rarely, wonderfully frank, but the certain point was there, and beyond that she would not go.

Was there anything beyond it? Harry said "No." Voted her dullish, and "cold like all blond women, with a touch, perhaps, of anaemia of the brain." But Bertha wouldn't agree with him; not yet, at any rate.

"No, the way she has of sitting with her head a little on one side, and smiling, has something behind it, Harry, and I must find out what that something is."

"Most likely it's a good stomach," answered Harry.

He made a point of catching Bertha's heels with replies of that kind . . . "liver frozen, my dear girl," or "pure flatulence," or "kidney disease," . . . and so on. For some strange reason Bertha liked this, and almost admired it in him very much.

She went into the drawing-room and lighted the fire; then, picking up the cushions, one by one, that Mary had disposed so carefully, she threw them back on to the chairs and the couches. That made all the difference; the room came alive at once. As she was about to throw the last one she surprised herself by suddenly hugging it to her, passionately, passionately. But it did not put out the fire in her bosom. Oh, on the contrary!

The windows of the drawing-room opened on to a balcony overlooking the garden. At the far end, against the wall, there was a tall, slender pear tree in fullest, richest bloom; it stood perfect, as though becalmed against the jade-green sky. Bertha couldn't help feeling, even from this distance, that it had not a single bud or a faded petal. Down below, in the garden beds, the red and yellow tulips, heavy with flowers, seemed to lean upon the dusk. A grey cat, dragging its belly, crept across the lawn, and a black one, its shadow, trailed after. The sight of them, so intent and so quick, gave Bertha a curious shiver.

"What creepy things cats are!" she stammered, and she turned away from the window and began walking up and down. . . .

How strong the jonquils smelled in the warm room. Too strong? Oh, no. And yet, as though overcome, she flung down on a couch and pressed her hands to her eyes.

"I'm too happy—too happy!" she murmured.

And she seemed to see on her eyelids the lovely pear tree with its wide open blossoms as a symbol of her own life.

Really—really—she had everything. She was young. Harry and she were as much in love as ever, and they got on together splendidly and were really good pals. She had an adorable baby. They didn't have to worry about money. They had this absolutely satisfactory house and garden. And friends—modern, thrilling friends, writers and painters and poets or people keen on social questions—just the kind of friends they wanted. And then there were books, and there was music, and she had found a wonderful little dressmaker, and they were going abroad in the summer, and their new cook made the most superb omelettes. . . .

"I'm absurd. Absurd!" She sat up; but she felt quite dizzy, quite drunk. It must have been the spring.

Yes, it was the spring. Now she was so tired she could not drag herself upstairs to dress.

A white dress, a string of jade beads, green shoes and stockings. It wasn't intentional. She had thought of this scheme hours before she stood at the drawing-room window.

Her petals rustled softly into the hall, and she kissed Mrs. Norman Knight, who was taking off the most amusing orange coat with a procession of black monkeys round the hem and up the fronts.

". . . Why! Why! Why is the middle-class so stodgy—so utterly without a sense of humour! My dear, it's only by a fluke that I am here at all—Norman being the protective fluke. For my darling monkeys so upset the train that it rose to a man and simply ate me with its eyes. Didn't laugh—wasn't amused—that I should have loved. No, just stared—and bored me through and through."

"But the cream of it was," said Norman, pressing a large tortoiseshell-rimmed monocle into his eye, "you don't mind me telling this, Face, do you?" (In their home and among their friends they called each other Face and Mug.) "The cream of it was when she, being full fed, turned to the woman beside her and said: 'Haven't you ever seen a monkey before?' "

"Oh, yes!" Mrs. Norman Knight joined in the laughter. "Wasn't that too absolutely creamy?"

And a funnier thing still was that now her coat was off she did look like a very intelligent monkey—who had even made that yellow silk dress out of scraped banana skins. And her amber ear-rings; they were like little dangling nuts.

"This is a sad, sad fall!" said Mug, pausing in front of Little B's perambulator. "When the perambulator comes into the hall—" and he waved the rest of the quotation away.

The bell rang. It was lean, pale Eddie Warren (as usual) in a state of acute distress.

"It *is* the right house, *isn't* it?" he pleaded.

"Oh, I think so—I hope so," said Bertha brightly.

"I have had such a *dreadful* experience with a taxi-man; he was *most* sinister. I couldn't get him to *stop*. The *more* I knocked and called the *faster* he went. And *in* the moonlight this *bizarre* figure with the *flattened* head *crouching* over the *lit-tle* wheel. . . ."

He shuddered, taking off an immense white silk scarf. Bertha noticed that his socks were white, too—most charming.

"But how dreadful!" she cried.

"Yes, it really was," said Eddie, following her into the drawingroom. "I saw myself *driving* through Eternity in a *timeless* taxi."

He knew the Norman Knights. In fact, he was going to write a play for N. K. when the theatre scheme came off.

"Well, Warren, how's the play?" said Norman Knight, dropping his monocle and giving his eye a moment in which to rise to the surface before it was screwed down again.

And Mrs. Norman Knight: "Oh, Mr. Warren, what happy socks!"

"I *am* so glad you like them," said he, staring at his feet. "They seem to have got so *much* whiter since the moon rose." And he turned his lean sorrowful young face to Bertha. "There *is* a moon, you know."

She wanted to cry: "I am sure there is—often—often!"

He really was a most attractive person. But so was Face, crouched before the fire in her banana skins, and so was Mug, smoking a cigarette and saying as he flicked the ash: "Why doth the bridegroom tarry?"

"There he is, now."

Bang went the front door open and shut. Harry shouted: "Hullo, you people. Down in five minutes." And they heard him swarm up the stairs. Bertha couldn't help smiling; she knew how he loved doing things at high pressure. What, after all, did an extra five minutes matter? But he would pretend to himself that they mattered beyond measure. And then he would make a great point of coming into the drawing-room, extravagantly cool and collected.

Harry had such a zest for life. Oh, how she appreciated it in him. And his passion for fighting—for seeking in everything that came up against him another test of his power and of his courage—that, too, she understood. Even when it made him just occasionally, to other people, who didn't know him well, a little ridiculous perhaps. . . . For there were moments when he rushed into battle where no battle was. . . . She talked and laughed and positively forgot until he had come in (just as she had imagined) that Pearl Fulton had not turned up.

"I wonder if Miss Fulton has forgotten?"

"I expect so," said Harry. "Is she on the 'phone?"

"Ah! There's a taxi, now," And Bertha smiled with that little air of proprietorship that she always assumed while her women finds were new and mysterious. "She lives in taxis."

"She'll run to fat if she does," said Harry coolly, ringing the bell for dinner. "Frightful danger for blond women."

"Harry—don't," warned Bertha, laughing up at him.

Came another tiny moment, while they waited, laughing and talking, just a trifle too much at their ease, a trifle too unaware. And then Miss Fulton, all in silver, with a silver fillet binding her pale blond hair, came in smiling, her head a little on one side.

"Am I late?"

"No, not at all," said Bertha. "Come along." And she took her arm and they moved into the dining-room.

What was there in the touch of that cool arm that could fan—fan—start blazing—blazing—the fire of bliss that Bertha did not know what to do with?

Miss Fulton did not look at her; but then she seldom did look at people directly. Her heavy eyelids lay upon her eyes and the strange half smile came and went upon her lips as though she lived by listening rather than seeing. But Bertha knew, suddenly, as if the longest, most intimate look had passed between them—as if they had said to each other: "You too?"—that Pearl Fulton, stirring the beautiful red soup in the grey plate, was feeling just what she was feeling.

And the others? Face and Mug, Eddie and Harry, their spoons rising and falling—dabbing their lips with their napkins, crumbling bread, fiddling with the forks and glasses and talking.

"I met her at the Alpha show—the weirdest little person. She'd not only cut off her hair, but she seemed to have taken a dreadfully good snip off her legs and arms and her neck and her poor little nose as well."

"Isn't she very *liée*[2] with Michael Oat?"

"The man who wrote *Love in False Teeth*?"

"He wants to write a play for me. One act. One man. Decides to commit suicide. Gives all the reasons why he should and why he shouldn't. And just as he has made up his mind either to do it or not to do it—curtain. Not half a bad idea."

"What's he going to call it—'Stomach Trouble'?"

"I *think* I've come across the *same* idea in a lit-tle French review, *quite* unknown in England."

No, they didn't share it. They were dears—dears—and she loved having them there, at her table, and giving them delicious food and wine. In fact, she longed to tell them how delightful they were, and what a decorative group they made, how they seemed to set one another off and how they reminded her of a play by Tchekof![3]

Harry was enjoying his dinner. It was part of his—well, not his nature, exactly, and certainly not his pose—his—something or other—to talk about food and to glory in his "shameless passion for the white flesh of the lobster" and "the green of pistachio ices—green and cold like the eyelids of Egyptian dancers."

When he looked up at her and said: "Bertha, this is a very admirable *soufflée!*" she almost could have wept with child-like pleasure.

Oh, why did she feel so tender towards the whole world tonight? Everything was good—was right. All that happened seemed to fill again her brimming cup of bliss.

And still, in the back of her mind, there was the pear tree. It would be silver now, in the light of poor dear Eddie's moon, silver as Miss Fulton, who sat there turning a tangerine in her slender fingers that were so pale a light seemed to come from them.

What she simply couldn't make out—what was miraculous—was how she should have guessed Miss Fulton's mood so exactly and so instantly. For she never doubted for a moment that she was right, and yet what had she to go on? Less than nothing.

"I believe this does happen very, very rarely between women. Never between men," thought Bertha. "But while I am making the coffee in the drawing-room perhaps she will 'give a sign.' "

What she meant by that she did not know, and what would happen after that she could not imagine.

While she thought like this she saw herself talking and laughing. She had to talk because of her desire to laugh.

"I must laugh or die."

But when she noticed Face's funny little habit of tucking something down the front of her bodice—as if she kept a tiny, secret hoard of nuts there, too—Bertha had to dig her nails into her hands—so as not to laugh too much.

---

[2] Intimate (French).

[3] Anton Chekhov (1860–1904), Russian dramatist.

It was over at last. And: "Come and see my new coffee machine," said Bertha.

"We only have a new coffee machine once a fortnight," said Harry. Face took her arm this time; Miss Fulton bent her head and followed after.

The fire had died down in the drawing-room to a red, flickering "nest of baby phoenixes," said Face.

"Don't turn up the light for a moment. It is so lovely." And down she crouched by the fire again. She was always cold . . . "without her little red flannel jacket, of course," thought Bertha.

At that moment Miss Fulton "gave the sign."

"Have you a garden?" said the cool, sleepy voice.

This was so exquisite on her part that all Bertha could do was to obey. She crossed the room, pulled the curtains apart, and opened those long windows.

"There!" she breathed.

And the two women stood side by side looking at the slender, flowering tree. Although it was so still it seemed, like the flame of a candle, to stretch up, to point, to quiver in the bright air, to grow taller and taller as they gazed—almost to touch the rim of the round, silver moon.

How long did they stand there? Both, as it were, caught in that circle of unearthly light, understanding each other perfectly, creatures of another world, and wondering what they were to do in this one with all this blissful treasure that burned in their bosoms and dropped, in silver flowers, from their hair and hands?

For ever—for a moment? And did Miss Fulton murmur: "Yes. Just *that*." Or did Bertha dream it?

Then the light was snapped on and Face made the coffee and Harry said: "My dear Mrs. Knight, don't ask me about my baby. I never see her. I shan't feel the slightest interest in her until she has a lover," and Mug took his eye out of the conservatory for a moment and then put it under glass again and Eddie Warren drank his coffee and set down the cup with a face of anguish as though he had drunk and seen the spider.

"What I want to do is to give the young men a show. I believe London is simply teeming with first-chop, unwritten plays. What I want to say to 'em is: 'Here's the theatre. Fire ahead.' "

"You know, my dear, I am going to decorate a room for the Jacob Nathans. Oh, I am so tempted to do a fried-fish scheme, with the backs of the chairs shaped like frying pans and lovely chip potatoes embroidered all over the curtains."

"The trouble with our young writing men is that they are still too romantic. You can't put out to sea without being seasick and wanting a basin. Well, why won't they have the courage of those basins?"

"A *dreadful* poem about a *girl* who was *violated* by a beggar *without* a nose in a lit-tle wood. . . ."

Miss Fulton sank into the lowest, deepest chair and Harry handed round the cigarettes.

From the way he stood in front of her shaking the silver box and saying abruptly: "Egyptian? Turkish? Virginian? They're all mixed up," Bertha realized that she not only bored him; he really disliked her. And she decided from the way Miss Fulton said: "No, thank you, I won't smoke," that she felt it, too, and was hurt.

"Oh, Harry, don't dislike her. You are quite wrong about her. She's wonderful, wonderful. And, besides, how can you feel so differently about someone who means so much to me. I shall try to tell you when we are in bed to-night what has been happening. What she and I have shared."

At those last words something strange and almost terrifying darted into Bertha's mind. And this something blind and smiling whispered to her: "Soon these people will go. The house will be quiet—quiet. The lights will be out. And you and he will be alone together in the dark room—the warm bed. . . ."

She jumped up from her chair and ran over to the piano.

"What a pity someone does not play!" she cried. "What a pity somebody does not play."

For the first time in her life Bertha Young desired her husband.

Oh, she'd loved him—she'd been in love with him, of course, in every other way, but just not in that way. And, equally, of course, she'd understood that he was different. They'd discussed it so often. It had worried her dreadfully at first to find that she was so cold, but after a time it had not seemed to matter. They were so frank with each other—such good pals. That was the best of being modern.

But now—ardently! ardently! The word ached in her ardent body! Was this what that feeling of bliss had been leading up to? But then then—

"My dear," said Mrs. Norman Knight, "you know our shame. We are the victims of time and train. We live in Hampstead. It's been so nice."

"I'll come with you into the hall," said Bertha. "I loved having you. But you must not miss the last train. That's so awful, isn't it?"

"Have a whisky, Knight, before you go?" called Harry.

"No, thanks, old chap."

Bertha squeezed his hand for that as she shook it.

"Good night, good-bye," she cried from the top step, feeling that this self of hers was taking leave of them for ever.

When she got back into the drawing-room the others were on the move.

". . . Then you can come part of the way in my taxi."

"I shall be *so* thankful *not* to have to face *another* drive *alone* after my *dreadful* experience."

"You can get a taxi at the rank just at the end of the street. You won't have to walk more than a few yards."

"That's a comfort. I'll go and put on my coat."

Miss Fulton moved towards the hall and Bertha was following when Harry almost pushed past.

"Let me help you."

Bertha knew that he was repenting his rudeness—she let him go. What a boy he was in some ways—so impulsive—so—simple.

And Eddie and she were left by the fire.

"I *wonder* if you have seen Bilks' *new* poem called *Table d'Hôte*," said Eddie softly. "It's *so* wonderful. In the last Anthology. Have you got a copy? I'd *so* like to *show* it to you. It begins with an *incredibly* beautiful line: 'Why Must it Always be Tomato Soup?' "

"Yes," said Bertha. And she moved noiselessly to a table opposite the drawing-room door and Eddie glided noiselessly after her. She picked up the little book and gave it to him; they had not made a sound.

While he looked it up she turned her head towards the hall. And she saw . . . Harry with Miss Fulton's coat in his arms and Miss Fulton with her back turned to him and her head bent. He tossed the coat away, put his hands on her shoulders and turned her violently to him. His lips said: "I adore you," and Miss Fulton laid her moonbeam fingers on his cheeks and smiled her sleepy smile. Harry's nostrils quivered; his lips curled back in a hideous grin while he whispered: "To-morrow," and with her eyelids Miss Fulton said: "Yes."

"Here it is," said Eddie. " 'Why Must it Always be Tomato Soup?' It's so *deeply* true, don't you feel? Tomato soup is so *dreadfully* eternal."

"If you prefer," said Harry's voice, very loud, from the hall, "I can phone you a cab to come to the door."

"Oh, no. It's not necessary," said Miss Fulton, and she came up to Bertha and gave her the slender fingers to hold.

"Good-bye. Thank you so much."

"Good-bye," said Bertha.

Miss Fulton held her hand a moment longer.

"Your lovely pear tree!" she murmured.

And then she was gone, with Eddie following, like the black cat following the grey cat.

"I'll shut up shop," said Harry, extravagantly cool and collected.

"Your lovely pear tree—pear tree—pear tree!"

Bertha simply ran over to the long windows.

"Oh, what is going to happen now?" she cried.

But the pear tree was as lovely as ever and as full of flower and as still.

QUESTIONS

1. The most important symbol is the pear tree. How do we know it is a symbol? Does Bertha perceive it as such? What does it symbolize?
2. Is the revelation at the end credible? Has the story prepared for it in any way?
3. Characterize Bertha. Can you believe in her as a human being?

A LITTLE CLOUD

James Joyce (1882–1941)

Eight years before he had seen his friend off at the North Wall and wished him godspeed. Gallaher had got on. You could tell that at once by his travelled air, his well-cut tweed suit, and fearless accent. Few fellows had talents like his and fewer still could remain unspoiled by such success. Gallaher's heart was in the right place and he had deserved to win. It was something to have a friend like that.

Little Chandler's thoughts ever since lunch-time had been of his meeting with Gallaher, of Gallaher's invitation and of the great city London where Gallaher lived. He was called Little Chandler because, though he was but slightly under the average stature, he gave one the idea of being a little man. His hands were white and small, his frame was fragile, his voice was quiet and his manners were refined. He took the greatest care of his fair silken hair and moustache and used perfume discreetly on his handkerchief. The half-moons of his nails were perfect and when he smiled you caught a glimpse of a row of childish white teeth.

As he sat at his desk in the King's Inns he thought what changes those eight years had brought. The friend whom he had known under a shabby and necessitous guise had become a brilliant figure on the London Press. He turned often from his tiresome writing to gaze out of the office window. The glow of a late autumn sunset covered the grass plots and walks. It cast a shower of kindly golden dust on the untidy nurses and decrepit old men who drowsed on the benches; it flickered upon all the moving figures—on the children who ran screaming along the gravel paths and on everyone who passed through the gardens. He watched the scene and thought of life; and (as always happened when he thought of life) he became sad. A gentle melancholy took possession of him. He felt how useless it was to struggle against fortune, this being the burden of wisdom which the ages had bequeathed to him.

He remembered the books of poetry upon his shelves at home. He had bought them in his bachelor days and many an evening, as he sat in the little room off the hall, he had been tempted to take one down from the bookshelf and read out something to his wife. But shyness had always held him back; and so the books had remained on their shelves. At times he repeated lines to himself and this consoled him.

When his hour had struck he stood up and took leave of his desk and of his fellow-clerks punctiliously. He emerged from under the feudal arch of the King's Inns, a neat modest figure, and walked swiftly down Henrietta Street. The golden sunset was waning and the air had grown sharp. A horde of grimy children populated the street. They stood or ran in the roadway or crawled up the steps before the gaping doors or squatted like mice upon the thresholds. Little Chandler gave them no thought. He picked his way deftly through all that minute vermin-like life and under the shadow of the gaunt spectral mansions in which the old nobility of Dublin had roistered. No memory of the past touched him, for his mind was full of a present joy.

He had never been in Corless's but he knew the value of the name. He knew that people went there after the theatre to eat oysters and drink liqueurs; and he had heard that the waiters there spoke French and German. Walking swiftly by at night he had seen cabs drawn up before the door and richly dressed ladies, escorted by cavaliers, alight and enter quickly. They wore noisy dresses and many wraps. Their faces were powdered and they caught up their dresses, when they touched earth, like alarmed Atalantas.[1] He had always passed without turning his head to look. It was his habit to walk swiftly in the street even by day and whenever he found himself in the city late at night he hurried on his way appre-

---

[1]Atalanta, swift-footed maiden of Greek myth, offered to marry any man who could run fast enough to defeat her in a race.

hensively and excitedly. Sometimes, however, he courted the causes of his fear. He chose the darkest and narrowest streets and, as he walked boldly forward, the silence that was spread about his footsteps troubled him, the wandering silent figures troubled him; and at times a sound of low fugitive laughter made him tremble like a leaf.

He turned to the right towards Capel Street. Ignatius Gallaher on the London Press! Who would have thought it possible eight years before? Still, now that he reviewed the past, Little Chandler could remember many signs of future greatness in his friend. People used to say that Ignatius Gallaher was wild. Of course, he did mix with a rakish set of fellows at that time, drank freely and borrowed money on all sides. In the end he had got mixed up in some shady affair, some money transaction: at least, that was one version of his flight. But nobody denied him talent. There was always a certain . . . something in Ignatius Gallaher that impressed you in spite of yourself. Even when he was out at elbows and at his wits' end for money he kept up a bold face. Little Chandler remembered (and the remembrance brought a slight flush of pride to his cheek) one of Ignatius Gallaher's sayings when he was in a tight corner:

—Half time, now, boys, he used to say light-heartedly. Where's my considering cap?

That was Ignatius Gallaher all out; and, damn it, you couldn't but admire him for it.

Little Chandler quickened his pace. For the first time in his life he felt himself superior to the people he passed. For the first time his soul revolted against the dull inelegance of Capel Street. There was no doubt about it: if you wanted to succeed you had to go away. You could do nothing in Dublin. As he crossed Grattan Bridge he looked down the river towards the lower quays and pitied the poor stunted houses. They seemed to him a band of tramps, huddled together along the river-banks, their old coats covered with dust and soot, stupefied by the panorama of sunset and waiting for the first chill of night to bid them arise, shake themselves and begone. He wondered whether he could write a poem to express his idea. Perhaps Gallaher might be able to get it into some London paper for him. Could he write something original? He was not sure what idea he wished to express but the thought that a poetic moment had touched him took life within him like an infant hope. He stepped onward bravely.

Every step brought him nearer to London, farther from his own sober inartistic life. A light began to tremble on the horizon of his mind. He was not so old—thirty-two. His temperament might be said to be just at the point of maturity. There were so many different moods and impressions that he wished to express in verse. He felt them within him. He tried to weigh his soul to see if it was a poet's soul. Melancholy was the dominant note of his temperament, he thought, but it was a melancholy tempered by recurrences of faith and resignation and simple joy. If he could give expression to it in a book of poems perhaps men would listen. He would never be popular: he saw that. He could not sway the crowd but he might appeal to a little circle of kindred minds. The English critics, perhaps, would recognize him as one of the Celtic school by reason of the melancholy tone of his poems; besides that, he would put in allusions. He began to invent sentences and phrases from the notices which his book would get. *Mr. Chandler has the gift of easy and graceful verse. . . . A wistful sadness pervades these poems. . . . The Celtic note.* It was a pity his name was not more Irish-looking. Perhaps it would be better to insert his mother's name before the surname: Thomas Malone Chandler, or better still: T. Malone Chandler. He would speak to Gallaher about it.

He pursued his revery so ardently that he passed his street and had to turn back. As he came near Corless's his former agitation began to overmaster him and he halted before the door in indecision. Finally he opened the door and entered.

The light and noise of the bar held him at the doorway for a few moments. He looked about him, but his sight was confused by the shining of many red and green wine-glasses. The bar seemed to him to be full of people and he felt that the people were observing him curiously. He glanced quickly to right and left (frowning slightly to make his errand appear serious), but when his sight cleared a little he saw that nobody had turned to look at him: and there, sure enough, was Ignatius Gallaher leaning with his back against the counter and his feet planted far apart.

—Hallo, Tommy, old hero, here you are! What is it to be? What will you have? I'm taking whisky: better stuff than we get across the water. Soda? Lithia?[2] No mineral? I'm the same. Spoils the flavour. . . . Here, *garçon*, bring us two halves of malt whisky, like a good fellow. . . . Well, and how have you been pulling along since I saw you last? Dear God, how old we're getting! Do you see any signs of aging in me—eh, what! A little grey and thin on the top—what?

Ignatius Gallaher took off his hat and displayed a large closely cropped head. His face was heavy, pale and clean-shaven. His eyes, which were of bluish slate-colour, relieved his unhealthy pallor and shone out plainly above the vivid orange tie he wore. Between these rival features the lips appeared very long and shapeless and colourless. He bent his head and felt with two sympathetic fingers the thin hair at the crown. Little Chandler shook his head as a denial. Ignatius Gallaher put on his hat again.

—It pulls you down, he said, Press life. Always hurry and scurry, looking for copy and sometimes not finding it: and then, always to have something new in your stuff. Damn proofs and printers, I say, for a few days. I'm deuced glad, I can tell you, to get back to the old country. Does a fellow good, a bit of a holiday. I feel a ton better since I landed again in dear dirty Dublin. . . . Here you are, Tommy. Water? Say when.

Little Chandler allowed his whisky to be very much diluted.

—You don't know what's good for you, my boy, said Ignatius Gallaher. I drink mine neat.

—I drink very little as a rule, said Little Chandler modestly. An odd half-one or so when I meet any of the old crowd: that's all.

—Ah, well, said Ignatius Gallaher, cheerfully, here's to us and to old times and old acquaintance.

They clinked glasses and drank the toast.

—I met some of the old gang to-day, said Ignatius Gallaher. O'Hara seems to be in a bad way. What's he doing?

—Nothing, said Little Chandler. He's gone to the dogs.

[2] A medicinal mineral water.

—But Hogan has a good sit, hasn't he?

—Yes; he's in the Land Commission.

—I met him one night in London and he seemed to be very flush. . . . Poor O'Hara! Boose, I suppose?

—Other things, too, said Little Chandler shortly.

Ignatius Gallaher laughed.

—Tommy, he said, I see you haven't changed an atom. You're the very same serious person that used to lecture me on Sunday mornings when I had a sore head and a fur on my tongue. You'd want to knock about a bit in the world. Have you never been anywhere, even for a trip?

—I've been to the Isle of Man, said Little Chandler.

Ignatius Gallaher laughed.

—The Isle of Man! he said. Go to London or Paris: Paris, for choice. That'd do you good.

—Have you seen Paris?

—I should think I have! I've knocked about there a little.

—And is it really so beautiful as they say? asked Little Chandler.

He sipped a little of his drink while Ignatius Gallaher finished his boldly.

—Beautiful? said Ignatius Gallaher, pausing on the word and on the flavour of his drink. It's not so beautiful, you know. Of course, it is beautiful. . . . But it's the life of Paris; that's the thing. Ah, there's no city like Paris for gaiety, movement, excitement. . . .

Little Chandler finished his whisky and, after some trouble, succeeded in catching the barman's eye. He ordered the same again.

—I've been to the Moulin Rouge,[3] Ignatius Gallaher continued when the barman had removed their glasses, and I've been to all the Bohemian cafés. Hot stuff! Not for a pious chap like you, Tommy.

Little Chandler said nothing until the barman returned with the two glasses: then he touched his friend's glass lightly and reciprocated the former toast. He was beginning to feel somewhat disillusioned. Gallaher's accent and way of expressing himself did not please him. There was something vulgar in his friend which he had not observed before. But perhaps it was only the result of living in London amid the bustle and competition of the Press. The old personal charm was still there under this new gaudy manner. And, after all, Gallaher had lived, he had seen the world. Little Chandler looked at his friend enviously.

—Everything in Paris is gay, said Ignatius Gallaher. They believe in enjoying life—and don't you think they're right? If you want to enjoy yourself properly you must go to Paris. And, mind you, they've a great feeling for the Irish there. When they heard I was from Ireland they were ready to eat me, man.

Little Chandler took four or five sips from his glass.

—Tell me, he said, is it true that Paris is so . . . immoral as they say?

Ignatius Gallaher made a catholic gesture with his right arm.

—Every place is immoral, he said. Of course you do find spicy bits in Paris. Go to one of the students' balls, for instance. That's lively, if you like, when the *co-cottes*[4] begin to let themselves loose. You know what they are, I suppose?

---

[3] Paris nightclub.
[4] "Loose women."

—I've heard of them, said Little Chandler.

Ignatius Gallaher drank off his whisky and shook his head.

—Ah, he said, you may say what you like. There's no woman like the Parisienne—for style, for go.

—Then it is an immoral city, said Little Chandler, with timid insistence—I mean, compared with London or Dublin?

—London! said Ignatius Gallaher. It's six of one and half-a-dozen of the other. You ask Hogan, my boy. I showed him a bit about London when he was over there. He'd open your eye. . . . I say, Tommy, don't make punch of that whisky: liquor up.

—No, really. . . .

—O, come on, another one won't do you any harm. What is it? The same again, I suppose?

—Well . . . all right.

—*François*, the same again. . . . Will you smoke, Tommy?

Ignatius Gallaher produced his cigar-case. The two friends lit their cigars and puffed at them in silence until their drinks were served.

—I'll tell you my opinion, said Ignatius Gallaher, emerging after some time from the clouds of smoke in which he had taken refuge, it's a rum world. Talk of immorality! I've heard of cases—what am I saying?—I've known them: cases of . . . immorality. . . .

Ignatius Gallaher puffed thoughtfully at his cigar and then, in a calm historian's tone, he proceeded to sketch for his friend some pictures of the corruption which was rife abroad. He summarized the vices of many capitals and seemed inclined to award the palm to Berlin. Some things he could not vouch for (his friends had told him), but of others he had had personal experience. He spared neither rank nor caste. He revealed many of the secrets of religious houses on the Continent and described some of the practices which were fashionable in high society and ended by telling, with details, a story about an English duchess—a story which he knew to be true. Little Chandler was astonished.

—Ah, well, said Ignatius Gallaher, here we are in old jog-along Dublin where nothing is known of such things.

—How dull you must find it, said Little Chandler, after all the other places you've seen!

—Well, said Ignatius Gallaher, it's a relaxation to come over here, you know. And, after all, it's the old country, as they say, isn't it? You can't help having a certain feeling for it. That's human nature. . . . But tell me something about yourself. Hogan told me you had . . . tasted the joys of connubial bliss. Two years ago, wasn't it?

Little Chandler blushed and smiled.

—Yes, he said. I was married last May twelve months.

—I hope it's not too late in the day to offer my best wishes, said Ignatius Gallaher. I didn't know your address or I'd have done so at the time.

He extended his hand, which Little Chandler took.

—Well, Tommy, he said, I wish you and yours every joy in life, old chap, and tons of money, and may you never die till I shoot you. And that's the wish of a sincere friend, an old friend. You know that?

—I know that, said Little Chandler.

—Any youngsters? said Ignatius Gallaher.

Little Chandler blushed again.

—We have one child, he said.

—Son or daughter?

—A little boy.

Ignatius Gallaher slapped his friend sonorously on the back.

—Bravo, he said, I wouldn't doubt you, Tommy.

Little Chandler smiled, looked confusedly at his glass and bit his lower lip with three childishly white front teeth.

—I hope you'll spend an evening with us, he said, before you go back. My wife will be delighted to meet you. We can have a little music and—

—Thanks awfully, old chap, said Ignatius Gallaher, I'm sorry we didn't meet earlier. But I must leave tomorrow night.

—To-night, perhaps . . .?

—I'm awfully sorry, old man. You see I'm over here with another fellow, clever young chap he is too, and we arranged to go to a little card-party. Only for that . . .

—O, in that case. . . .

—But who knows? said Ignatius Gallaher considerately. Next year I may take a little skip over here now that I've broken the ice. It's only a pleasure deferred.

—Very well, said Little Chandler, the next time you come we must have an evening together. That's agreed now, isn't it?

—Yes, that's agreed, said Ignatius Gallaher. Next year if I come, *parole d'honneur.*[5]

—And to clinch the bargain, said Little Chandler, we'll just have one more now.

Ignatius Gallaher took out a large gold watch and looked at it.

—Is it to be the last? he said. Because you know, I have an a.p.

—O, yes, positively, said Little Chandler.

—Very well, then, said Ignatius Gallaher, let us have another one as a *deoc an doruis*[6]—that's good vernacular for a small whisky, I believe.

Little Chandler ordered the drinks. The blush which had risen to his face a few moments before was establishing itself. A trifle made him blush at any time: and now he felt warm and excited. Three small whiskies had gone to his head and Gallaher's strong cigar had confused his mind, for he was a delicate and abstinent person. The adventure of meeting Gallaher after eight years, of finding himself with Gallaher in Corless's surrounded by lights and noise, of listening to Gallaher's stories and of sharing for a brief space Gallaher's vagrant and triumphant life, upset the equipoise of his sensitive nature. He felt acutely the contrast between his own life and his friend's, and it seemed to him unjust. Gallaher was his inferior in birth and education. He was sure that he could do something better than his friend had ever done, or could ever do, something higher than mere tawdry journalism if he only got the chance. What was it that stood in his way? His unfortunate timidity! He wished to vindicate himself in some way, to assert his manhood. He saw behind Gallaher's refusal of his invitation. Gallaher was

---

[5] "Word of honor."

[6] I.e., Irish Gaelic.

only patronizing him by his friendliness just as he was patronizing Ireland by his visit.

The barman brought their drinks. Little Chandler pushed one glass towards his friend and took up the other boldly.

—Who knows? he said, as they lifted their glasses. When you come next year I may have the pleasure of wishing long life and happiness to Mr and Mrs Ignatius Gallaher.

Ignatius Gallaher in the act of drinking closed one eye expressively over the rim of his glass. When he had drunk he smacked his lips decisively, set down his glass and said:

—No blooming fear of that, my boy. I'm going to have my fling first and see a bit of life and the world before I put my head in the sack—if I ever do.

—Some day you will, said Little Chandler calmly.

Ignatius Gallaher turned his orange tie and slate-blue eyes full upon his friend.

—You think so? he said

—You'll put your head in the sack, repeated Little Chandler stoutly, like everyone else if you can find the girl.

He had slightly emphasised his tone and he was aware that he had betrayed himself; but, though the colour had heightened in his cheek, he did not flinch from his friend's gaze. Ignatius Gallaher watched him for a few moments and then said:

—If ever it occurs, you may bet your bottom dollar there'll be no mooning and spooning about it. I mean to marry money. She'll have a good fat account at the bank or she won't do for me.

Little Chandler shook his head.

—Why, man alive, said Ignatius Gallaher, vehemently, do you know what it is? I've only to say the word and to-morrow I can have the woman and the cash. You don't believe it? Well, I know it. There are hundreds—what am I saying?—thousands of rich Germans and Jews, rotten with money, that'd only be too glad. . . . You wait a while, my boy. See if I don't play my cards properly. When I go about a thing I mean business, I tell you. You just wait.

He tossed his glass to his mouth, finished his drink and laughed loudly. Then he looked thoughtfully before him and said in a calmer tone:

—But I'm in no hurry. They can wait. I don't fancy tying myself up to one woman, you know.

He imitated with his mouth the act of tasting and made a wry face.

—Must get a bit stale, I should think, he said.

• • •

Little Chandler sat in the room off the hall, holding a child in his arms. To save money they kept no servant but Annie's young sister Monica came for an hour or so in the morning and an hour or so in the evening to help. But Monica had gone home long ago. It was a quarter to nine. Little Chandler had come home late for tea and, morever, he had forgotten to bring Annie home the parcel of coffee from Bewley's. Of course she was in a bad humour and gave him short answers. She said she would do without any tea but when it came near the time at which the shop at the corner closed she decided to go out herself for a quarter of a pound of tea and two pounds of sugar. She put the sleeping child deftly in his arms and said:

—Here. Don't waken him.

A little lamp with a white china shade stood upon the table and its light fell over a photograph which was enclosed in a frame of crumpled horn. It was Annie's photograph. Little Chandler looked at it, pausing at the thin tight lips. She wore the pale blue summer blouse which he had brought her home as a present one Saturday. It had cost him ten and elevenpence; but what an agony of nervousness it had cost him! How he had suffered that day, waiting at the shop door until the shop was empty, standing at the counter and trying to appear at his ease while the girl piled ladies' blouses before him, paying at the desk and forgetting to take up the odd penny of his change, being called back by the cashier, and, finally, striving to hide his blushes as he left the shop by examining the parcel to see if it was securely tied. When he brought the blouse home Annie kissed him and said it was very pretty and stylish; but when she heard the price she threw the blouse on the table and said it was a regular swindle to charge ten and elevenpence for that. At first she wanted to take it back but when she tried it on she was delighted with it, especially with the make of the sleeves, and kissed him and said he was very good to think of her.

Hm! . . .

He looked coldly into the eyes of the photograph and they answered coldly. Certainly they were pretty and the face itself was pretty. But he found something mean in it. Why was it so unconscious and lady-like? The composure of the eyes irritated him. They repelled him and defied him: there was no passion in them, no rapture. He thought of what Gallaher had said about rich Jewesses. Those dark Oriental eyes, he thought, how full they are of passion, of voluptuous longing! . . . Why had he married the eyes in the photograph?

He caught himself up at the question and glanced nervously around the room. He found something mean in the pretty furniture which he had bought for his house on the hire system. Annie had chosen it herself and it reminded him of her. It too was prim and pretty. A dull resentment against his life awoke within him. Could he not escape from his little house? Was it too late for him to try to live bravely like Gallaher? Could he go to London? There was the furniture still to be paid for. If he could only write a book and get it published, that might open the way for him.

A volume of Byron's poems lay before him on the table. He opened it cautiously with his left hand lest he should waken the child and began to read the first poem in the book:[7]

> Hushed are the winds and still the evening gloom,
>   Not e'en a Zephyr wanders through the grove,
> Whilst I return to view my Margaret's tomb
>   And scatter flowers on the dust I love.

He paused. He felt the rhythm of the verse about him in the room. How melancholy it was! Could he, too, write like that, express the melancholy of his soul

[7] The opening lines of Byron's "On The Death of a Young Lady."

in verse? There were so many things he wanted to describe: his sensation of a few hours before on Grattan Bridge, for example. If he could get back again into that mood. . . .

The child awoke and began to cry. He turned from the page and tried to hush it: but it would not be hushed. He began to rock it to and fro in his arms but its wailing cry grew keener. He rocked it faster while his eyes began to read the second stanza:

> Within this narrow cell reclines her clay,
> That clay where once . . .

It was useless. He couldn't read. He couldn't do anything. The wailing of the child pierced the drum of his ear. It was useless, useless! He was a prisoner for life. His arms trembled with anger and suddenly bending to the child's face he shouted:

—Stop!

The child stopped for an instant, had a spasm of fright and began to scream. He jumped up from his chair and walked hastily up and down the room with the child in his arms. It began to sob piteously, losing its breath for four or five seconds, and then bursting out anew. The thin walls of the room echoed the sound. He tried to soothe it but it sobbed more convulsively. He looked at the contracted and quivering face of the child and began to be alarmed. He counted seven sobs without a break between them and caught the child to his breast in fright. If it died! . . .

The door was burst open and a young woman ran in, panting.

—What is it? What is it? she cried.

The child, hearing its mother's voice, broke out into a paroxysm of sobbing.

—It's nothing, Annie . . . it's nothing. . . . He began to cry . . .

She flung her parcels on the floor and snatched the child from him.

—What have you done to him? she cried, glaring into his face.

Little Chandler sustained for one moment the gaze of her eyes and his heart closed together as he met the hatred in them. He began to stammer:

—It's nothing. . . . He . . . he began to cry. . . . I couldn't . . . I didn't do anything. . . . What?

Giving no heed to him she began to walk up and down the room, clasping the child tightly in her arms and murmuring:

—My little man! My little mannie! Was 'ou frightened, love? . . . There now, love! There now! . . . Lambabaun! Mamma's little lamb of the world! . . . There now!

Little Chandler felt his cheeks suffused with shame and he stood back out of the lamplight. He listened while the paroxysm of the child's sobbing grew less and less; and tears of remorse started to his eyes.

QUESTIONS

1. In a moment of metaphoric vision, Little Chandler sees the houses of Dublin as "a band of tramps, huddled together along the river-banks, their old coats covered with dust and soot. . . . " How does this vision and his reaction to it illuminate his situation?

2. Characterize Gallaher. Do we understand why Chandler envies him?
3. Is Chandler "a prisoner for life"? In what sense? Does he accept his condition at the end?

In "Lost in the Funhouse" we may trace allegories on three levels: the funhouse of adolescence, the funhouse of life, and the funhouse of art. Does the story work successfully on each of these levels and on the literal level as well?

LOST IN THE FUNHOUSE
John Barth   (1930–   )

For whom is the funhouse fun? Perhaps for lovers. For Ambrose it is *a place of fear and confusion.* He has come to the seashore with his family for the holiday, *the occasion of their visit is Independence Day, the most important secular holiday of the United States of America.* A single straight underline is the manuscript mark for italic type, *which in turn* is the printed equivalent to oral emphasis of words and phrases as well as the customary type for titles of complete works, not to mention. Italics are also employed, in fiction stories especially, for "outside," intrusive, or artificial voices, such as radio announcements, the texts of telegrams and newspaper articles, et cetera. They should be used *sparingly.* If passages originally in roman type are italicized by someone repeating them, it's customary to acknowledge the fact. *Italics mine.*

Ambrose was "at that awkward age." His voice came out high-pitched as a child's if he let himself get carried away; to be on the safe side, therefore, he moved and spoke with *deliberate calm* and *adult gravity.* Talking soberly of unimportant or irrelevant matters and listening consciously to the sound of your own voice are useful habits for maintaining control in this difficult interval. *En route* to Ocean City he sat in the back seat of the family car with his brother Peter, age fifteen, and Magda G_____, age fourteen, a pretty girl an exquisite young lady, who lived not far from them on B_____ Street in the town of D_____, Maryland. Initials, blanks, or both were often substituted for proper names in nineteenth-century fiction to enhance the illusion of reality. It is as if the author felt it necessary to delete the names for reasons of tact or legal liability. Interestingly, as with other aspects of realism, it is an *illusion* that is being enhanced, by purely artificial means. Is it likely, does it violate the principle of verisimilitude, that a thirteen-year-old boy could make such a sophisticated observation? A girl of fourteen is *the psychological coeval* of a boy of fifteen or sixteen; a thirteen-year-old boy, therefore, even one precocious in some other respects, might be three years *her emotional junior.*

Thrice a year—on Memorial, Independence, and Labor Days—the family visits Ocean City for the afternoon and evening. When Ambrose and Peter's father was their age, the excursion was made by train, as mentioned in the novel *The 42nd Parallel* by John Dos Passos. Many families from the same neighborhood used to travel together, with dependent relatives and often with Negro servants; schoolfuls of children swarmed through the railway cars; everyone shared everyone else's Maryland fried chicken, Virginia ham, deviled eggs, potato salad, beaten biscuits, iced tea. Nowadays (that is, in 19_____, the year of our story) the journey is made by automobile—more comfortably and quickly though without the extra fun though without the *camaraderie* of a general excursion. It's all part of the deterioration of American life, their father declares; Uncle Karl supposes that when the boys take *their* families to Ocean City for the holidays they'll fly in Autogiros. Their mother, sitting in the middle of the front seat like Magda in the second, only with her arms on the seat-back behind the men's shoulders, wouldn't want the good old days back again, the steaming trains and stuffy long dresses; on the other hand she can do without Autogiros, too, if she has to become a grandmother to fly in them.

Description of physical appearance and mannerisms is one of several standard methods of characterization used by writers of fiction. It is also important to "keep the senses operating"; when a detail from one of the five senses, say visual, is "crossed" with a detail from another, say auditory, the reader's imagination is oriented to the scene, perhaps unconsciously. This procedure may be compared to the way surveyors and navigators determine their positions by two or more compass bearings, a process known as triangulation. The brown hair on Ambrose's mother's forearms gleamed in the sun like. Though right-handed, she took her left arm from the seat-back to press the dashboard cigar lighter for Uncle Karl. When the glass bead in its handle glowed red, the lighter was ready for use. The smell of Uncle Karl's cigar smoke reminded one of. The fragrance of the ocean came strong to the picnic ground where they always stopped for lunch, two miles inland from Ocean City. Having to pause for a full hour almost within sound of the breakers was difficult for Peter and Ambrose when they were younger; even at their present age it was not easy to keep their anticipation, *stimulated by the briny spume*, from turning into short temper. The Irish author James Joyce, in his unusual novel entitled *Ulysses*, now available in this country, uses the adjectives *snot-green* and *scrotum-tightening* to describe the sea. Visual, auditory, tactile, olfactory, gustatory. Peter and Ambrose's father, while steering their black 1936 LaSalle sedan with one hand, could with the other remove the first cigarette from a white pack of Lucky Strikes and, more remarkably, light it with a match forefingered from its book and thumbed against the flint paper without being detached. The matchbook cover merely advertised U. S. War Bonds and Stamps. A fine metaphor, simile, or other figure of speech, in addition to its obvious "first-order" relevance to the thing it describes, will be seen upon reflection to have a second order of significance: it may be drawn from the *milieu* of the action, for example, or be particularly appropriate to the sensibility of the narrator, even hinting to the reader things of which the narrator is unaware; or it may cast further and subtler lights upon the thing it describes, sometimes ironically qualifying the more evident sense of the comparison.

To say that Ambrose's and Peter's mother was *pretty* is to accomplish nothing; the reader may acknowledge the proposition, but his imagination is not engaged. Besides, Magda was also pretty, yet in an altogether different way. Although she lived on B_____ Street she had very good manners and did better than average in school. Her figure was very well developed for her age. Her right hand lay casually on the plush upholstery of the seat, very near Ambrose's left leg, on which his own hand rested. The space between their legs, between her right and his left leg, was out of the line of sight of anyone sitting on the other side of Magda, as well as anyone glancing into the rear-view mirror. Uncle Karl's face resembled Peter's—rather, vice versa. Both had dark hair and eyes, short husky statures, deep voices. Magda's left hand was probably in a similar position on her left side. The boy's father is difficult to describe; no particular feature of his appearance or manner stood out. He wore glasses and was principal of a T_____ County grade school. Uncle Karl was a masonry contractor.

Although Peter must have known as well as Ambrose that the latter, because of his position in the car, would be the first to see the electrical towers of the power plant at V_____, the halfway point of their trip, he leaned forward and slightly toward the center of the car and pretended to be looking for them through the flat pinewoods and tuckahoe creeks along the highway. For as long as the boys could remember, "looking for the Towers" had been a feature of the first half of their excursions to Ocean City, "looking for the standpipe" of the second. Though the game was childish, their mother preserved the tradition of rewarding the first to see the Towers with a candy-bar or piece of fruit. She insisted now that Magda play the game; the prize, she said, was "something hard to get nowadays." Ambrose decided not to join in; he sat far back in his seat. Magda, like Peter, leaned forward. Two sets of straps were discernible through the shoulders of her sun dress; the inside right one, a brassiere-strap, was fastened or shortened with a small safety pin. The right armpit of her dress, presumably the left as well, was damp with perspiration. The simple strategy for being first to espy the Towers, which Ambrose had understood by the age of four, was to sit on the right-hand side of the car. Whoever sat there, however, had also to put up with the worst of the sun, and so Ambrose, without mentioning the matter, chose sometimes the one and sometimes the other. Not impossibly Peter had never caught on to the trick, or thought that his brother hadn't simply because Ambrose on occasion preferred shade to a Baby Ruth or tangerine.

The shade-sun situation didn't apply to the front seat, owing to the windshield; if anything the driver got more sun, since the person on the passenger side not only was shaded below by the door and dashboard but might swing down his sunvisor all the way too.

"Is that them?" Magda asked. Ambrose's mother teased the boys for letting Magda win, insinuating that "somebody [had] a girlfriend." Peter and Ambrose's father reached a long thin arm across their mother to butt his cigarette in the dashboard ashtray, under the lighter. The prize this time for seeing the Towers first was a banana. Their mother bestowed it after chiding their father for wasting a half-smoked cigarette when everything was so scarce. Magda, to take the prize, moved her hand from so near Ambrose's that he could have touched it as though accidentally. She offered to share the prize, things like that were so hard to find; but everyone insisted it was hers alone. Ambrose's mother sang an iambic trimeter couplet from a popular song, femininely rhymed:

> "What's good is in the Army;
> What's left will never harm me."

Uncle Karl tapped his cigar ash out the ventilator window; some particles were sucked by the slipstream back into the car through the rear window on the passenger side. Magda demonstrated her ability to hold a banana in one hand and peel it with her teeth. She still sat forward; Ambrose pushed his glasses back onto the bridge of his nose with his left hand, which he then negligently let fall to the seat cushion immediately behind her. He even permitted the single hair, gold, on the second joint of his thumb to brush the fabric of her skirt. Should she have sat back at that instant, his hand would have been caught under her.

Plush upholstery prickles uncomfortably through gabardine slacks in the July sun. The function of the *beginning* of a story is to introduce the principal characters, establish their initial relationships, set the scene for the main action, expose the background of the situation if necessary, plant motifs and foreshadowings where appropriate, and initiate the first complication or whatever of the "rising action." Actually, if one imagines a story called "The Funhouse," or "Lost in the Funhouse," the details of the drive to Ocean City don't seem especially relevant. The *beginning* should recount the events between Ambrose's first sight of the funhouse early in the afternoon and his entering it with Magda and Peter in the evening. The *middle* would narrate all relevant events from the time he goes in to the time he loses his way; middles have the double and contradictory function of delaying the climax while at the same time preparing the reader for it and fetching him to it. Then the *ending* would tell what Ambrose does while he's lost, how he finally finds his way out, and what everybody makes of the experience. So far there's been no real dialogue, very little sensory detail, and nothing in the way of a *theme*. And a long time has gone by already without anything happening; it makes a person wonder. We haven't even reached Ocean City yet: we will never get out of the funhouse.

The more closely an author identifies with the narrator, literally or metaphorically, the less advisable it is, as a rule, to use the first-person narrative viewpoint. Once three years previously the young people *aforementioned* played Niggers and Masters in the backyard; when it was Ambrose's turn to be Master and theirs to be Niggers Peter had to go serve his evening papers; Ambrose was afraid to punish Magda alone, but she led him to the whitewashed Torture Chamber between the woodshed and the privy in the Slaves Quarters; there she knelt sweating among bamboo rakes and dusty Mason jars, pleadingly embraced his knees, and while bees droned in the lattice as if on an ordinary summer afternoon, purchased clemency at a surprising price set by herself. Doubtless she remembered nothing of this event; Ambrose on the other hand seemed unable to forget the least detail of his life. He even recalled how, standing beside himself with awed impersonality in the reeky heat, he'd stared the while at an empty cigar box in which Uncle Karl kept stone-cutting chisels: beneath the words *El Producto*, a laureled, loose-toga'd lady regarded the sea from a marble bench; beside her, forgotten or not yet turned to, was a five-stringed lyre. Her chin reposed on the back of her right hand; her left depended negligently from the bench-arm. The lower half of scene and lady was peeled away; the words EXAMINED BY_____ were inked there into the wood. Nowadays cigar boxes are made of pasteboard. Ambrose wondered what Magda would have done, Ambrose wondered what Magda would do when she sat back on his hand as he resolved she should. Be angry. Make a teasing joke of it. Give no sign at all. For a long time she leaned forward, playing cow-poker with Peter against Uncle Karl and Mother and watching for the first sign of Ocean City. At nearly the same instant, picnic ground and Ocean City stand-pipe hove into view; an Amoco filling station on their side of the road cost Mother and Uncle Karl fifty cows and the game; Magda bounced back, clapping her right hand on Mother's right arm; Ambrose moved clear "in the nick of time."

At this rate our hero, at this rate our protagonist will remain in the funhouse forever. Narrative ordinarily consists of alternating dramatization and summarization. One symptom of nervous tension, paradoxically, is repeated and violent yawning; neither Peter nor Magda nor Uncle Karl nor Mother reacted in this manner. Although they were no longer small children, Peter and Ambrose were each given a dollar to spend on boardwalk amusements in addition to what money of their own they'd brought along. Magda too, though she protested she had ample spending money. The boys' mother made a little scene out of distributing the bills; she pretended that her sons and Magda were small children and cautioned them not to spend the sum too quickly or in one place. Magda promised with a merry laugh and, having both hands free, took the bill with her left. Peter laughed also and pledged in a falsetto to be a good boy. His imitation of a child was not clever. The boys' father was tall and thin, balding, fair-complexioned. Assertions of that sort are not effective; the reader may acknowledge the proposition, but. We should be much farther along than we are; something has gone wrong; not much of this preliminary rambling seems relevant. Yet everyone begins in the same place; how is it that most go along without difficulty but a few lose their way?

"Stay out from under the boardwalk," Uncle Karl growled from the side of his mouth. The boys' mother pushed his shoulder *in mock annoyance*. They were all standing before Fat May the Laughing Lady who advertised the funhouse. Larger than life, Fat May mechanically shook, rocked on her heels, slapped her thighs while recorded laughter—uproarious, female—came amplified from a hidden loudspeaker. It chuckled, wheezed, wept; tried in vain to catch its breath; tittered, groaned, exploded raucous and anew. You couldn't hear it without laughing yourself, no matter how you felt. Father came back from talking to a Coast-Guardsman on duty and reported that the surf was spoiled with crude oil from tankers recently torpedoed offshore. Lumps of it, difficult to remove, made tarry tidelines on the beach and stuck on swimmers. Many bathed in the surf nevertheless and came out speckled; others paid to use a municipal pool and only sunbathed on the beach. We would do the latter. We would do the latter. We would do the latter.

Under the boardwalk, matchbook covers, grainy other things. What is the story's theme? Ambrose is ill. He perspires in the dark passages; candied apples-on-a-stick, delicious-looking, disappointing to eat. Funhouses need men's and ladies' room at intervals. Others perhaps have also vomited in corners and corridors; may even have had bowel movements liable to be stepped in in the dark. The word *fuck* suggests suction and/or and/or flatulence. Mother and Father; grandmothers and grandfathers on both sides; great-grandmothers and great-grandfathers on four sides, et cetera. Count a generation as thirty years: in approximately the year when Lord Baltimore was granted charter to the province of Maryland by Charles I, five hundred twelve women—English, Welsh, Bavarian, Swiss—of every class and character, received into themselves the penises the intromittent organs of five hundred twelve men, ditto, in every circumstance and posture, to conceive the five hundred twelve ancestors of the two hundred fifty-six ancestors of the et cetera et cetera et cetera et cetera et cetera et cetera et cetera et cetera of the author, of the narrator, of this story, *Lost in the Funhouse*. In alleyways, ditches, canopy beds, pinewoods, bridal suites, ship's cabins, coach-and-fours, coaches-and-four, sultry toolsheds; on the cold sand under board-walks, littered with *El Producto* cigar butts, treasured with Lucky Strike cigarette stubs, Coca-Cola caps, gritty turds, cardboard lollipop sticks, matchbook covers warning that A Slip of the Lip Can Sink a Ship. The shluppish whisper, continuous as seawash round the globe, tidelike falls and rises with the circuit of dawn and dusk.

Magda's teeth. She *was* left-handed. Perspiration. They've gone all the way, through, Magda and Peter, they've been waiting for hours with Mother and Uncle Karl while Father searches for his lost son; they draw french-fried potatoes from a paper cup and shake their heads. They've named the children they'll one day have and bring to Ocean City on holidays. Can spermatozoa properly be thought of as male animalcules when there are no female spermatozoa? They grope through hot, dark windings, past Love's Tunnel's fearsome obstacles. Some perhaps lose their way.

Peter suggested then and there that they do the funhouse; he had been through it before, so had Magda, Ambrose hadn't and suggested, his voice cracking on account of Fat May's laughter, that they swim first. All were chuckling, couldn't help it; Ambrose's father, Ambrose's and Peter's father came up grinning like a lunatic with two boxes of syrup-coated popcorn, one for Mother, one for Magda; the men were to help themselves. Ambrose walked on Magda's right; being by nature left-handed, she carried the box in her left hand. Up front the situation was reversed.

"What are you limping for?" Magda inquired of Ambrose. He supposed in a husky tone that his foot had gone to sleep in the car. Her teeth flashed. "Pins and needles?" It was the honeysuckle on the lattice of the former privy that drew the bees. Imagine being stung there. How long is this going to take?

The adults decided to forgo the pool; but Uncle Karl insisted they change into swimsuits and do the beach. "He wants to watch the pretty girls," Peter teased, and ducked behind Magda from Uncle Karl's pretended wrath. "You've got all the pretty girls you need right here," Magda declared, and Mother said: "Now that's the gospel truth." Magda scolded Peter, who reached over her shoulder to sneak some popcorn. "Your brother and father aren't getting any." Uncle Karl wondered if they were going to have fireworks that night, what with the shortages. It wasn't the shortages, Mr. M____ replied; Ocean City had fireworks from pre-war. But it was too risky on account of the enemy submarines, some people thought.

"Don't seem like Fourth of July without fireworks," said Uncle Karl. The inverted tag in dialogue writing is still considered permissible with proper names or epithets, but sounds old-fashioned with personal pronouns. "We'll have 'em again soon enough," predicted the boys' father. Their mother declared she could do without fireworks: they reminded her too much of the real thing. Their father said all the more reason to shoot off a few now and again. Uncle Karl asked *rhetorically* who needed reminding, just look at people's hair and skin.

"The oil, yes," said Mrs. M____.

250

FICTION

Ambrose had a pain in his stomach and so didn't swim but enjoyed watching the others. He and his father burned red easily. Magda's figure was exceedingly well developed for her age. She too declined to swim, and got mad, and became angry when Peter attempted to drag her into the pool. She always swam, he insisted; what did she mean not swim? Why did a person come to Ocean City?

"Maybe I want to lay here with Ambrose," Magda teased.

Nobody likes a pedant.

"Aha," said Mother. Peter grabbed Magda by one ankle and ordered Ambrose to grab the other. She squealed and rolled over on the beach blanket. Ambrose pretended to help hold her back. Her tan was darker than even Mother's and Peter's. "Help out, Uncle Karl!" Peter cried. Uncle Karl went to seize the other ankle. Inside the top of her swimsuit, however, you could see the line where the sunburn ended and, when she hunched her shoulders and squealed again, one nipple's auburn edge. Mother made them behave themselves. "*You* should certainly know," she said to Uncle Karl. Archly. "That when a lady says she doesn't feel like swimming, a gentleman doesn't ask questions." Uncle Karl said excuse *him*; Mother winked at Magda; Ambrose blushed; stupid Peter kept saying "Phooey on *feel like!*" and tugging at Magda's ankle; then even he got the point, and cannonballed with a holler into the pool.

"I swear," Magda said, in mock *in feigned* exasperation.

The diving would make a suitable literary symbol. To go off the high board you had to wait in a line along the poolside and up the ladder. Fellows tickled girls and goosed one another and shouted to the ones at the top to hurry up, or razzed them for bellyfloppers. Once on the springboard some took a great while posing or clowning or deciding on a dive or getting up their nerve; others ran right off. Especially among the younger fellows the idea was to strike the funniest pose or do the craziest stunt as you fell, a thing that got harder to do as you kept on and kept on. But whether you hollered *Geronimo!* or *Sieg heil!*, held your nose or "rode a bicycle," pretended to be shot or did a perfect jacknife or changed your mind halfway down and ended up with nothing, it was over in two seconds, after all that wait. Spring, pose, splash. Spring, neat-o, splash. Spring, aw fooey, splash.

The grown-ups had gone on; Ambrose wanted to converse with Magda; she was remarkably well developed for her age; it was said that that came from rubbing with a turkish towel, and there were other theories. Ambrose could think of nothing to say except how good a diver Peter was, who was showing off for her benefit. You could pretty well tell by looking at their bathing suits and arm muscles how far along the different fellows were. Ambrose was glad he hadn't gone in swimming, the cold water shrank you up so. Magda pretended to be uninterested in the diving; she probably weighed as much as he did. If you knew your way around in the funhouse like your own bedroom, you could wait until a girl came along and then slip away without ever getting caught, even if her boyfriend was right with her. She'd think *he* did it! It would be better to be the boyfriend, and act outraged, and tear the funhouse apart.

Not act; *be*.

"He's a master diver," Ambrose said. In feigned admiration. "You really have to slave away at it to get that good." What would it matter anyhow if he asked her right out whether she remembered, even teased her with it as Peter would have?

There's no point in going farther; this isn't getting anybody anywhere; they haven't even come to the funhouse yet. Ambrose is off the track, in some new or old part of the place that's not supposed to be used; he strayed into it by some one-in-a-million chance, like the time the roller-coaster car left the tracks in the nineteen-teens against all the laws of physics and sailed over the boardwalk in the dark. And they can't locate him because they don't know where to look. Even the designer and operator have forgotten this other part, that winds around on itself like a whelk shell. That winds around the right part like the snakes on Mercury's caduceus. Some people, perhaps, don't "hit their stride" until their twenties, when the growing-up business is over and women appreciate other things besides wisecracks and teasing and strutting. Peter didn't have one-tenth the imagination *he* had, not one-tenth. Peter did this naming-their-children thing as a joke, making up names like Aloysius and Murgatroyd, but Ambrose knew *exactly* how it would feel to be married and have children of your own, and be a loving husband and father, and go comfortably to work in the mornings and to bed with your wife at night, and wake up with her there. With a breeze coming through the sash and birds and mockingbirds singing in the Chinese-cigar trees. His eyes watered, there aren't enough ways to say that. He would be quite famous in his line of work. Whether Magda was his wife or not, one evening when he was wise-lined and gray at the temples he'd smile gravely, at a fashionable dinner party, and remind her of his youthful passion. The time they went with his family to Ocean City; the *erotic fantasies* he used to have about her. How long ago it seemed, and childish! Yet tender, too, *n'est-ce pas?*[1] Would she have imagined that the world-famous whatever remembered how many strings were on the lyre on the bench beside the girl on the label of the cigar box he'd stared at in the toolshed at age ten while she, age eleven. Even then he had felt *wise beyond his years;* he'd stroked her hair and said in his deepest voice and correctest English, as to a dear child: "I shall never forget this moment."

But though he had breathed heavily, groaned as if ecstatic, what he'd really felt throughout was an odd detachment, as though someone else were Master. Strive as he might to be transported, he heard his mind take notes upon the scene: *This is what they call* passion. *I am experiencing it.* Many of the digger machines were out of order in the penny arcades and could not be repaired or replaced for the duration. Moreover the prizes, made now in USA, were less interesting than formerly, pasteboard items for the most part, and some of the machines wouldn't work on white pennies. The gypsy fortune-teller machine might have provided a foreshadowing of the climax of this story if Ambrose had operated it. It was even dilapidateder than most: the silver coating was worn off the brown metal handles, the glass windows around the dummy were cracked and taped, her kerchiefs and silks long-faded. If a man lived by himself, he could take a department-store mannequin with flexible joints and modify her in certain ways. *However*: by the time he was that old he'd have a real woman. There was a machine that stamped your name around a white-metal coin with a star in the middle: *A_____*. His son would be the second, and when the lad reached thirteen or so he would put a strong arm around his shoulder and tell him calmly: "It is perfectly normal. We have all been through it. It will not last forever." Nobody knew how to be what they were right. He'd smoke a pipe, teach his son

[1] "Is it not?" (French).

how to fish and softcrab, assure him he needn't worry about himself. Magda
would certainly give, Magda would certainly yield a great deal of milk, although
guilty of occasional solecisms. It don't taste so bad. Suppose the lights came on
now!

The day wore on. You think you're yourself, but there are other persons in you.
Ambrose gets hard when Ambrose doesn't want to, *and obversely.* Ambrose
watches them disagree; Ambrose watches him watch. In the funhouse mirror-
room you can't see yourself go on forever, because no matter how you stand,
your head gets in the way. Even if you had a glass periscope, the image of your
eye would cover up the thing you really wanted to see. The police will come;
there'll be a story in the papers. That must be where it happened. Unless he can
find a surprise exit, an unofficial backdoor or escape hatch opening on an alley,
say, and then stroll up to the family in front of the funhouse and ask where ever-
body's been; *he's* been out of the place for ages. That's just where it happened, in
that last lighted room: Peter and Magda found the right exit; he found one that
you weren't supposed to find and strayed off into the works somewhere. In a
perfect funhouse you'd be able to go only one way, like the divers off the high-
board; getting lost would be impossible; the doors and halls would work like
minnow traps or the valves in veins.

On account of German U-boats, Ocean City was "browned out": streetlights
were shaded on the seaward side; shop-windows and boardwalk amusement
places were kept dim, not to silhouette tankers and Liberty-ships for torpedoing.
In a short story about Ocean City, Maryland, during World War II, the author
could make use of the image of sailors on leave in the penny arcades and shooting galleries, sighting through the crosshairs of toy machine guns at swastika'd
subs, while out in the black Atlantic a U-boat skipper squints through his periscope at real ships outlined by the glow of penny arcades. After dinner the family strolled back to the amusement end of the boardwalk. The boys' father had
burnt red as always and was masked with Noxzema, a minstrel in reverse. The
grown-ups stood at the end of the boardwalk where the Hurricane of '33 had cut
an inlet from the ocean to Assawoman Bay.

"Pronounced with a long *o*," Uncle Karl reminded Magda with a wink. His
shirt sleeves were rolled up; Mother punched his brown biceps with the arrowed
heart on it and said his mind was naughty. Fat May's laugh came suddenly from
the funhouse, as if she'd just got the joke; the family laughed too at the coincidence. Ambrose went under the boardwalk to search for out-of-town matchbook
covers with the aid of his pocket flashlight; he looked out from the edge of the
North American continent and wondered how far their laughter carried over the
water. Spies in rubber rafts; survivors in lifeboats. If the joke had been beyond
his understanding, he could have said: *"The laughter was over his head."* And let
the reader see the serious wordplay on second reading.

He turned the flashlight on and then off at once even before the woman
whooped. He sprang away, heart athud, dropping the light. What had the man
grunted? Perspiration drenched and chilled him by the time he scrambled up to
the family. "See anything?" his father asked. His voice wouldn't come; he
shrugged and violently brushed sand from his pants legs.

"Let's ride the old flying horses!" Magda cried. I'll never be an author. It's
been forever already, everybody's gone home, Ocean City's deserted, the ghost-

crabs are tickling across the beach and down the littered cold streets. And the empty halls of clapboard hotels and abandoned funhouses. A tidal wave; an enemy air raid; a monster-crab swelling like an island from the sea. *The inhabitants fled in terror.* Magda clung to his trouser leg; he alone knew the maze's secret. "He gave his life that we might live," said Uncle Karl with a scowl of pain, as he. The fellow's hands had been tattooed; the woman's legs, the woman's fat white legs had. *An astonishing coincidence.* He yearned to tell Peter. He wanted to throw up for excitement. They hadn't even chased him. He wished he were dead.

One possible ending would be to have Ambrose come across another lost person in the dark. They'd match their wits together against the funhouse, struggle like Ulysses past obstacle after obstacle, help and encourage each other. Or a girl. By the time they found the exit they'd be closest friends, sweethearts if it were a girl; they'd know each other's inmost souls, be bound together *by the cement of shared adventure*; then they'd emerge into the light and it would turn out that his friend was a Negro. A blind girl. President Roosevelt's son. Ambrose's former archenemy.

Shortly after the mirror room he'd groped along a musty corridor, his heart already misgiving him at the absence of phosphorescent arrows and other signs. He'd found a crack of light—not a door, it turned out, but a seam between the plyboard wall panels—and squinting up to it, he spied a small old man, *in appearance not unlike* the photographs at home of Ambrose's late grandfather, nodding upon a stool beneath a bare, speckled bulb. A crude panel of toggle- and knife-switches hung beside the open fuse box near his head; elsewhere in the little room were wooden levers and ropes belayed to boat cleats. At the time, Ambrose wasn't lost enough to rap or call; later he couldn't find that crack. Now it seemed to him that he'd possibly dozed off for a few minutes somewhere along the way; certainly he was exhausted from the afternoon's sunshine and the evening's problems; he couldn't be sure he hadn't dreamed part or all of the sight. Had an old black wall fan droned like bees and shimmied two flypaper streamers? Had the funhouse operator—gentle, somewhat sad and tired-appearing, in expression not unlike the photographs at home of Ambrose's late Uncle Konrad—murmured in his sleep? Is there really such a person as Ambrose, or is he a figment of the author's imagination? Was it Assawoman Bay or Sinepuxent? Are there other errors of fact in this fiction? Was there another sound besides the little slap slap of thigh on ham, like water sucking at the chine-boards of a skiff?

When you're lost, the smartest thing to do is stay put till you're found, hollering if necessary. But to holler guarantees humiliation as well as rescue; keeping silent permits some saving of face—you can act surprised at the fuss when your rescuers find you and swear you weren't lost, if they do. What's more you might find your own way yet, *however belatedly*.

"Don't tell me your foot's still asleep!" Magda exclaimed as the three young people walked from the inlet to the area set aside for ferris wheels, carrousels, and other carnival rides, they having decided in favor of the vast and ancient merry-go-round instead of the funhouse. What a sentence, everything was wrong from the outset. People don't know what to make of him, he doesn't know what to make of himself, he's only thirteen, *athletically and socially inept*, not astonishingly bright, but there are antennae; he has . . . some sort of receivers in his head; things speak to him, he understands more than he should, the world winks at him through its objects, grabs grinning at his coat. Everybody else is in on some secret he doesn't know; they've forgotten to tell him. Through simple *procrastination* his mother put off his baptism until this year. Everyone else had it done as a baby; he'd assumed the same of himself, as had his mother, so she claimed, until it was time for him to join Grace Methodist-Protestant and the oversight came out. He was mortified, but pitched sleepless through his private catechizing, intimidated by the ancient mysteries, a thirteen year old would never say that, resolved to experience conversion like St. Augustine. When the water touched his brow and Adam's sin left him, he contrived by a strain like defecation to bring tears into his eyes—but felt nothing. There was some simple, radical difference about him; he hoped it was genius, feared it was madness, devoted himself to amiability and inconspicuousness. Alone on the seawall near his house he was seized by the terrifying transports he'd thought to find in toolshed, in Communion-cup. The grass was alive! The town, the river, himself, were not imaginary; time roared in his ears like wind; the world was *going on!* This part ought to be dramatized. The Irish author James Joyce once wrote. Ambrose M__ ___ is going to scream.

There is no *texture of rendered sensory detail*, for one thing. The faded distorting mirrors beside Fat May; the impossibility of choosing a mount when one had but a single ride on the great carrousel; the *vertigo attendant on his recognition* that Ocean City was worn out, the place of fathers and grandfathers, straw-boatered men and parasoled ladies survived by their amusements. Money spent, the three paused at Peter's insistence beside Fat May to watch the girls get their skirts blown up. The object was to tease Magda, who said: "I swear, Peter M_____, you've got a one-track mind! Amby and me aren't *interested* in such things." In the tumbling-barrel, too, just inside the Devil's-mouth entrance to the funhouse, the girls were upended and their boyfriends and others could see up their dresses if they cared to. Which was the whole point, Ambrose realized. Of the entire funhouse! If you looked around, you noticed that almost all the people on the boardwalk were paired off into couples except the small children; in a way, that was the whole point of Ocean City! If you had X-ray eyes and could see everything going on at that instant under the boardwalk and in all the hotel rooms and cars and alleyways, you'd realize that all that normally *showed*, like restaurants and dance halls and clothing and test-your-strength machines, was merely preparation and intermission. Fat May screamed.

Because he watched the goings-on from the corner of his eye, it was Ambrose who spied the half-dollar on the boardwalk near the tumbling-barrel. Losers weepers. The first time he'd heard some people moving through a corridor not far away, just after he'd lost sight of the crack of light, he'd decided not to call to them, for fear they'd guess he was scared and poke fun; it sounded like roughnecks; he'd hoped they'd come by and he could follow in the dark without their knowing. Another time he'd heard just one person, unless he imagined it, bumping along as if on the other side of the plywood; perhaps Peter coming back for him, or Father, or Magda lost too. Or the owner and operator of the funhouse. He'd called out once, as though merrily: "Anybody know where the heck we are?" But the query was too stiff, his voice cracked, when the sounds stopped he was terrified: maybe it was a queer who waited for fellows to get lost, or a long-haired filthy monster that lived in some cranny of the funhouse. He stood rigid for hours it seemed like, scarcely respiring. His future was shockingly clear, in outline. He tried holding his breath to the point of unconsciousness. There ought to be a button you could push to end your life absolutely without pain; disappear in a flick, like turning out a light. He would push it instantly! He despised Uncle Karl. But he despised his father too, for not being what he was supposed to be. Perhaps his father hated *his* father, and so on, and his son would hate him, and so on. Instantly!

Naturally he didn't have nerve enough to ask Magda to go through the funhouse with him. With incredible nerve and to everyone's surprise he invited Magda, quietly and politely, to go through the funhouse with him. "I warn you, I've never been through it before," he added, *laughing easily*; "but I reckon we can manage somehow. The important thing to remember, after all, is that it's meant to be a *fun*house; that is, a place of amusement. If people really got lost or injured or too badly frightened in it, the owner'd go out of business. There'd even be lawsuits. No character in a work of fiction can make a speech this long without interruption or acknowledgment from the other characters."

Mother teased Uncle Karl: "Three's a crowd, I always heard." But actually Ambrose was relieved that Peter now had a quarter too. Nothing was what it looked like. Every instant, under the surface of the Atlantic Ocean, millions of living animals devoured one another. Pilots were falling in flames over Europe; women were being forcibly raped in the South Pacific. His father should have taken him aside and said: "There is a simple secret to getting through the funhouse, as simple as being first to see the Towers. Here it is. Peter does not know it; neither does your Uncle Karl. You and I are different. Not surprisingly, you've often wished you weren't. Don't think I haven't noticed how unhappy your childhood has been! But you'll understand, when I tell you, why it had to be kept secret until now. And you won't regret not being like your brother and your uncle. *On the contrary!*" If you knew all the stories behind all the people on the boardwalk, you'd see that *nothing* was what it looked like. Husbands and wives often hated each other; parents didn't necessarily love their children; et cetera. A child took things for granted because he had nothing to compare his life to and everybody acted as if things were as they should be. Therefore each saw himself as the hero of the story, when the truth might turn out to be that he's the villain, or the coward. And there wasn't one thing you could do about it!

Hunchbacks, fat ladies, fools—that no one chose what he was was unbearable. In the movies he'd meet a beautiful young girl in the funhouse; they'd have hairs-breadth escapes from real dangers; he'd do and say the right things; she also; in the end they'd be lovers; their dialogue lines would match up; he'd be perfectly at ease; she'd not only like him well enough, she'd think he was *marvelous*. she'd lie awake thinking about *him*, instead of vice versa—the way *his* face looked in different lights and how he stood and exactly what he'd said—and yet that would be only one small episode in his wonderful life, among many many others. Not a *turning point* at all. What had happened in the toolshed was nothing. He hated, he loathed his parents! One reason for not writing a lost-in-the-funhouse story is that either everybody's felt what Ambrose feels, in which case it goes without saying, or else no normal person feels such things, in which case Ambrose is a freak. "Is anything more tiresome, in fiction, than the problems of sensitive adolescents?" And it's all too long and rambling, as if the author. For all a person knows the first time through, the end could be just around any corner; perhaps, *not impossibly* it's been within reach any number of times. On the other hand he may be scarcely past the start, with everything yet to get through, an intolerable idea.

Fill in: His father's raised eyebrows when he announced his decision to do the funhouse with Magda. Ambrose understands now, but didn't then, that his father was wondering whether he knew what the funhouse was *for*—especially since he didn't object, as he should have, when Peter decided to come along too. The ticket-woman, witchlike, mortifying him when inadvertently he gave her his name-coin instead of the half-dollar, then unkindly calling Magda's attention to the birthmark on his temple: "Watch out for him, girlie, he's a marked man!" She wasn't even cruel, he understood, only vulgar and insensitive. Somewhere in the world there was a young woman with such splendid understanding that she'd see him entire, like a poem or story, and find his words so valuable after all that when he confessed his apprehensions she would explain why they were in fact the very things that made him precious to her . . . and to Western Civilization! There was no such girl, the simple truth being. Violent yawns as they approached the mouth. Whispered advice from an old-timer on a bench near the barrel: "Go crabwise and ye'll get an eyeful without upsetting!" Composure vanished at the first pitch: Peter hollered joyously, Magda tumbled, shrieked, clutched her skirt; Ambrose scrambled crabwise, tight-lipped with terror, was soon out, watched his dropped name-coin slide among the couples. Shame-faced he saw that to get through expeditiously was not the point; Peter feigned assistance in order to trip Magda up, shouted "I see Christmas!" when her legs went flying. The old man, his latest betrayer, cacked approval. A dim hall then of black-thread cobwebs and recorded gibber: he took Magda's elbow to steady her against revolving discs set in the slanted floor to throw your feet out from under, and explained to her in a calm, deep voice his theory that each phase of the funhouse was triggered either automatically, by a series of photoelectric devices, or else manually by operators stationed at peepholes. But he lost his voice thrice as the discs unbalanced him; Magda was anyhow squealing; but at one point she clutched him about the waist to keep from falling, and her right cheek pressed for a moment against his belt-buckle. Heroically he drew her up, it was his chance to clutch her close as if for support and say: "I love you." He even put an arm lightly about the small of her back before a sailor-and-girl pitched into them from behind, sorely treading his left big toe and knocking Magda asprawl with them. The sailor's girl was a string-haired hussy with a loud laugh and light blue drawers; Ambrose realized that he wouldn't have said "I love you" anyhow, and was smitten with self-contempt. How much better it would be to be that common sailor! A wiry little Seaman 3rd, the fellow squeezed a girl to each side and stumbled hilarious into the mirror room, closer to Magda in thirty seconds than Ambrose had got in thirteen years. She giggled at something the fellow said to Peter; she drew her hair from her eyes with a movement so womanly it struck Ambrose's heart; Peter's smacking her backside then seemed particularly coarse. But Magda made a pleased indignant face and cried, "All right for *you*, mister!" and pursued Peter into the maze without a backward glance. The sailor followed after, leisurely, drawing his girl against his hip; Ambrose understood not only that they were all so relieved to be rid of his burdensome company that they didn't even notice his absence, but that he himself shared their relief. Stepping from the treacherous passage at last into the mirror-maze, he saw once again, more clearly than ever, how readily he deceived himself into supposing he was a person. He even foresaw, wincing at his dreadful self-knowledge, that he would repeat the deception, at ever-rarer intervals, all his wretched life, so fearful were the alternatives. Fame, madness, suicide; perhaps all three. It's not believable that so young a boy could articulate that reflection, and in fiction the merely true must always yield to the plausible. Moreover, the symbolism is in places heavy-footed. Yet Ambrose M_____ understood, as few adults do, that the famous lone-liness of the great was no popular myth but a general truth—furthermore, that it was as much cause as effect.

All the preceding except the last few sentences is exposition that should've been done earlier or interspersed with the present action instead of lumped to-gether. No reader would put up with so much with such *prolixity*. It's interesting that Ambrose's father, though presumably an intelligent man (as indicated by his role as grade-school principal), neither encouraged nor discouraged his sons at all in any way—as if he either didn't care about them or cared all right but didn't know how to act. If this fact should contribute to one of them's becoming a cele-brated but wretchedly unhappy scientist, was it a good thing or not? He too might someday face the question; it would be useful to know whether it had tor-tured his father for years, for example, or never once crossed his mind.

In the maze two important things happened. First, our hero found a name-coin someone else had lost or discarded: *AMBROSE,* suggestive of the famous lightship and of his late grandfather's favorite dessert, which his mother used to prepare on special occasions out of coconut, oranges, grapes, and what else. Sec-ond, as he wondered at the endless replication of his image in the mirrors, sec-ond, as he *lost himself in the reflection* that the necessity for an observer makes per-fect observation impossible, better make him eighteen at least, yet that would render other things unlikely, he heard Peter and Magda chuckling somewhere together in the maze. "Here!" "No here!" they shouted to each other; Peter said, "Where's Amby?" Magda murmured. "Amb?" Peter called. In a pleased, friendly voice. He didn't reply. The truth was, his brother was a *happy-go-lucky youngster* who'd've been better off with a regular brother of his own, but who seldom com-plained of his lot and was generally cordial. Ambrose's throat ached; there aren't enough different ways to say that. He stood quietly while the two young people giggled and thumped through the glittering maze, hurrah'd their discovery of its exit, cried out in joyful alarm at what next beset them. Then he set his mouth and followed after, as he supposed, took a wrong turn, strayed into the pass *wherein he lingers yet.*

The action of conventional dramatic narrative may be represented by a dia-gram called Freitag's Triangle:[2]

$$
\begin{array}{c}
B \\
A \diagup \diagdown C
\end{array}
$$

[2] See Gustave Freytag, *Technique of the Drama,* translated by Elias J. MacEwan, 1895.

or more accurately by a variant of that diagram:

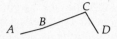

in which *AB* represents the exposition, *B* the introduction of conflict, *BC* the "rising action," complication, or development of the conflict, *C* the climax, or turn of the action, *CD* the dénouement, or resolution of the conflict. While there is no reason to regard this pattern as an absolute necessity, like many other conventions it became conventional because great numbers of people over many years learned by trial and error that it was effective; one ought not to forsake it, therefore, unless one wishes to forsake as well the effect of drama or has clear cause to feel that deliberate violation of the "normal" pattern can better can better effect that effect. This can't go on much longer; it can go on forever. He died telling stories to himself in the dark; years later, when that vast unsuspected area of the funhouse came to light, the first expedition found his skeleton in one of its labyrinthine corridors and mistook it for part of the entertainment. He died of starvation telling himself stories in the dark; but unbeknownst unbeknownst to him, an assistant operator of the funhouse, happening to overhear him, crouched just behind the plyboard partition and wrote down his every word. The operator's daughter, an exquisite young woman with a figure unusually well developed for her age, crouched just behind the partition and transcribed his every word. Though she had never laid eyes on him, she recognized that here was one of Western Culture's truly great imaginations, the eloquence of whose suffering would be an inspiration to unnumbered. And her heart was torn between her love for the misfortunate young man (yes, she loved him, though she had never laid though she knew him only—but how well!—through his words, and the deep, calm voice in which he spoke them) between her love et cetera and her womanly intuition that only in suffering and isolation could he give voice et cetera. Lone dark dying. Quietly she kissed the rough plyboard, and a tear fell upon the page. Where she had written in shorthand *Where she had written in shorthand* Where she had written in shorthand *Where she* et cetera. A long time ago we should have passed the apex of Freitag's Triangle and made brief work of the *dénouement*; the plot doesn't rise by meaningful steps but winds upon itself, digresses, retreats, hesitates, sighs, collapses, expires. The climax of the story must be its protagonist's discovery of a way to get through the funhouse. But he has found none, may have ceased to search.

What relevance does the war have to the story? Should there be fireworks outside or not?

Ambrose wandered, languished, dozed. Now and then he fell into his habit of rehearsing to himself the unadventurous story of his life, narrated from the third-person point of view, from his earliest memory parenthesis of maple leaves stirring in the summer breath of tidewater Maryland end of parenthesis to the present moment. Its principal events, on this telling, would appear to have been A, B, C, and D.

He imagined himself years hence, successful, married, at ease in the world, the trials of his adolescence far behind him. He has come to the seashore with his family for the holiday: how Ocean City has changed! But at one seldom at one ill-frequented end of the boardwalk a few derelict amusements survive from times gone by: the great carrousel from the turn of the century, with its monstrous griffins and mechanical concert band; the roller coaster rumored since 1916 to have been condemned; the mechanical shooting gallery in which only the image of our enemies changed. His own son laughs with Fat May and wants to know what a funhouse is; Ambrose hugs the sturdy lad close and smiles around his pipestem at his wife.

The family's going home. Mother sits between Father and Uncle Karl, who teases him good-naturedly who chuckles over the fact that the comrade with whom he'd fought his way shoulder to shoulder through the funhouse had turned out to be a blind Negro girl—to their mutual discomfort, as they'd opened their souls. But such are the walls of custom, which even. Whose arm is where? How must it feel. He dreams of a funhouse vaster by far than any yet constructed; but by then they may be out of fashion, like steamboats and excursion trains. Already quaint and seedy: the draperied ladies on the frieze of the carrousel are his father's father's mooncheeked dreams; if he thinks of it more he will vomit his apple-on-a-stick.

He wonders: will he become a regular person? Something has gone wrong; his vaccination didn't take; at the Boy-Scout initiation campfire he only pretended to be deeply moved, as he pretends to this hour that it is not so bad after all in the funhouse, and that he has a little limp. How long will it last? He envisions a truly astonishing funhouse, incredibly complex yet utterly controlled from a great central switchboard like the console of a pipe organ. Nobody had enough imagination. He could design such a place himself, wiring and all, and he's only thirteen years old. He would be its operator: panel lights would show what was up in every cranny of its cunning of its multifarious vastness; a switch-flick would ease this fellow's way, complicate that's, to balance things out; if anyone seemed lost or frightened, all the operator had to do was.

He wishes he had never entered the funhouse. But he has. Then he wishes he were dead. But he's not. Therefore he will construct funhouses for others and be their secret operator—though he would rather be among the lovers for whom funhouses are designed.

AFTER THE FAIR
Dylan Thomas (1914–1953)

The fair was over, the lights in the cocoanut stalls were put out, and the wooden horses stood still in the darkness, waiting for the music and the hum of the machines that would set them trotting forward. One by one, in every booth, the naphtha jets were turned down and the canvases pulled over the little gambling tables. The crowd went home, and there were lights in the windows of the caravans.

Nobody had noticed the girl. In her black clothes she stood against the side of the roundabouts, hearing the last feet tread upon the sawdust and the last voices die into the distance. Then, all alone on the deserted ground, surrounded by the shapes of wooden horses and cheap fairy boats, she looked for a place to sleep.

Now here and now there, she raised the canvas that shrouded the cocoanut stalls and peered into the warm darkness. She was frightened to step inside, and as a mouse scampered across the littered shavings on the floor, or as the canvas creaked and a rush of wind set it dancing, she ran away and hid again near the roundabouts. Once she stepped on the boards; the bells round a horse's throat jingled and were still; she did not dare breathe until all was quiet again and the darkness had forgotten the noise of the bells. Then here and there she went peeping for a bed, into each gondola, under each tent. But there was nowhere, nowhere in all the fair for her to sleep. One place was too silent, and in another was the noise of mice. There was straw in the corner of the Astrologer's tent, but it moved as she touched it; she knelt by its side and put out her hand; she felt a baby's hand upon her own.

Now there was nowhere; so slowly she turned towards the caravans, and reaching them where they stood on the outskirts of the field, found all but two to be unlit. She stood, clutching her empty bag, and wondering which caravan she should disturb. At last she decided to knock upon the window of the little, shabby one near her, and standing on tiptoes, she looked in. The fattest man she had ever seen was sitting in front of the stove, toasting a piece of bread. She tapped three times on the glass, then hid in the shadows. She heard him come to the top of the steps and call out Who? Who? but she dared not answer. Who? Who? he called again; she laughed at his voice which was as thin as he was fat. He heard her laughter and turned to where the darkness concealed her. First you tap, he said. Then you hide, then, by jingo, you laugh. She stepped into the circle of light, knowing she need no longer hide herself. A girl, he said, Come in and wipe your feet. He did not wait but retreated into his caravan, and she could do nothing but follow him up the steps and into the crowded room. He was seated again, and toasting the same piece of bread. Have you come in? He said, for his back was towards her. Shall I close the door? she asked, and closed it before he replied.

She sat on the bed and watched him toasting the bread until it burnt. I can toast better than you, she said. I don't doubt it, said the Fat Man. She watched him put down the charred toast upon a plate by his side, take another round of bread and hold that, too, in front of the stove. It burnt very quickly. Let me toast it for you, she said. Ungraciously he handed her the fork and the loaf. Cut it, he said, Toast it, and eat it, by jingo. She sat on the chair. See the dent you've made on my bed, said the Fat Man. Who are you to come in and dent my bed? My name is Annie, she told him. Soon all the bread was toasted and buttered, so she put it in the centre of the table and arranged two chairs. I'll have mine on the bed, said the Fat Man. You'll have it here.

When they had finished their supper, he pushed back his chair and stared at her across the table. I am the Fat Man, he said. My home is Treorchy; the Fortune Teller next door is Aberdare. I am nothing to do with the fair—I am Cardiff, she said. There's a town, agreed the Fat Man. He asked her why she had come away. Money, said Annie. I have one and three, said the Fat Man. I have nothing, said Annie.

Then he told her about the fair and the places he had been to and the people he had met. He told her his age and his weight and the names of his brothers and what he would call his son. He showed her a picture of Boston Harbour and the photograph of his mother who lifted weights. He told her how summer looked in Ireland. I've always been a fat man, he said, And now I'm *the* Fat Man; there's nobody to touch me for fatness. He told her of a heat wave in Sicily and of the Mediterranean Sea and of the wonders of the South stars. She told him of the baby in the Astrologer's tent.

That's the stars again, by jingo; looking at the stars doesn't do anybody any good.

The baby'll die, said Annie. He opened the door and walked out into the darkness. She looked about her but did not move, wondering if he had gone to fetch a policeman. It would never do to be caught by the policeman again. She stared through the open door into the inhospitable night and drew her chair closer to the stove. Better to be caught in the warmth, she said. But she trembled at the sound of the Fat Man approaching, and pressed her hands upon her thin breast, as he climbed up the steps like a walking mountain. She could see him smile in the darkness. See what the stars have done, he said, and brought in the Astrologer's baby in his arms.

After she had nursed it against her and it had cried on the bosom of her dress, she told him how she had feared his going. What should I be doing with a policeman? She told him that the policeman wanted her. What have you done for a policeman to be wanting you? She did not answer but took the child nearer again to her wasted breast. If it was money, I could have given you one and three, he said. Then he understood her and begged her pardon. I'm not quick, he told her. I'm just fat; sometimes I think I'm almost too fat. She was feeding the child; he saw her thinness. You must eat, Cardiff, he said.

Then the child began to cry. From a little wail its crying rose into a tempest of despair. The girl rocked it to and fro on her lap, but nothing soothed it. All the woe of a child's world flooded its tiny voice. Stop it, stop it, said the Fat Man, and the tears increased. Annie smothered it in kisses, but its wild cry broke on her lips like water upon rocks. We must do something, she said. Sing it a lullabee. She sang, but the child did not like her singing.

There's only one thing, said Annie, we must take it on the roundabouts. With the child's arm around her neck, she stumbled down the steps and ran towards the deserted fair, the Fat Man panting behind her. She found her way through the tents and stalls into the centre of the ground where the wooden horses stood waiting, and clambered up on to a saddle. Start the engine, she called out. In the distance the Fat Man could be heard cranking up the antique machine that drove the horses all the day into a wooden gallop. She heard the sudden spasmodic humming of the engine; the boards rattled under the horses' feet. She saw the Fat Man clamber up by her side, pull the central lever and climb on to the saddle of the smallest horse of all. As the roundabout started, slowly at first and slowly gaining speed, the child at the girl's breast stopped crying, clutched its hands together, and crowed with joy. The night wind tore through its hair, the music jangled in its ears. Round and round the wooden horses sped, drowning the cries of the wind with the beating of their wooden hooves.

And so the men from the caravans found them, the Fat Man and the girl in black with a baby in her arms, racing round and round on their mechanical steeds to the ever-increasing music of the organ.

QUESTIONS
1. "After the Fair" is a curiously cryptic story. How much of it can you explain?
2. Which elements are most difficult to understand? Do any seem at least partly symbolic?
3. The ending seems charged with symbolism. The wild ride on the roundabout, or merry-go-round, seems meant to carry a meaning not ordinarily carried by such rides. Is it possible to agree on what that meaning is?

CHAPTER 7

Theme

The desire to shape thought with a story is as old as storytelling. When Aesop's fox says of the grapes he cannot reach, "I thought those grapes were ripe, but I now see they are quite sour," the lesson is clear. Reading the Biblical parable of the Prodigal Son (Luke xv.:11–32), we stop to interpret: meaning is more important than plot or characterization. Although modern stories are not often as pointedly didactic as Aesop and the Bible, in most serious stories the ideas are vital. The *theme* of a story is its general subject (love, marriage, or death, for instance) or, frequently more important for criticism, its idea about the subject (love ennobles or debases, marriage fulfills or depletes, and so on). Some stories are dominated by theme; in others the ideas lie more subtly in the background.

In Ursula K. Le Guin's "The Ones Who Walk Away from Omelas," theme dominates. Introducing the story in her book *The Wind's Twelve Quarters*, she traces its origin to a passage in which the philosopher William James imagines a society "kept permanently happy on the one simple condition that a certain lost soul on the far-off edge of things should lead a life of lonely torment." Other influences included a road sign spelled backwards (Salem, Oregon), and the consideration that "salem" means "salaam," or "peace." Finally, Le Guin observes that the pronunciation of "Omelas" suggests "homme hèlas" (French for "man, alas").

THE ONES WHO WALK AWAY FROM OMELAS
Ursula K. Le Guin   (1929–   )

With a clamor of bells that set the swallows soaring, the Festival of Summer came to the city Omelas, bright-towered by the sea. The rigging of the boats in harbor sparkled with flags. In the streets between houses with red roofs and painted walls, between old moss-grown gardens and under avenues of trees, past great parks and public buildings, processions moved. Some were decorous: old people in long stiff robes of mauve and grey, grave master workmen, quiet, merry women carrying their babies and chatting as they walked. In other streets the music beat faster, a shimmering of gong and tambourine, and the people went dancing, the procession was a dance. Children dodged in and out, their high calls rising like the swallows' crossing flights over the music and the singing. All the processions wound towards the north side of the city, where on the great water-meadow called the Green Fields boys and girls, naked in the bright air, with mud-stained feet and ankles and long, lithe arms, exercised their restive horses before the race. The horses wore no gear at all but a halter without bit. Their manes were braided with streamers of silver, gold, and green. They flared their nostrils and pranced and boasted to one another; they were vastly excited, the horse being the only animal who has adopted our ceremonies as his own. Far off to the north and west the mountains stood up half encircling Omelas on her bay. The air of morning was so clear that the snow still crowning the Eighteen Peaks burned with white-gold fire across the miles of sunlit air, under the dark blue of the sky. There was just enough wind to make the banners that marked the racecourse snap and flutter now and then. In the silence of the broad green meadows one could hear the music winding through the city streets, farther and nearer and ever approaching, a cheerful faint sweetness of the air that from time to time trembled and gathered together and broke out into the great joyous clanging of the bells.

Joyous! How is one to tell about joy? How describe the citizens of Omelas?

They were not simple folk, you see, though they were happy. But we do not say the words of cheer much any more. All smiles have become archaic. Given a description such as this one tends to make certain assumptions. Given a description such as this one tends to look next for the King, mounted on a splendid stallion and surrounded by his noble knights, or perhaps in a golden litter borne by great-muscled slaves. But there was no king. They did not use swords, or keep slaves. They were not barbarians. I do not know the rules and laws of their society, but I suspect that they were singularly few. As they did without monarchy and slavery, so they also go on without the stock exchange, the advertisement, the secret police, and the bomb. Yet I repeat that these were not simple folk, not dulcet shepherds, noble savages, bland utopians. They were not less complex than us. The trouble is that we have a bad habit, encouraged by pedants and sophisticates, of considering happiness as something rather stupid. Only pain is intellectual, only evil interesting. This is the treason of the artist: a refusal to admit the banality of evil and the terrible boredom of pain. If you can't lick 'em, join 'em. If it hurts, repeat it. But to praise despair is to condemn delight, to embrace violence is to lose hold of everything else. We have almost lost hold; we can no longer describe a happy man, nor make any celebration of joy. How can I tell you about the people of Omelas? They were not naïve and happy children—though their children were, in fact, happy. They were mature, intelligent, passionate adults whose lives were not wretched. O miracle! but I wish I could describe it better. I wish I could convince you. Omelas sounds in my words like a city in a fairy tale, long ago and far away, once upon a time. Perhaps it would be best if you imagined it as your own fancy bids, assuming it will rise to the occasion, for certainly I cannot suit you all. For instance, how about technology? I think that there would be no cars or helicopters in and above the streets; this follows from the fact that the people of Omelas are happy people. Happiness is based on a just discrimination of what is necessary, what is neither necessary nor destructive, and what is destructive. In the middle category, however—that of the unnecessary but undestructive, that of comfort, luxury, exuberance, etc.—they could perfectly well have central heating, subway trains, washing machines, and all kinds of marvelous devices not yet invented here, floating light-sources, fuelless power, a cure for the common cold. Or they could have none of that: it doesn't matter. As you like it. I incline to think that people from towns up and down the coast have been coming in to Omelas during the last days before the Festival on very fast little trains and double-decked trams, and that the train station of Omelas is actually the handsomest building in town, though plainer than the magnificent Farmers' Market. But even granted trains, I fear that Omelas so far strikes some of you as goody-goody. Smiles, bells, parades, horses, bleh. If so, please add an orgy. If an orgy would help, don't hesitate. Let us not, however, have temples from which issue beautiful nude priests and priestesses already half in ecstasy and ready to copulate with any man or woman, lover or stranger, who desires union with the deep godhead of the blood, although that was my first idea. But really it would be better not to have any temples in Omelas—at least, not manned temples. Religion yes, clergy no. Surely the beautiful nudes can just wander about, offering themselves like divine soufflés to the hunger of the needy and the rapture of the flesh. Let them join the processions. Let tambourines be struck above the copulations, and the glory of desire be proclaimed upon the gongs, and (a not unimportant point) let the offspring of these delightful rituals be beloved and looked after by all. One thing I know there is none of in Omelas is guilt. But what else should there be? I thought at first there were no drugs, but that is puritanical. For those who like it, the faint insistent sweetness of *drooz* may perfume the ways of the city, *drooz* which first brings a great lightness and brilliance to the mind and limbs, and then after some hours a dreamy languor, and wonderful visions at last of the very arcana and inmost secrets of the Universe, as well as exciting the pleasure of sex beyond all belief; and it is not habit-forming. For more modest tastes I think there ought to be beer. What else, what else belongs in the joyous city? The sense of victory, surely, the celebration of courage. But as we did without clergy, let us do without soldiers. The joy built upon successful slaughter is not the right kind of joy; it will not do; it is fearful and it is trivial. A boundless and generous contentment, a magnanimous triumph felt not against some outer enemy but in communion with the finest and fairest in the souls of all men everywhere and the splendor of the world's summer: this is what swells the hearts of the people of Omelas, and the victory they celebrate is that of life. I really don't think many of them need to take *drooz*.

Most of the processions have reached the Green Fields by now. A marvelous smell of cooking goes forth from the red and blue tents of the provisioners. The faces of small children are amiably sticky; in the benign grey beard of a man a couple of crumbs of rich pastry are entangled. The youths and girls have mounted their horses and are beginning to group around the starting line of the course. An old woman, small, fat, and laughing, is passing out flowers from a basket, and tall young men wear her flowers in their shining hair. A child of nine or ten sits at the edge of the crowd, alone, playing on a wooden flute. People pause to listen, and they smile, but they do not speak to him, for he never ceases playing and never sees them, his dark eyes wholly rapt in the sweet, thin magic of the tune.

He finishes, and slowly lowers his hands holding the wooden flute.

As if that little private silence were the signal, all at once a trumpet sounds from the pavilion near the starting line: imperious, melancholy, piercing. The horses rear on their slender legs, and some of them neigh in answer. Sober-faced, the young riders stroke the horses' necks and soothe them, whispering, "Quiet,

quiet, there my beauty, my hope. . . ." They begin to form in rank along the start-ing line. The crowds along the racecourse are like a field of grass and flowers in the wind. The Festival of Summer has begun.

Do you believe? Do you accept the festival, the city, the joy? No? Then let me describe one more thing.

In a basement under one of the beautiful public buildings of Omelas, or per-haps in the cellar of one of its spacious private homes, there is a room. It has one locked door, and no window. A little light seeps in dustily between cracks in the boards, secondhand from a cobwebbed window somewhere across the cellar. In one corner of the little room a couple of mops, with stiff, clotted, foul-smelling heads, stand near a rusty bucket. The floor is dirt, a little damp to the touch, as cellar dirt usually is. The room is about three paces long and two wide: a mere broom closet or disused tool room. In the room a child is sitting. It could be a boy or a girl. It looks about six, but actually is nearly ten. It is feeble-minded. Perhaps it was born defective, or perhaps it has become imbecile through fear, malnutri-tion, and neglect. It picks its nose and occasionally fumbles vaguely with its toes or genitals, as it sits hunched in the corner farthest from the bucket and the two mops. It is afraid of the mops. It finds them horrible. It shuts its eyes, but it knows the mops are still standing there; and the door is locked; and nobody will come. The door is always locked; and nobody ever comes, except that some-times—the child has no understanding of time or interval—sometimes the door rattles terribly and opens, and a person, or several people, are there. One of them may come in and kick the child to make it stand up. The others never come close, but peer in at it with frightened, disgusted eyes. The food bowl and the water jug are hastily filled, the door is locked, the eyes disappear. The people at the door never say anything, but the child, who has not always lived in the tool room, and can remember sunlight and its mother's voice, sometimes speaks. "I will be good," it says. "Please let me out. I will be good!" They never answer. The child used to scream for help at night, and cry a good deal, but now it only makes a kind of whining, "eh-haa, eh-haa," and it speaks less and less often. It is so thin there are no calves to its legs; its belly protrudes; it lives on a half-bowl of corn meal and grease a day. It is naked. Its buttocks and thighs are a mass of festered sores, as it sits in its own excrement continually.

They all know it is there, all the people of Omelas. Some of them have come to see it, others are content merely to know it is there. They all know that it has to be there. Some of them understand why, and some do not, but they all under-stand that their happiness, the beauty of their city, the tenderness of their friend-ships, the health of their children, the wisdom of their scholars, the skill of their makers, even the abundance of their harvest and the kindly weathers of their skies, depend wholly on this child's abominable misery.

This is usually explained to children when they are between eight and twelve, whenever they seem capable of understanding; and most of those who come to see the child are young people, though often enough an adult comes, or comes back, to see the child. No matter how well the matter has been explained to them, these young spectators are always shocked and sickened at the sight. They feel disgust, which they had thought themselves superior to. They feel an-ger, outrage, impotence, despite all the explanations. They would like to do something for the child. But there is nothing they can do. If the child were brought up into the sunlight out of that vile place, if it were cleaned and fed and comforted, that would be a good thing, indeed; but if it were done, in that day and hour all the prosperity and beauty and delight of Omelas would wither and be destroyed. Those are the terms. To exchange all the goodness and grace of every life in Omelas for that single, small improvement: to throw away the happiness of thousands for the chance of the happiness of one: that would be to let guilt within the walls indeed.

The terms are strict and absolute; there may not even be a kind word spoken to the child.

Often the young people go home in tears, or in a tearless rage, when they have seen the child and faced this terrible paradox. They may brood over it for weeks or years. But as time goes on they begin to realize that even if the child could be released, it would not get much good of its freedom: a little vague pleasure of warmth and food, no doubt, but little more. It is too degraded and imbecile to know any real joy. It has been afraid too long ever to be free of fear. Its habits are too uncouth for it to respond to humane treatment. Indeed, after so long it would probably be wretched without walls about it to protect it, and darkness for its eyes, and its own excrement to sit in. Their tears at the bitter injustice dry when they begin to perceive the terrible justice of reality, and to accept it. Yet it is their tears and anger, the trying of their generosity and the acceptance of their helplessness, which are perhaps the true source of the splendor of their lives. Theirs is no vapid, irresponsible happiness. They know that they, like the child, are not free. They know compassion. It is the existence of the child, and their knowledge of its existence, that makes possible the nobility of their architecture, the poignancy of their music, the profundity of their science. It is because of the child that they are so gentle with children. They know that if the wretched one were not there snivelling in the dark, the other one, the fluteplayer, could make no joyful music as the young riders line up in their beauty for the race in the sunlight of the first morning of summer.

Now do you believe in them? Are they not more credible? But there is one more thing to tell, and this is quite incredible.

At times one of the adolescent girls or boys who go to see the child does not go home to weep or rage, does not, in fact, go home at all. Sometimes also a man or woman much older falls silent for a day or two, and then leaves home. These people go out into the street, and walk down the street alone. They keep walking, and walk straight out of the city of Omelas, through the beautiful gates. They keep walking across the farmlands of Omelas. Each one goes alone, youth or girl, man or woman. Night falls; the traveler must pass down village streets, between the houses with yellow-lit windows, and on out into the darkness of the fields. Each alone, they go west or north, towards the mountains. They go on. They leave Omelas, they walk ahead into the darkness, and they do not come back. The place they go towards is a place even less imaginable to most of us than the city of happiness. I cannot describe it at all. It is possible that it does not exist. But they seem to know where they are going, the ones who walk away from Omelas.

QUESTIONS

1. What, precisely, is this story trying to say?
2. Is it interesting apart from its message?

3. Describe the narrative perspective. What effects does it contribute to the story?
4. Can you imagine the place the people go to when they walk away from Omelas? What are its distinctive qualities?

HE

Katherine Anne Porter (1890–)

Life was very hard for the Whipples. It was hard to feed all the hungry mouths, it was hard to keep the children in flannels during the winter, short as it was: "God knows what would become of us if we lived north," they would say: keeping them decently clean was hard. "It looks like our luck won't never let up on us," said Mr. Whipple, but Mrs. Whipple was all for taking what was sent and calling it good, anyhow when the neighbors were in earshot. "Don't ever let a soul hear us complain," she kept saying to her husband. She couldn't stand to be pitied. "No, not if it comes to it that we have to live in a wagon and pick cotton around the country," she said, "nobody's going to get a chance to look down on us."

Mrs. Whipple loved her second son, the simple-minded one, better than she loved the other two children put together. She was forever saying so, and when she talked with certain of her neighbors, she would even throw in her husband and her mother for good measure.

"You needn't keep on saying it around," said Mr. Whipple, "you'll make people think nobody else has any feelings about Him but you."

"It's natural for a mother," Mrs. Whipple would remind him. "You know yourself it's more natural for a mother to be that way. People don't expect so much of fathers, some way."

This didn't keep the neighbors from talking plainly among themselves. "A Lord's pure mercy if He should die," they said. "It's the sin of the fathers," they agreed among themselves. "There's bad blood and bad doings somewhere, you can bet on that." This behind the Whipples' backs. To their faces everybody said, "He's not so bad off. He'll be all right yet. Look how He grows!"

Mrs. Whipple hated to talk about it, she tried to keep her mind off it, but every time anybody set foot in the house, the subject always came up, and she had to talk about Him first, before she could get on to anything else. It seemed to ease her mind. "I wouldn't have anything happen to Him for all the world, but it just looks like I can't keep Him out of mischief. He's so strong and active, He's always into everything; He was like that since He could walk. It's actually funny sometimes, the way He can do anything; it's laughable to see Him up to His tricks. Emly has more accidents; I'm forever tying up her bruises, and Adna can't fall a foot without cracking a bone. But He can do anything and not get a scratch. The preacher said such a nice thing once when he was here. He said, and I'll remember it to my dying day, 'The innocent walk with God—that's why He don't get hurt.' " Whenever Mrs. Whipple repeated these words, she always felt a warm pool spread in her breast, and the tears would fill her eyes, and then she could talk about something else.

He did grow and He never got hurt. A plank blew off the chicken house and struck Him on the head and He never seemed to know it. He had learned a few words, and after this He forgot them. He didn't whine for food as the other children did, but waited until it was given Him; He ate squatting in the corner, smacking and mumbling. Rolls of fat covered Him like an overcoat, and He could carry twice as much wood and water as Adna. Emly had a cold in the head most of the time—"she takes that after me," said Mrs. Whipple—so in bad weather they gave her the extra blanket off His cot. He never seemed to mind the cold.

Just the same, Mrs. Whipple's life was a torment for fear something might happen to Him. He climbed the peach trees much better than Adna and went skittering along the branches like a monkey, just a regular monkey. "Oh, Mrs. Whipple, you hadn't ought to let Him do that. He'll lose His balance sometime. He can't rightly know what He's doing."

Mrs. Whipple almost screamed out at the neighbor. "He *does* know what He's doing! He's as able as any other child! Come down out of there, you!" When He finally reached the ground she could hardly keep her hands off Him for acting like that before people, a grin all over His face and her worried sick about Him all the time.

"It's the neighbors," said Mrs. Whipple to her husband. "Oh, I do mortally wish they would keep out of our business. I can't afford to let Him do anything for fear they'll come nosing around about it. Look at the bees, now. Adna can't handle them, they sting him up so; I haven't got time to do everything, and now I don't dare let Him. But if He gets a sting He don't really mind."

"It's just because He ain't got sense enough to be scared of anything," said Mr. Whipple.

"You ought to be ashamed of yourself," said Mrs. Whipple, "talking that way about your own child. Who's to take up for Him if we don't, I'd like to know? He sees a lot that goes on, He listens to things all the time. And anything I tell Him to do He does it. Don't never let anybody hear you say such things. They'd think you favored the other children over Him."

"Well, now I don't, and you know it, and what's the use of getting all worked up about it? You always think the worst of everything. Just let Him alone, He'll get along somehow. He gets plenty to eat and wear, don't he?" Mr. Whipple suddenly felt tired out. "Anyhow, it can't be helped now."

Mrs. Whipple felt tired too, she complained in a tired voice. "What's done can't never be undone, I know that as good as anybody; but He's my child, and I'm not going to have people say anything. I get sick of people coming around saying things all the time."

In the early fall Mrs. Whipple got a letter from her brother saying he and his wife and two children were coming over for a little visit next Sunday week. "Put the big pot in the little one," he wrote at the end. Mrs. Whipple read this part out loud twice, she was so pleased. Her brother was a great one for saying funny things. "We'll just show him that's no joke," she said, "we'll just butcher one of the sucking pigs."

"It's a waste and I don't hold with waste the way we are now," said Mr. Whipple. "That pig'll be worth money by Christmas."

"It's a shame and a pity we can't have a decent meal's vittles once in a while when my own family comes to see us," said Mrs. Whipple. "I'd hate for his wife to go back and say there wasn't a thing in the house to eat. My God, it's better than buying up a great chance of meat in town. There's where you'd spend the money!"

"All right, do it yourself then," said Mr. Whipple. "Christamighty, no wonder we can't get ahead!"

The question was how to get the little pig away from his ma, a great fighter, worse than a Jersey cow. Adna wouldn't try it: "That sow'd rip my insides out all over the pen." "All right, old fraidy," said Mrs. Whipple, "He's not scared. Watch Him do it." And she laughed as though it was all a good joke and gave Him a little push towards the pen. He sneaked up and snatched the pig right away from the teat and galloped back and was over the fence with the sow raging at His heels. The little black squirming thing was screeching like a baby in a tantrum, stiffening its back and stretching its mouth to the ears. Mrs. Whipple took the pig with her face stiff and sliced its throat with one stroke. When He saw the blood He gave a great jolting breath and ran away. "But He'll forget and eat plenty, just the same," thought Mrs. Whipple. Whenever she was thinking, her lips moved making words. "He'd eat it all if I didn't stop Him. He'd eat up every mouthful from the other two if I'd let him."

She felt badly about it. He was ten years old now and a third again as large as Adna, who was going on fourteen. "It's a shame, a shame," she kept saying under her breath, "and Adna with so much brains!"

She kept on feeling badly about all sorts of things. In the first place it was the man's work to butcher; the sight of the pig scraped pink and naked made her sick. He was too fat and soft and pitiful-looking. It was simply a shame the way things had to happen. By the time she had finished it up, she almost wished her brother would stay at home.

Early Sunday morning Mrs. Whipple dropped everything to get Him all cleaned up. In an hour He was dirty again, with crawling under fences after a possum, and straddling along the rafters of the barn looking for eggs in the hayloft. "My Lord, look at you now after all my trying! And here's Adna and Emly staying so quiet. I get tired trying to keep you decent. Get off that shirt and put on another, people will say I don't half dress you!" And she boxed Him on the ears, hard. He blinked and blinked and rubbed His head, and His face hurt Mrs. Whipple's feelings. Her knees began to tremble, she had to sit down while she buttoned His shirt. "I'm just all gone before the day starts."

The brother came with his plump healthy wife and two great roaring hungry boys. They had a grand dinner, with the pig roasted to a crackling in the middle of the table, full of dressing, a pickled peach in his mouth and plenty of gravy for the sweet potatoes.

"This looks like prosperity all right," said the brother; "you're going to have to roll me home like I was a barrel when I'm done."

Everybody laughed out loud; it was fine to hear them laughing all at once around the table. Mrs. Whipple felt warm and good about it. "Oh, we've got six more of these; I say it's as little as we can do when you come to see us so seldom."

He wouldn't come into the dining room, and Mrs. Whipple passed it off very well. "He's timider than my other two," she said, "He'll just have to get used to you. There isn't everybody He'll make up with, you know how it is with some children, even cousins." Nobody said anything out of the way.

"Just like my Alfy here," said the brother's wife. "I sometimes got to lick him to make him shake hands with his own grandmammy."

So that was over, and Mrs. Whipple loaded up a big plate for Him first, before everybody. "I always say He ain't to be slighted, no matter who else goes without," she said, and carried it to Him herself.

"He can chin Himself on the top of the door," said Emly, helping along.

"That's fine, He's getting along fine," said the brother.

They went away after supper. Mrs. Whipple rounded up the dishes, and sent the children to bed and sat down and unlaced her shoes. "You see?" she said to Mr. Whipple. "That's the way my whole family is. Nice and considerate about everything. No out-of-the-way remarks—they *have* got refinement. I get awfully sick of people's remarks. Wasn't that pig good?"

Mr. Whipple said, "Yes, we're out three hundred pounds of pork, that's all. It's easy to be polite when you come to eat. Who knows what they had in their minds all along?"

"Yes, that's like you," said Mrs. Whipple. "I don't expect anything else from you. You'll be telling me next that my own brother will be saying around that we made Him eat in the kitchen! Oh, my God!" She rocked her head in her hands, a hard pain started in the very middle of her forehead. "Now it's all spoiled, and everything was so nice and easy. All right, you don't like them and you never did—all right, they'll not come here again soon, never you mind! But they *can't* say He wasn't dressed every lick as good as Adna—oh, honest, sometimes I wish I was dead!"

"I wish you'd let up," said Mr. Whipple. "It's bad enough as it is."

It was a hard winter. It seemed to Mrs. Whipple that they hadn't ever known anything but hard times, and now to cap it all a winter like this. The crops were about half of what they had a right to expect; after the cotton was in it didn't do much more than cover the grocery bill. They swapped off one of the plow horses, and got cheated, for the new one died of the heaves. Mrs. Whipple kept thinking all the time it was terrible to have a man you couldn't depend on not to get cheated. They cut down on everything, but Mrs. Whipple kept saying there are things you can't cut down on, and they cost money. It took a lot of warm clothes for Adna and Emly, who walked four miles to school during the three-months session. "He sets around the fire a lot, He won't need so much," said Mr. Whipple. "That's so," said Mrs. Whipple, "and when He does the outdoor chores He can wear your tarpaullion coat. I can't do no better, that's all."

In February He was taken sick, and lay curled up under His blanket looking very blue in the face and acting as if He would choke. Mr. and Mrs. Whipple did everything they could for Him for two days, and then they were scared and sent for the doctor. The doctor told them they must keep Him warm and give Him plenty of milk and eggs. "He isn't as stout as He looks, I'm afraid," said the doctor. "You've got to watch them when they're like that. You must put more cover onto Him, too."

"I just took off His big blanket to wash," said Mrs. Whipple, ashamed. "I can't stand dirt."

"Well, you'd better put it back on the minute it's dry," said the doctor, "or He'll have pneumonia."

Mr. and Mrs. Whipple took a blanket off their own bed and put His cot in by the fire. "They can't say we didn't do everything for Him," she said, "even to sleeping cold ourselves on His account."

When the winter broke He seemed to be well again, but He walked as if His feet hurt Him. He was able to run a cotton planter during the season.

"I got it all fixed up with Jim Ferguson about breeding the cow next time," said Mr. Whipple. "I'll pasture the bull this summer and give Jim some fodder in the fall. That's better than paying out money when you haven't got it."

"I hope you didn't say such a thing before Jim Ferguson," said Mrs. Whipple. "You oughtn't to let him know we're so down as all that."

"Godamighty, that ain't saying we're down. A man is got to look ahead some-times. He can lead the bull over today. I need Adna on the place."

At first Mrs. Whipple felt easy in her mind about sending Him for the bull. Adna was too jumpy and couldn't be trusted. You've got to be steady around ani-mals. After He was gone she started thinking, and after a while she could hardly bear it any longer. She stood in the lane and watched for Him. It was nearly three miles to go and a hot day, but He oughtn't to be so long about it. She shaded her eyes and stared until colored bubbles floated in her eyeballs. It was just like everything else in life, she must always worry and never know a mo-ment's peace about anything. After a long time she saw Him turn into the side lane, limping. He came on very slowly, leading the big hulk of an animal by a ring in the nose, twirling a little stick in His hand, never looking back or sideways, but coming on like a sleepwalker with His eyes half shut.

Mrs. Whipple was scared sick of bulls; she had heard awful stories about how they followed on quietly enough, and then suddenly pitched on with a bellow and pawed and gored a body to pieces. Any second now that black monster would come down on Him, my God, He'd never have sense enough to run.

She mustn't make a sound nor a move; she mustn't get the bull started. The bull heaved his head aside and horned the air at a fly. Her voice burst out of her in a shriek, and she screamed at Him to come on, for God's sake. He didn't seem to hear her clamor, but kept on twirling His switch and limping on, and the bull lumbered along behind him as gently as a calf. Mrs. Whipple stopped calling and ran towards the house, praying under her breath: "Lord, don't let anything hap-pen to Him. Lord, you *know* people will say we oughtn't to have sent Him. You *know* they'll say we didn't take care of Him. Oh, get Him home, safe home, safe home, and I'll look out for Him better! Amen."

She watched from the window while He led the beast in, and tied him up in the barn. It was no use trying to keep up, Mrs. Whipple couldn't bear another thing. She sat down and rocked and cried with her apron over her head.

From year to year the Whipples were growing poorer and poorer. The place just seemed to run down of itself, no matter how hard they worked. "We're los-ing our hold," said Mrs. Whipple. "Why can't we do like other people and watch for our best chances? They'll be calling us poor white trash next."

"When I get to be sixteen I'm going to leave," said Adna. "I'm going to get a job in Powell's grocery store. There's money in that. No more farm for me."

"I'm going to be a schoolteacher," said Emly. "But I've got to finish the eighth grade, anyhow. Then I can live in town. I don't see any chances here."

"Emly takes after my family," said Mrs. Whipple. "Ambitious every last one of them, and they don't take second place for anybody."

When fall came Emly got a chance to wait on table in the railroad eating-house in the town near by, and it seemed such a shame not to take it when the wages were good and she could get her food too, that Mrs. Whipple decided to let her take it, and not bother with school until the next session. "You've got plenty of time," she said. "You're young and smart as a whip."

With Adna gone too, Mr. Whipple tried to run the farm with just Him to help. He seemed to get along fine, doing His work and part of Adna's without noticing it. They did well enough until Christmas time, when one morning He slipped on the ice coming up from the barn. Instead of getting up He thrashed round and round, and when Mr. Whipple got to Him, He was having some sort of fit.

They brought Him inside and tried to make Him sit up, but He blubbered and rolled, so they put Him to bed and Mr. Whipple rode to town for the doctor. All the way there and back he worried about where the money was to come from: it sure did look like he had about all the troubles he could carry.

From then on He stayed in bed. His legs swelled up double their size, and the fits kept coming back. After four months, the doctor said, "It's no use, I think you'd better put Him in the County Home for treatment right away. I'll see about it for you. He'll have good care there and be off your hands."

"We don't begrudge Him any care, and I won't let Him out of my sight," said Mrs. Whipple. "I won't have it said I sent my sick child off among strangers."

"I know how you feel," said the doctor. "You can't tell me anything about that, Mrs. Whipple. I've got a boy of my own. But you'd better listen to me. I can't do anything more for Him, that's the truth."

Mr. and Mrs. Whipple talked it over a long time that night after they went to bed. "It's just charity," said Mrs. Whipple, "that's what we've come to, charity! I certainly never looked for this."

"We pay taxes to help support the place just like everybody else," said Mr. Whipple, "and I don't call that taking charity. I think it would be fine to have Him where He'd get the best of everything . . . and besides, I can't keep up with these doctor bills any longer."

"Maybe that's why the doctor wants us to send Him—he's scared he won't get his money," said Mrs. Whipple.

"Don't talk like that," said Mr. Whipple, feeling pretty sick, "or we won't be able to send Him."

"Oh, but we won't keep Him there long," said Mrs. Whipple. "Soon's He's better, we'll bring Him right back home."

"The doctor has told you and told you time and again He can't ever get better, and you might as well stop talking," said Mr. Whipple.

"Doctors don't know everything," said Mrs. Whipple, feeling almost happy. "But anyhow, in the summer Emly can come home for a vacation, and Adna can get down for Sundays: we'll all work together and get on our feet again, and the children will feel they've got a place to come to."

All at once she saw it full summer again, with the garden going fine, and new white roller shades up all over the house, and Adna and Emly home, so full of life, all of them happy together. Oh, it could happen, things would ease up on them.

They didn't talk before Him much, but they never knew just how much He understood. Finally the doctor set the day and a neighbor who owned a double-seated carryall offered to drive them over. The hospital would have sent an ambulance, but Mrs. Whipple couldn't stand to see Him going away looking so sick as all that. They wrapped Him in blankets, and the neighbor and Mr. Whipple lifted Him into the back seat of the carryall beside Mrs. Whipple, who had on her black shirt waist. She couldn't stand to go looking like charity.

"You'll be all right, I guess I'll stay behind," said Mr. Whipple. "It don't look like everybody ought to leave the place at once."

"Besides, it ain't as if He was going to stay forever," said Mrs. Whipple to the neighbor. "This is only for a little while."

They started away, Mrs. Whipple holding to the edges of the blankets to keep Him from sagging sideways. He sat there blinking and blinking. He worked His hands out and began rubbing His nose with His knuckles, and then with the end of the blanket. Mrs. Whipple couldn't believe what she saw; He was scrubbing away big tears that rolled out of the corners of His eyes. He sniveled and made a gulping noise. Mrs. Whipple kept saying, "Oh, honey, you don't feel so bad, do you? You don't feel so bad, do you?" for He seemed to be accusing her of something. Maybe He remembered that time she boxed His ears, maybe He had been scared that day with the bull, maybe He had slept cold and couldn't tell her about it; maybe He knew they were sending Him away for good and all because they were too poor to keep Him. Whatever it was, Mrs. Whipple couldn't bear to think of it. She began to cry, frightfully, and wrapped her arms tight around Him. His head rolled on her shoulder: she had loved Him as much as she possibly could, there were Adna and Emly who had to be thought of too, there was nothing she could do to make up to Him for His life. Oh, what a mortal pity He was ever born.

They came in sight of the hospital, with the neighbor driving very fast, not daring to look behind him.

QUESTIONS

1. Mrs. Whipple remembers that the preacher said, "The innocent walk with God—that's why He don't get hurt." Does the story support this idea?
2. What is gained by the narrative focus on Mrs. Whipple? Would anything be gained by allowing us to understand more directly what the boy sees and feels?
3. Which scenes are most vividly imagined? Do they add to the story's verisimilitude?
4. The subject matter here is poverty, motherhood, and retardation. What are some of the ideas suggested?

THE SEVENTH SALLY*
OR HOW TRURL'S OWN PERFECTION LED TO NO GOOD
Stanislaw Lem   (1921–   )

The Universe is infinite but bounded, and therefore a beam of light, in whatever direction it may travel, will after billions of centuries return—if powerful

* Translated by Michael Kandel.

enough—to the point of its departure; and it is no different with rumor, that flies about from star to star and makes the rounds of every planet. One day Trurl heard distant reports of two mighty constructor-benefactors, so wise and so accomplished that they had no equal; with this news he ran to Klapaucius, who explained to him that these were not mysterious rivals, but only themselves, for their fame had circumnavigated space. Fame, however, has this fault, that it says nothing of one's failures, even when those very failures are the product of a great perfection. And he who would doubt this, let him recall the last of the seven sallies[1] of Trurl, which was undertaken without Klapaucius, whom certain urgent duties kept at home at the time.

In those days Trurl was exceedingly vain, receiving all marks of veneration and honor paid to him as his due and a perfectly normal thing. He was heading north in his ship, as he was the least familiar with that region, and had flown through the void for quite some time, passing spheres full of the clamor of war as well as spheres that had finally obtained the perfect peace of desolation, when suddenly a little planet came into view, really more of a stray fragment of matter than a planet.

On the surface of this chunk of rock someone was running back and forth, jumping and waving his arms in the strangest way. Astonished by a scene of such total loneliness and concerned by those wild gestures of despair, and perhaps of anger as well, Trurl quickly landed.

He was approached by a personage of tremendous hauteur, iridium and vanadium all over and with a great deal of clanging and clanking, who introduced himself as Excelsius the Tartarian, ruler of Pancreon and Cyspenderora; the inhabitants of both these kingdoms had, in a fit of regicidal madness, driven His Highness from the throne and exiled him to this barren asteroid, eternally adrift among the dark swells and currents of gravitation.

Learning in turn the identity of his visitor, the deposed monarch began to insist that Trurl—who after all was something of a professional when it came to good deeds—immediately restore him to his former position. The thought of such a turn of events brought the flame of vengeance to the monarch's eyes, and his iron fingers clutched the air, as if already closing around the throats of his beloved subjects.

Now Trurl had no intention of complying with this request of Excelsius, as doing so would bring about untold evil and suffering, yet at the same time he wished somehow to comfort and console the humiliated king. Thinking a moment or two, he came to the conclusion that, even in this case, not all was lost, for it would be possible to satisfy the king completely—without putting his former subjects in jeopardy. And so, rolling up his sleeves and summoning up all his mastery, Trurl built the king an entirely new kingdom. There were plenty of towns, rivers, mountains, forests and brooks, a sky with clouds, armies full of derring-do, citadels, castles and ladies' chambers; and there were marketplaces, gaudy and gleaming in the sun, days of back-breaking labor, nights full of dancing and song until dawn, and the gay clatter of swordplay. Trurl also carefully set into this kingdom a fabulous capital, all in marble and alabaster, and assembled a council of hoary sages, and winter palaces and summer villas, plots, conspirators, false witnesses, nurses, informers, teams of magnificent steeds, and plumes waving crimson in the wind; and then he crisscrossed that atmosphere

[1] The first six sallies are recounted in *The Cyberiad*, the source of the present story.

with silver fanfares and twenty-one gun salutes, also threw in the necessary handful of traitors, another of heroes, added a pinch of prophets and seers, and one messiah and one great poet each, after which he bent over and set the works in motion, deftly making last-minute adjustments with his microscopic tools as it ran, and he gave the women of that kingdom beauty, the men—sullen silence and surliness when drunk, the officials—arrogance and servility, the astronomers—an enthusiasm for stars, and the children—a great capacity for noise. And all of this, connected, mounted and ground to precision, fit into a box, and not a very large box, but just the size that could be carried about with ease. This Trurl presented to Excelsius, to rule and have dominion over forever; but first he showed him where the input and output of his brand-new kingdom were, and how to program wars, quell rebellions, exact tribute, collect taxes, and also instructed him in the critical points and transition states of that microminiaturized society—in other words the maxima and minima of palace coups and revolutions—and explained everything so well, that the king, an old hand in the running of tyrannies, instantly grasped the directions and, without hesitation, while the constructor watched, issued a few trial proclamations, correctly manipulating the control knobs, which were carved with imperial eagles and regal lions. These proclamations declared a state of emergency, martial law, a curfew and a special levy. After a year had passed in the kingdom, which amounted to hardly a minute for Trurl and the king, by an act of the greatest magnanimity—that is, by a flick of the finger at the controls—the king abolished one death penalty, lightened the levy and deigned to annul the state of emergency, whereupon a tumultuous cry of gratitude, like the squeaking of tiny mice lifted by their tails, rose up from the box, and through its curved glass cover one could see, on the dusty highways and along the banks of lazy rivers that reflected the fluffy clouds, the people rejoicing and praising the great and unsurpassed benevolence of their sovereign lord.

And so, though at first he had felt insulted by Trurl's gift, in that the kingdom was too small and very like a child's toy, the monarch saw that the thick glass lid made everything inside seem large; perhaps too he dully understood that size was not what mattered here, for government is not measured in meters and kilograms, and emotions are somehow the same, whether experienced by giants or dwarfs—and so he thanked the constructor, if somewhat stiffly. Who knows, he might even have liked to order him thrown in chains and tortured to death, just to be safe—that would have been a sure way of nipping in the bud any gossip about how some common vagabond tinkerer presented a mighty monarch with a kingdom.

Excelsius was sensible enough, however, to see that this was out of the question, owing to a very fundamental disproportion, for fleas could sooner take their host into captivity than the king's army seize Trurl. So with another cold nod, he stuck his orb and scepter under his arm, lifted the box kingdom with a grunt, and took it to his humble hut of exile. And as blazing day alternated with murky night outside, according to the rhythm of the asteroid's rotation, the king, who was acknowledged by his subjects as the greatest in the world, diligently reigned, bidding this, forbidding that, beheading, rewarding—in all these ways incessantly spurring his little ones on to perfect fealty and worship of the throne.

As for Trurl, he returned home and related to his friend Klapaucius, not without pride, how he had employed his constructor's genius to indulge the autocratic aspirations of Excelsius and, at the same time, safeguard the democratic aspirations of his former subjects. But Klapaucius, surprisingly enough, had no words of praise for Trurl; in fact, there seemed to be rebuke in his expression.

"Have I understood you correctly?" he said at last. "You gave that brutal despot, that born slave master, that slavering sadist of a painmonger, you gave him a whole civilization to rule and have dominion over forever? And you tell me, moreover, of the cries of joy brought on by the repeal of a fraction of his cruel decrees! Trurl, how could you have done such a thing?!"

"You must be joking!" Trurl exclaimed. "Really, the whole kingdom fits into a box three feet by two by two and a half . . . it's only a model . . . "

"A model of what?"

"What do you mean, of what? Of a civilization, obviously, except that it's a hundred million times smaller."

"And how do you know there aren't civilizations a hundred million times larger than our own? And if there were, would ours then be a model? And what importance do dimensions have anyway? In that box kingdom, doesn't a journey from the capital to one of the corners take months—for those inhabitants? And don't they suffer, don't they know the burden of labor, don't they die?"

"Now just a minute, you know yourself that all these processes take place only because I programmed them, and so they aren't genuine. . . . "

"Aren't genuine? You mean to say the box is empty, and the parades, tortures and beheadings are merely an illusion?"

"Not an illusion, no, since they have reality, though purely as certain microscopic phenomena, which I produced by manipulating atoms," said Trurl. "The point is, these births, loves, acts of heroism and denunciations are nothing but the minuscule capering of electrons in space, precisely arranged by the skill of my nonlinear craft, which—"

"Enough of your boasting, not another word!" Klapaucius snapped. "Are these processes self-organizing or not?"

"Of course they are!"

"And they occur among infinitesimal clouds of electrical charge?"

"You know they do."

"And the phenomenological events of dawns, sunsets and bloody battles are generated by the concatenation of real variables?"

"Certainly."

"And are not we as well, if you examine us physically, mechanistically, statistically and meticulously, nothing but the minuscule capering of electron clouds? Positive and negative charges arranged in space? And is our existence not the result of subatomic collisions and the interplay of particles, though we ourselves perceive those molecular cartwheels as fear, longing, or meditation? And when you day-dream, what transpires within your brain but the binary algebra of connecting and disconnecting circuits, the continual meandering of electrons?"

"What, Klapaucius, would you equate our existence with that of an imitation kingdom locked up in some glass box?!" cried Trurl. "No, really, that's going too far! My purpose was simply to fashion a simulator of statehood, a model cybernetically perfect, nothing more!"

"Trurl! Our perfection is our curse, for it draws down upon our every endeavor no end of unforeseeable consequences!" Klapaucius said in a stentorian voice. "If an imperfect imitator, wishing to inflict pain, were to build himself a crude idol of wood or wax, and further give it some makeshift semblance of a sentient being, his torture of the thing would be a paltry mockery indeed! But consider a succession of improvements on this practice! Consider the next sculptor, who builds a doll with a recording in its belly, that it may groan beneath his blows; consider a doll which, when beaten, begs for mercy, no longer a crude idol, but a homeostat; consider a doll that sheds tears, a doll that bleeds, a doll that fears death, though it also longs for the peace that only death can bring! Don't you see, when the imitator is perfect, so must be the imitation, and the semblance becomes the truth, the pretense a reality! Trurl, you took an untold number of creatures capable of suffering and abandoned them forever to the rule of a wicked tyrant. . . . Trurl, you have committed a terrible crime!"

"Sheer sophistry!" shouted Trurl, all the louder because he felt the force of his friends's argument. "Electrons meander not only in our brains, but in phonograph records as well, which proves nothing, and certainly gives no grounds for such hypostatical analogies! The subjects of that monster Excelsius do in fact die when decapitated, sob, fight, and fall in love, since that is how I set up the parameters, but it's impossible to say, Klapaucius, that they feel anything in the process—the electrons jumping around in their heads will tell you nothing of that!"

"And if I were to look inside your head, I would also see nothing but electrons," replied Klapaucius. "Come now, don't pretend not to understand what I'm saying, I know you're not that stupid! A phonograph record won't run errands for you, won't beg for mercy or fall on its knees! You say there's no way of knowing whether Excelsius' subjects groan, when beaten, purely because of the electrons hopping about inside—like wheels grinding out the mimicry of a voice—or whether they really groan, that is, because they honestly experience the pain? A pretty distinction, this! No, Trurl, a sufferer is not one who hands you his suffering, that you may touch it, weigh it, bite it like a coin; a sufferer is one who behaves like a sufferer! Prove to me here and now, once and for all, that they do not feel, that they do not think, that they do not in any way exist as beings conscious of their enclosure between the two abysses of oblivion—the abyss before birth and the abyss that follows death—prove this to me, Trurl, and I'll leave you be! Prove that you only *imitated* suffering, and did not *create* it!"

"You know perfectly well that's impossible," answered Trurl quietly. "Even before I took my instruments in hand, when the box was still empty, I had to anticipate the possiblity of precisely such a proof—in order to rule it out. For otherwise the monarch of that kingdom sooner or later would have gotten the impression that his subjects were not real subjects at all, but puppets, marionettes. Try to understand, there was no other way to do it! Anything that would have destroyed in the littlest way the illusion of complete reality, would have also destroyed the importance, the dignity of governing, and turned it into nothing but a mechanical game. . . ."

"I understand, I understand all too well!" cried Klapaucius. "Your intentions were the noblest—you only sought to construct a kingdom as lifelike as possible, so similar to a real kingdom, that no one, absolutely no one, could ever tell the difference, and in this, I am afraid, you were successful! Only hours have passed since your return, but for them, the ones imprisoned in that box, whole centuries have gone by—how many beings, how many lives wasted, and all to gratify and feed the vanity of King Excelsius!"

Without another word Trurl rushed back to his ship, but saw that his friend was coming with him. When he had blasted off into space, pointed the bow between two great clusters of eternal flame and opened the throttle all the way, Klapaucius said:

"Trurl, you're hopeless. You always act first, think later. And now what do you intend to do when we get there?"

"I'll take the kingdom away from him!"

"And what will you do with it?"

"Destroy it!" Trurl was about to shout, but choked on the first syllable when he realized what he was saying. Finally he mumbled:

"I'll hold an election. Let them choose just rulers from among themselves."

"You programmed them all to be feudal lords or shiftless vassals. What good would an election do? First you'd have to undo the entire structure of the kingdom, then assemble from scratch. . . ."

"And where," exclaimed Trurl, "does the changing of structures end and the tampering with minds begin?!" Klapaucius had no answer for this, and they flew on in gloomy silence, till the planet of Excelsius came into view. As they circled it, preparing to land, they beheld a most amazing sight.

The entire planet was covered with countless signs of intelligent life. Microscopic bridges, like tiny lines, spanned every rill and rivulet, while the puddles, reflecting the stars, were full of microscopic boats like floating chips. . . . The night side of the sphere was dotted with glimmering cities, and on the day side one could make out flourishing metropolises, though the inhabitants themselves were much too little to observe, even through the strongest lens. Of the king there was not a trace, as if the earth had swallowed him up.

"He isn't here," said Trurl in an awed whisper. "What have they done with him? Somehow they managed to break through the walls of their box and occupy the asteroid. . . ."

"Look!" said Klapaucius, pointing to a little cloud no larger than a thimble and shaped like a mushroom; it slowly rose into the atmosphere. "They've discovered atomic energy. . . . And over there—you see that bit of glass? It's the remains of the box, they've made it into some sort of temple. . . ."

"I don't understand. It was only a model, after all. A process with a large number of parameters, a simulation, a mock-up for a monarch to practice on, with the necessary feedback, variables, multistats . . ." muttered Trurl, dumbfounded.

"Yes. But you made the unforgivable mistake of over-perfecting your replica. Not wanting to build a mere clocklike mechanism, you inadvertently—in your punctilious way—created that which was possible, logical and inevitable, that which became the very antithesis of a mechanism. . . ."

"Please no more!" cried Trurl. And they looked out upon the asteroid in silence, when suddenly something bumped their ship, or rather grazed it slightly. They saw this object, for it was illuminated by the thin ribbon of flame that issued from its tail. A ship, probably, or perhaps an artificial satellite, though remarkably similar to one of those steel boots the tyrant Excelsius used to wear. And when the constructors raised their eyes, they beheld a heavenly body shining high above the tiny planet—it hadn't been there previously—and they recognized, in that cold pale orb, the stern features of Excelsius himself, who had in this way become the Moon of the Microminians.

QUESTIONS

1. This story bears less immediate relationship to our everyday lives than some others in this collection. In what ways is its connection to us made most evident?
2. What are some of the most important ideas here?
3. Is this in any way a satire?

TO BUILD A FIRE

Jack London (1876–1916)

Day had broken cold and gray, exceedingly cold and gray, when the man turned aside from the main Yukon trail and climbed the high earth-bank, where a dim and little-travelled trail led eastward through the fat spruce timberland. It was a steep bank, and he paused for breath at the top, excusing the act to himself by looking at his watch. It was nine o'clock. There was no sun nor hint of sun, though there was not a cloud in the sky. It was a clear day, and yet there seemed an intangible pall over the face of things, a subtle gloom that made the day dark, and that was due to the absence of sun. This fact did not worry the man. He was used to the lack of sun. It had been days since he had seen the sun, and he knew that a few more days must pass before that cheerful orb, due south, should just peep above the sky line and dip immediately from view.

The man flung a look back along the way he had come. The Yukon lay a mile wide and hidden under three feet of ice. On top of this ice were as many feet of snow. It was all pure white, rolling in gentle undulations where the ice jams of the freeze-up had formed. North and south, as far as his eye could see, it was unbroken white, save for a dark hairline that curved and twisted from around the spruce-covered island to the south, and that curved and twisted away into the north, where it disappeared behind another spruce-covered island. This dark hairline was the trail—the main trail—that led south five hundred miles to the Chilcoot Pass, Dyea, and salt water; and that led north seventy miles to Dawson, and still on to the north a thousand miles to Nulato, and finally to St. Michael, on Bering Sea, a thousand miles and half a thousand more.

But all this—the mysterious, far-reaching hairline trail, the absence of sun from the sky, the tremendous cold, and the strangeness and weirdness of it all—made no impression on the man. It was not because he was long used to it. He was a newcomer in the land, a *chechaquo*, and this was his first winter. The trouble with him was that he was without imagination. He was quick and alert in the things of life, but only in the things, and not in the significances. Fifty degrees below zero meant eighty-odd degrees of frost. Such fact impressed him as being cold and uncomfortable, and that was all. It did not lead him to meditate upon his frailty as a creature of temperature, and upon man's frailty in general, able only to live within certain narrow limits of heat and cold; and from there on it did not lead him to the conjectural field of immortality and man's place in the universe. Fifty degrees below zero stood for a bite of frost that hurt and that must be guarded against by the use of mittens, ear flaps, warm moccasins, and thick socks. Fifty degrees below zero was to him just precisely fifty degrees below zero. That there should be anything more to it than that was a thought that never entered his head.

As he turned to go on, he spat speculatively. There was a sharp, explosive crackle that startled him. He spat again. And again, in the air, before it could fall to the snow, the spittle crackled. He knew that at fifty below spittle crackled on the snow, but this spittle had crackled in the air. Undoubtedly it was colder than fifty below—how much colder he did not know. But the temperature did not matter. He was bound for the old claim on the left fork of Henderson Creek, where the boys were already. They had come over across the divide from the Indian Creek country, while he had come the roundabout way to take a look at the possibilities of getting out logs in the spring from the islands in the Yukon. He would be in to camp by six o'clock; a bit after dark, it was true, but the boys would be there, a fire would be going, and a hot supper would be ready. As for lunch, he pressed his hand against the protruding bundle under his jacket. It was also under his shirt, wrapped up in a handkerchief and lying against the naked skin. It was the only way to keep the biscuits from freezing. He smiled agreeably to himself as he thought of those biscuits, each cut open and sopped in bacon grease, and each enclosing a generous slice of fried bacon.

He plunged in among the big spruce trees. The trail was faint. A foot of snow had fallen since the last sled had passed over, and he was glad he was without a sled, traveling light. In fact, he carried nothing but the lunch wrapped in the handkerchief. He was surprised, however, at the cold. It certainly was cold, he concluded, as he rubbed his numb nose and cheekbones with his mittened hand. He was a warm-whiskered man, but the hair on his face did not protect the high cheekbones and the eager nose that thrust itself aggressively into the frosty air.

At the man's heels trotted a dog, a big native husky, the proper wolf dog, gray-coated and without any visible or temperamental difference from its brother, the wild wolf. The animal was depressed by the tremendous cold. It knew that it was no time for traveling. Its instinct told it a truer tale than was told to the man by the man's judgment. In reality, it was not merely colder than fifty below zero; it was colder than sixty below, than seventy below. It was seventy-five below zero. Since the freezing point is thirty-two above zero, it meant that one hundred and seven degrees of frost obtained. The dog did not know anything about thermometers. Possibly in its brain there was no sharp consciousness of a condition of very cold such as was in the man's brain. But the brute had its instinct. It experienced a vague but menacing apprehension that subdued it and made it slink along at the man's heels, and that made it question eagerly every unwonted movement of the man as if expecting him to go into camp or to seek shelter somewhere and build a fire. The dog had learned fire, and it wanted fire, or else to burrow under the snow and cuddle its warmth away from the air.

The frozen moisture of its breathing had settled on its fur in a fine powder of frost, and especially were its jowls, muzzle, and eyelashes whitened by its crystalled breath. The man's red beard and mustache were likewise frosted, but more solidly, the deposit taking the form of ice and increasing with every warm, moist breath he exhaled. Also, the man was chewing tobacco, and the muzzle of ice held his lips so rigidly that he was unable to clear his chin when he expelled the juice. The result was that a crystal beard of the color and solidity of amber was increasing its length on his chin. If he fell down it would shatter itself, like glass, into brittle fragments. But he did not mind the appendage. It was the penalty all tobacco chewers paid in that country, and he had been out before in two cold snaps. They had not been so cold as this, he knew, but by the spirit thermometer at Sixty Mile he knew they had been registered at fifty below and at fifty-five.

He held on through the level stretch of woods for several miles, crossed a wide flat of nigger heads, and dropped down a bank to the frozen bed of a small stream. This was Henderson Creek, and he knew he was ten miles from the forks. He looked at his watch. It was ten o'clock. He was making four miles an hour, and he calculated that he would arrive at the forks at half-past twelve. He decided to celebrate that event by eating his lunch there.

The dog dropped in again at his heels, with a tail drooping discouragement, as the man swung along the creek bed. The furrow of the old sled trail was plainly visible, but a dozen inches of snow covered the marks of the last runners. In a month no man had come up or down that silent creek. The man held steadily on. He was not much given to thinking, and just then particularly he had nothing to think about save that he would eat lunch at the forks and that at six o'clock he would be in camp with the boys. There was nobody to talk to; and, had there been, speech would have been impossible because of the ice muzzle on his mouth. So he continued monotonously to chew tobacco and to increase the length of his amber beard.

Once in a while the thought reiterated itself that it was very cold and that he had never experienced such cold. As he walked along he rubbed his cheekbones and nose with the back of his mittened hand. He did this automatically, now and again changing hands. But, rub as he would, the instant he stopped his cheekbones went numb, and the following instant the end of his nose went numb. He was sure to frost his cheeks; he knew that, and experienced a pang of regret that he had not devised a nose strap of the sort Bud wore in cold snaps. Such a strap passed across the cheeks, as well, and saved them. But it didn't matter much, after all. What were frosted cheeks? A bit painful, that was all; they were never serious.

Empty as the man's mind was of thoughts, he was keenly observant, and he noticed the changes in the creek, the curves and bends and timber jams, and always he sharply noted where he placed his feet. Once, coming around a bend, he shied abruptly, like a startled horse, curved away from the place where he had been walking, and retreated several paces back along the trail. The creek he knew was frozen clear to the bottom—no creek could contain water in that arctic winter—but he knew also that there were springs that bubbled out from the hillsides and ran along under the snow and on top the ice of the creek. He knew that the coldest snaps never froze these springs, and he knew likewise their danger. They were traps. They hid pools of water under the snow that might be three inches deep, or three feet. Sometimes a skin of ice half an inch thick covered them, and in turn was covered by the snow. Sometimes there were alternate layers of water and ice skin, so that when one broke through he kept on breaking through for a while, sometimes wetting himself to the waist.

That was why he had shied in such panic. He had felt the give under his feet and heard the crackle of a snow-hidden ice skin. And to get his feet wet in such a temperature meant trouble and danger. At the very least it meant delay, for he would be forced to stop and build a fire, and under its protection to bare his feet while he dried his socks and moccasins. He stood and studied the creek bed and its banks, and decided that the flow of water came from the right. He reflected awhile, rubbing his nose and cheeks, then skirted to the left, stepping gingerly and testing the footing for each step. Once clear of the danger, he took a fresh chew of tobacco and swung along at his four-mile gait.

In the course of the next two hours he came upon several similar traps. Usually the snow above the hidden pools had a sunken, candied appearance that advertised the danger. Once again, however, he had a close call; and once, suspecting danger, he compelled the dog to go on in front. The dog did not want to go. It hung back until the man shoved it forward, and then it went quickly across the white, unbroken surface. Suddenly it broke through, floundered to one side, and got away to firmer footing. It had wet its forefeet and legs, and almost immediately the water that clung to it turned to ice. It made quick efforts to lick the ice off its legs, then dropped down in the snow and began to bite out the ice that had formed between the toes. This was a matter of instinct. To permit the ice to remain would mean sore feet. It did not know this. It merely obeyed the mysterious prompting that arose from the deep crypts of its being. But the man knew, having achieved a judgment on the subject, and he removed the mitten from his right hand and helped tear out the ice particles. He did not expose his fingers more than a minute, and was astonished at the swift numbness that smote them. It certainly was cold. He pulled on the mitten hastily, and beat the hand savagely across his chest.

At twelve o'clock the day was at its brightest. Yet the sun was too far south on its winter journey to clear the horizon. The bulge of the earth intervened between it and Henderson Creek, where the man walked under a clear sky at noon and cast no shadow. At half-past twelve, to the minute, he arrived at the forks of the creek. He was pleased at the speed he had made. If he kept it up, he would certainly be with the boys by six. He unbuttoned his jacket and shirt and drew forth his lunch. The action consumed no more than a quarter of a minute, yet in that brief moment the numbness laid hold of the exposed fingers. He did not put the mitten on, but, instead, struck the fingers a dozen sharp smashes against his leg. Then he sat down on a snow-covered log to eat. The sting that followed upon the striking of his fingers against his leg ceased so quickly that he was startled. He had had no chance to take a bite of biscuit. He struck the fingers repeatedly and returned them to the mitten, baring the other hand for the purpose of eating. He tried to take a mouthful, but the ice muzzle prevented. He had forgotten to build a fire and thaw out. He chuckled at his foolishness, and as he chuckled he noted the numbness creeping into the exposed fingers. Also, he noted that the stinging which had first come to his toes when he sat down was already passing away. He wondered whether the toes were warm or numb. He moved them inside the moccasins and decided that they were numb.

He pulled the mitten on hurriedly and stood up. He was a bit frightened. He stamped up and down until the stinging returned into the feet. It certainly was cold, was his thought. That man from Sulphur Creek had spoken the truth when telling how cold it sometimes got in the country. And he had laughed at him at the time! That showed one must not be too sure of things. There was no mistake about it, it *was* cold. He strode up and down, stamping his feet and threshing his arms, until reassured by the returning warmth. Then he got out matches and proceeded to make a fire. From the undergrowth, where high water of the previous spring had lodged a supply of seasoned twigs, he got his firewood. Working carefully from a small beginning, he soon had a roaring fire, over which he thawed the ice from his face and in the protection of which he ate his biscuits. For the moment the cold of space was outwitted. The dog took satisfaction in the fire, stretching out close enough for warmth and far enough away to escape being singed.

When the man had finished, he filled his pipe and took his comfortable time over a smoke. Then he pulled on his mittens, settled the ear flaps of his cap firmly about his ears, and took the creek trail up the left fork. The dog was disappointed and yearned back toward the fire. This man did not know cold. Possibly all the generations of his ancestry had been ignorant of cold, of real cold, of cold one hundred and seven degrees below freezing point. But the dog knew; all its ancestry knew, and it had inherited the knowledge. And it knew that it was not good to walk abroad in such fearful cold. It was the time to lie snug in a hole in the snow and wait for a curtain of cloud to be drawn across the face of outer space whence this cold came. On the other hand, there was no keen intimacy between the dog and the man. The one was the toil slave of the other, and the only caresses it had ever received were the caresses of the whip lash and of harsh and menacing throat sounds that threatened the whip lash. So the dog made no effort to communicate its apprehension to the man. It was not concerned in the welfare of the man; it was for its own sake that it yearned back toward the fire. But the man whistled, and spoke to it with the sound of whip lashes, and the dog swung in at the man's heels and followed after.

The man took a chew of tobacco and proceeded to start a new amber beard. Also, his moist breath quickly powdered with white his mustache, eyebrows, and lashes. There did not seem to be so many springs on the left fork of the Henderson, and for half an hour the man saw no signs of any. And then it happened. At a place where there were no signs, where the soft, unbroken snow seemed to advertise solidity beneath, the man broke through. It was not deep. He wet himself halfway to the knees before he floundered out to the firm crust.

He was angry, and cursed his luck aloud. He had hoped to get into camp with the boys at six o'clock, and this would delay him an hour, for he would have to build a fire and dry out his footgear. This was imperative at that low temperature—he knew that much; and he turned aside to the bank, which he climbed. On top, tangled in the underbrush about the trunks of several small spruce trees, was a highwater deposit of dry firewood—sticks and twigs, principally, but also larger portions of seasoned branches and fine dry last year's grasses. He threw down several large pieces on top of the snow. This served for a foundation and prevented the young flame from drowning itself in the snow it otherwise would melt. The flame he got by touching a match to a small shred of birch bark that he took from his pocket. This burned even more readily than paper. Placing it on the foundation, he fed the young flame with wisps of dry grass and with the tiniest dry twigs.

He worked slowly and carefully, keenly aware of his danger. Gradually, as the flame grew stronger, he increased the size of the twigs with which he fed it. He squatted in the snow, pulling the twigs out from their entanglement in the brush and feeding directly to the flame. He knew there must be no failure. When it is seventy-five below zero, a man must not fail in his first attempt to build a fire—that is, if his feet are wet. If his feet are dry, and he fails, he can run along the trail for half a mile and restore his circulation. But the circulation of wet and freezing feet cannot be restored by running when it is seventy-five below. No matter how fast he runs, the wet feet will freeze the harder.

All this the man knew. The old-timer on Sulphur Creek had told him about it the previous fall, and now he was appreciating the advice. Already all sensation had gone out of his feet. To build the fire he had been forced to remove his mittens, and the fingers had quickly gone numb. His pace of four miles an hour had kept his heart pumping blood to the surface of his body and to all the extremities. But the instant he stopped, the action of the pump eased down. The cold of space smote the unprotected tip of the planet, and he, being on that unprotected tip, received the full force of the blow. The blood of his body recoiled before it. The blood was alive, like the dog, and like the dog it wanted to hide away and cover itself up from the fearful cold. So long as he walked four miles an hour, he pumped that blood, willy-nilly, to the surface; but now it ebbed away and sank down into the recesses of his body. The extremities were the first to feel its absence. His wet feet froze the faster, and his exposed fingers numbed the faster, though they had not yet begun to freeze. Nose and cheeks were already freezing, while the skin of all his body chilled as it lost its blood.

But he was safe. Toes and nose and cheeks would be only touched by the frost, for the fire was beginning to burn with strength. He was feeding it with twigs the size of his finger. In another minute he would be able to feed it with branches the size of his wrist, and then he could remove his wet footgear, and, while it dried, he could keep his naked feet warm by the fire, rubbing them at first, of course, with snow. The fire was a success. He was safe. He remembered the advice of the old-timer on Sulphur Creek, and smiled. The old-timer had been very serious in laying down the law that no man must travel alone in the Klondike after fifty below. Well, here he was; he had had the accident; he was alone; and he had saved himself. Those old-timers were rather womanish, some of them, he thought. All a man had to do was to keep his head, and he was all right. Any man who was a man could travel alone. But it was surprising, the rapidity with which his cheeks and nose were freezing. And he had not thought his fingers could go lifeless in so short a time. Lifeless they were, for he could scarcely make them move together to grip a twig, and they seemed remote from his body and from him. When he touched a twig, he had to look and see whether or not he had hold of it. The wires were pretty well down between him and his finger ends.

All of which counted for little. There was the fire, snapping and crackling and promising life with every dancing flame. He started to untie his moccasins. They were coated with ice; the thick German socks were like sheaths of iron halfway to the knees; and the moccasin strings were like rods of steel all twisted and knotted as by some conflagration. For a moment he tugged with his numb fingers, then, realizing the follow of it, he drew his sheath knife.

But before he could cut the strings, it happened. It was his own fault or, rather, his mistake. He should not have built the fire under the spruce tree. He should have built it in the open. But it had been easier to pull the twigs from the brush and drop them directly on the fire. Now the tree under which he had done this carried a weight of snow on its boughs. No wind had blown for weeks, and each bough was fully freighted. Each time he had pulled a twig he had communicated a slight agitation to the tree—an imperceptible agitation, so far as he was concerned, but an agitation sufficient to bring about the disaster. High up in the tree one bough capsized its load of snow. This fell on the boughs beneath, capsizing them. This process continued, spreading out and involving the whole tree. It grew like an avalanche, and it descended without warning upon the man and the fire, and the fire was blotted out! Where it had burned was a mantle of fresh and disordered snow.

The man was shocked. It was as though he had just heard his own sentence of death. For a moment he sat and stared at the spot where the fire had been. Then he grew very calm. Perhaps the old-timer on Sulphur Creek was right. If he had only had a trail mate he would have been in no danger now. The trail mate could have built the fire. Well, it was up to him to build the fire over again, and this second time there must be no failure. Even if he succeeded, he would most likely lose some toes. His feet must be badly frozen by now, and there would be some time before the second fire was ready.

Such were his thoughts, but he did not sit and think them. He was busy all the time they were passing through his mind. He made a new foundation for a fire, this time in the open, where no treacherous tree could blot it out. Next he gathered dry grasses and tiny twigs from the high-water flotsam. He could not bring his fingers together to pull them out, but he was able to gather them by the handful. In this way he got many rotten twigs and bits of green moss that were undesirable, but it was the best he could do. He worked methodically, even collecting an armful of the larger branches to be used later when the fire gathered strength. And all the while the dog sat and watched him, a certain yearning wistfulness in its eyes, for it looked upon him as the fire provider, and the fire was slow in coming.

When all was ready, the man reached in his pocket for a second piece of birch bark. He knew the bark was there, and, though he could not feel it with his fingers, he could hear its crisp rustling as he fumbled for it. Try as he would, he could not clutch hold of it. And all the time, in his consciousness, was the knowledge that each instant his feet were freezing. This thought tended to put him in a panic, but he fought against it and kept calm. He pulled on his mittens with his teeth, and threshed his arms back and forth, beating his hands with all his might against his sides. He did this sitting down, and he stood up to do it; and all the while the dog sat in the snow, its wolf brush of a tail curled around warmly over its forefeet, its sharp wolf ears pricked forward intently as it watched the man. And the man, as he beat and threshed with his arms and hands, felt a great surge of envy as he regarded the creature that was warm and secure in its natural covering.

After a time he was aware of the first faraway signals of sensation in his beaten fingers. The faint tingling grew stronger till it evolved into a stinging ache that was excruciating, but which the man hailed with satisfaction. He stripped the mitten from his right hand and fetched forth the birch bark. The exposed fingers were quickly going numb again. Next he brought out his bunch of sulphur matches. But the tremendous cold had already driven the life out of his fingers. In his effort to separate one match from the others, the whole bunch fell in the snow. He tried to pick it out of the snow, but failed. The dead fingers could neither touch nor clutch. He was very careful. He drove the thought of his freezing feet, and nose, and cheeks, out of his mind, devoting his whole soul to the matches. He watched, using the sense of vision in place of that of touch, and when he saw his fingers on each side the bunch, he closed them—that is he willed to close them, for the wires were down, and the fingers did not obey. He pulled the mitten on the right hand, and beat it fiercely against his knee. Then, with both mittened hands, he scooped the bunch of matches, along with much snow, into his lap. Yet he was no better off.

After some manipulation he managed to get the bunch between the heels of his mittened hands. In this fashion he carried it to his mouth. The ice crackled and snapped when by a violent effort he opened his mouth. He drew the lower jaw in, curled the upper lip out of the way, scraped the bunch with his upper teeth in order to separate a match. He succeeded in getting one, which he dropped on his lap. He was no better off. He could not pick it up. Then he devised a way. He picked it up in his teeth and scratched in on his leg. Twenty times he scratched before he succeeded in lighting it. As it flamed he held it with his teeth to the birch bark. But the burning brimstone went up his nostrils and into his lungs, causing him to cough spasmodically. The match fell into the snow and went out.

The old-timer on Sulphur Creek was right, he thought in the moment of controlled despair that ensued: after fifty below, a man should travel with a partner. He beat his hands, but failed in exciting any sensation. Suddenly he bared both hands, removing the mittens with his teeth. He caught the whole bunch between the heels of his hands. His arm muscles not being frozen enabled him to press the hand heels tightly against the matches. Then he scratched the bunch along his leg. It flared into flame, seventy sulphur matches at once! There was no wind to blow them out. He kept his head to one side to escape the strangling fumes, and held the blazing bunch to the birch bark. As he so held it, he became aware of sensation in his hand. His flesh was burning. He could smell it. Deep down below the surface he could feel it. The sensation developed into pain that grew acute. And still he endured it, holding the flame of the matches clumsily to the bark that would not light readily because his own burning hands were in the way, absorbing most of the flame.

At last, when he could endure no more, he jerked his hands apart. The blazing matches fell sizzling into the snow, but the birch bark was alight. He began laying dry grasses and the tiniest twigs on the flame. He could not pick and choose, for he had to lift the fuel between the heels of his hands. Small pieces of rotten wood and green moss clung to the twigs, and he bit them off as well as he could with his teeth. He cherished the flame carefully and awkwardly. It meant life, and it must not perish. The withdrawal of blood from the surface of his body now made him begin to shiver, and he grew more awkward. A large piece of green moss fell squarely on the little fire. He tired to poke it out with his fingers, but his shivering frame made him poke too far, and he disrupted the nucleus of the little fire, the burning grasses and tiny twigs separating and scattering. He tried to poke them together again, but in spite of the tenseness of the effort, his shivering got away with him, and the twigs were hopelessly scattered. Each twig gushed a puff of smoke and went out. The fire provider had failed. As he looked apathetically about him, his eyes chanced on the dog, sitting across the ruins of the fire from him, in the snow, making restless, hunching movements, slightly lifting one forefoot and then the other, shifting its weight back and forth on them with wistful eagerness.

The sight of the dog put a wild idea into his head. He remembered the tale of the man, caught in a blizzard, who killed a steer and crawled inside the carcass, and so was saved. He would kill the dog and bury his hands in the warm body until the numbness went out of them. Then he could build another fire. He spoke to the dog, calling it to him; but in his voice was a strange note of fear that frightened the animal, who had never known the man to speak in such way before. Something was the matter, and its suspicious nature sensed danger—it knew not what danger, but somewhere, somehow, in its brain arose an apprehension of the man. It flattened its ears down at the sound of the man's voice, and its restless, hunching movements and the liftings and shiftings of its forefeet became more pronounced; but it would not come to the man. He got on his hands and knees and crawled toward the dog. This unusual posture again excited suspicion, and the animal sidled mincingly away.

The man sat up in the snow for a moment and struggled for calmness. Then he pulled on his mittens, by means of his teeth, and got upon his feet. He glanced down at first in order to assure himself that he was really standing up, for the absence of sensation in his feet left him unrelated to the earth. His erect position in itself started to drive the webs of suspicion from the dog's mind; and when he spoke peremptorily, with the sound of whip lashes in his voice, the dog rendered its customary allegiance and came to him. As it came within reaching distance the man lost his control. His arms flashed out to the dog, and he experienced genuine surprise when he discovered that his hands could not clutch, that there was neither bend nor feeling in the fingers. He had forgotten for the moment that they were frozen and that they were freezing more and more. All this happened quickly, and before the animal could get away, he encircled its body with his arms. He sat down in the snow, and in this fashion held the dog, while it snarled and whined and struggled.

But it was all he could do, hold its body encircled in his arms and sit there. He realized that he could not kill the dog. There was no way to do it. With his helpless hands he could neither draw nor hold his sheath knife nor throttle the animal. He released it, and it plunged wildly away, with tail between its legs, and still snarling. It halted forty feet away and surveyed him curiously, with ears sharply pricked forward.

The man looked down at his hands in order to locate them, and found them hanging on the ends of his arms. It struck him as curious that one should have to use his eyes in order to find out where his hands were. He began threshing his arms back and forth, beating the mittened hands against his sides. He did this for five minutes, violently, and his heart pumped enough blood up to the surface to put a stop to his shivering. But no sensation was aroused in the hands. He had an impression that they hung like weights on the ends of his arms, but when he tried to run the impression down, he could not find it.

A certain fear of death, dull and oppressive, came to him. This fear quickly became poignant as he realized that it was no longer a mere matter of freezing his fingers and toes, or of losing his hands and feet, but that it was a matter of life and death with the chances against him. This threw him into a panic, and he turned and ran up the creek bed along the old, dim trail. The dog joined in behind and kept up with him. He ran blindly, without intention, in fear such as he had never known in his life. Slowly, as he plowed and floundered through the snow, he began to see things again—the banks of the creek, the old timber jams, the leafless aspens, and the sky. The running made him feel better. He did not shiver. Maybe, if he ran on, his feet would thaw out; and, anyway, if he ran far enough, he would reach camp and the boys. Without doubt he would lose some fingers and toes and some of his face; but the boys would take care of him, and save the rest of him when he got there. And at the same time there was another thought in his mind that said he would never get to the camp and the boys; that it was too many miles away, that the freezing had too great a start on him, and that he would soon be stiff and dead. This thought he kept in the background and refused to consider. Sometimes it pushed itself forward and demanded to be heard, but he thrust it back and strove to think of other things.

It struck him as curious that he could run at all on feet so frozen that he could not feel them when they struck the earth and took the weight of his body. He seemed to himself to skim along above the surface, and to have no connection with the earth. Somewhere he had once seen a winged Mercury, and he wondered if Mercury felt as he felt when skimming over the earth.

His theory of running until he reached camp and the boys had one flaw in it: he lacked the endurance. Several times he stumbled, and finally he tottered, crumpled up, and fell. When he tried to rise, he failed. He must sit and rest, he decided, and next time he would merely walk and keep on going. As he sat and regained his breath, he noted that he was feeling quite warm and comfortable. He was not shivering, and it even seemed that a warm glow had come to this chest and trunk. And yet, when he touched his nose or cheeks, there was no sensation. Running would not thaw them out. Nor would it thaw out his hands and feet. Then the thought came to him that the frozen portions of his body must be extending. He tried to keep this thought down, to forget it, to think of something else; he was aware of the panicky feeling that it caused, and he was afraid of the panic. But the thought asserted itself, and persisted, until it produced a vision of his body totally frozen. This was too much, and he made another wild run along the trail. Once he slowed down to a walk, but the thought of the freezing extending itself made him run again.

And all the time the dog ran with him, at his heels. When he fell down a second time, it curled its tail over its forefeet and sat in front of him, facing him, curiously eager and intent. The warmth and security of the animal angered him, and he cursed it till it flattened down its ears appeasingly. This time the shivering came more quickly upon the man. He was losing in his battle with the frost. It was creeping into his body from all sides. The thought of it drove him on, but he ran no more than a hundred feet, when he staggered and pitched headlong. It was his last panic. When he had recovered his breath and control, he sat up and entertained in his mind the conception of meeting death with dignity. However, the conception did not come to him in such terms. His idea of it was that he had been making a fool of himself, running around like a chicken with its head cut off—such was the simile that occurred to him. Well, he was bound to freeze anyway, and he might as well take it decently. With this new-found peace of mind came the first glimmerings of drowsiness. A good idea, he thought, to sleep off to death. It was like taking an anesthetic. Freezing was not so bad as people thought. There were lots worse ways to die.

He pictured the boys finding his body next day. Suddenly he found himself with them, coming along the trail and looking for himself. And, still with them, he came around a turn in the trail and found himself lying in the snow. He did not belong with himself any more, for even then he was out of himself, standing with the boys and looking at himself in the snow. It certainly was cold, was his thought. When he got back to the States he could tell the folks what real cold was. He drifted on from this to a vision of the old-timer on Sulphur Creek. He could see him quite clearly, warm and comfortable, and smoking a pipe.

"You were right, old hoss; you were right," the man mumbled to the old-timer of Sulphur Creek.

Then the man drowsed off into what seemed to him the most comfortable and satisfying sleep he had ever known. The dog sat facing him and waiting. The brief day drew to a close in a long, slow twilight. There were no signs of a fire to be made, and, besides, never in the dog's experience had it known a man to sit like that in the snow and make no fire. As the twilight drew on, its eager yearning for the fire mastered it, and with a great lifting and shifting of forefeet, it whined softly, then flattened its ears down in anticipation of being chidden by the man. But the man remained silent. Later the dog whined loudly. And still later it crept close to the man and caught the scent of death. This made the animal bristle and back away. A little longer it delayed, howling under the stars that leaped and danced and shone brightly in the cold sky. Then it turned and trotted up the trail in the direction of the camp it knew, where were the other food providers and fire providers.

THE DREAM OF A RIDICULOUS MAN*

A FANTASTIC STORY

Fyodor Dostoyevsky (1821–1881)

I

I am a ridiculous man. They call me a madman now. That would be a distinct rise in my social position were it not that they still regard me as being as ridiculous as ever. But that does not make me angry any more. They are all dear to me now even while they laugh at me—yes, even then they are for some reason particularly dear to me. I shouldn't have minded laughing with them—not at myself, of course, but because I love them—had I not felt so sad as I looked at them. I feel sad because they do not know the truth, whereas I know it. Oh, how hard it is to be the only man to know the truth! But they won't understand that. No, they will not understand.

And yet in the past I used to be terribly distressed at appearing to be ridicu-

---

*Translated by David Magarshack.

lous. No, not appearing to be, but being. I've always cut a ridiculous figure. I suppose I must have known it from the day I was born. At any rate, I've known for certain that I was ridiculous ever since I was seven years old. Afterwards I went to school, then to the university, and—well—the more I learned, the more conscious did I become of the fact that I was ridiculous. So that for me my years of hard work at the university seem in the end to have existed for the sole purpose of demonstrating and proving to me, the more deeply engrossed I became in my studies, that I was an utterly absurd person. And as during my studies, so all my life. Every year the same consciousness that I was ridiculous in every way strengthened and intensified in my mind. They always laughed at me. But not one of them knew or suspected that if there were one man on earth who knew better than anyone else that he was ridiculous, that man was I. And this—I mean, the fact that they did not know it—was the bitterest pill for me to swallow. But there I was myself at fault. I was always so proud that I never wanted to confess it to anyone. No, I wouldn't do that for anything in the world. As the years passed, this pride increased in me so that I do believe that if ever I had by chance confessed it to any one I should have blown my brains out the same evening. Oh, how I suffered in the days of my youth from the thought that I might not myself resist the impulse to confess it to my schoolfellows. But ever since I became a man I grew for some unknown reason a little more composed in my mind, though I was more and more conscious of that awful characteristic of mine. Yes, most decidedly for some unknown reason, for to this day I have not been able to find out why that was so. Perhaps it was because I was becoming terribly disheartened owing to one circumstance which was beyond my power to control, namely, the conviction which was gaining upon me that nothing in the whole world *made any difference*. I had long felt it dawning upon me, but I was fully convinced of it only last year, and that, too, all of a sudden, as it were. I suddenly felt that it made *no* difference to me whether the world existed or whether nothing existed anywhere at all. I began to be acutely conscious that *nothing existed in my own lifetime*. At first I couldn't help feeling that at any rate in the past many things had existed; but later on I came to the conclusion that there had not been anything even in the past, but that for some reason it had merely seemed to have been. Little by little I became convinced that there would be nothing in the future, either. It was then that I suddenly ceased to be angry with people and almost stopped noticing them. This indeed disclosed itself in the smallest trifles. For instance, I would knock against people while walking in the street. And not because I was lost in thought—I had nothing to think about—I had stopped thinking about anything at that time: it made no difference to me. Not that I had found an answer to all the questions. Oh, I had not settled a single question, and there were thousands of them! But *it made no difference to me*, and all the questions disappeared.

And, well, it was only after that that I learnt the truth. I learnt the truth last November, on the third of November, to be precise, and every moment since then has been imprinted indelibly on my mind. It happened on a dismal evening, as dismal an evening as could be imagined. I was returning home at about eleven o'clock and I remember thinking all the time that there could not be a more dismal evening. Even the weather was foul. It had been pouring all day, and the rain too was the coldest and most dismal rain that ever was, a sort of menacing rain—I remember that—a rain with a distinct animosity towards people. But about eleven o'clock it had stopped suddenly, and a horrible dampness descended upon everything, and it became much damper and colder than when it had been raining. And a sort of steam was rising from everything, from every cobble in the street, and from every side-street if you peered closely into it from the street as far as the eye could reach. I could not help feeling that if the gaslight had been extinguished everywhere, everything would have seemed much more cheerful, and that the gaslight oppressed the heart so much just because it shed a light upon it all. I had had scarcely any dinner that day. I had been spending the whole evening with an engineer who had two more friends visiting him. I never opened my mouth, and I expect I must have got on their nerves. They were discussing some highly controversial subject, and suddenly got very excited over it. But it really did not make any difference to them. I could see that. I knew that their excitement was not genuine. So I suddenly blurted it out. "My dear fellows," I said, "you don't really care a damn about it, do you?" They were not in the least offended, but they all burst out laughing at me. That was because I had said it without meaning to rebuke them, but simply because it made no difference to me. Well, they realised that it made no difference to me, and they felt happy.

When I was thinking about the gaslight in the streets, I looked up at the sky. The sky was awfully dark, but I could clearly distinguish the torn wisps of cloud and between them fathomless dark patches. All of a sudden I became aware of a little star in one of those patches and I began looking at it intently. That was because the little star gave me an idea: I made up my mind to kill myself that night. I had made up my mind to kill myself already two months before and, poor as I am, I bought myself an excellent revolver and loaded it the same day. But two months had elapsed and it was still lying in the drawer. I was so utterly indifferent to everything that I was anxious to wait for the moment when I would not be so indifferent and then kill myself. Why—I don't know. And so every night during these two months I thought of shooting myself as I was going home. I was only waiting for the right moment. And now the little star gave me an idea, and I made up my mind then and there that it should *most certainly* be that night. But why the little star gave me the idea—I don't know.

And just as I was looking at the sky, this little girl suddenly grasped me by the elbow. The street was already deserted and there was scarcely a soul to be seen. In the distance a cabman was fast asleep on his box. The girl was about eight years old. She had a kerchief on her head, and she wore only an old, shabby little dress. She was soaked to the skin, but what stuck in my memory was her little torn wet boots. I still remember them. They caught my eye especially. She suddenly began tugging at my elbow and calling me. She was not crying, but saying something in a loud, jerky sort of voice, something that did not make sense, for she was trembling all over and her teeth were chattering from cold. She seemed to be terrified of something and she was crying desperately, "Mummy! Mummy!" I turned round to look at her, but did not utter a word and went on walking. But she ran after me and kept tugging at my clothes, and there was a sound in her voice which in very frightened children signifies despair. I know that sound. Though her words sounded as if they were choking her, I realised that her mother must be dying somewhere very near, or that something similar was happening to her, and that she had run out to call someone, to find someone who would help her mother. But I did not go with her; on the contrary, something made me drive her away. At first I told her to go and find a policeman. But she suddenly clasped her hands and, whimpering and gasping for breath, kept running at my side and would not leave me. It was then that I stamped my foot and shouted at her. She just cried, "Sir! Sir! . . ." and then she left me suddenly and rushed headlong across the road: another man appeared there and she evidently rushed from me to him.

I climbed to the fifth floor. I live apart from my landlord. We all have separate rooms as in an hotel. My room is very small and poor. My window is a semicircular skylight. I have a sofa covered with American cloth, a table with books on it, two chairs and a comfortable armchair, a very old armchair indeed, but low-seated and with a high back serving as a head-rest. I sat down in the armchair, lighted the candle, and began thinking. Next door in the other room behind the partition, the usual bedlam was going on. It had been going on since the day before yesterday. A retired army captain lived there, and he had visitors—six merry gentlemen who drank vodka and played faro with an old pack of cards. Last night they had a fight and I know that two of them were for a long time pulling each other about by the hair. The landlady wanted to complain, but she is dreadfully afraid of the captain. We had only one more lodger in our rooms, a thin little lady, the wife of an army officer, on a visit to Petersburg with her three little children who had all been taken ill since their arrival at our house. She and her children were simply terrified of the captain and they lay shivering and crossing themselves all night long, and the youngest child had a sort of nervous attack from fright. This captain (I know that for a fact) sometimes stops people on Nevsky Avenue and asks them for a few coppers, telling them he is very poor. He can't get a job in the Civil Service, but the strange thing is (and that's why I am telling you this) that the captain had never once during the month he had been living with us made me feel in the least irritated. From the very first, of course, I would not have anything to do with him, and he himself was bored with me the very first time we met. But however big a noise they raised behind their partition and however many of them there were in the captain's room, it makes no difference to me. I sit up all night and, I assure you, I don't hear them at all—so completely do I forget about them. You see, I stay awake all night till daybreak, and that has been going on for a whole year now. I sit up all night in the armchair at the table—doing nothing. I read books only in the daytime. At night I sit like that without even thinking about anything in particular: some thoughts wander in and out of my mind, and I let them come and go as they please. In the night the candle burns out completely.

I sat down at the table, took the gun out of the drawer, and put it down in front of me. I remember asking myself as I put it down, "Is it to be then?" and I replied with complete certainty, "It is!" That is to say, I was going to shoot myself. I knew I should shoot myself that night for certain. What I did not know was how much longer I should go on sitting at the table till I shot myself. And I should of course have shot myself, had it not been for the little girl.

II

You see, though nothing made any difference to me, I could feel pain, for instance, couldn't I? If anyone had struck me, I should have felt pain. The same was true so far as my moral perceptions were concerned. If anything happened to arouse my pity, I should have felt pity, just as I used to do at the time when things did make a difference to me. So I had felt pity that night: I should most decidedly have helped a child. Why then did I not help the little girl? Because of a thought that had occurred to me at the time: when she was pulling at me and calling me, a question suddenly arose in my mind and I could not settle it. It was an idle question, but it made me angry. What made me angry was the conclusion I drew from the reflection that if I had really decided to do away with myself that night, everything in the world should have been more indifferent to me than ever. Why then should I have suddenly felt that I was not indifferent and be sorry for the little girl? I remember that I was very sorry for her, so much so that I felt a strange pang which was quite incomprehensible in my position. I'm afraid I am unable better to convey that fleeting sensation of mine, but it persisted with me at home when I was sitting at the table, and I was very much irritated. I had not been so irritated for a long time past. One train of thought followed another. It was clear to me that so long as I was still a human being and not a meaningless cipher, and till I became a cipher, I was alive, and consequently able to suffer, be angry, and feel shame at my actions. Very well. But if, on the other hand, I were going to kill myself in, say, two hours, what did that little girl matter to me and what did I care for shame or anything else in the world? I was going to turn into a cipher, into an absolute cipher. And surely the realisation that I should soon cease to exist *altogether,* and hence everything would cease to exist, ought to have had some slight effect on my feeling of pity for the little girl or on my feeling of shame after so mean an action. Why after all did I stamp and shout so fiercely at the little girl? I did it because I thought that not only did I feel no pity, but that it wouldn't matter now if I were guilty of the most inhuman baseness, since in another two hours everything would become extinct. Do you believe me when I tell you that that was the only reason why I shouted like that? I am almost convinced of it now. It seemed clear to me that life and the world in some way or other depended on me now. It might almost be said that the world seemed to be created for me alone. If I were to shoot myself, the world would cease to exist—for me at any rate. To say nothing of the possibility that nothing would in fact exist for anyone after me and the whole world would dissolve as soon as my consciousness became extinct, would disappear in a twinkling like a phantom, like some integral part of my consciousness, and vanish without leaving a trace behind, for all this world and all these people exist perhaps only in my consciousness.

I remember that as I sat and meditated, I began to examine all these questions which thronged in my mind one after another from quite a different angle, and thought of something quite new. For instance, the strange notion occurred to me that if I had lived before on the moon or on Mars and had committed there the most shameful and dishonourable action that can be imagined, and had been so disgraced and dishonoured there as can be imagined and experienced only occasionally in a dream, a nightmare, and if, finding myself afterwards on earth, I had retained the memory of what I had done on the other planet, and moreover knew that I should never in any circumstances go back there—if that were to have happened, should I or should I not have felt, as I looked from the earth upon the moon, that *it made no difference* to me? Should I or should I not have felt ashamed of that action? The questions were idle and useless, for the gun was already lying before me and there was not a shadow of doubt in my mind that *it* was going to take place for certain, but they excited and maddened me. It seemed to me that I could not die now without having settled something first. The little girl, in fact, had saved me, for by these questions I put off my own execution.

Meanwhile things had grown more quiet in the captain's room: they had finished their card game and were getting ready to turn in for the night, and now were only grumbling and swearing at each other in a halfhearted sort of way. It was at that moment that I suddenly fell asleep in my armchair at the table, a thing that had never happened to me before.

I fell asleep without being aware of it at all. Dreams, as we all know, are very curious things: certain incidents in them are presented with quite uncanny vividness, each detail executed with the finishing touch of a jeweller, while others you leap across as though entirely unaware of, for instance, space and time. Dreams seem to be induced not by reason but by desire, not by the head but by the heart, and yet what clever tricks my reason has sometimes played on me in dreams! And furthermore what incomprehensible things happen to it in a dream. My brother, for instance, died five years ago. I sometimes dream about him: he takes a keen interest in my affairs, we are both very interested, and yet I know very well all through my dream that my brother is dead and buried. How is it that I am not surprised that, though dead, he is here beside me, doing his best to help me? Why does my reason accept all this without the slightest hesitation? But enough. Let me tell you about my dream. Yes, I dreamed that dream that night. My dream of the third of November. They are making fun of me now by saying that it was only a dream. But what does it matter whether it was a dream or not, so long as that dream revealed the Truth to me? For once you have recognised the truth and seen it, you know it is the one and only truth and that there can be no other, whether you are asleep or awake. But never mind. Let it be a dream, but remember that I had intended to cut short by suicide the life that means so much to us, and that my dream—my dream—oh, it revealed to me a new, grand, regenerated, strong life!

Listen.

III

I have said that I fell asleep imperceptibly and even while I seemed to be revolving the same thoughts again in my mind. Suddenly I dreamed that I picked up the gun and, sitting in my armchair, pointed it straight at my heart—at my heart, and not at my head. For I had firmly resolved to shoot myself through the head, through the right temple, to be precise. Having aimed the gun at my breast, I paused for a second or two, and suddenly my candle, the table and the wall began moving and swaying before me. I fired quickly.

In a dream you sometimes fall from a great height, or you are being murdered or beaten, but you never feel any pain unless you really manage somehow or other to hurt yourself in bed, when you feel pain and almost always wake up from it. So it was in my dream: I did not feel any pain, but it seemed as though with my shot everything within me was shaken and everything was suddenly extinguished, and a terrible darkness descended all around me. I seemed to have become blind and dumb. I was lying on something hard, stretched out full length on my back. I saw nothing and could not make the slightest movement.

All round me people were walking and shouting. The captain was yelling in his deep bass voice, the landlady was screaming and—suddenly another hiatus, and I was being carried in a closed coffin. I could feel the coffin swaying and I was thinking about it, and for the first time the idea flashed through my mind that I was dead, dead as a doornail, that I knew it, that there was not the least doubt about it, that I could neither see nor move, and yet I could feel and reason. But I was soon reconciled to that and, as usually happens in dreams, I accepted the facts without questioning them.

And now I was buried in the earth. They all went away, and I was left alone, entirely alone. I did not move. Whenever before I imagined how I should be buried in a grave, there was only one sensation I actually associated with the grave, namely, that of damp and cold. And so it was now. I felt that I was very cold, especially in the tips of my toes, but I felt nothing else.

I lay in my grave and, strange to say, I did not expect anything, accepting the idea that a dead man had nothing to expect as an incontestable fact. But it was damp. I don't know how long a time passed, whether an hour, or several days, or many days. But suddenly a drop of water, which had seeped through the lid of the coffin, fell on my closed left eye. It was followed by another drop a minute later, then after another minute by another drop, and so on. One drop every minute. All at once deep indignation blazed up in my heart, and I suddenly felt a twinge of physical pain in it. "That's my wound," I thought. "It's the shot I fired. There's a bullet there. . . ." And drop after drop still kept falling every minute on my closed eyelid. And suddenly I called (not with my voice, for I was motionless, but with the whole of my being) upon Him who was responsible for all that was happening to me:

"Whoever Thou art, and if anything more rational exists than what is happening here, let it, I pray Thee, come to pass here too. But if Thou are revenging Thyself for my senseless act of self-destruction by the infamy and absurdity of life after death, then know that no torture that may be inflicted upon me can ever equal the contempt which I shall go on feeling in silence, though my martyrdom last for aeons upon aeons!"

I made this appeal and was silent. The dead silence went on for almost a minute, and one more drop fell on my closed eyelid, but I knew, I knew and believed infinitely and unshakably that everything would without a doubt change immediately. And then my grave was opened. I don't know, that is, whether it was opened or dug open, but I was seized by some dark and unknown being and we found ouselves in space. I suddenly regained my sight. It was a pitch-black night. Never, never had there been such darkness! We were flying through space at a terrific speed and we had already left the earth behind us. I did not question the being who was carrying me. I was proud and waited. I was telling myself that I was not afraid, and I was filled with admiration at the thought that I was not afraid. I cannot remember how long we were flying, nor can I give you an idea of the time; it all happened as it always does happen in dreams when you leap over space and time and the laws of nature and reason, and only pause at the points which are especially dear to your heart. All I remember is that I suddenly beheld a little star in the darkness.

"Is that Sirius?" I asked, feeling suddenly unable to restrain myself, for I had made up my mind not to ask any questions.

"No," answered the being who was carrying me, "that is the same star you saw between the clouds when you were coming home."

I knew that its face bore some resemblance to a human face. It is a strange fact but I did not like that being, and I even felt an intense aversion for it. I had expected complete non-existence and that was why I had shot myself through the heart. And yet there I was in the hands of a being, not human of course, but which *was*, which existed. "So there is life beyond the grave!" I thought with the curious irrelevance of a dream, but at heart I remained essentially unchanged. "If I must *be* again," I thought, "and live again at someone's unalterable behest, I won't be defeated and humiliated!"

"You know I'm afraid of you and that's why you despise me," I said suddenly to my companion, unable to refrain from the humiliating remark with its implied admission, and feeling my own humiliation in my heart like the sharp prick of a needle.

He did not answer me, but I suddenly felt that I was not despised, that no one was laughing at me, that no one was even pitying me, and that our journey had a purpose, an unknown and mysterious purpose that concerned only me. Fear was steadily growing in my heart. Something was communicated to me from my silent companion—mutely but agonisingly—and it seemed to permeate my whole being. We were speeding through dark and unknown regions of space. I had long since lost sight of the constellations familiar to me. I knew that there were stars in the heavenly spaces whose light took thousands and millions of years to reach the earth. Possibly we were already flying through those spaces. I expected something in the terrible anguish that wrung my heart. And suddenly a strangely familiar and incredibly nostalgic feeling shook me to the very core: I suddenly caught sight of our sun! I knew that it could not possibly be *our* sun that gave birth to our earth, and that we were millions of miles away from our sun, but for some unknown reason I recognised with every fibre of my being that it was precisely the same sun as ours, its exact copy and twin. A sweet, nostalgic feeling filled my heart with rapture: the old familiar power of the same light which had given me life stirred an echo in my heart and revived it, and I felt the same life stirring within me for the first time since I had been in the grave.

"But if it is the sun, if it's exactly the same sun as ours," I cried, "then where is the earth?"

And my companion pointed to a little star twinkling in the darkness with an emerald light. We were making straight for it.

"But are such repetitions possible in the universe? Can that be nature's law? And if that is an earth there, is it the same earth as ours? Just the same poor, unhappy, but dear, dear earth, and beloved for ever and ever? Arousing like our earth the same poignant love for herself even in the most ungrateful of her children?" I kept crying, deeply moved by an uncontrollable, rapturous love for the dear old earth I had left behind.

The face of the poor little girl I had treated so badly flashed through my mind.

"You shall see it all," answered my companion, and a strange sadness sounded in his voice.

But we were rapidly approaching the planet. It was growing before my eyes. I could already distinguish the ocean, the outlines of Europe, and suddenly a strange feeling of some great and sacred jealousy blazed up in my heart.

"How is such a repetition possible and why? I love, I can only love the earth I've left behind, stained with my blood when, ungrateful wretch that I am, I extinguished my life by shooting myself through the heart. But never, never have I ceased to love that earth, and even on the night I parted from it I loved it perhaps more poignantly than ever. Is there suffering on this new earth? On our earth we can truly love only with suffering and through suffering! We know not how to love otherwise. We know no other love. I want suffering in order to love. I want and thirst this very minute to kiss, with tears streaming down my cheeks, the one and only earth I have left behind. I don't want, I won't accept life on any other! . . ."

But my companion had already left me. Suddenly, and without as it were being aware of it myself, I stood on this other earth in the bright light of a sunny day, fair and beautiful as paradise. I believe I was standing on one of the islands which on our earth form the Greek archipelago, or somewhere on the coast of the mainland close to this archipelago. Oh, everything was just as it is with us, except that everything seemed to be bathed in the radiance of some public festival and of some great and holy triumph attained at last. The gentle emerald sea softly lapped the shore and kissed it with manifest, visible, almost conscious love. Tall, beautiful trees stood in all the glory of their green luxuriant foliage, and their innumerable leaves (I am sure of that) welcomed me with their soft, tender rustle, and seemed to utter sweet words of love. The lush grass blazed with bright and fragrant flowers. Birds were flying in flocks through the air and, without being afraid of me, alighted on my shoulders and hands and joyfully beat against me with their sweet fluttering wings. And at last I saw and came to know the people of this blessed earth. They came to me themselves. They surrounded me. They kissed me. Children of the sun, children of their sun—oh, how beautiful they were! Never on our earth had I beheld such beauty in man. Only perhaps in our children during the very first years of their life could one have found a remote, though faint, reflection of this beauty. The eyes of these happy people shone with a bright lustre. Their faces were radiant with understanding and a serenity of mind that had reached its greatest fulfilment. Those faces were joyous; in the words and voices of these people there was a child-like gladness. Oh, at the first glance at their faces I at once understood all, all! It was an earth unstained by the Fall, inhabited by people who had not sinned and who lived in the same paradise as that in which, according to the legends of mankind, our first parents lived before they sinned, with the only difference that all the earth here was everywhere the same paradise. These people, laughing happily, thronged round me and overwhelmed me with their caresses; they took me home with them, and each of them was anxious to set my mind at peace. Oh, they asked me no questions, but seemed to know everything already (that was the impression I got), and they longed to remove every trace of suffering from my face as soon as possible.

IV

Well, you see, again let me repeat: All right, let us assume it was only a dream! But the sensation of the love of those innocent and beautiful people has remained with me for ever, and I can feel that their love is even now flowing out to me from over there. I have seen them myself. I have known them thoroughly and been convinced. I loved them and I suffered for them afterwards. Oh, I knew at once even all the time that there were many things about them I should never be able to understand. To me, a modern Russian progressive and a despicable citizen of Petersburg, it seemed inexplicable that, knowing so much, they knew nothing of our science, for instance. But I soon realised that their knowledge was derived from, and fostered by emotions other than those to which we were accustomed on earth, and that their aspirations, too, were quite different. They desired nothing. They were at peace with themselves. They did not strive to gain knowledge of life as we strive to understand it because their lives were full. But their knowledge was higher and deeper than the knowledge we derive from our science; for our science seeks to explain what life is and strives to understand it in order to teach others how to live, while they knew how to live without science. I understood that, but I couldn't understand their knowledge. They pointed out their trees to me, and I could not understand the intense love with which they looked on them; it was as though they were talking with beings like themselves. And, you know, I don't think I am exaggerating in saying that they talked with them! Yes, they had discovered their language, and I am sure the trees understood them. They looked upon all nature like that—the animals which lived peaceably with them and did not attack them, but loved them, conquered by their love for them. They pointed out the stars to me and talked to me about them in a way that I could not understand, but I am certain that in some curious way they communed with the stars in the heavens, not only in thought, but in some actual, living way. Oh, these people were not concerned whether I understood them or not; they loved me without it. But I too knew that they would never be able to understand me, and for that reason I hardly ever spoke to them about our earth. I merely kissed the earth on which they lived in their presence, and worshipped them without any words. And they saw that and let me worship them without being ashamed that I was worshipping them, for they themselves loved much. They did not suffer for me when, weeping, I sometimes kissed their feet, for in their hearts they were joyfully aware of the strong affection with which they would return my love. At times I asked myself in amazement how they had managed never to offend a person like me and not once arouse in a person like me a feeling of jealousy and envy. Many times I asked myself how I—a braggart and a liar—could refrain from telling them all I knew of science and philosophy, of which of course they had no idea? How it had never occurred to me to impress them with my store of learning, or impart my learning to them out of the love I bore them?

They were playful and high-spirited like children. They wandered about their beautiful woods and groves, they sang their beautiful songs, they lived on simple food—the fruits of their trees, the honey from their woods, and the milk of the animals that loved them. To obtain their food and clothes, they did not work very hard or long. They knew love and they begot children, but I never noticed in them those outbursts of *cruel* sensuality which overtake almost everybody on our earth, whether man or woman, and are the only source of almost every sin of our human race. They rejoiced in their new-born children as new sharers in their bliss. There were no quarrels or jealousy among them, and they did not even know what the words meant. Their children were the children of

them all, for they were all one family. There was scarcely any illness among
them, though there was death; but their old people died peacefully, as though
falling asleep, surrounded by the people who took leave of them, blessing them
and smiling at them, and themselves receiving with bright smiles the farewell
wishes of their friends. I never saw grief or tears on those occasions. What I did
see was love that seemed to reach the point of rapture, but it was a gentle, self-
sufficient, and contemplative rapture. There was reason to believe that they communicated with the departed after death, and that their earthly union was not
cut short by death. They found it almost impossible to understand me when I
questioned them about life eternal, but apparently they were so convinced of it
in their minds that for them it was no question at all. They had no places of worship, but they had a certain awareness of a constant, uninterrupted, and living
union with the Universe at large. They had no specific religions, but instead they
had a certain knowledge that when their earthly joy had reached the limits imposed upon it by nature, they—both the living and the dead—would reach a
state of still closer communion with the Universe at large. They looked forward
to that moment with joy, but without haste and without pining for it, as though
already possessing it in the vague stirrings of their hearts, which they communicated to each other.

In the evening, before going to sleep, they were fond of gathering together
and singing in melodious and harmonious choirs. In their songs they expressed
all the sensations the parting day had given them. They praised it and bade it
farewell. They praised nature, the earth, the sea, and the woods. They were also
fond of composing songs about one another, and they praised each other like
children. Their songs were very simple, but they sprang straight from the heart
and they touched the heart. And not only in their songs alone, but they seemed
to spend all their lives in perpetual praise of one another. It seemed to be a universal and all-embracing love for each other. Some of their songs were solemn
and ecstatic, and I was scarcely able to understand them at all. While understanding the words, I could never entirely fathom their meaning. It remained somehow beyond the grasp of my reason, and yet it sank unconsciously deeper and
deeper into my heart. I often told them that I had had a presentiment of it years
ago and that all that joy and glory had been perceived by me while I was still on
our earth as a nostalgic yearning, bordering at times on unendurably poignant
sorrow; that I had had a presentiment of them all and of their glory in the
dreams of my heart and in the reveries of my soul; that often on our earth I could
not look at the setting sun without tears. . . . That there always was a sharp pang
of anguish in my hatred of the men of our earth; why could I not hate them
without loving them too? why could I not forgive them? And in my love for
them, too, there was a sharp pang of anguish: why could I not love them without
hating them? They listened to me, and I could tell that they did not know what I
was talking about. But I was not sorry to have spoken to them of it, for I knew
that they appreciated how much and how anxiously I yearned for those I had
forsaken. Oh yes, when they looked at me with their dear eyes full of love, when
I realised that in their presence my heart, too, became as innocent and truthful as
theirs, I did not regret my inability to understand them, either. The sensation of
the fullness of life left me breathless, and I worshipped them in silence.

Oh, everyone laughs in my face now and everyone assures me that I could not possibly have seen and felt anything so definite, but was merely conscious of a sensation that arose in my own feverish heart, and that I invented all those details myself when I woke up. And when I told them that they were probably right, good Lord, what mirth that admission of mine caused and how they laughed at me! Why, of course, I was overpowered by the mere sensation of that dream and it alone survived in my sorely wounded heart. But none the less the real shapes and forms of my dream, that is, those I actually saw at the very time of my dream, were filled with such harmony and were so enchanting and beautiful, and so intensely true, that on awakening I was indeed unable to clothe them in our feeble words so that they were bound as it were to become blurred in my mind; so is it any wonder that perhaps unconsciously I was myself afterwards driven to make up the details which I could not help distorting, particularly in view of my passionate desire to convey some of them at least as quickly as I could. But that does not mean that I have no right to believe that it all did happen. As a matter of fact, it was quite possibly a thousand times better, brighter, and more joyful than I describe it. What if it was only a dream? All that couldn't possibly have been. And do you know, I think I'll tell you a secret: perhaps it was no dream at all! For what happened afterwards was so awful, so horribly true, that it couldn't possibly have been a mere coinage of my brain seen in a dream. Granted that my heart was responsible for my dream, but could my heart alone have been responsible for the awful truth of what happened to me afterwards? Surely my paltry heart and my vacillating and trivial mind could not have risen to such a revelation of truth! Oh, judge for yourselves: I have been concealing it all the time, but now I will tell you the whole truth. The fact is, I—corrupted them all!

V

Yes, yes, it ended in my corrupting them all! How it could have happened I do not know, but I remember it clearly. The dream encompassed thousands of years and left in me only a vague sensation of the whole. I only know that the cause of the Fall was I. Like a horrible trichina, like the germ of the plague infecting whole kingdoms, so did I infect with myself all that happy earth that knew no sin before me. They learnt to lie, and they grew to appreciate the beauty of a lie. Oh, perhaps, it all began *innocently*, with a jest, with a desire to show off, with amorous play, and perhaps indeed only with a germ, but this germ made its way into their hearts and they liked it. The voluptuousness was soon born, voluptuousness begot jealousy, and jealousy—cruelty. . . . Oh, I don't know, I can't remember, but soon, very soon the first blood was shed: they were shocked and horrified, and they began to separate and to shun one another. They formed alliances, but it was one against another. Recriminations began, reproaches. They came to know shame, and they made shame into a virtue. The conception of honour was born, and every alliance raised its own standard. They began torturing animals, and the animals ran away from them into the forests and became their enemies. A struggle began for separation, for isolation, for personality, for mine and thine. They began talking in different languages. They came to know sorrow, and they loved sorrow. They thirsted for suffering, and they said that Truth could only be attained through suffering. It was then that science made its appearance among them. When they became wicked, they began talking of brotherhood and humanity and understood the meaning of those ideas. When they became guilty of crimes, they invented justice, and drew up whole codes of law, and to ensure the carrying out of their laws they erected a guillotine. They only vaguely remembered what they had lost, and they would not believe that they ever were happy and innocent. They even laughed at the possibility of their former happiness and called it a dream. They could not even imagine it in any definite shape or form, but the strange and wonderful thing was that though they had lost faith in their former state of happiness and called it a fairy-tale, they longed so much to be happy and innocent once more that, like children, they succumbed to the desire of their hearts, glorified this desire, built temples, and began offering up prayers to their own idea, their own "desire," and at the same time firmly believed that it could not be realised and brought about, though they still worshipped it and adored it with tears. And yet if they could have in one way or another returned to the state of happy innocence they had lost, and if someone had shown it to them again and had asked them whether they desired to go back to it, they would certainly have refused. The answer they gave me was, "What if we are dishonest, cruel, and unjust? We *know* it and we are sorry for it, and we torment ourselves for it, and inflict pain upon ourselves, and punish ourselves more perhaps than the merciful Judge who will judge us and whose name we do not know. But we have science and with its aid we shall again discover truth, though we shall accept it only when we perceive it with our reason. Knowledge is higher than feeling, and the consciousness of life is higher than life. Science will give us wisdom. Wisdom will reveal to us the laws. And the knowledge of the laws of happiness is higher than happiness." That is what they said to me, and having uttered those words, each of them began to love himself better than anyone else, and indeed they could not do otherwise. Every one of them became so jealous of his own personality that he strove with might and main to belittle and humble it in others; and therein he saw the whole purpose of his life. Slavery made its appearance, even voluntary slavery: the weak eagerly submitted themselves to the will of the strong on condition that the strong helped them to oppress those who were weaker than themselves. Saints made their appearance, saints who came to these people with tears and told them of their pride, of their loss of proportion and harmony, of their lots of shame. They were laughed to scorn and stoned to death. Their sacred blood was spilt on the threshold of the temples. But then men arose who began to wonder how they could all be united again, so that everybody should, without ceasing to love himself best of all, not interfere with everybody else and so that all of them should live together in a society which would at least seem to be founded on mutual understanding. Whole wars were fought over this idea. All the combatants at one and the same time firmly believed that science, wisdom, and the instinct of self-preservation would in the end force mankind to unite into a harmonious and intelligent society, and therefore, to hasten matters, the "very wise" did their best to exterminate as rapidly as possible the "not so wise" who did not understand their idea, so as to prevent them from interfering with its triumph. But the instinct of self-preservation began to weaken rapidly. Proud and voluptuous men appeared who frankly demanded all or nothing. In order to obtain everything they did not hesitate to resort to violence, and if it failed—to suicide. Religions were founded to propagate the cult of non-existence and self-destruction for the sake of the everlasting peace in nothingness. At last these people grew weary of their senseless labours and suffering appeared on their faces, and these people proclaimed that suffering was beauty, for in suffering alone was there thought. They glorified suffering in their songs. I walked among them, wringing my hands and weeping over them, but I loved them perhaps more than before when there was no sign of suffering in their faces and when they were innocent and—oh, so beautiful! I loved the earth they had polluted even more than when it had been a paradise, and only because sorrow had made its appearance on it. Alas, I always loved sorrow and affliction, but only for myself, only for myself; for them I wept now, for I pitied them. I stretched out my hands to them, accusing, cursing, and despising myself. I told them that I alone was responsible for it all—I alone; that it was I who had brought them corruption, contamination, and lies! I implored them to crucify me, and I taught them how to make the cross. I could not kill myself; I had not the courage to do it; but I longed to receive martyrdom at their hands. I thirsted for martyrdom, I yearned for my blood to be shed to the last drop in torment and suffering. But they only laughed at me, and in the end they began looking upon me as a madman. They justified me. They said that they had got what they themselves wanted and that what was now could not have been otherwise. At last they told me that I was becoming dangerous to them and that they would lock me up in a lunatic asylum if I did not hold my peace. Then sorrow entered my soul with such force that my heart was wrung and I felt as though I were dying, and then—well, then I awoke.

It was morning, that is, the sun had not risen yet, but it was about six o'clock. When I came to, I found myself in the same armchair, my candle had burnt out, in the captain's room they were asleep, and silence, so rare in our house, reigned around. The first thing I did was to jump up in great amazement. Nothing like this had ever happened to me before, not even so far as the most trivial details were concerned. Never, for instance, had I fallen asleep like this in my armchair. Then, suddenly, as I was standing and coming to myself, I caught sight of my gun lying there ready and loaded. But I pushed it away from me at once! Oh, how I longed for life, life! I lifted up my hands and called upon eternal Truth— no, not called upon it, but wept. Rapture, infinite and boundless rapture intoxicated me. Yes, life and—preaching! I made up my mind to preach from that very moment and, of course, to go on preaching all my life. I am going to preach, I want to preach. What? Why, truth. For I have beheld truth, I have beheld it with mine own eyes, I have beheld it in all its glory!

And since then I have been preaching. Moreover, I love all who laugh at me more than all the rest. Why that is so, I don't know and I cannot explain, but let it be so. They say that even now I often get muddled and confused and that if I am getting muddled and confused now, what will be later on? It is perfectly true. I do get muddled and confused and it is quite possible that I shall be getting worse later. And, of course, I shall get muddled several times before I find out how to preach, that is, what words to use and what deeds to perform, for that is all very difficult! All this is even now as clear to me as daylight, but, pray, tell me who does not get muddled and confused? And yet all follow the same path, at least all strive to achieve the same thing, from the philosopher to the lowest criminal, only by different roads. It is an old truth, but this is what is new: I cannot even get very much muddled and confused. For I have beheld the Truth. I have beheld it and I know that people can be happy and beautiful without losing their ability to live on earth. I will not and I cannot believe that evil is the normal condition among men. And yet they all laugh at this faith of mine. But how can I help believing it? I have beheld it—the Truth—it is not as though I had invented it with my mind: I have beheld it, I have beheld it, and the *living image* of it has filled my soul for ever. I have beheld it in all its glory and I cannot believe that it cannot exist among men. So how can I grow muddled and confused? I shall of course lose my way and I'm afraid that now and again I may speak with words that are not my own, but not for long: the living image of what I beheld will always be with me and it will always correct me and lead me back on to the right path. Oh, I'm in fine fettle, and I am of good cheer. I will go on and on for a thousand years, if need be. Do you know, at first I did not mean to tell you that I corrupted them, but that was a mistake—there you have my first mistake! But Truth whispered to me that I was *lying*, and so preserved me and set me on the right path. But I'm afraid I do not know how to establish a heaven on earth, for I do not know how to put it into words. After my dream I lost the knack of putting things into words. At least, into the most necessary and most important words. But never mind, I shall go on and I shall keep on talking, for I have indeed beheld it with my own eyes, though I cannot describe what I saw. It is this the scoffers do not understand. "He had a dream," they say, "a vision, a hallucination!" Oh dear, is this all they have to say? Do they really think that is very clever? And how proud they are! A dream! What is a dream? And what about our life? Is that not a dream too? I will say more: even—yes, even if this never comes to pass, even if there never is a heaven on earth (that, at any rate, I can see very well!), even then I shall go on preaching. And really how simple it all is: in one day, *in one hour*, everything could be arranged at once! The main thing is to love your neighbour as yourself—that is the main thing, and that is everything, for nothing else matters. Once you do that, you will discover at once how everything can be arranged. And yet it is an old truth, a truth that has been told over and over again, but in spite of that it finds no place among men! "The consciousness of life is higher than life, the knowledge of happiness is higher than happiness"—that is what we have to fight against! And I shall, I shall fight against it! If only we all wanted it, everything could be arranged immediately.

And—I did find that little girl. . . . And I shall go on! I shall go on!

THE GOSPEL ACCORDING TO MARK*
Jorge Luis Borges (1899–   )

These events took place at La Colorada ranch, in the southern part of the township of Junín,[1] during the last days of March, 1928. The protagonist was a medical student named Baltasar Espinosa. We may describe him, for now, as one of the common run of young men from Buenos Aires, with nothing more noteworthy about him than an almost unlimited kindness and a capacity for public

---

*Translated by Norman Thomas di Giovanni in collaboration with the author.

[1] In Argentina, west of Buenos Aires.

speaking that had earned him several prizes at the English school in Ramos Mejía. He did not like arguing, and preferred having his listener rather than himself
in the right. Although he was fascinated by the probabilities of chance in any
game he played, he was a bad player because it gave him no pleasure to win. His
wide intelligence was undirected; at the age of thirty-three, he still lacked credit
for graduation, by one course—the course to which he was most drawn. His father, who was a freethinker (like all the gentlemen of his day), had introduced
him to the lessons of Herbert Spencer,[2] but his mother, before leaving on a trip
for Montevideo, once asked him to say the Lord's Prayer and make the sign of
the cross every night. Through the years, he had never gone back on that promise.

Espinosa was not lacking in spirit; one day, with more indifference than anger, he had exchanged two or three punches with a group of fellow-students
who were trying to force him to take part in a university demonstration. Owing
to an acquiescent nature, he was full of opinions, or habits of mind, that were
questionable: Argentina mattered less to him than a fear that in other parts of the
world people might think of us as Indians; he worshiped France but despised the
French; he thought little of Americans but approved the fact that there were tall
buildings, like theirs, in Buenos Aires; he believed the gauchos of the plains to
be better riders than those of hill or mountain country. When his cousin Daniel
invited him to spend the summer months out at La Colorada, he said yes at
once—not because he was really fond of the country, but more out of his natural
complacency and also because it was easier to say yes than to dream up reasons
for saying no.

The ranch's main house was big and slightly run-down; the quarters of the
foreman, whose name was Gutre, were close by. The Gutres were three: the father, an unusually uncouth son, and a daughter of uncertain paternity. They
were tall, strong, and bony, and had hair that was on the reddish side and faces
that showed traces of Indian blood. They were barely articulate. The foreman's
wife had died years before.

There in the country, Espinosa began learning things he never knew, or even
suspected—for example, that you do not gallop a horse when approaching settlements, and that you never go out riding except for some special purpose. In time,
he was to come to tell the birds apart by their calls.

After a few days, Daniel had to leave for Buenos Aires to close a deal on some
cattle. At most, this bit of business might take him a week. Espinosa, who was already somewhat weary of hearing about his cousin's incessant luck with women
and his tireless interest in the minute details of men's fashion, preferred staying
on at the ranch with his textbooks. But the heat was unbearable, and even the
night brought no relief. One morning at daybreak, thunder woke him. Outside,
the wind was rocking the Australian pines. Listening to the first heavy drops of
rain, Espinosa thanked God. All at once, cold air rolled in. That afternoon, the Salado overflowed its banks.

The next day, looking out over the flooded fields from the gallery of the main
house, Baltasar Espinosa thought that the stock metaphor comparing the pampa[3]

[2] Spencer (1820–1903) was an English philosopher and a proponent of scientific
determinism.
[3] Treeless plains.

to the sea was not altogether false—at least, not that morning—though W. H. Hudson[4] had remarked that the sea seems wider because we view it from a ship's deck and not from a horse or from eye level.

The rain did not let up. The Gutres, helped or hindered by Espinosa, the town dweller, rescued a good part of the livestock, but many animals were drowned. There were four roads leading to La Colorada; all of them were under water. On the third day, when a leak threatened the foreman's house, Espinosa gave the Gutres a room near the tool shed, at the back of the main house. This drew them all closer, they ate together in the big dining room. Conversation turned out to be difficult. The Gutres, who knew so much about country things, were hard put to it to explain them. One night, Espinosa asked them if people still remembered the Indian raids from back when the frontier command was located there in Junín. They told him yes, but they would have given the same answer to a question about the beheading of Charles I.[5] Espinosa recalled his father's saying that almost every case of longevity that was cited in the country was really a case of bad memory or of a dim notion of dates. Gauchos are apt to be ignorant of the year of their birth or of the name of the man who begot them.

In the whole house, there was apparently no other reading matter than a set of the *Farm Journal*, a handbook of veterinary medicine, a deluxe edition of the Uruguayan epic *Tabaré*, *a History of Shorthorn Cattle in Argentina*, a number of erotic or detective stories, and a recent novel called *Don Segundo Sombra*. Espinosa, trying in some way to bridge the inevitable after-dinner gap, read a couple of chapters of this novel to the Gutres, none of whom could read or write. Unfortunately, the foreman had been a cattle drover, and the doings of the hero, another cattle drover, failed to whet his interest. He said that the work was light, that drovers always traveled with a packhorse that carried everything they needed, and that, had he not been a drover, he would never have seen such far-flung places as the Laguna de Gómez, the town of Bragado, and the spread of the Núñez family in Chacabuco. There was a guitar in the kitchen; the ranch hands, before the time of the events I am describing, used to sit around in a circle. Someone would tune the instrument without ever getting around to playing it. This was known as a guitarfest.

Espinosa, who had grown a beard, began dallying in front of the mirror to study his new face, and he smiled to think how, back in Buenos Aires he would bore his friends by telling them the story of the Salado flood. Strangely enough, he missed places he never frequented and never would: a corner of Cabrera Street on which there was a mailbox; one of the cement lions of a gateway on Jujuy Street, a few blocks from the Plaza del Once; an old barroom with a tiled floor, whose exact whereabouts he was unsure of. As for his brothers and his father, they would already have learned from Daniel that he was isolated—etymologically, the word was perfect—by the floodwaters.

Exploring the house, still hemmed in by the watery waste, Espinosa came across an English Bible. Among the blank pages at the end, the Guthries—such was their original name—had left a handwritten record of their lineage. They were natives of Inverness;[6] had reached the New World, no doubt as common la-

---

[4] An English writer (1841–1922), born in Argentina.
[5] An English king, beheaded in 1649.
[6] In Scotland.

borers, in the early part of the nineteenth century; and had intermarried with Indians. The chronicle broke off sometime during the eighteen-seventies, when
they no longer knew how to write. After a few generations, they had forgotten
English; their Spanish, at the time Espinosa knew them, gave them trouble. They
lacked any religious faith, but there survived in their blood, like faint tracks, the
rigid fanaticism of the Calvinist and the superstitions of the pampa Indian.
Espinosa later told them of his find, but they barely took notice.

Leafing through the volume, his fingers opened it at the beginning of the
Gospel according to St. Mark. As an exercise in translation, and maybe to find
out whether the Gutres understood any of it, Espinosa decided to begin reading
them that text after their evening meal. It surprised him that they listened attentively, absorbed. Maybe the gold letters on the cover lent the book authority. It's
still there in their blood, Espinosa thought. It also occurred to him that the generations of men, throughout recorded time, have always told and retold two stories—that of a lost ship which searches the Mediterranean sea for a dearly loved
island, and that of a god who is crucified on Golgotha.[7] Remembering his lessons
in elocution from his schooldays in Ramos Mejía, Espinosa got to his feet when
he came to the parables.

The Gutres took to bolting their barbecued meat and their sardines so as not
to delay the Gospel. A pet lamb that the girl adored with a small blue ribbon had
injured itself on a strand of barbed wire. To stop the bleeding, the three had
wanted to apply a cobweb to the wound, but Espinosa treated the animal with
some pills. The gratitude that this treatment awakened in them took him aback.
(Not trusting the Gutres at first, he'd hidden away in one of his books the two
hundred and forty pesos he had brought with him.) Now, the owner of the place
away, Espinosa took over and gave timid orders, which were immediately
obeyed. The Gutres, as if lost without him, liked following him from room to
room and along the gallery that ran around the house. While he read to them, he
noticed that they were secretly stealing the crumbs he had dropped on the table.
One evening, he caught them unawares, talking about him respectfully, in very
few words.

Having finished the Gospel according to St. Mark, he wanted to read another
of the three Gospels that remained, but the father asked him to repeat the one he
had just read, so that they could understand it better. Espinosa felt that they were
like children, to whom repetition is more pleasing than variations or novelty.
That night—this is not to be wondered at—he dreamed of the Flood;[8] the hammer blows of the building of the Ark woke him up, and he thought that perhaps
they were thunder. In fact, the rain, which had let up, started again. The cold
was bitter. The Gutres had told him that the storm had damaged the roof of the
tool shed, and that they would show it to him when the beams were fixed. No
longer a stranger now, he was treated by them with special attention, almost to
the point of spoiling him. None of them liked coffee, but for him there was always a small cup into which they heaped sugar.

The new storm had broken out on a Tuesday. Thursday night, Espinosa was
awakened by a soft knock at his door, which—just in case—he always kept
locked. He got out of bed and opened it; there was the girl. In the dark he could

[7] Where Christ was crucified. See Mark xv.22.
[8] The story of the flood is told in Genesis, chapters 6–8.

hardly make her out, but by her footsteps he could tell she was barefoot, and moments later, in bed, that she must have come all the way from the other end of the house naked. She did not embrace him or speak a single word; she lay beside him, trembling. It was the first time she had known a man. When she left, she did not kiss him; Espinosa realized that he didn't even know her name. For some reason that he did not want to pry into, he made up his mind that upon returning to Buenos Aires he would tell no one about what had taken place.

The next day began like the previous ones, except that the father spoke to Espinosa and asked him if Christ had let Himself be killed so as to save all other men on earth. Espinosa, who was a freethinker but who felt committed to what he had read to the Gutres, answered, "Yes, to save everyone from Hell."

Gutre then asked, "What's Hell?"

"A place under the ground where souls burn and burn."

"And the Roman soldiers who hammered in the nails—were they saved too?"

"Yes," said Espinosa, whose theology was rather dim.

All along, he was afraid that the foreman might ask him about what had gone on the night before with his daughter. After lunch, they asked him to read the last chapters over again.

Espinosa slept a long nap that afternoon. It was a light sleep, disturbed by persistent hammering and by vague premonitions. Toward evening, he got up and went out onto the gallery. He said, as if thinking aloud, "The waters have dropped. It won't be long now."

"It won't be long now," Gutre repeated, like an echo.

The three had been following him. Bowing their knees to the stone pavement, they asked his blessing. Then they mocked at him, spat on him, and shoved him toward the back part of the house. The girl wept. Espinosa understood what awaited him on the other side of the door. When they opened it, he saw a patch of sky. A bird sang out. A goldfinch, he thought. The shed was without a roof; they had pulled down the beams to make the cross.

THE THROWER-AWAY*

Heinrich Böll (1917–)

For the last few weeks I have been trying to avoid people who might ask me what I do for a living. If I really had to put a name to my occupation, I would be forced to utter a word which would alarm people. So I prefer the abstract method of putting down my confession on paper.

Until recently I would have been prepared at any time to make an oral confession. I almost insisted. I called myself an inventor, a scholar, even a student, and, in the melodramatic mood of incipient intoxication, an unrecognized genius. I basked in the cheerful fame which a frayed collar can radiate; arrogantly, as if it were mine by right, I exacted reluctant credit from suspicious shopkeepers who watched margarine, ersatz coffee and cheap tobacco disappear into my pockets; I reveled in my unkempt appearance, and at breakfast, lunch and dinner I drank the nectar of Bohemian life: the bliss of knowing one is not conforming.

*Translated by Leila Vennewitz.

But for the past few weeks I have been boarding the streetcar every morning just before 7:30 at the corner of the Roonstrasse; like everyone else I meekly hold out my season ticket to the conductor. I have on a gray double-breasted suit, a striped shirt, a dark-green tie, I carry my sandwiches in a flat aluminum box and hold the morning paper, lightly rolled, in my hand. I look like a citizen who has managed to avoid introspection. After the third stop I get up to offer my seat to one of the elderly working women who have got on at the housing settlement. Having sacrificed my seat on the altar of social compassion, I continue to read the newspaper standing up, now and again letting myself be heard in the capacity of arbitrator when morning irritation is inclined to make people unjust. I correct the worst political and historical errors (by explaining, for instance, that there is a certain difference between SA and USA); as soon as anyone puts a cigarette to his lips I discreetly hold my lighter in front of his nose and, with the aid of the tiny but dependable flame, light his morning cigarette for him. Thus I complete the picture of a well-groomed fellow-citizen who is still young enough for people to say he "has nice manners."

I seem to have been successful in donning the mask which makes it impossible to ask me about my occupation. I am evidently taken for an educated businessman dealing in attactively packaged and agreeably smelling articles such as coffee, tea or spices, or in valuable small objects which are pleasing to the eye such as jewelry or watches; a man who practices his profession in a nice old-fashioned office with dark oil paintings of merchant forebears hanging on the walls, who phones his wife about ten, who knows how to imbue his apparently impassive voice with that hint of tenderness which betrays affection and concern. Since I also participate in the usual jokes and do not refrain from laughing when every morning at the Lohengrinstrasse the clerk from City Hall shouts out "When does the next swan leave?", since I do not withhold my comments concerning either the events of the day or the results of the football pools, I am obviously regarded as someone who, although prosperous (as can be seen from his suit material), has an attitude toward life which is deeply rooted in the principles of democracy. An air of integrity encases me the way the glass coffin encased Snow White.

When a passing truck provides the streetcar window with a background for a moment, I check up on the expression on my face: isn't it perhaps rather too pensive, almost verging on the sorrowful? I assiduously erase the remnants of brooding and do my best to give my face the expression I want it to wear: neither reserved nor familiar, neither superficial nor profound.

My camouflage seems to be successful, for when I get out at the Marienplatz and dive into the maze of streets in the Old Town, where there is no lack of nice old-fashioned offices, where notaries and lawyers abound, no one suspects that I pass through a rear entrance into the UBIA building—a firm that can boast of supporting 350 people and of insuring the lives of 400,000. The commissionaire greets me with a smile at the delivery entrance, I walk past him, go down to the basement, and start in on my work, which has to be completed by the time the employees come pouring into the office at 8:30. The activity that I pursue every morning between 8 and 8:30 in the basement of this respected establishment is devoted entirely to destruction. I throw away.

It took me years to invent my profession, to endow it with mathematical plausibility. I wrote treatises; graphs and charts covered—and still cover—the walls of my apartment. For years I climbed along abscissas and up ordinates, wallowed in theories, and savored the glacial ecstasy of solving formulas. Yet since practicing my profession and seeing my theories come to life, I am filled with a sense of sadness such as may come over a general who finds himself obliged to descend from the heights of strategy to the plains of tactics.

I enter my workroom, exchange my jacket for a gray smock, and immediately set to work. I open the mailbags which the commissionaire has already picked up earlier from the main post office, and I empty them into the two wooden bins which, constructed according to my design, hang to the right and left on the wall over my worktable. This way I only need to stretch out my hands, somewhat like a swimmer, and begin swiftly to sort the mail.

First I separate the circulars from the letters, a purely routine job, since a glance at the postage suffices. At this stage a knowledge of the postal tariff renders hesitation unnecessary. After years of practice I am able to complete this phase within half an hour, and by this time it is half past eight and I can hear the footsteps of the employees pouring into the offices overhead. I ring for the commissionaire, who takes the sorted letters to the various departments. It never fails to sadden me, the sight of the commissionaire carrying off in a metal tray the size of a briefcase the remains of what had once filled three mailbags. I might feel triumphant, for this, the vindication of my theory of throwing away, has for years been the objective of my private research; but, strangely enough, I do not feel triumphant. To have been right is by no means always a reason for rejoicing.

After the departure of the commissionaire there remains the task of examining the huge pile of printed matter to make sure it contains no letter masquerading behind the wrong postage, no bill mailed as a circular. This work is almost always superfluous, for the probity of the mailing public is nothing short of astounding. I must admit that here my calculations were incorrect: I had overestimated the number of postal defrauders.

Rarely has a post card, a letter or a bill sent as printed matter escaped my notice; about half past nine I ring for the commissionaire, who takes the remaining objects of my careful scrutiny to the departments.

The time has now come when I require some refreshment. The commissionaire's wife brings me my coffee, I take my sandwich out of the flat aluminum box, sit down for my break, and chat with the commissionaire's wife about her children. Is Alfred doing somewhat better in arithmetic? Has Gertrude been able to catch up in spelling? Alfred is not doing any better in arithmetic, whereas Gertrude has been able to catch up in spelling. Have the tomatoes ripened properly, are the rabbits plump, and was the experiment with the melons successful? The tomatoes have not ripened properly, but the rabbits are plump, while the experiment with the melons is still undecided. Serious problems, such as whether one should stock up on potatoes or not, matters of education, such as whether one should enlighten one's children or be enlightened by them, are the subjects of our intense consideration.

Just before eleven the commissionaire's wife leaves, and usually she asks me to let her have some travel folders. She is collecting them, and I smile at her enthusiasm, for I have retained tender memories of travel folders. As a child I also collected travel folders, I used to fish them out of my father's waste-paper basket.

Even as a boy it bothered me that my father would take mail from the mailman and throw it into the waste-paper basket without looking at it. This action wounded my innate propensity for economy: there was something that had been designed, set up, printed, put in an envelope, and stamped, that had passed through the mysterious channels by which the postal service actually causes our mail to arrive at our addresses; it was weighted with the sweat of the draftsman, the writer, the printer, the office boy who had stuck on the stamps; on various levels and in various tariffs it had cost money: all this only to end—without being deemed worthy of so much as a glance—in a waste-paper basket?

At the age of eleven I had already adopted the habit of taking out of the waste-paper basket, as soon as my father had left for the office, whatever had been thrown away. I would study it, sort it, and put it away in a chest which I used to keep toys in. Thus by the time I was twelve I already possessed an imposing collection of wine-merchants' catalogues, as well as prospectuses on naturopathy and natural history. My collection of travel folders assumed the dimensions of a geographical encyclopedia; Dalmatia was as familiar to me as the Norwegian fjords, Scotland as close as Zakopane, the forests of Bohemia soothed me while the waves of the Atlantic disquieted me; hinges were offered me, houses and buttons, political parties asked for my vote, charities for my money; lotteries promised me riches, religious sects poverty. I leave it to the reader's imagination to picture what my collection was like when at the age of seventeen, suddenly bored with it all, I offered my collection to a junk dealer who paid me 7 marks and 60 pfennigs for it.

Having finished school, I embarked in my father's footsteps and set my foot on the first rung of the civil service ladder. With the 7 marks and 60 pfennigs I bought a package of squared paper and three colored crayons, and my attempt to gain a foothold in the civil service turned into a laborious detour, for a happy thrower-away was slumbering in me while I filled the role of an unhappy junior clerk. All my free time was devoted to intricate calculations.

Stop-watch, pencil, slide-rule, squared paper, these were the props of my obsession; I calculated how long it took to open a circular of small, medium or large size, with or without pictures, give it a quick glance, satisfy oneself of its uselessness, and then throw it in the wastepaper basket, a process requiring a minimum of five seconds and a maximum of twenty-five; if the circular is at all attractive, either the text or the pictures, several minutes, often a quarter of an hour, must be allowed for this. By conducting bogus negotiations with printing firms, I also worked out the minimum production costs for circulars. Indefatigably I checked the results of my studies and adjusted them (it did not occur to me until two years later that the time of the cleaning-women who have to empty the waste-paper baskets had to be included in my calculations); I applied the results of my research to firms with ten, twenty, a hundred or more employees; and I arrived at results which an expert on economics would not have hesitated to describe as alarming.

Obeying my sense of loyalty, I began by offering my results to my superiors; although I had reckoned with the possibility of ingratitude, I was nevertheless shocked at the extent of that ingratitude. I was accused of neglecting my duties, suspected of nihilism, pronounced "a mental case," and discharged. To the great sorrow of my kind parents, I abandoned my promising career, began new ones, broke these off too, forsook the warmth of the parental hearth, and, as I have already said, eked out my existence as an unrecognized genius. I took pleasure in the humiliation of vainly peddling my invention, and spent years in a blissful state of being antisocial, so consistently that my punch-card in the central files which had long ago been punched with the symbol for "mental case" was now stamped with the confidential symbol for "antisocial."

In view of these circumstances, it can readily be imagined what a shock it was when the obviousness of my results at last became obvious to someone else—the manager of UBIA, how deeply humiliated I was to have to wear a dark-green tie, yet I must continue to go around in disguise as I am terrified of being found out. I try anxiously to give my face the proper expression when I laugh at the Lohengrin joke, since there is no greater vanity than that of the wags who populate the streetcar every morning. Sometimes, too, I am afraid the streetcar may be full of people who the previous day have done work which I am about to destroy that very morning: printers, typesetters, draftsmen, writers who compose the wording of advertisements, commercial artists, envelope stuffers, packers, apprentices of all kinds. From 6 to 8:30 every morning I ruthlessly destroy the products of respected paper mills, worthy printing establishments, brilliant commercial artists, the texts of talented writers; coated paper, glossy paper, copperplate, I take it all, just as it comes from the mailbag, and without the faintest sentimentality tie it up into handy bundles for the waste-paper dealer. In the space of one hour I destroy the output of 200 work-hours and save UBIA a further 100 hours, so that altogether (here I must lapse into my own jargon) I achieve a concentrate of 1:300.

When the commissionaire's wife leaves with the empty coffeepot and the travel folders, I knock off. I wash my hands, exchange my smock for my jacket, pick up the morning paper, and leave the UBIA building by the rear entrance. I stroll through the town and wonder how I can escape from tactics and get back into strategy. That which intoxicated me as a formula, I find disappointing, since it can be performed so easily. Strategy translated into action can be carried out by hacks. I shall probably establish schools for throwers-away. I may possibly also attempt to have throwers-away placed in post offices, perhaps even in printing establishments; an enormous amount of energy, valuable commodities, and intelligence could be utilized as well as postage saved; it might even be feasible to conceive, compose, and set brochures up in type but not print them. These are all problems still requiring a lot of study.

However, the mere throwing away of mail as such has almost ceased to interest me; any improvements on that level can be worked out by means of the basic formula. For a long time now I have been devoting my attention to calculations concerning wrapping paper and the process of wrapping: this is virgin territory where nothing has been done, here one can strive to spare humanity those unprofitable efforts under the burden of which it is groaning. Every day billions of throwing-away movements are made, energies are dissipated which, could they but be utilized, would suffice to change the face of the earth. It would be a great advantage if one were permitted to undertake experiments in department stores; should one dispense with the wrapping process altogether, or should one post an expert thrower-away right next to the wrapping table who unwraps what has just been wrapped and immediately ties the wrapping paper into bundles for the waste-paper dealer? These are problems meriting some thought. In any case it has struck me that in many shops the customers implore the clerk not to wrap the purchased article, but that they have to submit to having it wrapped. Clinics for nervous diseases are rapidly filling with patients who complain of an attack of nerves whenever they unwrap a bottle of perfume or a box of chocolates, or open a packet of cigarettes, and at the moment I am making an intensive study of a young man from my neighborhood who earned his living as a book reviewer but at times was unable to practice his profession because he found it impossible to undo the twisted wire tied around the parcel, and even when he did find himself equal to this physical exertion, he was incapable of penetrating the massive layer of gummed paper with which the corrugated paper is stuck together. The man appears deeply disturbed and has now gone over to reviewing the books unread and placing the parcels on his bookshelves without unwrapping them. I leave it to the reader's imagination to depict for himself the effect of such a case on our intellectual life.

While walking through the town between eleven and one I observe all sorts of details: I spend some time unobtrusively in the department stores, hovering around the wrapping tables; I stand in front of tobacco shops and pharmacies and note down minor statistics; now and again I even purchase something, so as to allow the senseless procedure to be performed on myself and to discover how much effort is required actually to take possession of the article one wishes to own.

So between eleven and one in my impeccable suit I complete the picture of a man who is sufficiently prosperous to afford a bit of leisure—who at about one o'clock enters a sophisticated little restaurant, casually chooses the most expensive meal, and scribbles some hieroglyphics on his beer coaster which could equally well be stock quotations or flights of poetry; who knows how to praise or decry the quality of the meat with arguments which betray the connoisseur to even the most blasé waiter; who, when it comes to choosing dessert, hesitates with a knowing air between cake, ice cream and cheese; and who finishes off his scribblings with a flourish which proves that they were stock quotations after all.

Shocked at the results of my calculations I leave the little restaurant. My expression becomes more and more thoughtful while I search for a small café where I can pass the time till three o'clock and read the evening paper. At three I re-enter the UBIA building by the rear door to take care of the afternoon mail, which consists almost exclusively of circulars. It is a matter of scarcely fifteen minutes to pick out the ten or twelve letters; I don't even have to wash my hands after it, I just brush them off, take the letters to the commissionaire, leave the building, and at the Marienplatz board the streetcar, glad that on the way home I do not need to laugh at the Lohengrin joke. When the dark tarpaulin of a passing truck makes a background for the streetcar window, I can see my face: it is relaxed, that is to say pensive, almost brooding, and I relish the fact that I do not have to put on any other face, for at this hour none of my morning fellow-travelers has finished work. I get out at the Roonstrasse, buy some fresh rolls, a piece of cheese or sausage, some ground coffee, and walk up to my little apartment, the walls of which are hung with graphs and charts, with hectic curves: between the abscissas and ordinates I capture the lines of a fever going up and up; not a single one of my curves goes down, not a single one of my formulas has the power to soothe me. I groan under the burden of my vision of economics, and while the water is boiling for the coffee I place my slide-rule, my notes, pencil and paper in readiness.

My apartment is sparsely furnished, it looks more like a laboratory. I drink my coffee standing up and hastily swallow a sandwich, the epicure I was at noon is now a thing of the past. Wash hands, light a cigarette, then I set my stop-watch and unwrap the nerve tonic I bought that morning on my stroll through the town: outer wrapping paper, cellophane covering, carton, inside wrapping paper, directions for use secured by a rubber band: thirty-seven seconds. The nervous energy consumed in unwrapping exceeds the nervous energy which the tonic promises to impart to me, but there may be subjective reasons for this which I shall disregard in my calculations. One thing is certain: the wrapping is worth more than the contents, and the cost of the twenty-five yellow tablets is out of all proportion to their value. But these are considerations verging on the moral aspect, and I would prefer to keep away from morality altogether. My field of speculation is one of pure economics.

Numerous articles are waiting to be unwrapped by me, many slips of paper are waiting to be evaluated; green, red, blue ink, everything is ready. It is usually late by the time I get to bed, and as I fall asleep I am haunted by my formulas, whole worlds of useless paper roll over me; some formulas explode like dynamite, the noise of the explosion sounds like a burst of laughter: it is my own, my laughter at the Lohengrin joke originating in my fear of the clerk from City Hall. Perhaps he has access to the punch-card file, has picked out my card, discovered that it contains not only the symbol for "mental case" but the second, more dangerous one for "antisocial." There is nothing more difficult to fill than a tiny hole like that in a punch-card; perhaps my laughter at the Lohengrin joke is the price I have to pay for my anonymity. I would not like to admit face to face what I find easier to do in writing: that I am a thrower-away.

THE FORD

W. S. Merwin (1927–)

Slides of his travels. I thought oh yes, and dismissed the enthusiasm in his voice, that clearly was begging for attention. The lights were on, so the slides were faint and translucent on the wall. Brought out in a hurry, with a touch of shyness, much of it false. There were other conversations going on. I listened here and there, for a moment, and so I missed the beginning of what he said about the pictures. I turned back to them only at the mention of the horses, the tone of the voices agreeing, saying, "There they are," and the slight pause that came after that, an intake of breath, a wave falling back.

Pale yellow wall, half dissolved by a diaphanous section of lit sky, some other time of day, maybe a winter noon, or summer in the far north, reflected in a surface that must be water, a water, a piece of shore beyond it, a river bank, so a river, part of a river, part of what could be seen of it from one spot, at one instant in the past. The wall gone from behind it. And there they were, the horses. A line of them, crossing from right to left, all bays—the slides were in color. There were nine or ten of the horses, in water almost to their bellies, and it looked as though there might be others behind, out of the picture. They had flat white cloths on their backs—blankets, or thin packs, it was impossible to say which, as everyone finally agreed after asking each other. He knew no more than the rest of us did. The horses were following a larger bay, several lengths ahead of them, who looked like a stallion, and had nothing at all on his back. There were no lines, traces, ropes, harness. The horses were travelling by themselves. Even on the wall they appeared to be moving, like smoke.

He said that he had not seen them when he took the picture. They weren't there, he said. He didn't see them. It was only after he got back, and had the rolls developed by the same special laboratory he always used, where they did good work, professional. Somebody asked the address.

He said it wasn't until he brought them home to look at with the projector that he saw the horses. It wasn't anything like a double exposure. There they were, wading the river, the legs out of sight in the water. Just in that one picture. Of the river. The only one of the river. He had thought he was just taking a picture of the river. Not even the river—that same building, from across the river.

"I know that place," one person said. "I asked about it once. All they had to say around there was that it had been there a long time. But it must have been something else. At one time."

I had scarcely noticed the building, on higher ground, looking no bigger that a single haycock, in the distance, to the left, well above the water and the horses. And as I looked harder, to make it out, the slide changed, and I saw the landscape across the river, no water, no horses. The landscape into which the horses would have been about to pass: stubble fields and unmown straw-gold meadows curving uphill into dark green woods, and in a clearing near the top, the same building, a little nearer but still small and doubtful. A cluster of roofs, and in the center a round tower, all the walls painted the red of barns, but darker, an ox-blood, dry blood, color—though it may have been the light at that time of day, or the distance, or the exposure, that made it look that shade. The slide changed again, and showed the wooden tower, much closer, with small windows on each floor. One roof, butted against it on the left, was clearly a habitation. Another wing, of corrugated iron, had been tacked against the tower at an angle, and was covered with tin, that had rusted. The dark red paint was peeling. The top of the tower rose in a point, like a hat. Another slide, taken from closer still, showed only the upper story of the house, and the top part of the tower. The curving rows of small windows, in sight of which the horses would pass. The windows looked as though lights were about to appear in them.

"Somebody living there?" one of the spectators asked.

"That's as near as I went," the man who had taken the picture said.

"I don't think anybody was actually living in it when I was there," said the one who had told them he knew the place. "But that was a few years ago."

"I was just taking pictures of that building," the man at the projector said. "I still don't know what it is."

"Looks like a farm," one of them said.

"Maybe at one time," another answered. "But it's not being used as a farm. The grass is too high."

"I wanted to get one picture of it from across the river," the man at the projector said again, now that they would understand. "And I never saw—"

"You'll have to go back," somebody said.

But the man said nothing. And then they started talking about where the horses were going, and where they might have got to, by then.

THE STORY OF BYRON THE BULB*

Thomas Pynchon (1937–)

Byron was to've been manufactured by Tungsram in Budapest. He would probably have been grabbed up by the ace salesman Géza Rózsavölgyi's father Sandor, who covered all the Transylvanian territory and had begun to go native enough to where the home office felt vaguely paranoid about him throwing some horrible spell on the whole operation if they didn't give him what he wanted. Actually he was a salesman who wanted his son to be a doctor, and that came true. But it may have been the bad witch-leery auras around Budapest that got the birth of Byron reassigned at the last minute to Osram, in Berlin. Reassigned, yes. There is a Bulb Baby Heaven, amiably satirized as if it was the movies or something, well Big *Business,* ha, ha! But don't let Them fool you, this *is* a bureaucracy first, and a Bulb Baby Heaven only as a sort of sideline. All overhead—yes, out of its own pocket the Company is springing for square leagues of organdy, hogsheads of IG Farben pink and blue Baby Dye, hundredweights of clever Siemens Electric Baby Bulb Pacifiers, giving the suckling Bulb the shape of 110-volt current without the least trickle of power. One way or another, these Bulb folks are in the business of providing the appearance of power, power against the night, without the reality.

Actually, B.B.H. is rather shabby. The brown rafters drip cobwebs. Now and then a roach shows up on the floor, and all the Babies try to roll over to look (being Bulbs they *seem* perfectly symmetrical, Skippy, but don't forget the contact at the top of the thread) going uh-guh! uhhhh-*guh!,* glowing feebly at the bewildered roach sitting paralyzed and squashable out on the bare boards, rushing, reliving the terror of some sudden blast of current out of nowhere and high overhead the lambent, all-seeing Bulb. In their innocence, the Baby Bulbs don't know what to make of this roach's abreaction—they feel his fright, but don't know what it is. They just want to be his friend. He's interesting and has good moves. Everybody's excited except for Byron, who considers the other Bulb Babies a bunch of saps. It is a constant struggle to turn their thoughts on anything meaningful. Hi there Babies, I'm Byron-the-Bulb! Here to sing a little song to you, that goes—

> Light-up, and shine, you—in-cande-scent Bulb Ba-bies!
> Looks-like ya got ra-bies
> Just lay there foamin' and a-screamin' like a buncha
>   little demons,
> I'm deliv'rin' unto you a king-dom of roa-ches,
> And no-thin' ap-proaches
> That joyful feelin' when-you're up-on the ceilin'
> Lookin' down—night and day—on the king-dom you sur-vey,
> They'll come out 'n' love ya till the break of dawn,
> But they run like hell when that light comes on!
> So shine on, Baby Bulbs, you're the wave of the fu-ture,
> And I'm here to recruit ya,
> In m'great crusade,
> Just sing along Babies—come-on-and-join-the-big-pa-rade!

*From Pynchon's novel *Gravity's Rainbow* (1973).

Trouble with Byron's he's an old, old soul, trapped inside the glass prison of a Baby Bulb. He hates this place, lying on his back waiting to get manufactured, nothing to listen to on the speakers but Charleston music, now and then an address to the Nation, what kind of a setup's that? Byron wants to get out of here and *into it*, needless to say he's been developing all kinds of nervous ailments, Baby Bulb Diaper Rash, which is a sort of corrosion on his screw threads, Bulb Baby Colic, a tight spasm of high resistance someplace among the deep loops of tungsten wire, Bulb Baby Hyperventilation, where it actually feels like his vacuum's been broken though there is no organic basis. . . .

When M-Day finally does roll around, you can bet Byron's elated. He has passed the time hatching some really insane grandiose plans—he's gonna organize all the Bulbs, see, get him a power base in Berlin, he's already hep to the Strobing Tactic, all you do is develop the knack (Yogic, almost) of shutting off and on at a rate close to the human brain's alpha rhythm, and you can actually trigger an *epileptic fit!* True. Byron has had a vision against the rafters of his ward, of 20 million Bulbs, all over Europe, at a given synchronizing pulse arranged by one of his many agents in the Grid, all these Bulbs beginning to strobe *together*, humans thrashing around the 20 million rooms like fish on the beaches of Perfect Energy—Attention, humans, this has been a warning to you. Next time, a few of us will *explode.* Ha-ha. Yes we'll unleash our *Kamikaze squads!* You've heard of the Kirghiz Light?[1] well that's the ass end of a firefly compared to what we're gonna—oh, you haven't heard of the—oh, well, too bad. Cause a few Bulbs, say a million, a mere 5% of our number, are more than willing to flame out in one grand burst instead of patiently waiting out their design hours. . . . So Byron dreams of his Guerrilla Strike Force, gonna get Herbert Hoover, Stanley Baldwin,[2] all of them, right in the face with one coordinated blast. . . .

Is Byron in for a rude awakening! There is already an organization, a human one, known as "Phoebus," the international light-bulb cartel, headquartered in Switzerland. Run pretty much by International GE, Osram, and Associated Electrical Industries of Britain, which are in turn owned 100%, 29% and 46%, respectively, by the General Electric Company in America. Phoebus fixes the prices and determines the operational lives of all the bulbs in the world, from Brazil to Japan to Holland (although Philips in Holland is the mad dog of the cartel, apt at any time to cut loose and sow disaster throughout the great Combination.) Given this state of general repression, there seems noplace for a newborn Baby Bulb to start but at the bottom.

But Phoebus doesn't know yet that Byron is immortal. He starts out his career at an all-girl opium den in Charlottenburg,[3] almost within sight of the statue of Wernher Siemens,[4] burning up in a sconce, one among many bulbs witnessing the more languorous forms of Republican[5] decadence. He gets to know all the

---

[1] A meteoric blast in Siberia on June 30, 1908 leveled forests over an area 60 to 100 kilometers in diameter. The Kirghiz are descendents of Asian nomads whose homeland was south and west of the blast area.

[2] U.S. president and British prime minister, in office concurrently in 1929.

[3] A district in West Berlin.

[4] Siemens (1816–1892) was a pioneer in applied electrical technology.

[5] The Weimar Republic was established in Germany in 1919 in the aftermath of World War 1. By 1929 Germany was rapidly moving toward the Nazi domination that in 1933 resulted in suspension of the constitution, giving Adolf Hitler virtually dictatorial powers.

bulbs in the place, Benito the Bulb over in the next sconce who's always planning an escape, Bernie down the hall in the toilet, who has all kinds of urolagnia
jokes to tell, his mother Brenda in the kitchen who talks of hashish hush puppies, dildos rigged to pump floods of paregoric orgasm to the capillaries of the
womb, prayers to Astarte and Lilith,[6] queen of the night, reaches into the true
Night of the Other, cold and naked on linoleum floors after days without sleep,
the dreams and tears become a natural state. . . .

One by one, over the months, the other bulbs burn out, and are gone. The
first few of these hit Byron hard. He's still a new arrival, still hasn't accepted his
immortality. But on through the burning hours he starts to learn about the transience of others: learns that loving them while they're here becomes easier, and
also more intense—to love as if each design-hour will be the last. Byron soon
enough becomes a Permanent Old-Timer. Others can recognize his immortality
on sight, but it's never discussed except in a general way, when folklore comes
flickering in from other parts of the Grid, tales of the Immortals, one in a kabba-
list's study in Lyons who's supposed to know magic, another in Norway outside
a warehouse facing arctic whiteness with a stoicism more southerly bulbs begin
strobing faintly just at the thought of. If other Immortals *are* out there, they remain silent. But it is a silence with much, perhaps, everything, in it.

After Love, then, Byron's next lesson is Silence.

As his burning lengthens toward 600 hours, the monitors in Switzerland begin to keep more of an eye on Byron. The Phoebus Surveillance Room is located
under a little-known Alp, a chilly room crammed full of German electro hardware, glass, brass, ebonite, and silver, massive terminal blocks shaggy with copper clips and screws, and a cadre of superclean white-robed watchers who wander meter to meter, light as snowdevils, making sure that nothing's going wrong,
that through no bulb shall the mean operating life be extended. You can imagine
what it would do to the market if *that* started happening.

Byron passes Surveillance's red-line at 600 hours, and immediately, as a matter of routine, he is checked out for filament resistance, burning temperature,
vacuum, power consumption. Everything's normal. Now Byron is to be checked
out every 50 hours hereafter. A soft chime will go off in the monitoring station
whenever it's time.

At 800 hours—another routine precaution—a Berlin agent is sent out to the
opium den to transfer Byron. She is wearing asbestos-lined kid gloves and seven-
inch spike heels, no not so she can fit in with the crowd, but so that she can
reach that sconce to unscrew Byron. The other bulbs watch, in barely subdued
terror. The word goes out along the Grid. At something close to the speed of
light, every bulb, Azos looking down the empty black Bakelite streets, Nitralam-
pen and Wotan Gs at night soccer matches, Just-Wolframs, Monowatts and Sir-
iuses, every bulb in Europe knows what's happened. They are silent with impotence, with surrender in the face of struggles they thought were all myth. We
can't help, this common thought humming through pastures of sleeping sheep,
down Autobahns and to the bitter ends of coaling piers in the North, *there's never
been anything we could do.* . . . Anyone shows us the meanest hope of transcending

----

[6] Astarte: Phoenician goddess of the moon and sexual love. Lilith: in Jewish folklore, the
first wife of Adam.

and the Committee on Incandescent Anomalies comes in and takes him away. Some do protest, maybe, here and there, but it's only information, glow-modulated, harmless, nothing close to the explosions in the faces of the powerful that Byron once envisioned, back there in his Baby ward, in his innocence.

He is taken to Neukölln, to a basement room, the home of a glassblower who is afraid of the night and who will keep Byron glowing and on watch over all the flint bowls, the griffins and flower-ships, ibexes in mid-leap, green spider-webs, somber ice deities. This is one of many so-called "control points," where suspicious bulbs can be monitored easily.

In less than a fortnight, a gong sounds along the ice and stone corridors of the Phoebus headquarters, and the faces swivel over briefly from their meters. Not too many gongs around here. Gongs are special. Byron has passed 1000 hours, and the procedure now is standard: the Committee on Incandescent Anomalies sends a hit man to Berlin.

But here something odd happens. Yes, damned odd. The plan is to smash up Byron and send him back right there in the shop to cullet[7] and batch—salvage the tungsten, of course—and let him be reincarnated in the glassblower's next project (a balloon setting out on a journey from the top of a white skyscraper). This wouldn't be too bad a deal for Byron—he knows as well as Phoebus does how many hours he has on him. Here in the shop he's watched enough glass being melted back into the structureless pool from which all glass forms spring and re-spring and wouldn't mind going through it himself. But he is trapped on the Karmic wheel.[8] The glowing orange batch is a taunt, a cruelty. There's no escape for Byron, he's doomed to an infinite regress of sockets and bulbsnatchers. In zips young Hansel Geschwindig, a Weimar street urchin—twirls Byron out of the ceiling into a careful pocket and Gessssschhhh*win*dig! out the door again. Darkness invades the dreams of the glassblower. Of all the unpleasantries his dreams grab in out of the night air, an extinguished light is the worst. Light, in his dreams, was always hope: the basic, mortal hope. As the contacts break helically away, hope turns to darkness, and the glassblower wakes sharply tonight crying. "Who? *Who?*"

Phoebus isn't exactly thrown into a frenzy. It's happened before. There is still a procedure to follow. It means more overtime for some employees, so there's that vague, full-boweled pleasure at the windfall, along with an equally vague excitement at the break in routine. You want high emotion, forget Phoebus. Their stonefaced search parties move out into the streets. They know more or less where in the city to look. They are assuming that no one among their consumers knows of Byron's immortality. So the data for *Non*-immortal Bulbsnatchings ought to apply also to Byron. And the data happen to hump up in poor sections, Jewish sections, drug, homosexual, prostitute, and magic sections of the capital. Here are the most logical bulbsnatchers, in terms of what the crime is. Look at all the propaganda. It's a *moral* crime. Phoebus discovered—one of the great undiscovered discoveries of our time—that consumers need to feel a sense of sin. That guilt, in proper invisible hands, is a most powerful weapon. In America, Lyle Bland and his psychologists had figures, expert testimony and money (money in

[7] Reduce to waste glass, to be remelted.
[8] The wheel of destiny, in accordance with the Hindu concept of Karma: an understanding of one's lot as the inescapable consequence of the acts of a previous existence.

the Puritan sense—an outward and visible O.K. on their intentions) enough to tip the Discovery of Guilt at the cusp between scientific theory and fact. Growth rates in later years were to bear Bland out (actually what bore Bland out was an honorary pallbearer sextet of all the senior members of Salitieri, Poore, Nash, De Brutus and Short, plus Lyle, Jr., who was sneezing. Buddy at the last minute decided to go see *Dracula*. He was better off). Of all the legacies Bland left around, the Bulbsnatching Heresy was perhaps his grandest. It doesn't just mean that somebody isn't buying a bulb. It also means that same somebody is not putting any power in that socket! It is a sin both against Phoebus and against the Grid. Neither one is about to let *that* get out of hand.

So, out go the Phoebus flatfoots, looking for the snatched Byron. But the urchin has already left town, gone to Hamburg, traded Byron to a Reeperbahn *prostitute* so he can *shoot up some morphine*—the young woman's customer tonight is a cost-accountant who likes to have light bulbs *screwed into his asshole*, and this john has also brought a little *hashish to smoke*, so by the time he leaves he's forgotten about Byron still there in his asshole—doesn't ever, in fact, find out, because when he finally gets around to sitting down (having stood up in trolleys all the way home) it's on his own home toilet and plop! there goes Byron in the water and flusssshhhh! away down the waste lines to the Elbe estuary. He is just round enough to get through smoothly all the way. For days he floats over the North Sea, till he reaches Helgoland, that red-and-white Napoleon pastry tipped in the sea. He stays there for a while at a hotel between the Hengst and the Mönch, till being brought back one day to the mainland by a very old priest who's been put hep to Byron's immortality in the course of a routine dream about the taste of a certain 1911 Hochheimer[9] . . . suddenly here's the great Berlin Eispalast, a booming, dim iron-trussed cavern, the smell of women in the blue shadows—perfumes, leathers, fur skating-costumes, ice-dust in the air, flashing legs, jutting haunches, desire in grippelike flashes, helplessness at the end of a crack-the-whip, rocketing through beams of sunlight choked with the powdered ice, and a voice in the blurred mirror underfoot saying, "Find the one who has performed this miracle. He is a saint. Expose him. Expose him. Expedite his canonization. . . ." The name is on a list the old man presently draws up of about a thousand tourists who've been in and out of Helgoland since Byron was found on the beach. The priest begins a search by train, footpath, and Hispano-Suiza, checking out each of the tourists on his list. But he gets no farther than Nürnberg, where his valise, with Byron wrapped inside in an alb, is ripped off by a transsectite, a Lutheran named Mausmacher who likes to dress up in Roman regalia. This Mausmacher, not content with standing in front of his own mirror making papal crosses, thinks it will be a really bizarre kick to go out to the Zeppelin field to a Nazi torchlight rally in full drag and walk around blessing people at random. Green torches flaring, red swastikas, twinkling brasses and Father Mausmacher, checking out tits 'n' asses, waistlines 'n' baskets, humming a clerical little tune, some Bach riff, smiling as he moves through the Sieg Heils[10] and choruses of "Die Fahne Hoch."[11] Unknown to him, Byron slides out of the stolen vestments

---

[9] A White Rhine wine.
[10] Nazi salutes—"Hail to vistory."
[11] A Nazi rallying song—"Raise the Flags."

onto the ground. He is then walked past by several hundred thousand boots and shoes, and not one so much as brushes him, natch. He is scavenged next day (the field now death-empty, columned, pale, streaked with long mudpuddles, morning clouds lengthening behind the gilded swastika and wreath) by a poor Jewish ragpicker, and taken on, on into another 15 years of preservation against chance and against Phoebus. He will be screwed into mother (Mutter) after mother, as the female threads of German light-bulb sockets are known, for some reason that escapes everybody.

The cartel have already gone over to Contingency Plan B, which assumes a seven-year statute of limitations, after which Byron will be considered legally burned out. Meanwhile, the personnel taken off of Byron's case are busy tracking a long-lived bulb that once occupied a socket on the porch of an army outpost in the Amazon jungle, Beatriz the Bulb, who has just been stolen, mysteriously by an Indian raiding party.

Through his years of survival, all these various rescues of Byron happen as if by accident. Whenever he can, he tries to instruct any bulbs nearby in the evil nature of Phoebus, and in the need for solidarity against the cartel. He has come to see how Bulb must move beyond its role as conveyor of light-energy alone. Phoebus has restricted Bulb to this one identity. "But there are other frequencies, above and below the visible band. Bulb can give heat. Bulb can provide energy for plants to grow, illegal plants, inside closets, for example. Bulb can penetrate the sleeping eye, and operate among the dreams of men." Some bulbs listened attentively—others thought of ways to fink to Phoebus. Some of the older anti-Byronists were able to fool with their parameters in systematic ways that would show up on the ebonite meters under the Swiss mountain: there were even a few self-immolations, hoping to draw the hit men down.

Any talk of Bulb's transcendence, of course, was clear subversion. Phoebus based everything on the bulb efficiency—the ratio of the usable power coming out, to the power put in. The Grid demanded that this ratio stay as small as possible. That way they got to sell more juice. On the other hand, low efficiency meant longer burning hours, and that cut into bulb sales for Phoebus. In the beginning Phoebus tried increasing filament resistance, reducing the hours of life on the sly and gradually—till the Grid noticed a fall-off in revenues, and started screaming. The two parties by and by reached an accord on a compromise bulb-life figure that would bring in enough money for both of them and to go fifty-fifty on the costs of the antibulbsnatching campaign. Along with a more subtle attack against those criminal souls who forswear bulbs entirely and use candles. Phoebus's long-standing arrangement with the Meat Cartel was to restrict the amount of tallow in circulation by keeping more fat in meat to be sold regardless of cardiac problems that might arise, and redirecting most of what was trimmed off into soap production. Soap in those days was a booming concern. Among the consumers, the Bland Institute had discovered deep feelings about shit. Even at that, meat and soap were minor interlocks to Phoebus. More important were items like tungsten. Another reason why Phoebus couldn't cut down bulb life too far. Too many tungsten filaments would eat into available stockpiles of the metal—China being the major world source, this also brought in very delicate questions of Eastern policy—and disturb the arrangement between General Electric and Krupp about how much tungsten carbide would be produced, where and

when and what the prices would be. The guidelines settled on were $37-$90 a
pound in Germany, $200-$400 a pound in U.S. This directly governed the production of machine tools, and thus all areas of light and heavy industry. When
the War came, some people thought it unpatriotic of GE to have given Germany
an edge like that. But nobody with any power. Don't worry.

Byron, as he burns on, sees more and more of this pattern. He learns how to
make contact with other kinds of electric appliances, in homes, in factories and
out in the streets. Each has something to tell him. The pattern gathers in his soul
(Seele, as the core of the earlier carbon filament was known in Germany), and the
grander and clearer it grows, the more desperate Byron gets. Someday he will
know everything, and still be as important as before. His youthful dreams of organizing all the bulbs in the world seem impossible now—the Grid is wide open,
all messages can be overheard, and there are more than enought traitors out on
the line. Prophets traditionally don't last long—they are either killed outright,
or given an accident serious enough to make them stop and think, and most often they do pull back. But on Byron has been visited an even better fate. He is
condemned to go on forever, knowing the truth and powerless to change anything. No longer will he seek to get off the wheel.[12] His anger and frustration
will grow without limit, and he will find himself, poor perverse bulb, enjoying
it. . . .

[12] Of Karma. See note 8.

CHAPTER 8

Longer Fiction

THE DEATH OF IVAN ILYCH*
Leo Tolstoy (1828–1910)

I

During an interval in the Melvinski trial in the large building of the Law Courts, the members and public prosecutor met in Ivan Egorovich Shebek's private room, where the conversation turned on the celebrated Krasovski case. Fëdor Vasilievich warmly maintained that it was not subject to their jurisdiction, Ivan Egorovich maintained the contrary, while Peter Ivanovich, not having entered into the discussion at the start, took no part in it but looked through the *Gazette* which had just been handed in.

"Gentlemen," he said, "Ivan Ilych has died!"

"You don't say so!"

"Here, read it yourself," replied Peter Ivanovich, handing Fëdor Vasilievich the paper still damp from the press. Surrounded by a black border were the words: "Praskovya Fëdorovna Goloviná, with profound sorrow, informs relatives and friends of the demise of her beloved husband Ivan Ilych Golovin, Member of the Court of Justice, which occurred on February the 4th of this year 1882. The funeral will take place on Friday at one o'clock in the afternoon."

Ivan Ilych had been a colleague of the gentlemen present and was liked by them all. He had been ill for some weeks with an illness said to be incurable. His post had been kept open for him, but there had been conjectures that in case of his death Alexeev might receive his appointment, and that either Vinnikov or Shtabel would succeed Alexeev. So on receiving the news of Ivan Ilych's death the first thought of each of the gentlemen in that private room was of the changes and promotions it might occasion among themselves or their acquaintances.

"I shall be sure to get Shtabel's place or Vinnikov's," thought Fëdor Vasilievich. "I was promised that long ago, and the promotion means an extra eight hundred rubles a year for me besides the allowance."

"Now I must apply for my brother-in-law's transfer from Kaluga," thought Peter Ivanovich. "My wife will be very glad and then she won't be able to say that I never do anything for her relations."

"I thought he would never leave his bed again," said Peter Ivanovich aloud. "It's very sad."

"But what really was the matter with him?"

* Translated by Louise and Aylmer Maude.

"The doctors couldn't say—at least they could, but each of them said something different. When last I saw him I thought he was getting better."

"And I haven't been to see him since the holidays. I always meant to go."

"Had he any property?"

"I think his wife had a little—but something quite trifling."

"We shall have to go to see her, but they live so terribly far away."

"Far away from you, you mean. Everything's far away from your place."

"You see, he never can forgive my living on the other side of the river," said Peter Ivanovich, smiling at Shebek. Then, still talking of the distances between different parts of the city, they returned to the Court.

Besides considerations as to the possible transfers and promotions likely to result from Ivan Ilych's death, the mere fact of the death of a near acquaintance aroused, as usual, in all who heard of it the complacent feeling that "it is he who is dead and not I."

Each one thought or felt, "Well, he's dead but I'm alive!" But the more intimate of Ivan Ilych's acquaintances, his so-called friends, could not help thinking also that they would now have to fulfil the very tiresome demands of propriety by attending the funeral service and paying a visit of condolence to the widow.

Fëdor Vasilievich and Peter Ivanovich had been his nearest acquaintances. Peter Ivanovich had studied law with Ivan Ilych and had considered himself to be under obligations to him.

Having told his wife at dinner-time of Ivan Ilych's death and of his conjecture that it might be possible to get her brother transferred to their circuit, Peter Ivanovich sacrificed his usual nap, put on his evening clothes, and drove to Ivan Ilych's house.

At the entrance stood a carriage and two cabs. Leaning against the wall in the hall downstairs near the cloak-stand was a coffin-lid covered with cloth of gold, ornamented with gold cord and tassels, that had been polished up with metal powder. Two ladies in black were taking off their fur cloaks. Peter Ivanovich recognized one of them as Ivan Ilych's sister, but the other was a stranger to him. His colleague Schwartz was just coming downstairs, but on seeing Peter Ivanovich enter he stopped and winked at him, as if to say: "Ivan Ilych has made a mess of things—not like you and me."

Schwartz's face with his Piccadilly whiskers and his slim figure in evening dress had as usual an air of elegant solemnity which contrasted with the playfulness of his character and had a special piquancy here, or so it seemed to Peter Ivanovich.

Peter Ivanovich allowed the ladies to precede him and slowly followed them upstairs. Schwartz did not come down but remained where he was, and Peter Ivanovich understood that he wanted to arrange where they should play bridge that evening. The ladies went upstairs to the widow's room, and Schwartz with seriously compressed lips but a playful look in his eyes, indicated by a twist of his eyebrows the room to the right where the body lay.

Peter Ivanovich, like everyone else on such occasions, entered feeling uncertain what he would have to do. All he knew was that at such times it is always safe to cross oneself. But he was not quite sure whether one should make obeisances while doing so. He therefore adopted a middle course. On entering the room he began crossing himself and made a slight movement resembling a bow. At the same time, as far as the motion of his head and arm allowed, he surveyed the room. Two young men—apparently nephews, one of whom was a high-school pupil—were leaving the room, crossing themselves as they did so. An old woman was standing motionless, and a lady with strangely arched eyebrows was saying something to her in a whisper. A vigorous, resolute Church Reader, in a frock-coat, was reading something in a loud voice with an expression that precluded any contradiction. The butler's assistant, Gerasim, stepping lightly in front of Peter Ivanovich, was strewing something on the floor. Noticing this, Peter Ivanovich was immediately aware of a faint odor of a decomposing body.

The last time he had called on Ivan Ilych, Peter Ivanovich had seen Gerasim in the study. Ivan Ilych had been particularly fond of him and he was performing the duty of a sick nurse.

Peter Ivanovich continued to make the sign of the cross, slightly inclining his head in an intermediate direction between the coffin, the Reader, and the icons on the table in a corner of the room. Afterwards, when it seemed to him that this movement of his arm in crossing himself had gone on too long, he stopped and began to look at the corpse.

The dead man lay, as dead men always lie, in a specially heavy way, his rigid limbs sunk in the soft cushions of the coffin, with the head forever bowed on the pillow. His yellow waxen brow with bald patches over his sunken temples was thrust up in the way peculiar to the dead, the protruding nose seeming to press on the upper lip. He was much changed and had grown even thinner since Peter Ivanovich had last seen him, but, as is always the case with the dead, his face was handsomer and above all more dignified than when he was alive. The expression on the face said that what was necessary had been accomplished, and accomplished rightly. Besides this there was in that expression a reproach and a warning to the living. This warning seemed to Peter Ivanovich out of place, or at least not applicable to him. He felt a certain discomfort and so he hurriedly crossed himself once more and turned and went out of the door—too hurriedly and too regardless of propriety, as he himself was aware.

Schwartz was waiting for him in the adjoining room with legs spread wide apart and both hands toying with his top-hat behind his back. The mere sight of that playful, well-groomed, and elegant figure refreshed Peter Ivanovich. He felt that Schwartz was above all these happenings and would not surrender to any depressing influences. His very look said that this incident of a church service for Ivan Ilych could not be a sufficient reason for infringing the order of the session—in other words, that it would certainly not prevent his unwrapping a new pack of cards and shuffling them that evening while a footman placed four fresh candles on the table: in fact, that there was no reason for supposing that this incident would hinder their spending the evening agreeably. Indeed he said this in a whisper as Peter Ivanovich passed him, proposing that they should meet for a game at Fëdor Vasilievich's. But apparently Peter Ivanovich was not destined to play bridge that evening. Praskovya Fëdorovna (a short, fat woman who despite all efforts to the contrary had continued to broaden steadily from her shoulders downwards and who had the same extraordinarily arched eyebrows as the lady who had been standing by the coffin), dressed all in black, her head covered with lace, came out of her own room with some other ladies, conducted them to the room where the dead body lay, and said: "The service will begin immediately. Please go in."

Schwartz, making an indefinite bow, stood still, evidently neither accepting nor declining this invitation. Praskovya Fëdorovna, recognizing Peter Ivanovich, sighed, went close up to him, took his hand, and said: "I know you were a true friend of Ivan Ilych . . ." and looked at him awaiting some suitable response. And Peter Ivanovich knew that, just as it had been the right thing to cross himself in that room, so what he had to do here was to press her hand, sigh, and say, "Believe me. . . ." So he did all this and as he did it felt that the desired result had been achieved: that both he and she were touched.

"Come with me. I want to speak to you before it begins," said the widow. "Give me your arm."

Peter Ivanovich gave her his arm and they went to the inner rooms, passing Schwartz, who winked at Peter Ivanovich compassionately.

"That does for our bridge! Don't object if we find another player. Perhaps you can cut in when you do escape," said his playful look.

Peter Ivanovich sighed still more deeply and despondently, and Praskovya Fëdorovna pressed his arm gratefully. When they reached the drawing-room, upholstered in pink cretonne and lighted by a dim lamp, they sat down at the table—she on a sofa and Peter Ivanovich on a low pouffe, the springs of which yielded spasmodically under his weight. Praskovya Fëdorovna had been on the point of warning him to take another seat, but felt that such a warning was out of keeping with her present condition and so changed her mind. As he sat down on the pouffe Peter Ivanovich recalled how Ivan Ilych had arranged this room and had consulted him regarding this pink cretonne with green leaves. The whole room was full of furniture and knick-knacks, and on her way to the sofa the lace of the widow's black shawl caught on the carved edge of the table. Peter Ivanovich rose to detach it, and the springs of the pouffe, relieved of his weight, rose also and gave him a push. The widow began detaching her shawl herself, and Peter Ivanovich again sat down, suppressing the rebellious springs of the pouffe under him. But the widow had not quite freed herself and Peter Ivanovich got up again, and again the pouffe rebelled and even creaked. When this was all over she took out a clean cambric handkerchief and began to weep. The episode with the shawl and the struggle with the pouffe had cooled Peter Ivanovich's emotions and he sat there with a sullen look on his face. This awkward situation was interrupted by Sokolov, Ivan Ilych's butler, who came to report that the plot in the cemetery that Praskovya Fëdorovna had chosen would cost two hundred rubles. She stopped weeping and, looking at Peter Ivanovich with the air of a victim, remarked in French that it was very hard for her. Peter Ivanovich made a silent gesture signifying his full conviction that it must indeed be so.

"Please smoke," she said in a magnanimous yet crushed voice, and turned to discuss with Sokolov the price of the plot for the grave.

Peter Ivanovich while lighting his cigarette heard her inquiring very circumstantially into the prices of different plots in the cemetery and finally decide which she would take. When that was done she gave instructions about engaging the choir. Sokolov then left the room.

"I look after everything myself," she told Peter Ivanovich, shifting the albums that lay on the table; and noticing that the table was endangered by his cigarette-ash, she immediately passed him an ashtray, saying as she did so: "I consider it an affectation to say that my grief prevents my attending to practical affairs. On the contrary, if anything can—I won't say console me, but—distract me, it is seeing to everything concerning him." She again took out her handker-chief as if preparing to cry, but suddenly, as if mastering her feeling, she shook herself and began to speak calmly. "But there is something I want to talk to you about."

Peter Ivanovich bowed, keeping control of the springs of the pouffe, which immediately began quivering under him.

"He suffered terribly the last few days."

"Did he?" said Peter Ivanovich.

"Oh, terribly! He screamed unceasingly, not for minutes but for hours. For the last three days he screamed incessantly. It was unendurable. I cannot understand how I bore it; you could hear him three rooms off. Oh, what I have suffered!"

"Is it possible that he was conscious all that time?" asked Peter Ivanovich.

"Yes," she whispered. "To the last moment. He took leave of us a quarter of an hour before he died, and asked us to take Volodya away."

The thought of the sufferings of this man he had known so intimately, first as a merry little boy, then as a school-mate, and later as a grown-up colleague, sud-denly struck Peter Ivanovich with horror, despite an unpleasant consciousness of his own and this woman's dissimulation. He again saw that brow, and that nose pressing down on the lip, and felt afraid for himself.

"Three days of frightful suffering and then death! Why, that might suddenly, at any time, happen to me," he thought, and for a moment felt terrified. But—he did not himself know how—the customary reflection at once occurred to him that this had happened to Ivan Ilych and not to him, and that it should not and could not happen to him, and that to think that it could would be yielding to de-pression which he ought not to do, as Schwartz's expression plainly showed. After which reflection Peter Ivanovich felt reassured, and began to ask with in-terest about the details of Ivan Ilych's death, as though death was an accident natural to Ivan Ilych but certainly not to himself.

After many details of the really dreadful physical sufferings Ivan Ilych had endured (which details he learnt only from the effect those sufferings had pro-duced on Praskovya Fëdorovna's nerves) the widow apparently found it neces-sary to get to business.

"Oh, Peter Ivanovich, how hard it is! How terribly, terribly hard!" and she again began to weep.

Peter Ivanovich sighed and waited for her to finish blowing her nose. When she had done so he said, "Believe me . . ." and she again began talking and brought out what was evidently her chief concern with him—namely, to ques-tion him as to how she could obtain a grant of money from the government on the occasion of her husband's death. She made it appear that she was asking Pe-ter Ivanovich's advice about her pension, but he soon saw that she already knew about that to the minutest detail, more even than he did himself. She knew how much could be got out of the government in consequence of her husband's death, but wanted to find out whether she could not possibly extract something more. Peter Ivanovich tried to think of some means of doing so, but after reflect-

ing for a while and, out of propriety, condemning the government for its nig-
gardliness, he said he thought that nothing more could be got. Then she sighed
and evidently began to devise means of getting rid of her visitor. Noticing this,
he put out his cigarette, rose, pressed her hand, and went out into the anteroom.

In the dining-room where the clock stood that Ivan Ilych had liked so much
and had bought at an antique shop, Peter Ivanovich met a priest and a few acquaintances who had come to attend the service, and he recognized Ivan Ilych's
daughter, a handsome young woman. She was in black and her slim figure appeared slimmer than ever. She had a gloomy, determined, almost angry expression, and bowed to Peter Ivanovich as though he were in some way to blame. Behind her, with the same offended look, stood a wealthy young man, an
examining magistrate, whom Peter Ivanovich also knew and who was her fiance,
as he had heard. He bowed mournfully to them and was about to pass into the
death-chamber, when from under the stairs appeared the figure of Ivan Ilych's
school boy son, who was extremely like his father. He seemed a little Ivan Ilych,
such as Peter Ivanovich remembered when they studied law together. His tear-
stained eyes had in them the look that is seen in the eyes of boys of thirteen or
fourteen who are not pure-minded. When he saw Peter Ivanovich he scowled
morosely and shamefacedly. Peter Ivanovich nodded to him and entered the
death-chamber. The service began: candles, groans, incense, tears, and sobs. Peter Ivanovich stood looking gloomily down at his feet. He did not look once at
the dead man, did not yield to any depressing influence, and was one of the first
to leave the room. There was no one in the anteroom, but Gerasim darted out of
the dead man's room, rummaged with his strong hands among the fur coats to
find Peter Ivanovich's, and helped him on with it.

"Well, friend Gerasim," said Peter Ivanovich, so as to say something. "It's a
sad affair, isn't it?"

"It's God's will. We shall all come to it some day," said Gerasim, displaying
his teeth—the even, white teeth of a healthy peasant—and, like a man in the
thick of urgent work, he briskly opened the front door, called the coachman,
helped Peter Ivanovich into the sledge, and sprang back to the porch as if in
readiness for what he had to do next.

Peter Ivanovich found the fresh air particularly pleasant after the smell of incense, the dead body, and carbolic acid.

"Where to, sir?" asked the coachman.

"It's not too late even now. . . . I'll call round on Fëdor Vasilievich."

He accordingly drove there and found them just finishing the first rubber, so
that it was quite convenient for him to cut in.

II

Ivan Ilych's life had been most simple and most ordinary and therefore most terrible.

He had been a member of the Court of Justice, and died at the age of forty-
five. His father had been an official who after serving in various ministries and
departments in Petersburg had made the sort of career which brings men to positions from which by reason of their long service they cannot be dismissed,
though they are obviously unfit to hold any responsible position, and for whom
therefore posts are specially created, which though fictitious carry salaries of

from six to ten thousand rubles that are not fictitious, and in receipt of which they live on to a great age.

Such was the Privy Councillor and superfluous member of various superfluous institutions, Ilya Epimovich Golovin.

He had three sons, of whom Ivan Ilych was the second. The eldest son was following in his father's footsteps only in another department, and was already approaching that stage in the service at which a similar sinecure would be reached. The third son was a failure. He had ruined his prospects in a number of positions and was now serving in the railway department. His father and brothers, and still more their wives, not merely disliked meeting him, but avoided remembering his existence unless compelled to do so. His sister had married Baron Greff, a Petersburg official of her father's type. Ivan Ilych was *le phénix de la famille*[1] as people said. He was neither as cold and formal as his elder brother nor as wild as the younger, but was a happy mean between them—an intelligent, polished, lively, and agreeable man. He had studied with his younger brother at the School of Law, but the latter had failed to complete the course and was expelled when he was in the fifth class. Ivan Ilych finished the course well. Even when he was at the School of Law he was just what he remained for the rest of his life: a capable, cheerful, good-natured, and sociable man, though strict in the fulfilment of what he considered to be his duty: and he considered his duty to be what was so considered by those in authority. Neither as a boy nor as a man was he a toady, but from early youth was by nature attracted to people of high station as a fly is drawn to the light, assimilating their ways and views of life and establishing friendly relations with them. All the enthusiasms of childhood and youth passed without leaving much trace on him; he succumbed to sensuality, to vanity, and latterly among the highest classes to liberalism, but always within limits which his instinct unfailingly indicated to him as correct.

At school he had done things which had formerly seemed to him very horrid and made him feel disgusted with himself when he did them; but when later on he saw that such actions were done by people of good position and that they did not regard them as wrong, he was able not exactly to regard them as right, but to forget about them entirely or not be at all troubled at remembering them.

Having graduated from the School of Law and qualified for the tenth rank of the civil service, and having received money from his father for his equipment, Ivan Ilych ordered himself clothes at Scharmer's, the fashionable tailor, hung a medallion inscribed *respice finem*[2] on his watch-chain, took leave of his professor and the prince who was patron of the school, had a farewell dinner with his comrades at Donon's first-class restaurant, and with his new and fashionable portmanteau, linen, clothes, shaving and other toilet appliances, and a travelling rug all purchased at the best shops, he set off for one of the provinces where, through his father's influence, he had been attached to the Governor as an official for special service.

In the province Ivan Ilych soon arranged as easy and agreeable a position for himself as he had had at the School of Law. He performed his official tasks, made his career, and at the same time amused himself pleasantly and decorously. Occa-

---

[1] "The phoenix [paragon] of the family."
[2] "Reflect on the end."

sionally he paid official visits to country districts, where he behaved with dignity both to his superiors and inferiors, and performed the duties entrusted to him, which related chiefly to the sectarians,[3] with an exactness and incorruptible honesty of which he could not but feel proud.

In official matters, despite his youth and taste for frivolous gaiety, he was exceedingly reserved, punctilious, and even severe; but in society he was often amusing and witty, and always good-natured, correct in his manner, and *bon enfant*,[4] as the Governor and his wife—with whom he was like one of the family—used to say of him.

In the province he had an affair with a lady who made advances to the elegant young lawyer, and there was also a milliner; and there were carousals with aides-de-camp who visited the district, and after-supper visits to a certain outlying street of doubtful reputation; and there was too some obsequiousness to his chief and even to his chief's wife, but all this was done with such a tone of good breeding that no hard names could be applied to it. It all came under the heading of the French saying: *"Il faut que jeunesse se passe."*[5] It was all done with clean hands, in clean linen, with French phrases, and above all among people of the best society and consequently with the approval of people of rank.

So Ivan Ilych served for five years and then came a change in his official life. The new and reformed judicial institutions were introduced, and new men were needed. Ivan Ilych became such a new man. He was offered the post of examining magistrate, and he accepted it though the post was in another province and obliged him to give up the connections he had formed and to make new ones. His friends met to give him a send-off; they had a group-photograph taken and presented him with a silver cigarette-case, and he set off to his new post.

As examining magistrate Ivan Ilych was just as *comme il faut*[6] and decorous a man, inspiring general respect and capable of separating his official duties from his private life, as he had been when acting as an official on special service. His duties now as examining magistrate were far more interesting and attractive than before. In his former position it had been pleasant to wear an undress uniform made by Scharmer, and to pass through the crowd of petitioners and officials who were timorously awaiting an audience with the Governor, and who envied him as with free and easy gait he went straight into his chief's private room to have a cup of tea and a cigarette with him. But not many people had been directly dependent on him—only police officials and the sectarians when he went on special missions—and he liked to treat them politely, almost as comrades, as if he were letting them feel that he who had the power to crush them was treating them in this simple, friendly way. There were then but few such people. But now, as an examining magistrate, Ivan Ilych felt that everyone without exception, even the most important and self-satisfied, was in his power, and that he need only write a few words on a sheet of paper with a certain heading, and this or that important, self-satisfied person would be brought before him in the role of an accused person or a witness, and if he did not choose to allow him to sit

[3] Religious dissenters.
[4] "Good fellow."
[5] "Youth will be served."
[6] "Correct."

down, would have to stand before him and answer his questions. Ivan Ilych never abused his power; he tried on the contrary to soften its expression, but the consciousness of it and of the possibility of softening its effect, supplied the chief interest and attraction of his office. In his work itself, especially in his examinations, he very soon acquired a method of eliminating all considerations irrelevant to the legal aspect of the case, and reducing even the most complicated case to a form in which it would be presented on paper only in its externals, completely excluding his personal opinion of the matter, while above all observing every prescribed formality. The work was new and Ivan Ilych was one of the first men to apply the new Code of 1864.[7]

On taking up the post of examining magistrate in a new town, he made new acquaintances and connections, placed himself on a new footing, and assumed a somewhat different tone. He took up an attitude of rather dignified aloofness towards the provincial authorities, but picked out the best circle of legal gentlemen and wealthy gentry living in the town and assumed a tone of slight dissatisfaction with the government, of moderate liberalism, and of enlightened citizenship. At the same time, without at all altering the elegance of his toilet, he ceased shaving his chin and allowed his beard to grow as it pleased.

Ivan Ilych settled down very pleasantly in this new town. The society there, which inclined towards opposition to the Governor, was friendly, his salary was larger, and he began to play *vint*,[8] which he found added not a little to the pleasure of life; for he had a capacity for cards, played good-humoredly, and calculated rapidly and astutely, so that he usually won.

After living there for two years he met his future wife, Praskovya Fëdorovna Mikhel, who was the most attractive, clever, and brilliant girl of the set in which he moved, and among other amusements and relaxations from his labors as examining magistrate, Ivan Ilych established light and playful relations with her.

While he had been an official on special service he had been accustomed to dance, but now as an examining magistrate it was exceptional for him to do so. If he danced now, he did it as if to show that though he served under the reformed order of things, and had reached the fifth official rank, yet when it came to dancing he could do it better than most people. So at the end of an evening he sometimes danced with Praskovya Fëdorovna, and it was chiefly during these dances that he captivated her. She fell in love with him. Ivan Ilych had at first no definite intention of marrying, but when the girl fell in love with him he said to himself: "Really, why shouldn't I marry?"

Praskovya Fëdorovna came of a good family, was not bad-looking, and had some little property. Ivan Ilych might have aspired to a more brilliant match, but even this was good. He had his salary, and she, he hoped, would have an equal income. She was well connected, and was a sweet, pretty, and thoroughly correct young woman. To say that Ivan Ilych married because he fell in love with Praskovya Fëdorovna and found that she sympathized with his views of life would be as incorrect as to say that he married because his social circle approved of the match. He was swayed by both these considerations: the marriage gave him per-

---

[7] The emancipation of the serfs in 1861 was followed by a thorough all-round reform of judicial proceedings. [L. and A. Maude]

[8] A form of bridge. [L. and A. Maude]

sonal satisfaction, and at the same time it was considered the right thing by the most highly placed of his associates.

So Ivan Ilych got married.

The preparations for marriage and the beginning of married life, with its conjugal caresses, the new furniture, new crockery, and new linen, were very pleasant until his wife became pregnant—so that Ivan Ilych had begun to think that marriage would not impair the easy, agreeable, gay, and always decorous character of his life, approved of by society and regarded by himself as natural, but would even improve it. But from the first months of his wife's pregnancy, something new, unpleasant, depressing, and unseemly, and from which there was no way of escape, unexpectedly showed itself.

His wife, without any reason—*de gaieté de coeur*[9] as Ivan Ilych expressed it to himself—began to disturb the pleasure and propriety of their life. She began to be jealous without any cause, expected him to devote his whole attention to her, found fault with everything, and made coarse and ill-mannered scenes.

At first Ivan Ilych hoped to escape from the unpleasantness of this state of affairs by the same easy and decorous relation to life that had served him heretofore: he tried to ignore his wife's disagreeable moods, continued to live in his usual easy and pleasant way, invited friends to his house for a game of cards, and also tried going out to his club or spending his evenings with friends. But one day his wife began upbraiding him so vigorously, using such coarse words, and continued to abuse him every time he did not fulfil her demands, so resolutely and with such evident determination not to give way till he submitted—that is, till he stayed at home and was bored just as she was—that he became alarmed. He now realized that matrimony—at any rate with Praskovya Fëdorovna—was not always conducive to the pleasures and amenities of life, but on the contrary often infringed both comfort and propriety, and that he must therefore entrench himself against such infringement. And Ivan Ilych began to seek for means of doing so. His official duties were the one thing that imposed upon Praskovya Fëdorovna, and by means of his official work and the duties attached to it he began struggling with his wife to secure his own independence.

With the birth of their child, the attempts to feed it and the various failures in doing so, and with the real and imaginary illnesses of mother and child, in which Ivan Ilych's sympathy was demanded but about which he understood nothing, the need of securing for himself an existence outside his family life became still more imperative.

As his wife grew more irritable and exacting and Ivan Ilych transferred the center of gravity of his life more and more to his official work, so did he grow to like his work better and become more ambitious than before.

Very soon, within a year of his wedding, Ivan Ilych had realized that marriage, though it may add some comforts to life, is in fact a very intricate and difficult affair towards which in order to perform one's duty, that is, to lead a decorous life approved of by society, one must adopt a definite attitude just as towards one's official duties.

And Ivan Ilych evolved such an attitude towards married life. He only required of it those conveniences—dinner at home, housewife, and bed—which it could give him, and above all that propriety of external forms required by public

---

[9] "Out of sheer wantonness."

opinion. For the rest he looked for light-hearted pleasure and propriety, and was very thankful when he found them, but if he met with antagonism and querulousness he at once retired into his separate fenced-off world of official duties, where he found satisfaction.

Ivan Ilych was esteemed a good official, and after three years was made Assistant Public Prosecutor. His new duties, their importance, the possibility of indicting and imprisoning anyone he chose, the publicity his speeches received, and the success he had in all these things, made his work still more attractive.

More children came. His wife became more and more querulous and ill-tempered, but the attitude Ivan Ilych had adopted towards his home life rendered him almost impervious to her grumbling.

After seven years' service in that town he was transferred to another province as Public Prosecutor. They moved, but were short of money and his wife did not like the place they moved to. Though the salary was higher the cost of living was greater, besides which two of their children died and family life became still more unpleasant for him.

Praskovya Fëdorovna blamed her husband for every inconvenience they encountered in their new home. Most of the conversations between husband and wife, especially as to the children's education, led to topics which recalled former disputes, and those disputes were apt to flare up again at any moment. There remained only those rare periods of amorousness which still came to them at times but did not last long. These were islets at which they anchored for a while and then again set out upon that ocean of veiled hostility which showed itself in their aloofness from one another. This aloofness might have grieved Ivan Ilych had he considered that it ought not to exist, but he now regarded the position as normal, and even made it the goal at which he aimed in family life. His aim was to free himself more and more from those unpleasantnesses and to give them a semblance of harmlessness and propriety. He attained this by spending less and less time with his family, and when obliged to be at home he tried to safeguard his position by the presence of outsiders. The chief thing however was that he had his official duties. The whole interest of his life now centered in the official world and that interest absorbed him. The consciousness of his power, being able to ruin anybody he wished to ruin, the importance, even the external dignity of his entry into court, or meetings with his subordinates, his success with superiors and inferiors, and above all his masterly handling of cases, of which he was conscious—all this gave him pleasure and filled his life, together with chats with his colleagues, dinners, and bridge. So that on the whole Ivan Ilych's life continued to flow as he considered it should do—pleasantly and properly.

So things continued for another seven years. His eldest daughter was already sixteen, another child had died, and only one son was left, a schoolboy and a subject of dissension. Ivan Ilych wanted to put him in the School of Law, but to spite him Praskovya Fëdorovna entered him at the High School. The daughter had been educated at home and had turned out well: the boy did not learn badly either.

III

So Ivan Ilych lived for seventeen years after his marriage. He was already a Public Prosecutor of long standing, and had declined several proposed transfers while awaiting a more desirable post, when an unanticipated and unpleasant oc-

currence quite upset the peaceful course of his life. He was expecting to be offered the post of presiding judge in a University town, but Happe somehow
came to the front and obtained the appointment instead. Ivan Ilych became irritable, reproached Happe, and quarrelled both with him and with his immediate
superiors—who became colder to him and again passed him over when other appointments were made.

This was in 1880, the hardest year of Ivan Ilych's life. It was then that it became evident on the one hand that his salary was insufficient for them to live on,
and on the other that he had been forgotten, and not only this, but that what was
for him the greatest and most cruel injustice appeared to others a quite ordinary
occurrence. Even his father did not consider it his duty to help him. Ivan Ilych
felt himself abandoned by everyone, and that they regarded his position with a
salary of 3,500 rubles as quite normal and even fortunate. He alone knew that
with the consciousness of the injustices done him, with his wife's incessant nagging, and with the debts he had contracted by living beyond his means, his position was far from normal.

In order to save money that summer he obtained leave of absence and went
with his wife to live in the country at her brother's place.

In the country, without his work, he experienced *ennui* for the first time in his
life, and not only *ennui* but intolerable depression, and he decided that it was impossible to go on living like that, and that it was necessary to take energetic measures.

Having passed a sleepless night pacing up and down the veranda, he decided
to go to Petersburg and bestir himself, in order to punish those who had failed to
appreciate him and to get transferred to another ministry.

Next day, despite many protests from his wife and her brother, he started for
Petersburg with the sole object of obtaining a post with a salary of five thousand
rubles a year. He was no longer bent on any particular department, or tendency,
or kind of activity. All he now wanted was an appointment to another post with
a salary of five thousand rubles, either in the administration, in the banks, with
the railways, in one of the Empress Marya's Institutions, or even in the customs—but it had to carry with it a salary of five thousand rubles and be in a ministry other than that in which they had failed to appreciate him.

And this quest of Ivan Ilych's was crowned with remarkable and unexpected
success. At Kursk an acquaintance of his, F. I. Ilyin, got into the first-class carriage, sat down beside Ivan Ilych, and told him of a telegram just received by the
Governor of Kursk announcing that a change was about to take place in the ministry: Peter Ivanovich was to be superseded by Ivan Semënovich.

The proposed change, apart from its significance for Russia, had a special significance for Ivan Ilych, because by bringing forward a new man, Peter Petrovich, and consequently his friend Zachar Ivanovich, it was highly favorable for
Ivan Ilych, since Zachar Ivanovich was a friend and colleague of his.

In Moscow this news was confirmed, and on reaching Petersburg Ivan Ilych
found Zachar Ivanovich and received a definite promise of an appointment in
his former department of Justice.

A week later he telegraphed to his wife: "Zachar in Miller's place. I shall receive appointment on presentation of report."

Thanks to this change of personnel, Ivan Ilych had unexpectedly obtained an appointment in his former ministry which placed him two stages above his former colleagues besides giving him five thousand rubles salary and three thousand five hundred rubles for expenses connected with his removal. All his ill humor towards his former enemies and the whole department vanished, and Ivan Ilych was completely happy.

He returned to the country more cheerful and contented than he had been for a long time. Praskovya Fëdorovna also cheered up and a truce was arranged between them. Ivan Ilych told of how he had been fêted by everybody in Petersburg, how all those who had been his enemies were put to shame and now fawned on him, how envious they were of his appointment, and how much everybody in Petersburg had liked him.

Praskovya Fëdorovna listened to all this and appeared to believe it. She did not contradict anything, but only made plans for their life in the town to which they were going. Ivan Ilych saw with delight that these plans were his plans, that he and his wife agreed, and that, after a stumble, his life was regaining its due and natural character of pleasant lightheartedness and decorum.

Ivan Ilych had come back for a short time only, for he had to take up his new duties on the 10th of September. Moreover, he needed time to settle into the new place, to move all his belongings from the province, and to buy and order many additional things: in a word, to make such arrangements as he had resolved on, which were almost exactly what Praskovya Fëdorovna too had decided one.

Now that everything had happened so fortunately, and that he and his wife were at one in their aims and moreover saw so little of one another, they got on together better than they had done since the first years of marriage. Ivan Ilych had thought of taking his family away with him at once, but the insistence of his wife's brother and her sister-in-law, who had suddenly become particularly amiable and friendly to him and his family, induced him to depart alone.

So he departed, and the cheerful state of mind induced by his success and by the harmony between his wife and himself, the one intensifying the other, did not leave him. He found a delightful house, just the thing both he and his wife had dreamt of. Spacious, lofty reception rooms in the old style, a convenient and dignified study, rooms for his wife and daughter, a study for his son—it might have been specially built for them. Ivan Ilych himself superintended the arrangements, chose the wallpapers, supplemented the furniture (preferably with antiques which he considered particularly *comme il faut*), and supervised the upholstering. Everything progressed and progressed and approached the ideal he had set himself: even when things were only half completed they exceeded his expectations. He saw what a refined and elegant character, free from vulgarity, it would all have when it was ready. On falling asleep he pictured to himself how the reception-room would look. Looking at the yet unfinished drawing-room he could see the fireplace, the screen, the what-not, the little chairs dotted here and there, the dishes and plates on the walls, and the bronzes, as they would be when everything was in place. He was pleased by the thought of how his wife and daughter, who shared his taste in this matter, would be impressed by it. They were certainly not expecting as much. He had been particularly successful in finding, and buying cheaply, antiques which gave a particularly aristocratic character to the whole place. But in his letter he intentionally understated everything in order to be able to surprise them. All this so absorbed him that his new duties—though he liked his official work—interested him less than he had expected. Sometimes he even had moments of absentmindedness during the Court Sessions, and would consider whether he should have straight or curved cornices for his curtains. He was so interested in it all that he often did things himself, rearranging the furniture, or rehanging the curtains. Once when mounting a stepladder to show the upholsterer, who did not understand, how he wanted the hangings draped, he made a false step and slipped, but being a strong and agile man he clung on and only knocked his side against the knob of the window frame. The bruised place was painful but the pain soon passed, and he felt particularly bright and well just then. He wrote: "I feel fifteen years younger." He thought he would have everything ready by September, but it dragged on till mid-October. But the result was charming not only in his eyes but to everyone who saw it.

In reality it was just what is usually seen in the houses of people of moderate means who want to appear rich, and therefore succeed only in resembling others like themselves: there were damasks, dark wood, plants, rugs, and dull and polished bronzes—all the things people of a certain class have in order to resemble other people of that class. His house was so like the others that it would never have been noticed, but to him it all seemed to be quite exceptional. He was very happy when he met his family at the station and brought them to the newly furnished house all lit up, where a footman in a white tie opened the door into the hall decorated with plants, and when they went on into the drawing-room and the study uttering exclamations of delight. He conducted them everywhere, drank in their praises eagerly, and beamed with pleasure. At tea that evening, when Praskovya Fëdorovna among other things asked him about his fall, he laughed and showed them how he had gone flying and had frightened the upholsterer.

"It's a good thing I'm a bit of an athlete. Another man might have been killed, but I merely knocked myself, just here; it hurts when it's touched, but it's passing off already—it's only a bruise."

So they began living in their new home—in which, as always happens, when they got thoroughly settled in they found they were just one room short—and with the increased income, which as always was just a little (some five hundred rubles) too little, but it was all very nice.

Things went particularly well at first, before everything was finally arranged and while something had still to be done: this thing bought, that thing ordered, another thing moved, and something else adjusted. Though there were some disputes between husband and wife, they were both so well satisfied and had so much to do that it all passed off without any serious quarrels. When nothing was left to arrange it became rather dull and something seemed to be lacking, but they were then making acquaintances, forming habits, and life was growing fuller.

Ivan Ilych spent his mornings at the law courts and came home to dinner, and at first he was generally in a good humor, though he occasionally became irritable just on account of his house. (Every spot on the tablecloth or the upholstery, and every broken window-blind string, irritated him. He had devoted so much trouble to arranging it all that every disturbance of it distressed him.) But on the whole his life ran its course as he believed life should do: easily, pleasantly, and decorously.

He got up at nine, drank his coffee, read the paper, and then put on his undress uniform and went to the law courts. There the harness in which he worked had already been stretched to fit him and he donned it without a hitch: petitioners, inquiries at the chancery, the chancery itself, and the sittings public and administrative. In all this the thing was to exclude everything fresh and vital, which always disturbs the regular course of official business, and to admit only official relations with people, and then only on official grounds. A man would come, for instance, wanting some information. Ivan Ilych, as one in whose sphere the matter did not lie, would have nothing to do with him: but if the man had some business with him in his official capacity, something that could be expressed on officially stamped paper, he would do everything, positively everything he could within the limits of such relations, and in doing so would maintain the semblance of friendly human relations, that is, would observe the courtesies of life. As soon as the official relations ended, so did everything else. Ivan Ilych possessed this capacity to separate his real life from the official side of affairs and not mix the two, in the highest degree, and by long practice and natural aptitude had brought it to such a pitch that sometimes, in the manner of a virtuoso, he would even allow himself to let the human and official relations mingle. He let himself do this just because he felt that he could at any time he chose resume the strictly official attitude again and drop the human relation. And he did it all easily, pleasantly, correctly, and even artistically. In the intervals between the sessions he smoked, drank tea, chatted a little about politics, a little about general topics, a little about cards, but most of all about official appointments. Tired, but with the feelings of a virtuoso—one of the first violins who has played his part in an orchestra with precision—he would return home to find that his wife and daughter had been out paying calls, or had a visitor, and that his son had been to school, had done his homework with his tutor, and was duly learning what is taught at High Schools. Everything was as it should be. After dinner, if they had no visitors, Ivan Ilych sometimes read a book that was being much discussed at the time, and in the evening settled down to work, that is, read official papers, compared the depositions of witnesses, and noted paragraphs of the Code applying to them. This was neither dull nor amusing. It was dull when he might have been playing bridge, but if no bridge was available it was at any rate better than doing nothing or sitting with his wife. Ivan Ilych's chief pleasure was giving little dinners to which he invited men and women of good social position, and just as his drawing-room resembled all other drawing-rooms so did his enjoyable little parties resemble all other such parties.

Once they even gave a dance. Ivan Ilych enjoyed it and everything went off well, except that it led to a violent quarrel with his wife about the cakes and sweets. Praskovya Fëdorovna had made her own plans, but Ivan Ilych insisted on getting everything from an expensive confectioner and ordered too many cakes, and the quarrel occurred because some of those cakes were left over and the confectioner's bill came to forty-five rubles. It was a great and disagreeable quarrel. Praskovya Fëdorovna called him "a fool and an imbecile," and he clutched at his head and made angry allusions to divorce.

But the dance itself had been enjoyable. The best people were there, and Ivan Ilych had danced with Princess Trufonova, a sister of the distinguished founder of the Society "Bear my Burden."

The pleasures connected with his work were pleasures of ambition; his social pleasures were those of vanity; but Ivan Ilych's greatest pleasure was playing bridge. He acknowledged that whatever disagreeable incident happened in his life, the pleasure that beamed like a ray of light above everything else was to sit down to bridge with good players, not noisy partners, and of course to four-handed bridge (with five players it was annoying to have to stand out, though one pretended not to mind), to play a clever and serious game (when the cards allowed it), and then to have supper and drink a glass of wine. After a game of bridge, especially if he had won a little (to win a large sum was unpleasant), Ivan Ilych went to bed in specially good humor.

So they lived. They formed a circle of acquaintances among the best people and were visited by people of importance and by young folk. In their views as to their acquaintances, husband, wife, and daughter were entirely agreed, and tacitly and unanimously kept at arm's length and shook off the various shabby friends and relations who, with much show of affection, gushed into the drawing-room with its Japanese plates on the walls. Soon these shabby friends ceased to obtrude themselves and only the best people remained in the Golovins' set.

Young men made up to Lisa, and Petrishchev, an examining magistrate and Dmitri Ivanovich Petrishchev's son and sole heir, began to be so attentive to her that Ivan Ilych had already spoken to Praskovya Fëdorovna about it, and considered whether they should not arrange a party for them, or get up some private theatricals.

So they lived, and all went well, without change, and life flowed pleasantly.

IV

They were all in good health. It could not be called ill health if Ivan Ilych sometimes said that he had a queer taste in his mouth and felt some discomfort in his left side.

But this discomfort increased and, though not exactly painful, grew into a sense of pressure in his side accompanied by ill humor. And his irritability became worse and worse and began to mar the agreeable, easy, and correct life that had established itself in the Golovin family. Quarrels between husband and wife became more and more frequent, and soon the ease and amenity disappeared and even the decorum was barely maintained. Scenes again became frequent, and very few of those islets remained on which husband and wife could meet without an explosion. Praskovya Fëdorovna now had good reason to say that her husband's temper was trying. With characteristic exaggeration she said he had always had a dreadful temper, and that it had needed all her good nature to put up with it for twenty years. It was true that now the quarrels were started by him. His bursts of temper always came just before dinner, often just as he began to eat his soup. Sometimes he noticed that a plate or dish was chipped, or the food was not right, or his son put his elbow on the table, or his daughter's hair was not done as he liked it, and for all this he blamed Praskovya Fëdorovna. At first she retorted and said disagreeable things to him, but once or twice he fell into such a rage at the beginning of dinner that she realized it was due to some physical derangement brought on by taking food, and so she restrained herself and did not answer, but only hurried to get the dinner over. She regarded this self-restraint as highly praiseworthy. Having come to the conclusion that her husband had a dreadful temper and made her life miserable, she began to feel sorry for herself, and the more she pitied herself the more she hated her husband. She began to wish he would die; yet she did not want him to die because then his salary would cease. And this irritated her against him still more. She considered herself dreadfully unhappy just because not even his death could save her, and though she concealed her exasperation, that hidden exasperation of hers increased his irritation also.

After one scene in which Ivan Ilych had been particularly unfair and after which he had said in explanation that he certainly was irritable but that it was due to his not being well, she said that if he was ill it should be attended to, and insisted on his going to see a celebrated doctor.

He went. Everything took place as he had expected and as it always does. There was the usual waiting and the important air assumed by the doctor, with which he was so familiar (resembling that which he himself assumed in court), and the sounding and listening, and the questions which called for answers that were foregone conclusions and were evidently unnecessary, and the look of importance which implied that "if only you put yourself in our hands we will arrange everything—we know indubitably how it has to be done, always in the same way for everybody alike." It was all just as it was in the law courts. The doctor put on just the same air towards him as he himself put on towards an accused person.

The doctor said that so-and-so indicated that there was so-and-so inside the patient, but if the investigation of so-and-so did not confirm this, then he must assume that and that. If he assumed that and that, then . . . and so on. To Ivan Ilych only one question was important: was his case serious or not? But the doctor ignored that inappropriate question. From his point of view it was not the one under consideration, the real question was to decide between a floating kidney, chronic catarrh, or appendicitis. It was not a question of Ivan Ilych's life or death, but one between a floating kidney and appendicitis. And that question the doctor solved brilliantly, as it seemed to Ivan Ilych, in favor of the appendix, with the reservation that should an examination of the urine give fresh indications the matter would be reconsidered. All this was just what Ivan Ilych had himself brilliantly accomplished a thousand times in dealing with men on trial. The doctor summed up just as brilliantly, looking over his spectacles triumphantly and even gaily at the accused. From the doctor's summing up Ivan Ilych concluded that things were bad, but that for the doctor, and perhaps for everybody else, it was a matter of indifference, though for him it was bad. And this conclusion struck him painfully, arousing in him a great feeling of pity for himself and of bitterness towards the doctor's indifference to a matter of such importance.

He said nothing of this, but rose, placed the doctor's fee on the table, and remarked with a sigh: "We sick people probably often put inappropriate questions. But tell me, in general, is this complaint dangerous, or not? . . ."

The doctor looked at him sternly over his spectacles with one eye, as if to say: "Prisoner, if you will not keep to the questions put to you, I shall be obliged to have you removed from the court."

"I have already told you what I consider necessary and proper. The analysis may show something more." And the doctor bowed.

Ivan Ilych went out slowly, seated himself disconsolately in his sledge, and drove home. All the way home he was going over what the doctor had said, trying to translate those complicated, obscure, scientific phrases into plain language and find in them an answer to the question: "Is my condition bad? Is it very bad? Or is there as yet nothing much wrong?" And it seemed to him that the meaning of what the doctor had said was that it was very bad. Everything in the streets seemed depressing. The cabmen, the houses, the passers-by, and the shops, were dismal. His ache, this dull gnawing ache that never ceased for a moment, seemed to have acquired a new and more serious significance from the doctor's dubious remarks. Ivan Ilych now watched it with a new and oppressive feeling.

He reached home and began to tell his wife about it. She listened, but in the middle of his account his daughter came in with her hat on, ready to go out with her mother. She sat down reluctantly to listen to this tedious story, but could not stand it long, and her mother too did not hear him to the end.

"Well, I am very glad," she said. "Mind now to take your medicine regularly. Give me the prescription and I'll send Gerasim to the chemist's." And she went to get ready to go out.

While she was in the room Ivan Ilych had hardly taken time to breathe, but he sighed deeply when she left it.

"Well," he thought, "perhaps it isn't so bad after all."

He began taking his medicine and following the doctor's directions, which had been altered after the examination of the urine. But then it happened that there was a contradiction between the indications drawn from the examination of the urine and the symptoms that showed themselves. It turned out that what was happening differed from what the doctor had told him, and that he had either forgotten, or blundered, or hidden something from him. He could not, however, be blamed for that, and Ivan Ilych still obeyed his orders implicitly and at first derived some comfort from doing so.

From the time of his visit to the doctor, Ivan Ilych's chief occupation was the exact fulfilment of the doctor's instructions regarding hygiene and the taking of medicine, and the observation of his pain and his excretions. His chief interests came to be people's ailments and people's health. When sickness, deaths, or recoveries were mentioned in his presence, especially when the illness resembled his own, he listened with agitation which he tried to hide, asked questions, and applied what he heard to his own case.

The pain did not grow less, but Ivan Ilych made efforts to force himself to think that he was better. And he could do this so long as nothing agitated him. But as soon as he had any unpleasantness with his wife, any lack of success in his official work, or held bad cards at bridge, he was at once acutely sensible of his disease. He had formerly borne such mischances, hoping soon to adjust what was wrong, to master it and attain success, or make a grand slam. But now every mischance upset him and plunged him into despair. He would say to himself: "There now, just as I was beginning to get better and the medicine had begun to take effect, comes this accursed misfortune, or unpleasantness. . . ." And he was furious with the mishap, or with the people who were causing the unpleasantness and killing him, for he felt that this fury was killing him but could not restrain it. One would have thought that it should have been clear to him that this exasperation with circumstances and people aggravated his illness, and that he ought therefore to ignore unpleasant occurrences. But he drew the very opposite conclusion: he said that he needed peace, and he watched for everything that might disturb it and became irritable at the slightest infringement of it. His condition was rendered worse by the fact that he read medical books and consulted doctors. The progress of his disease was so gradual that he could deceive himself when comparing one day with another—the difference was so slight. But when he consulted the doctors it seemed to him that he was getting worse, and even very rapidly. Yet despite this he was continually consulting them.

That month he went to see another celebrity, who told him almost the same as the first had done but put his questions rather differently, and the interview with this celebrity only increased Ivan Ilych's doubts and fears. A friend of a friend of his, a very good doctor, diagnosed his illness again quite differently from the others, and though he predicted recovery, his questions and suppositions bewildered Ivan Ilych still more and increased his doubts. A homoeopathist diagnosed the disease in yet another way, and prescribed medicine which Ivan Ilych took secretly for a week. But after a week, not feeling any improvement and having lost confidence both in the former doctor's treatment and in this one's, he became still more despondent. One day a lady acquaintance mentioned a cure effected by a wonder-working icon. Ivan Ilych caught himself listening attentively and beginning to believe that it had occurred. This incident alarmed him. "Has my mind really weakened to such an extent?" he asked himself. "Nonsense! It's all rubbish. I mustn't give way to nervous fears but having chosen a doctor must keep strictly to his treatment. That is what I will do. Now it's all settled. I won't think about it, but will follow the treatment seriously till summer, and then we shall see. From now there must be no more of this wavering!" This was easy to say but impossible to carry out. The pain in his side oppressed him and seemed to grow worse and more incessant, while the taste in his mouth grew stranger and stranger. It seemed to him that his breath had a disgusting smell, and he was conscious of a loss of appetite and strength. There was no deceiving himself: something terrible, new, and more important than anything before in his life, was taking place within him of which he alone was aware. Those about him did not understand or would not understand it, but thought everything in the world was going on as usual. That tormented Ivan Ilych more than anything. He saw that his household, especially his wife and daughter who were in a perfect whirl of visiting, did not understand anything of it and were annoyed that he was so depressed and so exacting, as if he were to blame for it. Though they tried to disguise it he saw that he was an obstacle in their path, and that his wife had adopted a definite line in regard to his illness and kept to it regardless of anything he said or did. Her attitude was this: "You know," she would say to her friends, "Ivan Ilych can't do as other people do, and keep to the treatment prescribed for him. One day he'll take his drops and keep strictly to his diet and go to bed in good time, but the next day unless I watch him he'll suddenly forget his medicine, eat sturgeon—which is forbidden—and sit up playing cards till one o'clock in the morning."

"Oh, come, when was that?" Ivan Ilych would ask in vexation. "Only once at Peter Ivanovich's."

"And yesterday with Shebek."

"Well, even if I hadn't stayed up, this pain would have kept me awake."

"Be that as it may you'll never get well like that, but will always make us wretched."

Praskovya Fëdorovna's attitude to Ivan Ilych's illness, as she expressed it both to others and to him, was that it was his own fault and was another of the annoyances he caused her. Ivan Ilych felt that this opinion escaped her involuntarily—but that did not make it easier for him.

At the law courts too, Ivan Ilych noticed, or thought he noticed, a strange attitude towards himself. It sometimes seemed to him that people were watching him inquisitively as a man whose place might soon be vacant. Then again, his friends would suddenly begin to chaff him in a friendly way about his low spirits, as if the awful, horrible, and unheard-of thing that was going on within him, incessantly gnawing at him and irresistibly drawing him away, was a very agreeable subject for jests. Schwartz in particular irritated him by his jocularity, vivacity, and *savoir-faire*, which reminded him of what he himself had been ten years ago.

Friends came to make up a set and they sat down to cards. They dealt, bending the new cards to soften them, and he sorted the diamonds in his hand and found he had seven. His partner said "No trumps" and supported him with two diamonds. What more could be wished for? It ought to be jolly and lively. They would make a grand slam. But suddenly Ivan Ilych was conscious of that gnawing pain, that taste in his mouth, and it seemed ridiculous that in such circumstances he should be pleased to make a grand slam.

He looked at his partner Mikhail Mikhaylovich, who rapped the table with his strong hand and instead of snatching up the tricks pushed the cards courteously and indulgently towards Ivan Ilych that he might have the pleasure of gathering them up without the trouble of stretching out his hand for them. "Does he think I am too weak to stretch out my arm?" thought Ivan Ilych, and forgetting what he was doing he over-trumped his partner, missing the grand slam by three tricks. And what was most awful of all was that he saw how upset Mikhail Mikhaylovich was about it but did not himself care. And it was dreadful to realize why he did not care.

They all saw that he was suffering, and said: "We can stop if you are tired. Take a rest." Lie down? No, he was not at all tired, and he finished the rubber. All were gloomy and silent. Ivan Ilych felt that he had diffused this gloom over them and could not dispel it. They had supper and went away, and Ivan Ilych was left alone with the consciousness that his life was poisoned and was poisoning the lives of others, and that this poison did not weaken but penetrated more and more deeply into his whole being.

With this consciousness, and with physical pain besides the terror, he must go to bed, often to lie awake the greater part of the night. Next morning he had to get up again, dress, go to the law courts, speak, and write; or if he did not go out, spend at home those twenty-four hours a day each of which was a torture. And he had to live thus all alone on the brink of an abyss, with no one who understood or pitied him.

V

So one month passed and then another. Just before the New Year his brother-in-law came to town and stayed at their house. Ivan Ilych was at the law courts and Praskovya Fëdorovna had gone shopping. When Ivan Ilych came home and entered his study he found his brother-in-law there—a healthy, florid man—unpacking his portmanteau himself. He raised his head on hearing Ivan Ilych's footsteps and looked up at him for a moment without a word. That stare told Ivan Ilych everything. His brother-in-law opened his mouth to utter an exclamation of surprise but checked himself, and that action confirmed it all.

"I have changed, eh?"

"Yes, there is a change."

And after that, try as he would to get his brother-in-law to return to the subject of his looks, the latter would say nothing about it. Praskovya Fëdorovna came home and her brother went out to her. Ivan Ilych locked the door and began to examine himself in the glass, first full face, then in profile. He took up a portrait of himself taken with his wife, and compared it with what he saw in the glass. The change in him was immense. Then he bared his arms to the elbow, looked at them, drew the sleeves down again, sat down on an ottoman, and grew blacker than night.

"No, no, this won't do!" he said to himself, and jumped up, went to the table, took up some law papers, and began to read them, but could not continue. He unlocked the door and went into the reception room. The door leading to the drawing-room was shut. He approached it on tiptoe and listened.

"No, you are exaggerating!" Praskovya Fëdorovna was saying.

"Exaggerating! Don't you see it? Why, he's a dead man! Look at his eyes—there's no light in them. But what is it that is wrong with him?"

"No one knows. Nikolaevich said something, but I don't know what. And Leshchetitsky[10] said quite the contrary...."

Ivan Ilych walked away, went to his own room, lay down, and began musing: "The kidney, a floating kidney." He recalled all the doctors had told him of how it detached itself and swayed about. And by an effort of imagination he tried to catch that kidney and arrest it and support it. So little was needed for this, it seemed to him. "No, I'll go to see Peter Ivanovich[11] again." He rang, ordered the carriage, and got ready to go.

"Where are you going, Jean?" asked his wife, with a specially sad and exceptionally kind look.

This exceptionally kind look irritated him. He looked morosely at her.

"I must go to see Peter Ivanovich."

He went to see Peter Ivanovich, and together they went to see his friend, the doctor. He was in, and Ivan Ilych had a long talk with him.

Reviewing the anatomical and physiological details of what in the doctor's opinion was going on inside him, he understood it all.

There was something, a small thing, in the vermiform appendix. It might all come right. Only stimulate the energy of one organ and check the activity of another, then absorption would take place and everything would come right. He got home rather late for dinner, ate his dinner, and conversed cheerfully, but could not for a long time bring himself to go back to work in his room. At last however, he went to his study and did what was necessary, but the consciousness that he had put something aside—an important, intimate matter which he

---

[10] *Nikolaevich, Leshchetitsky:* two doctors, the latter a celebrated specialist. [L. and A. Maude]

[11] *Peter Ivanovich:* That was the friend whose friend was a doctor. [L. and A. Maude]

would revert to when his work was done—never left him. When he had finished his work he remembered that this intimate matter was the thought of his vermiform appendix. But he did not give himself up to it, and went to the drawing-room for tea. There were callers there, including the examining magistrate who was a desirable match for his daughter, and they were conversing, playing the piano, and singing. Ivan Ilych, as Praskovya Fëdorovna remarked, spent that evening more cheerfully than usual, but he never for a moment forgot that he had postponed the important matter of the appendix. At eleven o'clock he said good-night and went to his bedroom. Since his illness he had slept alone in a small room next to his study. He undressed and took up a novel by Zola, but instead of reading it he fell into thought, and in his imagination that desired improvement in the vermiform appendix occurred. There was the absorption and evacuation and the re-establishment of normal activity. "Yes, that's it!" he said to himself. "One need only assist nature, that's all." He remembered his medicine, rose, took it, and lay down on his back watching for the beneficent action of the medicine and for it to lessen the pain. "I need only take it regularly and avoid all injurious influences. I am already feeling better, much better." He began touching his side: it was not painful to the touch. "There, I really don't feel it. It's much better already." He put out the light and turned on his side. . . . "The appendix is getting better, absorption is occurring." Suddenly he felt the old, familiar, dull, gnawing pain, stubborn and serious. There was the same familiar loathsome taste in his mouth. His heart sank and he felt dazed. "My God! My God!" he muttered. "Again, again! and it will never cease." And suddenly the matter presented itself in a quite different aspect. "Vermiform appendix! Kidney!" he said to himself. "It's not a question of appendix or kidney, but of life and . . . death. Yes, life was there and now it is going, going and I cannot stop it. Yes. Why deceive myself? Isn't it obvious to everyone but me that I'm dying, and that it's only a question of weeks, days . . . it may happen this moment. There was light and now there is darkness. I was here and now I'm going there! Where?" A chill came over him, his breathing ceased, and he felt only the throbbing of his heart.

"When I am not, what will there be? There will be nothing. Then where shall I be when I am no more? Can this be dying? No, I don't want to!" He jumped up and tried to light the candle, felt for it with trembling hands, dropped candle and candlestick on the floor, and fell back on his pillow.

"What's the use? It makes no difference," he said to himself, staring with wide-open eyes into the darkness. "Death. Yes, death. And none of them know or wish to know it, and they have no pity for me. Now they are playing." (He heard through the door the distant sound of a song and its accompaniment.) "It's all the same to them, but they will die too! Fools! I first, and they later, but it will be the same for them. And now they are merry . . . the beasts!"

Anger choked him and he was agonizingly, unbearably miserable. "It is impossible that all men have been doomed to suffer this awful horror!" He raised himself.

"Something must be wrong. I must calm myself—must think it all over from the beginning." And he again began thinking. "Yes, the beginning of my illness: I knocked my side, but I was still quite well that day and the next. It hurt a little, then rather more. I saw the doctors, then followed despondency and anguish, more doctors, and I drew nearer to the abyss. My strength grew less and I kept coming nearer and nearer, and now I have wasted away and there is no light in my eyes. I think of the appendix—but this is death! I think of mending the appendix, and all the while here is death! Can it really be death?" Again terror seized him and he gasped for breath. He leant down and began feeling for the matches, pressing with his elbow on the stand beside the bed. It was in his way and hurt him, he grew furious with it, pressed on it still harder, and upset it. Breathless and in despair he fell on his back, expecting death to come immediately.

Meanwhile the visitors were leaving. Praskovya Fëdorovna was seeing them off. She heard something fall and came in.

"What has happened?"

"Nothing. I knocked it over accidentally."

She went out and returned with a candle. He lay there panting heavily, like a man who has run a thousand yards, and stared upwards at her with a fixed look.

"What is it, Jean?"

"No . . . o . . . thing. I upset it." ("Why speak of it? She won't understand," he thought.)

And in truth she did not understand. She picked up the stand, lit his candle, and hurried away to see another visitor off. When she came back he still lay on his back, looking upwards.

"What is it? Do you feel worse?"

"Yes."

She shook her head and sat down.

"Do you know, Jean, I think we must ask Leshchetitsky to come and see you here."

This meant calling in the famous specialist, regardless of expense. He smiled malignantly and said "No." She remained a little longer and then went up to him and kissed his forehead.

While she was kissing him he hated her from the bottom of his soul and with difficulty refrained from pushing her away.

"Good-night. Please God you'll sleep."

"Yes."

VI

Ivan Ilych saw that he was dying, and he was in continual despair.

In the depth of his heart he knew he was dying, but not only was he not accustomed to the thought, he simply did not and could not grasp it.

The syllogism he had learnt from Kiezewetter's Logic: [12] "Caius is a man, men are mortal, therefore Caius is mortal," had always seemed to him correct as applied to Caius, but certainly not as applied to himself. That Caius—man in the abstract—was mortal, was perfectly correct, but he was not Caius, not an abstract man, but a creature quite, quite separate from all others. He had been little Vanya, with a mamma and a papa, with Mitya and Volodya, with the toys, a coachman and a nurse, afterwards with Katenka and with all the joys, griefs, and delights of childhood, boyhood, and youth. What did Caius know of the smell of

[12] Karl Kiezewetter, *Outline of Logic According to Kantian Principles.*

that striped leather ball Vanya had been so fond of? Had Caius kissed his mother's hand like that, and did the silk of her dress rustle so for Caius? Had he rioted like that at school when the pastry was bad? Had Caius been in love like that? Could Caius preside at a session as he did? "Caius really was mortal, and it was right for him to die; but for me, little Vanya, Ivan Ilych, with all my thoughts and emotions, it's altogether a different matter. It cannot be that I ought to die. That would be too terrible."

Such was his feeling.

"If I had to die like Caius I should have known it was so. An inner voice would have told me so, but there was nothing of the sort in me and I and all my friends felt that our case was quite different from that of Caius. And now here it is!" he said to himself. "It can't be. It's impossible! But here it is. How is this? How is one to understand it?"

He could not understand it, and tried to drive this false, incorrect, morbid thought away and to replace it by other proper and healthy thoughts. But that thought, and not the thought only but the reality itself, seemed to come and confront him.

And to replace that thought he called up a succession of others, hoping to find in them some support. He tried to get back into the former current of thoughts that had once screened the thought of death from him. But strange to say, all that had formerly shut off, hidden, and destroyed his consciousness of death, no longer had that effect. Ivan Ilych now spent most of his time in attempting to re-establish that old current. He would say to himself: "I will take up my duties again—after all I used to live by them." And banishing all doubts he would go to the law courts, enter into conversation with his colleagues, and sit carelessly as was his wont, scanning the crowd with a thoughtful look and leaning both his emaciated arms on the arms of his oak chair; bending over as usual to a colleague and drawing his papers nearer he would interchange whispers with him, and then suddenly raising his eyes and sitting erect would pronounce certain words and open the proceedings. But suddenly in the midst of those proceedings the pain in his side, regardless of the stage the proceedings had reached, would begin its own gnawing work. Ivan Ilych would turn his attention to it and try to drive the thought of it away, but without success. It would come and stand before him and look at him, and he would be petrified and the light would die out of his eyes, and he would again begin asking himself whether It alone was true. And his colleagues and subordinates would see with surprise and distress that he, the brilliant and subtle judge, was becoming confused and making mistakes. He would shake himself, try to pull himself together, manage somehow to bring the sitting to a close, and return home with the sorrowful consciousness that his judicial labors could not as formerly hide from him what he wanted them to hide, and could not deliver him from It. And what was worst of all was that It drew his attention to itself not in order to make him take some action but only that he should look at It, look it straight in the face: look at it and, without doing anything, suffer inexpressibly.

And to save himself from this condition Ivan Ilych looked for consolations—new screens—and new screens were found and for a while seemed to save him, but then they immediately fell to pieces or rather became transparent, as if It penetrated them and nothing could veil It.

In these latter days he would go into the drawing-room he had arranged—that drawing-room where he had fallen and for the sake of which (how bitterly ridiculous it seemed) he had sacrificed his life—for he knew that his illiness originated with that knock. He would enter and see that something had scratched the polished table. He would look for the cause of this and find that it was the bronze ornamentation of an album, that had got bent. He would take up the expensive album which he had lovingly arranged, and feel vexed with his daughter and her friends for their untidiness—for the album was torn here and there and some of the photographs turned upside down. He would put it carefully in order and bend the ornamentation back into position. Then it would occur to him to place all those things in another corner of the room, near the plants. He could call the footman, but his daughter or wife would come to help him. They would not agree, and his wife would contradict him, and he would dispute and grow angry. But that was all right, for then he did not think about *It. It* was invisible.

But then, when he was moving something himself, his wife would say: "Let the servants do it. You will hurt yourself again." And suddenly *It* would flash through the screen and he would see it. It was just a flash, and he hoped it would disappear, but he would involuntarily pay attention to his side. "It sits there as before, gnawing just the same!" And he could no longer forget *It,* but could distinctly see it looking at him from behind the flowers. "What is it all for?"

"It really is so! I lost my life over that curtain as I might have done when storming a fort. Is that possible? How terrible and how stupid. It can't be true! It can't, but it is."

He would go to his study, lie down, and again be alone with *It:* face to face with *It.* And nothing could be done with *It* except to look at it and shudder.

VII

How it happened it is impossible to say because it came about step by step, unnoticed, but in the third month of Ivan Ilych's illness, his wife, his daughter, his son, his acquaintances, the doctors, the servants, and above all he himself, were aware that the whole interest he had for other people was whether he would soon vacate his place, and at last release the living from the discomfort caused by his presence and be himself released from his sufferings.

He slept less and less. He was given opium and hypodermic injections of morphine, but this did not relieve him. The dull depression he experienced in a somnolent condition at first gave him a little relief, but only as something new, afterwards it became as distressing as the pain itself or even more so.

Special foods were prepared for him by the doctors' orders, but all those foods became increasingly distasteful and disgusting to him.

For his excretions also special arrangements had to be made, and this was a torment to him every time—a torment from the uncleanliness, the unseemliness, and the smell, and from knowing that another person had to take part in it.

But just through this most unpleasant matter, Ivan Ilych obtained comfort. Gerasim, the butler's young assistant, always came in to carry the things out. Gerasim was a clean, fresh peasant lad, grown stout on town food and always cheerful and bright. At first the sight of him, in his clean Russian peasant costume, engaged on that disgusting task embarrassed Ivan Ilych.

Once when he got up from the commode too weak to draw up his trousers, he dropped into a soft armchair and looked with horror at his bare, enfeebled thighs with the muscles so sharply marked on them.

Gerasim with a firm light tread, his heavy boots emitting a pleasant smell of tar and fresh winter air, came in wearing a clean Hessian apron, the sleeves of his print shirt tucked up over his strong, bare young arms; and refraining from looking at his sick master out of consideration for his feelings, and restraining the joy of life that beamed from his face, he went up to the commode.

"Gerasim!" said Ivan Ilych in a weak voice.

Gerasim started, evidently afraid he might have committed some blunder, and with a rapid movement turned his fresh, kind, simple young face which just showed the first downy signs of a beard.

"Yes, sir?"

"That must be very unpleasant for you. You must forgive me. I am helpless."

"Oh, why, sir," and Gerasim's eyes beamed and he showed his glistening white teeth, "what's a little trouble? It's a case of illness with you, sir."

And his deft strong hands did their accustomed task, and he went out of the room stepping lightly. Five minutes later he as lightly returned.

Ivan Ilych was still sitting in the same position in the armchair.

"Gerasim," he said when the latter had replaced the freshly-washed utensil. "Please come here and help me." Gerasim went up to him. "Lift me up. It is hard for me to get up, and I have sent Dmitri away."

Gerasim went up to him, grasped his master with his strong arms deftly but gently, in the same way that he stepped—lifted him, supported him with one hand, and with the other drew up his trousers and would have set him down again, but Ivan Ilych asked to be led to the sofa. Gerasim, without an effort and without apparent pressure, led him, almost lifting him, to the sofa and placed him on it.

"Thank you. How easily and well you do it all!"

Gerasim smiled again and turned to leave the room. But Ivan Ilych felt his presence such a comfort that he did not want to let him go.

"One thing more, please move up that chair. No, the other one—under my feet. It is easier for me when my feet are raised."

Gerasim brought the chair, set it down gently in place, and raised Ivan Ilych's legs on to it. It seemed to Ivan Ilych that he felt better while Gerasim was holding up his legs.

"It's better when my legs are higher," he said. "Place that cushion under them."

Gerasim did so. He again lifted the legs and placed them, and again Ivan Ilych felt better while Gerasim held his legs. When he set them down Ivan Ilych fancied he felt worse.

"Gerasim," he said. "Are you busy now?"

"Not at all, sir," said Gerasim, who had learnt from the townsfolk how to speak to gentlefolk.

"What have you still to do?"

"What have I to do? I've done everything except chopping the logs for tomorrow."

"Then hold my legs up a bit higher, can you?"

"Of course I can. Why not?" And Gerasim raised his master's legs higher and Ivan Ilych thought that in that position he did not feel any pain at all.

"And how about the logs?"

"Don't trouble about that, sir. There's plenty of time."

Ivan Ilych told Gerasim to sit down and hold his legs, and began to talk to him. And strange to say it seemed to him that he felt better while Gerasim held his legs up.

After that Ivan Ilych would sometimes call Gerasim and get him to hold his legs on his shoulders, and he liked talking to him. Gerasim did it all easily, willingly, simply, and with a good nature that touched Ivan Ilych. Health, strength, and vitality in other people were offensive to him, but Gerasim's strength and vitality did not mortify but soothed him.

What tormented Ivan Ilych most was the deception, the lie, which for some reason they all accepted, that he was not dying but was simply ill, and that he only need keep quiet and undergo a treatment and then something very good would result. He however knew that do what they would nothing would come of it, only still more agonizing suffering and death. This deception tortured him—their not wishing to admit what they all knew and what he knew, but wanting to lie to him concerning his terrible condition, and wishing and forcing him to participate in that lie. Those lies—lies enacted over him on the eve of his death and destined to degrade this awful, solemn act to the level of their visitings, their curtains, their sturgeon for dinner—were a terrible agony for Ivan Ilych. And strangely enough, many times when they were going through their antics over him he had been within a hairbreadth of calling out to them: "Stop lying! You know and I know that I am dying. Then at least stop lying about it!" But he had never had the spirit to do it. The awful, terrible act of his dying was, he could see, reduced by those about him to the level of a casual, unpleasant, and almost indecorous incident (as if someone entered a drawing-room diffusing an unpleasant odor) and this was done by that very decorum which he had served all his life long. He saw that no one felt for him, because no one even wished to grasp his position. Only Gerasim recognized it and pitied him. And so Ivan Ilych felt at ease only with him. He felt comforted when Gerasim supported his legs (sometimes all night long) and refused to go to bed, saying: "Don't you worry, Ivan Ilych. I'll get sleep enough later on," or when he suddenly became familiar and exclaimed: "If you weren't sick it would be another matter, but as it is, why should I grudge a little trouble?" Gerasim alone did not lie; everything showed that he alone understood the facts of the case and did not consider it necessary to disguise them, but simply felt sorry for his emaciated and enfeebled master. Once when Ivan Ilych was sending him away he even said straight out: "We shall all of us die, so why should I grudge a little trouble?"—expressing the fact that he did not think his work burdensome, because he was doing it for a dying man and hoped someone would do the same for him when his time came.

Apart from this lying, or because of it, what most tormented Ivan Ilych was that no one pitied him as he wished to be pitied. At certain moments after prolonged suffering he wished most of all (though he would have been ashamed to confess it) for someone to pity him as a sick child is pitied. He longed to be petted and comforted. He knew he was an important functionary, that he had a beard turning grey, and that therefore what he longed for was impossible, but still he longed for it. And in Gerasim's attitude towards him there was something akin to what he wished for, and so that attitude comforted him. Ivan Ilych wanted to weep, wanted to be petted and cried over, and then his colleague Shebek would come, and instead of weeping and being petted, Ivan Ilych would assume a serious, severe, and profound air, and by force of habit would express his opinion on a decision of the Court of Cassation and would stubbornly insist on that view. This falsity around him and within him did more than anything else to poison his last days.

VIII

It was morning. He knew it was morning because Gerasim had gone, and Peter the footman had come and put out the candles, drawn back one of the curtains, and begun quietly to tidy up. Whether it was morning or evening, Friday or Sunday, made no difference, it was all just the same: the gnawing, unmitigated, agonizing pain, never ceasing for an instant, the consciousness of life inexorably waning but not yet extinguished, the approach of that ever dreaded and hateful Death which was the only reality, and always the same falsity. What were days, weeks, hours, in such a case?

"Will you have some tea, sir?"

"He wants things to be regular, and wishes the gentlefolk to drink tea in the morning," thought Ivan Ilych, and only said "No."

"Wouldn't you like to move onto the sofa, sir?"

"He wants to tidy up the room, and I'm in the way. I am uncleanliness and disorder," he thought, and said only:

"No, leave me alone."

The man went on bustling about. Ivan Ilych stretched out his hand. Peter came up, ready to help.

"What is it, sir?"

"My watch."

Peter took the watch which was close at hand and gave it to his master.

"Half-past eight. Are they up?"

"No, sir, except Vladimir Ivanovich" (the son) "who has gone to school. Praskovya Fëdorovna ordered me to wake her if you asked for her. Shall I do so?"

"No, there's no need to." "Perhaps I'd better have some tea," he thought, and added aloud: "Yes, bring me some tea."

Peter went to the door, but Ivan Ilych dreaded being left alone. "How can I keep him here? Oh yes, my medicine." "Peter, give me my medicine." "Why not? Perhaps it may still do me some good." He took a spoonful and swallowed it. "No, it won't help. It's all tomfoolerly, all deception," he decided as soon as he became aware of the familiar, sickly, hopeless taste. "No, I can't believe in it any longer. But the pain, why this pain? If it would only cease just for a moment!" And he moaned. Peter turned towards him. "It's all right. Go and fetch me some tea."

Peter went out. Left alone Ivan Ilych groaned not so much with pain, terrible though that was, as from mental anguish. Always and forever the same, always these endless days and nights. If only it would come quicker! If only *what* would come quicker? Death, darkness? . . . No, no! Anything rather than death!

When Peter returned with the tea on a tray, Ivan Ilych stared at him for a time in perplexity, not realizing who and what he was. Peter was disconcerted by that look and his embarrassment brought Ivan Ilych to himself.

"Oh, tea! All right, put it down. Only help me to wash and put on a clean shirt."

And Ivan Ilych began to wash. With pauses for rest, he washed his hands and then his face, cleaned his teeth, brushed his hair, and looked in the glass. He was terrified by what he saw, especially by the limp way in which his hair clung to his pallid forehead.

While his shirt was being changed he knew that he would be still more frightened at the sight of his body, so he avoided looking at it. Finally he was ready. He drew on a dressing-gown, wrapped himself in a plaid, and sat down in the armchair to take his tea. For a moment he felt refreshed, but soon as he began to drink the tea he was again aware of the same taste, and the pain also returned. He finished it with an effort, and then lay down stretching out his legs, and dismissed Peter.

Always the same. Now a spark of hope flashes up, then a sea of despair rages, and always pain; always pain, always despair, and always the same. When alone he had a dreadful and distressing desire to call someone, but he knew beforehand that with others present it would be still worse. "Another dose of morphine—to lose consciousness. I will tell him, the doctor, that he must think of something else. It's impossible, impossible, to go on like this."

An hour and another pass like that. But now there is a ring at the door bell. Perhaps it's the doctor? It is. He comes in fresh, hearty, plump, and cheerful, with that look on his face that seems to say: "There now, you're in a panic about something, but we'll arrange it all for you directly!" The doctor knows this expression is out of place here, but he has put it on once for all and can't take it off—like a man who has put on a frock-coat in the morning to pay a round of calls.

The doctor rubs his hands vigorously and reassuringly.

"Brr! How cold it is! There's such a sharp frost; just let me warm myself!" he says, as if it were only a matter of waiting till he was warm, and then he would put everything right.

"Well now, how are you?"

Ivan Ilych feels that the doctor would like to say: "Well, how are our affairs?" but that even he feels that this would not do, and says instead: "What sort of a night have you had?"

Ivan Ilych looks at him as much as to say: "Are you really never ashamed of lying?" But the doctor does not wish to understand this question, and Ivan Ilych says: "Just as terrible as ever. The pain never leaves me and never subsides. If only something. . . ."

"Yes, you sick people are always like that. . . . There, now I think I am warm enough. Even Praskovya Fëdorovna, who is so particular, could find no fault with my temperature. Well, now I can say good-morning," and the doctor presses his patient's hand.

Then, dropping his former playfulness, he begins with a most serious face to examine the patient, feeling his pulse and taking his temperature, and then begins the sounding and auscultation.

Ivan Ilych knows quite well and definitely that all this is nonsense and pure deception, but when the doctor, getting down on his knee, leans over him, putting his ear first higher then lower, and performs various gymnastic movements over him with a significant expression on his face, Ivan Ilych submits to it all as he used to submit to the speeches of the lawyers, though he knew very well that they were all lying and why they were lying.

The doctor, kneeling on the sofa, is still sounding him when Praskovya Fëdorovna's silk dress rustles at the door and she is heard scolding Peter for not having let her know of the doctor's arrival.

She comes in, kisses her husband, and at once proceeds to prove that she has been up a long time already, and only owing to a misunderstanding failed to be there when the doctor arrived.

Ivan Ilych looks at her, scans her all over, sets against her the whiteness and plumpness and cleanness of her hands and neck, the gloss of her hair, and the sparkle of her vivacious eyes. He hates her with his whole soul. And the thrill of hatred he feels for her makes him suffer from her touch.

Her attitude towards him and his disease is still the same. Just as the doctor had adopted a certain relation to his patient which he could not abandon, so had she formed one towards him—that he was not doing something he ought to do and was himself to blame, and that she reproached him lovingly for this—and she could not now change that attitude.

"You see he doesn't listen to me and doesn't take his medicine at the proper time. And above all he lies in a position that is no doubt bad for him—with his legs up."

She described how he made Gerasim hold his legs up.

The doctor smiled with a contemptuous affability that said: "What's to be done? These sick people do have foolish fancies of that kind, but we must forgive them."

When the examination was over the doctor looked at his watch, and then Praskovya Fëdorovna announced to Ivan Ilych that it was of course as he pleased, but she had sent today for a celebrated specialist who would examine him and have a consultation with Michael Danilovich (their regular doctor).

"Please don't raise any objections. I am doing this for my own sake," she said ironically, letting it be felt that she was doing it all for his sake and only said this to leave him no right to refuse. He remained silent, knitting his brows. He felt that he was so surrounded and involved in a mesh of falsity that it was hard to unravel anything.

Everything she did for him was entirely for her own sake, and she told him she was doing for herself what she actually was doing for herself, as if that was so incredible that he must understand the opposite.

At half-past eleven the celebrated specialist arrived. Again the sounding began and the significant conversations in his presence and in another room, about the kidneys and the appendix, and the questions and answers, with such an air of importance that again, instead of the real question of life and death which now alone confronted him, the question arose of the kidney and appendix which were not behaving as they ought to and would now be attacked by Michael Danilovich and the specialist and forced to amend their ways.

The celebrated specialist took leave of him with a serious though not hopeless look, and in reply to the timid question Ivan Ilych, with eyes glistening with fear and hope, put to him as to whether there was a chance of recovery, said that he could not vouch for it but there was a possibility. The look of hope with which Ivan Ilych watched the doctor out was so pathetic that Praskovya Fëdorovna, seeing it, even wept as she left the room to hand the doctor his fee.

The gleam of hope kindled by the doctor's encouragement did not last long. The same room, the same pictures, curtains, wallpaper, medicine bottles, were all there, and the same aching suffering body, and Ivan Ilych began to moan. They gave him a subcutaneous injection and he sank into oblivion.

It was twilight when he came to. They brought him his dinner and he swallowed some beef tea with difficulty, and then everything was the same again and night was coming on.

After dinner, at seven o'clock, Praskovya Fëdorovna came into the room in evening dress, her full bosom pushed up by her corset, and with traces of powder on her face. She had reminded him in the morning that they were going to the theatre. Sarah Bernhardt was visiting the town and they had a box, which he had insisted on their taking. Now he had forgotten about it and her toilet offended him, but he concealed his vexation when he remembered that he had himself insisted on their securing a box and going because it would be an instructive and aesthetic pleasure for the children.

Praskovya Fëdorovna came in, self-satisfied but yet with a rather guilty air. She sat down and asked how he was, but, as he saw, only for the sake of asking and not in order to learn about it, knowing that there was nothing to learn—and then went on to what she really wanted to say: that she would not on any account have gone but that the box had been taken and Helen and their daughter were going, as well as Petrishchev (the examining magistrate, their daughter's fiancé), and that it was out of the question to let them go alone; but that she would have much preferred to sit with him for a while; and he must be sure to follow the doctor's orders while she was away.

"Oh, and Fëdor Petrovich" (the fiancé) would like to come in. May he? And Lisa?"

"All right."

Their daughter came in in full evening dress, her fresh young flesh exposed (making a show of that very flesh which in his own case caused so much suffering), strong, healthy, evidently in love, and impatient with illness, suffering, and death, because they interfered with her happiness.

Fëdor Petrovich came in too, in evening dress, his hair curled à la Capoul,[13] a tight stiff collar round his long sinewy neck, an enormous white shirtfront, and narrow black trousers tightly stretched over his strong thighs. He had one white glove tightly drawn on, and was holding his opera hat in his hand.

Following him the schoolboy crept in unnoticed, in a uniform, poor little fellow, and wearing gloves. Terribly dark shadows showed under his eyes, the meaning of which Ivan Ilych knew well.

His son had always seemed pathetic to him, and now it was dreadful to see the boy's frightened look of pity. It seemed to Ivan Ilych that Vasya was the only one besides Gerasim who understood and pitied him.

They all sat down and again asked how he was. A silence followed. Lisa asked

[13] A hair style named after Victor Capoul (1839–1924), a French singer.

her mother about the opera-glasses, and there was an altercation between mother and daughter as to who had taken them and where they had been put. This occasioned some unpleasantness.

Fëdor Petrovich inquired of Ivan Ilych whether he had ever seen Sarah Bernhardt. Ivan Ilych did not at first catch the question, but then replied: "No, have you seen her before?"

"Yes, in *Adrienne Lecouvreur*." [14]

Praskovya Fëdorovna mentioned some rôles in which Sarah Bernhardt was particularly good. Her daughter disagreed. Conversation sprang up as to the elegance and realism of of her acting—the sort of conversation that is always repeated and is always the same.

In the midst of the conversation Fëdor Petrovich glanced at Ivan Ilych and became silent. The others also looked at him and grew silent. Ivan Ilych was staring with glittering eyes straight before him, evidently indignant with them. This had to be rectified, but it was impossible to do so. The silence had to be broken, but for a time no one dared to break it and they all became afraid that the conventional deception would suddenly become obvious and the truth become plain to all. Lisa was the first to pluck up courage and break that silence, but by trying to hide what everybody was feeling, she betrayed it.

"Well, if we are going it's time to start," she said, looking at her watch, a present from her father, and with a faint and significant smile at Fëdor Petrovich relating to something known only to them. She got up with a rustle of her dress.

They all rose, said good-night, and went away.

When they had gone it seemed to Ivan Ilych that he felt better; the falsity had gone with them. But the pain remained—that same pain and that same fear that made everything monotonously alike, nothing harder and nothing easier. Everything was worse.

Again minute followed minute and hour followed hour. Everything remained the same and there was no cessation. And the inevitable end of it all became more and more terrible.

"Yes, send Gerasim here," he replied to a question Peter asked.

IX

His wife returned late at night. She came in on tiptoe, but he heard her, opened his eyes, and made haste to close them again. She wished to send Gerasim away and to sit with him herself, but he opened his eyes and said: "No, go away."

"Are you in great pain?"

"Always the same."

"Take some opium."

He agreed and took some. She went away.

Till about three in the morning he was in a state of stupefied misery. It seemed to him that he and his pain were being thrust into a narrow, deep black sack, but though they were pushed further and further in they could not be pushed to the bottom. And this, terrible enough in itself, was accompanied by suffering. He was frightened yet wanted to fall through the sack, he struggled

---

[14] A play by Eugène Scribe (1791–1861) and Ernest Legouvé (1807–1903), French playwrights.

but yet cooperated. And suddenly he broke through, fell, and regained consciousness. Gerasim was sitting at the foot of the bed dozing quietly and patiently, while he himself lay with his emaciated stockinged legs resting on Gerasim's shoulders; the same shaded candle was there and the same unceasing pain.

"Go away, Gerasim," he whispered.

"It's all right, sir. I'll stay a while."

"No. Go away."

He removed his legs from Gerasim's shoulders, turned sideways onto his arm, and felt sorry for himself. He only waited till Gerasim had gone into the next room and then restrained himself no longer but wept like a child. He wept on account of his helplessness, his terrible loneliness, the cruelty of man, the cruelty of God, and the absence of God.

"Why hast Thou done all this? Why hast Thou brought me here? Why, why dost Thou torment me so terribly?"

He did not expect an answer and yet wept because there was no answer and could be none. The pain again grew more acute, but he did not stir and did not call. He said to himself: "Go on! Strike me! But what is it for? What have I done to Thee? What is it for?"

Then he grew quiet and not only ceased weeping but even held his breath and became all attention. It was as though he were listening not to an audible voice but to the voice of his soul, to the current of thoughts arising within him.

"What is it you want?" was the first clear conception capable of expression in words, that he heard.

"What do you want? What do you want?" he repeated to himself.

"What do I want? To live and not to suffer," he answered.

And again he listened with such concentrated attention that even his pain did not distract him.

"To live? How?" asked his inner voice.

"Why, to live as I used to—well and pleasantly." the voice repeated.

"As you lived before, well and pleasantly?"

And in imagination he began to recall the best moments of his pleasant life. But strange to say none of those best moments of his pleasant life now seemed at all what they had then seemed—none of them except the first recollections of childhood. There, in childhood, there had been something really pleasant with which it would be possible to live if it could return. But the child who had experienced that happiness existed no longer, it was like a reminiscence of somebody else.

As soon as the period began which had produced the present Ivan Ilych, all that had then seemed joys now melted before his sight and turned into something trivial and often nasty.

And the further he departed from childhood and the nearer he came to the present the more worthless and doubtful were the joys. This began with the School of Law. A little that was really good was still found there—there was lightheartedness, friendship, and hope. But in the upper classes there had already been fewer of such good moments. Then during the first years of his official career, when he was in the service of the Governor, some pleasant moments again occurred; they were the memories of love for a woman. Then all became confused and there was still less of what was good; later on again there was still less that was good, and the further he went the less there was. His marriage, a mere accident, then the disenchantment that followed it, his wife's bad breath and the sensuality and hypocrisy: then that deadly official life and those preoccupations about money, a year of it, and two, and ten, and twenty, and always the same thing. And the longer it lasted the more deadly it became. "It is as if I had been going downhill while I imagined I was going up. And that is really what it was. I was going up in public opinion, but to the same extent life was ebbing away from me. And now it is all done and there is only death."

"Then what does it mean? Why? It can't be that life is so senseless and horrible. But if it really has been so horrible and senseless, why must I die and die in agony? There is something wrong!"

"Maybe I did not live as I ought to have done," it suddenly occurred to him. "But how could that be, when I did everything properly?" he replied, and immediately dismissed from his mind this, the sole solution of all the riddles of life and death, as something quite impossible.

"Then what do you want now? To live? Live how? Live as you lived in the law courts when the usher proclaimed 'The judge is coming!' The judge is coming, the judge!" he repeated to himself. "Here he is, the judge. But I am not guilty!" he exclaimed angrily. "What is it for?" And he ceased crying, but turning his face to the wall continued to ponder on the same question: Why, and for what purpose, is there all this horror? But however much he pondered he found no answer. And whenever the thought occurred to him, as it often did, that it all resulted from his not having lived as he ought to have done, he at once recalled the correctness of his whole life and dismissed so strange an idea.

X

Another fortnight passed. Ivan Ilych now no longer left his sofa. He would not lie in bed but lay on the sofa, facing the wall nearly all the time. He suffered ever the same unceasing agonies and in his loneliness pondered always on the same insoluble question: "What is this? Can it be that it is Death?" And the inner voice answered: "Yes, it is Death."

"Why these sufferings?" And the voice answered, "For no reason—they just are so." Beyond and besides this there was nothing.

From the very beginning of his illness, ever since he had first been to see the doctor, Ivan Ilych's life had been divided between two contrary and alternating moods: now it was despair and the expectation of this uncomprehended and terrible death, and now hope and an intently interested observation of the functioning of his organs. Now before his eyes there was only a kidney or an intestine that temporarily evaded its duty, and now only that incomprehensible and dreadful death from which it was impossible to escape.

These two states of mind had alternated from the very beginning of his illness, but the further it progressed the more doubtful and fantastic became the conception of the kidney, and the more real the sense of impending death.

He had but to call to mind what he had been three months before and what he was now, to call to mind with what regularity he had been going downhill, for every possibility of hope to be shattered.

Latterly during that loneliness in which he found himself as he lay facing the back of the sofa, a loneliness in the midst of a populous town and surrounded by numerous acquaintances and relations but that yet could not have been more complete anywhere—either at the bottom of the sea or under the earth—during that terrible loneliness Ivan Ilych had lived only in memories of the past. Pictures of his past rose before him one after another. They always began with what was nearest in time and then went back to what was most remote—to his childhood—and rested there. If he thought of the stewed prunes that had been offered him that day, his mind went back to the raw shrivelled French plums of his childhood, their peculiar flavor and the flow of saliva when he sucked their stones, and along with the memory of that taste came a whole series of memories of those days: his nurse, his brother, and their toys. "No, I mustn't think of that . . . . It is too painful," Ivan Ilych said to himself, and brought himself back to the present—to the button on the back of the sofa and the creases in its morocco. "Morocco is expensive, but it does not wear well: there had been a quarrel about it. It was a different kind of quarrel and a different kind of morocco that time when we tore father's portfolio and were punished, and mamma brought us some tarts. . . ." And again his thoughts dwelt on his childhood, and again it was painful and he tried to banish them and fix his mind on something else.

Then again together with that chain of memories another series passed through his mind—of how his illness had progressed and grown worse. There also the further back he looked the more life there had been. There had been more of what was good in life and more of life itself. The two merged together. "Just as the pain went on getting worse and worse, so my life grew worse and worse," he thought. "There is one bright spot there at the back, at the beginning of life, and afterwards all becomes blacker and blacker and proceeds more and more rapidly—in inverse ratio to the square of the distance from death," thought Ivan Ilych. And the example of a stone falling downwards with increasing velocity entered his mind. Life, a series of increasing sufferings, flies further and further towards its end—the most terrible suffering. "I am flying. . . ." He shuddered, shifted himself, and tried to resist, but was already aware that resistance was impossible, and again, with eyes weary of gazing but unable to cease seeing what was before them, he stared at the back of the sofa and waited—awaiting that dreadful fall and shock and destruction.

"Resistance is impossible!" he said to himself. "If I could only understand what it is all for! But that too is impossible. An explanation would be possible if it could be said that I have not lived as I ought to. But it is impossible to say that," and he remembered all the legality, correctitude, and propriety of his life. "That at any rate can certainly not be admitted," he thought, and his lips smiled ironically as if someone could see that smile and be taken in by it. "There is no explanation! Agony, death. . . . What for?"

XI

Another two weeks went by in this way and during that fortnight an event occurred that Ivan Ilych and his wife had desired. Petrishchev formally proposed. It happened in the evening. The next day Praskovya Fëdorovna came into her husband's room considering how best to inform him of it, but that very night there had been a fresh change for the worse in his condition. She found him still lying on the sofa but in a different position. He lay on his back, groaning and staring fixedly straight in front of him.

She began to remind him of his medicines, but he turned his eyes towards her with such a look that she did not finish what she was saying; so great an animosity, to her in particular, did that look express.

"For Christ's sake let me die in peace!" he said.

She would have gone away, but just then their daughter came in and went up to say good morning. He looked at her as he had done at his wife, and in reply to her inquiry about his health said dryly that he would soon free them all of himself. They were both silent and after sitting with him for a while went away.

"Is it our fault?" Lisa said to her mother. "It's as if we were to blame! I am sorry for papa, but why should we be tortured?"

The doctor came at his usual time. Ivan Ilych answered "Yes" and "No," never taking his angry eyes from him, and at last said: "You know you can do nothing for me, so leave me alone."

"We can ease your sufferings."

"You can't even do that. Let me be."

The doctor went into the drawing-room and told Praskovya Fëdorovna that the case was very serious and that the only resource left was opium to allay her husband's sufferings, which must be terrible.

It was true, as the doctor said, that Ivan Ilych's physical sufferings were terrible, but worse than the physical sufferings were his mental sufferings, which were his chief torture.

His mental sufferings were due to the fact that that night, as he looked at Gerasim's sleepy, good-natured face with its prominent cheekbones, the question suddenly occurred to him: "What if my whole life has really been wrong?"

It occurred to him that what had appeared perfectly impossible before, namely that he had not spent his life as he should have done, might after all be true. It occurred to him that his scarcely perceptible attempts to struggle against what was considered good by the most highly placed people, those scarcely noticeable impulses which he had immediately suppressed, might have been the real thing, and all the rest false. And his professional duties and the whole arrangement of his life and of his family, and all his social and official interests, might all have been false. He tried to defend all those things to himself and suddenly felt the weakness of what he was defending. There was nothing to defend.

"But if that is so," he said to himself, "and I am leaving this life with the consciousness that I have lost all that was given me and it is impossible to rectify it—what then?"

He lay on his back and began to pass his life in review in quite a new way. In the morning when he saw first his footman, then his wife, then his daughter, and then the doctor, their every word and movement confirmed to him the awful truth that had been revealed to him during the night. In them he saw himself—all that for which he had lived—and saw clearly that it was not real at all, but a terrible and huge deception which had hidden both life and death. This consciousness intensified his physical suffering tenfold. He groaned and tossed about, and pulled at his clothing which choked and stifled him. And he hated them on that account.

He was given a large dose of opium and became unconscious, but at noon his sufferings began again. He drove everybody away and tossed from side to side.

His wife came to him and said:

"Jean, my dear, do this for me. It can't do any harm and often helps. Healthy people often do it."

He opened his eyes wide.

"What? Take communion? Why? It's unnecessary! However. . . ."

She began to cry.

"Yes, do, my dear. I'll send for our priest. He is such a nice man."

"All right. Very well," he muttered.

When the priest came and heard his confession, Ivan Ilych was softened and seemed to feel a relief from his doubts and consequently from his sufferings, and for a moment there came a ray of hope. He again began to think of the vermiform appendix and the possibility of correcting it. He received the sacrament with tears in his eyes.

When they laid him down again afterwards he felt a moment's ease, and the hope that he might live awoke in him again. He began to think of the operation that had been suggested to him. "To live! I want to live!" he said to himself.

His wife came in to congratulate him after his communion, and when uttering the usual conventional words she added:

"You feel better, don't you?"

Without looking at her he said "Yes."

Her dress, her figure, the expression of her face, the tone of her voice, all revealed the same thing. "This is wrong, it is not as it should be. All you have lived for and still live for is falsehood and deception, hiding life and death from you." And as soon as he admitted that thought, his hatred and his agonizing physical suffering again sprang up, and with that suffering a consciousness of the unavoidable, approaching end. And to this was added a new sensation of grinding shooting pain and a feeling of suffocation.

The expression of his face when he uttered that "yes" was dreadful. Having uttered it, he looked her straight in the eyes, turned on his face with a rapidity extraordinary in his weak state and shouted:

"Go away! Go away and leave me alone!"

XII

From that moment the screaming began that continued for three days, and was so terrible that one could not hear it through two closed doors without horror. At the moment he answered his wife he realized that he was lost, that there was no return, that the end had come, the very end, and his doubts were still unsolved and remained doubts.

"Oh! Oh! Oh!" he cried in various intonations. He had begun by screaming "I won't!" and continued screaming on the letter O.

For three whole days, during which time did not exist for him, he struggled in that black sack into which he was being thrust by an invisible, resistless force. He struggled as a man condemned to death struggles in the hands of the executioner, knowing that he cannot save himself. And every moment he felt that despite all his efforts he was drawing nearer and nearer to what terrified him. He felt that his agony was due to his being thrust into that black hole and still more to his not being able to get right into it. He was hindered from getting into it by his conviction that his life had been a good one. That very justification of his life held him fast and prevented his moving forward, and it caused him most torment of all.

Suddenly some force struck him in the chest and side, making it still harder to breathe, and he fell through the hole and there at the bottom was a light. What had happened to him was like the sensation one sometimes experiences in a railway carriage when one thinks one is going backwards while one is really going forwards and suddenly becomes aware of the real direction.

"Yes, it was all not the right thing," he said to himself, "but that's no matter. It can be done. But what *is* the right thing?" he asked himself, and suddenly grew quiet.

This occurred at the end of the third day, two hours before his death. Just then his schoolboy son had crept softly in and gone up to the bedside. The dying man was still screaming desperately and waving his arms. His hand fell on the boy's head, and the boy caught it, pressed it to his lips, and began to cry.

At that very moment Ivan Ilych fell through and caught sight of the light, and it was revealed to him that though his life had not been what it should have been, this could still be rectified. He asked himself, "What *is* the right thing?" and grew still, listening. Then he felt that someone was kissing his hand. He opened his eyes, looked at his son, and felt sorry for him. His wife came up to him and he glanced at her. She was gazing at him open-mouthed, with undried tears on her nose and cheek and a despairing look on her face. He felt sorry for her too.

"Yes, I am making them wretched," he thought. "They are sorry, but it will be better for them when I die." He wished to say this but had not the strength to utter it. "Besides, why speak? I must act," he thought. With a look at his wife he indicated his son and said: "Take him away . . . sorry for him . . . sorry for you too. . . ." He tried to add, "Forgive me," but said "forgo" and waved his hand, knowing that He whose understanding mattered would understand.

And suddenly it grew clear to him that what had been oppressing him and would not leave him was all dropping away at once from two sides, from ten sides, and from all sides. He was sorry for them, he must act so as not to hurt them: release them and free himself from these sufferings. "How good and how simple!" he thought. "And the pain?" he asked himself. "What has become of it? Where are you, pain?"

He turned his attention to it.

"Yes, here it is. Well, what of it? Let the pain be."

"And death . . . where is it?"

He sought his former accustomed fear of death and did not find it. "Where is it? What death?" There was no fear because there was no death.

In place of death there was light.

"So that's what it is!" he suddenly exclaimed aloud. "What joy!"

To him all this happened in a single instant, and the meaning of that instant did not change. For those present his agony continued for another two hours. Something rattled in his throat, his emaciated body twitched, then the gasping and rattle became less and less frequent.

"It is finished!" said someone near him.

He heard these words and repeated them in his soul.

"Death is finished," he said to himself. "It is no more!"

He drew in a breath, stopped in the midst of a sigh, stretched out, and died.

THE SECRET SHARER

Joseph Conrad (1857–1924)

I

On my right hand there were lines of fishing-stakes resembling a mysterious system of half-submerged bamboo fences, incomprehensible in its division of the domain of tropical fishes, and crazy of aspect as if abandoned for ever by some nomad tribe of fishermen now gone to the other end of the ocean; for there was no sign of human habitation as far as the eye could reach. To the left a group of barren islets, suggesting ruins of stone walls, towers, and blockhouses, had its foundations set in a blue sea that itself looked solid, so still and stable did it lie below my feet; even the track of light from the westering sun shone smoothly, without that animated glitter which tells of an imperceptible ripple. And when I turned my head to take a parting glance at the tug which had just left us anchored outside the bar, I saw the straight line of the flat shore joined to the stable sea, edge to edge, with a perfect and unmarked closeness, in one levelled floor half brown, half blue under the enormous dome of the sky. Corresponding in their insignificance to the islets of the sea, two small clumps of trees, one on each side of the only fault in the impeccable joint, marked the mouth of the river Meinam[1] we had just left on the first preparatory stage of our homeward journey; and, far back on the inland level, a larger and loftier mass, the grove surrounding the great Paknam pagoda, was the only thing on which the eye could rest from the vain task of exploring the monotonous sweep of the horizon. Here and there gleams as of a few scattered pieces of silver marked the windings of the great river; and on the nearest of them, just within the bar, the tug steaming right into the land became lost to my sight, hull and funnel and masts, as though the impassive earth had swallowed her up without an effort, without a tremor. My eye followed the light cloud of her smoke, now here, now there, above the plain, according to the devious curves of the stream, but always fainter and farther away, till I lost it at last behind the mitre-shaped hill of the great pagoda. And then I was left alone with my ship, anchored at the head of the Gulf of Siam.

She floated at the starting-point of a long journey, very still in an immense stillness, the shadows of her spars flung far to the eastward by the setting sun. At that moment I was alone on her decks. There was not a sound in her—and around us nothing moved, nothing lived, not a canoe on the water, not a bird in the air, not a cloud in the sky. In this breathless pause at the threshold of a long passage we seemed to be measuring our fitness for a long and arduous enter-

[1] The Chao Phraya River, running through the heart of Bangkok, past the Paknam pagoda, and into the Gulf of Siam.

prise, the appointed task of both our existences to be carried out, far from all human eyes, with only sky and sea for spectators and for judges.

There must have been some glare in the air to interfere with one's sight, because it was only just before the sun left us that my roaming eyes made out beyond the highest ridge of the principal islet of the group something which did away with the solemnity of perfect solitude. The tide of darkness flowed on swiftly; and with tropical suddenness a swarm of stars came out above the shadowy earth, while I lingered yet, my hand resting lightly on my ship's rail as if on the shoulder of a trusted friend. But, with all that multitude of celestial bodies staring down at one, the comfort of quiet communion with her was gone for good. And there were also disturbing sounds by this time—voices, footsteps forward; the steward flitted along the maindeck, a busily ministering spirit; a hand-bell tinkled urgently under the poop-deck. . . .

I found my two officers waiting for me near the supper table, in the lighted cuddy. We sat down at once, and as I helped the chief mate, I said:

"Are you aware that there is a ship anchored inside the islands? I saw her mastheads above the ridge as the sun went down."

He raised sharply his simple face, overcharged by a terrible growth of whisker, and emitted his usual ejaculations: "Bless my soul, sir! You don't say so!"

My second mate was a round-cheeked, silent young man, grave beyond his years, I thought; but as our eyes happened to meet I detected a slight quiver on his lips. I looked down at once. It was not my part to encourage sneering on board my ship. It must be said, too, that I knew very little of my officers. In consequence of certain events of no particular significance, except to myself, I had been appointed to the command only a fortnight before. Neither did I know much of the hands forward. All these people had been together for eighteen months or so, and my position was that of the only stranger on board. I mention this because it has some bearing on what is to follow. But what I felt most was my being a stranger to the ship; and if all the truth must be told, I was somewhat of a stranger to myself. The youngest man on board (barring the second mate), and untried as yet by a position of the fullest responsibility, I was willing to take the adequacy of the others for granted. They had simply to be equal to their tasks; but I wondered how far I should turn out faithful to that ideal conception of one's own personality every man sets up for himself secretly.

Meanwhile the chief mate, with an almost visible effect of collaboration on the part of his round eyes and frightful whiskers, was trying to evolve a theory of the anchored ship. His dominant trait was to take all things into earnest consideration. He was of a painstaking turn of mind. As he used to say, he "liked to account to himself" for practically everything that came in his way, down to a miserable scorpion he had found in his cabin a week before. The why and the wherefore of that scorpion—how it got on board and came to select his room rather than the pantry (which was a dark place and more what a scorpion would be partial to), and how on earth it managed to drown itself in the inkwell of his writing-desk—had exercised him infinitely. The ship within the islands was much more easily accounted for; and just as we were about to rise from table he made his pronouncement. She was, he doubted not, a ship from home lately arrived. Probably she drew too much water to cross the bar except at the top of spring tides. Therefore she went into that natural harbour to wait for a few days in preference to remaining in an open roadstead.

"That's so," confirmed the second mate, suddenly, in his slightly hoarse voice. "She draws over twenty feet. She's the Liverpool ship *Sephora* with a cargo of coal. Hundred and twenty-three days from Cardiff." We looked at him in surprise.

"The tugboat skipper told me when he came on board for your letters, sir," explained the young man. "He expects to take her up the river the day after tomorrow."

After thus overwhelming us with the extent of his information he slipped out of the cabin. The mate observed regretfully that he "could not account for that young fellow's whims." What prevented him telling us all about it at once, he wanted to know.

I detained him as he was making a move. For the last two days the crew had had plenty of hard work, and the night before they had very little sleep. I felt painfully that I—a stranger—was doing something unusual when I directed him to let all hands turn in without setting an anchor-watch. I proposed to keep on deck myself till one o'clock or thereabouts. I would get the second mate to relieve me at that hour.

"He will turn out the cook and the steward at four," I concluded, "and then give you a call. Of course at the slightest sign of any sort of wind we'll have the hands up and make a start at once."

He concealed his astonishment. "Very well, sir." Outside the cuddy he put his head in the second mate's door to inform him of my unheard-of caprice to take a five hours' anchor-watch on myself. I heard the other raise his voice incredulously—"What? The Captain himself?" Then a few more murmurs, a door closed, then another. A few moments later I went on deck.

My strangeness, which had made me sleepless, had prompted that unconventional arrangement, as if I had expected in those solitary hours of the night to get on terms with the ship of which I knew nothing, manned by men of whom I knew very little more. Fast alongside a wharf, littered like any ship in port with a tangle of unrelated things, invaded by unrelated shore people, I had hardly seen her yet properly. Now, as she lay cleared for sea, the stretch of her main-deck seemed to me very fine under the stars. Very fine, very roomy for her size, and very inviting. I descended the poop and paced the waist, my mind picturing to myself the coming passage through the Malay Archipelago, down the Indian Ocean, and up the Atlantic. All its phases were familiar enough to me, every characteristic, all the alternatives which were likely to face me on the high seas—everything! . . . except the novel responsibility of command. But I took heart from the reasonable thought that the ship was like other ships, the men like other men, and that the sea was not likely to keep any special surprises expressly for my discomfiture.

Arrived at that comforting conclusion, I bethought myself of a cigar and went below to get it. All was still down there. Everybody at the after end of the ship was sleeping profoundly. I came out again on the quarter-deck, agreeably at ease in my sleeping-suit on that warm breathless night, barefooted, a glowing cigar in my teeth, and, going forward, I was met by the profound silence of the fore end of the ship. Only as I passed the door of the forecastle I heard a deep, quiet, trustful sigh of some sleeper inside. And suddenly I rejoiced in the great security of the sea as compared with the unrest of the land, in my choice of that untempted life presenting no disquieting problems, invested with an elementary moral beauty by the absolute straightforwardness of its appeal and by the singleness of its purpose.

The riding-light in the fore-rigging burned with a clear, untroubled, as if symbolic, flame, confident and bright in the mysterious shades of the night. Passing on my way aft along the other side of the ship, I observed that the rope side-ladder, put over, no doubt, for the master of the tug when he came to fetch away our letters, had not been hauled in as it should have been. I became annoyed at this, for exactitude in small matters is the very soul of discipline. Then I reflected that I had myself peremptorily dismissed my officers from duty, and by my own act had prevented the anchor-watch being formally set and things properly attended to. I asked myself whether it was wise ever to interfere with the established routine of duties even from the kindest of motives. My action might have made me appear eccentric. Goodness only knew how that absurdly whiskered mate would "account" for my conduct, and what the whole ship thought of that informality of their new captain. I was vexed with myself.

Not from compunction certainly, but, as it were mechanically, I proceeded to get the ladder in myself. Now a side-ladder of that sort is a light affair and comes in easily, yet my vigorous tug, which should have brought it flying on board, merely recoiled upon my body in a totally unexpected jerk. What the devil! . . . I was so astounded by the immovableness of that ladder that I remained stock-still, trying to account for it to myself like that imbecile mate of mine. In the end, of course, I put my head over the rail.

The side of the ship made an opaque belt of shadow on the darkling glassy shimmer of the sea. But I saw at once something elongated and pale floating very close to the ladder. Before I could form a guess a faint flash of phosphorescent light, which seemed to issue suddenly from the naked body of a man, flickered in the sleeping water with the elusive, silent play of summer lightning in a night sky. With a gasp I saw revealed to my stare a pair of feet, the long legs, a broad livid back immersed right up to the neck in a greenish cadaverous glow. One hand, awash, clutched the bottom rung of the ladder. He was complete but for the head. A headless corpse! The cigar dropped out of my gaping mouth with a tiny plop and a short hiss quite audible in the absolute stillness of all things under heaven. At that I suppose he raised up his face, a dimly pale oval in the shadow of the ship's side. But even then I could only barely make out down there the shape of his black-haired head. However, it was enough for the horrid, frostbound sensation which had gripped me about the chest to pass off. The moment of vain exclamations was past, too. I only climbed on the spare spar and leaned over the rail as far as I could, to bring my eyes nearer to that mystery floating alongside.

As he hung by the ladder, like a resting swimmer, the sea-lightning played about his limbs at every stir; and he appeared in it ghastly, silvery, fish-like. He remained as mute as a fish, too. He made no motion to get out of the water, either. It was inconceivable that he should not attempt to come on board, and strangely troubling to suspect that perhaps he did not want to. And my first words were prompted by just that troubled incertitude.

"What's the matter?" I asked in my ordinary tone, speaking down to the face upturned exactly under mine.

"Cramp," it answered, no louder. Then slightly anxious, "I say, no need to call any one."

"I was not going to," I said.

"Are you alone on deck?"

"Yes."

I had somehow the impression that he was on the point of letting go the ladder to swim away beyond my ken—mysterious as he came. But, for the moment, this being appearing as if he had risen from the bottom of the sea (it was certainly the nearest land to the ship) wanted only to know the time. I told him. And he, down there, tentatively:

"I suppose your captain's turned in?"

"I am sure he isn't," I said.

He seemed to struggle with himself, for I heard something like the low, bitter murmur of doubt. "What's the good?" His next words came out with a hesitating effort.

"Look here, my man. Could you call him out quietly?"

I thought the time had come to declare myself.

"*I* am the captain."

I heard a "By Jove!" whispered at the level of the water. The phosphorescence flashed in the swirl of the water all about his limbs, his other hand seized the ladder.

"My name's Leggatt."

The voice was calm and resolute. A good voice. The self-possession of that man had somehow induced a corresponding state in myself. It was very quietly that I remarked:

"You must be a good swimmer."

"Yes. I've been in the water practically since nine o'clock. The question for me now is whether I am to let go this ladder and go on swimming till I sink from exhaustion, or—to come on board here."

I felt this was no mere formula of desperate speech, but a real alternative in the view of a strong soul. I should have gathered from this that he was young; indeed, it is only the young who are ever confronted by such clear issues. But at this time it was pure intuition on my part. A mysterious communication was established already between us two—in the face of that silent, darkened tropical sea. I was young, too; young enough to make no comment. The man in the water began suddenly to climb up the ladder, and I hastened away from the rail to fetch some clothes.

Before entering the cabin I stood still, listening in the lobby at the foot of the stairs. A faint snore came through the closed door of the chief mate's room. The second mate's door was on the hook, but the darkness in there was absolutely soundless. He, too, was young and could sleep like a stone. Remained the steward, but he was not likely to wake up before he was called. I got a sleeping-suit out of my room and, coming back on deck, saw the naked man from the sea sitting on the main-hatch, glimmering white in the darkness, his elbows on his knees and his head in his hands. In a moment he had concealed his damp body in a sleeping-suit of the same grey-stripe pattern as the one I was wearing and followed me like my double on the poop. Together we moved right aft, barefooted, silent.

"What is it?" I asked in a deadened voice, taking the lighted lamp out of the binnacle, and raising it to his face.

"An ugly business."

He had rather regular features; a good mouth; light eyes under somewhat heavy, dark eyebrows; a smooth, square forehead; no growth on his cheeks; a small, brown moustache, and a well-shaped, round chin. His expression was concentrated, meditative, under the inspecting light of the lamp I held up to his face; such as a man thinking hard in solitude might wear. My sleeping-suit was just right for his size. A well-knit young fellow of twenty-five at most. He caught his lower lip with the edge of white, even teeth.

"Yes," I said, replacing the lamp in the binnacle. The warm, heavy tropical night closed upon his head again.

"There's a ship over there," he murmured.

"Yes, I know. The *Sephora*. Did you know of us?"

"Hadn't the slightest idea. I am the mate of her—" He paused and corrected himself. "I should say I *was*."

"Aha! Something wrong?"

"Yes. Very wrong indeed. I've killed a man."

"What do you mean? Just now?"

"No, on the passage. Weeks ago. Thirty-nine south. When I say a man—"

"Fit of temper," I suggested, confidently.

The shadowy, dark head, like mine, seemed to nod imperceptibly above the ghostly grey of my sleeping-suit. It was, in the night, as though I had been faced by my own reflection in the depths of a sombre and immense mirror.

"A pretty thing to have to own up to for a Conway[2] boy," murmured my double, distinctly.

"You're a Conway boy?"

"I am," he said, as if startled. Then, slowly . . . "Perhaps you too—"

It was so; but being a couple of years older I had left before he joined. After a quick interchange of dates a silence fell; and I thought suddenly of my absurd mate with his terrific whiskers and the "Bless my soul—you don't say so" type of intellect. My double gave me an inkling of his thoughts by saying: "My father's a parson in Norfolk. Do you see me before a judge and jury on that charge? For myself I can't see the necessity. There are fellows that an angel from heaven— And I am not that. He was one of those creatures that are just simmering all the time with a silly sort of wickedness. Miserable devils that have no business to live at all. He wouldn't do his duty and wouldn't let anybody else do theirs. But what's the good of talking! You know well enough the sort of ill-conditioned snarling cur—"

He appealed to me as if our experiences had been as identical as our clothes. And I knew well enough the pestiferous danger of such a character where there

[2] A British training ship.

are no means of legal repression. And I knew well enough also that my double
there was no homicidal ruffian. I did not think of asking him for details, and he
told me the story roughly in brusque, disconnected sentences. I needed no more.
I saw it all going on as though I were myself inside that other sleeping-suit.

"It happened while we were setting a reefed foresail, at dusk. Reefed foresail!
You understand the sort of weather. The only sail we had left to keep the ship
running; so you may guess what it had been like for days. Anxious sort of job,
that. He gave me some of his cursed insolence at the sheet. I tell you I was over-
done with this terrific weather that seemed to have no end to it. Terrific, I tell
you—and a deep ship. I believe the fellow himself was half crazed with funk. It
was no time for gentlemanly reproof, so I turned round and felled him like an
ox. He up and at me. We closed just as an awful sea made for the ship. All hands
saw it coming and took to the rigging, but I had him by the throat, and went on
shaking him like a rat, the men above us yelling, 'Look out! look out!' " Then a
crash as if the sky had fallen on my head. They say that for over ten minutes
hardly anything was to be seen of the ship—just the three masts and a bit of the
forecastle head and of the poop all awash driving along in a smother of foam. It
was a miracle that they found us, jammed together behind the forebits. It's clear
that I meant business, because I was holding him by the throat still when they
picked us up. He was black in the face. It was too much for them. It seems they
rushed us aft together, gripped as we were, screaming 'Murder!' like a lot of lunatics, and broke into the cuddy. And the ship running for her life, touch and go
all the time, any minute her last in a sea fit to turn your hair grey only a-looking
at it. I understand that the skipper, too, started raving like the rest of them. The
man had been deprived of sleep for more than a week, and to have this sprung
on him at the height of a furious gale nearly drove him out of his mind. I wonder
they didn't fling me overboard after getting the carcass of their precious ship-
mate out of my fingers. They had rather a job to separate us, I've been told. A sufficiently fierce story to make an old judge and a respectable jury sit up a bit. The
first thing I heard when I came to myself was the maddening howling of that
endless gale, and on that the voice of the old man. He was hanging on to my
bunk, staring into my face out of his sou'wester.

" 'Mr. Leggatt, you have killed a man. You can act no longer as chief mate of
this ship.' "

His care to subdue his voice made it sound monotonous. He rested a hand on
the end of the skylight to steady himself with, and all that time did not stir a
limb, so far as I could see. "Nice little tale for a quiet tea-party," he concluded in
the same tone.

One of my hands, too, rested on the end of the skylight; neither did I stir a
limb, so far as I knew. We stood less than a foot from each other. It occurred to
me that if old "Bless my soul—you don't say so" were to put his head up the
companion and catch sight of us, he would think he was seeing double, or imagine himself come upon a scene of weird witchcraft; the strange captain having a
quiet confabulation by the wheel with his own grey ghost. I became very much
concerned to prevent anything of the sort. I heard the other's soothing undertone.

"My father's a parson in Norfolk," it said. Evidently he had forgotten he had
told me this important fact before. Truly a nice little tale.

"You had better slip down into my stateroom now," I said, moving off stealth-ily. My double followed my movements; our bare feet made no sound; I let him in, closed the door with care, and, after giving a call to the second mate, returned on deck for my relief.

"Not much sign of any wind yet," I remarked when he approached.

"No, sir. Not much," he assented, sleepily, in his hoarse voice, with just enough deference, no more, and barely suppressing a yawn.

"Well, that's all you have to look out for. You have got your orders."

"Yes, sir."

I paced a turn or two on the poop and saw him take up his position face for-ward with his elbow in the ratlines of the mizzen-rigging before I went below. The mate's faint snoring was still going on peacefully. The cuddy lamp was burning over the table on which stood a vase with flowers, a polite attention from the ship's provision merchant—the last flowers we should see for the next three months at the very least. Two bunches of bananas hung from the beam symmetrically, one on each side of the rudder-casing. Everything was as before in the ship—except that two of her captain's sleeping-suits were simultaneously in use, one motionless in the cuddy, the other keeping very still in the captain's stateroom.

It must be explained here that my cabin had the form of the capital letter L the door being within the angle and opening into the short part of the letter. A couch was to the left, the bed-place to the right; my writing-desk and the chrono-meters' table faced the door. But any one opening it, unless he stepped right in-side, had no view of what I call the long (or vertical) part of the letter. It con-tained some lockers surmounted by a bookcase; and a few clothes, a thick jacket or two, caps, oilskin coat, and such like, hung on hooks. There was at the bottom of that part a door opening into my bath-room, which could be entered also di-rectly from the saloon. But that way was never used.

The mysterious arrival had discovered the advantage of this particular shape. Entering my room, lighted strongly by a big bulkhead lamp swung on gimbals above my writing-desk, I did not see him anywhere till he stepped out quietly from behind the coats hung in the recessed part.

"I heard somebody moving about, and went in there at once," he whispered.

I, too, spoke under my breath.

"Nobody is likely to come in here without knocking and getting permission."

He nodded. His face was thin and the sunburn faded, as though he had been ill. And no wonder. He had been, I heard presently, kept under arrest in his cabin for nearly seven weeks. But there was nothing sickly in his eyes or in his expression. He was not a bit like me, really; yet, as we stood leaning over my bed-place, whispering side by side, with our dark heads together and our backs to the door, anybody bold enough to open it stealthily would have been treated to the uncanny sight of a double captain busy talking in whispers with his other self.

"But all this doesn't tell me how you came to hang on to our side-ladder," I in-quired, in the hardly audible murmurs we used, after he had told me something more of the proceedings on board the *Sephora* once the bad weather was over.

"When we sighted Java Head I had had time to think all those matters out several times over. I had six weeks of doing nothing else, and with only an hour or so every evening for a tramp on the quarter-deck."

He whispered, his arms folded on the side of my bed-place, staring through the open port. And I could imagine perfectly the manner of this thinking out—a stubborn if not a steadfast operation; something of which I should have been perfectly incapable.

"I reckoned it would be dark before we closed with the land," he continued, so low that I had to strain my hearing, near as we were to each other, shoulder touching shoulder almost. "So I asked to speak to the old man. He always seemed very sick when he came to see me—as if he could not look me in the face. You know, that foresail saved the ship. She was too deep to have run long under bare poles. And it was I that managed to set it for him. Anyway, he came. When I had him in my cabin—he stood by the door looking at me as if I had the halter round my neck already—I asked him right away to leave my cabin door unlocked at night while the ship was going through Sunda Straits. There would be the Java coast within two or three miles, off Angier Point. I wanted nothing more. I've had a prize for swimming my second year in the Conway."

"I can believe it," I breathed out.

"God only knows why they locked me in every night. To see some of their faces you'd have thought they were afraid I'd go about at night strangling people. Am I a murdering brute? Do I look it? By Jove! If I had been he wouldn't have trusted himself like that into my room. You'll say I might have chucked him aside and bolted out, there and then—it was dark already. Well, no. And for the same reason I wouldn't think of trying to smash the door. There would have been a rush to stop me at the noise, and I did not mean to get into a confounded scrimmage. Somebody else might have got killed—for I would not have broken out only to get chucked back, and I did not want any more of that work. He refused, looking more sick than ever. He was afraid of the men, and also of that old second mate of his who had been sailing with him for years—a grey-headed old humbug; and his steward, too, had been with him devil knows how long—seventeen years or more—a dogmatic sort of loafer who hated me like poison, just because I was the chief mate. No chief mate ever made more than one voyage in the *Sephora*, you know. Those two old chaps ran the ship. Devil only knows what the skipper wasn't afraid of (all his nerve went to pieces altogether in that hellish spell of bad weather we had)—of what the law would do to him—of his wife, perhaps. Oh, yes! she's on board. Though I don't think she would have meddled. She would have been only too glad to have me out of the ship in any way. The 'brand of Cain'[3] business, don't you see. That's all right. I was ready enough to go off wandering on the face of the earth—and that was price enough to pay for an Abel of that sort. Anyhow, he wouldn't listen to me. 'This thing must take its course. I represent the law here.' He was shaking like a leaf. 'So you won't?' 'No!' 'Then I hope you will be able to sleep on that,' I said, and turned my back on him. 'I wonder that *you* can,' cries he, and locks the door.

---

[3] After Cain killed his brother Abel, the Lord made him "a fugitive and a vagabond" and then "the Lord set a mark upon Cain, lest any finding him should kill him" (Genesis iv.14–15).

"Well, after that, I couldn't. Not very well. That was three weeks ago. We have had a slow passage through the Java Sea; drifted about Carimata[4] for ten days. When we anchored here they thought, I suppose, it was all right. The nearest land (and that's five miles) is the ship's destination; the consul would soon set about catching me; and there would have been no object in bolting to these islets there. I don't suppose there's a drop of water on them. I don't know how it was, but to-night that steward, after bringing me my supper, went out to let me eat it, and left the door unlocked. And I ate it—all there was, too. After I had finished I strolled out on the quarter-deck. I don't know that I meant to do anything. A breath of fresh air was all I wanted, I believe. Then a sudden temptation came over me. I kicked off my slippers and was in the water before I had made up my mind fairly. Somebody heard the splash and they raised an awful hullabaloo. 'He's gone! Lower the boats! He's committed suicide! No, he's swimming.' Certainly I was swimming. It's not so easy for a swimmer like me to commit suicide by drowning. I landed on the nearest islet before the boat left the ship's side. I heard them pulling about in the dark, hailing, and so on, but after a bit they gave up. Everything quieted down and the anchorage became as still as death. I sat down on a stone and began to think. I felt certain they would start searching for me at daylight. There was no place to hide on those stony things—and if there had been, what would have been the good? But now I was clear of that ship, I was not going back. So after a while I took off all my clothes, tied them up in a bundle with a stone inside, and dropped them in the deep water on the outer side of that islet. That was suicide enough for me. Let them think what they liked, but I didn't mean to drown myself. I meant to swim till I sank—but that's not the same thing. I struck out for another of these little islands, and it was from that one that I first saw your riding-light. Something to swim for. I went on easily, and on the way I came upon a flat rock a foot or two above water. In the daytime, I dare say, you might make it out with a glass from your poop. I scrambled up on it and rested myself for a bit. Then I made another start. That last spell must have been over a mile."

His whisper was getting fainter and fainter, and all the time he stared straight out through the port-hole, in which there was not even a star to be seen. I had not interrupted him. There was something that made comment impossible in his narrative, or perhaps in himself; a sort of feeling, a quality, which I can't find a name for. And when he ceased, all I found was a futile whisper: "So you swam for our light?"

"Yes—straight for it. It was something to swim for. I couldn't see any stars low down because the coast was in the way, and I couldn't see the land, either. The water was like glass. One might have been swimming in a confounded thousand-feet deep cistern with no place for scrambling out anywhere; but what I didn't like was the notion of swimming round and round like a crazed bullock before I gave out; and as I didn't mean to go back . . . No. Do you see me being hauled back, stark naked, off one of these little islands by the scruff of the neck and fighting like a wild beast? Somebody would have got killed for certain, and I did not want any of that. So I went on. Then your ladder—"

"Why didn't you hail the ship?" I asked, a little louder.

[4] The Karimata islands, near Borneo.

He touched my shoulder lightly. Lazy footsteps came right over our heads and stopped. The second mate had crossed from the other side of the poop and might have been hanging over the rail, for all we knew.

"He couldn't hear us talking—could he?" My double breathed into my very ear, anxiously.

His anxiety was an answer, a sufficient answer, to the question I had put to him. An answer containing all the difficulty of that situation. I closed the port-hole quietly, to make sure. A louder word might have been overheard.

"Who's that?" he whispered then.

"My second mate. But I don't know much more of the fellow than you do."

And I told him a little about myself. I had been appointed to take charge while I least expected anything of the sort, not quite a fortnight ago. I didn't know either the ship or the people. Hadn't had the time in port to look about me or size anybody up. And as to the crew, all they knew was that I was appointed to take the ship home. For the rest, I was almost as much of a stranger on board as himself, I said. And at the moment I felt it most acutely. I felt that it would take very little to make me a suspect person in the eyes of the ship's company.

He had turned about meantime; and we, the two strangers in the ship, faced each other in identical attitudes.

"Your ladder—" he murmured, after a silence. "Who'd have thought of finding a ladder hanging over at night in a ship anchored out here! I felt just then a very unpleasant faintness. After the life I've been leading for nine weeks, anybody would have got out of condition. I wasn't capable of swimming round as far as your rudder-chains. And, lo and behold! there was a ladder to get hold of. After I gripped it I said to myself, 'What's the good?' When I saw a man's head looking over I thought I would swim away presently and leave him shouting—in whatever language it was. I didn't mind being looked at. I—I liked it. And then you speaking to me so quietly—as if you had expected me—made me hold on a little longer. It had been a confounded lonely time—I don't mean while swimming. I was glad to talk a little to somebody that didn't belong to the *Sephora*. As to asking for the captain, that was a mere impulse. It could have been no use, with all the ship knowing about me and the other people pretty certain to be round here in the morning. I don't know—I wanted to be seen, to talk with somebody, before I went on. I don't know what I would have said.... 'Fine night, isn't it?' or something of the sort."

"Do you think they will be round here presently?" I asked with some incredulity.

"Quite likely," he said, faintly.

He looked extremely haggard all of a sudden. His head rolled on his shoulders.

"H'm. We shall see then. Meantime get into that bed," I whispered. "Want help? There."

It was a rather high bed-place with a set of drawers underneath. This amazing swimmer really needed the lift I gave him by seizing his leg. He tumbled in, rolled over on his back, and flung one arm across his eyes. And then, with his face nearly hidden, he must have looked exactly as I used to look in that bed. I gazed upon my other self for a while before drawing across carefully the two green serge curtains which ran on a brass rod. I thought for a moment of pinning them together for greater safety, but I sat down on the couch, and once there I felt unwilling to rise and hunt for a pin. I would do it in a moment. I was extremely tired, in a peculiarly intimate way, by the strain of stealthiness, by the effort of whispering and the general secrecy of this excitement. It was three o'clock by now and I had been on my feet since nine, but I was not sleepy; I could not have gone to sleep. I sat there, fagged out, looking at the curtains, trying to clear my mind of the confused sensation of being in two places at once, and greatly bothered by an exasperating knocking in my head. It was a relief to discover suddenly that it was not in my head at all, but on the outside of the door. Before I could collect myself the words "Come in" were out of my mouth, and the steward entered with a tray, bringing in my morning coffee. I had slept, after all, and I was so frightened that I shouted, "This way! I am here, steward," as though he had been miles away. He put down the tray on the table next the couch and only then said, very quietly, "I can see you are here, sir." I felt him give me a keen look, but I dared not meet his eyes just then. He must have wondered why I had drawn the curtains of my bed before going to sleep on the couch. He went out, hooking the door open as usual.

I heard the crew washing decks above me. I knew I would have been told at once if there had been any wind. Calm, I thought, and I was doubly vexed. Indeed, I felt dual more than ever. The steward reappeared suddenly in the doorway. I jumped up from the couch so quickly that he gave a start.

"What do you want here?"

"Close your port, sir—they are washing decks."

"It is closed," I said, reddening.

"Very well, sir." But he did not move from the doorway and returned my stare in an extraordinary, equivocal manner for a time. Then his eyes wavered, all his expression changed, and in a voice unusually gentle, almost coaxingly:

"May I come in to take the empty cup away, sir?"

"Of course!" I turned my back on him while he popped in and out. Then I unhooked and closed the door and even pushed the bolt. This sort of thing could not go on very long. The cabin was as hot as an oven, too. I took a peep at my double, and discovered that he had not moved, his arm was still over his eyes; but his chest heaved; his hair was wet; his chin glistened with perspiration. I reached over him and opened the port.

"I must show myself on deck," I reflected.

Of course, theoretically, I could do what I liked, with no one to say nay to me within the whole circle of the horizon; but to lock my cabin door and take the key away I did not dare. Directly I put my head out of the companion I saw the group of my two officers, the second mate barefooted, the chief mate in long india-rubber boots, near the break of the poop, and the steward half-way down the poop-ladder talking to them eagerly. He happened to catch sight of me and dived, the second ran down on the main-deck shouting some order or other, and the chief mate came to meet me, touching his cap.

There was a sort of curiosity in his eye that I did not like. I don't know whether the steward had told them that I was "queer" only, or downright drunk, but I know the man meant to have a good look at me. I watched him coming with a smile which, as he got into point-blank range, took effect and froze his very whiskers. I did not give him time to open his lips.

"Square the yards by lifts and braces before the hands go to breakfast."

It was the first particular order I had given on board that ship; and I stayed on deck to see it executed, too. I had felt the need of asserting myself without loss of time. That sneering young cub got taken down a peg or two on that occasion, and I also seized the opportunity of having a good look at the face of every fore-mast man as they filed past me to go to the after braces. At breakfast time, eating nothing myself, I presided with such frigid dignity that the two mates were only too glad to escape from the cabin as soon as decency permitted; and all the time the dual working of my mind distracted me almost to the point of insanity. I was constantly watching myself, my secret self, as dependent on my actions as my own personality, sleeping in that bed, behind that door which faced me as I sat at the head of the table. It was very much like being mad, only it was worse because one was aware of it.

I had to shake him for a solid minute, but when at last he opened his eyes it was in the full possession of his senses, with an inquiring look.

"All's well so far," I whispered. "Now you must vanish into the bath-room."

He did so, as noiseless as a ghost, and then I rang for the steward, and facing him boldly, directed him to tidy up my stateroom while I was having my bath— "and be quick about it." As my tone admitted of no excuses, he said, "Yes, sir," and ran off to fetch his dust-pan and brushes. I took a bath and did most of my dressing, splashing, and whistling softly for the steward's edification, while the secret sharer of my life stood drawn up bolt upright in that little space, his face looking very sunken in daylight, his eyelids lowered under the stern, dark line of his eyebrows drawn together by a slight frown.

When I left him there to go back to my room the steward was finishing dust-ing. I sent for the mate and engaged him in some insignificant conversation. It was, as it were, trifling with the terrific character of his whiskers; but my object was to give him an opportunity for a good look at my cabin. And then I could at last shut, with a clear conscience, the door of my stateroom and get my double back into the recessed part. There was nothing else for it. He had to sit still on a small folding stool, half smothered by the heavy coats hanging there. We lis-tened to the steward going into the bath-room out of the saloon, filling the wa-ter-bottles there, scrubbing the bath, setting things to rights, whisk, bang, clat-ter—out again into the saloon—turn the key—click. Such was my scheme for keeping my second self invisible. Nothing better could be contrived under the circumstances. And there we sat; I at my writing-desk ready to appear busy with some papers, he behind me out of sight of the door. It would not have been pru-dent to talk in daytime; and I could not have stood the excitement of that queer sense of whispering to myself. Now and then, glancing over my shoulder, I saw him far back there, sitting rigidly on the low stool, his bare feet close together, his arms folded, his head hanging on his breast—and perfectly still. Anybody would have taken him for me.

I was fascinated by it myself. Every moment I had to glance over my shoulder. I was looking at him when a voice outside the door said:

"Beg pardon, sir."

"Well!" . . . I kept my eyes on him, and so when the voice outside the door an-nounced, "There's a ship's boat coming our way, sir," I saw him give a start—the first movement he had made for hours. But he did not raise his bowed head.

"All right. Get the ladder over."

I hesitated. Should I whisper something to him? But what? His immobility seemed to have been never disturbed. What could I tell him he did not know already? . . . Finally I went on deck.

II

The skipper of the *Sephora* had a thin red whisker all round his face, and the sort of complexion that goes with hair of that colour; also the particular, rather smeary shade of blue in the eyes. He was not exactly a showy figure; his shoulders were high, his stature but middling—one leg slightly more bandy than the other. He shook hands, looking vaguely around. A spiritless tenacity was his main characteristic, I judged. I behaved with a politeness which seemed to disconcert him. Perhaps he was shy. He mumbled to me as if he were ashamed of what he was saying; gave his name (it was something like Archbold—but at this distance of years I hardly am sure), his ship's name, and a few other particulars of that sort, in the manner of a criminal making a reluctant and doleful confession. He had had terrible weather on the passage out—terrible—terrible—wife aboard, too.

By this time we were seated in the cabin and the steward brought in a tray with a bottle and glasses. "Thanks! No." Never took liquor. Would have some water, though. He drank two tumblerfuls. Terrible thirsty work. Ever since daylight had been exploring the islands round his ship.

"What was that for—fun?" I asked, with an appearance of polite interest.

"No!" He sighed. "Painful duty."

As he persisted in his mumbling and I wanted my double to hear every word, I hit upon the notion of informing him that I regretted to say I was hard of hearing.

"Such a young man, too!" he nodded, keeping his smeary blue, unintelligent eyes fastened upon me. "What was the cause of it—some disease?" he inquired, without the least sympathy and as if he thought that, if so, I'd got no more than I deserved.

"Yes; disease," I admitted in a cheerful tone which seemed to shock him. But my point was gained, because he had to raise his voice to give me his tale. It is not worth while to record that version. It was just over two months since all this had happened, and he had thought so much about it that he seemed completely muddled as to its bearings, but still immensely impressed.

"What would you think of such a thing happening on board your own ship? I've had the *Sephora* for these fifteen years. I am a well-known shipmaster."

He was densely distressed—and perhaps I should have sympathised with him if I had been able to detach my mental vision from the unsuspected sharer of my cabin as though he were my second self. There he was on the other side of the bulkhead, four or five feet from us, no more, as we sat in the saloon. I looked politely at Captain Archbold (if that was his name), but it was the other I saw, in a grey sleeping-suit, seated on a low stool, his bare feet close together, his arms folded, and every word said between us falling into the ears of his dark head bowed on his chest.

"I have been at sea now, man and boy, for seven-and-thirty years, and I've never heard of such a thing happening in an English ship. And that it should be my ship. Wife on board, too."

I was hardly listening to him.

"Don't you think," I said, "that the heavy sea which, you told me, came aboard just then might have killed the man? I have seen the sheer weight of a sea kill a man very neatly, by simply breaking his neck."

"Good God!" he uttered, impressively, fixing his smeary blue eyes on me. "The sea! No man killed by the sea ever looked like that." He seemed positively scandalised at my suggestion. And as I gazed at him, certainly not prepared for anything original on his part, he advanced his head close to mine and thrust his tongue out at me so suddenly that I couldn't help starting back.

After scoring over my calmness in this graphic way he nodded wisely. If I had seen the sight, he assured me, I would never forget it as long as I lived. The weather was too bad to give the corpse a proper sea burial. So next day at dawn they took it up on the poop, covering its face with a bit of bunting; he read a short prayer, and then, just as it was, in its oilskins and long boots, they launched it amongst those mountainous seas that seemed ready every moment to swallow up the ship herself and the terrified lives on board of her.

"That reefed foresail saved you," I threw in.

"Under God—it did," he exclaimed fervently. "It was by a special mercy, I firmly believe, that it stood some of those hurricane squalls."

"It was the setting of that sail which—" I began.

"God's own hand in it," he interrupted me. "Nothing less could have done it. I don't mind telling you that I hardly dared give the order. It seemed impossible that we could touch anything without losing it, and then our last hope would have been gone."

The terror of that gale was on him yet. I let him go on for a bit, then said, casually—as if returning to a minor subject:

"You were very anxious to give up your mate to the shore people, I believe?"

He was. To the law. His obscure tenacity on that point had in it something incomprehensible and a little awful; something, as it were, mystical, quite apart from his anxiety that he should not be suspected of "countenancing any doings of that sort." Seven-and-thirty virtuous years at sea, of which over twenty of immaculate command, and the last fifteen in the *Sephora*, seemed to have laid him under some pitiless obligation.

"And you know," he went on, groping shamefacedly amongst his feelings, "I did not engage that young fellow. His people had some interest with my owners. I was in a way forced to take him on. He looked very smart, very gentlemanly, and all that. But do you know—I never liked him, somehow. I am a plain man. You see, he wasn't exactly the sort for the chief mate of a ship like the *Sephora*."

I had become so connected in thoughts and impressions with the secret sharer of my cabin that I felt as if I, personally, were being given to understand that I, too, was not the sort that would have done for the chief mate of a ship like the *Sephora*. I had no doubt of it in my mind.

"Not at all the style of man. You understand," he insisted, superfluously, looking hard at me.

I smiled urbanely. He seemed at a loss for a while.

"I suppose I must report a suicide."

"Beg pardon?"

"Sui-cide! That's what I'll have to write to my owners directly I get in."

"Unless you manage to recover him before to-morrow," I assented, dispassionately.... "I mean, alive."

He mumbled something which I really did not catch, and I turned my ear to him in a puzzled manner. He fairly bawled:

"The land—I say, the mainland is at least seven miles off my anchorage."

"About that."

My lack of excitement, of curiosity, of surprise, of any sort of pronounced interest, began to arouse his distrust. But except for the felicitous pretence of deafness I had not tried to pretend anything. I had felt utterly incapable of playing the part of ignorance properly, and therefore was afraid to try. It is also certain that he had brought some ready-made suspicions with him, and that he viewed my politeness as a strange and unnatural phenomenon. And yet how else could I have received him? Not heartily! That was impossible for psychological reasons, which I need not state here. My only object was to keep off his inquiries. Surlily? Yes, but surliness might have provoked a point-blank question. From its novelty to him and from its nature, punctilious courtesy was the manner best calculated to restrain the man. But there was the danger of his breaking through my defence bluntly. I could not, I think, have met him by a direct lie, also for psychological (not moral) reasons. If he had only known how afraid I was of his putting my feeling of identity with the other to the test! But, strangely enough—(I thought of it only afterwards)—I believe that he was not a little disconcerted by the reverse side of that weird situation, by something in me that reminded him of the man he was seeking—suggested a mysterious similitude to the young fellow he had distrusted and disliked from the first.

However that might have been, the silence was not very prolonged. He took another oblique step.

"I reckon I had no more than a two-mile pull to your ship. Not a bit more."

"And quite enough, too, in this awful heat," I said.

Another pause full of mistrust followed. Necessity, they say, is mother of invention, but fear, too, is not barren of ingenious suggestions. And I was afraid he would ask me point-blank for news of my other self.

"Nice little saloon, isn't it?" I remarked, as if noticing for the first time the way his eyes roamed from one closed door to the other. "And very well fitted out, too. Here, for instance," I continued, reaching over the back of my seat negligently and flinging the door open, "is my bath-room."

He made an eager movement, but hardly gave it a glance. I got up, shut the door of the bath-room, and invited him to have a look round, as if I were very proud of my accommodation. He had to rise and be shown round, but he went through the business without any raptures whatever.

"And now we'll have a look at my stateroom," I declared, in a voice as loud as I dared to make it, crossing the cabin to the starboard side with purposely heavy steps.

He followed me in and gazed around. My intelligent double had vanished. I played my part.

"Very convenient—isn't it?"

"Very nice. Very comf . . . " He didn't finish and went out brusquely as if to escape from some unrighteous wiles of mine. But it was not to be. I had been too frightened not to feel vengeful; I felt I had him on the run, and I meant to keep him on the run. My polite insistence must have had something menacing in it, because he gave in suddenly. And I did not let him off a single item; mate's room, pantry, storerooms, the very sail-locker which was also under the poop—he had to look into them all. When at last I showed him out on the quarter-deck he drew a long, spiritless sigh, and mumbled dismally that he must really be going back to his ship now. I desired my mate, who had joined us, to see to the captain's boat.

The man of whiskers gave a blast on the whistle which he used to wear hanging round his neck, and yelled, *"Sephora's* away!" My double down there in my cabin must have heard, and certainly could not feel more relieved than I. Four fellows came running out from somewhere forward and went over the side, while my own men, appearing on deck too, lined the rail. I escorted my visitor to the gangway ceremoniously, and nearly overdid it. He was a tenacious beast. On the very ladder he lingered, and in that unique, guiltily conscientious manner of sticking to the point:

"I say . . . you . . . you don't think that—"

I covered his voice loudly:

"Certainly not. . . . I am delighted. Goodbye."

I had an idea of what he meant to say, and just saved myself by the privilege of defective hearing. He was too shaken generally to insist, but my mate, close witness of that parting, looked mystified and his face took on a thoughtful cast. As I did not want to appear as if I wished to avoid all communication with my officers, he had the opportunity to address me.

"Seems a very nice man. His boat's crew told our chaps a very extraordinary story, if what I am told by the steward is true. I suppose you had it from the captain, sir?"

"Yes. I had a story from the captain."

"A very horrible affair—isn't it, sir?"

"It is."

"Beats all these tales we hear about murders in Yankee ships."

"I don't think it beats them. I don't think it resembles them in the least."

"Bless my soul—you don't say so! But of course I've no acquaintance whatever with American ships, not I, so I couldn't go against your knowledge. It's horrible enough for me. . . . But the queerest part is that those fellows seemed to have some idea the man was hidden aboard here. They had really. Did you ever hear of such a thing?"

"Preposterous—isn't it?"

We were walking to and fro athwart the quarter-deck. No one of the crew forward could be seen (the day was Sunday), and the mate pursued:

"There was some little dispute about it. Our chaps took offence. 'As if we would harbour a thing like that,' they said. 'Wouldn't you like to look for him in our coal-hole?' Quite a tiff. But they made it up in the end. I suppose he did drown himself. Don't you, sir?"

"I don't suppose anything."

"You have no doubt in the matter, sir?"

"None whatever."

I left him suddenly. I felt I was producing a bad impression, but with my double down there it was most trying to be on deck. And it was almost as trying to be below. Altogether a nerve-trying situation. But on the whole I felt less torn in two when I was with him. There was no one in the whole ship whom I dared take into my confidence. Since the hands had got to know his story, it would have been impossible to pass him off for any one else, and an accidental discovery was to be dreaded now more than ever. . . .

The steward being engaged in laying the table for dinner, we could talk only with our eyes when I first went down. Later in the afternoon we had a cautious try at whispering. The Sunday quietness of the ship was against us; the stillness of air and water around her was against us; the elements, the men were against us—everything was against us in our secret partnership; time itself—for this could not go on forever. The very trust in Providence was, I suppose, denied to his guilt. Shall I confess that this thought cast me down very much? And as to the chapter of accidents which counts for so much in the book of success, I could only hope that it was closed. For what favourable accident could be expected?

"Did you hear everything?" were my first words as soon as we took up our position side by side, leaning over my bed-place.

He had. And the proof of it was his earnest whisper, "The man told you he hardly dared to give the order."

I understood the reference to be to that saving foresail.

"Yes. He was afraid of it being lost in the setting."

"I assure you he never gave the order. He may think he did, but he never gave it. He stood there with me on the break of the poop after the maintopsail blew away, and whimpered about our last hope—positively whimpered about it and nothing else—and the night coming on! To hear one's skipper go on like that in such weather was enough to drive any fellow out of his mind. It worked me up into a sort of desperation. I just took it into my own hands and went away from him, boiling, and—But what's the use telling you? *You* know! . . . Do you think that if I had not been pretty fierce with them I should have got the men to do anything? Not it! The bo's'n perhaps? Perhaps! It wasn't a heavy sea—it was a sea gone mad! I suppose the end of the world will be something like that; and a man may have the heart to see it coming once and be done with it—but to have to face it day after day—I don't blame anybody. I was precious little better than the rest. Only—I was an officer of that old coal-wagon, anyhow—"

"I quite understand," I conveyed that sincere assurance into his ear. He was out of breath with whispering; I could hear him pant slightly. It was all very simple. The same strung-up force which had given twenty-four men a chance, at least, for their lives, had, in a sort of recoil, crushed an unworthy mutinous existence.

But I had no leisure to weigh the merits of the matter—footsteps in the saloon, a heavy knock. "There's enough wind to get under way with, sir." Here was the call of a new claim upon my thoughts and even upon my feelings.

"Turn the hands up," I cried through the door. "I'll be on deck directly."

I was going out to make the acquaintance of my ship. Before I left the cabin our eyes met—the eyes of the only two strangers on board. I pointed to the recessed part where the little camp-stool awaited him and laid my finger on my lips. He made a gesture—somewhat vague—a little mysterious, accompanied by a faint smile, as if of regret.

This is not the place to enlarge upon the sensations of a man who feels for the first time a ship move under his feet to his own independent word. In my case they were not unalloyed. I was not wholly alone with my command; for there was that stranger in my cabin. Or rather, I was not completely and wholly with her. Part of me was absent. That mental feeling of being in two places at once affected me physically as if the mood of secrecy had penetrated my very soul. Before an hour had elapsed since the ship had begun to move, having occasion to ask the mate (he stood by my side) to take a compass bearing of the Pagoda, I caught myself reaching up to his ear in whispers. I say I caught myself, but enough had escaped to startle the man. I can't describe it otherwise than by saying that he shied. A grave, preoccupied manner, as though he were in possession of some perplexing intelligence, did not leave him henceforth. A little later I moved away from the rail to look at the compass with such a stealthy gait that the helmsman noticed it—and I could not help noticing the unusual roundness of his eyes. These are trifling instances, though it's to no commander's advantage to be suspected of ludicrous eccentricities. But I was also more seriously affected. There are to a seaman certain words, gestures, that should in given conditions come as naturally, as instinctively as the winking of a menaced eye. A certain order should spring on to his lips without thinking; a certain sign should get itself made, so to speak, without reflection. But all unconscious alertness had abandoned me. I had to make an effort of will to recall myself back (from the cabin) to the conditions of the moment. I felt that I was appearing an irresolute commander to those people who were watching me more or less critically.

And, besides, there were the scares. On the second day out, for instance, coming off the deck in the afternoon (I had straw slippers on my bare feet) I stopped at the open pantry door and spoke to the steward. He was doing something there with his back to me. At the sound of my voice he nearly jumped out of his skin, as the saying is, and incidentally broke a cup.

"What on earth's the matter with you?" I asked, astonished.

He was extremely confused. "Beg your pardon, sir. I made sure you were in your cabin."

"You see I wasn't."

"No, sir. I could have sworn I had heard you moving in there not a moment ago. It's most extraordinary . . . very sorry, sir."

I passed on with an inward shudder. I was so identified with my secret double that I did not even mention the fact in those scanty, fearful whispers we exchanged. I suppose he had made some slight noise of some kind or other. It would have been miraculous if he hadn't at one time or another. And yet, haggard as he appeared, he looked always perfectly self-controlled, more than calm—almost invulnerable. On my suggestion he remained almost entirely in the bathroom, which, upon the whole, was the safest place. There could be really no shadow of an excuse for any one ever wanting to go in there, once the steward had done with it. It was a very tiny place. Sometimes he reclined on the floor, his legs bent, his head sustained on one elbow. At others I would find him on the camp-stool, sitting in his grey sleeping-suit and with his cropped dark hair like a patient, unmoved convict. At night I would smuggle him into my bed-place, and we would whisper together, with the regular footfalls of the officer of the watch passing and repassing over our heads. It was an infinitely miserable time. It was lucky that some tins of fine preserves were stowed in a locker in my stateroom; hard bread I could always get hold of; and so he lived on stewed chicken, pate de foie gras, asparagus, cooked oysters, sardines—on all sorts of abominable sham delicacies out of tins. My early morning coffee he always drank; and it was all I dared do for him in that respect.

Every day there was the horrible maneuvering to go through so that my room and then the bath-room should be done in the usual way. I came to hate the sight of the steward, to abhor the voice of that harmless man. I felt that it was he who would bring on the disaster of discovery. It hung like a sword over our heads.

The fourth day out, I think (we were then working down the east side of the Gulf of Siam, tack for tack, in light winds and smooth water)—the fourth day, I say, of this miserable juggling with the unavoidable, as we sat at our evening meal, that man, whose slightest movement I dreaded, after putting down the dishes ran up on deck busily. This could not be dangerous. Presently he came down again; and then it appeared that he had remembered a coat of mine which I had thrown over a rail to dry after having been wetted in a shower which had passed over the ship in the afternoon. Sitting stolidly at the head of the table I became terrified at the sight of the garment on his arm. Of course he made for my door. There was no time to lose.

"Steward," I thundered. My nerves were so shaken that I could not govern my voice and conceal my agitation. This was the sort of thing that made my terrifically whiskered mate tap his forehead with his forefinger. I had detected him using that gesture while talking on deck with a confidential air to the carpenter. It was too far to hear a word, but I had no doubt that this pantomime could only refer to the strange new captain.

"Yes, sir," the pale-faced steward turned resignedly to me. It was this maddening course of being shouted at, checked without rhyme or reason, arbitrarily chased out of my cabin, suddenly called into it, sent flying out of his pantry on incomprehensible errands, that accounted for the growing wretchedness of his expression.

"Where are you going with that coat?"

"To your room, sir."

"Is there another shower coming?"

"I'm sure I don't know, sir. Shall I go up again and see, sir?"

"No! never mind."

My object was attained, as of course my other self in there would have heard everything that passed. During this interlude my two officers never raised their eyes off their respective plates; but the lip of that confounded cub, the second mate, quivered visibly.

I expected the steward to hook my coat on and come out at once. He was very slow about it; but I dominated my nervousness sufficiently not to shout after him. Suddenly I became aware (it could be heard plainly enough) that the fellow for some reason or other was opening the door of the bath-room. It was the end. The place was literally not big enough to swing a cat in. My voice died in my throat and I went stony all over. I expected to hear a yell of surprise and terror, and made a movement, but had not the strength to get on my legs. Everything remained still. Had my second self taken the poor wretch by the throat? I don't know what I could have done next moment if I had not seen the steward come out of my room, close the door, and then stand quietly by the sideboard.

"Saved," I thought. "But, no! Lost! Gone! He was gone!"

I laid my knife and fork down and leaned back in my chair. My head swam. After a while, when sufficiently recovered to speak in a steady voice, I instructed my mate to put the ship round at eight o'clock himself.

"I won't come on deck," I went on. "I think I'll turn in, and unless the wind shifts I don't want to be disturbed before midnight. I feel a bit seedy."

"You did look middling bad a little while ago," the chief mate remarked without showing any great concern.

They both went out, and I stared at the steward clearing the table. There was nothing to be read on that wretched man's face. But why did he avoid my eyes I asked myself. Then I thought I should like to hear the sound of his voice.

"Steward!"

"Sir!" Startled as usual.

"Where did you hang up that coat?"

"In the bath-room, sir." The usual anxious tone. "It's not quite dry yet, sir."

For some time longer I sat in the cuddy. Had my double vanished as he had come? But of his coming there was an explanation, whereas his disappearance would be inexplicable. . . . I went slowly into my dark room, shut the door, lighted the lamp, and for a time dared not turn round. When at last I did I saw him standing bolt-upright in the narrow recessed part. It would not be true to say I had a shock, but an irresistible doubt of his bodily existence flitted through my mind. Can it be, I asked myself, that he is not visible to other eyes than mine? It was like being haunted. Motionless, with a grave face, he raised his hands slightly at me in a gesture which meant clearly, "Heavens! what a narrow escape!" Narrow indeed. I think I had come creeping quietly as near insanity as any man who has not actually gone over the border. That gesture restrained me, so to speak.

The mate with the terrific whiskers was now putting the ship on the other tack. In the moment of profound silence which follows upon the hands going to their stations I heard on the poop his raised voice: "Hard alee!" and the distant shout of the order repeated on the maindeck. The sails, in that light breeze, made but a faint fluttering noise. It ceased. The ship was coming round slowly; I held my breath in the renewed stillness of expectation; one wouldn't have thought that there was a single living soul on her decks. A sudden brisk shout, "Mainsail haul!" broke the spell, and in the noisy cries and rush overhead of the men running away with the main-brace we two, down in my cabin, came together in our usual position by the bed-place.

He did not wait for my question. "I heard him fumbling here and just managed to squat myself down in the bath," he whispered to me. "The fellow only opened the door and put his arm in to hang the coat up. All the same—"

"I never thought of that," I whispered back, even more appalled than before at the closeness of the shave, and marvelling at that something unyielding in his character which was carrying him through so finely. There was no agitation in his whisper. Whoever was being driven distracted, it was not he. He was sane. And the proof of his sanity was continued when he took up the whispering again.

"It would never do for me to come to life again."

It was something that a ghost might have said. But what he was alluding to was his old captain's reluctant admission of the theory of suicide. It would obviously serve his turn—if I had understood at all the view which seemed to govern the unalterable purpose of his action.

"You must maroon me as soon as ever you can get amongst these islands off the Cambodge[5] shore," he went on.

"Maroon you! We are not living in a boy's adventure tale," I protested. His scornful whispering took me up.

"We aren't indeed! There's nothing of a boy's tale in this. But there's nothing else for it. I want no more. You don't suppose I am afraid of what can be done to me? Prison or gallows or whatever they may please. But you don't see me coming back to explain such things to an old fellow in a wig and twelve respectable tradesmen, do you? What can they know whether I am guilty or not—or of *what* I am guilty, either? That's my affair. What does the Bible say?[6] 'Driven off the face of the earth.' Very well. I am off the face of the earth now. As I came at night so I shall go."

"Impossible!" I murmured. "You can't."

"Can't? . . . Not naked like a soul on the Day of Judgment. I shall freeze on to this sleeping-suit. The Last Day is not yet—and . . . you have understood thoroughly. Didn't you?"

I felt suddenly ashamed of myself. I may say truly that I understood—and my hesitation in letting that man swim away from my ship's side had been a mere sham sentiment, a sort of cowardice.

"It can't be done now till next night," I breathed out. "The ship is on the offshore tack and the wind may fail us."

"As long as I know that you understand," he whispered. "But of course you do. It's a great satisfaction to have got somebody to understand. You seem to have been there on purpose." And in the same whisper, as if we two whenever we talked had to say things to each other which were not fit for the world to hear, he added, "It's very wonderful."

We remained side by side talking in our secret way—but sometimes silent or just exchanging a whispered word or two at long intervals. And as usual he stared through the port. A breath of wind came now and again into our faces. The ship might have been moored in dock, so gently and on an even keel she slipped through the water, that did not murmur even at our passage, shadowy and silent like a phantom sea.

At midnight I went on deck, and to my mate's great surprise put the ship round on the other tack. His terrible whiskers flitted round me in silent criticism. I certainly should not have done it if it had been only a question of getting out of that sleepy gulf as quickly as possible. I believe he told the second mate, who relieved him, that it was a great want of judgment. The other only yawned. That intolerable cub shuffled about so sleepily and lolled against the rails in such a slack, improper fashion that I came down on him sharply.

"Aren't you properly awake yet?"

"Yes, sir! I am awake."

[5] Cambodian.
[6] Of Cain (Genesis iv.14).

"Well, then, be good enough to hold yourself as if you were. And keep a look-out. If there's any current we'll be closing with some islands before daylight."

The east side of the gulf is fringed with islands, some solitary, others in groups. On the blue background of the high coast they seem to float on silvery patches of calm water, arid and grey, or dark green and rounded like clumps of evergreen bushes, with the larger ones, a mile or two long, showing the outlines of ridges, ribs of grey rock under the dank mantle of matted leafage. Unknown to trade, to travel, almost to geography, the manner of life they harbour is an unsolved secret. There must be villages—settlements of fishermen at least—on the largest of them, and some communication with the world is probably kept up by native craft. But all that forenoon, as we headed for them, fanned along by the faintest of breezes, I saw no sign of man or canoe in the field of the telescope I kept on pointing at the scattered group.

At noon I gave no orders for a change of course, and the mate's whiskers became much concerned and seemed to be offering themselves unduly to my notice. At last I said:

"I am going to stand right in. Quite in—as far as I can take her."

The stare of extreme surprise imparted an air of ferocity also to his eyes, and he looked truly terrific for a moment.

"We're not doing well in the middle of the gulf," I continued, casually. "I am going to look for the land breezes to-night."

"Bless my soul! Do you mean, sir, in the dark amongst the lot of all them islands and reefs and shoals?"

"Well—if there are any regular land breezes at all on this coast one must get close inshore to find them, mustn't one?"

"Bless my soul!" he exclaimed again under his breath. All that afternoon he wore a dreamy, contemplative appearance which in him was a mark of perplexity. After dinner I went into my stateroom as if I meant to take some rest. There we two bent our dark heads over a half-unrolled chart lying on my bed.

"There," I said. "It's got to be Koh-ring. I've been looking at it ever since sunrise. It has got two hills and a low point. It must be inhabited. And on the coast opposite there is what looks like the mouth of a biggish river—with some town, no doubt, not far up. It's the best chance for you that I can see."

"Anything. Koh-ring let it be."

He looked thoughtfully at the chart as if surveying chances and distances from a lofty height—and following with his eyes his own figure wandering on the blank land of Cochin-China,[7] and then passing off that piece of paper clean out of sight into uncharted regions. And it was as if the ship had two captains to plan her course for her. I had been so worried and restless running up and down that I had not had the patience to dress that day. I had remained in my sleeping-suit, with straw slippers and a soft floppy hat. The closeness of the heat in the gulf had been most oppressive, and the crew were used to see me wandering in that airy attire.

"She will clear the south point as she heads now," I whispered into his ear. "Goodness only knows when, though, but certainly after dark. I'll edge her in to half a mile, as far as I may be able to judge in the dark—"

[7] South Vietnam.

"Be careful," he murmured, warningly—and I realised suddenly that all my future, the only future for which I was fit, would perhaps go irretrievably to pieces in any mishap to my first command.

I could not stop a moment longer in the room. I motioned him to get out of sight and made my way on the poop. That unplayful cub had the watch. I walked up and down for a while thinking things out, then beckoned him over.

"Send a couple of hands to open the two quarter-deck ports," I said, mildly.

He actually had the impudence, or else so forgot himself in his wonder at such an incomprehensible order, as to repeat:

"Open the quarter-deck ports! What for, sir?"

"The only reason you need concern yourself about is because I tell you to do so. Have them opened wide and fastened properly."

He reddened and went off, but I believe made some jeering remark to the carpenter as to the sensible practice of ventilating a ship's quarter-deck. I know he popped into the mate's cabin to impart the fact to him because the whiskers came on deck, as it were by chance, and stole glances at me from below—for signs of lunacy or drunkenness, I suppose.

A little before supper, feeling more restless than ever, I rejoined, for a moment, my second self. And to find him sitting so quietly was surprising, like something against nature, inhuman.

I developed my plan in a hurried whisper.

"I shall stand in as close as I dare and then put her round. I will presently find means to smuggle you out of here into the sail-locker, which communicates with the lobby. But there is an opening, a sort of square for hauling the sails out, which gives straight on the quarter-deck and which is never closed in fine weather, so as to give air to the sails. When the ship's way is deadened in stays and all the hands are aft at the main-braces you will have a clear road to slip out and get overboard through the open quarter-deck port. I've had them both fastened up. Use a rope's end to lower yourself into the water so as to avoid a splash—you know. It could be heard and cause some beastly complication."

He kept silent for a while, then whispered, "I understand."

"I won't be there to see you go," I began with an effort. "The rest . . . I only hope I have understood, too."

"You have. From first to last"—and for the first time there seemed to be a faltering, something strained in his whisper. He caught hold of my arm, but the ringing of the supper bell made me start. He didn't though; he only released his grip.

After supper I didn't come below again till well past eight o'clock. The faint, steady breeze was loaded with dew; and the wet, darkened sails held all there was of propelling power in it. The night, clear and starry, sparkled darkly, and the opaque, lightless patches shifting slowly against the low stars were the drifting islets. On the port bow there was a big one more distant and shadowily imposing by the great space of sky it eclipsed.

On opening the door I had a back view of my very own self looking at a chart. He had come out of the recess and was standing near the table.

"Quite dark enough," I whispered.

He stepped back and leaned against my bed with a level, quiet glance. I sat on the couch. We had nothing to say to each other. Over our heads the officer of the watch moved here and there. Then I heard him move quickly. I knew what that meant. He was making for the companion; and presently his voice was outside my door.

"We are drawing in pretty fast, sir. Land looks rather close."

"Very well," I answered. "I am coming on deck directly."

I waited till he was gone out of the cuddy, then rose. My double moved too. The time had come to exchange our last whispers, for neither of us was ever to hear each other's natural voice.

"Look here!" I opened a drawer and took out three sovereigns. "Take this anyhow. I've got six and I'd give you the lot, only I must keep a little money to buy some fruit and vegetables for the crew from native boats as we go through Sunda Straits."

He shook his head.

"Take it," I urged him, whispering desperately. "No one can tell what—"

He smiled and slapped meaningly the only pocket of the sleeping-jacket. It was not safe, certainly. But I produced a large old silk handkerchief of mine, and tying the three pieces of gold in a corner, pressed it on him. He was touched, I suppose, because he took it at last and tied it quickly round his waist under the jacket, on his bare skin.

Our eyes met; several seconds elapsed, till, our glances still mingled, I extended my hand and turned the lamp out. Then I passed through the cuddy, leaving the door of my room wide open. . . . "Steward!"

He was still lingering in the pantry in the greatness of his zeal, giving a rub-up to a plated cruet stand the last thing before going to bed. Being careful not to wake up the mate, whose room was opposite, I spoke in an undertone.

He looked round anxiously. "Sir!"

"Can you get me a little hot water from the galley?"

"I am afraid, sir, the galley fire's been out for some time now."

"Go and see."

He flew up the stairs.

"Now," I whispered, loudly, into the saloon—too loudly, perhaps, but I was afraid I couldn't make a sound. He was by my side in an instant—the double captain slipped past the stairs—through a tiny dark passage . . . a sliding door. We were in the sail-locker, scrambling on our knees over the sails. A sudden thought struck me. I saw myself wandering barefooted, bareheaded, the sun beating on my dark poll. I snatched off my floppy hat and tried hurriedly in the dark to ram it on my other self. He dodged and fended off silently. I wonder what he thought had come to me before he understood and suddenly desisted. Our hands met gropingly, lingered united in a steady, motionless clasp for a second. . . . No word was breathed by either of us when they separated. I was standing quietly by the pantry door when the steward returned.

"Sorry, sir. Kettle barely warm. Shall I light the spirit-lamp?"

"Never mind."

I came out on deck slowly. It was now a matter of conscience to shave the land as close as possible—for now he must go overboard whenever the ship was put in stays. Must! There could be no going back for him. After a moment I walked over to leeward and my heart flew into my mouth at the nearness of the land on the bow. Under any other circumstances I would not have held on a minute longer. The second mate had followed me anxiously.

I looked on till I felt I could command my voice.

"She will weather," I said then in a quiet tone.

"Are you going to try that, sir?" he stammered out incredulously.

I took no notice of him and raised my tone just enough to be heard by the helmsman.

"Keep her good full."

"Good full, sir."

The wind fanned my cheek, the sails slept, the world was silent. The strain of watching the dark loom of the land grow bigger and denser was too much for me. I had shut my eyes—because the ship must go closer. She must! The stillness was intolerable. Were we standing still?

When I opened my eyes the second view started my heart with a thump. The black southern hill of Koh-ring seemed to hang right over the ship like a towering fragment of the everlasting night. On that enormous mass of blackness there was not a gleam to be seen, not a sound to be heard. It was gliding irresistibly towards us and yet seemed already within reach of the hand. I saw the vague figures of the watch grouped in the waist, gazing in awed silence.

"Are you going on, sir?" inquired an unsteady voice at my elbow.

I ignored it. I had to go on.

"Keep her full. Don't check her way. That won't do now," I said, warningly.

"I can't see the sails very well," the helmsman answered me, in strange, quavering tones.

Was she close enough? Already she was, I won't say in the shadow of the land, but in the very blackness of it, already swallowed up as it were, gone too close to be recalled, gone from me altogether.

"Give the mate a call," I said to the young man who stood at my elbow as still as death. "And turn all hands up."

My tone had a borrowed loudness reverberated from the height of the land. Several voices cried out together: "We are all on deck, sir."

Then stillness again, with the great shadow gliding closer, towering higher, without a light, without a sound. Such a hush had fallen on the ship that she might have been a bark of the dead floating in slowly under the very gate of Erebus.

"My God! Where are we?"

It was the mate moaning at my elbow. He was thunderstruck, and as it were deprived of the moral support of his whiskers. He clapped his hands and absolutely cried out, "Lost!"

"Be quiet," I said, sternly.

He lowered his tone, but I saw the shadowy gesture of his despair. "What are we doing here?"

"Looking for the land wind."

He made as if to tear his hair, and addressed me recklessly.

"She will never get out. You have done it, sir. I knew it'd end in something like this. She will never weather, and you are too close now to stay. She'll drift ashore before she's round. O my God!"

I caught his arm as he was raising it to batter his poor devoted head, and shook it violently.

"She's ashore already," he wailed, trying to tear himself away.

"Is she? . . . Keep good full there!"

"Good full, sir," cried the helmsman in a frightened, thin, child-like voice.

I hadn't let go the mate's arm and went on shaking it. "Ready about, do you hear? You go forward"—shake—"and stop there"—shake—"and hold your noise"—shake—"and see these head-sheets properly overhauled"—shake, shake—shake.

And all the time I dared not look towards the land lest my heart should fail me. I released my grip at last and he ran forward as if fleeing for dear life.

I wondered what my double there in the sail-locker thought of this commotion. He was able to hear everything—and perhaps he was able to understand why, on my conscience, it had to be thus close—no less. My first order "Hard alee!" re-echoed ominously under the towering shadow of Koh-ring as if I had shouted in a mountain gorge. And then I watched the land intently. In that smooth water and light wind it was impossible to feel the ship coming-to. No! I could not feel her. And my second self was making now ready to slip out and lower himself overboard. Perhaps he was gone already . . . ?

The great black mass brooding over our very mast-heads began to pivot away from the ship's side silently. And now I forgot the secret stranger ready to depart, and remembered only that I was a total stranger to the ship. I did not know her. Would she do it? How was she to be handled?

I swung the mainyard and waited helplessly. She was perhaps stopped, and her very fate hung in the balance, with the black mass of Koh-ring like the gate of the everlasting night towering over her taffrail. What would she do now? Had she way on her yet? I stepped to the side swiftly, and on the shadowy water I could see nothing except a faint phosphorescent flash revealing the glassy smoothness of the sleeping surface. It was impossible to tell—and I had not learned yet the feel of my ship. Was she moving? What I needed was something easily seen, a piece of paper, which I could throw overboard and watch. I had nothing on me. To run down for it I didn't dare. There was no time. All at once my strained, yearning stare distinguished a white object floating within a yard of the ship's side. White on the black water. A phosphorescent flash passed under it. What was that thing? . . . I recognised my own floppy hat. It must have fallen off his head . . . and he didn't bother. Now I had what I wanted—the saving mark for my eyes. But I hardly thought of my other self, now gone from the ship, to be hidden for ever from all friendly faces, to be a fugitive and a vagabond on the earth, with no brand of the curse on his sane forehead to stay a slaying hand . . . too proud to explain.

And I watched the hat—the expression of my sudden pity for his mere flesh. It had been meant to save his homeless head from the dangers of the sun. And now—behold—it was saving the ship, by serving me for a mark to help out the ignorance of my strangeness. Ha! It was drifting forward, warning me just in time that the ship had gathered sternway.

"Shift the helm," I said in a low voice to the seaman standing still like a statue.

The man's eyes glistened wildly in the binnacle light as he jumped round to the other side and spun round the wheel.

I walked to the break of the poop. On the over-shadowed deck all hands stood by the forebraces waiting for my order. The stars ahead seemed to be gliding from right to left. And all was so still in the world that I heard the quiet remark, "She's round," passed in a tone of intense relief between two seamen.

"Let go and haul."

The foreyards ran round with a great noise, amidst cheery cries. And now the frightful whiskers made themselves heard giving various orders. Already the ship was drawing ahead. And I was alone with her. Nothing! no one in the world should stand now between us, throwing a shadow on the way of silent knowledge and mute affection, the perfect communion of a seaman with his first command.

Walking to the taffrail, I was in time to make out, on the very edge of a darkness thrown by a towering black mass like the very gateway of Erebus—yes, I was in time to catch an evanescent glimpse of my white hat left behind to mark the spot where the secret sharer of my cabin and of my thoughts, as though he were my second self, had lowered himself into the water to take his punishment: a free man, a proud swimmer striking out for a new destiny.

Writing About Fiction

Narration is in the past tense: "It happened," "she said," "I thought I would die." The storyteller is recalling the past, as we all must when we tell the merest anecdote about ourselves, how we smashed a fender or lost our credit cards. And the telling makes the listener see it again, feel how it was. In general, the more immediate the past, the more realistic the story, with the tale becoming more fanciful as it moves back in time toward that fairyland beyond the deep end of history—more "romantic," as we say, since it moves toward those Bohemias of knights and ladies, giants and fays, projected into our imaginative habits by the great romances of the Middle Ages. Realism is the here and now, the past so immediate as to seem just last week. Romance is the far away and the long ago, the exotic in place and time, whether in the past or in some future trek among the stars. Realism is the hard realities, grim or wry or amusing, and essentially ironic—the way it is as against the way we wish it were. Romance is wish fulfillment, difficulties overcome with happiness ever after. The blends, of course, are infinite, as wishes and facts work their ironic ways. In writing about fiction, we should ponder the blend. How realistically detailed is it? How much enters of the romantic wish to start low and end high and happy everafter? How realistically are the wishes cut down to size?

The Author's Voice

As the narrator tells his tale, his voice conveys his point of view with every word. He is sad. He is smiling. He is passionately involved in his tale. He is seeing it with godlike detachment. And as he speaks, or writes as if he is speaking, he takes us with him, putting us precisely in the position he is taking, giving us his point of view. The author's voice is thus present even when he never says "I think" or calls us "dear Reader." We catch the author's amused, ironic point of view, and we hear her individual authorial voice immediately, as Jane Austen opens *Pride and Prejudice*: "It is a truth universally acknowledged, that a single man in possession of a good fortune must be in want of a wife." That truth is, of course, no more universal than the opinions of mothers with marriageable daughters. The author's voice continues even as she mimics for us the voices of her characters:

> "My dear Mr. Bennet," said his lady to him one day, "have you heard that Netherfield Park is to let at last?"
> Mr. Bennet replied that he had not.

The author is reporting what she wants us to know. She reports speeches in that natural narrative mimicry we can all detect around us as our friends tell us what a stupid boss said or how a roommate demanded privacy. Or she summarizes silences and thoughts as she sees fit. And in a very few more lines, she not only has sketched her basic situation but has given us the personalities of the talkative Mrs. Bennet and the taciturn Mr. Bennet, who understands his wife thoroughly, teases her unbeknownst, and lets her have her way. All this is in Jane Austen's unmistakable narrative voice, leading us on in quiet ironic amusement with no explanations necessary.

When we write about fiction, as when we write about poetry or the drama, we simply fill in the implied explanations. Whatever we have to explain about a story, whatever detail we may lift up to examine, we had best get our bearings by determining the point of view and considering its effect and by trying to define for ourselves the tone of the writer's voice. Is it sad, light hearted, ironic, grim, or weary? What does it imply about how the story will end? In the writer's voice, we can probably detect immediately whether the ending will be happy or tragic, or perhaps just quizzical.

The Narrative Modes

The narrator tells his story in one of two ways, in the third person or in the first: "she said" or "I said." In the third person, he is an *omniscient narrator*, knowing everything and telling us just as much and just as little as he wishes before he unfolds everything to its end. He may show his characters mostly from the outside, with very little report of what they are thinking or feeling, or he may report the tumbling thoughts and impressions in their silent stream of consciousness. In a common form of limited omniscience, he may tell us events only from his main character's viewpoint, as if he were almost at her side, letting us into her thoughts only. Less limited, he may tell the story from several viewpoints, as he contrasts one view with another. Third-person omniscience is the main narrative impulse that started once upon a time around some prehistoric campfire and persists through the complexities of Joyce and Beckett. As you read, notice whose inner life the author opens for us, and whose he never enters.

The other way to tell a story is in the first person. In comparison to third-person narration, first-person narrative is a new comer. It rose to competitive prominence in the eighteenth century, as the individual, and individual consciousness, rose in the world. It is more complex than it appears. Since the first-person narrator cannot know, omnisciently, what goes on in other people's minds or in other places—he is an actor within the reality of the story and cannot move beyond it—the author must consequently exclude all information the actor–narrator could not realistically know. Since the narrator knows how things turned out, the author must also realistically balance the innocence, uncertainties, and suspense of the narrator's former experience, about which he is now telling us, against the evidence before us that he survived, well seasoned, to tell the tale.

As you read a first-person narrative, check the plausibility of the narrator's knowing what he knows and the author's ingenuity in getting the information to him. "I learned this much later from a friend of a friend" may show the author working a little too hard and unskillfully. A traditional western tall tale illustrates the dilemma of first-person narration. A cowboy is telling about how he hunted a mountain lion along a narrow ledge on a cliff. The ledge narrows to nothing. "I heard a noise behind me, turned, and knocked the rifle out of my hands. It was the lion getting ready to spring." "What happened then?" his excited audience asks. "He ate me up," says the cowboy.

To retain the immediacy of the first person and solve the dilemmas of information and survival, first-person narration has evolved three varieties: (1) first person as protagonist, (2) first person as participant, (3) first person as observer. The second two may combine in various ways, as in Kipling's "The Man Who Would Be King" where the newspaperman who tells us the story, a first-person observer, is joined by Carnehan, first-person participant, who is necessary to bring us the details of Dravot's end. Both the secondary participant and the mere observer take on personalities of their own to make them interesting and plausible, and again we can observe the author's skill in piecing his information together seamlessly, or his awkwardness in leaving too many seams showing. Emily Brontë's skill with Mr. Lockwood and Nelly Dean, the two first-person observers who also participate in her *Wuthering Heights,* is nothing less than brilliant and will reward anyone's careful study. The first-person narrator's personality, indeed, may be more significant than the story he tells, as when Anderson's first-person protagonist in "I'm a Fool" unconsciously underlines the poignancy in the impossible gap between social classes by demonstrating to us that he is fully qualified for the class he cannot join and fully worthy of the girl he can never see again, though he himself thinks he is not.

Thus first-person narration frequently generates dramatic irony through the personality and the imperceptions of the speaker. Just as the tone of the author's voice in third-person narration conveys a sense of the omniscient narrator's personality and attitude, so the first-person narrator positions himself, and us, in relation to the events he tells. If he is ignorant of their implications, like the loquacious barber in Lardner's "Haircut," we have dramatic irony at its fullest: the self-confident speaker does not perceive the whole meaning of what he says, pleased with himself as he displays his ignorance; and through his imperception the events hit us between the eyes with ironic force. So as you explain what needs to be said about a story or novel, take into account whether it is in a form of omniscient third person or in some version of the first, and the effect of these different ways of telling on the story's impact and point.

Irony

Since irony is such a pervasive element of storytelling, and in poetry and drama as well, recognizing its varieties will help you describe a story for your readers, and explain its force. In general, irony is the perception of a clash between appearance and reality, between *seems* and *is*. Its many shades fall into three varieties: (1) verbal, (2) dramatic, and (3) situational.

1. Verbal irony—saying something contrary to what it means. The appearance is what the words say; the reality is the contrary thing they mean. Both speaker and listener are aware of the contrast, mutually understanding the situation and each other. "A marvelous time" means a boring time. "A great guy" is a petty sniveler. "A truth universally acknowledged" is a self-interested opinion. I must know that the party was boring to get the irony in your "marvelous." I must know it is raining to get the irony in your "What a great day for a picnic!" Speaker and listener enjoy a silent compact. We are in cahoots. This silent ironic understanding may flow between author and reader, as it does between us and Jane Austen. Or it may flow between characters within a story, which the reader enjoys by listening in.

2. Dramatic irony—saying or doing something unaware of its full meaning. Dramatic irony, named for its frequency in drama, is verbal irony with the speaker's awareness erased. Someone says "This is the happiest day of my life," and we in the audience, and perhaps some of the people on stage, know that his mortgage has been foreclosed and his family wiped out at the intersection. When someone goes to open a door and the audience shouts "No! No!," knowing the disaster awaiting, we have dramatic irony in action alone. Dramatic irony may combine with verbal irony when two characters exchange hidden meanings and a third character understands only the surface of what they say, or, better, when two characters exchange verbal ironies, enjoying what they think

is superior knowledge, while we, the audience, know how blind they are to the awful truth. Furthermore, fiction and the drama abound in a kind of retrospective dramatic irony, as, looking back, we realize that the speaker's "happiest day of my life" is now being rendered painfully or comically ironic. When in Act I, Hamlet tells his father's ghost that he will sweep to his revenge with wings as swift as meditation or the thoughts of love, we find his words gathering more and more dramatic irony as he dawdles on and on through most of the play.

3. Situational irony—events turning to the opposite of what we expect or what should be (also called circumstantial irony and the irony of fate). It rains on the Weather Bureau's annual picnic. The new car is totalled leaving the dealer's. The new outfit is spattered with oil. The ironic situation—the *ought* upended by the *is*—is integral with dramatic irony. We need the ironic situation to turn the speaker's unknowing words ironic. Situational irony is the very essence of both comedy and tragedy. The young lovers run into the worst possible luck, until everything clears up happily. The most noble spirit goes to his death, while the featherheads survive.

To describe for your readers how any one, or several, of these ironies works is almost a paper in itself. You could probably write a book, if you had the time, on a thesis like "The central point of *Hamlet* is the ironic difference between human intentions and their outcome." You could, indeed, apply that thesis very effectively to any number of stories—"The Man Who Would Be King," "Bliss," "A Little Cloud," for instance. Or try "This story illustrates the irony that each limited human view thinks it sees everything."

The Figurative Dimension

Style, of course, is a function of the author's voice, and you will have already gauged him as terse and grim, playfully ornate, or deadly serious. If you are interested in style, you can write a good paper on the author's peculiar habits, favorite words, the way his sentences hang in customary patterns. But the likeliest topics are his figures of speech: his metaphors, his symbols, and perhaps, his allegorical dimension.

A metaphor speaks of something in terms of something else, of a woman as a tree with slender limbs, or of a tree as a woman with a nest of robins in her hair. *Metaphor*, in Greek, means *transfer* in Latin. English has taken both words straight (*meta* equals *trans*; *phor* equals *fer*). Transferring characteristics from one thing to another is the essence of the metaphorical process, through which we see a thing more vividly, with meaning added—we see how it strikes the writer's imagination. Metaphor is an *as if*: presenting something *as if* it were something else. It is not a two-way equation. The good writer will make clear which is the real object and which the figurative. If you cannot tell whether this woman is like a tree or this tree is like a woman, the writer has failed, and you have something to report. The *as if* must be clear in symbols and allegories as well.

· The metaphorical transfer operates in four ways:

1. Simile:
   She is *like* a tree.
   She swayed *as* a tree sways.
   She stood firm, *as if* she were a tree.

2. Plain Metaphor:
   She is a tree.

3. Implied Metaphor:
   She stood firm, as if rooted in granite.
   She swayed in the wind, her hair fluttering like leaves.

4. Dead Metaphor:
   Her limbs are long.

If the writer is a particularly good metaphorist, he will revive the dead metaphors of everyday speech by adding further metaphorical details: "Her limbs are long, supple as aspen, strong as oak."

You can analyze a writer's metaphors to great advantage, noting which kind he prefers, whether he revives his dead metaphors or lets them pass unnoticed, and where his imagination ranges for his figurative terms. Carolyn Spurgeon long ago illuminated the special savagery of Shakespeare's *King Lear* by pointing to the prevalence, in this play only, of metaphors concerning beasts tearing each other apart. Metaphors vivify an author's meaning, illustrating, as if by pictures, how he sees his people and their dealings. Joyce Cary's "Evangelist" (p. 210) is a neat and amusing study of how metaphors illustrate our moods. You can write a good paper on that one.

Symbols take the metaphorical process a step farther. Some physical object—a rose, a cloud—comes to represent a cluster of meanings arising from its natural characteristics. A rose comes to represent beauty, freshness, and transitoriness, perhaps also thorns behind beauty, in human life. A cloud symbolizes a gathering storm. The title of James Joyce's "A Little Cloud," for instance, brings a symbolic dimension to a story by alluding to the familiar Biblical "Behold, there ariseth a little cloud out of the sea, like a man's hand," which soon blackens all the heavens with a storm (1 Kings xviii.44). Explaining what symbols imply makes a good paper. For instance, you might like to explain how the tree in Katharine Mansfield's "Bliss" (p. 225) gathers symbolic significance.

Allegory is a kind of extended symbolizing, in which the story runs parallel to some deeper contest implied beneath it. Edmund Spenser's *Faerie Queen*, for instance, allegorizes in its questing knights and imprisoned maidens the struggles of the human soul toward virtue, while it also idealizes Queen Elizabeth's court—a kind of three-decker omnibus. Modern fiction has nothing so elaborate—except that Joyce's fantastic *Finnegans Wake*, and his *Ulysses* too, are a species of allegory—but even less steamy modern fiction frequently takes on an allegorical dimension. Hawthorne's "My Kinsman, Major Molineux" is unusually allegorical, with two allegorical layers ironically at odds: the one, a journey of youth toward worldly self-reliance, the other, an apparent journey across the river Styx to Hell itself, which is actually both colonial America and the everyday political world after all. Perhaps this is a quadruple-decker. Spelling it out would make a very good paper.

Theme

In the end, we need to explain a story's theme. What *is* the point? The author gives us the details, involves us in the experience, then leaves us pondering. We need to explain what all this means, if we are to grasp the story fully and appreciate its details. The story has told of us, under different names. But what were we supposed to perceive about ourselves? This is the ultimate task of writing about fiction.

The story may mean several things. Different people will take different threads as the most important. We may disagree diametrically as to the meaning, like the two knights, looking at different sides of the shield by the road, who fought to death over whether it was gold or silver. The theme of that story would seem to be: look at both sides of the question and don't be too cocky about your opinion. But stories, which can be as many-sided as diamonds, will draw differing explanations, and we can write about them almost inexhaustibly as we see one facet then another and add to our understanding of a cumulative theme. Even picking one facet, such as, let us say, "The Significance of Dark and Light in 'My Kinsman, Major Molineux,'" will lead us to determine and to suggest to our readers what it all adds up to.

In writing about fiction, you come to understand it and enjoy it as you can in no other way. Seeking explanations is exploring. Writing is a voyage of discovery. You dig up the riches and put them on display. So make yourself a proposition. Assert in a sentence what you want to explain, and then describe and quote and summarize the details of the story that illustrate your point. Your thesis might put the story's unstated point into words: "The real point of Joyce's story is the price of self-delusion." Or it might focus on a significant detail: "The hat at the end of 'The Secret Sharer' symbolically summarizes the story's most important theme."

The figurative hats of any story invite your explanation, and your paper. Every story emanates unstated implications. These are what the physical details *mean*. These are what you explain in your paper. They may display the irony of human ambitions or of dreams, as in the very different stories, "The Chaser," "The Man Who Would Be King," and "I'm a Fool." They may be stories of initiation, like "The Secret Sharer." Initiation into what? What values? What assumptions? Through what kind of perilous journey? The story's whole impact may depend on how it is told, by a bitter or a kindly omniscient awareness, by a cocky or humble first person. The central character may learn something ("Bliss") or may learn very little ("Halfway to the Moon"). Any of these implications can engage your curiosity and crystalize into a paper.

Whatever you choose to write about, the procedure is the same. You open your paper with some introductory remarks to situate your reader:

> Hawthorne's "My Kinsman, Major Molineux" concerns a young country boy in colonial America. He comes to a city, which seems to be Boston, to look up an influential relative and start a career.

Or you might orient your reader from another direction:

> Fitzgerald's "Babylon Revisited" at first seems nothing more than a tale of a man beset by domestic difficulty. We discover that Charlie Wales has lost his wife through death and his daughter to his in-laws.

Give your reader a few more details, then set your thesis: "Hawthorne's real theme is self-reliance," or "By the end we understand the story to be not only of Charlie Wales, but also of the twenties, just before and after the crash."

This introduces your paper. Now start a new paragraph and describe and quote and explain until you feel that you have fully shown your reader what you mean. Your story will have been in the past tense, of course: "It was near nine o'clock of a moonlight evening...." Your description will be in the present tense:

> It is nearly nine o'clock when Robin crosses the ferry. The evening is fully lit by the moon, as we are reminded throughout the story at crucial points.

To repeat, your quotations will come from the story exactly as they are: everything in the past tense, except, of course, the dialogue, followed by the narrative past: " 'Now, truly, I am in luck,' replied Robin." Your description will be in the present: "Robin replies that he is truly in luck," or " 'Now, truly, I am in luck,' Robin replies"—since here you are quoting only Robin's words, and not including Hawthorne's narrative "replied Robin."

When you have put all your evidence before your reader, write a concluding paragraph to sum up your point and drive it home, and your paper is done. But don't forget a title that will head your reader toward what you are going to show: "The theme of self-reliance in 'My Kinsman, Major Molineux' "; "The Babylon of 'Babylon Revisited'."

Poetry

On Poetry

Sound

A poet has to accept the language given to him at birth, so we have first to ask what the peculiar strengths and difficulties of the English language are, as a medium of poetry. First, it is a heavily accented language (French critics speak of "the British thump"); second, it has a high proportion of consonants to vowels; third, most of the words in common use, including most of the words of native English origin, are monosyllables or near monosyllables; and fourth, it has very few inflections. There are other characteristics that will emerge in the more specific commentaries, but these will do to go on with. All four, of course, are closely interconnected.

Every monosyllable has a separate accent, however slight, and because the English language is so heavily accented, and so full of consonants as well, the effect is like that of riding a bucking and plunging horse that is capable of great speed and power if brought under control or of merely running away with its rider if not. Partly because of the lack of inflections, English is very full of such phrases as "the house," "by him," "when I," "of love," "to be," and the like. These phrases are iambic (short–long) in rhythm, and help to make iambic the normal meter for English poetry:

> When I consider how my light is spent (Milton: "On His Blindness").
> And I with thee will choose to live (Milton: "Il Penseroso").

The first line quoted is iambic pentameter, or five iambic feet; the second iambic tetrameter, or four feet. The iambic pentameter has been the backbone of English poetry from Chaucer to our own day, but tetrameters or octosyllabics are used a good deal too, especially when high speed is wanted. Longer lines than the pentameter are seldom used for long poems, because in English the rhythm is apt to get clattery and turn into doggerel when there are too many beats in a line, especially if rhyme is added. In fact, anything unusual that a poet does to his rhythm or rhyme, in English, is likely to sound obtrusive, to call more attention to itself than would normally be wanted. So such unusual features, when we find them in competent poets, are being used for special effects.

At the beginning of *Paradise Lost,* Milton describes the expelling of Satan from heaven thus:

> Hurled headlong flaming from the ethereal sky.

The rhythm of "headlong flaming" is trochaic (long–short), because the trochaic is a "falling" rhythm and is also a more energetic rhythm in English than the more usual iambic. We notice too that the use of a long word ("ethereal") makes the rhythm lighter because, with the heavy accent in English, a long word brings in a ripple of unaccented syllables. This principle, that the longer words in English (mostly borrowed from Greek or Latin) lighten the rhythm because of their lightly stressed syllables, meets us everywhere: in Cummings' "O sweet spontaneous earth," in Wordsworth's "From high to low doth dissolution climb," in Whitman's "A reminiscence sing," and so on.

Special effect poems in unusual rhythms include Tennyson's "Charge of the Light Brigade," where the prevailing rhythm is dactylic (long–short–short), because the theme is a cavalry charge. In this passage from Swinburne's "Atalanta in Calydon" an anapestic rhythm (short–short–long) mingles with the iambic one, and goes with the sense of bursting energy that the poem celebrates:

> When the hounds of spring are on winter's traces,
>   The mother of months in meadow or plain
> Fills the shadows and windy places
>   With lisp of leaves and ripple of rain.

In the second and fourth lines there is also a heavy alliteration (beginning with the same letter) in the texture: this again is there to mark the driving power of emerging life in the spring.

The same principles apply to rhyme. Most rhymes are very resonant in English, and even the simplest double rhymes, like the "traces–places" rhyme above, are generally used rather sparingly. Triple rhymes usually belong to light verse, as in Byron's

> But O! ye lords of ladies intellectual,
> Inform us truly: have they not henpecked you all?

where the poet is writing deliberate or intentional doggerel. In Hopkins' sonnet, "That Nature is a Heraclitean Fire," we find such rhymes as "resurrection–dejection–deck shone." Here again what would be in other contexts doggerel rhymes are being used for a special reason: they go with the complex and syncopated rhythm of the poem.

Poetry is language used with the greatest possible intensity, and one obvious way in which it can express intensity is in its movement and sound. Poetry is never very far from dancing and singing or from other energetic actions like marching and horseback riding, and, as already suggested, English is an excellent vehicle for high speeds. Thus Edith Sitwell:

> Nobody comes to give him his rum but the
> Rim of the sky hippopotamus-glum
> Enhances the chances to bless with a benison
> Alfred Lord Tennyson crossing the bar laid. . .

Here the movement is so fast that it drags the meaning along after it: there is a meaning, and the words will eventually make some sense, but the meaning can wait. Here we are in the world of the nursery rhyme, where the bouncing rhythm is what carries the poem. We may notice two things in particular. First, a very emphatic rhyme scheme cuts across the arrangement of the lines, which gives a syncopated rhythm suggesting the jazz rhythms popular in the 1920s, which the poem is in part imitating. Second, while there is a rolling dactylic meter, there are also four main beats or accents to the line.

This four-beat line is the most primitive measure in English: it is the rhythm of Old English poetry, where as a rule the first three beats alliterate to increase the emphasis, as in the adaptation of the Old English poem "The Seafarer" by Ezra Pound:

> Chill its chains are; chafing sighs
> Hew my heart round and hunger begot
> Mere-weary mood. Lest man know not. . .

It is also the rhythm of most nursery rhymes, and of most ballads. The ballad is often in a four-lined stanza with four and three accents alternating (or, counting by syllables, eight–six–eight–six, the "common meter" of hymnbooks). This is really a continuous four-beat line with a rest at the end of every other line. Thus in "Sir Patrick Spens":

> The kíng síts in Dumfeŕling tówn,
> Drińking the bloód-red wíne: (rest)
> "O whére will Í get goód sailór
> To sáil this shíp of miñe?" (rest).

Originally the ballad (from the Latin *ballare*, to dance; cf. "ball") had a background of dancing as well as singing, and for dancing one needs a continuous rhythm.

After English poetry adopted meters in the Middle Ages, the old four-beat rhythm could still be heard as a secondary rhythm syncopating against it. If we look at Hamlet's famous "to be or not to be" soliloquy on the page, we see iambic pentameter lines; but if we listen to an actor speaking the lines on a stage, we also hear something like this:

> To BE or NOT to be, THAT is the QUEStion:
> WHEther 'tis NOBler in the MIND to SUFfer
> The SLINGS and ARrows of outRAGEous FORtune,
> Or TAKE up ARMS against a SEA of TROUBles. . .

The conflict of the two rhythms against each other, in Shakespeare as elsewhere, is largely what provides the subtlety and complexity of what we hear. In a high-speed poem like Browning's "How They Brought the Good News from Ghent to Aix," the speed comes from both the anapestic meter and the heavy accent of the four main beats:

> I sprang to the stirrup, and Joris, and he;
> I galloped, Dirck galloped, we galloped all three;
> "Good speed!" cried the watch, as the gatebolts undrew;
> "Speed!" echoed the wall to us galloping through. . .

But of course poetry has to have its andante and adagio movements as well. In the stopped couplets of Dryden or Pope, the iambic pentameter takes charge, and the four beats we heard in Hamlet's soliloquy fade into the background:

> Tim'rous by nature, of the Rich in awe,
> I come to Counsel learned in the Law:
> You'll give me, like a friend both sage and free,
> Advice; and (as you use) without a Fee.

We can still hear the four main stresses, but a strict meter and rhyme scheme controls them. If such verse as this (from Pope's "Imitation of the First Satire of the Second Book of Horace") is read aloud to us, we have a sense of constantly fulfilled expectation. If we hear the line "You'll give me, like a friend both sage and free," we don't know what the next line will be, but we do know that it will be an impeccable iambic pentameter, with the last word a perfect rhyme to "free." Such strict meter and rhyme give the effect of *wit*, of high intelligence in full control of its material. Similarly with E. A. Robinson's "Richard Cory":

> So on we worked, and waited for the light,
>> And went without the meat, and cursed the bread;
> And Richard Cory, one calm summer night,
>> Went home and put a bullet through his head.

The punch line is surprising, but, once we have had the surprise, inevitable. Such a combination of relaxed easy movement and deadly accuracy would be impossible without the firmly established meter and rhyme.

The capacity of English for high speed has also something to do with the fact that, because it has so few inflections, it is dependent on a fixed word order. If we hear someone say at a station, "When does go this train?" there is no disturbance of logical order, but we know that the speaker's native language is not English. The skeleton of word order is the sequence subject–predicate–object, as in "John loves Mary," where *John* is the subject, *loves* the predicate, and *Mary* the object. "Mary loves John" is clearly a different statement, and "John Mary loves" means nothing because it could mean both. In Latin we would normally say "Johannes Mariam amat," but we could rearrange the words in any order, because the *m* on the word *Mariam* shows that that is the object whatever the order. Latin verse often seems to the student who is accustomed to the unvarying linear drive of English from subject through predicate to object, like a very tangled ball of yarn. In Gray's "Elegy in a Country Churchyard" we read:

> The boast of heraldry, the pomp of power,
>> And all that beauty, all that wealth e'er gave,
> Awaits alike th' inevitable hour. . .

Here the *s* on "awaits" shows that "hour" is the subject and the first two lines the object. It is very unusual to alter the word order in this way, but in such a slow and meditative movement it is perhaps appropriate sometimes to pause and rearrange our impressions of the words.

In still slower movements we become more aware of such features of English as its clusters of consonants. In the passage given in this book from Pope's "Essay on Criticism," Pope gives examples of how to vary the speed and rhythm to fit the subject being talked about, and says:

> When Ajax strives some rock's vast weight to throw,
> The line too labours, and the words move slow.

What makes the first line laborious is the number of consonants we have to stop and spit out before we can go on to the next word. If we are to read poetry with an ear as sharp as Pope's, we have to be conscious of every sound. If we try to introduce "ghost story," "wasp's nest," or "priest's stole" into ordinary conversation, we soon realize how much eliding, or cutting out of consonants, we do; but we cannot read poetry in this way. Thus in Ben Jonson's little song beginning:

> Slow, slow, fresh fount, keep time with my salt tears

there are two *t*'s in "salt tears," not one, and getting them both out will bring us down to the speed Jonson wants.

The same song goes on:

> Droop herbs and flowers
> Fall grief in showers

Here we come back to something noted earlier: that monosyllables have separate accents and thus slow down the rhythm. In a passage just before the one quoted from Pope's "Essay on Criticism," Pope gives horrible examples of bad ways to write and cautions against an overuse of monosyllables with this one:

> And ten low words oft creep in one dull line.

The trouble with this line is not the ten monosyllables but the ten heavy stressed accents: such a line has no rhythm at all. So when Milton is describing the scenery of hell, he says:

> Rocks, caves, lakes, fens, bogs, dens, and shades of death
> (*Paradise Lost*, Book 2, 621)

Both the rhythm and the harsh discordant inner rhyme "fens–dens" tell our ears that the scenery of hell is not attractive.

Monosyllables, however, are very useful to a skilful poet. Even in an unobtrusive line like Shakespeare's "When icicles hang by the wall,"

we should notice how the lively anapestic meter can still "hang" the
icicle for a suspended instant. Or, again, placing two heavy accents,
usually monosyllables, together in the middle of a line (called a spondee), can often give the effect of something ominous or foreboding, as
in a wonderful little poem written by Sir Thomas Wyatt at the beginning of the sixteenth century:

> Perchaunce thee lie withered and old
> These winter nights that are so cold,
> Plaining in vain unto the moon:
> Thy wishes then dare not be told.

On the other hand, the absence of inflectional endings means that
English can seldom manage the gentle caressing rhythm that we find
so often in, say, German lyrics. In the Middle English that Chaucer
used there were still a large number of such endings, and modern
English can seldom match the lightness of such lines in Chaucer as

> And trewély to tellen atté lasté.

or

> And whan we weren eséd atté besté.

Writing lyrics in English is like carving in oak: it can be done all right,
but we need to allow for the toughness of the medium. In Housman's
A Shropshire Lad we have:

> With rue my heart is laden
> For golden friends I had,
> For many a rose-lipt maiden
> And many a lightfoot lad.

The delicate charm needed is skilfully brought out, but the curiously
old-fashioned words used show that the poet is not finding it easy.

So far we have dealt with poetry that is also verse, that is, has certain
features like a regularly recurring rhythm that can be identified. But
we can have verse that is not acceptable as poetry, or what we usually
call doggerel, and we can have poetry in "free verse," with none of
these specific features. If we look at, say, Whitman's "Dalliance of the
Eagles," we can see that the furious gyrating and twisting movement is
just as effective without a metrical framework. In other free verse, such
as we have in William Carlos Williams, we can see what makes it "poetry" if we look at what the arrangement of lines on the page does to
our reading of it. There is no continuous linear movement through the

syntax of one sentence after another, as in prose: the rhythm keeps returning on itself, driving towards its own center, forcing us to grasp
the total meaning of the words.

Meaning

We said a moment ago that poetry is language used with the greatest
possible intensity, and this means, first of all, that in reading poetry
we have to step up the intensity of our reading, beginning with the
movements and sounds. In prose, or more specifically nonliterary
prose, there is a low-keyed intensity, because the words are being used
to describe something else. In poetry the words exist for their own
sake, and the primary relation of each word, including nouns and
verbs, is to the other words, not to the things or actions they describe.
In this world, surrounded as we are with such masses of verbiage,
mostly passing for prose, we get feelings of panic about the amount of
material we have to "cover." We have to start reading poetry by dismissing this panic. Reading poetry is a technique of meditation: we
must keep reading and rereading the same poem for quite a while before its real intensity will emerge.

When it does, we can begin to see that poetry is *figured* speech, made
up of patterns of words that bring things together in ways that would
be quite impossible if the writer were trying to describe something in
experience. The most frequent of these figures are metaphor (this is
that), simile (this is like that), and metonymy (this is put for that). We
have metaphor in Shakespeare's:

> Thou that art now the world's fresh ornament,
> And only herald of the gaudy spring.

We have simile in T. S. Eliot's:

> When the evening is spread out against the sky
> Like a patient etherized upon a table.

We have metonymy in Dylan Thomas':

> The force that through the green fuse drives the flower.

These figures are not decorative or ornamental; they are modes of
thinking. A great poet is a great thinker too, but he does not think
conceptually or in ideas like a philosopher: he thinks in images, and

sets these images beside one another or on top of each other, leaving it to us to make the connections. We said that the metaphor usually takes the form "this is that," but Ezra Pound says that real metaphor just puts things together, as in his little two-line poem "In a Station of the Metro":

> The apparition of these faces in the crowd,
> Petals on a wet, black bough.

We may feel that this is not good grammar, and that we need some predicate in between, such as "is," "is like," "reminds me of," "suggests to me," "is linked in my mind with," or whatever; but it is clear that as soon as we have put one down we have ruined the poem. Similarly:

> O Western wind, when wilt thou blow,
> The small rain down can rain?
> Christ, if my love were in my arms,
> And I in my bed again!

Here the juxtaposing of uncomfortable weather and comfortable bed is easier to follow; it is not a logical connection, but an emotional connection of a kind we have all had in some form or other. The important thing is that the poem simply presents the two images: it does not talk about them, still less about the relation between them.

Thinking in metaphor, simile, and metonymy is in some ways a primitive way of thinking; it has no relation to telling the "truth" as we usually understand truth, where we put a body of words up against something it's supposed to describe and say it's "true" if it's an adequate counterpart of that something. It's because of the primitive nature of poetic thinking that all literatures, in all human societies, begin with poetry: prose develops only much later. But while it's primitive it's also extremely concentrated. Suppose I were writing an essay about eighteenth-century England and were trying to explain how the common-sense philosophy of John Locke helped to establish the cultural climate out of which the Industrial Revolution emerged. This revolution brought in new inventions, like the spinning jenny, but also other things like mass migrations, exploitation, and imperialism, which had very little to do with common sense. As I keep writing, it may occur to me that there is a grotesque analogy here with the Biblical story of the fall of man, with Adam so well adjusted to this world until, with the creation of Eve from his body, another person, and consequently a human community, a wholly unexpected complication, emerged in which he lost that world. But the more I labor at this analogy, the more strained and unconvincing it would get; my readers couldn't follow it, and I would finally have to cut it: one can't do this kind of thing in prose. Yeats, in poetry, can say it all in twenty syllables or so:

> Locke sank into a swoon,
> The garden died:
> God took the spinning-jenny
> Out of his side.

Or, again, Hopkins writes of the instability of all things, and of how, for him, the resurrection of Christ establishes something permanent and solid in the middle of it. He ends:

> This Jack, joke, poor potsherd, patch, matchwood, immortal diamond. . .

Heraclitus said that everything was in a state of flux, a constant flowing or burning, so that one very central image of his pessimistic philosophy (he was called the weeping philosopher) would be a burnt match. If we held the opposite view, that there was something in reality that did not disintegrate, about the best image we could use would be a diamond, the hardest known substance and as precious as the match is the opposite. Yet both match and diamond are made of the same substance, namely carbon, just as the physical body of man ("potsherd" because it's compared in the Bible to a potter's vessel) is of the same substance as the spiritual body that enters the resurrection. Hopkins wrote the poem out of a profound belief in the resurrection. We don't have to share the belief to respond to the poem, but we do have to see that the belief is imaginatively possible.

The greater intensity of poetry as compared with prose, we said, is partly a greater intensity of sound: that is why rhyme, alliteration, pun, and assonance (similarity of sound) belong to it. Such resemblances of sound are accidents in a language until a poet uses them; then they become elements of design. Here we have "jack–joke," "patch–match," diamond as gem and diamond as suit in a pack of cards. The "jack" in cards, also called knave or valet (servant), suggests man in his ordinary state, of no use except as a servant of God and usually unreliable as that. When Pope describes a card game in his long mock-epic "The Rape of the Lock," he says

> The Knave of Diamonds tries his wily arts,

indicating that this particular card has a shifty reputation in card lore. The sound link between jack and joke turns up another card, the joker or fool (the fool was often called "patch" in Shakespeare's day). In the background, not in the poem, but within its range of allusions, is the contrast between ordinary man, weak and suggestible, and the invincible man Christ: Paul calls them the first and second Adam. The Greek word *adamas*, unconquerable, is the origin of our word diamond.

Poetry, we see, can be endlessly allusive. If you try to write poetry, you will soon find that the kind of poetry you produce will depend entirely on what kind of poetry you have read and will be full of echoes of it. You may be expressing your ideas or emotions, but you can never express them directly: they must go inside some poetic structure, or what is called a convention. Young poets usually gather in groups and write like each other, but as they get older they strike their individual roots into literature and learn more and more from the poets of the past. But the notion that they can write outside the framework of the literary tradition itself is pure illusion, and all great poets gave it up long before they became great poets. When Yeats tells, for the thousandth time in poetry, the classical myth of Leda and the swan, and says

> A shudder in the loins engenders there
> The broken wall, the burning roof and tower
> And Agamemnon dead

he is indirectly telling us that, because Homer wrote about the Trojan War, at the beginning of our literary tradition, that is the most important war for readers of poetry to know about, and the word "Agamemnon" can fall on our ears with a resonant crash that no less familiar name can match. True, Whitman urged his Muse to "migrate from Greece and Ionia" on the ground that we had heard enough about the Trojan War, and come to "a better, fresher, busier sphere" in the United States. But fortunately, Whitman's real Muse made him write like a poet and ignored his advertising copy. The *content* of poetry constantly changes, but its inner structure does not, just as a new baby is always a different individual but never constitutes a different species.

The allusiveness of poetry is a by-product of the fact that the study of literature is as coherent and systematic as the study of any other subject. Just as every genuine discovery in science is true because it is consistent with other genuine discoveries, so every great work of the imagination is imaginatively consistent with other works in the same medium. Even so, this allusiveness in poetry may put some of us off. Why, we may say, should we have to look up so many references? O.K., they may be part of our cultural heritage, and it may be very interesting to see how classical and Biblical stories and echoes from earlier poets are used in poetry, but, with so complicated a world facing us in this century, is it really worth so much time and effort to learn a special elitist language?

Some poets are explicitly allusive, like Milton, or like Eliot or Yeats in our day. They make us look things up and consult footnotes, and we find ourselves rapidly getting an education in comparative mythology, religion, and literature. Others, like Wordsworth or Robert Frost, keep their language as free of special reference as they can, and they are the ones who may give us a clue to the question we're looking at. We notice that some poems—we might call them emblematic poems—set up a single central image and stare hard at it, as, to take random examples, Blake does with his tiger and worm-eaten rose, W. C. Williams with his red wheelbarrow, or Whitman with his live-oaks in Louisiana. Sometimes the poet tells us that the image is the distilled essence of an intense experience, as Rossetti does in "The Woodspurge." The poet doesn't use these images as a pretext for talking about something else, as is done in certain kinds of allegory, where the "real" meaning is something different. If we look at Robert Frost's poem, "Stopping by Woods on a Snowy Evening," long enough and hard enough, we begin to see that it is collecting a great variety of experiences into that single, solemn, hushed moment. But we can't say, for instance, "the poem is really about death," because it is, just as really, about stopping by woods on a snowy evening. It's as though the central image of the poem had been placed in a reverberating sound chamber and were expressing some kind of infinite resonance in its very concrete and specific theme.

Explicitly allusive poems, then, like Milton's "Lycidas" or Eliot's "Prufrock," create a resonance by their allusions against everything else we've read in literature, as well as an infinite amount that we haven't. (This goes for the poet too, who hasn't read the poems written after his death that echo him, and that he echoes by anticipation.) Such poems tell us that the whole world of literature is one gigantic imaginative body, and that studying literature is entering into that body of human imaginative experience, not just reading one thing after another. But implicit allusion, like that of Frost's poem, raises an even bigger question.

Wallace Stevens has a poem called "Description Without Place," a long and very difficult poem, which says that man does not live directly in the world of nature, like animals and plants—he lives within his own constructs of the world. These constructs, in their totality, are what we call cultures or civilizations. They are what, as Stevens says, make everything that we see in Spain look Spanish. A great deal of these constructs consists of words, and at the center of it all is the body of words we call poetry. Because the metaphors and images and analogies of poetry are what tell us most clearly that we cannot see or understand or act or feel except from within the human construct that we entered at birth. Nature knows nothing of up or down, of inside or outside, of beginning or ending, of before and not yet. All these are notions we impose on nature. It is the poets who keep reducing our experience to these simple and essential things, and they who lead us to the engine room of creation, the energy and intensity of the constructing process itself.

CHAPTER 1

Types of Poems

Lyric

Think of a lyre. It is a stringed instrument, a small harp. The poet knows how to play a bit, and he is trying to find on it the sounds that will suit his emotional state. He hums as he plays, seeking a rhythm and a melody, and begins to find words that can express his feelings even better than his notes. As he plays, the music becomes secondary, and he discovers he is creating a poem. The words become more interesting. Perhaps he lays the lyre aside and continues working with the rhythm of the language alone and the subtly musical variations of the words themselves.

The poet is a lyrist, or a lyricist. His poem is a lyric. He is indulging in probably the most ancient form of poetic composition. He may have lived in ancient Greece, or Anglo–Saxon England, or the Australian Bush of the early twentieth century—or he may live today in an apartment in the Bronx, a condominium in Ann Arbor, a tract house in Phoenix, or a farmhouse outside of Fargo. The poetic impulse knows no limits in time or space. As a maker of lyrics, the poet is attempting to express his own deep-seated feelings. He tries the words and the rhythms one way, then another, and so again and again until he is satisfied. The process may be easy, or it may take weeks or years. Between times he goes about his other business. Somewhere along the way he recites the poem to a friend or prints it on a sheet or in a book. If it is good enough—if enough people like it—it becomes a part of the shared artistic heritage of humanity and finds renewed expression down the years in the throats and minds of countless people who never knew the maker. Consider the following lyric:

> Western wind, when wilt thou blow,
> The small rain down can rain?
> Christ, if my love were in my arms,
> And I in my bed again! 4

The poem comes from England in the fifteenth century. As with many fine lyrics, nobody knows now who wrote it, but it has delighted numerous readers and listeners. Read it several times, trying to recapture the feeling of the individual who made it. What is there in these few words that he liked and that so many since him have admired? Start simply with the pleasure in the reading. Find some delight in the way the words move in your throat or sound in your mind. Try to imagine yourself the maker. The poem is your poem. What are you trying to say? What do you like best about the way you have said it?

Perhaps this particular poem holds no delight for you. Perhaps you can make no sense of it at all. If so, your case is not unusual, and not without remedy. Not all poems are for all people, any more than all paintings are, or all music or all movies or all automobiles. Leave this poem and go on to another. You may want to return to this one later. Perhaps you will see it differently after you have read some others that you find more immediately appealing. Perhaps other individuals who have admired this poem are in some way wrong about it, but if your mind is inquisitive you will want to return to it from time to time in order to discover whether you can yet see it as they do.

Meanwhile, try this one:

Waly, Waly, Love Be Bonny

O waly,[1] waly, up the bank,
   And waly, waly, down the brae,[2]
And waly, waly, yon burn[3] side,
   Where I and my love were wont to gae.[4]   4

I leant my back upon an oak,
   I thought it was a trusty tree;
But first it bent, and then it broke,
   Just as my love proved false to me.   8

O waly, waly, love is bonny,
   A little while when it is new;
But when it's old, it waxes cold,
   And fades away like morning dew.   12

O wherefore should I busk[5] my head?
   O wherefore should I comb my hair?
For my true love has me forsook,
   And says he'll never love me more.   16

[1] Woefully.
[2] Steep bank.
[3] Brook.
[4] Go.
[5] Dress.

Now Arthur's Seat[6] shall be my bed,
   The sheets shall ne'er be filled by me:
Saint Anthony's well[7] shall be my drink,
   Since my true love has forsaken me.   20

Martinmas[8] wind, when wilt thou blow,
   And shake the green leaves off the tree?
O gentle death, when wilt thou come?
   For of my life I am weary.   24

'Tis not the frost, that freezes fell,[9]
   Nor blowing snow's inclemency;
'Tis not such cold that makes me cry,
   But my love's heart grown cold to me.   28

When we came in by Glasgow town,
   We were a comely sight to see,
My love was clad in black velvet,
   And I myself in cramasie.[10]   32

But had I wist,[11] before I kissed,
   That love had been so ill to win,
I'd locked my heart in a case of gold,
   And pinned it with a silver pin.   36

And oh! if my young babe were born,
   And set upon the nurse's knee,
And I my self were dead and gone:
   For a maid again I'll never be.   40

[6] A hill outside Edinburgh.
[7] Near Arthur's Seat.
[8] Feast of St. Martin, November 11.
[9] Cruelly.
[10] Crimson.
[11] Known.

"Waly, Waly" is another old poem, longer than "Western Wind," and, depending upon a number of matters peculiar to you as an individual, perhaps more immediately attractive or more puzzling still. Like "Western Wind" it is anonymous, its author no longer known. We can assume that it was already old in the eighteenth century when it was first printed. It has experienced a large part of its popularity as a folk song, being passed down orally in singing families and communities until well into the twentieth century. In the form in which we have printed it (we have modernized some of the lines), it is obviously Scottish, but in other versions it loses its evidence of that particular locality and becomes localized elsewhere, or nowhere. In other versions, it loses some stanzas or picks up others.

You have probably already noticed that the sixth stanza contains some haunting echoes of "Western Wind." Did this poet know the other poem? He may have, but, if not, he at least seems familiar with the same ways of thinking, aware of the same poetic conventions, attuned to the same rhythms. Here is an interesting point: Poems reflect upon one another. The more we read, the more easily we understand and enjoy them, having accumulated the means to compare each new poem intelligently with a large number of others.

Does the sixth stanza here reflect any light upon the single stanza of "Western Wind"? What is the poet trying to convey? It seems clear that the speaker, weary of life, is asking for death. But what has that to do with "Martinmas wind" and with shaking the leaves off the tree? A dictionary will tell us that Martinmas comes each year on November 11. A wind on that day would blow the leaves off the trees that are soon going to lose them anyway, because winter is coming. The speaker seems to be asking for winter to come more quickly and seems to be associating winter with death. This is not a difficult or unusual association. We can easily imagine moods that might find expression in these words. We write the words, try them different ways, set them to music, and find we are pleased. We have written a lyric.

Let us return briefly to "Western Wind." The similarities in the lines suggest similar things happening in the poem. If the Martinmas wind that shakes the leaves from the trees is a harbinger of winter, is the western wind that brings small rain also suggesting a season? What season? We might put ourselves in the poet's place and try to understand the emotion he desires to convey. He didn't say "north wind" or "east wind," for those winds would presumably not express his feeling. Not "south wind" either. Each of those winds would bring a different kind of weather. If you live in the country almost anywhere in North America, and are observant of natural phenomena, or if you are a meteorologist, you have noticed yourself what this English poet had observed centuries ago in the similar weather patterns of his country. The west wind brings the light rains ("the small rain") of spring. "April showers bring May flowers." The poet wants the spring because he wants his loved one in his arms again. Have they been separated in some way that will end in the spring, or is he merely playing upon the natural association of spring and love? He doesn't say.

The poem "Waly, Waly" covers more ground. In this poem the speaker wants not love, but death. The poem asks not for spring, but winter. Why? The other stanzas help to fill in the story. Although not all of its details are clear, we know enough to summarize the outline.

By the end of the fourth stanza, we have discovered that the speaker is a woman and by the end of the final stanza we know why she wants to die. We also know why she looks forward to a later rather than immediate death. She respects the life of her unborn child. She wants to see it safely cared for. And then she asks for relief from her shame and sorrow. We have called this a lyric rather than a narrative poem, yet it is also a narrative, a story in small, dramatic scope. Every lyric, indeed, is a brief dramatic statement from some larger life's story at which we can only guess from the emotions expressed and the details given.

If we consider "Waly, Waly" from another perspective, we will notice that some stanzas contribute nothing to the story but express the speaker's emotion in different ways, as if she were trying one way of making poetry out of her feelings and then another. With this hint and that, obliquely she circles round the situation, each time adding to, or qualifying, our understanding of her emotions. Obviously if we want greater compression or want to stick more closely to the story, we can leave out some of the stanzas. This is exactly what some versions of "Waly, Waly" do. Just as obviously, if we wish to dwell upon the emotion or clarify the story we can add another stanza or two. Such changes are part of the folk process. In some songs related to this one, for example, the stanza about the oak is coupled with one about a rose:

> I put my finger to the bush
>   To pluck a rose of fairest kind;
> The thorn it pricked me at a touch,
>   And O, I left that rose behind.

This stanza does not appear in the version of "Waly, Waly" we have used. If you were a poet, would you put it in or leave it out? What would you gain or lose? We must balance fullness of statement against the power of compression. Our opinions may differ. The extreme compression of "Western Wind," for instance, may be either an advantage or a disadvantage. Some people believe it a fragment of a lost folk song.

Here is another anonymous Scottish song.

The Bonny Earl of Murray*

> Ye highlands and ye lowlands,
>   Oh! where have ye been?
> They have slain the Earl of Murray,
>   And have laid him on the green.   4
>
> Now woe be to thee, Huntley!
>   And wherefore did ye so?
> I bade you bring him with you,
>   But forbade you him to slay.   8

*Francis J. Child, *English and Scottish Popular Ballads*, 181A. We have normalized the spelling.

He was a braw[1] gallant,
　　And he rode at the ring;
And the bonny Earl of Murray,
　　Oh! he might have been a king.　　　　　　　　12

He was a braw gallant,
　　And he played at the ball;
And the bonny Earl of Murray
　　Was the flower among them all.　　　　　　　　16

He was a braw gallant,
　　And he played at the glove;
And the bonny Earl of Murray,
　　Oh! he was the Queen's love.　　　　　　　　20

Oh! long will his lady
　　Look o'er the Castle Downe,[2]
Ere she see the Earl of Murray
　　Come sounding through the town.　　　　　　　　24

---

[1] Brave.
[2] Doune Castle, belonging to the Earl of Murray (or Moray).

Like "Waly, Waly" the poem has obviously a story lying behind it, but the poet seems less concerned with telling the story than with communicating his feelings about it. We can, if we wish, look up the details, for the story is based in historical fact. The "Bonny Earl of Murray" died mysteriously at Donibristle on February 7, 1592. But myriads of people have found this folksong attractive without knowing the history. We can do the same. We can see that a man named Huntley has killed the Earl of Murray. We can see that the Earl was admired for his athletic prowess and that he was loved by the queen (was Huntley jealous?). We can see that the Earl might, in time, have been a king. This is all we learn, but probably all we need to know.

But who is the anonymous speaker and exactly what emotion is he trying to express? In "Western Wind" and "Waly, Waly," the speaker was the center of events as far as we could see into them: the man in love, the girl betrayed. Is this speaker someone close to the Earl of Murray, perhaps a friend or relation? Not according to anything we can be sure of in the poem. He appears to have been a person in command, though his orders not to slay the Earl were disobeyed. From his position of authority, he speaks to all Scots ("Ye highlands and ye lowlands") and implies that all are involved in the guilt ("Oh! where have ye been?") and now share the sense of loss. He seems, in short, to address himself to a country mourning a national hero. He wants to remind his people of a promise now lost for the whole nation ("he might have been a king").

He wants also to remind them of the personal dimensions of a national tragedy:

>Oh! long will his lady
>Look o'er the Castle Downe,
>Ere she see the Earl of Murray
>Come sounding through the town.

We do not need to live in Scotland in the sixteenth century to appreciate these emotions.

Let us change the mood. Lyrics, as we are beginning to see, appear often to be one form or another of lamentation. The poet, in solitude, desires something he does not have or wishes to undo something now past correction. Human emotions in solitude often take just that turn. But other emotions are possible. Lyrics can celebrate the poet's entire satisfaction with the current state of his affairs, or they can suggest, as the next one does, that even if he has lost something, he has not lost everything. There are more fish than one in the sea. Or, in the language of "The Brazos River," there are more rivers than one in Texas.

The Brazos River

We crossed the broad Pecos, we forded the Nueces,
We swum the Guadalupe, we followed the Brazos,
Red River runs rusty, the Wichita clear,
But down by the Brazos I courted my dear.   4

    Then la, la, la, lee, lee, lee, give me your hand,
    La, la, la, lee, lee, lee, give me your hand,
    La, la, la, lee, lee, lee, give me your hand,
    There's a-many a river that waters the land.   8

The fair Angelina runs glossy and gliding,
The crooked Colorado runs weaving and winding,
And the slow San Antonio, it courses the plain,
But I never will walk by the Brazos again.   12

    Then la, la, la, lee, lee, lee, pole the boat on,
    La, la, la, lee, lee, lee, pole the boat on,
    La, la, la, lee, lee, lee, pole the boat on,
    My Brazos River sweetheart has left me and gone.   16

She kissed me, she hugged me, she called me her dandy,
The Trinity's muddy, the Brazos quicksandy,
She hugged me, she kissed me, she called me her own,
But down by the Brazos she left me alone.   20

Then la, la, la, lee, lee, lee, give me your hand,
La, la, la, lee, lee, lee, give me your hand,
La, la, la, lee, lee, lee, give me your hand,
The Trinity's muddy, but the Brazos quicksand.   24

The girls of Little River, they're plump and they're pretty,
The Sabine and the Sulphur have many a beauty,
On the banks of the Natchez there's girls by the score,
And down by the Brazos I'll wander no more.   28

Then la, la, la, lee, lee, lee, give me your hand,
La, la, la, lee, lee, lee, give me your hand,
La, la, la, lee, lee, lee, give me your hand,
There's a-many a river that waters the land.   32

To this point we have been illustrating our concepts with anonymous poems. For lyrics this is easy to do, because the lyric is in its essence a simple outpouring of emotion. All people have emotions and many have sat or wandered by themselves, trying to shape their feelings into poems. Many people not otherwise known as poets have created works that passed into the anonymous stream of oral tradition because other people liked them and kept them alive. But a number of the best lyrics in English have been created by people who established reputations as poets, and whose names are therefore available to us. Let us examine a few.

Loveliest of Trees, the Cherry Now

A. E. Housman   (1859–1936)

Loveliest of trees, the cherry now
Is hung with bloom along the bough,
And stands about the woodland ride
Wearing white for Eastertide.   4

Now, of my threescore years and ten,
Twenty will not come again,
And take from seventy springs a score,
It only leaves me fifty more.   8

And since to look at things in bloom
Fifty springs are little room,
About the woodlands I will go
To see the cherry hung with snow.   12

Like the poems that we have already examined, Housman's is mostly concerned with the speaker's emotional response to his situation. In some respects, both the situation and the emotion seem quite simple. It is spring. The speaker tells us the cherry trees are in bloom. The speaker is twenty years old, and he expects to live fifty more years, until he has reached the normal human expectancy of "threescore years and ten." Through the simple subtraction that he performs for us, we see that he thinks of fifty years as a short time ("It *only* leaves me fifty more"); we begin to see, in other words, that the source of his emotion is his sense of how short life is, of how little time he has left. He feels a sense of loss, but it is followed by a sense of recovery. In the last stanza, he seems to be saying that since time is short, he will use it well by doing the things he most enjoys. This is a poem of mixed emotions, like "The Brazos River": something has been lost, but much remains. Yet the emotions here seem much more subtly mixed than they are in "The Brazos River."

The cherry is not for this speaker just any tree. It is the "Loveliest of trees." We may not agree with him, but we know what he means. We can share his emotional response to cherry trees in bloom in the spring. Just so, we did not know the Earl of Murray, but we have observed the death of other men that we admired and that the nation looked up to. The poem moves us because it touches our emotions in ways similar to the way that the original experience touched the poet. All poetry acts upon us this way (or it does not act upon us at all). We have felt similar emotions in comparable experiences. We read the poem, and it becomes our poem because it says something to us that we would have liked to have said ourselves, if not about cherry trees, about other things cherished. The poem is a concrete expression of abstract truths we have all responded to. We are surrounded by things that we love. Life is short. We can make the most of our time by spending it at those activities that bring life's beauty home to us.

The last word, "snow," is a puzzle to some readers, but need not be. The two most obvious possibilities of meaning do not contradict but support one another. As a first possibility, the word may carry its ordinary, literal meaning. The poet says that since fifty springs provide such a limited time to enjoy the cherries, he will visit them in the winter as well, when they are covered not with blossoms, but with snow. In other words, he will take full advantage of all his human opportunities to enjoy their beauty. As a second possibility, the poet may not mean real snow, but may intend the word in a figurative or metaphoric sense. The blossoms, as the first stanza makes clear, are white. In the last line he may be telling us that they make the trees look as though they were "hung with snow." The message is essentially the same. Given his awareness of the shortness of life, he will expend his present moments enjoying the beauty of the trees and the wonder and mystery of life they represent.

But why does the poet end a poem about spring with an ambiguous reference to snow? The poem, we may say, is not about spring. It is about the brevity of life. Blossoms remind us of spring and youth (when we are twenty—or were, or soon will be). Snow reminds us of winter and death (when we shall have run out our threescore years and ten). In one brilliant word at the end of the poem the poet reminds us of both our hopes and our human limitations. For this effect it does not matter whether the snow is literal or figurative, since the fundamental image is the same and in either case it is played off against the blossoms.

Faced with a knowledge of the shortness of our lives, most of us will not spend our time wandering in cherry orchards, either in spring or in winter, but we can respond to the desire to grasp at fleeting beauty and vitality. The poet's experience of looking at blossoms and being reminded of snow becomes for us a fitting response to life's brevity. We, too, are moved by the thought that lies behind the bittersweet double image.

Although the word "snow" may be read both with a literal and a metaphoric sense, both readings are consistent with the poetic effect of the other lines. Both affirm the poet's desire to extract all the enjoyment he can from the fleeting moments of his existence. The poem is memorable because its clear and effective communication is not hurt but assisted by the ambiguity of the last word. An accomplished reader of poetry learns to welcome the enrichment of such extended meanings without using their existence as an excuse to believe that a poem can mean anything he wants it to.

When a poem is well made, momentary delight turns sometimes into a lifelong possession. Not all our emotions are serious. Not all moments that we treasure are of earth-shaking importance.

Maid of Athens, Ere We Part

George Gordon, Lord Byron   (1788–1824)

Ζωή μου, σᾶς ἀγαπῶ.

1

Maid of Athens, ere we part,
Give, oh give me back my heart!
Or, since that has left my breast,
Keep it now, and take the rest!
Hear my vow before I go,
Ζωή μου, σᾶς ἀγαπῶ.[1]   6

2

By those tresses unconfined,
Wooed by each Ægean wind;

---

[1] It means, "My life, I love you!" [Byron]. Say "Zo-ay mo sas agatho."

By those lids whose jetty fringe
Kiss thy soft cheeks' blooming tinge;
By those wild eyes like the roe,
Ζωή μου, σᾶς ἀγαπῶ.   12

3

By that lip I long to taste;
By that zone-encircled waist;
By all the token-flowers that tell
What words can never speak so well;
By love's alternate joy and woe,
Ζωή μου, σᾶς ἀγαπῶ.   18

4

Maid of Athens! I am gone:
Think of me, sweet! when alone.
Though I fly to Istambol,
Athens holds my heart and soul:
Can I cease to love thee? No!
Ζωή μου, σᾶς ἀγαπῶ.   24

Did the poet feel as strongly about the Maid of Athens as his words suggest? Perhaps he did, but this poem also conveys the strong sense of delight that the poet must have felt in making it. The poem is not so much a lament as a celebration. Responding to the music, we find ourselves celebrating with him. You don't know Greek? That doesn't matter. It is easy to imagine what fun it must have been to work into a poem in English the rhythms and sounds of the Maid's own language. Many a reader, if he possessed the knowledge and the skill, would be happy to do the same.

The grass at our feet and the clouds overhead, if seen clearly, can supply the emotion for a lyric.

Cut Grass

Philip Larkin (1922–   )

Cut grass lies frail:
Brief is the breath
Mown stalks exhale.
Long, long the death   4

It dies in the white hours
Of young-leafed June
With chestnut flowers,
With hedges snowlike strewn,   8

White lilac bowed,
Lost lanes of Queen Anne's lace,
And that high-builded cloud
Moving at summer's pace.   12

Emotion is fundamental to the lyric, but the emotion is heightened by the form. If we look back over the lyrics already presented, we see that all were subjected to rigid control of meter and rhyme. Like the lyre player, the poet must discover the pitch and rhythm, the words and arrangements that will present his idea most memorably. At times he may discover that a form as exacting as the sonnet will serve him admirably:

Composed Upon Westminster Bridge, September 3, 1802

William Wordsworth (1770–1850)

Earth has not anything to show more fair:
Dull would he be of soul who could pass by
A sight so touching in its majesty:
This City now doth, like a garment, wear   4
The beauty of the morning; silent, bare,
Ships, towers, domes, theatres, and temples lie
Open unto the fields, and to the sky;
All bright and glittering in the smokeless air.   8
Never did sun more beautifully steep
In his first splendour, valley, rock, or hill;
Ne'er saw I, never felt, a calm so deep!
The river glideth at his own sweet will: 12
Dear God! the very houses seem asleep;
And all that mighty heart is lying still!

A lesser poet could not achieve this effect in a form so difficult. Wordsworth, despite the sonnet's complicated demands of rhyme and meter, has managed to keep his emotion pure and create a poem that sings with a stately music. At its best, indeed, the sonnet turns out to be a remarkably useful lyric form.

Although written by a highly sophisticated modern poet, the following lyric is in a style much like that of the anonymous lyrics with which we began.

Down by the Salley Gardens

W. B. Yeats (1865–1939)

Down by the salley[1] gardens my love and I did meet;
She passed the salley gardens with little snow-white feet.

---
[1] Willow.

She bid me take love easy, as the leaves grow on the tree;
But I, being young and foolish, with her would not agree.   4
In a field by the river my love and I did stand,
And on my leaning shoulder she laid her snow-white hand.
She bid me take life easy, as the grass grows on the weirs;[2]
But I was young and foolish, and now am full of tears.   8

[2] Milldams.

What are we to make of this? Like the folk poets, Yeats leaves much of his story untold. He wants less to tell a story than to express a state of mind, to find the words that will convey his emotion. Has he succeeded? Does the music in his lines bring his feelings home to us? Does omitting the details heighten the force of the tears? We probably care lastingly for the lives of strangers only as we find them relevant through the magic of art. The lyrist gives his emotion a form that makes it tangible to others. If he cannot do that, he sings only to himself.

Narrative

A *narrative poem* is a story in verse. The impulse to tell stories this way is as old as human memory. Like the lyric impulse, the narrative impulse is fundamental to human nature. The teller is originally also a singer. He wishes to give his story a form, and his meters help other singers to remember it and pass it along, just as they enchant his listeners. As the centuries wear on, the words may outlast the music. And, as with the lyrics, poets may engage in the sounds and rhythms of the words alone.

The first five of the following poems are, again, anonymous folksongs. The last three were written by poets whose names we know. All have a story to tell and tell it in different ways.

Edward*

"Why does your brand[1] so drop with blood,
               Edward, Edward?
Why does your brand so drop with blood,
    And why so sad gang[2] ye, O?"   4
"O I have killed my hawk so good,
               Mother, Mother.
O I have killed my hawk so good,
    And I had no more but he, O."   8

*Francis J. Child, *English and Scottish Popular Ballads*, 13B. We have normalized the spelling.
[1] Sword.
[2] Go.

"Your hawk's blood was never so red,
                    Edward, Edward.
Your hawk's blood was never so red,
    My dear son I tell thee, O."   12
"O I have killed my red-roan steed,
                 Mother, Mother.
O I have killed my red-roan steed,
    That erst[3] was so fair and free, O."   16

"Your steed was old, and ye have got more,
                    Edward, Edward.
Your steed was old, and ye have got more,
    Some other dule[4] ye drie,[5] O."   20
"O I have killed my father dear,
                 Mother, Mother.
O I have killed my father dear,
    Alas, and woe is me, O!"   24

"And what penance will ye drie for that,
                    Edward, Edward?
And what penance will ye drie for that?
    My dear son, now tell me, O."   28
"I'll set my feet in yonder boat,
                 Mother, Mother.
I'll set my feet in yonder boat,
    And I'll fare over the sea, O."   32

"And what will ye do with your towers and your hall,
                    Edward, Edward?
And what will ye do with your towers and your hall,
    That were so fair to see, O?"   36
"I'll let them stand till they down fall,
                 Mother, Mother.
I'll let them stand till they down fall,
    For here never more may I be, O."   40

"And what will ye leave to your bairns[6] and your wife,
                    Edward, Edward?
And what will ye leave to your bairns and your wife,
    When ye gang over the sea, O?"   44
"The world's room, let them beg through life,
                 Mother, Mother.

[3] Once.
[4] Sorrow.
[5] Suffer.
[6] Children.

The world's room, let them beg through life,
    For them never more will I see, O."   48

"And what will ye leave to your own mother dear,
    Edward, Edward?
And what will ye leave to your own mother dear?
    My dear son, now tell me, O."   52
"The curse of hell from me shall ye bear,
    Mother, Mother.
The curse of hell from me shall ye bear,
    Such counsels ye gave to me, O."   56

The story of Edward is much older than even the Scottish version printed here, existing in a number of languages other than English. Its roots are in the Middle Ages, but it lives on with twentieth-century folk-singers, both British and American.

Where is its staying power? Certainly, the story itself is engaging. Edward has killed his father, but we don't know that at the outset. The manner of telling is part of the attraction; it is a succession of suspenses. The listener wonders until the end of the third stanza why Edward's sword is dripping with blood. He also may wonder why the mother seems unperturbed on learning that her son has killed her husband. She merely asks him what penance he will do. Only in the last line does the poet tell us (if we are alert) why she was not upset, or even surprised. The elements of a mystery are heightened first by the horror of patricide, then by the further horror of the mother's instigation. There is no punishment for such wickedness—or is there? The son says "I'll set my feet in yonder boat, / and I'll fare over the sea, O." Among some ancient seafaring peoples the normal punishment for murder was to be set upon the open sea in an oarless boat. The son accepts his punishment. But the mother? How calmly she asks about the blood on the sword. How willingly she lets the son go to his judgment. How eagerly she asks what he will leave behind. The poem is an intense study of character.

We could say more. Notice the abruptness of the beginning. Notice the repetition. Notice the rhythm of the lines. The poem is entirely dialogue, wholly the mother's questions and the son's answers. Are any of these elements important? They are if they help us to feel the effect of the poem, if they help to locate it among our memorable literary experiences.

Another ancient poem tells a story of the jealousy of two sisters.

The Two Sisters

There was an old man in the North Countrie,
    Bow down, bow down.

There was an old man in the North Countrie,
And he had daughters, one, two, three.   4
    Love will be true, true to my love,
    Love will be true to you.

There was a young man came courting there,
And he did choose the youngest fair.   8

He gave to the youngest a gay gold ring,
And to the oldest not a single thing.

He gave to the youngest a beaver hat,
And the oldest she thought hard of that.   12

"Sister, O sister, let's walk the sea shore,
To see the ships come sailing o'er."

They were walking along on yonder sea-brim
When the oldest shoved the youngest in.   16

"O sister, O sister, hand me your hand,
And you may have my house and land."

"O sister, O sister, hand me your glove,
And you may have my own true love."   20

"I'll neither hand you hand nor glove,
For all I want is your true love."

So down she sank and away she swam
Until she reached the old mill dam.   24

The miller threw out his old grab-hook
And pulled the fair maiden out of the brook.

"O miller, O miller, here's three gold rings,
If you'll take me to my father's again."   28

He up with her fingers and off with her rings
And threw her back in the brook again.

The miller was hung at his mill gate
For drowning of my sister Kate.   32

Although this song, too, exists in some fine Scottish versions, this is a
version from North America. What is the story? Are any elements un-
clear? Does it bear any resemblances to "Edward"? Both are family tragedies, for instance. Does this have any bearing on their enduring popularity? Are other elements particularly worthy of comment?

Sir Patrick Spens*

The king sits in Dumferling town,
    Drinking the blood-red wine:
"O where will I get good sailor,
    To sail this ship of mine?"   4

Up and spoke an elderly knight,
    Sat at the king's right knee:
"Sir Patrick Spens is the best sailor
    That sails upon the sea."   8

The king has written a braid[1] letter,
    And signed it with his hand,
And sent it to Sir Patrick Spens,
    Was walking on the sand.   12

The first line that Sir Patrick read,
    A loud laugh laughed he;
The next line that Sir Patrick read,
    The tear blinded his eye.   16

"O who is this has done this deed,
    This ill deed done to me,
To send me out this time o' the year,
    To sail upon the sea!   20

"Make haste, make haste, my merry men all,
    Our good ship sails the morn."
"O say not so, my master dear,
    For I fear a deadly storm.   24

"Late late yestreen I saw the new moon,
    With the old moon in her arm,
And I fear, I fear, my dear master,
    That we will come to harm."   28

O our Scots nobles were right loath
    To wet their cork-heeled shoon,[2]
But long o'er all the play were played,
    Their hats they swam aboon.[3]   32

*Child 58A. We have normalized the spelling.
  [1] Informal.
  [2] Shoes.
  [3] Above.

O long, long may their ladies sit,
    With their fans into their hand,
Or e'er they see Sir Patrick Spens
    Come sailing to the land.   36

O long, long may the ladies stand,
    With their gold combs in their hair,
Waiting for their own dear lords,
    For they'll see them no more.   40

Half o'er, half o'er to Aberdour,
    It's fifty fathoms deep,
And there lies good Sir Patrick Spens,
    With the Scots lords at his feet.   44

What is the story? Sir Patrick Spens put to sea at his king's command, despite his misgivings and the warning of one of his followers, and went down with his ship and his men. Why should we care? We can't care, in fact—not unless it is a good story, well told, with some relationship to our own lives. Does it have these qualities? We have no king we must obey, but can imagine ourselves doing something against our better judgment out of loyalty to another. We can imagine a tragedy ensuing. In this sense, we can participate in the story of Sir Patrick Spens, can understand his bravery, and can sympathize with his fate. If we judge it a good story, and well told, we will return to it again and again, as others have before us. Thousands of ships have gone down in various seas. Few are remembered so vividly.

Part of the poet's power is his grim sense of irony. The best sailor in the kingdom drowns. His men are loath to wet even the heels of their shoes in such a bad season, but their hats swim fifty fathoms overhead before they are through. Their ladies will wait long, he says in grim understatement, meaning they will wait forever. Stanzas 9 and 10 enhance the tragedy memorably by turning to the ladies ashore. We may remember, however, that an almost identical stanza ends "The Bonny Earl of Murray." We don't need to ask which came first; the question is probably beyond answering in any case. A more interesting question is whether "Sir Patrick Spens" needs to work this traditional formula twice, or whether once, as in "The Bonny Earl of Murray," would have been enough.

Queen Eleanor's Confession*

Queen Eleanor was a sick woman,
    And afraid that she should die;

*Child 156; text from Thomas Percy, *Reliques of Ancient English Poetry*. We have normalized the spelling.

Then she sent for two friars of France
    To speak with her speedily. 4

The king called down his nobles all,
    By one, by two, by three;
"Earl Marshall, I'll go shrive[1] the queen,
    And thou shalt wend[2] with me." 8

"A boon, a boon,"[3] quoth Earl Marshall,
    And fell on his bended knee,
"That whatsoever Queen Eleanor say,
    No harm thereof may be." 12

"I'll pawn my lands," the king then cried,
    "My scepter, crown, and all,
That whatsoever Queen Eleanor says,
    No harm thereof shall fall. 16

"Do thou put on a friar's coat,
    And I'll put on another;
And we will to Queen Eleanor go,
    Like friar and his brother." 20

Thus both attired then they go:
    When they came to Whitehall,[4]
The bells did ring, and the choristers sing,
    And the torches did light them all. 24

When that they came before the queen
    They fell on their bended knee;
"A boon, a boon, our gracious queen,
    That you sent so hastily." 28

"Are you two friars of France," she said,
    "As I suppose you be?
But if you are two English friars,
    You shall hang on the gallows tree." 32

"We are two friars of France," they said,
    "As you suppose we be;
We have not been at any mass,
    Since we came from the sea." 36

"The first vile thing that ever I did
    I will to you unfold:

[1] Receive confession of.
[2] Go.
[3] A favor.
[4] A former London palace.

Earl Marshall had my maidenhead,
    Beneath this cloth of gold."   40

"That's a vile sin," then said the king,
    "May God forgive it thee!"
"Amen, amen," quoth Earl Marshall;
    With a heavy heart spoke he.   44

"The next vile thing that ever I did,
    To you I'll not deny:
I made a box of poison strong,
    To poison King Henry."   48

"That's a vile sin," then said the king,
    "May God forgive it thee!"
"Amen, amen," quoth Earl Marshall;
    "And I wish it so may be."   52

"The next vile thing that ever I did,
    To you I will discover:
I poisoned fair Rosamond,[5]
    All in fair Woodstock bower."   56

"That's a vile sin," then said the king,
    "May God forgive it thee!"
"Amen, amen," quoth Earl Marshall;
    "And I wish it so may be."   60

"Do you see yonder's little boy,
    A tossing of the ball?
That is Earl Marshall's eldest son
    And I love him the best of all.   64

"Do you see yonder's little boy,
    A catching of the ball?
That is King Henry's youngest son,
    And I love him the worst of all.   68

"His head is fashioned like a bull;
    His nose is like a boar—"
"No matter for that," King Henry cried,
    "I love him the better, therefore."   72

The king pulled off his friar's coat,
    And appeared all in red.
She shrieked, and cried, and wrung her hands,
    And said she was betrayed.   76

---

[5] Rosamond Clifford. King Henry II (1133–1189) built her a "bower," or cottage, at Woodstock, near the present site of Blenheim Palace.

The king looked over his left shoulder,
  And a grim look looked he:
"Earl Marshall," he said, "but for my oath,
  Or hanged thou shouldst be."   80

Queen Eleanor of Aquitaine married Henry II of England in 1152, but the poem was probably composed much later, and the story is, as Bishop Percy observes, "altogether fabulous." The tale of a husband's disguising himself to hear his wife's deathbed confession is traditional, and a part of the fun here arises from the poet's decision to place his story in a royal court rather than among more common people.

The next story is more common, both in events and in setting. There are numerous murdered girls in folksongs. This poem appears to be based on a murder in North Carolina at the beginning of the nineteenth century.

Poor Omie

A story to you I'll tell of little Omie Wise,
How she got deluded by John Lewis's lies.

He told her to meet him all at Adams Spring,
The money he would bring her and other fine things.   4

Little Omie went to meet him all at old Adams Spring,
No money did he bring her nor other fine things.

So hop up behind me and away we will go
Back down to the river where the deep waters flow.   8

Says: John Lewis, John Lewis, please tell me your mind;
Do you mean to marry me or leave me behind?

Little Omie, Little Omie, says: I'll tell you my mind;
My mind is to drown you and leave you behind.   12

Says: John Lewis, John Lewis, please spare my sweet life,
I'll go out a-begging if I can't be your wife.

I'll not have no pity, neither will I spare your life,
You will not go out begging, neither will you be my wife.   16

O he beat her, then he banged her till she could scarcely go;
Lord, he threw her in the river where the deep waters flow.

He jumped up on his pony, Lord, away he did ride,
The screams of his darling ride all on by his side.   20

Two little boys were fishing just at the break of morn,
They spied poor Omie's body come floating along.

They threw their nets around her and drew her to shore,
O then poor Omie's body was to hunt for no more.   24

They arrested John Lewis, they arrested him to-day,
They buried poor little Omie down in the cold clay.

My name is John Lewis, my name I'll never deny,
I murdered my own true lover and her name is Omie Wise.   28

My name is John Lewis, my name I'll never deny,
I murdered my own true lover; I'll never reach the sky.

Literary poets have frequently attempted to capture the anonymous ballad for their own, sometimes with greater sophistication in subject matter and technique, as in the following poem.

The Rime of the Ancient Mariner

Samuel Taylor Coleridge   (1772–1834)

Argument

How a Ship, having first sailed to the Equator, was driven by Storms to the cold Country towards the South Pole; how the Ancient Mariner cruelly and in contempt of the laws of hospitality killed a Seabird and how he was followed by many and strange Judgements: and in what manner he came back to his own Country.

Part I

An ancient Mariner meet-eth three Gallants bidden to a wedding-feast, and de-taineth one.

It is an ancient Mariner,
And he stoppeth one of three.
'By thy long grey beard and glittering eye,
Now wherefore stopp'st thou me?

The Bridegroom's doors are opened wide,   5
And I am next of kin;
The guests are met, the feast is set:
May'st hear the merry din.'

He holds him with his skinny hand,
'There was a ship,' quoth he.   10
'Hold off! unhand me, grey-beard loon!'
Eftsoons[1] his hand dropt he.

The Wedding-Guest is spellbound by the eye of the old seafaring man, and constrained to hear his tale.

He holds him with his glittering eye—
The Wedding-Guest stood still,
And listens like a three years' child: 15
The Mariner hath his will.

---

[1] Immediately.

The Wedding-Guest sat on a stone:
He cannot choose but hear;
And thus spake on that ancient man,
The bright-eyed Mariner.   20

**The Mariner tells how the
ship sailed southward with
a good wind and fair
weather, till it reached the
line.**

'The ship was cheered, the harbour cleared,
Merrily did we drop
Below the kirk,[2] below the hill,
Below the lighthouse top.

The Sun came up upon the left,   25
Out of the sea came he!
And he shone bright, and on the right
Went down into the sea.

Higher and higher every day,
Till over the mast at noon[3]—'   30
The Wedding-Guest here beat his breast,
For he heard the loud bassoon.

**The Wedding-Guest hear-
eth the bridal music; but
the Mariner continueth his
tale.**

The bride hath paced into the hall,
Red as a rose is she;
Nodding their heads before her goes   35
The merry minstrelsy.

The Wedding-Guest he beat his breast,
Yet he cannot choose but hear;
And thus spake on that ancient man,
The bright-eyed Mariner.   40

**The ship driven by a storm
toward the south pole.**

And now the STORM-BLAST came, and he
Was tyrannous and strong:
He struck with his o'ertaking wings,
And chased us south along.

With sloping masts and dipping prow,   45
As who pursued with yell and blow
Still treads the shadow of his foe,
And forward bends his head,
The ship drove fast, loud roared the blast,
And southward aye we fled.   50

And now there came both mist and snow,
And it grew wondrous cold:
And ice, mast-high, came floating by,
As green as emerald.

[2] Church.
[3] When the ship has reached the equator, or "line."

The land of ice, and of
fearful sounds where no
living thing was to be
seen.

And through the drifts the snowy clifts   55
Did send a dismal sheen:
Nor shapes of men nor beasts we ken[4]—
The ice was all between.

The ice was here, the ice was there,
The ice was all around: 60
It cracked and growled, and roared and howled,
Like noises in a swound![5]

Till a great sea-bird, called
the Albatross, came
through the snow-fog and
was received with great
joy and hospitality.

At length did cross an Albatross,
Thorough the fog it came;
As if it had been a Christian soul,   65
We hailed it in God's name.

It ate the food it ne'er had eat,
And round and round it flew.
The ice did split with a thunder-fit;
The helmsman steered us through!   70

And lo! the Albatross
proveth a bird of good
omen, and followeth the
ship as it returned northward through fog and
floating ice.

And a good south wind sprung up behind;
The Albatross did follow,
And every day, for food or play,
Came to the mariner's hollo!

In mist or cloud, on mast or shroud,[6]   75
It perched for vespers[7] nine;
Whiles all the night, through fog-smoke white,
Glimmered the white Moon-shine.'

The ancient Mariner
inhospitably killeth the
pious bird of good omen.

'God save thee, ancient Mariner!
From the fiends, that plague thee thus!—   80
Why look'st thou so?'—With my cross-bow
I shot the Albatross.

Part II
The Sun now rose upon the right:
Out of the sea came he,
Still hid in mist, and on the left   85
Went down into the sea.

And the good south wind still blew behind,
But no sweet bird did follow,
Nor any day for food or play
Came to the mariners' hollo!   90

[4] See.
[5] Swoon.
[6] The set of ropes supporting the mast.
[7] Evenings.

His shipmates cry out
against the ancient Mari-
ner, for killing the bird of
good luck.

And I had done a hellish thing,
And it would work 'em woe:
For all averred, I had killed the bird
That made the breeze to blow.
Ah wretch! said they, the bird to slay,   95
That made the breeze to blow!

But when the fog cleared
off, they justify the same,
and thus make themselves
accomplices in the crime.

Nor dim nor red, like God's own head,
The glorious Sun uprist:
Then all averred, I had killed the bird
That brought the fog and mist.   100
'Twas right, said they, such birds to slay,
That bring the fog and mist.

The fair breeze continues;
the ship enters the Pacific
Ocean, and sails north-
ward, even till it reaches
the Line.

The fair breeze blew, the white foam flew,
The furrow followed free;
We were the first that ever burst   105
Into that silent sea.

The ship hath been sud-
denly becalmed.

Down dropt the breeze, the sails dropt down,
'Twas sad as sad could be;
And we did speak only to break
The silence of the sea!   110

All in a hot and copper sky,
The bloody Sun, at noon,
Right up above the mast did stand,
No bigger than the Moon.

Day after day, day after day,   115
We stuck, nor breath nor motion;
As idle as a painted ship
Upon a painted ocean.

And the Albatross begins
to be avenged.

Water, water, every where,
And all the boards did shrink;   120
Water, water, every where,
Nor any drop to drink.

The very deep did rot: O Christ!
That ever this should be!
Yea, slimy things did crawl with legs   125
Upon the slimy sea.

About, about, in reel and rout
The death-fires[8] danced at night;
The water, like a witch's oils,
Burnt green, and blue and white.   130

[8] Corposants, or St. Elmo's fire: glowing balls of electricity sometimes appearing on a ship's masts.

A Spirit had followed them; one of the invisible inhabitants of this planet, neither departed souls nor angels; concerning whom the learned Jew, Josephus, and the Platonic Constantinopolitan, Michael Psellus, may be consulted. They are very numerous, and there is no climate or element without one or more.

And some in dreams assuréd were
Of the Spirit that plagued us so;
Nine fathom deep he had followed us
From the land of mist and snow.

And every tongue, through utter drought,   135
Was withered at the root;
We could not speak, no more than if
We had been choked with soot.

The shipmates, in their sore distress, would fain throw the whole guilt on the ancient Mariner: in sign whereof they hang the dead sea-bird round his neck.

Ah! well a-day! what evil looks
Had I from old and young!   140
Instead of the cross, the Albatross
About my neck was hung.

Part III

There passed a weary time. Each throat
Was parched, and glazed each eye.
A weary time! a weary time!   145
How glazed each weary eye,
When looking westward, I beheld
A something in the sky.

The ancient Mariner beholdeth a sign in the element afar off.

At first it seemed a little speck,
And then it seemed a mist;   150
It moved and moved, and took at last
A certain shape, I wist.[9]

A speck, a mist, a shape, I wist!
And still it neared and neared:
As if it dodged a water-sprite,   155
It plunged and tacked and veered.

At its nearer approach, it seemeth him to be a ship; and at a dear ransom he freeth his speech from the bonds of thirst.

With throats unslaked, with black lips baked,
We could nor laugh nor wail;
Through utter drought all dumb we stood!
I bit my arm, I sucked the blood,   160
And cried, A sail! a sail!

A flash of joy;

With throats unslaked, with black lips baked,
Agape they heard me call:
Gramercy![10] they for joy did grin,
And all at once their breath drew in,   165
As they were drinking all.

[9] Knew.
[10] Great thanks.

And horror follows. For can it be a ship that comes onward without wind or tide?

See! see! (I cried) she tacks no more!
Hither to work us weal;[11]
Without a breeze, without a tide,
She steadies with upright keel!   170

The western wave was all a-flame.
The day was well nigh done!
Almost upon the western wave
Rested the broad bright Sun;
When that strange shape drove suddenly   175
Betwixt us and the Sun.

It seemeth him but the skeleton of a ship.

And straight the Sun was flecked with bars,
(Heaven's Mother send us grace!)
As if through a dungeon-grate he peered
With broad and burning face.   180

And its ribs are seen as bars on the face of the setting Sun.

Alas! (thought I, and my heart beat loud)
How fast she nears and nears!
Are those *her* sails that glance in the Sun,
Like restless gossameres[12]?

The Spectre-Woman and her Deathmate, and no other on board the skeleton ship.

Are those *her* ribs through which the Sun   185
Did peer, as through a grate?
And is that Woman all her crew?
Is that a DEATH? and are there two?
Is DEATH that woman's mate?

Like vessel, like crew! Death and Life-in-Death have diced for the ship's crew, and she (the latter) winneth the ancient Mariner.

Her lips were red, *her* looks were free,   190
Her locks were yellow as gold:
Her skin was as white as leprosy,
The Night-mare LIFE-IN-DEATH was she,
Who thicks man's blood with cold.

The naked hulk alongside came,   195
And the twain were casting dice;
'The game is done! I've won! I've won!'
Quoth she, and whistles thrice.

No twilight within the courts of the Sun.

The Sun's rim dips; the stars rush out:
At one stride comes the dark;   200
With far-heard whisper, o'er the sea,
Off shot the spectre-bark.

At the rising of the Moon,

We listened and looked sideways up!
Fear at my heart, as at a cup,

---

[11] Good.
[12] Filmy cobwebs floating in air.

My life-blood seemed to sip!   205
The stars were dim, and thick the night,
The steersman's face by his lamp gleamed white;
From the sails the dew did drip—
Till clomb above the eastern bar
The hornéd Moon, with one bright star   210
Within the nether tip.

One after another,

One after one, by the star-dogged Moon,
Too quick for groan or sigh,
Each turned his face with a ghastly pang,
And cursed me with his eye.   215

**His shipmates
drop down dead.**

Four times fifty living men,
(And I heard nor sigh nor groan)
With heavy thump, a lifeless lump,
They dropped down one by one.

**But Life-in-Death begins
her work on the ancient
Mariner.**

The souls did from their bodies fly,—   220
They fled to bliss or woe!
And every soul, it passed me by,
Like the whizz of my cross-bow!

Part IV

**The Wedding-Guest fear-
eth that a Spirit is talking
to him;**

'I fear thee, ancient Mariner!
I fear thy skinny hand!   225
And thou art long, and lank, and brown,
As is the ribbed sea-sand.

I fear thee and thy glittering eye,
And thy skinny hand, so brown.'—

**But the ancient Mariner as-
sureth him of his bodily
life, and proceedeth to relate his horrible penance.**

Fear not, fear not, thou Wedding-Guest!   230
This body dropt not down.

Alone, alone, all, all alone,
Alone on a wide wide sea!
And never a saint took pity on
My soul in agony.   235

**He despiseth the creatures
of the calm,**

The many men, so beautiful!
And they all dead did lie:
And a thousand thousand slimy things
Lived on; and so did I.

**And envieth that *they*
should live, and so many
lie dead.**

I looked upon the rotting sea,   240
And drew my eyes away;
I looked upon the rotting deck,
And there the dead men lay.

I looked to heaven, and tried to pray;
But or ever a prayer had gusht,   245
A wicked whisper came, and made
My heart as dry as dust.

I closed my lids, and kept them close,
And the balls like pulses beat;
For the sky and the sea, and the sea and the sky   250
Lay like a load on my weary eye,
And the dead were at my feet.

But the curse liveth for him in the eye of the dead men.

The cold sweat melted from their limbs,
Nor rot nor reek did they:
The look with which they looked on me   255
Had never passed away.

An orphan's curse would drag to hell
A spirit from on high;
But oh! more horrible than that
Is the curse in a dead man's eye!   260
'Seven days, seven nights, I saw that curse,
And yet I could not die.

In his loneliness and fixedness he yearneth towards the journeying Moon, and the stars that still sojourn, yet still move onward; and every where the blue sky belongs to them, and is there appointed rest, and their native country and their own natural homes, which they enter unannounced, as lords that are certainly expected and yet there is a silent joy at their arrival.
By the light of the Moon he beholdeth God's creatures of the great calm.

The moving Moon went up the sky,
And no where did abide:
Softly she was going up,   265
And a star or two beside—

Her beams bemocked the sultry main,
Like April hoar-frost spread;
But where the ship's huge shadow lay,
The charmèd water burnt alway   270
A still and awful red.

Beyond the shadow of the ship,
I watched the water-snakes:
They moved in tracks of shining white,
And when they reared, the elfish light   275
Fell off in hoary flakes.

Within the shadow of the ship
I watched their rich attire:
Blue, glossy green, and velvet black,
They coiled and swam; and every track   280
Was a flash of golden fire.

Their beauty and their happiness.

O happy living things! no tongue
Their beauty might declare:

He blesseth them in his heart.

A spring of love gushed from my heart,
And I blessed them unaware: 285
Sure my kind saint took pity on me,
And I blessed them unaware.

The spell begins to break.

The self-same moment I could pray;
And from my neck so free
The Albatross fell off, and sank   290
Like lead into the sea.

Part V

Oh sleep! it is a gentle thing,
Beloved from pole to pole!
To Mary Queen the praise be given!
She sent the gentle sleep from Heaven,   295
That slid into my soul.

By grace of the holy Mother, the ancient Mariner is refreshed with rain.

The silly[13] buckets on the deck,
That had so long remained,
I dreamt that they were filled with dew;
And when I awoke, it rained.   300

My lips were wet, my throat was cold,
My garments all were dank;
Sure I had drunken in my dreams,
And still my body drank,

I moved, and could not feel my limbs: 305
I was so light—almost
I thought that I had died in sleep,
And was a blessèd ghost.

He heareth sounds and seeth strange sights and commotions in the sky and the element.

And soon I heard a roaring wind:
It did not come anear;   310
But with its sound it shook the sails,
That were so thin and sere.[14]

The upper air burst into life!
And a hundred fire-flags sheen,[15]
To and fro they were hurried about!   315
And to and fro, and in and out,
The wan stars danced between.

And the coming wind did roar more loud,
And the sails did sigh like sedge;[16]

[13] Simple, plain.
[14] Dried.
[15] Shone. The "fire-flags" are the aurora australis, streamers of lights in the skies of the Southern Hemisphere, comparable to the aurora borealis, or northern lights, of the Northern Hemisphere.
[16] A coarse, grass-like planet.

And the rain poured down from one black cloud;   320
The Moon was at its edge.

The thick black cloud was cleft, and still
The Moon was at its side:
Like waters shot from some high crag,
The lightning fell with never a jag,   325
A river steep and wide.

The bodies of the ship's crew are inspirited, and the ship moves on;

The loud wind never reached the ship,
Yet now the ship moved on!
Beneath the lightning and the Moon
The dead men gave a groan.   330

They groaned, they stirred, they all uprose,
Nor spake, nor moved their eyes:
It had been strange, even in a dream,
To have seen those dead men rise.

The helmsman steered, the ship moved on;   335
Yet never a breeze up-blew;
The mariners all 'gan work the ropes,
Where they were wont to do;
They raised their limbs like lifeless tools—
We were a ghastly crew.   340

The body of my brother's son
Stood by me, knee to knee:
The body and I pulled at one rope,
But he said nought to me.

But not by the souls of the men, nor by daemons of earth or middle air, but by a blessed troop of angelic spirits, sent down by the invocation of the guardian saint.

'I fear thee, ancient Mariner!'   345
Be calm, thou Wedding-Guest!
'Twas not those souls that fled in pain,
Which to their corses[17] came again,
But a troop of spirits blest:

For when it dawned—they dropped their arms,   350
And clustered round the mast;
Sweet sounds rose slowly through their mouths,
And from their bodies passed.

Around, around, flew each sweet sound,
Then darted to the Sun;   355
Slowly the sounds came back again,
Now mixed, now one by one.

[17] Bodies.

Sometimes a-dropping from the sky
I heard the sky-lark sing;
Sometimes all little birds that are,   360
How they seemed to fill the sea and air
With their sweet jargoning![18]

And now 'twas like all instruments,
Now like a lonely flute;
And now it is an angel's song,   365
That makes the heavens be mute.

It ceased; yet still the sails made on
A pleasant noise till noon,
A noise like of a hidden brook
In the leafy month of June,   370
That to the sleeping woods all night
Singeth a quiet tune.

Till noon we quietly sailed on,
Yet never a breeze did breathe:
Slowly and smoothly went the ship,   375
Moved onward from beneath.

The lonesome Spirit from the south-pole carries on the ship as far as the Line, in obedience to the angelic troop, but still requireth vengeance.

Under the keel nine fathom deep,
From the land of mist and snow,
The spirit slid: and it was he
That made the ship to go.   380
The sails at noon left off their tune,
And the ship stood still also.

The Sun, right up above the mast,
Had fixed her to the ocean:
But in a minute she 'gan stir,   385
With a short uneasy motion—
Backwards and forwards half her length
With a short uneasy motion.

Then like a pawing horse let go,
She made a sudden bound: 390
It flung the blood into my head,
And I fell down in a swound.

How long in that same fit I lay,
I have not to declare;
But ere my living life returned,   395

[18] Twittering.

The Polar Spirit's fellow-
daemons, the invisible inhabitants of the element,
take part in his wrong; and
two of them relate, one to
the other, that penance
long and heavy for the ancient Mariner hath been
accorded to the Polar Spirit, who returneth south-
ward.

I heard and in my soul discerned
Two voices in the air.

'Is it he?' quoth one, 'Is this the man?
By him who died on cross,
With his cruel bow he laid full low   400
The harmless Albatross.

The spirit who bideth by himself
In the land of mist and snow,
He loved the bird that loved the man
Who shot him with his bow.'   405

The other was a softer voice,
As soft as honey-dew:
Quoth he, 'The man hath penance done,
And penance more will do.'

Part VI

FIRST VOICE
'But tell me, tell me! speak again,   410
Thy soft response renewing—
What makes that ship drive on so fast?
What is the ocean doing?'

SECOND VOICE
'Still as a slave before his lord,
The ocean hath no blast;   415
His great bright eye most silently
Up to the Moon is cast—

If he may know which way to go;
For she guides him smooth or grim.
See, brother, see! how graciously   420
She looketh down on him.'

FIRST VOICE
'But why drives on that ship so fast,
Without or wave or wind?'

The Mariner hath been
cast into a trance; for the
angelic power causeth the
vessel to drive northward
faster than human life
could endure.

SECOND VOICE
'The air is cut away before,
And closes from behind.   425

Fly, brother, fly! more high, more high!
Or we shall be belated:
For slow and slow that ship will go,
When the Mariner's trance is abated.'

The supernatural motion is retarded; the Mariner awakes, and his penance begins anew.

I woke, and we were sailing on 430
As in a gentle weather:
'Twas night, calm night, the moon was high;
The dead men stood together.

All stood together on the deck,
For a charnel-dungeon[19] fitter: 435
All fixed on me their stony eyes,
That in the Moon did glitter.

The pang, the curse, with which they died,
Had never passed away:
I could not draw my eyes from theirs, 440
Nor turn them up to pray.

The curse is finally expiated.

And now this spell was snapt: once more
I viewed the ocean green,
And looked far forth, yet little saw
Of what had else been seen— 445

Like one, that on a lonesome road
Doth walk in fear and dread,
And having once turned round walks on,
And turns no more his head;
Because he knows, a frightful fiend 450
Doth close behind him tread.

But soon there breathed a wind on me,
Nor sound nor motion made:
Its path was not upon the sea,
In ripple or in shade. 455

It raised my hair, it fanned my cheek
Like a meadow-gale of spring—
It mingled strangely with my fears,
Yet it felt like a welcoming.

Swiftly, swiftly flew the ship, 460
Yet she sailed softly too:
Sweetly, sweetly blew the breeze—
On me alone it blew.

And the ancient Mariner beholdeth his native country.

Oh! dream of joy! is this indeed
The light-house top I see? 465
Is this the hill? is this the kirk?
Is this mine own countree?

[19] Tomb enclosure.

We drifted o'er the harbour-bar,
And I with sobs did pray—
O let me be awake, my God!   470
Or let me sleep alway.

The harbour-bay was clear as glass,
So smoothly it was strewn!
And on the bay the moonlight lay,
And the shadow of the Moon.   475

The rock shone bright, the kirk no less,
That stands above the rock:
The moonlight steeped in silentness
The steady weathercock.

And the bay was white with silent light,   480
Till rising from the same,

**The angelic spirits leave
the dead bodies,**

Full many shapes, that shadows were,
In crimson colours came.

**And appear in their own
forms of light.**

A little distance from the prow
Those crimson shadows were: 485
I turned my eyes upon the deck—
Oh, Christ! what saw I there!

Each corse lay flat, lifeless and flat,
And, by the holy rood![20]
A man all light, a seraph-man,[21]   490
On every corse there stood.

This seraph-band, each waved his hand:
It was a heavenly sight!
They stood as signals to the land,
Each one a lovely light;   495

This seraph-band, each waved his hand,
No voice did they impart—
No voice; but oh! the silence sank
Like music on my heart.

But soon I heard the dash of oars,   500
I heard the Pilot's cheer;
My head was turned perforce away
And I saw a boat appear.

[20] Cross.
[21] Seraph: an angel of the highest rank.

The Pilot and the Pilot's boy,
I heard them coming fast: 505
Dear Lord in Heaven! it was a joy
The dead men could not blast.[22]

I saw a third—I heard his voice:
It is the Hermit good!
He singeth loud his godly hymns   510
That he makes in the wood.
He'll shrive[23] my soul, he'll wash away
The Albatross's blood.

Part VII

The Hermit of the Wood,

This Hermit good lives in that wood
Which slopes down to the sea.   515
How loudly his sweet voice he rears!
He loves to talk with marineres
That come from a far countree.

He kneels at morn, and noon, and eve—
He hath a cushion plump: 520
It is the moss that wholly hides
The rotted old oak-stump.

The skiff-boat neared: I heard them talk,
'Why, this is strange, I trow!
Where are those lights so many and fair,   525
That signal made but now?'

Approacheth the ship with wonder.

'Strange, by my faith!' the Hermit said—
'And they answered not our cheer!
The planks looked warped! and see those sails,
How thin they are and sere!   530
I never saw aught like to them,
Unless perchance it were

Brown skeletons of leaves that lag
My forest-brook along;
When the ivy-tod[24] is heavy with snow,   535
And the owlet whoops to the wolf below,
That eats the she-wolf's young.'

'Dear Lord! it hath a fiendish look—
(The Pilot made reply)

[22] Blight, wither.
[23] Hear confession of.
[24] Ivy clump.

I am a-feared'—'Push on, push on!'   540
Said the Hermit cheerily.

The boat came closer to the ship,
But I nor spake nor stirred;
The boat came close beneath the ship,
And straight a sound was heard.   545

The ship suddenly sinketh. Under the water it rumbled on,
Still louder and more dread:
It reached the ship, it split the bay;
The ship went down like lead.

The ancient Mariner is saved in the Pilot's boat. Stunned by that loud and dreadful sound,   550
Which sky and ocean smote,
Like one that hath been seven days drowned
My body lay afloat;
But swift as dreams, myself I found
Within the Pilot's boat.   555

Upon the whirl, where sank the ship,
The boat spun round and round;
And all was still, save that the hill
Was telling of the sound.

I moved my lips—the Pilot shrieked   560
And fell down in a fit;
The holy Hermit raised his eyes,
And prayed where he did sit.

I took the oars: the Pilot's boy,
Who now doth crazy go,   565
Laughed loud and long, and all the while
His eyes went to and fro.
'Ha! ha!' quoth he, 'full plain I see,
The Devil knows how to row.'

And now, all in my own countree,   570
I stood on the firm land!
The Hermit stepped forth from the boat,
And scarcely he could stand.

The ancient Mariner earnestly entreateth the Hermit to shrive him; and the penance of life falls on him. 'O shrive me, shrive me, holy man!'
The Hermit crossed his brow.[25]   575
'Say, quick,' quoth he, 'I bid thee say—
What manner of man art thou?'

[25] Made the sign of the cross on his forehead.

Forthwith this frame of mine was wrenched
With a woful agony,
Which forced me to begin my tale;   580
And then it left me free.

Since then, at an uncertain hour,
That agony returns:
And till my ghastly tale is told,
This heart within me burns.   585

I pass, like night, from land to land;
I have strange power of speech;
That moment that his face I see,
I know the man that must hear me:
To him my tale I teach.   590

What loud uproar bursts from that door!
The wedding-guests are there:
But in the garden-bower the bride
And bride-maids singing are:
And hark the little vesper bell,   595
Which biddeth me a prayer!

O Wedding-Guest! this soul hath been
Alone on a wide wide sea:
So lonely 'twas, that God himself
Scarce seeméd there to be.   600

O sweeter than the marriage-feast,
'Tis sweeter far to me,
To walk together to the kirk
With a goodly company!—

To walk together to the kirk,   605
And all together pray,
While each to his great Father bends,
Old men, and babes, and loving friends
And youths and maidens gay!

Farewell, farewell! but this I tell   610
To thee, thou Wedding-Guest!
He prayeth well, who loveth well
Both man and bird and beast.

He prayeth best, who loveth best
All things both great and small;   615
For the dear God who loveth us,
He made and loveth all.

The Mariner, whose eye is bright,
Whose beard with age is hoar,
Is gone: and now the Wedding-Guest 620
Turned from the bridegroom's door.

He went like one that hath been stunned,
And is of sense forlorn:
A sadder and a wiser man,
He rose the morrow morn. 625

There is not much to the story of Richard Cory. You can easily retell it. But can you retell so memorably?

Richard Cory

Edwin Arlington Robinson (1869–1935)

Whenever Richard Cory went down town,
We people on the pavement looked at him:
He was a gentleman from sole to crown,
Clean favored, and imperially slim. 4

And he was always quietly arrayed,
And he was always human when he talked;
But still he fluttered pulses when he said,
"Good-morning," and he glittered when he walked. 8

And he was rich—yes, richer than a king—
And admirably schooled in every grace:
In fine, we thought that he was everything
To make us wish that we were in his place. 12

So on we worked, and waited for the light,
And went without the meat, and cursed the bread.
And Richard Cory, one calm summer night,
Went home and put a bullet through his head. 16

Here is a very different kind of narrative verse:

Hurt Hawks

Robinson Jeffers (1887–1962)

I

The broken pillar of the wing jags from the clotted shoulder,
The wing trails like a banner in defeat,
No more to use the sky forever but live with famine

And pain a few days: cat nor coyote
Will shorten the week of waiting for death, there is game with-
    out talons.   5
He stands under the oak-bush and waits
The lame feet of salvation; at night he remembers freedom
And flies in a dream, the dawns ruin it.
He is strong and pain is worse to the strong, incapacity is worse.
The curs of the day come and torment him   10
At distance, no one but death the redeemer will humble that
    head,
The intrepid readiness, the terrible eyes.
The wild God of the world is sometimes merciful to those
That ask mercy, not often to the arrogant.
You do not know him, you communal people, or you have for-
    gotten him;   15
Intemperate and savage, the hawk remembers him;
Beautiful and wild, the hawks, and men that are dying, remember
    him.

II

I'd sooner, except the penalties, kill a man than a hawk; but the
    great redtail
Had nothing left but unable misery
From the bone too shattered for mending, the wing that trailed
    under his talons when he moved.   20
We had fed him six weeks, I gave him freedom,
He wandered over the foreland hill and returned in the evening,
    asking for death,
Not like a beggar, still eyed with the old
Implacable arrogance. I gave him the lead gift in the twilight.
    What fell was relaxed,
Owl-downy, soft feminine feathers; but what   25
Soared: the fierce rush: the night-herons by the flooded river
    cried fear at its rising
Before it was quite unsheathed from reality.

What is the story here? The poem lacks the insistent rhythm and rhyme of the usual narrative poem. Does it lose or gain? What does the subject have to do with the form? The poet, of course, wants to do more than merely tell a story in verse. The story means something to him. He has an emotion, an attitude, or a thought he wishes to convey. His poem is not simply narrative, any more than lyric poems are simply lyric.

The narrative or the lyric element dominates some poems and serves lesser roles in others. Similarly, some poems are more descriptive, others more discursive or thoughtful, more interested in ideas. Something of "Hurt Hawks" is descriptive, something discursive. Other poems emphasize one or the other of these elements, but nothing seems quite as fundamental to poetry as the lyric or the narrative impulse.

CHAPTER 2

The Poem as Drama

Situation

Many poems revolve around a situation inherently dramatic. Sometimes the poet has experienced or observed an event that he wishes to record in verse. Sometimes he has imagined an event. His poem may take the form of a complete narrative or an incident presented in isolation, or it may amount to no more than the expression of an emotion for which the reader may infer an active cause. As readers we may classify the poem as narrative, lyric, descriptive, discursive, or by such other designations as we find helpful, yet if the poem was worth writing the poet was probably driven to it by an inner need, something like the need to dramatize.

The poem comes to us as a verbal communication, but as we first approach it we cannot be certain either that the voice is the poet's or that it is addressed to us as readers. Perhaps the poet has invented a voice other than his own. Perhaps he has written a love poem or a letter to a patron. In any event, we may suppose that something has happened to prompt this communication at this time. We can define the dramatic situation if we can answer three questions: Who speaks the words of the poem? To whom is the poem addressed? Under what circumstances is the poem spoken? Careful and complete answers to these questions will frequently take us a long way into understanding.

The Walk

Thomas Hardy   (1840–1928)

You did not walk with me
Of late to the hill-top tree
  By the gated ways,
  As in earlier days;   4
  You were weak and lame,
  So you never came,
And I went alone, and I did not mind,
Not thinking of you as left behind.   8

I walked up there to-day
Just in the former way;

> Surveyed around
> The familiar ground   12
> By myself again:
> What difference, then?
>   Only that underlying sense
> Of the look of a room on returning thence.   16

Who speaks the poem? Perhaps the poet, at least someone long in the habit of walking to a tree at the top of a hill. To whom is the poem addressed? Clearly not directly to the reader, but to a "you" who used to walk up the hill also, a "you" who later became too "weak and lame" for the habitual walk. In what circumstances is the poem spoken? Something has happened to make a difference in the lives of the two people, although the speaker still takes his habitual walk, just as he had been doing "of late," without the "you." "What difference, then?" he asks and then answers himself: "Only that underlying sense / Of the look of a room on returning thence." One question prompts another in the mind of the reader. Why should the room look different? Most obviously, if the person is no longer there. The poem radiates a sense of loss, and probably refers to the final loss of death. The speaker communicates his anguish over the loss of a loved one, someone no longer able to greet him on his return. He speaks in the form of an *apostrophe*, an address either to an inanimate object or an individual not present to receive the communication.

If we want completely to answer the question: "To whom is the poem addressed?" we will probably now add that, although it is an apostrophe addressed directly to the "you," it is also addressed indirectly to the sympathetic ear of the reader, asking him to share in the emotion. On the evidence of the poem, we cannot say much more than this. We cannot identify for certain the sex of either the speaker or the "you." We cannot even be sure of a death, although we may feel it strongly, since the person addressed may simply have gone away—as the result of a quarrel, say, or to enter a hospital. The poem obtains its power from what it says and also from what it does not say. By attempting to provide careful and complete answers to the three questions that define its dramatic situation, we are forced a long way into the complexities of a poem that looks quite simple on the surface.

If we remain unsatisfied with answers we derive from the poem itself, we may examine its connection with the life of the poet, Thomas Hardy. So doing, we discover "The Walk" to be one of a number of frankly autobiographical poems Hardy wrote in his seventies, not long after the death of Emma Hardy, to whom he had been married for almost 40 years. Such knowledge defines the situation more precisely than is apparent in the poem alone. Does our added understanding make the poem in any way a different or a better work of art?

In the next poem, little question of an autobiographical basis arises.
The poet has imagined a verbal exchange between a redwood tree and a
person.

Kind

A. R. Ammons (1926–)

I can't understand it
  said the giant redwood
    I have attained height and distant view,
    am easy with time,

and yet you search the   5
wood's edge
for weeds
that find half-dark room in margins
  of stone
  and are   10
as everybody knows
  here and gone in a season

  O redwood I said in this matter
I may not be able to argue from reason
but preference sends me stooping   15
seeking
  the least,
  as finished as you
  and with a flower

Who speaks? A redwood tree and a person, with the person reporting
the conversation. To whom do they speak? To each other (and the reader
as auditor). Under what circumstances do they speak? The person has
displayed his fascination with weeds rather than trees and has been
asked to explain himself. By means of his fable, Ammons suggests something about one individual's preference for small and transient perfections over loftier things.

Not Waving But Drowning

Stevie Smith   (1902–1971)

Nobody heard him, the dead man,
But still he lay moaning:
I was much further out than you thought
And not waving but drowning.   4

Poor chap, he always loved larking
And now he's dead
It must have been too cold for him his heart gave way,
They said.   8

Oh, no no no, it was too cold always
(Still the dead one lay moaning)
I was much too far out all my life
And not waving but drowning.   12

Here are the words of three speakers: a narrator, a dead man, and a collective "they." The narrator speaks to the reader, and the "they" speak to each other. The most important speaker, however, is the dead man, who speaks to the "they" but is heard only by the narrator and the reader. The point of the poem is the failure of communication. The dead man was misunderstood as he was drowning, just as he had been misunderstood (and therefore "drowning") all his life.

Robert Frost's "Home Burial" extends a dramatic situation to a length in which it possesses the complications of a miniature stage play.

Home Burial

Robert Frost (1874–1963)

He saw her from the bottom of the stairs
Before she saw him. She was starting down,
Looking back over her shoulder at some fear.
She took a doubtful step and then undid it
To raise herself and look again. He spoke   5
Advancing toward her: "What is it you see
From up there always?—for I want to know."
She turned and sank upon her skirts at that,
And her face changed from terrified to dull.
He said to gain time: "What is it you see?"   10
Mounting until she cowered under him.
"I will find out now—you must tell me, dear."
She, in her place, refused him any help,
With the least stiffening of her neck and silence.
She let him look, sure that he wouldn't see,   15
Blind creature; and awhile he didn't see.
But at last he murmured, "Oh," and again, "Oh."

"What is it—what?" she said.
                              "Just that I see."

"You don't," she challenged. "Tell me what it is."

"The wonder is I didn't see at once.   20
I never noticed it from here before.
I must be wonted to it—that's the reason.
The little graveyard where my people are!
So small the window frames the whole of it.
Not so much larger than a bedroom, is it?   25
There are three stones of slate and one of marble,
Broad-shouldered little slabs there in the sunlight
On the sidehill. We haven't to mind *those*.
But I understand: it is not the stones,
But the child's mound—"
                                "Don't, don't, don't,
     don't," she cried.   30

She withdrew, shrinking from beneath his arm
That rested on the banister, and slid downstairs;
And turned on him with such a daunting look,
He said twice over before he knew himself:
"Can't a man speak of his own child he's lost?"   35

"Not you!—Oh, where's my hat? Oh, I don't need it!
I must get out of here. I must get air.—
I don't know rightly whether any man can."

"Amy! Don't go to someone else this time.
Listen to me. I won't come down the stairs."   40
He sat and fixed his chin between his fists.
"There's something I should like to ask you, dear."

"You don't know how to ask it."
                                "Help me, then."

Her fingers moved the latch for all reply.

"My words are nearly always an offense.   45
I don't know how to speak of anything
So as to please you. But I might be taught,
I should suppose. I can't say I see how.
A man must partly give up being a man
With womenfolk. We could have some arrangement   50
By which I'd bind myself to keep hands off
Anything special you're a-mind to name.
Though I don't like such things 'twixt those that love.
Two that don't love can't live together without them.
But two that do can't live together with them."   55
She moved the latch a little. "Don't—don't go.
Don't carry it to someone else this time.

Tell me about it if it's something human.
Let me into your grief. I'm not so much
Unlike other folks as your standing there   60
Apart would make me out. Give me my chance.
I do think, though, you overdo it a little.
What was it brought you up to think it the thing
To take your mother-loss of a first child.
So inconsolably—in the face of love.   65
You'd think his memory might be satisfied—"

"There you go sneering now!"
                        "I'm not, I'm not!
You make me angry. I'll come down to you.
God, what a woman! And it's come to this,
A man can't speak of his own child that's dead."   70

"You can't because you don't know how to speak.
If you had any feelings, you that dug
With your own hand—how could you?—his little grave;
I saw you from that very window there,
Making the gravel leap and leap in air,   75
Leap up, like that, like that, and land so lightly
And roll back down the mound beside the hole.
I thought, Who is that man? I didn't know you.
And I crept down the stairs and up the stairs
To look again, and still your spade kept lifting.   80
Then you came in. I heard your rumbling voice
Out in the kitchen, and I don't know why,
But I went near to see with my own eyes.
You could sit there with the stains on your shoes
Of the fresh earth from your own baby's grave   85
And talk about your everyday concerns.
You had stood the spade up against the wall
Outside there in the entry, for I saw it."

"I shall laugh the worst laugh I ever laughed.
I'm cursed. God, if I don't believe I'm cursed."   90

"I can repeat the very words you were saying:
'Three foggy mornings and one rainy day
Will rot the best birch fence a man can build.'
Think of it, talk like that at such a time!
What had how long it takes a birch to rot   95
To do with what was in the darkened parlor?
You *couldn't* care! The nearest friends can go
With anyone to death, comes so far short

They might as well not try to go at all.
No, from the time when one is sick to death,   100
One is alone, and he dies more alone.
Friends make pretense of following to the grave,
But before one is in it, their minds are turned
And making the best of their way back to life
And living people, and things they understand. 105
But the world's evil. I won't have grief so
If I can change it. Oh, I won't, I won't!"

"There, you have said it all and you feel better.
You won't go now. You're crying. Close the door.
The heart's gone out of it: why keep it up?   110
Amy! There's someone coming down the road!"

"*You*—oh, you think the talk is all. I must go—
Somewhere out of this house. How can I make you—"

"If—you—do!" She was opening the door wider.
"Where do you mean to go? First tell me that. 115
I'll follow and bring you back by force. I *will!*—"

In the next selection the poet, Alexander Pope, speaks in his own
voice, playfully consulting his lawyer, William Fortescue, as to the risks
of satire.

[A Question of Libel]
FROM "THE FIRST SATIRE OF THE SECOND BOOK OF HORACE"
Alexander Pope (1688–1744)

P. There are (I scarce can think it, but am told)
There are to whom my Satire seems too bold,
Scarce to wise *Peter*[1] complaisant enough,
And something said of *Chartres*[2] much too rough.
The Lines are weak, another's pleas'd to say, 5
Lord *Fanny*[3] spins a thousand such a Day.
Tim'rous by Nature, of the Rich in awe,
I come to Council learned in the Law.
You'll give me, like a Friend both sage and free,
Advice; and (as you use) without a Fee. 10

---

[1] Peter Walter (1664?–1746), a wealthy and unscrupulous money lender; the model for Henry Fielding's Peter Pounce in *Joseph Andrews* (1742).
[2] Francis Chartres (1675–1732), a wealthy gambler, drunkard, and libertine who supported Pope's principal political enemy, Sir Robert Walpole, the Prime Minister.
[3] Pope's name for John Hervey, Baron Hervey of Ickworth, an ally of Robert Walpole and the queen's confidant.

*F.*I'd write no more.
     *P.*Not write? but then I *think*,
And for my Soul I cannot sleep a wink.
I nod in Company, I wake at Night,
Fools rush into my Head, and so I write.

 *F.*You could not do a worse thing for your Life.   15
Why, if the Nights seem tedious—take a Wife;
Or rather truly, if your Point be Rest,
Lettuce and Cowslip Wine; *Probatum est.*[4]

* * *

 *P.*Each Mortal has his Pleasure: None deny
Scarsdale his Bottle, *Darty* his Ham-Pye;[5]   20

* * *

I love to pour out all myself, as plain
As downright *Shippen*, or as old *Montagne.*[6]
In them, as certain to be lov'd as seen,
The Soul stood forth, nor kept a Thought within;
In me what Spots (for Spots I have) appear,   25
Will prove at least the Medium must be clear.
In this impartial Glass, my Muse intends
Fair to expose myself, my Foes, my Friends;
Publish the present Age, but where my Text
Is Vice too high, reserve it for the next: 30
My Foes shall wish my Life a longer date,
And ev'ry Friend the less lament my Fate.
 My Head and Heart thus flowing thro' my Quill,
Verse-man or Prose-man, term me which you will,
Papist or Protestant, or both between,   35
Like good *Erasmus*[7] in an honest Mean,
In Moderation placing all my Glory,
While Tories call me Whig, and Whigs a Tory.

* * *

 Then learned Sir! (to cut the Matter short)
What-e'er my Fate, or well or ill at Court,   40

---

[4] A lawyer's phrase: "It has been proved."
[5] *Scarsdale*: Nicholas Leke, fourth Earl of Scarsdale (1682–1736), a heavy drinker who had helped impeach Pope's friend Henry St. John, Viscount Bolingbroke; *Darty*: Charles Dartineuf (1664–1737), an epicure and a friend of Swift.
[6] *Shippen*: William Shippen (1673–1753), a member of Parliament whose integrity was admired by all parties; *Montagne*: Michel de Montaigne (1533–1592), a French essayist.
[7] Desiderius Erasmus (1466–1536), a Dutch humanist who lectured at Cambridge and settled in England; he urged moderation on both sides when Martin Luther rebelled against the established church.

Whether old Age, with faint, but chearful Ray,
Attends to gild the Evening of my Day,
Or Death's black Wing already be display'd
To wrap me in the Universal Shade;
Whether the darken'd Room to muse invite,   45
Or whiten'd Wall provoke the Skew'r to write,
In Durance, Exile, Bedlam, or the Mint,[8]
Like *Lee* or *Budgell*,[9] I will Rhyme and Print.
    F.Alas young Man! your Days can ne'r be long,
In Flow'r of Age you perish for a Song!   50
Plums, and Directors,[10] *Shylock*[11] and his Wife,
Will club their Testers, now, to take your Life![12]
    P.What? arm'd for *Virtue* when I point the Pen,
Brand the bold Front of shameless, guilty Men,
Dash the proud Gamester in his gilded Car,   55
Bare the mean Heart that lurks beneath a Star;[13]
Can there be wanting to defend Her Cause,
Lights of the Church, or Guardians of the Laws?
Could pension'd *Boileau*[14] lash in honest Strain
Flatt'rers and Bigots ev'n in *Louis*' Reign?   60
Could Laureate *Dryden*[15] Pimp and Fry'r engage,
Yet neither *Charles* nor *James* be in a Rage?
And I not strip the Gilding off a Knave,
Un-plac'd, un-pension'd, no Man's Heir, or Slave?
I will, or perish in the gen'rous Cause.   65
Hear this, and tremble! you, who 'scape the Laws.
Yes, while I live, no rich or noble knave
Shall walk the World, in credit, to his grave.
To VIRTUE ONLY AND HER FRIENDS, A FRIEND,

---

[8] "Prison, exile, the madhouse, or poverty." The Mint was a district in Southwark, south of the Thames, where debtors were exempt from arrest; it was named from the mint that existed there in Henry VIII's time.

[9] *Lee*: Nathaniel Lee (1653?–1692), a tragic playwright who was confined to Bedlam as insane, where he is said to have written a tragedy consisting of twenty-five acts; *Budgell*: Eustace Budgell (1686–1737), Addison's cousin, a contributor to *The Spectator* and a writer of epilogues and poems.

[10] A "plum" was slang for £100,000, or any large sum, usually ill-gotten; hence, a man who had made a "plum." "Directors" refers to those of the South Sea Company, organized in 1711 to trade with Spanish America and eventually taking over the national debt at a profit, which made many people rich in the wild speculation before the market crashed in 1720. One of the directors, Sir John Blunt, whom Pope mentions in his *Epistle to Bathurst*, was also a director of The Charitable Corporation for the Relief of the Poor, which he used for a notorious swindle.

[11] Pope's name for Charles Douglas, Earl of Selkirk (1663–1739), an unpopular Scottish peer whom Pope seems to see as a usurer.

[12] Put their sixpences together to hire an assassin.

[13] The badge of knighthood.

[14] Nicolas Boileau Despréaux (1636–1711), a French satirist and critic who had a pension from Louis XIV.

[15] John Dryden (1631–1700), Poet Laureate under Charles II and his brother and successor, James II. His play, *The Spanish Friar* (1680), satirized the Catholics in the character of Friar Dominick, who was a pimp. Protestant Charles approved it, but his brother James, a Catholic, banned it when he was on the throne.

The World beside may murmur, or commend.   70
Know, all the distant Din that World can keep
Rolls o'er my *Grotto*,[16] and but sooths my sleep.
There, my Retreat the best Companions grace,
Chiefs, out of War, and Statesmen, out of Place.
There *St. John*[17] mingles with my friendly Bowl,   75
The Feast of Reason and the Flow of Soul:
And He,[18] whose Lightning pierc'd th' *Iberian*[19] Lines,
Now, forms my Quincunx,[20] and now ranks my Vines,
Or tames the Genius of the stubborn Plain,
Almost as quickly, as he conquer'd *Spain*.   80
    Envy must own, I live among the Great,
No Pimp of Pleasure, and no Spy of State,
With Eyes that pry not, Tongue that ne'er repeats,
Fond to spread Friendships, but to cover Heats,
To help who want, to forward who excel;   85
This, all who know me, know; who love me, tell;
And who unknown defame me, let them be
Scriblers or Peers, alike are *Mob* to me.
This is my Plea, on this I rest my Cause—
What saith my Council learned in the Laws?   90
    *F.*Your Plea is good. But still I say, beware!
Laws are explain'd by Men—so have a care.
It stands on record, that in *Richard*'s Times
A Man was hang'd for very honest Rhymes.[21]
Consult the Statute: *quart.* I think it is,   95
Edwardi Sext. or *prim. & quint. Eliz:*[22]

---

[16] The road from London, the seat of worldly power, to Hampton Court, its elegant country home, ran directly behind Pope's house at Twickenham. Pope connected his house with his garden beyond the road by tunneling under it and making the tunnel a grotto, with fountains and side rooms, where he did much of his writing and entertained his friends, and, if this line is literally true, sometimes slept or napped.

[17] Henry St. John, Viscount Bolingbroke (1678–1751), Secretary of State under Queen Anne, was impeached for treason by George I, whose accession he had opposed, and fled to France in 1715. He was pardoned in 1723 but was forbidden his seat in the House of Lords and lived in semiretirement. Ten years Pope's senior and a nobleman, he influenced Pope's writing and thought considerably. Even the elegant Chesterfield praised his "flowing happiness of expression" in conversation.

[18] Charles Mordaunt, third Earl of Peterborough and first Earl of Monmouth (1658–1735), the "Chief, out of War," who captured Barcelona in 1705 and Valencia, with a small force of cavalry and infantry, in 1706, but retired from politics and the army on George I's accession (1714). An enthusiastic gardener.

[19] Spanish.

[20] A planting of five trees in a square with one in the middle.

[21] In the reign of Richard III (1483–1485), a poet named Collingbourne was hanged for writing:

> The catte, the ratte and Lovell our dogge
> Rulyth all England under a hogge.

The cat was Sir William Catesby, Speaker of the House of Commons; the rat, Sir Richard Ratcliff, one of Richard's right-hand men; Lovell, Viscount Francis Lovell, Richard's strongest supporter and Lord Chamberlain.

[22] The statutes on libel, numbered among the acts of Edward VI and Elizabeth I: "the fourth of Edward VI," "the first and fifth of Elizabeth."

See *Libels, Satires*—here you have it—read.
   P.Libels and *Satires!* lawless Things indeed!
But grave *Epistles*,[23] bringing Vice to light,
Such as a *King* might read, a *Bishop* write,
Such as Sir *Robert*[24] would approve—   100
                    *F.*Indeed?
The Case is alter'd—you may then proceed.
In such a Cause the Plaintiff will be hiss'd,
My Lords the Judges laugh, and you're dismiss'd.

[23] Horace, whom Pope is imitating, wrote both "Satires" and more friendly "Epistles."
[24] Walpole, the Prime Minister, Pope's political enemy, who could not complain openly at the exposure of vice.

The dramatic situation in the next poem is largely a dream, but not entirely.

Dream Barker

Jean Valentine (1934–)

We met for supper in your flat-bottomed boat.
I got there first: in a white dress: I remember
Wondering if you'd come. Then you shot over the bank,
A Virgilian[1] Nigger Jim,[2] and poled us off
To a little sea-food barker's cave you knew.   5

What'll you have? you said. Eels hung down,
Bamboozled claws hung up from the crackling weeds.
The light was all behind us. To one side
In a dish of ice was a shell shaped like a sand-dollar
But worked with Byzantine blue and gold. *What's that?*   10

Well, I've never seen it before, you said,
And I don't know how it tastes.
Oh well, said I, *if it's bad,*
I'm not too hungry, are you? We'd have the shell . . .
I know just how you feel, you said   15

And asked for it; we held out our hands.
Six Dollars! barked the barker, *For This Beauty!*
We fell down laughing in your flat-bottomed boat,

And then I woke up: in a white dress:
Dry as a bone on dry land, Jim,   20
Bone dry, old, in a dry land, Jim, my Jim.

[1] Of the Roman poet Virgil (70–19 B.C.).
[2] From Twain's *Huckleberry Finn.*

In the following poem an old man speaks to any listener, or to the reader. How do we know he is old? What experience has prompted the poem?

The Brothers

Edwin Muir   (1887–1959)

Last night I watched my brothers play,
The gentle and the reckless one,
In a field two yards away.
For half a century they were gone
Beyond the other side of care   5
To be among the peaceful dead.
Even in a dream how could I dare
Interrogate that happiness
So wildly spent yet never less?

For still they raced about the green   10
And were like two revolving suns;
A brightness poured from head to head,
So strong I could not see their eyes
Or look into their paradise.
What were they doing, the happy ones?   15
Yet where I was they once had been.

I thought, How could I be so dull,
Twenty thousand days ago,
Not to see they were beautiful?
I asked them, Were you really so   20
As you are now, that other day?
And the dream was soon away.

For then we played for victory
And not to make each other glad.
A darkness covered every head,   25
Frowns twisted the original face,
And through that mask we could not see
The beauty and the buried grace.

I have observed in foolish awe
The dateless mid-days of the law   30
And seen indifferent justice done
By everyone on everyone.
And in a vision I have seen
My brothers playing on the green.

In the next poem, from an Omaha Indian ritual, a priest apostrophizes the sun, moon, and stars. The ceremony is called "Introduction of the Child to the Cosmos."

Ho! Ye Sun, Moon, Stars

Ho! Ye Sun, Moon, Stars, all ye that
   move in the heavens,
   I bid you hear me!
Into your midst has come a new life.
   Consent ye, I implore!   5
Make its path smooth, that it may reach
   the brow of the first hill!

Ho! Ye Winds, Clouds, Rain, Mist, all ye that
   move in the air,
   I bid you hear me!   10
Into your midst has come a new life.
   Consent ye, I implore!
Make its path smooth, that it may reach
   the brow of the second hill!

Ho! Ye Hills, Valleys, Rivers, Lakes, Trees,   15
   Grasses, all ye of the earth,
   I bid you hear me!
Into your midst has come a new life.
   Consent ye, I implore!
Make its path smooth, that it may reach   20
   the brow of the third hill!

Ho! Ye Birds, great and small, that fly in the air,
Ho! Ye Animals, great and small, that dwell
   in the forest,
Ho! Ye Insects that creep among the grasses   25
   and burrow in the ground—
   I bid you hear me!
Into your midst has come a new life.
   Consent ye, I implore!
Make its path smooth, that it may reach   30
   the brow of the fourth hill!

Ho! All ye of the heavens, all ye of the air,
   all ye of the earth:
   I bid you hear me!
Into your midst has come a new life.   35
   Consent ye, consent ye all, I implore!
Make its path smooth—then shall it travel
   beyond the four hills!

As a final example of how understanding the dramatic situation can assist one to an understanding of the whole poem, consider the following lines by Thom Gunn.

Moly
Thom Gunn (1929–)

Nightmare of beasthood, snorting, how to wake.
I woke. What beasthood skin she made me take?

Leathery toad that ruts for days on end,
Or cringing dribbling dog, man's servile friend,   4

Or cat that prettily pounces on its meat,
Tortures it hours, then does not care to eat:

Parrot, moth, shark, wolf, crocodile, ass, flea.
What germs, what jostling mobs there were in me.   8

    These seem like bristles, and the hide is tough.
No claw or web here: each foot ends in hoof.

Into what bulk has method disappeared?
Like ham, streaked. I am gross—grey, gross, flap-eared.   12

The pale-lashed eyes my only human feature.
My teeth tear, tear. I am the snouted creature

That bites through anything, root, wire, or can.
If I was not afraid I'd eat a man.   16

Oh a man's flesh already is in mine.
Hand and foot poised for risk. Buried in swine.

    I root and root, you think that it is greed,
It is, but I seek out a plant I need.   20

Direct me, gods, whose changes are all holy,
To where it flickers deep in grass, the moly:

Cool flesh of magic in each leaf and shoot,
From milky flower to the black forked root.   24

From this fat dungeon I could rise to skin
And human title, putting pig within.

I push my big grey wet snout through the green,
Dreaming the flower I have never seen.   28

First we need to recall the Circe episode in book 10 of Homer's *Odyssey*, since Gunn assumes a common knowledge of this famous incident.

The beautiful Circe turned Odysseus's men to swine, though they retained their human minds; Odysseus was protected from her enchantment by the magic herb moly, which was given to him by the messenger
of the gods, Hermes. In "Moly," Gunn imagines the story from a perspective different from Homer's.

Character

Any poem rooted in an inherently dramatic situation projects the character of the speaker, but the poet heightens the characterization when he
presents a speaker markedly different from himself. He deliberately dra-
matizes, evoking character for its own sake. Usually, he presents only
one speaker, revealing himself through his language, his speech patterns, his way of looking at the world. The poet then speaks through the
mask of experiences not his own, projecting himself, like a dramatist,
into a different personality. Such a mask, or adopted identity, is sometimes called a *persona*.

A male writer may adopt the character (or persona) of a woman, or a
woman of a man. A young man may adopt the character of an old one, or
a brave man of a coward, or an honest man of a thief. A twentieth-century English writer may adopt the character of an ancient Greek warrior
changed by enchantment into a pig, as Thom Gunn does in "Moly." The
possibilities are as limitless as the human imagination. This section presents a series of these dramatizations, as the speakers reveal themselves
through their various voices.

Ulysses

Alfred, Lord Tennyson   (1809–1892)

It little profits that an idle king,
By this still hearth, among these barren crags,
Matched with an agèd wife, I mete and dole
Unequal laws unto a savage race,
That hoard, and sleep, and feed, and know not me.   5
I cannot rest from travel: I will drink
Life to the lees:[1] all times I have enjoyed
Greatly, have suffered greatly, both with those
That loved me, and alone; on shore, and when
Through scudding drifts the rainy Hyades[2]   10
Vext the dim sea: I am become a name;
For always roaming with a hungry heart

---

[1] Sediment at the bottom of a wine glass or bottle.
[2] A constellation associated, in rising, with rain.

Much have I seen and known; cities of men
And manners, climates, councils, governments,
Myself not least, but honoured of them all;   15
And drunk delight of battle with my peers,
Far on the ringing plains of windy Troy.
I am a part of all that I have met;
Yet all experience is an arch wherethrough
Gleams that untravelled world, whose margin fades   20
For ever and for ever when I move.
How dull it is to pause, to make an end,
To rust unburnished, not to shine in use!
As though to breathe were life. Life piled on life
Were all too little, and of one to me   25
Little remains: but every hour is saved
From that eternal silence, something more,
A bringer of new things; and vile it were
For some three suns to store and hoard myself,
And this gray spirit yearning in desire   30
To follow knowledge like a sinking star,
Beyond the utmost bound of human thought.

    This is my son, mine own Telemachus,
To whom I leave the sceptre and the isle—
Well-loved of me, discerning to fulfil   35
This labour, by slow prudence to make mild
A rugged people, and through soft degrees
Subdue them to the useful and the good.
Most blameless is he, centred in the sphere
Of common duties, decent not to fail   40
In offices of tenderness, and pay
Meet adoration to my household gods,
When I am gone. He works his work, I mine.

    There lies the port; the vessel puffs her sail:
There gloom the dark broad seas. My mariners,   45
Souls that have toiled, and wrought, and thought with me—
That ever with a frolic welcome took
The thunder and the sunshine, and opposed
Free hearts, free foreheads—you and I are old;
Old age hath yet his honour and his toil;   50
Death closes all: but something ere the end,
Some work of noble note, may yet be done,
Not unbecoming men that strove with Gods.
The lights begin to twinkle from the rocks.
The long day wanes: the slow moon climbs: the deep   55

Moans round with many voices. Come, my friends,
'Tis not too late to seek a newer world.
Push off, and sitting well in order smite
The sounding furrows; for my purpose holds
To sail beyond the sunset, and the baths   60
Of all the western stars, until I die.
It may be that the gulfs will wash us down:
It may be we shall touch the Happy Isles,
And see the great Achilles, whom we knew.
Though much is taken, much abides; and though   65
We are not now that strength which in old days
Moved earth and heaven; that which we are, we are;
One equal temper of heroic hearts,
Made weak by time and fate, but strong in will
To strive, to seek, to find, and not to yield.   70

The speaker is Ulysses himself, and we can define him further by considering the time and place from which he speaks. An old man, he has long since completed his wandering journey home, won back his wife, and regained his throne. Tennyson takes up where Homer's *Odyssey* left off. He imagines himself Ulysses. Given Ulysses's history and temperament, how would he respond to his aging in Ithaca? The poem presents Tennyson's answer. In what lines does Ulysses most clearly indicate his attitude toward his past, his present, and his future? Would it be possible to suggest that Tennyson selected the character of Ulysses not simply to reveal the personality of one imagined individual, but to create through him a memorable example of a human type? What type?

My Last Duchess[1]
FERRARA
Robert Browning   (1812–1889)

That's my last Duchess painted on the wall,
Looking as if she were alive. I call
That piece a wonder, now: Frà Pandolf's hands
Worked busily a day, and there she stands.
Will 't please you sit and look at her? I said   5
'Frà Pandolf' by design, for never read
Strangers like you that pictured countenance,
The depth and passion of its earnest glance,

[1] Alfonso II, a sixteenth-century Duke of Ferrara, in Italy, negotiated a second marriage after the death of his first young wife. Browning imagined the details and also, apparently, the painter, Frà Pandolf, and the sculptor, Claus of Innsbruck.

But to myself they turned (since none puts by
The curtain I have drawn for you, but I)   10
And seemed as they would ask me, if they durst,
How such a glance came there; so, not the first
Are you to turn and ask thus. Sir, 't was not
Her husband's presence only, called that spot
Of joy into the Duchess' cheek: perhaps   15
Frà Pandolf chanced to say 'Her mantle laps
'Over my lady's wrist too much,' or 'Paint
'Must never hope to reproduce the faint
'Half-flush that dies along her throat:' such stuff
Was courtesy, she thought, and cause enough   20
For calling up that spot of joy. She had
A heart—how shall I say?—too soon made glad,
Too easily impressed; she liked whate'er
She looked on, and her looks went everywhere.
Sir, 't was all one! My favour at her breast,   25
The dropping of the daylight in the West,
The bough of cherries some officious fool
Broke in the orchard for her, the white mule
She rode with round the terrace—all and each
Would draw from her alike the approving speech,   30
Or blush, at least. She thanked men,—good! but thanked
Somehow—I know not how—as if she ranked
My gift of a nine-hundred-years-old name
With anybody's gift. Who'd stoop to blame
This sort of trifling? Even had you skill   35
In speech—(which I have not)—to make your will
Quite clear to such an one, and say, 'Just this
'Or that in you disgusts me; here you miss,
'Or there exceed the mark'—and if she let
Herself be lessoned so, nor plainly set   40
Her wits to yours, forsooth, and made excuse,
—E'en then would be some stooping; and I choose
Never to stoop. Oh sir, she smiled, no doubt,
Whene'er I passed her; but who passed without
Much the same smile? This grew; I gave commands;   45
Then all smiles stopped together. There she stands
As if alive. Will 't please you rise? We'll meet
The company below, then. I repeat,
The Count your master's known munificence
Is ample warrant that no just pretence   50
Of mine for dowry will be disallowed;

Though his fair daughter's self, as I avowed
At starting, is my object. Nay, we'll go
Together down, sir. Notice Neptune, though,
Taming a sea-horse, thought a rarity,   55
Which Claus of Innsbruck cast in bronze for me!

"My Last Duchess" is one of Browning's several distinctive *dramatic monologues*. Browning has imagined not only a character and a situation, but a listener other than the reader. In Tennyson's "Ulysses" the character speaks in *soliloquy*, addressing himself only, or, as in a play by Shakespeare, speaking his thoughts aloud to clarify his motives or explain himself to the playgoing audience. In "My Last Duchess," however, the Duke of Ferrara addresses his remarks not to himself or to us, but to another imagined figure who silently shares the stage with him.

"My Last Duchess" is a fine illustration of an obvious truth: a speaker is not always aware of the effect of his words. The Duke obviously has a high opinion of himself, but his words reveal a man neither poet nor reader can admire. What is repellent about him? What details reveal his attitudes? Where do our attitudes differ? Here is what we call *dramatic irony*: a character's words or acts have implications opposite to what he assumes or intends. Dramatic irony is the frequent effect of first-person narration, as here, when the Duke asserts himself in his "I" and "my." What can we infer about his imagined listener? Are we to assume that he says nothing at all?

In the next two poems, the poets, both male, adopt the identity of females. Is each poem successful in projecting a sense of a human individual separate from the poet? To whom is each poem addressed? What are the circumstances out of which each voice speaks? How should we characterize each speaker?

The River-Merchant's Wife: A Letter

Ezra Pound (1885–1972)

While my hair was still cut straight across my forehead
I Played about the front gate, pulling flowers.
You came by on bamboo stilts, playing horse,
You walked about my seat, playing with blue plums.
And we went on living in the village of Chōkan: 5
Two small people, without dislike or suspicion.

At fourteen I married My Lord you.
I never laughed, being bashful.
Lowering my head, I looked at the wall.
Called to, a thousand times, I never looked back.   10

At fifteen I stopped scowling,
I desired my dust to be mingled with yours
Forever and forever and forever.
Why should I climb the look out?

At sixteen you departed,   15
You went into far Ku-tō-en, by the river of swirling eddies,
And you have been gone five months.
The monkeys make sorrowful noise overhead.

You dragged your feet when you went out.
By the gate now, the moss is grown, the different mosses,   20
Too deep to clear them away!
The leaves fall early this autumn, in wind.
The paired butterflies are already yellow with August
Over the grass in the West garden;
They hurt me. I grow older.   25
If you are coming down through the narrows of the river Kiang,
Please let me know beforehand,
And I will come out to meet you
          As far as Chō-fū-Sa.

                 By Rihaku (Li T'ai Po)

The Lost Children

Randall Jarrell   (1914–1965)

Two little girls, one fair, one dark,
One alive, one dead, are running hand in hand
Through a sunny house. The two are dressed
In red and white gingham, with puffed sleeves and sashes.
They run away from me . . . But I am happy;   5
When I wake I feel no sadness, only delight.
I've seen them again, and I am comforted
That, somewhere, they still are.

It is strange
To carry inside you someone else's body;   10
To know it before it's born;
To see at last that it's a boy or girl, and perfect;
To bathe it and dress it; to watch it
Nurse at your breast, till you almost know it
Better than you know yourself—better than it knows itself.   15
You own it as you made it.
You are the authority upon it.

But as the child learns
To take care of herself, you know her less.
Her accidents, adventures are her own,   20
You lose track of them. Still, you know more
About her than anyone *except* her.

Little by little the child in her dies.
You say, "I have lost a child, but gained a friend."
You feel yourself gradually discarded.   25
She argues with you or ignores you
Or is kind to you. She who begged to follow you
Anywhere, just so long as it was you,
Finds follow the leader no more fun.
She makes few demands; you are grateful for the few.   30

The young person who writes once a week
Is the authority upon herself.
She sits in my living room and shows her husband
My albums of her as a child. He enjoys them
And makes fun of them. I look too   35
And I realize the girl in the matching blue
Mother-and-daughter dress, the fair one carrying
The tin lunch box with the half-pint thermos bottle
Or training her pet duck to go down the slide
Is lost just as the dark one, who is dead, is lost.   40
But the world in which the two wear their flared coats
And the hats that match, exists so uncannily
That, after I've seen its pictures for an hour,
I believe in it: the bandage coming loose
One has in the picture of the other's birthday,   45
The castles they are building, at the beach for asthma.
I look at them and all the old sure knowledge
Floods over me, when I put the album down
I keep saying inside: "I *did* know those children.
I braided those braids. I was driving the car   50
The day that she stepped in the can of grease
We were taking to the butcher for our ration points.[1]
I *know* those children. I know all about them.
Where are they?"

I stare at her and try to see some sign   55
Of the child she was. I can't believe there isn't any.
I tell her foolishly, pointing at the picture,
That I keep wondering where she is.

[1] During World War II certain foods were rationed in the United States, and cans of kitchen grease
were saved for exchange.

She tells me, "Here I am."
                Yes, and the other
Isn't dead, but has everlasting life . . .   60
The girl from next door, the borrowed child,
Said to me the other day, "You like children so much,
Don't you want to have some of your own?"
I couldn't believe that she could say it.
I thought: "Surely you can look at me and see them."   65

When I see them in my dreams I feel such joy.
If I could dream of them every night!

When I think of my dream of the little girls
It's as if we were playing hide-and-seek.
The dark one   70
Looks at me longingly, and disappears;
The fair one stays in sight, just out of reach
No matter where I reach. I am tired
As a mother who's played all day, some rainy day.
I don't want to play it any more, I don't want to,   75
But the child keeps on playing, so I play.

Our last example is the longest and in some respects the most difficult. The speaker is J. Alfred Prufrock; a reader will understand much in
the poem when he begins to see Prufrock as a personality with a past, a
present, and a future. Prufrock speaks to a "you" who may be difficult to
define, but Eliot evidently parallels Prufrock's speech with the speech in
Italian he quotes as his epigraph (both Guido and Prufrock may be seen
as describing their private hells to listeners they believe condemned to
similar fates). Finally, the conditions that prompt Prufrock to speak become more clear when we consider that Eliot has given the poem a
pointedly ironic title; this "love song" contains little that most people
would call "love."

The Love Song of J. Alfred Prufrock

T. S. Eliot   (1888–1965)

> *S'io credessi che mia risposta fosse*
> *a persona che mai tornasse al mondo,*
> *questa fiamma staria senza più scosse.*
> *Ma per ciò che giammai di questo fondo*
> *non tornò vivo alcun, s'i'odo il vero,*
> *senza tema d'infamia ti rispondo.*[1]

[1] In Dante's *Inferno* the poet, a visitor to Hell, has asked Guido da Montefeltro, whose soul burns in
eternal flame, who he is and how he came there. The Italian lines given here begin Guido's reply: "If I
believed my answer were to one who might return to the world, this flame would shake [because I
would speak] no more. But since, if I hear true, none ever came alive from this abyss, I answer you
without fear of infamy" (xxvii, 61–66).

Let us go then, you and I,
When the evening is spread out against the sky
Like a patient etherised upon a table;
Let us go, through certain half-deserted streets,
The muttering retreats   5
Of restless nights in one-night cheap hotels
And sawdust restaurants with oyster-shells:
Streets that follow like a tedious argument
Of insidious intent
To lead you to an overwhelming question. . .   10
Oh, do not ask, 'What is it?'
Let us go and make our visit.

In the room the women come and go
Talking of Michelangelo.[2]

The yellow fog that rubs its back upon the window-panes,   15
The yellow smoke that rubs its muzzle on the window-panes,
Licked its tongue into the corners of the evening,
Lingered upon the pools that stand in drains,
Let fall upon its back the soot that falls from chimneys,
Slipped by the terrace, made a sudden leap,   20
And seeing that it was a soft October night,
Curled once about the house and fell asleep.

And indeed there will be time
For the yellow smoke that slides along the street
Rubbing its back upon the window-panes;   25
There will be time, there will be time
To prepare a face to meet the faces that you meet;
There will be time to murder and create,
And time for all the works and days[3] of hands
That lift and drop a question on your plate;   30
Time for you and time for me,
And time yet for a hundred indecisions,
And for a hundred visions and revisions,
Before the taking of a toast and tea.

In the room the women come and go   35
Talking of Michelangelo.

And indeed there will be time
To wonder, 'Do I dare?' and, 'Do I dare?'
Time to turn back and descend the stair,
With a bald spot in the middle of my hair—   40

[2] Michelangelo created; these people talk.
[3] *Works and Days*, by Hesiod (eighth century B.C.), an account of agricultural labor.

(They will say: 'How his hair is growing thin!')
My morning coat, my collar mounting firmly to the chin,
My necktie rich and modest, but asserted by a simple pin—
(They will say: 'But how his arms and legs are thin!')
Do I dare   45
Disturb the universe?
In a minute there is time
For decisions and revisions which a minute will reverse.

For I have known them all already, known them all—
Have known the evenings, mornings, afternoons,   50
I have measured out my life with coffee spoons;
I know the voices dying with a dying fall[4]
Beneath the music from a farther room.
    So how should I presume?

And I have known the eyes already, known them all—   55
The eyes that fix you in a formulated phrase,
And when I am formulated, sprawling on a pin,
When I am pinned and wriggling on the wall,
Then how should I begin
To spit out all the butt-ends of my days and ways?   60
    And how should I presume?

And I have known the arms already, known them all—
Arms that are braceleted and white and bare
(But in the lamplight, downed with light brown hair!)
Is it perfume from a dress   65
That makes me so digress?
Arms that lie along a table, or wrap about a shawl.
    And should I then presume?
    And how should I begin?

                        •   •   •

Shall I say, I have gone at dusk through narrow streets   70
And watched the smoke that rises from the pipes
Of lonely men in shirt-sleeves, leaning out of windows? . . .

I should have been a pair of ragged claws
Scuttling across the floors of silent seas.

                        •   •   •

And the afternoon, the evening, sleeps so peacefully!   75
Smoothed by long fingers,

---

[4] Cf. Shakespeare, *Twelfth Night*, Act I, Scene 1, lines 1–4: "If music be the food of love, play on. / Give me excess of it, that, surfeiting, / The appetite may sicken, and so die. / That strain again! It had a dying fall." Music, love, and romance are distant from Prufrock, in "a farther room."

Asleep . . . tired . . . or it malingers,
Stretched on the floor, here beside you and me.
Should I, after tea and cakes and ices,
Have the strength to force the moment to its crisis?   80
But though I have wept and fasted, wept and prayed,
Though I have seen my head (grown slightly bald) brought in
    upon a platter,[5]
I am no prophet—and here's no great matter;
I have seen the moment of my greatness flicker,
And I have seen the eternal Footman hold my coat, and snicker,   85
And in short, I was afraid.

And would it have been worth it, after all,
After the cups, the marmalade, the tea,
Among the porcelain, among some talk of you and me,
Would it have been worth while,   90
To have bitten off the matter with a smile,
To have squeezed the universe into a ball[6]
To roll it towards some overwhelming question,
To say: 'I am Lazarus, come from the dead,[7]
Come back to tell you all, I shall tell you all'—   95
If one, settling a pillow by her head,
    Should say: 'That is not what I meant at all.
    That is not it, at all.'

And would it have been worth it, after all,
Would it have been worth while,   100
After the sunsets and the dooryards and the sprinkled streets,
After the novels, after the teacups, after the skirts that trail along
    the floor—
And this, and so much more?—
It is impossible to say just what I mean!
But as if a magic lantern threw the nerves in patterns on a
    screen: 105
Would it have been worth while
If one, settling a pillow or throwing off a shawl,
And turning toward the window, should say:
    'That is not it at all,
    That is not what I meant, at all.'   110

• • •

[5] Like John the Baptist. See Mark vi, 17–28; Matthew xiv, 3–11.
[6] Cf. Andrew Marvell's "To His Coy Mistress": 'Let us roll all our strength and all / Our sweetness up into one ball, / And tear our pleasures with rough strife / Through the iron gates of life."
[7] John xi, 1–44 tells of Christ's raising Lazarus from the dead. Another Lazarus appears in Luke xvi, 19–31, where the passage ends: "If they hear not Moses and the prophets, neither will they be persuaded, though one rose from the dead."

No! I am not Prince Hamlet,[8] nor was meant to be;
Am an attendant lord, one that will do
To swell a progress, start a scene or two,
Advise the prince; no doubt, an easy tool,
Deferential, glad to be of use,   115
Politic, cautious, and meticulous;
Full of high sentence,[9] but a bit obtuse;
At times, indeed, almost ridiculous—
Almost, at times, the Fool.

I grow old . . . I grow old . . .   120
I shall wear the bottoms of my trousers rolled.

Shall I part my hair behind? Do I dare to eat a peach?
I shall wear white flannel trousers, and walk upon the beach.
I have heard the mermaids singing, each to each.

I do not think that they will sing to me.   125

I have seen them riding seaward on the waves
Combing the white hair of the waves blown back
When the wind blows the water white and black.

We have lingered in the chambers of the sea
By sea-girls wreathed with seaweed red and brown   130
Till human voices wake us, and we drown.

[8] Prufrock considers himself like Shakespeare's Hamlet in procrastination but not in action. In the play of life he is not a tragic hero but a Polonius, Rosencrantz, or Guildenstern—perhaps even the stock comic character, the Fool.
[9] Sententiousness, pomposity.

CHAPTER 3

Language

Denotation and Connotation

The *denotation* of a word is its direct reference, its dictionary definition. It is the thing the word stands for, a concept without emotional coloring. The *connotation* is the feeling or emotion aroused in the mind of speaker or listener. Certain words possess powerful connotations for most people, though the precise feelings aroused may vary with the individual using them: *God, Hiroshima, love, Communist*. Others are more simply denotative (*chair, street*), though even these may be connotative for some people: *dog* and *cat* may be emotional words for people afraid of animals. Careful control of connotations is vital to poetry. As readers, we must be alert to the meanings of words, but we must also observe the associations the poet evokes.

Through images of estate and garden the following poem contrasts the emotional satisfactions of possession with the pain of irretrievable loss.

Those Hours When Happy Hours Were My Estate
Edna St. Vincent Millay   (1892–1950)

Those hours when happy hours were my estate,—
Entailed, as proper, for the next in line,
Yet mine the harvest, and the title mine—
Those acres, fertile, and the furrow straight,   4
From which the lark would rise—all of my late
Enchantments, still, in brilliant colours, shine,
But striped with black, the tulip, lawn and vine,
Like gardens looked at through an iron gate.   8
Yet not as one who never sojourned there
I view the lovely segments of a past
I lived with all my senses, well aware
That this was perfect, and it would not last: 12
I smell the flower, though vacuum-still the air;
I feel its texture, though the gate is fast.

The speaker has, in fact, not lost a garden. What has she lost? What words and phrases serve most powerfully to convey her feelings through their connotations?

In the next poem we start with associations suggested by the name "Iona." An island, scarcely three miles long, off the west coast of Scotland, it remained a powerful center of Celtic culture for three centuries after St. Columba established a mission there in 563. Vast numbers of kings, chieftains, and holy men were buried in its rocky soil.

Iona: The Graves of the Kings
Robinson Jeffers (1887–1962)

I wish not to lie here.
There's hardly a plot of earth not blessed for burial, but here
One might dream badly.   3

In beautiful seas a beautiful
And sainted island, but the dark earth so shallow on the rock
Gorged with bad meat.   6

Kings buried in the lee of the saint,
Kings of fierce Norway, blood-boltered[1] Scotland, bitterly dreaming
Treacherous Ireland.   9

Imagine what delusions of grandeur.
What suspicion-agonized eyes, what jellies of arrogance and terror
This earth has absorbed.   12

[1] Blood-spattered. A "bolter" is a sieve, or a cloth used for sifting. Cf. "blood-boltered Banquo," Shakespeare's *Macbeth*, iv, i, 123.

What is the emotional force of the line "Gorged with bad meat"? What attitude does it suggest toward the kings buried on Iona? How is that attitude supported elsewhere in the poem?

Shakespeare was a master both of precise meanings and of vital associations. In the following poem the speaker denies to his mistress the beauty usually associated with roses and perfumes, but does he mean that she is not beautiful?

My Mistress' Eyes Are Nothing Like the Sun
William Shakespeare (1564–1616)

My mistress' eyes are nothing like the sun;
Coral is far more red than her lips' red:
If snow be white, why then her breasts are dun;

If hairs be wires, black wires grow on her head.   4
I have seen roses damask'd, red and white,
But no such roses see I in her cheeks;
And in some perfumes is there more delight
Than in the breath that from my mistress reeks.   8
I love to hear her speak, yet well I know
That music hath a far more pleasing sound:
I grant I never saw a goddess go,—
My mistress, when she walks, treads on the ground: 12
   And yet, by heaven, I think my love as rare
   As any she belied with false compare.

William Carlos Williams, too, could play that game. The woman described by his speaker is more like a weed than an anemone, but does the comparison make her less beautiful?

Queen-Ann's-Lace

William Carlos Williams (1883–1963)

Her body is not so white as
anemone petals nor so smooth—nor
so remote a thing. It is a field
of the wild carrot taking
the field by force; the grass   5
does not raise above it.
Here is no question of whiteness,
white as can be, with a purple mole
at the center of each flower.
Each flower is a hand's span   10
of her whiteness. Wherever
his hand has lain there is
a tiny purple blemish. Each part
is a blossom under his touch
to which the fibres of her being   15
stem one by one, each to its end,
until the whole field is a
white desire, empty, a single stem,
a cluster, flower by flower,
a pious wish to whiteness gone over—   20
or nothing.

In still another description of a lovely woman, the following speaker plays with some mildly off-color double meanings ("Love likes a gander, and adores a goose"), but that is only part of the fun.

I Knew a Woman

Theodore Roethke   (1908–1963)

I knew a woman, lovely in her bones,
When small birds sighed, she would sigh back at them;
Ah, when she moved, she moved more ways than one:
The shapes a bright container can contain!
Of her choice virtues only gods should speak,   5
Or English poets who grew up on Greek
(I'd have them sing in chorus, cheek to cheek).

How well her wishes went! She stroked my chin,
She taught me Turn, and Counter-turn, and Stand;
She taught me Touch, that undulant white skin;   10
I nibbled meekly from her proffered hand;
She was the sickle; I, poor I, the rake,
Coming behind her for her pretty sake
(But what prodigious mowing we did make).

Love likes a gander, and adores a goose: 15
Her full lips pursed, the errant note to seize;
She played it quick, she played it light and loose;
My eyes, they dazzled at her flowing knees;
Her several parts could keep a pure repose,
Or one hip quiver with a mobile nose   20
(She moved in circles, and those circles moved).

Let seed be grass, and grass turn into hay:
I'm martyr to a motion not my own;
What's freedom for? To know eternity.
I swear she cast a shadow white as stone.   25
But who would count eternity in days?
These old bones live to learn her wanton ways:
(I measure time by how a body sways).

What is the usual denotation of "container"? Does the word ordinarily have any significant connotation? What meanings and associations does it have here? What other words and phrases lend important effects to the poem through their associations?

The last two poems in this section deal with death, almost invariably an emotional subject. Observe which words work most powerfully by association.

The Raid

Brother Antoninus (William Everson)   (1912–   )

They came out of the sun undetected,
Who had lain in the thin ships
All night long on the cold ocean,
Watched Vega[1] down, the Wain[2] hover,
Drank in the weakening dawn their brew,   5
And sent the lumbering death-laden birds
Level along the decks.

They came out of the sun with their guns geared,
Saw the soft and easy shape of that island
Laid on the sea,   10
An unwakening woman,
Its deep hollows and its flowing folds
Veiled in the garlands of its morning mists.
Each of them held in his aching eyes the erotic image,
And then tipped down,   15
In the target's trance,
In the ageless instant of the long descent,
And saw sweet chaos blossom below,
And felt in that flower the years release.

The perfect achievement.   20
They went back toward the sun crazy with joy,
Like wild birds weaving,
Drunkenly stunting;
Passed out over edge of that injured island,
Sought the rendezvous on the open sea   25
Where the ships would be waiting.

None were there.
Neither smoke nor smudge;
Neither spar nor splice nor rolling raft.
Only the wide waiting waste,   30
That each of them saw with intenser sight
Than he ever had spared it,
Who circled that spot,
The spent gauge caught in its final flutter,
And straggled down on their wavering wings   35
From the vast sky,

[1] A bright star.
[2] The seven bright stars in the Big Dipper.

From the endless spaces,
Down at last for the low hover,
And the short quick quench of the sea.

Lady Lazarus[1]

Sylvia Plath   (1932–1963)

I have done it again.
One year in every ten
I manage it—   3

A sort of walking miracle, my skin
Bright as a Nazi lampshade,[2]
My right foot   6

A paperweight,
My face a featureless, fine
Jew linen.   9

Peel off the napkin
O my enemy.
Do I terrify?—   12

The nose, the eye pits, the full set of teeth?
The sour breath
Will vanish in a day.   15

Soon, soon the flesh
The grave cave ate will be
At home on me   18

And I a smiling woman.
I am only thirty.
And like the cat I have nine times to die.   21

This is Number Three.
What a trash
To annihilate each decade.   24

What a million filaments.
The peanut-crunching crowd
Shoves in to see   27

Them unwrap me hand and foot—
The big strip tease.
Gentlemen, ladies,   30

[1] Jesus raised Lazarus from the dead (John xi, 1–44).
[2] Made of skin from a death camp victim.

These are my hands,
My knees.
I may be skin and bone,   33

Nevertheless, I am the same, identical woman.
The first time it happened I was ten.
It was an accident.   36

The second time I meant
To last it out and not come back at all.
I rocked shut   39

As a seashell.
They had to call and call
And pick the worms off me like sticky pearls.   42

Dying
Is an art, like everything else.
I do it exceptionally well.   45

I do it so it feels like hell.
I do it so it feels real.
I guess you could say I've a call.   48

It's easy enough to do it in a cell.
It's easy enough to do it and stay put.
It's the theatrical   51

Comeback in broad day
To the same place, the same face, the same brute
Amused shout: 54

"A miracle!"
That knocks me out.
There is a charge   57

For the eyeing of my scars, there is a charge
For the hearing of my heart—
It really goes.   60

And there is a charge, a very large charge,
For a word or a touch
Or a bit of blood   63

Or a piece of my hair or my clothes.
So, so, Herr Doktor.
So, Herr Enemy.   66

I am your opus,
I am your valuable,
The pure gold baby   69

That melts to a shriek.
I turn and burn.
Do not think I underestimate your great concern.   72

Ash, ash—
You poke and stir.
Flesh, bone, there is nothing there—   75

A cake of soap,
A wedding ring,
A gold filling.   78

Herr God, Herr Lucifer,
Beware
Beware.   81

Out of the ash
I rise with my red hair
And I eat men like air.   84

Allusion

An *allusion* is a reference to something outside the work and not entirely explained within it. When a poet alludes to something, he ordinarily expects the reader to catch the reference and understand its use. If he describes a teacher as "a Socrates" or an acquaintance as "a Judas," he expects the reader to see a wise and quizzical schoolmaster or a treacherous friend. Most allusions, like those to Socrates and Judas, refer to the most widely shared heritage of Western culture: Greek and Roman myths, the Bible, Shakespeare, memorable historical events. But other sources are possible, from philosophers to scientists, from priests to Oriental prophets. The writer may allude to his own life, or the lives of his friends and acquaintances. Allusions may, in other words, be easy or difficult, obvious or obscure.

Allusions are not limited to poetry, but appear in all forms of written or oral communication, from novels and sermons to private letters and conversations at cocktail parties. Because poetry is, however, a more condensed form of communication than other forms, the allusions sometimes require particularly close attention. In each of the poems of this section, the reader loses a major part of the communication if he does not understand the relevance of one or more central allusions.

Terence, This Is Stupid Stuff

A. E. Housman (1859–1936)

'Terence, this is stupid stuff:
You eat your victuals fast enough;
There can't be much amiss, 'tis clear,
To see the rate you drink your beer.
But oh, good Lord, the verse you make,   5
It gives a chap the belly-ache.
The cow, the old cow, she is dead;
It sleeps well, the horned head:
We poor lads, 'tis our turn now
To hear such tunes as killed the cow.   10
Pretty friendship 'tis to rhyme
Your friends to death before their time
Moping melancholy mad:
Come, pipe a tune to dance to, lad.'
      Why, if 'tis dancing you would be,   15
There's brisker pipes than poetry.
Say, for what were hop-yards meant,
Or why was Burton built on Trent?
Oh many a peer[1] of England brews
Livelier liquor than the Muse,   20
And malt does more than Milton can
To justify God's ways to man.
Ale, man, ale's the stuff to drink
For fellows whom it hurts to think:
Look into the pewter pot   25
To see the world as the world's not.
And faith, 'tis pleasant till 'tis past:
The mischief is that 'twill not last.
Oh I have been to Ludlow[2] fair
And left my necktie God knows where,   30
And carried half-way home, or near,
Pints and quarts of Ludlow beer:
Then the world seemed none so bad,
And I myself a sterling lad;
And down in lovely muck I've lain,   35
Happy till I woke again.
Then I saw the morning sky:
Heigho, the tale was all a lie;
The world, it was the old world yet,

---

[1] Nobleman. Wealth from breweries sometimes led to peerages.
[2] A Shropshire market town.

I was I, my things were wet,   40
And nothing now remained to do
But begin the game anew.
    Therefore, since the world has still
Much good, but much less good than ill,
And while the sun and moon endure   45
Luck's a chance, but trouble's sure,
I'd face it as a wise man would,
And train for ill and not for good.
'Tis true, the stuff I bring for sale
Is not so brisk a brew as ale: 50
Out of a stem that scored[3] the hand
I wrung it in a weary land.
But take it: if the smack is sour,
The better for the embittered hour;
It should do good to heart and head   55
When your soul is in my soul's stead;
And I will friend you, if I may,
In the dark and cloud day.

    There was a king reigned in the East:
There, when kings will sit to feast,   60
They get their fill before they think
With poisoned meat and poisoned drink.
He gathered all that springs to birth
From the many-venomed earth;
First a little, thence to more,   65
He sampled all her killing store;
And easy, smiling, seasoned sound,
Sate the king when healths went round.
They put arsenic in his meat
And stared aghast to watch him eat;   70
They poured strychnine in his cup
And shook to see him drink it up:
They shook, they stared as white's their shirt:
Them it was their poison hurt.
—I tell the tale that I heard told.   75
Mithridates, he died old.

[3] Scratched, cut.

In this poem the most important allusion is to Mithridates, a king whose story is told in Pliny's *Natural History*. Perhaps because he fears Mithridates will not be familiar to his readers, Housman recapitulates the story in the last section of the poem, making the allusion largely self-explanatory. He leaves it to the reader, however, to perceive the relationship between Mithridates and the rest of the poem. Other allusions help to clarify the attitude toward life upon which the relationship rests. Burton upon Trent is an English town famous for its breweries. The allusion to Milton ("And malt does more than Milton can/To justify God's ways to man") reminds us that in the opening lines of *Paradise Lost* Milton says he wrote the poem to "justify the ways of God to men." The line "Terence, this is stupid stuff" also involves an allusion: Terence was a Latin comic dramatist (ca. 190–159 B.C.), and Housman was Professor of Latin at Cambridge. Terence's reputation for a polished Latin style may have prompted Housman's choice of this pseudonym for himself. The poem gains force when read in its original position near the end of a volume of poems that are not comic, but "moping melancholy mad," Housman's *A Shropshire Lad*. A good dictionary or encyclopedia will usually clarify such allusions as "Mithridates" and "Terence," but the opening lines of "Terence, This is Stupid Stuff" are more immediately clear to those who have already savored Housman in the poems preceding it.

The following poem is enriched by knowledge of Homer's *Odyssey*.

Ulysses

Robert Graves   (1895–   )

> To the much-tossed Ulysses, never done
>   With woman whether gowned as wife or whore,
> Penelope and Circe seemed as one:
> She like a whore made his lewd fancies run,
>   And wifely she a hero to him bore.   5
>
> Their counter-changings terrified his way:
>   They were the clashing rocks, Symplegades,
> Scylla and Charybdis too were they;
> Now they were storms frosting the sea with spray
>   And now the lotus island's drunken ease.   10
>
> They multiplied into the Sirens' throng,
>   Forewarned by fear of whom he stood bound fast
> Hand and foot helpless to the vessel's mast,
> Yet would not stop his ears: daring their song
>   He groaned and sweated till that shore was past.   15
>
> One, two and many: flesh had made him blind,
>   Flesh had one pleasure only in the act,
> Flesh set one purpose only in the mind—
> Triumph of flesh and afterwards to find
>   Still those same terrors wherewith flesh was racked.   20

His wiles were witty and his fame far known,
Every king's daughter sought him for her own,
    Yet he was nothing to be won or lost.
    All lands to him were Ithaca: love-tossed
He loathed the fraud, yet would not bed alone.   25

Penelope was the wife of Ulysses; Circe, an enchantress whose attractions kept him for a year from continuing his journey homeward. In the mind of Ulysses, as Graves portrays him, they stand for two extremes of woman, "wife or whore," but seem also "as one." By identifying with woman the difficulties that Ulysses met in his wanderings (Symplegades, Scylla, Charybdis, storms, the lotus island, and the Sirens), Graves makes the *Odyssey* into a metaphoric voyage by a man "love-tossed," who "loathed the fraud, yet would not bed alone."

The title of the next poem fixes the scene in a museum of fine arts. The first few lines present a generalization about the "Old Masters" that is specifically illustrated in two paintings by Pieter Breughel.

Musée des Beaux Arts

W. H. Auden   (1907–1973)

About suffering they were never wrong,
The Old Masters: how well they understood
Its human position; how it takes place
While someone else is eating or opening a window or just walking
    dully along;   5
How, when the aged are reverently, passionately waiting
For the miraculous birth, there always must be
Children who did not specially want it to happen, skating
On a pond at the edge of the wood:
They never forgot   10
That even the dreadful martyrdom must run its course
Anyhow in a corner, some untidy spot
Where the dogs go on with their doggy life and the torturer's horse
Scratches its innocent behind on a tree.

In Breughel's *Icarus*, for instance: how everything turns away   15
Quite leisurely from the disaster; the ploughman may
Have heard the splash, the forsaken cry,
But for him it was not an important failure; the sun shone
As it had to on the white legs disappearing into the green
Water; and the expensive delicate ship that must have seen   20
Something amazing, a boy falling out of the sky,
Had somewhere to get to and sailed calmly on.

Auden refers to Breughel's "The Massacre of the Innocents" and "The Fall of Icarus," but he evokes the paintings in sufficient detail for our understanding. We do need, however, to know something of the Icarus of ancient Greek myth: a boy who flew too near the sun on wings of feathers and wax, which the sun melted, plunging him into the sea.

The Second Coming

W. B. Yeats (1865–1939)

Turning and turning in the widening gyre
The falcon cannot hear the falconer;
Things fall apart; the centre cannot hold;
Mere anarchy is loosed upon the world,
The blood-dimmed tide is loosed, and everywhere   5
The ceremony of innocence is drowned;
The best lack all conviction, while the worst
Are full of passionate intensity.

Surely some revelation is at hand;
Surely the Second Coming is at hand.   10
The Second Coming! Hardly are those words out
When a vast image out of *Spiritus Mundi*
Troubles my sight: somewhere in sands of the desert
A shape with lion body and the head of a man,
A gaze blank and pitiless as the sun,   15
Is moving its slow thighs, while all about it
Reel shadows of the indignant desert birds.
The darkness drops again; but now I know
That twenty centuries of stony sleep
Were vexed to nightmare by a rocking cradle,   20
And what rough beast, its hour come round at last,
Slouches towards Bethlehem to be born?

The most important allusion here is to the widespread belief that God will appear on earth once more, in a "Second Coming." The speaker of this poem suggests that the Second Coming will present mankind not with a god of love, like the first coming, but a god of wrath. In the "gyre" Yeats describes a widening cone similar to the path of an upward-flying falcon, but similar also to his own image for the periodic movement of history, from one gyre into another opposing one. In the term *"Spiritus Mundi"* he suggests that his vision derives from a "Spirit of the World," an ever-present, animating principle.

Frequently, as here, the reader needs not only to identify the allusion, but to understand it in the poet's particular focus. The traditional joyous

Second Coming contrasts in violent irony with Yeats's vision in his poem. In the next two sets of poems, Yeats similarly requires identification first, and then an understanding of how he uses the allusions.

Two Songs from a Play

W. B. Yeats (1865–1939)

I

I saw a staring virgin stand
Where holy Dionysus[1] died,
And tear the heart out of his side,
And lay the heart upon her hand   4
And bear that beating heart away;
And then did all the Muses sing
Of Magnus Annus[2] at the spring,
As though God's death were but a play.   8

Another Troy[3] must rise and set,
Another lineage feed the crow,
Another Argo's painted prow
Drive to a flashier bauble yet.[4]   12
The Roman Empire stood appalled:
It dropped the reigns of peace and war
When that fierce virgin and her Star[5]
Out of the fabulous darkness called.   16

II

In pity for man's darkening thought
He walked that room and issued thence
In Galilean turbulence;[6]
The Babylonian starlight brought   20

A fabulous, formless darkness in;
Odour of blood when Christ was slain
Made all Platonic[7] tolerance vain
And vain all Doric[8] discipline.   24

Everything that man esteems
Endures a moment or a day.

[1] Greek god of vegetation and wine.
[2] A great or long year.
[3] Scene of the Trojan War.
[4] Jason sought the Golden Fleece in a ship called the Argo.
[5] Mary and the Star of Bethlehem.
[6] Jesus began his miracles in Galilee during a time of disorder.
[7] Plato, a Greek philosopher (427–347 B.C.).
[8] A Greek architectural style characterized by simplicity of form.

Love's pleasure drives his love away,
The painter's brush consumes his dreams;   28
The herald's cry, the soldier's tread
Exhaust his glory and his might:
Whatever flames upon the night
Man's own resinous heart has fed.   32

In the above lines, we need to know not simply who Plato was, but
what "Platonic tolerance" might be; we need not simply to define "Doric," but "Doric discipline." So, too, Yeats's attitude toward the "virgin"
(Mary) is not everybody's attitude. As in all good poems, each line and
phrase reflects upon and is affected by the preceding lines and phrases
and ultimately by the entire poem that surrounds it. The allusions feed
understanding but do not by themselves create it. In a general way, the
idea of history in "Two Songs from a Play" is summed up in the concluding stanza. The earlier lines become considerably more transparent
when we see each of the allusions as an example pointing toward the
truths that begin and end the last stanza.

Fragments

W. B. Yeats   (1865–1939)

I

Locke sank into a swoon;
The Garden died;
God took the spinning-jenny
Out of his side.   4

II

Where got I that truth?
Out of a medium's mouth,
Out of nothing it came,
Out of the forest loam,   8
Out of dark night where lay
The crowns of Nineveh.

The first stanza alludes to the Garden of Eden and the story in Genesis
of how God created Eve from the rib of the sleeping Adam. It alludes
also to the British philosopher John Locke (1632–1704) and to the invention of the spinning jenny. Why does the speaker consider Locke to be
like Adam, why is the creation of the spinning jenny analogous to the
creation of Eve, and why does the Garden die? Locke asserted that all
knowledge came through the senses rather than from intuition or divine

revelation; the spinning jenny is in a sense the mother of the industrial age; with their coming died both the Garden of Eden and the garden of an agricultural economy. Nineveh was the site of a civilization that died centuries before the birth of Locke; the allusion helps make the point that the modern world has doomed itself to mere sensory knowledge and technology, cutting itself off from natural and supernatural realms, and heading for the night that engulfs all civilizations.

Irony

All irony entails a reversal either of meaning or of expectation. An individual says or does something opposite to what he would normally be expected to say or do. Although ironies can be compounded in some of the most complicated and subtle effects in literature, they generally fall into one of three categories: verbal ironies, situational ironies, and dramatic ironies.

A *verbal irony* occurs when someone says the opposite of what he means. He comes in dripping rainwater on the carpet and says "It's lovely weather outside." Verbal ironies depend on their context. The rainstorm makes the "lovely" ironic. And so the poet will control the *context* in his language, the surroundings that will turn a "lovely" into a "dreadful."

A *situational irony* occurs when something happens that is opposite to what was intended or normally expected. A swimmer attempting a rescue is drowned, but the drowning nonswimmer is pulled to shore and survives; it rains on the Weather Bureau's picnic; the noble prince is killed, but the court nonentities survive unscathed.

A *dramatic irony* occurs when a character says or does something in ironic ignorance of the facts, which the audience, sharing the author's wider perspective, knows, or senses to be, in opposition. When Oedipus, the great riddle solver, says he will find the unknown murderer, a thrill of ironic horror runs through the audience, who knows that he himself is the killer he seeks. When Jack Benny smiles blissfully as he fiddles, the audience dies with laughter at the musical atrocity.

Ironies vary from bitter to hilarious, from tragic to comic, and occur in all the subtleties of human attitudes between. They are also frequently complex. All dramatic ironies require a situational irony, where *ought to be* clashes with *is*, for instance. And a speaker may say an intentional verbal irony that is also a dramatic irony in his ignorance of all the facts. He may call a stormy day "lovely" in deliberate irony and not know that everything he owns has perished in the flood. In discussing irony, we must distinguish the differing perspectives and contexts of knowledge that produce the oppositions; we must know from what point of view the irony appears.

The Trees in the Garden Rained Flowers

Stephen Crane   (1871–1900)

The trees in the garden rained flowers.
Children ran there joyously.
They gathered the flowers
Each to himself.
Now there were some   5
Who gathered great heaps—
Having opportunity and skill—
Until, behold, only chance blossoms
Remained for the feeble.
Then a little spindling tutor   10
Ran importantly to the father, crying:
"Pray, come hither!
See this unjust thing in your garden!"
But when the father had surveyed,
He admonished the tutor: 15
"Not so, small sage!
This thing is just.
For, look you,
Are not they who possess the flowers
Stronger, bolder, shrewder   20
Than they who have none?
Why should the strong—
The beautiful strong—
Why should they not have the flowers?"

Upon reflection, the tutor bowed to the ground.   25
"My Lord," he said,
"The stars are displaced
By this towering wisdom."

The words attributed to the tutor at the end of the poem are clearly ironic from the perspective of the author and the reader, but are they ironic to the tutor as well? Does the tutor mean what he says, or does he mean something different? If the reader knew more about the tutor, he would know whether he might accept the father's explanation or speak ironically. But all we have to go on is the gross exaggeration: what the father has said is hardly "towering wisdom," and the stars are not displaced by it. The irony is so sharp we can hardly believe the tutor is not aware of it. But can we be sure?

The Convergence of the Twain

(LINES ON THE LOSS OF THE "TITANIC")

Thomas Hardy   (1840–1928)

I

In a solitude of the sea
Deep from human vanity,
And the Pride of Life that planned her, stilly couches she.   3

II

Steel chambers, late the pyres
Of her salamandrine[1] fires,
Cold currents thrid,[2] and turn to rhythmic tidal lyres.   6

III

Over the mirrors meant
To glass the opulent
The sea-worm crawls—grotesque, slimed, dumb, indifferent.   9

IV

Jewels in joy designed
To ravish the sensuous mind
Lie lightless, all their sparkles bleared and black and blind.   12

V

Dim moon-eyed fishes near
Gaze at the gilded gear
And query: "What does this vaingloriousness down here?" . . .   15

VI

Well: while was fashioning
This creature of cleaving wing,
The Immanent Will that stirs and urges everything   18

VII

Prepared a sinister mate
For her—so gaily great—
A Shape of Ice, for the time far and dissociate.   21

---

[1] Hardy associates aquatic salamanders with the mythical salamanders that could live in fire.
[2] Thread.

VIII

And as the smart ship grew
In stature, grace, and hue,
In shadowy silent distance grew the Iceberg too.   24

IX

Alien they seemed to be:
No mortal eye could see
The intimate welding of their later history.   27

X

Or sign that they were bent
By paths coincident
On being anon twin halves of one august event.   30

XI

Till the Spinner of the Years
Said "Now!" And each one hears,
And consummation comes, and jars two hemispheres.   33

The British White Star liner *Titanic*, on her maiden voyage, collided
with an iceberg and sank on the night of April 14, 1912. What ironies
does the poem associate with her sinking?

1887

A. E. Housman   (1859–1936)

From Clee to heaven the beacon burns,
   The shires have seen it plain,
From north and south the sign returns
   And beacons burn again.   4

Look left, look right, the hills are bright,
   The dales are light between,
Because 'tis fifty years to-night
   That God has saved the Queen.   8

Now, when the flames they watch not towers
   About the soil they trod,
Lads, we'll remember friends of ours
   Who shared the work with God.   12

To skies that knit their heartstrings right,
   To fields that bred them brave,
The saviors come not home to-night:
   Themselves they could not save.   16

It dawns in Asia, tombstones show
    And Shropshire names are read;
And the Nile spills his overflow
    Beside the Severn's dead.   20

We pledge in peace by farm and town
    The Queen they served in war,
And fire the beacons up and down
    The land they perished for.   24

'God save the Queen' we living sing,
    From height to height 'tis heard;
And with the rest your voices ring,
    Lads of the Fifty-third.   28

Oh, God will save her, fear you not:
    Be you the men you've been,
Get you the sons your fathers got,
    And God will save the Queen.   32

In 1887, Great Britain celebrated Queen Victoria's fiftieth year on the throne. For the speaker of this poem the slogan "God save the Queen" is tinged with irony. Why? What is the nature of the irony? In what lines does it become most apparent?

Dulce et Decorum Est

Wilfred Owen (1893–1918)

Bent double, like old beggars under sacks,
Knock-kneed, coughing like hags, we cursed through sludge,
Till on the haunting flares we turned our backs,
And towards our distant rest began to trudge.
Men marched asleep. Many had lost their boots,   5
But limped on, blood-shod. All went lame, all blind;
Drunk with fatigue; deaf even to the hoots
Of gas-shells dropping softly behind.

Gas! GAS! Quick, boys!—An ecstasy of fumbling,
Fitting the clumsy helmets just in time,   10
But someone still was yelling out and stumbling
And floundering like a man in fire or lime.—
Dim through the misty panes and thick green light,
As under a green sea, I saw him drowning.

In all my dreams before my helpless sight   15
He plunges at me, guttering, choking, drowning.

If in some smothering dreams, you too could pace
Behind the wagon that we flung him in,
And watch the white eyes writhing in his face,
His hanging face, like a devil's sick of sin;   20
If you could hear, at every jolt, the blood
Come gargling from the froth-corrupted lungs,
Bitter as the cud
Of vile, incurable sores on innocent tongues,—
My friend, you would not tell with such high zest   25
To children ardent for some desperate glory,
The old Lie: Dulce et decorum est
Pro patria mori.

Although the verbal ironist says the opposite of what he means, he does not lie. He does not intend to deceive a listener, but rather to drive home a truth through indirection. Those who can translate the Latin title of this poem ("sweet and fitting it is") see an obvious ironic distance between the title and the horrible description of gas warfare that follows. At the end of the poem, Owen presents the Latin expanded into a more full quotation from the poet Horace ("Sweet and fitting it is to die for one's country") and calls it a lie. From the perspective of the speaker of this poem, it is a lie when it is spoken straight and meant to be believed; it is ironic when what is meant is "It is *not* sweet and fitting to die for one's country," as the poem attempts to demonstrate. The meaning depends upon who is speaking and what attitude he wishes to communicate.

Naming of Parts

Henry Reed   (1914–   )

To-day we have naming of parts. Yesterday,
We had daily cleaning. And to-morrow morning,
We shall have what to do after firing. But to-day,
To-day we have naming of parts. Japonica
Glistens like coral in all of the neighbouring gardens,
    And to-day we have naming of parts.   6

This is the lower sling swivel. And this
Is the upper sling swivel, whose use you will see,
When you are given your slings. And this is the piling swivel,
Which in your case you have not got. The branches
Hold in the gardens their silent, eloquent gestures,
    Which in our case we have not got.   12

This is the safety-catch, which is always released
With an easy flick of the thumb. And please do not let me
See anyone using his finger. You can do it quite easy
If you have any strength in your thumb. The blossoms
Are fragile and motionless, never letting anyone see
      Any of them using their finger.   18

And this you can see is the bolt. The purpose of this
Is to open the breech, as you see. We can slide it
Rapidly backwards and forwards: we call this
Easing the spring. And rapidly backwards and forwards
The early bees are assaulting and fumbling the flowers:
      They call it easing the Spring.   24

They call it easing the Spring: it is perfectly easy
If you have any strength in your thumb: like the bolt,
And the breech, and the cocking-piece, and the point of balance,
Which in our case we have not got; and the almond-blossom
Silent in all of the gardens and the bees going backwards and forwards,
      For to-day we have naming of parts.   30

There are two voices in this poem. Whose are they? Identify the lines that each speaks. Where are the ironies? Are the ironies apparent to both speakers?

CHAPTER 4

Traditional Themes

A *theme* is a recurring element of subject matter, a connective thread that sews together a number of other elements. A *theme* is also an insistent idea, a thought about the subject matter and not simply the matter itself. In some poems, subject matter and thought about subject matter are essentially the same. In discussing others, however, precise distinctions between *thematic material* and *thematic idea* are helpful. In a poem about death, for instance, the thematic material might be recurring references to dead leaves or withered flowers or the scent of chrysanthemums, and the thematic idea might be that death is a release, or a termination of all existence.

Because subjects and ideas are limited, poets have returned frequently to a limited number of traditional thematic materials and ideas. The poet's experience may be new to him, of course. His writing may convey the excitement of discovery and the joys of emotional enlargement and intellectual enlightenment. A poem, said Robert Frost, "begins in delight and ends in wisdom." Yet, in a broad sense, innumerable writers have produced the delight and wisdom before. The new particulars illustrate the old truths anew and lead us to realize them anew. Great poetry celebrates both the new and the old at the same time. We can see a poem both in its own time and place and in the wider context of all times and places. The greater the poem, the more surely it joins the timeless company of the great ones on similar themes, and any thematic grouping will enhance our pleasure and understanding.

The poems that follow illustrate a number of common poetic themes. In some, the prevailing subject matter provides the most important link; in others, the prevailing ideas.

Where Are the Snows of Yesteryear?

Ubi sunt qui ante nos fuerunt? wrote the medieval poets, again and again— "Where are those who were before us?" And *ubi sunt* has come to designate the whole group of poems lamenting the irrecoverable past. Each of the following poems asks the same question, by implication if not explicitly. The answers vary, of course, but the lamenting question remains, perhaps ultimately unanswerable.

The Ruin[1]

Wondrous this masonry   wasted by Fate!
Giant-built battlements   shattered and broken!
The roofs are in ruin,   the towers are wrecked,
The frost-covered bastions   battered and fallen.
Rime[2] whitens mortar;   the cracking walls   5
Have sagged and toppled,   weakened by Time.
The clasp of earth   and the clutch of the grave
Grip the proud builders,   long perished and gone,
While a hundred generations   have run.
Hoary with lichen   and ruddy of hue   10
This wall has outlasted,   unshaken by storm,
Reign after reign;   now ravaged and wrecked
The lofty arch   is leveled in ruin. . . .
     Firmly the builder   laid the foundations,
Cunningly bound them   with iron bands;   15
Stately the palaces,   splendid the baths,
Towers and pinnacles   pointing on high;
Many a mead-hall   rang with their revelry,
Many a court   with the clangor of arms,
Till Fate the all-leveling   laid them low.   20
A pestilence rose   and corpses were rife,
And death laid hold   on the warrior-host.
     Then their bulwarks were broken,   their fortresses fell,
The hands to restore them   were helpless and still.
Desolate now are the courts,   and the dome,   25
With arches discolored,   is stripped of its tiles.
Where of old once the warrior   walked in his pride,
Gleaming with gold   and wanton with wine,
Splendidly shining   in glittering mail,
The structure lies fallen   and scattered in ruin.   30
Around him he saw   a treasure of silver,
Riches of pearl   and precious stones,
In a shining city   of far-flung sway.
There stood courts of stone,   with a gushing spring
Of boiling water   in welling floods,   35
And a wall embosomed   in gleaming embrace
The spot where the hot baths   burst into air.

Translated by Charles W. Kennedy

---

[1] This anonymous Old English poem presumably describes the Roman ruins at Bath.
[2] Frost.

Ubi Sunt Qui Ante Nos Fuerunt?

Were beth they biforen us weren,	Where are those that were before us,
Houndes ladden and hauekes beren	Hounds led and hawks bore,
And hadden feld and wode?	And had field and wood?
The riche levedies in hoere bour,	The rich ladies in their bowers,
That wereden gold in hoere tressour,	That wore gold in their coiffures,
With hoere brightte rode,	With their bright faces,

6

Eten and drounken and maden hem glad;	Ate and drank and made themselves glad;
Hoere lif was al with gamen i-lad;	Their lives were all with pleasure led;
Men keneleden hem beforen;	Men knelt before them;
They beren hem wel swithe heye—	They bore themselves right haughtily—
And in a twincling of an eye	And in the twinkling of an eye
Hoere soules weren forloren.	Their souls were lost.

12

Were is that lawing and that song,	Where is that laughter and that song,
That trayling and that proude yong,	Those trailing garments and that proud gait,
Tho hauekes and tho houndes?	Those hawks and those hounds?
Al that joye is went away;	All that joy has gone away;
That wele is comen to welaway,	That wealth has come to wellaway,
To manie harde stoundes.	To many hard times.

18

Hoere paradis hy nomen here,	Their paradise they took here,
And nou they lien in helle i-fere—	And now they lie in hell together—
The fuir hit brennes hevere.	The fire it burns ever.
Long is ay and long is ho,	Long is aye and long is always,
Long is wy and long is wo—	Long is alas and long is woe—
Thennes ne cometh they nevere.	Thence they shall come never.

24

Dreghy here, man, thenne if thou wilt,	Endure here, man, then if thou wilt,
A luitel pine, that me the bit.	The little pain that thou art bid.
Withdrau thine eyses ofte.	Put away thy comforts often.
They thi pine be ounrede,	Though thy pain be hard,
And thou thenke on thi mede,	If thou consider thy reward,
Hit sal the thinken softe.	Thou shalt think it soft.

30

If that fend, that foule thing,	If that fiend, that foul thing,
Thorou wikke roun, thorou fals egging,	Through wicked counsel, through false tempting,
Nethere the haveth i-cast,	Downward hast thee cast,
Oup, and be god chaunpioun!	Up, and be a good champion!
Stond, ne fal namore adoun	Stand, and fall no more adown
For a luytel blast.	For a little blast.

36

Thou tak the rode to thi staf	Take thou the cross for thy staff,
And thenk on him that thereonne yaf	And think on Him that thereon gave
His lif that wes so lef.	His life that was so lief.
He hit yaf for the; thou yelde hit him	He gave it for thee; repay it to Him
Ayein his fo. That staf thou nim	Against His foe. Take thou that staff
And wrek him of that thef.	And avenge Him on that thief.

42

Of rightte bileve thou nim that sheld	Of right belief take thou the shield,
The wiles that thou best in that feld.	While thou art in the field;
Thin hond to strenkthen fonde	Seek to strengthen thy hand,
And kep thy fo with staves ord	And keep thy foe at staff's end,
And do that traytre seien that word.	And make that traitor say surrender.
Biget that murie londe	Attain that pleasant land.

48

Thereinne is day withouten night,	Therein is day without night,
Withouten ende strenkthe and might,	Strength without end, and might,
And wreche of everich fo,	And vengeance on every foe;
Mid god himselwen eche lif	With God himself eternal life,
And pes and rest withoute strif,	And peace and rest without strife,
Wele withouten wo.	Well-being without woe. 54
Mayden moder, hevene quene,	Maiden mother, heaven's queen,
Thou might and const and owest to bene	Thou might and can and ought to be
Oure sheld ayein the fende,	Our shield against the fiend.
Help ous sunne for to flen	Help us sin to flee,
That we moten thi sone i-seen	That we may thy son see
In joye withouten hende.	In joy without end. 60

Translated by George Perkins

The Ballad of Dead Ladies

François Villon   (1431– ?)

Tell me now in what hidden way is
    Lady Flora[1] the lovely Roman?
Where's Hipparchia,[2] and where is Thais,[3]
    Neither of them the fairer woman?   4
    Where is Echo,[4] beheld of no man,
Only heard on river and mere,—
    She whose beauty was more than human? . . .
But where are the snows of yester-year?   8

Where's Héloise,[5] the learned nun,
    For whose sake Abeillard, I ween,
Lost manhood and put priesthood on?
    (From Love he won such dule and teen[6]!)   12
    And where, I pray you, is the Queen
Who willed that Buridan should steer
    Sewed in a sack's mouth down the Seine[7]? . . .
But where are the snows of yester-year?   16

White Queen Blanche,[8] like a queen of lilies,
    With a voice like any mermaiden—
Bertha Broadfoot, Beatrice, Alice,[9]

---

[1] A courtesan mentioned by Juvenal.
[2] Identity uncertain.
[3] A courtesan who followed Alexander the Great.
[4] Nymph of Greek myth, who pined away for unrequited love, leaving only a voice.
[5] Héloise and Abélard: famous twelfth-century lovers.
[6] Servitude and grief.
[7] According to legend, Buridan (a fourteenth-century professor at the University of Paris) paid in this manner for his love of Jeanne de Navarre.
[8] Blanche de Castille.
[9] Three heroines of *Hervi de Metz*, a medieval *chanson de geste*.

And Ermengarde the lady of Maine,[10]—   20
And that good Joan[11] whom Englishmen
At Rouen doomed and burned her there,—
Mother of God, where are they then? . . .
But where are the snows of yester-year?   24

Nay, never ask this week, fair lord,
Where they are gone, nor yet this year,
Except with this for an overword,—
But where are the snows of yester-year?   28

Translated by D. G. Rossetti

[10] Twelfth-century heiress of the French province.
[11] Of Arc.

With Rue My Heart Is Laden
A. E. Housman   (1859–1936)

With rue my heart is laden
For golden friends I had,
For many a rose-lipt maiden
And many a lightfoot lad.   4

By brooks too broad for leaping
The lightfoot boys are laid;
The rose-lipt girls are sleeping
In fields where roses fade.   8

Calmly We Walk Through This April's Day
Delmore Schwartz   (1913–1966)

Calmly we walk through this April's day,
Metropolitan poetry here and there,
In the park sit pauper and *rentier*,[1]
The screaming children, the motor-car
Fugitive about us, running away,   5
Between the worker and the millionaire
Number provides all distances,
It is Nineteen Thirty-Seven now,
Many great dears are taken away,
What will become of you and me   10

[1] A stockholder.

(This is the school in which we learn . . .)
Besides the photo and the memory?
(. . . that time is the fire in which we burn.)

(This is the school in which we learn . . .)
What is the self amid this blaze?   15
What am I now that I was then
Which I shall suffer and act again,
The theodicy[2] I wrote in my high school days
Restored all life from infancy,
The children shouting are bright as they run   20
(This is the school in which they learn . . .)
Ravished entirely in their passing play!
(. . . that time is the fire in which they burn.)

Avid its rush, that reeling blaze!
Where is my father and Eleanor?   25
Not where are they now, dead seven years,
But what they were then?
               No more? No more?
From Nineteen-Fourteen to the present day,
Bert Spira and Rhoda consume, consume
Not where they are now (where are they now?)   30
But what they were then, both beautiful;
Each minute bursts in the burning room,
The great globe reels in the solar fire,
Spinning the trivial and unique away.
(How all things flash! How all things flare!)   35
What am I now that I was then?
May memory restore again and again
The smallest color of the smallest day:
Time is the school in which we learn,
Time is the fire in which we burn.   40

[2] A vindication of God's permitting evil to exist.

The Vanity of Human Wishes

We never cease wishing, though we wish in vain, and what we gain we may lose, or not like after all. We can be certain of nothing except the passing of time and of life. These ideas have been common in poetry from earliest times: "Vanity of vanities, saith the Preacher, vanity of vanities; all is vanity" (Eccles. i.2).

What If a Day, or a Month, or a Year

Thomas Campion   (1567–1620)

What if a day, or a month, or a year
Crown thy delights with a thousand sweet contentings?
Cannot a chance of a night or an hour
Cross thy desires with as many sad tormentings?   4
  Fortune, honor, beauty, youth
  Are but blossoms dying;
  Wanton pleasure, doting love,
  Are but shadows flying.   8
  All our joys are but toys,
  Idle thoughts deceiving;
  None have power of an hour
  In their lives' bereaving.   12

Earth's but a point to the world, and a man
Is but a point to the world's compared ceinture:[1]
Shall then a point of a point be so vain
As to triumph in a seely[2] points adventure?   16
  All is hazard that we have,
  There is nothing biding;
  Days of pleasure are like streams
  Through fair meadows gliding.   20
  Weal and woe, time doth go,
  Time is never turning:
  Secret fates guide our states,
  Both in mirth and mourning.   24

[1] Belt, girdle.
[2] Wretched.

A Litany in Time of Plague

Thomas Nashe   (1567–1601)

Adieu, farewell, earth's bliss;
This world uncertain is;
Fond[1] are life's lustful joys;
Death proves them all but toys;
None from his darts can fly;   5
I am sick, I must die.
    Lord, have mercy on us!

[1] Foolish.

Rich men, trust not in wealth,
Gold cannot buy you health;
Physic himself must fade. 10
All things to end are made,
The plague full swift goes by;
I am sick, I must die
   Lord, have mercy on us!

Beauty is but a flower 15
Which wrinkles will devour;
Brightness falls from the air;
Queens have died young and fair;
Dust hath closed Helen's[2] eye.
I am sick, I must die. 20
   Lord, have mercy on us!

Strength stoops unto the grave,
Worms feed on Hector[3] brave;
Swords may not fight with fate,
Earth still holds ope her gate. 25
"Come, come!" the bells do cry.
I am sick, I must die.
   Lord, have mercy on us.

Wit with his wantonness
Tasteth death's bitterness; 30
Hell's executioner
Hath no ears for to hear
What vain art can reply.
I am sick, I must die.
   Lord, have mercy on us. 35

Haste, therefore, each degree,
To welcome destiny;
Heaven is our heritage,
Earth but a player's stage;
Mount we unto the sky. 40
I am sick, I must die.
   Lord, have mercy on us.

[2] Helen of Troy.
[3] A Trojan hero.

A Palinode[1]

Edmund Bolton   (c. 1575–c. 1633)

As withereth the primrose by the river,
As fadeth summer's sun from gliding fountains,
As vanisheth the light-blown bubble ever,
As melteth snow upon the mossy mountains: 4
So melts, so vanisheth, so fades, so withers
The rose, the shine, the bubble, and the snow,
Of praise, pomp, glory, joy, which short life gathers,
Fair praise, vain pomp, sweet glory, brittle joy.   8
The withered primrose by the mourning river,
The faded summer's sun from weeping fountains,
The light-blown bubble, vanishéd for ever,
The molten snow upon the naked mountains,   12
   Are emblems that the treasures we uplay
   Soon wither, vanish, fade, and melt away.

For as the snow, whose lawn did overspread
Th' ambitious hills which giant-like did threat   16
To pierce the heaven with their aspiring head,
Naked and bare doth leave their craggy seat;
Whenas the bubble, which did empty fly
The dalliance of the undiscernéd wind   20
On whose calm rolling waves it did rely,
Hath shipwreck made where it did dalliance find;
And when the sunshine which dissolved the snow,
Colored the bubble with a pleasant vary,[2]   24
And made the rathe[3] and timely primrose grow,
Swarth[4] clouds withdrawn, which longer time do tarry:
   Oh, what is praise, pomp, glory, joy, but so
   As shine by fountains, bubbles, flowers, or snow?   28

[1] A song of retraction or recantation.
[2] Variation.
[3] Eager.
[4] Dark, swarthy.

The Vanity of Human Wishes
THE TENTH SATIRE OF JUVENAL IMITATED
Samuel Johnson   (1709–1784)

Let Observation[1] with extensive view,
Survey mankind, from China to Peru;

[1] Johnson personifies his general terms in accordance with the visually figurative mode current in his time.

Remark each anxious toil, each eager strife,
And watch the busy scenes of crowded life;
Then say how Hope and Fear, Desire and Hate,   5
O'erspread with snares the clouded maze of Fate,
Where wavering man, betrayed by venturous Pride,
To tread the dreary paths without a guide,
As treacherous phantoms in the mist delude,
Shuns fancied ills, or chases airy good;   10
How rarely Reason guides the stubborn choice,
Rules the bold hand, or prompts the suppliant voice;
How nations sink, by darling schemes oppressed,
When Vengeance listens to the fool's request.
Fate wings with every wish th' afflictive dart,   15
Each gift of nature, and each grace of art,
With fatal heat impetuous courage glows,
With fatal sweetness elocution flows.
Impeachment stops the speaker's powerful breath,
And restless fire precipitates on death.[2]   20
   But scarce observed, the knowing and the bold
Fall in the general massacre of gold;[3]
Wide-wasting pest! that rages unconfined,
And crowds with crimes the records of mankind;
For gold his sword the hireling ruffian draws,   25
For gold the hireling judge distorts the laws;
Wealth heaped on wealth, nor truth nor safety buys,
The dangers gather as the treasures rise.
   Let History tell where rival kings command,
And dubious title shakes the madded land,   30
When statues glean the refuse of the sword.[4]
How much more safe the vassal than the lord;
Low skulks the hind beneath the rage of power,
And leaves the wealthy traitor in the Tower.[5]
Untouched his cottage, and his slumbers sound,   35
Though Confiscation's vultures hover round.
   The needy traveler, serene and gay,
Walks the wild heath, and sings his toil away.
Does envy seize thee? crush th' upbraiding joy,
Increase his riches and his peace destroy;   40
Now fears in dire vicissitude invade.[6]

---

[2] "And the speaker's restless fire precipitates him onto (on toward) death," because he can no longer express his fiery elocution (?).
[3] Here Johnson begins to organize humanity's vain goals into sections, beginning with "Gold."
[4] When the king's edicts expropriate whatever is left from the sword's reaping.
[5] The peasant, by sulking low, is unnoticed, but the wealthy lord is accused of treason and imprisoned in the Tower of London, while all he owns is confiscated by the king.
[6] "Now fears invade every change in the landscape, and every change is dire."

The rustling brake[7] alarms, and quivering shade,
Nor light nor darkness bring his pain relief,
One shows the plunder, and one hides the thief.
    Yet still one general cry the skies assails,   45
And gain and grandeur load the tainted gales;[8]
Few know the toiling statesman's fear or care,
Th' insidious rival and the gaping heir.
    Once more, Democritus,[9] arise on earth,
With cheerful wisdom and instructive mirth,   50
See motley[10] life in modern trappings dressed,
And feed with varied fools th' eternal jest:
Thou who couldst laugh where want enchained caprice.
Toil crushed conceit, and man was of a piece;
Where wealth unloved without a mourner died,   55
And scarce a sycophant was fed by pride,
Where ne'er was known the form of mock debate,
Or seen a new-made mayor's unwieldy state;[11]
Where change of favorites made no change of laws,
And senates heard before they judged a cause;   60
How wouldst thou shake at Britain's modish tribe,
Dart the quick taunt, and edge the piercing gibe!
Attentive truth and nature to descry,
And pierce each scene with philosophic eye.
    To thee were solemn toys or empty show,   65
The robes of pleasure and the veils of woe:
All aid the farce, and all thy mirth maintain,
Whose joys are causeless, or whose griefs are vain.
    Such was the scorn that filled the sage's mind,
Renewed at every glance on humankind: 70
How just that scorn ere yet thy voice declare,[12]
Search every state, and canvass every prayer.
    Unnumbered suppliants crowd Preferment's gate,[13]
Athirst for wealth, and burning to be great;
Delusive Fortune hears th' incessant call,   75

[7] Thicket.
[8] Now Johnson's topic shifts to "Gain and Grandeur."
[9] Democritus (c. 460–350) founded atomic theory and the first system of ethics, which proposed a moderate "cheerfulness" as the highest good, whence the erroneous label "the laughing philosopher" arose. Robert Burton introduces his *Anatomy of Melancholy* (1628) with Democritus, "a little wearish old man, very melancholy by nature," who would sometimes walk down to the harbor from his study in the suburbs "and laugh heartily at such variety of ridiculous objects, which there he saw."
[10] The patchwork suit of a king's fool.
[11] The ornate golden coach in which each new Lord Mayor of London rides in the annual ceremony of installation, as well as his garments, is unwieldy. The coach still in use, a four-tonner, was built in 1757, eight years after Johnson's poem.
[12] "Before you declare how just that scorn is."
[13] Preferment: a generalized personification for any nobleman able to bestow "preferment"—positions in church, government, or the military—among the suppliants who crowd his gate.

They mount, they shine, evaporate, and fall.
On every stage the foes of peace attend,
Hate dogs their flight, and insult mocks their end.
Love ends with hope, the sinking statesman's door
Pours in the morning worshipper no more: 80
For growing names the weekly scribbler lies,
To growing wealth the dedicator flies,
From every room descends the painted face,
That hung the bright palladium of the place,[14]
And smoked in kitchens, or in auctions sold,   85
To better features yields the frame of gold;
For now no more we trace in every line
Heroic worth, benevolence divine:
The form distorted justifies the fall,
And detestation rids th' indignant wall.   90
    But will not Britain hear the last appeal,
Sign her foes' doom, or guard her favorites' zeal?
Through Freedom's sons no more remonstrance rings,
Degrading nobles and controlling kings;
Our supple tribes[15] repress their patriot throats,   95
And ask no questions but the price of votes;
With weekly libels and septennial ale.[16]
Their wish is full to riot and to rail.
    In full-blown dignity, see Wolsey[17] stand,
Law in his voice, and fortune in his hand: 100
To him the church, the realm, their powers consign,
Through him the rays of regal bounty shine,
Turned by his nod the stream of honor flows,[18]
His smile alone security bestows:
Still to new heights his restless wishes tower,   105
Claim leads to claim, and power advances power;
Till conquest unresisted ceased to please,

[14] The Palladium, an archaic wooden image of Pallas Athena about three feet high, which safeguarded Troy while it was within the city. Odysseus and Diomedes stole it from the temple to prepare for Troy's fall. Here the statesman's portrait is his palladium in every room, relegated to the kitchen or the auction, or cut from the frame, when he falls.

[15] Voters: each tribe in Rome had one vote.

[16] Parliament was bound to an election at least septennially: every seventh year. Candidates bribed with ale as well as money.

[17] Now Johnson's topic is "Power," with Cardinal John Wolsey (c. 1475–1530), Henry VIII's first adviser, heading the list. He promoted secret trials by the Star Chamber and plundered the monasteries on Henry's behalf. When he fell from power he retired to his nominal archbishopric of York, where he had never been, with a huge annual pension of £1000. But he was soon summoned to London for treason, and died on the way. In Shakespeare's *Henry VIII*, Wolsey turns his possessions over to the king "To the last penny"—hence, probably, Johnson's erroneous "monastic rest"—and says that if he had served God half as well as the king, the king would not now "Have left me naked to mine enemies" (III.ii.452–57).

[18] England's ruler is still called "the fount of honour" in the dispensing of titles.

And rights submitted, left him none to seize.
At length his sovereign frowns—the train of state
Mark the keen glance, and watch the sign to hate.   110
Where'er he turns he meets a stranger's eye,
His suppliants scorn him, and his followers fly;
At once is lost the pride of aweful state,
The golden canopy, the glittering plate,
The regal palace, the luxurious board,   115
The liveried army, and the menial lord.
With age, with cares, with maladies oppressed,
He seeks the refuge of monastic rest.
Grief aids disease, remembered folly stings,
And his last sighs reproach the faith of kings.   120
    Speak thou, whose thoughts at humble peace repine,
Shall Wolsey's wealth, with Wolsey's end, be thine?
Or liv'st thou now, with safer pride content,
The wisest justice on the banks of Trent?[19]
For why did Wolsey near the steeps of fate,   125
On weak foundations raise th' enormous weight?
Why but to sink beneath misfortune's blow,
With louder ruin[20] to the gulfs below?
    What gave great Villiers to th' assassin's knife,
And fixed disease on Harley's closing life?   130
What murdered Wentworth, and what exiled Hyde,[21]
By kings protected, and to kings allied?
What but their wish indulged in courts to shine,
And power too great to keep, or to resign?
    When first the college rolls receive his name,   135
The young enthusiast quits his ease for fame;[22]
Through all his veins the fever of renown
Burns from the strong contagion of the gown:[23]

---

[19] A Justice of the Peace by the Trent river, which empties into the Humber in Wolsey's Yorkshire, would hold a very small and rural post: the part-time job of a country squire.

[20] A pun on Latin *ruina*, a falling down (Wimsatt, p. 60).

[21] George Villiers, first Duke of Buckingham (1592–1628), close friend and leading minister to both James I and his son, Charles I, was stabbed to death by an officer who was disgruntled about pay and promotion when Parliament declared him a public enemy following a long series of military disasters. Robert Harley, first Earl of Oxford (1661–1724), Queen Anne's chief minister, lost favor just before her death, owing to indecision and illness, and was impeached and imprisoned by her successor, George I. Thomas Wentworth, first Earl of Strafford (1523–1641), another friend of Charles I, was accused of treason and executed by Parliament. Edward Hyde, first Earl of Clarendon (1609–1674), Charles II's Lord Chancellor and father-in-law to Charles's brother, the future James II, was impeached in 1667, fled to France, was banished, and died in exile, twice asking fruitlessly to return and die in England. Charles resented his elderly minister, especially because of his failure to procure him Frances Stuart as a mistress.

[22] "Fame" is now the topic.

[23] The Oxford scholar's academic gown, which is like the cloak Hercules's estranged wife, Dejeneira, sent him: loaded with poison that burst into flames and killed him. Nessus, the centaur, had carried Dejeneira across a river for Hercules, then raped her. Hercules shot him from across the river with a poisoned arrow. The dying Nessus soaked a cloak in his poisoned blood and gave it to Dejeneira as the sure means of regaining an unfaithful husband.

O'er Bodley's dome[24] his future labors spread.
And Bacon's mansion trembles o'er his head.[25]   140
Are these thy views? proceed, illustrious youth,
And Virtue guard thee to the throne of Truth!
Yet should thy soul indulge the generous heat,
Till captive Science yields her last retreat;
Should Reason guide thee with her brightest ray,   145
And pour on misty Doubt resistless day;
Should no false Kindness lure to loose delight,
Nor Praise relax, nor Difficulty fright;
Should tempting Novelty thy cell refrain,
And Sloth effuse her opiate fumes in vain;   150
Should Beauty blunt on fops her fatal dart,
Nor claim the triumph of a lettered heart;
Should no disease they torpid veins invade,
Nor Melancholy's phantoms haunt thy shade;
Yet hope not life from grief or danger free,   155
Nor think the doom of man reversed for thee:
Deign on the passing world to turn thine eyes,
And pause awhile from letters, to be wise:
There mark what ills the scholar's life assail,
Toil, envy, want, the patron, and the jail.   160
See nations slowly wise, and meanly just,
To buried merit raise the tardy bust.
If dreams yet flatter, once again attend,
Hear Lydiat's life, and Galileo's end.[26]

    Nor deem, when Learning her last prize bestows,   165
The glittering eminence exempt from foes:
See when the vulgar 'scape, despised or awed,
Rebellion's vengeful talons seize on Laud.[27]
From meaner minds, though smaller fines content,
The plundered palace or sequestered rent;   170
Marked out by dangerous parts[28] he meets the shock,
And fatal Learning leads him to the block:
Around his tomb let Art and Genius weep,
But hear his death, ye blockheads, hear and sleep.

[24] The Bodleian Library, Oxford.
[25] Oxford students kept the tradition that the room where Friar Roger Bacon (c. 1214–1294) lived and studied, which was over a passageway, would tremble when a greater scholar walked beneath.
[26] Thomas Lydiat (1572–1646), a mathematician jailed for debt; Galileo Galilei (1564–1642), a physical astronomer confined to house arrest for his belief that the earth orbited the sun.
[27] William Laud (1573–1645), Archbishop of Canterbury (the supreme bishop of England), reformed the educational system at Oxford when Charles I appointed him chancellor in reward for zealous and often cruel political activity. He fell under the executioner's ax by order of the Puritan Parliament that eventually executed Charles as well. His tomb is at his Oxford college, St. John's, which he had refurbished with new buildings.
[28] Abilities.

The festal blazes, the triumphal show,[29]   175
The ravished standard, and the captive foe,
The senate's thanks, the gazette's pompous tale,
With force resistless o'er the brave prevail.
Such bribes the rapid Greek[30] o'er Asia whirled,
For such the steady Romans shook the world;   180
For such in distant lands the Britons shine,
And stain with blood the Danube or the Rhine;
This power has Praise, that Virtue scarce can warm.
Till Fame supplies the universal charm.
Yet Reason frowns on War's unequal game,   185
Where wasted nations raise a single name.
And mortgaged states their grandsires wreaths regret,
From age to age in everlasting debt;
Wreaths which at last the dear-bought right convey
To rust on medals, or on stones decay.   190
      On what foundation stands the warrior's pride,
How just his hopes let Swedish Charles[31] decide;
A frame of adamant, a soul of fire,
No dangers fright him, and no labors tire;
O'er love, o'er fear, extends his wide domain,   195
Unconquered lord of pleasure and of pain;
No joys to him pacific scepters yield,
War sounds the trump, he rushes to the field;
Behold surrounding kings their power combine,
And one capitulate, and one resign;[32]   200
Peace courts his hand, but spreads her charms in vain;
"Think nothing gained," he cries. "till nought remain,
"On Moscow's walls till Gothic standards fly,
"And all be mine beneath the polar sky."
The march begins in military state,   205
And nations on his eye suspended wait;
Stern Famine guards the solitary coast,
And Winter barricades the realms of Frost;
He comes, not want and cold his course delay;—
Hide, blushing Glory, hide Pultowa's day:[33]   210
The vanquished hero leaves his broken bands,
And shows his miseries in distant lands;

[29] Here "Glory" becomes the topic.
[30] Alexander the Great (356–323 B.C.), "rapid" for both speed and rapacity.
[31] Charles XII of Sweden (1682–1718), king at 15, victor against greatly superior numbers of Danes, Russians, Poles, and Saxons at 17.
[32] Frederick IV of Denmark capitulated in 1700 during Charles's first fiery campaign. In 1705, at 21, Charles forced the deposition of Augustus II of Poland.
[33] In his Russian campaign, a disaster like Napoleon's in the next century, Charles met defeat at Poltava on June 26, 1709, after surviving Europe's harshest winter in a century, so cold that wood wouldn't burn in the open and spittle froze in midair.

Condemned a needy supplicant to wait,
While ladies interpose, and slaves debate.[34]
But did not Chance at length her error mend?   215
Did no subverted empire mark his end?
Did rival monarchs give the fatal wound?
Or hostile millions press him to the ground?
His fall was destined to a barren strand,
A petty fortress, and a dubious hand;[35]   220
He left the name, at which the world grew pale,
To point a moral, or adorn a tale.

    All times their scenes of pompous woes afford,
From Persia's tyrant to Bavaria's lord."[36]
In gay hostility, and barbarous pride,   225
With half mankind embattled at his side,
Great Xerxes comes to seize the certain prey,
And starves exhausted regions in his way;[37]
Attendant Flattery counts his myriads o'er,
Till counted myriads soothe his pride no more;   230
Fresh praise is tried till madness fires his mind,
The waves he lashes, and enchains the wind;
New powers are claimed, new powers are still bestowed,
Till rude Resistance lops the spreading god;
The daring Greeks deride the martial show,   235
And heap their valleys with the gaudy foe;
Th' insulted sea with humbler thoughts he gains,
A single skiff to speed his flight remains;
Th' incumbered oar scarce leaves the dreaded coast
Through purple billows and a floating host.   240

    The bold Bavarian in a luckless hour,
Tries the dread summits of Caesarean power,[38]

---

[34] Charles, with only 1500 cavalry left from 24,000, and 20,000 infantry, took refuge in Turkey, where for more than four years he tried to stir up support against Russia.

[35] Besieging Fredricksten, Norway, hoping to gain territory amd renewed leverage, Charles was killed by a bullet in the head while observing the fortress from his front trench. Later, some believed his own troops had shot him.

[36] Xerxes (c. 519–465 B.C.); Charles Albert, Elector of Bavaria (1697–1745).

[37] Xerxes invaded Greece in 480 B.C. to avenge the defeat of his father, Darius I, at Marathon (490 B.C.). He hoped to make certain of victory by building a double bridge of boats across the Hellespont, cutting a canal across the isthmus behind Mt. Athos and caching supplies along his intended route, and then invading with a huge army and navy of Persians and allies. But the battered Greeks finally defeated his fleet at Salamis (September 28, 480), and weather smashed his bridge of boats—at which he is said to have ordered the waves chained and whipped.

[38] Charles Albert was elected Emperor of the Holy Roman Empire, becoming Charles VII (1740–1745) in opposition to Francis I, husband of Maria Theresa of Austria, eldest daughter and Hapsburg heiress of Emperor Charles VI (and future mother of Marie Antoinette). Young, beautiful, and dramatic, she had earlier gotten Austria's share in partitioning Poland with Frederick the Great, who said *Elle pleurait et prenait toujours* ("She's always weeping and taking"). She and her allies fought Charles and his allies in the War of the Austrian Succession (1740-1748), in which he was frequently beaten, ill, and neglected among the war's wider territorial issues. Charles died, only to be succeeded by Maria Theresa's husband, Francis I.

With unexpected legions bursts away,
And sees defenseless realms receive his sway;
Short sway! fair Austria spreads her mournful charms,   245
The queen, the beauty, sets the world in arms;
From hill to hill the beacon's rousing blaze
Spreads wide the hope of plunder and of praise;
The fierce Croatian, and the wild Hussar,
And all the sons of ravage crowd the war;   250
The baffled prince in honor's flattering bloom
Of hasty greatness finds the fatal doom,
His foes' derision, and his subjects' blame,
And steals to death from anguish and from shame.
　　Enlarge my life with multitude of days,[39]   255
In health, in sickness, this the suppliant prays;
Hides from himself his state, and shuns to know,
That life protracted is protracted woe.
Time hovers o'er, impatient to destroy,
And shuts up all the passages of joy: 260
In vain their gifts the bounteous seasons pour,
The fruit autumnal, and the vernal flower,
With listless eyes the dotard views the store,
He views, and wonders that they please no more;
Now pall the tasteless meats and joyless wines,   265
And Luxury with sighs her slave resigns.
Approach, ye minstrels, try the soothing strain,
Diffuse the tuneful lenitives of pain:
No sounds, alas, would touch th' impervious ear,
Though dancing mountains witnessed Orpheus near;[40]   270
Nor lute nor lyre his feeble powers attend,
Nor sweeter music of a virtuous friend,
But everlasting dictates crowd his tongue,
Perversely grave, or positively wrong.
The still returning tale, and lingering jest,   275
Perplex the fawning niece and pampered guest,
While growing hopes scarce awe the gathering sneer,
And scarce a legacy can bribe to hear;
The watchful guests still hint the last offense,
The daughter's petulance, the son's expense,   280
Improve his heady rage with treacherous skill,
And mold his passions till they make his will.
　　Unnumbered maladies his joints invade,

[39] "Longevity" becomes the topic.
[40] Orpheus, the mythical singer and lyrist, traditionally could move beasts, trees, and rocks, and halt streams, to listen. Johnson's dancing mountains are his own.

Lay siege to life and press the dire blockade;
But unextinguished Avarice still remains,   285
And dreaded losses aggravate his pains;
He turns, with anxious heart and crippled hands,
His bonds of debt, and mortgages of lands;
Or views his coffers with suspicious eyes,
Unlocks his gold, and counts it till he dies.   290
    But grant the virtues of a temperate prime,
Bless with an age exempt from scorn or crime;
An age that melts with unperceived decay,
And glides in modest innocence away;
Whose peaceful day Benevolence endears,   295
Whose night congratulating Conscience cheers;
The general favorite as the general friend:
Such age there is, and who shall wish its end?
    Yet even on this her load Misfortune flings,
To press the weary minutes' flagging wings: 300
New sorrow rises as the day returns,
A sister sickens, or a daughter mourns.
Now kindred Merit fills the sable bier,
Now lacerated Friendship claims a tear.
Year chases year, decay pursues decay,   305
Still drops some joy from withering life away;
New forms arise, and different views engage,
Superfluous lags the veteran on the stage,
Till pitying Nature signs the last release,
And bids afflicted worth retire to peace.   310
    But few there are whom hours like these await,
Who set unclouded in the gulfs of Fate.
From Lydia's monarch should the search descend,
By Solon cautioned to regard his end,[41]
In life's last scene what prodigies surprise,   315
Fears of the brave, and follies of the wise?
From Marlborough's eyes the streams of dotage flow,
And Swift expires a driveler and a show.[42]
    The teeming mother, anxious for her race,
Begs for each birth the fortune of a face:[43]   320

[41] Croesus, the fabulously wealthy King of Lydia (560–546), was allegedly warned by Solon, the Greek, that Nemesis would bring the usual gods' punishment for excessive wealth and power. Cyrus the Great of Persia conquered him and, by some probably fanciful accounts, burned him alive on a pyre of his riches. (It is more likely that he became a governor under Cyrus.)

[42] John Churchill, Duke of Marlborough (1650–1722), supreme allied commander against the French died at 72, an invalid for five years after two strokes in 1716. Jonathan Swift (1667–1745) was insane and senile, with some lucid moments, for his last three years, dying at 78; but he was hardly "a show," as he would have been if confined to a public institution.

[43] "Beauty" becomes the topic.

Yet Vane could tell what ills from beauty spring;
And Sedley cursed the form that pleased a king.[44]
Ye nymphs of rosy lips and radiant eyes,
Whom Pleasure keeps too busy to be wise,
Whom joys with soft varieties invite,   325
By day the frolic, and the dance by night,
Who frown with Vanity, who smile with Art,
And ask the latest fashion of the heart,
What care, what rules your heedless charms shall save,
Each nymph your rival, and each youth your slave?   330
Against your fame with fondness hate combines,
The rival batters, and the lover mines,
With distant voice neglected Virtue calls,
Less heard and less, the faint remonstrance falls;
Tired with contempt, she quits the slippery reign,   335
And Pride and Prudence take her seat in vain.
In crowd at once, where none the pass defend,
The harmless Freedom, and the private Friend.
The guardians yield, by force superior plied;
By Interest, Prudence,[45] and by Flattery, Pride.   340
Now Beauty falls betrayed, despised, distressed,
And hissing Infamy proclaims the rest.
        Where then shall Hope and Fear their objects find?
Must dull suspense corrupt the stagnant mind?
Must helpless man, in ignorance sedate,   345
Roll darkling down the torrent of his fate?
Must no dislike alarm, no wishes rise,
No cries attempt the mercies of the skies?
Inquirer, cease, petitions yet remain,
Which heaven may hear, nor deem religion vain.   350
Still raise for good the supplicating voice,
But leave to heaven the measure and the choice,
Safe in His power, whose eyes discern afar
The secret ambush of a specious prayer.
Implore His aid, in His decisions rest,   355
Secure whate'er He gives, He gives the best.
Yet when the sense of sacred presence fires,
And strong devotion to the skies aspires,
Pour forth thy fervors for a healthful mind,
Obedient passions, and a will resigned;   360

---

[44] Anne Vane (1705–1736) was the mistress of the unpleasant and unpopular Frederick, Prince of Wales, George II's eldest son. She died at 31, unrewarded. James II made his mistress Catharine Sedley (1657–1717) Countess of Dorchester after he became king, but he soon dropped her.
[45] Self-interest unseats Prudence.

For love, which scarce collective man can fill:[46]
For patience sovereign o'er transmuted ill;
For faith, that panting for a happier seat,
Counts death kind Nature's signal of retreat:
These goods for man the laws of heaven ordain,   365
These goods He grants, who grants the power to gain;
With these celestial Wisdom calms the mind,
And makes the happiness she does not find.

[46] "Pray for God's love, which is so vast that the whole of mankind together can hardly fill it."

Elegy Written in a Country Churchyard
Thomas Gray   (1716–1771)

The curfew tolls the knell of parting day,
  The lowing herd wind slowly o'er the lea,[1]
The plowman homeward plods his weary way,
  And leaves the world to darkness and to me.   4

Now fades the glimmering landscape on the sight,
  And all the air a solemn stillness holds,
Save where the beetle wheels his droning flight,
  And drowsy tinklings lull the distant folds;   8

Save that from yonder ivy-mantled tower
  The moping owl does to the moon complain
Of such, as wandering near her secret bower,
  Molest her ancient solitary reign.   12

Beneath those rugged elms, that yew tree's shade,
  Where heaves the turf in many a moldering heap,
Each in his narrow cell forever laid,
  The rude forefathers of the hamlet sleep.   16

The breezy call of incense-breathing Morn,
  The swallow twittering from the straw-built shed,
The cock's shrill clarion, or the echoing horn,[2]
  No more shall rouse them from their lowly bed.   20

For them no more the blazing hearth shall burn,
  Or busy housewife ply her evening care;
No children run to lisp their sire's return,
  Or climb his knees the envied kiss to share.   24

[1] Pasture.
[2] Hunter's horn.

Oft did the harvest to their sickle yield,
    Their furrow oft the stubborn glebe[3] has broke;
How jocund did they drive their team afield!
    How bowed the woods beneath their sturdy stroke!   28

Let not Ambition mock their useful toil,
    Their homely joys, and destiny obscure;
Nor Grandeur hear with a disdainful smile
    The short and simple annals of the poor.   32

The boast of heraldry, the pomp of power,
    And all that beauty, all that wealth e'er gave,
Awaits alike the inevitable hour.
    The paths of glory lead but to the grave.   36

Nor you, ye proud, impute to these the fault,
    If Memory o'er their tomb no trophies[4] raise,
Where through the long-drawn aisle and fretted[5] vault
    The pealing anthem swells the note of praise.   40

Can storied urn or animated bust[6]
    Back to its mansion call the fleeting breath?
Can Honor's voice provoke[7] the silent dust,
    Or Flattery soothe the dull cold ear of Death?   44

Perhaps in this neglected spot is laid
    Some heart once pregnant with celestial fire;
Hands that the rod of empire might have swayed,
    Or waked to ecstasy the living lyre.   48

But Knowledge to their eyes her ample page
    Rich with the spoils of time did ne'er unroll;
Chill Penury repressed their noble rage,
    And froze the genial current of the soul.   52

Full many a gem of purest ray serene,
    The dark unfathomed caves of ocean bear:
Full many a flower is born to blush unseen,
    And waste its sweetness on the desert air.   56

Some village Hampden,[8] that with dauntless breast
    The little tyrant of his fields withstood;

---

[3] Soil.
[4] For example, memorials celebrating the triumphs of military heroes.
[5] Ornamented with intersecting bars.
[6] An urn with a narrative epitaph or a lifelike bust.
[7] Call forth.
[8] John Hampden (1597–1643), a hero of the English Civil War.

Some mute inglorious Milton[9] here may rest,
    Some Cromwell[10] guiltless of his country's blood.   60

The applause of listening senates to command,
    The threats of pain and ruin to despise,
To scatter plenty o'er a smiling land,
    And read their history in a nation's eyes,   64

Their lot forbade: nor circumscribed alone
    Their growing virtues, but their crimes confined;
Forbade to wade through slaughter to a throne,
    And shut the gates of mercy on mankind,   68

The struggling pangs of conscious truth to hide,
    To quench the blushes of ingenuous shame,
Or heap the shrine of Luxury and Pride
    With incense kindled at the Muse's flame.   72

Far from the madding crowd's ignoble strife,
    Their sober wishes never learned to stray;
Along the cool sequestered vale of life
    They kept the noiseless tenor of their way.   76

Yet even these bones from insult to protect
    Some frail memorial still erected nigh,
With uncouth rhymes and shapeless sculpture decked,
    Implores the passing tribute of a sigh.   80

Their name, their years, spelt by the unlettered Muse,
    The place of fame and elegy supply:
And many a holy text around she strews,
    That teach the rustic moralist to die.   84

For who to dumb Forgetfulness a prey,
    This pleasing anxious being e'er resigned,
Left the warm precincts of the cheerful day,
    Nor cast one longing lingering look behind?   88

On some fond breast the parting soul relies,
    Some pious drops the closing eye requires;
Even from the tomb the voice of Nature cries,
    Even in our ashes live their wonted fires.   92

For thee, who mindful of the unhonored dead
    Dost in these lines their artless tale relate;

[9] John Milton (1608–1674), an English poet.
[10] Oliver Cromwell (1599–1658), a soldier and statesman.

If chance, by lonely contemplation led,
 Some kindred spirit shall inquire thy fate,   96

Haply some hoary-headed swain may say,
 "Oft have we seen him at the peep of dawn
Brushing with hasty steps the dews away
 To meet the sun upon the upland lawn.   100

"There at the foot of yonder nodding beech
 That wreathes its old fantastic roots so high,
His listless length at noontide would he stretch,
 And pore upon the brook that babbles by.   104

"Hard by yon wood, now smiling as in scorn,
 Muttering his wayward fancies he would rove,
Now drooping, woeful wan, like one forlorn,
 Or crazed with care, or crossed in hopeless love. 108

"One morn I missed him on the customed hill,
 Along the heath and near his favorite tree;
Another came; nor yet beside the rill,
 Nor up the lawn, nor at the wood was he;   112

"The next with dirges due in sad array
 Slow through the churchway path we saw him borne.
Approach and read (for thou canst read) the lay,
 Graved on the stone beneath yon aged thorn."   116

The Epitaph

Here rests his head upon the lap of Earth
 A youth to Fortune and to Fame unknown.
Fair Science[11] *frowned not on his humble birth,*
 And Melancholy marked him for her own.   120

Large was his bounty, and his soul sincere,
 Heaven did a recompense as largely send:
He gave to Misery all he had, a tear,
 He gained from Heaven ('twas all he wished) a friend. 124

No farther seek his merits to disclose,
 Or draw his frailties from their dread abode
(There they alike in trembling hope repose),
 The bosom of his Father and his God.   128

[11] Learning.

Hamatreya[1]

Ralph Waldo Emerson   (1803–1882)

Bulkeley, Hunt, Willard, Hosmer, Meriam, Flint,[2]
Possessed the land which rendered to their toil
Hay, corn, roots, hemp, flax, apples, wool and wood.
Each of these landlords walked amidst his farm,
Saying, ' 'Tis mine, my children's and my name's.   5
How sweet the west wind sounds in my own trees!
How graceful climb those shadows on my hill!
I fancy these pure waters and the flags
Know me, as does my dog: we sympathize;
And, I affirm, my actions smack of the soil.'   10
Where are these men? Asleep beneath their grounds:
And strangers, fond as they, their furrows plough.
Earth laughs in flowers, to see her boastful boys
Earth-proud, proud of the earth which is not theirs;
Who steer the plough, but cannot steer their feet   15
Clear of the grave.
They added ridge to valley, brook to pond,
And sighed for all that bounded their domain;
'This suits me for a pasture; that's my park;
We must have clay, lime, gravel, granite-ledge,   20
And misty lowland, where to go for peat.
The land is well,—lies fairly to the south.
'T is good, when you have crossed the sea and back,
To find the sitfast acres where you left them.'
Ah! the hot owner sees not Death, who adds   25
Him to his land, a lump of mould the more.
Hear what the Earth says:—

Earth-Song

'Mine and yours;
Mine, not yours.
Earth endures;   30
Stars abide—
Shine down in the old sea;
Old are the shores;

---

[1] The poem is based on a passage in the *Vishnu Purana*, a Hindu religious work, in which Maitreya (Hamatreya) is taught an "Earth Song" similar to Emerson's.
[2] Early settlers of Concord, Mass.

But where are old men?
I who have seen much,   35
Such have I never seen.

'The lawyer's deed
Ran sure,
In tail,
To them, and to their heirs   40
Who shall succeed,
Without fail,
Forevermore.

'Here is the land,
Shaggy with wood,   45
With its old valley,
Mound and flood.
But the heritors?—

Fled like the flood's foam.
The lawyer, and the laws,   50
And the kingdom,
Clean swept herefrom.

'They called me theirs,
Who so controlled me;
Yet every one   55
Wished to stay, and is gone,
How am I theirs,
If they cannot hold me,
But I hold them?'

When I heard the Earth-song   60
I was no longer brave;
My avarice cooled
Like lust in the chill of the grave.

Back

Weldon Kees (1914–1955)

Much cry and little wool:
I have come back
As empty-handed as I went.   3

Although the woods were full,
And past the track
The heavy boughs were bent   6

Down to my knees with fruit
Ripe for a still life, I had meant
My trip as a search for stones.   9

But the beach was bare
Except for the drying bones
Of a fish, shells, an old wool   12

Shirt, a rubber boot,
A strip of lemon rind.
They were not what I had in mind: 15

It was merely stones.
Well, the days are full.
This day at least is spent.   18

Much cry and little wool:
I have come back
As empty-handed as I went.   21

Seize the Day

Carpe diem, quam minimum credula postero—"seize today, and trust tomorrow little"—wrote Horace (*Odes* I, xi, 8), giving a name and an attitude to a whole class of poems: *carpe diem*. Since life is short, we must grasp what pleasures we have. This is the poetry of youth, especially of the youth persuading his girl to join him.

Lesbia
(CATULLUS NO. 5)
Catullus (84?–54? B.C.)

Let's live, my Lesbia, and love.
For sour old murmurs we won't give
One cent. Suns set and still can rise,
But once our little daylight dies   4
We sleep one never-ending night.
Give me a thousand kisses straight,
Then a hundred, then another
Thousand with a hundred smother.   8
Thousands, a hundred—thousands more
We'll make, mix, and forget before

Some evil eye gets envious,
Knowing how many times we kiss.[1]   12

Translated by Sheridan Baker

[1] Knowing the exact number of anything enabled a person to *invidere*: to envy and to cast an evil eye, bringing bad luck. So Catullus not only rushes his thousands and hundreds, but also wants the lovers themselves to lose count, to be doubly safe (and doubly happy). In prose, line for line, this famous poem translates: "Let us live, my Lesbia, and let us love./ And let us estimate the murmurs of the severe old people at one [very small coin]./ Suns can set (die) and come back:/ For us, when once the brief light sets (dies),/ One perpetual night must be slept./ Gimme a thousand kisses,* then a hundred,/ Then another thousand, then a second hundred,/ Then all the way to another thousand, then a hundred,/ Then, when we will have made many thousands,/ We will stir them all to confusion, so we will not know,/ Or so someone bad cannot look with the evil eye,/ When he will know how many there are of kisses."

---

*Catullus's *Da mi basia mille* is apparently intimate slang, with *basia*, for *kisses*, appearing for the first time in recorded Latin.

My Sweetest Lesbia*

Thomas Campion   (1567–1620)

My sweetest Lesbia, let us live and love,
And, though the sager sort our deeds reprove,
Let us not weigh them: heaven's great lamps do dive
Into their west, and straight again revive,
But, soon as once set is our little light,
Then must we sleep one ever-during night.   6

If all would lead their lives in love like me,
Then bloody swords and armor should not be;
No drum nor trumpet peaceful sleeps should move,
Unless alarm came from the camp of love:
But fools do live, and waste their little light,
And seek with pain their ever-during night.   12

When timely death my life and fortune ends,
Let not my hearse be vexed with mourning friends,
But let all lovers, rich in triumph, come,
And with sweet pastimes grace my happy tomb;
And, Lesbia, close up thou my little light,
And crown with love my ever-during night.   18

*Based upon and partly translated from Catullus No. 5, with some influence from Propertius.

Fragment

ON THE BACK OF THE MS. OF CANTO I.

George Gordon, Lord Byron (1788–1824)

I would to Heaven that I were so much clay,
    As I am blood, bone, marrow, passion, feeling—
Because at least the past were passed away,
    And for the future—(but I write this reeling,
Having got drunk exceedingly to-day,
    So that I seem to stand upon the ceiling)
I say—the future is a serious matter—
And so—for God's sake—hock[1] and soda-water!   8

[1] White Rhine wine.

To the Virgins, to Make Much of Time

Robert Herrick (1591–1624)

Gather ye rosebuds while ye may,
    Old time is still a-flying:
And this same flower that smiles today,
    Tomorrow will be dying.   4

The glorious lamp of heaven, the sun,
    The higher he's a-getting;
The sooner will his race be run,
    And nearer he's to setting.   8

That age is best which is the first,
    When youth and blood are warmer;
But being spent, the worse, and worst
    Times, still succeed the former.   12

Then be not coy, but use your time;
    And while ye may, go marry:
For having lost but once your prime,
    You may forever tarry.   16

Corinna's Going A-Maying

Robert Herrick (1591–1624)

Get up! get up for shame! the blooming morn
Upon her wings presents the god unshorn.[1]

[1] Apollo, god of the sun, with his streaming rays.

See how Aurora[2] throws her fair
Fresh-quilted colors through the air:
Get up, sweet slug-a-bed, and see   5
The dew bespangling herb and tree.
Each flower has wept and bowed toward the east
Above an hour since, yet you not dressed;
    Nay, not so much as out of bed?
    When all the birds have matins[3] said,   10
    And sung their thankful hymns, 'tis sin,
    Nay, profanation to keep in,
Whenas a thousand virgins on this day
Spring, sooner than the lark, to fetch in May.[4]

Rise, and put on your foliage, and be seen   15
To come forth, like the springtime, fresh and green,
    And sweet as Flora.[5] Take no care
    For jewels for your gown or hair;
    Fear not; the leaves will strew
    Gems in abundance upon you;   20
Besides, the childhood of the day has kept,
Against you come, some orient pearls[6] unwept;
    Come and receive them while the light
    Hangs on the dew-locks of the night,
    And Titan[7] on the eastern hill   25
    Retires himself, or else stands still
Till you come forth. Wash, dress, be brief in praying:
Few beads[8] are best when once we go a-Maying.

Come, my Corinna, come; and, coming, mark
How each field turns a street, each street a park   30
    Made green and trimmed with trees; see how
    Devotion gives each house a bough
    Or branch: each porch, each door ere this,
    An ark, a tabernacle is,[9]
Made up of whitethorn neatly interwove,   35
As if here were those cooler shades of love.
    Can such delights be in the street
    And open fields, and we not see 't?

---

[2] Goddess of the dawn.
[3] Morning prayers.
[4] Boughs of hawthorn ("whitethorn," l. 35) were traditionally gathered as May Day decorations for streets and houses.
[5] Goddess of flowers.
[6] Pearls from the East.
[7] The sun.
[8] Prayers.
[9] Each decorated porch or door is like a place of religious shelter or worship.

Come, we'll abroad; and let's obey
The proclamation made for May,   40
And sin no more, as we have done, by staying;
But, my Corinna, come, let's go a-Maying.

There's not a budding boy or girl this day
But is got up and gone to bring in May;
 A deal of youth, ere this, is come   45
 Back, and with whitethorn laden home.
 Some have dispatched their cakes and cream
 Before that we have left to dream;
And some have wept and wooed, and plighted troth,
And chose their priest, ere we can cast off sloth.   50
 Many a green-gown has been given,
 Many a kiss, both odd and even;
 Many a glance, too, has been sent
 From out the eye, love's firmament;
Many a jest told of the keys betraying   55
This night, and locks picked; yet we're not a-Maying.

Come, let us go while we are in our prime,
And take the harmless folly of the time.
 We shall grow old apace, and die
 Before we know our liberty.   60
 Our life is short, and our days run
 As fast away as does the sun;
And, as a vapor or a drop of rain
Once lost, can ne'er be found again;
 So when or you or I are made   65
 A fable, song, or fleeting shade,
 All love, all liking, all delight
 Lies drowned with us in endless night.
Then while time serves, and we are but decaying,
Come, my Corinna, come, let's go a-Maying.   70

To His Coy Mistress
Andrew Marvell (1621–1678)

Had we but world enough, and time,
This coyness, lady, were no crime.
We would sit down, and think which way
To walk, and pass our long love's day.
Thou by the Indian Ganges' side   5
Should'st rubies find: I by the tide
Of Humber would complain. I would

Love you ten years before the flood:
And you should, if you please, refuse
Till the conversion of the Jews.   10
My vegetable love should grow
Vaster then empires, and more slow.
An hundred years should go to praise
Thine eyes, and on thy forehead gaze.
Two hundred to adore each breast: 15
But thirty thousand to the rest.
An age at least to every part,
And the last age should show your heart.
For, lady, you deserve this state;
Nor would I love at lower rate.   20
      But at my back I always hear
Time's winged chariot hurrying near:
And yonder all before us lie
Deserts of vast eternity.
Thy beauty shall no more be found;   25
Nor, in thy marble vault, shall sound
My echoing song: then worms shall try
That long preserved virginity:
And your quaint honor turn to dust;
And into ashes all my lust.   30
The grave's a fine and private place,
But none I think do there embrace.
      Now therefore, while the youthful hue
Sits on thy skin like morning dew,
And while thy willing soul transpires   35
At every pore with instant fires,
Now let us sport us while we may;
And now, like amorous birds of prey,
Rather at once our time devour,
Than languish in his slow-chapped power.   40
Let us roll all our strength, and all
Our sweetness, up into one ball:
And tear our pleasures with rough strife,
Thorough the iron gates of life.
Thus, though we cannot make our sun   45
Stand still, yet we will make him run.

The Ecstasy
John Donne (1572–1631)

Where, like a pillow on a bed,
    A pregnant bank swelled up to rest

The violet's reclining head,
    Sat we two, one another's best.
Our hands were firmly cemented   5
    With a fast balm, which thence did spring.
Our eye-beams twisted, and did thread
    Our eyes upon one double string;
So to intergraft our hands, as yet
    Was all our means to make us one;   10
And pictures in our eyes to get
    Was all our propagation.
As 'twixt two equal armies, Fate
    Suspends uncertain victory,
Our souls (which to advance their state,   15
    Were gone out) hung 'twixt her and me.
And whilst our souls negotiate there,
    We like sepulchral statues lay;
All day the same our postures were,
    And we said nothing all the day.   20
If any, so by love refined
    That he soul's language understood,
And by good love were grown all mind,
    Within convenient distance stood,
He (though he know not which soul spake,   25
    Because both meant, both spake the same)
Might thence a new concoction take,
    And part far purer than he came.
This ecstasy doth unperplex,
    We said, and tell us what we love;   30
We see by this it was not sex;
    We see we saw not what did move;[1]
But as all several[2] souls contain
    Mixture of things, they know not what,
Love these mixed souls doth mix again,   35
    And makes both one, each this and that.
A single violet transplant.
    The strength, the color, and the size
(All which before was poor, and scant)
    Redoubles still, and multiplies.   40
When love, with one another so
    Interinanimates two souls,
That abler soul, which thence doth flow,
    Defects of loneliness controls.

[1] We did not understand what motivated us.
[2] Separate.

We then, who are this new soul, know,   45
    Of what we are composed, and made,
For, th' atomies[3] of which we grow,
    Are souls, whom no change can invade.
But O alas, so long, so far
    Our bodies why do we forbear?   50
They are ours, though they are not we; we are
    The intelligences, they the sphere.[4]
We owe them thanks because they thus,
    Did us to us at first convey,
Yielded their forces, sense, to us,   55
    Nor are dross to us, but allay.[5]
On man heaven's influence works not so
    But that it first imprints the air,
So soul into the soul may flow,
    Though it to body first repair.   60
As our blood labors to beget
    Spirits as like souls as it can,
Because such fingers need to knit
    That subtle knot which makes us man:
So must pure lovers' souls descend   65
    T' affections, and to faculties
Which sense may reach and apprehend;
    Else a great Prince in prison lies.
To our bodies turn we then, that so
    Weak men on love revealed may look;   70
Love's mysteries in souls do grow,
    But yet the body is his book.
And if some lover, such as we,
    Have heard this dialogue of one,
Let him still mark us; he shall see   75
    Small change when we are to bodies gone.

[3] Atoms.
[4] As the spheres of Ptolemaic astronomy were believed to be governed by "intelligences," so we govern our bodies.
[5] A "dross" is an impurity in a mixture; an "allay" (alloy) strengthens it.

Love

"All you need is love," sang the Beatles, giving new impetus to a sentiment ages old. But what is love, and how do we distinguish true from false?

As You Came from the Holy Land*

As you came from the holy land
    Of Walsingham,[1]
Met you not with my true love,
    By the way as you came?   4

"How should I know your true love
    That have met many a one
As I came from the holy land,
    That have come, that have gone?"   8

She is neither white nor brown,
    But as the heavens fair;
There is none hath her form so divine,
    On the earth, in the air.   12

"Such a one did I meet, good sir,
    With angel-like face,
Who like a nymph, like a queen, did appear
    In her gait, in her grace."   16

She hath left me here alone,
    All alone unknown,
Who sometime loved me as her life,
    And called me her own.   20

"What is the cause she hath left thee alone,
    And a new way doth take,
That sometime did thee love as herself,
    And her joy did thee make?"   24

I have loved her all my youth,
    But now am old as you see;
Love liketh not the falling fruit,
    Nor the withered tree.   28

For love is a careless child,
    And forgets promise past;
He is blind, he is deaf, when he list,[2]
    And in faith never fast.   32

His desire is fickle found,
    And a trustless joy;
He is won with a world of despair,
    And is lost with a toy.   36

* Sometimes attributed to Sir Walter Raleigh (c. 1552–1618).
[1] The shrine of Our Lady of Walsingham.
[2] Wants, desires.

"Such is the love of womenkind,
  Or the word 'love' abused,
Under which many childish desires
  And conceits are excused.   40

"But love, it is a durable fire
  In the mind ever burning,
Never sick, never dead, never cold,
  From itself never turning."   44

Over the Hills and Far Away[1]

John Gay (1685–1732)

MACHEATH: Were I laid on Greenland's coast,
            And in my arms embraced my lass,
            Warm amidst eternal frost,
            Too soon the half year's night would pass.   4

POLLY: Were I sold on Indian soil,
            Soon as the burning day was closed,
            I could mock the sultry toil,
            When on my charmer's breast reposed.   8

MACHEATH: And I would love you all the day,
POLLY: Every night would kiss and play,
MACHEATH: If with me you'd fondly stray
POLLY: Over the hills and far away.   12

[1] In this song from *The Beggar's Opera* (1728), Macheath, the outlaw, and Polly, his beloved, sing of the love they might share if things were different.

When Faces Called Flowers

E. E. Cummings (1894–1962)

when faces called flowers float out of the ground
and breathing is wishing and wishing is having—
but keeping is downward and doubting and never
—it's april(yes,april;my darling)it's spring!
yes the pretty birds frolic as spry as can fly   5
yes the little fish gambol as glad as can be
(yes the mountains are dancing together)

when every leaf opens without any sound
and wishing is having and having is giving—
but keeping is doting and nothing and nonsense   10
—alive;we're alive,dear:it's(kiss me now)spring!

now the pretty birds hover so she and so he
now the little fish quiver so you and so i
(now the mountains are dancing,the mountains)

when more than was lost has been found has been found   15
and having is giving and giving is living—
but keeping is darkness and winter and cringing
—it's spring(all our night becomes day)o,it's spring!
all the pretty birds dive to the heart of the sky
all the little fish climb through the mind of the sea   20
(all the mountains are dancing;are dancing)

Song

Sir John Suckling   (1609–1642)

Why so pale and wan fond lover?
        Prithee why so pale?
Will, when looking well can't move her,
        Looking ill prevail?
        Prithee why so pale?   5

Why so dull and mute young sinner?
        Prithee why so mute?
Will, when speaking well can't win her,
        Saying nothing do't?
        Prithee why so mute?   10

Quit, quit, for shame, this will not move,
        This cannot take her;
If of her self she will not love,
        Nothing can make her:
        The Devil take her!   15

Song: To Celia

Ben Jonson   (1573–1637)

Drink to me only with thine eyes,
And I will pledge with mine;
Or leave a kiss but in the cup,
And I'll not look for wine.   4
The thirst that from the soul doth rise,
Doth ask a drink divine:
But might I of Jove's nectar sup,
I would not change for thine.   8

I sent thee late a rosy wreath,
Not so much honoring thee,
As giving it a hope, that there
It could not withered be.   12
But thou thereon did'st only breathe,
And sent'st it back to me;
Since when it grows and smells, I swear,
Not of itself, but thee.   16

To My Dear and Loving Husband

Anne Bradstreet   (c. 1612–1672)

If ever two were one, then surely we.
If ever man were loved by wife, then thee;
If ever wife was happy in a man,
Compare with me, ye women, if you can.   4
I prize thy love more than whole mines of gold
Or all the riches that the East doth hold.
My love is such that rivers cannot quench,
Nor ought but love from thee, give recompense.   8
Thy love is such I can no way repay,
The heavens reward thee manifold, I pray.
Then while we live, in love let's so persevere
That when we live no more, we may live ever.   12

John Anderson My Jo

Robert Burns   (1759–1796)

John Anderson my jo,[1] John,
  When we were first acquent,[2]
Your locks were like the raven,
  Your bonny brow was brent;[3]   4
But now your brow is beld,[4] John,
  Your locks are like the snow,
But blessings on your frosty pow,[5]
  John Anderson, my jo.   8

John Anderson my jo, John,
  We clamb[6] the hill thegither,[7]

[1] Sweetheart.
[2] Acquainted.
[3] Smooth, unwrinkled.
[4] Bald.
[5] Head.
[6] Climbed.
[7] Together.

And mony a canty[8] day, John,
   We've had wi' ane anither;   12
Now we maun[9] totter down, John,
   And hand in hand we'll go,
And sleep thegither at the foot,
   John Anderson, my jo.   16

[8] Jolly.
[9] Must.

They Flee from Me

Thomas Wyatt (1503–1542)

They flee from me, that sometime did me seek,
With naked foot stalking in my chamber.
I have seen them, gentle, tame, and meek,
That now are wild, and do not remember
That sometime they put themselves in danger   5
To take bread at my hand; and now they range,
Busily seeking with a continual change.

Thanked be Fortune it hath been otherwise,
Twenty times better; but once in special,
In thin array, after a pleasant guise,   10
When her loose gown from her shoulders did fall,
And she me caught in her arms long and small,
And therewith all sweetly did me kiss
And softly said, "Dear heart, how like you this?"

It was no dream, I lay broad waking.   15
But all is turned, thorough my gentleness,
Into a strange fashion of forsaking;
And I have leave to go, of her goodness,
And she also to use newfangleness.
But since that I so kindely[1] am served,   20
I fain would know what she hath deserved.

[1] "Naturally," an older meaning, but with an ironic pun on the modern meaning of "kindly."

Love Among the Ruins

Robert Browning (1812–1889)

I

Where the quiet-colored end of evening smiles,
   Miles and miles

On the solitary pastures where our sheep
   Half-asleep   4
Tinkle homeward thro' the twilight, stray or stop
   As they crop—
Was the site once of a city great and gay,
   (So they say)   8
Of our country's very capital, its prince
   Ages since
Held his court in, gathered councils, wielding far
   Peace or war.   12

II

Now,—the country does not even boast a tree,
   As you see,
To distinguish slopes of verdure, certain rills
   From the hills   16
Intersect and give a name to, (else they run
   Into one)
Where the domed and daring palace shot its spires
   Up like fires   20
O'er the hundred-gated circuit of a wall
   Bounding all,
Made of marble, men might march on nor be pressed,
   Twelve abreast.   24

III

And such plenty and perfection, see, of grass
   Never was!
Such a carpet as, this summer time, o'erspreads
   And embeds   28
Every vestige of the city, guessed alone,
   Stock or stone—
Where a multitude of men breathed joy and woe
   Long ago;   32
Lust of glory pricked their hearts up, dread of shame
   Struck them tame;
And that glory and that shame alike, the gold
   Bought and sold.   36

IV

Now,—the single little turret that remains
   On the plains,
By the caper[1] overrooted, by the gourd
   Overscored,   40

[1] A Mediterranean bush. Its green flower buds are pickled for salads and sauces.

While the patching houseleek's[2] head of blossom winks
    Through the chinks—
Marks the basement whence a tower in ancient time
    Sprang sublime,   44
And a burning ring, all round, the chariots traced
    As they raced,
And the monarch and his minions and his dames
    Viewed the games.   48

V

And I know, while thus the quiet-colored eve
    Smiles to leave
To their folding, all our many-tinkling fleece
    In such peace,   52
And the slopes and rills in undistinguished grey
    Melt away—
That a girl with eager eyes and yellow hair
    Waits me there   56
In the turret whence the charioteers caught soul
    For the goal,
When the king looked, where she looks now, breathless, dumb
    Till I come.   60

VI

But he looked upon the city, every side,
    Far and wide,
All the mountains topped with temples, all the glades'
    Colonnades,   64
All the causeys,[3] bridges, aqueducts,—and then,
    All the men!
When I do come, she will speak not, she will stand,
    Either hand   68
On my shoulder, give her eyes the first embrace
    Of my face,
Ere we rush, ere we extinguish sight and speech
    Each on each.   72

VII

In one year they sent a million fighters forth
    South and North,
And they built their gods a brazen pillar high
    As the sky,   76

[2] A plant related to the onion.
[3] Causeways.

Yet reserved a thousand chariots in full force—
    Gold, of course.
Oh heart! oh blood that freezes, blood that burns!
    Earth's returns   80
For whole centuries of folly, noise and sin!
    Shut them in,
With their triumphs and their glories and the rest!
    Love is best!   84

Love Is Not All

Edna St. Vincent Millay (1892–1950)

Love is not all: it is not meat nor drink
Nor slumber nor a roof against the rain;
Nor yet a floating spar to men that sink
And rise and sink and rise and sink again;   4
Love can not fill the thickened lung with breath,
Nor clean the blood, nor set the fractured bone;
Yet many a man is making friends with death
Even as I speak, for lack of love alone.   8
It well may be that in a difficult hour,
Pinned down by pain and moaning for release,
Or nagged by want past resolution's power,
I might be driven to sell your love for peace,   12
Or trade the memory of this night for food.
It well may be. I do not think I would.

Age

Youth passes away, and age brings other problems. Although the subject
matter in the following poems is in a broad sense the same, the ideas it
generates are by no means identical.

Sailing to Byzantium[1]

W. B. Yeats (1865–1939)

I

That[2] is no country for old men. The young
In one another's arms, birds in the trees

---

[1] The ancient name for the modern Istanbul. Byzantium here symbolizes a time and place devoted to the permanence of art and artifice as opposed to the transience of "Whatever is begotten, born, and dies."
[2] The country, presumably Ireland, that the speaker leaves behind.

—Those dying generations—at their song,
The salmon-falls, the mackerel-crowded seas,   4
Fish, flesh, or fowl, commend all summer long
Whatever is begotten, born, and dies.
Caught in that sensual music all neglect
Monuments of unageing intellect.   8

II

An aged man is but a paltry thing,
A tattered coat upon a stick, unless
Soul clap its hands and sing, and louder sing
For every tatter in its mortal dress,   12
Nor is there singing school but studying
Monuments of its own magnificence;
And therefore I have sailed the seas and come
To the holy city of Byzantium.   16

III

O sages standing in God's holy fire
As in the gold mosaic of a wall,
Come from the holy fire, perne in a gyre,[3]
And be the singing-masters of my soul.   20
Consume my heart away; sick with desire
And fastened to a dying animal
It knows not what it is; and gather me
Into the artifice of eternity.   24

IV

Once out of nature I shall never take
My bodily form from any natural thing,
But such a form as Grecian goldsmiths make
Of hammered gold and gold enamelling   28
To keep a drowsy Emperor awake;
Or set upon a golden bough to sing[4]
To lords and ladies of Byzantium
Of what is past, or passing, or to come.   32

[3] To move in a gyrating motion like a perne (sometimes "pirn"), or weaver's bobbin.
[4] Yeats had read "that in the Emperor's palace at Byzantium was a tree made of gold and silver, and artificial birds that sang."

That Time of Year Thou Mayst in Me Behold

William Shakespeare (1565–1616)

That time of year thou mayst in me behold
When yellow leaves, or none, or few, do hang
Upon those boughs which shake against the cold,
Bare ruined choirs, where late the sweet birds sang.   4
In me thou see'st the twilight of such day
As after sunset fadeth in the west;
Which by and by black night doth take away,
Death's second self, that seals up all in rest.   8
In me thou see'st the glowing of such fire,
That on the ashes of his youth doth lie,
As the deathbed whereon it must expire
Consumed with that which it was nourished by.   12
    This thou perceiv'st, which makes thy love more strong,
    To love that well which thou must leave ere long.

Survivor

Archibald MacLeish (1892–)

On an oak in autumn
there'll always be
one leaf left at the top of the tree
that won't let go with the rest and rot—
won't cast loose and skitter and sail   5
and end in a puddle of rain in a swale
and fatten the earth and be fruitful . . .

                        No,
it won't and it won't and it won't let go.
It rattles a kind of a jig tattoo,   10
a telegrapher's tattle that *will* get through
like an SOS from a struggling ship
over and over, a dash and a skip.

You cover your head with your quilt and still
that telegrapher's key on Conway hill   15
calls to Polaris.[1]

      I can spell:
I know what it says . . . I know too well.
I pull my pillow over my ear
but I hear.   20

[1] The North Star.

The Ivy Crown[1]

William Carlos Williams   (1883–1963)

The whole process is a lie,
       unless,
              crowned by excess,
it break forcefully,
       one way or another,   5
              from its confinement—
or find a deeper well.
       Antony and Cleopatra[2]
          were right;
they have shown   10
       the way. I love you
          or I do not live
at all.

Daffodil time
       is past. This is   15
           summer, summer!
the heart says,
       and not even the full of it.
          No doubts
are permitted—   20
       though they will come
          and may
before our time
       overwhelm us.
          We are only mortal   25
but being mortal
       can defy our fate.
          We may
by an outside chance
       even win! We do not   30
          look to see
jonquils and violets
       come again
          but there are,
still,   35
       the roses!

---

[1] From *Journey to Love*, published in 1955, when Williams was 72, and addressed to his wife of many years, Florence (Flossie).
[2] Famous as older lovers.

Romance has no part in it.
          The business of love is
                    cruelty *which*,
by our wills,   40
          we transform
                    to live together.
It has its seasons,
          for and against,
                    whatever the heart   45
fumbles in the dark
          to assert
                    toward the end of May.
Just as the nature of briars
          is to tear flesh,   50
                    I have proceeded
through them.
          Keep
                    the briars out,
they say.   55
          You cannot live
                    and keep free of
briars.

Children pick flowers.
          Let them.   60
                    Though having them
in hand
          they have no further use for them
                    but leave them crumpled
at the curb's edge.   65
At our age the imagination
          across the sorry facts
                    lifts us
to make roses
          stand before thorns.   70
                    Sure
love is cruel
          and selfish
                    and totally obtuse—
at least, blinded by the light,   75
          young love is.
                    But we are older,
I to love
          and you to be loved,
                    we have,   80

                    no matter how,
                            by our wills survived
                                    to keep
                    the jeweled prize
                            always   85
                                    at our finger tips.
            We will it so
                    and so it is
                            past all accident.

Good-bye My Fancy!
Walt Whitman (1819–1892)

Good-bye my Fancy!
Farewell dear mate, dear love!
I'm going away, I know not where,
Or to what fortune, or whether I may ever see you again,
So Good-bye my Fancy.   5
Now for my last—let me look back a moment;
The slower fainter ticking of the clock is in me,
Exit, nightfall, and soon the heart-thud stopping.

Long have we lived, joy'd, caress'd together;
Delightful!—now separation—Good-bye my Fancy.   10

Yet let me not be too hasty,
Long indeed have we lived, slept, filter'd, become really blended
        into one;
Then if we die we die together, (yes, we'll remain one,)
If we go anywhere we'll go together to meet what happens,
May-be we'll be better off and blither, and learn something,   15
May-be it is yourself now really ushering me to the true songs,
        (who knows?)
May-be it is you the mortal knob really undoing, turning—so
        now finally,
Good-bye—and hail! my Fancy.   20

Mutability

All things flow. You can never put your foot in the same river twice.
These observations, paraphrased from the Greek philosopher Heraclitus,
are essential to the concept of *mutability* (a word that derives from the
Latin word for *change*). You can never put your foot in the same river
twice because the river will change, will become a different river, even

as you take your foot from the water and put it back. The same law applies, as poets have frequently observed, to all things accessible to the five senses. What should be our response to a world in which change may be our only constant? Can we somehow escape the law of mutability? Are there planes of existence, beyond the reach of our senses, not subject to earthly change? Poems on mutability provide a variety of responses.

Mutability

William Wordsworth (1770–1850)

From low to high doth dissolution climb,
And sink from high to low, along a scale
Of awful notes, whose concord shall not fail;
A musical but melancholy chime,   4
Which they can hear who meddle not with crime,
Nor avarice, nor over-anxious care.
Truth fails not; but her outward forms that bear
The longest date do melt like frosty rime,   8
That in the morning whitened hill and plain
And is no more; drop like the tower sublime
Of yesterday, which royally did wear
His crown of weeds, but could not even sustain   12
Some casual shout that broke the silent air,
Or the unimaginable touch of Time.

How Many Paltry, Foolish, Painted Things

Michael Drayton (1563–1631)

How many paltry, foolish, painted things,
That now in coaches trouble every street,
Shall be forgotten, whom no poet sings,
Ere they be well wrapped in their winding sheet?   4
Where I to thee eternity shall give,
When nothing else remaineth of these days,
And Queens hereafter shall be glad to live
Upon the alms of thy superfluous praise;   8
Virgins and matrons reading these my rimes,
Shall be so much delighted with thy story,
That they shall grieve, they lived not in these times,
To have seen thee, their sexes only glory: 12
    So shalt thou fly above the vulgar throng,
    Still to survive in my immortal song.

Death, Be Not Proud

John Donne (1572–1631)

Death, be not proud, though some have called thee
Mighty and dreadful, for thou art not so;
For those whom thou think'st thou dost overthrow
Die not, poor Death, nor yet canst thou kill me.   4
From rest and sleep, which but thy pictures be,
Much pleasure; then from thee much more must flow,
And soonest our best men with thee do go,
Rest of their bones, and soul's delivery.   8
Thou art slave to fate, chance, kings, and desperate men,
And dost with poison, war, and sickness dwell,
And poppy[1] or charms can make us sleep as well
And better than thy stroke; why swell'st thou then?   12
One short sleep last, we wake eternally
And death shall be no more; Death, thou shalt die.

[1] The opium poppy.

To the Stone-Cutters

Robinson Jeffers (1887–1962)

Stone-cutters fighting time with marble, you foredefeated
Challengers of oblivion
Eat cynical earnings, knowing rock splits, records fall down,
The square-limbed Roman letters
Scale in the thaws, wear in the rain. The poet as well   5
Builds his monument mockingly;
For man will be blotted out, the blithe earth die, the brave sun
Die blind and blacken to the heart:
Yet stones have stood for a thousand years, and pained thoughts
    found
The honey of peace in old poems.   10

The River

Hart Crane (1889–1932)

Stick your patent name on a signboard[1]
brother—all over—going west—young man

[1] The first eighteen lines present a montage of the sights and sounds of the twentieth century, many in the form of billboards as they might be glimpsed from the speeding Twentieth-Century Limited (an express passenger train that ran for years between New York and Chicago). Brand names, radio, vaudeville all play their part. Bert Williams was a famed black entertainer.

Tintex—Japalac—Certain-teed Overalls ads
and lands sakes! under the new playbill ripped
in the guaranteed corner—see Bert Williams what?   5
Minstrels when you steal a chicken just
save me the wing for if it isn't
Erie it ain't for miles around a
Mazda—and the telegraphic night coming on Thomas

a Ediford—and whistling down the tracks   10
a headlight rushing with the sound—can you
imagine—while an EXPRESS makes time like
SCIENCE—COMMERCE and the HOLYGHOST
RADIO ROARS IN EVERY HOME WE HAVE THE NORTHPOLE
WALLSTREET AND VIRGINBIRTH WITHOUT STONES OR   15
WIRES OR EVEN RUNning brooks connecting ears
and no more sermons windows flashing roar
breathtaking—as you like it . . . eh?
      So the 20th Century—so
whizzed the Limited—roared by and left   20
three men, still hungry on the tracks, ploddingly
watching the tail lights wizen and converge, slipping gimleted and neatly out of sight.

                          •   •   •

The last bear, shot drinking in the Dakotas
Loped under wires that span the mountain stream.   25
Keen instruments, strung to a vast precision
Bind town to town and dream to ticking dream.
But some men take their liquor slow—and count
—Though they'll confess no rosary nor clue—
The river's minute by the far brook's year.   30
Under a world of whistles, wires and steam
Caboose-like they go ruminating through
Ohio, Indiana—blind baggage—
To Cheyenne tagging . . . Maybe Kalamazoo.

Time's rendings, time's blendings they construe   35
As final reckonings of fire and snow;
Strange bird-wit, like the elemental gist
Of unwalled winds they offer, singing low
My Old Kentucky Home and Casey Jones,
Some Sunny Day. I heard a road-gang chanting so.   40
And afterwards, who had a colt's eyes—one said,
"Jesus! Oh I remember watermelon days!" And sped
High in a cloud of merriment, recalled

"—And when my Aunt Sally Simpson smiled," he drawled—
"It was almost Louisiana, long ago."   45
"There's no place like Booneville though, Buddy,"
One said, excising a last burr from his vest,
"—For early trouting." Then peering in the can,
"—But I kept on the tracks." Possessed, resigned,
He trod the fire down pensively and grinned,   50
Spreading dry shingles of a beard . . . .
                                             Behind.
My father's cannery works I used to see
Rail-squatters ranged in nomad raillery,
The ancient men—wifeless or runaway
Hobo-trekkers that forever search   55
An empire wilderness of freight and rails.
Each seemed a child, like me, on a loose perch,
Holding to childhood like some termless play.
John, Jake or Charley, hopping the slow freight
—Memphis to Tallahassee—riding the rods,   60
Blind fists of nothing, humpty-dumpty clods.

Yet they touch something like a key perhaps.
From pole to pole across the hills, the states
—They know a body[2] under the wide rain;
Youngsters with eyes like fjords, old reprobates   65
With racetrack jargon,—dotting immensity
They lurk across her, knowing her yonder breast
Snow-silvered, sumac-stained or smoky blue—
Is past the valley-sleepers, south or west.
—As I have trod the rumorous midnights, too,   70

And past the circuit of the lamp's thin flame
(O Nights that brought me to her body bare!)
Have dreamed beyond the print that bound her name.
Trains sounding the long blizzards out—I heard
Wail into distances I knew were hers.   75
Papooses crying on the wind's long mane
Screamed redskin dynasties that fled the brain,
—Dead echoes! But I knew her body there,
Time like a serpent down her shoulder, dark,
And space, an eaglet's wing, laid on her hair.   80

Under the Ozarks, domed by Iron Mountain,
The old gods of the rain lie wrapped in pools

[2] In *The Bridge*, a long poem of which "The River" forms one section, the American land is imaged as the body of Pocahontas, our first heroine.

Where eyeless fish curvet a sunken fountain
And re-descend with corn from querulous crows.
Such pilferings make up their timeless eatage,   85
Propitiate them for their timber torn
By iron, iron—always the iron dealt cleavage!
They doze now, below axe and powder horn.

And Pullman breakfasters glide glistening steel
From tunnel into field—iron strides the dew—   90
Straddles the hill, a dance of wheel on wheel.
You have a half-hour's wait at Siskiyou,
Or stay the night and take the next train through.
Southward, near Cairo passing, you can see
The Ohio merging,—borne down Tennessee;   95
And if it's summer and the sun's in dusk
Maybe the breeze will lift the River's musk
—As though the waters breathed that you might know
Memphis Johnny, Steamboat Bill, Missouri Joe.
Oh, lean from the window, if the train slows down,   100
As though you touched hands with some ancient
        clown,
—A little while gaze absently below
And hum Deep River with them while they go.

Yes, turn again and sniff once more—look see,
O Sheriff, Brakeman and Authority—   105
Hitch up your pants and crunch another quid,
For you, too, feed the River timelessly.
And few evade full measure of their fate;
Always they smile out eerily what they seem.
I could believe he joked at heaven's gate—   110
Dan Midland[3]—jolted from the cold brake-beam.

Down, down—born pioneers in time's despite,
Grimed tributaries to an ancient flow—
They win no frontier by their wayward plight,
But drift in stillness, as from Jordan's brow.   115

You will not hear it as the sea; even stone
Is not more hushed by gravity . . . But slow,
As loth to take more tribute—sliding prone
Like one whose eyes were buried long ago

The River, spreading, flows—and spends your dream.   120
What are you, lost within this tideless spell?

[3] A famous hobo.

You are your father's father, and the stream—
A liquid theme that floating niggers swell.

Damp tonnage and alluvial march of days—
Nights turbid, vascular with silted shale   125
And roots surrendered down of moraine clays:
The Mississippi drinks the farthest dale.

O quarrying passion, undertowed sunlight!
The basalt surface drags a jungle grace
Ochreous and lynx-barred in lengthening might;   130
Patience! and you shall reach the biding place!

Over De Soto's bones[4] the freighted floors
Throb past the City storied of three thrones.
Down two more turns the Mississippi pours
(Anon tall ironsides up from salt lagoons)   135

And flows within itself, heaps itself free.
All fades but one thin skyline 'round . . . Ahead
No embrace opens but the stinging sea;
The River lifts itself from its long bed,

Poised wholly on its dream, a mustard glow   140
Tortured with history, its one will—flow!
—The Passion spreads in wide tongues, choked and
      slow,
Meeting the Gulf, hosannas silently below.

[4] Hernando DeSoto (c. 1500–1542) was buried in the Mississippi River near the later site of New Orleans, "the City storied of three thrones" of Spain, France, and England.

As I Ebb'd with the Ocean of Life

Walt Whitman (1819–1892)

1

As I ebb'd with the ocean of life,
As I wended the shores I know,
As I walk'd where the ripples continually wash you Paumanok,[1]
Where they rustle up hoarse and sibilant,
Where the fierce old mother[2] endlessly cries for her castaways,   5
I musing late in the autumn day, gazing off southward,
Held by this electric self out of the pride of which I utter poems,
Was seiz'd by the spirit that trails in the lines underfoot,

[1] Indian name for Long Island, where Whitman was born.
[2] The sea.

The rim, the sediment that stands for all the water and all the land of the
     globe.

Fascinated, my eyes reverting from the south, dropt, to follow those slender
     windrows,   10
Chaff, straw, splinters of wood, weeds, and the sea-gluten,
Scum, scales from shining rocks, leaves of salt-lettuce, left by the tide,
Miles walking, the sound of breaking waves the other side of me,
Paumanok there and then as I thought the old thought of likenesses,[3]
These you presented to me you fish-shaped island,   15
As I wended the shores I know,
As I walk'd with that electric self seeking types.

2

As I wend to the shores I know not,
As I list to the dirge, the voice of men and women wreck'd,
As I inhale the impalpable breezes that set in upon me,   20
As the ocean so mysterious rolls toward me closer and closer,
I too but signify at the utmost a little wash'd-up drift,
A few sands and dead leaves to gather,
Gather, and merge myself as part of the sands and drift.

O baffled, balk'd, bent to the very earth,   25
Oppress'd with myself that I have dared to open my mouth,
Aware now that amid all that blab whose echoes recoil upon me I have not
     once had the least idea who or what I am,
But that before all my arrogant poems the real Me stands yet untouch'd,
     untold, altogether unreach'd,
Withdrawn far, mocking me with mock-congratulatory signs and bows,
With peals of distant ironical laughter at every word I have written,   30
Pointing in silence to these songs, and then to the sand beneath.

I perceive I have not really understood anything, not a single object, and that
     no man ever can,
Nature here in sight of the sea taking advantage of me to dart upon me and
     sting me,
Because I have dared to open my mouth to sing at all.

3

You oceans both, I close with you,   35
We murmur alike reproachfully rolling sands and drift, knowing not why,
These little shreds indeed standing for you and me and all.

You friable[4] shore with trails of debris,

---

[3] Correspondences between man and nature, the "types" of line 17.
[4] Easily crumbled.

You fish-shaped island, I take what is underfoot,
What is yours is mine my father.[5]   40

I too Paumanok,
I too have bubbled up, floated the measureless float, and been wash'd on
    your shores,
I too am but a trail of drift and debris,
I too leave little wrecks upon you, you fish-shaped island.

I throw myself upon your breast my father,   45
I cling to you so that you cannot unloose me,
I hold you so firm till you answer me something.

Kiss me my father,
Touch me with your lips as I touch those I love,
Breathe to me while I hold you close the secret of the murmuring I envy. 50

4

Ebb, ocean of life, (the flow will return,)
Cease not your moaning you fierce old mother,
Endlessly cry for your castaways, but fear not, deny not me,
Rustle not up so hoarse and angry against my feet as I touch you or gather
    from you.

I mean tenderly by you and all,   55
I gather for myself and for this phantom looking down where we lead, and
    following me and mine.

Me and mine, loose windrows, little corpses,
Froth, snowy white, and bubbles,
(See, from my dead lips the ooze exuding at last,
See, the prismatic colors glistening and rolling,)   60
Tufts of straw, sands, fragments,
Buoy'd hither from many moods, one contradicting another,
From the storm, the long calm, the darkness, the swell,
Musing, pondering, a breath, a briny tear, a dab of liquid or soil,
Up just as much out of fathomless workings fermented and thrown,   65
A limp blossom or two, torn, just as much over waves floating, drifted at
    random,
Just as much for us that sobbing dirge of Nature,
Just as much whence we come that blare of the cloud-trumpets,
We, capricious, brought hither we know not whence, spread out before you,
You up there walking or sitting,   70
Whoever you are, we too lie in drifts at your feet.

[5] Paumanok (Long Island).

Directive

Robert Frost (1874–1963)

Back out of all this now too much for us,
Back in a time made simple by the loss
Of detail, burned, dissolved, and broken off
Like graveyard marble sculpture in the weather,
There is a house that is no more a house   5
Upon a farm that is no more a farm
And in a town that is no more a town.
The road there, if you'll let a guide direct you
Who only has at heart your getting lost,
May seem as if it should have been a quarry—   10
Great monolithic knees the former town
Long since gave up pretense of keeping covered.
And there's a story in a book about it:
Besides the wear of iron wagon wheels
The ledges show lines ruled southeast-northwest,   15
The chisel work of an enormous Glacier
That braced his feet against the Arctic Pole.
You must not mind a certain coolness from him
Still said to haunt this side of Panther Mountain.
Nor need you mind the serial ordeal   20
Of being watched from forty cellar holes
As if by eye pairs out of forty firkins.[1]
As for the woods' excitement over you
That sends light rustle rushes to their leaves,
Charge that to upstart inexperience.   25
Where were they all not twenty years ago?
They think too much of having shaded out
A few old pecker-fretted apple trees.
Make yourself up a cheering song of how
Someone's road home from work this once was,   30
Who may be just ahead of you on foot
Or creaking with a buggy load of grain.
The height of the adventure is the height
Of country where two village cultures faded
Into each other. Both of them are lost.   35
And if you're lost enough to find yourself
By now, pull in your ladder road behind you
And put a sign up CLOSED to all but me.
Then make yourself at home. The only field

[1] Small wooden tubs.

Now left's no bigger than a harness gall.   40
First there's the children's house of make-believe,
Some shattered dishes underneath a pine,
The playthings in the playhouse of the children.
Weep for what little things could make them glad.
Then for the house that is no more a house,   45
But only a belilaced cellar hole,
Now slowly closing like a dent in dough.
This was no playhouse but a house in earnest.
Your destination and your destiny's
A brook that was the water of the house,   50
Cold as a spring as yet so near its source,
Too lofty and original to rage.
(We know the valley streams that when aroused
Will leave their tatters hung on barb and thorn.)
I have kept hidden in the instep arch   55
Of an old cedar at the waterside
A broken drinking goblet like the Grail[2]
Under a spell so the wrong ones can't find it,
So can't get saved, as Saint Mark says they mustn't.[3]
(I stole the goblet from the children's playhouse.)   60
Here are your waters and your watering place.
Drink and be whole again beyond confusion.

[2] The cup Christ drank from at the Last Supper.
[3] See Mark xvi.16.

Death

Death is the final constant. It serves as the ultimate common denominator, eventually reducing all living things to the same condition. How should we as humans confront the death of others? In what way should we contemplate the fact of our own end?

The Exequy[1]

Henry King (1592–1669)

Accept, thou shrine of my dead saint,
Instead of dirges, this complaint;
And for sweet flowers to crown thy hearse,
Receive a strew of weeping verse
From thy grieved friend, whom thou might'st see   5
Quite melted into tears for thee.

[1] Funeral rite.

Dear loss! since thy untimely fate
My task hath been to meditate
On thee, on thee; thou art the book,
The library whereon I look,   10
Though almost blind. For thee, loved clay,
I languish out, not live, the day,
Using no other exercise
But what I practice with mine eyes;
By which wet glasses I find out   15
How lazily time creeps about
To one that mourns: this, only this,
My exercise and business is.
So I compute the weary hours
With sighs dissolvéd into showers.   20

Nor wonder if my time go thus
Backward and most preposterous;
Thou hast benighted me, thy set
This eve of blackness did beget,
Who wast my day, though overcast   25
Before thou hadst thy noontide passed;
And I remember must in tears,
Thou scarce hadst seen so many years
As day tells hours. By thy clear sun
My love and fortune first did run;   30
But thou wilt never more appear
Folded within my hemisphere,
Since both thy light and motiön
Like a fled star is fallen and gone;
And 'twixt me and my soul's dear wish   35
An earth now interposéd is,
Which such a strange eclipse doth make
As ne'er was read in almanac.
I could allow thee for a time
To darken me and my sad clime;   40
Were it a month, a year, or ten,
I would thy exile live till then,
And all that space my mirth adjourn,
So thou wouldst promise to return;
And putting off thy ashy shroud,   45
At length disperse this sorrow's cloud.

But woe is me! the longest date
Too narrow is to calculate
These empty hopes; never shall I

Be so much blest as to descry   50
A glimpse of thee, till that day come
Which shall the earth to cinders doom,
And a fierce fever must calcine[2]
The body of this world—like thine,
My little world! That fit of fire   55
Once off, our bodies shall aspire
To our souls' bliss; then we shall rise
And view ourselves with clearer eyes
In that calm region where no night
Can hide us from each other's sight.   60

Meantime, thou hast her, earth: much good
May my harm do thee. Since it stood
With heaven's will I might not call
Her longer mine, I give thee all
My short-lived right and interest   65
In her whom living I loved best;
With a most free and bounteous grief
I give thee what I could not keep.
Be kind to her, and prithee look
Thou write into thy doomsday book   70
Each parcel of this rarity
Which in thy casket shrined doth lie.
See that thou make thy reckoning straight,
And yield her back again by weight;
For thou must audit on thy trust   75
Each grain and atom of this dust,
As thou wilt answer Him that lent,
Not gave thee, my dear monument.
So close the ground, and 'bout her shade
Black curtains draw; my bride is laid.   80

Sleep on, my love, in thy cold bed,
Never to be disquieted!
My last good-night! Thou wilt not wake
Till I thy fate shall overtake;
Till age, or grief, or sickness must   85
Marry my body to that dust
It so much loves; and fill the room
My heart keeps empty in thy tomb.
Stay for me there; I will not fail
To meet thee in that hollow vale.   90
And think not much of my delay;

---

[2] Burn to ashes.

I am already on the way,
And follow thee with all the speed
Desire can make, or sorrows breed.
Each minute is a short degree,   95
And every hour a step towards thee.
At night when I betake to rest,
Next morn I rise nearer my west
Of life, almost by eight hours' sail,
Than when sleep breathed his drowsy gale.   100

Thus from the sun my bottom[3] steers,
And my day's compass downward bears;
Nor labor I to stem the tide
Through which to thee I swiftly glide.

'Tis true, with shame and grief I yield,   105
Thou like the van[4] first took'st the field,
And gotten hast the victory
In thus adventuring to die
Before me, whose more years might crave
A just precédence in the grave.   110
But hark! my pulse like a soft drum
Beats my approach, tells thee I come;
And slow howe'er my marches be,
I shall at last sit down by thee.

The thought of this bids me go on,   115
And wait my dissolutiön
With hope and comfort. Dear (forgive
The crime), I am content to live
Divided, with but half a heart,
Till we shall meet and never part.   120

[3] Vessel.
[4] Vanguard.

Lycidas

John Milton (1608–1674)

*In this Monody[1] the Author bewails a learned Friend, unfortu-
nately drowned in his passage from Chester on the Irish Seas,
1637; and by occasion, foretells the ruin of our corrupted Clergy,
then in their height.*

[1] A lament or dirge sung by a single voice. Milton writes in the form of a *pastoral elegy*, drawing his
imagery from an idyllic vision of a shepherd's life, in a tradition dating from classical antiquity. The
friend was Edward King, who had been a fellow student with Milton at Cambridge.

Yet once more, O ye laurels,[2] and once more,
Yet myrtles brown, with ivy never sere,[3]
I come to pluck your berries harsh and crude,
And with forced fingers rude
Shatter your leaves before the mellowing year.   5
Bitter constraint and sad occasion dear
Compels me to disturb your season due;
For Lycidas is dead, dead ere his prime,
Young Lycidas, and hath not left his peer.
Who would not sing for Lycidas? he knew   10
Himself to sing, and build the lofty rhyme.
He must not float upon his watery bier
Unwept, and welter to the parching wind,
Without the meed[4] of some melodious tear.
    Begin, then, Sisters[5] of the sacred well   15
That from beneath the seat of Jove doth spring;
Begin, and somewhat loudly sweep the string.
Hence with denial vain and coy excuse:
So may some gentle Muse
With lucky words favour my destined urn,   20
And as he passes turn,
And bid fair peace be to my sable shroud!
    For we were nursed upon the self-same hill,
Fed the same flock, by fountain, shade, and rill;
Together both, ere the high lawns appeared   25
Under the opening eyelids of the Morn,
We drove a-field, and both together heard
What time the grey-fly winds her sultry horn,
Battening[6] our flocks with the fresh dews of night,
Oft till the star that rose at evening bright   30
Toward heaven's descent had sloped his westering wheel.
Meanwhile the rural ditties were not mute;
Tempered to th' oaten flute,
Rough Satyrs danced, and Fauns with cloven heel
From the glad sound would not be absent long;   35
And old Damaetas[7] loved to hear our song.
    But, oh! the heavy change, now thou art gone,

---

[2] Laurel, myrtle, and ivy, all evergreen, were traditional materials for poetic garlands, symbolic of inspiration.
[3] Withered.
[4] Reward.
[5] The Muses, who were associated with the sacred well of Aganippe, at the foot of Mt. Helicon.
[6] Fattening.
[7] A conventional pastoral name, though Milton may have had in mind a particular Cambridge tutor.

Now thou art gone and never must return!
Thee, Shepherd, thee the woods and desert caves,
With wild thyme and the gadding[8] vine o'ergrown,   40
And all their echoes, mourn.
The willows, and the hazel copses green,
Shall now no more be seen
Fanning their joyous leaves to thy soft lays.
As killing as the canker to the rose,   45
Or taint-worm to the weanling herds that graze,
Or frost to flowers, that their gay wardrobe wear,
When first the white-thorn blows;[9]
Such, Lycidas, thy loss to shepherd's ear.
  Where were ye, Nymphs, when the remorseless deep   50
Closed o'er the head of your loved Lycidas?
For neither were ye playing on the steep
Where your old bards, the famous Druids,[10] lie,
Nor on the shaggy top of Mona high,
Nor yet where Deva spreads her wizard stream.   55
Ay me! I fondly[11] dream
"Had ye been there,"... for what could that have done?
What could the Muse herself that Orpheus[12] bore,
The Muse herself, for her enchanting son,
Whom universal nature did lament,   60
When, by the rout that made the hideous roar,
His gory visage down the stream was sent,
Down the swift Hebrus to the Lesbian shore?
  Alas! what boots[13] it with uncessant care
To tend the homely, slighted, shepherd's trade,   65
And strictly meditate the thankless Muse?
Were it not better done, as others use,
To sport with Amaryllis in the shade,
Or with the tangles of Neaera's hair?[14]
Fame is the spur that the clear spirit doth raise   70
(That last infirmity of noble mind)
To scorn delights and live laborious days;

[8] Wandering.
[9] Blossoms.
[10] The Druids, Celtic priests, were buried on the "steep" of Kerig-y-Druidion in Wales. Mona is the Isle of Anglesey and Deva the River Dee (counted "wizard" or magic by the local inhabitants). All are near the site of King's drowning.
[11] Foolishly.
[12] Calliope, Muse of epic poetry, was the mother of Orpheus, whose music was fabled for its power over nature. Orpheus was torn apart by screaming Maenads, who threw his head into the River Hebrus, whence it floated to Lesbos.
[13] Profits.
[14] Amaryllis and Neaera: conventional pastoral names.

But the fair guerdon[15] when we hope to find,
And think to burst out into sudden blaze,
Comes the blind Fury with th' abhorrèd shears,   75
And slits the thin-spun life.[16] "But not the praise,"
Phoebus[17] replied, and touched my trembling ears:
"Fame is no plant that grows on mortal soil,
Nor in the glistering foil[18]
Set off to the world, nor in broad rumour lies,   80
But lives and spreads aloft by those pure eyes
And perfect witness of all-judging Jove;
As he pronounces lastly on each deed,
Of so much fame in Heaven expect thy meed."

   O fountain Arethuse, and thou honoured flood,   85
Smooth-sliding Mincius,[19] crowned with vocal reeds,
That strain I heard was of a higher mood.
But now my oat[20] proceeds,
And listens to the Herald of the Sea,[21]
That came in Neptune's plea.   90
He asked the waves, and asked the felon winds,
What hard mishap hath doomed this gentle swain?
And questioned every gust of rugged wings
That blows from off each beakèd promontory.
They knew not of his story;   95
And sage Hippotades[22] their answer brings,
That not a blast was from his dungeon strayed:
The air was calm, and on the level brine
Sleek Panopè[23] with all her sisters played.
It was that fatal and perfidious bark,   100
Built in th' eclipse, and rigged with curses dark,
That sunk so low that sacred head of thine.

   Next, Camus,[24] reverend sire, went footing slow,
His mantle hairy, and his bonnet sedge,[25]
Inwrought with figures dim, and on the edge   105

[15] Reward.
[16] Atropos, one of the three Fates, cut the thread of a person's life after her sisters had spun and measured it.
[17] Phoebus Apollo, god of poetic inspiration.
[18] Setting, often for an inferior gem.
[19] Arethuse: fountain in Sicily associated with the poet Theocritus; Mincius: river in Italy associated with the poet Virgil.
[20] Oaten pipe; song.
[21] Triton, who pleads Neptune's innocence in the death of King.
[22] Aeolus, god of the winds.
[23] A sea nymph.
[24] God of the river Cam; hence, a representative of Cambridge University.
[25] Marsh grass.

Like to that sanguine flower[26] inscribed with woe.
"Ah! who hath reft," quoth he, "my dearest pledge?"
Last came, and last did go,
The Pilot of the Galilean Lake;[27]
Two massy keys he bore of metals twain   110
(The golden opes, the iron shuts amain).
He shook his mitred locks,[28] and stern bespake:—
"How well could I have spared for thee, young swain,
Enow of such as, for their bellies' sake,
Creep, and intrude, and climb into the fold!   115
Of other care they little reckoning make
Than how to scramble at the shearers' feast,
And shove away the worthy bidden guest.
Blind mouths! that scarce themselves know how to hold
A sheep-hook, or have learnt aught else the least   120
That to the faithful herdman's art belongs!
What recks it them? What need they? They are sped,
And, when they list,[29] their lean and flashy songs
Grate on their scrannel[30] pipes of wretched straw;
The hungry sheep look up, and are not fed,   125
But, swoln with wind and the rank mist they draw,
Rot inwardly, and foul contagion spread;
Besides what the grim wolfe with privy[31] paw
Daily devours apace, and nothing said.
But that two-handed engine at the door[32]   130
Stands ready to smite once, and smite no more,"
        Return, Alpheus,[33] the dread voice is past
That shrunk thy streams; return, Sicilian-Muse,
And call the vales, and bid them hither cast
Their bells and flowerets of a thousand hues.   135
Ye valleys low, where the mild whispers use
Of shades, and wanton winds, and gushing brooks,
On whose fresh lap the swart star[34] sparely looks,
Throw hither all your quaint enamelled eyes,
That on the green turf suck the honeyed showers,   140
And purple all the ground with vernal flowers.

[26] The hyacinth, with bloody marks AI AI ("Alas, alas") commemorating the accidental death of the youthful Hyancinthus at the hands of Apollo.
[27] St. Peter, who holds the keys to Heaven.
[28] He wears a bishop's miter.
[29] Choose.
[30] Meager.
[31] Secret, with an allusion to Roman Catholicism.
[32] An instrument of death, though the specific meaning is obscure.
[33] A river god who loved Arethusa.
[34] Sirius, the Dog Star, thought to have a "swart," or dark, malignant influence in late summer.

Bring the rathe[35] primrose that forsaken dies,
The tufted crow-toe, and pale jessamine,
The white pink, and the pansy freaked with jet,
The glowing violet,   145
The musk rose, and the well-attired woodbine,
With cowslips wan that hang the pensive head,
And every flower that sad embroidery wears;
Bid amaranthus[36] all his beauty shed,
And daffadillies fill their cups with tears,   150
To strew the laureate hearse where Lycid lies.
For so, to interpose a little ease,
Let our frail thoughts dally with false surmise.
Ay me! whilst thee the shores and sounding seas
Wash far away, where'er thy bones are hurled;   155
Whether beyond the stormy Hebrides,[37]
Where thou perhaps under the whelming tide
Visit'st the bottom of the monstrous world;
Or whether thou, to our moist vows denied,
Sleep'st by the fable of Bellerus[38] old,   160
Where the great Vision of the guarded mount[39]
Looks toward Namancos and Bayona's hold.
Look homeward, Angel, now, and melt with ruth:[40]
And, O ye dolphins, waft the hapless youth.
Weep no more, woeful shepherds, weep no more,   165
For Lycidas, your sorrow, is not dead,
Sunk though he be beneath the watery floor.
So sinks the day-star in the ocean bed,
And yet anon repairs his drooping head,
And tricks his beams, and with new-spangled ore   170
Flames in the forehead of the morning sky:
So Lycidas sunk low, but mounted high,
Through the dear might of him that walked the waves,[41]
Where, other groves and other streams along,
With nectar pure his oozy locks he laves,[42]   175
And hears the unexpressive nuptial song,
In the blest kingdoms meek of joy and love.
There entertain him all the Saints above,

[35] Early.
[36] A legendary flower supposed never to fade.
[37] Off the coast of Scotland, at the northern end of the Irish Sea.
[38] A legendary giant supposed to be buried at Land's End, Cornwall.
[39] From St. Michael's Mount at the tip of Cornwall, the archangel gazes toward Namancos and Bayona, strongholds of Catholicism in northern Spain.
[40] Pity.
[41] Christ.
[42] Bathes.

In solemn troops, and sweet societies,
That sing, and singing in their glory move,   180
And wipe the tears for ever from his eyes.
Now, Lycidas, the shepherds weep no more;
Henceforth thou art the Genius of the shore,
In thy large recompense, and shalt be good
To all that wander in that perilous flood.   185

    Thus sang the uncouth[43] swain to th' oaks and rills,
While the still morn went out with sandals grey:
He touched the tender stops of various quills,
With eager thought warbling his Doric[44] lay;
And now the sun had stretched out all the hills,   190
And now was dropped into the western bay;
At last he rose, and twitched his mantle blue:
To-morrow to fresh woods, and pastures new.

[43] Unlettered.
[44] Simple, pastoral.

On the University Carrier[1]

John Milton   (1608–1674)

*Who sickened in the time of his vacancy,[2] being forbid to go to
London, by reason of the plague.*

Here lies old Hobson, Death hath broke his girt,
And here, alas, hath laid him in the dirt,
Or else the ways being foul, twenty to one,
He's here stuck in a slough,[3] and overthrown.
'Twas such a shifter,[4] that if truth were known,   5
Death was half glad when he had got him down;
For he had any time this ten years full,
Dodged with him, betwixt Cambridge and The Bull.[5]
And surely, Death could never have prevailed,
Had not his weekly course of carriage failed;   10
But lately finding him so long at home,
And thinking now his journey's end was come,
And that he had taken up his latest inn,

[1] Thomas Hobson for years made weekly trips between Cambridge and London, carrying letters, parcels, and passengers. His death at 86 removed a figure that had become legendary to Cambridge students: the phrase "Hobson's choice" refers to his practice of requiring a person renting a horse from him to take the one that stood nearest the door.
[2] Leisure.
[3] A muddy or swampy place.
[4] Trickster.
[5] A London inn.

In the kind office of a chamberlain[6]
Showed him to his room where he must lodge that night,   15
Pulled off his boots, and took away the light:
If any ask for him, it shall be said,
"Hobson has supped, and's newly gone to bed."

[6] Attendant in a bedchamber.

Andrée Rexroth

Kenneth Rexroth (1905–)

Mt. Tamalpais[1]

The years have gone. It is spring
Again. Mars and Saturn will
Soon come on, low in the West,
In the dusk. Now the evening
Sunlight makes hazy girders   5
Over Steep Ravine above
The waterfalls. The winter
Birds from Oregon, robins
And varied thrushes, feast on
Ripe toyon and madroñe[2]   10
Berries. The robins sing as
The dense light falls.
      Your ashes
Were scattered in this place. Here
I wrote you a farewell poem,   15
And long ago another,
A poem of peace and love,
Of the lassitude of a long
Spring evening in youth. Now
It is almost ten years since   20
You came here to stay. Once more,
The pussy willows that come
After the New Year in this
Outlandish land are blooming.
There are deer and raccoon tracks   25
In the same places. A few
New sand bars and cobble beds
Have been left where erosion
Has gnawed deep into the hills.
The rounds of life are narrow.   30

[1] A mountain overlooking San Francisco Bay.
[2] Evergreens with red berries.

War and peace have past like ghosts.
The human race sinks towards
Oblivion. A bittern[3]
Calls from the same rushes where
You heard one on our first year   35
In the West; and where I heard
One again in the year
Of your death.

Kings River Canyon[4]

My sorrow is so wide
I cannot see across it;
And so deep I shall never
Reach the bottom of it.
The moon sinks through deep haze,   5
As though the Kings River Canyon
Were filled with fine, warm, damp gauze.
Saturn gleams through the thick light
Like a gold, wet eye; nearby,
Antares[5] glows faintly,   10
Without sparkle. Far overhead,
Stone shines darkly in the moonlight—
Lookout Point, where we lay
In another full moon, and first
Peered down into this canyon.   15
Here we camped, by still autumnal
Pools, all one warm October.
I baked you a bannock[6] birthday cake.
Here you did your best paintings—
Innocent, wondering landscapes.   20
Very few of them are left
Anywhere. You destroyed them
In the terrible trouble
Of your long sickness. Eighteen years
Have passed since that autumn.   25
There was no trail here then.
Only a few people knew
How to enter this canyon.
We were all alone, twenty
Miles from anybody;   30

[3] Heronlike bird with a booming cry.
[4] In Southern California.
[5] A bright red star.
[6] A thick, flat griddle cake of oatmeal or barley.

A young husband and wife,
Closed in and wrapped about
In the quiet autumn,
In the sound of quiet water,
In the turning and falling leaves,   35
In the wavering of innumerable
Bats from the caves, dipping
Over the odorous pools
Where the great trout drowsed in the evenings.

Eighteen years have been ground   40
To pieces in the wheels of life.
You are dead. With a thousand
Convicts they have blown a highway
Through Horseshoe Bend. Youth is gone,
That only came once. My hair   45
Is turning grey and my body
Heavier. I too move on to death.
I think of Henry King's stilted
But desolated *Exequy*,[7]
Of Yuan Chen's great poem,[8]   50
Unbearably pitiful;
Alone by the Spring river
More alone than I had ever
Imagined I would ever be,
I think of Frieda Lawrence,[9]   55
Sitting alone in New Mexico,
In the long drought, listening
For the hiss of the milky Isar,[10]
Over the cobbles, in a lost Spring.

[7] Henry King (1592–1669), an English poet. His *Exequy* is a funeral poem for his wife.
[8] Yuan Chen (779–831), a Chinese poet. In his "Three Dreams at Chiang-ling" a husband dreams of his dead wife.
[9] Widow of the novelist D. H. Lawrence.
[10] An Austrian river, flowing through the land of Frieda Lawrence's birth.

Burial

Alice Walker   (1944–   )

I

They have fenced in the dirt road
that once led to Wards Chapel
A.M.E.[1] church,

[1] African Methodist Episcopalian.

and cows graze
among the stones that   5
mark my family's graves.
The massive oak is gone
from out the church yard,
but the giant space is left
unfilled;   10
despite the two-lane blacktop
that slides across
the old, unalterable
roots.

II

Today I bring my own child here;   15
to this place where my father's
grandmother rests undisturbed
beneath the Georgia sun,
above her the neatstepping hooves
of cattle.   20
Here the graves soon grow back into the land.
Have been known to sink. To drop open without
warning. To cover themselves with wild ivy,
blackberries. Bittersweet and sage.
No one knows why. No one asks.   25
When Burning Off Day comes, as it does
some years,
the graves are haphazardly cleared and snakes
hacked to death and burned sizzling
in the brush .... The odor of smoke, oak   30
leaves, honeysuckle.
Forgetful of geographic resolutions as birds,
the farflung young fly South to bury
the old dead.

III

The old women move quietly up   35
and touch Sis Rachel's face.
"Tell Jesus I'm coming," they say.
"Tell Him I ain't goin' to *be*
long."

My grandfather turns his creaking head   40
away from the lavender box.
He does not cry. But looks afraid.

For years he called her "Woman";
shortened over the decades to
" 'Oman."
On the cut stone for " 'Oman's" grave
he did not notice
they had misspelled her name.

(The stone reads *Racher Walker*—not "Rachel"—
Loving Wife, Devoted Mother.)

IV

As a young woman, who had known her? Tripping
eagerly, "loving wife," to my grandfather's
bed. Not pretty, but serviceable. A hard
worker, with rough, moist hands. Her own two
babies dead before she came.
Came to seven children.
To aprons and sweat.
Came to quiltmaking.
Came to canning and vegetable gardens
big as fields.
Came to fields to plow.
Cotton to chop.
Potatoes to dig.
Came to multiple measles, chickenpox,
and croup.
Came to water from springs.
Came to leaning houses one story high.
Came to rivalries. Saturday night battles.
Came to straightened hair, Noxzema, and
feet washing at the Hardshell Baptist church.
Came to zinnias around the woodpile.
Came to grandchildren not of her blood
whom she taught to dip snuff without
sneezing.

Came to death blank, forgetful of it all.

When he called her " 'Oman" she no longer
listened. Or heard, or knew, or felt.

V

It is not until I see my first grade teacher
review her body that I cry.
Not for the dead, but for the gray in my

first grade teacher's hair. For memories
of before I was born, when teacher and
grandmother loved each other; and later
above the ducks made of soap and the orange-
legged chicks Miss Reynolds drew over   85
my own small hand
on paper with wide blue lines.

VI

Not for the dead, but for memories. None of
them sad. But seen from the angle of her
death.

In Memory of W. B. Yeats
(D. JAN. 1939)

W. H. Auden   (1907–1973)

I

He disappeared in the dead of winter:
The brooks were frozen, the airports almost deserted,
And snow disfigured the public statues;
The mercury sank in the mouth of the dying day.
What instruments we have agree   5
The day of his death was a dark cold day.

Far from his illness
The wolves ran on through the evergreen forests,
The peasant river was untempted by the fashionable quays;[1]
By mourning tongues   10
The death of the poet was kept from his poems.

But for him it was his last afternoon as himself,
An afternoon of nurses and rumours;
The provinces of his body revolted,
The squares of his mind were empty,   15
Silence invaded the suburbs,
The current of his feeling failed; he became his admirers.

Now he is scattered among a hundred cities
And wholly given over to unfamiliar affections,
To find his happiness in another kind of wood   20
And be punished under a foreign code of conscience.
The words of a dead man
Are modified in the guts of the living.

[1] Paved landing places for loading ships.

But in the importance of noise of to-morrow
When the brokers are roaring like beasts on the floor of the Bourse,[2]   25
And the poor have the sufferings to which they are fairly accustomed,
And each in the cell of himself is almost convinced of his freedom,
A few thousand will think of this day
As one thinks of a day when one did something slightly unusual.
What instruments we have agree   30
The day of his death was a dark cold day.

II

You were silly like us; your gift survived it all:
The parish of rich women, physical decay,
Yourself. Mad Ireland hurt you into poetry.
Now Ireland has her madness and her weather still,   35
For poetry makes nothing happen: it survives
In the valley of its making where executives
Would never want to tamper, flows on south
From ranches of isolation and the busy griefs,
Raw towns that we believe and die in; it survives,   40
A way of happening, a mouth.

III

Earth, receive an honoured guest:
William Yeats is laid to rest.
Let the Irish vessel lie
Emptied of its poetry.   45

In the nightmare of the dark
All the dogs of Europe bark,
And the living nations wait,
Each sequestered in its hate;

Intellectual disgrace   50
Stares from every human face,
And the seas of pity lie
Locked and frozen in each eye.

Follow, poet, follow right
To the bottom of the night,   55
With your unconstraining voice
Still persuade us to rejoice;

With the farming of a verse
Make a vineyard of the curse,
Sing of human unsuccess   60
In a rapture of distress;

[2] Stock exchange.

In the deserts of the heart
Let the healing fountain start,
In the prison of his days
Teach the free man how to praise.   65

Out of the Cradle Endlessly Rocking

Walt Whitman   (1819–1892)

Out of the cradle endlessly rocking,
Out of the mocking-bird's throat, the musical shuttle,
Out of the Ninth-month[1] midnight,
Over the sterile sands and the fields beyond, where the child
    leaving his bed wander'd alone, bareheaded, barefoot,
Down from the shower'd halo,   5
Up from the mystic play of shadows twining and twisting as if
    they were alive,
Out from the patches of briers and blackberries,
From the memories of the bird that chanted to me,
From your memories sad brother,[2] from the fitful risings and
    fallings I heard,
From under that yellow half-moon late-risen and swollen as if with
    tears,   10
From those beginning notes of yearning and love there in the
    mist,
From the thousand responses of my heart never to cease,
From the myriad thence-arous'd words,
From the word stronger and more delicious than any,
From such as now they start the scene revisiting,   15
As a flock, twittering, rising, or overhead passing,
Borne hither, ere all eludes me, hurriedly,
A man, yet by these tears a little boy again,
Throwing myself on the sand, confronting the waves,
I, chanter of pains and joys, uniter of here and hereafter,   20
Taking all hints to use them, but swiftly leaping beyond them,
A reminiscence sing

Once Paumanok,[3]
When the lilac-scent was in the air and Fifth-month grass was
    growing,
Up this seashore in some briers,   25
Two feather'd guests from Alabama, two together,

[1] The Quaker name for September.
[2] The bird.
[3] The Indian name for Long Island, where Whitman was born.

And their nest, and four light-green eggs spotted with brown,
And every day the he-bird to and fro near at hand,
And every day the she-bird crouch'd on her nest; silent, with
   bright eyes,
And every day I, a curious boy, never too close, never disturbing
   them,   30
Cautiously peering, absorbing, translating.

Shine! shine! shine![4]
Pour down your warmth, great sun!
While we bask, we two together.

Two together!   35
Winds blow south, or winds blow north,
Day come white, or night come black,
Home, or rivers and mountains from home,
Singing all time, minding no time,
While we two keep together.   40

Till of a sudden,
May-be kill'd, unknown to her mate,
One forenoon the she-bird crouch'd not on the nest,
Nor return'd that afternoon, nor the next,
Nor ever appear'd again.   45

And thenceforward all summer in the sound of the sea,
And at night under the full of the moon in calmer weather,
Over the hoarse surging of the sea,
Or flitting from brier to brier by day,
I saw, I heard at intervals the remaining one, the he-bird,   50
The solitary guest from Alabama.

Blow! blow! blow!
Blow up sea-winds along Paumanok's shore;
I wait and I wait till you blow my mate to me.

Yes, when the stars glisten'd,   55
All night long on the prong of a moss-scallop'd stake,
Down almost amid the slapping waves,
Sat the lone singer wonderful causing tears.

He call'd on his mate,
He pour'd forth the meanings which I of all men know.   60

Yes my brother I know,
The rest might not, but I have treasur'd every note,
For more than once dimly down to the beach gliding,

---

[4] Here and later, the songs of the bird, as translated by the poet, appear in italics.

Silent, avoiding the moonbeams, blending myself with the shadows,
Recalling now the obscure shapes, the echoes, the sounds and
    sights after their sorts,   65
The white arms out in the breakers tirelessly tossing,
I, with bare feet, a child, the wind wafting my hair,
Listen'd long and long.

Listen'd to keep, to sing, now translating the notes,
Following you my brother.   70

Soothe! soothe! soothe!
Close on its wave soothes the wave behind,
And again another behind embracing and lapping, every one close,
But my love soothes not me, not me.

Low hangs the moon, it rose late,   75
It is lagging—O I think it is heavy with love, with love.

O madly the sea pushes upon the land,
With love, with love.

O night! do I not see my love fluttering out among the breakers?
What is that little black thing I see there in the white?   80

Loud! loud! loud!
Loud I call to you, my love!
High and clear I shoot my voice over the waves,
Surely you must know who is here, is here,
You must know who I am, my love.   85

Low-hanging moon!
What is that dusky spot in your brown yellow?
O it is the shape, the shape of my mate!
O moon do not keep her from me any longer.

Land! land! O land!   90
Whichever way I turn, O I think you could give me my mate
    back again if you only would,
For I am almost sure I see her dimly whichever way I look.

O rising stars!
Perhaps the one I want so much will rise, will rise with some
    of you.

O throat! O trembling throat!   95
Sound clearer through the atmosphere!
Pierce the woods, the earth,
Somewhere listening to catch you must be the one I want.

Shake out carols!
Solitary here, the night's carols! 100
Carols of lonesome love! death's carols!
Carols under that lagging, yellow, waning moon!
O under that moon where she droops almost down into the sea!
O reckless despairing carols.

But soft! sink low! 105
Soft! let me just murmur,
And do you wait a moment you husky-nois'd sea,
For somewhere I believe I heard my mate responding to me,
So faint, I must be still, be still to listen,
But not altogether still, for then she might not come immediately 110
to me.

Hither my love!
Here I am! here!
With this just-sustain'd note I announce myself to you,
This gentle call is for you my love, for you.

Do not be decoy'd elsewhere, 115
That is the whistle of the wind, it is not my voice,
That is the fluttering, the fluttering of the spray,
Those are the shadows of leaves.

O darkness! O in vain!
O I am very sick and sorrowful. 120

O brown halo in the sky near the moon, drooping upon the sea!
O troubled reflection in the sea!
O throat! O throbbing heart!
And I singing uselessly, uselessly all the night.

O past! O happy life! O songs of joy! 125
In the air, in the woods, over fields,
Loved! loved! loved! loved! loved!
But my mate no more, no more with me!
We two together no more.

The aria sinking, 130
All else continuing, the stars shining,
The winds blowing, the notes of the bird continuous echoing,
With angry moans the fierce old mother[5] incessantly moaning,
On the sands of Paumanok's shore gray and rustling,

---

[5] The sea.

The yellow half-moon enlarged, sagging down, drooping, the face
    of the sea almost touching,   135
The boy ecstatic, with his bare feet the waves, with his hair the
    atmosphere dallying,
The love in the heart long pent, now loose, now at last tumultu-
    ously bursting,
The aria's meaning, the ears, the soul, swiftly depositing,
The strange tears down the cheeks coursing,
The colloquy[6] there, the trio, each uttering,   140
The undertone, the savage old mother incessantly crying,
To the boy's soul's questions sullenly timing, some drown'd secret
    hissing,
To the outsetting bard.

Demon or bird! (said the boy's soul,)
Is it indeed toward your mate you sing? or is it really to me?   145
For I, that was a child, my tongue's use sleeping, now I have
    heard you,
Now in a moment I know what I am for, I awake,
And already a thousand singers, a thousand songs, clearer, louder
    and more sorrowful than yours,
A thousand warbling echoes have started to life within me, never
    to die.

O you singer solitary, singing by yourself, projecting me,   150
O solitary me listening, never more shall I cease perpetuating
    you,
Never more shall I escape, never more the reverberations,
Never more the cries of unsatisfied love be absent from me,
Never again leave me to be the peaceful child I was before what
    there in the night,
By the sea under the yellow and sagging moon,   155
The messenger there arous'd, the fire, the sweet hell within,
The unknown want, the destiny of me.

O give me the clew! (it lurks in the night here somewhere,)
O if I am to have so much, let me have more!

A word then, (for I will conquer it,)   160
The word final, superior to all,
Subtle, sent up—what is it?—I listen;
Are you whispering it, and have been all the time, you sea-
    waves?
Is that it from your liquid rims and wet sands?

[6] Discourse.

Whereto answering, the sea,   165
Delaying not, hurrying not,
Whisper'd me through the night, and very plainly before day-
    break,
Lisp'd to me the low and delicious word death,
And again death, death, death, death,
Hissing melodious, neither like the bird nor like my arous'd child's
    heart,   170
But edging near as privately for me rustling at my feet,
Creeping thence steadily up to my ears and laving me softly all
    over,
Death, death, death, death, death.

Which I do not forget,
But fuse the song of my dusky demon and brother,   175
That he sang to me in the moonlight on Paumanok's gray beach,
With the thousand responsive songs at random,
My own songs awaked from that hour,
And with them the key, the word up from the waves,
The word of the sweetest song and all songs,   180
That strong and delicious word which, creeping to my feet,
(Or like some old crone rocking the cradle, swathed in sweet
    garments, bending aside,)
The sea whisper'd me.

CHAPTER 5

Elements of Technique

Images: The Primary Vision

An *image* is an imitation. The word derives from the Latin *imago*, meaning a copy or a likeness. A painting is an image, and so is a statue. A poem, too, is an image. It is an imitation of life, with the poet's perceptions made accessible to the perceptions of others by means of the sensual responses shared by all humans.

Because it is an imitation, an *image* is also an appeal to the senses. The painter constructs his imitation almost entirely in terms of the sense of sight. He creates a *visual image* that makes his conception permanently accessible to the perceptions of others. The sculptor appeals to the senses of sight and touch, creating both visual and *tactile images*. The musician appeals primarily to the sense of hearing, creating *auditory images*. Because the poet uses language as his medium, he may extend his use of imagery further than the painter, the sculptor, or the musician. In addition to visual, tactile, and auditory imagery, he may also use imagery that appeals to our senses of smell and taste. Whenever we discover such an appeal in a poem we may speak of the imagery involved. As a rule, however, the two most common images found in poems are those of sound and sight. *Auditory imagery* is important in poetry because sound is a necessary part of the spoken word. *Visual imagery* is still more important because it is through the eyes that we as humans take in the largest portion of our knowledge of the world.

Occasionally a poet will create the effect of a poem almost exclusively with visual imagery.

The Red Wheelbarrow
William Carlos Williams (1883–1963)

so much depends
upon

a red wheel
barrow

>   glazed with rain
>   water
>
>   beside the white
>   chickens.   8

This poem is almost, but not quite, a painting in words. Putting aside for the moment the provocative beginning, "so much depends upon . . ." we are struck by the almost exclusively visual nature of the images that follow. Williams has carefully excluded a number of sensory experiences that might have given the images qualities less like those of a painting and more like those of most poems. He uses no words that evoke the sounds of the chickens as they go clucking about their business (perhaps they are making no sounds) or the sound of the rain as it drums upon the wheelbarrow and drips from its edges (perhaps it has stopped raining). He evokes no smell of the barnyard or of the ozone that accompanies the rain. The limitations of the imagery suggest an impressionistic painting: the emphasis is on bright color and the arrangement of forms. Yet the poem is clearly something different from a painting. Although Williams has told us there are chickens present, he has not told us how many, as the painter must do, or what kind they are (except that they are white) or even whether they are hens or roosters. He has told us that the wheelbarrow is red, but beyond that he has not specified its size or shape or whether it is wooden or metal.

Images in poetry are almost always more suggestive than explicit, springing to life when the words expand in the mind of the reader. The ability to read poetry well involves the ability to respond actively to the signals verbalized by the poet. We have seen chickens, wheelbarrows, and rain. The poet gives us the signals that require us to put these elements together in a composition. But why? What does it mean? Williams has introduced the images with the statement that so much depends upon them, but what exactly does that statement mean? Does the poem suggest that as humans we are in some way dependent upon our ability to visualize the world about us? To transmit that vision to others? Whatever the poem means, it makes us aware, as all good art does, that our responses to the world are changed when we view it through the eyes of another. We see things then that we hadn't seen before. The world becomes for us not simply what we make of it in our own direct contact with it; it becomes also a world shaped for us in the images, or the "imitations," of others.

What the poet sees is not necessarily what we would see if we were standing in his place. We might look long and intently at a barnyard without seeing it the way that Williams asks us to see it in his poem. The life that the poet imitates is partly the life external to his mental processes, but it is also partly the life that goes on within his head. An image may spring from a direct sensory experience (Williams may have seen the chickens, the wheelbarrow, and the rain), or it may be uncovered from the storehouse of the poet's mind (Williams may have only been thinking about those things). The word *imagination* is related to the word *image* in this important fundamental sense. The poet's imagination is his ability to imitate life both externally, as it appears to others, and internally, as he conceives of it within the recesses of his mind. As readers who reconstitute the images from the words of the poem, we share in the imaginative processes of the poet. Our minds are opened and enlightened as his has been. Our imaginations are enlivened and our lives enriched through contact with a mental process different from our own, and perhaps deeper and richer.

Within the longer poem that follows the imagery is still heavily visual.

A Flock of Guinea Hens Seen from a Car

Eudora Welty (1909–)

The lute and the pear are your half sisters,
The mackerel moon a full first cousin,
And you were born to appear seemly, even when running on
    guinea legs,
As maiden-formed, as single-minded as raindrops,
Ellipses, small homebodies of great orbits (little knots
    at the back like apron strings),   5
Perfected, sealed off, engraved like a dozen perfect
    consciences,
As egglike as the eggs you know best, triumphantly
    speckled . . .
But fast!
Side-eyed with emancipation, no more lost than a string
    of pearls are lost from one another,
You cross the road in the teeth of Pontiacs   10
As over a threshold, into waving, gregarious grasses,
Welcome wherever you go—the Guinea Sisters.

Bobbins with the threads of innumerable visits behind you,
As light on your feet
As the daughters[1] of Mr. Barrett of Wimpole Street,   15
Do you ever wonder where Africa has fled?

---

[1] The poet Elizabeth Barrett Browning and her sisters.

Is the strangeness of your origins packed tight in those
    little nutmeg heads, so ceremonious,
        partly naked?
Is there time to ask each other what became of the family
    wings?

Do you dream?
Princess of Dapple,   20
Princess of Moonlight,
Princess of Conch,
Princess of Guinealand,
Though you roost in the care of S. Thomas Truly, Rt. 1
(There went his mailbox flying by),   25
The whole world knows you've never yet given up the secret
    of where you've hidden your nests.

Which images come closest to describing the scene as it might appear to any objective viewer? Which images seem most to belong to the subjective reaction of the poet herself? Consider the first two lines:

The lute and the pear are your half sisters,
The mackerel moon a full first cousin, . . .

Although there are no lutes or pears literally present in the scene the poet describes, as seen from her car, the mental images of lutes and pears share a likeness of shape that makes them "half sisters" to the guinea hens; although we as readers may have no clear idea of the shape of guinea hens before we read this line, we begin to see a picture as we complete it. With the introduction of the mackerel moon in the second line we begin to understand something of the coloration of the hens (they are barred like a "mackerel moon"). The images are both external and internal at the same time. The poet has seen what we would see but has forced us to perceive it also in the way that it appears in her mind. Do other images in the poem also operate in this way, requiring us to respond to what the poet has seen and also to what she has been reminded of?

Since in fact we rarely stand in the place where the poet has stood, we are often in our reading confronted with instances wherein we cannot be certain which elements of a poem possessed an objective existence and which were manufactured by the poet. Yet by a curious paradox the distinction between objective reality and subjective reality that existed before the creation of the poem ceases to be of serious importance once the poem has come into being. Once an image has been fixed in a poem by the imagination of the poet it possesses the same artistic reality as any other image in the poem. The lute and the pear and the guinea hens share forever the relationship created by the poet. If she has used her imagination well, these images will become a part of our experience (perhaps even a larger part than real lutes, real pears, or real guinea hens).

The effect of imagery is to fix a perceptual moment, taking it outside of time and giving it the lasting quality of art. All experiences available to our senses are subject to change—except the images of art.

In the following poem the poet takes an experience common in the country and gives it an existence more memorable to many people than the similar experiences they themselves have had. Long after one has forgotten what it felt like—or might have felt like—to pick apples, reading this poem can make the experience come to life again.

After Apple-Picking

Robert Frost   (1874–1963)

My long two-pointed ladder's sticking through a tree
Toward heaven still,
And there's a barrel that I didn't fill
Beside it, and there may be two or three
Apples I didn't pick upon some bough.   5
But I am done with apple-picking now.
Essence of winter sleep is on the night,
The scent of apples: I am drowsing off.
I cannot rub the strangeness from my sight
I got from looking through a pane of glass   10
I skimmed this morning from the drinking trough
And held against the world of hoary grass.
It melted, and I let it fall and break.
But I was well
Upon my way to sleep before it fell,   15
And I could tell
What form my dreaming was about to take.
Magnified apples appear and disappear,
Stem end and blossom end,
And every fleck of russet showing clear.   20
My instep arch not only keeps the ache;
It keeps the pressure of a ladder-round.
I feel the ladder sway as the boughs bend.
And I keep hearing from the cellar bin
The rumbling sound   25
Of load on load of apples coming in.
For I have had too much
Of apple-picking: I am overtired

Of the great harvest I myself desired.
There were ten thousand thousand fruit to touch,   30
Cherish in hand, lift down, and not let fall.
For all
That struck the earth,
No matter if not bruised or spiked with stubble,
Went surely to the cider-apple heap   35
As of no worth.
One can see what will trouble
This sleep of mine, whatever sleep it is.
Were he not gone,
The woodchuck could say whether it's like his   40
Long sleep, as I describe its coming on,
Or just some human sleep.

Again, the greater part of the imagery is visual. Here, however, there are also some effective tactile images, or appeals to the sense of touch. Where are they? Note also how we are invited to hear "from the cellar bin / The rumbling sound / Of load on load of apples coming in."

Frost derives his imagery almost exclusively from the immediate experience, straying only so far as a dream about apples and a question whether the woodchuck's hibernating sleep is like the sleep the narrator feels "coming on." In "On the Ice Islands" William Cowper creates shining images of icebergs but derives much of the imagery from sources far removed from the immediate visual subject.

On the Ice Islands Seen Floating in the German Ocean

William Cowper   (1731–1800)

What portents, from what distant region, ride,
Unseen till now in ours, the astonished tide?
In ages past, old Proteus,[1] with his droves
Of sea-calves, sought the mountains and the groves:
But now, descending whence of late they stood,   5
Themselves the mountains seem to rove the flood.
Dire times were they, full-charged with human woes;
And these, scarce less calamitous than those.
What view we now? More wondrous still! Behold!
Like burnished brass they shine, or beaten gold;   10
And all around the pearl's pure splendour show,
And all around the ruby's fiery glow.
Come they from India? where the burning earth,
All-bounteous, gives her richest treasures birth;

[1] A sea god.

And where the costly gems, that beam around   15
The brows of mightiest potentates, are found?
No. Never such a countless dazzling store
Had left unseen the Ganges' peopled shore.
Rapacious hands, and ever-watchful eyes,
Should sooner far have marked and seized the prize.   20
Whence sprang they then? Ejected have they come
From Vesuvius', or from Ætna's[2] burning womb?
Thus shine they self-illumed, or but display
The borrowed splendours of a cloudless day?
With borrowed beams they shine. The gales that breathe   25
Now land-ward, and the current's force beneath,
Have borne them nearer: and the nearer sight,
Advantaged more, contemplates them aright.
Their lofty summits, crested high, they show,
With mingled sleet and long-incumbent snow.   30
The rest is ice. Far hence, where, most severe,
Bleak winter well-nigh saddens all the year,
Their infant growth began. He bade arise
Their uncouth forms, portentous in our eyes.
Oft as, dissolved by transient suns, the snow   35
Left the tall cliff, to join the flood below,
He caught and curdled, with a freezing blast,
The current, ere it reached the boundless waste.
By slow degrees uprose the wondrous pile,
And long-successive ages rolled the while;   40
Till, ceaseless in its growth, it claimed to stand
Tall as its rival mountains on the land.
Thus stood—and, unremovable by skill
Or force of man, had stood the structure still;
But that, tho' firmly fixt, supplanted yet   45
By pressure of its own enormous weight,
It left the shelving beach—and, with a sound
That shook the bellowing waves and rocks around,
Self-launched, and swiftly, to the briny wave,
As if instinct with strong desire to lave,[3]   50
Down went the ponderous mass. So bards of old,
How Delos[4] swam the Ægean deep, have told.
But not of ice was Delos. Delos bore
Herb, fruit, and flower. She, crowned with laurel, wore,
E'en under wintry skies, a summer smile;   55

[2] Italian volcanoes.
[3] Bathe.
[4] An island sacred to Apollo; the legendary land of his birth.

And Delos was Apollo's favorite isle.
But, horrid wanderers of the deep, to you
He deems Cimmerian[5] darkness only due.
Your hated birth he deigned not to survey,
But, scornful, turned his glorious eyes away.   60
Hence! Seek your home; no longer rashly dare
The darts of Phoebus,[6] and a softer air;
Lest ye regret, too late, your native coast,
In no congenial gulf for ever lost!

[5] Of the mythical people described by Homer as living in mist and darkness.
[6] Apollo.

List the images that you consider to be not immediately present. Some
serve a descriptive purpose: they help to clarify the picture of the icebergs. What purposes are served by the others?

On Seeing the Elgin Marbles

John Keats   (1795–1821)

My spirit is too weak—mortality
   Weighs heavily on me like unwilling sleep,
   And each imagined pinnacle and steep
Of godlike hardship tells me I must die   4
Like a sick eagle looking at the sky.
   Yet 'tis a gentle luxury to weep
   That I have not the cloudy winds to keep
Fresh for the opening of the morning's eye.   8
Such dim-conceivèd glories of the brain
   Bring round the heart an undescribable feud;
So do these wonders a most dizzy pain,
   That mingles Grecian grandeur with the rude   12
Wasting of old Time, with a billowy main,
   A sun, a shadow of a magnitude.

The Elgin Marbles are a collection of statuary and friezes from the
Parthenon at Athens, brought to England by Lord Elgin at the beginning
of the nineteenth century and put on public display in the British Museum. It might seem odd at first sight that Keats chose to write a poem
about them without ever giving any clear idea what they look like. But is
it odd? Is the subject the marbles themselves or the poet's emotions on
seeing them, or his thoughts about something else? When does he actually begin talking about the marbles? Identify the images. Is the eagle
important as an eagle or as the representation of an idea? Does "mortality / Weighs heavily on me" convey an image? If it does, what is its ef-

fect? What are we to make of the collection of images at the end: "a billowy main, / A sun, a shadow of a magnitude"?

Much visual imagery is essentially *static*: the pictures stand suspended in time, frozen in inactivity like paintings or photographs. In *kinetic imagery* a sense of motion is important, as it is in the movies, first called "motion pictures," or cinema (*cinema* and *kinetic* come from the same Greek root). Strong kinetic imagery of approaching darkness is essential to the success of the following poem.

You, Andrew Marvell
Archibald MacLeish   (1892–   )

And here face down beneath the sun
And here upon earth's noonward height
To feel the always coming on
The always rising of the night: 4

To feel creep up the curving east
The earthy chill of dusk and slow
Upon those under lands the vast
And ever climbing shadow grow   8

And strange at Ecbatan[1] the trees
Take leaf by leaf the evening strange
The flooding dark about their knees
The mountains over Persia change   12

And now at Kermanshah the gate
Dark empty and the withered grass
And through the twilight now the late
Few travelers in the westward pass   16

And Baghdad darken and the bridge
Across the silent river gone
And through Arabia the edge
Of evening widen and steal on   20

And deepen on Palmyra's street
The wheel rut in the ruined stone
And Lebanon fade out and Crete
High through the clouds and overblown   24

And over Sicily the air
Still flashing with the landward gulls

---

[1] From Ecbatan, a city in ancient Persia, to Spain and Africa, the poet's mind moves westward with the sun, passing over sites of ancient civilizations.

And loom and slowly disappear
The sails above the shadowy hulls   28

And Spain go under and the shore
Of Africa the gilded sand
And evening vanish and no more
The low pale light across that land   32

Nor now the long light on the sea:

And here face downward in the sun
To feel how swift how secretly
The shadow of the night comes on . . .   36

Although kinetic imagery is not as insistent in the following poem as
it is in "You, Andrew Marvell," in a number of places it is important.

Mr. Flood's Party
Edwin Arlington Robinson (1869–1935)

Old Eben Flood, climbing alone one night
Over the hill between the town below
And the forsaken upland hermitage
That held as much as he should ever know   4
On earth again of home, paused warily.
The road was his with not a native near;
And Eben, having leisure, said aloud,
For no man else in Tilbury Town to hear: 8

"Well, Mr. Flood, we have the harvest moon
Again, and we may not have many more;
The bird is on the wing, the poet[1] says,
And you and I have said it here before.   12
Drink to the bird." He raised up to the light
The jug that he had gone so far to fill,
And answered huskily: "Well, Mr. Flood,
Since you propose it, I believe I will."   16

Alone, as if enduring to the end
A valiant armor of scarred hopes outworn,
He stood there in the middle of the road
Like Roland's[2] ghost winding a silent horn.   20
Below him, in the town among the trees,

---

[1] Edward Fitzgerald, in *The Rubáiyát of Omar Khayyâm*: "Come, fill the Cup, and in the Fire of Spring/Your Winter-garment of Repentence fling:/The Bird of Time has but a little way/To flutter— and the Bird is on the wing."
[2] A romantic hero killed at Roncesvalles in 778; Winding: blowing.

Where friends of other days had honored him,
A phantom salutation of the dead
Rang thinly till old Eben's eyes were dim.   24

Then, as a mother lays her sleeping child
Down tenderly, fearing it may awake,
He set the jug down slowly at his feet
With trembling care, knowing that most things break;   28
And only when assured that on firm earth
It stood, as the uncertain lives of men
Assuredly did not, he paced away,
And with his hand extended paused again: 32

"Well, Mr. Flood, we have not met like this
In a long time; and many a change has come
To both of us, I fear, since last it was
We had a drop together. Welcome home!"   36
Convivially returning with himself,
Again he raised the jug up to the light;
And with an acquiescent quaver said:
"Well, Mr. Flood, if you insist, I might.   40

"Only a very little, Mr. Flood—
For auld lang syne. No more, sir; that will do."
So, for the time, apparently it did,
And Eben evidently thought so too;   44
For soon amid the silver loneliness
Of night he lifted up his voice and sang,
Secure, with only two moons listening,
Until the whole harmonious landscape rang—   48

"For auld lang syne." The weary throat gave out,
The last word wavered, and the song was done.
He raised again the jug regretfully
And shook his head, and was again alone.   52
There was not much that was ahead of him,
And there was nothing in the town below—
Where strangers would have shut the many doors
That many friends had opened long ago.   56

List some of the most important kinetic images. How much do they
contribute to the total success of the poem?

Consider the uses and effects of the various kinds of imagery in the
following poems.

The Waterfall

Henry Vaughan   (1622–1695)

With what deep murmurs through time's silent stealth
Doth thy transparent, cool and watery wealth
      Here flowing fall,
      And chide, and call,
As if his liquid, loose retinue stayed   5
Lingering, and were of this steep place afraid,
      The common pass
      Where, clear as glass,
      All must descend
      Not to an end: 10
But quickened by this deep and rocky grave,
Rise to a longer course more bright and brave.
Dear stream! dear bank, where often I
Have sat, and pleased my pensive eye,
Why, since each drop of thy quick[1] store   15
Runs thither, whence it flowed before,
Should poor souls fear a shade or night,
Who came sure from a sea of light?
Or since those drops are all sent back
So sure to thee, that none doth lack,   20
Why should frail flesh doubt any more
That what God takes, He'll not restore?
O useful element and clear!
My sacred wash and cleanser[2] here,
My first consigner unto those   25
Fountains of life, where the lamb goes?
What sublime truths, and wholesome themes,
Lodge in thy mystical, deep streams!
Such as dull man can never find
Unless that Spirit lead his mind,   30
Which first upon thy face did move,
And hatched all with his quickening love.
As this loud brook's incessant fall
In streaming rings restagnates all,
Which reach by course the bank, and then   35
Are no more seen, just so pass men.

[1] Living.
[2] By baptism.

O my invisible estate,
My glorious liberty, still late!
Thou art the channel my soul seeks,
Not this with cataracts and creeks.   40

The Conspirators

Frederic Prokosch (1908–   )

And if the dead, and the dead
Of spirit now join, and in their horrifying ritual
Proceed till at last with oriental grace
End their concluding dance with the candles guttering,
The cymbals sobbing, the wind harassing the curtains,   5
The chill from the flood embracing the golden stairway.
The scent devoured and the bowls blown clean of incense:

Ah then, farewell, sweet northern music;
No longer the flight of the mind across the continents,
The dazzling flight of our words across the tempestuous   10
Black, or the firelit recital of a distant battle.

No. All that we loved is lost, if the intricate
Languor of recollected centuries
Descends in its terrible sweetness on our limbs.
No shot will echo; no fire; no agonizing   15
Cry will resound in the city's thickets: only,
The ivy falling gently across the bridges,
The larches piercing the roofs, the reclining steeples,
The cellars rich with the agony of the reptiles,
The contemplative worms, the victorious rodents,   20
And at last, the climax entrancingly serene,
The inconclusive note drowned on the ascendant:
Our lovely shapes in marble still shine through the greenery,
Our exquisite silver bones still glide with the glaciers
That split our familiar hills, still fall with the avalanche   25
And weaving their vast wing's thunder over the Indies
The birds, the birds, sob for the time of man.

Morning Song

Sylvia Plath (1932–1963)

Love set you going like a fat gold watch.
The midwife slapped your footsoles, and your bald cry
Took its place among the elements.

Our voices echo, magnifying your arrival. New statue.
In a drafty museum, your nakedness   5
Shadows our safety. We stand round blankly as walls.

I'm no more your mother
Than the cloud that distils a mirror to reflect its own slow
Effacement at the wind's hand.

All night your moth-breath   10
Flickers among the flat pink roses. I wake to listen:
A far sea moves in my ear.

One cry, and I stumble from bed, cow-heavy and floral
In my Victorian nightgown.
Your mouth opens clean as a cat's. The window square   15

Whitens and swallows its dull stars. And now you try
Your handful of notes;
The clear vowels rise like balloons.

The Bear on the Delhi Road

Earle Birney   (1904–   )

Unreal   tall as a myth
by the road the Himalayan bear
is beating the brilliant air
with his crooked arms
About him two men   bare   5
spindly as locusts   leap

One pulls on a ring
in the great soft nose   His mate
flicks   flicks with a stick
up at the rolling eyes   10

They have not led him here
down from the fabulous hills
to this bald alien plain
and the clamorous world   to kill
but simply to teach him to dance   15

They are peaceful both   these spare
men of Kashmir   and the bear
alive is their living   too
If   far on the Delhi way
around him galvanic they dance   20
it is merely to wear   wear

from his shaggy body the tranced
wish forever to stay
only an ambling bear
four-footed in berries   25

It is no more joyous for them
in this hot dust to prance
out of reach of the praying claws
sharpened to paw for ants
in the shadows of deodars   30
It is not easy to free
myth from reality
or rear this fellow up
to lurch   lurch with them
in the tranced dancing of men   35

Carentan O Carentan[1]

Louis Simpson   (1923–   )

Trees in the old days used to stand
And shape a shady lane
Where lovers wandered hand in hand
Who came from Carentan.   4

This was the shining green canal
Where we came two by two
Walking at combat-interval.
Such trees we never knew.   8

The day was early June, the ground
Was soft and bright with dew.
Far away the guns did sound,
But here the sky was blue.   12

The sky was blue, but there a smoke
Hung still above the sea
Where the ships together spoke
To towns we could not see.   16

Could you have seen us through a glass
You would have said a walk
Of farmers out to turn the grass,
Each with his own hay-fork.   20

The watchers in their leopard suits[2]
Waited till it was time,

[1] A French port town, the site of a severe battle on June 8–12, 1944, a few days after D-Day.
[2] Camouflage uniforms.

And aimed between the belt and boot
And let the barrel climb.   24

I must lie down at once, there is
A hammer at my knee.
And call it death or cowardice,
Don't count again on me.   28

Everything's all right, Mother,
Everyone gets the same
At one time or another.
It's all in the game.   32

I never strolled, nor ever shall,
Down such a leafy lane.
I never drank in a canal,
Nor ever shall again.   36

There is a whistling in the leaves
And it is not the wind,
The twigs are falling from the knives
That cut men to the ground.   40

Tell me, Master-Sergeant,
The way to turn and shoot.
But the Sergeant's silent
That taught me how to do it.   44

O Captain, show us quickly
Our place upon the map.
But the Captain's sickly
And taking a long nap.   48

Lieutenant, what's my duty,
My place in the platoon?
He too's a sleeping beauty,
Charmed by that strange tune.   52

Carentan O Carentan
Before we met with you
We never yet had lost a man
Or known what death could do.   56

Heat

H. D. [Hilda Doolittle]   (1886–1961)

O wind, rend open the heat,
    cut apart the heat,
    rend it to tatters.

Fruit cannot drop
through this thick air—   5
fruit cannot fall into heat
that presses up and blunts
the points of pears
and rounds the grapes.

Cut the heat—   10
plough through it,
turning it on either side
of your path.

The Cool Web

Robert Graves (1895–)

Children are dumb to say how hot the day is,
How hot the scent is of the summer rose,
How dreadful the black wastes of evening sky,
How dreadful the tall soldiers drumming by.   4

But we have speech, to chill the angry day,
And speech, to dull the rose's cruel scent.
We spell away the overhanging night,
We spell away the soldiers and the fright.   8

There's a cool web of language winds us in,
Retreat from too much joy or too much fear:
We grow sea-green at last and coldly die
In brininess and volubility.   12

But if we let our tongues lose self-possession,
Throwing off language and its watery clasp
Before our death, instead of when death comes,
Facing the wide glare of the children's day,   16
Facing the rose, the dark sky and the drums
We shall go mad no doubt and die that way.

Metaphor: The Double Vision

A *metaphor* is an implied comparison between objects that are in important respects dissimilar. It is a form of imagery and is therefore, like an
image, rooted in a sensual perception that is usually visual.

In its simple form an image carries no metaphor. The poet implies no
comparison, forces no double response. Complex images, however, tend
toward metaphor. Suggesting a likeness between two essentially unlike

objects, or between a physical object and an abstraction, the poet creates a double vision that serves as one of the chief ingredients of most successful poems.

There Is a Garden in Her Face

Thomas Campion (1567–1620)

There is a garden in her face,
Where roses and white lillies grow;
   A heavenly paradise is that place,   3
Wherein all pleasant fruits do flow.
   There cherries grow, which none may buy
   Till "Cherry ripe" themselves do cry.[1]   6

Those cherries fairly do enclose
Of orient pearl a double row,
   Which when her lovely laughter shows,   9
They look like rosebuds filled with snow.
   Yet them nor peer nor prince can buy,
   Till "Cherry ripe" themselves do cry.   12

Her eyes like angels watch them still;
Her brows like bended bows do stand,
   Threatening with piercing frowns to kill   15
All that attempt with eye or hand
   Those sacred cherries to come nigh,
   Till "Cherry ripe" themselves do cry.   18

[1] Until they cry out like street vendors, announcing goods for sale.

The controlling metaphor in this poem implies a comparison between a girl's face and a garden. From the double vision of garden and face, we extract qualities shared by both, so that we see (although the poet has not stated) the elements of a face and the elements of roses, lilies, and cherries that may reasonably be compared. Through the shorthand of metaphor, we perceive two images simultaneously and also perceive the relationship between the two.

A *simile* is a stated comparison, usually using *like* and *as*, between objects that are in important respects dissimilar. Had Campion chosen to make his garden comparisions in the form of similes he would have found metrical ways to say "her complexion is like roses and lilies" and "her lips are like cherries." Indeed, he did choose to write some of the poem in simile form: "Her eyes like angels" and "Her brows like bended bows."

The simile is really a more explicit kind of metaphor, one that states what the metaphor merely implies. Both are double visions, making comparisons where none are immediately obvious.

Dissimilarity is important in the comparison made by either metaphor or simile. When we say of a girl that "Her lips are like her sister's" and "She has her mother's eyes," we have stated one comparison and implied another, but we have created neither simile nor metaphor. The poetic effect of both comes from the surprise of seeing an unexpected resemblance. Some metaphors have become *conventional* through use, however, and carry no great surprise; others are *unconventional*, and remain surprising in their originality.

About an Excavation

Charles Reznikoff (1894–   )

About an excavation
a flock of bright red lanterns
has settled.   3

This poem illustrates admirably the essential double vision of metaphor. We see a group of red lanterns, but we also see a flock of birds. The poem is a record of that isolated double perception. If the perception had been single, the poet might have written:

About an excavation
a flock of birds
has settled.

Or, alternatively:

About an excavation
a number of bright red lanterns
have been placed.

Each of these revisions presents an image. Reznikoff's poem implies a comparison by presenting two images simultaneously. The metaphor in this poem is less conventional than the metaphors in the Campion poem. Do you find the metaphors in both poems successful?

Because the poet shares with other humans the ability to perceive externally and internally at the same time, images in poetry have a way of turning into metaphors. The poet compares what he sees to what he has seen, what exists to what he imagines could exist, what is real to what he believes to be ideal. Looking back at those poems presented under the heading "Images: The Primary Vision" one could discover a number of lines to illustrate this tendency. Robert Graves' "The Cool Web," for example, mixes the single vision of hot days, summer roses, evening skies, and tall soldiers with the more complicated double vision of "a cool web of language" to make a statement about the protective nature of verbal communication. Sylvia Plath's "Morning Song" begins with a vision of a baby that has been set "going like a fat gold watch" and develops a number of its later images through the same double vision of metaphor. The poem that follows is a particularly interesting example of how the single image tends to expand into a double vision.

Always Begin Where You Are

Thomas Hornsby Ferril (1896–)

Always begin right here where you are
And work out from here:
If adrift, feel the feel of the oar in the oarlock first,
If saddling a horse let your right knee slug   4
The belly of the horse like an uppercut,
Then cinch his suck,
Then mount and ride away
To any dream deserving the sensible world.   8

None of the images of rowing or riding, taken by themselves, goes far toward implying a comparison. Taken side by side, they imply a comparison with each other (rowing is like riding), but the poet wants us to see more than that. "Always begin right here where you are," he says, "And work out from here." The images, in other words, are metaphoric examples for any endeavor. By the time we finish the poem, we know that the horse we "mount and ride away / To any dream deserving the sensible world" is no physical horse we can find in any pasture.

A metaphor always has two terms. Something is being compared to something else. Yet sometimes the second term has been left vague, as when Ferril requires the reader to imagine other activities to compare to rowing and riding. Sometimes both terms are clear, but the likeness is obscure, as perhaps in the baby's "moth-breath" of Plath's "Morning Song."

A *riddle* is a form of metaphor in which one term is expressed and the other left for guessing.

Consider the following children's riddle:

Twenty white horses on a red hill:
Now they prance,
Now they dance,
Now they stand still.

A reader adept at riddles will sense a clue in the unlikely "red hill." What may be compared to white horses on a red hill? What moves and stands still "Now"? The answer is teeth and gums. The child's twenty teeth (the twenty "milk teeth" before the molars arrive) move as he speaks the riddle and stand still when he ceases speaking. Poets do not often speak in riddles, but at times they approach the riddle form.

The Haunted Palace

Edgar Allan Poe   (1809–1849)

In the greenest of our valleys
  By good angels tenanted,
Once a fair and stately palace—
  Radiant palace—reared its head.   4
In the monarch Thought's dominion—
  It stood there!
Never seraph spread a pinion
  Over fabric half so fair!   8

Banners yellow, glorious, golden,
  On its roof did float and flow,
(This—all this—was in the olden
  Time long ago,)   12
And every gentle air that dallied,
  In that sweet day,
Along the ramparts plumed and pallid,
  A wingéd odor went away.   16

Wanderers in that happy valley,
  Through two luminous windows, saw
Spirits moving musically,
  To a lute's well-tuned law,   20
Round about a throne where, sitting,
  Porphyrogene,[1]
In state his glory well befitting,
  The ruler of the realm was seen.   24

And all with pearl and ruby glowing
  Was the fair palace door,
Through which came flowing, flowing, flowing,
  And sparkling evermore,   28
A troop of Echoes, whose sweet duty
  Was but to sing,
In voices of surpassing beauty,
  The wit and wisdom of their king.   32

But evil things, in robes of sorrow,
  Assailed the monarch's high estate.

[1] A Greek-derived name, "born to the purple," or to royalty.

> (Ah, let us mourn!—for never morrow
>   Shall dawn upon him desolate!)   36
> And round about his home the glory
>   That blushed and bloomed,
> Is but a dim-remembered story
>   Of the old time entombed.   40
>
> And travellers, now, within that valley,
>   Through the red-litten windows see
> Vast forms, that move fantastically
>   To a discordant melody,   44
> While, like a ghastly rapid river,
>   Through the pale door
> A hideous throng rush out forever
>   And laugh—but smile no more.   48

Poe inserted this poem into his story "The Fall of the House of Usher"
as a way of underlining one of the main themes. Readers sometimes miss
the point, for although they respond well enough to the main imagery
they fail to see the intended metaphoric comparison. For such readers
the poem remains an unperceived and unsolved riddle. The palace is, of
course, a human head. The banners are hair, the windows eyes, the door
the mouth, and so on. The most important description is not of a palace
but of insanity.

A *personification* is a metaphor that gives human qualities to something
not human. Personification serves frequently as a way of providing objective existence for an abstraction.

Since There's No Help, Come Let Us Kiss and Part

Michael Drayton   (1563–1631)

> Since there's no help, come let us kiss and part;
> Nay, I have done, you get no more of me,
> And I am glad, yea, glad with all my heart
> That thus so cleanly I myself can free;   4
> Shake hands for ever, cancel all our vows,
> And when we meet any time again,
> Be it not seen in either of our brows
> That we one jot of former love retain.   8
> Now at the last gasp of Love's latest breath,
> When, his pulse failing, Passion speechless lies,
> When Faith is kneeling by his bed of death,
> And Innocence is closing up his eyes,   12
>   Now if thou wouldst, when all have given him over,
>   From death to life thou mightst him yet recover.   14

Here, in lines 9 through 12, the abstract idea that love is not quite at an end is made concrete by a series of personifications grouped to create a deathbed scene. Faith and innocence attend like humans at the side of dying love. Unfortunately, they have not the power, as the last line makes clear, of the real person to whom the lines are addressed. Personifications are common in poetry as they are in everyday language. When we say that Justice is blind or Fate is cruel we have personified those two abstractions. Even the least poetic among us sometimes see the sun as smiling or dark clouds as frowning.

An *extended metaphor* is a metaphor expanded at length. The fundamental comparison behind "Justice is blind" could easily be extended by creating a set of images running through several sentences. The author of the following poem has created an extended metaphor by elaborating a set of images over the first 16 lines and then suggesting a set of parallels in the rest of the poem.

Calenture[1]

Alastair Reid (1926–)

He never lives to tell,
but other men bring back the tale
of how, after days of gazing at the sea
unfolding itself incessantly and greenly—
hillsides of water crested with clouds of foam—   5
heavy with a fading dream of home,
he climbs aloft one morning and, looking down,
cries out at seeing a different green,
farms, woods, grasslands, an extending plain,
hazy meadows, a long tree-fledged horizon,   10
swallows flashing in the halcyon sun,
his ship riding in deep rippling grain,
the road well-known to him, the house, the garden,
figures at the gate, till, dazed by his passion,
he suddenly climbs down and begins to run.   15
Stunned by his joy, the others watch him drown.

Such calenture, they say,
is not unknown in lovers long at sea,

yet such a like fever did she make in me,
this green-leaved summer morning, that I,   20
seeing her confirm a wish made lovingly,
felt gate, trees, grass, birds, garden glimmer over,

[1]A delirium in which sailors in tropic seas are said to desire to jump into the sea, which they imagine to be green fields.

a ripple cross her face, the sky quiver,
the cropped lawn sway in waves, the house founder,
the light break into flecks, the path shimmer,   25
till, seeing her eyes clear and true at the center,
I walked toward her on the flowering water.

A *mixed metaphor* is usually a mistake, with several physical impossi-
bilities clashing their images together. If we were to write "the web of
fate rolled blindly in its iron groove," we would probably communicate
little beyond an insensitivity to language. Yet mixed metaphors are not
unknown to good poetry. An important element of the metaphoric vision is a sense of how each metaphor relates to the communication of the
rest of the poem: a poet possessing that sense may use fundamentally
different images to support and not undermine one another.

Question

May Swenson   (1919–)

Body my house
my horse my hound
what will I do
when you are fallen

Where will I sleep   5
How will I ride
What will I hunt
Where can I go
without my mount
all eager and quick   10
How will I know
in thicket ahead
is danger or treasure
when Body my good
bright dog is dead   15

How will it be
to lie in the sky
without roof or door
and wind for an eye

With cloud for shift   20
how will I hide?

Within the first seven words the poet tells us that the body is like a
house, a horse, and a hound. Yet she manages to extend these fundamentally unlike images into an affecting and unified whole.

Shine, Perishing Republic

Robinson Jeffers   (1887–1962)

While this America settles in the mould of its vulgarity, heav-
    ily thickening to empire,
And protest, only a bubble in the molten mass, pops and sighs out,
    and the mass hardens,   4

I sadly smiling remember that the flower fades to make fruit, the
    fruit rots to make earth.
Out of the mother; and through the spring exultances, ripeness
    and decadence; and home to the mother.   8

You making haste haste on decay: not blameworthy; life is good,
    be it stubbornly long or suddenly
A mortal splendor: meteors are not needed less than mountains:
    shine, perishing republic.   12

But for my children, I would have them keep their distance from
    the thickening center; corruption
Never has been compulsory, when the cities lie at the monster's
    feet there are left the mountains.   16

And boys, be in nothing so moderate as in love of man, a clever
    servant, insufferable master.
There is the trap that catches noblest spirits, that caught—they
    say—God, when he walked on earth.   20

In this poem, Jeffers wrote the first stanza around a volcanic metaphor, shifted in the second to flowers and fruit, shifted again in the
third to meteors and mountains. Each metaphor is one way of expressing
his vision of America; although the basic image shifts from stanza to
stanza, each has the effect of building upon and clarifying the one that
has gone before.

The double vision of metaphor is allied to the duality fundamental to
all *figurative language:* language that communicates a meaning other than
that conveyed by the literal sense of the words. Although we speak of
roses in a girl's cheeks, we do not mean that she literally has plants
growing out of the side of her face. Similarly, other forms of figurative
language require the reader or listener to maintain a double understanding, balancing what we have said against what we have not said. *Over-
statement,* or *hyperbole* ("hie–PER–bo–lee"), communicates by exaggeration, as when we say: "I've told you a thousand times" but mean we have
said it three or four. In *understatement,* we say much less than we hope
will be understood, as when we say "It will be to your advantage to listen well," meaning some disaster will occur if you don't. When we use

litotes ("lie–TOTE–ees"), we affirm one meaning by negating a contrary one, as when we say we have attended "not a few" movies in our time. Poets may support the primary vision of the image and the double vision of the metaphor by hyperbole, understatement, or litotes, attaching them to the sensory experience of the poem. These figures, however, are generally less important to the total effect than either image or metaphor.

In *metonymy*, one thing stands for another associated with it: we speak of the wishes of "the oval office," but mean the wishes of the president. Metonymy is often ranked in importance with metaphor and simile as one of three primary figures. A subordinate figure, *synecdoche*, makes a part stand for a whole: we speak of "wheels," but mean "automobile." Both are kinds of metaphor, of course, and they are sometimes difficult to keep distinct. Consider, for example, Shakespeare's phrase "rosy lips and cheeks" in the following sonnet:

Let Me Not to the Marriage of True Minds

William Shakespeare (1564–1616)

Let me not to the marriage of true minds
Admit impediments.   Love is not love
Which alters when it alteration finds,
Or bends with the remover to remove: 4
O, no! it is an ever-fixed mark,
That looks on tempests and is never shaken;
It is the star to every wandering bark,
Whose worth's unknown, although his height be taken.   8
Love's not Time's fool, though rosy lips and cheeks
Within his bending sickle's compass come;
Love alters not with his brief hours and weeks,
But bears it out even to the edge of doom.   12
      If this be error, and upon me proved,
      I never writ, nor no man ever loved.

The "rosy lips and cheeks" are a part of the body that Time, personified, cuts down with "his bending sickle": considered in this way, the phrase is an excellent example of synecdoche. But because Time is a metaphor and the action of his sickle metaphoric, we may also suggest that "rosy lips and cheeks" stand for or are associated with youth and health: considered in this way the phrase looks like metonymy. The label is finally not important provided that we understand the metaphoric double vision that operates throughout the poem to underscore its meaning.

The poems that follow in this section have been selected to illustrate some of the possibilities of metaphor.

An Ode: To Himself

Ben Jonson   (1573–1637)

Where dost thou careless lie,
　　Buried in ease and sloth?
Knowledge that sleeps doth die;   3
And this security,
　　It is the common moth
That eats on wits and arts, and oft destroys them both.   6

Are all the Aonian springs
　　Dried up? Lies Thespia[1] waste?
Doth Clarius'[2] harp want strings,   9
That not a nymph now sings?
　　Or droop they, as disgraced
To see their seats and bowers by chattering pies[3] defaced?   12

If hence thy silence be,
　　As 'tis too just a cause,
Let this thought quicken thee: 15
Minds that are great and free,
　　Should not on fortune pause;
'Tis crown enough to virtue still, her own applause.   18

What though the greedy fry[4]
　　Be taken with false baits
Of worded balladry,   21
And think it poesie?
　　They die with their conceits,
And only piteous scorn upon their folly waits.   24

Then take in hand thy lyre,
　　Strike in thy proper strain;
With Japhet's[5] line, aspire   27
Sol's[6] chariot for new fire
　　To give the world again;
Who aided him, will thee, the issue of Jove's brain.   30

And since our dainty age
　　Cannot endure reproof,

---

[1] The Aonian springs and the town of Thespia were both sacred to the muses.
[2] Apollo's (from his place of worship in Claros).
[3] Magpies.
[4] Young fishes.
[5] Iapetus, father of Prometheus, who stole fire from the gods.
[6] The sun's.

Make not thyself a page   33
  To that strumpet, the stage;
    But sing high and aloof,
Safe from the wolf's black jaw, and the dull ass's hoof.   36

The Windhover[1]
TO CHRIST OUR LORD
Gerard Manley Hopkins (1844–1889)

I caught this morning morning's minion,[2] king-
  dom of daylight's dauphin,[3] dapple-dawn-drawn Falcon, in
    his riding
Of the rolling level underneath him steady air, and striding
High there, how he rung upon the rein[4] of a wimpling[5] wing   4
In his ecstasy! then off, off forth on swing,
  As a skate's heel sweeps smooth on a bow-bend: the hurl and
    gliding
  Rebuffed the big wind. My heart in hiding
Stirred for a bird,—the achieve of, the mastery of the thing!   8

Brute beauty and valour and act, oh, air, pride, plume, here
  Buckle! AND the fire that breaks from thee then, a billion
Times told lovelier, more dangerous, O my chevalier![6]

No wonder of it: shéer plód makes plough down sillion[7]   12
Shine, and blue-bleak embers, ah my dear,
  Fall, gall themselves, and gash gold-vermilion.

[1] The kestrel, a bird that can hover against the wind.
[2] Favorite.
[3] Heir to the throne of France.
[4] Like a horse running in rings at the end of a rein.
[5] Rippling.
[6] Christ.
[7] Furrow.

A Red, Red Rose
Robert Burns (1759–1796)

O my Luve's like a red, red rose,
  That's newly sprung in June;
O my Luve's like the melodie
  That's sweetly play'd in tune.—   4

As fair art thou, my bonie lass,
  So deep in luve am I;

And I will luve thee still, my Dear,
    Till a'[1] the seas gang[2] dry.—   8

Till a' the seas gang dry, my Dear,
    And the rocks melt wi' the sun:
I will luve thee still, my Dear,
    While the sands o' life shall run.—   12

And fare thee weel, my only Luve!
    And fare thee weel, a while!
And I will come again, my Luve,
    Tho' it were ten thousand mile!—   16

[1] All.
[2] Go.

She Walks in Beauty

George Gordon, Lord Byron (1788–1824)

I

She walks in Beauty, like the night
    Of cloudless climes and starry skies;
And all that's best of dark and bright
    Meet in her aspect and her eyes:
Thus mellowed to that tender light
    Which Heaven to gaudy day denies.   6

II

One shade the more, one ray the less,
    Had half impaired the nameless grace
Which waves in every raven tress,
    Or softly lightens o'er her face;
Where thoughts serenely sweet express,
    How pure, how dear their dwelling-place.   12

III

And on that cheek, and o'er that brow,
    So soft, so calm, yet eloquent,
The smiles that win, the tints that glow,
    But tell of days in goodness spent,
A mind at peace with all below,
    A heart whose love is innocent!   18

When Daffodils Begin to Peer

William Shakespeare (1564–1616)

When daffodils begin to peer,
  With heigh, the doxy[1] over the dale!
Why, then comes in the sweet o' the year,
  For the red blood reigns in the winter's pale.[2]   4

The white sheet bleaching on the hedge,
  With hey, the sweet birds, O how they sing!
Doth set my pugging[3] tooth on edge,
  For a quart of ale is a dish for a king.   8

The lark, that tirra-lyra chants,
  With heigh, with heigh, the thrush and the jay!
Are summer songs for me and my aunts,[4]
  While we lie tumbling in the hay.   12

[1] Wench.
[2] Paleness; also, area of authority.
[3] Thieving.
[4] Prostitutes.

After Great Pain, a Formal Feeling Comes

Emily Dickinson (1830–1886)

After great pain, a formal feeling comes—
The Nerves sit ceremonious, like Tombs—
The stiff Heart questions was it He, that bore,
And Yesterday, or Centuries before?

The Feet, mechanical, go round—
Of Ground, or Air, or Ought[1]—
A Wooden way
Regardless grown,
A Quartz contentment, like a stone—

This is the Hour of Lead—
Remembered, if outlived,
As Freezing persons, recollect the Snow—
First—Chill—then Stupor—then the letting go—

[1] Nothing; or, perhaps, obligation.

The Force That Through the Green Fuse Drives the Flower

Dylan Thomas   (1914–1953)

The force that through the green fuse drives the flower
Drives my green age; that blasts the roots of trees
Is my destroyer.
And I am dumb to tell the crooked rose
My youth is bent by the same wintry fever.   5

The force that drives the water through the rocks
Drives my red blood; that dries the mouthing streams
Turns mine to wax.
And I am dumb to mouth unto my veins
How at the mountain spring the same mouth sucks.   10

The hand that whirls the water in the pool
Stirs the quicksand; that ropes the blowing wind
Hauls my shroud sail.
And I am dumb to tell the hanging man
How of my clay is made the hangman's lime.   15

The lips of time leech to the fountain head;
Love drips and gathers, but the fallen blood
Shall calm her sores.
And I am dumb to tell a weather's wind
How time has ticked a heaven round the stars.   20

And I am dumb to tell the lover's tomb
How at my sheet goes the same crooked worm.

A Valediction:[1] Forbidding Mourning

John Donne   (1572–1631)

As virtuous men pass mildly away,
    And whisper to their souls to go,
Whilst some of their sad friends do say
    The breath goes now, and some say, No;   4

So let us melt, and make no noise,
    No tear-floods, nor sigh-tempests move:
'Twere profanation of our joys
    To tell the laity our love.   8

Moving of th' earth[2] brings harms and fears,
    Men reckon what it did and meant;

[1] Farewell.
[2] An earthquake.

But trepidation of the spheres,[3]
    Though greater far, is innocent.[4]   12

Dull sublunary[5] lovers' love
    (Whose soul is sense[6]) cannot admit
Absence, because it doth remove
    Those things which elemented[7] it.   16

But we by a love so much refined
    That our selves know not what it is,
Inter-assuréd of the mind,
    Care less, eyes, lips, and hands to miss.   20

Our two souls therefore, which are one,
    Though I must go, endure not yet
A breach,[8] but an expansion,
    Like gold to airy thinness beat.   24

If they be two, they are two so
    As stiff twin compasses[9] are two;
Thy soul, the fixed foot, makes no show
    To move, but doth, if th' other do.   28

And though it in the center sit,
    Yet when the other far doth roam,
It leans and hearkens after it,
    And grows erect, as that comes home.   32

Such wilt thou be to me, who must
    Like th' other foot, obliquely run;
Thy firmness makes my circle just,
    And makes me end where I begun.   36

[3] In Ptolemaic astronomy, the spheres supported the stars, planets, sun, and moon.
[4] Not sinister.
[5] Beneath the moon, earthly. Contrasted with the lovers of the poem, whose love is higher and greater.
[6] The love of ordinary lovers has its essence in the senses.
[7] Composed.
[8] Break.
[9] Instrument for drawing circles.

Symbol and Allegory

The double vision of metaphor originates in the human desire to see connections between disparate elements of earthly phenomena. The same human search for correspondences leads us into the still more complicated realms of allegory and symbol.

[From] Endymion: Book I

John Keats   (1795–1821)

A thing of beauty is a joy for ever:
Its loveliness increases; it will never
Pass into nothingness, but still will keep
A bower[1] quiet for us, and a sleep
Full of sweet dreams, and health, and quiet breathing.   5
Therefore, on every morrow, are we wreathing
A flowery band to bind us to the earth,
Spite of despondence, of the inhuman dearth
Of noble natures, of the gloomy days,
Of all the unhealthy and o'er-darkened ways   10
Made for our searching—yes, in spite of all,
Some shape of beauty moves away the pall[2]
From our dark spirits. Such the sun, the moon,
Trees, old and young, sprouting a shady boon
For simple sheep; and such are daffodils   15
With the green world they live in; and clear rills[3]
That for themselves a cooling covert[4] make
'Gainst the hot season; the mid-forest brake,[5]
Rich with a sprinkling of fair musk-rose[6] blooms;
And such too is the grandeur of the dooms[7]   20
We have imagined for the mighty dead,
All lovely tales that we have heard or read—
An endless fountain of immortal drink,
Pouring unto us from the heaven's brink.

Nor do we merely feel these essences   25
For one short hour; no, even as the trees
That whisper round a temple become soon
Dear as the temple's self, so does the moon,
The passion poesy, glories infinite,
Haunt us till they become a cheering light   30
Unto our souls, and bound to us so fast
That, whether there be shine or gloom o'ercast,
They always must be with us, or we die.

[1] Rustic cottage, retreat.
[2] Funeral covering.
[3] Small brooks.
[4] Hidden nook.
[5] Thicket.
[6] A Mediterranean rose, usually white.
[7] Destinies.

Within these lines Keats asserts the value of natural beauty:

> ... daffodils
> With the green world they live in; and clear rills
> That for themselves a cooling covert make
> 'Gainst the hot season. . . .

He reminds us also of our heritage of literature:

> ... the grandeur of the dooms
> We have imagined for the mighty dead;
> All lovely tales that we have heard or read—
> An endless fountain of immortal drink,
> Pouring unto us from the heaven's brink.

Fundamental to the argument is the idea that both the natural objects of the world and the created objects of art possess meanings deeper and more complex than their surface appearance. A daffodil is no more than a beautiful flower, but it is also an eternal vindication of a principle of beauty that lies behind the visible surface of the world. A tale that "we have imagined" is no more than a tale, but it is also part of "an endless fountain of immortal drink," connected with eternal principles.

The poet who writes about a daffodil but insists upon the larger meaning that lies behind the flower has created a *symbol*. The poet who tells a story but who reminds us of some other more permanent story has created an *allegory*.

An *allegory* is a narrative in which concrete events, explicitly stated, imply a more general and abstract set of events. In the medieval play *Everyman* the events carry an allegorical significance connected with the lives of all men. In Dante's *Inferno* the poet journeys to a Hell fraught with implications for readers on earth. The allegorical significance of the following poem is strongly suggested in the last stanza:

To a Waterfowl
William Cullen Bryant (1794–1878)

> Whither, midst falling dew,
> While glow the heavens with the last steps of day:
> Far, through their rosy depths, dost thou pursue
> Thy solitary way?
>
> Vainly the fowler's eye
> Might mark thy distant flight to do thee wrong,

4

As, darkly seen against the crimson sky,
    Thy figure floats along.   8

    Seek'st thou the plashy brink
Of weedy lake, or marge of river wide,
Or where the rocking billows rise and sink
    On the chafed ocean-side?   12

    There is a Power whose care
Teaches thy way along that pathless coast—
The desert and illimitable air—
    Lone wandering, but not lost.   16

    All day thy wings have fanned,
At that far height, the cold, thin atmosphere,
Yet stoop not, weary, to the welcome land,
    Though the dark night is near.   20

    And soon that toil shall end;
Soon shalt thou find a summer home, and rest,
And scream among thy fellows; reeds shall bend,
    Soon, o'er thy sheltered nest.   24

    Thou'rt gone, the abyss of heaven
Hath swallowed up thy form; yet, on my heart
Deeply has sunk the lesson thou hast given,
    And shall not soon depart.   28

    He who, from zone to zone,
Guides through the boundless sky thy certain flight,
In the long way that I must tread alone,
    Will lead my steps aright.   32

In what way does each element of the bird's situation parallel the situation of the "I" who narrates the poem?

Not all writers announce their allegorical intent.

Whoso List to Hunt

Thomas Wyatt (1503–1542)

Whoso list[1] to hunt, I know where is an hind,
    But as for me, alas, I may no more;
    The vain travail hath wearied me so sore,
    I am of them that farthest come behind.   4
Yet may I by no means my wearied mind
    Draw from the deer, but as she fleeth afore

---

[1] Wishes.

Fainting I follow; I leave off therefore,
Since in a net I seek to hold the wind.   8
Who list her hunt, I put him out of doubt,
　As well as I, may spend his time in vain.
　And graven with diamonds in letters plain,
There is written her fair neck round about,   12
　"*Noli me tangere*,[2] for Caesar's I am,
　And wild for to hold, though I seem tame."

[2] Touch me not.

This seems to be something more than a poem about a man hunting a
deer. Scholars have suggested that it may refer to Wyatt's interest in
Anne Boleyn, who became wife to Henry VIII. Are there hints within
the poem of this or similar meaning?

All stories are, in a sense, allegories, since their particular events imply things we recognize as generally valid in human experience. But we
also recognize as true allegories those narratives, like Wyatt's poem, that
clearly imply a secondary or larger set of events, even though we cannot
be sure whether the writer is implying some specific affair or a more
generalized human predicament.

Stopping by Woods on a Snowy Evening
Robert Frost (1874–1963)

Whose woods these are I think I know.
His house is in the village, though;
He will not see me stopping here
To watch his woods fill up with snow.   4

My little horse must think it queer
To stop without a farmhouse near
Between the woods and frozen lake
The darkest evening of the year.   8

He gives his harness bells a shake
To ask if there is some mistake.
The only other sound's the sweep
Of easy wind and downy flake.   12

The woods are lovely, dark, and deep,
But I have promises to keep,
And miles to go before I sleep,
And miles to go before I sleep.   16

The strongest hint at larger meanings within this poem comes at the end. The first "miles to go before I sleep" presumably means no more than it says, yet in the repetition some readers perceive another meaning for "sleep": the sleep of death. From this hint, we may look back at the other lines and extract a consistent pattern of allegory. Frost, as it happens, is reported as insisting that he did not intend a reference to death. But he seems to have created something of an allegory without intending it. What details would support an allegorical reading?

Not all allegories are clear and consistent. Sometimes it is easier and more accurate to speak of allegorical passages or allegorical tendencies than it is to describe a carefully conceived allegorical scheme that runs through the whole.

A *symbol* is an object or act that carries a meaning more complicated than is evident in its ordinary significance. A bird is ordinarily only a bird, but the American eagle on the Presidential seal symbolizes governmental power, with perhaps some freedom and farsightedness included. Handing a key to someone ordinarily signifies nothing more than convenience, but as part of the ritual greeting a visiting dignitary it is symbolic. The eagle and the ceremony are *conventional symbols:* objects or acts invested with complicated meanings widely understood. Conventional symbols form an important part of everyday communication.

Writers, of course, employ these conventional symbols, as well as a wide range of *natural symbols,* often related to the conventional ones. A sunrise naturally suggests hope, a new birth, a new beginning; a sunset naturally suggests death. The sun stands for life; darkness, for confusion or death; a star, for guidance, constancy, and hope; pools and fountains, for sustenance; the sea, for eternity; tides, for change. Moreover, a writer can draw on such natural associations to create new symbols, as when Melville invests the white whale with an eerie majesty symbolizing some natural force that man cannot, and should not, conquer.

The Sick Rose

William Blake   (1757–1827)

> O rose, thou art sick:
> The invisible worm
> That flies in the night,
> In the howling storm,   4
> Has found out thy bed
> Of crimson joy;
> And his dark secret love
> Does thy life destroy.   8

Both the rose and the worm carry symbolic meanings. Are they in some way extensions of natural symbols? What ideas do they represent?

The Portent[1]

Herman Melville (1819–1891)

Hanging from the beam,
   Slowly swaying (such the law),
Gaunt the shadow on your green,
   Shenandoah!   4
The cut is on the crown
(Lo, John Brown),
And the stabs shall heal no more.

Hidden in the cap   8
   Is the anguish none can draw;
So your future veils its face,
   Shenandoah!
But the streaming beard is shown   12
(Weird[2] John Brown),
The meteor of the war.

[1] An omen, especially of evil. The abolitionist John Brown led an attack on Harper's Ferry, Virginia (now West Virginia), on October 16, 1859. After a trial in Charles Town (in the Shenandoah valley), he was hanged on December 2, 1859.
[2] Supernatural; suggestive of things to come.

What does the hanging of John Brown symbolize? What elements within the poem support the symbolism?

In Just-

E. E. Cummings (1894–1962)

in Just-
spring   when the world is mud-
luscious the little
lame balloonman   5

whistles   far   and wee

and eddieandbill come
running from marbles and
piracies and it's   10
spring

when the world is puddle-wonderful

the queer
old balloonman whistles
far   and   wee
and bettyandisbel come dancing   15
from hop-scotch and jump-rope and

it's
spring
and
     the   20

          goat-footed

balloonMan   whistles
far
and
wee   25

Among the elements associated with spring in this poem, the balloon man is so insistently stressed as to suggest something larger than himself. We learn progressively, through incremental repetition not unlike that of folk ballads, that he is little, lame, queer, old, and goat footed. Finally, he is oddly capitalized a "balloonMan."

Symbols and allegories tend to shade into one another, since both share the metaphorical process—something represented by something else. An allegory is really a story of symbols in action, an animated tapestry, with ladies on white horses, symbolizing Virtue, rescued from dragons, symbolizing Evil, by Red Cross Knights, symbolizing ultimate Truth. The line between symbol and allegory is difficult to distinguish when the correspondences are few and the narrative slight. A symbol resembles a metaphor, but a symbol represents an abstract idea, or several, like Virtue or Beauty, and a metaphor presents one physical thing in terms of another, a woman as a moonlit poplar branch, for instance. And the two frequently merge, since the woman, like a poplar branch, also symbolizes beauty—either vaguely or specifically, according to the author's emphasis.

Use the terms *metaphor, allegory,* and *symbol* to discuss the following poems.

Hymn to Cynthia[1]

Ben Jonson   (1573–1637)

Queen and huntress, chaste and fair,
Now the sun is laid to sleep,
Seated in thy silver chair,
State in wonted manner keep:
     Hesperus[2] entreats thy light,
     Goddess excellently bright.   6

---

[1] Diana, goddess of the moon; also traditionally a name for Queen Elizabeth I.
[2] The evening star.

Earth, let not thy envious shade
Dare itself to interpose;
Cynthia's shining orb was made
Heaven to clear, when day did close:
　　Bless us then with wished sight,
　　Goddess excellently bright.　　　　　　　　　　12

Lay thy bow of pearl apart,
And thy crystal-shining quiver;
Give unto the flying hart[3]
Space to breathe, how short soever:
　　Thou that mak'st a day of night,
　　Goddess excellently bright.　　　　　　　　　　18

[3] Male deer.

The Chambered Nautilus[1]

Oliver Wendell Holmes　(1809–1894)

This is the ship of pearl, which, poets feign,
　　Sails the unshadowed main,—
　　The venturous bark that flings
On the sweet summer wind its purpled wings
In gulfs enchanted, where the Siren[2] sings,　　　　5
　　And coral reefs lie bare,
Where the cold sea-maids rise to sun their stream-
　　　　ing hair.

Its webs of living gauze no more unfurl;
　　Wrecked is the ship of pearl!
　　And every chambered cell,　　　　　　　　　　10
Where its dim dreaming life was wont to dwell,
As the frail tenant shaped his growing shell,
　　Before thee lies revealed,—
Its irised[3] ceiling rent, its sunless crypt unsealed!

Year after year beheld the silent toil　　　　　　　15
　　That spread his lustrous coil;
　　Still, as the spiral grew,
He left the past year's dwelling for the new,

[1] The pearly nautilus of the South Pacific builds a spiral shell, adding a chamber each year. The ancients believed it could erect a membrane as a sail.
[2] A mythical creature, half woman, half bird, that lured men to their death with its song.
[3] Rainbowed.

Stole with soft step its shining archway through,
    Built up its idle door,   20
Stretched in his last-found home, and knew the old no more.

Thanks for the heavenly message brought by thee,
    Child of the wandering sea,
    Cast from her lap, forlorn!
From thy dead lips a clearer note is born   25
Than ever Triton[4] blew from wreathèd horn!
    While on mine ear it rings,
Through the deep caves of thought I hear a voice
        that sings:—

Build thee more stately mansions, O my soul,
    As the swift seasons roll!   30
    Leave thy low-vaulted past!
Let each new temple, nobler than the last,
Shut thee from heaven with a dome more vast,
    Till thou at length art free,
Leaving thine outgrown shell by life's unresting
        sea!   35

[4] Sea god. Cf. Wordsworth's sonnet "The World Is Too Much With Us," last line: "Or hear old Triton blow his wreathèd horn."

Sound

Language communicates not alone through images and ideas, but also through sounds and rhythms. Some speakers move us more by their delivery than their arguments. We respond to some writing more for its music than its thought. Poetry especially communicates through patterns of sound and rhythm.

Rhyme, like all of these patterns, depends on repetition with variation, matching the ends of words, with a difference: *be, see; sat, hat; contend, offend.* A couplet rhyming *sore* and *soar* leaves us unfulfilled, unless the poet wants to amuse us with a clinker. Most rhymes are *masculine,* matching the accented final syllable: *hate, fate; report, contort. Feminine rhyme (double rhyme)* adds an unstressed syllable: *candy, dandy.* Three syllables make a *triple rhyme: ratified, stratified.* These rhymes have been *exact rhymes,* but poets sometimes use *slant rhymes (off rhymes, approximate rhymes),* like these: *hate, heat; candy, Cindy; ratified, satisfied.* These are called *eye rhymes* when the words look alike but sound slanted: *move, love.* Sometimes we need to speak of *end rhyme,* at the line-ends, to distinguish it from *initial rhyme* at the beginning, or *internal rhyme* somewhere between.

The Marshes of Glynn
Sidney Lanier (1842–1881)

Glooms of the live-oaks, beautiful-braided and woven
With intricate shades of the vines that myriad-cloven
   Clamber the forks of the multiform boughs,—
      Emerald twilights,—
        Virginal shy lights,   5
Wrought of the leaves to allure to the whisper of vows,
When lovers pace timidly down through the green colon-
          nades
   Of the dim sweet woods, of the dear dark woods,
    Of the heavenly woods and glades,
That run to the radiant marginal sand-beach within   10
   The wide sea-marshes of Glynn;—

Beautiful glooms, soft dusks in the noon-day fire,—
Wildwood privacies, closets of lone desire,
Chamber from chamber parted with wavering arras of
        leaves,—
Cells for the passionate pleasure of prayer to the soul that
        grieves,   15
   Pure with a sense of the passing of saints through the wood,
   Cool for the dutiful weighing of ill with good;—

O braided dusks of the oak and woven shades of the vine,
While the riotous noon-day sun of the June-day long did shine,
Ye held me fast in your heart and I held you fast in mine;   20
   But now when the noon is no more, and riot is rest,
   And the sun is a-wait at the ponderous gate of the West,
      And the slant yellow beam down the wood-aisle doth seem
      Like a lane into heaven that leads from a dream,—
Ay, now, when my soul all day hath drunken the soul of the oak,   25
And my heart is at ease from men, and the wearisome sound
        of the stroke
Of the scythe of time and the trowel of trade is low,
And belief overmasters doubt, and I know that I know,
And my spirit is grown to a lordly great compass within,
That the length and the breadth and the sweep of the
        marshes of Glynn   30
Will work me no fear like the fear they have wrought me
      of yore
   When length was fatigue, and when breadth was but bitter-
       ness sore,
    And when terror and shrinking and dreary unnamable pain

Drew over me out of the merciless miles of the plain,—
    Oh, now, unafraid, I am fain to face   35
        The vast sweet visage of space.
    To the edge of the wood I am drawn, I am drawn,
Where the gray beach glimmering runs, as a belt of the dawn,
        For a mete and a mark
        To the forest-dark:—   40
            So:
    Affable live-oak, leaning low,—
    Thus—with your favor—soft, with a reverent hand,
    (Not lightly touching your person, Lord of the land!)
    Bending your beauty aside, with a step I stand   45
        On the firm-packed sand,
           Free
    By a world of marsh that borders a world of sea.
Sinuous southward and sinuous northward the shimmering
        band
Of the sand-beach fastens the fringe of the marsh to the folds
        of the land.   50
Inward and outward to northward and southward the beach-
        lines linger and curl
As a silver-wrought garment that clings to and follows the firm sweet limbs
        of a girl.
Vanishing, swerving, evermore curving again into sight,
Softly the sand-beach wavers away to a dim gray looping of
        light.
And what if behind me to westward the wall of the woods
        stands high?   55
The world lies east: how ample, the marsh and the sea and
        the sky!
A league and a league of marsh-grass, waist-high, broad in
        the blade,
Green, and all of a height, and unflecked with a light or a
        shade,
    Stretch leisurely off, in a pleasant plain,
    To the terminal blue of the main.   60

    Oh, what is abroad in the marsh and the terminal sea?
    Somehow my soul seems suddenly free

    From the weighing of fate and the sad discussion of sin,
    By the length and the breadth and the sweep of the marshes
        of Glynn.
Ye marshes, how candid and simple and nothing-withholding
        and free   65

Ye publish yourselves to the sky and offer yourselves to the
        sea!
Tolerant plains, that suffer the sea and the rains and the sun,
Ye spread and span like the catholic man who hath mightily
        won
    God out of knowledge and good out of infinite pain
    And sight out of blindness and purity out of a stain.   70
As the marsh-hen secretly builds on the watery sod,
Behold I will build me a nest on the greatness of God:
I will fly in the greatness of God as the marsh-hen flies
In the freedom that fills all the space 'twixt the marsh and
        the skies:
By so many roots as the marsh-grass sends in the sod   75
I will heartily lay me a-hold on the greatness of God:
Oh, like to the greatness of God is the greatness within
The range of the marshes, the liberal marshes of Glynn.

And the sea lends large, as the marsh: lo, out of his plenty
        the sea
Pours fast: full soon the time of the flood-tide must be:
    Look how the grace of the sea doth go   80
About and about through the intricate channels that flow
        Here and there,
        Everywhere,
Till his waters have flooded the uttermost creeks and the low-
        lying lanes,
    And the marsh is meshed with a million veins,   85
That like as with rosy and silvery essences flow
    In the rose-and-silver evening glow.
        Farewell, my lord Sun!
The creeks overflow: a thousand rivulets run
'Twixt the roots of the sod; the blades of the marsh-grass
        stir;   90
Passeth a hurrying sound of wings that westward whirr;
Passeth, and all is still, and the currents cease to run;
        And the sea and the marsh are one.

    How still the plains of the waters be!
    The tide is in his ecstasy.   95
    The tide is at his highest height:
        And it is night.

And now from the Vast of the Lord will the waters of sleep
    Roll in on the souls of men,
    But who will reveal to our waking ken   100

> The forms that swim and the shapes that creep
> Under the waters of sleep?
> And I would I could know what swimmeth below when the tide comes in
> On the length and the breadth of the marvellous marshes
> of Glynn.

Along with much end rhyme and internal rhyme, "The Marshes of Glynn" also illustrates three other important poetic sound effects. *Alliteration* repeats initial sounds: the sound of *p* in "passionate pleasure of prayer." *Consonance* repeats inner or end consonants: the *n* sound in "noon-day sun of the June-day long did shine." *Assonance* repeats the middles, rhyming the vowels: the *i* sounds in "firm sweet limbs of a girl."

The following sonnet is a treasure house of alliteration, consonance, and assonance.

God's Grandeur

Gerard Manley Hopkins   (1844–1889)

> The world is charged with the grandeur of God.
>   It will flame out, like shining from shook foil;
>   It gathers to a greatness, like the ooze of oil
> Crushed. Why do men then now not reck[1] his rod?   4
> Generations have trod, have trod, have trod;
>   And all is seared with trade; bleared, smeared with toil;
>   And wears man's smudge and shares man's smell: the soil
> Is bare now, nor can foot feel, being shod.   8
>
> And for all this, nature is never spent;
>   There lives the dearest freshness deep down things;
> And though the last lights off the black West went
>   Oh, morning, at the brown brink eastward, springs—   12
> Because the Holy Ghost over the bent
>   World broods with warm breast and with ah! bright wings.

[1] Take heed of.

Whatever its combination of rhyme or other sounds, skillful poetry displays a union of sound and sense, as the melody of sounds seems to support what is being said.

[From] Essay on Criticism

Alexander Pope   (1668–1744)

> True ease in writing comes from art, not chance,
>   As those move easiest who have learned to dance.

'Tis not enough no harshness gives offence,
The sound must seem an Echo to the sense: 4
Soft is the strain when Zephyr gently blows,
And the smooth stream in smoother nunbers flows;
But when loud surges lash the sounding shore,
The hoarse, rough verse should like the torrent roar: 8
When Ajax strives some rock's vast weight to throw,
The line too labours, and the words move slow;
Not o, when swift Camilla scours the plain,
Flies o'er th' unbending corn, and skims along the main.   12

Pope supports his meaning with the sounds of his lines. Zephyr blows, the stream flows, the torrent roars, Ajax strives, and Camilla scours—all in lines suited in sound to their varied activities. Notice how the lines linked by rhyme are also linked by thought, and how the rhymes underscore meaning in these skillful *rhymed couplets*. Note also how alliteration, like rhyme, can link concepts and underscore meaning—"soft . . . strain," "smooth stream," "loud . . . lash"—and how the consonance "strain when" blends with the assonance on *e* in "when Zephyr gently." What is the effect of the assonance in "loud . . . sounding"? The repeated *m*'s ("smooth stream in smoother numbers") and the flowing varied *o* sounds from *aw* to *oh* to *oo* ("soft . . . blows . . . smooth") are all part of this musical inner rhyming that underlines the sense and illustrates Pope's point.

These pleasing combinations of sound are called *euphony*. The opposite—harsh, jarring, or discordant sounds—is called *cacophony*. Pope's lines on Ajax approach cacophony; certainly they are less euphonious than his lines on Zephyr.

Isolate the sound elements that contribute to the euphony of the following poem.

The Splendor Falls

Alfred, Lord Tennyson   (1809–1892)

The splendor falls on castle walls
    And snowy summits old in story:
The long light shakes across the lakes,   3
    And the wild cataract leaps in glory.
Blow, bugle, blow, set the wild echoes flying,
Blow, bugle; answer, echoes, dying, dying, dying.   6

    O hark, O hear! how thin and clear,
        And thinner, clearer, farther going!
    O sweet and far from cliff and scar   9
        The horns of Elfland faintly blowing!

Blow, let us hear the purple glens replying:
Blow, bugle; answer, echoes, dying, dying, dying.   12

    O love, they die in yon rich sky,
       They faint on hill or field or river:
    Our echoes roll from soul to soul,   15
       And grow for ever and for ever.
Blow, bugle, blow, set the wild echoes flying,
And answer, echoes, answer, dying, dying, dying.   18

Onomatopoeia is a word sounding like its meaning: the "buzz" of a bee, the "clop, clop" of horses' hooves, the "sizzling" of bacon in a skillet. Does onomatopoeia contribute to the effect of "The Splendor Falls"?

The poems that follow are especially memorable for their varied sound effects.

Dover Beach

Matthew Arnold   (1822–1888)

The sea is calm to-night.
The tide is full, the moon lies fair
Upon the straits;—on the French coast the light
Gleams and is gone; the cliffs of England stand,
Glimmering and vast, out in the tranquil bay.   5
Come to the window, sweet is the night-air!

Only, from the long line of spray
Where the sea meets the moon-blanched land,
Listen! you hear the grating roar
Of pebbles which the waves draw back, and fling,   10
At their return, up the high strand,
Begin, and cease, and then again begin,
With tremulous cadence slow, and bring
The eternal note of sadness in.

Sophocles long ago   15
Heard it on the Ægæan, and it brought
Into his mind the turbid ebb and flow
Of human misery;[1] we
Find also in the sound a thought,
Hearing it by this distant northern sea.   20

The Sea of Faith
Was once, too, at the full, and round earth's shore

---

[1] Cf. *Antigone*, II, 583–591.

Lay like the folds of a bright girdle furled.
But now I only hear
Its melancholy, long, withdrawing roar,   25
Retreating, to the breath
Of the night-wind, down the vast edges drear
And naked shingles[2] of the world.

Ah, love, let us be true
To one another! for the world, which seems   30
To lie before us like a land of dreams,
So various, so beautiful, so new,
Hath really neither joy, nor love, nor light,

Nor certitude, nor peace, nor help for pain;
And we are here as on a darkling[3] plain   35
Swept with confused alarms of struggle and flight,
Where ignorant armies clash by night.

[2] Pebbly beaches.
[3] Becoming dark.

Felix Randal

Gerard Manley Hopkins (1844–1889)

Felix Randal the farrier,[1] O is he dead then? my duty all ended,
Who have watched his mould of man, big-boned and hardy-handsome
Pining, pining, till time when reason rambled in it and some
Fatal four disorders, fleshed there, all contended?   4

Sickness broke him. Impatient, he cursed at first, but mended
Being anointed and all; though a heavenlier heart began some
Months earlier, since I had our sweet reprieve and ransom
Tendered to him.[2] Ah well, God rest him all road ever he offended!   8

This seeing the sick endears them to us, us too it endears.
My tongue had taught thee comfort, touch had quenched thy tears,
Thy tears that touched my heart, child, Felix, poor Felix Randal;

How far from then forethought of, all thy more boisterous years,   12
When thou at the random grim forge, powerful amidst peers,
Didst fettle[3] for the great grey drayhorse his bright and battering sandal!

[1] Blacksmith.
[2] Had confessed him and given him absolution (Hopkins was a priest).
[3] Prepare.

Batter My Heart, Three-Personed God

John Donne (1572–1631)

Batter my heart, three-personed God; for You
As yet but knock, breathe, shine, and seek to mend;
That I may rise and stand, o'erthrow me, and bend
Your force to break, blow, burn, and make me new.   4
I, like an usurped town, to another due,[1]
Labor to admit You, but oh, to no end;
Reason, Your viceroy in me, me should defend,
But is captived, and proves weak or untrue.   8
Yet dearly I love You, and would be loved fain,[2]
But am betrothed unto Your enemy.
Divorce me, untie or break that knot again;
Take me to You, imprison me, for I,   12
Except You enthrall me, never shall be free,
Nor ever chaste, except You ravish me.

[1] Owed.
[2] Joyfully.

Slow, Slow, Fresh Fount

Ben Jonson (1573–1637)

Slow, slow, fresh fount, keep time with my salt tears;
Yet slower yet, O faintly gentle springs;
List to the heavy part the music bears:
    Woe weeps out her division when she sings.
     Droop, herbs and flowers,   5
     Fall, grief, in showers;
     Our beauties are not ours:
     Oh, could I still
(Like melting snow upon some craggy hill)
     Drop, drop, drop, drop   10
Since nature's pride is now a withered daffodil.

Sir Beelzebub

Edith Sitwell (1887–1964)

When
Sir
Beelzebub[1] called for his syllabub[2] in the hotel in Hell

[1] A devil; Satan.
[2] A drink or dessert made of milk or cream, curdled with wine, cider, or, in this instance, rum.

Where Proserpine[3] first fell,
Blue as the gendarmerie[4] were the waves of the sea   5

(Rocking and shocking the bar-maid).

Nobody comes to give him his rum but the
Rim of the sky hippopotamus-glum
Enhances the chances to bless with a benison[5]
Alfred Lord Tennyson[6] crossing the bar laid   10
With cold vegetation from pale deputations
Of temperance workers (all signed In Memoriam)
Hoping with glory to trip up the Laureate's feet

(Moving in classical metres) . . .

Like Balaclava,[7] the lava came down from the   15
Roof, and the sea's blue wooden gendarmerie
Took them in charge while Beelzebub roared for his rum.

. . . None of them come!

[3] Persephone, who was carried to the underworld by Hades.
[4] Police.
[5] Blessing.
[6] Poet laureate. His "Crossing the Bar" is a poem on death, "In Memoriam" an elegy for a friend.
[7] In the Crimea, scene of the battle that occasioned Tennyson's "The Charge of the Light Brigade."

I Like to See It Lap the Miles

Emily Dickinson   (1830–1886)

I like to see it lap the Miles—
And lick the Valleys up—
And stop to feed itself at Tanks—
And then—prodigious step

Around a Pile of Mountains—   5
And supercilious peer
In Shanties—by the sides of Roads—
And then a Quarry pare

To fit its Ribs
And crawl between   10
Complaining all the while
In horrid—hooting stanza—
Then chase itself down Hill—

And neigh like Boanerges[1]—
Then—punctual as a Star　　　　　　　　　　　15
Stop—docile and omnipotent
At its own stable door—

[1] A surname meaning "sons of thunder," given by Christ to James and John (Mark iii.17); any loud preacher.

I Hear an Army Charging Upon the Land

James Joyce　(1882–1941)

I hear an army charging upon the land
　　And the thunder of horses plunging, foam about their knees.
Arrogant, in black armour, behind them stand,
　　Disdaining the reins, with fluttering whips, the charioteers.　　4

They cry unto the night their battlename:
　　I moan in sleep when I hear afar their whirling laughter.
They cleave the gloom of dreams, a blinding flame,
　　Clanging, clanging upon the heart as upon an anvil.　　8

They come shaking in triumph their long green hair:
　　They come out of the sea and run shouting by the shore.
My heart, have you no wisdom thus to despair?
　　My love, my love, my love, why have you left me alone?　　12

Break, Break, Break

Alfred, Lord Tennyson　(1809–1892)

Break, break, break,
　　On thy cold gray stones, O Sea!
And I would that my tongue could utter
　　The thoughts that arise in me.　　4

O well for the fisherman's boy,
　　That he shouts with his sister at play!
O well for the sailor lad,
　　That he sings in his boat on the bay!　　8

And the stately ships go on
　　To their haven under the hill;
But O for the touch of a vanished hand,
　　And the sound of a voice that is still!　　12

Break, break, break,
　　At the foot of thy crags, O Sea!
But the tender grace of a day that is dead
　　Will never come back to me.　　16

Death & Co.

Sylvia Plath   (1932–1963)

Two, of course there are two.
It seems perfectly natural now—
The one who never looks up, whose eyes are lidded
And balled, like Blake's,[1]
Who exhibits   5

The birthmarks that are his trademark—
The scald scar of water,
The nude
Verdigris[2] of the condor.
I am red meat. His beak   10

Claps sidewise: I am not his yet.
He tells me how badly I photograph.
He tells me how sweet
The babies look in their hospital
Icebox, a simple   15

Frill at the neck,
Then the flutings of their Ionian[3]
Death-gowns,
Then two little feet.
He does not smile or smoke.   20

The other does that,
His hair long and plausive.
Bastard
Masturbating a glitter,
He wants to be loved.   25

I do not stir.
The frost makes a flower,
The dew makes a star,
The dead bell,
The dead bell.   30

Somebody's done for.

[1] Like eyes in engravings by William Blake.
[2] Greenish blue (of the condor's head and neck).
[3] Grooved like an Ionic column.
[4] Applauding.

Meter

Language is characterized by units of time and stress. Some words and
syllables take longer than others to pronounce; we pause for emphasis or

clarity; we stress some words and syllables more than others. *Meter* organizes these elements of time and stress. Rhyme, alliteration, assonance, and other sound elements are as notes to the melody for which the meter provides the rhythm.

Iambic pentameter—the ten-syllable line of five iambic feet ($\cup -$)—has been the dominant English meter for centuries, as poet after poet since Chaucer adopted it for his own time and idiom. It captures English sound and syntax easily and naturally. Shakespeare's dramatic passages in this meter resound as verse, but they resound also as speech. Frost's New England farmers speak in ten-syllable verse remarkably close to the colloquial conversation of their nonversified neighbors. *Blank verse,* or unrhymed iambic pentameter, imitates speech particularly well. Much of Frost is blank verse. Shakespeare's plays, too, are blank verse, except for occasional passages of prose or song or when a rhymed couplet brings the audience up sharp to close a scene: ". . . . The play's the thing/ Wherein I'll catch the conscience of the King." Blank verse works well, also, for meditative poems such as the following.

Lines

COMPOSED A FEW MILES ABOVE TINTERN ABBEY,[1] ON REVISITING
THE BANKS OF THE WYE DURING A TOUR. JULY 13, 1798

William Wordsworth (1770–1850)

Five years have past; five summers, with the length
Of five long winters! and again I hear
These waters, rolling from their mountain-springs
With a soft inland murmur.—Once again
Do I behold these steep and lofty cliffs,   5
That on a wild secluded scene impress
Thoughts of more deep seclusion; and connect
The landscape with the quiet of the sky.
The day is come when I again repose
Here, under this dark sycamore, and view   10
These plots of cottage-ground, these orchard-tufts,
Which at this season, with their unripe fruits,
Are clad in one green hue, and lose themselves
'Mid groves and copses.[2] Once again I see
These hedge-rows, hardly hedge-rows, little lines   15
Of sportive wood run wild: these pastoral farms,
Green to the very door; and wreaths of smoke
Sent up, in silence, from among the trees!

[1] Ruined medieval abbey in Monmouthshire in the valley of the river Wye.
[2] Thickets.

With some uncertain notice, as might seem
Of vagrant dwellers in the houseless woods,   20
Or of some Hermit's cave, where by his fire
The Hermit sits alone.

     These beauteous forms,
Through a long absence, have not been to me
As is a landscape to a blind man's eye: 25
But oft, in lonely rooms, and 'mid the din
Of towns and cities, I have owed to them
In hours of weariness, sensations sweet,
Felt in the blood, and felt along the heart;
And passing even into my purer mind,   30
With tranquil restoration:—feelings too
Of unremembered pleasure: such, perhaps,
As have no slight or trivial influence
On that best portion of a good man's life,
His little, nameless, unremembered, acts   35
Of kindness and of love. Nor less, I trust,
To them I may have owed another gift,
Of aspect more sublime; that blessed mood
In which the burthen of the mystery,
In which the heavy and the weary weight   40
Of all this unintelligible world,
Is lightened:—that serene and blessed mood,
In which the affections gently lead us on,—
Until, the breath of this corporeal frame
And even the motion of our human blood   45
Almost suspended, we are laid asleep
In body, and become a living soul:
While with an eye made quiet by the power
Of harmony, and the deep power of joy,
We see into the life of things.   50
        If this
Be but a vain belief, yet, oh! how oft—
In darkness and amid the many shapes
Of joyless daylight; when the fretful stir
Unprofitable, and the fever of the world,   55
Have hung upon the beatings of my heart—
How oft, in spirit, have I turned to thee,
O sylvan Wye! thou wanderer thro' the woods,
How often has my spirit turned to thee!

  And now, with gleams of half-extinguished thought,   60
With many recognitions dim and faint,

And somewhat of a sad perplexity,
The picture of the mind revives again:
While here I stand, not only with the sense
Of present pleasure, but with pleasing thoughts   65
That in this moment there is life and food
For future years. And so I dare to hope,
Though changed, no doubt, from what I was when first
I came among these hills; when like a roe
I bounded o'er the mountains, by the sides   70
Of the deep rivers, and the lonely streams,
Wherever nature led: more like a man
Flying from something that he dreads than one
Who sought the thing he loved. For nature then
(The coarser pleasures of my boyish days,   75
And their glad animal movements all gone by)
To me was all in all.—I cannot paint
What then I was. The sounding cataract
Haunted me like a passion: the tall rock,
The mountain, and the deep and gloomy wood,   80
Their colours and their forms, were then to me
An appetite; a feeling and a love,
That had no need of a remoter charm,
By thought supplied, nor any interest
Unborrowed from the eye.—That time is past,   85
And all its aching joys are now no more,
And all its dizzy raptures. Not for this
Faint I, nor mourn nor murmur; other gifts
Have followed; for such loss, I would believe,
Abundant recompense. For I have learned   90
To look on nature, not as in the hour
Of thoughtless youth; but hearing oftentimes
The still, sad music of humanity,
Nor harsh nor grating, though of ample power
To chasten and subdue. And I have felt   95
A presence that disturbs me with the joy
Of elevated thoughts; a sense sublime
Of something far more deeply interfused,
Whose dwelling is the light of setting suns,
And the round ocean and the living air,   100
And the blue sky, and in the mind of man:
A motion and a spirit, that impels
All thinking things, all objects of all thought,
And rolls through all things. Therefore am I still
A lover of the meadows and the woods,   105

And mountains; and of all that we behold
From this green earth; of all the mighty world
Of eye, and ear,—both what they half create,
And what perceive; well pleased to recognise
In nature and the language of the sense   110
The anchor of my purest thoughts, the nurse,
The guide, the guardian of my heart, and soul
Of all my moral being.
                 Nor perchance,
If I were not thus taught, should I the more   115
Suffer my genial spirits to decay:
For thou art with me here upon the banks
Of this fair river; thou my dearest Friend,[3]
My dear, dear Friend; and in thy voice I catch
The language of my former heart, and read   120
My former pleasures in the shooting lights
Of thy wild eyes. Oh! yet a little while
May I behold in thee what I was once,
My dear, dear Sister! and this prayer I make,
Knowing that Nature never did betray   125
The heart that loved her; 'tis her privilege,
Through all the years of this our life, to lead
From joy to joy: for she can so inform
The mind that is within us, so impress
With quietness and beauty, and so feed   130
With lofty thoughts, that neither evil tongues,
Rash judgments, nor the sneers of selfish men,
Nor greetings where no kindness is, nor all
The dreary intercourse of daily life,
Shall e'er prevail against us, or disturb   135
Our cheerful faith, that all which we behold
Is full of blessings. Therefore let the moon
Shine on thee in thy solitary walk;
And let the misty mountain-winds be free
To blow against thee: and, in after years,   140
When these wild ecstasies shall be matured
Into a sober pleasure; when thy mind
Shall be a mansion for all lovely forms,
Thy memory be as a dwelling-place
For all sweet sounds and harmonies; oh! then,   145
If solitude, or fear, or pain, or grief,
Should be thy portion, with what healing thoughts

---

[3] Wordsworth's sister Dorothy.

Of tender joy wilt thou remember me,
And these my exhortations! Nor, perchance—
If I should be where I no more can hear   150
Thy voice, nor catch from thy wild eyes these gleams
Of past existence—wilt thou then forget
That on the banks of this delightful stream
We stood together; and that I, so long
A worshipper of Nature, hither came   155
Unwearied in that service: rather say
With warmer love—oh! with far deeper zeal
Of holier love. Nor wilt thou then forget,
That after many wanderings, many years
Of absence, these steep woods and lofty cliffs,   160
And this green pastoral landscape, were to me
More dear, both for themselves and for thy sake!

We *scan* a line of verse by marking its metrical feet:

$$\cup \; - \mid \cup \; - \mid \cup \; - \mid \cup \; - \mid \cup \; - \mid$$
Five years have past; five sum-mers with the length

Scan a number of lines of "Tintern Abbey," indicating the stress pattern
and its variations within the regular ten syllables of each line. Regular
iambic lines have ten syllables stressed in a strict iambic pattern:

$$\cup - \mid \cup - \mid \cup - \mid \cup - \mid \cup - \mid$$

Irregular lines vary the stress pattern, and some poets add or subtract
one or more syllables. But Wordsworth, like other masters of the iambic
line, achieves great flexibility within his ten-syllable, five-stress pattern
by his pauses and by substituting stresses, as in:

$$\cup \; \cup \mid - \; - \mid \cup \; - \mid \cup \; - \mid \cup - \mid$$
With a soft in-land mur-mur. Once again

Adding rhyme to iambic pentameter heightens the pleasures and
forces of perceived structure. Pope favored the *heroic couplet*: a rhymed
couplet of iambic pentameter, frequently closing the thought on the
rhyme of the second line. The following lines introduce his long poem
"An Essay on Man."

[The Wild Garden][1]

Alexander Pope (1688–1744)

Awake, my St. John! leave all meaner things
To low ambition, and the pride of Kings.

---

[1] *An Essay on Man*, I, 1–16. Henry St. John, Viscount Bolingbroke, Secretary of State under Queen
Anne, had been deposed and attainted for treason by George I.

Let us (since Life can little more supply
Than just to look about us and to die)   4
Expatiate free o'er all this scene of Man;
A mighty maze! but not without a plan;
A Wild, where weeds and flowers promiscuous shoot,
Or Garden, tempting with forbidden fruit.   8
Together let us beat this ample field,
Try what the open, what the covert yield;
The latent tracts, the giddy heights explore
Of all who blindly creep, or sightless soar;   12
Eye Nature's walks, shoot Folly as it flies,
And catch the Manners living as they rise;
Laugh where we must, be candid where we can;
But vindicate the ways of God to Man.   16

The sonnet, too, uses iambic pentameter, adding to the demands of meter the demands of a complicated rhyme scheme:

When I Have Fears That I May Cease to Be

John Keats   (1795–1821)

When I have fears that I may cease to be
  Before my pen has gleaned my teeming brain,
Before high-pilèd books, in charactery,[1]
  Hold like rich garners the full ripened grain;   4
When I behold, upon the night's starred face,
  Huge cloudy symbols of a high romance,
And think that I may never live to trace
  Their shadows with the magic hand of chance;   8
And when I feel, fair creature of an hour,
  That I shall never look upon thee more,
Never have relish in the fairy power
  Of unreflecting love; then on the shore   12
Of the wide world I stand alone and think
Till love and fame to nothingness do sink.

[1] The characters, or letters, on the pages.

Besides iambic pentameter, iambic lines of three or four feet (*trimeter* and *tetrameter*) are also favorites, with the quicker movement of the six or eight syllables frequently underscored by rhyme.

My Papa's Waltz

Theodore Roethke   (1908–1963)

The whiskey on your breath
Could make a small boy dizzy;
But I hung on like death:
Such waltzing was not easy.   4

We romped until the pans
Slid from the kitchen shelf;
My mother's countenance
Could not unfrown itself.   8

The hand that held my wrist
Was battered on one knuckle;
At every step you missed
My right ear scraped a buckle.   12

You beat time on my head
With a palm caked hard by dirt,
Then waltzed me off to bed
Still clinging to your shirt.   16

Here the insistent beat of the iambic feet mimics the rhythm of a
dance (three steps to the line, in a kind of drunken waltz time). Notice
the small irregularities of meter in the feminine rhymes of "dizzy" and
"easy," "knuckle" and "buckle." The effect supports the slightly woozy
exuberance. "Slid" in the sixth line has a *rhetorical stress*, an emphasis
from meaning rather than meter, again swinging along the tipsy effect.

Often a poet varies his effect with lines markedly different from the
prevailing meter.

La Belle Dame Sans Merci

John Keats   (1795–1821)

I

Oh, what can ail thee, knight-at-arms,
Alone and palely loitering?
The sedge has withered from the lake,
And no birds sing!   4

II

Oh, what can ail thee, knight-at-arms,
So haggard and so woe-begone?
The squirrel's granary is full,
And the harvest's done.   8

III

I see a lily on thy brow,
  With anguish moist and fever-dew,
And on thy cheek a fading rose
  Fast withereth too.   12

IV

I met a lady in the meads
  Full beautiful, a fairy's child,
Her hair was long, her foot was light,
  And her eyes were wild.   16

V

I made a garland for her head,
  And bracelets too, and fragrant zone;
She looked at me as she did love,
  And made sweet moan.   20

VI

I set her on my pacing steed,
  And nothing else saw all day long;
For sidelong would she bend, and sing
  A fairy's song.   24

VII

She found me roots of relish sweet,
  And honey wild, and manna dew;
And sure in language strange she said,
  'I love thee true'.   28

VIII

She took me to her elfin grot,
  And there she wept, and sighed full sore,
And there I shut her wild wild eyes
  With kisses four.   32

IX

And there she lullèd me asleep,
  And there I dreamed—Ah! woe betide!—
The latest dream I ever dreamed
  On the cold hill side.   36

X

I saw pale kings, and princes too,
  Pale warriors, death-pale were they all;

They cried—'La belle Dame sans merci
  Hath thee in thrall!'   40

XI

I saw their starved lips in the gloam
  With horrid warning gapèd wide,
And I awoke, and found me here
  On the cold hill side.   44

XII

And this is why I sojourn here,
  Alone and palely loitering,
Though the sedge is withered from the lake,
  And no birds sing.   48

Here the first three lines of each stanza are fairly regular iambic tetrameter. The fourth line closes each stanza curtly with a number of variations on a basic iambic *dimeter* (line of only two feet).

In the following poem, the poet has forced a common meter into an unusual effect by ending almost every line with a feminine rhyme.

The War-Song of Dinas Vawr

Thomas Love Peacock   (1785–1866)

The mountain sheep are sweeter,
But the valley sheep are fatter;
We therefore deemed it meeter[1]
To carry off the latter.   4
We made an expedition;
We met a host, and quelled it;
We forced a strong position,
And killed the men who held it.   8

On Dyfed's richest valley,
Where herds of kine[2] were browsing,
We made a mighty sally,
To furnish our carousing.   12
Fierce warriors rushed to meet us;
We met them, and o'erthrew them:
They struggled hard to beat us;
But we conquered them, and slew them.   16

As we drove our prize at leisure,
The king marched forth to catch us:

[1] More suitable.
[2] Cattle.

His rage surpassed all measure,
But his people could not match us.   20
He fled to his hall-pillars;
And, ere our force we led off,
Some sacked his house and cellars,
While others cut his head off.   24

We there, in strife bewild'ring,
Spilt blood enough to swim in:
We orphaned many children,
And widowed many women.   28
The eagles and the ravens
We glutted with our foemen;
The heroes and the cravens,
The spearmen and the bowmen.   32

We brought away from battle,
And much their land bemoaned them,
Two thousand head of cattle,
And the head of him who owned them: 36
Ednyfed, king of Dyfed,
His head was borne before us;
His wine and beasts supplied our feasts,
And his overthrow, our chorus.   40

The meter is the iambic trimeter of Roethke's "My Papa's Waltz," but the effect carries to extremes the metrical point in Roethke's rhymes on "dizzy" and "knuckle." Feminine rhymes require an extra syllable after the last stress, varying the meter without destroying it. But here their appearance in every line but one (that line, the penultimate, expands the meter to iambic tetrameter) undercuts the basic meter and helps to mock the tradition of heroic war songs.

The following poem, a serious account of heroic adventure, also makes good use of trimeter, but varies the line in a significantly different way.

To the Cambro-Britons and Their Harp:
HIS BALLAD OF AGINCOURT[1]

Michael Drayton   (1563–1631)

Fair stood the wind for France,
When we our sails advance,
Nor now to prove our chance,
    Longer will tarry;   4

[1] Where the English, under King Henry V, defeated the French in 1415 on October 25, St. Crispin's Day.

But putting to the main
At Kaux, the mouth of Seine,
With all his martial train,
    Landed King Harry.   8

And taking many a fort,
Furnished in warlike sort,
Marcheth towards Agincourt,
    In happy hour;   12
Skirmishing day by day
With those that stopped his way,
Where the French gen'ral lay
    With all his power.   16

Which in his height of pride,
King Henry to deride,
His ransom to provide
    To the King sending;   20
Which he neglects the while
As from a nation vile,
Yet with an angry smile
    Their fall portending.   24

And turning to his men,
Quoth our brave Henry then:
Though they to one be ten,
    Be not amazed.   28
Yet have we well begun,
Battles so bravely won
Have ever to the sun
    By fame been raised.   32

And for myself, quoth he,
This my full rest shall be,
England ne'er mourn for me,
    Nor more esteem me;   36
Victor I will remain,
Or on this earth lie slain,
Never shall she sustain
    Loss to redeem me.   40

Poitiers and Crecy[2] tell,
When most their pride did swell,
Under our swords they fell;
    No less our skill is   44

[2] Sites of earlier English victories in the Hundred Years' War.

Than when our grandsire great,
Claiming the regal seat
By many a warlike feat,
    Lopped the French lilies.   48

The Duke of York so dread
The eager vaward[3] led;
With the main Henry sped
    Amongst his henchmen.   52
Excester[4] had the rear,
A braver man not there,
Oh Lord, how hot they were
    On the false Frenchmen!   56

They now to fight are gone,
Armor on armor shone,
Drum now to drum did groan,
    To hear was wonder,   60
That with cries they make
The very earth did shake,
Trumpet to trumpet spake,
    Thunder to thunder.   64

Well it thine age became,
Oh noble Erpingham,
Which didst the signal aim
    To our hid forces;   68
When from a meadow by,
Like a storm suddenly,
The English archery
    Struck the French horses.   72

With Spanish yew so strong,
Arrows a cloth-yard long,
That like to serpents stung,
    Piercing the weather;   76
None from his fellow starts,
But playing manly parts,
And like true English hearts,
    Stuck close together.   80

When down their bows they threw,
And forth their bilboes[5] drew,

[3] Vanguard.
[4] Exeter.
[5] Swords.

And on the French they flew,
    Not one was tardy;   84
Arms were from shoulders sent,
Scalps to the teeth were rent,
Down the French peasants went;
    Our men were hardy.   88

This while our noble King,
His broad sword brandishing,
Down the French host did ding,
    As to o'erwhelm it;   92
And many a deep wound lent,
His arms with blood besprent,
And many a cruel dent
    Bruiséd his helmet.   96

Gloster, that Duke so good,
Next of the royal blood,
For famous England stood
    With his brave brother;   100
Clarence, in steel so bright,
Though but a maiden knight,
Yet in that furious fight,
    Scarce such another.   104

Warwick in blood did wade,
Oxford the foe invade,
And cruel slaughter made,
    Still as they ran up;   108
Suffolk his ax did ply,
Beaumont and Willoughby
Bare them right doughtily,
    Ferrers and Fanhope.   112

Upon Saint Crispin's day
Fought was this noble fray,
Which fame did not delay
    To England to carry;   116
Oh, when shall English men
With such acts fill a pen,
Or England breed again
    Such a King Harry?   120

Here the six trimeter lines of each stanza end with the stress of masculine rhymes. But something else is going on. Drayton evidently wants to
imitate the warlike ballads of the Welsh harpers (Cambro–Britons), but,

being an able classicist, he invents an English version of the Sapphic stanza, originated in Greek by Sappho and followed in Latin by Catullus. Thus, Drayton gives his three long lines the downhill thrust of Latin by starting often with a *trochee* ($-\cup$), and he ends each set of four lines with the characteristic short dimeter of the Sapphic, a *dactyl* ($-\cup\cup$) and a trochee: $-\cup\cup|-\cup|$. His stanza, which has become famous, is really two Sapphic stanzas, Anglicized and rhymed in trimeter, with the two dimeter lines also rhymed. The original Sapphic line was unrhymed, and the long lines were five-footers, all with the trochaic "downhill" movement.

L. E. Sissman recalls the glory of Agincourt by playfully celebrating a modern victory in Drayton's meter and stanza.

Henley, July 4: 1914–1964

L. E. Sissman   (1928–1976)

Fifty years after Capt. Leverett Saltonstall's Harvard junior varsity became the first American eight to win the Grand Challenge Cup at Henley in England, Saltonstall . . . will lead his crew back to the scene of its triumph. Every man who pulled an oar in the victorious 1914 Harvard crew, as well as the coxswain, is not only alive but is preparing to return to Henley on July 1. They will take to a shell again on the picturesque Thames course during the forthcoming regatta.

—THE NEW YORK TIMES

Fair stands the wind again
For nine brave Harvard men
Sung by both tongue and pen,
    Sailing for Henley   4
Fifty years after they
Won the great rowing fray
On Independence Day,
    Boyish and manly.   8

On Independence Day
Fifty light years away
They took the victor's bay
    From mighty Britain.   12
They were a City joke
Till they put up the stroke
And their strong foemen broke,
    As it is written.   16

Leverett Saltonstall
Is the first name of all

That noble roll we call,
    That band of brothers.   20
Curtis, Talcott, and Meyer,
Morgan and Lund set fire
To England's funeral pyre,
    They and three others.   24

That young and puissant crew
Quickened their beat and flew
Past all opponents, who
    Watched them in wonder.   28
Fifty years later, we
See them across the sea
Echo that memory
    Like summer thunder.   32

Fair stands the wind again;
Thames, bear them softly, then.
Far came these rowing men
    In every weather.   36
What though their stroke has slowed?
(How long they all have rowed!)
Oarsmen, accept our ode,
    Blades of a feather.   40

Tennyson had done something similar, earlier and more earnestly.

The Charge of the Light Brigade[1]
Alfred, Lord Tennyson   (1809–1892)

I

Half a league, half a league,
    Half a league onward,
All in the valley of Death
    Rode the six hundred.
'Forward, the Light Brigade!   5
Charge for the guns!' he said:
Into the valley of Death
    Rode the six hundred.

[1] The charge took place in the Crimea, October 25, 1854, as a result of a mistake in orders. Although the meter is similar to that in Drayton's "To the Cambro-Britons," Tennyson said the poem "was not in my mind; my poem is dactylic."

II

'Forward, the Light Brigade!'
Was there a man dismayed?   10
Not though the soldier knew
   Some one had blundered:
Their's not to make reply,
Their's not to reason why,
Their's but to do and die: 15
Into the valley of Death
   Rode the six hundred.

III

Cannon to right of them,
Cannon to left of them,
Cannon in front of them   20
   Volleyed and thundered;
Stormed at with shot and shell,
Boldly they rode and well,
Into the jaws of Death,
Into the mouth of Hell   25
   Rode the six hundred.

IV

Flashed all their sabres bare,
Flashed as they turned in air
Sabring the gunners there,
Charging an army, while   30
   All the world wondered;
Plunged in the battery-smoke
Right through the line they broke;
Cossack and Russian
Reeled from the sabre-stroke   35
   Shattered and sundered.
Then they rode back, but not
   Not the six hundred.

V

Cannon to right of them,
Cannon to left of them,   40
Cannon behind them
   Volleyed and thundered;
Stormed at with shot and shell,
While horse and hero fell,

They that had fought so well   45
Came through the jaws of Death,
Back from the mouth of Hell,
All that was left of them,
    Left of six hundred.

VI

When can their glory fade?   50
O the wild charge they made!
    All the world wondered.
Honour the charge they made!
Honour the Light Brigade,
    Noble six hundred!   55

Which is the more successful user of this stanza, Sissman or Tennyson? Why?

In "The Dance," William Carlos Williams gets some interesting effects from dactyls.

The Dance

William Carlos Williams (1883–1963)

In Breughel's[1] great picture, The Kermess,[2]
the dancers go round, they go round and
around, the squeal and the blare and the
tweedle of bagpipes, a bugle and fiddles   4
tipping their bellies (round as the thick-
sided glasses whose wash they impound)
their hips and their bellies off balance
to turn them. Kicking and rolling about   8
the Fair Grounds, swinging their butts, those
shanks must be sound to bear up under such
rollicking measures, prance as they dance
in Breughel's great picture, The Kermess.   12

[1] Pieter Breughel (1520?–1569), a Flemish painter.
[2] Fair.

The poem may look irregular at first, with its syllable count per line varying from eight to eleven and its stresses from three to four. But as we look closer we observe that Williams has organized his metrics not by the line, but running throughout the poem on the dactylic beat of ONE, two, three, as in a waltz. The poem starts off beat, comes in on the beat on the first syllable of "Breughel" and carries through with fair consistency, swinging from line to line in the measured time of music. This is a quicker, more rollicking dance than Roethke's.

Pauses greatly affect meter. An *end-stopped* line ends in a pause enforced by syntax, ordinarily indicated by punctuation. A *run-on* line ends with no syntactical pause, running the meaning of the phrase into the next line, without punctuation, to create an effect called *enjambment*. The first and third lines in "Frost at Midnight," immediately below, are end stopped, the second run on, creating an enjambment between lines two and three. A *caesura* is a syntactical pause within a line, indicated by punctuation: the second line in "Frost at Midnight" contains one caesura and the third line three. A poem with few caesuras and many end-stopped lines has a much more regular (and even monotonous) effect than a poem with many caesuras and many run-on lines.

Frost at Midnight

Samuel Taylor Coleridge   (1772–1834)

The frost performs its secret ministry,
Unhelped by any wind. The owlet's cry
Came loud—and hark, again! loud as before.
The inmates of my cottage, all at rest,
Have left me to that solitude, which suits   5
Abstruser musings: save that at my side
My cradled infant[1] slumbers peacefully.
'Tis calm indeed! so calm, that it disturbs
And vexes meditation with its strange
And extreme silentness. Sea, hill, and wood,   10
This populous village! Sea, and hill, and wood,
With all the numberless goings-on of life,
Inaudible as dreams! the thin blue flame
Lies on my low-burnt fire, and quivers not;
Only that film,[2] which fluttered on the grate,   15
Still flutters there, the sole unquiet thing.
Methinks, its motion in this hush of nature
Gives it dim sympathies with me who live,
Making it a companionable form,
Whose puny flaps and freaks the idling Spirit   20
By its own moods interprets, every where
Echo or mirror seeking of itself,
And makes a toy of Thought.

[1] Coleridge's son Hartley.
[2] The film on the grate, called a "stranger," was supposed to foretell the arrival of a friend.

But O! how oft,
How oft, at school, with most believing mind,
Presageful,[3] have I gazed upon the bars,   25
To watch that fluttering *stranger*! and as oft
With unclosed lids, already had I dreamt
Of my sweet birth-place, and the old church-tower,
Whose bells, the poor man's only music, rang
From morn to evening, all the hot Fair-day,   30
So sweetly, that they stirred and haunted me
With a wild pleasure, falling on mine ear
Most like articulate sounds of things to come!
So gazed I, till the soothing things, I dreamt,
Lulled me to sleep, and sleep prolonged my dreams!   35
And so I brooded all the following morn,
Awed by the stern preceptor's face, mine eye
Fixed with mock study on my swimming book:
Save if the door half opened, and I snatched
A hasty glance, and still my heart leaped up,   40
For still I hoped to see the *stranger's* face,
Townsman, or aunt, or sister more beloved,
My play-mate when we both were clothed alike!

Dear Babe, that sleepest cradled by my side,
Whose gentle breathings, heard in this deep calm,   45
Fill up the interspersèd vacancies
And momentary pauses of the thought!
My babe so beautiful! it thrills my heart
With tender gladness, thus to look at thee,
And think that thou shalt learn far other lore,   50
And in far other scenes! For I was reared
In the great city, pent 'mid cloisters dim,
And saw nought lovely but the sky and stars.
But *thou*, my babe! shalt wander like a breeze
By lakes and sandy shores, beneath the crags   55
Of ancient mountain, and beneath the clouds,
Which image in their bulk both lakes and shores
And mountain crags: so shalt thou see and hear
The lovely shapes and sounds intelligible
Of that eternal language, which thy God   60
Utters, who from eternity doth teach
Himself in all, and all things in himself.

[3] Foretelling.

Great universal Teacher! he shall mould
Thy spirit, and by giving make it ask.

Therefore all seasons shall be sweet to thee,   65
Whether the summer clothe the general earth
With greenness, or the redbreast sit and sing
Betwixt the tufts of snow on the bare branch
Of mossy apple-tree, while the nigh thatch
Smokes in the sun-thaw; whether the eave-drops fall   70
Heard only in the trances of the blast,
Or if the secret ministry of frost
Shall hang them up in silent icicles,
Quietly shining to the quiet Moon.

The conversational quality of this poem is enhanced by variations in the stress patterns, by extra syllables (lines 11 and 12, for instance), and by frequent caesuras and run-on lines. At the same time, the thought and the images are carefully controlled. Observe, for example, how the owlet's cry at the beginning is thrust into the memory because it comes in a line extended by the pauses of three caesuras, because the "loud" is repeated and twice stressed, as the sound echoes the sense, and because the second stress on "loud" disturbs the normal meter of the line:

$$\cup\;\;-\;|\;\cup\;\;-\;|\;\cup\;-\;|\;-\;\cup\;|\;\cup\;-\;|$$
Came loud—and hark, again: loud as before.

Long, slow lines such as "Lulled me to sleep, and sleep prolonged my dreams!" interact effectively with the relatively few brisker lines such as "Echo or mirror seeking of itself." An occasional initial stress varies the pattern at the beginnings of lines, just as a feminine ending does at times at the ends.

The twentieth century has characteristically experimented, frequently returning to traditional forms while inventing new ones. As early as 1875, Gerard Manley Hopkins was experimenting with what he called *sprung rhythm*, in which the stress count is regular, but the unstressed syllables vary in number. Similarly, William Carlos Williams's *variable foot* is a verse unit with one stress, but an indeterminate number of unstressed syllables. Marianne Moore writes *syllabic verse*, ignoring stress and counting only syllables. Her "No Swan So Fine," for example, sets up a pattern of syllable counts in the first stanza (7/8/6/8/8/5/9/) that she repeats almost precisely in the second stanza.

No Swan So Fine

Marianne Moore (1887–1972)

"No water so still as the
    dead fountains of Versailles."[1] No swan,
with swart blind look askance
and gondoliering legs, so fine
    as the chintz china one with fawn-   5
brown eyes and toothed gold
collar on to show whose bird it was.

Lodged in the Louis Fifteenth
    candelabrum-tree-of cockscomb-
tinted buttons, dahlias,   10
sea urchins, and everlastings,
    it perches on the branching foam
of polished sculptured
flowers—at ease and tall. The king is dead.

[1] A quotation taken by Moore from a magazine article. The palace at Versailles, built by Louis XIV, has many fountains.

In the last line of the poem, Moore allows herself the metrical variation of one extra syllable. That is also the only line with two caesuras. Does the resultant lengthening of the line serve any purpose?

Like Moore, Dylan Thomas at times used a rigid syllable count to determine the shape of his stanzas. In the following poem, he also allowed himself some minor variations from the pattern.

Poem in October

Dylan Thomas (1914–1953)

It was my thirtieth year to heaven
Woke to my hearing from harbour and neighbour wood
And the mussel pooled and the heron
        Priested shore
        The morning beckon   5
With water praying and call of seagull and rook
And the knock of sailing boats on the net webbed wall
        Myself to set foot
        That second
In the still sleeping town and set forth.   10

My birthday began with the water-
Birds and the birds of the winged trees flying my name

Above the farms and the white horses
   And I rose
     In rainy autumn 15
And walked abroad in a shower of all my days.
High tide and the heron dived when I took the road
   Over the border
     And the gates
Of the town closed as the town awoke. 20

A springful of larks in a rolling
Cloud and the roadside bushes brimming with whistling
   Blackbirds and the sun of October
     Summery
   On the hill's shoulder. 25
Here were fond climates and sweet singers suddenly
Come in the morning where I wandered and listened
   To the rain wringing
     Wind blow cold
In the wood faraway under me. 30

Pale rain over the dwindling harbour
And over the sea wet church the size of a snail
   With its horns through mist and the castle
     Brown as owls
   But all the gardens 35
Of spring and summer were blooming in the tall tales
Beyond the border and under the lark full cloud.
   There could I marvel
     My birthday
Away but the weather turned around. 40

It turned away from the blithe country
And down the other air and the blue altered sky
   Streamed again a wonder of summer
     With apples
   Pears and red currants 45
And I saw in the turning so clearly a child's
Forgotten mornings when he walked with his mother
   Through the parables
     Of sun light
And the legends of the green chapels 50

And the twice told fields of infancy
That his tears burned my cheeks and his heart moved in mine.
   These were the woods the river and sea
     Where a boy

In the listening   55
Summertime of the dead whispered the truth of his joy
To the trees and the stones and the fish in the tide.
    And the mystery
        Sang alive
Still in the water and singingbirds.   60

And there could I marvel my birthday
Away but the weather turned around. And the true
    Joy of the long dead child sang burning
        In the sun.
    It was my thirtieth   65
Year to heaven stood there then in the summer noon
Though the town below lay leaved with October blood.
    O may my heart's truth
        Still be sung
On this high hill in a year's turning.   70

Free verse discards all restrictions of stress and syllable-count. Lines are organized only by the poet's "feel" for his rhythm or by some largely subjective standard, as when Allen Ginsberg wrote of his "Howl" that each line is "a single breath unit." Generally, the "free verse" poets have subscribed to T. S. Eliot's dictum, "No verse is free for the man who wants to do a good job," even though they have not always been able to explain their methods.

CHAPTER 6

Traditional Forms

The *form* of a poem is the shape dictated by its structural elements: the meter, the number of lines, the *rhyme scheme* (the pattern of repetition made by the rhyme words), and the characteristic *stanza* (fixed number of lines, with a particular rhyme scheme, repeated as a unit). Of the traditional forms, the ballad and the sonnet have been especially popular. The villanelle and the sestina are much rarer.

Ballad

A *ballad* is a song that tells a story. A *folk ballad* (or *traditional ballad*) has been shaped by oral transmission: the words of the original composer have been modified as the song has been passed from one singer to another so that the song is finally a collaboration of numerous forgotten singers.[1] A *broadside ballad* is one commemorating some local atrocity, printed on one side of a sheet of paper, and hawked in the streets like newspapers. Broadside ballads are usually cruder than folk ballads, which have been worn smooth by oral transmission. A *literary ballad* is written by a sophisticated poet in imitation of folk or broadside ballads.

"The Wife of Usher's Well" illustrates the traditional *ballad stanza*: four lines, the first and third in iambic tetrameter, without rhyme, and the second and fourth in iambic trimeter, with rhyme. This 4/3/4/3 iambic stanza, rhyming *abcb*, is the most common ballad stanza, enduring for centuries on both sides of the Atlantic and widely adapted in lyric poetry, hymns, greeting cards, and popular songs.

The Wife of Usher's Well

There lived a wife at Usher's Well,
    And a wealthy wife was she;
She had three stout and stalwart sons,
    And sent them oer the sea.   4

---

[1] For English folk ballads, the basic source is Francis J. Child, *The English and Scottish Popular Ballads*. For American folk ballads see such collections as Alan Lomax, *The Folksongs of North America*; Vance Randolph, *Ozark Folksongs*; Newman Ivey White, *The Frank C. Brown Collection of North Carolina Folklore*.

They hadna been a week from her,
   A week but barely ane,
When word came to the carline[1] wife
   That her three sons were gane.   8

They hadna been a week from her,
   A week but barely three,
When word came to the carlin wife
   That her sons she'd never see.   12

'I wish the wind may never cease,
   Nor fashes[2] in the flood,
Till my three sons come hame to me,
   In earthly flesh and blood'   16

It fell about the Martinmass,[3]
   When nights are lang and mirk,[4]
The carlin wife's three sons came hame,
   And their hats were o the birk.[5]   20

It neither grew in syke[6] nor ditch,
   Nor yet in ony sheugh;[7]
But at the gates of Paradise,
   That birk grew fair eneugh.   24

'Blow up the fire, my maidens,
   Bring water from the well;
For a' my house shall feast this night,
   Since my three sons are well.'   28

And she has made to them a bed,
   She's made it large and wide,
And she's taen[8] her mantle her about,
   Sat down at the bed-side.   32

Up then the crew the red, red cock,
   And up and crew the gray;
The eldest to the youngest said,
   'T is time we were away.   36

The cock he hadna crawd but once,
   And clapped his wings at a',

[1] Old woman, witch.
[2] Troubles.
[3] Feast of St. Martin, November 11.
[4] Dark.
[5] Birch.
[6] Grove.
[7] Dell.
[8] Taken.

When the youngest to the eldest said,
　Brother, we must awa.   40

'The cock doth craw, the day~doth daw,
　The channerin[9] worm doth chide;
Gin[10] we be mist[11] out o our place,
　A sair[12] pain we maun[13] bide.   44

'Fare ye weel, my mother dear !
　Fareweel to barn and byre ![14]
And fare ye weel, the bonny lass
　That kindles my mother's fire !   48

[9] Plaintive.
[10] If.
[11] Missed.
[12] Sore.
[13] Must.
[14] Cow shed.

　With its consistent feminine rhymes, "Barbara Allan" illustrates the flexibility of the traditional ballad stanza. Like "The Wife of Usher's Well" and most other traditional ballads, "Barbara Allan" includes lines that scan awkwardly in reading but move well with the music when sung.

Barbry Ellen[1]

All in the merry month of May,
　When the green buds they were swelling,
Young William Green on his death-bed lay,
　For the love of Barbry Ellen.   4

He sent his servant to the town,
　To the place where she was dwelling,
Saying, my master bids you come,
　If your name is Barbry Ellen.   8

Then slowly, slowly she got up,
　And slowly came she nigh him,
And when she pulled the curtains back,
　Young man, I think you're dying.   12

O yes, I'm sick, I'm very very sick,
　And I never will be any better,
Until I have the love of one,
　The love of Barbry Ellen.   16

[1] This version of "Barbara Allan" (Child 84) was collected in Pine Mountain, Kentucky in 1916.

O don't you remember in yonder town,
 In the place where you were dwelling,
You drank the health of the ladies all around,
 But you slighted Barbry Ellen.   20

O yes, I remember in yonder town,
 In the place where I was dwelling,
I drank the health of the ladies all around,
 But my love was to Barbry Ellen.   24

He turned his pale face to the wall,
 And death was in him dwelling.
Adieu, adieu, my kind friends all,
 Be kind to Barbry Ellen.   28

As she was going through the field,
 She heard the death bells knelling,
And every stroke they seemed to say,
 Hard-hearted Barbry Ellen.   32

She looked east, she looked west,
 And saw the pale corpse coming.
Go bring him here and lay him down,
 And let me look upon him.   36

The more she looked, the more she grieved,
 Until she burst out crying.
Go take him away, go take him away,
 For I am now a-dying.   40

O Mother, O Mother, come make my bed,
 Come make it soft and narrow;
Sweet William died for me today,
 I'll die for him tomorrow.   44

O Father, O Father, come dig my grave,
 O dig it deep and narrow;
Sweet William died for love of me,
 And I will die for sorrow.   48

They buried her in the old churchyard,
 And William's grave was nigh her,
And out of his grave there grew a red rose,
 And out of hers a briar.   52

They grew and grew to the old church tower,
 And they could not grow any higher,
They grew and grew till they tied love knots,
 And the rose wrapped round the briar. 56

Although scanning in iambs 4/3/4/3, the essential beat of a traditional ballad is really 4/4/4/4, with the three-beat line sometimes filled out
with an "Oh" or a "Ho." Thus here the last syllable of each trimeter line,
unstressed in reading, picks up an extra beat from the music:

$$\cup \; -| \cup \; - | \cup -| \cup -|$$
I'll die for him tomorrow   .

This nonverbal stress may be called a *rhythmic stress*. The background
music also lets the lines with ten or eleven syllables, rather than the
eight of a standard iambic tetrameter line, slip easily into the same four-
beat pattern.

As I Walked Out One Evening

W. H. Auden   (1907–1973)

As I walked out one evening,
  Walking down Bristol Street,
The crowds upon the pavement
  Were fields of harvest wheat.   4

And down by the brimming river
  I heard a lover sing
Under an arch of the railway:
  'Love has no ending.   8

'I'll love you, dear, I'll love you
  Till China and Africa meet,
And the river jumps over the mountain
  And the salmon sing in the street,   12

'I'll love you till the ocean
  Is folded and hung up to dry
And the seven stars go squawking
  Like geese about the sky.   16

The years shall run like rabbits,
  For in my arms I hold
The Flower of the Ages,
  And the first love of the world.'   20

But all the clocks in the city
  Began to whirr and chime:
'O let not Time deceive you,
  You cannot conquer Time.   24

'In the burrows of the Nightmare
  Where Justice naked is,

Time watches from the shadow
    And coughs when you would kiss.   28

'In headaches and in worry
    Vaguely life leaks away,
And Time will have his fancy
    To-morrow or to-day.   32

'Into many a green valley
    Drifts the appalling snow;
Time breaks the threaded dances
    And the diver's brilliant bow.   36

'O plunge your hands in water,
    Plunge them in up to the wrist;
Stare, stare in the basin
    And wonder what you've missed.   40

'The glacier knocks in the cupboard,
    The desert sighs in the bed,
And the crack in the tea-cup opens
    A lane to the land of the dead.   44

'Where the beggars raffle the banknotes
    And the Giant is enchanting to Jack,
And the Lily-white Boy is a Roarer,
    And Jill goes down on her back.   48

'O look, look in the mirror,
    O look in your distress;
Life remains a blessing
    Although you cannot bless.   52

'O stand, stand at the window
    As the tears scald and start;
You shall love your crooked neighbour
    With your crooked heart.'   56

It was late, late in the evening,
    The lovers they were gone;
The clocks had ceased their chiming,
    And the deep river ran on.   60

In this literary ballad a highly sophisticated poet has adapted the techniques of the folk poet to his own use. In normal scansion the first and third lines of each stanza would be considered iambic trimeter, with feminine endings:

◡ –| ◡   – | ◡   –   ◡ |
As I walked out one evening;

◡   – | ◡ –| ◡   –   ◡ |
The crowds upon the pavement.

Yet so common is the traditional folk stanza and so careful is Auden's adaptation that the lines can easily be seen as iambic tetrameter, with rhythmic stress dictated by a silent melody:

◡ –| ◡   – | ◡   – | ◡   – |
As I walked out one evening [oh];

◡   – | ◡ –| ◡   – | ◡   – |
The crowds upon the pavement [ho].

Many traditional ballads fill out the full 4/4/4/4 beat, as does E. E. Cummings in the following poem.

Anyone Lived in a Pretty How Town
E. E. Cummings (1894–1962)

anyone lived in a pretty how town
(with up so floating many bells down)
spring summer autumn winter
he sang his didn't his danced his did.   4

Women and men(both little and small)
cared for anyone not at all
they sowed their isn't they reaped their same
sun moon stars rain   8

children guessed(but only a few
and down they forgot as up they grew
autumn winter spring summer)
that noone loved him more by more   12

when by now and tree by leaf
she laughed his joy she cried his grief
bird by snow and stir by still
anyone's any was all to her   16

someones married their everyones
laughed their cryings and did their dance
(sleep wake hope and then)they
said their nevers they slept their dream   20

stars rain sun moon
(and only the snow can begin to explain

how children are apt to forget to remember
with up so floating many bells down)   24

one day anyone died i guess
(and noone stooped to kiss his face)
busy folk buried them side by side
little by little and was by was   28

all by all and deep by deep
and more by more they dream their sleep
noone and anyone earth by april
wish by spirit and if by yes.   32

Women and men(both dong and ding)
summer autumn winter spring
reaped their sowing and went their came
sun moon stars rain   36

Like Auden and the folk poets, Cummings uses his insistent rhythms
to fill out some lines with rhythmic stress:

$$\cup \; - \; | \cup \quad - \; | \cup \quad - \; | \cup \quad - \; |$$
sun   moon   stars   rain.

Other irregularities vary slightly without greatly changing the fundamental four-beat rhythm.

One of the most accomplished contemporary ballad makers, Woody
Guthrie in the next song extended the basic four-stress pattern to accommodate a melodic line with a ONE-two-three beat:

$$\cup \; | \; - \; \cup \; \cup \; | \; - \; \cup \; \cup \; | \; - \; \cup \; \cup \; | \; - \; \cup \; \cup \; |$$
The crops are all in and the peaches are rotting   .

Considered by itself, the verbal structure has the effect of an irregular
dactylic tetrameter.

Plane Wreck at Los Gatos [1]

Woody Guthrie (1912–1967)

The crops are all in and the peaches are rotting,
The oranges are piled in their creosote dumps;
You're flying them back to the Mexican border
To pay all their money to wade back again.   4

---

[1] On January 28, 1948, a plane crash in California killed twenty-eight migrant workers being de-
ported to Mexico.

Refrain:

      Goodbye to my Juan, Goodbye Rosalita;
      Adiós mes amigos, Jesús and Marie,
      You won't have a name when you ride the big airplane:
      And all they will call you will be deportee.   8

My father's own father he waded that river;
They took all the money he made in his life;
My brothers and sisters come working the fruit trees
And they rode the truck till they took down and died.   12

Some of us are illegal and some are not wanted,
Our work contract's out and we have to move on;
Six hundred miles to that Mexico border,
They chase us like outlaws, like rustlers, like thieves.   16

We died in your hills, we died in your deserts,
We died in your valleys and died on your plains;
We died 'neath your trees and we died in your bushes,
Both sides of this river we died just the same.   20

The sky plane took fire over Los Gatos Canyon,
A fireball of lightning and shook all our hills.
Who are all these friends all scattered like dry leaves?
The radio says they are just deportees.   24

Is this the best way we can grow our big orchards?
Is this the best way we grow our good fruit?
To fall like dry leaves to rot on my topsoil
And be called by no name except deportees?   28

The last two poems in this section show the influence of the traditional ballad stanza, though they also show considerable variation from it.

A Runnable Stag

John Davidson   (1857–1909)

    When the pods went pop on the broom, green broom,[1]
      And apples began to be golden-skinned,
    We harboured[2] a stag in the Priory[3] coomb,[4]
      And we feathered[5] his trail up-wind, up-wind,

[1] A shrub of the pea family.
[2] Traced.
[3] Monastery or nunnery.
[4] Small valley.
[5] Set the hounds on.

We feathered his trail up-wind—   5
  A stag of warrant, a stag, a stag,
  A runnable stag, a kingly crop,
  Brow, bay and tray[6] and three on top,
  A stag, a runnable stag.

Then the huntsman's horn rang yap, yap, yap,   10
  And 'Forwards' we heard the harbourer[7] shout;
But 'twas only a brocket[8] that broke a gap
  In the beechen underwood, driven out,
  From the underwood antlered out
    By warrant and might of the stag, the stag,   15
    The runnable stag, whose lordly mind
    Was bent on sleep, though beamed[9] and tined
    He stood, a runnable stag.

So we tufted the covert[10] till afternoon
  With Tinkerman's Pup and Bell-of-the-North;[11]   20
And hunters were sulky and hounds out of tune
  Before we tufted the right stag forth,
  Before we tufted him forth,
    The stag of warrant, the wily stag,
    The runnable stag with his kingly crop,   25
    Brow, bay and tray and three on top,
    The royal and runnable stag.

It was Bell-of-the-North and Tinkerman's Pup
  That stuck to the scent till the copse was drawn.[12]
'Tally ho! tally ho!' and the hunt was up,   30
  The tufters whipped and the pack laid on,
  The resolute pack laid on,
    And the stag of warrant away at last,
    The runnable stag, the same, the same,
    His hoofs on fire, his horns like flame,   35
    A stag, a runnable stag.

'Let your gelding be: if you check or chide
He stumbles at once and you're out of the hunt;
For three hundred gentlemen, able to ride,
  On hunters accustomed to bear the brunt,   40

---

[6] Brow, bay and tray: first, second, and third branches of a stag's horns.
[7] The person charged with tracing the stag.
[8] A two-year-old stag.
[9] Having fourth-year horns, or tines.
[10] Beat the undergrowth.
[11] Names of the hounds.
[12] The wood was searched.

Accustomed to bear the brunt,
    Are after the runnable stag, the stag,
    The runnable stag with his kingly crop,
    Brow, bay and tray and three on top,
      The right, the runnable stag.'   45

By perilous paths in coomb and dell,
    The heather, the rocks, and the river-bed,
The pace grew hot, for the scent lay well,
    And a runnable stag goes right ahead,
    The quarry went right ahead—   50
      Ahead, ahead, and fast and far;
      His antlered crest, his cloven hoof,
      Brow, bay and tray and three aloof,
      The stag, the runnable stag.

For a matter of twenty miles and more,   55
    By the densest hedge and the highest wall,
Through herds of bullocks he baffled the lore
    Of harbourer, huntsman, hounds and all,
    Of harbourer, hounds and all—
      The stag of warrant, the wily stag,   60
      For twenty miles, and five and five,
      He ran, and he never was caught alive,
      This stag, this runnable stag.

When he turned at bay in the leafy gloom,
    In the emerald gloom where the brook ran deep,   65
He heard in the distance the rollers[13] boom,
    And he saw in a vision of peaceful sleep,
    In a wonderful vision of sleep,
      A stag of warrant, a stag, a stag,
      A runnable stag in a jewelled bed,   70
      Under the sheltering ocean dead,
      A stag, a runnable stag.

So a fateful hope lit up his eye,
    And he opened his nostrils wide again,
And he tossed his branching antlers high   75
    As he headed the hunt down the Charlock glen,
    As he raced down the echoing glen,
      For five miles more, the stag, the stag,
      For twenty miles, and five and five,
      Not to be caught now, dead or alive,   80
      The stag, the runnable stag.

[13] Waves, billows.

Three hundred gentlemen, able to ride,
  Three hundred horses as gallant and free,
Behind him escape on the evening tide,
  Far out till he sank in the Severn Sea,[14]   85
  Till he sank in the depths of the sea—
    The stag, the buoyant stag, the stag
    That slept at last in a jewelled bed
    Under the sheltering ocean spread,
    The stag, the runnable stag.   90

[14] At the mouth of the Severn River, between Gloucestershire and Monmouthshire, England.

Recruiting Drive

Charles Causley (1917–)

Under the willow the willow
  I heard the butcher-bird sing,
*Come out you fine young fellow
  From under your mother's wing.*   4
*I'll show you the magic garden
  That hangs in the beamy air,
The way of the lynx and the angry Sphinx
  And the fun of the freezing fair.*   8

*Lie down lie down with my daughter
  Beneath the Arabian tree,
Gaze on your face in the water
  Forget the scribbling sea.*   12
*Your pillow the nine bright shiners
  Your bed the spilling sand,
But the terrible toy of my lily-white boy
  Is the gun in his innocent hand.*   16

You must take off your clothes for the doctor
  And stand as straight as a pin,
His hand of stone on your white breast-bone
  Where the bullets all go in.   20
They'll dress you in lawn and linen
  And fill you with Plymouth gin,
O the devil may wear a rose in his hair
  I'll wear my fine doe-skin.   24

My mother weeps as I leave her
  But I tell her it won't be long,
The murderers wail in Wandsworth Gaol[1]

[1] A London prison.

But I shoot a more popular song.   28
  Down in the enemy country
    Under the enemy tree
There lies a lad whose heart has gone bad
    Waiting for me, for me.   32

He says I have no culture
  And that when I've stormed the pass
I shall fall on the farm with a smoking arm
    And ravish his bonny lass.   36
Under the willow the willow
  Death spreads her dripping wings
And caught in the snare of the bleeding air
    The butcher-bird sings, sings, sings.   40

Sonnets, villanelles, and sestinas, unlike ballads, are tightly controlled forms.

Sonnet

A *sonnet* is 14 lines of iambic pentameter, with either of two rhyme schemes, the *Shakespearean sonnet*, composed of three *quatrains* and a *couplet*, rhyming *abab cdcd efef gg;* and the *Italian* (or *Petrarchan*) *sonnet*, composed of an *octave*, rhyming *abba abba*, and a *sestet*, rhyming *cde cde* or in some variant pattern. Some writers, of course, have tried other schemes, but most have had their say by mastering the rules of the Shakespearean or Italian game.

Although Shakespeare's three quatrains and a couplet provide three natural containers for thought, and a conclusion, he frequently kept the larger division of octave and sestet found in the earlier Italian sonnet. In "Shall I Compare Thee to a Summer's Day," note how the first two quatrains, the octave, set up the thought, and how the last six lines, the sestet, resolve the question, beginning with "But" at the turn. The final couplet gives the resolution a strong conclusion.

Shall I Compare Thee to a Summer's Day?

William Shakespeare (1564–1616)

Shall I compare thee to a summer's day?
Thou art more lovely and more temperate:
Rough winds do shake the darling buds of May,
And summer's lease hath all too short a date: 4
Sometime too hot the eye of heaven shines,
And often is his gold complexion dimmed;
And every fair from fair sometime declines,

By chance, or nature's changing course untrimmed;   8
But thy eternal summer shall not fade,
Nor lose possession of that fair thou ow'st,[1]
Nor shall death brag thou wander'st in his shade,
When in eternal lines to time thou grow'st;   12
    So long as men can breathe, or eyes can see,
    So long lives this, and this gives life to thee.

[1] Ownest.

Other poets have worked out further blendings of Shakespearean and Italian patterns.

To Sleep

John Keats (1795–1821)

O soft embalmer of the still midnight,
    Shutting with careful fingers and benign
Our gloom-pleased eyes, embowered from the light,
    Enshaded in forgetfulness divine: 4
O soothest Sleep! If so it please thee, close,
    In midst of this thine hymn, my willing eyes,
Or wait the 'Amen', ere thy poppy[1] throws
    Around my bed its lulling charities.   8
Then save me, or the passèd day will shine
Upon my pillow, breeding many woes;
    Save me from curious conscience, that still hoards
Its strength for darkness, burrowing like a mole;   12
    Turn the key deftly in the oilèd wards,[2]
And seal the hushèd casket of my soul.

[1] The opium poppy.
[2] The ridges of a lock that allow a particular key to pass, but not others.

Leda and the Swan[1]

W. B. Yeats (1865–1939)

A sudden blow: the great wings beating still
Above the staggering girl, her thighs caressed
By the dark webs, her nape caught in his bill,
He holds her helpless breast upon his breast.   4

How can those terrified vague fingers push
The feathered glory from her loosening thighs?

[1] Leda, raped by Zeus in the form of a swan, later gave birth to Helen of Troy and Clytemnestra.

And how can body, laid in that white rush,
But feel the strange heart beating where it lies? 8

A shudder in the loins engenders there
The broken wall, the burning roof and tower[2]
And Agamemnon dead.[3]
                    Being so caught up,
So mastered by the brute blood of the air, 12
Did she put on his knowledge with his power
Before the indifferent beak could let her drop?

[2] The destruction of Troy, in a war fought over Helen.
[3] Killed by his wife Clytemnestra.

Design

Robert Frost (1874–1963)

I found a dimpled spider, fat and white,
On a white heal-all,[1] holding up a moth
Like a white piece of rigid satin cloth—
Assorted characters of death and blight 4
Mixed ready to begin the morning right,
Like the ingredients of a witches' broth—
A snow-drop spider, a flower like a froth,
And dead wings carried like a paper kite. 8

What had that flower to do with being white,
The wayside blue and innocent heal-all?
What brought the kindred spider to that height,
Then steered the white moth thither in the night? 12
What but design of darkness to appall?—
If design govern in a thing so small.

[1] A flower that is usually blue.

Here are some more representative sonnets to illustrate the possibilities of the form. The last one, by Hopkins, is the extravagant variation of an unusual poet.

When in Disgrace with Fortune and Men's Eyes

William Shakespeare (1564–1616)

When in disgrace with fortune and men's eyes
I all alone beweep my outcast state,
And trouble deaf heaven with my bootless[1] cries,

[1] Useless, unrewarding.

And look upon myself, and curse my fate,   4
Wishing me like to one more rich in hope,
Featured like him, like him with friends possessed,
Desiring this man's art, and that man's scope,
With what I most enjoy contented least;   8
Yet in these thoughts myself almost despising,
Haply I think on thee,—and then my state,
Like to the lark at break of day arising
From sullen earth, sings hymns at heaven's gate;   12
    For thy sweet love remembered such wealth brings
    That then I scorn to change my state with kings.

What Lips My Lips Have Kissed

Edna St. Vincent Millay (1892–1950)

What lips my lips have kissed, and where, and why,
I have forgotten, and what arms have lain
Under my head till morning; but the rain
Is full of ghosts tonight, that tap and sigh   4
Upon the glass and listen for reply,
And in my heart there stirs a quiet pain
For unremembered lads that not again
Will turn to me at midnight with a cry.   8
Thus in the winter stands the lonely tree,
Nor knows what birds have vanished one by one,
Yet knows its boughs more silent than before:
I cannot say what loves have come and gone,   12
I only know that summer sang in me
A little while, that in me sings no more.

The World Is Too Much with Us

William Wordsworth (1770–1850)

The world is too much with us; late and soon,
Getting and spending, we lay waste our powers:
Little we see in Nature that is ours;
We have given our hearts away, a sordid boon![1]   4
This Sea that bares her bosom to the moon;
The winds that will be howling at all hours,
And are up-gathered now like sleeping flowers;
For this, for everything, we are out of tune;   8
It moves us not.—Great God! I'd rather be

[1] Gift.

A Pagan suckled in a creed outworn;
So might I, standing on this pleasant lea,[2]
Have glimpses that would make me less forlorn;   12
Have sight of Proteus[3] rising from the sea;
Or hear old Triton blow his wreathèd horn.

[2] Meadow.
[3] Proteus and Triton: sea gods.

When Serpents Bargain for the Right to Squirm

E. E. Cummings   (1894–1962)

when serpents bargain for the right to squirm
and the sun strikes to gain a living wage—
when thorns regard their roses with alarm
and rainbows are insured against old age   4

when every thrush may sing no new moon in
if all screech-owls have not okayed his voice
—and any wave signs on the dotted line
or else an ocean is compelled to close   8

when the oak begs permission of the birch
to make an acorn—valleys accuse their
mountains of having altitude—and march
denounces april as a saboteur   12

then we'll believe in that incredible
unanimal mankind(and not until)

Dear, Why Make You More of a Dog than Me?

Sir Philip Sidney   (1554–1586)

Dear, why make you more of a dog than me?
If he do love, I burn, I burn in love;
If he wait well, I never thence would move;
If he be fair, yet but a dog can be.   4
Little he is, so little worth is he;
He barks, my songs thine own voice oft doth prove;
Bidden, perhaps he fetcheth thee a glove,
But I, unbid, fetch even my soul to thee.   8
Yet, while I languish, him that bosom clips,[1]
That lap doth lap, nay lets, in spite of spite,

[1] Embraces.

This sour-breathed mate taste of those sugared lips.
Alas, if you grant only such delight   12
     To witless things, then Love, I hope, since wit
Becomes a clog,[2] will soon ease me of it.

[2] A wooden block attached to a man's or animal's leg to prevent straying.

Bright Star! Would I Were Steadfast as Thou Art

John Keats (1795–1821)

Bright star! Would I were steadfast as thou art—
     Not in lone splendour hung aloft the night
And watching, with eternal lids apart,
     Like nature's patient, sleepless eremite,[1]   4
The moving waters at their priestlike task
     Of pure ablution[2] round earth's human shores,
Or gazing on the new soft-fallen mask
     Of snow upon the mountains and the moors;   8
No—yet still steadfast, still unchangeable,
     Pillowed upon my fair love's ripening breast,
To feel for ever its soft fall and swell,
     Awake for ever in a sweet unrest,   12
Still, still to hear her tender-taken breath,
And so live ever—or else swoon to death.

[1] Hermit.
[2] Washing, especially as a religious ceremony.

Spelt from Sibyl's[1] Leaves

Gerard Manley Hopkins (1844–1889)

Earnest, earthless, equal, attuneable, | vaulty, voluminous, . . . stupendous
Evening strains to be tíme's vást, | womb-of-all, home-of-all, hearse-of-all night.
Her fond yellow hornlight[2] wound to the west, | her wild hollow hoarlight hung
     to the height
Waste; her earliest stars, earlstars, | stárs principal, overbend us,   4
Fíre-féaturing heaven. For earth | her being has unbound; her dapple is at an end, as-
tray or aswarm, all throughther,[3] in throngs; | self ín self steepèd and páshed[4]—
     qúite

[1] Sibyl: a prophetess or oracle. The sonnet is in sprung rhythm, with eight feet to the line, and, according to Hopkins, should be performed in "loud, leisurely, poetical (not rhetorical) recitation, with long rests, long dwells on the rhyme and other marked syllables, and so on."
[2] In his journal Hopkins wrote of the "horned rays" of the setting sun.
[3] Through other (Scots): pell-mell.
[4] Smashed.

Disremembering, dísmémbering | áll now. Heart, you round[5] me right
With: Óur évening is over us; óur night | whélms, whélms, ánd will end us.   8
Only the beakleaved boughs dragonish | damask[6] the tool-smooth bleak light; black,
Ever so black on it. Óur tale, O óur oracle! | Lét life, wáned, ah lét life wind
Off hér once skéined stained véined varíety | upon, áll on twó spools; párt, pen, páck[7]
Now her áll in twó flocks, twó folds—black, white; | right, wrong; reckon but, reck but, mind   12
But thése two; wáre[8] of a wórld where bút these | twó tell, each off the óther; of a rack
Where, selfwrung, selfstrung, sheathe–and shelterless, | thóughts agáinst thoughts ín groans grínd.

[5] Counsel, advise.
[6] Make a pattern on.
[7] Part, pen, pack; sort out, as sheep.
[8] Aware.

Villanelle

A *villanelle* has five *tercets* (three-line stanzas) and a quatrain, all on two rhymes repeated in an *aba* pattern, with the last stanza *abaa*. The whole first and third lines are repeated alternately, as the final lines of stanzas two, three, four, and five, and together to conclude the quatrain. A difficult form, it is seldom written with success. Of the following examples, the first is in iambic trimeter, the others in iambic pentameter.

The House on the Hill
Edwin Arlington Robinson   (1869–1935)

They are all gone away,
   The House is shut and still,
   There is nothing more to say.   3

Through broken walls and gray
   The winds blow bleak and shrill.
   They are all gone away.   6

Nor is there one to-day
   To speak them good or ill:
   There is nothing more to say.   9

Why is it then we stray
   Around the sunken sill?
   They are all gone away,   12

And our poor fancy-play
    For them is wasted skill:
There is nothing more to say.   15

There is ruin and decay
    In the House on the Hill:
They are all gone away,
There is nothing more to say.   18

Do Not Go Gentle into That Good Night
Dylan Thomas (1914–1953)

Do not go gentle into that good night,
Old age should burn and rave at close of day;
Rage, rage against the dying of the light.   3

Though wise men at their end know dark is right,
Because their words had forked no lightning they
Do not go gentle into that good night.   6

Good men, the last wave by, crying how bright
Their frail deeds might have danced in a green bay,
Rage, rage against the dying of the light.   9

Wild men who caught and sang the sun in flight,
And learn, too late, they grieved it on its way,
Do not go gentle into that good night.   12

Grave men, near death, who see with blinding sight
Blind eyes could blaze like meteors and be gay,
Rage, rage against the dying of the light.   15

And you, my father, there on the sad height,
Curse, bless, me now with your fierce tears, I pray.
Do not go gentle into that good night.   18
Rage, rage against the dying of the light.

The Waking
Theodore Roethke (1908–1963)

I wake to sleep, and take my waking slow.
I feel my fate in what I cannot fear.
I learn by going where I have to go.   3

We think by feeling. What is there to know?
I hear my being dance from ear to ear.
I wake to sleep, and take my waking slow.   6

Of those so close beside me, which are you?
God bless the Ground! I shall walk softly there,
And learn by going where I have to go. 9

Light takes the Tree; but who can tell us how?
The lowly worm climbs up the winding stair;
I wake to sleep, and take my waking slow. 12

Great Nature has another thing to do
To you and me; so take the lively air,
And, lovely, learn by going where to go. 15

This shaking keeps me steady. I should know.
What falls away is always. And is near.
I wake to sleep, and take my waking slow. 18
I learn by going where I have to go.

Sestina

The *sestina* is still more complex than the villanelle. Consequently, it is seldom attempted. It has 6 six-line stanzas and a three-line *envoy*, or conclusion. Instead of rhyme, it ends the lines of each stanza with the same six words. Within the three lines of the envoy the six key words are repeated again, three within the lines and three at the ends.

In its strict form, the sestina interweaves the repeated words systematically. After the first stanza establishes the key words, each succeeding stanza rearranges the end words of the one preceding, beginning with the last, then following with the first, then the fifth, second, fourth, and third. In Kipling's "Sestina of the Tramp-Royal," therefore, the order of the end words for the first three stanzas is: *all, world, good, long, done, die | die, all, done, world, along, good | good, die, long, all, world, done.* Save for the minor substitution in two places of "along" for "long," the sestina follows through in strict form until the end. In the envoy, Kipling follows a pattern that repeats the first three words of the sixth stanza in order in the middle of the lines (*world, long, die*) and the last three in order at the ends (*done, good, all*).

Sestina of the Tramp-Royal
Rudyard Kipling (1865–1936)

Speakin' in general, I 'ave tried 'em all—
The 'appy roads that take you o'er the world.
Speakin' in general, I 'ave found them good 3

For such as cannot use one bed too long,
But must get 'ence, the same as I 'ave done,
An' go observin' matters till they die.   6

What do it matter where or 'ow we die,
So long as we've our 'ealth to watch ĭt all—
The different ways that different things are done,   9
An' men an' women lovin' in this world;
Takin' our chances as they come along,
An' when they ain't, pretendin' they are good?   12

In cash or credit—no, it aren't no good;
You 'ave to 'ave the 'abit or you'd die,
Unless you lived your life but one day long,   15
Nor didn't prophesy nor fret at all,
But drew your tucker[1] some'ow from the world,
An' never bothered what you might ha' done.   18

But, Gawd, what things are they I 'aven't done?
I've turned my 'and to most, an' turned it good,
In various situations round the world—   21
For 'im that doth not work must surely die;
But that's no reason man should labour all
'Is life on one same shift—life's none so long.   24

Therefore, from job to job I've moved along.
Pay couldn't 'old me when my time was done,
For something in my 'ead upset it all,   27
Till I 'ad dropped whatever 'twas for good,
An', out at sea, be'eld the dock-lights die,
An' met my mate—the wind that tramps the world!   30

It's like a book, I think, this bloomin' world,
Which you can read and care for just so long,
But presently you feel that you will die   33
Unless you get the page you're readin' done,
An' turn another—likely not so good;
But what you're after is to turn 'em all.   36

Gawd bless this world! Whatever she 'ath done—
Excep' when awful long—I've found it good.
So write, before I die, " 'E liked it all!"   39

---

[1] Daily rations.

In the next sestina, the writer has abandoned the strict order of repetition, but kept the general form.

Rink Keeper's Sestina

Hockey, hockey

George Draper (1942–   )

Call me Zamboni.[1] Nights my job is hockey.
I make the ice and watch the kids take slapshots
At each other. They act like Esposito,[2]   3
As tough in the slot as Phil, as wild with fury
In fights. Their coaches tell me this is pleasure.
But it isn't pleasure. What it is, is Hockey.   6

Now let me tell you what I mean by Hockey.
I mean the fights. I mean young kids in fury,
And all these coaches yelling for more slapshots.   9
I tell you, blood is spilled here. This is pleasure?
It seems to me the coaches should teach hockey,
Not how to act like Schultz or Esposito.   12

Look, I have nothing against Phil Esposito.
He's one of the greats, no question, it's a pleasure
To watch him play. My point is, why teach fury?   15
If I know life (at least if I know hockey),
Then fury's here to stay. We don't need Hockey
To tell us that, we don't need fights and slapshots.   18

Like yesterday. I heard a coach yell, "Slapshots!
Take slapshots, son! You think Phil Esposito
Hangs back? And hit! And hit again! That's hockey!"   21
But he was wrong. The kid was ten. That's Hockey.
You could tell the boy admired his coach's fury.
It won't be long before he hits with pleasure.   24

Sure, I'm no saint. I know. I've gotten pleasure
From fury, too, like any man. And hockey
At times gets changed around in me to Hockey.   27
I've yelled for blood at Boston Garden. Slapshots?
They've thrilled me. I've seen men clobber Esposito
And loved it when he hit them back with fury.   30

But you know what? Before these days of fury,
When indoor rinks were just a gleam in Hockey
Fanatics' eyes, there was no greater pleasure   33
Than winter mornings. Black ice. (Esposito

---

[1] Inventor of a machine that renews or "makes" the ice in ice-skating rinks.
[2] Like Schultz (below), a National Hockey League player.

Knew days like this as a boy.) Some friends. No slapshots,
But a clear, cold sky. Choose teams. Drop the puck. Play hockey.   36

Yes, before big Hockey (sorry, Esposito),
Before the fury and all the blazing slapshots,
We had great pleasure outdoors playing hockey.   39

CHAPTER 7

Free Forms

Poems in *free forms* follow no established pattern. Lines loosely metrical or in free verse vary in length; rhymes follow no regular order or are missing entirely; groupings of lines, if they exist, are without regular stanzaic form.

A Man Said to the Universe

Stephen Crane   (1871–1900)

A man said to the universe:
"Sir, I exist!"
"However," replied the universe,
"The fact has not created in me
A sense of obligation."   5

The Purse-Seine

Robinson Jeffers   (1887–1962)

Our sardine fishermen work at night in the dark of the moon; daylight or moon-
    light
They could not tell where to spread the net, unable to see the phosphorescence
    of the shoals of fish.
They work northward from Monterey, coasting Santa Cruz; off New Year's Point
    or off Pigeon Point
The look-out man will see some lakes of milk-color light on the sea's night-pur-
    ple; he points, and the helmsman
Turns the dark prow, the motorboat circles the gleaming shoal and drifts out her
    seine-net. They close the circle   5
And purse the bottom of the net, then with great labor haul it in.

                                  I cannot tell you
How beautiful the scene is, and a little terrible, then, when the crowded fish
Know they are caught, and wildly beat from one wall to the other of their clos-
    ing destiny the phosphorescent
Water to a pool of flame, each beautiful slender body sheeted with flame, like a
    live rocket

679

A comet's tail wake of clear yellow flame; while outside the narrowing   10
Floats and cordage of the net great sea-lions come up to watch, sighing in the
    dark; the vast walls of night
Stand erect to the stars.

                    Lately I was looking from a night mountain-top
On a wide city, the colored splendor, galaxies of light: how could I help but re-
    call the seine-net
Gathering the luminous fish? I cannot tell you how beautiful the city appeared,
    and a little terrible.
I thought, We have geared the machines and locked all together into interdepen-
    dence; we have built the great cities; now   15
There is no escape. We have gathered vast populations incapable of free survival,
    insulated
From the strong earth, each person in himself helpless, on all dependent. The
    circle is closed, and the net
Is being hauled in. They hardly feel the cords drawing, yet they shine already.
    The inevitable mass-disasters
Will not come in our time nor in our children's, but we and our children
Must watch the net draw narrower, government take all powers—or revolution,
    and the new government   20
Take more than all, add to kept bodies kept souls—or anarchy, the mass-disas-
    ters.

           These things are Progress;
Do you marvel our verse is troubled or frowning, while it keeps its reason? Or it
    lets go, lets the mood flow
In the manner of the recent young men into mere hysteria, splintered gleams,
    crackled laughter. But they are quite wrong.
There is no reason for amazement: surely one always knew that cultures decay,
    and life's end is death.

A Supermarket in California
Allen Ginsberg   (1926–   )

    What thoughts I have of you tonight, Walt Whitman,[1] for I walked down the
sidestreets under the trees with a headache self-conscious looking at the full
moon.
    In my hungry fatigue, and shopping for images, I went into the neon fruit su-
permarket, dreaming of your enumerations!
    What peaches and what penumbras! Whole families shopping at night! Aisles
full of husbands! Wives in the avocados, babies in the tomatoes!—and you, Gar-
cia Lorca,[2] what were you doing down by the watermelons?

[1] An American poet (1819–1892).
[2] A Spanish poet (1899–1936).

I saw you, Walt Whitman, childless, lonely old grubber, poking among the meats in the refrigerator and eyeing the grocery boys.

I heard you asking questions of each: Who killed the pork chops? What price bananas? Are you my Angel?   5

I wandered in and out of the brilliant stacks of cans following you, and followed in my imagination by the store detective.

We strode down the open corridors together in our solitary fancy tasting artichokes, possessing every frozen delicacy, and never passing the cashier.

Where are we going, Walt Whitman? The doors close in an hour. Which way does your beard point tonight?

(I touch your book and dream of our odyssey in the supermarket and feel absurd.)

Will we walk all night through solitary streets? The trees add shade to shade, lights out in the houses, we'll both be lonely.   10

Will we stroll dreaming of the lost America of love past blue automobiles in driveways, home to our silent cottage?

Ah, dear father, graybeard, lonely old courage-teacher, what America did you have when Charon[3] quit poling his ferry and you got out on a smoking bank and stood watching the boat disappear on the black waters of Lethe?[4]

[3] Charon transported dead souls over the river Styx.
[4] River of forgetfulness.

The Far Field

Theodore Roethke   (1908–1963)

1

I dream of journeys repeatedly:
Of flying like a bat deep into a narrowing tunnel,
Of driving alone, without luggage, out a long peninsula,
The road lined with snow-laden second growth,
A fine dry snow ticking the windshield,   5
Alternate snow and sleet, no on-coming traffic,
And no lights behind, in the blurred side-mirror,
The road changing from glazed tarface to a rubble of stone,
Ending at last in a hopeless sand-rut,
Where the car stalls,   10
Churning in a snowdrift
Until the headlights darken.

2

At the field's end, in the corner missed by the mower,
Where the turf drops off into a grass-hidden culvert,
Haunt of the cat-bird, nesting-place of the field-mouse,   15

Not too far away from the ever-changing flower-dump,
Among the tin cans, tires, rusted pipes, broken machinery,—
One learned of the eternal;
And in the shrunken face of a dead rat, eaten by rain and ground-beetles
(I found it lying among the rubble of an old coal bin)   20
And the tom-cat, caught near the pheasant-run,
Its entrails strewn over the half-grown flowers,
Blasted to death by the night watchman.

I suffered for birds, for young rabbits caught in the mower,
My grief was not excessive.   25
For to come upon warblers in early May
Was to forget time and death:
How they filled the oriole's elm, a twittering restless cloud, all one morning,
And I watched and watched till my eyes blurred from the bird shapes,—
Cape May, Blackburnian, Cerulean,—   30
Moving, elusive as fish, fearless,
Hanging, bunched like young fruit, bending the end branches,
Still for a moment,
Then pitching away in half-flight,
Lighter than finches,   35
While the wrens bickered and sang in the half-green hedgerows,
And the flicker drummed from his dead tree in the chicken-yard.

—Or to lie naked in sand,
In the silted shallows of a slow river,
Fingering a shell,   40
Thinking:
Once I was something like this, mindless,
Or perhaps with another mind, less peculiar;
Or to sink down to the hips in a mossy quagmire;
Or, with skinny knees, to sit astride a wet log,   45
Believing:
I'll return again,
As a snake or a raucous bird,
Or, with luck, as a lion.

I learned not to fear infinity,   50
The far field, the windy cliffs of forever,
The dying of time in the white light of tomorrow,
The wheel turning away from itself,
The sprawl of the wave,
The on-coming water.   55

3

The river turns on itself,
The tree retreats into its own shadow.

I feel a weightless change, a moving forward
As of water quickening before a narrowing channel
When banks converge, and the wide river whitens;   60
Or when two rivers combine, the blue glacial torrent
And the yellowish-green from the mountainy upland,—
At first a swift rippling between rocks,
Then a long running over flat stones
Before descending to the alluvial plain,   65
To the clay banks, and the wild grapes hanging from the elmtrees.
The slightly trembling water
Dropping a fine yellow silt where the sun stays;
And the crabs bask near the edge,
The weedy edge, alive with small snakes and bloodsuckers,—   70
I have come to a still, but not a deep center,
A point outside the glittering current;
My eyes stare at the bottom of a river,
At the irregular stones, iridescent sandgrains,
My mind moves in more than one place,   75
In a country half-land, half-water.

I am renewed by death, thought of my death,
The dry scent of a dying garden in September,
The wind fanning the ash of a low fire.
What I love is near at hand,   80
Always, in earth and air.

                              4

The lost self changes,
Turning toward the sea,
A sea-shape turning around,—
An old man with his feet before the fire,   85
In robes of green, in garments of adieu.

A man faced with his own immensity
Wakes all the waves, all their loose wandering fire.
The murmur of the absolute, the why
Of being born fails on his naked ears.   90
His spirit moves like monumental wind
That gentles on a sunny blue plateau.
He is the end of things, the final man.

All finite things reveal infinitude:
The mountain with its singular bright shade   95
Like the blue shine on freshly frozen snow,
The after-light upon ice-burdened pines;
Odor of basswood on a mountain-slope,
A scent beloved of bees;

Silence of water above a sunken tree:
The pure serene of memory in one man,—
A ripple widening from a single stone
Winding around the waters of the world.

100

CHAPTER 8

Time and Place

Many poems stand forth comparatively free of specific indications of birth. Others are closely tied to a particular event, a way of life, a manner of thought peculiar to the poet or his time. Although we are often tempted to read poems in isolation, relating them as best we can to our own vision of the world, we sometimes gain much by an effort to enter into another time, another place, another human circumstance.

The Secular Masque[1]

John Dryden (1631–1700)

[*Enter* JANUS]

JANUS.	Chronos, Chronos, mend thy pace,	
	An hundred times the rolling sun	
	Around the radiant belt has run	
	In his revolving race.	
	Behold, behold, the goal in sight,	5
	Spread thy fans, and wing thy flight.	

[*Enter* CHRONOS, *with a scythe in his hand and a great globe on his back, which he sets down at his entrance*]

CHRONOS.	Weary, weary of my weight,	
	Let me, let me drop my freight,	
	And leave the world behind.	
	I could not bear	10
	Another year	
	The load of humankind.	

[1] Dryden wrote this to celebrate the new century, ushered in by New Year's Day, 1700 (which was also to be the year of Dryden's death, on May 1, 1700). Dryden's cast consists of the following:

JANUS—two faced-god of the year, and of doorways, who looks behind and before, to past and future, and ushers in the new year, and from whom January takes its name.
CHRONOS—god of time, who set the Fates going; our Father Time, with the scythe that mows us down. His carrying the world seems to be Dryden's invention.
MOMUS—god of ridicule.
DIANA—goddess of the moon (and month), the virgin huntress. The new moon's silver bow suggests her hunting bow.
MARS—god of war.
VENUS—goddess of love.

[*Enter* MOMUS *laughing*]

MOMUS.   Ha! ha! ha! Ha! ha! ha! well hast thou done
                     To lay down thy pack
                     And lighten thy back.   15
                The world was a fool e'er since it begun,
                And since neither Janus nor Chronos nor I
                     Can hinder the crimes
                     Or mend the bad times,
                'Tis better to laugh than to cry.   20
CHO. OF ALL 3. 'Tis better to laugh than to cry.
JANUS.   Since Momus comes to laugh below,
                     Old Time begin the show,
                That he may see in every scene
                What changes in this age have been.   25
CHRONOS.   Then Goddess of the Silver Bow begin.

[*Horns or hunting music within*]

[*Enter* DIANA]

DIANA.   With horns and with hounds I waken the day,
                And hie to my woodland walks away;
                I tuck up my robe, and am buskin'd soon,
                And tie to my forehead a waxing moon.   30
                I course the fleet stag, unkennel the fox,
                And chase the wild goats o'er summits of rocks;
                With shouting and hooting we pierce thro' the sky,
                And Echo turns hunter and doubles the cry.
CHO. OF ALL.   With shouting and hooting we pierce through the sky,   35
                And Echo turns hunter and doubles the cry.
JANUS.   Then our age was in its prime,
CHRONOS.   Free from rage,
DIANA.   And free from crime.
MOMUS.   A very merry, dancing, drinking,   40
                Laughing, quaffing, and unthinking time.
CHO. OF ALL.   Then our age was in its prime,
                Free from rage, and free from crime,
                A very merry, dancing, drinking,
                Laughing, quaffing, and unthinking time.   45

[*Dance of* DIANA'S *attendants*]

[*Enter* MARS]

MARS.   Inspire the vocal brass,[2] inspire;
                The world is past its infant age:
                     Arms and honour,
                     Arms and honour,
                Set the martial mind on fire,   50

[2] The trumpets of war, "vocal" because they call the troops to battle.

And kindle manly rage.
Mars has looked the sky to red;
And peace, the lazy good, is fled.
Plenty, peace, and pleasure fly;
   The sprightly green   55
In woodland-walks no more is seen;
The sprightly green has drunk the Tyrian dye.[3]

CHO. OF ALL.   Plenty, peace, etc.
MARS.   Sound the trumpet, beat the drum,
   Through all the world around;
    Sound a reveille, sound, sound,   60
The warrior god is come.
CHO. OF ALL.   Sound the trumpet, etc.
MOMUS.   Thy sword within the scabbard keep,
   And let mankind agree;
Better the world were fast asleep   65
   Than kept awake by thee.
The fools are only thinner,
   With all our cost and care;
But neither side a winner,
   For things are as they were.   70
CHO. OF ALL.   The fools are only, etc.

[Enter VENUS]

VENUS.   Calms appear, when storms are past;
Love will have his hour at last:
Nature in my kindly care;
Mars destroys, and I repair;   75
Take me, take me, while you may,
Venus comes not ev'ry day.
CHO. OF ALL.   Take her, take her, etc.
CHRONOS.   The world was then so light,
I scarcely felt the weight;   80
Joy ruled the day, and love the night.
But since the Queen of Pleasure[4] left the ground,
   I faint, I lag,
   And feebly drag
The pond'rous orb around.   85
MOMUS.
  pointing)
  to DIANA }   Thy chase had a beast in view;
  to MARS,
  to VENUS.   Thy wars brought nothing about;
   Thy lovers were all untrue.
JANUS.   'Tis well an old age is out,   90

All, all, of a piece throughout;

---

[3] Dryden's metaphor for blood, which stains the grass. Tyrian dye was a crimson purple made from the glands of the murex, a Mediterranean mollusk. It was much valued by the Greeks and Romans, and was shipped from the Phoenician seaport of Tyre.
[4] Venus.

CHRONOS.   And time to begin a new.
CHO. OF ALL.   All, all, of a piece throughout;
                Thy chase had a beast in view;
                Thy wars brought nothing about;
                Thy lovers were all untrue.   95
                'Tis well an old age is out,
                And time to begin a new.

[*Dance of huntsmen, nymphs, warriors and lovers.*]

September 1, 1939[1]

W. H. Auden   (1907–1973)

I sit in one of the dives
Of Fifty-Second Street[2]
Uncertain and afraid
As the clever hopes expire
Of a low dishonest decade:[3]   5
Waves of anger and fear
Circulate over the bright
And darkened lands of the earth,
Obsessing our private lives;
The unmentionable odour of death   10
Offends the September night.

Accurate scholarship can
Unearth the whole offence
From Luther[4] until now
That has driven a culture mad,   15
Find what occurred at Linz,[5]
What huge imago made
A psychopathic god:
I and the public know
What all schoolchildren learn,   20
Those to whom evil is done[6]
Do evil in return.

[1] The date on which Hitler's panzer tanks rolled into Poland and launched World War II.
[2] New York City.
[3] The decade of the 1930s was "low" because of the worldwide Great Depression and also "low" and "dishonest" in rationalizing Hitler's national and international crimes with such "clever hopes" as those with which Britain's Neville Chamberlain and France's Edouard Daladier agreed at Munich (September 30, 1938) to give Hitler his way with Czechoslovakia in exchange for what they thought was "peace in our time," as Chamberlain phrased it from the *Book of Common Prayer*, "Evening Prayer."
[4] Martin Luther (c. 1483–1546), founder of the Lutheran Church and, as Auden sees it, initiator of German nationalism in his protestant break with Rome.
[5] The capital of Upper Austria, in the vicinity of which Hitler grew up and where he made his first major speech.
[6] Contrary to Auden's assumption, Hitler had a somewhat pampered though lonely youth.

Exiled Thucydides[7] knew
All that a speech can say
About Democracy,   25
And what dictators do,
The elderly rubbish they talk
To an apathetic grave;
Analysed all in his book,
The enlightenment driven away,   30
The habit-forming pain,
Mismanagement and grief:
We must suffer them all again.

Into his neutral air
Where blind skyscrapers use   35
Their full height to proclaim
The strength of Collective Man,
Each language pours its vain
Competitive excuse:
But who can live for long   40
In an euphoric dream;
Out of the mirror they stare,
Imperialism's face
And the international wrong.

Faces along the bar   45
Cling to their average day:
The lights must never go out,
The music must always play,
All the conventions conspire
To make this fort assume   50
The furniture of home;
Lest we should see where we are,
Lost in a haunted wood,
Children afraid of the night
Who have never been happy or good.   55

The windiest militant trash
Important Persons shout
Is not so crude as our wish:
What mad Nijinsky wrote
About Diaghilev[8]   60

---

[7] A Greek historian (c. 460–403 B.C.), author of the unfinished *History of the Peloponnesian War*, exiled for twenty years when his Athenian fleet failed to thwart the capture of a city. He analyzes Athens's claims to empire and the democracy that continued uninhibited in all the Greek states. The speeches he constructs for the leaders of both sides are notable.

[8] Vaslav Nijinsky (1890–1950), a Russian ballet dancer, wrote to Sergei Diaghilev (1872–1929), his producer, that he, Nijinsky, loved the whole world whereas Diaghilev loved only himself.

Is true of the normal heart;
For the error bred in the bone
Of each woman and each man
Craves what it cannot have,
Not universal love   65
But to be loved alone.

From the conservative dark
Into the ethical life
The dense commuters come,
Repeating their morning vow,   70
'I *will* be true to the wife,
I'll concentrate more on my work',
And helpless governors wake
To resume their compulsory game:
Who can release them now,   75
Who can reach the deaf,
Who can speak for the dumb?

All I have is a voice
To undo the folded lie,
The romantic lie in the brain   80
Of the sensual man-in-the-street
And the lie of Authority
Whose buildings grope the sky:
There is no such thing as the State
And no one exists alone;   85
Hunger allows no choice
To the citizen or the police;
We must love one another or die.

Defenceless under the night
Our world in stupor lies;   90
Yet, dotted everywhere,
Ironic points of light
Flash out wherever the Just
Exchange their messages:
May I, composed like them   95
Of Eros and of dust,
Beleaguered by the same
Negation[9] and despair,
Show an affirming flame.

---

[9] Auden puns on the League of Nations, the congress of countries established in 1920 to affirm the Peace of Versailles concluding World War I, which, as World War II sadly demonstrated, had failed of its hopes to legitimatize worldwide peace.

Little Gidding

T. S. Eliot   (1888–1965)

I

Midwinter spring is its own season
Sempiternal though sodden towards sundown,
Suspended in time, between pole and tropic.
When the short day is brightest, with frost and fire,
The brief sun flames the ice, on pond and ditches,   5
In windless cold that is the heart's heat,
Reflecting in a watery mirror
A glare that is blindness in the early afternoon.
And glow more intense than blaze of branch, or brazier,
Stirs the dumb spirit: no wind, but pentecostal fire[1]   10
In the dark time of the year. Between melting and freezing
The soul's sap quivers. There is no earth smell
Or smell of living thing. This is the spring time
But not in time's covenant. Now the hedgerow
Is blanched for an hour with transitory blossom   15
Of snow, a bloom more sudden
Than that of summer, neither budding nor fading,
Not in the scheme of generation.
Where is the summer, the unimaginable
Zero summer?

        If you came this way,   20
Taking the route you would be likely to take
From the place you would be likely to come from,
If you came this way in may time, you would find the hedges
White again, in May, with voluptuary sweetness.
It would be the same at the end of the journey,   25
If you came at night like a broken king,[2]
If you came by day not knowing what you came for,
It would be the same, when you leave the rough road
And turn behind the pig-sty to the dull façade
And the tombstone. And what you thought you came for   30
Is only a shell, a husk of meaning
From which the purpose breaks only when it is fulfilled
If at all. Either you had no purpose

---

[1] On the feast of the Pentecost, Christ's apostles were confronted with "a sound from heaven as of a rushing mighty wind . . . . And there appeared unto them cloven tongues like as of fire . . . . And they were all filled with the Holy Ghost, and began to speak with other tongues, as the Spirit gave them utterance" (Acts ii. 2–4). Pentecost (or Whitsunday) is celebrated in May or June, seven Sundays after Easter.

[2] Charles I is supposed to have visited Little Gidding after his final defeat.

Or the purpose is beyond the end you figured
And is altered in fulfilment. There are other places[3]   35
Which also are the world's end, some at the sea jaws,
Or over a dark lake, in a desert or a city—
But this is the nearest, in place and time,
Now and in England.

            If you came this way,
Taking any route, starting from anywhere,   40
At any time or at any season,
It would always be the same: you would have to put off
Sense and notion. You are not here to verify,
Instruct yourself, or inform curiosity
Or carry report. You are here to kneel   45
Where prayer has been valid. And prayer is more
Than an order of words, the conscious occupation
Of the praying mind, or the sound of the voice praying.
And what the dead had no speech for, when living,
They can tell you, being dead: the communication   50
Of the dead is tongued with fire beyond the language of the living.
Here, the intersection of the timeless moment
Is England and nowhere. Never and always.

II

Ash on an old man's sleeve
Is all the ash the burnt roses leave.   55
Dust in the air suspended
Marks the place where a story ended.
Dust inbreathed was a house—
The wall, the wainscot and the mouse.
The death of hope and despair,   60
    This is the death of air.

There are flood and drouth
Over the eyes and in the mouth,
Dead water and dead sand
Contending for the upper hand.   65
The parched eviscerate soil
Gapes at the vanity of toil,
Laughs without mirth.
    This is the death of earth.

Water and fire succeed   70
The town, the pasture and the weed.

---

[3] Eliot had in mind several specific places of religious refuge: the holy islands of Iona and Lindis-farne (off the coasts of Scotland and England), the lake at Glendalough (Ireland), the desert associated with St. Anthony of Egypt, the city of Padua in Italy.

Water and fire deride
The sacrifice that we denied.
Water and fire shall rot
The marred foundations we forgot, 75
Of sanctuary and choir.
 This is the death of water and fire.

In the uncertain hour before the morning[4]
 Near the ending of interminable night
 At the recurrent end of the unending 80
After the dark dove with the flickering tongue
 Had passed below the horizon of his homing
 While the dead leaves still rattled on like tin
Over the asphalt where no other sound was
 Between three districts whence the smoke arose 85
 I met one walking, loitering and hurried
As if blown towards me like the metal leaves
 Before the urban dawn wind unresisting.
 And as I fixed upon the down-turned face
That pointed scrutiny with which we challenge 90
 The first-met stranger in the waning dusk
 I caught the sudden look of some dead master
Whom I had known, forgotten, half recalled
 Both one and many; in the brown baked features
 The eyes of a familiar compound ghost 95
Both intimate and unidentifiable.
 So I assumed a double part, and cried
 And heard another's voice cry: 'What! are *you* here?'[5]
Although we were not. I was still the same,
 Knowing myself yet being someone other— 100
 And he a face still forming; yet the words sufficed
To compel the recognition they preceded.
 And so, compliant to the common wind,
 Too strange to each other for misunderstanding,
In concord at this intersection time 105
 Of meeting nowhere, no before and after,
 We trod the pavement in a dead patrol.
I said: 'The wonder that I feel is easy,
 Yet ease is cause of wonder. Therefore speak:
 I may not comprehend, may not remember.' 110

---

[4] Eliot wrote "This section of a poem . . . cost me far more time and trouble and vexation than any passage of the same length that I have ever written." His intention was to create "the nearest equivalent to a canto of the *Inferno* or the *Purgatorio,* in style as well as content, that I could achieve."

[5] The line recalls Dante's meeting in Hell with Brunetto Latini, his former teacher (*Inferno,* XV). Latini's prediction of Dante's future ill treatment at the hands of his countrymen parallels Eliot's fears concerning the lasting value and acceptance of his own work.

And he: 'I am not eager to rehearse
   My thoughts and theory which you have forgotten.
   These things have served their purpose: let them be.
So with your own, and pray they be forgiven
   By others, as I pray you to forgive   115
   Both bad and good. Last season's fruit is eaten
And the fullfed beast shall kick the empty pail.
   For last year's words belong to last year's language
   And next year's words await another voice.
But, as the passage now presents no hindrance   120
   To the spirit unappeased and peregrine
   Between two worlds become much like each other,
So I find words I never thought to speak
   In streets I never thought I should revisit
   When I left my body on a distant shore.   125
Since our concern was speech, and speech impelled us
   To purify the dialect of the tribe[6]
   And urge the mind to aftersight and foresight,
Let me disclose the gifts reserved for age
   To set a crown upon your lifetime's effort.   130
   First, the cold friction of expiring sense
Without enchantment, offering no promise
   But bitter tastelessness of shadow fruit
   As body and soul begin to fall asunder.
Second, the conscious impotence of rage   135
   At human folly, and the laceration
   Of laughter at what ceases to amuse.
And last, the rending pain of re-enactment
   Of all that you have done, and been; the shame
   Of motives late revealed, and the awareness   140
Of things ill done and done to others' harm
   Which once you took for exercise of virtue.
   Then fools' approval stings, and honour stains.
From wrong to wrong the exasperated spirit
   Proceeds, unless restored by that refining fire   145
   Where you must move in measure, like a dancer.'[7]
The day was breaking. In the disfigured street
   He left me, with a kind of valediction,
   And faded on the blowing of the horn.[8]

---

[6] Translating "Donner un sens plus pur aux mots de la tribu" from Stéphane Mallarmé's "Le Tombeau d'Edgar Poe," the line defines an ambition shared by many poets, including Dante and Yeats.
[7] The spirit moving "in measure" in a "refining fire" recalls especially "Sailing to Byzantium" and "Byzantium," by Yeats, the poet who in Eliot's time wrote most memorably of the problems of aging. Cf. also "Vacillation." Yeats had died in 1939.
[8] The All Clear signal. The ghost of Hamlet's father disappears in similar fashion: "It faded on the crowing of the cock" (Hamlet, I, i, 157).

III

There are three conditions which often look alike[9]   150
Yet differ completely, flourish in the same hedgerow:
Attachment to self and to things and to persons, detachment
From self and from things and from persons; and, growing between them,
    indifference
Which resembles the others as death resembles life,
Being between two lives—unflowering, between   155
The live and the dead nettle. This is the use of memory:
For liberation—not less of love but expanding
Of love beyond desire, and so liberation
From the future as well as the past. Thus, love of a country
Begins as attachment to our own field of action   160
And comes to find that action of little importance
Though never indifferent. History may be servitude,
History may be freedom. See, now they vanish,
The faces and places, with the self which, as it could, loved them,
    To become renewed, transfigured, in another pattern.   165

Sin is Behovely, but
All shall be well, and
All manner of thing shall be well.[10]
If I think, again, of this place,
And of people, not wholly commendable,   170
Of no immediate kin or kindness,
But some of peculiar genius,
All touched by a common genius,
United in the strife which divided them;
If I think of a king at nightfall,[11]   175
Of three men, and more, on the scaffold
And a few who died forgotten
In other places, here and abroad,
And of one who died blind and quiet,[12]
Why should we celebrate   180
These dead men more than the dying?
It is not to ring the bell backward
Nor is it an incantation
To summon the spectre of a Rose.[13]

[9] The thought here owes much to the *Bhagavad-Gita*, which Eliot considered "the next greatest philosophical poem" to *The Divine Comedy*. See especially, in the translation by Swami Prabhavananda and Christopher Isherwood, parts V, VI, XIV, XVIII.

[10] Three lines from *Revelations of Divine Love*, by Dame Julian of Norwich, a fourteenth-century English mystic. Her vision shows the pain resulting from sin as a necessary step toward self-knowledge.

[11] Charles I.

[12] John Milton.

[13] Specifically, the rose, in various forms, long associated with the English royalty dethroned with the beheading of Charles I (1649). The reference recalls, however, the rose's traditional symbolic value as an emblem of earthly beauty (cf. l. 55) and its use, in Dante and at the end of this poem, as a symbol of eternity.

We cannot revive old factions   185
We cannot restore old policies
Or follow an antique drum.
These men, and those who opposed them
And those whom they opposed
Accept the constitution of silence   190
And are folded in a single party.
Whatever we inherit from the fortunate
We have taken from the defeated
What they had to leave us—a symbol:
A symbol perfected in death.   195
And all shall be well and
All manner of thing shall be well
By the purification of the motive
In the ground of our beseeching.[14]

IV

The dove descending breaks the air   200
With flame of incandescent terror
Of which the tongues declare
The one discharge from sin and error.
The only hope, or else despair
  Lies in the choice of pyre or pyre—   205
  To be redeemed from fire by fire.

Who then devised the torment? Love.
Love is the unfamiliar Name
Behind the hands that wove
The intolerable shirt of flame   210
Which human power cannot remove.[15]
  We only live, only suspire
  Consumed by either fire or fire.

V

What we call the beginning is often the end[16]
And to make an end is to make a beginning.   215
The end is where we start from. And every phrase
And sentence that is right (where every word is at home,
Taking its place to support the others,

[14] Dame Julian, after fifteen years of searching, discovered that "the ground of our beseeching" is "Love," Cf. l. 207.
[15] Deianira hoped to regain the love of her husband, Hercules, by giving him a shirt stained with the blood of Nessus. The shirt burst into flames, adhering to the skin as Hercules tore at it. Badly burned, he had himself immolated on a funeral pyre.
[16] Cf. "In my beginning is my end" and "In my end is my beginning," the first and last words of Eliot's East Coker.

The word neither diffident nor ostentatious,
An easy commerce of the old and the new,   220
The common word exact without vulgarity,
The formal word precise but not pedantic,
The complete consort dancing together)
Every phrase and every sentence is an end and a beginning,
Every poem an epitaph. And any action   225
Is a step to the block, to the fire, down the sea's throat
Or to an illegible stone: and that is where we start.
We die with the dying:
See, they depart, and we go with them.
We are born with the dead: 230
See, they return, and bring us with them.
The moment of the rose and the moment of the yew-tree[17]
Are of equal duration. A people without history
Is not redeemed from time, for history is a pattern
Of timeless moments. So, while the light fails   235
On a winter's afternoon, in a secluded chapel
History is now and England.

With the drawing of this Love and the voice of this Calling[18]

We shall not cease from exploration
And the end of all our exploring   240
Will be to arrive where we started
And know the place for the first time.
Through the unknown, remembered gate
When the last of earth left to discover
Is that which was the beginning;   245
At the source of the longest river
The voice of the hidden waterfall
And the children in the apple-tree
Not known, because not looked for
But heard, half-heard, in the stillness   250
Between two waves of the sea.
Quick now, here, now, always—[19]
A condition of complete simplicity
(Costing not less than everything)
And all shall be well and   255

[17] Simply, the rose is a symbol of transient life, the yew-tree a symbol of death.
[18] A line from an anonymous fourteenth-century religious work, *The Cloud of Unknowing.* The book takes its title from the "cloud" that surrounds human effort, save as God's light breaks through. Cf. the darkness and pentecostal fire of this poem.
[19] By repeating here the third-from-the-last line of the first *Quartet, Burnt Norton,* Eliot stresses an idea that is important to all four poems and to his work as a whole. All times meet in the present moment, which is the moment of intersection with eternity.

All manner of thing shall be well
When the tongues of flame are in-folded
Into the crowned knot of fire
And the fire and the rose are one.[20]

[20] Cf. Dante's *Paradiso,* XXXIII, in which all the disparate elements of the universe are gathered by the force of love into "un semplice lume," one simple flame. Dante's lines, wrote Eliot, attain "the highest point that poetry has ever reached or ever can reach."

The fourth of T. S. Eliot's *Four Quartets, Little Gidding* is the last major poem of one of the twentieth century's most accomplished poets. Eliot was fifty-four in 1942, when *Little Gidding* was first published. Undergirding the poem is a carefully nurtured poetic skill first apparent twenty-five years earlier in *Prufrock and Other Observations.* Supporting it also is a philosophic and religious stance thoughtfully developed in a number of prose essays and shaped in poetic form especially vivid in *The Waste Land, Ash-Wednesday* and the three earlier *Quartets. Little Gidding* is in addition constructed solidly upon the conditions of the immediate time and place in which it was written. In 1942 Eliot lived and worked in wartime in a London that had learned to accept the explosions and fires of German bombs as a recurring part of ordinary existence. Out of the materials of incoherence and despair Eliot built a shapely monument of affirmation.

Although the atmosphere of World War II surrounds the poem, the confusion and destruction enter its lines directly only in the second section of part II, where an air raid warden on a dawn patrol "After the dark dove with the flickering tongue / Had passed below the horizon of his homing" meets and converses with a "dead master" in the calm preceding the blowing of the All Clear signal. The rest of the poem builds toward and falls away from this structural midpoint. The poem's beginning takes us miles into the English countryside and centuries into the past; the end takes us out of time and place entirely, enfolding all that has happened and will happen into "the fire and the rose" of eternity.

I

In Part I the poet meditates upon a midwinter visit to Little Gidding, the site of an Anglican religious community founded in 1625 and destroyed by Puritans not long after. In the nineteenth century a chapel was erected there. Into this now peaceful setting, seventy-five miles from London, the narrator has come seeking in a place "where prayer has been valid" a respite from the turmoil of his everyday existence. In passages structurally kin (as the entire poem is) to the repetitions and thematic variations of a formal musical composition, the narrator considers the visit from three different perspectives.

The first twenty lines spring from the observation that the sun sometimes shines at its brightest even in the darkest days of winter, flaming in reflection from the ice. The snow mimics spring, forming blossoms on the hedges. In this spring which is not spring, ("not in time's convenant"), the narrator perceives the religious symbolism of "pentecostal fire / In the dark time of the year." These lines anticipate, thematically, the dark time in the second section of Part II: the dive bombers attacking London. The question "Where is the summer, the unimaginable / Zero summer?" applies to the destruction of Little Gidding, the bombing of London, and to the dark, midwinter time of an aging poet.

In the next group of lines the narrator adopts a "you" perspective, inviting the reader's participation in the meditation. "If you came this way" he says to himself, and also to the reader made sympathetic by the universal appeal of the problem with which the poem begins, "you would find the hedges / White again, in May." Then, paradoxically, you would find the same "If you came at night." The brightness that flames in midwinter, we begin to understand, is symbolic of a brightness not easily enclosed in any particular "husk of meaning." We travel to places like Little Gidding for reasons that we do not fully understand, seeking to fulfill purposes that are "altered in fulfillment." In other times we might have sought answers in places other than this particular "world's end," but this one is convenient and will serve.

The next section is more general in its description of need and more specific in its suggestion of remedy. It does not matter where you come from or when you come. All the world's problems drive toward one solution: the validity of the kind of prayer that breaks through the boundaries of sense to arrive at "the intersection of the timeless moment" that is "never and always." Through prayerful communion with the dead, we learn that

> . . . what the dead had no speech for, when living,
> They can tell you, being dead: the communication
> Of the dead is tongued with fire beyond the language of the living.

Reminding us of the inadequacy of language to deal effectively with our most deeply felt needs, the narrator prepares us for his pre-dawn meeting with the dead master.

II

Part II begins with a lyric on the death of the four elements that the ancients saw as the structural building blocks of the universe: air, earth, water, and fire. In three carefully metered and rhyming stanzas, the poet describes the end of those attributes of existence that humans care most for, both those that possess physical being (roses, houses, eyes and mouths, towns and pastures) and those that exist as abstract ambitions or fears (hope, despair, toil, sacrifice). The key word is the "vanity" of the second stanza, carrying with it centuries of Biblical and literary associations. "Vanity of vanities, saith the Preacher, vanity of vanities; all is vanity" (Eccles. i.2). The reader steeped in Eliot will see in the symbols of the passage a number of insistent echoes from earlier poems: the "lonely men in shirt-sleeves" of *The Love Song of J. Alfred Prufrock,* the dust and watery death of *The Waste Land,* the Rose, the Garden, and the sand of *Ash-Wednesday,* the rose-garden and dust of *Burnt Norton,* the house, wainscot, and mouse of *East Coker,* the "ground swell" of the sea and the "significant soil" of *The Dry Salvages*. Eliot here mourns and at the same celebrates the termination of all things earthly, including his own poetic endeavor in his lifetime.

The air raid section follows. Walking before dawn through streets deserted in the wake of the latest bombing, the narrator meets and converses with "some dead master," a composite figure modeled upon Dante, Yeats, and other individuals important to Eliot. The section moves in three-line units of careful iambic pentameter, with alternate feminine and masculine endings: not precisely the *terza rima* of Dante's *Divine Comedy*, but a meticulous adaptation to suit the requirements of twentieth-century English. The darkness before dawn, the surrounding smoke, the timeless meeting with an individual recognized and yet not recognized evoke especially the atmosphere of the *Inferno*, in which Dante converses with individuals long dead. After the death of the world contemplated in the preceding lyric, these lines compel the narrator to consider the death of his poetic voice (for "next year's words await another voice") and turn his attention to the disappointments of age. Faced with "expiring sense," "the conscious impotence of rage," and "the rending pain of re-enactment / Of all that you have done, and been," the aging poet can be restored to vitality only by the "refining fire" of eternity, celebrated in both Eastern and Western religions, that envelops and transcends the fires of this temporal world.

III

In the first section of Part III Eliot summarizes some of the most important teachings of the *Bhagavad-Gita*, the Hindu religious text that served him also as a major source for the discussion that dominates the last half of *The Dry Salvages*, setting the stage in that work for the intellectual and religious stance of *Little Gidding*. In the lines of this poem there is no direct reference to the plight of Arjuna or the response of Krishna, but instead a transformation of Eastern teachings to suit a Western setting. The "three conditions which often look alike" characterize reactions theoretically possible to the poet contemplating the memory of the destroyed Anglican religious community, the present reality of the bombing of London, and his own inevitable aging and death. Between the sensual "attachment to self and to things and to persons" characteristic of much earthly life and the spiritual detachment necessary as a preparation for eternal salvation, there lies the emptiness of indifference, "which resembles the others as death resembles life." Only by retaining a delicate tension between love for "faces and places" and acceptance of the knowledge that ultimately "they vanish" can we learn to accept "our own field of action" as necessary to an eternal order "renewed, transfigured, in another pattern."

All things come to the same end and that end is good. That, in essence, is the message of the second section of Part III, but it includes also the important corollary that all things tending toward that end are also good because they are part of a timeless order inscrutable to humans encapsulated in the particulars of their times and places. "Sin is Behovely": so wrote the fourteenth-century English mystic Julian of Norwich, meaning by that phrase that sin, too, has a necessary place in the Divine Plan. In the lines that follow, the poet applies that thought to the war that long ago destroyed Little Gidding, preparing himself and the reader for the application of it, in Part IV, to the bombing of London in his own time. Charles I is the king we are asked to remember. He was beheaded, just as Little Gidding was destroyed, in the civil and religious strife that tore England apart in the seventeenth century. Others died as he did, publicly, "on the scaffold," while still others "died forgotten." Milton, a poet much embroiled in politics, "died blind and quiet." Yet Eliot asks us to consider that however much we regret the past we cannot change it: "We cannot revive old factions / We cannot restore old policies." More important, the men who followed their different opinions to destructive ends in the seventeenth century now "Accept the constitution of silence / And are folded in a single party." The rose, symbolic in life of English factionalism, stands in death as a symbol of the perfection of eternity. In the last two lines of this section the poet adds an important qualification to the idea that "All shall be well": the motives of our human actions must be purified through prayers arising from love.

IV

In the first of these two lyric stanzas Eliot returns to the London of 1942. Applying the lesson of the preceding section, he merges the image of the bombers with the image of the Pentecostal Holy Ghost, with its "tongues like as of fire" (Acts ii.3). We may be redeemed from earthly fire only by the fire of God's love. The second stanza enforces the point. Hercules' "intolerable shirt of flame," although intended as a gift of human love, caused him a pain relieved only when he placed himself upon his own funeral pyre. The public fires of London and the private fires of Hercules are as one in the all-consuming, all-redeeming fire of eternity. Man's only hope, as opposed to his otherwise inevitable despair, resides in his ability to make an active choice of the eternal fire that offers "The one discharge from sin and error."

V

Defining his choices through his words, the poet seeks always that identification with the timeless that came to the apostles when, inspired with the Holy Ghost, they began to "speak with other tongues" (Acts ii.4). Caught in the here and now, he strives toward the wisdom half-grasped in the speech of the dead master, that "communication" of Part I that "is tongued with fire beyond the language of the living." Struggling toward truth, he discovers that "Every phrase and every sentence is an end and a beginning, / Every poem an epitaph." Paradoxically, humanity can reach through to eternity only by living each moment now, for it is only within time that we come to know the timeless. "We die with the dying. . . . We are born with the dead." At the end of the first section of Part V, the light that bursts forth in midwinter in Little Gidding at the beginning of the poem now "fails" on that same "winter's afternoon," but only to remind the poet that there is no escaping from the present. "History is now and England."

Nor is there any escaping from the work of the present. The "Love" and "Calling" in a line borrowed from a fourteenth-century religious work foreshadow the active commitment required of us in the poem's summation. Just as all time is one time, so all movement forward takes us but to the place where we began. Eliot here echoes earlier movements in the *Four Quartets:* the gate into the rose-garden remembered from *Burnt Norton,* the concern with beginnings and ends that runs through *East Coker,* the sea waves of *The Dry Salvages.* More generally, the lines remind us of all beginnings: the children we once were, the voices of waterfalls heard but not yet seen, the sources of rivers—indeed, we should probably be reminded of the garden of Eden that was the world's first garden. In "the stillness / Between two waves," we are reminded of the silence and stability of eternity. Finally, "all shall be well" not in our earthly time, but in that time to come when all beginnings and endings and all manners of expression and activity "are in-folded / Into the crowned knot of fire / And the fire and the rose are one."

CHAPTER 9

The Popular Muse

Some poems reach audiences—or are aimed at audiences—larger than those that respond to other poems. Folksongs are an ancient form of popular music, often imitated by the Tin Pan Alley and Nashville tunesmiths of our day. Broadside ballads once responded to a thirst for sensational news akin to that now exploited by the tabloids at the supermarket check-outs. Often a particular poet or poem expresses a fundamental spirit for an entire generation. Not all popular poems are literary successes, though some may be. Not all outlast the time that gave them their greatest popularity, though some do.

In each of the following, is it possible to see the qualities of widespread appeal necessary to make a poem popular? Some have not remained so. Others, though popular today, may not last to tomorrow. Do any deserve to?

The Minstrel Boy

Thomas Moore   (1779–1852)

The minstrel boy to the war is gone,
  In the ranks of death you'll find him;
His father's sword he has girded on,
  And his wild harp slung behind him.—   4
"Land of song !" said the warrior bard,
  "Tho' all the world betrays thee,
"*One* sword, at least, thy rights shall guard,
  "*One* faithful harp shall praise thee!"   8

The minstrel fell!—but the foeman's chain
  Could not bring his proud soul under;
The harp he loved ne'er spoke again
  For he tore its chords asunder;   12
And said, "No chains shall sully thee,
  "Thou soul of love and bravery!
"Thy songs were made for the pure and free,
  "They shall never sound in slavery."   16

703

Eleanor Rigby

John Lennon   (1940–   )
and Paul McCartney   (1942–   )

Ah, look at all the lonely people!
Ah, look at all the lonely people!

Eleanor Rigby
Picks up the rice in the church where a wedding has been,
Lives in a dream,   5
Waits at the window
Wearing the face that she keeps in a jar by the door.
Who is it for?

All the lonely people,
Where do they all come from?   10
All the lonely people,
Where do they all belong?

Father McKenzie,
Writing the words of a sermon that no one will hear—
No one comes near.   15
Look at him working,
Darning his socks in the night when there's nobody there.
What does he care?

All the lonely people,
Where do they all come from?   20
All the lonely people,
Where do they all belong?

Eleanor Rigby
Died in the church and was buried along with her name.
Nobody came.   25
Father McKenzie,
Wiping the dirt from his hands as he walks from the grave—
No one was saved.

All the lonely people,
Where do they all come from?   30
All the lonely people,
Where do they all belong?

Ah, look at all the lonely people!
Ah, look at all the lonely people!

Excelsior

Henry Wadsworth Longfellow (1807–1882)

The shades of night were falling fast,
As through an Alpine village passed
A youth, who bore, 'mid snow and ice,
A banner with the strange device,
     Excelsior![1]   5

His brow was sad; his eye beneath,
Flashed like a falchion[2] from its sheath,
And like a silver clarion rung
The accents of that unknown tongue,
     Excelsior!   10

In happy homes he saw the light
Of household fires gleam warm and bright;
Above, the spectral glaciers shone,
And from his lips escaped a groan,
     Excelsior!   15

"Try not the Pass!" the old man said;
"Dark lowers the tempest overhead,
The roaring torrent is deep and wide!"
And loud that clarion voice replied,
     Excelsior!   20

"Oh stay," the maiden said, "and rest
Thy weary head upon this breast!"
A tear stood in his bright blue eye,
But still he answered, with a sigh,
     Excelsior!   25

"Beware the pine-tree's withered branch!
Beware the awful avalanche!"
This was the peasant's last Good-night,
A voice replied, far up the height,
     Excelsior!   30

At break of day, as heavenward
The pious monks of Saint Bernard
Uttered the oft-repeated prayer,
A voice cried through the startled air,
     Excelsior!   35

[1] Higher (Latin).
[2] Sword.

A traveller, by the faithful hound,
Half-buried in the snow was found,
Still grasping in his hand of ice
That banner with the strange device,
   Excelsior!   40

There in the twilight cold and gray,
Lifeless, but beautiful, he lay,
And from the sky, serene and far,
A voice fell, like a falling star,
   Excelsior!   45

[From] The Rubáiyát of Omar Khayyám

Translated by Edward FitzGerald[1]   (1809–1883)

I

Awake! for Morning in the Bowl of Night
Has flung the Stone that puts the Stars to Flight:
  And Lo! the Hunter of the East has caught
The Sultán's Turret in a Noose of Light.   (1st)[2]   4

III

And, as the Cock crew, those who stood before
The Tavern shouted—"Open then the Door!
  "You know how little while we have to stay,
"And, once departed, may return no more."   (1st)   8

VII

Come, fill the Cup, and in the Fire of Spring
Your Winter-garment of Repentence fling:
  The Bird of Time has but a little way
To flutter—and the Bird is on the Wing.   (2nd)   12

XII

Here with a little Bread beneath the Bough,
A Flask of Wine, a Book of Verse—and Thou

[1] FitzGerald (1809–1883), except for five of his childhood years and a year of his youth in Paris, never left England. He had already translated some Persian poets when his friend, Professor E. B. Cowell, an orientalist, discovered in the Bodleian Library, Oxford, a manuscript of Omar Khayyám (d. 1123 or 1132), written in deep purple ink dusted with gold. This "rubáiyát"—which means simply "quatrainiad"—FitzGerald translated into English quatrains that no subsequent translator has equaled. He expanded and revised his first edition of 75 quatrains (1859) into a second of 110 (1868). He trimmed this to a third edition of 101 (1872), polishing further for a fourth (1879).

Our selections follow the order of the second edition. The roman numerals indicate the stanza in the edition shown in parenthesis. But we have overruled the poet, as popularity has frequently done too, in preferring some of his earlier versions. *Khayyám* means "the tentmaker."

[2] FitzGerald's note: "Flinging a stone into the cup was the signal for 'To horse!' in the desert."

Beside me singing in the Wilderness—
Oh, Wilderness were Paradise enow!   (2nd)[3]   16

XIII

Some for the Glories of This World; and some
Sigh for the Prophet's Paradise to come;
   Ah, take the Cash and let the Credit go,
Nor heed the rumble of a distant Drum!   (3rd)   20

XXI

Ah, my Beloved, fill the Cup that clears
TO-DAY of past Regrets and future Fears:
   To-morrow! Why, To-morrow I may, be
Myself with Yesterday's Sev'n thousand Years.   (2nd)[4]   24

XXVII

Myself when young did eagerly frequent
Doctor and Saint, and heard great argument
   About it and about: but evermore
Came out by the same door where in I went.   (3rd)   28

XXXII

Into the Universe, and *Why* not knowing
Nor *Whence,* like Water willy-nilly flowing;
   And out of it, as Wind along the Waste,
I know not *Whither,* willy-nilly blowing.   (2nd)   32

XL

For I remember stopping by the way
To watch a Potter thumping his wet Clay:
   And with its all-obliterated Tongue
It murmur'd—"Gently, Brother, gently, pray!"   (2nd)   36

XLVIII

While the Rose blows along the River Brink,
With old Khayyám the Ruby Vintage drink:

---

[3] The popular version of this most famous of Omar's quatrains is that of the third edition, reading:

> A Book of Verses underneath the Bough,
> A Jug of Wine, a Loaf of Bread—and Thou . . .

But the first line loses some metrical verve, and FitzGerald loses Omar's point by swelling his bit of bread to a loaf, and his flask to a jug. Omar says that a modest supply of earth's bounties, with friendship, can make a desert surpass the Sultan's palace. FitzGerald's third edition also drops the "Here," so characteristic of Omar's here and now.

[4] FitzGerald's note: "A thousand years to each Planet."

And when the Angel with his darker Draught
Draws up to Thee—take that, and do not shrink.   (1st)   40

XLIII

The Grape that can with Logic absolute
The Two-and-Seventy jarring Sects confute:
    The subtle Alchemist that in a Trice
Life's leaden Metal into Gold transmute.   (1st)   44

XLVII

And fear not lest Existence closing *your*
Account, should lose, or know the type no more;
    The Eternal Sáki from the Bowl has pour'd
Millions of Bubbles like us, and will pour.   (2nd)   48

XXXVIII

One Moment in Annihilation's Waste,
One Moment, of the Well of Life to taste—
    The Stars are setting and the Caravan
Starts for the Dawn of Nothing—Oh, make haste!   (1st)[5]   52

LV

You know, my Friends, with what a brave Carouse
I made a Second Marriage in my house;
    Divorced old barren Reason from my Bed,
And took the Daughter of the Vine to Spouse.   (3rd)   56

LXIII

Why, be this Juice the growth of God, who dare
Blaspheme the twisted tendril as a Snare?
    A Blessing, we should use it, should we not?
And if a Curse—why, then, Who set it there?   (2nd)   60

LXVI

Oh threats of Hell and Hopes of Paradise!
One thing at least is certain—*This* Life flies:
    One thing is certain and the rest is lies;
The Flower that once is blown for ever dies.   (2nd)   64

LXIX

But helpless Pieces of the Game He plays
Upon this Chequer-board of Nights and Days;

---

[5] FitzGerald's note: "The caravan travelling by night (after their New Year's Day of the vernal equinox) by command of Mohammed, I believe."

Hither and thither moves, and checks, and slays,
And one by one back in the Closet lays. (3rd) 68

LXXVI

The Moving Finger writes; and, having writ,
Moves on: nor all your Piety nor Wit
  Shall lure it back to cancel half a Line,
Nor all your Tears wash out a Word of it. (2nd) 72

LXXII

And that inverted Bowl they call The Sky,
Whereunder crawling coop'd we live and die,
  Lift not your hands to *It* for help—for It
As impotently moves as you or I. (4th) 76

LXXXI

Oh, Thou, who Man of baser Earth didst make,
And ev'n with Paradise devise the Snake:
  For all the Sin wherewith the Face of Man
Is blacken'd—Man's forgiveness give—and take! (3rd) 80

XCVIII

Ah, with the Grape my fading Life provide,
And wash my Body whence the Life has died,
  And lay me, shrouded in the living Leaf,
By some not unfrequented Garden-side. (2nd) 84

CI

Indeed the Idols I have loved so long
Have done my credit in Men's eye much wrong:
  Have drown'd my Glory in a shallow Cup,
And sold my Reputation for a Song. (2nd) 88

XCV

And much as Wine has play'd the Infidel,
And robb'd me of my Robe of Honour—Well,
  I wonder often what the Vintners buy
One half so precious as the stuff they sell. (3rd) 92

LXXII

Alas, that Spring should vanish with the Rose!
That Youth's sweet-scented Manuscript should close!
  The Nightingale that in the Branches sang,
Ah, whence, and whither flown again, who knows! (1st) 96

XCIX

Ah Love! could you and I with Him conspire
To grasp this sorry Scheme of Things entire,
　　Would we not shatter it to bits—and then
Re-mould it nearer to the Heart's Desire!　　　　(3rd)　　100

LXXIV

Ah, Moon of my Delight, who know'st no wane,
The Moon of Heav'n is rising once again:
　　How oft hereafter rising shall she look
Through this same Garden after me—in vain!　　　　(1st)　　104

LXXV

And when Thyself with shining Foot shall pass
Among the Guests Star-scattered on the Grass,
　　And in thy joyous Errand reach the Spot
Where I made one—turn down an empty Glass!　　　　(1st)　　108

Tamâm Shud[6]

[6] It is completed.

Non Sum Qualis Eram Bonae Sub Regno Cynarae[1]

Ernest Dowson　(1867–1900)

Last night, ah, yesternight, betwixt her lips and mine
There fell thy shadow, Cynara! thy breath was shed
Upon my soul between the kisses and the wine;　　　　　3
And I was desolate and sick of an old passion,
　　Yea, I was desolate and bowed my head:
I have been faithful to thee, Cynara! in my fashion.　　6

All night upon mine heart I felt her warm heart beat,
Night-long within mine arms in love and sleep she lay;
Surely the kisses of her bought red mouth were sweet;　　9
But I was desolate and sick of an old passion,
　　When I awoke and found the dawn was gray:
I have been faithful to thee, Cynara! in my fashion.　　12

I have forgot much, Cynara! gone with the wind,
Flung roses, roses riotously with the throng,
Dancing, to put thy pale, lost lilies out of mind;　　15
But I was desolate and sick of an old passion,

[1] "I am not as I was under the reign of the good Cynara," Horace, *Odes*, IV, I, lines 3–4.

　　Yea, all the time, because the dance was long:
　I have been faithful to thee, Cynara! in my fashion.　　　18

　I cried for madder music and for stronger wine,
　But when the feast is finished and the lamps expire,
　Then falls thy shadow, Cynara! the night is thine;　　　21
　And I am desolate and sick of an old passion,
　　Yea hungry for the lips of my desire:
　I have been faithful to thee, Cynara! in my fashion.　　　24

The Man with the Hoe
WRITTEN AFTER SEEING MILLET'S WORLD-FAMOUS PAINTING[1]

Edwin Markham　(1852–1940)

God made man in His own image,
in the image of God made He him.

GENESIS

Bowed by the weight of centuries he leans
Upon his hoe and gazes on the ground,
The emptiness of ages in his face,
And on his back the burden of the world.
Who made him dead to rapture and despair,　　　5
A thing that grieves not and that never hopes,
Stolid and stunned, a brother to the ox?
Who loosened and let down this brutal jaw?
Whose was the hand that slanted back this brow?
Whose breath blew out the light within this brain?　　　10
Is this the Thing the Lord God made and gave
To have dominion over sea and land;
To trace the stars and search the heavens for power;
To feel the passion of Eternity?
Is this the Dream He dreamed who shaped the suns　　　15
And marked their ways upon the ancient deep?
Down all the stretch of Hell to its last gulf
There is no shape more terrible than this—
More tongued with censure of the world's blind greed—
More filled with signs and portents for the soul—　　　20
More fraught with menace to the universe.

What gulfs between him and the seraphim![2]
Slave of the wheel of labor, what to him
Are Plato and the swing of Pleiades?[3]

[1] Jean François Millet (1814–1875).
[2] The highest order of angels.
[3] Stars in the constellation Taurus.

What the long reaches of the peaks of song,   25
The rift of dawn, the reddening of the rose?

Through this dread shape the suffering ages look;
Time's tragedy is in that aching stoop;
Through this dread shape humanity betrayed,
Plundered, profaned and disinherited,   30
Cries protest to the Judges of the World,
A protest that is also prophecy.

O masters, lords and rulers in all lands,
Is this the handiwork you give to God,
This monstrous thing distorted and soul-quenched?   35
How will you ever straighten up this shape;
Touch it again with immortality;
Give back the upward looking and the light;
Rebuild in it the music and the dream;
Make right the immemorial infamies,   40
Perfidious wrongs, immedicable⁴ woes?

O masters, lords and rulers in all lands,
How will the Future reckon with this Man?
How answer his brute question in that hour
When whirlwinds of rebellion shake the world?   45
How will it be with kingdoms and with kings—
With those who shaped him to the thing he is—
When this dumb Terror shall reply to God,
After the silence of the centuries?

⁴ Incurable.

A Psalm of Life

Henry Wadsworth Longfellow   (1807–1882)

Tell me not, in mournful numbers,
    Life is but an empty dream!—
For the soul is dead that slumbers,
    And things are not what they seem.   4

Life is real! Life is earnest!
    And the grave is not its goal;
Dust thou art, to dust returnest,
    Was not spoken of the soul.   8

Not enjoyment, and not sorrow,
    Is our destined end or way;

But to act, that each to-morrow
    Find us farther than to-day.   12

Art is long, and Time is fleeting,
    And our hearts, though stout and brave,
Still, like muffled drums, are beating
    Funeral marches to the grave.   16

In the world's broad field of battle,
    In the bivouac of Life,
Be not like dumb, driven cattle!
    Be a hero in the strife!   20

Trust no Future, howe'er pleasant!
    Let the dead Past bury its dead!
Act,—act in the living Present!
    Heart within, and God o'erhead!   24

Lives of great men all remind us
    We can make our lives sublime,
And, departing, leave behind us
    Footprints on the sands of time;   28

Footprints, that perhaps another,
    Sailing o'er life's solemn main,
A forlorn and shipwrecked brother,
    Seeing, shall take heart again.   32

Let us, then, be up and doing,
    With a heart for any fate;
Still achieving, still pursuing,
    Learn to labor and to wait.   36

The New Colossus[1]

Emma Lazarus   (1849–1887)

Not like the brazen giant of Greek fame,
With conquering limbs astride from land to land;
Here at our sea-washed, sunset gates shall stand
A mighty woman with a torch, whose flame   4
Is the imprisoned lightning, and her name
Mother of Exiles. From her beacon-hand
Glows world-wide welcome; her mild eyes command
The air-bridged harbor that twin cities frame.   8
"Keep, ancient lands, your storied pomp!" cries she

[1] Written in 1883 and later inscribed on a tablet at the base of the Statue of Liberty.

With silent lips. "Give me your tired, your poor,
Your huddled masses yearning to breathe free,
The wretched refuse of your teeming shore.   12
Send these, the homeless, tempest-tost to me,
I lift my lamp beside the golden door!"

CHAPTER 10

Poems for Study

When April with Its Sweet Showers[1]

Geoffrey Chaucer (c. 1343–1400)

Whan that Aprill with his shoures soote
The droghte of March hath perced to the roote,
And bathed every veyne in swich licour
Of which vertu engendred is the flour;   4
When Zephirus eek with his sweete breeth
Inspired hath in every holt and heeth
The tendre croppes, and the yonge sonne
Hath in the Ram his halve cours yronne,   8
And smale foweles maken melodye,
That slepen al the nyght with open yë
(So priketh hem nature in hir corages),—
Thanne longen folk to goon on pilgrimages,   12
And palmeres for to seken straunge strondes,
To ferne halwes, kowthe in sondry londes;
And specially from every shires ende
Of Engelond to Caunterbury they wende,   16
The hooly blisful martir for to seke,
That hem hath holpen whan that they were seeke.

[1] The opening lines of the General Prologue to *The Canterbury Tales:* "When April with its sweet showers / The drought of March has pierced to the root, / And bathed every vein in such liquor / Of which virtue engendered is the flower; / When Zephyrus, also, with his sweet breath / Inspired has in every wood and heath / The tender shoots, and the young sun / Has in the Ram his half course run, / And small birds make melody, / That sleep all night with open eye / (So nature pricks them in their hearts),— / Then folk long to go on pilgrimages, / And palmers to seek strange shores, / To far shrines, known in sundry lands; / And specially from every shire's end / Of England to Canterbury they wend, / The holy, blissful martyr for to seek, / Who had helped them when they were sick."

Zephyrus: the west wind. The Ram: sign of the Zodiac; Aries. Palmers: so called because pilgrims wore palm branches as a sign they had been to the Holy Land. Blissful martyr: St. Thomas à Becket, murdered at Canterbury in 1170.

When Daisies Pied

William Shakespeare (1564–1616)

When daisies pied, and violets blue,
And lady-smocks all silver-white,

And cuckoo-buds of yellow hue
   Do paint the meadows with delight,   4
The cuckoo then on every tree
Mocks married men;[1] for thus sings he,
         "Cuckoo;
Cuckoo, cuckoo"—O word of fear,
Unpleasing to a married ear!   8

When shepherds pipe on oaten straws,
   And merry larks are ploughmen's clocks;
When turtles tread,[2] and rooks and daws,
   And maidens bleach their summer smocks,   12
The cuckoo then on every tree
Mocks married men; for thus sings he,
         "Cuckoo;
Cuckoo, cuckoo"—O word of fear,
Unpleasing to a married ear!   16

[1] Because his song suggests the word *cuckold.*
[2] Turtle-doves mate.

When Icicles Hang by the Wall

William Shakespeare   (1564–1616)

When icicles hang by the wall,
   And Dick the shepherd blows his nail,
And Tom bears logs into the hall,
   And milk comes frozen home in pail;
When blood is nipped, and ways be foul,
Then nightly sings the staring owl,
        "Tu-whit, tu-who!"—
A merry note,
While greasy Joan doth keel[1] the pot.

When all aloud the wind doth blow,
   And coughing drowns the parson's saw,[2]
And birds sit brooding in the snow,
   And Marian's nose looks red and raw;
When roasted crabs[3] hiss in the bowl,
Then nightly sings the staring owl,
        "Tu-whit, tu-who!"—
A merry note,
While greasy Joan doth keel the pot.

[1] Stir.
[2] Platitude.
[3] Crab apples.

Hark, Hark, the Lark

William Shakespeare (1564–1616)

Hark, hark, the lark at heaven's gate sings,
    And Phoebus gins[1] arise,
His steeds to water at those springs
    On chaliced[2] flowers that lies;
And winking Mary-buds[3] begin to ope their golden eyes;   5
With every thing that pretty is, my lady sweet, arise:
             Arise, arise!

[1] The sun begins to.
[2] Cup-shaped.
[3] Marigold buds.

Fear No More the Heat o' the Sun

William Shakespeare (1564–1616)

Fear no more the heat o' the sun,
Nor the furious winter's rages,
Thou thy worldly task hast done,   3
Home art gone, and ta'en thy wages.
Golden lads and girls all must,
As chimney-sweepers, come to dust.   6
Fear no more the frown o' the great,
Thou art past the tyrant's stroke;
Care no more to clothe and eat,   9
To thee the reed is as the oak.
The sceptre, learning, physic,[1] must
All follow this and come to dust.   12

Fear no more the lightning-flash.
Nor th' all-dreaded thunder-stone.[2]
Fear not slander, censure rash.   15
Thou hast finished joy and moan.
All lovers young, all lovers must
Consign to thee and come to dust.   18
No exorciser harm thee.
Nor no witchcraft charm thee.
Ghost unlaid forbear thee.   21
Nothing ill come near thee.
Quiet consummation have,
And renowned be thy grave.   24

[1] Medical science.
[2] Thunderbolt.

Blow, Blow, Thou Winter Wind

William Shakespeare (1564–1616)

Blow, blow, thou winter wind,
Thou art not so unkind
    As man's ingratitude;
Thy tooth is not so keen,
Because thou art not seen,   5
    Although thy breath be rude.
Heigh-ho, sing heigh-ho! unto the green holly,
Most friendship is feigning, most loving mere folly.
Then heigh-ho, the holly!
    This life is most jolly.   10

Freeze, freeze, thou bitter sky,
That dost not bite so nigh
    As benefits forgot;
Though thou the waters warp,
Thy sting is not so sharp   15
    As friend remembered not.
Heigh-ho, sing heigh-ho! etc.

Still to Be Neat

Ben Jonson (1573–1637)

Still to be neat, still to be dressed,
As you were going to a feast;
Still to be powdered, still perfumed: 3
Lady, it is to be presumed,
Though art's hid causes are not found,
All is not sweet, all is not sound.   6

Give me a look, give me a face,
That makes simplicity a grace;
Robes loosely flowing, hair as free: 9
Such sweet neglect more taketh me
Than all the adulteries of art:
They strike mine eyes, but not my heart.   12

Call for the Robin Redbreast and the Wren

John Webster (1580–1625)

Call for the robin redbreast and the wren,
Since o'er shady groves they hover,

And with leaves and flowers do cover
The friendless bodies of unburied men. 4
Call unto his funeral dole[1]
The ant, the field mouse, and the mole,
To rear him hillocks that shall keep him warm,
And, when gay tombs are robbed, sustain no harm; 8
But keep the wolf far thence, that's foe to men,
For with his nails he'll dig them up again.

[1] Lamentation.

Delight in Disorder

Robert Herrick (1591–1674)

A sweet disorder in the dress
Kindles in clothes a wantonness.
A lawn[1] about the shoulders thrown
Into a fine distraction; 4
An erring lace, which here and there
Enthralls the crimson stomacher;[2]
A cuff neglectful, and thereby
Ribbons to flow confusedly; 8
A winning wave, deserving note,
In a tempestuous petticoat;
A careless shoestring, in whose tie
I see a wild civility; 12
Do more bewitch me than when art
Is too precise in every part.

[1] Shawl of fine linen.
[2] An ornamental cloth worn over the chest.

The Bad Season Makes the Poet Sad

Robert Herrick (1591–1674)

Dull to myself, and almost dead to these
My many fresh and fragrant mistresses,
Lost to all music now, since everything
Puts on the semblance here of sorrowing. 4
Sick is the land to th' heart; and doth endure
More dangerous faintings by her desp'rate cure.
But if that golden age would come again,
And Charles[1] here rule, as he before did reign, 8

[1] Charles I, beheaded 1649.

If smooth and unperplexed the seasons were,
As when the sweet Maria[2] livéd here,
I should delight to have my curls half drowned
In Tyrian dews, and head with roses crowned.   12
And once more yet (ere I am laid out dead)
Knock at a star with my exalted head.

[2] Henrietta Maria, Charles's Queen.

The Pulley

George Herbert   (1593–1633)

When God at first made man,
Having a glass of blessings standing by,
"Let us," said he, "pour on him all we can:
Let the world's riches, which dispersed lie,
    Contract into a span."   5

So strength first made a way;
Then beauty flowed, then wisdom, honor, pleasure:
When almost all was out, God made a stay,
Perceiving that, alone of all his treasure,
    Rest in the bottom lay.   10

"For if I should," said he,
"Bestow this jewel also on my creature,
He would adore my gifts instead of me,
And rest in Nature, not the God of Nature:
    So both should losers be.   15

"Yet let him keep the rest,
But keep them with repining restlesness:
Let him be rich and weary, that at least,
If goodness lead him not, yet weariness
    May toss him to my breast."   20

Song

Edmund Waller   (1607–1687)

Go, lovely rose!
Tell her that wastes her time and me
    That now she knows,
When I resemble[1] her to thee,
How sweet and fair she seems to be.   5

[1] Compare.

Tell her that's young,
And shuns to have her graces spied,
   That hadst thou sprung
In deserts, where no men abide,
Thou must have uncommended died.   10

   Small is the worth
Of beauty from the light retired;
   Bid her come forth,
Suffer herself to be desired,
And not blush so to be admired.   15

   Then die! that she
The common fate of all things rare
   May read in thee;
How small a part of time they share
That are so wondrous sweet and fair!   20

On His Having Arrived at the Age of Twenty-Three

John Milton (1608–1674)

How soon hath Time, the subtle thief of youth,
   Stolen on his wing my three-and-twentieth year!
   My hasting days fly on with full career,
But my late spring no bud or blossom shew'th.[1]   4
Perhaps my semblance might deceive the truth
   That I to manhood am arrived so near;
   And inward ripeness doth much less appear,
That some more timely-happy spirits endu'th.[2]   8
Yet, be it less or more, or soon or slow,
   It shall be still in strictest measure even[3]
   To that same lot, however mean or high,
Toward which Time leads me, and the will of Heaven,   12
   All is, if I have grace to use it so,
   As ever in my great Task-Master's eye.

[1] Showeth.
[2] Endow, clothe.
[3] Equal.

Song

Sir John Suckling (1609–1672)

No, no, fair heretic, it needs must be
   But an ill love in me,
   And worse for thee.

For were it in my power
To love thee now this hour   5
   More than I did the last,
'Twould then so fall
   I might not love at all.
Love that can flow, and can admit increase,
Admits as well an ebb, and may grow less.   10

True love is still the same; the torrid zones
   And those more frigid ones,
   It must not know;
For love, grown cold or hot,
Is lust or frienship, not   15
   The thing we have;
For that's a flame would die,
   Held down or up too high.
Then think I love more than I can express,
And would love more, could I but love thee less.   20

His Metrical Prayer: Before Execution[1]

James Graham   (1612–1650)

Let them bestow on every airth[2] a limb;
Open all my veins, that I may swim
To thee my Maker, in that crimson lake;
Then place my par-boiled head upon a stake;   4
Scatter my ashes, strew them in the air:
Lord since thou know'st where all these atoms are,
I'm hopeful thou'lt recover once my dust,
And confident thou'lt raise me with the just.   8

---

[1] James Graham, Marquis of Montrose, was hanged, disembowelled, and dismembered. His intestines were burned and his remains distributed throughout Scotland.
[2] Compass point.

The Picture of Little T. C. in a Prospect of Flowers

Andrew Marvell   (1621–1678)

See with what simplicity
This nymph begins her golden days!

In the green grass she loves to lie,
And there with her fair aspect tames 4
The wilder flowers, and gives them names;
But only with the roses plays,
    And them does tell
What color best becomes them, and what smell. 8

Who can foretell for what high cause
This darling of the gods was born?
Yet this is she whose chaster laws
The wanton Love shall one day fear, 12
And, under her command severe,
See his bow broke and ensigns torn.
    Happy who can
Appease this virtuous enemy of man! 16

O then let me in time compound¹
And parley with those conquering eyes,
Ere they have tried their force to wound;
Ere with their glancing wheels they drive 20
In triumph over hearts that strive,
And them that yield but more despise:
    Let me be laid
Where I may see thy glories from some shade. 24

Meantime, whilst every verdant thing
Itself does at the beauty charm,
Reform the errors of the spring;
Make that the tulips may have share 28
Of sweetness, seeing they are fair;
And roses of their thorns disarm;
    But most procure
That violets may a longer age endure. 32

But, O young beauty of the woods,
Whom nature courts with fruits and flowers,
Gather the flowers, but spare the buds,
Lest Flora,² angry at thy crime 36
To kill her infants in their prime,
Do quickly make the example yours;
    And ere we see,
Nip in the blossom all our hopes and thee. 40

¹ Bargain.
² Goddess of flowers.

Whilst Alexis Lay Pressed

John Dryden (1631–1700)

Whilst *Alexis* lay pressed
  In her arms he loved best,
With his hands round her neck,
  And his head on her breast,
He found the fierce pleasure too hasty to stay,   5
And his soul in the tempest just flying away.

When *Celia* saw this,
  With a sigh, and a kiss,
She cried, Oh my dear, I am robbed of my bliss;
'Tis unkind to your love, and unfaithfully done,   10
To leave me behind you, and die all alone.

The youth, though in haste,
  And breathing his last,
In pity died slowly, while she died more fast;
Till at length she cried, Now, my dear, now let us go,   15
Now die, my *Alexis*, and I will die too.

Thus intranced they did lie,
  Till *Alexis* did try
To recover new breath, that again he might die:
Then often they did; but the more they did so,   20
The nymph died more quick, and the shepherd
  more slow.

Harvest Home

John Dryden (1631–1700)

Your hay it is mowed, and your corn is reaped;
Your barns will be full, and your hovels heaped:
  Come, my boys, come;
  Come, my boys, come;
And merrily roar out Harvest Home.   5

Chorus. Come, my boys, come, &c.

We ha' cheated the parson, we'll cheat him again,
For why should a blockhead ha' one in ten?[1]
  One in ten,
  One in ten,
For why should a blockhead ha' one in Ten?   10

---

[1] A tithe; one-tenth of a person's annual production given to the clergy.

For prating so long like a book-learned sot,
Till pudding and dumpling burn to pot,
   Burn to pot,
   Burn to pot,
Till pudding and dumpling burn to pot.   15

Chorus. Burn to pot, etc.

We'll toss off our ale till we canno' stand,
And hoigh for the honor of old *England:*
   Old *England,*
   Old *England,*
And hoigh for the honor of Old *England.*   20

Chorus. Old *England,* etc.

[Man]*

Alexander Pope (1688–1744)

Know then thyself, presume not God to scan;
The proper study of mankind is Man.
Placed on this isthmus of a middle state,
A being darkly wise, and rudely great: 4
With too much knowledge for the sceptic side,
With too much weakness for the stoic's pride,
He hangs between; in doubt to act, or rest,
In doubt to deem himself a god, or beast;   8
In doubt his mind or body to prefer,
Born but to die, and reasoning but to err;
Alike in ignorance, his reason such,
Whether he thinks too little, or too much: 12
Chaos of thought and passion, all confused;
Still by himself abused, or disabused;
Created half to rise, and half to fall;
Great lord of all things, yet a prey to all;   16
Sole judge of truth, in endless error hurled:
The glory, jest, and riddle of the world!

* *An Essay on Man,* II, 1–18.

Ode

ON A DISTANT PROSPECT[1] OF
ETON COLLEGE

Thomas Gray (1716–1771)

Ye distant spires, ye antique towers,
That crown the watery glade,

[1] View.

Where grateful Science still adores
Her Henry's[2] holy shade;
And ye, that from the stately brow 5
Of Windsor's heights the expanse below
Of grove, of lawn, of mead survey,
Whose turf, whose shade, whose flowers among
Wanders the hoary Thames along
His silver-winding way. 10

Ah happy hills, ah pleasing shade,
Ah fields beloved in vain,
Where once my careless childhood strayed,
A stranger yet to pain!
I feel the gales, that from ye blow, 15
A momentary bliss bestow,
As waving fresh their gladsome wing,
My weary soul they seem to soothe,
And, redolent of joy and youth,
To breathe a second spring. 20

Say, Father Thames, for thou hast seen
Full many a sprightly race
Disporting on thy margent green
The paths of pleasure trace,
Who foremost now delight to cleave 25
With pliant arm thy glassy wave?
The captive linnet which enthrall?[3]
What idle progeny succeed[4]
To chase the rolling circle's[5] speed,
Or urge the flying ball? 30

While some on earnest business bent
Their murmuring labors ply
'Gainst graver hours, that bring constraint
To sweeten liberty:
Some bold adventurers disdain 35
The limits of their little reign,
And unknown regions dare descry:[6]
Still as they run they look behind,
They hear a voice in every wind,
And snatch a fearful joy. 40

[2] Henry VI, founder of Eton.
[3] Which boys imprison linnets?
[4] Take the place of earlier schoolboys.
[5] Hoop.
[6] Discover.

Gay hope is theirs by fancy fed,
Less pleasing when possessed;
The tear forgot as soon as shed,
The sunshine of the breast:
Theirs buxom health of rosy hue,   45
Wild wit, invention ever-new,
And lively cheer of vigor born;
The thoughtless day, the easy night,
The spirits pure, the slumbers light,
That fly the approach of morn.   50

Alas, regardless of their doom,
The little victims play!
No sense have they of ills to come,
Nor care beyond today:
Yet see how all around 'em wait   55
The ministers of human fate,
And black Misfortune's baleful train!
Ah, show them where in ambush stand
To seize their prey the murderous band!
Ah, tell them, they are men!   60

These shall the fury Passions tear,
The vultures of the mind,
Disdainful Anger, pallid Fear,
And Shame that skulks behind;
Or pining Love shall waste their youth,   65
Or Jealousy with rankling tooth,
That inly gnaws the secret heart,
And Envy wan, and faded Care,
Grim-visaged comfortless Despair,
And Sorrow's piercing dart.   70

Ambition this[7] shall tempt to rise,
Then whirl the wretch from high,
To bitter Scorn a sacrifice,
And grinning Infamy.
The stings of Falsehood those[8] shall try,   75
And hard Unkindness' altered eye,
That mocks the tear it forced to flow;
And keen Remorse with blood defiled,
And moody Madness laughing wild
Amid severest woe.   80

[7] This one.
[8] Those others.

Lo, in the vale of years beneath
A grisly troop are seen,
The painful family of Death,
More hideous than their queen:
This racks the joints, this fires the veins,   85
That every laboring sinew strains,
Those in the deeper vitals rage:
Lo, Poverty, to fill the band,
That numbs the soul with icy hand,
And slow-consuming Age.   90

To each his sufferings: all are men,
Condemned alike to groan,
The tender for another's pain;
The unfeeling for his own.
Yet ah! why should they know their fate?   95
Since sorrow never comes too late,
And happiness too swiftly flies.
Thought would destroy their paradise.
No more; where ignorance is bliss,
'Tis folly to be wise.   100

Of Jeoffry, His Cat

Christopher Smart   (1722–1771)

For I will consider my Cat Jeoffry.

For he is the servant of the Living God, duly and daily serving him.

For at the first glance of the glory of God in the East he worships in his
way.

For is this done by wreathing his body seven times round with elegant
quickness.

For then he leaps up to catch the musk, which is the blessing of God upon
his prayer.   5

For he rolls upon prank to work it in.

For having done duty and received blessing he begins to consider himself.

For this he performs in ten degrees.

For first he looks upon his fore-paws to see if they are clean.

For secondly he kicks up behind to clear away there.   10

For thirdly he works it upon stretch with the fore paws extended.

For fourthly he sharpens his paws by wood.

For fifthly he washes himself.

For sixthly he rolls upon wash.

For Seventhly he fleas himself, that he may not be interrupted upon the beat.   15

For Eightly he rubs himself against a post.

For Ninthly he looks up for his instructions.

For Tenthly he goes in quest of food.
For having considered God and himself he will consider his neighbor.
For if he meets another cat he will kiss her in kindness. 20
For when he takes his prey he plays with it to give it chance.
For one mouse in seven escapes by his dallying.
For when his day's work is done his business more properly begins.
For he keeps the Lord's watch in the night against the adversary.
For he counteracts the powers of darkness by his electrical skin & glaring eyes. 25
For he counteracts the Devil, who is death, by brisking about the life.
For in his morning orisons[1] he loves the sun and the sun loves him.
For he is of the tribe of Tiger.
For the Cherub Cat is a term of the Angel Tiger.
For he has the subtlety and hissing of a serpent, which in goodness he
    suppresses. 30
For he will not do destruction, if he is well-fed, neither will he spit without
    provocation.
For he purrs in thankfulness, when God tells him he's a good Cat.
For he is an instrument for the children to learn benevolence upon.
For every house is incomplete without him & a blessing is lacking in the spirit.
For the Lord commanded Moses concerning the cats at the departure of the
    Children of Israel from Egypt.[2] 35
For every family had one cat at least in the bag.
For the English Cats are the best in Europe.
For he is the cleanest in the use of his fore-paws of any quadruped.
For the dexterity of his defense is an instance of the love of God to him
    exceedingly.
For he is the quickest to his mark of any creature. 40
For he is tenacious of his point.
For he is a mixture of gravity and waggery.
For he knows that God is his Saviour.
For there is nothing sweeter than his peace when at rest.
For there is nothing brisker than his life when in motion. 45
For he is of the Lord's poor and so indeed is he called by benevolence
    perpetually—Poor Jeoffry! poor Jeoffry! the rat has bit thy throat.
For I bless the name of the Lord Jesus that Jeoffry is better.
For the divine spirit comes about his body to sustain it in complete cat.
For his tongue is exceeding pure so that it has in purity what it wants
    in music.
For he is docile and can learn certain things. 50
For he can set up with gravity which is patience upon approbation.
For he can fetch and carry, which is patience in employment.
For he can jump over a stick which is patience upon proof positive.
For he can spraggle upon waggle at the word of command.

[1] Prayers.
[2] Smart adds cats to the Biblical account.

For he can jump from an eminence into his master's bosom.   55
For he can catch the cork and toss it again.
For he is hated by the hypocrite and miser.
For the former is affraid of detection.
For the latter refuses the charge.
For he camels his back to bear the first notion of business.   60
For he is good to think on, if a man would express himself neatly.
For he made a great figure in Egypt for his signal services.
For he killed the Icneumon-rat very pernicious by land.
For his ears are so acute that they sting again.
For from this proceeds the passing quickness of his attention.   65
For by stroking of him I have found out electricity.
For I perceived God's light about him both wax and fire.
For the Electrical fire is the spiritual substance, which God sends from heaven
    to sustain the bodies both of man and beast.
For God has blessed him in the variety of his movements.
For, tho he cannot fly, he is an excellent clamberer.   70
For his motions upon the face of the earth are more than any other
    quadruped.
For he can tread to all the measures upon the music.
For he can swim for life.
For he can creep.

When Lovely Woman Stoops to Folly

Oliver Goldsmith   (1730–1774)

When lovely woman stoops to folly,
    And finds too late that men betray,
What charm can soothe her melancholy,
    What art can wash her guilt away?   4

The only art her guilt to cover,
    To hide her shame from every eye,
To give repentance to her lover,
    And wring his bosom—is to die.   8

The Clod and the Pebble

William Blake   (1757–1827)

'Love seeketh not itself to please,
Nor for itself hath any care,
But for another gives its ease
And builds a Heaven in Hell's despair.'   4

    So sang a little clod of clay,
    Trodden with the cattle's feet;

But a pebble of the brook
Warbled out these meters meet: 8

'Love seeketh only self to please,
To bind another to its delight,
Joys in another's loss of ease,
And builds a Hell in Heaven's despite.'   12

Mad Song
William Blake   (1757–1827)

The wild winds weep,
   And the night is a-cold;
Come hither, Sleep,
   And my griefs infold: 4
But lo! the morning peeps
   Over the eastern steeps,
And the rustling birds of dawn
The earth do scorn.   8

Lo! to the vault
   Of pavéd heaven,
With sorrow fraught
   My notes are driven: 12
They strike the ear of night,
   Make weep the eyes of day;
They make mad the roaring winds,
   And the tempests play.   16

Like a fiend in a cloud
   With howling woe,
After night I do crowd,
   And with night will go;   20
I turn my back to the east,
From whence comforts have increased;
For light doth seize my brain
With frantic pain.   24

The Tiger
William Blake   (1757–1827)

Tiger, tiger, burning bright
In the forests of the night,
What immortal hand or eye
Could frame thy fearful symmetry?   4

In what distant deeps or skies
Burnt the fire of thine eyes?
On what wings dare he aspire?
What the hand dare seize the fire?   8

And what shoulder and what art
Could twist the sinews of thy heart?
And when thy heart began to beat,
What dread hand? And what dread feet?   12

What the hammer? What the chain?
In what furnace was thy brain?
What the anvil? What dread grasp
Dare its deadly terrors clasp?   16

When the stars threw down their spears
And watered Heaven with their tears,
Did he smile his work to see?
Did he who made the Lamb make thee?   20

Tiger, tiger, burning bright
In the forests of the night,
What immortal hand or eye
Dare frame thy fearful symmetry?   24

And Did Those Feet[1]
William Blake   (1757–1827)

And did those feet in ancient time
Walk upon England's mountains green?
And was the holy Lamb of God
On England's pleasant pastures seen?   4

And did the Countenance Divine
Shine forth upon our clouded hills?
And was Jerusalem builded here,
Among these dark Satanic Mills?[2]   8

Bring me my Bow of burning gold:
Bring me my Arrows of desire:
Bring me my Spear: O clouds unfold!
Bring me my Chariot of fire!   12

[1] The feet of Jesus, who was believed by some to have visited England in the company of Joseph of
Arimathea. The poem is from the preface to Blake's prophetic poem *Milton*.
[2] Millstones as symbolic of society; the mills of the industrial revolution.

I will not cease from Mental Fight,
Nor shall my Sword sleep in my hand,
Till we have built Jerusalem
In England's green & pleasant Land. 16

Ah, Sunflower

William Blake (1757–1827)

Ah, sunflower, weary of time,
Who countest the steps of the sun,
Seeking after that sweet golden clime
Where the traveller's journey is done; 4

Where the youth pined away with desire
And the pale virgin shrouded in snow
Arise their graves and aspire
Where my sunflower wishes to go. 8

London

William Blake (1757–1827)

I wander through each chartered street
Near where the chartered Thames does flow,
And mark in every face I meet
Marks of weakness, marks of woe. 4

In every cry of every man,
In every infant's cry of fear,
In every voice, in every ban,
The mind-forged manacles I hear— 8

How the chimney-sweeper's cry
Every blackening church appalls,
And the hapless soldier's sigh
Runs in blood down palace walls; 12

But most through midnight streets I hear
How the youthful harlot's curse
Blasts the new-born infant's tear
And blights with plagues the marriage hearse. 16

Mock on, Mock on, Voltaire, Rousseau![1]

William Blake   (1757–1827)

Mock on, mock on, Voltaire, Rousseau!
Mock on, mock on—'Tis all in vain!
You throw the sand against the wind,
And the wind blows it back again.   4

And every sand becomes a gem
Reflected in the beams divine;
Blown back they blind the mocking eye,
But still in Israel's paths they shine.   8

The atoms of Democritus
And Newton's particles of light[2]
Are sands upon the Red Sea shore,
Where Israel's tents do shine so bright.   12

[1] Symbols, to Blake, of eighteenth-century skepticism.
[2] Democritus held atoms to be the primary materials of the universe. Newton thought light was composed of particles.

To a Mouse

ON TURNING HER UP IN HER NEST, WITH THE PLOUGH,
NOVEMBER, 1785

Robert Burns   (1759–1796)

Wee, sleeket, cowran,[1] tim'rous *beastie*,
O, what a panic's in thy breastie!
Thou need na start awa sae hasty,   3
    Wi' bickering brattle![2]
I wad be laith to rin[3] an' chase thee,
    Wi' murd'ring *pattle!*[4]   6

I'm truly sorry Man's dominion
Has broken Nature's social union,
An' justifies that ill opinion,   9
    Which makes thee startle,
At me, thy poor, earth-born companion,
    An' *fellow-mortal!*   12

[1] Sleek, cowering.
[2] Anxious chiding.
[3] Would be loath to run.
[4] Ploughstaff.

I doubt na, whyles,[5] but thou may *thieve;*
What then? poor beastie, thou maun[6] live!
A *daimen-icker* in a *thrave*[7]   15
   'S a sma' request:
I'll get a blessin wi' the lave,[8]
   An' never miss't!   18

Thy wee-bit *housie,* too, in ruin!
It's silly wa's[9] the win's are strewin!
An' naething, now, to big[10] a new ane,   21
   O' foggage[11] green!
An' bleak *December's winds* ensuin,
   Baith snell[12] an' keen!   24

Thou saw the fields laid bare an' waste,
An' weary *Winter* comin fast,
An' cozie here, beneath the blast,   27
   Thou thought to dwell,
Till crash! the cruel *coulter*[13] passed
   Out thro' thy cell.   30

That wee-bit heap o' leaves an' stibble,
Has cost thee monie a weary nibble!
Now thou's turn'd out, for a' thy trouble,   33
   But house or hald,[14]
To thole[15] the Winter's *sleety dribble,*
   An *cranreuch*[16] cauld!   36

But Mousie, thou art no thy-lane,[17]
In proving *foresight* may be vain:
The best laid schemes o' *Mice* an' *Men,*   39
   Gang aft agley,[18]
An' lea'e us nought but grief an' pain,
   For promis'd joy!   42

[5] At times.
[6] Must.
[7] Stray ear in a sheaf.
[8] Remainder.
[9] Feeble walls.
[10] Build.
[11] Foliage.
[12] Sharp.
[13] Plough blade.
[14] Without house or holding.
[15] Endure.
[16] Frosty.
[17] Not alone.
[18] Go oft awry.

Still, thou art blest, compar'd wi' *me!*
The *present* only toucheth thee:
But Och! I *backward* cast my e'e,   45
   On prospects drear!
An' *forward*, tho' I canna *see*,
   I *guess* an' *fear!*   48

To a Louse

ON SEEING ONE ON A LADY'S BONNET AT CHURCH
Robert Burns   (1759–1796)

Ha! whare ye gaun, Ye crowlan ferlie![1]
Your impudence protects you sairly:[2]
I canna say but ye strunt rarely,   3
   Owre *gawze* and *lace;*
Tho' faith, I fear ye dine but sparely,
   On sic a place.   6

Ye ugly, creepan, blastet wonner,[3]
Detested, shunn'd, by saunt an' sinner,
How daur ye set your fit[4] upon her,   9
   Sae fine a *Lady!*
Gae somewhere else and seek you dinner,
   On some poor body.   12

Swith, in some beggar's haffet squattle;[5]
There ye may creep, and sprawl, and sprattle,
Wi' ither kindred, jumping cattle,   15
   In shoals and nations;
Whare *horn* nor *bane*[6] ne'er daur unsettle,
   Your thick plantations.   18

Now haud[7] you there, ye're out o' sight,
Below the fatt'rels,[8] snug and tight,
Na faith ye yet! ye'll no be right,   21
   Till ye've got on it,
The vera tapmost, towrin height
   O' *Miss's bonnet.*   24

[1] Crawling wonder.
[2] Sorely.
[3] Wonder.
[4] Foot.
[5] Off! in some beggar's whisker squat.
[6] Horn nor bone [comb].
[7] Hold.
[8] Ribbons.

My sooth! right bauld[9] ye set your nose out,
As plump an' gray as onie grozet:[10]
O for some rank, mercurial rozet,[11]　　　　　　　　27
　　Or fell, red smeddum,[12]
I'd gie you sic a heart does o't,
　　Wad dress your droddum![13]　　　　　　　　　30

I wad na been surpriz'd to spy
You on an auld wife's *flainen toy*;[14]
Or aiblins[15] some bit duddie[16] boy,　　　　　　33
　　On 's *wylecoat*;[17]
But Miss's fine *Lunardi*,[18] fye!
　　How daur ye do't?　　　　　　　　　　　　36

O *Jenny* dinna toss your head,
An' set your beauties a' abread![19]
Ye little ken[20] what cursed speed　　　　　　　39
　　The blastie's[21] makin!
Thae[22] *winks* and *finger-ends*, I dread,
　　Are notice takin!　　　　　　　　　　　　42

O wad some Pow'r the giftie gie[23] us
To see oursels as others see us!
It wad frae monie a blunder free us　　　　　　45
　　An' foolish notion:
What airs in dress an' gait wad lea'e us,
　　And ev' n Devotion!　　　　　　　　　　　48

[9] Bold.
[10] Gooseberry.
[11] Resin.
[12] Powder.
[13] Backside.
[14] Flannel cap.
[15] Perhaps.
[16] Small, ragged.

[17] Waistcoat.
[18] Bonnet.
[19] All abroad.
[20] Know.
[21] Dwarf's.
[22] Those.
[23] Gift give.

The Banks o' Doon

Robert Burns　(1759–1796)

Ye flowery banks o' bonie Doon,
　　How can ye blume sae fair;
How can ye chant, ye little birds,
　　And I sae fu' o' care!　　　　　　　　　　4

Thou'll break my heart, thou bonie bird
   That sings upon the bough;
Thou minds[1] me o' the happy days
   When my fause[2] luve was true.   8

Thou'll break my heart, thou bonie bird
   That sings beside thy mate;
For sae I sat, and sae I sang,
   And wist[3] na o' my fate.   12

Aft hae I rov'd by bonie Doon,
   To see the wood-bine twine,
And ilka bird sang o' its love,
   And sae did I o' mine.   16

Wi' lightsome heart I pu'd[4] a rose
   Frae aff its thorny tree,
And my fause luver staw[5] the rose,
   But left the thorn wi' me.   20

Wi' lightsome heart I pu'd a rose,
   Upon a morn in June:
And sae I flourish'd on the morn,
   And sae was pu'd or[6] noon!   24

[1] Reminds.
[2] False.
[3] Knew.
[4] Pulled.
[5] Stole.
[6] Before.

She Dwelt Among the Untrodden Ways

William Wordsworth (1770–1850)

She dwelt among the untrodden ways
   Beside the springs of Dove,
A Maid whom there were none to praise
   And very few to love: 4

A violet by a mossy stone
   Half hidden from the eye!
—Fair as a star, when only one
   Is shining in the sky.   8

She lived unknown, and few could know
   When Lucy ceased to be;
But she is in her grave, and, oh,
   The difference to me!   12

A Slumber Did My Spirit Seal

William Wordsworth (1770–1850)

A slumber did my spirit seal;
   I had no human fears:
She seemed a thing that could not feel
   The touch of earthly years.   4

No motion has she now, no force;
   She neither hears nor sees;
Rolled round in earth's diurnal[1] course,
   With rocks, and stones, and trees.   8

[1] Daily.

Ode

INTIMATIONS OF IMMORTALITY FROM RECOLLECTIONS
OF EARLY CHILDHOOD

William Wordsworth (1770–1850)

The Child is father of the Man;
And I could wish my days to be
Bound each to each by natural piety.[1]

I

There was a time when meadow, grove, and stream,
The earth, and every common sight,
   To me did seem
   Apparelled in celestial light,
The glory and the freshness of a dream.   5
It is not now as it hath been of yore;—
   Turn wheresoe'er I may,
     By night or day,
The things which I have seen I now can see no more.

[1] The last three lines of Wordsworth's "My Heart Leaps Up."

II

The Rainbow comes and goes,   10
And lovely is the Rose,
The Moon doth with delight

Look round her when the heavens are bare;

Waters on a starry night
Are beautiful and fair;   15

The sunshine is a glorious birth;
But yet I know, where'er I go,
That there hath past away a glory from the earth.

III

Now, while the birds thus sing a joyous song,

And while the young lambs bound   20
As to the tabor's² sound,

To me alone there came a thought of grief:
A timely utterance gave that thought relief,

And I again am strong:

The cataracts blow their trumpets from the steep;
No more shall grief of mine the season wrong;   25
I hear the Echoes through the mountains throng,
The Winds come to me from the fields of sleep,

And all the earth is gay;
Land and sea
Give themselves up to jollity,   30
And with the heart of May

Doth every Beast keep holiday;—

Thou Child of Joy,

Shout round me, let me hear thy shouts, thou happy Shep-
herd-boy!

IV

Ye blessed Creatures, I have heard the call   35

Ye to each other make; I see

The heavens laugh with you in your jubilee;

My heart is at your festival,
My head hath its coronal,³

The fulness of your bliss, I feel—I feel it all.   40

Oh evil day! if I were sullen
While Earth herself is adorning,
This sweet May-morning,

---

² A small drum.
³ Crown of flowers.

And the Children are culling
    On every side,   45
In a thousand valleys far and wide,
    Fresh flowers; while the sun shines warm,
And the Babe leaps up on his Mother's arm:—
    I hear, I hear, with joy I hear!
    —But there's a Tree, of many, one,   50
A single Field which I have looked upon,
Both of them speak of something that is gone:
    The Pansy at my feet
    Doth the same tale repeat:
Whither is fled the visionary gleam?   55
Where is it now, the glory and the dream?

V

Our birth is but a sleep and a forgetting:
The Soul that rises with us, our life's Star,
    Hath had elsewhere its setting,
    And cometh from afar: 60
    Not in entire forgetfulness,
    And not in utter nakedness,
But trailing clouds of glory do we come
    From God, who is our home:
Heaven lies about us in our infancy!   65
Shades of the prison-house begin to close
    Upon the growing Boy,
        But He
Beholds the light, and whence it flows,
    He sees it in his joy;   70
The Youth, who daily farther from the east
    Must travel, still is Nature's Priest,
    And by the vision splendid
    Is on his way attended;
At length the Man perceives it die away,
And fade into the light of common day.   75

VI

Earth fills her lap with pleasures of her own;
Yearnings she hath in her own natural kind,
And, even with something of a Mother's mind,
    And no unworthy aim,
    The homely[4] Nurse doth all she can   80

---

[4] Simple, unpretentious.

To make her Foster-child, her Inmate Man,
    Forget the glories he hath known,
And that imperial palace whence he came.

VII

Behold the Child among his new-born blisses,
A six years' Darling of a pigmy size!   85
See, where 'mid work of his own hand he lies,
Frettied by sallies of his mother's kisses,
With light upon him from his father's eyes!
See, at his feet, some little plan or chart,
Some fragment from his dream of human life,   90
Shaped by himself with newly-learned art;
    A wedding or a festival,
    A mourning or a funeral;
      And this hath now his heart,
    And unto this he frames his song: 95
      Then will he fit his tongue
To dialogues of business, love, or strife;
    But it will not be long
    Ere this be thrown aside,
    And with new joy and pride   100
The little Actor cons another part;
Filling from time to time his "humorous stage"[5]
With all the Persons, down to palsied Age,
That Life brings with her in her equipage;
    As if his whole vocation   105
    Were endless imitation.

VIII

Thou, whose exterior semblance doth belie,
    Thy Soul's immensity;
Thou best Philosopher, who yet dost keep
Thy heritage, thou Eye among the blind,   110
That, deaf and silent, read'st the eternal deep,
Haunted for ever by the eternal mind,—
    Mighty Prophet! Seer blest!
    On whom those truths do rest,
Which we are toiling all our lives to find,   115
In darkness lost, the darkness of the grave;
Thou, over whom thy Immortality
Broods like the Day, a Master o'er a Slave,

---

[5] Displaying the "humors," or characteristic temperaments, of people.

A Presence which is not to be put by;
Thou little Child, yet glorious in the might   120
Of heaven-born freedom on thy being's height,
Why with such earnest pains dost thou provoke
The years to bring the inevitable yoke,
Thus blindly with thy blessedness at strife?
Full soon thy Soul shall have her earthly freight,   125
And custom lie upon thee with a weight,
Heavy as frost, and deep almost as life!

IX

    O joy! that in our embers
    Is something that doth live,
    That nature yet remembers   130
    What was so fugitive!
The thought of our past years in me doth breed
Perpetual benediction: not indeed
For that which is most worthy to be blest;
Delight and liberty, the simple creed   135
Of Childhood, whether busy or at rest,
With new-fledged hope still fluttering in his breast:—
    Not for these I raise
    The song of thanks and praise;
    But for those obstinate questionings   140
    Of sense and outward things,
    Fallings from us, vanishings;
    Blank misgivings of a Creature
Moving about in worlds not realised,
High instincts before which our mortal Nature   145
Did tremble like a guilty Thing surprised:
    But for those first affections,
    Those shadowy recollections,
    Which, be they what they may,
Are yet the fountain light of all our day,   150
Are yet a master light of all our seeing;
    Uphold us, cherish, and have power to make
Our noisy years seem moments in the being
Of the eternal Silence: truths that wake,
    To perish never;   155
Which neither listlessness, nor mad endeavour,
    Nor Man nor Boy,
Nor all that is at enmity with joy,
Can utterly abolish or destroy!
    Hence in a season of calm weather   160

Though inland far we be,
Our Souls have sight of that immortal sea
Which brought us hither,
Can in a moment travel thither,
And see the Children sport upon the shore,   165
And hear the mighty waters rolling evermore.

X

Then sing, ye Birds, sing, sing a joyous song!
And let the young Lambs bound
As to the tabor's sound!
We in thought will join your throng,
Ye that pipe and ye that play,   170
Ye that through your hearts to-day
Feel the gladness of the May!
What though the radiance which was once so bright
Be now for ever taken from my sight,
Though nothing can bring back the hour   175
Of splendour in the grass, of glory in the flower;
We will grieve not, rather find
Strength in what remains behind;
In the primal sympathy
Which having been must ever be;   180
In the soothing thoughts that spring
Out of human suffering;
In the faith that looks through death,
In years that bring the philosophic mind.

XI

And O, ye Fountains, Meadows, Hills, and Groves,   185
Forebode not any severing of our loves!
Yet in my heart of hearts I feel your might;
I only have relinquished one delight
To live beneath your more habitual sway.
I love the Brooks which down their channels fret,   190
Even more than when I tripped lightly as they;
The innocent brightness of a new-born Day
Is lovely yet;
The Clouds that gather round the setting sun
Do take a sober colouring from an eye   195
That hath kept watch o'er man's mortality;
Another race hath been, and other palms are won.

Thanks to the human heart by which we live,
Thanks to its tenderness, its joys, and fears,
To me the meanest flower that blows[6] can give 200
Thoughts that do often lie too deep for tears.

[6] Blooms.

Kubla Khan[1]

Samuel Taylor Coleridge (1772–1834)

In Xanadu did Kubla Khan
A stately pleasure-dome decree:
Where Alph, the sacred river, ran
Through caverns measureless to man
    Down to a sunless sea. 5
So twice five miles of fertile ground
With walls and towers were girdled round:
And there were gardens bright with sinuous rills,[2]
Where blossomed many an incense-bearing tree;
And here were forests ancient as the hills, 10
Enfolding sunny spots of greenery.

But oh! that deep romantic chasm which slanted
Down the green hill athwart a cedarn cover!
A savage place! as holy and enchanted
As e'er beneath a waning moon was haunted 15
By woman wailing for her demon-lover![3]
And from this chasm, with ceaseless turmoil seething,
As if this earth in fast thick pants were breathing,
A mighty fountain momently was forced:
Amid whose swift half-intermitted burst 20
Huge fragments vaulted like rebounding hail,
Or chaffy grain beneath the thresher's flail:
And 'mid these dancing rocks at once and ever
It flung up momently the sacred river.
Five miles meandering with a mazy motion 25
Through wood and dale the sacred river ran,
Then reached the caverns measureless to man,
And sank in tumult to a lifeless ocean:
And 'mid this tumult Kubla heard from far

[1] Kubla Khan was a thirteenth-century Mongol ruler, but the place names and most of the supporting details are imaginary. Coleridge said he composed the poem in a drug-induced dream.
[2] Small brooks.
[3] The demon lover is common in folklore and folksong.

Ancestral voices prophesying war!   30
 The shadow of the dome of pleasure
 Floated midway on the waves;
 Where was heard the mingled measure
 From the fountain and the caves.
It was a miracle of rare device,   35
A sunny pleasure-dome with caves of ice!

 A damsel with a dulcimer
 In a vision once I saw:
 It was an Abyssinian maid,
 And on her dulcimer she played,   40
 Singing of Mount Abora.
 Could I revive within me
 Her symphony and song,
 To such a deep delight 'twould win me,
That with music loud and long,   45
I would build that dome in air,
That sunny dome! those caves of ice!
And all who heard should see them there,
And all should cry, Beware! Beware!
His flashing eyes, his floating hair!   50
Weave a circle round him thrice,[4]
And close your eyes with holy dread,
For he on honey-dew hath fed,
And drunk the milk of Paradise.

[4] A charm against intrusion.

So We'll Go No More A-Roving

George Gordon, Lord Byron   (1788–1824)

So we'll go no more a-roving
 So late into the night,
Though the heart be still as loving,
 And the moon be still as bright.   4

For the sword outwears its sheath,
 And the soul wears out the breast,
And the heart must pause to breathe,
 And Love itself have rest.   8

Though the night was made for loving,
 And the day returns too soon,
Yet we'll go no more a-roving
 By the light of the moon.   12

Ode to the West Wind

Percy Bysshe Shelley   (1792–1822)

1

O wild West Wind, thou breath of Autumn's being,
Thou, from whose unseen presence the leaves dead
Are driven, like ghosts from an enchanter fleeing,

Yellow, and black, and pale, and hectic red,
Pestilence-stricken multitudes: O thou,   5
Who chariotest to their dark wintry bed

The wingéd seeds, where they lie cold and low,
Each like a corpse within its grave, until
Thine azure sister of the Spring shall blow

Her clarion[1] o'er the dreaming earth, and fill   10
(Driving sweet buds like flocks to feed in air)
With living hues and odors plain and hill:

Wild Spirit, which are moving everywhere;
Destroyer and preserver; hear, oh, hear!

2

Thou on whose stream, mid the steep sky's commotion,   15
Loose clouds like earth's decaying leaves are shed,
Shook from the tangled boughs of Heaven and Ocean,

Angels of rain and lightning: there are spread
On the blue surface of thine aëry surge,
Like the bright hair uplifted from the head   20

Of some fierce Maenad,[2] even from the dim verge
Of the horizon to the zenith's height,
The locks of the approaching storm. Thou dirge

Of the dying year, to which this closing night
Will be the dome of a vast sepulcher,   25
Vaulted with all they congregated might

Of vapors, from whose solid atmosphere
Black rain, and fire, and hail will burst: oh, hear!

3

Thou who didst waken from his summer dreams
The blue Mediterranean, where he lay,   30
Lulled by the coil of his crystálline streams,

[1] Trumpet.
[2] A female worshiper of Bacchus; a frenzied, dancing woman.

Beside a pumice isle in Baiae's bay,[3]
And saw in sleep old palaces and towers
Quivering within the wave's intenser day,

All overgrown with azure moss and flowers   35
So sweet, the sense faints picturing them! Thou
For whose path the Atlantic's level powers

Cleave themselves into chasms, while far below
The sea-blooms and the oozy woods which wear
The sapless foliage of the ocean, know   40

Thy voice, and suddenly grow gray with fear,
And tremble and despoil themselves: oh, hear!

4

If I were a dead leaf thou mightest bear;
If I were a swift cloud to fly with thee;
A wave to pant beneath thy power, and share   45

The impulse of thy strength, only less free
Than thou, O uncontrollable! If even
I were as in my boyhood, and could be

The comrade of thy wanderings over Heaven,
As then, when to outstrip thy skyey speed   50
Scarce seem a vision; I would ne'er have striven

As thus with thee in prayer in my sore need.
Oh, lift me as a wave, a leaf, a cloud!
I fall upon the thorns of life! I bleed!

A heavy weight of hours has chained and bowed   55
One too like thee: tameless, and swift, and proud.

5

Make me thy lyre,[4] even as the forest is:
What if my leaves are falling like its own!
The tumult of thy mighty harmonies

Will take from both a deep, autumnal tone,   60
Sweet though in sadness. Be thou, Spirit fierce,
My spirit! Be thou me, impetuous one!

Drive my dead thoughts over the universe
Like withered leaves to quicken a new birth!
And, by the incantation of this verse,   65

---

[3] Near Naples.
[4] An aeolian harp (or lyre) plays when the wind blows over its strings.

Scatter, as from an unextinguished hearth
Ashes and sparks, my words among mankind!
Be through my lips to unawakened earth

The trumpet of a prophecy! O Wind,
If Winter comes, can Spring be far behind!   70

I Am

John Clare   (1793–1864)

I am: yet what I am none cares or knows,
   My friends forsake me like a memory lost;
I am the self-consumer of my woes,
   They rise and vanish in oblivious host,
Like shades in love and death's oblivion lost;   5
And yet I am, and live with shadows tossed
Into the nothingness of scorn and noise,
   Into the living sea of waking dreams,
Where there is neither sense of life nor joys,
   But the vast shipwreck of my life's esteems;   10
And e'en the dearest—that I loved the best—
Are strange—nay, rather stranger than the rest.
I long for scenes where man has never trod,
   A place where woman never smiled or wept;
There to abide with my Creator, God,   15
   And sleep as I in childhood sweetly slept:
Untroubling and untroubled where I lie,
The grass below—above, the vaulted sky.

Badger

John Clare   (1793–1864)

When midnight comes a host of dogs and men
Go out and track the badger to his den,
And put a sack within the hole, and lie
Till the old grunting badger passes by.   4
He comes and hears—they let the strongest loose.
The old fox hears the noise and drops the goose.
The poacher shoots and hurries from the cry,
And the old hare half wounded buzzes by.   8
They get a forkèd stick to bear him down
And clap the dogs and take him to the town,
And bait him all the day with many dogs,
And laugh and shout and fright the scampering hogs.   12

He runs along and bites at all he meets:
They shout and hollo down the noisy streets.

He turns about to face the loud uproar
And drives the rebels to their very door.   16
The frequent stone is hurled where'er they go;
When badgers fight, then every one's a foe.
The dogs are clapped and urged to join the fray;
The badger turns and drives them all away.   20
Though scarcely half as big, demure and small,
He fights with dogs for hours and beats them all.
The heavy mastiff, savage in the fray,
Lies down and licks his feet and turns away.   24
The bulldog knows his match and waxes cold,
The badger grins and never leaves his hold.
He drives the crowd and follows at their heels
And bites them through—the drunkard swears and reels.   28

The frighted women take the boys away,
The blackguard laughs and hurries on the fray.
He tries to reach the woods; an awkward race,
But sticks and cudgels quickly stop the chase.   32
He turns again and drives the noisy crowd
And beats the many dogs in noises loud.
He drives away and beats them every one,
And then they loose them all and set them on.   34
He falls as dead and kicked by boys and men,
Then starts and grins and drives the crowd again;
Till kicked and torn and beaten out he lies
And leaves his hold and cackles, groans, and dies.   36

Gypsies

John Clare   (1793–1864)

The snow falls deep; the forest lies alone;
The boy goes hasty for his load of brakes,[1]
Then thinks upon the fire and hurries back;
The gypsy knocks his hands and tucks them up,   4
And seeks his squalid camp, half hid in snow,
Beneath the oak which breaks away the wind,
And bushes close in snow like hovel warm;
There tainted mutton wastes upon the coals,   8
And the half-wasted dog squats close and rubs,

---

[1] Brushwood.

Then feels the heat too strong, and goes aloof;
He watches well, but none a bit can spare,
And vainly waits the morsel thrown away.   12
'Tis thus they live—a picture to the place,
A quiet, pilfering, unprotected race.

On First Looking into Chapman's Homer[1]

John Keats   (1795–1821)

Much have I travelled in the realms of gold,
    And many goodly states and kingdoms seen;
    Round many western islands have I been
Which bards in fealty[2] to Apollo[3] hold.   4
Oft of one wide expanse had I been told
    That deep-browed Homer ruled as his demesne;[4]
    Yet did I never breathe its pure serene
Till I heard Chapman speak out loud and bold.   8
Then felt I like some watcher of the skies
    When a new planet swims into his ken;
Or like stout Cortez when with eagle eyes
    He stared at the Pacific, and all his men   12
Looked at each other with a wild surmise—
    Silent, upon a peak in Darien.[5]

[1] The translation of Homer by George Chapman, an Elizabethan poet.
[2] Allegiance.
[3] God of the sun and also music and poetry.
[4] Domain.
[5] Keats confused Cortez with Balboa, who first saw the Pacific from a "peak in Darien" (Panama).

Ode to a Nightingale

John Keats   (1795–1821)

I

My heart aches, and a drowsy numbness pains
    My sense, as though of hemlock[1] I had drunk,
Or emptied some dull opiate to the drains
    One minute past, and Lethe-wards[2] had sunk.
'Tis not through envy of thy happy lot,   5
    But being too happy in thine happiness—
        That thou, light-wingèd Dryad[3] of the trees,
            In some melodious plot

[1] Poisonous herb.
[2] Toward the river of forgetfulness in Hades.
[3] Wood nymph.

Of beechen green, and shadows numberless,
    Singest of summer in full-throated ease.   10

II

Oh, for a draught of vintage that hath been
    Cooled a long age in the deep-delvèd earth,
Tasting of Flora and the country green,
    Dance, and Provençal song, and sunburnt mirth!
Oh, for a beaker full of the warm South,   15
    Full of the true, the blushful Hippocrene,[4]
      With beaded bubbles winking at the brim,
        And purple-stainèd mouth,
That I might drink, and leave the world unseen,
    And with thee fade away into the forest dim—   20

III

Fade far away, dissolve, and quite forget
    What thou among the leaves hast never known,
The weariness, the fever, and the fret
    Here, where men sit and hear each other groan;
Where palsy shakes a few, sad, last gray hairs,   25
    Where youth grows pale, and spectre-thin, and dies;
      Where but to think is to be full of sorrow
        And leaden-eyed despairs;
Where Beauty cannot keep her lustrous eyes,
    Or new Love pine at them beyond to-morrow.   30

IV

Away! away! For I will fly to thee,
    Not charioted by Bacchus and his pards,[5]
But on the viewless wings of Poesy,
    Though the dull brain perplexes and retards.
Already with thee! Tender is the night,   35
    And haply the Queen-Moon is on her throne,
      Clustered around by all her starry fays;[6]
        But here there is no light,
Save what from heaven is with the breezes blown
    Through verdurous[7] glooms and winding mossy ways.   40

[4] A sacred spring on Mount Helicon.
[5] Bacchus, god of wine, was sometimes depicted with leopards.
[6] Fairies.
[7] Green-foliaged.

V

I cannot see what flowers are at my feet,
    Nor what soft incense hangs upon the boughs,
But, in embalmèd darkness, guess each sweet
    Wherewith the seasonable month endows
The grass, the thicket, and the fruit-tree wild—   45
    White hawthorn, and the pastoral eglantine;
        Fast-fading violets covered up in leaves;
            And mid-May's eldest child,
    The coming musk-rose, full of dewy wine,
        The murmurous haunt of flies on summer eves.   50

VI

Darkling,[8] I listen; and, for many a time
    I have been half in love with easeful Death,
Called him soft names in many a musèd rhyme,
    To take into the air my quiet breath;
Now more than ever seems it rich to die,   55
    To cease upon the midnight with no pain,
        While thou art pouring forth thy soul abroad
            In such an ecstasy.
    Still wouldst thou sing, and I have ears in vain—
        To thy high requiem become a sod.   60

VII

Thou wast not born for death, immortal Bird!
    No hungry generations tread thee down;
The voice I hear this passing night was heard
    In ancient days by emperor and clown:
Perhaps the self-same song that found a path   65
    Through the sad heart of Ruth, when, sick for home,
        She stood in tears amid the alien corn;[9]
            The same that oft-times hath
    Charmed magic casements, opening on the foam
    Of perilous seas in fairy lands forlorn.   70

VIII

Forlorn! The very word is like a bell
    To toll me back from thee to my sole self!
Adieu! The fancy cannot cheat so well
    As she is famed to to, deceiving elf.

[8] In the dark.
[9] Cf. Ruth ii. 3.

Adieu! adieu! Thy plaintive anthem fades   75
    Past the near meadows, over the still stream,
        Up the hill-side; and now 'tis buried deep
        In the next valley-glades:
    Was it a vision, or a waking dream?
        Fled is that music . . . Do I wake or sleep?   80

Ode on a Grecian Urn

John Keats   (1795–1821)

I

Thou still unravished bride of quietness,
    Thou foster-child of silence and slow time,
Sylvan[1] historian, who canst thus express
    A flowery tale more sweetly than our rhyme!
What leaf-fringed legend haunts about thy shape   5
    Of deities or mortals, or of both,
        In Tempe or the dales of Arcady?[2]
    What men or gods are these? What maidens loath?
What mad pursuit? What struggle to escape?
        What pipes and timbrels?[3] What wild ecstasy?   10

II

Heard melodies are sweet, but those unheard
    Are sweeter; therefore, ye soft pipes, play on;
Not to the sensual ear, but, more endeared,
    Pipe to the spirit ditties of no tone.
Fair youth beneath the trees, thou canst not leave   15
Thy song, nor ever can those trees be bare;
        Bold lover, never, never canst thou kiss,
Though winning near the goal—yet do not grieve:
        She cannot fade, though thou hast not thy bliss,
        For ever wilt thou love, and she be fair!   20

III

Ah, happy, happy boughs, that cannot shed
    Your leaves, nor ever bid the spring adieu;
And, happy melodist, unwearièd,
    For ever piping songs for ever new!
More happy love, more happy, happy love!   25

---

[1] Woodland.
[2] Tempe: a valley in Greece; Arcady: Arcadia, Greek state associated with a pastoral ideal.
[3] Small drums.

For ever warm and still to be enjoyed,
    For ever panting, and for ever young—
All breathing human passion far above,
    That leaves a heart high-sorrowful and cloyed,
        A burning forehead, and a parching tongue.   30

IV

Who are these coming to the sacrifice?
    To what green altar, O mysterious priest,
Lead'st thou that heifer lowing at the skies,
    And all her silken flanks with garlands dressed?
What little town by river or sea shore,   35
    Or mountain-built with peaceful citadel,
        Is emptied of this folk, this pious morn?
And, little town, thy streets for evermore
    Will silent be; and not a soul to tell
        Why thou art desolate can e'er return.   40

V

O Attic[4] shape! Fair attitude! With brede[5]
    Of marble men and maidens overwrought,
With forest branches and the trodden weed—
    Thou, silent form, dost tease us out of thought
As doth eternity. Cold pastoral!   45
    When old age shall this generation waste,
        Thou shalt remain, in midst of other woe
Than ours, a friend to man, to whom thou say'st,
    'Beauty is truth, truth beauty'—that is all
        Ye know on earth, and all ye need to know.   50

[4] From the region of Athens.
[5] Interwoven pattern; braid.

Ode on Melancholy

John Keats   (1795–1821)

I

No, no, go not to Lethe,[1] neither twist
    Wolf's-bane,[2] tight-rooted, for its poisonous wine;
Nor suffer thy pale forehead to be kissed
    By nightshade, ruby grape of Proserpine;[3]

[1] The river of forgetfulness.
[2] A common poisonous plant, as is nightshade, l. 4.
[3] Persephone, queen of the underworld.

Make not your rosary of yew-berries,[4]   5
   Nor let the beetle, nor the death-moth be
      Your mournful Psyche,[5] nor the downy owl
A partner in your sorrow's mysteries;
   For shade to shade will come too drowsily,
      And drown the wakeful anguish of the soul.   10

II

But when the melancholy fit shall fall
   Sudden from heaven like a weeping cloud,
That fosters the droop-headed flowers all,
   And hides the green hill in an April shroud;
Then glut thy sorrow on a morning rose,   15
   Or on the rainbow of the salt sand-wave,
      Or on the wealth of globèd peonies;
Or if thy mistress some rich anger shows,
   Imprison her soft hand, and let her rave,
      And feed deep, deep upon her peerless eyes.   20

III

She dwells with Beauty—Beauty that must die;
   And Joy, whose hand is ever at his lips
Bidding adieu; and aching Pleasure nigh,
   Turning to poison while the bee-mouth sips.
Aye, in the very temple of Delight   25
   Veiled Melancholy has her sovran shrine,
      Though seen of none save him whose strenuous
      tongue
Can burst Joy's grape against his palate fine;
His soul shall taste the sadness of her might,
      And be among her cloudy trophies hung.   30

[4] Symbolic of death.
[5] Psyche: The soul often pictured as a butterfly, in mourning for her lost lover, Cupid.

To Autumn
John Keats (1795–1821)

I

Season of mists and mellow fruitfulness,
   Close bosom friend of the maturing sun,
Conspiring with him how to load and bless
   With fruit the vines that round the thatch-eaves run:
To bend with apples the mossed cottage-trees,   5
   And fill all fruit with ripeness to the core;

To swell the gourd, and plump the hazel shells
With a sweet kernel; to set budding more,
And still more, later flowers for the bees,
Until they think warm days will never cease,   10
  For summer has o'er-brimmed their clammy cells.

II

Who hath not seen thee oft amid thy store?[1]
  Sometimes whoever seeks abroad may find
Thee sitting careless on a granary floor,
  Thy hair soft-lifted by the winnowing wind;   15
Or on a half-reaped furrow sound asleep,
  Drowsed with the fume of poppies, while thy hook[2]
    Spares the next swath and all its twinèd flowers;
And sometimes like a gleaner[3] thou dost keep
Steady thy laden head across a brook;   20
Or by a cider-press, with patient look,
  Thou watchest the last oozings hours by hours,

III

Where are the songs of spring? Aye, where are they?
  Think not of them, thou hast thy music too—
While barrèd clouds bloom the soft-dying day,   25
  And touch the stubble-plains with rosy hue.
Then in a wailful choir the small gnats mourn
  Among the river sallows,[4] borne aloft
    Or sinking as the light wind lives or dies;
And full-grown lambs loud bleat from hilly bourn;[5]   30
  Hedge-crickets sing; and now with treble soft
The red-breast whistles from a garden-croft;[6]
  And gathering swallows twitter in the skies.

[1] Abundance.
[2] Sickle.
[3] One who gathers after reapers.
[4] Willows.
[5] Field.
[6] Enclosed field, kitchen garden.

Song by Isbrand

Thomas Lovell Beddoes (1803–1849)

Squats on a toad-stool under a tree
  A bodiless childfull of life in the gloom,
Crying with frog voice, "What shall I be?
Poor unborn ghost, for my mother killed me

Scarcely alive in her wicked womb.   5
What shall I be? shall I creep to the egg
   That's cracking asunder yonder by Nile,
      And with eighteen toes,
      And a snuff-taking nose,
   Make an Egyptian crocodile?   10
   Sing, "Catch a mummy by the leg
   And crunch him with an upper jaw,
   Wagging tail and clenching claw;
   Take a bill-full from my craw,
   Neighbour raven, caw, O caw,   15
   Grunt, my crocky, pretty maw!"

'Swine, shall I be one? 'Tis a dear dog;
   But for a smile, and kiss, and pout,
   I much prefer *your* black-lipped snout,
     Little, gruntless, fairy hog,   20
     Godson of the hawthorn hedge.
   For, when Ringwood snuffs me out,
     And 'gins my tender paunch to grapple,
     Sing, " 'Twixt your ankles visage wedge,
      And roll up like an apple."   25
'Serpent Lucifer, how do you do?
Of your worms and your snakes I'd be one or two
   For in this dear planet of wool and of leather
'Tis pleasant to need no shirt, breeches or shoe,
   And have arm, leg, and belly together.   30
   Then aches your head, or are you lazy?
   Sing, "Round your neck your belly wrap,
   Tail-a-top, and make your cap
     Any bee and daisy."

'I'll not be a fool, like the nightingale   35
Who sits up all midnight without any ale,
   Making a noise with his nose;
Nor a camel, although 'tis a beautiful back;
Nor a duck, notwithstanding the music of quack
   And the webby, mud-patting toes.   40
I'll be a new bird with the head of an ass,
   Two pigs' feet, two men's feet, and two of a hen;
Devil-winged; dragon-bellied; grave-jawed, because
     grass
   Is a beard that's soon shaved, and grows seldom
     again
     Before it is summer; so cow all the rest;   45
     The new Dodo is finished. O! come to my nest.'

Chaucer

Henry Wadsworth Longfellow (1807–1882)

An old man in a lodge within a park;
　The chamber walls depicted all around
　With portraitures of huntsman, hawk, and hound,
　And the hurt deer. He listeneth to the lark, 4
Whose song comes with the sunshine through the dark
　Of painted glass in leaden lattice bound;
　He listeneth and he laugheth at the sound,
　Then writeth in a book like any clerk. 8
He is the poet of the dawn, who wrote
　The Canterbury Tales, and his old age
　Made beautiful with song; and as I read
I hear the crowing cock, I hear the note 12
　Of lark and linnet, and from every page
　Rise odors of ploughed field or flowery mead.[1]

---

[1] Meadow.

To Helen

Edgar Allan Poe (1809–1849)

Helen, thy beauty is to me
　Like those Nicéan barks of yore,
That gently, o'er a perfumed sea,
　The weary, way-worn wanderer bore
　To his own native shore. 5

On desperate seas long wont to roam,
　Thy hyacinth hair, thy classic face,
Thy Naiad[1] airs have brought me home
　To the glory that was Greece,
And the grandeur that was Rome. 10

Lo! in yon brilliant window-niche
　How statue-like I see thee stand,
The agate lamp within thy hand!
Ah, Psyche, from the regions which
　Are Holy-Land! 15

---

[1] Water nymph.

Annabel Lee

Edgar Allan Poe (1809–1849)

It was many and many a year ago,
      In a kingdom by the sea,
That a maiden there lived whom you may know
      By the name of Annabel Lee;—
And this maiden she lived with no other thought   5
      Than to love and be loved by me.

She was a child and I was a child,
      In this kingdom by the sea,
But we loved with a love that was more than love—
      I and my Annabel Lee—   10
With a love that the wingéd seraphs of Heaven
      Coveted her and me.

And this was the reason that, long ago,
      In this kingdom by the sea,
A wind blew out of a cloud by night   15
      Chilling my Annabel Lee;
So that her high-born kinsmen came
      And bore her away from me,
To shut her up in a sepulchre
      In this kingdom by the sea.   20

The angels, not half so happy in Heaven,
      Went envying her and me:—
Yes! that was the reason (as all men know,
      In this kingdom by the sea)
That the wind came out of the cloud, chilling   25
      And killing my Annabel Lee.

But our love it was stronger by far than the love
      Of those who were older than we—
      Of many far wiser than we—
And neither the angels in Heaven above   30
      Nor the demons down under the sea
Can ever dissever my soul from the soul
      Of the beautiful Annabel Lee:—

For the moon never beams without bringing me dreams
      Of the beautiful Annabel Lee;   35
And the stars never rise but I see the bright eyes
      Of the beautiful Annabel Lee;

And so, all the night-tide, I lie down by the side
Of my darling, my darling, my life and my bride
　　　In her sepulchre there by the sea—　　40
　　　In her tomb by the side of the sea.

The Eagle

Alfred, Lord Tennyson　(1809–1892)

He clasps the crag with crookèd hands;
Close to the sun in lonely lands,
Ringed with the azure world, he stands.　　3

The wrinkled sea beneath him crawls;
He watches from his mountain walls,
And like a thunderbolt he falls.　　6

The Bishop Orders His Tomb at Saint Praxed's Church
ROME, 15—

Robert Browning　(1812–1889)

Vanity, saith the preacher, vanity![1]
Draw round my bed: is Anselm keeping back?
Nephews—sons mine . . . ah, God, I know not! Well—
She, men would have to be your mother once,
Old Gandolf[2] envied me, so fair she was!　　5
What's done is done, and she is dead beside,
Dead long ago, and I am Bishop since,
And as she died so must we die ourselves,
And thence ye may perceive the world's a dream.
Life, how and what is it? As here I lie　　10
In this state-chamber, dying by degrees,
Hours and long hours in the dead night, I ask
'Do I live, am I dead?' Peace, peace seems all.
Saint Praxed's ever was the church for peace;
And so, about this tomb of mine. I fought　　15
With tooth and nail to save my niche, ye know:
—Old Gandolf cozened[3] me, despite my care;
Shrewd was that snatch from out the corner South
He graced his carrion with, God curse the same!
Yet still my niche is not so cramped but thence　　20
One sees the pulpit o' the epistle-side,

[1] Cf. Eccles. i. 2.
[2] An imagined person, like the speaker.
[3] Cheated.

And somewhat of the choir, those silent seats,
And up into the aery dome where live
The angels, and a sunbeam's sure to lurk:
And I shall fill my slab of basalt there,   25
And 'neath my tabernacle take my rest,
With those nine columns round me, two and two,
The odd one at my feet where Anselm stands:
Peach-blossom marble all, the rare, the ripe
As fresh-poured red wine of a mighty pulse.   30
—Old Gandolf with his paltry onion-stone,
Put me where I may look at him! True peach,
Rosy and flawless: how I earned the prize!
Draw close: that conflagration of my church
—What then? So much was saved if aught were missed!   35
My sons, ye would not be my death? Go dig
The white-grape vineyard where the oil-press stood,
Drop water gently till the surface sink,
And if ye fine . . . Ah God, I know not, I! . . .
Bedded in store of rooten fig-leaves soft,   40
And corded up in a tight olive-frail,[4]
Some lump, ah God, of *lapis lazuli*,[5]
Big as a Jew's head cut off at the nape,
Blue as a vein o'er the Madonna's breast . . .
Sons, all have I bequeathed you, villas, all,   45
That brave Frascati[6] villa with its bath,
So, let the blue lump poise between my knees,
Like God the Father's globe on both his hands
Ye worship in the Jesu Church so gay,
For Gandolf shall not choose but see and burst!   50
Swift as a weaver's shuttle fleet our years:
Man goeth to the grave, and where is he?
Did I say basalt for my slab, sons? Black—
'T was ever antique-black I meant! How else
Shall ye contrast my frieze to come beneath?   55
The bas-relief in bronze ye promised me,
Those Pans and Nymphs ye wot of, and perchance
Some tripod, thyrsus,[7] with a vase or so,
The Saviour at his sermon on the mount,
Saint Praxed in a glory,[8] and one Pan   60
Ready to twitch the Nymph's last garment off,

[4] Olive basket.
[5] A valuable blue stone.
[6] A wealthy Roman suburb.
[7] Staff.
[8] Gold rays, signifying sanctity.

And Moses with the tables[9] . . . but I know
Ye mark me not! What do they whisper thee,
Child of my bowels, Anselm? Ah, ye hope
To revel down my villas while I gasp   65
Bricked o'er with beggar's mouldy travertine[10]
Which Gandolf from his tomb-top chuckles at!
Nay, boys, ye love me—all of jasper, then!
'T is jasper ye stand pledged to, lest I grieve
My bath must needs be left behind, alas!   70
One block, pure green as a pistachio-nut,
There's plenty jasper somewhere in the world—
And have I not Saint Praxed's ear to pray
Horses for ye, and brown Greek manuscripts,
And mistresses with great smooth marbly limbs?   75
—That's if ye carve my epitaph aright,
Choice Latin, picked phrase, Tully's[11] every word,
No gaudy ware like Gandolf's second line—
Tully, my masters? Ulpian[12] serves his need!
And then how I shall lie through centuries,   80
And hear the blessed mutter of the mass,
And see God made and eaten all day long,[13]
And feel the steady candle-flame, and taste
Good strong thick stupefying incense-smoke!
For as I lie here, hours of the dead night,   85
Dying in state and by such slow degrees,
I fold my arms as if they clasped a crook,[14]
And stretch my feet forth straight as stone can point,
And let the bedclothes, for a mortcloth,[15] drop
Into great laps and folds of sculptor's-work: 90
And as yon tapers dwindle, and strange thoughts
Grow, with a certain humming in my ears,
About the life before I lived this life,
And this life too, popes, cardinals and priests,
Saint Praxed at his sermon on the mount,   95
Your tall pale mother with her talking eyes,
And new-found agate urns as fresh as day,
And marble's language, Latin pure, discreet,
—Aha, ELUCESCEBAT[16] quoth our friend?

[9] Tablets with the Ten Commandments.
[10] Inexpensive limestone.
[11] Marcus Tullius Cicero, an esteemed stylist.
[12] A later Latin writer.
[13] Through transubstantiation; in the Eucharist.
[14] Bishop's crozier.
[15] Cloth used as covering for a body or coffin.
[16] "He was illustrious"; but the bishop thinks the verb form not up to Tully's standard.

No Tully, said I, Ulpian at the best! 100
Evil and brief hath been my pilgrimage.
All *lapis*, all, sons! Else I give the Pope
My villas! Will ye ever eat my heart?
Ever your eyes were as a lizard's quick
They glitter like your mother's for my soul, 105
Or ye would heighten my impoverished frieze,
Piece out its starved design, and fill my vase
With grapes, and add a vizor and a Term,[17]
And to the tripod ye would tie a lynx
That in his struggle throws the thyrsus down, 110
To comfort me on my entablature[18]
Whereon I am to lie till I must ask
'Do I live, am I dead?' There, leave me, there!
For ye have stabbed me with ingratitude
To death—ye wish it—God, ye wish it! Stone— 115
Gritstone, a-crumble! Clammy squares which sweat
As if the corpse they keep were oozing through—
And no more *lapis* to delight the world!
Well go! I bless ye. Fewer tapers there,
But in a row: and, going, turn your backs 120
—Ay, like departing altar-ministrants,
And leave me in my church, the church for peace,
That I may watch at leisure if he leers—
Old Gandolf, at me, from his onion-stone,
As still he envied me, so fair she was! 125

[17] Pillar.
[18] Raised platform.

Home-Thoughts, from Abroad

Robert Browning   (1812–1889)

I

Oh, to be in England
Now that April's there,
And whoever wakes in England
Sees, some morning, unaware, 4
That the lowest boughs and the brushwood sheaf
Round the elm-tree bole are in tiny leaf,
While the chaffinch sings on the orchard bough
In England—now! 8

II

And after April, when May follows,
And the whitethroat builds, and all the swallows!

Hark, where my blossomed pear-tree in the hedge
Leans to the field and scatters on the clover 12
Blossoms and dewdrops—at the bent spray's edge—
That's the wise thrush; he sings each song twice over,
Lest you should think he never could recapture
The first fine careless rapture! 16
And though the fields look rough with hoary dew
All will be gay when noontide wakes anew
The buttercups, the little children's dower
—Far brighter than this gaudy melon-flower! 20

I Saw in Louisiana a Live-Oak Growing

Walt Whitman (1819–1892)

I saw in Louisiana a live-oak growing,
All alone stood it and the moss hung down from the branches,
Without any companion it grew there uttering joyous leaves of
    dark green,
And its look, rude, unbending, lusty, made me think of myself,
But I wonder'd how it could utter joyous leaves standing alone
    there without its friend near, for I knew I could not, 5
And I broke off a twig with a certain number of leaves upon it,
    and twined around it a little moss,
And brought it away, and I have placed it in sight in my room,
It is not needed to remind me as of my own dear friends,
(For I believe lately I think of little else than of them,)
Yet it remains to me a curious token, it makes me think of manly
    love; 10
For all that, and though the live-oak glistens there in Louisiana
    solitary in a wide flat space,
Uttering joyous leaves all its life without a friend a lover near,
I know very well I could not.

The Wound-Dresser

Walt Whitman (1819–1892)

1

An old man bending I come among new faces,
Years looking backward resuming in answer to children,
Come tell us old man, as from young men and maidens that love me,
(Arous'd and angry, I'd thought to beat the alarum, and urge relentless war,
But soon my fingers fail'd me, my face droop'd and I resign'd myself, 5
To sit by the wounded and soothe them, or silently watch the dead;)
Years hence of these scenes, of these furious passions, these chances,

Of unsurpass'd heroes (was one side so brave? the other was equally brave;)
Now be witness again, paint the mightiest armies of earth,
Of those armies so rapid so wondrous what saw you to tell us?   10
What stays with you latest and deepest? of curious panics,
Of hard-fought engagements or sieges tremendous what deepest remains?

2

O maidens and young men I love and that love me,
What you ask of my days those the strangest and sudden your talking recalls,
Soldier alert I arrive after a long march cover'd with sweat and dust,   15
In the nick of time I come, plunge in the fight, loudly shout in the rush of suc-
          cessful charge,
Enter the captur'd works—yet lo, like a swift-running river they fade,
Pass and are gone they fade—I dwell not on soldiers' perils or soldiers' joys,
(Both I remember well—many the hardships, few the joys, yet I was content.)

But in silence, in dreams' projections,   20
While the world of gain and appearance and mirth goes on,
So soon what is over forgotten, and waves wash the imprints off the sand,
With hinged knees returning I enter the doors, (while for you up there,
Whoever you are, follow without noise and be of strong heart.)

Bearing the bandages, water and sponge,   25
Straight and swift to my wounded I go,
Where they lie on the ground after the battle brought in,
Where their priceless blood reddens the grass the ground,
Or to the rows of the hospital tent, or under the roof'd hospital,
To the long rows of cots up and down each side I return,   30
To each and all one after another I draw near, not one do I miss,
An attendant follows holding a tray, he carries a refuse pail,
Soon to be fill'd with clotted rags and blood, emptied, and fill'd again.

I onward go, I stop,
With hinged knees and steady hand to dress wounds,   35
I am firm with each, the pangs are sharp yet unavoidable,
One turns to me his appealing eyes—poor boy! I never knew you,
Yet I think I could not refuse this moment to die for you, if that would save you.

3

On, on I go, (open doors of time! open hospital doors!)
The crush'd head I dress, (poor crazed hand tear not the bandage away,)   40
The neck of the cavalry-man with the bullet through and through I examine,
Hard the breathing rattles, quite glazed already the eye yet life struggles hard,
(Come sweet death! be persuaded O beautiful death!
In mercy come quickly.)

From the stump of the arm, the amputated hand, 45
I undo the clotted lint, remove the slough,[1] wash off the matter and blood,
Back on his pillow the soldier bends with curv'd neck and side-falling head,
His eyes are closed, his face is pale, he dares not look on the bloody stump,
And has not yet look'd on it.

I dress a wound in the side, deep, deep, 50
But a day or two more, for see the frame all wasted and sinking,
And the yellow-blue countenance see

I dress the perforated shoulder, the foot with the bullet-wound,
Cleanse the one with a gnawing and putrid gangrene, so sickening, so offensive,
While the attendant stands behind aside me holding the tray and pail. 55

I am faithful, I do not give out,
The fractur'd thigh, the knee, the wound in the abdomen,
These and more I dress with impassive hand, (yet deep in my breast a fire, a
    burning flame.)

4

Thus in silence in dreams' projections,
Returning, resuming, I thread my way through the hospitals, 60
The hurt and wounded I pacify with soothing hand,
I sit by the restless all the dark night, some are so young,
Some suffer so much, I recall the experience sweet and sad,
(Many a soldier's loving arms about his neck have cross'd and rested,
Many a soldier's kiss dwells on these bearded lips.) 65

---

[1] Shed skin or tissue.

The Dalliance of the Eagles

Walt Whitman (1819–1892)

Skirting the river road, (my forenoon walk, my rest,)
Skyward in air a sudden muffled sound, the dalliance of the eagles,
The rushing amorous contact high in space together,
The clinching interlocking claws, a living, fierce, gyrating wheel,
Four beating wings, two beaks, a swirling mass tight grappling, 5
In tumbling turning clustering loops, straight downward falling,
Till o'er the river pois'd, the twain yet one, a moment's lull,
A motionless still balance in the air, then parting, talons loosing,
Upward again on slow-firm pinions slanting, their separate diverse flight,
She hers, he his, pursuing. 10

To Marguerite

Matthew Arnold (1822–1888)

Yes! in the sea of life enisled,
With echoing straits between us thrown,
Dotting the shoreless watery wild,   3
We mortal millions live *alone*.
The islands feel the enclasping flow,
And then their endless bounds they know.   6

But when the moon their hollows lights,
And they are swept by balms of spring,
And in their glens, on starry nights,   9
The nightingales divinely sing;
And lovely notes, from shore to shore,
Across the sounds and channels pour—   12

Oh! then a longing like despair
Is to their farthest caverns sent;
For surely once, they feel, we were   15
Parts of a single continent!
Now round us spreads the watery plain—
Oh might our marges meet again!   18

Who order'd, that their longing's fire
Should be, as soon as kindled, cool'd?
Who renders vain their deep desire?—   21
A God, a God their severance ruled!
And bade betwixt their shores to be
The unplumb'd, salt, estranging sea.   24

The Woodspurge

Dante Gabriel Rossetti (1828–1882)

The wind flapped loose, the wind was still,
Shaken out dead from tree and hill;
I had walked on at the wind's will,—
I sat now, for the wind was still.   4

Between my knees my forehead was,—
My lips, drawn in, said not Alas!
My hair was over in the grass,
My naked ears heard the day pass.   8

My eyes, wide open, had the run
Of some ten weeds to fix upon;

Among those few out of the sun,
The woodspurge flowered, three cups in one. 12

From perfect grief there need not be
Wisdom or even memory;
One thing then learnt remains to me—
The woodspurge has a cup of three. 16

The Heart Asks Pleasure—First

Emily Dickinson (1830–1886)

The Heart asks Pleasure—first—
And then—Excuse from Pain—
And then—those little Anodynes
That deaden suffering— 4

And then—to go to sleep—
And then—if it should be
The will of its Inquisitor
The privilege to die— 8

When the Hounds of Spring Are on Winter's Traces

Algernon Charles Swinburne (1834–1909)

When the hounds of spring are on winter's traces,
The mother of months[1] in meadow or plain
Fills the shadows and windy places
With lisp of leaves and ripple of rain; 4
And the brown bright nightingale[2] amorous
Is half assuaged for Itylus,
For the Thracian ships and the foreign faces,
The tongueless vigil, and all the pain. 8

Come with bows bent and with emptying of quivers,
Maiden most perfect, lady of light,
With a noise of winds and many rivers,
With a clamour of waters, and with might; 12
Bind on thy sandals, O thou most fleet,
Over the splendour and speed of thy feet;
For the faint east quickens, the wan west shivers,
Round the feet of the day and the feet of the night. 16

[1] Diana (Artemis), the huntress, goddess of the moon and, hence, "mother of months."
[2] Philomela was raped by Tereus, king of Thrace, who cut out her tongue so that she could not tell her sister Procne, his wife. Procne, however, found out and in revenge served Tereus a meal cooked from the flesh of his son Itylus. The gods changed Philomela into the nightingale and Procne into the sparrow, while Tereus became the hawk, who pursues them. The story is told in Ovid, *Metamorphoses*, VI.

Where shall we find her, how shall we sing to her,
    Fold our hands round her knees, and cling?
O that man's heart were as fire and could spring to her,
    Fire, or the strength of the streams that spring!   20
For the stars and the winds are unto her
As raiment, as songs of the harp-player;
For the risen stars and the fallen cling to her,
    And the southwest-wind and the west-wind sing.   24

For winter's rains and ruins are over,
    And all the season of snows and sins;
The days dividing lover and lover,
    The light that loses, the night that wins;   28
And time remembered is grief forgotten,
And frosts are slain and flowers begotten,
And in green underwood and cover
    Blossom by blossom the spring begins.   32

The full streams feed on flower of rushes,
    Ripe grasses trammel a travelling foot,
The faint fresh flame of the young year flushes
    From leaf to flower and flower to fruit;   36
And fruit and leaf are as gold and fire,
And the oat[3] is heard above the lyre,
And the hoofèd heel of a satyr[4] crushes
    The chestnut-husk at the chestnut-root.   40

And Pan[5] by noon and Bacchus[6] by night,
    Fleeter of foot than the fleet-foot kid,
Follows with dancing and fills with delight
    The Maenad and the Bassarid[7];   44
And soft as lips that laugh and hide
The laughing leaves of the trees divide,
And screen from seeing and leave in sight
    The god pursuing, the maiden hid.   48

The ivy falls with the Bacchanal's hair
    Over her eyebrows hiding her eyes;
The wild vine slipping down leaves bare
    Her bright breast shortening into sighs;   52

---

[3] Reed pipe.
[4] A demigod, part man, part horse.
[5] God of shepherds, part goat.
[6] God of wine.
[7] Followers of Pan and Bacchus.

The wild vine slips with the weight of its leaves,
But the berried ivy catches and cleaves
To the limbs that glitter, the feet that scare
    The wolf that follows, the fawn that flies.   56

I Look into My Glass

Thomas Hardy (1840–1928)

I look into my glass,
And view my wasting skin,
And say, "Would God it came to pass
My heart had shrunk as thin!"   4

For then, I, undistrest
By hearts grown cold to me,
Could lonely wait my endless rest
With equanimity.   8

But Time, to make me grieve,
Part steals, lets part abide;
And shakes this fragile frame at eve
With throbbings of noontide.   12

The Self-Unseeing

Thomas Hardy (1840–1928)

Here is the ancient floor,
Footworn and hollowed and thin,
Here was the former door
Where the dead feet walked in.   4

She sat here in her chair,
Smiling into the fire;
He who played stood there,
Bowing it higher and higher.   8

Childlike, I danced in a dream;
Blessings emblazoned that day;
Everything glowed with a gleam;
Yet we were looking away!   12

In Tenebris[1]

Thomas Hardy   (1840–1928)

"Percussion sum sicut foenum, et aruit cor meum."[2]

—PSALM cii.

Wintertime nighs;
But my bereavement-pain
It cannot bring again:
    Twice no one dies.

        4

Flower-petals flee;
But, since it once hath been,
No more that severing scene
    Can harrow me.

        8

Birds faint in dread:
I shall not lose old strength
In the lone frost's black length:
    Strength long since fled!

        12

Leaves freeze to dun;
But friends can not turn cold
This season as of old
    For him with none.

        16

Tempests may scath;[3]
But love can not make smart
Again this year his heart
    Who no heart hath.

        20

Black is night's cope;[4]
But death will not appal
One who, past doubtings all,
    Waits in unhope.

        24

[1] In darkness.
[2] "My heart is smitten, and withered like grass."
[3] Scathe, injure.
[4] Priest's vestment, covering.

Channel Firing

Thomas Hardy   (1840–1928)

That night your great guns, unawares,
Shook all our coffins as we lay,

And broke the chancel window-squares,
We thought it was the Judgment-day 4

And sat upright. While drearisome
Arose the howl of wakened hounds:
The mouse let fall the altar-crumb,
The worms drew back into the mounds, 8

The glebe[1] cow drooled. Till God called, "No;
It's gunnery practice out at sea
Just as before you went below;
The world is as it used to be: 12

"All nations striving to make
Red war yet redder. Mad as hatters
They do no more for Christés sake
Than you who are helpless in such matters. 16

"That this is not the judgment-hour
For some of them's a blessed thing,
For if it were they'd have to scour
Hell's floor for so much threatening. . . . 20

"Ha, ha. It wil be warmer when
I blow the trumpet (if indeed
I ever do; for you are men,
And rest eternal sorely need)." 24

So down we lay again. "I wonder,
Will the world ever saner be,"
Said one, "than when He sent us under
In our indifferent century!" 28

And many a skeleton shook his head.
"Instead of preaching forty year,"
My neighbor Parson Thirdly said,
"I wish I had stuck to pipes and beer." 32

Again the guns disturbed the hour,
Roaring their readiness to avenge,
As far inland as Stourton Tower,
And Camelot, and starlit Stonehenge.[2] 36

[1] Land belonging to a parish church.
[2] Stourton Tower: the so-called "Arthur's Tower" on the National Trust estate of Stourhead, near Mere, Wiltshire; Camelot: seat of King Arthur's court, sometimes thought to be in Somerset; Stonehenge: ancient stone circle near Amesbury, Wiltshire.

The Impercipient [1]
(AT A CATHEDRAL SERVICE)

Thomas Hardy   (1840–1928)

That with this bright believing band
    I have no claim to be,
That faiths by which my comrades stand   3
    Seem fantasies to me,
And mirage-mists their Shining Land,
    Is a strange destiny.   6

Why thus my soul should be consigned
    To infelicity,
Why always I must feel as blind   9
    To sights my brethren see,
Why joys they've found I cannot find,
    Abides a mystery.   12

Since heart of mine knows not that ease
    Which they know; since it be
That He who breathes All's Well to these   15
    Breathes no All's-Well to me,
My lack might move their sympathies
    And Christian charity!   18

I am like a gazer who should mark
    An inland company
Standing upfingered, with, "Hark! hark!   21
    The glorious distant sea!"
And feel, "Alas, 'tis but yon dark
    And wind-swept pine to me!"   24

Yet I would bear my shortcomings
    With meet tranquillity,
But for the charge that blessed things   27
    I'd liefer not have be.
O, doth a bird deprived of wings
    Go earth-bound wilfully!   30

•   •   •

Enough. As yet disquiet clings
    About us. Rest shall we.

[1] A person unable to perceive.

Pied[1] Beauty

Gerard Manley Hopkins   (1844–1889)

Glory be to God for dappled things—
   For skies of couple-colour as a brinded[2] cow;
     For rose-moles all in stipple upon trout that swim;
Fresh-firecoal chestnut-falls; finches' wings;
   Landscape plotted and pieced—fold, fallow,[3] and plough;   5
     And áll trádes, their gear and tackle and trim.

All things counter, original, spare, strange;
   Whatever is fickle, freckled (who knows how?)
     With swift, slow; sweet, sour; adazzle, dim;
He fathers-forth whose beauty is past change: 10
               Praise him.

[1] Variegated; colored with spots or patches.
[2] Brindled; streaked or spotted.
[3] Fold: an enclosure for animals; fallow: uncultivated land.

As Kingfishers Catch Fire, Dragonflies Draw Flame

Gerard Manley Hopkins   (1844–1889)

As kingfishers catch fire,[1] dragonflies draw flame;
   As tumbled over rim in roundy wells
   Stones ring; like each tucked[2] string tells, each hung bell's
Bow swung finds tongue to fling out broad its name;   4
Each mortal thing does one thing and the same:
   Deals out that being indoors each one dwells;[3]
   Selves[4]—goes itself; *myself* it speaks and spells,
Crying *What I do is me: for that I came.*   8

I say more: the just man justices;
   Keeps gráce: thát keeps all his goings graces;
   Acts in God's eye what in God's eye he is—
   Chríst. For Christ plays in ten thousand places,   12
Lovely in limbs, and lovely in eyes not his
   To the Father through the features of men's faces.

[1] Reflecting sunlight.
[2] Pulled.
[3] Establishes the essence that lives within itself.
[4] Identifies itself.

To an Athlete Dying Young

A. E. Housman (1859–1936)

The time you won your town the race
We chaired you through the market-place;
Man and boy stood cheering by,
And home we brought you shoulder-high.   4

To-day, the road all runners come,
Shoulder-high we bring you home,
And set you at your threshold down,
Townsman of a stiller town.   8

Smart lad, to slip betimes away
From fields where glory does not stay
And early though the laurel[1] grows
It withers quicker than the rose.   12

Eyes the shady night has shut
Cannot see the record cut,
And silence sounds no worse than cheers
After earth has stopped the ears: 16

Now you will not swell the rout[2]
Of lads that wore their honours out,
Runners whom renown outran
And the name died before the man.   20

So set, before its echoes fade,
The fleet foot on the sill of shade,
And hold to the low lintel[3] up
The still-defended challenge-cup.   24

And round that early-laurelled head
Will flock to gaze the strengthless dead,
And find unwithered on its curls
The garland briefer than a girl's.   28

[1] Used to crown winners of athletic events.
[2] Crowd.
[3] Crosspiece over a door.

On Wenlock Edge the Wood's in Trouble

A. E. Housman (1859–1936)

On Wenlock Edge[1] the wood's in trouble;
His forest fleece the Wrekin[2] heaves;

[1] A ridge in Shropshire.
[2] A hill in Shropshire.

The gale, it plies the saplings double,
    And thick on Severn[3] snow the leaves.   4

'Twould blow like this through holt and hanger[4]
    When Uricon[5] the city stood:
'Tis the old wind in the old anger,
    But then it threshed another wood.   8

Then, 'twas before my time, the Roman
    At yonder heaving hill would stare:
The blood that warms an English yeoman,
    The thoughts that hurt him, they were there.   12

There, like the wind through woods in riot,
    Through him the gale of life blew high;
The tree of man was never quiet:
    Then 'twas the Roman, now 'tis I.   16

The gale, it plies the saplings double,
    It blows so hard, 'twill soon be gone:
To-day the Roman and his trouble
    Are ashes under Uricon.   20

[3] A Shropshire river.
[4] Woods and wooded slopes.
[5] A Roman city near where Shrewsbury now stands.

From Far, from Eve and Morning

A. E. Housman (1859–1936)

From far, from eve and morning
    And yon twelve-winded sky,
The stuff of life to knit me
    Blew hither: here am I.   4

Now—for a breath I tarry
    Nor yet disperse apart—
Take my hand quick and tell me,
    What have you in your heart.   8

Speak now, and I will answer;
    How shall I help you, say;
Ere to the wind's twelve quarters
    I take my endless way.   12

Epitaph on an Army of Mercenaries

A. E. Housman (1859–1936)

These, in the day when heaven was falling,
  The hour when earth's foundations fled,
Followed their mercenary calling
  And took their wages and are dead.   4

Their shoulders held the sky suspended;
  They stood, and earth's foundations stay;
What God abandoned, these defended,
  And saved the sum of things for pay.   8

The Chestnut Casts His Flambeaux

A. E. Housman (1859–1936)

The chestnut casts his flambeaux,[1] and the flowers
  Stream from the hawthorn on the wind away,
The doors clap to, the pane is blind with showers.
  Pass me the can, lad; there's an end of May.   4

There's one spoilt spring to scant our mortal lot,
  One season ruined of our little store.
May will be fine next year as like as not:
  Oh ay, but then we shall be twenty-four.   8

We for a certainty are not the first
  Have sat in taverns while the tempest hurled
Their hopeful plans to emptiness, and cursed
  Whatever brute and blackguard made the world.   12

It is in truth iniquity on high
  To cheat our sentenced souls of aught they crave,
And mar the merriment as you and I
  Fare on our long fool's-errand to the grave.   16

Iniquity it is; but pass the can.
  My lad, no pair of kings our mothers bore;
Our only portion is the estate of man:
  We want the moon, but we shall get no more.   20

If here to-day the cloud of thunder lours[2]
  To-morrow it will hie on far behests;
The flesh will grieve on other bones than ours
  Soon, and the soul will mourn in other breasts.   24

[1] Torches; here, blossoms.
[2] Lowers, scowls.

The troubles of our proud and angry dust
　Are from eternity, and shall not fail.
Bear them we can, and if we can we must.
　Shoulder the sky, my lad, and drink your ale.   28

The Night Is Freezing Fast

A. E. Housman   (1859–1936)

The night is freezing fast,
　To-morrow comes December;
　　And winterfalls of old   3
Are with me from the past;
　And chiefly I remember
　　How Dick would hate the cold.   6

Fall, winter, fall; for he,
　Prompt hand and headpiece clever,
　　Has woven a winter robe,   9
And made of earth and sea
　His overcoat for ever,
　　And wears the turning globe.   12

The Song of the Banjo

Rudyard Kipling   (1865–1936)

You couldn't pack a Broadwood half a mile—
　You mustn't leave a fiddle in the damp—
You couldn't raft an organ up the Nile,
　And play it in an Equatorial swamp.   4
I travel with the cooking-pots and pails—
　I'm sandwiched 'tween the coffee and the pork—
And when the dusty column checks and tails,
　You should hear me spur the rearguard to a walk!   8

　With my *"Pilly-willy-winky-winky-popp!"*
　　[Oh, it's any tune that comes into my head!]
　So I keep 'em moving forward till they drop;
　　So I play 'em up to water and to bed.   12

In the silence of the camp before the fight,
　When it's good to make your will and say your prayer,
You can hear my *strumpty-tumpty* overnight,
　Explaining ten to one was always fair.   16
I'm the Prophet of the Utterly Absurd,
　Of the Patently Impossible and Vain—

And when the Thing that Couldn't has occurred,
   Give me time to change my leg and go again.   20

    With my *"Tumpa-tumpa-tumpa-tumpa-tump!"*
      In the desert where the dung-fed camp-smoke curled.
    There was never voice before us till I led our lonely chorus,
      I—the war-drum of the White Man round the world!   24

By the bitter road the Younger Son must tread,
   Ere he win to hearth and saddle of his own,—
'Mid the riot of the shearers at the shed,
   In the silence of the herder's hut alone—   28
In the twilight, on a bucket upside down,
   Hear me babble what the weakest won't confess—
I am Memory and Torment—I am Town!
   I am all that ever went with evening dress!   32

    With my *"Tunka-tunka-tunka-tunka-tunk!"*
      [So the lights—the London Lights—grow near and plain!]
    So I rowel[1] 'em afresh towards the Devil and the Flesh,
      Till I bring my broken rankers home again.   36

In desire of many marvels over sea,
   Where the new-raised tropic city sweats and roars,
I have sailed with Young Ulysses from the quay
   Till the anchor rumbled down on stranger shores.   40
He is blooded to the open and the sky,
   He is taken in a snare that shall not fail,
He shall hear me singing strongly, till he die,
   Like the shouting of a backstay in a gale.   44

    With my *"Hya! Heeya! Heeya! Hullah! Haul!"*
      [Oh, the green that thunders aft along the deck!]
    Are you sick o' towns and men? You must sign and sail again,
      For it's "Johnny Bowlegs, pack your kit and trek!"   48

Through the gorge that gives the stars at noon-day clear—
   Up the pass that packs the scud beneath our wheel—
Round the bluff that sinks her thousand fathom sheer—
   Down the valley with our guttering brakes asqueal: 52
Where the trestle groans and quivers in the snow,
   Where the many-shedded levels loop and twine,
Hear me lead my reckless children from below
   Till we sing the Song of Roland to the pine!   56

[1] Spur.

With my *"Tinka-tinka-tinka-tinka-tink!"*
   [Oh, the axe has cleared the mountain, croup and crest!]
And we ride the iron stallions down to drink,
   Through the cañons to the waters of the West!   60

And the tunes that mean so much to you alone—
   Common tunes that make you choke and blow your nose—
Vulgar tunes that bring the laugh that brings the groan—
   I can rip your very heartstrings out with those;   64
With the feasting, and the folly, and the fun—
   And the lying, and the lusting, and the drink,
And the merry play that drops you, when you're done,
   To the thoughts that burn like irons if you think.   68

With my *"Plunka-lunka-lunka-lunka-lunk!"*
   Here's a trifle on account of pleasure past,
   Ere the wit that made you win gives you eyes to see your sin
     And—the heavier repentance at the last!   72

Let the organ moan her sorrow to the roof—
   I have told the naked stars the Grief of Man!
Let the trumpet snare the foeman to the proof—
   I have known Defeat, and mocked it as we ran!   76
My bray ye may not alter nor mistake
   When I stand to jeer the fatted Soul of Things,
But the Song of Lost Endeavour that I make,
   Is it hidden in the twanging of the strings?   80

With my *"Ta-ra-rara-rara-ra-ra-rrrp!"*
   [Is it naught to you that hear and pass me by?]
But the word—the word is mine, when the order moves the line
   And the lean, locked ranks go roaring down to die!   84

The grandam of my grandam was the Lyre—
   [Oh, the blue below the little fisher-huts!]
That the Stealer stooping beachward filled with fire,
   Till she bore my iron head and ringing guts!   88
By the wisdom of the centuries I speak—
   To the tune of yestermorn I set the truth—
I, the joy of life unquestioned—I, the Greek—
   I, the everlasting Wonder-song of Youth!   92

With my *"Tinka-tinka-tinka-tinka-tink!"*
   [What d'ye lack, my noble masters! What d'ye lack?]
So I draw the world together link by link:
   Yea, from Delos up to Limerick[2] and back!   96

[2] From ancient Greece to modern Ireland; from odes to limericks.

The Lake Isle of Innisfree

W. B. Yeats (1865–1939)

I will arise and go now, and go to Innisfree,[1]
And a small cabin build there, of clay and wattles made:
Nine bean-rows will I have there, a hive for the honeybee,
And live alone in the bee-loud glade.   4

And I shall have some peace there, for peace comes dropping slow,
Dropping from the veils of the morning to where the cricket sings;
There midnight's all a glimmer, and noon a purple glow,
And evening full of the linnet's wings.   8

I will arise and go now, for always night and day
I hear lake water lapping with low sounds by the shore;
While I stand on the roadway, or on the pavements grey,
I hear it in the deep heart's core.   12

[1] An island in Lough Gill, near Sligo, Ireland.

When You Are Old

W. B. Yeats (1865–1939)

When you are old and grey and full of sleep,
And nodding by the fire, take down this book,
And slowly read, and dream of the soft look
Your eyes had once, and of their shadows deep;   4

How many loved your moments of glad grace,
And loved your beauty with love false or true,
But one man loved the pilgrim soul in you,
And loved the sorrows of your changing face;   8

And bending down beside the glowing bars,
Murmur, a little sadly, how Love fled
And paced upon the mountains overhead
And hid his face amid a crowd of stars.   12

A Prayer for My Daughter[1]

W. B. Yeats (1865–1939)

Once more the storm is howling, and half hid
Under this cradle-hood and coverlid
My child sleeps on. There is no obstacle
But Gregory's wood and one bare hill

[1] Anne Butler Yeats, born February 26, 1919.

Whereby the haystack- and roof-levelling wind,   5
Bred on the Atlantic, can be stayed;
And for an hour I have walked and prayed
Because of the great gloom that is in my mind.

I have walked and prayed for this young child an hour
And heard the sea-wind scream upon the tower,   10
And under the arches of the bridge, and scream
In the elms above the flooded stream;
Imagining in excited reverie
That the future years had come,
Dancing to a frenzied drum,   15
Out of the murderous innocence of the sea.

May she be granted beauty and yet not
Beauty to make a stranger's eye distraught,
Or hers before a looking-glass, for such,
Being made beautiful overmuch,   20
Consider beauty a sufficient end,
Lose natural kindness and maybe
The heart-revealing intimacy
That chooses right, and never find a friend.

Helen[2] being chosen found life flat and dull   25
And later had much trouble from a fool,
While that great Queen,[3] that rose out of the spray,
Being fatherless could have her way
Yet chose a bandy-leggèd smith for man.
It's certain that fine women eat   30
A crazy salad with their meat
Whereby the Horn of Plenty is undone.

In courtesy I'd have her chiefly learned;
Hearts are not had as a gift but hearts are earned
By those that are not entirely beautiful;   35
Yet many, that have played the fool
For beauty's very self, has charm made wise,
And many a poor man that has roved,
Loved and thought himself beloved,
From a glad kindness cannot take his eyes.   40

May she become a flourishing hidden tree
That all her thoughts may like the linnet be,
And have no business but dispensing round
Their magnanimities of sound,

[2] Helen of Troy, for whom the Trojan War was fought.
[3] Aphrodite sprang out of sea foam. She married Hephaestus, a blacksmith.

Nor but in merriment begin a chase,   45
Nor but in merriment a quarrel.
O may she live like some green laurel
Rooted in one dear perpetual place.

My mind, because the minds that I have loved,
The sort of beauty that I have approved,   50
Prosper but little, has dried up of late,
Yet knows that to be choked with hate
May well be of all evil chances chief.
If there's no hatred in a mind
Assault and battery of the wind   55
Can never tear the linnet from the leaf.

An intellectual hatred is the worst,
So let her think opinions are accursed.
Have I not seen the loveliest woman born[4]
Out of the mouth of Plenty's horn,   60
Because of her opinionated mind
Barter that horn and every good
By quiet natures understood
For an old bellows full of angry wind?

Considering that, all hatred driven hence,   65
The soul recovers radical innocence
And learns at last that it is self-delighting,
Self-appeasing, self-affrighting,
And that its own sweet will is Heaven's will;
She can, though every face should scowl   70
And every windy quarter howl
Or every bellows burst, be happy still.

And may her bridegroom bring her to a house
Where all's accustomed, ceremonious;
For arrogance and hatred are the wares   75
Peddled in the thoroughfares.
How but in custom and in ceremony
Are innocence and beauty born?
Ceremony's a name for the rich horn,
And custom for the spreading laurel tree.   80

[4] Maud Gonne, a vocal Irish patriot, long loved by Yeats.

Among School Children

W. B. Yeats   (1865–1939)

I

I walk through the long schoolroom questioning;
A kind old nun in a white hood replies;
The children learn to cipher and to sing,
To study reading-books and history,   4
To cut and sew, be neat in everything
In the best modern way—the children's eyes
In momentary wonder stare upon
A sixty-year-old smiling public man.   8

II

I dream of a Ledaean[1] body, bent
Above a sinking fire, a tale that she
Told of a harsh reproof, or trivial event
That changed some childish day to tragedy—   12
Told, and it seemed that our two natures blent
Into a sphere from youthful sympathy,
Or else, to alter Plato's parable,[2]
Into the yolk and white of the one shell.   16

III

And thinking of that fit of grief or rage
I look upon one child or t'other there
And wonder if she stood so at that age—
For even daughters of the swan can share   20
Something of every paddler's heritage—
And had that colour upon cheek or hair,
And thereupon my heart is driven wild:
She stands before me as a living child.   24

IV

Her present image floats into the mind—
Did Quattrocento[3] finger fashion it
Hollow of cheek as though it drank the wind
And took a mess of shadows for its meat?   28
And I though never of Ledaean kind

---

[1] As beautiful as Leda, loved by Zeus.

[2] In the *Symposium* it is suggested that human males and females were once one complete unit. Through love they try to reunite.

[3] The fifteenth century in Italy, a time of great artistic activity.

Had pretty plumage once—enough of that,
Better to smile on all that smile, and show
There is a comfortable kind of old scarecrow.   32

V

What youthful mother, a shape upon her lap
Honey of generation had betrayed,
And that must sleep, shriek, struggle to escape
As recollection or the drug decide,   36
Would think her son, did she but see that shape
With sixty or more winters on its head,
A compensation for the pang of his birth,
Or the uncertainty of his setting forth?   40

VI

Plato thought nature but a spume that plays
Upon a ghostly paradigm of things;[4]
Solider Aristotle played the taws
Upon the bottom of a king of kings;[5]   44
World-famous golden-thighed Pythagoras[6]
Fingered upon a fiddle-stick or strings
What a star sang and careless Muses heard:
Old clothes upon old sticks to scare a bird.   48

VII

Both nuns and mothers worship images,
But those the candles light are not as those
That animate a mother's reveries,
But keep a marble or a bronze repose.   52
And yet they too break hearts—O Presences
That passion, piety or affection knows,
And that all heavenly glory symbolise—
O self-born mockers of man's enterprise;   56

VIII

Labour is blossoming or dancing where
The body is not bruised to pleasure soul,
Nor beauty born out of its own despair,
Nor blear-eyed wisdom out of midnight oil.   60

---

[4] Plato taught that things in nature are but imperfect copies of ideal forms.
[5] Aristotle was tutor to Alexander the Great.
[6] Pythagorus emphasized mathematical relationships in music and in the universe.

O chestnut-tree, great-rooted blossomer,
Are you the leaf, the blossom or the bole?
O body swayed to music, O brightening glance,
How can we know the dancer from the dance?　64

After Long Silence

W. B. Yeats　(1865–1939)

Speech after long silence; it is right,
All other lovers being estranged or dead,
Unfriendly lamplight hid under its shade,
The curtains drawn upon unfriendly night,　4
That we descant and yet again descant
Upon the supreme theme of Art and Song:
Bodily decrepitude is wisdom; young
We loved each other and were ignorant.　8

The Circus Animals' Desertion

W. B. Yeats　(1865–1939)

I

I sought a theme and sought for it in vain,
I sought it daily for six weeks or so.
Maybe at last, being but a broken man,
I must be satisfied with my heart, although　4
Winter and summer till old age began
My circus animals were all on show,
Those stilted boys, that burnished chariot,
Lion and woman and the Lord knows what.　8

II

What can I but enumerate old themes?
First that sea-rider Oisin[1] led by the nose
Through three enchanted islands, allegorical dreams,
Vain gaiety, vain battle, vain repose,　12
Themes of the embittered heart, or so it seems,
That might adorn old songs or courtly shows;
But what cared I that set him on to ride,
I, starved for the bosom of his faery bride?　16

[1] From Yeats's poem *The Wanderings of Oisin.*

And then a counter-truth filled out its play,
The Countess Cathleen[2] was the name I gave it;
She, pity-crazed, had given her soul away,
But masterful Heaven had intervĕned to save it.   20
I thought my dear[3] must her own soul destroy,
So did fanaticism and hate enslave it,
And this brought forth a dream and soon enough
This dream itself had all my thought and love.   24

And when the Fool and Blind Man[4] stole the bread
Cuchulain fought the ungovernable sea;
Heart-mysteries there, and yet when all is said
It was the dream itself enchanted me: 28
Character isolated by a deed
To engross the present and dominate memory.
Players and painted stage took all my love,
And not those things that they were emblems of.   32

III

Those masterful images because complete
Grew in pure mind, but out of what began?
A mound of refuse or the sweepings of a street,
Old kettles, old bottles, and a broken can,   36
Old iron, old bones, old rags, that raving slut
Who keeps the till. Now that my ladder's gone,
I must lie down where all the ladders start,
In the foul rag-and-bone shop of the heart.   40

[2] A play by Yeats.
[3] Maud Gonne, whom Yeats loved but lost.
[4] Characters, like Cuchulain, from Yeats's play *On Baile's Strand*.

The Mill

Edwin Arlington Robinson   (1869–1935)

The miller's wife had waited long,
    The tea was cold, the fire was dead;
And there might yet be nothing wrong
    In how he went and what he said: 4
"There are no millers any more,"
    Was all that she had heard him say:
And he had lingered at the door
    So long that it seemed yesterday.   8

Sick with a fear that had no form
    She knew that she was there at last;

And in the mill there was a warm
    And mealy fragrance of the past.   12
What else there was would only seem
    To say again what he had meant;
And what was hanging from a beam
    Would not have heeded where she went.   16

And if she thought it followed her,
    She may have reasoned in the dark
That one way of the few there were
    Would hide her and would leave no mark: 20
Black water, smooth above the weir
    Like starry velvet in the night,
Though ruffled once, would soon appear
    The same as ever to the sight.   24

Mending Wall

Robert Frost   (1874–1963)

Something there is that doesn't love a wall,
That sends the frozen-ground-swell under it
And spills the upper boulders in the sun,
And makes gaps even two can pass abreast.
The work of hunters is another thing: 5
I have come after them and made repair
Where they have left not one stone on a stone,
But they would have the rabbit out of hiding,
To please the yelping dogs. The gaps I mean,
No one has seen them made or heard them made,   10
But at spring mending-time we find them there.
I let my neighbor know beyond the hill;
And on a day we meet to walk the line
And set the wall between us once again.
We keep the wall between us as we go.   15
To each the boulders that have fallen to each.
And some are loaves and some so nearly balls
We have to use a spell to make them balance:
"Stay where you are until our backs are turned!"
We wear our fingers rough with handling them.   20
Oh, just another kind of outdoor game,
One on a side. It comes to little more:
There where it is we do not need the wall:
He is all pine and I am apple orchard.
My apple trees will never get across   25

And eat the cones under his pines, I tell him.
He only says, "Good fences make good neighbors."
Spring is the mischief in me, and I wonder
If I could put a notion in his head:
"*Why* do they make good neighbors? Isn't it   30
Where there are cows? But here there are no cows.
Before I built a wall I'd ask to know
What I was walling in or walling out,
And to whom I was like to give offense.
Something there is that doesn't love a wall,   35
That wants it down." I could say "Elves" to him,
But it's not elves exactly, and I'd rather
He said it for himself. I see him there,
Bringing a stone grasped firmly by the top
In each hand, like an old-stone savage armed.   40
He moves in darkness as it seems to me,
Not of woods only and the shade of trees.
He will not go behind his father's saying,
And he likes having thought of it so well
He says again, "Good fences make good neighbors."   45

Dust of Snow

Robert Frost   (1874–1963)

> The way a crow
> Shook down on me
> The dust of snow
> From a hemlock tree   4
>
> Has given my heart
> A change of mood
> And saved some part
> Of a day I had rued.   8

Two Tramps in Mud Time

Robert Frost   (1874–1963)

Out of the mud two strangers came
And caught me splitting wood in the yard.
And one of them put me off my aim
By hailing cheerily "Hit them hard!"   4
I knew pretty well why he dropped behind
And let the other go on a way.
I knew pretty well what he had in mind:
He wanted to take my job for pay.   8

Good blocks of oak it was I split,
As large around as the chopping block;
And every piece I squarely hit
Fell splinterless as a cloven rock.   12
The blows that a life of self-control
Spares to strike for the common good,
That day, giving a loose to my soul,
I spent on the unimportant wood.   16

The sun was warm but the wind was chill.
You know how it is with an April day
When the sun is out and the wind is still,
You're one month on in the middle of May.   20
But if you so much as dare to speak,
A cloud comes over the sunlit arch,
A wind comes off a frozen peak,
And you're two months back in the middle of March.   24

A bluebird comes tenderly up to alight
And turns to the wind to unruffle a plume,
His song so pitched as not to excite
A single flower as yet to bloom.   28
It is snowing a flake: and he half knew
Winter was only playing possum.
Except in color he isn't blue,
But he wouldn't advise a thing to blossom.   32

The water for which we may have to look
In summertime with a witching wand,
In every wheelrut's now a brook,
In every print of a hoof a pond.   36
Be glad of water, but don't forget
The lurking frost in the earth beneath
That will steal forth after the sun is set
And show on the water its crystal teeth.   40

The time when most I loved my task
These two must make me love it more
By coming with what they came to ask.
You'd think I never had felt before   44
The weight of an ax-head poised aloft,
The grip on earth of outspread feet,
The life of muscles rocking soft
And smooth and moist in vernal heat.   48

Out of the woods two hulking tramps
(From sleeping God knows where last night,

But not long since in the lumber camps).
They thought all chopping was theirs of right.   52
Men of the woods and lumberjacks,
They judged me by their appropriate tool.
Except as a fellow handled an ax
They had no way of knowing a fool.   56

Nothing on either side was said.
They knew they had but to stay their stay
And all their logic would fill my head:
As that I had no right to play   60
With what was another man's work for gain.
My right might be love but theirs was need.
And where the two exist in twain
Theirs was the better right—agreed.   64

But yield who will to their separation,
My object in living is to unite
My avocation and my vocation
As my two eyes make one in sight.   68
Only where love and need are one,
And the work is play for mortal stakes,
Is the deed ever really done
For Heaven and the future's sakes.   72

Fire and Ice

Robert Frost (1874–1963)

Some say the world will end in fire,
Some say in ice.
From what I've tasted of desire
I hold with those who favor fire.   4
But if it had to perish twice,
I think I know enough of hate
To say that for destruction ice
Is also great   8
And would suffice.

Once by the Pacific

Robert Frost (1874–1963)

The shattered water made a misty din.
Great waves looked over others coming in,
And thought of doing something to the shore

That water never did to land before.   4
The clouds were low and hairy in the skies,
Like locks blown forward in the gleam of eyes.
You could not tell, and yet it looked as if
The shore was lucky in being backed by cliff,   8
The cliff in being backed by continent;
It looked as if a night of dark intent
Was coming, and not only a night, an age.
Someone had better be prepared for rage.   12
There would be more than ocean-water broken
Before God's last *Put out the Light* was spoken.

Anecdote of the Jar

Wallace Stevens   (1879–1955)

I placed a jar in Tennessee,
And round it was, upon a hill.
It made the slovenly wilderness
Surround that hill.   4

The wilderness rose up to it,
And sprawled around, no longer wild.
The jar was round upon the ground
And tall and of a port in air.   8

It took dominion everywhere.
The jar was gray and bare.
It did not give of bird or bush,
Like nothing else in Tennessee.   12

The Snow Man

Wallace Stevens   (1879–1955)

One must have a mind of winter
To regard the frost and the boughs
Of the pine-trees crusted with snow;   3

And have been cold a long time
To behold the junipers shagged with ice,
The spruces rough in the distant glitter   6

Of the January sun; and not to think
Of any misery in the sound of the wind,
In the sound of a few leaves,   9

Which is the sound of the land
Full of the same wind
That is blowing in the same bare place   12

For the listener, who listens in the snow,
And, nothing himself, beholds
Nothing that is not there and the nothing that is.   15

The Idea of Order at Key West

Wallace Stevens   (1879–1955)

She sang beyond the genius of the sea.
The water never formed to mind or voice,
Like a body wholly body, fluttering
Its empty sleeves; and yet its mimic motion
Made constant cry, caused constantly a cry,   5
That was not ours although we understood,
Inhuman, of the veritable ocean.

The sea was not a mask. No more was she.
The song and water were not medleyed sound
Even if what she sang was what she heard,   10
Since what she sang was uttered word by word.
It may be that in all her phrases stirred
The grinding water and the gasping wind;
But it was she and not the sea we heard.

For she was the maker of the song she sang.   15
The ever-hooded, tragic-gestured sea
Was merely a place by which she walked to sing.
Whose spirit is this? we said, because we knew
It was the spirit that we sought and knew
That we should ask this often as she sang.   20

If it was only the dark voice of the sea
That rose, or even colored by many waves;
If it was only the outer voice of sky
And cloud, of the sunken coral water-walled,
However clear, it would have been deep air,   25
The heaving speech of air, a summer sound
Repeated in a summer without end
And sound alone. But it was more than that,
More even than her voice, and ours, among
The meaningless plungings of water and the wind,   30
Theatrical distances, bronze shadows heaped
On high horizons, mountainous atmospheres
Of sky and sea.

It was her voice that made
The sky acutest at its vanishing.
She measured to the hour its solitude.   35
She was the single artificer of the world
In which she sang. And when she sang, the sea,
Whatever self it had, became the self
That was her song, for she was the maker. Then we,
As we beheld her striding there alone,   40
Knew that there never was a world for her
Except the one she sang and, singing, made.

Ramon Fernandez[1], tell me, if you know,
Why, when the singing ended and we turned
Toward the town, tell why the glassy lights,   45
The lights in the fishing boats at anchor there,
As the night descended, tilting in the air,
Mastered the night and portioned out the sea,
Fixing emblazoned zones and fiery poles,
Arranging, deepening, enchanting night.   50

Oh! Blessed rage for order, pale Ramon,
The maker's rage to order words of the sea,
Words of the fragrant portals, dimly-starred,
And of ourselves and of our origins,
In ghostlier demarcations, keener sounds.   55

[1] Although there was a French literary critic by this name (1894–1944), Stevens
wrote that he intended it as an invention.

Of Modern Poetry

Wallace Stevens   (1879–1955)

The poem of the mind in the act of finding
What will suffice. It has not always had
To find: the scene was set; it repeated what
Was in the script.
                     Then the theatre was changed
To something else. Its past was a souvenir.   5

It has to be living, to learn the speech of the place.
It has to face the men of the time and to meet
The women of the time. It has to think about war
And it has to find what will suffice. It has
To construct a new stage. It has to be on that stage   10
And, like an insatiable actor, slowly and
With meditation, speak words that in the ear,
In the delicatest ear of the mind, repeat,

Exactly, that which it wants to hear, at the sound
Of which, an invisible audience listens,   15
Not to the play, but to itself, expressed
In an emotion as of two people, as of two
Emotions becoming one. The actor is
A metaphysician in the dark, twanging
An instrument, twanging a wiry string that gives   20
Sounds passing through sudden rightnesses, wholly
Containing the mind, below which it cannot descend,
Beyond which it has no will to rise.
                                        It must
Be the finding of a satisfaction, and may
Be of a man skating, a woman dancing, a woman   25
Combing. The poem of the act of the mind.

The Sparrow
(TO MY FATHER)

William Carlos Williams   (1883–1963)

This sparrow
          who comes to sit at my window
                    is a poetic truth
more than a natural one.
          His voice,   5
                    his movements,
his habits—
          how he loves to
                    flutter his wings
in the dust—   10
          all attest it;
                    granted, he does it
to rid himself of lice
          but the relief he feels
                    makes him   15
cry out lustily—
          which is a trait
                    more related to music
than otherwise.
          Wherever he finds himself   20
                    in early spring,
on back streets
          or beside palaces,
                    he carries on

unaffectedly   25
        his amours.
               It begins in the egg,
his sex genders it:
        What is more pretentiously
               useless   30
or about which
        we more pride ourselves?
               It leads as often as not
to our undoing.
        The cockerel, the crow   35
               with their challenging voices
cannot surpass
        the insistence
               of his cheep!
Once   40
        at El Paso
               toward evening,
I saw—and heard!—
        ten thousand sparrows
               who had come in from   45
the desert
        to roost. They filled the trees
               of a small park. Men fled
(with ears ringing!)
        from their droppings,   50
               leaving the premises
to the alligators
        who inhabit
               the fountain. His image
is familiar   55
        as that of the aristocratic
               unicorn, a pity
there are not more oats eaten
        nowadays
               to make living easier   60
for him.
        At that,
               his small size,
keen eyes,
        serviceable beak   65
               and general truculence
assure his survival—
        to say nothing
               of his innumerable

brood.   70
                  Even the Japanese
                          know him
and have painted him
          sympathetically,
                  with profound insight   75
into his minor
          characteristics.
                  Nothing even remotely
subtle
          about his lovemaking.   80
                  He crouches
before the female,
          drags his wings,
                  waltzing,
throws back his head   85
          and simply—
                  yells! The din
is terrific.
          The way he swipes his bill
                  across a plank   90
to clean it,
          is decisive.
                  So with everything
he does. His coppery
          eyebrows   95
                  give him the air
of being always
          a winner—and yet
                  I saw once,
the female of his species   100
          clinging determinedly
                  to the edge of
a water pipe,
          catch him
                  by his crown-feathers   105
to hold him
          silent,
                  subdued,
hanging above the city streets
          until   110
                  she was through with him.
What was the use
          of that?
                  She hung there

herself,   115
                    puzzled at her success.
                              I laughed heartily.
         Practical to the end,
                    it is the poem
                              of his existence   120
         that triumphed
                    finally;
                              a wisp of feathers
         flattened to the pavement,
                    wings spread symmetrically   125
                              as if in flight,
         the head gone,
                    the black escutcheon of the breast
                              undecipherable,
         an effigy of a sparrow,   130
                    a dried wafer only,
                              left to say
         and it says it
                    without offense,
                              beautifully;   135
         This was I,
                    a sparrow.
                              I did my best;
         farewell.

Snake

D. H. Lawrence   (1885–1930)

A snake came to my water-trough
On a hot, hot day, and I in pyjamas for the heat,
To drink there.

In the deep, strange-scented shade of the great dark carob tree
I came down the steps with my pitcher   5
And must wait, must stand and wait, for there he was at
    the trough before me.

He reached down from a fissure in the earth-wall in the
    gloom
And trailed his yellow-brown slackness soft-bellied down,
    over the edge of the stone trough
And rested his throat upon the stone bottom,
And where the water had dripped from the tap, in a small
    clearness,   10
He sipped with his straight mouth,

Softly drank through his straight gums, into his slack long body,
Silently.

Someone was before me at my water-trough,
And I, like a second comer, waiting.   15

He lifted his head from his drinking, as cattle do,
And looked at me vaguely, as drinking cattle do,
And flickered his two-forked tongue from his lips, and
      mused a moment,
And stooped and drank a little more,
Being earth-brown, earth-golden from the burning bowels
      of the earth   20
On the day of Sicilian July, with Etna[1] smoking.

The voice of my education said to me
He must be killed,
For in Sicily the black, black snakes are innocent, the gold
      are venomous.

And voices in me said, If you were a man   25
You would take a stick and break him now, and finish
      him off.

But must I confess how I liked him,
How glad I was he had come like a guest in quiet, to drink
      at my water-trough
And depart peaceful, pacified, and thankless,
Into the burning bowels of this earth?   30

Was it cowardice, that I dared not kill him?
Was it perversity, that I longed to talk to him?
Was it humility, to feel so honoured?
I felt so honoured.

And yet those voices: 35
If you were not afraid, you would kill him!

And truly I was afraid, I was most afraid,
But even so, honoured still more
That he should seek my hospitality
From out the dark door of the secret earth.   40

He drank enough
And lifted his head, dreamily, as one who has drunken,
And flickered his tongue like a forked night on the air, so black;

---

[1] A volcanic mountain in eastern Sicily.

Seeming to lick his lips,
And looked around like a god, unseeing, into the air,   45
And slowly turned his head,
And slowly, very slowly, as if thrice adream,
Proceeded to draw his slow length curving round
And climb again the broken bank of my wall-face.

And as he put his head into that dreadful hole,   50
And as he slowly drew up, snake-easing his shoulders, and
    entered farther,
A sort of horror, a sort of protest against his withdrawing
    into that horrid black hole,
Deliberately going into the blackness, and slowly drawing
    himself after,
Overcame me now his back was turned.

I looked round, I put down my pitcher,   55
I picked up a clumsy log
And threw it at the water-trough with a clatter.

I think it did not hit him,
But suddenly that part of him that was left behind convulsed
    in undignified haste,
Writhed like lightning, and was gone   60
Into the black hole, the earth-lipped fissure in the wall-front,
At which, in the intense still noon, I stared with fascination.

And immediately I regretted it.
I thought how paltry, how vulgar, what a mean act!
I despised myself and the voices of my accursed human education.   65

And I thought of the albatross,[2]
And I wished he would come back, my snake.

For he seemed to me again like a king,
Like a king in exile, uncrowned in the underworld,
Now due to be crowned again.   70

And so, I missed my chance with one of the lords
Of life.
And I have something to expiate;
A pettiness.

---

[2] In Coleridge's *Rime of the Ancient Mariner*.

The Ship of Death[1]

D. H. Lawrence   (1885–1930)

I

Now it is autumn and the falling fruit
and the long journey towards oblivion.

The apples falling like great drops of dew
to bruise themselves an exit from themselves.

And it is time to go, to bid farewell   5
to one's own self, and find an exit
from the fallen self.

II

Have you built your ship of death, O have you?
O build your ship of death, for you will need it.

The grim frost is at hand, when the apples will fall   10
thick, almost thundrous, on the hardened earth.

And death is on the air like a smell of ashes!
Ah! can't you smell it?

And in the bruised body, the frightened soul
finds itself shrinking, wincing from the cold   15
that blows upon it through the orifices.

III

And can a man his own quietus make
with a bare bodkin?[2]

With daggers, bodkins, bullets, man can make
a bruise or break of exit for his life: 20
but is that a quietus, O tell me, is it quietus?

Surely not so! for how could murder, even self-murder
ever a quietus make?

IV

O let us talk of quiet that we know,
that we can know, the deep and lovely quiet   25
of a strong heart at peace!

How can we this, our own quietus, make?

---

[1] Ancient peoples sometimes buried with their dead small ships provisioned for the trip to the other world. Lawrence had observed the practice in Etruscan tombs.

[2] Cf. *Hamlet*, III, 1, 75–76; Quietus: release from life. Bodkin: dagger.

V

Build then the ship of death, for you must take
the longest journey, to oblivion.
And die the death, the long and painful death   30
that lies between the old self and the new.

Already our bodies are fallen, bruised, badly bruised,
already our souls are oozing through the exit
of the cruel bruise.

Already the dark and endless ocean of the end   35
is washing in through the breaches of our wounds,
already the flood is upon us.

Oh build your ship of death, your little ark
and furnish it with food, with little cakes, and wine
for the dark flight down oblivion.   40

VI

Piecemeal the body dies, and the timid soul
has her footing washed away, as the dark flood rises.

We are dying, we are dying, we are all of us dying
and nothing will stay the death-flood rising within us
and soon it will rise on the world, on the outside world.   45

We are dying, we are dying, piecemeal our bodies are dying
and our strength leaves us,
and our soul cowers naked in the dark rain over the flood,
cowering in the last branches of the tree of our life.

VII

We are dying, we are dying, so all we can do   50
is now to be willing to die, and to build the ship
of death to carry the soul on the longest journey.

A little ship, with oars and food
and little dishes, and all accoutrements
fitting and ready for the departing soul.   55

Now launch the small ship, now as the body dies
and life departs, launch out, the fragile soul
in the fragile ship of courage, the ark of faith
with its store of food and little cooking pans
and change of clothes,   60
upon the flood's black waste
upon the waters of the end

upon the sea of death, where still we sail
darkly, for we cannot steer, and have no port.

There is no port, there is nowhere to go   65
only the deepening blackness darkening still
blacker upon the soundless, ungurgling flood
darkness at one with darkness, up and down
and sideways utterly dark, so there is no direction any more.
And the little ship is there; yet she is gone.   70
She is not seen, for there is nothing to see her by.
She is gone! gone! and yet
somewhere she is there.
Nowhere!

VIII
And everything is gone, the body is gone   75
completely under, gone, entirely gone.
The upper darkness is heavy as the lower,
between them the little ship
is gone
she is gone.   80

It is the end, it is oblivion.

IX
And yet out of eternity, a thread
separates itself on the blackness,
a horizontal thread
that fumes a little with pallor upon the dark.   85

Is it illusion? or does the pallor fume
A little higher?
Ah wait, wait, for there's the dawn,
the cruel dawn of coming back to life
out of oblivion.

Wait, wait, the little ship   90
drifting, beneath the deathly ashy grey
of a flood-dawn.

Wait, wait! even so, a flush of yellow
and strangely, O chilled wan soul, a flush of rose.

A flush of rose, and the whole thing starts again.   95

X

The flood subsides, and the body, like a worn sea-shell
emerges strange and lovely.
And the little ship wings home, faltering and lapsing
on the pink flood,
and the frail soul steps out, into her house again   100
filling the heart with peace.

Swings the heart renewed with peace
even of oblivion.

Oh build your ship of death, oh build it!
for you will need it.   105
For the voyage of oblivion awaits you.

Prophecy

Elinor Wylie   (1885–1928)

I shall lie hidden in a hut
    In the middle of an alder wood,
With the back door blind and bolted shut,
    And the front door locked for good.   4

I shall lie folded like a saint,
    Lapped in a scented linen sheet,
On a bedstead striped with bright-blue paint,
    Narrow and cold and neat.   8

The midnight will be glassy black
    Behind the panes, with wind about
To set his mouth against a crack
    And blow the candle out.   12

Bells for John Whiteside's Daughter

John Crowe Ransom   (1888–1974)

There was such speed in her little body,
And such lightness in her footfall,
It is no wonder her brown study[1]
Astonishes us all.   4

[1] Deep absorption, reverie.

Her wars were bruited in our high window.
We looked among orchard trees and beyond
Where she took arms against her shadow,
Or harried unto the pond   8

The lazy geese, like a snow cloud
Dripping their snow on the green grass,
Tricking and stopping, sleepy and proud,
Who cried in goose, Alas,   12

For the tireless heart within the little
Lady with rod that made them rise
From their noon apple-dreams and scuttle
Goose-fashion under the skies!   16

But now go the bells, and we are ready,
In one house we are sternly stopped
To say we are vexed at her brown study,
Lying so primly propped.   20

Blue Girls

John Crowe Ransom   (1888–1974)

Twirling your blue skirts, travelling the sward
Under the towers of your seminary,
Go listen to your teachers old and contrary
Without believing a word.   4

Tie the white fillets then about your hair
And think no more of what will come to pass
Than bluebirds that go walking on the grass
And chattering on the air.   8

Practise your beauty, blue girls, before it fail;
And I will cry with my loud lips and publish
Beauty which all our power shall never establish,
It is so frail.   12

For I could tell you a story which is true;
I know a woman with a terrible tongue,
Blear eyes fallen from blue,
All her perfections tarnished—yet it is not long   16
Since she was lovelier than any of you.

Winter Remembered

John Crowe Ransom (1888–1974)

Two evils, monstrous either one apart,
Possessed me, and were long and loath at going:
A cry of Absence, Absence, in the heart,
And in the wood the furious winter blowing.   4

Think not, when fire was bright upon my bricks,
And past the tight boards hardly a wind could enter,
I glowed like them, the simple burning sticks,
Far from my cause, my proper heat and center.   8

Better to walk forth in the frozen air
And wash my wound in the snows; that would be healing;
Because my heart would throb less painful there,
Being caked with cold, and past the smart of feeling.   12

And where I walked, the murderous winter blast
Would have this body bowed, these eyeballs streaming,
And though I think this heart's blood froze not fast
It ran too small to spare one drop for dreaming.   16

Dear love, these fingers that had known your touch,
And tied our separate forces first together,
Were ten poor idiot fingers not worth much,
Ten frozen parsnips hanging in the weather.   20

Tetélestai[1]

Conrad Aiken (1889–1973)

I

How shall we praise the magnificence of the dead,
The great man humbled, the haughty brought to dust?
Is there a horn we should not blow as proudly
For the meanest of us all, who creeps his days,
Guarding his heart from blows, to die obscurely?   5
I am no king, have laid no kingdoms waste,
Taken no princes captive, led no triumphs
Of weeping women through long walls of trumpets;
Say rather, I am no one, or an atom;
Say rather, two great gods, in a vault of starlight,   10
Play ponderingly at chess, and at the game's end
One of the pieces, shaken, falls to the floor
And runs to the darkest corner; and that piece

---

[1] Christ's last word (in Greek), as given in John xix.30: "It is finished."

Forgotten there, left motionless, is I . . .
Say that I have no name, no gifts, no power,   15
Am only one of millions, mostly silent;
One who came with eyes and hands and a heart,
Looked on beauty, and loved it, and then left it.
Say that the fates of time and space obscured me,
Led me a thousand ways to pain, bemused me,   20
Wrapped me in ugliness; and like great spiders
Dispatched me at their leisure . . . Well, what then?
Should I not hear, as I lie down in dust,
The horns of glory blowing above my burial?

II

Morning and evening opened and closed above me: 25
Houses were built above me; trees let fall
Yellowing leaves upon me, hands of ghosts;
Rain has showered its arrows of silver upon me
Seeking my heart; winds have roared and tossed me;
Music in long blue waves of sound has borne me   30
A helpless weed to shores of unthought silence;
Time, above me, within me, crashed its gongs
Of terrible warning, sifting the dust of death;
And here I lie. Blow now your horns of glory
Harshly over my flesh, you trees, you waters!   35
You stars and suns, Canopus, Deneb, Rigel,[2]
Let me, as I lie down, here in this dust,
Hear, far off, your whispered salutation!
Roar now above my decaying flesh, you winds,
Whirl out your earth-scents over this body, tell me   40
Of ferns and stagnant pools, wild roses, hillsides!
Anoint me, rain, let crash your silver arrows
On this hard flesh! I am the one who named you,
I lived in you, and now I die in you.
I your son, your daughter, treader of music,   45
Lie broken, conquered . . . Let me not fall in silence.

III

I, the restless one; the circler of circles;
Herdsman and roper of stars, who could not capture
The secret of self; I who was tyrant to weaklings,
Striker of children; destroyer of women; corrupter   50
Of innocent dreamers, and laugher at beauty; I,
Too easily brought to tears and weakness by music,

[2] Bright stars in the constellations Argus, Cygnus, and Orion.

Baffled and broken by love, the helpless beholder
Of the war in my heart of desire with desire, the struggle
Of hatred with love, terror with hunger; I 55
Who laughed without knowing the cause of my laughter, who grew
Without wishing to grow, a servant to my own body;
Loved without reason the laughter and flesh of a woman,
Enduring such torments to find her! I who at last
Grow weaker, struggle more feebly, relent in my purpose, 60
Choose for my triumph an easier end, look backward
At earlier conquests; or, caught in the web, cry out
In a sudden and empty despair, 'Tetélestai!'
Pity me, now! I, who was arrogant, beg you!
Tell me, as I lie down, that I was courageous. 65
Blow horns of victory now, as I reel and am vanquished.
Shatter the sky with trumpets above my grave.

IV

. . . Look! this flesh how it crumbles to dust and is blown!
These bones, how they grind in the granite of frost and are nothing!
This skull, how it yawns for a flicker of time in the darkness, 70
Yet laughs not and sees not! It is crushed by a hammer of sunlight,
And the hands are destroyed . . . Press down through the leaves of
    the jasmine,
Dig through the interlaced roots—nevermore will you find me;
I was no better than dust, yet you cannot replace me . . .
Take the soft dust in your hand—does it stir: does it sing? 75
Has it lips and a heart? Does it open its eyes to the sun?
Does it run, does it dream, does it burn with a secret, or tremble
In terror of death? Or ache with tremendous decisions? . . .
Listen! . . . It says: 'I lean by the river. The willows
Are yellowed with bud. White clouds roar up from the south 80
And darken the ripples; but they cannot darken my heart,
Nor the face like a star in my heart! . . . Rain falls on the water
And pelts it, and rings it with silver. The willow trees glisten,
The sparrows chirp under the eaves; but the face in my heart
Is a secret of music . . . I wait in the rain and am silent.' 85
Listen again! . . . It says: 'I have worked, I am tired,
The pencil dulls in my hand: I see through the window
Walls upon walls of windows with faces behind them,
Smoke floating up to the sky, an ascension of sea-gulls.
I am tired. I have struggled in vain, my decision was fruitless, 90
Why then do I wait? with darkness, so easy, at hand! . . .
But tomorrow, perhaps . . . I will wait and endure till tomorrow!' . . .
Or again: 'It is dark. The decision is made. I am vanquished

By terror of life. The walls mount slowly about me
In coldness. I had not the courage. I was forsaken.   95
I cried out, was answered by silence . . . Tetélestai . . . !'

<h2 style="text-align:center">V.</h2>

Hear how it babbles!—Blow the dust out of your hand,
With its voices and visions, tread on it, forget it, turn homeward
With dreams in your brain . . . This, then, is the humble,
    the nameless,—
The lover, the husband and father, the struggler with shadows,   100
The one who went down under shoutings of chaos, the weakling
Who cried his 'forsaken!' like Christ on the darkening hilltop![3] . . .
This, then, is the one who implores, as he dwindles to silence,
A fanfare of glory . . . And which of us dares to deny him?

[3] See Matthew xxvii.46; Mark xv.34.

This Beast That Rends Me

Edna St. Vincent Millay   (1892–1950)

This beast that rends me in the sight of all,
This love, this longing, this oblivious thing,
That has me under as the last leaves fall,
Will glut, will sicken, will be gone by spring.   4
The wound will heal, the fever will abate,
The knotted hurt will slacken in the breast;
I shall forget before the flickers mate
Your look that is today my east and west.   8
Unscathed, however, from a claw so deep
Though I should love again I shall not go:
Along my body, waking while I sleep,
Sharp to the kiss, cold to the hand as snow,   12
The scar of this encounter like a sword
Will lie between me and my troubled lord.

Since Feeling Is First

E. E. Cummings   (1894–1962)

since feeling is first
who pays any attention
to the syntax of things
will never wholly kiss you;

wholly to be a fool   5
while Spring is in the world

my blood approves,
and kisses are a better fate
than wisdom
lady i swear by all flowers. Don't cry   10
—the best gesture of my brain is less than
your eyelids' flutter which says

we are for each other: then
laugh, leaning back in my arms
for life's not a paragraph   15

And death i think is no parenthesis

If You Can't Eat You Got To

E. E. Cummings   (1894–1962)

If you can't eat you got to

smoke and we aint got
nothing to smoke:come on kid

let's go to sleep
if you can't smoke you got to   5

Sing and we aint got

nothing to sing; come on kid
let's go to sleep

if you can't sing you got to
die and we aint got   10

Nothing to die;come on kid

let's go to sleep
if you can't die you got to

dream and we aint got
nothing to dream(come on kid   15

Let's go to sleep)

O Sweet Spontaneous

E. E. Cummings   (1894–1962)

O sweet spontaneous
earth how often have
the
doting

                    fingers of   5
prurient philosophers pinched
and
poked

thee
, has the naughty thumb   10
of science prodded
thy

        beauty   . how
often have religions taken
thee upon their scraggy knees   15
squeezing and

buffeting thee that thou mightest conceive
gods
        (but
true   20

to the incomparable
couch of death thy
rhythmic
lover

        thou answerest   25

them only with

                spring)

After I Had Worked All Day

Charles Reznikoff   (1894–   )

After I had worked all day at what I earn my living,
I was tired. Now my own work has lost another day,
I thought, but began slowly,
and slowly my strength came back to me.
Surely, the tide comes in twice a day.   5

Obit on Parnassus

F. Scott Fitzgerald   (1896–1940)

Death before forty's no bar. Lo!
    These had accomplished their feats:
Chatterton, Burns, and Kit Marlowe,
    Byron and Shelley and Keats.   4

Death, the eventual censor,
    Lays for the forties, and so
Took off Jane Austen and Spenser,
    Stevenson, Hood, and poor Poe.   8

You'll leave a better-lined wallet
    By reaching the end of your rope
After fifty, like Shakespeare and Smollett,
    Thackeray, Dickens, and Pope.   12

Try for the sixties—but say, boy,
    That's when the tombstones were built on
Butler and Sheridan, the play boy,
    Arnold and Coleridge and Milton.   16

Three score and ten—the tides rippling
    Over the bar; slip the hawser.
Godspeed to Clemens and Kipling,
    Swinburne and Browning and Chaucer.   20

Some staved the debt off but paid it
    At eighty—that's after the law.
Wordsworth and Tennyson made it,
    And Meredith, Hardy, and Shaw.   24

But, Death, while you make up your quota,
    Please note this confession of candor—
That I wouldn't give an iota
    To linger till ninety, like Landor.   28

To Be Sung on the Water

Louise Bogan   (1897–1970)

Beautiful, my delight,
Pass, as we pass the wave.
Pass, as the mottled night
Leaves what it cannot save,
Scattering dark and bright.   5

Beautiful, pass and be
Less than the guiltless shade
To which our vows were said;
Less than the sound of the oar
To which our vows were made,—   10
Less than the sound of its blade
Dipping the stream once more.

To Brooklyn Bridge

Hart Crane (1899–1932)

How many dawns, chill from his rippling rest
The seagull's wings shall dip and pivot him,
Shedding white rings of tumult, building high
Over the chained bay waters Liberty—   4

Then, with inviolate curve, forsake our eyes
As apparitional as sails that cross
Some page of figures to be filed away;
—Till elevators drop us from our day . . .   8

I think of cinemas, panoramic sleights
With multitudes bent toward some flashing scene
Never disclosed, but hastened to again,
Foretold to other eyes on the same screen;   12

And Thee,[1] across the harbor, silver-paced
As though the sun took step of thee, yet left
Some motion ever unspent in thy stride,—
Implicitly thy freedom staying thee!   16

Out of some subway scuttle, cell or loft
A bedlamite[2] speeds to thy parapets,
Tilting there momently, shrill shirt ballooning,
A jest falls from the speechless caravan.   20

Down Wall,[3] from girder into street noon leaks,
A rip-tooth of the sky's acetylene;
All afternoon the cloud-flown derricks turn . . .
Thy cables breathe the North Atlantic still.   24

And obscure as that heaven of the Jews,
Thy guerdon[4] . . . Accolade thou dost bestow
Of anonymity time cannot raise:
Vibrant reprieve and pardon thou dost show.   28

O harp and altar, of the fury fused,
(How could mere toil align thy choiring strings!)
Terrific threshold of the prophet's pledge,
Prayer of pariah,[5] and the lover's cry,—   32

[1] The bridge.
[2] Mad person.
[3] Wall Street, in Manhattan, near the bridge.
[4] Reward
[5] Outcast.

Again the traffic lights that skim thy swift
Unfractioned idiom, immaculate sigh of stars,
Beading thy path—condense eternity:
And we have seen night lifted in thine arms.   36

Under thy shadow by the piers I waited;
Only in darkness is thy shadow clear.
The City's fiery parcels all undone,
Already snow submerges an iron year . . .   40

O Sleepless as the river under thee,
Vaulting the sea, the prairies' dreaming sod,
Unto us lowliest sometime sweep, descend
And of the curveship lend a myth to God.   44

Ode to the Confederate Dead

Allen Tate   (1899–1979)

Row after row with strict impunity
The headstones yield their names to the element,
The wind whirrs without recollection;
In the riven troughs the splayed leaves
Pile up, of nature the casual sacrament   5
To the seasonal eternity of death;
Then driven by the fierce scrutiny
Of heaven to their election in the vast breath,
They sough[1] the rumour of mortality.

Autumn is desolation in the plot   10
Of a thousand acres where these memories grow
From the inexhaustible bodies that are not
Dead, but feed the grass row after rich row.
Think of the autumns that have come and gone!—
Ambitious November with the humors of the year,   15
With a particular zeal for every slab,
Staining the uncomfortable angels that rot
On the slabs, a wing chipped here, an arm there:
The brute curiosity of an angel's stare
Turns you, like them, to stone,   20
Transforms the heaving air
Till plunged to a heavier world below
You shift your sea-space blindly
Heaving, turning like the blind crab.

[1] Sound.

Dazed by the wind, only the wind   25
The leaves flying, plunge

You know who have waited by the wall
The twilight certainty of an animal,
Those midnight restitutions of the blood
You know—the immitigable² pines, the smoky frieze   30
Of the sky, the sudden call: you know the rage,
The cold pool left by the mounting flood,
Of muted Zeno and Parmenides.³
You who have waited for the angry resolution
Of those desires that should be yours tomorrow,   35
You know the unimportant shrift⁴ of death
And praise the vision
And praise the arrogant circumstance
Of those who fall
Rank upon rank, hurried beyond decision—   40
Here by the sagging gate, stopped by the wall.

Seeing, seeing only the leaves
Flying, plunge and expire

Turn your eyes to the immoderate past,
Turn to the inscrutable infantry rising   45
Demons out of the earth—they will not last.
Stonewall, Stonewall,⁵ and the sunken fields of hemp,
Shiloh, Antietam, Malvern Hill, Bull Run.⁶
Lost in that orient of the thick-and-fast
You will curse the setting sun.   50

Cursing only the leaves crying
Like an old man in a storm

You hear the shout, the crazy hemlocks point
With troubled fingers to the silence which
Smothers you, a mummy, in time.

                            The hound bitch   55
Toothless and dying, in a musty cellar
Hears the wind only.

---

² Unchanging.
³ Eleatic philosophers, who held change to be illusory, and permanent "being" the only reality.
⁴ Absolution, confession.
⁵ Stonewall Jackson (1824–1863), Confederate general.
⁶ Civil War battles.

               Now that the salt of their blood
Stiffens the saltier oblivion of the sea,
Seals the malignant purity of the flood,
What shall we who count our days and bow   60
Our heads with a commemorial woe
In the ribboned coats of grim felicity,
What shall we say of the bones, ŭnclean,
Whose verdurous anonymity will grow?
The ragged arms, the ragged heads and eyes   65
Lost in these acres of the insane green?
The gray lean spiders come, they come and go;
In a tangle of willows without light
The singular screech-owl's tight
Invisible lyric seeds the mind   70
With the furious murmur of their chivalry.

    We shall say only the leaves
    Flying, plunge and expire

We shall say only the leaves whispering
In the improbable mist of nightfall   75
That flies on multiple wing;
Night is the beginning and the end
And in between the ends of distraction
Waits mute speculation, the patient curse
That stones the eyes, or like the jaguar leaps   80
For his own image in a jungle pool, his victim.
What shall we say who have knowledge
Carried to the heart? Shall we take the act
To the grave? Shall we, more hopeful, set up the grave
In the house? The ravenous grave?

                  Leave now   85
The shut gate and the decomposing wall:
The gentle serpent, green in the mulberry bush,
Riots with his tongue through the hush—
Sentinel of the grave who counts us all!

The Zebras

Roy Campbell   (1901–1957)

From the dark woods that breathe of fallen showers,
Harnessed with level rays in golden reins,
The zebras draw the dawn across the plains

Wading knee-deep among the scarlet flowers.   4
The sunlight, zithering their flanks with fire,
Flashes between the shadows as they pass
Barred with electric tremors through the grass
Like wind along the gold strings of a lyre.   8

Into the flushed air snorting rosy plumes
That smoulder round their feet in drifting fumes,
With dove-like voices call the distant fillies,
While round the herds the stallion wheels his flight,   12
Engine of beauty volted with delight,
To roll his mare among the trampled lilies.

Only the Polished Skeleton

Countee Cullen   (1903–1946)

The heart has need of some deceit
    To make its pistons rise and fall;
For less than this it would not beat,
    Nor flush the sluggish vein at all.   4

With subterfuge and fraud the mind
    Must fend and parry thrust for thrust,
With logic brutal and unkind
    Beat off the onslaughts of the dust.   8

Only the polished skeleton,
    Of flesh relieved and pauperized,
Can rest at ease and think upon
    The worth of all it so despised.   12

The Fury of Aerial Bombardment

Richard Eberhart   (1904–   )

You would think the fury of aerial bombardment
Would rouse God to relent; the infinite spaces
Are still silent. He looks on shock-pried faces.
History, even, does not know what is meant.   4

You would feel that after so many centuries
God would give man to repent; yet he can kill
As Cain could, but with multitudinous will,
No farther advanced than in his ancient furies.   8

Was man made stupid to see his own stupidity?
Is God by definition indifferent, beyond us all?
Is the eternal truth man's fighting soul
Wherein the Beast ravens in its own avidity?   12

Of Van Wettering I speak, and Averill,
Names on a list, whose faces I do not recall
But they are gone to early death, who late in school
Distinguished the belt feed lever from the belt holding pawl.[1]   16

---

[1] Machinegun parts.

The Sunlight on the Garden

Louis MacNeice (1907–1963)

The sunlight on the garden
Hardens and grows cold,
We cannot cage the minute   3
Within its nets of gold,
When all is told
We cannot beg for pardon.   6

Our freedom as free lances
Advances towards its end;
The earth compels, upon it   9
Sonnets and birds descend;
And soon, my friend,
We shall have no time for dances.   12

The sky was good for flying
Defying the church bells
And every evil iron   15
Siren and what it tells:
The earth compels,
We are dying, Egypt, dying[1]   18

And not expecting pardon,
Hardened in heart anew,
But glad to have sat under   21
Thunder and rain with you,
And grateful too
For sunlight on the garden.   24

---

[1] Cf. Antony to Cleopatra, "I am dying, Egypt, dying," *Antony and Cleopatra*, IV, xv, 41.

Icarus [1]

Stephen Spender   (1909–   )

He will watch the hawk with an indifferent eye
   Or pitifully;
Nor on those eagles that so feared him, now   3
   Will strain his brow;
Weapons men use, stone, sling and strong-thewed bow
   He will not know.   6

This aristocrat, superb of all instinct,
   With death close linked
Had paced the enormous cloud, almost had won   9
   War on the sun;
Till now, like Icarus mid-ocean-drowned,
   Hands, wings, are found.   12

[1] Flying on wings of wax and feathers too close to the sun, he fell into the sea and drowned, when the sun melted the wax.

Montana Pastoral

J. V. Cunningham   (1911–   )

I am no shepherd of a child's surmises.
I have seen fear where the coiled serpent rises,

Thirst where the grasses burn in early May
And thistle, mustard, and the wild oat stay.   4

There is dust in this air. I saw in the heat
Grasshoppers busy in the threshing wheat.

So to this hour. Through the warm dusk I drove
To blizzards sifting on the hissing stove,   8

And found no images of pastoral will,
But fear, thirst, hunger, and this huddled chill.

Coffee

J. V. Cunningham   (1911–   )

When I awoke with cold
And looked for you, my dear,
And the dusk inward rolled,
Not light or dark, but drear,   4

Unabsolute, unshaped,
That no glass can oppose,
I fled not to escape
Myself, but to transpose.   8

I have so often fled
Wherever I could drink
Dark coffee and there read
More than a man would think   12

That I say I waste time
For contemplation's sake:
In an uncumbered clime
Minute inductions wake,   16

Insight flows in my pen.
I know nor fear nor haste.
Time is my own again.
I waste it for the waste.   20

Dream Songs: 14

John Berryman   (1914–1972)

Life, friends, is boring. We must not say so.
After all, the sky flashes, the great sea yearns,
we ourselves flash and yearn,   3
and moreover my mother told me as a boy
(repeatedly) 'Ever to confess you're bored
means you have no   6

Inner Resources.' I conclude now I have no
inner resources, because I am heavy bored.
Peoples bore me,   9
literature bores me, especially great literature,
Henry bores me, with his plights & gripes
as bad as achilles,[1]   12

who loves people and valiant art, which bores me.
And the tranquil hills, & gin, look like a drag
and somehow a dog   15
has taken itself & its tail considerably away
into mountains or sea or sky, leaving
behind: me, wag.   18

---

[1] Achilles is often sulky in Homer's *Iliad*.

Rescue the Dead
David Ignatow   (1914–   )

Finally, to forgo love is to kiss a leaf,
is to let rain fall nakedly upon your head,
is to respect fire,
is to study man's eyes and his gestures
as he talks,   5
is to set bread upon the table
and a knife discreetly by,
is to pass through crowds
like a crowd of oneself.
Not to love is to live.   10

To love is to be led away
into a forest where the secret grave
is dug, singing, praising darkness
under the trees.

To live is to sign your name,   15
is to ignore the dead,
is to carry a wallet
and shake hands.

To love is to be a fish.
My boat wallows in the sea.   20
You who are free,
rescue the dead.

The Death of the Ball Turret Gunner
Randall Jarrell   (1914–1965)

From my mother's sleep I fell into the State,
And I hunched in its belly till my wet fur froze.
Six miles from earth, loosed from its dream of life,
I woke to black flak and the nightmare fighters.
When I died they washed me out of the turret with a hose.

The Hunchback in the Park
Dylan Thomas   (1914–1953)

The hunchback in the park
A solitary mister
Propped between trees and water   3

From the opening of the garden lock
That lets the trees and water enter
Until the Sunday sombre bell[1] at dark   6

Eating bread from a newspaper
Drinking water from the chained cup
That the children filled with gravel   9
In the fountain basin where I sailed my ship
Slept at night in a dog kennel
But nobody chained him up.   12

Like the park birds he came early
Like the water he sat down
And Mister they called Hey mister   15
The truant boys from the town
Running when he had heard them clearly
On out of sound   18

Past lake and rockery
Laughing when he shook his paper
Hunchbacked in mockery   21
Through the loud zoo of the willow groves
Dodging the park keeper
With his stick that picked up leaves.   24

And the old dog sleeper
Alone between nurses and swans
While the boys among willows   27
Made the tigers jump out of their eyes
To roar on the rockery stones
And the groves were blue with sailors   30

Made all day until bell time
A woman figure without fault
Straight as a young elm   33
Straight and tall from his crooked bones
That she might stand in the night
After the locks and chains   36

All night in the unmade park
After the railings and shrubberies
The birds the grass the trees the lake   39
And the wild boys innocent as strawberries
Had followed the hunchback
To his kennel in the dark.   42

[1] Signifying the closing of the park.

The Bean Eaters

Gwendolyn Brooks   (1917–   )

They eat beans mostly, this old yellow pair.
Dinner is a casual affair.
Plain chipware on a plain and creaking wood,
Tin flatware.   4

Two who are Mostly Good.
Two who have lived their day,
But keep on putting on their clothes
And putting things away.   8

And remembering . . .
Remembering, with twinklings and twinges,
As they lean over the beans in their rented back room that
    is full of beads and receipts and dolls and cloths,   12
    tobacco crumbs, vases and fringes.

We Real Cool

Gwendolyn Brooks   (1917–   )

The Pool Players.
Seven at the Golden Shovel.

    We real cool. We
    Left school. We

    Lurk late. We
    Strike straight. We   4

    Sing sin. We
    Thin gin. We

    Jazz June. We
    Die soon.   8

Skunk Hour
(FOR ELIZABETH BISHOP)[1]

Robert Lowell   (1917–1977)

Nautilus Island's hermit
heiress still lives through winter in her Spartan cottage;
her sheep still graze above the sea.   3
Her son's a bishop. Her farmer

---

[1] An American poet born in 1911. Lowell wrote that he modeled the poem on her "The Armadillo," which is dedicated to him.

is first selectman in our village;
she's in her dotage.   6

Thirsting for
the hierarchic privacy
of Queen Victoria's century,   9
she buys up all
the eyesores facing her shore,
and lets them fall.   12

The season's ill—
we've lost our summer millionaire,
who seemed to leap from an L. L. Bean[2]   15
catalogue. His nine-knot yawl
was auctioned off to lobstermen.
A red fox stain covers Blue Hill.   18

And now our fairy
decorator brightens his shop for fall;
his fishnet's filled with orange cork,   21
orange, his cobbler's bench and awl;
there is no money in his work,
he'd rather marry.   24

One dark night,
my Tudor Ford climbed the hill's skull;
I watched for love-cars. Lights turned down,   27
they lay together, hull to hull,
where the graveyard shelves on the town. . . .
My mind's not right.   30

A car radio bleats,
"Love, O careless Love. . . ."[3] I hear
my ill-spirit sob in each blood cell,   33
as if my hand were at its throat. . . .
I myself am hell;[4]
nobody's here—   36

only skunks, that search
in the moonlight for a bite to eat.
They march on their soles up Main Street: 39
white stripes, moonstruck eyes' red fire
under the chalk-dry and spar spire
of the Trinitarian Church.   42

[2] A Maine dealer in sporting goods and clothing.
[3] From the folk song "Careless Love," the lament of a pregnant girl.
[4] Like Milton's Satan in *Paradise Lost*: "Which way I fly is Hell; myself am Hell" (IV, 75).

I stand on top
of our back steps and breathe the rich air—
a mother skunk with her column of kittens swills the garbage pail. 45
She jabs her wedge-head in a cup
of sour cream, drops her ostrich tail,
and will not scare.   48

Church Going

Philip Larkin   (1922–   )

Once I am sure there's nothing going on
I step inside, letting the door thud shut.
Another church: matting, seats, and stone,
And little books; sprawlings of flowers, cut
For Sunday, brownish now; some brass and stuff   5
Up at the holy end; the small neat organ;
And a tense, musty, unignorable silence,
Brewed God knows how long. Hatless, I take off
My cycle-clips in awkward reverence,

Move forward, run my hand around the font.   10
From where I stand, the roof looks almost new—
Cleaned, or restored? Someone would know: I don't.
Mounting the lectern, I peruse a few
Hectoring[1] large-scale verses, and pronounce
'Here endeth' much more loudly than I'd meant.   15
The echoes snigger briefly. Back at the door
I sign the book, donate an Irish sixpence,
Reflect the place was not worth stopping for.

Yet stop I did: in fact I often do,
And always end much at a loss like this,   20
Wondering what to look for; wondering, too,
When churches fall completely out of use
What we shall turn them into, if we shall keep
A few cathedrals chronically on show,
Their parchment, plate and pyx[2] in locked cases,   25
And let the rest rent-free to rain and sheep.
Shall we avoid them as unlucky places?

Or, after dark, will dubious women come
To make their children touch a particular stone;
Pick simples[3] for a cancer; or on some   30
Advised night see walking a dead one?

---

[1] Bullying, threatening.
[2] Container for the Eucharist wafer.
[3] Medicinal herbs.

Power of some sort or other will go on
In games, in riddles, seemingly at random;
But superstition, like belief, must die,
And what remains when disbelief has gone? 35
Grass, weedy pavement, brambles, buttress, sky,

A shape less recognisable each week,
A purpose more obscure. I wonder who
Will be the last, the very last, to seek
This place for what it was; one of the crew 40
That tap and jot and know what rood-lofts[4] were?
Some ruin-bibber, randy for antique,
Or Christmas-addict, counting on a whiff
Of gown-and-bands and organ-pipes and myrrh?
Or will he be my representative, 45

Bored, uninformed, knowing the ghostly silt
Dispersed, yet tending to this cross of ground
Through suburb scrub because it held unspilt
So long and equably what since is found
Only in separation—marriage, and birth, 50
And death, and thoughts of these—for whom was built
This special shell? For, though I've no idea
What this accoutred frowsty[5] barn is worth,
It pleases me to stand in silence here;

A serious house on serious earth it is, 55
In whose blent air all our compulsions meet,
Are recognised, and robed as destinies.
And that much never can be obsolete,
Since someone will forever be surpising
A hunger in himself to be more serious, 60
And gravitating with it to this ground,
Which, he once heard, was proper to grow wise in,
If only that so many dead lie round.

[4] Church galleries, located over the rood screen.
[5] Musty.

Poetry of Departures

Philip Larkin (1922–)

Sometimes you hear, fifth-hand,
As epitaph:
He chucked up everything
And just cleared off,
And always the voice will sound 4

Certain you approve
This audacious, purifying,
Elemental move.   8

And they are right, I think.
We all hate home
And having to be there:
I detest my room,   12
Its specially-chosen junk,
The good books, the good bed,
And my life, in perfect order:
So to hear it said   16

He walked out on the whole crowd
Leaves me flushed and stirred,
Like *Then she undid her dress*
Or *Take that you bastard;*   20
Surely I can, if he did?
And that helps me stay
Sober and industrious.
But I'd go today,   24

Yes, swagger the nut-strewn roads,
Crouch in the fo'c'sle[1]
Stubbly with goodness, if
It weren't so artificial,   28
Such a deliberate step backwards
To create an object:
Books; china; a life
Reprehensibly perfect.   32

[1] The forecastle, location of the sailors' quarters on a merchant ship.

Cherrylog Road

James Dickey   (1923–   )

Off Highway 106
At Cherrylog Road I entered
The '34 Ford without wheels,   3
Smothered in kudzu,[1]
With a seat pulled out to run
Corn whiskey down from the hills,   6

And then from the other side
Crept into an Essex
With a rumble seat of red leather   9

[1] A rambling, viny plant.

And then out again, aboard
A blue Chevrolet, releasing
The rust from its other color,   12

Reared up on three building blocks.
None had the same body heat;
I changed with them inward, toward   15
The weedy heart of the junkyard,
For I knew that Doris Holbrook
Would escape from her father at noon   18

And would come from the farm
To seek parts owned by the sun
Among the abandoned chassis,   21
Sitting in each in turn
As I did, leaning forward
As in a wild stock-car race   24

In the parking lot of the dead.
Time after time, I climbed in
And out the other side, like   27
An envoy or movie star
Met at the station by crickets.
A radiator cap raised its head,   30

Become a real toad or a kingsnake
As I neared the hub of the yard,
Passing through many states,   33
Many lives, to reach
Some grandmother's long Pierce-Arrow
Sending platters of blindness forth   36

From its nickel hubcaps
And spilling its tender upholstery
On sleepy roaches,   39
The glass panel in between
Lady and colored driver
Not all the way broken out,   42

The back-seat phone
Still on its hook.
I got in as though to exclaim,   45
"Let us go to the orphan asylum,
John; I have some old toys
For children who say their prayers."   48

I popped with sweat as I thought
I heard Doris Holbrook scrape
Like a mouse in the southern-state sun   51

That was eating the paint in blisters
From a hundred car tops and hoods.
She was tapping like code,   54

Loosening the screws,
Carrying off headlights,
Sparkplugs, bumpers,   57
Cracked mirrors and gear-knobs,
Getting ready, already,
To go back with something to show   60

Other than her lips' new trembling
I would hold to me soon, soon,
Where I sat in the ripped back seat   63
Talking over the interphone,
Praying for Doris Holbrook
To come from her father's farm   66

And to get back there
With no trace of me on her face
To be seen by her red-haired father   69
Who would change, in the squalling barn,
Her back's pale skin with a strop,
Then lay for me   72

In a bootlegger's roasting car
With a string-triggered 12-gauge shotgun
To blast the breath from the air.   75
Not cut by the jagged windshields,
Through the acres of wrecks she came
With a wrench in her hand,   78

Through dust where the blacksnake dies
Of boredom, and the beetle knows
The compost has no more life.   81
Someone outside would have seen
The oldest car's doors inexplicably
Close from within: 84

I held her and held her and held her,
Convoyed at terrific speed
By the stalled, dreaming traffic around us,   87
So the blacksnake, stiff
With inaction, curved back
Into life, and hunted the mouse   90

With deadly overexcitement,
The beetles reclaimed their field
As we clung, glued together,   93

With the hooks of the seat springs
Working through to catch us red-handed
Amidst the gray breathless batting   96

That burst from the seat at our backs.
We left by separate doors
Into the changed, other bodies   99
Of cars, she down Cherrylog Road
And I to my motorcycle
Parked like the soul of the junkyard   102

Restored, a bicycle fleshed
With power, and tore off
Up Highway 106, continually   105
Drunk on the wind in my mouth,
Wringing the handlebar for speed,
Wild to be wreckage forever.   108

The Skein

Carolyn Kizer   (1925–)

Moonlight through my gauze curtains
Turns them to nets for snaring wild birds,
Turns them into woven traps, into shrouds.
The old, restless grief keeps me awake.
I wander around, holding a scarf or shawl;   5
In the muffled moonlight I wander around
Folding it carefully, shaking it out again.
Everyone says my old lover is happy.
I wish they said he was coming back to me.
I hesitate here, my scarf like a skein of yarn   10
Binding my two hands loosely
        that would reach for paper and pen.

So I memorize these lines,
Dew on the scarf, dappling my nightdress also.
O love long gone, it is raining in our room!   15
So I memorize these lines,
        without salutation, without close.

Down at the Docks

Kenneth Koch   (1925–)

Down at the docks
Where everything is sweet and inclines
At night

To the sound of canoes   4
I planted a maple tree
And every night
Beneath it I studied the cosmos
Down at the docks.   8

Sweet ladies, listen to me.
The dock is made of wood
The maple tree's not made of wood
It is wood   12
Wood comes from it
As music comes from me
And from this mandolin I've made
Out of the maple tree.   16

Jealous gentlemen, study how
Wood comes from the maple
Then devise your love
So that it seems   20
To come from where
All is it yet something more
White spring flowers and leafy bough
Jealous gentlemen.   24

Arrogant little waves
Knocking at the dock
It's for you I've made this chanson
For you and that big dark blue.   28

To Christ Our Lord

Galway Kinnell (1927–   )

The legs of the elk punctured the snow's crust
And wolves floated lightfooted on the land
Hunting Christmas elk living and frozen;
Inside snow melted in a basin, and a woman basted
A bird spread over coals by its wings and head.   5

Snow had sealed the windows; candles lit
The Christmas meal. The Christmas grace chilled
The cooked bird, being long-winded and the room cold.
During the words a boy thought, is it fitting
To eat this creature killed on the wing?   10

He had killed it himself, climbing out
Alone on snowshoes in the Christmas dawn,
The fallen snow swirling and the snowfall gone,

Heard its throat scream as the rifle shouted,
Watched it drop, and fished from the snow the dead.   15

He had not wanted to shoot. The sound
Of wings beating into the hushed air
Had sitrred his love, and his fingers
Froze in his gloves, and he wondered,
Famishing, could he fire? Then he fired.   20

Now the grace praised his wicked act. At its end
The bird on the plate
Stared at his stricken appetite.
There had been nothing to do but surrender,
To kill and to eat; he ate as he had killed, with wonder.   25

At night on snowshoes on the drifting field
He wondered again, for whom had love stirred?
The stars glittered on the snow and nothing answered.
Then the Swan spread her wings, cross of the cold north,
The pattern and mirror of the acts of earth.   30

Grandmother Watching at Her Window

W. S. Merwin (1927–   )

There was always the river or the train
Right past the door, and someone might be gone
Come morning. When I was a child I mind
Being held up at a gate to wave
Good-bye, good-bye to I didn't know who,   5
Gone to the War, and how I cried after.
When I married I did what was right
But I knew even that first night
That he would go. And so shut my soul tight
Behind my mouth, so he could not steal it   10
When he went. I brought the children up clean
With my needle, taught them that stealing
Is the worst sin; knew if I loved them
They would be taken away, and did my best
But must have loved them anyway   15
For they slipped through my fingers like stitches.
Because God loves us always, whatever
We do. You can sit all your life in churches
And teach your hands to clutch when you pray
And never weaken, but God loves you so dearly   20
Just as you are, that nothing you are can stay,
But all the time you keep going away, away.

Evening

James Wright (1927–)

I called him to come in,
The wide lawn darkened so.
Laughing, he held his chin
And hid beside a bush.   4
The light gave him a push;
Shadowy grass moved slow.
He crept on agile toes
Under a sheltering rose.   8

His mother, still beyond
The bare porch and the door,
Called faintly, out of sound,
And vanished with her voice.   12
I caught his curious eyes
Measuring me, and more—
The light dancing behind
My shoulder in the wind.   16

Then, struck beyond belief
By the child's voice I heard,
I saw his hair turn leaf,
His dancing toes divide   20
To hoofs on either side,
One hand become a bird.
Startled, I held my tongue
To hear what note he sang.   24

Where was the boy gone now?
I stood on the grass, alone.
Swung from the apple bough,
The bees ignored my cry.   28
A dog roved past, and I
Turned up a sinking stone,
But found beneath no more
Than grasses dead last year.   32

Suddenly, lost and cold,
I knew the yard lay bare.
I longed to touch and hold
My child, my talking child,   36
Laughing or tame or wild,
Solid in light and air,
The supple hands, the face
To fill that barren place.   40

Slowly, the leaves descended,
The birds resolved to hands;
Laugh, and the charm was ended,
The hungry boy stepped forth.   44
He stood on the hard earth,
Like one who understands
Fairy and ghost, but less
Our human loneliness.   48

Then, on the withering lawn
He walked beside my arm.
Trees and the sun were gone,
Everything gone but us.   52
His mother sang in the house,
And kept our supper warm,
And loved us, God knows how,
The wide earth darkened so.   56

Marriage

Gregory Corso   (1930–   )

Should I get married? Should I be good?
Astound the girl next door with my velvet suit and faustus hood?
Don't take her to movies but to cemeteries
tell all about werewolf bathtubs and forked clarinets
then desire her and kiss and all the preliminaries   5
and she going just so far and I understanding why
not getting angry saying You must feel! It's beautiful to feel!
Instead take her in my arms lean against an old crooked tombstone
and woo her the entire night the constellations in the sky—

When she introduces me to her parents   10
back straightened, hair finally combed, strangled by a tie,
should I sit knees together on their 3rd degree sofa
and not ask Where's the bathroom?
How else to feel other than I am,
often thinking Flash Gordon soap—   15
O how terrible it must be for a young man
seated before a family and the family thinking
We never saw him before! He wants our Mary Lou!
After tea and homemade cookies they ask What do you do for a living?

Should I tell them? Would they like me then?   20
Say All right get married, we're losing a daughter
but we're gaining a son—
And should I then ask Where's the bathroom?

O God, and the wedding! All her family and her friends
and only a handful of mine all scroungy and bearded   25
just wait to get at the drinks and food—
And the priest! he looking at me as if I masturbated
asking me Do you take this woman for your lawful wedded wife?
And I trembling what to say say Pie Glue?
I kiss the bride all those corny men slapping me on the back   30
She's all yours, boy! Ha-ha-ha!
And in their eyes you could see some obscene honeymoon going on—

Then all that absurd rice and clanky cans and shoes
Niagara Falls! Hordes of us! Husbands! Wives! Flowers! Chocolates!

All streaming into cozy hotels   35
All going to do the same thing tonight
The indifferent clerk he knowing what was going to happen
The lobby zombies they knowing what
The whistling elevator man he knowing
The winking bellboy knowing   40
Everybody knowing! I'd be almost inclined not to do anything!
Stay up all night! Stare that hotel clerk in the eye!
Screaming: I deny honeymoon! I deny honeymoon!
running rampant into those almost climactic suites
yelling Radio belly! Cat shovel!   45
O I'd live in Niagara forever! in a dark cave beneath the Falls
I'd sit there the Mad Honeymooner
devising ways to break marriages, a scourge of bigamy
a saint of divorce—
But I should get married I should be good   50
How nice it'd be to come home to her
and sit by the fireplace and she in the kitchen
aproned young and lovely wanting my baby
and so happy about me she burns the roast beef
and comes crying to me and I get up from my big papa chair   55
saying Christmas teeth! Radiant brains! Apple deaf!
God what a husband I'd make! Yes, I should get married!
So much to do! like sneaking into Mr Jones' house late at night
and cover his golf clubs with 1920 Norwegian books
Like hanging a picture of Rimbaud on the lawnmower   60
like pasting Tannu Tuva postage stamps all over the picket fence
like when Mrs Kindhead comes to collect for the Community Chest
grab her and tell her There are unfavorable omens in the sky!
And when the mayor comes to get my vote tell him
When are you going to stop people killing whales!   65

And when the milkman comes leave him a note in the bottle
Penguin dust, bring me penguin dust, I want penguin dust—

Yet if I should get married and it's Connecticut and snow
and she gives birth to a child and I am sleepless, worn,
up for nights, head bowed against a quiet window, the past behind me,   70
finding myself in the most common of situations a trembling man
knowledged with responsibility not twig-smear nor Roman coin soup—
O what would that be like!
Surely I'd give it for a nipple a rubber Tacitus
For a rattle a bag of broken Bach records   75
Tack Della Francesca all over its crib
Sew the Greek alphabet on its bib
And build for its playpen a roofless Parthenon

No, I doubt I'd be that kind of father
not rural not snow no quiet window   80
but hot smelly tight New York City
seven flights up, roaches and rats in the walls
a fat Reichian wife screeching over potatoes Get a job!
And five nose running brats in love with Batman
And the neighbors all toothless and dry haired   85
like those hag masses of the 18 century
all wanting to come in and watch TV
The landlord wants his rent
Grocery store Blue Cross Gas & Electric Knights of Columbus
Impossible to lie back and dream Telephone snow, ghost parking—   90
No! I should not get married I should never get married!
But—imagine If I were married to a beautiful sophisticated woman
tall and pale wearing an elegant black dress and long black gloves
holding a cigarette holder in one hand and a highball in the other
and we lived high up in a penthouse with a huge window   95
from which we could see all of New York and ever farther on clearer days
No, can't imagine myself married to that pleasant prison dream—

O but what about love? I forget love
not that I am incapable of love
it's just that I see love as odd as wearing shoes—   100
I never wanted to marry a girl who was like my mother
And Ingrid Bergman was always impossible
And there's maybe a girl now but she's already married
And I don't like men and—
but there's got to be somebody!   105
Because what if I'm 60 years old and not married,
all alone in a furnished room with pee stains on my underwear
and everybody else is married! All the universe married but me!

Ah, yet well I know that were a woman possible as I am possible
then marriage would be possible—   110
Like SHE in her lonely alien gaud waiting her Egyptian lover
so I wait—bereft of 2,000 years and the bath of life.

Second Glance at a Jaguar

Ted Hughes   (1930–   )

Skinful of bowls, he bowls them,
The hip going in and out of joint, dropping the spine
With urgency of his hurry
Like a cat going along under thrown stones, under cover,
Glancing sideways, running   5
Under his spine. A terrible, stump-legged waddle
Like a thick Aztec disemboweller,
Club-swinging, trying to grind some square
Socket between his hind legs round,
Carrying his head like a brazier of spilling embers,   10
And the black bit of his mouth, he takes it
Between his back teeth, he has to wear his skin out,
He swipes a lap at the water-trough as he turns,
Swivelling the ball of his heel on the polished spot,
Showing his belly like a butterfly,   15
At every stride he has to turn a corner
In himself and correct it. His head
Is like the worn-down stump of another whole jaguar,
His body is just the engine shoving it forward,
Lifting the air up and shoving on under,   20
The weight of his fangs hanging the mouth open,
Bottom jaw combing the ground. A gorged look,
Gangster, club-tail lumped along behind gracelessly,
He's wearing himself to heavy ovals,
Muttering some mantra,[1] some drum-song of murder   25
To keep his rage brightening, making his skin
Intolerable, spurred by the rosettes, the cain-brands,
Wearing the spots off from the inside,
Rounding some revenge. Going like a prayer-wheel,
The head dragging forward, the body keeping up,   30
The hind legs lagging. He coils, he flourishes
The blackjack tail as if looking for a target,
Hurrying through the underworld, soundless.

[1] Mystic word used in Hindu or Buddhist ritual or meditation.

Daddy

Sylvia Plath (1932–1963)

You do not do, you do not do
Any more, black shoe
In which I have lived like a foot
For thirty years, poor and white,
Barely daring to breathe or Achoo.   5

Daddy, I have had to kill you.
You died before I had time—
Marble-heavy, a bag full of God,
Ghastly statue with one grey toe
Big as a Frisco seal   10

And a head in the freakish Atlantic
Where it pours bean green over blue
In the waters off beautiful Nauset.
I used to pray to recover you.
Ach, du.[1]   15

In the German tongue, in the Polish town
Scraped flat by the roller
Of wars, wars, wars.
But the name of the town is common.
My Polack friend   20

Says there are a dozen or two.
So I never could tell where you
Put your foot, your root,
I never could talk to you.
The tongue stuck in my jaw.   25

It stuck in a barb wire snare.
Ich,[2] ich, ich, ich,
I could hardly speak.
I thought every German was you.
And the language obscene   30

An engine, an engine
Chuffing me off like a Jew.
A Jew to Dachau, Auschwitz, Belsen.[3]
I began to talk like a Jew.
I think I may well be a Jew.   35

[1] Ah, you (German).
[2] I (German).
[3] Death camps in World War II.

The snows of the Tyrol, the clear beer of Vienna
Are not very pure or true.
With my gypsy ancestress and my weird luck
And my Taroc[4] pack and my Taroc pack
I may be a bit of a Jew.   40

I have always been scared of *you*,
With your Luftwaffe,[5] your gobbledygoo.
And your neat moustache
And your Aryan eye, bright blue.
Panzer-man,[6] panzer-man, O You—   45

Not God but a swastika
So black no sky could squeak through.
Every woman adores a Fascist,
The boot in the face, the brute
Brute heart of a brute like you.   50

You stand at the blackboard, daddy,
In the picture I have of you,
A cleft in your chin instead of your foot
But no less a devil for that, no not
Any less the black man who   55

Bit my pretty red heart in two.
I was ten when they buried you.
At twenty I tried to die
And get back, back, back to you.
I thought even the bones would do.   60

But they pulled me out of the sack,
And they stuck me together with glue.
And then I knew what to do.
I made a model of you,
A man in black with a Meinkampf[7] look   65

And a love of the rack and the screw.
And I said I do, I do.
So daddy, I'm finally through.
The black telephone's off at the root,
The voices just can't worm through.   70

If I've killed one man, I've killed two—
The vampire who said he was you

[4] Fortune-telling cards; frequently spelled "Tarot."
[5] German Air Force.
[6] Soldier in an armored division.
[7] Adolf Hitler's autobiography was called *Mein Kampf* ("My Struggle").

And drank my blood for a year,
Seven years, if you want to know.
Daddy, you can lie back now.   75

There's a stake in your fat black heart
And the villagers never liked you.
They are dancing and stamping on you.
They always *knew* it was you.
Daddy, daddy, you bastard, I'm through.   80

Uncle Dog: The Poet at 9

Robert Sward (1933–)

I did not want to be old Mr.
Garbage man, but uncle dog
Who rode sitting beside him.   3

Uncle dog had always looked
To me to be truck-strong
Wise-eyed, a cur-like Ford   6

Of a dog. I did not want
To be Mr. Garbage man because
All he had was cans to do.   9

Uncle dog sat there me-beside-him
Emptying nothing. Barely even
Looking from garbage side to side: 12

Like rich people in the backseats
Of chauffeur-cars, only shaggy
In an unwagging tall-scrawny way.   15

Uncle dog belonged any just where
He sat, but old Mr. Garbage man
Had to stop at everysingle can.   18

I thought. I did not want to be Mr.
Everybody calls them that first.
A dog is said, Dog! Or by name.   21

I would rather be called Rover
Than Mr. And sit like a tough
Smart mongrel beside a garbage man.   24

Uncle dog always went to places
Unconcerned, without no hurry.
Independent like some leashless   27

Toot. Honorable among scavenger
Can-picking dogs. And with a bitch
At every other can. And meat: 30

His for the barking. Oh, I wanted
To be uncle dog—sharp, high fox-
Eared, cur-Ford truck-faced   33

With his pick of the bones.
A doing, truckman's dog
And not a simple child-dog   36

Nor friend to man, but an uncle
Traveling, and to himself—
And a bitch at every second can.   39

Smudging

Diane Wakoski (1937–   )

*Smudging is the term used for lighting small oil fires in the
orange groves at night when the temperatures are too low, to
keep the leaves and fruit warm, so as not to lose the crop.*

I come out of a California orange grove
the way a meteor might be
plucked out of an Arizona desert. The icy origins
of genes
could easily be   ·   5
flaming ones
                    And in my head
those red-hot rocks
shake down into a bed of
coals, oranges roll off the shelves,   10
amber sticks on the roof of my mouth,
honey glistens in glass jars, the combs full of music
—all in the back of my head / the gold
of the small loops in my ears
is the sound of a king cobra crossing the rocks,   15
tigers walk across my lips / the gold is
in my head. It is the honeysuckle of an island.
This gold is in your house;
I sleep in your bed at night
and love you,   20
            but the firelight from those smudging pots flickers
against my eyes, burned by the eclipse this year,
and reminds me:

When I was five years old, we lived on the
edge of Orange County, in an orange grove,   25
in a small two-room house with a sagging
screened porch. Outside the kitchen at
night when it was near frosting, the
immigrant laborers would build fires in the
smudge pots to keep the trees from freezing.   30
The poetry of dew-points would be on the
news each night, and after we went to bed,
the flickering of these fires would embroider
the windows, and the sounds of voices
talking in Spanish and laughing over their   35
tequila bottles would wander into the
windows like turning lawn sprinklers.
Our doors had locks that opened with
skeleton keys. You could purchase them in
dime stores. The flimsy jambs and lintels   40
could have been pushed down by children, and
my mother was not at all secure in her
plain whiteness. Those voices frightened
her. My father was never home. I was a
child with a father who was a sailor, a   45
child who did not even know what a fishing
rod looked like. My mother stood up in
agony, all night, in the dark, every night
there was smudging and the Chicanos were
sitting on our steps laughing, drinking, or   50
under the kitchen window, talking.
Orange groves in California
are the boundaries
of my childhood.
Nights   55
       when the temperatures hovered
near the mouth of frost
on the thermometer /
pots of glowing oil
tended by dark Mexicans   60
on dark nights
in the dark rows of the dark-leaved trees. Each orange shining
like a cold sour gold anger
on the bushy tough arms
of the tree.   65
       I remember those hard knots
of light

that turned into the fruit
for dew-soaked breakfasts.
But it was the smudge pots   70
burning
like old lamps in a dim room,
warming the trees
glowing in the orchards
as I passed on asphalt highways   75
unable to talk
that reminded me
of my own unripe sour tight
globular fruit
hopefully ripening,   80
hopefully not killed off
by a frost.
Even now,
my leaves like toes
reach out   85
for warmth. Cold
nights and city
streets
have no glowing smudge pots
to leave traces   90
of soot
on the leaves and golden finally-ripe
oranges.
You are
the man with big hands,   95
the man whose brain
numbers every piece of hardware,
and who knows how to use any tool. A mechanic
you always come home dirty,
as if some flame had   100
been smudging you,
keeping your tender leaves from
low temperatures,
and I who grew up in a little house
frightened of soot and angry   105
at the voices of men in the night,
long for you
with all the mystery of my childhood.
You threw me out once
for a whole year,   110

and I felt that all the masculinity I knew about was gone:
   saw blades humming through stiff wood,
   the hand that threaded wire into place and made light,
   the soaking parts of motorcycles and cars which
   were sloshed free of old dirt and put meticulously back   115
   into now running
   machines,
   the hands and mind which could fix the shower
   or the furnace if either
   didn't work.   120
That year
I sought sunshine,
looked for men who could work in a foundry,
who were not afraid to touch hot metal.
And I was the orange   125
who began to love the dark groves at night,
the dewy shake of the leaves,
and who believed these burnings in the night
were part of a ritual
that might someday be understood.   130
And from the little girl who read fairy tales,
I have grown into the woman
in them, the one who steps magically out
of those fragrant orange peels,
into your house,   135
next to your side. I sort your dirty smudged work clothes
for the laundromat and long for the sun.
You are the voices in those dark nights, laughing on the front steps
into that clear fiery tequila;
and always there will be part of the child shivering in me   140
inside, knowing my mother feared something
that I must also fear,
her husband who left her alone for the salty ocean.
My father who walked away from me;
and then there is the part of me, that golden fruit growing on   145
the orange tree outside in the orchard,
searching for the warmth of the smudge pot,
and it is that part of me that takes your hand confidently
as we walk down the street and listens to your deep voice telling
stories.   150
Thank god for our visions.
That in our heads
we play many roles. There is part of me that trembles,

and part of me that reaches for warmth,
and part of me that breaks open   155
like mythic fruit,
the golden orange every prince will fight
to own.

I Am a Cowboy in the Boat of Ra

Ishmael Reed (1938–   )

*'The devil must be forced to reveal any such physical evil
(potions, charms fetishes, etc.) still outside the body
and these must be burned.'* (Rituale Romanum, *published
1947, endorsed by the coat-of-arms and introductory
letter from Francis Cardinal Spellman)*

I am a cowboy in the boat of Ra,[1]
sidewinders in the saloons of fools
bit my forehead   like   O
the untrustworthiness of Egyptologists
who do not know their trips. Who was that   5
dog-faced man? they asked, the day I rode
from town.

School marms with halitosis cannot see
the Nefertiti[2] fake chipped on the run by slick
germans, the hawk behind Sonny Rollins'[3] head or   10
the ritual beard of his axe; a longhorn winding
its bells thru the Field of Reeds.

I am a cowboy in the boat of Ra. I bedded
down with Isis,[4] Lady of the Boogaloo, dove
down deep in her horny, stuck up her Wells-Far-ago   15
in daring midday getaway. 'Start grabbing the
blue', I said from top of my double crown.

I am a cowboy in the boat of Ra. Ezzard Charles[5]
of the Chisholm Trail. Took up the bass but they
blew off my thunb. Alchemist in ringmanship but a   20
sucker for the right cross.

I am a cowboy in the boat of Ra. Vamoosed from
the temple i bide my time. The price on the wanted

---

[1] Egyptian sun god.
[2] Egyptian queen of the fourteenth century B.C.
[3] A jazz musician.
[4] Goddess of fertility.
[5] Formerly world heavyweight boxing champion.

poster was a-going down, outlaw alias copped my stance
and moody greenhorns were making me dance;   25
   while my mouth's
shooting iron got its chambers jammed.

I am a cowboy in the boat of Ra. Boning-up in
the ol West i bide my time. You should see
me pick off these tin cans whippersnappers. I   30
write the motown long plays for the comeback of
Osiris.[6] Make them up when stars stare at sleeping
steer out here near the campfire. Women arrive
on the backs of goats and throw themselves on
my Bowie.[7]   35

I am a cowboy in the boat of Ra. Lord of the lash,
the Loup Garou[8] Kid. Half breed son of Pisces and
Aquarius.[9] I hold the souls of men in my pot. I do
the dirty boogie with scorpions. I make the bulls
keep still and was the first swinger to grape the taste.   40

I am a cowboy in his boat. Pope Joan[10] of the
Ptah[11] Ra. C/mere a minute willya doll?
Be a good girl and
bring me my Buffalo horn of black powder
bring me my headdress of black feathers   45
bring me my bones of Ju-Ju[12] snake
go get my eyelids of red paint.
Hand me my shadow

I'm going into town after Set[13]

I am a cowboy in the boat of Ra   50

look out Set   here i come Set
to get Set   to sunset Set
to unseat Set   to Set down Set

               usurper of the Royal couch
               imposter RAdio of Moses' bush[14]   55
               party pooper O hater of dance
               vampire outlaw of the milky way

[6] God of the underworld, husband of Isis.
[7] Hunting knife.
[8] Werewolf.
[9] Signs of the zodiac.
[10] A fictitious female pope.
[11] Chief god of ancient Memphis.
[12] Magic charm.
[13] Egyptian god of evil.
[14] Cf. Genesis iii.2.

Writing About Poetry

Poetry lifts language from everyday talk into its full potentiality. It calls our attention to the unnoticed meanings and images in words, to the half-heard chimes of sound, and the unconscious rhythms in the sentences we speak as we breathe. It recalls the primitive alliance of language with song and dance and celebration. It reflects, in its structures, the recurring natural order we sense in our surrounding world. And it concentrates these things in cryptic ways with the magical challenge of ancient riddles. Hence writing about poetry is the challenge of laying out in plain prose this concentration of dynamics and meanings.

As with people, we may like a poem on first meeting, one feature or another seeming attractive. But to appreciate its full synthesis of image, sound, rhythm, structure, and meaning, its full personality and being, requires a little longer acquaintance. We may choose one feature or another for our essay, as we assert and explain its significance, but we must know it as part of the whole to understand its significance at all. So let us look at the various features poets draw on to achieve their poems—sounds, images, and sense.

Sense

Whatever in a poem attracts us, we want most to make sense of it, explaining its attractions and its meaning. All poems are, in a general way, riddles. What am I? What do I mean? And many poems are specifically versions of this primitive and enduring word game, as when Emily Dickinson writes "I like to see it lap the Miles," and goes on to make clear, without ever saying so directly, that her *it* is a train.

The plain sense behind any figurative writing also teases us like the answer to a riddle, and poets play sense against sense in a myriad of ways. Here is Pope, in a seriously playful appeal to his friend to consider the human condition, to "Expatiate free o'er all this scene of Man." Immediately he is punning, playing one sense of *expatiate*, "to expound at length," against its literal sense, "to amble about through space." Then he expands this literal sense into a fanciful picture of two gentlemen roaming around a country estate for a bit of shooting, and the features of English landscaping—its shrubbery planted in mazes, its walks, gardens, and open fields—become a metaphor for the world itself:

> Expatiate free o'er all this scene of Man;
> A mighty maze! but not without a plan;

> A Wild, where weeds and flow'rs promiscuous shoot,
> Or Garden, tempting with forbidden fruit . . . .
> Eye Nature's walks, shoot Folly as it flies,
> And catch the Manners living as they rise;
> Laugh where we must, be candid where we can;
> But vindicate the ways of God to Man.

The lively play of meanings in this passage accounts for much of its appeal—the intellectual satisfaction of "getting the idea," of seeing the answer to the small implied riddles. A maze is precisely a tight series of paths between high hedges that seems aimlessly puzzling but actually is cleverly planned, and this is just like God's world, says Pope. The wild side of man's nature, with its promiscuity, contrasts with his civilized and orderly life, with its forbidden fruit, like the Garden of man's first fall. Man's folly is like that of the partridge, which rises for the hunter's gun when it might have stayed hidden. The different "manners" of people are like smaller birds caught by net, not so cruelly satirized as the bigger follies. And to "catch the living manners" is exactly what a writer, or a painter (and Pope was a bit of both), does in his art—in the poem he is now writing. He wittily acknowledges that we must laugh, in self-protection, at those things we cannot help (one remembers Pope's own dwarfed stature and humped back, and his brave wit at his own expense, "this long disease, my life"). Then he enjoys the simple intellectual fun in the reiteration of *"can*did where we *can.*" Finally, the whole poem is a kind of playful resonance of meanings, as Pope recalls Milton's *Paradise Lost*, which had famously set out to "justify the ways of God to men."

ALLUSION

Allusion, which means "a playing with," is probably the poet's broadest play of meanings. What he is saying takes its broadest sense in the context of some larger, more familiar, more established body of sense. You can see this when Housman, playing on the mere coincidence of sound in *malt* and *Milt*, also alludes, like Pope, to *Paradise Lost:*

> And malt does more than Milton can
> To justify God's ways to man.

Allusions may thus echo some well-known literary work and use it directly, or ironically, as a meaningful background, or they may call up other familiar contexts, as with Pope's "Garden."

But as the writer tries to make sense of a poem's sly and cryptic ways, he must sometimes dig for allusions not readily at hand. Shelley's "Ozymandias" immediately prompts this kind of curiosity. To what is Shelley alluding? The poem makes a certain clear sense without bothering, but that final key to the riddle tempts us. Here is the poem we start with:

Ozymandias

I met a traveller from an antique land
Who said: Two vast and trunkless legs of stone
Stand in the desert . . . Near them, on the sand,
Half sunk, a shattered visage lies, whose frown,
And wrinkled lip, and sneer of cold command,
Tell that its sculptor well those passions read
Which yet survive, stamped on these lifeless things,
The hand that mocked them, and the heart that fed:
And on the pedestal these words appear:
"My name is Ozymandias, king of kings:
Look on my works, ye Mighty, and despair!"
Nothing beside remains. Round the decay
Of that colossal wreck, boundless and bare
The lone and level sands stretch far away.

Who was Ozymandias? Was there an Ozymandias? *The Oxford Companion to English Literature* tells us that "The Ramesseum (of Rameses II) at Thebes is called by Diodorus Siculus (i.47 et seq.) the tomb of Ozymandias." An unabridged dictionary will tell us that Rameses II lived from 1324–1258 B.C. *The Encyclopedia Britannica* (11th ed.) says that in his 67 years of reign he "filled all Egypt and Nubia with his own monuments" and that the "excavation of the rock temple of Abu Simbel and the completion of the great hall of Karnak were his greatest achievements." In the delta at the mouth of the Nile, "a colossus of the king placed here was over 90 ft. in height, exceeding in scale even the greatest of the Theban colossi which he had erected in his mortuary temple of the Ramesseum."

He was a big builder, all right, but Shelley's point about the ruin time has wrought on such gigantic pride is blunted by our knowledge that Abu Simbel and more than a little of the temple at Karnak still stand. Was Shelley mistaken? Or did he change the picture to emphasize his point? We now need to know what Shelley knew, and several scholars have spent considerable time to find out. Johnstone Parr identifies this statue of Ozymandias as one of three colossi at Thebes, each one cut from solid stone, by the sculptor Memnon (note Shelley's effective play on the word *colossal*). Parr quotes a translation of Diodorus, the Sicilian Greek historian who saw the statue in the first century B.C., when it was still intact:

> One of these, made in a sitting posture, is the greatest in all Egypt. . . . In so great a work there is not to be discerned the least flaw, or any other blemish.
>
> Upon it there is this inscription:—"I am Osymandyas, king of kings; if any would know how great I am, and where I lie, let him excel me in any of my works"[1]

[1] Johnstone Parr, "Shelley's *Ozymandias*," *Keats-Shelley Journal*, 6 (1957), p. 31.

This translation of the epitaph had first appeared in 1700 and had been quoted frequently enough—once in the *Encyclopedia Britannica* of 1812, six years before Shelley's poem—for Parr to suspect "that the arrogant epitaph . . . had become virtually a commonplace."[2] But long before Shelley's time, the huge 60-foot colossus had tumbled, leaving nothing but the torso, a piece of a foot, a wholly obliterated face, and no sign of an inscription whatever, but with columns of the temple and other fragments of statues in the vicinity. Where Shelley derives his details—including the empty sands and the two standing legs of stone, whereas the statue had been seated, and the trunk, not the legs, survived—remains to be found.

H. M. Richmond supplies the answer.[3] Shelley and his friend Horatio H. Smith had been looking through Richard Pococke's *A Description of the East* (1742), a two-volume work with engraved illustrations. Pococke simply says that the statue "is broke off about the middle of the trunk" and gives measurements of the head, shoulders, and the foot.[4] But from pictures of several other ruined statues, Shelley and Smith both evolved their poetic images of the ruined fragments of colossal pride and the sands of time. Shelley published his sonnet in Leigh Hunt's *Examiner* on January 11, 1818, and Hunt printed Smith's companion piece in the following issue, February 1:

On a Stupendous Leg of Granite, Discovered Standing by Itself in the Deserts of Egypt, with the Inscription Inserted Below

In Egypt's sandy silence, all alone,
    Stands a gigantic leg, which far off throws
    The only shadow that the desert knows.
"I am great Ozymandias," saith the stone,
    "The king of kings: this mighty city shows
The wonders of my hand." The city's gone!
    Nought but the leg remaining to disclose
The site of that forgotten Babylon.

We wonder, and some hunter may express
Wonder like ours, when thro' the wilderness,
    Where London *stood*, holding the wolf in chace,
He meets some fragment huge, and stops to guess
    What powerful, but unrecorded, race,
    Once dwelt in that annihilated place.

[2] *Ibid*, p. 34.
[3] H. M. Richmond, "Ozymandias and the Travelers," *Keats–Shelley Journal*, 11 (1962), pp. 65–71.
[4] Parr, "Shelley's *Ozymandias*," p. 32.

EXPLICATION

We could well explicate—"lay out the pleats of"—one or both of these poems in an essay, explaining as fully as possible the sense of what they are saying, and, better still, trying to demonstrate that one is superior to the other in its impact, in its psychological depth, in its poetic skill. We would begin in the usual way of inquiry, putting questions to the poem and seeing what answers we could find. Is the poet a lover of meter and sounds, and in what way? What are his images, his metaphors? What is he alluding to, if anything? What does he say, really? What does he mean? To what effect, for instance, do Shelley and Smith both introduce a visitor discovering something memorable? From your answers you can form an essay about, let us say, "The Importance of Shelley's Traveler." Give it a try.

One feature of Shelley's poem has aroused debate in class, and occasionally in print. Here we may need to *paraphrase*—writing out our own prose translation—to help us decide exactly what Shelley means when he speaks of the shattered face

>   ... whose frown,
> And wrinkled lip, and sneer of cold command,
> Tell that its sculptor well those passions read
> Which yet survive, stamped on these lifeless things,
> The hand that mocked them, and the heart that fed:

To whom does that hand and heart belong? To Ozymandias or to the sculptor? Some vote for the sculptor:

> Then we have the deliberate diminuendo of the lines about the sculptor, with the involved grammar, the gentle speculation and the archaic *mocked* (for *mimicked*) creating an olde-worlde air.[5]

This reading assumes that the sculptor's skillful hand mimicked in stone the passions behind the frown and the sneering lip. But does the sculptor's heart feed those passions? Perhaps—as he imagines them and recreates them in stone.

Nevertheless, the alternate choice seems to fit the involved grammar more closely, as we paraphrase it, filling in the implications as we understand them:

> ... whose frown, wrinkled lip, and arrogant and contemptuous sneer show that the sculptor knew very well the passions, which he has stamped on these lifeless fragments: arrogance, lust for power, contempt for rivals, passions that survive down to this day in all too many people. The sculptor knew very well the king's hand, which mocked those same passions in his rivals, and the king's cold and haughty heart, which fed those passions in himself.

[5]Desmond King-Hele, *Shelley, His Thought and Work*, 2nd ed. (Teaneck, Rutherford, Madison: Fairleigh Dickinson University Press, 1971), p. 94.

The words remain as Shelley wrote them, and we cannot ask him what he meant. The best we can do is to spell out the possible meanings, and, if we can, guess at the one that seems most likely. Since the epitaph is directed in a mighty sneer at "ye Mighty," asking them to "Look on my works," which suggests a mocking gesture of the hand, the second possibility seems to hold the higher likelihood.

So writing about poetry is answering the puzzles that attract you as you read, explaining the delights, and persuading your own readers that your answers make the best and fullest sense. You write about poetry to explain what is there to understand and enjoy, and the process of writing will in fact unfold further dimensions in your own understanding, and increase your own enjoyment.

Images

Shelley has made his point with images—quite literally a shattered stone image, but also sands, a frown, a wrinkled lip. Images are simply physical things we can see, or touch, or smell. The physical images represent abstract qualities, and each of the qualities—desolation, displeasure, scorn—joins to convey the poet's meaning: human pride is colossally futile. Thus the images, the physical items, represent some more general idea.

SYMBOLS

Even the most pictorial description shares this representative—this symbolizing—function. A poet may simply describe what he sees, and wants us to see, as when William Carlos Williams writes about

> a red wheel
> barrow
>
> glazed with rain
> water
>
> beside the white
> chickens.

But then we see that even such bare description symbolizes something, for Williams begins this strange little poem with:

> so much depends
> upon

Williams does not say (perhaps could not say) what that *so much* is. But he does seem to find the things of this world meaningful—symbolizing something beyond themselves. He certainly is suggesting something about rural life, the natural world, labor (perhaps), the repose of a still life, perhaps, or the sheer vividness of one's perceptions in moments of heightened awareness. But the point for the moment is that poetic pictures are symbolic, whether they are sheer description, as here, or whether they are more conventionally presented as symbols. And in writing about the poem we must find, or surmise, however conjecturally, the meaning these symbols convey.

Some things have acquired conventional symbolic meanings, as one or another of their natural qualities has caught the human imagination. A garden, for instance, is naturally pleasant, peaceful, hopeful, as grass and buds declare again and again life's renewal. The ancient Golden Age and the Biblical Eden both pictured a garden of perpetual spring. Any garden in literature will have this natural suggestiveness, and the author will very likely, and indeed naturally, add some touch to remind us that all gardens reflect something of the Garden of Eden. A snake, for instance, will inevitably symbolize the dangers in beautiful gardens and will bring to mind the most famous of snakes in the grass, Satan himself, who, disguised as a serpent, destroyed the Garden's innocent bliss.

The dove is another natural symbol, long made traditional in literature. Doves—white, soft, and cooy—flocked around the temples of Venus, the Greek goddess of love, as her own sacred birds. Thus the dove naturally seems to symbolize Love. When Noah sends out a dove from the Ark, and the dove returns with an olive leaf to show that trees are emerging, both the dove and the olive come to symbolize the peace that follows God's wrathful flood. Love naturally has transposed into peace. Next, in the New Testament, when John baptizes Jesus in the Jordan River: "Lo, the heavens were opened unto him, and he saw the Spirit of God descending like a dove, and lighting upon him: and lo a voice from heaven, saying, This is my beloved Son, in whom I am well pleased" (Matt. 3:16–17). Pagan Love has become the Spirit of God—which is Love, for his beloved Son. Finally, in the minds of Christian symbolizers, the dove becomes associated with the tongues of fire that descended on the apostles at the Pentecost—50 days after Easter and Christ's resurrection—filling them with the Holy Ghost (God's Spirit) and affirming the resurrection to the skeptical bystanders. In thousands of paintings and stained-glass windows, and through centuries of Bible reading, the dove, and the fire, become fixed as symbols for the Holy Spirit, for Love, and the peace that passeth understanding, emphasized in literature and thought in one aspect or another—a symbol so universal indeed that it is now also the dominant symbol in Communist countries for peace and community. Christianity, indeed, has so thoroughly imbued Western culture through the centuries, that even the obviously non-Christian writers of the twentieth century cannot resist returning again and again to characters symbolically analogous to Christ, to crosses, and other traditional symbols.

One Christian symbol in particular shows how a natural suggestiveness deepens into a symbol, the more men think about it: the fish. Again, ancient societies chose the fish as a token of fertility, perhaps from some more primitive intuition that life, and the salty fecundity of woman, had emerged from the sea. Venus, goddess of love, we will remember, rose from the sea. Again, Christian history and thought projected an ancient symbol into higher significance, and again by natural association. Christ's apostles were fishermen. Christ is soon helping them bring in a tremendous catch, soon punning that he will be a fisher of men, soon feeding a multitude with a few loaves and fishes. Soon the fish becomes a symbol for Christ's spiritual fertility, and becomes an acronym, a secret sign, for the early Christian underground. The *ichthus*, a fish drawn in Roman catacombs and on tombstones (from the Greek word for fish, *ichthys*) was taken as the initial sounds of the Latinized Greek phrase for "Jesus Christ, Son of God, Savior": *Iēsous* CH*ristos*, TH*eou* HY*ios*, *Soter*—ICHTHYS. So the fish symbolizes Christ and his spiritual power. And any fish, like any garden, in a story or poem, may well carry these symbolic implications. Our job as writers about literature is to decide whether the writer intended them, or whether a fish is simply a fish and nothing more.

METAPHOR
When we move to metaphor, we usually find the writer's intentions unmistakable: to picture something in terms of something else to make the idea more visible. *Similes* spell the comparison out, with *like, as,* or *as if:*

> Laura stretched her gleaming neck
> Like a rush-imbedded swan,
> Like a lily from the beck

The plain metaphor makes the analogy in one leap: "She *is* a swan, a lily." The implied metaphor gives her swanlike or lilylike qualities without naming *swan* or *lily*. "O so white: O so soft: . . . is she!" writes Jonson, after mentioning the lily and swansdown. The implied metaphor seems often like a pun, because ordinary words suddenly project their pictorial potential, as when Shakespeare says: "And summer's *lease* hath all too short a *date*," and we get the sudden picture of Summer as a person renting a house with a short lease. Implied metaphors can be wonderfully compounded, as when, in another poem, Shakespeare shifts his picture in a kind of montage: an old man with shaking limbs is like a barren tree in autumn with its boughs shaking in the cold wind, and the tree's bare limbs, deserted by birds, are like a ruined choir loft in one of the monastic chapels ruined by Henry VIII, where the choirboys used to sing like birds:

> That time of year thou mayst in me behold
> When yellow leaves, or none, or few, do hang
> Upon those boughs which shake against the cold,
> Bare ruin'd choirs, where late the sweet birds sang.

Metaphors may also be compounded with symbols, as in that most amazing of poems, Gerard Manley Hopkins's "The Windhover," where the windhover, a type of falcon, wings stretched against the sky, symbolizes Christ on the cross as well as Christ as Prince of Morning, Heir to the Kingdom of Heaven, and as a chivalric knight gloriously riding and managing his horse:

> I caught this morning morning's minion, king-
>   dom of daylight's dauphin, dapple-dawn-drawn Falcon, in
>   his riding
> Of the rolling level underneath him steady air, and striding
> High there, how he rung upon the rein of a wimpling wing
> In his ecstasy! . . .

And even another metaphor has burst into the picture, since the curved wing of the falcon is like the curving fabric of a nun's or monk's wimple, or hood, fluttering on either side of the face.

The poet's fancy can even invert the metaphor, so that the real becomes the fancied and the fancied the real, as in this stanza by Ebenezer Jones where the fancied flame of autumn becomes the actuality, and the actual crocus becomes the *as if*. The figurative flame is like the crocus, rather than the crocus being like a flame, and the concentration on the beautiful flower itself is startingly intense.

> And the woodland haunter
> Shall not cease to saunter
>   When, far down some glade,
> Of the great world's burning,
> One soft flame upturning,
> Seems, to his discerning,
>   Crocus in the shade.

Sounds

> *Hickory dickory dock*
>
> *Fee fie foe fum*

Sounds strike us first. We enjoy them in themselves, even when they mean nothing. Poetry, as in these nursery rhymes, calls forth for our en-

joyment the sounds of language, those chiming variations, especially
when they also imitate the rhythms we know as we breathe, or walk, or
clap our hands in time. So let us say that the sounds of poetry consist in
rhyme and meter: (1) sounds matched to each other, and (2) the rhythms
of language matched to measured time.

RHYME

We may segregate the rhyming sounds of poetry into *alliteration, assonance, consonance, full rhyme,* and *reiteration.* All are repetitions, in which
we enjoy the similarities among the differences in language.

1. *Alliteration.* First sounds of words (or of accented syllables) the same:
   "a *L*ittle *L*ost a*lL*iteration."

> Western *w*ind, when *w*ilt thou blow

(The *hw* sound of *wh*en comes close, and indeed is identical, a full alliteration, in some pronunciations.)
2. *Assonance.* Middle vowel sounds the same: sm*o*ky l*oa*m; gl*a*d r*a*g; h*o*t
   r*o*d.

> Ere sh*e* s*ee* the E*a*rl of M*u*rray
> Come s*ou*nding through the t*ow*n

(Sh*e* s*ee* th*e* makes a triple assonance, if we say "thee" for *the*; E*a*rl/
M*u*rray shows how similar sounds, not spelling, make the assonance.)
3. *Consonance.* End-consonant sounds the same in words or syllables but
   vowels different (called "slant rhyme" when rhymed at line-ends):
   bored/third, supple/apple, cried/bleed, love/over.

> When*as* in si*lks* my *J*ulia goes

4. *Reiteration.* The same word repeated, often with different force:

> *Tiger, Tiger,* burning bright
> *Then, then* (me thinks) how sweetly flowes
> Of hammered *gold* and *gold* enameling

5. *Rhyme.* Words ending in the same sound: *bird/third,* usually at line-
   ends ("Does it rhyme?"). Slant rhyme (*bird/soared*) also counts as
   "rhyme" at line-ends, and may even include approximations like *cob/
   rap* or *cot/mad.*

A poet frequently orchestrates all or most of these rhyming-sounds
together, sometimes stressing one sound in different combinations to
augment his meaning, as Robert Herrick does the *s* sounds in the poem
below, which seem to suggest the sound of water and the liquid sound
of silks rubbing together:

Whenas in silks my *Julia* goes,
Then, then (me thinks) how sweetly flowes
That liquefaction of her clothes.

Next, when I cast mine eyes and see
That brave Vibration each way free;
O how that glittering taketh me!

The reiterated *then* and the end-rhymes are obvious. But note the alliter-
ated *th*'s (*Then, then, thinks*), the *l*'s (*-ly, flowes, liquefaction*), and the *br*'s in
brave and *-brations* that also combine in assonance with *way*. Other asso-
nances are *in–silks, me–sweetly, That–faction, -tion–of, Next–when, cast–and,
I–mine–eyes, each–free*. Consonance appears in *Whenas–goes, sil–Jul, then–
thin, when–mine*, and merges with alliteration in *brave–vibration* and *glittering–taketh*. The way Herrick's sounds flow and echo probably eludes
precise demonstration, as when the *a* in *that* deepens to *brave* and then
squeezes up into the *ee*'s of *each* and *free* or as *o* flows into *-ow*, as if one
were hearing the different vowels recited. With the swishing *s*'s underlining the silken image, we can only point in admiration to Herrick's or-
chestrated sounds as we attempt to explain, to our readers, the total effect of this little poem.

METER
Meter is the drummer in the poetic band: *rattity–tat–ta–tat–ta–tat.* Or
perhaps we should say that meter is the bass drum's steady beat, with the
snare drum's *rattity–tat* marking its varieties, as in the opening line of
Andrew Marvell's "To His Coy Mistress": *"Had we but world enough and
time"—rattity–tat–ta–tat–ta–tat.* This is *iambic* meter, which has predomi-
nated in English for over four hundred years. Three other meters—*anapestic, trochaic, dactylic*—lend iambic an occasional foot, for variety, and
produce a few poems.

Modern verse is predominantly "free," with no regular pattern. And
some modern poets have tried other systems in place of the four traditional meters, writing "syllabic verse" in which all lines have a predeter-
mined number of syllables but no regular beat, or "rhythmic verse,"
with, say, three beats to each line of loosely varying numbers of syllables. Others have tried *spatial patterns,* grouping their words on the page
to look like keys or locomotives, or scattering them around to suggest
swooping pigeons or sheer dramatic pause and emphasis. When writing
about a poem, we should at least consider whether our readers need to
know if it has a metrical pattern or no pattern, and what that pattern is.

Dipodic Verse
Sometimes looking like free verse, dipodic ("two-footed") verse survives from Old English poetry in a light-hearted rocking meter, with

two half lines, each with two stresses falling among scattered light syllables. Nursery rhymes picked up the pattern:

$$\breve{} \quad - \,|\breve{}\;\breve{}\; - \;\breve{}\; \| \;\breve{}\quad - \,|\breve{}\;\breve{}\; - \,|$$
There was an old woman who lived in a shoe.

$$\breve{}\quad - \,|\breve{}\;\;\breve{}\;\breve{}\; - \;\;\breve{}\;\|\breve{}\;\; - \,|\;\breve{}\;\;\breve{}\;\;\breve{}\;\;\breve{}\; - \,|$$
She had so many children she didn't know what to do.

From this emerged a more patterned light verse, which will scan in alternating heavy and light iambic feet ($\breve{}\,-$): ta–DA, ta–da, ta–DA, ta–da:

$$\breve{}\quad - \;|\breve{}\; - \,|\breve{}-|\breve{}\; - \;\|\breve{}-|\breve{}\; - \;|\breve{}-|\breve{}\; - \;|$$
Go down to Kew in lilac-time, in lilac-time, in lilac-time

But it really rollicks better when read more quickly in the old dipodic
way, with the lighter heavies falling in with the lights (tap your foot to
the accented syllables):

$$\breve{}\quad - \;|\breve{}\;\;\breve{}\;\;\breve{}\; -\breve{}\;\;\breve{}\;\|\breve{}\; -\breve{}\;\;\breve{}\;|\breve{}\; -\breve{}\;\;\breve{}\;|$$
Go down to Kew in lilac-time, in lilac-time, in lilac-time

$$\breve{}\quad - \;|\breve{}\;\;\breve{}\;\;\breve{}\; -\breve{}\;\;\breve{}\;\|\breve{}\; -|\breve{}\;\;\breve{}\;\;\breve{}\;\; - \;\;\breve{}\;|$$
Go down to Kew in lilac-time (it isn't far from London!)

$$\breve{}\quad -|\;\breve{}\;\;\;\breve{}\;\;\breve{}\;\; - \;\;\breve{}\;\breve{}\;\|\;\breve{}\;\; - \;|\breve{}\;\;\breve{}\;\;\breve{}\;\; - \;\breve{}\;\;\breve{}\;|$$
And you shall wander hand in hand with love in summer's wonderland

$$\breve{}\quad - \;|\breve{}\;\;\breve{}\;\;\breve{}\; -\breve{}\;\;\breve{}\;\|\breve{}\; -|\breve{}\;\;\breve{}\;\;\breve{}\;\; - \;\;\breve{}\;|$$
Go down to Kew in lilac-time (it isn't far from London)!
Alfred Noyes, "The Barrel-Organ"

Noyes's refrain illustrates another trait of dipodics: to slow down the
two-footed run at the end, with a three-stressed, and more conventional,
pattern. We can keep on running, as in the scansion above, but we will
probably slow down to conventional iambics:

$$\breve{}\; -|\breve{}\; - \;|\;\breve{}\;\; - \;\;\breve{}\;|$$
it isn't far from London

Regular Meters

Most metrical poems will be in iambics, with feet from the other three
meters occasionally substituted for variety. Here are the four regular meters:

RISING METERS

Iambic: $\breve{}\,-$
Anapestic: $\breve{}\;\breve{}\,-$

FALLING METERS

Trochaic: $-\,\breve{}$
Dactylic: $-\,\breve{}\;\breve{}$

The number of these metrical units, or feet, in a line also gives the verse a name:

> 1 foot: monometer
> 2 feet: dimeter
> 3 feet: trimeter
> 4 feet: tetrameter
> 5 feet: pentameter
> 6 feet: hexameter
> 7 feet: heptameter

Thus we have *iambic tetrameter*, lines of four iambic feet, or *dactylic hexameter*, lines of six dactylic feet. All meters will show some variations, substituting other kinds of feet, but the dominant foot is usually easily recognizable—indeed, *must* be recognizable for us to say, "This is an iambic pentameter poem," or "This is an anapestic poem in stanzas of two tetrameter lines and a dimeter." *Scansion*—marking off the feet—will help your analysis:

IAMBIC TETRAMETER

– ͜ | ͜ – | ͜ – | ͜ – |
Had we but world enough and time

ANAPESTIC TETRAMETER

͜ – | ͜ ͜ – | ͜ – | ͜ ͜ – |
The pop-lars are felled; farewell to the shade

͜ ͜ – | ͜ ͜ – | ͜ ͜ – | ͜ ͜ – |
And the whis-pering sound of the cool colonade!
William Cowper, "The Poplar Field"

TROCHAIC TETRAMETER

– ͜ | – ͜ | – ͜ | – ͜ |
Tell me not in mournful numbers
Longfellow, "A Psalm of Life"

DACTYLIC HEXAMETER

– ͜ ͜ | – ͜ ͜ | – ͜ ͜ | – ͜ ͜ | – ͜ ͜ | – ͜ |
This is the forest prim-eval. The murmuring pines and the hemlocks

– ͜ ͜ | – ͜ ͜ |
Bearded with moss. . . .
Longfellow, "Evangeline"

SCANSION

Scanning the lines of a poem—marking off the beat and its variations in metrical feet—helps you to perceive the metrical sound effects, and to describe their striking features. The regular iambic pentameter line—ten syllables, five stresses—scans like this:

u – | u   – | u   – | u – | u   – |
What oft was thought, but ne'er so well expressed

The iambic also regularly admits an extra light syllable at the line-end, a "feminine ending" (the regular one is "masculine"), giving the five-stress line an occasional eleventh syllable:

–   u | u   – | u – | u – | u – u |
Like to the lark at break of day arising.

Scanning will tune your ear to the way in which meter underlines certain of the slurred syllables of speech, lifting them into metrical regularity, as the poet imposes his will on language and stretches out its latent accents in metrical pleasure. Each of the following lines, in ordinary speech, would have only four stresses:

True Wít is *Náture* to advántage drést

And leáves the wórld to dárkness and to mé

Deép in the shády sádness of a vále

But each of the poets (Pope, Gray, Keats), in the context of his other lines and regular beat, stretches them into iambic meter:

u   –| u –| u –| u – | u   – |
True Wit is Nature to advantage drest

u   – | u   – | u – | u   – | u – |
And leaves the world to darkness and to me

–   u | u – | u – | u –| u – |
Deep in the sha- dy sad- ness of a vale

In reading them metrically, we lift into meter, just slightly, the otherwise unaccented syllables *to, and, of*. Keats and Yeats (and others) can even extrude iambic pentameter from ordinarily three-stressed lines, showing how this kind of mastery is most pleasing when exerted on big polysyllabic words. Each of the following lines would show only three stresses in ordinary speech (*sun, shad-, mag*, and *Mon-, own, -nif-*). But the meaning seems to emerge with the beat as the poets stretch them out along the metrical frame:

u – | u – | u –| u – | u – |
A sun—a shad- ow of a mag- nitude.

–   u | u –| u   – | u –| u – |
Monuments of his own magnif- icence

Thus scansion identifies the metrical pattern for you, and leads you to discern the poet's mastery in bending his language to the pleasures of meter.

By scanning, you will discover that iambic has three regular variations:

Inverted foot: | – ∪ | (a trochee)
Spondee: | – – |
Ionic double-foot: | ∪ ∪ | – – |

We have already seen how frequently the inverted foot begins an iambic line: *Had we but world; Like to the lark; Monuments of.* The spondee is rarer, but see how it energizes Dylan Thomas's iambic line:

∪   – | ∪   – | ∪   – | –   – | ∪   – |
The force that through the green fuse drives the flower

Some lines from Housman's "To an Athlete Dying Young" will show nicely how the inverted foot and the double ionic can vary the iambic march without missing a beat:

∪ – | ∪ – | ∪ – | ∪   – |
So set, before its echoes fade,

∪   – | – ∪ | ∪ – | ∪   – |
The fleet foot on the sill of shade,

∪   – | ∪ ∪ | –   – | ∪ – |
And hold to the low lintel up

∪   – | ∪ – | ∪   – | ∪   – |
The still-defended challenge-cup.

Some writers like an extra ("hypermetric") light syllable. Others hold their iambics close, allowing only the three regular variations. The punctuation also varies the meter, of course, either in mid-line caesuras or at endline, as when a conductor momentarily suspends his baton in mid-air and the orchestra pauses, before resuming the beat. Scanning will tell you what kind of a metrist you have, so you can describe his metrical bent, and the way his sound-effects flow and twirl over the march of his meter.

RHYME SCHEME

Ultimately, through rhyme, the pleasures of sound fall into larger patterns. As with meter, we can enjoy variations only as we perceive and enjoy a regular rhyming pattern, skipping away and touching base. To see the regularity and enjoy the release, we must first detect the pattern. Conversely, we must assure ourselves that another poem, apparently unrhymed or in altogether free verse, derives its pleasures elsewhere. So we discover rhyme scheme by assigning letters to the sounds at line-ends:

> O long, long may the ladies stand,   *a*
> With their gold combs in their hair,   *b*
> Waiting for their own dear lords,   *c*
> For they'll see them no more.   *b*

This is a typical *ballad stanza*, from "Sir Patrick Spens," a quatrain of alternate iambic tetrameters and trimeters rhymed *abcb*.

Marking the scheme in longer stanzas, especially freely rhyming stanzas, can reveal a pattern otherwise not noticed, as the apparently casual flow of language chimes into patterns metrical and stanzaic:

> Laura stretched her gleaming neck   *a*
> Like a rush-embedded swan,   *b*
> Like a lily from the beck,   *a*
> Like a moonlit poplar branch,   *c*
> Like a vessel at the launch   *c*
> When its last restraint is gone.   *b*
>
> *Christina Rossetti, "Goblin Market"*

You will notice that *branch/launch* looks like a consonance, a "slant rhyme," though it may have rhymed exactly in the poet's pronunciation. Marking the rhyme scheme will thus bring out unnoticed slant rhymes and even more remote approximations.

> That is no country for old men. The young   *a*
> In one another's arms, birds in the trees,   *b*
> —Those dying generations—at their song,   *a*
> The salmon-falls, the mackerel-crowded seas,   *b*
> Fish, flesh, or fowl, commend all summer long   *a*
> Whatever is begotten, born, and dies.   *b*
> Caught in that sensual music all neglect   *c*
> Monuments of unageing intellect.   *c*
>
> *Yeats, "Sailing to Byzantium"*

In marking the rhymes, we are surprised to discover how simple and straightforward Yeats's stanzaic scheme is, and as we move through the poem (see p. 542), we can admire how confidently (and characteristically) he can force a rhyme to keep his sense and his pattern both, even rhyming *magnificence* with *dress*, for instance:

> ... and louder sing   *a*
> For every tatter in its mortal dress,   *b*
> Nor is there singing school but studying   *a*
> Monuments of its own magnificence   *b*

Or, more conventionally, *wall/soul/animal:*

> O sages standing in God's holy fire   *a*
> As in the gold mosaic of a wall,   *b*
> Come from the holy fire, perne in a gyre,   *a*
> And be the singing-masters of my soul.   *b*
> Consume my heart away; sick with desire   *a*
> And fastened to a dying animal   *b*
> It knows not what it is. . . .

CONVENTIONAL PATTERNS

The rhyming lines of poetry, then, fall into many patterns—many of them generated as the poet writes his first stanza then matches his following stanzas to it, as both Keats and Yeats frequently did. But, in addition to the ballad stanza from folk tradition, three other patterns have proved basic to English poetry.

Tetrameter Couplet (iambics)

> The grave's a fine and private place,
> But none, I think do there embrace.
> *Marvell, "To His Coy Mistress"*

The Closed Couplet

Also called the heroic couplet, balanced couplet, and pentameter couplet, this classic unit is at its best when thoughts are balanced against each other in lines and half-lines, as they are in Sir John Denham's famous address to the River Thames:

> O could I flow like thee, and make thy stream
> My great example, as it is my theme.
> Tho' deep, yet clear; tho' gentle, yet not dull;
> Strong, without rage; without o'erflowing, full.
> *Sir John Denham, "Cooper's Hill"*

The Sonnet

The sonnet is probably the most durable large form in English verse, the form challenging both the poet and the person writing about him. Thomas Wyatt, soon followed by his friend Henry Howard, the Earl of

Surrey, introduced the sonnet into English about 1530 by translating Pe-
trarch's Italian sonnets (written two centuries earlier) and then imitating
the form in over thirty sonnets of his own. The *Petrarchan* pattern divides its fourteen lines into an *octave* of eight lines, in which the poet
poses some problem, and a *sestet*, of six, in which he reaches some solution. The octave is two quatrains rhymed *abba*. The sestet is two triads
rhymed *cde cde*, with variations allowed, such as *cde dce*, or even *cddc ee*,
which, with its final couplet, moves toward Shakespeare. But however
the poet arranges the three rhymes in his sestet, he limits himself to five
rhymes only. Here is Milton's famous sonnet on his blindness, in which
he "paragraphs" his quatrains and triads to emphasize his Petrarchan
pattern:

On His Blindness

When I consider how my light is spent,	*a*
Ere half my days, in this dark world and wide,	*b*
And that one Talent which is death to hide,	*b*
Lodg'd with me useless, though my Soul more bent	*a*
To serve therewith my Maker, and present	*a*
My true account, lest he returning chide;	*b*
Doth God exact day-labour, light denied,	*b*
I fondly ask; But patience to prevent	*a*
That murmur, soon replies, God doth not need	*c*
Either man's work or his own gifts; who best	*d*
Bear his mild yoke, they serve him best, his state	*e*
Is Kingly. Thousands at his bidding speed	*c*
And post o'er Land and Ocean without rest:	*d*
They also serve who only stand and wait.	*e*

Shakespeare loosened up the Petrarchan pattern into three quatrains
and a summative couplet, affording himself seven rhymes instead of
five, since rhymes are harder to find in English than in Italian. He frequently keeps the Petrarchan turn of idea from octave to sestet (see pp.
667–668), but just as frequently does not, as in this famous example:

When to the Sessions of Sweet Silent Thought

When to the sessions of sweet silent thought	*a*
I summon up remembrance of things past,	*b*
I sigh the lack of many a thing I sought,	*a*
And with old woes new wail my dear time's waste.	*b*
Then can I drown an eye, unus'd to flow,	*c*
For precious friends hid in death's dateless night,	*d*

And weep afresh love's long since cancell'd woe, c
And moan the expense of many a vanish'd sight. d
Then can I grieve at grievances foregone, e
And heavily from woe to woe tell o'er f
The sad account of fore-bemoaned moan e
Which I new pay as if not paid before. f
   But if the while I think on thee, dear friend, g
   All losses are restor'd and sorrows end. g

In summary, by marking rhyme-scheme and meter, you can grasp and explain a poet's stanzaic pattern, within which all the smaller harmonics and larger rhythms of phrasing are also working. Here is a poem of Ben Jonson's, celebrating the beauty of his "Charis," a lady of the court otherwise unknown. His stanza is a masterpiece of variety within order, which is the essence of our pleasure in the sounds of poetry. He alternates anapestic and iambic trimeters for four lines, contrasting the meters further by consistent feminine endings on his iambic lines. In his next four lines, he shifts to couplets of long and short lines, first blending the two meters in two lines (aided by his feminine iambic ending), and then again contrasting iambic and anapestic in his two short lines. His concluding couplet locks home his basic anapestic trimeter with an extra iambic foot. His last stanza is worth the whole poem, but we cannot appreciate it fully without the first two, which it culminates:

Her Triumph

See the chariot at hand here of Love a

Wherein my lady rideth: b

Each that drawes is a swan, or a dove, a

And well the carre Love guideth. b

As she goes, all hearts doe duty c

Unto her beauty; c

And enamour'd, doe wish, so they might d

But enjoy such a sight, d

That they still were to run by her side, e

Through swords, through seas, whether she would ride. e

```
  U  U   -  | U  U   -  | U   U   - |
Doe but looke on her eyes; they doe light          a

    U  U |  -     -  ³ | U   -  U|
 All that Loves world compriseth:                  b

  U   U    -  | U  U    -  | U U   -  |
Doe but looke on her haire; it is bright            a

    U   -  | -    U ⁴ | U  -  U|
  As Loves starre when it riseth:                  b

  U   U    -  | U  -| U    -    U|
Doe but marke, her forhead's smoother              c

        U    -  | U   -    U |
    Then words that sooth her:                      c

  U   U   -| U  U    -   | U  U   - |
And from her arched browes, such a grace           d

      U    U -| U    U   - |
    Sheds itselfe through the face,                 d

  U U -| U   U   -  | U  U  -|
As alone there triumphs to the life                e

 U  U   -  | U U   -  | U U -| U  U   -  ⁵ |
All the gaine, all the good, of the elements strife.  e
```

```
      U    U   -  | U U   -  | U U    - |
    Have you seen but a bright lillie grow,          a

  U  -| U    -  | U     -    U|
Before rude hands have touch'd it?                   b

      U  U    -   | U  U  -| U U    - |
    Ha' you mark'd but the fall o'the snow           a

  U  -| U    -  | U      -     U|
Before the soyle hath smutch'd it?                   b

  U   U   -| U   -  | U  -  U|
Ha' you felt the wooll of bever?                     c

      U    -  | U   - U|
    Or swans downe ever?                             c

  U   U    -   | U U   -| U U    - |
Or have smelt o'the bud o'the brier?                 d

        U    -  | U U   -|
    Or the nard in the fire?                         d

  U   U  -| U   U   -| U  U    - |
Or have tasted the bag of the bee?                   e

  U U    -   | U U   -| U U    -  | U -|
O so white! O so soft! O so sweet is she!            e
```

Ben Jonson, from "A Celebration of Charis"

Jonson has followed his intricate pattern in meter and rhyme scheme in all three of his stanzas, substituting only five feet (marked in light numerals) in the total of eighty-seven. *(Unto* in the sixth line was probably accented on *to,* like *until* and *upon,* and the meter forces emphasis on the second syllable of *triumphs.)* Substitutions 3 and 4 are regular iambic ones (ionic doubleton and inverted foot) stressing *Loves world* and *Loves starre.* And we might want to read *rude hands* and *downe ev—* as regular spondees. But the first two obvious substitutions trade iambs for the anapests of the pattern *(through swords, through seas).* And the fifth *(elements)* throws a compensating anapest back into the balance. See how the last line of the last stanza synthesizes this metrical balancing. Here are the three last lines:

$$\overset{\cup}{}\ \ \overset{-}{}\ |\ \overset{\cup}{}\ \ \overset{-}{}\ |\ \overset{\cup}{}\ \overset{\cup}{}\ \overset{-}{}\ |\ \overset{\cup}{}\ \ \overset{-}{}\ |$$
Through swords, through seas, whether she would ride.

$$\overset{\cup}{}\ \overset{\cup}{}\ \overset{-}{}\ |\overset{\cup}{}\ \overset{\cup}{}\ \overset{-}{}\ |\overset{\cup}{}\ \overset{\cup}{}\overset{-}{}|\overset{\cup}{}\ \overset{\cup}{}\ \overset{-}{}\ |$$
All the gaine, all the good, of the elements strife.

$$\overset{\cup}{}\ \overset{\cup}{}\ \overset{-}{}\ |\overset{\cup}{}\ \overset{\cup}{}\ \overset{-}{}\ |\overset{\cup}{}\ \overset{\cup}{}\ \overset{-}{}\ |\overset{\cup}{}\overset{-}{}\ |$$
O so white! O so soft! O so sweet is she!

The poem really is a triumph. The last stanza moves from the conventional figures of Love and doves and arched brows to original natural ones, like unsmutched snow and beaver's fur, and its long last line summarizes the meter (regular, but varied by the exclamations) as it also summarizes whiteness, softness, and sweetness in the order they have been gathering—all ending with the iambic emphasis on the superlative *she* of Jonson's adoration.

Writing the Paper

Since you cannot write about everything, pick some detail or angle you found interesting or, better, delightful. Decide whether you want to concentrate on one poem or several related ones. Read your poems over a few times, exploring your interest, then write yourself a thesis—a proposition to guide both you and your reader. As always, you simply turn your personal response into a general fact, changing "I like Ben Jonson's metaphors" into "Ben Jonson makes his attitude toward writing vivid through a surprising variety of metaphors." You do the same with your preferences for poems. You change "I like Donne's better than Marvell's" to "Donne's 'The Ecstasy' is a deeper and more spiritual poem than Marvell's 'To His Coy Mistress.'"

Once you have a thesis, your major problem is solved. As with fiction, or the drama, or anything, for that matter, you then introduce your reader to your subject, leading him down to your thesis in three or four sentences:

   Although John Donne's "The Ecstasy" and Andrew Marvell's "To His Coy Mistress" may seem at first to have little in common, they are actually on the same subject. Both are love poems. Both were written in the seventeenth century. Both . . . . Both . . . . But, all in all, Donne's poem is the deeper of the two, the more spiritual, the more meaningful.

If you like Marvell's poem better—and many people do—make a case for it instead, on whatever terms are convincing: its clarity, its force, its irony, its imaginative wit.

   Now, after ending your introductory paragraph with your thesis, you bring in your evidence and write it out for the rest of your paper, describing, quoting, explaining, bringing in anything that will support your thesis and convince your reader. You may wish to bring in historical or biographical evidence, researching the background, as the scholars did with Shelley's "Ozymandias." You could do a considerable research paper on "The Bonny Earl of Murray," for instance, beginning in the encyclopedia with "MURRAY" (or "MORAY," James Stuart or Stewart, c. 1531–1570) and pointing out the differences between balladry and fact. Anything that interests you will make a paper interesting to others too.

SUGGESTIONS FOR WRITING

Lyric

1. Compare "Waly, Waly" and Yeats's "Down By the Salley Gardens," a true folk lyric and an imitation. How are the themes alike, how different? What is the story implied behind the details of each? What do the poets gain by omitting them? For your thesis, you might assert something about the advantages of condensation.
2. Compare Byron's "Maid of Athens" and Poe's "To Helen." Note the effect of Byron's Greek refrain ("My life, I love you").

Narrative

1. Explain the point of "Hurt Hawks."
2. Explore irony (see p. 495) in one or more narrative poems ("Sir Patrick Spens," "Richard Cory").

The Poem as Drama

1. Explain the situation and its force in one poem (Valentine's "Dream Barker," Muir's "The Brothers," Gunn's "Moly").

Denotation and Connotation

1. Explain the double meanings and the humor in "I Knew a Woman." Can you reconcile this playfulness with a sincere love? You might

bring in Shakespeare's "My Mistress' Eyes" and Campion's "There Is a Garden in Her Face."
2. Study the force of particular words and their associations in one poem ("Lady Lazarus"—*it, lampshade, cat, strip tease, skin and bone;* "The Raid"—*sun, cold ocean, birds, woman, sea*).

Allusion

1. What is the effect of Housman's Terence, Milton, and Mithridates; Graves's Ulysses, or the like?
2. Trace out the allusive context of Auden's "Musée des Beaux Arts," Yeats's "Second Coming" or his "Two Songs."

Irony

1. Who is the better ironist, Shelley or Smith, in their sonnets on Ozymandias (pp. 850–851).
2. Explicate the irony in a poem by Crane, Hardy, Housman, Owen, or Reed (pp. 496–501).

Traditional Themes

1. Compare Emerson and Gray on the vanity of human wishes.
2. Compare one or more of the *carpe diem* poems (Campion, Herrick, Marvell, Donne, pp. 528–534) with Catullus's "Lesbia."
3. Compare Browning's "Love Among the Ruins" with Millay's "Love Is Not All."
4. Compare a poem concerning bereavement (Rexroth's "Andrée Rexroth") with one concerning death in less personal terms (Auden, Whitman, pp. 572–579).

Images and Metaphors

1. Explain the effect of a dominant image—Welty's guinea hens, Frost's apples, Keats's marbles.
2. Explicate the metaphors, and their effect, in any highly metaphorical poem (Reid's "Calenture," Swenson's "Question," Jonson's "Ode: To Himself," Hopkins's "Windhover").

Symbol and Allegory

1. Explain a dominant symbol (Keats's flowery band in "Endymion," Bryant's waterfowl, Blake's rose).
2. Trace out the allegory in Holmes's "The Chambered Nautilus" or Cummings's "In Just—."

Sound

1. See how, or if, the sound echoes the sense in a poem you like, first scanning, then noting alliteration, assonance, consonance, and reiteration.
2. Compare the sounds and their effectiveness in "Dover Beach" and "Break, Break, Break."
3. See how Tennyson or Sissman, or both, derive their effects from the Drayton poem that they imitate (pp. 641–648).

Traditional Forms

1. Show what advantages Auden or Cummings draws from the traditional ballad.
2. Taking Shakespeare as the primary sonneteer, what advantages do one of the moderns—Millay, Cummings, Yeats, Frost, Hopkins—draw from the sonnet form?

The Popular Muse

1. Attack or defend one of the poems in this section, perhaps bringing in another for illustration: one of the ballads to put beside "Eleanor Rigby," for instance.
2. Explain the popularity of one of the poems in this section. Perhaps you will want to consider its history, or the life and times of the author.

Drama

On Drama

Spectacle

The word "theater" is derived from a Greek word meaning *to see*, and this indicates that the basis of what goes on in a theater is spectacle, something to look at. The words in themselves often have a secondary function. Many, if not most, major developments of drama have been closely associated with music, where singing frequently takes over from speaking, and sometimes music and spectacle converge in the dance so that words get squeezed out altogether. In any case it is spectacle that has been the most popular feature of drama in all ages and cultures. If we start to read Shakespeare's plays, for instance, in what scholars regard as their chronological order, we find, very early on, three plays on the Wars of the Roses in the reign of Henry VI, and a tragedy called *Titus Andronicus*. If our only contact with these plays is through reading, we may find the Henry VI plays rather dull, and *Titus Andronicus* in particular almost childishly grotesque and horrible. Yet whenever any dramatic company works up enough nerve to give these plays a proper production, we discover that they can be made into superb pieces of spectacular theater. We have to realize, then, that Shakespeare was not educating himself through written texts, as we do for the most part, but through experience with audiences who wanted, and were ready to respond to, spectacle.

Later on, Shakespeare began his *Henry V* with a prologue apologizing for not giving his audience more spectacle, and what may be his last play, *Henry VIII*, again seems rather a dull play to read, because it is really a costume piece, a historical panorama with long processions of noblemen in full parade dress. So while an excellent film can be made of Shakespeare's *Henry V* (and of most of his other plays too), still, if Shakespeare's theater had possessed the resources of the modern cinema, it is clear that we should never have had Shakespeare. The more spectacular the play, the less important the words are, and an audience, unless it is a specially educated audience, will not listen long if there is not enough to see. It's sometimes said that this emphasis on the visual is peculiar to Western culture: it's been suggested that when we say we listen "to" music, the word *to* indicates that we're putting even music into a visual and spatial context. But the emphasis on spectacle is quite as marked in Oriental drama too.

Through most of its history the verbal drama has been squeezed between musical forms on the one hand (opera, ballet, revue), and spectacular ones on the other (pantomime, circus, masque), which, as already noted, often combine to reduce the verbal content still further. One comedy by the best of the Roman dramatists, Terence, was not played through on its first performance, because the audience went out during the intermission to watch a rope-dancing act, and failed to return. In later Roman times, when such circus entertainment had expanded into gladiatorial battles and chariot races, serious drama seems to have disappeared from stage almost altogether. If stage drama is not crowded out today by the competition of movies, television, and ball games, that is partly because of the efforts made by books like this one to stress the importance of verbal education and partly out of a need for greater variety. The most popular dramatic forms, because they are mass produced, tend to be highly conventionalized: this is true of sitcoms and similar stereotyped dramatic forms in television, as it was of their predecessors in radio and cinema a generation or so ago, when they were the most popular forms. It is not much wonder if we find a tendency on the part of playwrights to nag and scold their audiences for wanting something more lowbrow; this tendency has run through the history of drama from Aristophanes to Bernard Shaw and beyond. We may assume that a parallel tendency to say "nothing ever happens in these new-fangled plays; they're all just a lot of talk" has recurred in audiences for the same length of time.

Dramatic Roles

But there are some very profound and central human experiences that only verbal drama can express. We might begin by looking at two types of these experiences in particular. In the first place, we act out dramatic roles constantly in our own lives. Someone we know comes into our room, and we instantly adopt a role that is based on our knowledge of his character and the way he talks. He leaves, and we start dramatizing ourselves to ourselves, like Hamlet: if we aren't consciously talking to ourselves, as he did, we are unconsciously throwing our minds into some sort of inner dialogue. Cutting out all the babble and chatter that goes on inside us takes a high degree of concentration and mental discipline, and all this chatter is dramatic in one way or another. Some people speak of a "persona" as the part of ourselves that expresses the social aspect of our life: the word means mask, and refers to the fact that in the plays of ancient Greece the actors wore masks. The phrase *dramatis personae*, before the list of characters at the beginning of a play, originally meant "the masks to be used for the performance." But we don't have just one mask: we have any number of them, and it's highly significant that our words *person* and *personality* come from the same dramatic metaphor. They suggest that we can never take a mask off and show the "real self" underneath. There's nothing under a "persona" except another persona: there's no core to that onion. The Greek equivalent of persona is *hypocrites*, from which our word *hypocrite* comes. This sounds bad, and suggests that if we are better people we can remove all deceitful disguises and speak with utter sincerity and truthfulness. Perhaps we can, but when we do we are entering into a dramatic role of sincerity and are wearing *that* mask.

So one of the things drama does is to reflect back to us the dramas we carry on with each other and with ourselves. When we first come upon the dialogue in Albee's *American Dream*, we might assume, if we were unaccustomed to this kind of drama, that all the characters were simply insane. But if we listen closely to the interaction of the things we say with the things that are also in our minds that we don't say, along with an occasional echo of things we don't dare say to ourselves or even consciously think, we might hear something not so very different. And we have all gone through conversations that seemed to us so pointless and meaningless, with so many empty clichés mechanically spoken whether they related to anything else said or not, as to make the dialogue in Ionesco's *Bald Soprano* sound like the soberest realism.

Our second type of dramatic experience is an extension of the same principle to the characters in a play, who are so often locked inside subdramas of their own, so that the play we are watching often becomes a bundle of subsidiary dramas. Take the conclusion of Strindberg's *Miss Julie*, a dialogue between two people, Miss Julie herself and Jean, the valet who has seduced her. Miss Julie goes out and kills herself at the end of the play because she feels that fate or God or circumstances or the class structure of nineteenth-century Sweden, or whatever, has woven an ironic drama around her in which she has the role of a sacrificial victim, and she kills herself in obedience to the role she assumes she's cast in. The valet then hears his master's bell ring, and says that behind his master's hand there's something else moving the hand. That something else is presumably his subdramatist, setting a role for him to go on living, at least through the mess of Julie's death. However we interpret the words of his final speech, they make it clear that there's no simple situation involved where Strindberg merely writes a play and an audience merely listens to it. There's a group of intermediate dramas, some of them within the characters and some of them within our own previous experiences, and it's the interactions of all these that make up the whole drama. Admittedly, the dramatist who is shaping Miss Julie's life into a suicide is a pretty corny dramatist and is really not God or fate or Sweden but Miss Julie herself. In other words both she and Jean are projecting their inner dramas on something outside them. That doesn't, however, reflect on Strindberg, who had the ability to create Miss Julie and Jean both as characters and as the subdramatists of their own lives.

Illusion and Irony

It's also important that when we assume a dramatic role in relation to someone else we become partly a dramatic construct of that someone else. Anyone who has thrown himself into a set role, like Willy Loman in *Death of a Salesman*, is in danger of suddenly realizing that he's not sure whether he's himself or merely a kind of ventriloquist's dummy, an echo of what other people or other people's values have made out of him. Something similar is the reason for the neurotic snoopiness of the people in Pirandello's *It Is So! (If You Think So)*. It drives them up the wall to think that there may be something about the Ponza family that they can't get to the bottom of once and for all and establish the truth about by documentary or other "certain" forms of evidence. Because, of course, if there is no tangible reality in those lives to be clutched and grasped, there is no such reality in their own lives either. One character, Laudisi, understands that we don't see or touch reality directly: we gradually learn something about it by bouncing illusions off against each other.

Similarly, in Shakespeare's *The Tempest*, at the beginning of the second act, we find Antonio and Sebastian in a state of giggling hysteria that gradually turns venomous as they plot to murder Alonso when he's asleep. They plot this because they're realists, because this is the kind of thing you do in the real world to get on and get ahead. Earlier, when Gonzalo says that the island is fresh and green, they see it realistically as totally barren. Later the hero, Ferdinand, sees the masque put on by Ariel and the other spirits working for Prospero, which is of course an illusion, like all dramatic performances. By the end of the play we realise that these notions of reality and illusion are exactly the opposite of those being presented by the play itself. The masque symbolizes a far profounder reality than actual existence ever affords; the squalid plot of Antonio and Sebastian shows that they are the ones who are plunged in illusion. And on top of that we have Prospero's speech after the masque, pointing out that the difference between reality and illusion is itself an illusion, what we call reality being simply an illusion that lasts a little longer.

One form of drama that has been popular at various times is the puppet play, where we can see that the movements and sounds of the characters are being produced by somebody else offstage. But of course human actors are to some degree puppets also, considering how much authors and directors have to do with their acting. Audiences, again, are always in a state of greater freedom than the characters on the stage, simply because they are able to walk out of the theater; and in the great majority of plays they know more about what is going on in the whole action of the play than the characters on the stage are supposed to know. All this makes for the situation that we call irony, where the spectator knows more than the participator.

Irony is an obvious source of the comic: in many comedies we find a type of character that Shakespeare's friend and contemporary Ben Jonson called a "humor," a character like a miser or hypochondriac or snob or jealous husband or father or glutton or pedant, who is identified with a single leading characteristic and can't do anything not connected with exhibiting it. Such characters are funny because they have made themselves into puppets, mechanically responding to every stimulus in the same way. Most of Molière's plays are constructed on this principle, where a father forbids a son or daughter to marry the person he or she wants to marry because the father is obsessed with his "humor": In *The Physician in Spite of Himself* this principle is played down, and the father is simply being obstinate about getting his daughter married to a rich man, but the action of the play follows the usual setup. The characters in *The Cherry Orchard* are also humors, wandering around in a daze created by their own dreams and snobberies. Lyubov, who compulsively gives too much money to beggars because she resents the fact that she's not wealthy anymore and can't afford to, is the central humor of the play.

But irony is a feature of tragedy also. In *Oedipus Rex* the audience already knows the outlines of the story and so keeps anticipating all the horrific discoveries that Oedipus makes about himself. In *Macbeth,* there's a prophecy that no man born of woman can kill Macbeth, but then Macduff was the result of a Caesarian operation, and so wasn't really born of a woman at all. It sounds like a poor joke, and gives us a glimpse into the sheer idiocy of the world that Macbeth has committed himself to. In *Death of a Salesman,* again, the audience, while it may not know the end of that particular story, still does know that Willy Loman's version of the American dream is a lot of nonsense, and that no good can come of pursuing it.

In general, there's a broad division between tragedy and comedy, which is mainly a difference in endings: a tragedy traditionally ends in the death or disaster of the central character and a comedy with some kind of party, such as a wedding. The pervading mood of tragedy is likely to be sombre and that of comedy festive, but we can have tragedies full of wit and humor, like *Romeo and Juliet,* or "black" comedies that seem very gloomy or bitter. The original idea was that tragedy showed us death and comedy showed us a passage through, if not actual death, at least something quite ominous, to renewed life.

In Aristophanes' *Lysistrata* the women barricade the Acropolis, and the chorus of old men scrambles up with wood to set the place on fire, so as either to roast the women alive or smoke them out. They are too old to be drafted for military service or to be affected by the sexual strike, but the intensity of their hatred for the women who want to intervene in public affairs long enough to stop the war with Sparta is not just good fun. This is "Old" Comedy, and was succeeded on the stage by "New" Comedy, where, usually, a young man wants a young woman, is opposed by his or her father, but finally gets her. He is often helped, in Roman comedies, by a clever slave, who may be threatened with anything from flogging to crucifixion by the father. We notice how, even in the very light-hearted farce of Molière, when the hero gets the heroine from under the nose of her father through the aid of Sganarelle, Sganarelle is led away to be hanged.

Tragedy usually focuses on a heroic figure, of greater authority or
articulateness than we have. Tragedy is an event: it does not depend
on the moral quality of the hero. The hero may be the mature and
responsible Oedipus, utterly unconscious of anything he could have
done to provoke the wrath of the gods, or he may be loaded down
with the foulest crimes, like Macbeth. The one thing he must be is a
hero, somebody worth writing a tragedy about. Willy Loman may not
be what we ordinarily think of as a hero, but, as his wife says, small
men can get just as exhausted as big ones, and however absurd his
values may be he has fought hard for them. And, in the sight of
watching angels or someone equally removed from the human scene,
his values might be much less absurd than Macbeth's ambition.

Is the final meaning of drama, then, simply that everything is illusion
and that nothing is real? Not quite. We notice that Oedipus keeps
driving himself through the most agonizing self-discoveries because,
as he says, he is determined to find out who he is. In *Death of a
Salesman*, Biff says of his father: "He never knew who he was," but
he's reached a profounder level of insight himself when he says of
himself simply "I'm nothing, Pop." Macbeth, after his last hope has
failed him, is threatened with the negative dramatic role of being
made "the show and gaze o' th' time," and he realizes that whatever
he has done his identity is still that of a warrior. At the end of *The
Tempest*, Gonzalo says that "all of us [found] ourselves when no man
was his own." At the end of a play, then, there is often left behind
some sense of identity that has been attained by somebody, in
however perverse a way, and this sense of identity, a reality that can
only be pointed to by illusion, seems to be what is really underneath
all the masks and stage paint and lighting. Sometimes a character in
the play attains it; sometimes, as in *The Cherry Orchard*, nobody does.
In that case the gaining of a sense of identity is a job for the people in
the audience, as Prospero indicates when he says, in the Epilogue to
The Tempest, the play's over; I've done what I can; now it's all yours.

CHAPTER 1

Tragedy

The Greek Theater

Imagine yourself an actor and playwright. As the "wright" you will make the play (not write it), just as a wheelwright and wainwright used to make wheels and wagons. Your tools are words, actors, and whatever physical support the budget will allow: costumes, perhaps, and a painted backdrop or two. You have been asked to provide a play to highlight the spring festival your university holds annually in its football stadium. You will use one end of the stadium. You will stand near the goal line and face the 14 thousand spectators the stadium can seat from the curve at the end to the line at your right and left. At your back will be a structure of wood and canvas to serve as setting and as a place to change costumes, but you will have no curtains, no electric lights, and no microphones. You will step out in daylight, before thousands, and hold their attention for three or four hours. It won't be easy.

But it can be done. Or at least it once was done regularly in ancient Greece, for what we have described is essentially an ancient Greek theater. Unless your stadium is among the largest in the country you won't be able to seat 14 thousand people at one end, but the theater of Dionysus at Athens held approximately that number. Other theaters in the ancient world accommodated perhaps as many as 50 thousand. All were open to the sky, illuminated naturally by daylight. A *skene* (from which comes our word *scene*), originally a tent or wooden hut, faced the semicircle of seats.

How will you make all those people hear? How will you get their attention and keep them interested? The *skene* will help to enclose your voice in the amphitheater, but your play will do best with speeches suited to public declamation; you won't want to write any intimate, whispery passages. Perhaps you will invent some mechanical magnification. Your players could wear masks cleverly constructed to serve as sounding boards or megaphones. But will the people in the back rows be able to see? Perhaps the masks could enlarge facial features, emphasizing emotional attributes. The actors might be physically heightened by elevated shoes, or clogs. The play then will not want much movement, but will depend upon strong, easily projected emotions and large, unmistakable

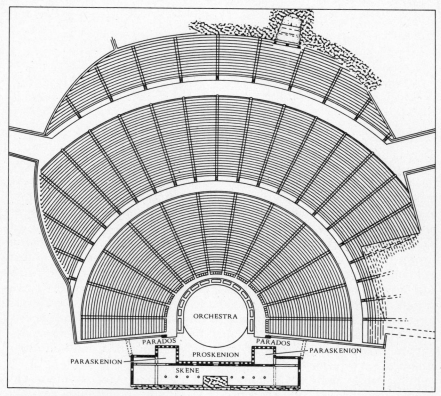

Theater of Dionysus, Fourth Century B.C.
(Adapted from Dörpfeld and Reisch, *Griechische Theater*, 1896)

gestures. For subject matter, you may well decide upon some familiar story, with characters everyone knows, a dean or a football hero or a recent president of the United States. If you take a new story, you will want to keep it simple. You will reach your audience more easily that way, but to keep them with you perhaps you had better throw in a chorus and some dancing.

You have reinvented Greek theater. Unfortunately, it is not likely to work well for you, for the theatrical *conventions* of today are far different from those of Sophocles' day. Your audience is accustomed to the psychological isolation of a seat in a darkened theater, looking upon a brightly lit stage or screen. Greek theater was communal, festive, religious. Your audience wants the novelty of a new story. Greek audiences wanted endless variations on stories known since childhood. Your audience wants close-ups and electronic amplification. Greek audiences wanted the magic of painted masks and the ritual affirmations of choral interludes.

You can read *Oedipus Rex* as you would any nondramatic work of literature, recreating its images upon the stage of your mind as you do the
images of a poem or a story. But you are much more free than you are
with a poem or a story to imagine how the actors look and move and
how the setting surrounding them appears: all the physical details made
concrete in a production. Develop your imagination as you may, you can
never experience the play quite the way its first audiences did, but you
can sense its ancient greatness if you imagine the Greek stage: the masks,
the declamatory voices, the sweeping gestures, the bright blue Mediterranean sky above, the shared responses of thousands. Or you can stage
the play in your mind in a darkened twentieth-century theater, either
with living actors or with pictures projected upon a screen; done well it
retains its power to move deeply. Among literary genres, only the play
has quite this protean nature, taking a large part of its identity from its
production. To read a play well is to become part stage manager, part actor, and part audience.

OEDIPUS REX*

Sophocles   (496?–406 B.C.)

PERSONS REPRESENTED

OEDIPUS	MESSENGER
A PRIEST	SHEPHERD OF LAÏOS
CREON	SECOND MESSENGER
TEIRESIAS	CHORUS OF THEBAN ELDERS
IOCASTÊ	

*The Scene: Before the palace of Oedipus, King of Thebes. A central door and two lateral
doors open onto a platform which runs the length of the façade. On the platform, right
and left, are altars; and three steps lead down into the "orchestra," or chorus-ground. At
the beginning of the action these steps are crowded by Suppliants[1] who have brought
branches and chaplets of olive leaves and who lie in various attitudes of despair. Oedipus
enters.*

Prologue[2]

OEDIPUS: My children, generations of the living
In the line of Kadmos,[3] nursed at his ancient hearth:
Why have you strewn yourselves before these altars
In supplication, with your boughs and garlands?
The breath of incense rises from the city   5
With a sound of prayer and lamentation.

---

*English version by Dudley Fitts and Robert Fitzgerald.

[1] Persons entreating favors.
[2] Introduction, or foreword to the action.
[3] Cadmus, legendary Phoenician founder of the city of Thebes. Here, as in the names Iocastê (Jo-
casta) and Laïos (Laius), Fitts and Fitzgerald prefer spellings more like the Greek than are the usual
English forms.

                                              Children,
I would not have you speak through messengers,
And therefore I have come myself to hear you—
I, Oedipus, who bear the famous name.
(To a Priest.) You, there, since you are eldest in the company,
Speak for them all, tell me what preys upon you,   10
Whether you come in dread, or crave some blessing:
Tell me, and never doubt that I will help you
In every way I can; I should be heartless
Were I not moved to find you suppliant here.

PRIEST: Great Oedipus, O powerful King of Thebes!   15
You see how all the ages of our people
Cling to your altar steps: here are boys
Who can barely stand alone, and here are priests
By weight of age, as I am a priest of God,
And young men chosen from those yet unmarried;   20
As for the others, all that multitude,
They wait with olive chaplets in the squares,
At the two shrines of Pallas,⁴ and where Apollo⁵
Speaks in the glowing embers.
                                    Your own eyes
Must tell you: Thebes is in her extremity   25
And can not lift her head from the surge of death.
A rust consumes the buds and fruits of the earth;
The herds are sick; children die unborn,
And labor is vain. The god of plague and pyre
Raids like detestable lightning through the city,   30
And all the house of Kadmos is laid waste,
All emptied, and all darkened: Death alone
Battens upon the misery of Thebes.

You are not one of the immortal gods, we know;
Yet we have come to you to make our prayer   35
As to the man of all men best in adversity
And wisest in the ways of God. You saved us
From the Sphinx,⁶ that flinty singer, and the tribute
We paid to her so long; yet you were never
Better informed than we, nor could we teach you: 40
It was some god breathed in you to set us free.

Therefore, O mighty King, we turn to you:
Find us our safety, find us a remedy,

---

⁴ Pallas Athena, goddess of wisdom.
⁵ Phoebus Apollo, the sun god. At his shrine, fortunes were told in a variety of ways, including from embers.
⁶ A monster with female head and the body of a lion. She had terrorized Thebes, killing all who could not answer her riddle ("What goes on four legs in the morning, two at noon, three in the evening?"). Oedipus answered correctly, "Man" (as a baby, an adult, and in age supported by a cane), and destroyed the monster.

Whether by counsel of the gods or men.
A king of wisdom tested in the past   45
Can act in a time of troubles, and act well.
Noblest of men, restore
Life to your city! Think how all men call you
Liberator for your triumph long ago;
Ah, when your years of kingship are remembered,   50
Let them not say *We rose, but later fell*—
Keep the State from going down in the storm!
Once, years ago, with happy augury,
You brought us fortune; be the same again!
No man questions your power to rule the land: 55
But rule over men, not over a dead city!
Ships are only hulls, citadels are nothing,
When no life moves in the empty passageways.
OEDIPUS: Poor children! You may be sure I know
  All that you longed for in your coming here.   60
  I know that you are deathly sick; and yet,
  Sick as you are, not one is as sick as I.
  Each of you suffers in himself alone
  His anguish, not another's; but my spirit
  Groans for the city, for myself, for you.   65

  I was not sleeping, you are not waking me.
  No, I have been in tears for a long while
  And in my restless thought walked many ways.
  In all my search, I found one helpful course,
  And that I have taken: I have sent Creon,   70
  Son of Menoikeus, brother of the Queen,
  To Delphi, Apollo's place of revelation,
  To learn there, if he can,
  What act or pledge of mine may save the city.
  I have counted the days, and now, this very day,   75
  I am troubled, for he has overstayed his time.
  What is he doing? He has been gone too long.
  Yet whenever he comes back, I should do ill
  To scant whatever hint the god may give.
PRIEST: It is a timely promise. At this instant   80
  They tell me Creon is here.
OEDIPUS: O Lord Apollo!
  May his news be fair as his face is radiant!
PRIEST: It could not be otherwise: he is crowned with bay,
  The chaplet is thick with berries.
OEDIPUS: We shall soon know;
  He is near enough to hear us now.

  (Enter Creon)

                        O Prince: 85
Brother: son of Menoikeus:

What answer do you bring us from the god?
CREON: It is favorable. I can tell you, great afflictions
   Will turn out well, if they are taken well.
OEDIPUS: What was the oracle? These vague words   90
   Leave me still hanging between hope and fear.
CREON: Is it your pleasure to hear me with all these
   Gathered around us? I am prepared to speak,
   But should we not go in?
OEDIPUS: Let them all hear it.
   It is for them I suffer, more than for myself.   95
CREON: Then I will tell you what I heard at Delphi.
   In plain words
   The god commands us to expel from the land of Thebes
   An old defilement that it seems we shelter.
   It is a deathly thing, beyond expiation.   100
   We must not let it feed upon us longer.
OEDIPUS: What defilement? How shall we rid ourselves of it?
CREON: By exile or death, blood for blood. It was
   Murder that brought the plague-wind on the city.
OEDIPUS: Murder of whom? Surely the god has named him?   105
CREON: My lord: long ago Laïos was our king,
   Before you came to govern us.
OEDIPUS: I know;
   I learned of him from others; I never saw him.
CREON: He was murdered; and Apollo commands us now
   To take revenge upon whoever killed him.   110
OEDIPUS: Upon whom? Where are they? Where shall we find a clue
   To solve that crime, after so many years?
CREON: Here in this land, he said.
                  If we make enquiry,
   We may touch things that otherwise escape us.
OEDIPUS: Tell me: Was Laïos murdered in his house,   115
   Or in the fields, or in some foreign country?
CREON: He said he planned to make a pilgrimage.
   He did not come home again.
OEDIPUS: And was there no one,
   No witness, no companion, to tell what happened?
CREON: They were all killed but one, and he got away   120
   So frightened that he could remember one thing only.
OEDIPUS: What was that one thing? One may be the key
   To everything, if we resolve to use it.
CREON: He said that a band of highwaymen attacked them,
   Outnumbered them, and overwhelmed the King.   125
OEDIPUS: Strange, that a highwayman should be so daring—
   Unless some faction here bribed him to do it.
CREON: We thought of that. But after Laïos' death
   New troubles arose and we had no avenger.
OEDIPUS: What troubles could prevent your hunting down the killers?   130

CREON: The riddling Sphinx's song
    Made us deaf to all mysteries but her own.
OEDIPUS: Then once more I must bring what is dark to light.
    It is most fitting that Apollo shows,
    As you do, this compunction for the dead. 135
    You shall see how I stand by you, as I should,
    To avenge the city and the city's god,
    And not as though it were for some distant friend,
    But for my own sake, to be rid of evil.
    Whoever killed King Laïos might—who knows?— 140
    Decide at any moment to kill me as well.
    By avenging the murdered king I protect myself.
    Come, then, my children: leave the altar steps,
    Lift up your olive boughs!
                One of you go
    And summon the people of Kadmos to gather here. 145
    I will do all that I can; you may tell them that.

(Exit a Page)

    So, with the help of God,
    We shall be saved—or else indeed we are lost.
PRIEST: Let us rise, children. It was for this we came,
    And now the King has promised it himself. 150
    Phoibos has sent us an oracle; may he descend
    Himself to save us and drive out the plague.

(Exeunt Oedipus and Creon into the palace by the central door. The Priest and the Suppliants disperse right and left. After a short pause the Chorus enters the orchestra.)

Parodos[7]

Strophe[8] 1

CHORUS: What is God singing in his profound
    Delphi of gold and shadow?
    What oracle for Thebes, the sunwhipped city?
    Fear unjoints me, the roots of my heart tremble.
    Now I remember, O Healer, your power, and wonder; 5
    Will you send doom like a sudden cloud, or weave it
    Like nightfall of the past?
    Speak, speak to us, issue of holy sound:
    Dearest to our expectancy: be tender!

Antistrophe 1

    Let me pray to Athenê, the immortal daughter of Zeus, 10
    And to Artemis[9] her sister
    Who keeps her famous throne in the market ring,
    And to Apollo, bowman at the far butts of heaven—

[7] An entrance song delivered by the chorus.
[8] A song accompanied by a dance right to left. The *antistrophe* accompanies a dance back again.
[9] Goddess of the moon and hunting.

O gods, descend! Like three streams leap against
The fires of our grief, the fires of darkness;   15
Be swift to bring us rest!

As in the old time from the brilliant house
Of air you stepped to save us, come again!

Now our afflictions have no end,
Now all our stricken host lies down   20
And no man fights off death with his mind;

The noble plowland bears no grain,
And groaning mothers can not bear—

See, how our lives like birds take wing,
Like sparks that fly when a fire soars,   25
To the shore of the god of evening.

The plague burns on, it is pitiless,
Though pallid children laden with death
Lie unwept in the stony ways,

And old gray women by every path   30
Flock to the strand about the altars

There to strike their breasts and cry
Worship of Phoibos in wailing prayers:
Be kind, God's golden child!

There are no swords in this attack by fire,   35
No shields, but we are ringed with cries.
Send the besieger plunging from our homes
Into the vast sea-room of the Atlantic
Or into the waves that foam eastward of Thrace—
For the day ravages what the night spares—   40
Destroy our enemy, lord of the thunder!
Let him be riven by lightning from heaven!

Phoibos Apollo, stretch the sun's bowstring,
That golden cord, until it sing for us,
Flashing arrows in heaven!
                              Artemis, Huntress,   45
Race with flaring lights upon our mountains!

O scarlet god, O golden-banded brow,
O Theban Bacchos in a storm of Maenads[10],

(Enter Oedipus, center)

[10] Bacchus, god of wine and revelry, with female attendants.

Whirl upon Death, that all the Undying hate!
Come with blinding cressets, come in joy!   50

Scene I

OEDIPUS: Is this your prayer? It may be answered. Come,
    Listen to me, act as the crisis demands,
    And you shall have relief from all these evils.

Until now I was a stranger to this tale,
As I had been a stranger to the crime.   5
Could I track down the murderer without a clue?
But now, friends,
As one who became a citizen after the murder,
I make this proclamation to all Thebans:
If any man knows by whose hand Laïos, son of Labdakos,   10
Met his death, I direct that man to tell me everything,
No matter what he fears for having so long withheld it.
Let it stand as promised that no further trouble
Will come to him, but he may leave the land in safety.

Moreover: If anyone knows the murderer to be foreign,   15
Let him not keep silent: he shall have his reward from me.
However, if he does conceal it; if any man
Fearing for his friend or for himself disobeys this edict,
Hear what I propose to do:

I solemnly forbid the people of this country,   20
Where power and throne are mine, ever to receive that man
Or speak to him, no matter who he is, or let him
Join in sacrifice, lustration, or in prayer.
I decree that he be driven from every house,
Being, as he is, corruption itself to us: the Delphic   25
Voice of Zeus has pronounced this revelation.
Thus I associate myself with the oracle
And take the side of the murdered king.

As for the criminal, I pray to God—
Whether it be a lurking thief, or one of a number—   30
I pray that that man's life be consumed in evil and wretchedness.
And as for me, this curse applies no less
If it should turn out that the culprit is my guest here,
Sharing my hearth.
                    You have heard the penalty.
I lay it on you now to attend to this   35
For my sake, for Apollo's, for the sick
Sterile city that heaven has abandoned.
Suppose the oracle had given you no command:
Should this defilement go uncleansed for ever?
You should have found the murderer: your king,   40
A noble king, had been destroyed!

Now I,

Having the power that he held before me,
Having his bed, begetting children there
Upon his wife, as he would have, had he lived—
Their son would have been my children's brother,   45
If Laïos had had luck in fatherhood!
(But surely ill luck rushed upon his reign)—
I say I take the son's part, just as though
I were his son, to press the fight for him
And see it won! I'll find the hand that brought   50
Death to Labdakos' and Polydoros' child,
Heir of Kadmos' and Agenor's line.
And as for those who fail me,
May the gods deny them the fruit of the earth,
Fruit of the womb, and may they rot utterly!   55
Let them be wretched as we are wretched, and worse!

For you, for loyal Thebans, and for all
Who find my actions right, I pray the favor
Of justice, and of all the immortal gods.
CHORAGOS[11]: Since I am under oath, my lord, I swear   60
I did not do the murder, I can not name
The murderer. Might not the oracle
That has ordained the search tell where to find him?
OEDIPUS: An honest question. But no man in the world
Can make the gods do more than the gods will.   65
CHORAGOS: There is one last expedient—
OEDIPUS: Tell me what it is.
Though it seem slight, you must not hold it back.
CHORAGOS: A lord clairvoyant to the lord Apollo,
As we all know, is the skilled Teiresias.
One might learn much about this from him, Oedipus.   70
OEDIPUS: I am not wasting time:
Creon spoke of this, and I have sent for him—
Twice, in fact; it is strange that he is not here.
CHORAGOS: The other matter—that old report—seems useless.
OEDIPUS: Tell me. I am interested in all reports.   75
CHORAGOS: The King was said to have been killed by highwaymen.
OEDIPUS: I know. But we have no witnesses to that.
CHORAGOS: If the killer can feel a particle of dread,
Your curse will bring him out of hiding!
OEDIPUS: No.
The man who dared that act will fear no curse.   80

(Enter the blind seer Teiresias, led by a Page)

CHORAGOS: But there is one man who may detect the criminal.
This is Teiresias, this is the holy prophet
In whom, alone of all men, truth was born.

---

[11] Leader of the chorus.

OEDIPUS: Teiresias: seer: student of mysteries,
    Of all that's taught and all that no man tells,   85
    Secrets of Heaven and secrets of the earth:
    Blind though you are, you know the city lies
    Sick with plague; and from this plague, my lord,
    We find that you alone can guard or save us.

    Possibly you did not hear the messengers?   90
    Apollo, when we sent to him,
    Sent us back word that this great pestilence
    Would lift, but only if we established clearly
    The identity of those who murdered Laïos.
    They must be killed or exiled.
                           Can you use   95
    Birdflight or any art of divination
    To purify yourself, and Thebes, and me
    From this contagion? We are in your hands.
    There is no fairer duty
    Than that of helping others in distress.   100
TEIRESIAS: How dreadful knowledge of the truth can be
    When there's no help in truth! I knew this well,
    But did not act on it: else I should not have come.
OEDIPUS: What is troubling you? Why are your eyes so cold?
TEIRESIAS: Let me go home. Bear your own fate, and I'll   105
    Bear mine. It is better so: trust what I say.
OEDIPUS: What you say is ungracious and unhelpful
    To your native country. Do not refuse to speak.
TEIRESIAS: When it comes to speech, your own is neither temperate
    Nor opportune. I wish to be more prudent.   110
OEDIPUS: In God's name, we all beg you—
TEIRESIAS: You are all ignorant.
    No; I will never tell you what I know.
    Now it is my misery; then, it would be yours.
OEDIPUS: What! You do know something, and will not tell us?
    You would betray us all and wreck the State?   115
TEIRESIAS: I do not intend to torture myself, or you.
    Why persist in asking? You will not persuade me.
OEDIPUS: What a wicked old man you are! You'd try a stone's
    Patience! Out with it! Have you no feeling at all?
TEIRESIAS: You call me unfeeling. If you could only see   120
    The nature of your own feelings . . .
OEDIPUS: Why,
    Who would not feel as I do? Who could endure
    Your arrogance toward the city?
TEIRESIAS: What does it matter!
    Whether I speak or not, it is bound to come.
OEDIPUS: Then, if "it" is bound to come, you are bound to tell me.   125
TEIRESIAS: No, I will not go on. Rage as you please.
OEDIPUS: Rage? Why not!

                    And I'll tell you what I think:
        You planned it, you had it done, you all but
        Killed him with your own hands: if you had eyes,
        I'd say the crime was yours, and yours alone.   130
TEIRESIAS: So? I charge you, then,
        Abide by the proclamation you have made:
        From this day forth
        Never speak again to these men or to me;
        You yourself are the pollution of this country.   135
OEDIPUS: You dare say that! Can you possibly think you have
        Some way of going free, after such insolence?
TEIRESIAS: I have gone free. It is the truth sustains me.
OEDIPUS: Who taught you shamelessness? It was not your craft.
TEIRESIAS: You did. You made me speak. I did not want to.   140
OEDIPUS: Speak what? Let me hear it again more clearly.
TEIRESIAS: Was it not clear before? Are you tempting me?
OEDIPUS: I did not understand it. Say it again.
TEIRESIAS: I say that you are the murderer whom you seek.
OEDIPUS: Now twice you have spat out infamy. You'll pay for it!   145
TEIRESIAS: Would you care for more? Do you wish to be really angry?
OEDIPUS: Say what you will. Whatever you say is worthless.
TEIRESIAS: I say you live in hideous shame with those
        Most dear to you. You can not see the evil.
OEDIPUS: It seems you can go on mouthing like this for ever.   150
TEIRESIAS: I can, if there is power in truth.
OEDIPUS: There is:
        But not for you, not for you,
        You sightless, witless, senseless, mad old man!
TEIRESIAS: You are the madman. There is no one here
        Who will not curse you soon, as you curse me.   155
OEDIPUS: You child of endless night! You can not hurt me
        Or any other man who sees the sun.
TEIRESIAS: True: it is not from me your fate will come.
        That lies within Apollo's competence,
        As it is his concern.
OEDIPUS: Tell me: 160
        Are you speaking for Creon, or for yourself?
TEIRESIAS: Creon is no threat. You weave your own doom.
OEDIPUS: Wealth, power, craft of statesmanship!
        Kingly position, everywhere admired!
        What savage envy is stored up against these,   165
        If Creon, whom I trusted, Creon my friend,
        For this great office which the city once
        Put in my hands unsought—if for this power
        Creon desires in secret to destroy me!

        He has brought this decrepit fortune-teller, this   170
        Collector of dirty pennies, this prophet fraud—
        Why, he is no more clairvoyant than I am!

Tell us:
Has your mystic mummery ever approached the truth?
When that hellcat the Sphinx was performing here,
What help were you to these people?   175
Her magic was not for the first man who came along:
It demanded a real exorcist. Your birds—
What good were they? or the gods, for the matter of that?
But I came by,
Oedipus, the simple man, who knows nothing—   180
I thought it out for myself, no birds helped me!
And this is the man you think you can destroy,
That you may be close to Creon when he's king!
Well, you and your friend Creon, it seems to me,
Will suffer most. If you were not an old man,   185
You would have paid already for your plot.
CHORAGOS: We can not see that his words or yours
Have been spoken except in anger, Oedipus,
And of anger we have no need. How can God's will
Be accomplished best? That is what most concerns us.   190
TEIRESIAS: You are a king. But where argument's concerned
I am your man, as much a king as you.
I am not your servant, but Apollo's.
I have no need of Creon to speak for me.

Listen to me. You mock my blindness, do you?   195
But I say that you, with both your eyes, are blind:
You can not see the wretchedness of your life,
Nor in whose house you live, no, nor with whom.
Who are your father and mother? Can you tell me?
You do not even know the blind wrongs   200
That you have done them, on earth and in the world below.
But the double lash of your parents' curse will whip you
Out of this land some day, with only night
Upon your precious eyes.
Your cries then—where will they not be heard?   205
What fastness of Kithairon will not echo them?
And that bridal-descant of yours—you'll know it then,
The song they sang when you came here to Thebes
And found your misguided berthing.
All this, and more, that you can not guess at now,   210
Will bring you to yourself among your children.

Be angry, then. Curse Creon. Curse my words.
I tell you, no man that walks upon the earth
Shall be rooted out more horribly than you.
OEDIPUS: Am I to bear this from him?—Damnation   215
Take you! Out of this place! Out of my sight!
TEIRESIAS: I would not have come at all if you had not asked me.
OEDIPUS: Could I have told that you'd talk nonsense, that

You'd come here to make a fool of yourself, and of me?
TEIRESIAS: A fool? Your parents thought me sane enough.   220
OEDIPUS: My parents again!—Wait: who were my parents?
TEIRESIAS: This day will give you a father, and break your heart.
OEDIPUS: Your infantile riddles! Your damned abracadabra!
TEIRESIAS: You were a great man once at solving riddles.
OEDIPUS: Mock me with that if you like; you will find it true.   225
TEIRESIAS: It was true enough. It brought about your ruin.
OEDIPUS: But if it saved this town?
TEIRESIAS (to the Page):   Boy, give me your hand.
OEDIPUS: Yes, boy; lead him away.
                                   —While you are here
    We can do nothing. Go; leave us in peace.
TEIRESIAS: I will go when I have said what I have to say.   230
    How can you hurt me? And I tell you again:
    The man you have been looking for all this time,
    The damned man, the murderer of Laïos,
    That man is in Thebes. To your mind he is foreignborn,
    But it will soon be shown that he is a Theban,   235
    A revelation that will fail to please.
                                   A blind man,
    Who has his eyes now; a penniless man, who is rich now;
    And he will go tapping the strange earth with his staff;
    To the children with whom he lives now he will be
    Brother and father—the very same; to her   240
    Who bore him, son and husband—the very same
    Who came to his father's bed, wet with his father's blood.

    Enough. Go think that over.
    If later you find error in what I have said,
    You may say that I have no skill in prophecy.   245

(Exit Teiresias, led by his Page. Oedipus goes into the palace.)

Ode[12] I

CHORUS: The Delphic stone of prophecies
    Remembers ancient regicide
    And a still bloody hand.
    That killer's hour of flight has come.
    He must be stronger than riderless   5
    Coursers of untiring wind,
    For the son of Zeus[13] armed with his father's thunder
    Leaps in lightning after him;
    And the Furies[14] follow him, the sad Furies.

[12] A choral song.
[13] Apollo was a son of Zeus.
[14] Avenging spirits.

Antistrophe 1

Holy Parnassos' peak of snow   10
Flashes and blinds that secret man,
That all shall hunt him down:
Though he may roam the forest shade
Like a bull gone wild from pasture
To rage through glooms of stone.   15
Doom comes down on him; flight will not avail him;
For the world's heart calls him desolate,
And the immortal Furies follow, for ever follow.

Strophe 2

But now a wilder thing is heard
From the old man skilled at hearing Fate in the wingbeat of a bird.   20
Bewildered as a blown bird, my soul hovers and can not find
Foothold in this debate, or any reason or rest of mind.
But no man ever brought—none can bring
Proof of strife between Thebes' royal house,
Labdakos' line, and the son of Polybos,[15]   25
And never until now has any man brought word
Of Laïos dark death staining Oedipus the King.

Antistrophe 2

Divine Zeus and Apollo hold
Perfect intelligence alone of all tales ever told;
And well though this diviner works, he works in his own night;   30
No man can judge that rough unknown or trust in second sight,
For wisdom changes hands among the wise.
Shall I believe my great lord criminal
At a raging word that a blind old man let fall?
I saw him, when the carrion woman faced him of old,   35
Prove his heroic mind! These evil words are lies.

Scene II

CREON: Men of Thebes:
    I am told that heavy accusations
    Have been brought against me by King Oedipus.

    I am not the kind of man to bear this tamely.

    If in these present difficulties   5
    He holds me accountable for any harm to him
    Through anything I have said or done—why, then,
    I do not value life in this dishonor.
    It is not as though this rumor touched upon
    Some private indiscretion. The matter is grave.   10
    The fact is that I am being called disloyal
    To the State, to my fellow citizens, to my friends.

---

[15] Oedipus is at this point thought to be a son of Polybos, who had adopted him as a baby. His true
father, Laïos, was of "Labdakos' line."

CHORAGOS: He may have spoken in anger, not from his mind.
CREON: But did you not hear him say I was the one
    Who seduced the old prophet into lying?   15
CHORAGOS: The thing was said; I do not know how seriously.
CREON: But you were watching him! Were his eyes steady?
    Did he look like a man in his right mind?
CHORAGOS: I do not know.
    I can not judge the behavior of great men.
    But here is the King himself.

(Enter Oedipus)

OEDIPUS: So you dared come back.   20
    Why? How brazen of you to come to my house,
    You murderer!
                 Do you think I do not know
    That you plotted to kill me, plotted to steal my throne?
    Tell me, in God's name: am I coward, a fool,
    That you should dream you could accomplish this?   25
    A fool who could not see your slippery game?
    A coward, not to fight back when I saw it?
    You are the fool, Creon, are you not? hoping
    Without support or friends to get a throne?
    Thrones may be won or bought: you could do neither.   30
CREON: Now listen to me. You have talked; let me talk, too.
    You can not judge unless you know the facts.
OEDIPUS: You speak well: there is one fact; but I find it hard
    To learn from the deadliest enemy I have.
CREON: That above all I must dispute with you.   35
OEDIPUS: That above all I will not hear you deny.
CREON: If you think there is anything good in being stubborn
    Against all reason, then I say you are wrong.
OEDIPUS: If you think a man can sin against his own kind
    And not be punished for it, I say you are mad.   40
CREON: I agree. But tell me: what have I done to you?
OEDIPUS: You advised me to send for that wizard, did you not?
CREON: I did. I should do it again.
OEDIPUS: Very well. Now tell me:
    How long has it been since Laïos—
CREON: What of Laïos?
OEDIPUS: Since he vanished in that onset by the road?   45
CREON: It was long ago, a long time.
OEDIPUS: And this prophet,
    Was he practicing here then?
CREON: He was; and with honor, as now.
OEDIPUS: Did he speak of me at that time?
CREON: He never did;
    At least, not when I was present.
OEDIPUS: But . . . the enquiry?
    I suppose you held one?

CREON: We did, but we learned nothing.   50
OEDIPUS: Why did the prophet not speak against me then?
CREON: I do not know; and I am the kind of man
  Who holds his tongue when he has no facts to go on.
OEDIPUS: There's one fact that you know, and you could tell it.
CREON: What fact is that? If I know it, you shall have it.   55
OEDIPUS: If he were not involved with you, he could not say
  That it was I who murdered Laïos.
CREON: If he says that, you are the one that knows it!—
  But now it is my turn to question you.
OEDIPUS: Put your questions. I am no murderer.   60
CREON: First then: You married my sister?
OEDIPUS: I married your sister.
CREON: And you rule the kingdom equally with her?
OEDIPUS: Everything that she wants she has from me.
CREON: And I am the third, equal to both of you?
OEDIPUS: That is why I call you a bad friend.   65
CREON: No. Reason it out, as I have done.
  Think of this first. Would any sane man prefer
  Power, with all a king's anxieties,
  To that same power and the grace of sleep?
  Certainly not I.   70
  I have never longed for the king's power—only his rights.
  Would any wise man differ from me in this?
  As matters stand, I have my way in everything
  With your consent, and no responsibilities.
  If I were king, I should be a slave to policy.   75

  How could I desire a scepter more
  Than what is now mine—untroubled influence?
  No, I have not gone mad; I need no honors,
  Except those with the perquisites I have now.
  I am welcome everywhere; every man salutes me,   80
  And those who want your favor seek my ear,
  Since I know how to manage what they ask.
  Should I exchange this ease for that anxiety?
  Besides, no sober mind is treasonable.
  I hate anarchy   85
  And never would deal with any man who likes it.

  Test what I have said. Go to the priestess
  At Delphi, ask if I quoted her correctly.
  And as for this other thing: if I am found
  Guilty of treason with Teiresias,   90
  Then sentence me to death! You have my word
  It is a sentence I should cast my vote for—
  But not without evidence!
                        You do wrong
  When you take good men for bad, bad men for good.
  A true friend thrown aside—why, life itself   95

Is not more precious!
          In time you will know this well:
For time, and time alone, will show the just man,
Though scoundrels are discovered in a day.
CHORAGOS: This is well said, and a prudent man would ponder it.
    Judgments too quickly formed are dangerous.   100
OEDIPUS: But is he not quick in his duplicity?
    And shall I not be quick to parry him?
    Would you have me stand still, hold my peace, and let
    This man win everything, through my inaction?
CREON: And you want—what is it, then? To banish me?   105
OEDIPUS: No, not exile. It is your death I want,
    So that all the world may see what treason means.
CREON: You will persist, then? You will not believe me?
OEDIPUS: How can I believe you?
CREON: Then you are a fool.
OEDIPUS: To save myself?
CREON: In justice, think of me.   110
OEDIPUS: You are evil incarnate.
CREON: But suppose that you are wrong?
OEDIPUS: Still I must rule.
CREON: But not if you rule badly.
OEDIPUS: O city, city!
CREON: It is my city, too!
CHORAGOS: Now, my lords, be still. I see the Queen,
    Iocastê, coming from her palace chambers;   115
    And it is time she came, for the sake of you both.
    This dreadful quarrel can be resolved through her.

    (Enter Iocastê)

IOCASTÊ: Poor foolish men, what wicked din is this?
    With Thebes sick to death, is it not shameful
    That you should rake some private quarrel up?   120
    (To Oedipus) Come into the house.
                    —And you, Creon, go now:
    Let us have no more of this tumult over nothing.
CREON: Nothing? No, sister: what your husband plans for me
    Is one of two great evils: exile or death.
OEDIPUS: He is right.
               Why, woman, I have caught him squarely   125
    Plotting against my life.
CREON: No! Let me die
    Accurst if ever I have wished you harm!
IOCASTÊ: Ah, believe it, Oedipus!
    In the name of the gods, respect this oath of his
    For my sake, for the sake of these people here!   130

                                 Strophe 1
CHORAGOS: Open your mind to her, my lord. Be ruled by her, I beg you!

OEDIPUS: What would you have me do?
CHORAGOS: Respect Creon's word. He has never spoken like a fool,
   And now he has sworn an oath.
OEDIPUS: You know what you ask?
CHORAGOS: I do.
OEDIPUS: Speak on, then.
CHORAGOS: A friend so sworn should not be baited so,   135
   In blind malice, and without final proof.
OEDIPUS: You are aware, I hope, that what you say
   Means death for me, or exile at the least.

                                     Strophe 2

CHORAGOS: No, I swear by Helios, first in Heaven!
   May I die friendless and accurst,   140
   The worst of deaths, if ever I meant that!
   It is the withering fields
   That hurt my sick heart;
   Must we bear all these ills,
   And now your bad blood as well?   145
OEDIPUS: Then let him go. And let me die, if I must,
   Or be driven by him in shame from the land of Thebes.
   It is your unhappiness, and not his talk,
   That touches me.
               As for him—
   Wherever he is, I will hate him as long as I live.   150
CREON: Ugly in yielding, as you were ugly in rage!
   Natures like yours chiefly torment themselves.
OEDIPUS: Can you not go? Can you not leave me?
CREON: I can.
   You do not know me; but the city knows me,
   And in its eyes I am just, if not in yours.   155

(Exit Creon)

                                 Antistrophe 1

CHORAGOS: Lady Iocastê, did you not ask the King to go to his chambers?
IOCASTÊ: First tell me what has happened.
CHORAGOS: There was suspicion without evidence; yet it rankled
   As even false charges will.
IOCASTÊ: On both sides?
CHORAGOS: On both.
IOCASTÊ: But what was said?
CHORAGOS: Oh let it rest, let it be done with!   160
   Have we not suffered enough?
OEDIPUS: You see to what your decency has brought you:
   You have made difficulties where my heart saw none.

                                   Antistrophe 2

CHORAGOS: Oedipus, it is not once only I have told you—
   You must know I should count myself unwise   165

To the point of madness, should I now forsake you—
You, under whose hand,
In the storm of another time,
Our dear land sailed out free.
But now stand fast at the helm!   170
IOCASTÊ: In God's name, Oedipus, inform your wife as well:
    Why are you so set in this hard anger?
OEDIPUS: I will tell you, for none of these men deserves
    My confidence as you do. It is Creon's work,
    His treachery, his plotting against me.   175
IOCASTÊ: Go on, if you can make this clear to me.
OEDIPUS: He charges me with the murder of Laïos.
IOCASTÊ: Has he some knowledge? Or does he speak from hearsay?
OEDIPUS: He would not commit himself to such a charge,
    But he has brought in that damnable soothsayer   180
    To tell his story.
IOCASTÊ: Set your mind at rest.
    If it is a question of soothsayers, I tell you
    That you will find no man whose craft gives knowledge
    Of the unknowable.
                        Here is my proof:

An oracle was reported to Laïos once   185
(I will not say from Phoibos himself, but from
His appointed ministers, at any rate)
That his doom would be death at the hands of his own son—
His son, born of his flesh and of mine!

Now, you remember the story: Laïos was killed   190
By marauding strangers where three highways meet;
But his child had not been three days in this world
Before the King had pierced the baby's ankles
And left him to die on a lonely mountainside.

Thus, Apollo never caused that child   195
To kill his father, and it was not Laïos' fate
To die at the hands of his son, as he had feared.
This is what prophets and prophecies are worth!
Have no dread of them.
                        It is God himself
Who can show us what he wills, in his own way.   200
OEDIPUS: How strange a shadowy memory crossed my mind,
    Just now while you were speaking; it chilled my heart.
IOCASTÊ: What do you mean? What memory do you speak of?
OEDIPUS: If I understand you, Laïos was killed
    At a place where three roads meet.
IOCASTÊ: So it was said;   205
    We have no later story.
OEDIPUS: Where did it happen?
IOCASTÊ: Phokis, it is called: at a place where the Theban Way
    Divides into the roads toward Delphi and Daulia.

OEDIPUS: When?

IOCASTÊ: We had the news not long before you came
  And proved the right to your succession here.   210

OEDIPUS: Ah, what net has God been weaving for me?

IOCASTÊ: Oedipus! Why does this trouble you?

OEDIPUS: Do not ask me yet.
  First, tell me how Laïos looked, and tell me
  How old he was.

IOCASTÊ: He was tall, his hair just touched
  With white; his form was not unlike your own.   215

OEDIPUS: I think that I myself may be accurst
  By my own ignorant edict.

IOCASTÊ: You speak strangely.
  It makes me tremble to look at you, my King.

OEDIPUS: I am not sure that the blind man can not see.
  But I should know better if you were to tell me—   220

IOCASTÊ: Anything—though I dread to hear you ask it.

OEDIPUS: Was the King lightly escorted, or did he ride
  With a large company, as a ruler should?

IOCASTÊ: There were five men with him in all: one was a herald;
  And a single chariot, which he was driving.   225

OEDIPUS: Alas, that makes it plain enough!

                      But who—
  Who told you how it happened?

IOCASTÊ: A household servant,
  The only one to escape.

OEDIPUS: And is he still
  A servant of ours?

IOCASTÊ: No; for when he came back at last
  And found you enthroned in the place of the dead king,   230
  He came to me, touched my hand with his, and begged
  That I would send him away to the frontier district
  Where only the shepherds go—
  As far away from the city as I could send him.
  I granted his prayer; for although the man was a slave,   235
  He had earned more than this favor at my hands.

OEDIPUS: Can he be called back quickly?

IOCASTÊ: Easily.
  But why?

OEDIPUS: I have taken too much upon myself
  Without enquiry; therefore I wish to consult him.

IOCASTÊ: Then he shall come.

                  But am I not one also   240
  To whom you might confide these fears of yours?

OEDIPUS: That is your right; it will not be denied you,
  Now least of all; for I have reached a pitch
  Of wild foreboding. Is there anyone
  To whom I should sooner speak?   245
  Polybos of Corinth is my father.

My mother is a Dorian: Meropê.
I grew up chief among the men of Corinth
Until a strange thing happened—
Not worth my passion, it may be, but strange.   250
At a feast, a drunken man maundering in his cups
Cries out that I am not my father's son!

I contained myself that night, though I felt anger
And a sinking heart. The next day I visited
My father and mother, and questioned them. They stormed,   255
Calling it all the slanderous rant of a fool;
And this relieved me. Yet the suspicion
Remained always aching in my mind;
I knew there was talk; I could not rest;
And finally, saying nothing to my parents,   260
I went to the shrine at Delphi.
The god dismissed my question without reply;
He spoke of other things.
                        Some were clear,
Full of wretchedness, dreadful, unbearable:
As, that I should lie with my own mother, breed   265
Children from whom all men would turn their eyes;
And that I should be my father's murderer.

I heard all this, and fled. And from that day
Corinth to me was only in the stars
Descending in that quarter of the sky,   270
As I wandered farther and farther on my way
To a land where I should never see the evil
Sung by the oracle. And I came to this country
Where, so you say, King Laïos was killed.

I will tell you all that happened there, my lady.   275

There were three highways
Coming together at a place I passed;
And there a herald came towards me, and a chariot
Drawn by horses, with a man such as you describe
Seated in it. The groom leading the horses   280
Forced me off the road at his lord's command;
But as this charioteer lurched over towards me
I struck him in my rage. The old man saw me
And brought his double goad down upon my head
As I came abreast.
                        He was paid back, and more!   285
Swinging my club in this right hand I knocked him
Out of his car, and he rolled on the ground.
                                        I killed him.

I killed them all.
Now if that stranger and Laïos were—kin,

Where is a man more miserable than I?   290
More hated by the gods? Citizen and alien alike
Must never shelter me or speak to me—
I must be shunned by all.
                And I myself
Pronounced this malediction upon myself!

Think of it: I have touched you with these hands,   295
These hands that killed your husband. What defilement!

Am I all evil, then? It must be so,
Since I must flee from Thebes, yet never again
See my own countrymen, my own country,
For fear of joining my mother in marriage   300
And killing Polybos, my father.
                Ah,
If I was created so, born to this fate,
Who could deny the savagery of God?

O holy majesty of heavenly powers!
May I never see that day! Never!   305
Rather let me vanish from the race of men
Than know the abomination destined me!
CHORAGOS: We too, my lord, have felt dismay at this.
    But there is hope: you have yet to hear the shepherd.
OEDIPUS: Indeed, I fear no other hope is left me.   310
IOCASTÊ: What do you hope from him when he comes?
OEDIPUS: This much:
    If his account of the murder tallies with yours,
    Then I am cleared.
IOCASTÊ: What was it that I said
    Of such importance?
OEDIPUS: Why "marauders," you said,
    Killed the King, according to this man's story.   315
    If he maintains that still, if there were several,
    Clearly the guilt is not mine: I was alone.
    But if he says one man, singlehanded, did it,
    Then the evidence all points to me.
IOCASTÊ: You may be sure that he said there were several;   320
    And can he call back that story now? He can not.
    The whole city heard it as plainly as I.
    But suppose he alters some detail of it:
    He can not ever show that Laïos' death
    Fulfilled the oracle: for Apollo said   325
    My child was doomed to kill him; and my child—
    Poor baby!—it was my child that died first.

No. From now on, where oracles are concerned,
    I would not waste a second thought on any.
OEDIPUS: You may be right.
                But come: let someone go   330

For the shepherd at once. This matter must be settled.
IOCASTÊ: I will send for him.
    I would not wish to cross you in anything,
    And surely not in this.—Let us go in.

(Exeunt into the palace)

Ode II

Strophe 1

CHORUS: Let me be reverent in the ways of right,
    Lowly the paths I journey on;
    Let all my words and actions keep
    The laws of the pure universe
    From highest Heaven handed down.   5
    For Heaven is their bright nurse,
    Those generations of the realms of light;
    Ah, never of mortal kind were they begot,
    Nor are they slaves of memory, lost in sleep:
    Their Father is greater than Time, and ages not.   10

Antistrophe 1

    The tyrant is a child of Pride
    Who drinks from his great sickening cup
    Recklessness and vanity,
    Until from his high crest headlong
    He plummets to the dust of hope.   15
    That strong man is not strong.
    But let no fair ambition be denied;
    May God protect the wrestler for the State
    In government, in comely policy,
    Who will fear God, and on His ordinance wait.   20

Strophe 2

    Haughtiness and the high hand of disdain
    Tempt and outrage God's holy law;
    And any mortal who dares hold
    No immortal Power in awe
    Will be caught up in a net of pain: 25
    The price for which his levity is sold.
    Let each man take due earnings, then,
    And keep his hands from holy things,
    And from blasphemy stand apart—
    Else the crackling blast of heaven   30
    Blows on his head, and on his desperate heart;
    Though fools will honor impious men,
    In their cities no tragic poet sings.

Antistrophe 2

    Shall we lose faith in Delphi's obscurities,
    We who have heard the world's core   35

Discredited, and the sacred wood
Of Zeus at Elis praised no more?
The deeds and the strange prophecies
Must make a pattern yet to be understood.
Zeus, if indeed you are lord of all,   40
Throned in light over night and day,
Mirror this in your endless mind:
Our masters call the oracle
Words on the wind, and the Delphic vision blind!
Their hearts no longer know Apollo,   45
And reverence for the gods has died away.

Scene III

(Enter Iocastê)

IOCASTÊ: Princes of Thebes, it has occurred to me
To visit the altars of the gods, bearing
These branches as a suppliant, and this incense.
Our King is not himself: his noble soul
Is overwrought with fantasies of dread,   5
Else he would consider
The new prophecies in the light of the old.
He will listen to any voice that speaks disaster,
And my advice goes for nothing.

(She approaches the altar, right)

                                        To you, then, Apollo,
Lycean lord, since you are nearest, I turn in prayer.   10
Receive these offerings, and grant us deliverance
From defilement. Our hearts are heavy with fear
When we see our leader distracted, as helpless sailors
Are terrified by the confusion of their helmsman.

(Enter Messenger)

MESSENGER: Friends, no doubt you can direct me: 15
Where shall I find the house of Oedipus,
Or, better still, where is the King himself?
CHORAGOS: It is this very place, stranger; he is inside.
This is his wife and mother of his children.
MESSENGER: I wish her happiness in a happy house,   20
Blest in all the fulfillment of her marriage.
IOCASTÊ: I wish as much for you: your courtesy
Deserves a like good fortune. But now, tell me:
Why have you come? What have you to say to us?
MESSENGER: Good news, my lady, for your house and your husband. 25
IOCASTÊ: What news? Who sent you here?
MESSENGER: I am from Corinth.
The news I bring ought to mean joy for you,
Though it may be you will find some grief in it.

IOCASTÊ: What is it? How can it touch us in both ways?
MESSENGER: The people of Corinth, they say,   30
   Intend to call Oedipus to be their king.
IOCASTÊ: But old Polybos—is he not reigning still?
MESSENGER: No. Death holds him in his sepulchre.
IOCASTÊ: What are you saying? Polybos is dead?
MESSENGER: If I am not telling the truth, may I die myself.   35
IOCASTÊ (to a Maidservant): Go in, go quickly; tell this to your master.

   O riddlers of God's will, where are you now!
   This was the man whom Oedipus, long ago,
   Feared so, fled so, in dread of destroying him—
   But it was another fate by which he died.   40

   (Enter Oedipus, center)

OEDIPUS: Dearest Iocastê, why have you sent for me?
IOCASTÊ: Listen to what this man says, and then tell me
   What has become of the solemn prophecies.
OEDIPUS: Who is this man? What is his news for me?
IOCASTÊ: He has come from Corinth to announce your father's death!   45
OEDIPUS: Is it true, stranger? Tell me in your own words.
MESSENGER: I can not say it more clearly: the King is dead.
OEDIPUS: Was it by treason? Or by an attack of illness?
MESSENGER: A little thing brings old men to their rest.
OEDIPUS: It was sickness, then?
MESSENGER: Yes, and his many years.   50
OEDIPUS: Ah!
   Why should a man respect the Pythian hearth,[16] or
   Give heed to the birds that jangle above his head?
   They prophesied that I should kill Polybos,
   Kill my own father; but he is dead and buried,   55
   And I am here—I never touched him, never,
   Unless he died of grief for my departure,
   And thus, in a sense, through me. No. Polybos
   Has packed the oracles off with him underground.
   They are empty words.
IOCASTÊ: Had I not told you so?   60
OEDIPUS: You had; it was my faint heart that betrayed me.
IOCASTÊ: From now on never think of those things again.
OEDIPUS: And yet—must I not fear my mother's bed?
IOCASTÊ: Why should anyone in this world be afraid,
   Since Fate rules us and nothing can be foreseen?   65
   A man should live only for the present day.

   Have no more fear of sleeping with your mother:
   How many men, in dreams, have lain with their mothers!
   No reasonable man is troubled by such things.

[16]The shrine at Delphi, where a priestess spoke with inspiration from the god Apollo.

OEDIPUS: That is true, only—   70
   If only my mother were not still alive!
   But she is alive. I can not help my dread.
IOCASTÊ: Yet this news of your father's death is wonderful.
OEDIPUS: Wonderful. But I fear the living woman.
MESSENGER: Tell me, who is this woman that you fear?   75
OEDIPUS: It is Meropê, man; the wife of King Polybos.
MESSENGER: Meropê? Why should you be afraid of her?
OEDIPUS: An oracle of the gods, a dreadful saying.
MESSENGER: Can you tell me about it or are you sworn to silence?
OEDIPUS: I can tell you, and I will.   80
   Apollo said through his prophet that I was the man
   Who should marry his own mother, shed his father's blood
   With his own hands. And so, for all these years
   I have kept clear of Corinth, and no harm has come—
   Though it would have been sweet to see my parents again.   85
MESSENGER: And is this the fear that drove you out of Corinth?
OEDIPUS: Would you have me kill my father?
MESSENGER: As for that
   You must be reassured by the news I gave you.
OEDIPUS: If you could reassure me, I would reward you.
MESSENGER: I had that in mind, I will confess: I thought   90
   I could count on you when you returned to Corinth.
OEDIPUS: No: I will never go near my parents again.
MESSENGER: Ah, son, you still do not know what you are doing—
OEDIPUS: What do you mean? In the name of God tell me!
MESSENGER: —If these are your reasons for not going home.   95
OEDIPUS: I tell you, I fear the oracle may come true.
MESSENGER: And guilt may come upon you through your parents?
OEDIPUS: That is the dread that is always in my heart.
MESSENGER: Can you not see that all your fears are groundless?
OEDIPUS: How can you say that? They are my parents, surely?   100
MESSENGER: Polybos was not your father.
OEDIPUS: Not my father?
MESSENGER: No more your father than the man speaking to you.
OEDIPUS: But you are nothing to me!
MESSENGER: Neither was he.
OEDIPUS: Then why did he call me son?
MESSENGER: I will tell you:
   Long ago he had you from my hands, as a gift.   105
OEDIPUS: Then how could he love me so, if I was not his?
MESSENGER: He had no children, and his heart turned to you.
OEDIPUS: What of you? Did you buy me? Did you find me by chance?
MESSENGER: I came upon you in the crooked pass of Kithairon.
OEDIPUS: And what were you doing there?
MESSENGER: Tending my flocks.   110
OEDIPUS: A wandering shepherd?
MESSENGER: But your savior, son, that day.

OEDIPUS: From what did you save me?
MESSENGER: Your ankles should tell you that.
OEDIPUS: Ah, stranger, why do you speak of that childhood pain?
MESSENGER: I cut the bonds that tied your ankles together.
OEDIPUS: I have had the mark as long as I can remember.   115
MESSENGER: That was why you were given the name you bear.
OEDIPUS: God! Was it my father or my mother who did it?
     Tell me!
MESSENGER: I do not know. The man who gave you to me
     Can tell you better than I.   120
OEDIPUS: It was not you that found me, but another?
MESSENGER: It was another shepherd gave you to me.
OEDIPUS: Who was he? Can you tell me who he was?
MESSENGER: I think he was said to be one of Laïos' people.
OEDIPUS: You mean the Laïos who was king here years ago?   125
MESSENGER: Yes; King Laïos; and the man was one of his herdsmen.
OEDIPUS: Is he still alive? Can I see him?
MESSENGER: These men here
     Know best about such things.
OEDIPUS: Does anyone here
     Know this shepherd that he is talking about?
     Have you seen him in the fields, or in the town?   130
     If you have, tell me. It is time things were made plain.
CHORAGOS: I think the man he means is that same shepherd
     You have already asked to see. Iocastê perhaps
     Could tell you something.
OEDIPUS: Do you know anything
     About him, Lady? Is he the man we have summoned?   135
     Is that the man this shepherd means?
IOCASTÊ: Why think of him?
     Forget this herdsman. Forget it all.
     This talk is a waste of time.
OEDIPUS: How can you say that,
     When the clues to my true birth are in my hands?
IOCASTÊ: For God's love, let us have no more questioning!   140
     Is your life nothing to you?
     My own is pain enough for me to bear.
OEDIPUS: You need not worry. Suppose my mother a slave,
     And born of slaves: no baseness can touch you.
IOCASTÊ: Listen to me, I beg you: do not do this thing!   145
OEDIPUS: I will not listen; the truth must be made known.
IOCASTÊ: Everything that I say is for your own good!
OEDIPUS: My own good
     Snaps my patience, then; I want none of it.
IOCASTÊ: You are fatally wrong! May you never learn who you are!
OEDIPUS: Go, one of you, and bring the shepherd here.   150
     Let us leave this woman to brag of her royal name.

IOCASTÊ: Ah, miserable!
That is the only word I have for you now.
That is the only word I can ever have.

(Exit into the palace)

CHORAGOS: Why has she left us, Oedipus? Why has she gone   155
In such a passion of sorrow? I fear this silence:
Something dreadful may come of it.
OEDIPUS: Let it come!
However base my birth, I must know about it.
The Queen, like a woman, is perhaps ashamed
To think of my low origin. But I   160
Am a child of Luck; I can not be dishonored.
Luck is my mother; the passing months, my brothers,
Have seen me rich and poor.
                              If this is so,
How could I wish that I were someone else?
How could I not be glad to know my birth?   165

Ode III

Strophe

CHORUS: If ever the coming time were known
To my heart's pondering,
Kithairon, now by Heaven I see the torches
At the festival of the next full moon,
And see the dance, and hear the choir sing   5
A grace to your gentle shade:
Mountain where Oedipus was found,
O mountain guard of a noble race!
May the god who heals us lend his aid,
And let that glory come to pass   10
For our king's cradling-ground.

Antistrophe

Of the nymphs that flower beyond the years,
Who bore you, royal child,
To Pan of the hills or the timberline Apollo,
Cold in delight where the upland clears,   15
Or Hermês for whom Kyllenê's[17] heights are piled?
Or flushed as evening cloud,
Great Dionysos, roamer of mountains,
He—was it he who found you there,

---

[17] The mountain birthplace of Hermês, messenger of the gods.

And caught you up in his own proud   20
Arms from the sweet god-ravisher
Who laughed by the Muses' fountains?

Scene IV

OEDIPUS: Sirs: though I do not know the man,
    I think I see him coming, this shepherd we want:
    He is old, like our friend here, and the men
    Bringing him seem to be servants of my house.
    But you can tell, if you have ever seen him.   5

(Enter Shepherd escorted by servants)

CHORAGOS: I know him, he was Laïos' man. You can trust him.
OEDIPUS: Tell me first, you from Corinth: is this the shepherd
    We were discussing?
MESSENGER: This is the very man.
OEDIPUS *(to Shepherd)*: Come here. No, look at me. You must answer
    Everything I ask.—You belonged to Laïos?   10
SHEPHERD: Yes: born his slave, brought up in his house.
OEDIPUS: Tell me: what kind of work did you do for him?
SHEPHERD: I was a shepherd of his, most of my life.
OEDIPUS: Where mainly did you go for pasturage?
SHEPHERD: Sometimes Kithairon, sometimes the hills near-by.   15
OEDIPUS: Do you remember ever seeing this man out there?
SHEPHERD: What would he be doing there? This man?
OEDIPUS: This man standing here. Have you ever seen him before?
SHEPHERD: No. At least, not to my recollection.
MESSENGER: And that is not strange, my lord. But I'll refresh   20
    His memory: he must remember when we two
    Spent three whole seasons together, March to September,
    On Kithairon or thereabouts. He had two flocks;
    I had one. Each autumn I'd drive mine home
    And he would go back with his to Laïos' sheepfold.—   25
    Is this not true, just as I have described it?
SHEPHERD: True, yes; but it was all so long ago.
MESSENGER: Well, then: do you remember, back in those days
    That you gave me a baby boy to bring up as my own?
SHEPHERD: What if I did? What are you trying to say?   30
MESSENGER: King Oedipus was once that little child.
SHEPHERD: Damn you, hold your tongue!
OEDIPUS: No more of that!
    It is your tongue needs watching, not this man's.
SHEPHERD: My King, my Master, what is it I have done wrong?
OEDIPUS: You have not answered his question about the boy.   35
SHEPHERD: He does not know . . . He is only making trouble . . .
OEDIPUS: Come, speak plainly, or it will go hard with you.

SHEPHERD: In God's name, do not torture an old man!
OEDIPUS: Come here, one of you; bind his arms behind him.
SHEPHERD: Unhappy king! What more do you wish to learn?   40
OEDIPUS: Did you give this man the child he speaks of?
SHEPHERD: I did.
    And I would to God I had died that very day.
OEDIPUS: You will die now unless you speak the truth.
SHEPHERD: Yet if I speak the truth, I am worse than dead.
OEDIPUS: Very well; since you insist upon delaying—   45
SHEPHERD: No! I have told you already that I gave him the boy.
OEDIPUS: Where did you get him? From your house? From somewhere else?
SHEPHERD: Not from mine, no. A man gave him to me.
OEDIPUS: Is that man here? Do you know whose slave he was?
SHEPHERD: For God's love, my King, do not ask me any more!   50
OEDIPUS: You are a dead man if I have to ask you again.
SHEPHERD: Then . . . Then the child was from the palace of Laïos.
OEDIPUS: A slave child? or a child of his own line?
SHEPHERD: Ah, I am on the brink of dreadful speech!
OEDIPUS: And I of dreadful hearing. Yet I must hear.   55
SHEPHERD: If you must be told, then . . .
                         They said it was Laïos' child,
    But it is your wife who can tell you about that.
OEDIPUS: My wife!—Did she give it to you?
SHEPHERD: My lord, she did.
OEDIPUS: Do you know why?
SHEPHERD: I was told to get rid of it.
OEDIPUS: An unspeakable mother!
SHEPHERD: There had been prophecies . . .   60
OEDIPUS: Tell me.
SHEPHERD: It was said that the boy would kill his own father.
OEDIPUS: Then why did you give him over to this old man?
SHEPHERD: I pitied the baby, my King,
    And I thought that this man would take him far away
    To his own country.
                  He saved him—but for what a fate!   65
    For if you are what this man says you are,
    No man living is more wretched than Oedipus.
OEDIPUS: Ah God!
    It was true!
          All the prophecies!
               —Now,
    O Light, may I look on you for the last time!   70
    I, Oedipus,
    Oedipus, damned in his birth, in his marriage damned,
    Damned in the blood he shed with his own hand!

(He rushes into the palace)

Ode IV

CHORUS: Alas for the seed of men.

What measure shall I give these generations
That breathe on the void and are void
And exist and do not exist?

Who bears more weight of joy   5
Than mass of sunlight shifting in images,
Or who shall make his thought stay on
That down time drifts away?

Your splendor is all fallen.

O naked brow of wrath and tears,   10
O change of Oedipus!
I who say your days call no man blest—
Your great days like ghósts góne.

That mind was a strong bow.
Deep, how deep you drew it then, hard archer,   15
At a dim fearful range,
And brought dear glory down!

You overcame the stranger—
The virgin with her hooking lion claws—
And though death sang, stood like a tower   20
To make pale Thebes take heart.

Fortress against our sorrow!

Divine king, giver of laws,
Majestic Oedipus!
No prince in Thebes had ever such renown,   25
No prince won such grace of power.

And now of all men ever known
Most pitiful is this man's story:
His fortunes are most changed, his state
Fallen to a low slave's   30
Ground under bitter fate.

O Oedipus, most royal one!
The great door that expelled you to the light
Gave at night—ah, gave night to your glory:
As to the father, to the fathering son.   35

All understood too late.

How could that queen whom Laïos won,
The garden that he harrowed at his height,
Be silent when that act was done?

Antistrophe 2

But all eyes fail before time's eye,   40
All actions come to justice there.
Though never willed, though far down the deep past,
Your bed, your dread sirings,
Are brought to book at last.
Child by Laïos doomed to die,   45
Then doomed to lose that fortunate little death,
Would God you never took breath in this air
That with my wailing lips I take to cry:

For I weep the world's outcast.

I was blind, and now I can tell why: 50
Asleep, for you had given ease of breath
To Thebes, while the false years went by.

Exodos[18]

(Enter, from the palace, Second Messenger)

SECOND MESSENGER: Elders of Thebes, most honored in this land,
What horrors are yours to see and hear, what weight
Of sorrow to be endured, if, true to your birth,
You venerate the line of Labdakos!
I think neither Istros nor Phasis, those great rivers,   5
Could purify this place of the corruption
It shelters now, or soon must bring to light—
Evil not done unconsciously, but willed.

The greatest griefs are those we cause ourselves.
CHORAGOS: Surely, friend, we have grief enough already;   10
What new sorrow do you mean?
SECOND MESSENGER: The Queen is dead.
CHORAGOS: Iocastê? Dead? But at whose hand?
SECOND MESSENGER: Her own.
The full horror of what happened, you can not know,
For you did not see it; but I, who did, will tell you
As clearly as I can how she met her death.   15

When she had left us,
In passionate silence, passing through the court,

---

[18] Final scene.

She ran to her apartment in the house,
Her hair clutched by the fingers of both hands.
She closed the doors behind her; then, by that bed   20
Where long ago the fatal son was conceived—
That son who should bring about his father's death—
We heard her call upon Laïos, dead so many years,
And heard her wail for the double fruit of her marriage,
A husband by her husband, children by her child.   25

Exactly how she died I do not know:
For Oedipus burst in moaning and would not let us
Keep vigil to the end: it was by him
As he stormed about the room that our eyes were caught.
From one to another of us he went, begging a sword,   30
Cursing the wife who was not his wife, the mother
Whose womb had carried his own children and himself.
I do not know: it was none of us aided him,
But surely one of the gods was in control!
For with a dreadful cry   35
He hurled his weight, as though wrenched out of himself,
At the twin doors: the bolts gave, and he rushed in.
And there we saw her hanging, her body swaying
From the cruel cord she had noosed about her neck.
A great sob broke from him, heartbreaking to hear,   40
As he loosed the rope and lowered her to the ground.

I would blot out from my mind what happened next!
For the King ripped from her gown the golden brooches
That were her ornament, and raised them, and plunged them down
Straight into his own eyeballs, crying, "No more,   45
No more shall you look on the misery about me,
The horrors of my own doing! Too long you have known
The faces of those whom I should never have seen,
Too long been blind to those for whom I was searching!
From this hour, go in darkness!" And as he spoke,   50
He struck at his eyes—not once, but many times;
And the blood spattered his beard,
Bursting from his ruined sockets like red hail.
So from the unhappiness of two this evil has sprung,
A curse on the man and woman alike. The old   55
Happiness of the house of Labdakos
Was happiness enough: where is it today?
It is all wailing and ruin, disgrace, death—all
The misery of mankind that has a name—   60
And it is wholly and for ever theirs.
CHORAGOS: Is he in agony still? Is there no rest for him?
SECOND MESSENGER: He is calling for someone to lead him to the gates
So that all the children of Kadmos may look upon
His father's murderer, his mother's—no,

I can not say it!
                    And then he will leave Thebes,   65
Self-exiled, in order that the curse
Which he himself pronounced may depart from the house.
He is weak, and there is none to lead him,
So terrible is his suffering.
                              But you will see:
Look, the doors are opening; in a moment   70
You will see a thing that would crush a heart of stone.

(The central door is opened; Oedipus, blinded, is led in)

CHORAGOS: Dreadful indeed for men to see.
    Never have my own eyes
    Looked on a sight so full of fear.

    Oedipus!   75
    What madness came upon you, what daemon
    Leaped on your life with heavier
    Punishment than a mortal man can bear?
    No: I can not even
    Look at you, poor ruined one.   80
    And I would speak, question, ponder,
    If I were able. No.
    You make me shudder.
OEDIPUS: God. God.
    Is there a sorrow greater?   85
    Where shall I find harbor in this world?
    My voice is hurled far on a dark wind.
    What has God done to me?
CHORAGOS: Too terrible to think of, or to see.

                                                          Strophe 1
OEDIPUS: O cloud of night,   90
    Never to be turned away: night coming on,
    I can not tell how: night like a shroud!

    My fair winds brought me here.
                              Oh God. Again
    The pain of the spikes where I had sight,
    The flooding pain   95
    Of memory, never to be gouged out.
CHORAGOS: This is not strange.
    You suffer it all twice over, remorse in pain,
    Pain in remorse.

                                                      Antistrophe 1
OEDIPUS: Ah dear friend   100
    Are you faithful even yet, you alone?
    Are you still standing near me, will you stay here,
    Patient, to care for the blind?

                                          The blind man!
          Yet even blind I know who it is attends me,
          By the voice's tone—   105
          Though my new darkness hide the comforter.
CHORAGOS: Oh fearful act!
          What god was it drove you to rake black
          Night across your eyes?

                                                        Strophe 2
OEDIPUS: Apollo. Apollo. Dear   110
          Children, the god was Apollo.
          He brought my sick, sick fate upon me.
          But the blinding hand was my own!
          How could I bear to see
          When all my sight was horror everywhere?   115
CHORAGOS: Everywhere; that is true.
OEDIPUS: And now what is left?
          Images? Love? A greeting even,
          Sweet to the senses? Is there anything?
          Ah, no, friends: lead me away.   120
          Lead me away from Thebes.
                                    Lead the great wreck
          And hell of Oedipus, whom the gods hate.
CHORAGOS: Your fate is clear, you are not blind to that.
          Would God you had never found it out!

                                                        Antistrophe 2
OEDIPUS: Death take the man who unbound   125
          My feet on that hillside
          And delivered me from death to life! What life?
          If only I had died,
          This weight of monstrous doom
          Could not have dragged me and my darlings down.   130
CHORAGOS: I would have wished the same.
OEDIPUS: Oh never to have come here
          With my father's blood upon me! Never
          To have been the man they call his mother's husband!
          Oh accurst! Oh child of evil,   135
          To have entered that wretched bed—
                                    the selfsame one!
          More primal than sin itself, this fell to me.
CHORAGOS: I do not know how I can answer you.
          You were better dead than alive and blind.
OEDIPUS: Do not counsel me any more. This punishment   140
          That I have laid upon myself is just.
          If I had eyes,
          I do not know how I could bear the sight
          Of my father, when I came to the house of Death,

Or my mother: for I have sinned against them both   145
So vilely that I could not make my peace
By strangling my own life.
       Or do you think my children,
Born as they were born, would be sweet to my eyes?
Ah never, never! Nor this town with its high walls,
Nor the holy images of the gods.
        For I,   150
Thrice miserable!—Oedipus, noblest of all the line
Of Kadmos, have condemned myself to enjoy
These things no more, by my own malediction
Expelling that man whom the gods declared
To be a defilement in the house of Laïos.   155
After exposing the rankness of my own guilt,
How could I look men frankly in the eyes?
No, I swear it,
If I could have stifled my hearing at its source,
I would have done it and made all this body   160
A tight cell of misery, blank to light and sound:
So I should have been safe in a dark agony
Beyond all recollection.
      Ah Kithairon!
Why did you shelter me? When I was cast upon you,
Why did I not die? Then I should never   165
Have shown the world my execrable birth.

Ah Polybos! Corinth, city that I believed
The ancient seat of my ancestors: how fair
I seemed, your child! And all the while this evil
Was cancerous within me!
       For I am sick   170
In my daily life, sick in my origin.

O three roads, dark ravine, woodland and way
Where three roads met: you, drinking my father's blood,
My own blood, spilled by my own hand: can you remember
The unspeakable things I did there, and the things   175
I went on from there to do?
       O marriage, marriage!
The act that engendered me, and again the act
Performed by the son in the same bed—
         Ah, the net
Of incest, mingling fathers, brothers, sons,
With brides, wives, mothers: the last evil   180
That can be known by men: no tongue can say
How evil!
    No. For the love of God, conceal me
Somewhere far from Thebes; or kill me; or hurl me
Into the sea, away from men's eyes for ever.

Come, lead me. You need not fear to touch me.   185
Of all men, I alone can bear this guilt.

(Enter Creon)

CHORAGOS: We are not the ones to decide; but Creon here
    May fitly judge of what you ask. He only
    Is left to protect the city in your place.
OEDIPUS: Alas, how can I speak to him? What right have I   190
    To beg his courtesy whom I have deeply wronged?
CREON: I have not come to mock you, Oedipus,
    Or to reproach you either.
    (To Attendants)   —You, standing there:
    If you have lost all respect for man's dignity,
    At least respect the flame of Lord Helios: 195
    Do not allow this pollution to show itself
    Openly here, an affront to the earth
    And Heaven's rain and the light of day. No, take him
    Into the house as quickly as you can.
    For it is proper   200
    That only the close kindred see his grief.
OEDIPUS: I pray you in God's name, since your courtesy
    Ignores my dark expectation, visiting
    With mercy this man of all men most execrable:
    Give me what I ask—for your good, not for mine.   205
CREON: And what is it that you would have me do?
OEDIPUS: Drive me out of this country as quickly as may be
    To a place where no human voice can ever greet me.
CREON: I should have done that before now—only,
    God's will had not been wholly revealed to me.   210
OEDIPUS: But his command is plain: the parricide
    Must be destroyed. I am that evil man.
CREON: That is the sense of it, yes; but as things are,
    We had best discover clearly what is to be done.
OEDIPUS: You would learn more about a man like me?   215
CREON: You are ready now to listen to the god.
OEDIPUS: I will listen. But it is to you
    That I must turn for help. I beg you, hear me.

    The woman in there—
    Give her whatever funeral you think proper: 220
    She is your sister.
                —But let me go, Creon!
    Let me purge my father's Thebes of the pollution
    Of my living here, and go out to the wild hills,
    To Kithairon, that has won such fame with me,
    The tomb my mother and father appointed for me,   225
    And let me die there, as they willed I should.
    And yet I know

Death will not ever come to me through sickness
Or in any natural way: I have been preserved
For some unthinkable fate. But let that be.   230
As for my sons, you need not care for them.
They are men, they will find some way to live.
But my poor daughters, who have shared my table,
Who never before have been parted from their father—
Take care of them, Creon; do this for me.   235
And will you let me touch them with my hands
A last time, and let us weep together?
Be kind, my lord,
Great prince, be kind!
                    Could I but touch them,
They would be mine again, as when I had my eyes.   240

(Enter Antigone and Ismene, attended)

Ah, God!
Is it my dearest children I hear weeping?
Has Creon pitied me and sent my daughters?
CREON: Yes, Oedipus: I knew that they were dear to you
In the old days, and know you must love them still.   245
OEDIPUS: May God bless you for this—and be a friendlier
Guardian to you than he has been to me!

Children, where are you?
Come quickly to my hands: they are your brother's—
Hands that have brought your father's once clear eyes   250
To this way of seeing—
                    Ah dearest ones,
I had neither sight nor knowledge then, your father
By the woman who was the source of his own life!
And I weep for you—having no strength to see you—
I weep for you when I think of the bitterness   255
That men will visit upon you all your lives.
What homes, what festivals can you attend
Without being forced to depart again in tears?
And when you come to marriageable age,
Where is the man, my daughters, who would dare   260
Risk the bane that lies on all my children?
Is there any evil wanting? Your father killed
His father; sowed the womb of her who bore him;
Engendered you at the fount of his own existence!
That is what they will say of you.
                    Then, whom   265
Can you ever marry? There are no bridegrooms for you,
And your lives must wither away in sterile dreaming.
O Creon, son of Menoikeus!
You are the only father my daughters have,

Since we, their parents, are both of us gone for ever.   270
They are your own blood: you will not let them
Fall into beggary and loneliness;
You will keep them from the miseries that are mine!
Take pity on them; see, they are only children,
Friendless except for you. Promise me this,   275
Great Prince, and give me your hand in token of it.

(Creon clasps his right hand)

Children:
I could say much, if you could understand me,
But as it is, I have only this prayer for you:
Live where you can, be as happy as you can—   280
Happier, please God, than God has made your father!
CREON: Enough. You have wept enough. Now go within.
OEDIPUS: I must; but it is hard.
CREON: Times eases all things.
OEDIPUS: But you must promise . . .
CREON: Say what you desire.
OEDIPUS: Send me from Thebes!
CREON: God grant that I may!   285
OEDIPUS: But since God hates me . . .
CREON: No, he will grant your wish.
OEDIPUS: You promise?
CREON: I can not speak beyond my knowledge.
OEDIPUS: Then lead me in.
CREON: Come now, and leave your children.
OEDIPUS: No! Do not take them from me!
CREON: Think no longer
That you are in command here, but rather think   290
How, when you were, you served your own destruction.

(Exeunt into the house all but the Chorus; the Choragos chants directly to the audience)

CHORAGOS: Men of Thebes: look upon Oedipus.

This is the king who solved the famous riddle
And towered up, most powerful of men.
No mortal eyes but looked on him with envy,   295
Yet in the end ruin swept over him.
Let every man in mankind's frailty
Consider his last day; and let none
Presume on his good fortune until he find
Life, at his death, a memory without pain.   300

Greek Tragedy

Oedipus Rex, one of the first and greatest tragedies, is the play Aristotle had most immediately in mind in his famous definition:

Tragedy, then, is an imitation of an action that is serious, complete, and of a certain magnitude; in language embellished with each kind of artistic ornament, the several kinds being found in separate parts of the play; in the form of action, not of narrative; through pity and fear effecting the proper purgation of these emotions.

(S. H. Butcher translation)

Aristotle's definition, in his *Poetics,* has remained central to the Western world's understanding of tragedy for over two thousand years. However we envision *Oedipus Rex,* as we play it on the stage in our mind, we will want to ask ourselves what in it has transcended the particulars of time and space.

Certainly the action is serious. Oedipus murders his father, marries his mother and begets children, discovers his history, blinds himself, and goes into exile. All this the audience already knew, since Sophocles took the *story* (the chronological set of events upon which the play is based) from the common ground of Greek myth. The story, we may say, was inherently tragic, but it was not a tragedy until Sophocles put his playwright's hand to it. A tragedy, in other words, is an author's shaping of serious events into meaningful art. Our business as students is to examine the constituent elements.

For Aristotle, the most important element was *plot,* which we may define as the author's arrangement of the events of the story. Although the story of Oedipus begins with a prophecy made at his birth, Sophocles confines his plot to the day Oedipus discovers his identity. All springs from Oedipus's promise to discover and punish the murderer of Laïos. The events are compressed into a *unified plot*: a chain in which each single event is the necessary or probable result of an event that has gone before. Only at the end does the chain terminate. This compressed sense of inevitability lies at the heart of Greek tragedy. Once the chain of events has begun, it moves link by iron link to its inescapable conclusion. Another kind of arrangement, not in the Greek view suitable for tragedy, is the *episodic plot*: a series of events not logically linked to one another by necessity or probability.[1]

Two important elements of plot are reversal and recognition. *Reversal* (Greek *Peripeteia*) is a change of fortune, from good to bad in tragedy, from bad to good in comedy. Although Oedipus still lives at the end of the play, his fortunes are horribly reversed. For Aristotle, *reversal of intention* is most important: Oedipus intends to triumph, but ironically ruins himself. Similarly, the messenger intends to be helpful, but only hastens the tragic revelation by telling Oedipus that King Polybos was not

---

[1] Writers on tragedy have sometimes emphasized the *three unities* of plot, time, and place, though Aristotle emphasizes only plot. Unity of time and place follow naturally from a unified plot—showing all action at one place during one span of time—a concept arising from the limited staging possibilities of the Greek theater, though it was often an ideal of later writers, particularly in seventeenth-century France, whose theaters were actually more versatile. Unities of time and place (and sometimes even plot) were considerably less important in the fluid Elizabethan theater.

his father. And Oedipus's search for the murderer discloses only himself. Twinned naturally with reversal is *discovery* or *recognition* (Greek *anagnorisis*), when a character comes into knowledge about himself, his associates, or his place in the world. Oedipus's discovery of who he is profoundly alters his sense of self, his relation to his family and countrymen, and his understanding of his place in the universe.

Character is for Aristotle next in importance to plot. A complex summary of all that an individual is and does, character in literary works tends to be most meaningful when it helps define a significant *choice*, which turns the plot. As Aristotle expresses it: "Character is that which reveals moral purpose, showing what kinds of things a man chooses or avoids." Many literary works use *stock characters, flat characters,* or *type characters,* people whose choices will be obvious from their simple positions or personalities: the boastful soldier, the gambler with a heart of gold, the hypocritical preacher. Others use *individualized characters* or *round characters,* personalities we must understand in depth before we can understand how they function. Oedipus may at first seem flat, easily defined by his pride, his stubbornness, or his hasty judgment, but the more we consider him, the more we perceive a complexity that defies easy summary. To understand the play, we must ask why Oedipus makes his choices. To say simply that he was fated will not do, since prediction is not necessarily predestination. The oracle foresaw that, being the kind of man he was, he would act in a given way in a particular situation. In Oedipus we can see the vital part character plays in forging the links of probability and necessity in a relentlessly unified plot. The events are probable or necessary because the character is so defined that he can act in no other way.

A tragic character must be *good* in his moral purposes; he must intend to do right. In Greek tragedy he is also noble, so that his moral purposes affect all society. The tragic irony occurs when his good intentions misfire. Out of this come the tragic emotions of pity and fear: *pity,* the emotion we experience as witnesses to undeserved misfortune, and *fear,* the emotion aroused when the misfortune occurs to a person like ourselves. Yet although the person is good, he cannot be spotless. He must in some degree be responsible for his fate through a *tragic flaw* in his character or an *error of judgment* (alternative translations of the Greek *hamartia*). Although we blame Oedipus in part for what happens, we cannot blame him totally or we do not pity him. Although we admire him, we cannot consider him perfect, or we lose the tragic emotion of fear. (The essential goodness of the hero, it should be added, like other elements of the Aristotelian formula, does not apply equally well to other tragedies: for example, Shakespeare's *Macbeth.* The noble position common to the heroes of Sophocles and Shakespeare is diminished or nonexistent in the heroes of nineteenth- and twentieth-century tragedy.)

In his definition of tragedy, Aristotle stresses the importance for the audience of *catharsis* (or *purgation*) of the emotions of pity and fear. Watching the play, we release pent-up emotions; we leave the theater healthier than we went in. Not all writers have agreed upon the benefits of tragedy, or even that there are any benefits. For the Greeks, however, the experience was clearly communal, rooted in religious ritual and fostered by a shared vision of man's place in the eternal scheme of things.

Even in its most Grecian elements, the Greek theater provides a way of seeing and a vocabulary that helps us understand the plays of later cultures. The *chorus*, for example, is hardly ever used again. Yet later playwrights frequently use a *chorus character*, a person who, like the Greek chorus, stands apart from the passions of the play and verbalizes the judgment of an intelligent, compassionate bystander. So, too, the Greeks had a derrick on top of the skene to lower a god out of the heavens, when necessary. The term *deus ex machina* ("god out of the machine") now describes any unlikely solution to a problem, as if the author were intervening from heaven. In its entirety, the Greek vision of tragedy remains a necessary starting point for understanding later tragic visions of the Western world down to our own day.

The Elizabethan Theater

To imagine the size of the Globe theater in London, where Shakespeare produced many of his plays, consider first the dimensions of a Greek theater. Within that huge amphiteater, seating tens of thousands, was the *orchestra*, a circular acting area 85 feet in diameter.[2] Shakespeare's Globe was an octagonal building of approximately the size of the Greek orchestra. Elizabethan actors and audiences shared the space Greek spectators viewed from their many ranks of seats. From one side of the English octagon, the stage jutted into the midst of the standees (the *groundlings*), so that the actors played to an audience almost surrounding them. Up the other seven sides of the octagon were three levels of galleries, for those who could pay a bit more for a loftier view of the proceedings. Although perhaps two to three thousand spectators could cram into the Globe, the farthest seat in the house was perhaps only 60 feet from center stage. The galleries and stage were roofed, the rest open to the sky.

With such a stage, the playwright will want no masks, unless for comedies. Every gesture, every grimace will be clearly visible, though the playwright may wish to underline them in dialogue for those off to the side. No clogs will be wanted here; the actors in their natural dimen-

[2] In the Theater of Dionysus at Athens up to the middle of the fifth century B.C., when it was reduced to 65 feet.

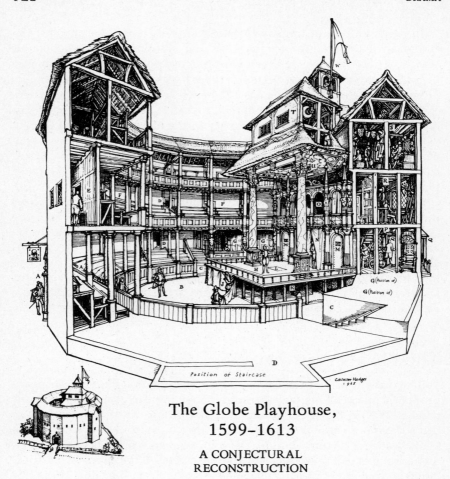

The Globe Playhouse, 1599–1613

A CONJECTURAL RECONSTRUCTION

AA	Main entrance	MM	Stage doors
B	The Yard	N	Curtained 'place behind the stage'
CC	Entrances to lowest gallery	O	Gallery above the stage, used as required sometimes by musicians, sometimes by spectators, and often as part of the play
D	Entrances to staircase and upper galleries		
E	Corridor serving the different sections of the middle gallery		
		P	Back-stage area (the tiring-house)
F	Middle gallery ('Twopenny Rooms')	Q	Tiring-house door
G	'Gentlemen's Rooms' or 'Lords' Rooms'	R	Dressing-rooms
H	The stage	S	Wardrobe and storage
J	The hanging being put up round the stage	T	The hut housing the machine for lowering enthroned gods, etc., to the stage
K	The 'Hell' under the stage		
L	The stage trap, leading down to the Hell	U	The 'Heavens'
		W	Hoisting the playhouse flag

The Globe Theater, London, 1599–1613

(From *The Globe Restored* by C. Walter Hodges, published by Oxford University Press)

sions will be large enough for this stage. With the actors freed from clogs and masks, and clearly distinguishable by face, the playwright will write for freer movement and more variety of tone, introducing numerous extra characters. A theater of such intimacy will, of course, have its own problems. It may demand some swordplay to stir the audience up from time to time, some *comic relief* to give them a break from the tension of tragedy, an occasional direct address from actor to audience in at least partial acknowledgment that they stand so close.

An important feature of the Globe theater, unlike anything in the Greek (save for the occasional *deus ex machina*), was the three stories of its height. On the first level, behind the stage, a curtained inner stage allowed for bedroom exchanges or death scenes that did not necessitate dragging a corpse offstage. On either side of this curtained area were doors for entrances and exits to and from the main stage. A trap door midstage allowed for the appearance of devils and ghosts. On the second level, a gallery provided another acting area and behind that was a second inner stage. On either side of the gallery, windows provided still more acting space. On the third level was a musicians' gallery, perhaps occasionally used for acting.

Not much of this was the invention of the moment. The general plan had evolved over centuries by way of medieval pageant wagons and performances in inn yards and marketplaces, as had the playwright's way of using it and the audience's manner of responding. The net result, by the time of Shakespeare, was a theatrical experience of remarkable fluidity. To change a scene, the actors merely left one acting area as another group appeared on another. Thus quickly the action moves from Scotland to England, say, or from Rome to Alexandria. If necessary, a word or an item of costume will fix a new scene in the imaginations of the audience. Frequently, no precise idea of place is necessary: in the turmoil of battle, for example, the scene may change several times within minutes without the audience knowing or much caring precisely where each incident occurs. In such a theater, the unities of time and place may seem irrelevant. Even unity of plot seems challenged.

Just as we cannot experience the Greek theater, we can never experience the theater of Shakespeare exactly as his first audiences did, although some theaters seek to duplicate the Globe playhouse (we can reproduce the theater, but not the audience). As we read the play, we set the stage in our minds: the Globe theater as we imagine it, the vastly different fluidity of the motion picture, or the twentieth-century stage in any of its variations. Always we seek to provide the fullest scope for the dramatic potential in the playwright's words.

MACBETH*

William Shakespeare   (1564–1616)

NAMES OF THE ACTORS

DUNCAN, King of Scotland

MALCOLM ⎱ his sons
DONALBAIN ⎰

MACBETH
BANQUO
MACDUFF
LENNOX
ROSS   ⎱ noblemen of Scotland
MENTEITH
ANGUS
CAITHNESS

FLEANCE, son to Banquo
SIWARD, Earl of Northumberland
YOUNG SIWARD, his son
SEYTON, an officer attending
   on Macbeth
BOY, son to Macduff

A CAPTAIN
AN ENGLISH DOCTOR
A SCOTTISH DOCTOR
A PORTER
AN OLD MAN
THREE MURDERERS
LADY MACBETH
LADY MACDUFF
A GENTLEWOMAN, attending on
   Lady Macbeth
THE WEIRD SISTERS
HECATE
THE GHOST OF BANQUO
APPARITIONS
LORDS, OFFICERS, SOLDIERS, MESSENGERS,
   ATTENDANTS

Scene: Scotland and England

I, i   (*Thunder and lightning. Enter three Witches.*)

1. WITCH: When shall we three meet again
   In thunder, lightning, or in rain?
2. WITCH: When the hurlyburly's done,
   When the battle's lost and won.
3. WITCH: That will be ere the set of sun.
1. WITCH: Where the place?
2. WITCH: Upon the heath.
3. WITCH: There to meet with Macbeth.
1. WITCH: I come, Graymalkin!   8
2. WITCH: Paddock calls.   9
3. WITCH: Anon!
ALL: Fair is foul, and foul is fair.
         Hover through the fog and filthy air.   (*Exeunt*)

I, ii   (*Alarum within. Enter King [Duncan], Malcolm, Donalbain, Lennox,
             with Attendants, meeting a bleeding Captain.*)

KING:
   What bloody man is that? He can report,

---

* Edited, with notes, by Alfred Harbage.

I, i An open place   **8** *Graymalkin* her familiar spirit, a gray cat   **9** *Paddock* a toad; *Anon* at once.

As seemeth by his plight, of the revolt
The newest state
MALCOLM: This is the sergeant   3
Who like a good and hardy soldier fought
'Gainst my captivity. Hail, brave friend!
Say to the King the knowledge of the broil
As thou didst leave it.
CAPTAIN: Doubtful it stood,
As two spent swimmers that do cling together
And choke their art. The merciless Macdonwald
(Worthy to be a rebel, for to that
The multiplying villainies of nature
Do swarm upon him) from the Western Isles   12
Of kerns and gallowglasses is supplied;   13
And Fortune, on his damnèd quarrel smiling,
Showed like a rebel's whore. But all's too weak:
For brave Macbeth (well he deserves that name),
Disdaining Fortune, with his brandished steel,
Which smoked with bloody execution,
Like valor's minion carved out his passage   19
Till he faced the slave;
Which ne'er shook hands nor bade farewell to him,
Till he unseamed him from the nave to th' chops   22
And fixed his head upon our battlements.
KING:
O valiant cousin! worthy gentleman!
CAPTAIN:
As whence the sun 'gins his reflection
Shipwracking storms and direful thunders break,
So from that spring whence comfort seemed to come
Discomfort swells. Mark, King of Scotland, mark.
No sooner justice had, with valor armed,
Compelled these skipping kerns to trust their heels
But the Norweyan lord, surveying vantage,   31
With furbished arms and new supplies of men,
Began a fresh assault.
KING: Dismayed not this
Our captains, Macbeth and Banquo?
CAPTAIN: Yes,
As sparrows eagles, or the hare the lion.
If I say sooth, I must report they were
As cannons overcharged with double cracks,   37
So they doubly redoubled strokes upon the foe.
Except they meant to bathe in reeking wounds,

I, ii A field near Forres 3 *sergeant* so designated, apparently, as a staff-officer; he ranks as a captain
12 *Western Isles* Hebrides (and Ireland?) 13 *kerns* Irish bush-fighters; *gallowglasses* Irish regulars, armored infantrymen 19 *minion* darling 22 *nave* navel 31 *surveying vantage* seeing opportunity
37 *cracks* explosives

Or memorize another Golgotha,   40
I cannot tell—
But I am faint; my gashes cry for help.
KING:
    So well thy words become thee as thy wounds,
    They smack of honor both. Go get him surgeons.

(Exit Captain, attended)

(Enter Ross and Angus)
    Who comes here?
MALCOLM: The worthy Thane of Ross.   45
LENNOX:
    What a haste looks through his eyes! So should he look
    That seems to speak things strange.   47
ROSS: God save the King!
KING:
    Whence cam'st thou, worthy Thane?
ROSS: From Fife, great King,
    Where the Norweyan banners flout the sky
    And fan our people cold.
    Norway himself, with terrible numbers,
    Assisted by that most disloyal traitor
    The Thane of Cawdor, began a dismal conflict,   53
    Till that Bellona's bridegroom, lapped in proof,   54
    Confronted him with self-comparisons,   55
    Point against point rebellious, arm 'gainst arm,
    Curbing his lavish spirit: and to conclude,
    The victory fell on us.
KING: Great happiness!
ROSS: That now
    Sweno, the Norways' king, craves composition;   59
    Nor would we deign him burial of his men
    Till he disbursed, at Saint Colme's Inch,   61
    Ten thousand dollars to our general use.   62
KING:
    No more that Thane of Cawdor shall deceive
    Our bosom interest. Go pronounce his present death   64
    And with his former title greet Macbeth.
ROSS:
    I'll see it done.
KING:
    What he hath lost noble Macbeth hath won.   *(Exeunt)*

---

40 *memorize another Golgotha* make memorable as another 'place of the dead' **45** *Thane* a Scottish lord
47 *seems to* seems about to   **53** *dismal* ominous   **54** *Bellona* goddess of war; *lapped in proof* clad in proven
armor   **55** *self-comparisons* cancelling powers   **59** *composition* terms of surrender   **61** *Inch* island   **62** *dollars* Spanish or Dutch coins   **64** *bosom interest* heart's trust

I, iii   *(Thunder. Enter the three Witches.)*

1. WITCH: Where hast thou been, sister?
2. WITCH: Killing swine.
3. WITCH: Sister, where thou?
1. WITCH: A sailor's wife had chestnuts in her lap
   And mounched and mounched and mounched.
   'Give me,' quoth I.
   'Aroint thee, witch!' the rump-fed ronyon cries.   6
   Her husband's to Aleppo gone, master o' th' Tiger:
   But in a sieve I'll thither sail
   And, like a rat without a tail,
   I'll do, I'll do, and I'll do.
2. WITCH: I'll give thee a wind.
1. WITCH: Th' art kind.
3. WITCH: And I another.
1. WITCH: I myself have all the other,
   And the very ports they blow,   15
   All the quarters that they know
   I' th' shipman's card.   17
   I'll drain him dry as hay.
   Sleep shall neither night nor day
   Hang upon his penthouse lid.   20
   He shall live a man forbid.   21
   Weary sev' nights, nine times nine,
   Shall he dwindle, peak, and pine.
   Though his bark cannot be lost,
   Yet it shall be tempest-tost.
   Look what I have.
2. WITCH: Show me, show me.
1. WITCH: Here I have a pilot's thumb,
   Wracked as homeward he did come.

   (Drum within)

3. WITCH: A drum, a drum!
   Macbeth doth come.
ALL: The weird sisters, hand in hand,   32
   Posters of the sea and land,   33
   Thus do go about, about,
   Thrice to thine, and thrice to mine,
   And thrice again, to make up nine.
   Peace! The charm's wound up.

   (Enter Macbeth and Banquo)

I, iii A heath **6** *Aroint thee* get thee gone; *rump-fed ronyon* fat-rumped scab   **15** *very ports they blow* i.e.
their power to blow ships to ports   **17** *card* compass card   **2** *penthouse lid* eyelid   **21** *forbid* accursed
32 *weird* fate-serving   **33** *Posters* swift travellers

MACBETH:
> So foul and fair a day I have not seen.

BANQUO:
> How far is't called to Forres? What are these,
> So withered and so wild in their attire
> That look not like th' inhabitants o' th' earth
> And yet are on't? Live you, or are you aught
> That man may question? You seem to understand me,   43
> By each at once her choppy finger laying   44
> Upon her skinny lips. You should be women,
> And yet your beards forbid me to interpret
> That you are so.

MACBETH: Speak, if you can. What are you?

1. WITCH:
> All hail, Macbeth! Hail to thee, Thane of Glamis!

2. WITCH:
> All hail, Macbeth! Hail to thee, Thane of Cawdor!

3. WITCH:
> All hail, Macbeth, that shalt be King hereafter!

BANQUO:
> Good sir, why do you start and seem to fear
> Things that do sound so fair? I' th' name of truth,
> Are ye fantastical, or that indeed   53
> Which outwardly ye show? My noble partner
> You greet with present grace and great prediction   55
> Of noble having and of royal hope,
> That he seems rapt withal. To me you speak not.   57
> If you can look into the seeds of time   58
> And say which grain will grow and which will not,
> Speak then to me, who neither beg nor fear
> Your favors nor your hate.

1. WITCH: Hail!

2. WITCH: Hail!

3. WITCH: Hail!

1. WITCH:
> Lesser than Macbeth, and greater.

2. WITCH:
> Not so happy, yet much happier.   66

3. WITCH:
> Thou shalt get kings, though thou be none.   67
> So all hail, Macbeth and Banquo!

1. WITCH:
> Banquo and Macbeth, all hail!

MACBETH:
> Stay, you imperfect speakers, tell me more: 70

---

43 *question* confer with   **44** *choppy* chapped **53** *fantastical* creatures of fantasy   **55** *grace* honor   **57** *rapt withal* spellbound at the thought   **58** *seeds of time* genesis of events   **66** *happy* fortunate   **67** *get* beget **70** *imperfect* incomplete

By Sinel's death I know I am Thane of Glamis,   71
But how of Cawdor? The Thane of Cawdor lives,
A prosperous gentleman; and to be King
Stands not within the prospect of belief,
No more than to be Cawdor. Say from whence
You owe this strange intelligence, or why
Upon this blasted heath you stop our way
With such prophetic greeting. Speak, I charge you.

                                         (Witches vanish)

BANQUO:
The earth hath bubbles as the water has,
And these are of them. Whither are they vanished?
MACBETH:
Into the air, and what seemed corporal melted   81
As breath into the wind. Would they had stayed!
BANQUO:
Were such things here as we do speak about?
Or have we eaten on the insane root   84
That takes the reason prisoner?
MACBETH:
Your children shall be kings.
BANQUO: You shall be King.
MACBETH:
And Thane of Cawdor too. Went it not so?
BANQUO:
To th' selfsame tune and words. Who's here?

(Enter Ross and Angus)

ROSS:
The King hath happily received, Macbeth,
The news of thy success; and when he reads   90
Thy personal venture in the rebels' fight,
His wonders and his praises do contend   92
Which should be thine or his. Silenced with that,
In viewing o'er the rest o' th' selfsame day,
He finds thee in the stout Norweyan ranks,
Nothing afeard of what thyself didst make,
Strange images of death. As thick as tale   97
Came post with post, and every one did bear   98
Thy praises in his kingdom's great defense
And poured them down before him.
ANGUS: We are sent
To give thee from our royal master thanks;

---

71 *Sinel* i.e. Macbeth's father   81 *corporal* corporeal   84 *insane* madness-inducing   90 *reads* considers
92-93 *His wonders . . . or his* i.e. dumbstruck admiration makes him keep your praises to himself
97 *thick as tale* i.e. as fast as they can be counted   98 *post with post* messenger after messenger

Only to herald thee into his sight,
Not pay thee.

ROSS:
And for an earnest of a greater honor,
He bade me, from him, call thee Thane of Cawdor;
In which addition, hail, most worthy Thane,   106
For it is thine.

BANQUO: What, can the devil speak true?

MACBETH:
The Thane of Cawdor lives. Why do you dress me
In borrowed robes?

ANGUS: Who was the Thane lives yet,
But under heavy judgment bears that life
Which he deserves to lose. Whether he was combined   111
With those of Norway, or did line the rebel   112
With hidden help and vantage, or that with both   113
He labored in his country's wrack. I know not:
But treasons capital, confessed and proved,
Have overthrown him.

MACBETH (aside):   Glamis, and Thane of Cawdor—
The greatest is behind   117
(To Ross and Angus) Thanks for your pains.

(Aside to Banquo)

Do you not hope your children shall be kings,
When those that gave the Thane of Cawdor to me
Promised no less to them?

BANQUO (to Macbeth):   That, trusted home,   120
Might yet enkindle you unto the crown,
Besides the Thane of Cawdor. But 'tis strange:
And oftentimes, to win us to our harm,
The instruments of darkness tell us truths,
Win us with honest trifles, to betray's
In deepest consequence.—   126
Cousins, a word, I pray you.   127

MACBETH (aside):   Two truths are told,
As happy prologues to the swelling act   128
Of the imperial theme.—I thank you, gentlemen.—

(Aside)

This supernatural soliciting   130
Cannot be ill, cannot be good. If ill,
Why hath it given me earnest of success,
Commencing in a truth? I am Thane of Cawdor.

---

106 *addition* title 111 *combined* leagued 112 *line* support 113 *vantage* assistance 117 *is behind* is to come 120 *home* all the way 126 *deepest consequence* i.e. in the vital sequel 127 *Cousins* i.e. fellow lords 128-29 *swelling act . . . imperial theme* i.e. stately drama of rise to sovereignty 130 *soliciting* inviting, beckoning

If good, why do I yield to that suggestion
Whose horrid image doth unfix my hair
And make my seated heart knock at my ribs   136
Against the use of nature? Present fears   137
Are less than horrible imaginings.
My thought, whose murder yet is but fantastical,   139
Shakes so my single state of man that function   140
Is smothered in surmise and nothing is
But what is not.

BANQUO: Look how our partner's rapt.   142

MACBETH *(aside)*:
If chance will have me King, why chance may crown me
Without my stir.

BANQUO: New honors come upon him,
Like our strange garments, cleave not to their mould   145
But with the aid of use.

MACBETH *(aside)*:   Come what come may,
Time and the hour runs through the roughest day.

BANQUO:
Worthy Macbeth, we stay upon your leisure.

MACBETH:
Give me your favor. My dull brain was wrought   149
With things forgotten. Kind gentlemen, your pains
Are regist'red where every day I turn
The leaf to read them. Let us toward the King.

(Aside to Banquo):

Think upon what hath chanced, and at more time,
The interim having weighed it, let us speak
Our free hearts each to other.   155

BANQUO: Very gladly.

MACBETH:
Till then, enough.—Come, friends.

                                                   (Exeunt)

I, iv   *(Flourish. Enter King [Duncan], Lennox, Malcolm, Donalbain,
             and Attendants.)*

KING:
Is execution done on Cawdor? Are not
Those in commission yet returned?   2

MALCOLM: My liege,
They are not yet come back. But I have spoke
With one that saw him die; who did report

---

136 *seated* fixed **137** *use* way **139** *fantastical* imaginary **140** *single* unaided, weak; *function* normal
powers **142** *rapt* bemused **145** *strange* new **149** *favor* pardon **155** *Our free hearts* our thoughts freely **I, iv** A field near Forres as before, or a place in the palace itself **2** *in commission* commissioned to
carry out the execution

That very frankly he confessed his treasons,
Implored your Highness' pardon, and set forth
A deep repentance. Nothing in his life
Became him like the leaving it. He died
As one that had been studied in his death   9
To throw away the dearest thing he owed   10
As 'twere a careless trifle.

KING: There's no art
To find the mind's construction in the face.
He was a gentleman on whom I built
An absolute trust.

(Enter Macbeth, Banquo, Ross, and Angus)

                    O worthiest cousin,
The sin of my ingratitude even now
Was heavy on me. Thou art so far before   16
That swiftest wing of recompense is slow
To overtake thee. Would thou hadst less deserved,
That the proportion both of thanks and payment   19
Might have been mine! Only I have left to say,
More is thy due than more than all can pay.

MACBETH:
The service and the loyalty I owe,
In doing it pays itself. Your Highness' part
Is to receive our duties, and our duties
Are to your throne and state children and servants,
Which do but what they should by doing everything
Safe toward your love and honor.   27

KING: Welcome hither.
I have begun to plant thee and will labor   28
To make thee full of growing. Noble Banquo,
That hast no less deserved nor must be known
No less to have done so, let me enfold thee
And hold thee to my heart.

BANQUO: There if I grow,
The harvest is your own.

KING: My plenteous joys,
Wanton in fullness, seek to hide themselves   34
In drops of sorrow. Sons, kinsmen, thanes,
And you whose places are the nearest, know
We will establish our estate upon
Our eldest, Malcolm, whom we name hereafter
The Prince of Cumberland; which honor must
Not unaccompanied invest him only,
But signs of nobleness, like stars, shall shine
On all deservers. From hence to Inverness,
And bind us further to you.

9 *studied* rehearsed **10** *owed* owned **16** *before* ahead in deserving **19** *proportion* preponderance
27 *safe* fitting **28** *plant* nurture **34** *Wanton* unrestrained

MACBETH:
> The rest is labor which is not used for you.
> I'll be myself the harbinger, and make joyful
> The hearing of my wife with your approach;
> So, humbly take my leave.

KING: My worthy Cawdor!

MACBETH (*aside*):
> The Prince of Cumberland—that is a step
> On which I must fall down or else o'erleap,
> For in my way it lies. Stars, hide your fires;
> Let not light see my black and deep desires.
> The eye wink at the hand; yet let that be   52
> Which the eye fears, when it is done, to see.

> > > > > > > (*Exit*)

KING:
> True, worthy Banquo: he is full so valiant,
> And in his commendations I am fed;
> It is a banquet to me. Let's after him,
> Whose care is gone before to bid us welcome.
> It is a peerless kinsman.

> > > > > > (*Flourish. Exeunt*)

I, v   (*Enter Macbeth's Wife, alone, with a letter*)

LADY: (*reads*) 'They met me in the day of success; and I have learned by the
perfect'st report they have more in them than mortal knowledge. When
I burned in desire to question them further, they made themselves air,
into which they vanished. Whiles I stood rapt in the wonder of it, came
missives from the King, who all-hailed me Thane of Cawdor, by which   5
title, before, these weird sisters saluted me, and referred me to the coming on of time with "Hail, King that shalt be!" This have I thought good
to deliver thee, my dearest partner of greatness, that thou mightst not
lose the dues of rejoicing by being ignorant of what greatness is promised thee. Lay it to thy heart, and farewell.'

> Glamis thou art, and Cawdor, and shalt be
> What thou art promised. Yet do I fear thy nature.
> It is too full o' th' milk of human kindness
> To catch the nearest way. Thou wouldst be great,
> Art not without ambition, but without
> The illness should attend it. What thou wouldst highly,   16
> That wouldst thou holily; wouldst not play false,
> And yet wouldst wrongly win. Thou'ldst have, great Glamis,
> That which cries 'Thus thou must do' if thou have it;
> And that which rather thou dost fear to do
> Than wishest should be undone. Hie thee hither,
> That I may pour my spirits in thine ear

---

52 *wink at the hand* blind itself to what the hand does   **I, v** Within Macbeth's castle at Inverness   **5** *missives* messengers   **16** *illness* ruthlessness

And chastise with the valor of my tongue
All that impedes thee from the golden round   24
Which fate and metaphysical aid doth seem   25
To have thee crowned withal.   26
(Enter Messenger)   What is your tidings?
MESSENGER:
The King comes here to-night.
LADY: Thou'rt mad to say it!
Is not thy master with him? who, were't so,
Would have informed for preparation.
MESSENGER:
So please you, it is true. Our Thane is coming.
One of my fellows had the speed of him,
Who, almost dead for breath, had scarcely more   32
Than would make up his message.
LADY: Give him tending;
He brings great news.   *(Exit Messenger)*
                       The raven himself is hoarse
That croaks the fatal entrance of Duncan
Under my battlements. Come, you spirits
That tend on mortal thoughts, unsex me here,   37
And fill me from the crown to the toe top-full
Of direst cruelty. Make thick my blood;
Stop up th' access and passage to remorse,   40
That no compunctious visitings of nature   41
Shake my fell purpose nor keep peace between   42
Th' effect and it. Come to my woman's breasts
And take my milk for gall, you murd'ring ministers,   44
Wherever in your sightless substances   45
You wait on nature's mischief. Come, thick night,   46
And pall thee in the dunnest smoke of hell,   47
That my keen knife see not the wound it makes,
Nor heaven peep through the blanket of the dark
To cry 'Hold, hold!'
(Enter Macbeth) Great Glamis! worthy Cawdor!
Greater than both, by the all-hail hereafter!
Thy letters have transported me beyond
This ignorant present, and I feel now   53
The future in the instant.
MACBETH: My dearest love,
Duncan comes here to-night.
LADY: And when goes hence?
MACBETH:
To-morrow, as he purposes.

---

24 *round* crown   **25** *metaphysical* supernatural   **26** *withal* with   **32** *breath* want of breath   **37** *mortal* deadly   **40** *remorse* pity   **41** *nature* natural feeling   **42** *fell* fierce   **42-43** *keep peace . . . and it* i.e. lull it from achieving its end   **44** *for gall* in exchange for gall; *ministers* agents   **45** *sightless* invisible   **46** *wait on* aid   **47** *pall thee* shroud thyself; *dunnest* darkest   **53** *ignorant* i.e. ordinarily unaware

LADY: O, never
  Shall sun that morrow see!
  Your face, my Thane, is as a book where men
  May read strange matters. To beguile the time,   59
  Look like the time; bear welcome in your eye,   60
  Your hand, your tongue; look like th' innocent flower,
  But be the serpent under't. He that's coming
  Must be provided for; and you shall put
  This night's great business into my dispatch,   64
  Which shall to all our nights and days to come
  Give solely sovereign sway and masterdom.

MACBETH:
  We will speak further.

LADY: Only look up clear.   67
  To alter favor ever is to fear.   68
  Leave all the rest to me.   *(Exeunt)*

I, vi   *(Hautboys and torches. Enter King [Duncan], Malcolm, Donalbain,*
       Banquo, Lennox, Macduff, Ross, Angus, and Attendants.)

KING:
  This castle hath a pleasant seat. The air   1
  Nimbly and sweetly recommends itself
  Unto our gentle senses.   3

BANQUO: This guest of summer,
  The temple-haunting martlet, does approve   4
  By his loved mansionry that the heaven's breath   5
  Smells wooingly here. No jutty, frieze,   6
  Buttress, nor coign of vantage, but this bird   7
  Hath made his pendent bed and procreant cradle.   8
  Where they most breed and haunt, I have observed
  The air is delicate.

(Enter Lady Macbeth)

KING: See, see, our honored hostess!
  The love that follows us sometime is our trouble,   11
  Which still we thank as love. Herein I teach you
  How you shall bid God 'ield us for your pains   13
  And thank us for your trouble.

LADY: All our service
  In every point twice done, and then done double,
  Were poor and single business to contend
  Against those honors deep and broad wherewith

---

59 *beguile the time* make sly use of the occasion   **60** *Look like the time* play up to the occasion   **64** *dispatch* swift management   **67** *look up clear* appear untroubled   **68** *alter favor* change countenance; *fear* incur risk   **I, vi** At the portal of Inverness **s.d.** *Hautboys* oboes **1** *seat* site **3** *gentle* soothed **4** *temple-haunting* nesting in church spires; *martlet* martin, swallow; *approve* prove **5** *loved mansionry* beloved nests **6** *jutty* projection **7** *coign of vantage* convenient corner **8** *procreant* breeding **11-12** *The love . . . as love* the love that sometimes inconveniences us we still hold precious **13** *God 'ield us* God reward me

Your Majesty loads our house. For those of old,
And the late dignities heaped up to them,
We rest your hermits.   20
KING: Where's the Thane of Cawdor?
We coursed him at the heels and had a purpose
To be his purveyor; but he rides well,   22
And his great love, sharp as his spur, hath holp him
To his home before us. Fair and noble hostess,
We are your guest to-night.
LADY: Your servants ever
Have theirs, themselves, and what is theirs, in compt,   26
To make their audit at your Highness' pleasure,
Still to return your own.   28
KING: Give me your hand.
Conduct me to mine host; we love him highly
And shall continue our graces towards him.
By your leave, hostess.   (Exeunt)

I, vii   (Hautboys. Torches. Enter a Sewer, and divers Servants with dishes
             and service over the stage. Then enter Macbeth.)

MACBETH:
If it were done when 'tis done, then 'twere well   1
It were done quickly. If th' assassination
Could trammel up the consequence, and catch   3
With his surcease success, that but this blow   4
Might be the be-all and the end-all—; here,
But here upon this bank and shoal of time,
We'ld jump the life to come. But in these cases   7
We still have judgment here, that we but teach
Bloody instructions, which, being taught, return   9
To plague th' inventor. This even-handed justice
Commends th' ingredience of our poisoned chalice
To our own lips. He's here in double trust:
First, as I am his kinsman and his subject,
Strong both against the deed; then, as his host,
Who should against his murderer shut the door,
Not bear the knife myself. Besides, this Duncan
Hath borne his faculties so meek, hath been   17
So clear in his great office, that his virtues   18
Will plead like angels, trumpet-tongued against
The deep damnation of his taking-off;
And pity, like a naked new-born babe

---

20 *hermits* beadsmen   22 *purveyor* advance agent of supplies   26 *Have theirs* have their servants; *what is theirs* their possessions; *in compt* in trust   28 *Still* always   **I, vii** The courtyard of Inverness from which open the chambers of the castle   **s.d.** *Sewer* chief waiter   1 *done* done with   3 *trammel up the consequence* enclose the consequences in a net   4 *his surcease* its (the assassination's) completion; *success* all that follows   7 *jump* risk   9 *instructions* lessons   17 *faculties* powers   18 *clear* untainted

Striding the blast, or heaven's cherubin horsed
Upon the sightless couriers of the air,   23
Shall blow the horrid deed in every eye
That tears shall drown the wind. I have no spur
To prick the sides of my intent, but only
Vaulting ambition, which o'erleaps itself
And falls on th' other—

(Enter Lady Macbeth)

                    How now? What news?
LADY:
He has almost supped. Why have you left the chamber?
MACBETH:
Hath he asked for me?
LADY: Know you not he has?
MACBETH:
We will proceed no further in this business.
He hath honored me of late, and I have bought   32
Golden opinions from all sorts of people,
Which would be worn now in their newest gloss,
Not cast aside so soon.
LADY: Was the hope drunk
Wherein you dressed yourself? Hath it slept since?
And wakes it now to look so green and pale   37
At what it did so freely? From this time
Such I account thy love. Art thou afeard
To be the same in thine own act and valor
As thou art in desire? Wouldst thou have that
Which thou esteem'st the ornament of life,
And live a coward in thine own esteem,
Letting 'I dare not' wait upon 'I would,'
Like the poor cat i' th' adage?   45
MACBETH: Prithee peace!
I dare do all that may become a man;
Who dares do more is none.
LADY: What beast was't then
That made you break this enterprise to me?   48
When you durst do it, then you were a man;
And to be more than what you were, you would
Be so much more the man. Nor time nor place
Did then adhere, and yet you would make both.   52
They have made themselves, and that their fitness now   53
Does unmake you. I have given suck, and know
How tender 'tis to love the babe that milks me:
I would, while it was smiling in my face,

---

23 *sightless couriers* invisible coursers (the winds)   **32** *bought* acquired   **37** *green* bilious   **45** *cat i' th' adage* (who wants the fish but doesn't want to get its paws wet)   **48** *break* broach   **52** *adhere* lend themselves to the occasion   **53** *that their fitness* their very fitness

Have plucked my nipple from his boneless gums
And dashed the brains out, had I so sworn as you
Have done to this.
MACBETH: If we should fail?
LADY: We fail?
But screw your courage to the sticking place   60
And we'll not fail. When Duncan is asleep
(Whereto the rather shall his day's hard journey
Soundly invite him), his two chamberlains
Will I with wine and wassail so convince   64
That memory, the warder of the brain,
Shall be a fume, and the receipt of reason   66
A limbeck only. When in swinish sleep   67
Their drenchèd natures lies as in a death,
What cannot you and I perform upon
Th' unguarded Duncan? what not put upon
His spongy officers, who shall bear the guilt
Of our great quell?   72
MACBETH: Bring forth men-children only;
For thy undaunted mettle should compose   73
Nothing but males. Will it not be received,
When we have marked with blood those sleepy two
Of his own chamber and used their very daggers,
That they have done't?
LADY: Who dares receive it other,   77
As we shall make our griefs and clamor roar
Upon his death?
MACBETH: I am settled, and bend up
Each corporal agent to this terrible feat.
Away, and mock the time with fairest show;   81
False face must hide what the false heart doth know.

                                                            (Exeunt)

II, i   *(Enter Banquo, and Fleance, with a torch before him)*

BANQUO:
How goes the night, boy?
FLEANCE:
The moon is down; I have not heard the clock.
BANQUO:
And she goes down at twelve.
FLEANCE: I take't, 'tis later, sir.
BANQUO:
Hold, take my sword. There's husbandry in heaven;   4

---

60 *sticking place* notch (holding the string of a crossbow cranked taut for shooting)   **64** *convince* overcome   **66** *receipt* container   **67** *limbeck* cap of a still (to which the fumes rise)   **72** *quell* killing   **73** *mettle* vital substance   **77** *other* otherwise   **81** *mock* delude   **II, i** The same   **4** *husbandry* economy

Their candles are all out. Take thee that too.
A heavy summons lies like lead upon me,   6
And yet I would not sleep. Merciful powers,
Restrain in me the cursèd thoughts that nature
Gives way to in repose.

(Enter Macbeth, and a Servant with a torch)

                              Give me my sword!
Who's there?
MACBETH:
    A friend.
BANQUO:
    What, sir, not yet at rest? The King's abed.
    He hath been in unusual pleasure and
    Sent forth great largess to your offices.   14
    This diamond he greets your wife withal
    By the name of most kind hostess, and shut up   16
    In measureless content.
MACBETH: Being unprepared,
    Our will became the servant to defect,   18
    Which else should free have wrought.
BANQUO: All's well.
    I dreamt last night of the three weird sisters.
    To you they have showed some truth.
MACBETH: I think not of them.
    Yet when we can entreat an hour to serve,
    We would spend it in some words upon that business,
    If you would grant the time.
BANQUO: At your kind'st leisure.
MACBETH:
    If you shall cleave to my consent, when 'tis,   25
    It shall make honor for you.
BANQUO: So I lose none
    In seeking to augment it, but still keep
    My bosom franchished and allegiance clear,   28
    I shall be counselled.   29
MACBETH: Good repose the while.
BANQUO:
    Thanks, sir. The like to you.

                              (Exeunt Banquo [and Fleance])

MACBETH:
    Go bid thy mistress, when my drink is ready,
    She strike upon the bell. Get thee to bed. *(Exit Servant)*
    Is this a dagger which I see before me,

---

6 *summons* signal to sleep   **14** *largess to your offices* gratuities to your household departments   **16** *shut up* concluded   **18** *will* good will; *defect* deficient means   **25** *cleave . . . when 'tis* favor my cause at the proper time   **28** *franchised* free from guilt   **29** *counselled* open to persuasion

The handle toward my hand? Come, let me clutch thee!
I have thee not, and yet I see thee still.
Art thou not, fatal vision, sensible
To feeling as to sight? or art thou but
A dagger of the mind, a false creation
Proceeding from the heat-oppressèd brain?
I see thee yet, in form as palpable
As this which now I draw.
Thou marshall'st me the way that I was going,
And such an instrument I was to use.
Mine eyes are made the fools o' th' other senses,
Or else worth all the rest. I see thee still,
And on thy blade and dudgeon gouts of blood,   46
Which was not so before. There's no such thing.
It is the bloody business which informs   48
Thus to mine eyes. Now o'er the one half-world
Nature seems dead, and wicked dreams abuse   50
The curtained sleep. Witchcraft celebrates
Pale Hecate's offerings; and withered murder,   52
Alarumed by his sentinel, the wolf,   53
Whose howl's his watch, thus with his stealthy pace,
With Tarquin's ravishing strides, towards his design   55
Moves like a ghost. Thou sure and firm-set earth,
Hear not my steps which way they walk, for fear
Thy very stones prate of my whereabout
And take the present horror from the time,   59
Which now suits with it. Whiles I threat, he lives;
Words to the heat of deeds too cold breath gives.

A bell rings.

I go, and it is done. The bell invites me.
Hear it not, Duncan, for it is a knell
That summons thee to heaven, or to hell.   *(Exit)*

II, ii   *(Enter Lady Macbeth)*

LADY:
That which hath made them drunk hath made me bold:
What hath quenched them hath given me fire. Hark!
    Peace!
It was the owl that shrieked, the fatal bellman   3
Which gives the stern'st good-night. He is about it.

---

46 *dudgeon* wooden hilt; *gouts* blobs   **48** *informs* creates impressions   **50** *abuse* deceive   **52** *Hecate's offerings* worship of Hecate (Goddess of sorcery)   **53** *Alarumed* given the signal   **55** *Tarquin* Roman tyrant, ravisher of Lucrece   **59-60** *take . . . suits with it* delay, by prating, the commission of the deed at this suitably horrible moment (?), reduce, by breaking the silence, the suitable horror of this moment (?)   **II, ii 3-4** *fatal bellman . . .good-night* i.e. like the night-watch cry to felons scheduled for execution in the morning

The doors are open, and the surfeited grooms
Do mock their charge with snores. I have drugged their possets,   6
That death and nature do contend about them
Whether they live or die.

MACBETH: *(within)*:   Who's there? What, ho?

LADY:

Alack, I am afraid they have awaked,
And 'tis not done! Th' attempt, and not the deed,
Confounds us. Hark! I laid their daggers ready—   11
He could not miss 'em. Had he not resembled
My father as he slept, I had done't.
(Enter Macbeth)   My husband!

MACBETH:

I have done the deed. Didst thou not hear a noise?

LADY:

I heard the owl scream and the crickets cry
Did not you speak?

MACBETH: When?

LADY: Now.

MACBETH: As I descended?

LADY: Ay.

MACBETH: Hark!
Who lies i' th' second chamber?

LADY: Donalbain.

MACBETH: This is a sorry sight.

LADY:

A foolish thought, to say a sorry sight.

MACBETH:

There's one did laugh in's sleep, and one cried 'Murder!'
That they did wake each other. I stood and heard them.   23
But they did say their prayers and addressed them
Again to sleep.

LADY: There are two lodged together.

MACBETH:

One cried 'God bless us!' and 'Amen!' the other,
As they had seen me with these hangman's hands,   27
List'ning their fear. I could not say 'Amen!'
When they did say 'God bless us!'

LADY: Consider it not so deeply.

MACBETH:

But wherefore could not I pronounce 'Amen'?
I had most need of blessing, and 'Amen'
Stuck in my throat.

LADY: These deeds must not be thought
After these ways; so, it will make us mad.

---

6 *possets* bedtime drinks   **11** *Confounds* ruins   **23** *That* so that   **27** *hangman's hands* i.e. bloody, like an executioner's

MACBETH:

> Methought I heard a voice cry 'Sleep no more!
> Macbeth does murder sleep'—the innocent sleep,
> Sleep that knits up the ravelled sleave of care,   36
> The death of each day's life, sore labor's bath,
> Balm of hurt minds, great nature's second course,   38
> Chief nourisher in life's feast.

LADY: What do you mean?

MACBETH:

> Still it cried 'Sleep no more!' to all the house;
> 'Glamis hath murdered sleep, and therefore Cawdor
> Shall sleep no more, Macbeth shall sleep no more.'

LADY:

> Who was it that thus cried? Why, worthy Thane,
> You do unbend your noble strength to think   44
> So brainsickly of things. Go get some water
> And wash this filthy witness from your hand.   46
> Why did you bring these daggers from the place?
> They must lie there: go carry them and smear
> The sleepy grooms with blood.

MACBETH: I'll go no more.

> I am afraid to think what I have done;
> Look on't again I dare not.

LADY: Infirm of purpose!

> Give me the daggers. The sleeping and the dead
> Are but as pictures. 'Tis the eye of childhood   53
> That fears a painted devil. If he do bleed,
> I'll gild the faces of the grooms withal,   55
> For it must seem their guilt.   (Exit)

(Knock within)

MACBETH:

> Whence is that knocking?
> How is't with me when every noise appals me?
> What hands are here? Ha! they pluck out mine eyes.
> Will all great Neptune's ocean wash this blood
> Clean from my hand? No, this my hand will rather
> The multitudinous seas incarnadine,   61
> Making the green one red.   62

(Enter Lady Macbeth)

LADY:

> My hands are of your color, but I shame
> To wear a heart so white. *(Knock)* I hear a knocking
> At the south entry. Retire we to our chamber.

36 *knits up . . . sleave* smooths out the tangled skein   38 *second course* i.e. sleep, after food   44 *unbend* relax   46 *witness* evidence   53 *as pictures* like pictures (since without motion)   55 *gild* paint   61 *incarnadine* redden   62 *one* uniformly

A little water clears us of this deed.
How easy is it then! Your constancy
Hath left you unattended.   68
(Knock)   Hark! more knocking.
Get on your nightgown, lest occasion call us   69
And show us to be watchers. Be not lost   70
So poorly in your thoughts.   71
MACBETH:
To know my deed, 'twere best not know myself.
(Knock)
Wake Duncan with thy knocking! I would thou couldst.

(Exeunt)

II, iii   *(Enter a Porter. Knocking within.)*

PORTER: Here's a knocking indeed! If a man were porter of hell gate, he
    should have old turning the key. *(Knock.)* Knock, knock, knock. Who's   2
    there, i' th' name of Belze-bub? Here's a farmer that hanged himself on   3
    th' expectation of plenty. Come in time! Have napkins enow about you;   4
    here you'll sweat for't. *(Knock.)* Knock, knock. Who's there, in th' other
    devil's name? Faith, here's an equivocator, that could swear in both the   6
    scales against either scale; who committed treason enough for God's
    sake, yet could not equivocate to heaven. O come in, equivocator.
    (Knock.) Knock, knock, knock. Who's there? Faith, here's an English tai-
    lor come hither for stealing out of a French hose. Come in, tailor. Here   10
    you may roast your goose. *(Knock.)* Knock, knock. Never at quiet! What   11
    are you?—But this place is too cold for hell. I'll devil-porter it no fur-
    ther. I had thought to have let in some of all professions that go the
    primrose way to th' everlasting bonfire. *(Knock.)* Anon, anon! *(Opens
    the way.)* I pray you remember the porter.

(Enter Macduff and Lennox)

MACDUFF:
    Was it so late, friend, ere you went to bed,
    That you do lie so late?
PORTER: Faith, sir, we were carousing till the second cock; and drink, sir, is 18
    a great provoker of three things.
MACDUFF: What three things does drink especially provoke?
PORTER: Marry, sir, nose-painting, sleep, and urine. Lechery, sir, it pro-
    vokes, and unprovokes: it provokes the desire, but it takes away the per-
    formance. Therefore much drink may be said to be an equivocator with
    lechery: it makes him, and it mars him; it sets him on, and it takes him

---

68 *unattended* deserted   **69** *nightgown* dressing gown   **70** *watchers* i.e. awake   **71** *poorly* weakly   **II, iii**
2 *old* much   **3** *farmer* i.e. one who has hoarded crops   **4** *expectation of plenty* prospect of a crop surplus
(which will lower prices);   *enow* enough   **6** *equivocator* (usually considered an allusion to the Jesuits
tried for political conspiracy)   **10** *French hose* close-fitting breeches   **11** *roast your goose* heat your press-
ing-iron   **18** *second cock* second cockcrow (3 a.m.)

off; it persuades him, and disheartens him; makes him stand to, and not
stand to; in conclusion, equivocates him in a sleep, and, giving him   26
the lie, leaves him.

MACDUFF: I believe drink gave thee the lie last night.   28

PORTER: That it did, sir, i' the very throat on me; but I requited him for his
lie; and, I think, being too strong for him, though he took up my legs
sometime, yet I made a shift to cast him.   31

MACDUFF: Is thy master stirring?

(Enter Macbeth)

Our knocking has awaked him: here he comes.

LENNOX:
Good morrow, noble sir.

MACBETH: Good morrow, both.

MACDUFF:
Is the King stirring, worthy Thane?

MACBETH: Not yet.

MACDUFF:
He did command me to call timely on him;   36
I have almost slipped the hour.   37

MACBETH: I'll bring you to him.

MACDUFF:
I know this is a joyful trouble to you;
But yet 'tis one.

MACBETH:
The labor we delight in physics pain.   40
This is the door.

MACDUFF: I'll make so bold to call,
For 'tis my limited service   42

                                                              (Exit Macduff)

LENNOX:
Goes the King hence to-day?

MACBETH: He does; he did appoint so.

LENNOX:
The night has been unruly. Where we lay,
Our chimneys were blown down; and, as they say,
Lamentings heard i' th' air, strange screams of death,
And prophesying, with accents terrible,
Of dire combustion and confused events   48
New hatched to th' woeful time. The obscure bird   49
Clamored the livelong night. Some say the earth
Was feverous and did shake.

MACBETH: 'Twas a rough night.

---

26 *stand to* stand his guard   **28** *gave thee the lie* called you a liar (i.e. unable to stand)   **31** *cast* throw
36 *timely* early   **37** *slipped* let slip   **40** *physics pain* cures trouble   **42** *limited* appointed   **48** *combustion* tumult   **49** *obscure bird* i.e. the owl

LENNOX:
  My young remembrance cannot parallel
  A fellow to it.

  (Enter Macduff)

MACDUFF
  O horror, horror, horror! Tongue nor heart
  Cannot conceive nor name thee!
MACBETH AND LENNOX: What's the matter?
MACDUFF:
  Confusion now hath made his masterpiece: 56
  Most sacrilegious murder hath broke ope
  The Lord's anointed temple and stole thence
  The life o' th' building!
MACBETH: What is't you say? the life?
LENNOX:
  Mean you his Majesty?
MACDUFF:
  Approach the chamber and destroy your sight
  With a new Gorgon. Do not bid me speak.   62
  See, and then speak yourselves.

                              (Exeunt Macbeth and Lennox)

                              Awake, awake!
  Ring the alarum bell! Murder and treason!
  Banquo and Donalbain! Malcolm, awake!
  Shake off this downy sleep, death's counterfeit,
  And look on death itself. Up, up, and see
  The great doom's image. Malcolm! Banquo!   68
  As from your graves rise up and walk like sprites
  To countenance this horror. Ring the bell!   70

  (Bell rings. Enter Lady Macbeth.)

LADY:
  What's the business,
  That such a hideous trumpet calls to parley
  The sleepers of the house? Speak, speak!
MACDUFF: O gentle lady,
  'Tis not for you to hear what I can speak:
  The repetition in a woman's ear   75
  Would murder as it fell.
  (Enter Banquo)   O Banquo, Banquo,
  Our royal master's murdered!
LADY: Woe, alas!
  What, in our house?

56 *Confusion* destruction   62 *a new Gorgon* a new Medusa (capable of turning the beholder's eyes to stone)   68 *great doom's image* resemblance of the day of judgment   70 *countenance* appear in keeping with   75 *repetition* recital

BANQUO: Too cruel anywhere.
Dear Duff, I prithee contradict thyself
And say it is not so.

(Enter Macbeth, Lennox, and Ross)

MACBETH:
Had I but died an hour before this chance,
I had lived a blessèd time; for from this instant
There's nothing serious in mortality: 83
All is but toys. Renown and grace is dead,   84
The wine of life is drawn, and the mere lees   85
Is left this vault to brag of.   86

(Enter Malcolm and Donalbain)

DONALBAIN:
What is amiss?
MACBETH: You are, and do not know't.
The spring, the head, the fountain of your blood
Is stopped, the very source of it is stopped.
MACDUFF:
Your royal father's murdered.
MALCOLM: O, by whom?
LENNOX:
Those of his chamber, as it seemed, had done't.
Their hands and faces were all badged with blood;   92
So were their daggers, which unwiped we found
Upon their pillows. They stared and were distracted.
No man's life was to be trusted with them.
MACBETH:
O, yet I do repent me of my fury
That I did kill them
MACDUFF: Wherefore did you so?
MACBETH:
Who can be wise, amazed, temp'rate and furious,   98
Loyal and neutral, in a moment? No man.
The expedition of my violent love   100
Outrun the pauser, reason. Here lay Duncan,
His silver skin laced with his golden blood;
And his gashed stabs looked like a breach in nature
For ruin's wasteful entrance: there, the murderers,
Steeped in the colors of their trade, their daggers
Unmannerly breeched with gore. Who could refrain   106
That had a heart to love, and in that heart
Courage to make 's love known?
LADY: Help me hence, ho!

---

83 *serious in mortality* worthwhile in human life   **84** *toys* trifles   **85** *lees* dregs   **86** *vault* wine-vault
92 *badged* marked   **98** *amazed* confused   **100** *expedition* haste   **106** *Unmannerly . . . gore* crudely wearing
breeches of blood; *refrain* restrain oneself

MACDUFF:
  Look to the lady.
MALCOLM *(aside to Donalbain)*:
                    Why do we hold our tongues,   109
  That most may claim this argument for ours?   110
DONALBAIN *(to Malcolm)*:
  What should be spoken here,
  Where our fate, hid in an auger hole,   112
  May rush and seize us? Let's away:
  Our tears are not yet brewed.
MALCOLM *(to Donalbain)*:   Nor our strong sorrow
  Upon the foot of motion.
BANQUO: Look to the lady.   115

                    (Lady Macbeth is carried out)

  And when we have our naked frailties hid,   116
  That suffer in exposure, let us meet
  And question this most bloody piece of work,   118
  To know it further. Fears and scruples shake us.   119
  In the great hand of God I stand, and thence
  Against the undivulged pretense I fight   121
  Of treasonous malice.
MACDUFF: And so do I.
ALL: So all.
MACBETH:
  Let's briefly put on manly readiness
  And meet i' th' hall together.
ALL: Well contented.

          (Exeunt all but Malcolm and Donalbain)

MALCOLM:
  What will you do? Let's not consort with them.
  To show an unfelt sorrow is an office
  Which the false man does easy. I'll to England.
DONALBAIN:
  To Ireland I. Our separated fortune
  Shall keep us both the safer. Where we are
  There's daggers in men's smiles; the near in blood,   130
  The nearer bloody.
MALCOLM: This murderous shaft that's shot
  Hath not yet lighted, and our safest way
  Is to avoid the aim. Therefore to horse,
  And let us not be dainty of leave-taking
  But shift away. There's warrant in that theft   135
  Which steals itself when there's no mercy left.   *(Exeunt)*

---

109 *Look to* look after **110** *argument for ours* topic as chiefly our concern **112** *auger hole* i.e. any tiny cranny **115** *Upon the foot of motion* yet in motion **116** *frailties hid* bodies clothed **118** *question* discuss **119** *scruples* doubts **121** *undivulged pretense* secret stratagems **130** *near* nearer **135** *warrant* justification

II, iv   *(Enter Ross with an Old Man)*

OLD MAN:

 Threescore and ten I can remember well;
 Within the volume of which time I have seen
 Hours dreadful and things strange, but this sore night
 Hath trifled former knowings.   4

ROSS: Ha, good father,
 Thou seest the heavens, as troubled with man's act,   5
 Threatens his bloody stage. By th' clock 'tis day,
 And yet dark night strangles the travelling lamp.   7
 Is't night's predominance, or the day's shame,   8
 That darkness does the face of earth entomb
 When living light should kiss it?

OLD MAN: 'Tis unnatural,
 Even like the deed that's done. On Tuesday last
 A falcon, tow'ring in her pride of place,   12
 Was by a mousing owl hawked at and killed.   13

ROSS:

 And Duncan's horses (a thing most strange and certain),   14
 Beauteous and swift, the minions of their race,   15
 Turned wild in nature, broke their stalls, flung out,   16
 Contending 'gainst obedience, as they would make
 War with mankind.

OLD MAN: 'Tis said they eat each other.   18

ROSS:

 They did so, to th' amazement of mine eyes
 That looked upon't.
 (Enter Macduff) Here comes the good Macduff.
 How goes the world, sir, now?

MACDUFF: Why, see you not?

ROSS:

 Is't known who did this more than bloody deed?

MACDUFF:

 Those that Macbeth hath slain.

ROSS: Alas the day,
 What good could they pretend?   24

MACDUFF: They were suborned.
 Malcolm and Donalbain, the King's two sons,
 Are stol'n away and fled, which puts upon them
 Suspicion of the deed.

ROSS: 'Gainst nature still.
 Thriftless ambition, that will ravin up   28

II, iv Outside Inverness castle **4** *trifled former knowings* made former experiences seem trifling **5** *man's act* the human drama **7** *travelling lamp* i.e. of Phoebus, the sun **8** *predominance* supernatural ascendancy **12** *tow'ring* soaring **13** *mousing* i.e. ordinarily preying on mice; *hawked at* swooped upon **14** *certain* significant **15** *minions* darlings **16** *flung out* lunged about **18** *eat* ate **24** *pretend* expect; *suborned* bribed **28** *Thriftless* wasteful; *ravin up* bolt, swallow

Thine own live's means! Then 'tis most like
The sovereignty will fall upon Macbeth.
MACDUFF:
He is already named, and gone to Scone
To be invested.   32
ROSS: Where is Duncan's body?
MACDUFF:
Carried to Colmekill,
The sacred storehouse of his predecessors
And guardian of their bones.
ROSS: Will you to Scone?
MACDUFF:
No, cousin, I'll to Fife.
ROSS: Well, I will thither.
MACDUFF:
Well, may you see things well done there. Adieu,
Lest our old robes sit easier than our new!
ROSS:
Farewell, father.
OLD MAN:
God's benison go with you, and with those   40
That would make good of bad, and friends of foes.

                                                    (*Exeunt omnes*)

III, i   (*Enter Banquo*)

BANQUO:
Thou hast it now—King, Cawdor, Glamis, all,
As the weird women promised; and I fear
Thou play'dst most foully for't. Yet it was said   3
It should not stand in thy posterity,   4
But that myself should be the root and father
Of many kings. If there come truth from them
(As upon thee, Macbeth, their speeches shine),   7
Why, by the verities on thee made good,
May they not be my oracles as well
And set me up in hope? But hush, no more!   10

(*Sennet sounded. Enter Macbeth as King, Lady [Macbeth], Lennox, Ross,
Lords, and Attendants.*)

MACBETH:
Here's our chief guest.
LADY: If he had been forgotten,
It had been as a gap in our great feast,
And all-thing unbecoming.   13

32 *invested* crowned   40 *benison* blessing   **III, i** Within the royal palace (at Forres)   3 *foully* cheating-
ly   4 *stand* continue as a legacy   7 *shine* are brilliantly substantiated   10 s.d. *Sennet* trumpet salute
13 *all-thing* altogether

MACBETH:
   To-night we hold a solemn supper, sir,   14
   And I'll request your presence.
BANQUO: Let your Highness
   Command upon me, to the which my duties
   Are with a most indissoluble tie
   For ever knit.
MACBETH: Ride you this afternoon?
BANQUO:
   Ay, my good lord.
MACBETH:
   We should have else desired your good advice
   (Which still hath been both grave and prosperous)   21
   In this day's council; but we'll take to-morrow.
   Is't far you ride?
BANQUO:
   As far, my lord, as will fill up the time
   'Twixt this and supper. Go not my horse the better,   25
   I must become a borrower of the night   26
   For a dark hour or twain.
MACBETH: Fail not our feast.
BANQUO:
   My lord, I will not.
MACBETH:
   We hear our bloody cousins are bestowed
   In England and in Ireland, not confessing
   Their cruel parricide, filling their hearers
   With strange invention. But of that to-morrow,   32
   When therewithal we shall have cause of state   33
   Craving us jointly. Hie you to horse. Adieu,
   Till you return at night. Goes Fleance with you?
BANQUO:
   Ay, my good lord. Our time does call upon's.
MACBETH:
   I wish your horses swift and sure of foot,
   And so I do commend you to their backs.
   Farewell.   *(Exit Banquo)*
   Let every man be master of his time
   Till seven at night. To make society
   The sweeter welcome, we will keep ourself
   Till supper time alone. While then, God be with you!   43

                  (Exeunt Lords and others)

   Sirrah, a word with you. Attend those men   44
   Our pleasure?

---

14 *solemn* state   **21** *still* always; *prosperous* profitable   **25** *Go not my horse the better* i.e. unless my horse goes faster than anticipated   **26** *borrower of* i.e. borrower of time from   **32** *invention* falsehoods   **33-34** *cause . . . jointly* state business requiring our joint attention   **43** *While* until   **44** *Sirrah* form used in addressing inferiors; *Attend* await

SERVANT:
  They are, my lord, without the palace gate.
MACBETH:
  Bring them before us.   *(Exit Servant)*
  To be thus is nothing, but to be safely thus—   48
  Our fears in Banquo stick deep,   49
  And in his royalty of nature reigns that
  Which would be feared. 'Tis much he dares;   51
  And to that dauntless temper of his mind
  He hath a wisdom that doth guide his valor
  To act in safety. There is none but he
  Whose being I do fear; and under him
  My genius is rebuked, as it is said   56
  Mark Antony's was by Caesar. He chid the sisters
  When first they put the name of King upon me,
  And bade them speak to him. Then, prophet-like,
  They hailed him father to a line of kings.
  Upon my head they placed a fruitless crown
  And put a barren sceptre in my gripe,   62
  Thence to be wrenched with an unlineal hand,
  No son of mine succeeding. If't be so,
  For Banquo's issue have I filed my mind;   65
  For them the gracious Duncan have I murdered;
  Put rancors in the vessel of my peace   67
  Only for them, and mine eternal jewel   68
  Given to the common enemy of man   69
  To make them kings—the seeds of Banquo kings.
  Rather than so, come, Fate, into the list,   71
  And champion me to th' utterance! Who's there?   72

(Enter Servant and two Murderers)

  Now go to the door and stay there till we call.

                              (Exit Servant)

  Was it not yesterday we spoke together?
MURDERERS:
  It was, so please your Highness.
MACBETH: Well then, now
  Have you considered of my speeches? Know
  That it was he, in the times past, which held you
  So under fortune, which you thought had been   78
  Our innocent self. This I made good to you
  In our last conference, passed in probation with you   80
  How you were borne in hand, how crossed; the   81
    instruments;

48 *but* unless   **49** *in Banquo* about Banquo; *stick deep* are deeply imbedded in me   **51** *would be* deserves to be   **56** *genius is rebuked* controlling spirit is daunted   **62** *gripe* grasp   **65** *filed* defiled   **67** *rancors* bitter enmities   **68** *jewel* soul   **69** *common enemy of man* i.e. Satan   **71** *list* lists, field of combat   **72** *champion . . . utterance* engage with me to the death   **78** *under fortune* out of favor with fortune   **80** *passed in probation* reviewed the evidence   **81** *borne in hand* manipulated; *crossed* thwarted; *instruments* agents

Who wrought with them; and all things else that might
To half a soul and to a notion crazed   83
Say 'Thus did Banquo.'
1. MURDERER: You made it known to us.
MACBETH:
I did so; and went further, which is now
Our point of second meeting. Do you find   86
Your patience so predominant in your nature
That you can let this go? Are you so gospelled   88
To pray for this good man and for his issue,
Whose heavy hand hath bowed you to the grave
And beggared yours for ever?
1. MURDERER: We are men, my liege.
MACBETH:
Ay, in the catalogue ye go for men,   92
As hounds and greyhounds, mongrels, spaniels, curs,
Shoughs, water-rugs, and demi-wolves are clept   94
All by the name of dogs. The valued file   95
Distinguishes the swift, the slow, the subtle,
The housekeeper, the hunter, every one   97
According to the gift which bounteous nature
Hath in him closed, whereby he does receive   99
Particular addition, from the bill   100
That writes them all alike; and so of men.
Now, if you have a station in the file,
Not i' th' worst rank of manhood, say't;
And I will put that business in your bosoms   104
Whose execution takes your enemy off,
Grapples you to the heart and love of us,
Who wear our health but sickly in his life,
Which in his death were perfect.
2. MURDERER: I am one, my liege,
Whom the vile blows and buffets of the world
Have so incensed that I am reckless what
I do to spite the world.
1. MURDERER: And I another,
So weary with disasters, tugged with fortune,
That I would set my life on any chance   113
To mend it or be rid on't.
MACBETH: Both of you
Know Banquo was your enemy.
MURDERERS: True, my lord.
MACBETH:
So is he mine, and in such bloody distance   116
That every minute of his being thrusts

83 *half a soul* a halfwit; *notion* mind   86 *Our point of* the point of our   88 *gospelled* tamed by gospel precepts   92 *catalogue* inventory, classification   94 *Shoughs* shaggy pet dogs; *water-rugs* long-haired water-
dogs; *clept* named   95 *valued file* classification according to valuable traits   97 *housekeeper* watchdog
99 *closed* invested   100 *addition, from the bill* distinction, contrary to the listing   104 *in your bosoms* in
your trust   113 *set* risk   116 *distance* enmity

Against my near'st of life; and though I could   118
With barefaced power sweep him from my sight
And bid my will avouch it, yet I must not,   120
For certain friends that are both his and mine,   121
Whose loves I may not drop, but wail his fall   122
Who I myself struck down. And thence it is
That I to your assistance do make love,
Masking the business from the common eye
For sundry weighty reasons.
2. MURDERER: We shall, my lord,
Perform what you command us.
1. MURDERER: Though our lives—
MACBETH:
Your spirits shine through you. Within this hour at most
I will advise you where to plant yourselves,
Acquaint you with the perfect spy o' th' time   130
The moment on't, for't must be done to-night
And something from the palace (always thought   132
That I require a clearness); and with him,   133
To leave no rubs nor botches in the work,   134
Fleance his son, that keeps him company,
Whose absence is no less material to me
Than is his father's, must embrace the fate
Of that dark hour. Resolve yourselves apart;
I'll come to you anon.
MURDERERS: We are resolved, my lord.
MACBETH:
I'll call upon you straight. Abide within.
It is concluded. Banquo, thy soul's flight,
If it find heaven, must find it out to-night.   *(Exeunt)*

III, ii   *(Enter Macbeth's Lady and a Servant)*

LADY:
Is Banquo gone from court?
SERVANT:
Ay, madam, but returns again to-night.
LADY:
Say to the King I would attend his leisure
For a few words.
SERVANT: Madam, I will.   *(Exit)*
LADY: Naught's had, all's spent,
Where our desire is got without content.
'Tis safer to be that which we destroy
Than by destruction dwell in doubtful joy.

---

118 *near'st of life* vital parts   **120** *avouch* justify   **121** *For* because of   **122** *wail I* must wail   **130** *with the perfect spy o' th' time* by means of a perfect look-out (?), with precise timing (?)   **132** *thought* borne in mind   **133** *clearness* alibi   **134** *rubs* defects   **III, ii** The same

(Enter Macbeth)

How now, my lord? Why do you keep alone,
Of sorriest fancies your companions making,   9
Using those thoughts which should indeed have died
With them they think on? Things without all remedy   11
Should be without regard. What's done is done.

MACBETH:
We have scorched the snake, not killed it.   13
She'll close and be herself, whilst our poor malice   14
Remains in danger of her former tooth.
But let the frame of things disjoint, both the worlds   16
  suffer,
Ere we will eat our meal in fear, and sleep
In the affliction of these terrible dreams
That shake us nightly. Better be with the dead,
Whom we, to gain our peace, have sent to peace,
Than on the torture of the mind to lie   21
In restless ecstasy. Duncan is in his grave;   22
After life's fitful fever he sleeps well.
Treason has done his worst: nor steel nor poison,
Malice domestic, foreign levy, nothing,   25
Can touch him further.

LADY: Come on.
Gentle my lord, sleek o'er your rugged looks;
Be bright and jovial among your guests to-night.

MACBETH:
So shall I, love; and so, I pray, be you.
Let your remembrance apply to Banquo;   30
Present him eminence both with eye and tongue: 31
Unsafe the while, that we must lave   32
Our honors in these flattering streams
And make our faces vizards to our hearts,   34
Disguising what they are.

LADY: You must leave this.

MACBETH:
O, full of scorpions is my mind, dear wife!
Thou know'st that Banquo, and his Fleance, lives.

LADY:
But in them Nature's copy's not eterne: 38

MACBETH:
There's comfort yet; they are assailable.
Then be thou jocund. Ere the bat hath flown
His cloistered flight, ere to black Hecate's summons

---

9 *sorriest* most contemptible   **11** *all remedy* any form of remedy   **13** *scorched* slashed   **14** *close* heal; *poor malice* feeble opposition   **16** *frame of things disjoint* structure of the universe collapse; *both the worlds* i.e. heaven and earth   **21** *torture* rack   **22** *ecstasy* frenzy   **25** *Malice domestic* civil war   **30** *remembrance* i.e. awareness of the necessity   **31** *Present him eminence* exalt him   **32** *lave* dip   **34** *vizards* masks   **38** *Nature's copy* Nature's copyhold, lease on life

The shard-borne beetle with his drowsy hums   42
Hath rung night's yawning peal, there shall be done
A deed of dreadful note.
LADY: What's to be done?
MACBETH:
Be innocent of the knowledge, dearest chuck,
Till thou applaud the deed. Come, seeling night,   46
Scarf up the tender eye of pitiful day,   47
And with thy bloody and invisible hand
Cancel and tear to pieces that great bond   49
Which keeps me pale. Light thickens, and the crow
Makes wing to th' rooky wood.   51
Good things of day begin to droop and drowse,
Whiles night's black agents to their preys do rouse.
Thou marvell'st at my words, but hold thee still;
Things bad begun make strong themselves by ill.
So prithee go with me.   *(Exeunt)*

III, iii   *(Enter three Murderers)*

1. MURDERER:
But who did bid thee join with us?
3. MURDERER: Macbeth.
2. MURDERER:
He needs not our mistrust, since he delivers   2
Our offices and what we have to do   3
To the direction just.
1. MURDERER: Then stand with us.
The west yet glimmers with some streaks of day.
Now spurs the lated traveller apace   6
To gain the timely inn, and near approaches
The subject of our watch.
3. MURDERER: Hark, I hear horses.
BANQUO *(within)*
Give us a light there, ho!
2. MURDERER: Then 'tis he: the rest
That are within the note of expectation   10
Already are i' th' court.
1. MURDERER: His horses go about.
3. MURDERER:
Almost a mile; but he does usually,
So all men do, from hence to th' palace gate
Make it their walk.

---

42 *shard-borne* borne on scaly wings   46 *seeling* sewing together the eyelids (from falconry)   47 *Scarf up* blindfold   49 *great bond* i.e. Banquo's lease on life (with suggestion also of the bond of human feeling)   51 *rooky* harboring rooks   **III, iii** An approach to the palace   2 *He needs not our mistrust* i.e. we need not mistrust this man   3 *offices* duties   6 *lated* belated   10 *within the note of expectation* on the list of those expected (invited)

(Enter Banquo and Fleance, with a torch)

2. MURDERER:
A light, a light!
3. MURDERER: 'Tis he.
1. MURDERER: Stand to't.
BANQUO:
It will be rain to-night.
1. MURDERER: Let it come down!
BANQUO:
O, treachery! Fly, good Fleance, fly, fly, fly!

(Exit Fleance)

Thou mayst revenge—O slave!

(Banquo slain)

3. MURDERER:
Who did strike out the light?
1. MURDERER: Was't not the way?   19
3. MURDERER:
There's but one down: the son is fled.
2. MURDERER:
We have lost best half of our affair.
1. MURDERER:
Well, let's away, and say how much is done.   *(Exeunt)*

III, iv   *(Banquet prepared. Enter Macbeth, Lady [Macbeth],*
Ross, Lennox, Lords, and Attendants.)

MACBETH:
You know your own degrees—sit down: 1
At first and last the hearty welcome.
LORDS:
Thanks to your Majesty.
MACBETH:
Ourself will mingle with society   4
And play the humble host.
Our hostess keeps her state, but in best time   6
We will require her welcome.
LADY:
Pronounce it for me, sir, to all our friends,
For my heart speaks they are welcome.

(Enter First Murderer)

MACBETH:
See, they encounter thee with their hearts' thanks.   10
Both sides are even. Here I'll sit i' th' midst.

---

19 *Was't not the way* i.e. was it not the right thing to do   **III, iv** The hall of the palace   **1** *degrees* relative rank, order of precedence   **4** *society* the company   **6** *keeps her state* remains seated in her chair of state   **10** *encounter* greet

Be large in mirth; anon we'll drink a measure
The table round.

(Goes to Murderer)

There's blood upon thy face.
MURDERER: 'Tis Banquo's then.
MACBETH:
'Tis better thee without than he within.
Is he dispatched?
MURDERER: My lord, his throat is cut:
That I did for him.
MACBETH: Thou are the best o' th' cut-throats.
Yet he's good that did the like for Fleance:
If thou didst it, thou art the nonpareil.
MURDERER:
Most royal sir, Fleance is 'scaped.
MACBETH *(aside)*:
Then comes my fit again. I had else been perfect;   21
Whole as the marble, founded as the rock,   22
As broad and general as the casing air.   23
But now I am cabined, cribbed, confined, bound in   24
To saucy doubts and fears.—But Banquo's safe?   25
MURDERER:
Ay, my good lord. Safe in a ditch he bides,
With twenty trenchèd gashes on his head,   27
The least a death to nature.
MACBETH: Thanks for that.—

(Aside)

There the grown serpent lies; the worm that's fled   29
Hath nature that in time will venom breed,
No teeth for th' present.—Get thee gone. To-morrow
We'll hear ourselves again.   *(Exit Murderer)*   32
LADY: My royal lord,
You do not give the cheer. The feast is sold   33
That is not often vouched, while 'tis a-making,   34
'Tis given with welcome. To feed were best at home;   35
From thence, the sauce to meat is ceremony: 36
Meeting were bare without it.   37

(Enter the Ghost of Banquo, and sits in Macbeth's place)

MACBETH: Sweet remembrancer!
Now good digestion wait on appetite,
And health on both!

---

21 *perfect* sound of health   **22** *founded* solidly based   **23** *broad and general* unconfined; *casing* enveloping   **24** *cribbed* boxed in   **25** *saucy* insolent   **27** *trenchèd* deep, trench-like   **29** *worm* serpent   **32** *hear
ourselves* confer   **33** *cheer* tokens of convivial hospitality; *sold* i.e. not freely given   **34** *vouched*
sworn   **35** *To feed . . . home* i.e. mere eating is best done at home   **36** *meat* food   **37** *bare* barren, pointless; *remembrancer* prompter

LENNOX: May't please your Highness sit.
MACBETH:
 Here had we now our country's honor roofed
 Were the graced person of our Banquo present—
 Who may I rather challenge for unkindness   42
 Than pity for mischance!
ROSS: His absence, sir,
 Lays blame upon his promise. Please't your Highness
 To grace us with your royal company?
MACBETH:
 The table's full.
LENNOX: Here is a place reserved, sir.
MACBETH:
 Where?
LENNOX:
 Here, my good lord. What is't that moves your
  Highness?
MACBETH:
 Which of you have done this?
LORDS: What, my good lord?
MACBETH:
 Thou canst not say I did it. Never shake
 Thy gory locks at me.
ROSS:
 Gentlemen, rise. His Highness is not well.
LADY:
 Sit, worthy friends. My lord is often thus,
 And hath been from his youth. Pray you keep seat.
 The fit is momentary; upon a thought
 He will again be well. If much you note him,
 You shall offend him and extend his passion.   57
 Feed, and regard him not.—Are you a man?
MACBETH:
 Ay, and a bold one, that dare look on that
 Which might appal the devil.
LADY: O proper stuff!
 This is the very painting of your fear.
 This is the air-drawn dagger which you said   62
 Led you to Duncan. O, these flaws and starts   63
 (Impostors to true fear) would well become   64
 A woman's story at a winter's fire,
 Authorized by her grandam. Shame itself!   66
 Why do you make such faces? When all's done,
 You look but on a stool.
MACBETH: Prithee see there!
 Behold! Look! Lo!—How say you?

---

42 *Who may ... challenge* whom I hope I may reprove 57 *extend his passion* prolong his seizure 62 *air-drawn* fashioned of air 63 *flaws* outbursts 64 *Impostors to true fear* (i.e. because they are authentic signs of false or unjustified fear) 66 *Authorized* sanctioned

Why, what care I? If thou canst nod, speak too.
If charnel houses and our graves must send
Those that we bury back, our monuments   72
Shall be the maws of kites.   *(Exit Ghost)*   73
LADY   What, quite unmanned in folly?
MACBETH:
If I stand here, I saw him.
LADY: Fie, for shame!
MACBETH:
Blood hath been shed ere now, i' th' olden time,
Ere humane statute purged the gentle weal;   76
Ay, and since too, murders have been performed
Too terrible for the ear. The time has been
That, when the brains were out, the man would die,
And there an end. But now they rise again,
With twenty mortal murders on their crowns,   81
And push us from our stools. This is more strange
Than such a murder is.
LADY: My worthy lord,
Your noble friends do lack you.
MACBETH: I do forget.
Do not muse at me, my most worthy friends:
I have a strange infirmity, which is nothing
To those that know me. Come, love and health to all!
Then I'll sit down. Give me some wine, fill full.

(Enter Ghost)

I drink to th' general joy o' th' whole table,
And to our dear friend Banquo, whom we miss.
Would he were here! To all, and him, we thirst,   91
And all to all.
LORDS: Our duties, and the pledge.
MACBETH:
Avaunt, and quit my sight! Let the earth hide thee!
Thy bones are marrowless, thy blood is cold;
Thou has no speculation in those eyes   95
Which thou dost glare with!
LADY: Think of this, good peers,
But as a thing of custom. 'Tis no other.
Only it spoils the pleasure of the time.
MACBETH:
What man dare, I dare.
Approach thou liked the rugged Russian bear,
The armed rhinoceros, or th' Hyrcan tiger;   101
Take any shape but that, and my firm nerves

---

72 *monuments* i.e. our only tombs   **73** *maws of kites* bellies of ravens   **76** *purged the gentle weal* i.e. purged
the state of savagery   **81** *murders on their crowns* murderous gashes on their heads   **91** *thirst* are eager to
drink   **92** *all to all* let everyone drink to everyone   **95** *speculation* intelligence, power of rational observation   **101** *Hyrcan* from Hyrcania, anciently a region near the Caspian Sea

Shall never tremble. Or be alive again
And dare me to the desert with thy sword.   104
If trembling I inhabit then, protest me   105
The baby of a girl. Hence, horrible shadow!   106
Unreal mock'ry, hence!   *(Exit Ghost)*
                            Why, so; being gone,
I am a man again. Pray you sit still.

LADY:
You have displaced the mirth, broke the good meeting
With most admired disorder.   110

MACBETH: Can such things be,
And overcome us like a summer's cloud   111
Without our special wonder? You make me strange   112
Even to the disposition that I owe,
When now I think you can behold such sights
And keep the natural ruby of your cheeks
When mine is blanched with fear.   116

ROSS: What sights, my lord?

LADY:
I pray you speak not: he grows worse and worse;
Question enrages him. At once, good night.
Stand not upon the order of your going,
But go at once.

LENNOX: Good night and better health
Attend his Majesty.

LADY: A kind good night to all.   *(Exeunt Lords)*

MACBETH:
It will have blood, they say: blood will have blood.
Stones have been known to move and trees to speak;
Augures and understood relations have   124
By maggot-pies and choughs and rooks brought forth   125
The secret'st man of blood. What is the night?

LADY:
Almost at odds with morning, which is which.

MACBETH:
How say'st thou, that Macduff denies his person
At our great bidding?

LADY: Did you send to him, sir?

MACBETH:
I hear it by the way; but I will send.   130
There's not a one of them but in his house
I keep a servant fee'd. I will to-morrow   132
(And betimes I will) to the weird sisters.   133

---

104 *the desert* a solitary place   **105** *If trembling I inhabit* if I tremble   **106** *The baby of a girl* a baby girl
110 *admired* wondered at   **111** *overcome us* come over us   **112-13** *You make . . . I owe* you oust me from
my proper role (as a brave man)   **116** *blanched* made pale   **124** *Augures* auguries; *relations* utterances
125 *maggot-pies* magpies; *choughs* jackdaws (capable of 'utterances,' as are magpies and rooks)   **130** *by the*
way casually   **132** *fee'd* paid to spy   **133** *betimes* speedily

More shall they speak, for now I am bent to know   134
By the worst means the worst. For mine own good
All causes shall give way. I am in blood
Stepped in so far that, should I wade no more,
Returning were as tedious as go o'er.
Strange things I have in head, that will to hand,
Which must be acted ere they may be scanned.   140
LADY:
  You lack the season of all natures, sleep.   141
MACBETH:
  Come, we'll to sleep. My strange and self-abuse   142
Is the initiate fear that wants hard use.   143
We are yet but young in deed.   *(Exeunt)*
III, v   *(Thunder. Enter the three Witches, meeting Hecate.)*
1. WITCH:
  Why, how now, Hecate? You look angerly.
HECATE:
  Have I not reason, beldams as you are,   2
Saucy and overbold? How did you dare
To trade and traffic with Macbeth
In riddles and affairs of death;
And I, the mistress of your charms,
The close contriver of all harms,   7
Was never called to bear my part
Or show the glory of our art?
And, which is worse, all you have done
Hath been but for a wayward son,
Spiteful and wrathful, who, as others do,
Loves for his own ends, not for you.
But make amends now: get you gone
And at the pit of Acheron   15
Meet me i' th' morning. Thither he
Will come to know his destiny.
Your vessels and your spells provide,
Your charms and everything beside.
I am for th' air. This night I'll spend
Unto a dismal and a fatal end.
Great business must be wrought ere noon.
Upon the corner of the moon
There hangs a vap'rous drop profound;   24
I'll catch it ere it come to ground:
And that, distilled by magic sleights,   26
Shall raise such artificial sprites   27

---

134 *bent* inclined, determined   **140** *ere they may be scanned* i.e. without being closely studied   **141** *season* seasoning, preservative   **142** *self-abuse* delusion   **143** *initiate fear* beginner's fear; *wants hard use* lacks toughening practice   **III, v** An open place (an interpolated scene, by a different author)   **2** *beldams* old crones   **7** *close* secret   **15** *Acheron* a river of Hades   **24** *profound* weighty   **26** *sleights* devices   **27** *artificial sprites* spirits created by magic arts

As by the strength of their illusion
Shall draw him on to his confusion.
He shall spurn fate, scorn death, and bear
His hopes 'bove wisdom, grace, and fear:
And you all know security   32
Is mortals' chiefest enemy.

(Music, and a song)

Hark! I am called. My little spirit, see,
Sits in a foggy cloud and stays for me.   *(Exit)*

(Sing within, 'Come away, come away,' etc.)

1. WITCH:
   Come, let's make haste: she'll soon be back again.

                                                              (Exeunt)

III, vi   *(Enter Lennox and another Lord)*

LENNOX:
My former speeches have but hit your thoughts,   1
Which can interpret farther. Only I say   2
Things have been strangely borne. The gracious Duncan
Was pitied of Macbeth. Marry, he was dead.
And the right valiant Banquo walked too late;
Whom, you may say (if't please you) Fleance killed,
For Fleance fled. Men must not walk too late.
Who cannot want the thought how monstrous   8
It was for Malcolm and for Donalbain
To kill their gracious father? Damnèd fact,   10
How it did grieve Macbeth! Did he not straight,
In pious rage, the two delinquents tear
That were the slaves of drink and thralls of sleep?   13
Was not that nobly done? Ay, and wisely too,
For 'twould have angered any heart alive
To hear the men deny't. So that I say
He has borne all things well; and I do think   17
That, had he Duncan's sons under his key
(As, an't please heaven, he shall not), they should find 19
What 'twere to kill a father. So should Fleance.
But peace! for from broad words, and 'cause he failed   21
His presence at the tyrant's feast, I hear
Macduff lives in disgrace. Sir, can you tell
Where he bestows himself?
LORD: The son of Duncan,
From whom this tyrant holds the due of birth,   25

---

32 *security* over-confidence   **III, vi** Any meeting place in Scotland   **1** *My former speeches* what I have
just said; *hit* matched   **2** *interpret farther* draw further conclusions   **8** *cannot want the thought* can
avoid thinking   **10** *fact* deed   **13** *thralls* slaves   **17** *borne* carried off   **19** *an't* if it   **21** *from broad words*
through plain speaking   **25** *due of birth* birthright

Lives in the English court, and is received
Of the most pious Edward with such grace
That the malevolence of fortune nothing
Takes from his high respect. Thither Macduff   29
Is gone to pray the holy King upon his aid   30
To wake Northumberland and warlike Siward;   31
That by the help of these (with Him above
To ratify the work) we may again
Give to our tables meat, sleep to our nights,
Free from our feasts and banquets bloody knives,
Do faithful homage and receive free honors—   36
All which we pine for now. And this report
Hath so exasperate the King that he
Prepares for some attempt of war.
LENNOX: Sent he to Macduff?
LORD:
He did; and with an absolute 'Sir, not I,'
The cloudy messenger turns me his back   41
And hums, as who should say, 'You'll rue the time
That clogs me with this answer.'   43
LENNOX: And that well might
Advise him to a caution t' hold what distance   44
His wisdom can provide. Some holy angel
Fly to the court of England and unfold
His message ere he come, that a swift blessing
May soon return to this our suffering country
Under a hand accursed!
LORD: I'll send my prayers with him.

                                                          (Exeunt)

IV, i   *(Thunder. Enter the three Witches.)*
1. WITCH: Thrice the brinded cat hath mewed.   1
2. WITCH: Thrice, and once the hedge-pig whined.
3. WITCH: Harper cries.—'Tis time, 'tis time!   3
1. WITCH: Round about the cauldron go;
   In the poisoned entrails throw.
   Toad, that under cold stone
   Days and nights has thirty-one
   Swelt'red venom, sleeping got,   8
   Boil thou first i' th' charmèd pot.
ALL: Double, double, toil and trouble,
   Fire burn and cauldron bubble.
2. WITCH: Fillet of a fenny snake,   12
   In the cauldron boil and bake;

---

29 *his high respect* high respect for him   30 *upon his aid* upon Malcolm's behalf   31 *wake* arouse; *North-umberland* (English country bordering Scotland)   36 *free* untainted   41 *cloudy* angry   43 *clogs* encumbers   44–45 *Advise him . . . can provide* warn him to keep at as safe a distance as he can devise   IV i, A cave (cf. III, v, 15)   1 *brinded* brindled, stripped   3 *Harpier* (name of familiar spirit, suggestive of harpy)   8 *Swelt'red venom, sleeping got* exuded venom formed while sleeping   12 *fenny* swamp

Eye of newt, and toe of frog,
Wool of bat, and tongue of dog,
Adder's fork, and blindworm's sting,   16
Lizard's leg, and howlet's wing—
For a charm of pow'rful trouble
Like a hell-broth boil and bubble.
ALL: Double, double, toil and trouble
Fire burn and cauldron bubble.
3. WITCH: Scale of dragon, tooth of wolf,
Witch's mummy, maw and gulf   23
Of the ravined salt-sea shark,   24
Root of hemlock digged i' th' dark,
Liver of blaspheming Jew,
Gall of goat, and slips of yew
Silvered in the moon's eclipse,
Nose of Turk, and Tartar's lips,
Finger of birth-strangled babe
Ditch-delivered by a drab   31
Make the gruel thick and slab.   32
Add thereto a tiger's chaudron   33
For th' ingredience of our cauldron.
ALL: Double, double, toil and trouble,
Fire burn and cauldron bubble.
2. WITCH: Cool it with a baboon's blood,
Then the charm is firm and good.   38

(Enter Hecate and the other three Witches)

HECATE: O, well done! I commend your pains,
And every one shall share i' th' gains.
And now about the cauldron sing
Like elves and fairies in a ring,
Enchanting all that you put in.

(Music and a song, 'Black spirits,' etc.)

                                          (Exeunt Hecate and singers)
2. WITCH: By the pricking of my thumbs,   44
Something wicked this way comes.
Open locks,
Whoever knocks!

(Enter Macbeth)

MACBETH:
How now, you secret, black, and midnight hags,
What is't you do?
ALL: A deed without a name.

---

16 *blindworm* a lizard, popularly supposed poisonous   **23**   *mummy* mummified flesh; *maw and gulf*
stomach and gullet   **24** *ravined* insatiable   **31** *drab* harlot   **32**   *slab* sticky   **33** *chaudron* guts   **38 s.d.—**
43 s.d. (an interpolation)   **44** *By* i.e. I know by

MACBETH:

    I conjure you by that which you profess,
    Howe'er you come to know it, answer me.
    Though you untie the winds and let them fight
    Against the churches, though the yesty waves   53
    Confound and swallow navigation up,   54
    Though bladed corn be lodged and trees blown down,   55
    Though castles topple on their warders' heads,
    Though palaces and pyramids do slope   57
    Their heads to their foundations, though the treasure
    Of Nature's germains tumble all together   59
    Even till destruction sicken, answer me   60
    To what I ask you.
1. WITCH: Speak.
2. WITCH: Demand.
3. WITCH: We'll answer.
1. WITCH:
    Say if th' hadst rather hear it from our mouths
    Or from our masters.
MACBETH: Call 'em. Let me see 'em.
1. WITCH: Pour in sow's blood, that hath eaten
    Her nine farrow; grease that's sweaten   65
    From the murderer's gibbet throw
    Into the flame.
ALL: Come, high or low,
    Thyself and office deftly show!   68

(Thunder. First Apparition, an Armed Head.)

MACBETH:
    Tell me, thou unknown power—
1. WITCH: He knows thy thought:
    Hear his speech, but say thou naught.
1. APPARITION:
    Macbeth, Macbeth, Macbeth, beware Macduff!
    Beware the Thane of Fife! Dismiss me.—Enough.

(He descends)

MACBETH:
    Whate'er thou art, for thy good caution thanks:
    Thou hast harped my fear aright. But one word more—   74
1. WITCH:
    He will not be commanded. Here's another,
    More potent than the first.

(Thunder. Second Apparition, a Bloody Child.)

---

53 *yesty* yeasty, foamy   **54** *Confound* destroy   **55** *bladed corn be lodged* ripe grain be beaten to earth   **57** *slope* incline   **59** *Nature's germains* seeds of creation   **60** *sicken* shall surfeit   **65** *nine farrow* litter of nine   **68** *office* function   **74** *harped* hit the tune of

2. APPARITION:
   Macbeth, Macbeth, Macbeth—
MACBETH:
   Had I three ears, I'ld hear thee.
2. APPARITION:
   Be bloody, bold, and resolute! Laugh to scorn
   The pow'r of man, for none of woman born
   Shall harm Macbeth.   *(Descends)*
MACBETH:
   Then live, Macduff,—what need I fear of thee?
   But yet I'll make assurance double sure
   And take a bond of fate. Thou shalt not live;   84
   That I may tell pale-hearted fear it lies
   And sleep in spite of thunder.

   (Thunder. Third Apparition, a Child Crowned, with a tree in his hand.)

                          What is this
   That rises like the issue of a king
   And wears upon his baby-brow the round   88
   And top of sovereignty?
ALL: Listen, but speak not to't.
3. APPARITION:
   Be lion-mettled, proud, and take no care
   Who chafes, who frets, or where conspirers are!
   Macbeth shall never vanquished be until
   Great Birnam Wood to high Dunsinane Hill
   Shall come against him.   *(Descends)*
MACBETH: That will never be.
   Who can impress the forest, bid the tree   95
   Unfix his earth-bound root? Sweet bodements, good!   96
   Rebellious dead rise never till the Wood
   Of Birnam rise, and our high-placed Macbeth
   Shall live the lease of nature, pay his breath   99
   To time and mortal custom. Yet my heart   100
   Throbs to know one thing. Tell me, if your art
   Can tell so much: Shall Banquo's issue ever   102
   Reign in this kingdom?
ALL: Seek to know no more.
MACBETH:
   I will be satisfied. Deny me this,
   And an eternal curse fall on you! Let me know.
   Why sinks that cauldron? and what noise is this?   106

   (Hautboys)

1. WITCH: Show!
2. WITCH: Show!

---

84 *take a bond of* secure a guarantee from   **88** *round* crown   **95** *impress* conscript   **96** *bodements* prophecies   **99** *lease of nature* i.e. the full life-span   **100** *mortal custom* normal death   **102** *issue* offspring   **106** *noise* music

3. WITCH: Show!
ALL: Show his eyes, and grieve his heart!
    Come like shadows, so depart!

(A show of eight Kings and Banquo, last [King] with a glass in his hand)

MACBETH:
    Thou art too like the spirit of Banquo. Down!
    Thy crown does sear mine eyeballs. And thy hair,
    Thou other gold-bound brow, is like the first.
    A third is like the former. Filthy hags,
    Why do you show me this? A fourth? Start, eyes!   116
    What, will the line stretch out to th' crack of doom?
    Another yet? A seventh? I'll see no more.
    And yet the eighth appears, who bears a glass
    Which shows me many more; and some I see
    That twofold balls and treble sceptres carry.   121
    Horrible sight! Now I see 'tis true;
    For the blood-boltered Banquo smiles upon me   123
    And points at them for his. What? Is this so?
1. WITCH: Ay, sir, all this is so. But why   125
    Stands Macbeth thus amazedly?
    Come, sisters, cheer we up his sprites   127
    And show the best of our delights.
    I'll charm the air to give a sound
    While you perform your antic round,   130
    That this great king may kindly say
    Our duties did his welcome pay.

(Music. The Witches dance, and vanish.)

MACBETH:
    Where are they? Gone? Let this pernicious hour
    Stand aye accursèd in the calendar!
    Come in, without there!

(Enter Lennox)

LENNOX: What's your Grace's will?
MACBETH:
    Saw you the weird sisters?
LENNOX: No, my lord.
MACBETH:
    Came they not by you?
LENNOX: No indeed, my lord.
MACBETH:
    Infected be the air whereon they ride,
    And damned all those that trust them! I did hear
    The galloping of horse. Who was't came by?

---

116 *Start* bulge **121** *twofold balls and treble sceptres* (English coronation insignia) **123** *blood-boltered* matted with blood **125-32** (an interpolation) **127** *sprites* spirits **130** *antic round* grotesque circular dance

LENNOX:
　'Tis two or three, my lord, that bring you word
　Macduff is fled to England.
MACBETH: Fled to England?
LENNOX:
　Ay, my good lord.
MACBETH *(aside)*:
　Time, thou anticipat'st my dread exploits.   144
　The flighty purpose never is o'ertook   145
　Unless the deed go with it. From this moment
　The very firstlings of my heart shall be   147
　The firstlings of my hand. And even now,
　To crown my thoughts with acts, be it thought and done:
　The castle of Macduff I will surprise,
　Seize upon Fife, give to th' edge o' th' sword
　His wife, his babes, and all unfortunate souls
　That trace him in his line. No boasting like a fool;   153
　This deed I'll do before this purpose cool.
　But no more sights!—Where are these gentlemen?
　Come, bring me where they are.   *(Exeunt)*

IV, ii   *(Enter Macduff's Wife, her Son, and Ross)*

WIFE:
　What had he done to make him fly the land?
ROSS:
　You must have patience, madam.   2
WIFE: He had none.
　His flight was madness. When our actions do not,
　Our fears do make us traitors.
ROSS: You know not   4
　Whether it was his wisdom or his fear.
WIFE:
　Wisdom? To leave his wife, to leave his babes,
　His mansion and his titles in a place
　From whence himself does fly? He loves us not,
　He wants the natural touch. For the poor wren   9
　(The most diminutive of birds) will fight,
　Her young ones in her nest, against the owl.
　All is the fear and nothing is the love,
　As little is the wisdom, where the flight
　So runs against all reason.
ROSS: My dearest coz,   14
　I pray you school yourself. But for your husband,
　He is noble, wise, judicious, and best knows

---

144 *anticipat'st* forestall   **145** *flighty* fleeting   **147-48** *firstlings . . . my hand* i.e. I shall act at the moment I
feel the first impulse   **153** *trace* follow; *line* family line   **IV, ii** Within the castle at Fife   **2** *patience* self-
control   **4** *traitors* i.e. traitors to ourselves   **9** *wants* lacks   **14** *coz* cousin, kinswoman

The fits o' th' season. I dare not speak much further,   17
But cruel are the times when we are traitors
And do not know ourselves; when we hold rumor   19
From what we fear, yet know not what we fear
But float upon a wild and violent sea
Each way and none. I take my leave of you.
Shall not be long but I'll be here again.
Things at the worst will cease, or else climb upward   24
To what they were before.—My pretty cousin,
Blessing upon you!

WIFE:
Fathered he is, and yet he's fatherless.

ROSS:
I am so much a fool, should I stay longer
It would be my disgrace and your discomfort.   29
I take my leave at once.   *(Exit)*

WIFE: Sirrah, your father's dead;
And what will you do now? How will you live?

SON:
As birds do, mother.

WIFE: What, with worms and flies?

SON:
With what I get, I mean; and so do they.

WIFE:
Poor bird! thou'dst never fear the net nor lime,   34
The pitfall nor the gin.   35

SON:
Why should I, mother? Poor birds they are not set for.
My father is not dead for all your saying.

WIFE:
Yes, he is dead. How wilt thou do for a father?

SON: Nay, how will you do for a husband?

WIFE: Why, I can buy me twenty at any market.

SON: Then you'll buy 'em to sell again.   41

WIFE:
Thou speak'st with all thy wit; and yet, i' faith,   42
With wit enough for thee.

SON:
Was my father a traitor, mother?

WIFE: Ay, that he was!

SON: What is a traitor?

WIFE: Why, one that swears and lies.

SON: And be all traitors that do so?

WIFE: Every one that does so is a traitor and must be hanged.

SON: And must they all be hanged that swear and lie?

---

17 *fits o' th' season* present disorders   **19** *know ourselves* know ourselves to be so   **19-20** *hold rumor . . . we fear* are credulous in accordance with our fears   **24** *will cease* i.e. must cease descending   **29** *would be my* would be to my (i.e. his weeping)   **34** *lime* birdlime   **35** *gin* trap   **41** *sell* betray   **42-43** *Thou speak'st . . . for thee* i.e. you use all the intelligence you have, and it is quite enough.

WIFE: Every one.

SON: Who must hang them?

WIFE: Why, the honest men.

SON: Then the liars and swearers are fools, for there are liars and
swearers enow to beat the honest men and hang up them.   55

WIFE: Now God help thee, poor monkey! But how wilt thou do for a
father?

SON: If he were dead, you'ld weep for him. If you would not, it were
a good sign that I should quickly have a new father.

WIFE: Poor prattler, how thou talk'st!

(Enter a Messenger)

MESSENGER:

    Bless you, fair dame! I am not to you known,

    Though in your state of honor I am perfect.   62

    I doubt some danger does approach you nearly.   63

    If you will take a homely man's advice,   64

    Be not found here. Hence with your little ones!

    To fright you thus methinks I am too savage;

    To do worse to you were fell cruelty,   67

    Which is too nigh your person. Heaven preserve you!

    I dare abide no longer.   *(Exit)*

WIFE: Whither should I fly?

    I have done no harm. But I remember now

    I am in this earthly world, where to do harm

    Is often laudable, to do good sometime

    Accounted dangerous folly. Why then, alas,

    Do I put up that womanly defense

    To say I have done no harm?

    (Enter Murderers)   What are these faces?

MURDERER:

    Where is your husband?

WIFE:

    I hope in no place so unsanctified

    Where such as thou mayst find him.

MURDERER: He's a traitor.

SON:

    Thou liest, thou shag-eared villain!   79

MURDERER: What, you egg!

    (Stabs him) Young fry of treachery!   80

SON: He has killed me, mother.

    Run away, I pray you! *(Dies)*

---

55 *enow* enough   **62** *in your state . . . perfect* I am informed of your noble identity   **63** *doubt* fear   **64**
homely plain   **67-68** *To do worse . . . your person* i.e. not to frighten you were to do worse, expose you to
that fierce cruelty which is impending   **79** *shag-eared* i.e. with shaggy hair falling about the ears   **80**
fry spawn

(Exit [Wife,] crying 'Murder!'
[pursued by Murderers])

IV, iii   *(Enter Malcolm and Macduff)*

MALCOLM:
  Let us seek out some desolate shade, and there
  Weep our sad bosoms empty.
MACDUFF: Let us rather
  Hold fast the mortal sword and, like good men,   3
  Bestride our downfall'n birthdom. Each new morn   4
  New widows howl, new orphans cry, new sorrows
  Strike heaven on the face, that it resounds
  As if it felt with Scotland and yelled out
  Like syllable of dolor.   8
MALCOLM: What I believe, I'll wail;
  What know, believe; and what I can redress,
  As I shall find the time to friend, I will   10
  What you have spoke, it may be so perchance.
  This tyrant, whose sole name blisters our tongues,   12
  Was once thought honest; you have loved him well;
  He hath not touched you yet. I am young; but something   14
  You may deserve of him through me, and wisdom   15
  To offer up a weak, poor, innocent lamb
  T' appease an angry god.
MACDUFF:
  I am not treacherous.
MALCOLM: But Macbeth is.
  A good and virtuous nature may recoil   19
  In an imperial charge. But I shall crave your pardon.
  That which you are, my thoughts cannot transpose: 21
  Angels are bright still though the brightest fell;   22
  Though all things foul would wear the brows of grace,
  Yet grace must still look so.
MACDUFF: I have lost my hopes.
MALCOLM:
  Perchance even there where I did find my doubts.
  Why in that rawness left you wife and child,   26
  Those precious motives, those strong knots of love,
  Without leave-taking? I pray you,
  Let not my jealousies be your dishonors,   29
  But mine own safeties. You may be rightly just
  Whatever I shall think.

IV, iii The grounds of the King's palace in England   **3** *mortal* deadly   **4** *Bestride* i.e. stand over protectively; *birthdom* place of birth   **8** *Like syllable of dolor* a similar cry of pain   **10** *time to friend* time propitious   **12** *sole name* very name   **14** *young* i.e. young and inexperienced   **15** *wisdom* i.e. it may be wise   **19-20** *recoil . . . imperial charge* reverse itself under royal pressure   **21** *transpose* alter   **22** *the brightest* i.e. Lucifer   **26** *rawness* unprotected state   **29** *jealousies* suspicions

MACDUFF: Bleed, bleed, poor country!
  Great tyranny, lay thou thy basis sure,   32
  For goodness dare not check thee; wear thou thy wrongs,
  The title is affeered! Fare thee well, lord.   34
  I would not be the villain that thou think'st
  For the whole space that's in the tyrant's grasp
  And the rich East to boot.
MALCOLM: Be not offended.
  I speak not as in absolute fear of you.   38
  I think our country sinks beneath the yoke.
  It weeps, it bleeds, and each new day a gash
  Is added to her wounds. I think withal   41
  There would be hands uplifted in my right;
  And here from gracious England have I offer
  Of goodly thousands. But, for all this,
  When I shall tread upon the tyrant's head
  Or wear it on my sword, yet my poor country
  Shall have more vices than it had before,
  More suffer, and more sundry ways than ever,
  By him that shall succeed.
MACDUFF: What should he be?
MALCOLM:
  It is myself I mean, in whom I know
  All the particulars of vice so grafted   51
  That, when they shall be opened, black Macbeth   52
  Will seem as pure as snow, and the poor state
  Esteem him as a lamb, being compared
  With my confineless harms.   55
MACDUFF: Not in the legions
  Of horrid hell can come a devil more damned
  In evils to top Macbeth.
MALCOLM: I grant him bloody,
  Luxurious, avaricious, false, deceitful,   58
  Sudden, malicious, smacking of every sin   59
  That has a name. But there's no bottom, none,
  In my voluptuousness. Your wives, your daughters,
  Your matrons, and your maids could not fill up
  The cistern of my lust; and my desire
  All continent impediments would o'erbear   64
  That did oppose my will. Better Macbeth
  Than such an one to reign.
MACDUFF: Boundless intemperance
  In nature is a tyranny. It hath been   67
  Th' untimely emptying of the happy throne

---

32 *basis* foundation   **34** *affeered* confirmed by law   **38** *absolute* complete   **41** *withal* furthermore   **51** *particulars* varieties; *grafted* implanted   **52** *opened* revealed   **55** *confineless harms* unlimited vices   **58** *Luxurious* lecherous   **59** *Sudden* violent   **64** *continent* containing, restraining   **67** *In nature* in one's nature

And fall of many kings. But fear not yet
To take upon you what is yours. You may
Convey your pleasures in a spacious plenty 71
And yet seem cold—the time you may so hoodwink.
We have willing dames enough. There cannot be
That vulture in you to devour so many
As will to greatness dedicate themselves,
Finding it so inclined.

MALCOLM: With this there grows
In my most ill-composed affection such 77
A stanchless avarice that, were I King, 78
I should cut off the nobles for their lands,
Desire his jewels, and this other's house,
And my more-having would be as a sauce
To make me hunger more, that I should forge 82
Quarrels unjust against the good and loyal,
Destroying them for wealth.

MACDUFF: This avarice
Sticks deeper, grows with more pernicious root
Than summer-seeming lust, and it hath been 86
The sword of our slain kings. Yet do not fear. 87
Scotland hath foisons to fill up your will 88
Of your mere own. All these are portable, 89
With other graces weighted.

MALCOLM:
But I have none. The king-becoming graces,
As justice, verity, temp'rance, stableness,
Bounty, perseverance, mercy, lowliness, 93
Devotion, patience, courage, fortitude,
I have no relish of them, but abound 95
In the division of each several crime, 96
Acting in many ways. Nay, had I pow'r, I should
Pour the sweet milk of concord into hell,
Uproar the universal peace, confound 99
All unity on earth.

MACDUFF: O Scotland, Scotland!

MALCOLM:
If such a one be fit to govern, speak.
I am as I have spoken.

MACDUFF: Fit to govern?
No, not to live! O nation miserable,
With an untitled tyrant bloody-sceptred,
When shalt thou see thy wholesome days again,
Since that the truest issue of thy throne

---

71 *Convey* obtain by stealth   77 *ill-composed affection* disordered disposition   78 *stanchless* insatiable   82 *forge* fabricate   86 *summer-seeming* i.e. seasonal, transitory   87 *sword of our slain* cause of death of our   88-89 *foisons . . . mere own* riches of your own enough to satisfy you   89 *portable* bearable   93 *lowliness* humility   95 *relish* trace   96 *division* subdivisions   99 *Uproar* blast

By his own interdiction stands accursed   107
And does blaspheme his breed? Thy royal father
Was a most sainted king; the queen that bore thee,
Oft'ner upon her knees than on her feet,
Died every day she lived. Fare thee well.   111
These evils thou repeat'st upon thyself
Hath banished me from Scotland. O my breast,
Thy hope ends here!

MALCOLM: Macduff, this noble passion,
Child of integrity, hath from my soul
Wiped the black scruples, reconciled my thoughts   116
To thy good truth and honor. Devilish Macbeth
By many of these trains hath sought to win me   118
Into his power; and modest wisdom plucks me   119
From over-credulous haste; but God above
Deal between thee and me, for even now
I put myself to thy direction and
Unspeak mine own detraction, here abjure
The taints and blames I laid upon myself
For strangers to my nature. I am yet   125
Unknown to woman, never was forsworn,
Scarcely have coveted what was mine own,
At no time broke my faith, would not betray
The devil to his fellow, and delight
No less in truth than life. My first false speaking
Was this upon myself. What I am truly,   131
Is thine and my poor country's to command;
Whither indeed, before thy here-approach,
Old Siward with ten thousand warlike men
Already at a point was setting forth.   135
Now we'll together; and the chance of goodness   136
Be like our warranted quarrel! Why are you silent?

MACDUFF:
Such welcome and unwelcome things at once
'Tis hard to reconcile.

(Enter a Doctor)

MALCOLM:
Well, more anon. Comes the King forth, I pray you?   140
DOCTOR:
Ay, sir. There are a crew of wretched souls
That stay his cure. Their malady convinces   142
The great assay of art; but at his touch,   143

---

107 *interdiction* curse   **11** *Died* i.e. turned away from this life   **116** *scruples* doubts   **118** *trains* plots
119 *modest* cautious; *plucks* holds   **125** *For* as   **131** *upon* against   **135** *at a point* armed   **136–37** *the
chance . . . warranted quarrel* i.e. let the chance of success equal the justice of our cause   **140** *anon* soon
142 *stay* await; *convinces* baffles   **143** *assay of art* resources of medical science

Such sanctity hath heaven given his hand,
They presently amend.

MALCOLM: I thank you, doctor.   *(Exit Doctor)*

MACDUFF:
What's the disease he means?

MALCOLM: 'Tis called the evil.   146
A most miraculous work in this good King,
Which often since my here-remain in England
I have seen him do: how he solicits heaven
Himself best knows, but strangely-visited people,   150
All swol'n and ulcérous, pitiful to the eye,
The mere despair of surgery, he cures,   152
Hanging a golden stamp about their necks,   153
Put on with holy prayers; and 'tis spoken,
To the succeeding royalty he leaves
The healing benediction. With this strange virtue,
He hath a heavenly gift of prophecy,
And sundry blessings hang about his throne
That speak him full of grace.

(Enter Ross)

MACDUFF: See who comes here.

MALCOLM:
My countryman; but yet I know him not.

MACDUFF:
My ever gentle cousin, welcome hither.

MALCOLM:
I know him now. Good God betimes remove   162
The means that makes us strangers!

ROSS: Sir, amen.

MACDUFF:
Stands Scotland where it did?

ROSS: Alas, poor country,
Almost afraid to know itself. It cannot
Be called our mother but our grave, where nothing   166
But who knows nothing is once seen to smile:
Where signs and groans, and shrieks that rent the air,
Are made, not marked; where violent sorrow seems   169
A modern ecstasy. The dead man's knell   170
Is there scarce asked for who, and good men's lives   171
Expire before the flowers in their caps,
Dying or ere they sicken.

---

146 *evil* scrofula (king's evil) **150** *strangely-visited* unusually afflicted **152** *mere* utter **153** *stamp* coin **162** *betimes* quickly **166** *nothing* no one **169** *marked* noticed **170** *modern ecstasy* commonplace emotion **171** *Is there ... for who* scarcely calls forth an inquiry about identity

MACDUFF: O, relation   173
  Too nice, and yet too true!   174
MALCOLM: What's the newest grief?
ROSS:
  That of an hour's age doth hiss the speaker;   175
  Each minute teems a new one.   176
MACDUFF: How does my wife?
ROSS:
  Why, well.
MACDUFF:
  And all my children?
ROSS: Well too.
MACDUFF:
  The tyrant has not battered at their peace?
ROSS:
  No, they were well at peace when I did leave 'em.
MACDUFF:
  Be not a niggard of your speech. How goes't?
ROSS:
  When I came hither to transport the tidings
  Which I have heavily borne, there ran a rumor   182
  Of many worthy fellows that were out,   183
  Which was to my belief witnessed the rather   184
  For that I saw the tyrant's power afoot.
  Now is the time of help. Your eye in Scotland
  Would create soldiers, make our women fight
  To doff their dire distresses.
MALCOLM: Be't their comfort
  We are coming thither. Gracious England hath
  Lent us good Siward and ten thousand men,
  An older and a better soldier none
  That Christendom gives out.   192
ROSS: Would I could answer
  This comfort with the like. But I have words
  That would be howled out in the desert air,
  Where hearing should not latch them.   195
MACDUFF: What concern they,
  The general cause or is it a fee-grief   196
  Due to some single breast?   197
ROSS: No mind that's honest
  But in it shares some woe, though the main part
  Pertains to you alone.
MACDUFF: If it be mine,
  Keep it not from me; quickly let me have it.

---

173 *relation report*   **174** *nice* precise   **175** *doth hiss the speaker* causes the speaker to be hissed (for stale repetition)   **176** *teems* brings forth   **182** *heavily borne* sadly carried   **183** *out* up in arms   **184** *witnessed* attested   **192** *gives out* reports   **195** latch catch hold of   **196** *fee-grief* i.e. a grief possessed in private **197** *Due* belonging

Ross:

   Let not your ears despise my tongue for ever,
   Which shall possess them with the heaviest sound
   That ever yet they heard.

Macduff: Humh! I guess at it.

Ross:

   Your castle is surprised, your wife and babes   204
   Savagely slaughtered. To relate the manner
   Were, on the quarry of these murdered deer,   206
   To add the death of you.

Malcolm: Merciful heaven!

   What, man! Ne'er pull your hat upon your brows.
   Give sorrow words. The grief that does not speak   209
   Whispers the o'erfraught heart and bids it break.   210

Macduff:

   My children too?

Ross: Wife, children, servants, all
   That could be found.

Macduff: And I must be from thence?
   My wife killed too?

Ross: I have said.

Malcolm: Be comforted.

   Let's make us med'cines of our great revenge
   To cure this deadly grief.

Macduff:

   He has no children. All my pretty ones?
   Did you say all? O hell-kite! All?
   What, all my pretty chickens and their dam
   At one fell swoop?

Malcolm:

   Dispute it like a man.   220

Macduff: I shall do so;

   But I must also feel it as a man.
   I cannot but remember such things were
   That were most precious to me. Did heaven look on
   And would not take their part? Sinful Macduff,
   They were all struck for thee! Naught that I am,   225
   Not for their own demerits but for mine
   Fell slaughter on their souls. Heaven rest them now!

Malcolm:

   Be this the whetstone of your sword. Let grief
   Convert to anger; blunt not the heart, enrage it.

Macduff:

   O, I could play the woman with mine eyes
   And braggart with my tongue. But, gentle heavens,
   Cut short all intermission. Front to front   232

204 *surprised* attacked **206** *quarry* heap of game **209** *speak* speak aloud **210** *Whispers* whispers to **220** *Dispute* revenge **225** *Naught* wicked **232** *intermission* interval; *Front to front* face to face

Bring thou this fiend of Scotland and myself.
Within my sword's length set him. If he scape,
Heaven forgive him too!
MALCOLM: This tune goes manly.
Come, go we to the King. Our power is ready;   236
Our lack is nothing but our leave. Macbeth   237
Is ripe for shaking, and the pow'rs above
Put on their instruments. Receive what cheer you may.   239
The night is long that never finds the day.   (Exeunt)

V, i   (Enter a Doctor of Physic and a Waiting Gentlewoman)

DOCTOR: I have two nights watched with you, but can perceive no truth in
your report. When was it she last walked?
GENTLEWOMAN: Since his Majesty went into the field I have seen her rise
from her bed, throw her nightgown upon her, unlock her closet, take   4
forth paper, fold it, write upon't, read it, afterwards seal it, and again return to bed; yet all this while in a most fast sleep.
DOCTOR: A great perturbation in nature, to receive at once the benefit of
sleep and do the effects of watching! In this slumb'ry agitation, besides   8
her walking and other actual performances, what (at any time) have you
heard her say?
GENTLEWOMAN: That, sir, which I will not report after her.
DOCTOR: You may to me, and 'tis most meet you should.   12
GENTLEWOMAN: Neither to you nor any one, having no witness to confirm
my speech.

(Enter Lady Macbeth, with a taper)

Lo you, here she comes! This is her very guise, and, upon my life, fast   15
asleep! Observe her; stand close.   16
DOCTOR: How came she by that light?
GENTLEWOMAN: Why, it stood by her. She has light by her continually. 'Tis
her command.
DOCTOR: You see her eyes are open.
GENTLEWOMAN: Ay, but their sense are shut.   21
DOCTOR: What is it she does now? Look how she rubs her hands.
GENTLEWOMAN: It is an accustomed action with her, to seem thus washing
her hands. I have known her continue in this a quarter of an hour.
LADY: Yet here's a spot.
DOCTOR: Hark, she speaks. I will set down what comes from her, to satisfy
my remembrance the more strongly.
LADY: Out, damned spot! Out, I say! One—two—why then 'tis time to do't.
Hell is murky. Fie, my lord, fie! a soldier and afeard? What need we fear
who knows it, when none can call our power to accompt? Yet who   30
would have thought the old man to have had so much blood in him?

---

236 *power* army   **237** *Our lack . . . our leave* i.e. nothing remains but to say farewell   **239** *Put on their in-*
struments urge on their agents   **V, i** Within Macbeth's castle at Dunsinane   **4** *nightgown* dressing gown;
closet a chest, or desk   **8** *do the effects of watching* act as if awake   **12** *meet* fitting   **15** *guise* habit
16 *close* concealed   **21** *sense* powers of sensation   **30** *call our power to accompt* call to account anyone so
powerful as we

DOCTOR: Do you mark that?

LADY: The Thane of Fife had a wife. Where is she now? What, will these hands ne'er be clean? No more o' that, my lord, no more o' that! You mar all with this starting.   35

DOCTOR: Go to, go to! You have known what you should not.

GENTLEWOMAN: She has spoke what she should not, I am sure of that. Heaven knows what she has known.

LADY: Here's the smell of the blood still. All the perfumes of Arabia will not sweeten this little hand. Oh, oh, oh!

DOCTOR: What a sigh is there! The heart is sorely charged.   41

GENTLEWOMAN: I would not have such a heart in my bosom for the dignity of the whole body.

DOCTOR: Well, well, well.

GENTLEWOMAN: Pray God it be, sir.

DOCTOR: This disease is beyond my practice. Yet I have known those which   46
have walked in their sleep who have died holily in their beds.

LADY: Wash your hands, put on your nightgown, look not so pale! I tell you yet again, Banquo's buried. He cannot come out on's grave.

DOCTOR: Even so?

LADY: To bed, to bed! There's knocking at the gate. Come, come, come, come, give me your hand! What's done cannot be undone. To bed, to bed, to bed!

(Exit)

DOCTOR: Will she go now to bed?

GENTLEWOMAN: Directly.

DOCTOR:
Foul whisp'rings are abroad. Unnatural deeds
Do breed unnatural troubles. Infected minds
To their deaf pillows will discharge their secrets.
More needs she the divine than the physician.
God, God forgive us all! Look after her;
Remove from her the means of all annoyance,   61
And still keep eyes upon her. So good night.
My mind she has mated, and amazed my sight.   63
I think, but dare not speak.

GENTLEWOMAN: Good night, good doctor.

(Exeunt)

V, ii   *(Drum and Colors. Enter Menteith, Caithness,*
              Angus, Lennox, Soldiers.)

MENTEITH:
The English pow'r is near, led on by Malcolm,
His uncle Siward, and the good Macduff.
Revenges burn in them; for their dear causes

---

35 *starting* startled movements   **41** *charged* laden   **46** *practice* professional competence   **61** *annoyance*
self-injury   **63** *mated* bemused   **V, ii** Open country near Birnam Wood and Dunsinane

Would to the bleeding and the grim alarm   4
Excite the mortified man.   5
ANGUS: Near Birnam Wood
Shall we well meet them; that way are they coming.   6
CAITHNESS:
Who knows if Donalbain be with his brother?
LENNOX:
For certain, sir, he is not. I have a file   8
Of all the gentry. There is Siward's son
And many unrough youths that even now   10
Protest their first of manhood.   11
MENTEITH: What does the tyrant?
CAITHNESS:
Great Dunsinane he strongly fortifies.
Some say he's mad; others, that lesser hate him,
Do call it valiant fury; but for certain
He cannot buckle his distempered cause   15
Within the belt of rule.   16
ANGUS: Now does he feel
His secret murders sticking on his hands.
Now minutely revolts upbraid his faith-breach.   18
Those he commands move only in command,
Nothing in love. Now does he feel his title
Hang loose about him, like a giant's robe
Upon a dwarfish thief.
MENTEITH: Who then shall blame
His pestered senses to recoil and start,   23
When all that is within him does condemn
Itself for being there?
CAITHNESS: Well, march we on
To give obedience where 'tis truly owed.
Meet we the med'cine of the sickly weal;   27
And with him pour we in our country's purge
Each drop of us.
LENNOX: Or so much as it needs
To dew the sovereign flower and drown the weeds.   30
Make we our march towards Birnam.   *(Exeunt, marching)*

V, iii   *(Enter Macbeth, Doctor, and Attendants)*

MACBETH:
Bring me no more reports. Let them fly all!
Till Birnam Wood remove to Dunsinane,
I cannot taint with fear. What's the boy, Malcolm?   3

---

4 *bleeding* blood of battle   **5** *Excite* incite; *mortified* dead   **6** *well* surely   **8** *file* list   **10** *unrough* unbeard-
ed   **11** *Protest* assert   **15** *distempered* disease-swollen   **16** *rule* reason   **18** *minutely* every minute; *revolts*
rebellions   **23** *pestered* tormented   **27** *med'cine* cure (i.e. Malcolm); *weal* commonwealth   **30** *dew* water   **V, iii** Within Dunsinane Castle   **3** *taint* become tainted

Was he not born of woman? The spirits that know
All mortal consequences have pronounced me thus: 5
'Fear not, Macbeth. No man that's born of woman
Shall e'er have power upon thee.' Then fly, false thanes,
And mingle with the English epicures.   8
The mind I sway by and the heart I bear   9
Shall never sag with doubt nor shake with fear.

(Enter Servant)

The devil damn thee black, thou cream-faced loon!   11
Where got'st thou that goose look?
SERVANT:
There is ten thousand—
MACBETH: Geese, villain?
SERVANT: Soldiers, sir.
MACBETH:
Go prick thy face and over-red thy fear,   14
Thou lily-livered boy. What soldiers, patch?   15
Death of thy soul! those linen cheeks of thine
Are counsellors to fear. What soldiers, whey-face?
SERVANT:
The English force, so please you.
MACBETH:
Take thy face hence.   *(Exit Servant)*
                Seyton!—I am sick at heart,
When I behold—Seyton, I say!—This push   20
Will cheer me ever, or disseat me now.
I have lived long enough. My way of life
Is fall'n into the sear, the yellow leaf,   23
And that which should accompany old age,
As honor, love, obedience, troops of friends,
I must not look to have; but, in their stead,
Curses not loud but deep, mouth-honor, breath,
Which the poor heart would fain deny, and dare not.
Seyton!

(Enter Seyton)

SEYTON:
What's your gracious pleasure?
MACBETH: What news more?
SEYTON:
All is confirmed, my lord, which was reported.
MACBETH:
I'll fight till from my bones my flesh be hacked.
Give me my armor.

5 *consequences* sequence of events   8 *English epicures* (i.e. as compared with the austerely-living Scots)
9 *sway* direct myself   11 *loon* lout   14 *over-red thy fear* i.e. paint red over your fearful pallor   15 *patch*
fool   20 *push* struggle   23 *sear* dry, withered

SEYTON: 'Tis not needed yet.

MACBETH:

I'll put it on.

Send out moe horses, skirr the country round,   35

Hang those that talk of fear. Give me mine armor.

How does your patient, doctor?

DOCTOR: Not so sick, my lord,

As she is troubled with thick-coming fancies

That keep her from her rest.

MACBETH   Cure her of that!

Canst thou not minister to a mind diseased,

Pluck from the memory a rooted sorrow,

Raze out the written troubles of the brain,   42

And with some sweet oblivious antidote   43

Cleanse the stuffed bosom of that perilous stuff   44

Which weighs upon the heart?

DOCTOR: Therein the patient

Must minister to himself.

MACBETH:

Throw physic to the dogs, I'll none of it!   47

Come, put mine armor on. Give me my staff.

Seyton, send out. —Doctor, the thanes fly from me.—

Come, sir, dispatch. —If thou couldst, doctor, cast   50

The water of my land, find her disease,

And purge it to a sound and pristine health,

I would applaud thee to the very echo,

That should applaud again.—Pull't off, I say.—

What rhubarb, senna, or what purgative drug

Would scour these English hence? Hear'st thou of them?

DOCTOR:

Ay, my good lord. Your royal preparation

Makes us hear something.

MACBETH: Bring it after me!   58

I will not be afraid of death and bane   59

Till Birnam Forest come to Dunsinane.

Exeunt (all but the Doctor)

DOCTOR:

Were I from Dunsinane and clear,

Profit again should hardly draw me here.   *(Exit)*

V, iv   *(Drum and Colors. Enter Malcolm, Siward,*
             Macduff, Siward's Son, Menteith, Caithness,
             Angus, [Lennox, Ross,] and Soldiers, marching.)

---

35 *moe* more; *skirr* scour   **42** *Raze* erase   **43** *oblivious antidote* opiate, medicine of forgetfulness   **44**
stuffed choked up   **47** *physic* medicine   **50** *dispatch* hasten   **50-51** *cast . . . water* analyze the urine   **58** *it*
i.e. the remainder of the armor   **59** *bane* destruction   **V, iv** Birnam Wood

MALCOLM:
Cousins, I hope the days are near at hand
That chambers will be safe.   2
MENTEITH: We doubt it nothing.
SIWARD:
What wood is this before us?
MENTEITH: The Wood of Birnam.
MALCOLM:
Let every soldier hew him down a bough
And bear't before him. Thereby shall we shadow
The numbers of our host and make discovery   6
Err in report of us.
SOLDIERS: It shall be done.
SIWARD:
We learn no other but the confident tyrant
Keeps still in Dunsinane and will endure
Our setting down before't.
MALCOLM: 'Tis his main hope,
For where there is advantage to be gone   11
Both more and less have given him the revolt,   12
And none serve with him but constrainèd things
Whose hearts are absent too.
MACDUFF: Let our just censures   14
Attend the true event, and put we on   15
Industrious soldiership.
SIWARD: The time approaches
That will with due decision make us know
What we shall say we have and what we owe.
Thoughts speculative their unsure hopes relate,   19
But certain issue strokes must arbitrate—   20
Towards which advance the war.   *(Exeunt, marching)*   21

V, v   *(Enter Macbeth, Seyton, and Soldiers, with Drum
                and Colors)*

MACBETH:
Hang out our banners on the outward walls.
The cry is still, 'They come!' Our castle's strength   2
Will laugh a siege to scorn. Here let them lie
Till famine and the ague eat them up.
Were they not forced with those that should be ours,   5
We might have met them dareful, beard to beard,
And beat them backward home.
(A cry within of women.)   What is that noise?

---

2 *That chambers* when sleeping-chambers; *nothing* not at all   6 *discovery* i.e. reports by scouts   11 *advantage* opportunity   12 *more and less* high and low   14 *just censures* impartial judgment   15 *Attend* await; *put we on* let us put on   19 *relate* convey   20 *certain issue* the definite outcome; *arbitrate* decide   21 *war* army V, v Within Dunsinane Castle   2 *still* always   5 *forced* reinforced

SEYTON:
It is the cry of women, my good lord.   *(Exit)*
MACBETH:
I have almost forgot the taste of fears.
The time has been my senses would have cooled
To hear a night-shriek, and my fell of hair   11
Would at a dismal treatise rouse and stir   12
As life were in't. I have supped full with horrors.
Direness, familiar to my slaughterous thoughts,   14
Cannot once start me.   15
(Enter Seyton)   Wherefore was that cry?
SEYTON:
The Queen, my lord, is dead.
MACBETH:
She should have died hereafter:
There would have been a time for such a word.
To-morrow, and to-morrow, and to-morrow
Creeps in this petty pace from day to day
To the last syllable of recorded time,
And all our yesterdays have lighted fools
The way to dusty death. Out, out, brief candle!
Life's but a walking shadow, a poor player
That struts and frets his hour upon the stage
And then is heard no more. It is a tale
Told by an idiot, full of sound and fury,
Signifying nothing.

(Enter a Messenger)

Thou com'st to use thy tongue: thy story quickly!
MESSENGER:
Gracious my lord,
I should report that which I say I saw,   31
But know not how to do't.
MACBETH: Well, say, sir.
MESSENGER:
As I did stand my watch upon the hill,
I looked toward Birnam, and anon methought
The wood began to move.
MACBETH: Liar and slave!
MESSENGER:
Let me endure your wrath if't be not so.
Within this three mile may you see it coming.
I say, a moving grove.
MACBETH: If thou speak'st false,
Upon the next tree shalt thou hang alive
Till famine cling thee. If thy speech be sooth,   40

11 *fell* pelt   **12** *treatise* story   **14** *Direness* horror   **15** *start me* make me start   **31** *say* i.e. affirm   **40** *cling* shrivel; *sooth* truth

I care not if thou dost for me as much.
I pull in resolution, and begin   42
To doubt th' equivocation of the fiend,   43
That lies like truth. 'Fear not, till Birnam Wood
Do come to Dunsinane!' and now a wood
Comes toward Dunsinane. Arm, arm, and out!
If this which he avouches does appear,   47
There is nor flying hence nor tarrying here.
I 'gin to be aweary of the sun,
And wish th' estate o' th' world were now undone.
Ring the alarum bell! Blow wind, come wrack,
At least we'll die with harness on our back.   *(Exeunt)*   52

V, vi   *(Drum and Colors. Enter Malcolm, Siward,*
                 Macduff, and their Army, with boughs.)

MALCOLM:
    Now near enough. Your leavy screens throw down
    And show like those you are. You, worthy uncle,
    Shall with my cousin, your right noble son,
    Lead our first battle. Worthy Macduff and we   4
    Shall take upon's what else remains to do,
    According to our order.   6
SIWARD: Fare you well.
    Do we but find the tyrant's power to-night,   7
    Let us be beaten if we cannot fight.
MACDUFF:
    Make all our trumpets speak, give them all breath,
    Those clamorous harbingers of blood and death.

                            (Exeunt. Alarums continued.)

V, vii   *(Enter Macbeth)*

MACBETH:
    They have tied me to a stake. I cannot fly,
    But bear-like I must fight the course. What's he   2
    That was not born of woman? Such a one
    Am I to fear, or none.

    (Enter Young Siward)

YOUNG SIWARD:
    What is thy name?
MACBETH: Thou'lt be afraid to hear it.

---

42 *pull in* curb, check   **43** *doubt* suspect; *equivocation* double-talk   **47** *avouches* affirms   **52** *harness* armor   **V, vi** Fields outside Dunsinane Castle   **4** *battle* battalion   **6** *order* battleplan   **7** *power* forces   **V, vii** The same   **2** *course* attack (like a bear tied to a stake and baited by dogs or men)

YOUNG SIWARD:
　No, though thou call'st thyself a hotter name
　Than any is in hell.
MACBETH:　　　　　　　　My name's Macbeth.
YOUNG SIWARD:
　The devil himself could not pronounce a title
　More hateful to mine ear.
MACBETH:　　　　　　　　No, nor more fearful.
YOUNG SIWARD:
　Thou liest, abhorrèd tyrant! With my sword
　I'll prove the lie thou speak'st.

(Fight, and Young Siward slain)

MACBETH:　　　　　　　　Thou wast born of woman.
　But swords I smile at, weapons laugh to scorn,
　Brandished by man that's of a woman born.　　　　　*(Exit)*

(Alarums. Enter Macduff.)

MACDUFF:
　That way the noise is. Tyrant, show thy face!
　If thou beest slain and with no stroke of mine,
　My wife and children's ghosts will haunt me still.
　I cannot strike at wretched kerns, whose arms   17
　Are hired to bear their staves. Either thou, Macbeth,   18
　Or else my sword with an unbattered edge
　I sheathe again undeeded. There thou shouldst be: 20
　By this great clatter one of greatest note
　Seems bruited. Let me find him, Fortune,   22
　And more I beg not!　　　　　　　　　*(Exit. Alarums)*

(Enter Malcolm and Siward)

SIWARD:
　This way, my lord. The castle's gently rend'red: 24
　The tyrant's people on both sides do fight,
　The noble thanes do bravely in the war,
　The day almost itself professes yours   27
　And little is to do.
MALCOLM:　　　　　　　　We have met with foes
　That strike beside us.
SIWARD:　　　　　　　　Enter, sir, the castle.   29

　　　　　　　　　　　　　　　　　(Exeunt. Alarum)

---

17 *kerns* soldiers of meanest rank　**18** *staves* spears　**20** *undeeded* not glorified by deeds　**22** *bruited* reported　**24** *rend'red* surrendered　**27** *itself professes* declares itself　**29** *beside us* at our side (?), without trying to hit us (?)

V, viii   *(Enter Macbeth)*

MACBETH:

    Why should I play the Roman fool and die
    On mine own sword? Whiles I see lives, the gashes   2
    Do better upon them.

    (Enter Macduff)

MACDUFF: Turn, hellhound, turn!

MACBETH:

    Of all men else I have avoided thee.
    But get thee back! My soul is too much charged   5
    With blood of thine already.

MACDUFF: I have no words;

    My voice is in my sword, thou bloodier villain
    Than terms can give thee out!

    (Fight. Alarum.)

MACBETH: Thou losest labor.

    As easy mayst thou the intrenchant air   9
    With thy keen sword impress as make me bleed.   10
    Let fall thy blade on vulnerable crests.
    I bear a charmed life, which must not yield
    To one of woman born.

MACDUFF: Despair thy charm,   13

    And let the angel whom thou still hast served   14
    Tell thee, Macduff was from his mother's womb
    Untimely ripped.

MACBETH:

    Accursèd be that tongue that tells me so,
    For it hath cowed my better part of man!   18
    And be these juggling fiends no more believed,
    That palter with us in a double sense,   20
    That keep the word of promise to our ear
    And break it to our hope. I'll not fight with thee.

MACDUFF:

    Then yield thee, coward,
    And live to be the show and gaze o' th' time.   24
    We'll have thee, as our rarer monsters are,   25
    Painted upon a pole, and underwrit   26
    'Here may you see the tyrant.'

MACBETH: I will not yield,

    To kiss the ground before young Malcolm's feet

V, viii 2 *lives* living bodies   **5** *charged* burdened   **9** *intrenchant* incapable of being trenched (gashed)
10 *impress* leave a mark on   **13** *Despair* despair of   **14** *angel* i.e. of the host of Lucifer; *still* always   **18**
better part of man most manly side   **20** *palter* quibble   **24** *gaze* sight   **25** *monsters* freaks   **26** *Painted upon
a pole* pictured on a showman's banner

And to be baited with the rabble's curse.
Though Birnam Wood be come to Dunsinane,
And thou opposed, being of no woman born,
Yet I will try the last. Before my body
I throw my warlike shield. Lay on, Macduff,
And damned be him that first cries 'Hold, enough!'   34

> (Exeunt fighting. Alarums.
> [Re-]enter fighting, and Macbeth slain.
> [Exit Macduff])

(Retreat and flourish. Enter, with Drum and Colors,
Malcolm, Siward, Ross, Thanes, and Soldiers.)

MALCOLM:
I would the friends we miss were safe arrived.
SIWARD:
Some must go off, and yet, by these I see,   36
So great a day as this is cheaply bought.
MALCOLM:
Macduff is missing, and your noble son.
ROSS:
Your son, my lord, has paid a soldier's debt.
He only lived but till he was a man,
The which no sooner had his prowess confirmed
In the unshrinking station where he fought   42
But like a man he died.
SIWARD: Then he is dead?
ROSS:
Ay, and brought off the field. Your cause of sorrow
Must not be measured by his worth, for then
It hath no end.
SIWARD: Had he his hurts before?
ROSS:
Ay, on the front.
SIWARD: Why then, God's soldier be he.
Had I as many sons as I have hairs,
I would not wish them to a fairer death:
And so his knell is knolled.
MALCOLM: He's worth more sorrow,
And that I'll spend for him.
SIWARD: He's worth no more.
They say he parted well and paid his score,
And so, God be with him. Here comes newer comfort.   52

(Enter Macduff, with Macbeth's head)

---

34 s.d. Exeunt . . . slain (after this action the scene apparently shifts to within Dunsinane Castle, cf. V, vii,
29) **36** go off perish; these i.e. these here assembled **42** unshrinking station place from which he did not
retreat **52** parted departed; score reckoning

MACDUFF:
    Hail, King, for so thou art. Behold where stands
    Th' usurper's cursèd head. The time is free.   55
    I see thee compassed with thy kingdom's pearl,   56
    That speak my salutation in their minds,
    Whose voices I desire aloud with mine—
    Hail, King of Scotland!
ALL: Hail, King of Scotland!

(Flourish)

MALCOLM:
    We shall not spend a large expense of time
    Before we reckon with your several loves   61
    And make us even with you. My Thanes and kinsmen,   62
    Henceforth be Earls, the first that ever Scotland
    In such an honor named. What's more to do
    Which would be planted newly with the time—   65
    As calling home our exiled friends abroad
    That fled the snares of watchful tyranny,
    Producing forth the cruel ministers   68
    Of this dead butcher and his fiend-like queen,
    Who (as 'tis thought) by self and violent hands   70
    Took off her life—this, and what needful else
    That calls upon us, by the grace of Grace
    We will perform in measure, time, and place.   73
    So thanks to all at once and to each one,
    Whom we invite to see us crowned at Scone.

(Flourish. Exeunt omnes.)

55 *free* released from tyranny   **56** *compassed* surrounded   **61** *reckon* come to an accounting   **62** *make us even with you* repay you   **65** *would be planted newly with the time* i.e. should be done at the outset of this new era   **68** *ministers* agents   **70** *self and violent* her own violent   **73** *in measure* with decorum; *time, and place* at the proper time and place

As a tragedy, *Macbeth* strikes different chords from *Oedipus Rex*. The Elizabethan theater, the expectations of the audience, and the genius of Shakespeare combined to produce an idea of tragedy different from the Greeks'. Nevertheless, there are fundamental similarities. To sharpen our understanding, we may wish to consider some questions:

1. Does *Macbeth* have a unified plot? Is each incident between beginning and end the necessary or probable result of a previous incident?
2. Do some episodes seem to lie outside the chain of necessity? For example, we might question the porter at the gate at the beginning of act 2, scene 3. Do any of the scenes with the witches seem superfluous? If some incidents seem unnecessary to the plot, can they be justified on some other ground?

3. Does the plot contain a reversal? Does it contain a reversal of intention? Are there more reversals than one? Where?
4. Does the play contain a recognition? More than one? Where? Is there a recognition that extends beyond simple identity (for example, the discovery that Macduff is not "of woman born") to suggest a new understanding of man's place in society or the universe?
5. Is Macbeth in any sense a "good" character, or is he simply the villain some think? Lady Macbeth? If we understand them as villains, can we find any redeeming features in either of them? Does either have a tragic flaw?
6. If we feel pity for undeserved misfortune and fear for a misfortune for someone like us, do we feel either pity or fear for Macbeth or Lady Macbeth? Do we feel these emotions for others in the play?
7. Does Macbeth make significant choices? Do we understand his motivations? Are Macbeth and Lady Macbeth rounded characters? Is Macbeth responsible for his own downfall, or is he a victim of the gods?
8. Do the witches function in any way like the oracle in *Oedipus Rex?* Are they important in different ways?

Answers to some of these questions may provoke considerable debate in the classroom, as they have among scholars.

Despite their differences, both *Oedipus Rex* and *Macbeth* deal seriously with serious matters, as all tragedies must. Both question the extent to which humans control their fates, but both hold humanity accountable for its actions. Both support a vision of an ordered universe, with tragedy resulting from an attempted disruption, a willful kicking against fate. In both, transgression brings death or exile, as society heals its wound by casting out the offender. Both engage the audience in a spectacle both moving and thought provoking, an amalgamation of heart and mind. Both suggest the heights to which man may aspire, and the depths to which he may fall. Later tragedies contain most of the same ingredients, although twentieth-century plays frequently take a more chaotic view of the universe and of man's place in it.

Because tragedies are plays, and plays language, they share common literary elements. *Theme* is obviously important. In comparing *Oedipus Rex* and *Macbeth*, we might want to observe how the theme of ambition is handled. Clearly, the same thematic material would be used differently in a comedy. Because both plays are in verse, both use the techniques of verse: rhythm, sound, imagery, and metaphor. Both, for example, stress blood, physically present on stage and memorably supported in language. Other important images abound. Shakespeare's language, especially, is probably the richest in metaphor ever written. As storytellers, both playwrights had to master *exposition*: the unfolding of events both past and present necessary to understanding plot development.

Shakespeare's exposition comes mostly in his early scenes; Sophocles' plot in the present serves also as his exposition of the past. Similarly, both had to provide a *denouement*: an untying of the knotted threads of the plot after its high point, or *climax*.

CHAPTER 2

Comedy, Satire, and Romance

Diametrically opposed to tragedy is comedy, the upturned mirth of the comic mask as opposed to tragedy's downturned mouth. As tragedies provoke tears, comedies provoke laughter. In both tragedy and comedy we see ourselves, made slightly more noble or slightly more ridiculous than in real life, but recognizable all the same. This fundamental reality of vision binds the two together around the twin poles of emotion and intellect. On the tragic side, the tug is toward emotion, on the comic toward intellect. But in the end, we are both moved and rendered thoughtful about the human predicament.

In comedy the emphasis on laughter sometimes complicates plot at the expense of character, or, alternatively, stresses character at the expense of plot. Frequently, however, the interplay between plot and character is as important as it is in tragedy. The comic hero, only a little less noble than ourselves, embroils himself in comic entanglements that are in large degree of his own making, the result of choices arising from his personality. Like the tragic hero, he is buffeted by incidents that suggest an unkind Fate, but the uninvolved bystander is not so sure that he has not engendered them. Whereas in tragedy the hero is at the end removed from society through death or exile, the comic hero is at the end embraced by a society that has threatened to cast him out.

Below the horizontal axis of tragedy and comedy, lies the realm of *satire*. Herein the fundamental reality of the tragic–comic vision is subordinated to the desire to expose men and their institutions to ridicule and contempt. Both tragedy and comedy move sometimes in this direction, becoming *satiric tragedy* or *satiric comedy*. Above the tragic–comic axis lies *romance*. Herein the fundamental reality of the tragic–comic vision is subordinated to sentimental wish fulfillment. Moving in this direction, tragedy and comedy become *romantic tragedy* and *romantic comedy*. Just as the common element binding tragedy and comedy is a vision of the real, so the common element binding satire and romance is a vision of the ideal, either directly or ironically expressed. When the characters of a comedy or tragedy seem abstractions of human types, rather than round-

994

ed, individualized human beings, we begin to suspect elements either of romance or satire. When the play denigrates these human abstractions as falling ironically short of the ideal that we hope for in this world, we have satire. When it elevates them toward an ideal that in this world we only aspire to, we have romance. Adopting the mythic vision of the Bible, we may say that satire directs our attention toward man's demonic, romance toward his angelic potential.

Because tragedy and comedy reside with us in the world that nestles between the unrealized ideal above and its ironic alternative below, they have throughout history seemed more central to the human experience than either romance or satire. Comedy, indeed, has always taken to itself large elements of romance and satire. The great classics of comedy, however, are constructed around a central core of realistic truth.

Lysistrata

Aristophanes was the undisputed master of Greek Old Comedy, a form that flourished in Athens for about a century, beginning a generation before his birth and ending with his death. Like Greek tragedy, Old Comedy was performed before thousands in the huge theater of Dionysus during the annual Dionysian festivals. It was shaped by the physical theater as well as by the festive ritual. The actors wore grotesque comic masks and ludicrously padded costumes, including large leather phalluses for the male characters. All parts, male and female, were played by men, with the women distinguished by their masks and long gowns. Within these conventions, Aristophanes commented astutely on the human situation. *Lysistrata* was especially timely when first performed in 411 B.C. After thirty years of war between Athens and Sparta, broken only by one short truce, Aristophanes imagined the women of both sides conspiring for the peace that had eluded the politicians.

LYSISTRATA*
Aristophanes   (Ca. 447-380 B.C.)

CHARACTERS

LYSISTRATA ⎫
KALONIKE ⎬ Athenian women
MYRRHINA ⎭
LAMPITO, a Spartan woman
CHORUS OF OLD MEN
CHORUS OF WOMEN
ATHENIAN COMMISSIONER

OLD MARKET-WOMEN
CINESIAS, an Athenian, husband
  of Myrrhina
SPARTAN HERALD
SPARTAN AMBASSADORS
ATHENIAN AMBASSADORS

* Translated by Donald Sutherland.

(A street in Athens before daylight)

LYSISTRATA: If anyone had asked them to a festival
    of Aphrodite[1] or of Bacchus[2] or of Pan,[3]
    you couldn't get through Athens for the tambourines,
    but now there's not one solitary woman here.
    Except my next-door neighbor. Here she's coming out.   5
    Hello, Kalonike.
KALONIKE: Hello, Lysistrata.
    What are you so upset about? Don't scowl so, dear.
    You're less attractive when you knit your brows and glare.
LYSISTRATA: I know, Kalonike, but I am smoldering
    with indignation at the way we women act.   10
    Men think we are so gifted for all sorts of crime
    that we will stop at nothing—
KALONIKE: Well, we are, by Zeus!
LYSISTRATA: —but when it comes to an appointment here with me
    to plot and plan for something really serious
    they lie in bed and do not come.
KALONIKE: They'll come, my dear.   15
    You know what trouble women have in going out:
    one of us will be wrapped up in her husband still,
    another waking up the maid, or with a child
    to put to sleep, or give its bath, or feed its pap.
LYSISTRATA: But they had other more important things to do than those.   20
KALONIKE: What ever is it, dear Lysistrata?
    What have you called us women all together for?
    How much of a thing is it?
LYSISTRATA: Very big.
KALONIKE: And thick?
LYSISTRATA: Oh very thick indeed.
KALONIKE: Then *how* can we be late?
LYSISTRATA: That's not the way it is. Or we would all be here.   25
    But it is something I have figured out myself
    and turned and tossed upon for many a sleepless night.
KALONIKE: It must be something slick you've turned and tossed
    upon!
LYSISTRATA: So slick that the survival of all Greece depends
    upon the women.
KALONIKE: On the women? In that case   30
    poor Greece has next to nothing to depend upon.
LYSISTRATA: Since now it's we who must decide affairs of state:
    either there is to be no Spartan left alive—
KALONIKE: A very good thing too, if none were left, by Zeus!
LYSISTRATA: —and every living soul in Thebes to be destroyed—   35
KALONIKE: Except the eels![4] Spare the delicious eels of Thebes!

---

[1] Goddess of love and beauty.
[2] God of wine and revelry.
[3] God of fields and forests.
[4] Considered a delicacy.

LYSISTRATA: —and as for Athens—I can't bring myself to say
    the like of that for us. But just think what I mean!
    Yet if the women meet here as I told them to
    from Sparta, Thebes, and all of their allies,   40
    and we of Athens, all together we'll save Greece.
KALONIKE: What reasonable thing could women ever do,
    or glorious, we who sit around all prettied up
    in flowers and scandalous saffron-yellow gowns,
    groomed and draped to the ground in oriental stuffs   45
    and fancy pumps?
LYSISTRATA: And those are just the very things
    I count upon to save us—wicked saffron gowns,
    perfumes and pumps and rouge and sheer transparent frocks.
KALONIKE: But what use can they be?
LYSISTRATA: So no man in our time
    will raise a spear against another man again—   50
KALONIKE: I'll get a dress dyed saffron-yellow, come what may!
LYSISTRATA: —nor touch a shield—
KALONIKE: I'll slip into the sheerest gown!
LYSISTRATA: —nor so much as a dagger—
KALONIKE: I'll buy a pair of pumps!
LYSISTRATA: So don't you think the women should be here by now?
KALONIKE: I don't. They should have *flown* and got here long ago.   55
LYSISTRATA: You'll see, my dear. They will, like good Athenians,
    do everything too late. But from the coastal towns
    no woman is here either, nor from Salamis.
KALONIKE: I'm certain those from Salamis have crossed the strait:
    they're always straddling *something* at this time of night.   60
LYSISTRATA: Not even those I was expecting would be first
    to get here, from Acharnae, from so close to town,
    not even they are here.
KALONIKE: But one of them, I know,
    is under way, and three sheets to the wind, by now.
    But look—some women are approaching over there.   65
LYSISTRATA: And over here are some, coming this way—
KALONIKE: Phew! Phew!
    Where are they from?
LYSISTRATA: Down by the marshes.
KALONIKE: Yes, by Zeus!
    It smells as if the bottoms had been all churned up!

(Enter Myrrhina, and others)

MYRRHINA: Hello Lysistrata. Are we a little late?
    What's that? Why don't you speak?
LYSISTRATA: I don't think much of you,   70
    Myrrhina, coming to this business only now.
MYRRHINA: Well, I could hardly find my girdle in the dark.
    If it's so urgent, tell us what it is. We're here.

KALONIKE: Oh no. Let's wait for just a little while until
the delegates from Sparta and from Thebes arrive.   75
LYSISTRATA: You show much better judgment.

(Enter Lampito, and others)

                                        Here comes Lampito!
LYSISTRATA: Well, darling Lampito! My dearest Spartan friend!
How very sweet, how beautiful you look! That fresh
complexion! How magnificent your figure is!
Enough to crush a bull!
LAMPITO: Ah shorely think Ah could.[5]   80
Ah take mah exacise. Ah jump and thump mah butt.
KALONIKE: And really, what a handsome set of tits you have!
LAMPITO: You feel me ovah lahk a cow fo sacrafahce!
LYSISTRATA: And this other young thing—where ever is *she* from?
LAMPITO: She's prominent, Ah sweah, in Thebes—a delegate   85
ample enough.
LYSISTRATA: By Zeus, she represent Thebes well,
having so trim a ploughland.
KALONIKE: Yes, by Zeus, she does!
There's not a weed of all her field she hasn't plucked.
LYSISTRATA: And who's the other girl?
LAMPITO: Theah's nothing small, Ah sweah,
or tahght about her folks in Corinth.
KALONIKE: No, by Zeus!—   90
to judge by this side of her, nothing small or tight.
LAMPITO: But who has called togethah such a regiment
of all us women?
LYSISTRATA: Here I am. I did.
LAMPITO: Speak up,
just tell us what you want.
KALONIKE: Oh yes, by Zeus, my dear,   95
do let us know what the important business is!
LYSISTRATA: Let me explain it, then. And yet . . . before I do . . .
I have one little question.
KALONIKE: Anything you like.
LYSISTRATA: Don't you all miss the fathers of your little ones,
your husbands who have gone away to war? I'm sure
you all have husbands in the armies far from home.   100
KALONIKE: Mine's been away five months in Thrace—a general's
guard,
posted to see his general does not desert.
MYRRHINA: And mine has been away in Pylos seven whole months.
LAMPITO: And mahn, though he does get back home on leave
sometahms,
no soonah has he come than he is gone again.   105

---

[5] A comic southern accent here represents the Doric of the original. Other translators have tried
Northern British, Scots, and American hillbilly.

LYSISTRATA: No lovers either. Not a sign of one is left.
　　For since our eastern allies have deserted us
　　they haven't sent a single six-inch substitute
　　to serve as leatherware replacement for our men.
　　Would you be willing, then, if I thought out a scheme,   110
　　to join with me to end the war?
KALONIKE:　　　　　　　　　　　　　Indeed I would,
　　even if I had to pawn this very wrap-around
　　and drink up all the money in one day, I would!
MYRRHINA: And so would I, even if I had to see myself
　　split like a flounder, and give half of me away!   115
LAMPITO: And so would Ah! Ah'd climb up Mount Taÿgetos
　　if Ah just had a chance of seeing peace from theah!
LYSISTRATA: Then I will tell you. I may now divulge my plan.
　　Women of Greece!—if we intend to force the men
　　to make a peace, we must abstain . . .
KALONIKE:　　　　　　　　　　　　　From what? Speak out!   120
LYSISTRATA: But will you do it?
KALONIKE:　　　　　　　　We will, though death should be the price!
LYSISTRATA: Well then, we must abstain utterly from the prick.
　　Why do you turn your backs? Where are you off to now?
　　And you—why pout and make such faces, shake your heads?
　　Why has your color changed? Why do you shed those tears?   125
　　Will you do it or will you not? Why hesitate?
KALONIKE: I will not do it. Never. Let the war go on!
MYRRHINA: Neither will I. By Zeus, no! Let the war go on!
LYSISTRATA: How can you say so, Madam Flounder, when just
　　now
　　you were declaiming you would split yourself in half?   130
KALONIKE: Anything else you like, anything! If I must
　　I'll gladly walk through fire. That, rather than the prick!
　　Because there's nothing like it, dear Lysistrata.
LYSISTRATA: How about you?
MYRRHINA:　　　　　　　　　　I too would gladly walk through fire.
LYSISTRATA: Oh the complete depravity of our whole sex!   135
　　It is no wonder tragedies are made of us,
　　we have such unrelenting unity of mind!
　　But you, my friend from Sparta, dear, if you alone
　　stand by me, only you, we still might save the cause.
　　Vote on my side!
LAMPITO:　　　　　　They'ah hahd conditions, mahty hahd,   140
　　to sleep without so much as the fo'skin of one . . .
　　but all the same . . . well . . . yes. We need peace just as bad.
LYSISTRATA: Oh dearest friend!—the one real woman of them all!
KALONIKE: And if we really should abstain from what you say—
　　which Heaven forbid!—do you suppose on that account   145
　　that peace might come to be?
LYSISTRATA:　　　　　　　　　　　I'm absolutely sure.
　　If we should sit around, rouged and with skins well creamed,

with nothing on but a transparent negligé,
and come up to them with our deltas plucked quite smooth,
and, once our men get stiff and want to come to grips,   150
we do not yield to them at all but just hold off,
they'll make a truce in no time. There's no doubt of that.

LAMPITO: We say in Spahta that when Menelaos[6] saw
  Helen's ba'e apples he just tossed away his swo'd.

KALONIKE: And what, please, if our husbands just toss us away?   155

LYSISTRATA: Well, you have heard the good old saying: Know Thyself.

KALONIKE: It isn't worth the candle. I hate cheap substitutes.
  But what if they should seize and drag us by brute force
  into the bedroom?

LYSISTRATA: Hang onto the doors!

KALONIKE: And if—
  they beat us?   160

LYSISTRATA: Then you must give in, but nastily,
  and do it badly. There's no fun in it by force.
  And then, just keep them straining. They will give it up
  in no time—don't you worry. For never will a man
  enjoy himself unless the woman coincides.

KALONIKE: If both of you are for this plan, then so are we.   165

LAMPITO: And we of Spahta shall persuade ouah men to keep
  the peace sinceahly and with honah in all ways,
  but how could anyone pe'suade the vulgah mob
  of Athens not to deviate from discipline?

LYSISTRATA: Don't worry, we'll persuade our men. They'll keep
  the peace.   170

LAMPITO: They won't, so long as they have battleships afloat
  and endless money sto'ed up in the Pahthenon.[7]

LYSISTRATA: But that too has been carefully provided for:
  we shall take over the Acropolis[8] today.
  The oldest women have their orders to do that: 175
  while we meet here, they go as if to sacrifice
  up there, but really seizing the Acropolis.

LAMPITO: All should go well. What you say theah is very smaht.

LYSISTRATA: In that case, Lampito, what are we waiting for?
  Let's take an oath, to bind us indissolubly.   180

LAMPITO: Well, just you show us what the oath is. Then we'll
  sweah.

LYSISTRATA: You're right. Where is that lady cop?

(To the armed Lady Cop looking around for a Lady Cop)

                                          What do you think
you're looking for? Put down your shield in front of us,
there, on its back, and someone get some scraps of gut.

---

[6] Husband of Helen of Troy.
[7] A war reserve fund had been kept for years in the Parthenon.
[8] The fortified upper part of Athens, including the Parthenon.

KALONIKE: Lysistrata, what in the world do you intend   185
   to make us take an oath on?
LYSISTRATA: What? Why, on a shield,
   just as they tell me some insurgents in a play
   by Aeschylus[9] once did, with a sheep's blood and guts.
KALONIKE: Oh *don't*, Lysistrata, don't swear upon a *shield*,
   not if the oath has anything to do with peace!   190
LYSISTRATA: Well then, what *will* we swear on? Maybe we should get
   a white horse somewhere, like the Amazons, and cut
   some bits of gut from it.
KALONIKE: *Where* would we get a horse?
LYSISTRATA: But what kind of an oath *is* suitable for us?
KALONIKE: By Zeus, I'll tell you if you like. First we put down   195
   a big black drinking-cup, face up, and then we let
   the neck of a good jug of wine bleed into it,
   and take a solemn oath to—add no water in.
LAMPITO: Bah Zeus, Ah jest can't tell you how Ah lahk that oath!
LYSISTRATA: Someone go get a cup and winejug from inside.   200

   (Kalonike goes and is back in a flash)

KALONIKE: My dears, my dearest dears—how's *this* for pottery?
   You feel good right away, just laying hold of it.
LYSISTRATA: Well, set it down, and lay your right hand on this pig.
   O goddess of Persuasion, and O Loving-cup,
   accept this victim's blood! Be gracious unto us.   205
KALONIKE: It's not anaemic, and flows clear. Those are good signs.
LAMPITO: What an aroma, too! Bah Castah[10] it *is* sweet!
KALONIKE: My dears, if you don't mind—I'll be the first to swear.
LYSISTRATA: By Aphrodite, no! If you had drawn first place
   by lot—but now let all lay hands upon the cup.   210
   Yes, Lampito—and now, let one of you repeat
   for all of you what I shall say. You will be sworn
   by every word she says, and bound to keep this oath:
   No lover and no husband and no man on earth—
KALONIKE: No lover and no husband and no man on earth—   215
LYSISTRATA: *shall e'er approach me with his penis up.* Repeat.
KALONIKE: shall e'er approach me with his penis up. Oh dear,
   my knees are buckling under me, Lysistrata!
LYSISTRATA: *and I shall lead an unlaid life alone at home,*   220
KALONIKE: and I shall lead an unlaid life alone at home,
LYSISTRATA: *wearing a saffron gown and groomed and beautified*
KALONIKE: wearing a saffron gown and groomed and beautified
LYSISTRATA: *so that my husband will be all on fire for me*
KALONIKE: so that my husband will be all on fire for me
LYSISTRATA: *but I will never willingly give in to him*   225
KALONIKE: but I will never willingly give in to him

---

[9] A Greek tragic playwright (525–456 B.C.).
[10] Castor, son of Leda and Zeus.

LYSISTRATA: *and if he tries to force me to against my will*
KALONIKE: and if he tries to force me to against my will
LYSISTRATA: *I'll do it badly and not wiggle in response*
KALONIKE: I'll do it badly and not wiggle in response   230
LYSISTRATA: *nor toward the ceiling will I lift my Persian pumps*
KALONIKE: nor toward the ceiling will I lift my Persian pumps
LYSISTRATA: *nor crouch down as the lions on cheese-graters do*
KALONIKE: nor crouch down as the lions on cheese-graters do
LYSISTRATA: *and if I keep my promise, may I drink of this—*   235
KALONIKE: and if I keep my promise, may I drink of this—
LYSISTRATA: *but if I break it, then may water fill the cup!*
KALONIKE: but if I break it, then may water fill the cup!
LYSISTRATA: Do you all swear to this with her?
ALL: We do, by Zeus!
LYSISTRATA: I'll consecrate our oath now.
KALONIKE: Share alike, my dear,   240
   so we'll be friendly to each other from the start.
LAMPITO: What was that screaming?
LYSISTRATA: That's what I was telling you:
   the women have already seized the Parthenon
   and the Acropolis. But now, dear Lampito
   return to Sparta and set things in order there—   245
   but leave these friends of yours as hostages with us—
   And let *us* join the others in the citadel
   and help them bar the gates.
KALONIKE: But don't you think the men
   will rally to the rescue of the citadel,
   attacking us at once?
LYSISTRATA: They don't worry me much: 250
   they'll never bring against us threats or fire enough
   to force open the gates, except upon our terms.
KALONIKE: Never by Aphrodite! Or we'd lose our name
   for being battle-axes and unbearable!

*(Exeunt. The scene changes to the Propylaea[11] of the Acropolis. A chorus of very old
men struggles slowly in, carrying logs and firepots.)*

ONE OLD MAN: Lead on! O Drakës, step by step, although your   255
                          shoulder's aching
                    and under this green olive log's great weight
                          your back be breaking!
ANOTHER: Eh, life is long but always has
                          more surprises for us!   260
                    Now who'd have thought we'd live to hear
                          this, O Strymodorus?—
                    The wives we fed and looked upon
                    as helpless liabilities
                    now dare to occupy the Parthenon,   265

---

[11] The roofed gateway on the west side of the Acropolis.

> our whole Acropolis, for once they seize
> the Propylaea, straightway
> they lock and bar the gateway.

CHORUS: Let's rush to the Acropolis with due precipitation
and lay these logs down circlewise, till presently we turn them   270
into one mighty pyre to make a general cremation
of all the women up there—eh! with our own hands we'll burn
    them,
the leaders and the followers, without discrimination!

AN OLD MAN: They'll never have the laugh on me!
> Though I may not look it,   275
> I rescued the Acropolis
>   when the Spartans took it
> about a hundred years ago.
> We laid a siege that kept their king
> six years unwashed, so when I made him throw   280
> his armor off, for all his blustering,
> in nothing but his shirt he
> looked very very dirty.

CHORUS: How strictly I besieged the man! These gates were all
    invested
with seventeen ranks of armored men all equally ferocious!   285
Shall women—by Euripides[12] and all the gods detested—
not be restrained—with me on hand—from something so
    atrocious?
They shall!—or may our trophies won at Marathon[13] be bested!
> But we must go a long way yet
>   up that steep and winding road   290
> before we reach the fortress where we want to get.
> How shall we ever drag this load,
>   lacking pack-mules, way up there?
> I can tell you that my shoulder has caved in beyond
>   repair!
>   Yet we must trudge ever higher,   295
>   ever blowing on the fire,
> so its coals will still be glowing when we get where we
>   are going
>   Fooh! Fooh!
>   Whoo! I choke!
>   What a smoke!   300

> Lord Herakles![14] How fierce it flies
> out against me from the pot!

---

[12] A Greek tragic playwright (Ca. 485–406 B.C.).
[13] Where the Athenians defeated the Persians in 490 B.C., almost eighty years before the first performance of *Lysistrata*.
[14] Hercules, son of Zeus and Alcmene.

and like a rabid bitch it bites me in the eyes!
It's female fire, or it would not
scratch my poor old eyes like this.   305
Yet undaunted we must onward, up the high Acropolis
where Athena's temple stands
fallen into hostile hands.
O my comrades! shall we ever have a greater need to
save her?
Fooh! Fooh!   310
Whoo! I choke!
What a smoke!

FIRST OLD MAN: Well, thank the gods, I see the fire is yet alive
and waking!
SECOND OLD MAN: Why don't we set our lumber down right here
in handy batches,
then stick a branch of grape-vine in the pot until it catches   315
THIRD OLD MAN: and hurl ourselves against the gate with battering and shaking?
FIRST OLD MAN: and if the women won't unbar at such an ultimatum
we'll set the gate on fire and then the smoke will suffocate 'em.
SECOND OLD MAN: Well, let's put down our load. Fooh fooh, what
smoke! But blow as needed!
THIRD OLD MAN: Your ablest generals *these* days would not carry
wood like *we* did.   320
SECOND OLD MAN: At last the lumber ceases grinding my poor
back to pieces!
THIRD OLD MAN: These are your orders, Colonel Pot: wake up
the coals and bid them
report here and present to me a torch lit up and flaring.
FIRST OLD MAN: O Victory, be with us! If you quell the women's
daring
we'll raise a splendid trophy of how you and we undid them!   325

(A Chorus of middle-aged women appears in the offing)

A WOMAN: I think that I perceive a smoke in which appears a
flurry
of sparks as of a lighted fire. Women, we'll have to hurry!

CHORUS OF WOMEN:
Oh fleetly fly, oh swiftly flit,
my dears, e'er Kalykë be lit
and with Kritylla swallowed up alive   330
in flames which the gales dreadfully drive
and deadly old men fiercely inflate!
Yet one thing I'm afraid of: will I not arrive too late?
for filling up my water-jug has been no easy matter
what with the crowd at the spring in the dusk and the
clamor and pottery clatter.   335

        Pushed as I was, jostled by slave-
        women and sluts marked with a brand
        yet with my jug firmly in hand
        here I have come, hoping to save
            my burning friends and brave,   340

        for certain windy, witless, old,
        and wheezy fools, so I was told,
     with wood some tons in weight crept up this path,
        not having in mind heating a bath
        but uttering threats, vowing they will   345
    consume those nasty women into cinders on grill!
    But O Athena! never may I see my friends igniting!
    Nay!—let them save all the cities of Greece and their
        people from folly and fighting!
        Goddess whose crest flashes with gold,   350
        they were so bold taking your shrine
        only for this—Goddess who hold
        Athens—for *this* noble design,
        braving the flames, calling on you
        to carry water too!   355

(One of the old men urinates noisily)

CHORUS OF WOMEN: Be still! What was that noise? Aha! Oh,
    wicked and degraded!
Would any good religious men have ever done what *they* did?
CHORUS OF MEN: Just look! It's a surprise-attack! Oh, dear, we're
    being raided   360
by swarms of them below us when we've got a swarm above us!
CHORUS OF WOMEN: Why panic at the sight of us? This is not
    many of us.
We number tens of thousands but you've hardly seen a fraction.
CHORUS OF MEN: O Phaidrias, shall they talk so big and we not
    take some action?   365
Oh, should we not be bashing them and splintering our lumber?

(The old men begin to strip for combat)

CHORUS OF WOMEN: Let us, too, set our pitchers down, so they will not encumber
    our movements if these gentlemen should care to offer battle.
CHORUS OF MEN: Oh someone should have clipped their jaws—twice, thrice, until
    they rattle—
    (as once the poet put it)—then we wouldn't hear their prating.   370
CHORUS OF WOMEN: Well, here's your chance. Won't someone hit me? Here I
    stand, just waiting!
No other bitch will ever grab your balls, the way I'll treat you!
CHORUS OF MEN: Shut up—or I will drub you so old age will never reach you!
CHORUS OF WOMEN: Won't anyone step and lay one finger on Stratyllis?
CHORUS OF MEN: And if we pulverize her with our knuckles, will you kill us?   375

CHORUS OF WOMEN: No, only chew your lungs out and your innards and your eyes, sir.

CHORUS OF MEN: How clever is Euripides! There is no poet wiser:
he says indeed that women are the worst of living creatures.

CHORUS OF WOMEN: Now is the time, Rhodippe: let us raise our brimming pitchers.

CHORUS OF MEN: Why come up here with water, you, the gods' abomination? 380

CHORUS OF WOMEN: And why come here with fire, you tomb? To give yourself cremation?

CHORUS OF MEN: To set your friends alight upon a pyre erected for them.

CHORUS OF WOMEN: And so we brought our water-jugs. Upon your pyre we'll pour them.

CHORUS OF MEN: *You'll* put my fire out?

CHORUS OF WOMEN: Any time! You'll see there's nothing to it.   385

CHORUS OF MEN: I think I'll grill you right away, with just this torch to do it!

CHORUS OF WOMEN: Have you some dusting-powder? Here's your wedding-bath all ready.

CHORUS OF MEN: *You'll* bathe me, garbage that you are?

CHORUS OF WOMEN: Yes, bridegroom, just hold steady!

CHORUS OF MEN: Friends, you have heard her insolence—

CHORUS OF WOMEN: I'm free-born, not your slave, sir.   390

CHORUS OF MEN: I'll have this noise of yours restrained—

CHORUS OF WOMEN: Court's out—so be less grave, sir.

CHORUS OF MEN: Why don't you set her hair on fire!

CHORUS OF WOMEN: Oh, Water, be of service!

CHORUS OF MEN: Oh woe is me!

CHORUS OF WOMEN: Was it too hot?

CHORUS OF MEN: Oh, stop! What *is* this? Hot? Oh no!

CHORUS OF WOMEN: I'm watering you to make you grow.   395

CHORUS OF MEN: I'm withered from this chill I got!

CHORUS OF WOMEN: You've got a fire, so warm yourself. You're trembling: are you nervous?

(Enter a Commissioner, escorted by four Scythian policemen with bows and quivers slung on their backs)

COMMISSIONER: Has the extravagance of women broken out
into full fury, with their banging tambourines
and constant wailings for their oriental gods,   400
and on the roof-tops their Adonis[15] festival,
which I could hear myself from the Assembly once?
For while Demostratos—that numbskull—had the floor,
urging an expedition against Sicily,
his wife was dancing and we heard her crying out   405
"Weep for Adonis!"—so the expedition failed
with such an omen. When the same Demostratos
was urging that we levy troops from our allies

---

[15] A handsome young man of myth, loved by Aphrodite. He was killed by a wild boar.

his wife was on the roof again, a little drunk:
"Weep for Adonis! Beat your breast!" says she. At that, 410
he gets more bellicose, that god-Damn-ox-tratos.
To this has the incontinence of women come!

CHORUS OF MEN: You haven't *yet* heard how outrageous they can be!
With other acts of violence, these women here
have showered us from their jugs, so now we are reduced 415
to shaking out our shirts as if we'd pissed in them.

COMMISSIONER: Well, by the God of Waters, what do you expect?
When we ourselves conspire with them in waywardness
and give them good examples of perversity
such wicked notions naturally sprout in them. 420
We go into a shop and say something like this:
"Goldsmith, about that necklace you repaired: last night
my wife was dancing, when the peg that bolts the catch
fell from its hole. I have to sail for Salamis,
but if you have the time, by all means try to come 425
towards evening, and put in the peg she needs."
Another man says to a cobbler who is young
and has no child's-play of a prick, "Cobbler," he says,
"her sandal-strap is pinching my wife's little toe,
which is quite delicate. So please come by at noon 430
and stretch it for her so it has a wider play."
Such things as that result of course in things like this:
when I, as a Commissioner, have made a deal
to fit the fleet with oars and need the money now,
I'm locked out by these women from the very gates. 435
But it's no use just standing here. Bring on the bars,
so I can keep these women in their proper place.
What are *you* gaping at, you poor unfortunate?
Where are *you* looking? Only seeing if a bar
is open yet downtown? Come, drive these crowbars in 440
under the gates on that side, pry away, and I
will pry away on this.

(Lysistrata comes out)

LYSISTRATA: No need to pry at all.
I'm coming out, of my own will. What use are bars?
It isn't bolts and bars we need so much as brains.

COMMISSIONER: Really, you dirty slut? Where is that officer? 445
Arrest her, and tie both her hands behind her back.

LYSISTRATA: By Artemis,[16] just let him lift a hand at me
and, public officer or not, you'll hear him howl.

COMMISSIONER: You let her scare you? Grab her round the middle, you.
Then *you* go help him and between you get her tied. 450

(Kalonike comes out)

[16] Goddess of the moon and hunting.

KALONIKE: By Artemis, if you just lay one hand on her
I have a mind to trample the shit out of you.
COMMISSIONER: It's out already! Look! Now where's the other one?
Tie up *that* woman first. She babbles, with it all.

(*Myrrhina comes out*)

MYRRHINA: By Hecatë,[17] if you just lay a hand on her   455
you'll soon ask for a cup—to get your swellings down!

(*The policeman dashes behind the Commissioner and clings to him for protection*)

COMMISSIONER: What happened? Where's that bowman, now? Hold onto *her!*

(*He moves quickly away downhill*)

I'll see that none of you can get away through here!
LYSISTRATA: By Artemis, you come near her and I'll bereave
your head of every hair! You'll weep for each one, too.   460
COMMISSIONER: What a calamity! This one has failed me too.
But never must we let ourselves be overcome
by women. All together now, O Scythians!—
let's march against them in formation!
LYSISTRATA: You'll find out
that inside there we have four companies   465
of fighting women perfectly equipped for war.
COMMISSIONER: Charge! Turn their flanks, O Scythians! and tie their hands!
LYSISTRATA: O allies—comrades—women! Sally forth and fight!
O vegetable vendors, O green-grocery-
grain-garlic-bread-bean-dealers and inn-keepers all!   470

(*A group of fierce Old Market-Women, carrying baskets of vegetables, spindles, etc.
emerges. There is a volley of vegetables. The Scythians are soon routed.*)

Come pull them, push them, smite them, smash them into bits!
Rail and abuse them in the strongest words you know!
Halt, Halt! Retire in order! We'll forego the spoils!
COMMISSIONER: (*tragically, like say Xerxes*[18]) Oh what reverses have
my bowmen undergone!
LYSISTRATA: But what did you imagine? Did you think you came   475
against a pack of slaves? Perhaps you didn't know
that women can be resolute?
COMMISSIONER: I know they can—
above all when they spot a bar across the way.
CHORUS OF MEN: Commissioner of Athens, you are spending words unduly,
to argue with these animals, who only roar the louder,   480
or don't you know they showered us so coldly and so cruelly,
and in our undershirts at that, and furnished us no powder?

---

[17] Goddess of the moon and witchcraft.
[18] A king of Persia, defeated by the Greeks at the decisive naval battle at Salamis in 480 B.C.

CHORUS OF WOMEN: But beating up your neighbor is inevitably bringing
    a beating on yourself, sir, with your own eyes black and bloody.
    I'd rather sit securely like a little girl demurely   485
    not stirring up a single straw nor harming anybody,
    So long as no one robs my hive and rouses me to stinging.
CHORUS OF MEN: How shall we ever tame these brutes? We cannot
    tolerate
    the situation further, so we must investigate
        this occurrence and find   490
        with what purpose in mind
    they profane the Acropolis, seize it, and lock
    the approach to this huge and prohibited rock,
        to our holiest ground!
    Cross-examine them! Never believe one word   495
        they tell you—refute them, confound them!
    We must get to the bottom of things like this
    and the circumstances around them.
COMMISSIONER: Yes indeed! and I want to know first one thing:
        just *why* you committed this treason,   500
    barricading the fortress with locks and bars—
        I insist on knowing the reason.
LYSISTRATA: To protect all the money up there from you—
    you'll have nothing to fight for without it.
COMMISSIONER: You think it is *money* we're fighting for?   505
LYSISTRATA: All the troubles we have are about it.
    It was so Peisander[19] and those in power
        of his kind could embezzle the treasure
    that they cooked up emergencies all the time.
        Well, let them, if such is their pleasure,   510
    but they'll never get into this money again,
        though you men should elect them to spend it.
COMMISSIONER: And just what will *you* do with it?
LYSISTRATA: Can you ask?
    Of course we shall superintend it.
COMMISSIONER: You will superintend the treasury, *you!*?   515
LYSISTRATA: And why should it strike you so funny?
    when we manage our houses in everything
        and it's we who look after your money.
COMMISSIONER: But it's not the same thing!
LYSISTRATA: Why not?
COMMISSIONER: It's war,
    and *this* money must pay the expenses.   520
LYSISTRATA: To begin with, you needn't be waging war.
COMMISSIONER: To survive, we don't need our
    defenses?

[19] A contemporary politician, frequently attacked for corruption.

LYSISTRATA: You'll survive: we shall save you.
COMMISSIONER: Who? You?
LYSISTRATA: Yes, we.
COMMISSIONER: You absolutely disgust me.
LYSISTRATA: You may like it or not, but you *shall* be saved.   525
COMMISSIONER: I protest!
LYSISTRATA: If you care to, but, trust me,
   this has got to be done all the same.
COMMISSIONER: It has?
      It's illegal, unjust, and outrageous!
LYSISTRATA: We must save you, sir.
COMMISSIONER: Yes? And if I refuse?
LYSISTRATA: You will much the more grimly engage us.   530
COMMISSIONER: And whence does it happen that war and peace
      are fit matters for women to mention?
LYSISTRATA: I will gladly explain—
COMMISSIONER: And be quick, or else
      you'll be howling!
LYSISTRATA: Now, just pay attention
   and keep your hands to yourself, if you can!   535
COMMISSIONER: But I can't. You can't think how I suffer
   from holding them back in my anger!
AN OLD WOMAN: Sir—
   if you don't you will have it much rougher.
COMMISSIONER: You may croak that remark to yourself, you hag!
      Will *you* do the explaining?
LYSISTRATA: I'll do it.   540
   Heretofore we women in time of war
      have endured very patiently through it,
   putting up with whatever you men might do,
      for never a peep would you let us
   deliver on your unstatesmanly acts   545
      no matter how much they upset us,
   but we knew very well, while we sat at home,
      when you'd handled a big issue poorly,
   and we'd ask you then, with a pretty smile
      though our heart would be grieving us sorely,   550
   "And what were the terms for a truce, my dear,
      you drew up in assembly this morning?"
   "And what's it to you?" says our husband, "Shut up!"
      —so, as ever, at this gentle warning
   I of course would discreetly shut up.
KALONIKE: Not me!   555
      You can bet I would never be quiet!
COMMISSIONER: I'll bet, if you weren't, you were beaten up.
LYSISTRATA: I'd shut up, and I do not deny it,
   but when plan after plan was decided on,

so bad we could scarcely believe it,   560
I would say "This last is so mindless, dear,
    I cannot think how you achieve it!"
And then he would say, with a dirty look,
    "Just you think what your spindle is for, dear,
or your head will be spinning for days on end—   565
    let the *men* attend to the war, dear."
COMMISSIONER: By Zeus, *he* had the right idea!
LYSISTRATA: You fool!
    Right ideas were quite out of the question,
when your reckless policies failed, and yet
    we never could make a suggestion.   570
And lately we heard you say so yourselves:
    in the streets there'd be someone lamenting:
"There's not one man in the country now!"
    —and we heard many others assenting.
After that, we conferred through our deputies   575
    and agreed, having briefly debated,
to act in common to save all Greece
    at once—for why should we have waited?
So now, when we women are talking sense,
    if you'll only agree to be quiet   580
and to listen to us as we did to you,
    you'll be very much edified by it.
COMMISSIONER: *You* will edify *us!* I protest!
LYSISTRATA: Shut up!
COMMISSIONER: *I'm* to shut up and listen, you scum, you?!
    Sooner death! And a veil on your head at that!   585
LYSISTRATA: We'll fix that. It may really become you:
do accept this veil as a present from me.
    Drape it modestly—so—round your head, do you see?
And now—*not* a word more, sir.
KALONIKE: Do accept this dear little wool-basket, too!   590
    Hitch your girdle and card! Here are beans you may chew
the way all of the nicest Athenians do—
    and the *women* will see to the war, sir!

CHORUS OF WOMEN: Oh women, set your jugs aside and keep a
    closer distance:
our friends may need from us as well some resolute assistance.   595

    Since never shall I weary of the stepping of the dance
    nor will my knees of treading, for these ladies I'll advance
        anywhere they may lead,
        and they're daring indeed,
    they have wit, a fine figure, and boldness of heart,   600
    they are prudent and charming, efficient and smart,
        patriotic and brave!

But, O manliest grandmothers, onward now!
    And you matronly nettles, don't waver!
but continue to bristle and rage, my dears,   605
    for you've still got the wind in your favor!

(The Chorus of Women and the Old Market-Women join)

LYSISTRATA: But if only the spirit of tender Love
    and the power of sweet Aphrodite
were to breathe down over our breasts and thighs
    an attraction both melting and mighty,   610
and infuse a pleasanter rigor in men,
    raising only their cudgels of passion,
then I think we'd be known throughout all of Greece
    as makers of peace and good fashion.
COMMISSIONER: Having done just what?
LYSISTRATA: Well, first of all   615
    we shall certainly make it unlawful
to go madly to market in armor.
AN OLD MARKET-WOMAN: Yes!
    By dear Aphrodite, it's awful!
LYSISTRATA: For now, in the midst of the pottery-stalls   620
    and the greens and the beans and the garlic,
men go charging all over the market-place
    in full armor and beetling and warlike.
COMMISSIONER: They must do as their valor impels them to!
LYSISTRATA: But it makes a man only look funny   625
    to be wearing a shield with a Gorgon's[20] head
    and be wanting sardines for less money.
OLD MARKET-WOMEN: Well, I saw a huge cavalry-captain once
    on a stallion that scarcely could hold him,
pouring into his helmet of bronze a pint   630
    of pea-soup an old woman had sold him,
and a Thracian who, brandishing shield and spear
    like some savage Euripides staged once,
when he'd frightened a vendor of figs to death,
    gobbled up all her ripest and aged ones.   635
COMMISSIONER: And how, on the international scale,
    can you straighten out the enormous
confusion among all the states of Greece?
LYSISTRATA: Very easily.
COMMISSIONER: How? Do inform us.
LYSISTRATA: When our skein's in a tangle we take it thus   640
    on our spindles, or haven't you seen us?—
one on this side and one on the other side,
    and we work out the tangles between us.

---

[20] The Gorgons of Greek myth were three sisters with snakes for hair. Medusa was the most famous
of them.

And that is the way we'll undo this war,
    by exchanging ambassadors, whether   645
you like it or not, one from either side,
    and we'll work out the tangles together.
COMMISSIONER: Do you really think that with wools and skeins
    and just being able to spin you
can end these momentous affairs, you fools?   650
LYSISTRATA: With any intelligence in you
you statesmen would govern as we work wool,
    and in everything Athens would profit.
COMMISSIONER: How so? Do tell.
LYSISTRATA: First, you take raw fleece
    and you wash the beshittedness off it: 655
just so, you should first lay the city out
    on a washboard and beat out the rotters
and pluck out the sharpers like burrs, and when
    you find tight knots of schemers and plotters
who are out for key offices, card them loose,   660
    but best tear off their heads in addition.
Then into one basket together card
    all those of a good disposition
be they citizens, resident aliens, friends,
    an ally or an absolute stranger,   665
even people in debt to the commonwealth,
    you can mix them all in with no danger.
And the cities which Athens has colonized—
    by Zeus, you should try to conceive them
as so many shreddings and tufts of wool   670
    that are scattered about and not leave them
to lie around loose, but from all of them
    draw the threads in here, and collect them
into one big ball and then weave a coat
    for the people, to warm and protect them.   675
COMMISSIONER: Now, isn't this awful? They treat the state
    like wool to be beaten and carded,
who have nothing at all to do with war!
LYSISTRATA: Yes we do, you damnable hard-head!
We have none of your honors but we have more   680
    then double your sufferings by it.
First of all, we bear sons whom you send to war.
COMMISSIONER: Don't bring up our old sorrows! Be quiet!
LYSISTRATA: And now, when we ought to enjoy ourselves,
    making much of our prime and our beauty,   685
we are sleeping alone because all the men
    are away on their soldierly duty.
But never mind *us*—when young girls grow old
    in their bedrooms with no men to share them.
COMMISSIONER: You seem to forget that men, too, grow old.   690

LYSISTRATA: By Zeus, but you cannot compare them!
When a man gets back, though he be quite gray,
    he can wed a young girl in a minute,
    but the season of woman is very short:
        she must take what she can while she's in it.   695
And you know she must, for when it's past,
    although you're not awfully astute, you're
aware that no man will marry her then
    and she sits staring into the future.
COMMISSIONER: But he who can raise an erection still—   700
LYSISTRATA: Is there some good reason you don't drop dead?
We'll sell you a coffin if you but will.
Here's a string of onions to crown your head
and I'll make a honey-cake large and round
you can feed to Cerberus[21] underground!   705
FIRST OLD MARKET-WOMAN: Accept these few fillets of leek from
    me!
SECOND OLD MARKET-WOMAN: Let me offer you these for your
    garland, sir!
LYSISTRATA: What now? Do you want something else you see?
Listen! Charon's[22] calling his passenger—
will you catch the ferry or still delay   710
when his other dead want to sail away?
COMMISSIONER: Is it not downright monstrous to treat *me* like this?
By Zeus, I'll go right now to the Commissioners
and show myself in evidence, just as I am!

    (He begins to withdraw with dignity and his four Scythian policemen)

LYSISTRATA: Will you accuse us of not giving you a wake?   715
But your departed spirit will receive from us
burnt offerings in due form, two days from now at dawn!

    (Lysistrata with the other women goes into the Acropolis. The Commissioner etc.
    have left. The male chorus and the mixed female chorus are alone.)

CHORUS OF MEN: No man now dare fall to drowsing, if he wishes
    to stay free!
Men, let's strip and gird ourselves for this eventuality!

        To me this all begins to have a smell   720
            of bigger things and larger things as well:
      most of all I sniff a tyranny afoot. I'm much afraid
           certain secret agents of the Spartans may have come,
           meeting under cover here, in Cleisthenes's home,
      instigating those damned women by deceit to make a raid   725
           upon our treasury and that great sum
           the city paid my pension from.

---

[21] The three-headed dog guarding the gate of Hades.
[22] Charon ferried the dead across the River Styx to Hades.

Sinister events already!—think of lecturing the state,
women as they are, and prattling on of things like shields of
    bronze,
even trying hard to get us reconciled to those we hate—   730
those of Sparta, to be trusted like a lean wolf when it yawns!
All of this is just a pretext, men, for a dictatorship—
but to me they shall not dictate! Watch and ward! A sword I'll
    hide
underneath a branch of myrtle; through the agora[23] I'll slip,
following Aristogeiton, backing the tyrannicide!   735

*(The Old Men pair off to imitate the gestures of the famous group
    statue of the tyrannicides Harmodius and Aristogeiton[24])*

Thus I'll take my stand beside him! Now my rage is goaded raw
I'm as like as not to clip this damned old woman on the jaw!
CHORUS OF WOMEN: Your own mother will not know you when
      you come home, if you do!
Let us first, though, lay our things down, O my dear old friends
    and true.
        For now, O fellow-citizens, we would   740
        consider what will do our city good.
Well I may, because it bred me up in wealth and elegance:
      letting me at seven help with the embroidering
      of Athena's mantle, and at ten with offering
cakes and flowers. When I was grown and beautiful I had my
    chance   745
      to bear her baskets, at my neck a string
      of figs, and proud as anything.

Must I not, then, give my city any good advice I can?
Need you hold the fact against me that I was not born a man,
when I offer better methods than the present ones, and when   750
I've a share in this economy, for I contribute men?
But, you sad old codgers, *yours* is forfeited on many scores:
you have drawn upon our treasure dating from the Persian wars,
what they call grampatrimony, and you've paid no taxes back.
Worse, you've run it nearly bankrupt, and the prospect's pretty
    black.   755
Have you anything to answer? Say you were within the law
and I'll take this rawhide boot and clip you one across the jaw!
CHORUS OF MEN: Greater insolence than ever!—
        that's the method that she calls
        "better"—if you would believe her.   760
But this threat must be prevented! Every man with both his balls
must make ready—take our shirts off, for a man must reek of
    male

---

[23] Assembly place.
[24] Memorialized for their part in overthrowing the tyrant Hippias, who ruled from 527 to 510 B.C.

outright—not wrapped up in leafage like an omelet for sale!

> Forward and barefoot: we'll do it again
> to the death, just as when we resisted   765
> tyranny out at Leipsydrion, when
> we really existed!

> Now or never we must grow
> young again and, sprouting wings
> over all our bodies, throw   770
> off this heaviness age brings!

For if any of us give them even just a little hold
nothing will be safe from their tenacious grasp. They are so bold
they will soon build ships of war and, with exorbitant intent,
send such navies out against us as Queen Artemisia[25] sent.   775
But if they attack with horse, our knights we might as well delete:
nothing rides so well as woman, with so marvelous a seat,
never slipping at the gallop. Just look at those Amazons
in that picture in the Stoa, from their horses bringing bronze
axes down on men. We'd better grab *these* members of the sex   780
one and all, arrest them, get some wooden collars on their necks!

CHORUS OF WOMEN: By the gods, if you chagrin me
> or annoy me, if you dare,
> I'll turn loose the sow that's in me
till you rouse the town to help you with the way I've done your
> hair!   785
Let us too make ready, women, and our garments quickly doff
so we'll smell like women angered fit to bite our fingers off!

> Now I am ready: let one of the men
> come against me, and *he'll* never hanker
> after a black bean or garlic again: 790
> no woman smells ranker!

> Say a single unkind word,
> I'll pursue you till you drop,
> as the beetle did the bird.
> My revenge will never stop!   795

Yet you will not worry me so long as Lampito's alive
and my noble friends in Thebes and other cities still survive.
You'll not overpower us, even passing seven decrees or eight,
you, poor brutes, whom everyone and everybody's neighbors hate.
Only yesterday I gave a party, honoring Hecatë,   800
but when I invited in the neighbor's child to come and play,
such a pretty thing from Thebes, as nice and quiet as you please,
just an eel, they said she couldn't, on account of your decrees.
You'll go on forever passing such decrees without a check
till somebody takes you firmly by the leg and breaks your neck!   805

---

[25] Artemisia fought with the Persians against the Greeks at Salamis in 480 B.C.

(Lysistrata comes out. The Chorus of Women addresses her in the manner of trage-dy.)

Oh Queen of this our enterprise and all our hopes,
wherefore in baleful brooding hast thou issued forth?
LYSISTRATA: The deeds of wicked women and the female mind discourage me and
    set me pacing up and down.
CHORUS OF WOMEN: What's that? What's that you say?
LYSISTRATA: The truth, alas, the truth!   810
CHORUS OF WOMEN: What is it that's so dreadful? Tell it to your friends.
LYSISTRATA: A shameful thing to tell and heavy not to tell.
CHORUS OF WOMEN: Oh, never hide from me misfortune that is ours!
LYSISTRATA: To put it briefly as I can, we are in heat.
CHORUS OF WOMEN: Oh Zeus!
LYSISTRATA: Why call on Zeus? This is the way
   things are.   815
At least it seems I am no longer capable
of keeping them from men. They are deserting me.
This morning I caught one of them digging away
to make a tunnel to Pan's grotto down the slope,
another letting herself down the parapet   820
with rope and pulley, and another climbing down
its sheerest face, and yesterday was one I found
sitting upon a sparrow with a mind to fly
down to some well-equipped whoremaster's place in town.
Just as she swooped I pulled her backward by the hair.   825
They think of every far-fetched excuse they can
for going home. And here comes one deserter now.
You there, where are you running?
FIRST WOMAN: I want to go home,
   because I left some fine Milesian wools at home
   that must be riddled now with moths.
LYSISTRATA: Oh, damn your moths!   830
   Go back inside.
FIRST WOMAN: But I shall come back right away,
   just time enough to stretch them out upon my bed.
LYSISTRATA: Stretch nothing out, and don't you go away at all.
FIRST WOMAN: But shall I let my wools be ruined?
LYSISTRATA: If you must.
SECOND WOMAN: Oh miserable me! I sorrow for the flax   835
   I left at home unbeaten and unstripped!
LYSISTRATA: One more—
   wanting to leave for stalks of flax she hasn't stripped.
   Come back here!
SECOND WOMAN: But, by Artemis, I only want
   to strip my flax. Then I'll come right back here again.
LYSISTRATA: Strip me no strippings! If you start this kind of thing   840
   some other woman soon will want to do the same.
THIRD WOMAN: O lady Artemis, hold back this birth until
   I can get safe to some unconsecrated place!

LYSISTRATA: What is this raving?

THIRD WOMAN: I'm about to have a child.

LYSISTRATA: But you weren't pregnant yesterday.

THIRD WOMAN: I am today. 845
    Oh, send me home this instant, dear Lysistrata,
    so I can find a midwife.

LYSISTRATA: What strange tale is this?
    What is this hard thing you have here?

THIRD WOMAN: The child is male.

LYSISTRATA: By Aphrodite, no! You obviously have
    some hollow thing of bronze. I'll find out what it is. 850
    You silly thing!—you have Athena's helmet here—
    and claiming to be pregnant!

THIRD WOMAN: So I am, by Zeus!

LYSISTRATA: In that case, what's the helmet for?

THIRD WOMAN: So if the pains
    came on me while I'm still up here, I might give birth
    inside the helmet, as I've seen the pigeons do. 855

LYSISTRATA: What an excuse! The case is obvious. Wait here.
    I want to show this bouncing baby helmet off.

(She passes the huge helmet around the Chorus of Women)

SECOND WOMAN: But I can't even sleep in the Acropolis,
    not for an instant since I saw the sacred snake!

FOURTH WOMAN: The owls are what are killing *me*. How can I sleep 860
    with their eternal whit-to-whoo-to-whit-to-whoo?

LYSISTRATA: You're crazy! Will you stop this hocus-pocus now?
    No doubt you miss your husbands: don't you think that they
    are missing us as much? I'm sure the nights they pass
    are just as hard. But, gallant comrades, do bear up, 865
    and face these gruelling hardships yet a little while.
    There is an oracle that says we'll win, if we
    only will stick together. Here's the oracle.

CHORUS OF WOMEN: Oh, read us what it says!

LYSISTRATA: Keep silence, then and hear:

"Now when to one high place are gathered the fluttering swallows, 870
Fleeing the Hawk and the Cock however hotly it follows,
Then will their miseries end, and that which is over be under:
Thundering Zeus will decide.

A WOMAN: Will *we* lie on top now, I wonder?

LYSISTRATA: *But if the Swallows go fighting each other and spring-*
    ing and winging
    Out of the holy and high sanctuary, then people will never 875
    Say there was any more dissolute bitch of a bird whatsoever.

A WOMAN: The oracle is clear, by Zeus!

LYSISTRATA: By *all* the gods!
    So let us not renounce the hardships we endure.

But let us go back in. Indeed, my dearest friends,
it would be shameful to betray the oracle.   880

   (Exeunt into the Acropolis)

CHORUS OF MEN: Let me tell you a story I heard one day
         when I was a child:
There was once a young fellow Melanion by name
who refused to get married and ran away
         to the wild.   885
         To the mountains he came
         and inhabited there
            in a grove
         and hunted the hare
         both early and late   890
         with nets that he wove
         and also a hound
and he never came home again, such was his hate,
         all women he found
         so nasty, and we   895
         quite wisely agree.
     Let us kiss you, dear old dears!
CHORUS OF WOMEN: With no onions, you'll shed tears!
CHORUS OF MEN: I mean, lift my leg and *kick.*
CHORUS OF WOMEN: My, you wear your thicket thick!   900
CHORUS OF MEN: Great Myronides[26] was rough
         at the front and black enough
         in the ass to scare his foes.
            Just ask anyone who knows:
            it's with hair that wars are won—   905
         take for instance Phormion.[27]
CHORUS OF WOMEN: Let me tell you a story in answer to
         Melanion's case.
There is now a man, Timon,[28] who wanders around
in the wilderness, hiding his face from view   910
         in a place
         where the brambles abound
         so he looks like a chip
         off a Fury,[29]
         curling his lip.   915
         Now Timon retired
         in hatred and pure
         contempt of all men
and he cursed them in words that were truly inspired
         again and again   920
         but women he found

---

[26] An Athenian general, fifth century B.C.
[27] Athenian admiral, fifth century B.C.
[28] A semilegendary character, the original of Shakespeare's *Timon of Athens.*
[29] The Furies were female avengers, with snakelike hair, who punished evil-doers.

    delightful and sound.
  Would you like your jaw repaired?
CHORUS OF MEN: Thank you, no. You've got me scared.
CHORUS OF WOMEN: Let me jump and kick it though.   925
CHORUS OF MEN: You will let your man-sack show.
CHORUS OF WOMEN: All the same you wouldn't see,
        old and gray as I may be,
        any superfluity
           of unbarbered hair on me: 930
        it is plucked and more, you scamp,
        since I singe it with a lamp!

   (Enter Lysistrata on the wall)

LYSISTRATA: Women, O women, come here quickly, here to me!
WOMEN: Whatever is it? Tell me! What's the shouting for?
LYSISTRATA: I see a man approaching, shaken and possessed,   935
  seized and inspired by Aphrodite's power.
   O thou, of Cyprus, Paphos, and Cythera, queen!
  continue straight along this way you have begun!
A WOMAN: Whoever he is, where is he?
LYSISTRATA: Near Demeter's[30] shrine.
A WOMAN: Why yes, by Zeus, he is. Who ever can he be?   940
LYSISTRATA: Well, look at him. Do any of you know him?
MYRRHINA: Yes.
  I do. He's my own husband, too, Cinesias.
LYSISTRATA: Then it's your duty now to turn him on a spit,
  cajole him and make love to him and not make love,
  to offer everything, short of those things of which   945
  the wine-cup knows.
MYRRHINA: I'll do it, don't you fear.
LYSISTRATA: And I
  will help you tantalize him. I will stay up here
  and help you roast him slowly. But now, disappear!

   (Enter Cinesias)

CINESIAS: Oh how unfortunate I am, gripped by what spasms,
  stretched tight like being tortured on a wheel!   950
LYSISTRATA: Who's there? Who has got this far past the sentries?
CINESIAS: I.
LYSISTRATA: A man?
CINESIAS: A man, for sure.
LYSISTRATA: Then clear away from here.
CINESIAS: Who're you, to throw me out?
LYSISTRATA: The look-out for the day.
CINESIAS: Then, for the gods' sake, call Myrrhina out for me.
LYSISTRATA: You don't say! Call Myrrhina out! And who are you?   955

---

[30] Goddess of agriculture.

CINESIAS: Her husband. I'm Cinesias Paionides.

LYSISTRATA: Well, my dear man, hello! Your name is not unknown
    among us here and not without a certain fame,
    because your wife has it forever on her lips.
    She can't pick up an egg or quince but she must say: 960
    Cinesias would enjoy it so!

CINESIAS: How wonderful!

LYSISTRATA: By Aphrodite, yes. And if we chance to talk
    of husbands, your wife interrupts and says the rest
    are nothing much compared to her Cinesias.

CINESIAS: Go call her.

LYSISTRATA: Will you give me something if I do?   965

CINESIAS: Indeed I will, by Zeus, if it is what you want.
    I can but offer what I have, and I have this.

LYSISTRATA: Wait there. I will go down and call her.

CINESIAS: Hurry up!
    because I find no charm whatever left in life
    since she departed from the house. I get depressed   970
    whenever I go into it, and everything
    seems lonely to me now, and when I eat my food
    I find no taste in it at all—because I'm stiff.

MYRRHINA (offstage): I love him, how I love him! But he doesn't
    want
    my love! (on wall) So what's the use of calling me to him?   975

CINESIAS: My sweet little Myrrhina, why do you act like that?
    Come down here.

MYRRHINA: There? By Zeus, I certainly will not.

CINESIAS: Won't you come down, Myrrhina, when I'm calling
    you?

MYRRHINA: Not when you call me without needing anything.

CINESIAS: Not needing anything? I'm desperate with need.   980

MYRRHINA: I'm going now.

CINESIAS: Oh, no! No, don't go yet! At least
    you'll listen to the baby. Call your mammy, you.

BABY: Mammy mammy mammy!

CINESIAS: What's wrong with you? Have you no pity on your child
    when it is six days now since he was washed or nursed?   985

MYRRHINA: Oh, I have pity. But his father takes no care
    of him.

CINESIAS: Come down, you flighty creature, for the child.

MYRRHINA: Oh, what it is to be a mother! I'll come down,
    for what else can I do?

    (Myrrhina exits to reenter below)

CINESIAS: It seems to me she's grown
    much younger, and her eyes have a more tender look.
    Even her being angry with me and her scorn   990
    are just the things that pain me with the more desire.

MYRRHINA: Come let me kiss you, dear sweet little baby mine,
with such a horrid father. Mammy loves you, though.

CINESIAS: But why are you so mean? Why do you listen to   995
those other women, giving me such pain?—And you,
you're suffering yourself.

MYRRHINA: Take your hands off of me!

CINESIAS: But everything we have at home, my things and yours,
you're letting go to pieces.

MYRRHINA: Little do I care!

CINESIAS: Little you care even if your weaving's pecked apart   1000
and carried off by chickens?

MYRRHINA (bravely):   Little I care, by Zeus!

CINESIAS: You have neglected Aphrodite's rituals
for such a long time now. Won't you come back again?

MYRRHINA: Not I, unless you men negotiate a truce
and make an end of war.

CINESIAS: Well, if it's so decreed,   1005
we will do even that.

MYRRHINA: Well, if it's so decreed,
I will come home again. Not now. I've sworn I won't.

CINESIAS: All right, all right. But now lie down with me once more.

MYRRHINA: No! No!—yet I don't say I'm not in love with you.

CINESIAS: You love me? Then why not lie down, Myrrhina dear?   1010

MYRRHINA: Don't be ridiculous! Not right before the child!

CINESIAS: By Zeus, of course not. Manes, carry him back home.
There now. You see the baby isn't in your way.
Won't you lie down?

MYRRHINA: But *where*, you rogue, just where
is one to do it?

CINESIAS: Where? Pan's grotto's a fine place.   1015

MYRRHINA: But how could I come back to the Acropolis
in proper purity?

CINESIAS: Well, there's a spring below
the grotto—you can very nicely bathe in that.

(Ekkyklema[31] *or inset-scene with grotto)*

MYRRHINA: And then I'm under oath. What if I break my vows?

CINESIAS: Let me bear all the blame. Don't worry about your oath.   1020

MYRRHINA: Wait here, and I'll go get a cot for us.

CINESIAS: No no,
the ground will do.

MYRRHINA: No, by Apollo! Though you *are*
so horrid, I can't have you lying on the ground. *(Leaves)*

CINESIAS: You know, the woman loves me—*that's* as plain as day.

MYRRHINA: There. Get yourself in bed and I'll take off my clothes.   1025
Oh, what a nuisance! I must go and get a mat.

---

[31] A movable or revolving platform sometimes used as a supplement to the more famous stage machine, the *mēchanē*, or derrick.

CINESIAS: What for? I don't need one
MYRRHINA: Oh yes, by Artemis!
  On the bare cords? How ghastly!
CINESIAS: Let me kiss you now.
MYRRHINA: Oh, very well.
CINESIAS: Wow! Hurry, hurry and come back.

  (Myrrhina leaves. A long wait.)

MYRRHINA: Here is the mat. Lie down now, while I get undressed.   1030
  Oh, what a nuisance! You don't have a pillow, dear.
CINESIAS: But I don't need one, not one bit!
MYRRHINA: By Zeus, *I* do!

  (Leaves)

CINESIAS: Poor prick, the service around here is terrible!
MYRRHINA: Sit up, my dear, jump up! Now I've got everything.
CINESIAS: Indeed you have. And now, my golden girl, come here.   1035
MYRRHINA: I'm just untying my brassiere. Now don't forget:
  about that treaty—you won't disappoint me, dear?
CINESIAS: By Zeus, no! On my life!
MYRRHINA: You have no blanket, dear.
CINESIAS: By Zeus, I do not need one. I just want to screw.
MYRRHINA: Don't worry, dear, you will. I'll be back right away.   1040

  (Leaves)

CINESIAS: This number, with her bedding, means to murder me.
MYRRHINA: Now raise yourself upright.
CINESIAS: But *this* is upright now!
MYRRHINA: Wouldn't you like some perfume?
CINESIAS: By Apollo, no!
MYRRHINA: By Aphrodite, yes! You must—like it or not.

  (Leaves)

CINESIAS: Lord Zeus! Just let the perfume spill! That's all I ask!   1045
MYRRHINA: Hold out your hand. Take some of this and rub it on.
CINESIAS: This perfume, by Apollo, isn't sweet at all.
  It smells a bit of stalling—not of wedding nights!
MYRRHINA: I brought the *Rhodian* perfume! How absurd of me!
CINESIAS: It's fine! Let's keep it.
MYRRHINA: You *will* have your little joke.   1050

  (Leaves)

CINESIAS: Just let me at the man who first distilled perfumes!
MYRRHINA: Try this, in the long vial.
CINESIAS: I've got one like it, dear.
  But don't be tedious. Lie down. And please don't bring
  anything more.
MYRRHINA *(going)*: That's what I'll do, by Artemis!
  I'm taking off my shoes. But dearest, don't forget   1055

you're going to vote for peace.
CINESIAS: I will consider it.
  She has destroyed me, murdered me, that woman has!
  On top of which she's got me skinned and gone away!
  What shall I do? Oh, whom shall I screw,
  cheated of dear Myrrhina, the first   1060
  beauty of all, a creature divine?
  How shall I tend this infant of mine?
  Find me a pimp: it has to be nursed!

CHORUS OF MEN: *(in tragic style, as if to Prometheus or Andromeda[32] bound)*
              In what dire woe, how heavy-hearted
              I see thee languishing, outsmarted!   1065
                I pity thee, alas I do.
              What kidney could endure such pain,
              what spirit could, what balls, what back,
              what loins, what sacroiliac,
              if they came under such a strain   1070
              and never had a morning screw?
CINESIAS: O Zeus! the twinges! Oh, the twitches!
CHORUS OF MEN: And this is what she did to you,
              that vilest, hatefullest of bitches!
CINESIAS: Oh nay, by Zeus, she's dear and sweet!   1075
CHORUS OF MEN: How can she be? She's vile, O Zeus, she's vile!
              Oh treat her, Zeus, like so much wheat—
              O God of Weather, hear my prayer—
              and raise a whirlwind's mighty blast
              to roll her up into a pile   1080
              and carry her into the sky
              far up and up and then at last
              drop her and land her suddenly
              astride that pointed penis there!

*(The ekkyklema turns, closing the inset-scene. Enter, from opposite
sides, a Spartan and an Athenian official.)*

SPARTAN: Wheah is the Senate-house of the Athenians?   1085
  Ah wish to see the chaihman. Ah have news fo him.
ATHENIAN: And who are you? Are you a Satyr or a man?
SPARTAN: Ah am a herald, mah young friend, yes, by the gods,
  and Ah have come from Sparta to negotiate.
ATHENIAN: And yet you come here with a spear under your arm?   1090
SPARTAN: Not Ah, bah Zeus, not Ah!
ATHENIAN: Why do you turn around?
  Why throw your cloak out so in front? Has the long trip
  given you a swelling?
SPARTAN: Ah do think the man is queah!
ATHENIAN: But you have an erection, oh you reprobate!

[32] The mythical hero and heroine, respectively, of Aeschylus' *Prometheus Bound* and Euripides' lost play *Andromeda*.

SPARTAN: Bah Zeus, Ah've no sech thing! And don't you fool
    around!   1095
ATHENIAN: And what have you got there?
SPARTAN: A Spahtan scroll-stick, suh.
ATHENIAN: Well, if it is, *this* is a Spartan scroll-stick, too.
    But look, I know what's up; you can tell *me* the truth.
    Just how are things with you in Sparta: tell me that.
SPARTAN: Theah is uprising in all Spahta. Ouah allies   1100
    are all erect as well. We need ouah milkin'-pails.
ATHENIAN: From where has this great scourge of frenzy fallen on
      you?
    From Pan?
SPARTAN: No, Ah think Lampito began it all,
    and then, the othah women throughout Spahta joined
    togethah, just lahk at a signal fo a race,   1105
    and fought theah husbands off and drove them from theah cunts.
ATHENIAN: So, how're you getting on?
SPARTAN: We suffah. Through the town
    we walk bent ovah as if we were carrying
    lamps in the wind. The women will not let us touch
    even theah berries, till we all with one acco'd   1110
    have made a peace among the cities of all Greece.
ATHENIAN: This is an international conspiracy
    launched by the women! Now I comprehend it all!
    Return at once to Sparta. Tell them they must send
    ambassadors fully empowered to make peace.   1115
    And our Assembly will elect ambassadors
    from our side, when I say so, showing them this prick.
SPARTAN: Ah'll run! Ah'll flah! Fo all you say is excellent!
CHORUS OF MEN: No wild beast is more impossible than woman is
    to fight,
    nor is fire, nor has the panther such unbridled appetite!   1120
CHORUS OF WOMEN: Well you know it, yet you go on warring with
    me without end,
    when you might, you cross-grained creature, have me as a trusty
    friend.
CHORUS OF MEN: Listen: I will never cease from hating women
    till I die!
CHORUS OF WOMEN: Any time you like. But meanwhile is there
    any reason why
    I should let you stand there naked, looking so ridiculous?   1125
    I am only coming near you, now, to slip your coat on, thus.
CHORUS OF MEN: That was very civil of you, very kind to treat
    me so,
    when in such uncivil rage I took it off a while ago.
CHORUS OF WOMEN: Now you're looking like a man again, and
    not ridiculous.
    If you hadn't hurt my feelings, I would not have made a fuss,   1130
    I would even have removed that little beast that's in your eye.

CHORUS OF MEN: *That* is what was hurting me! Well, won't you
    take my ring to pry
back my eyelid? Rake the beast out. When you have it, let me see,
for some time now it's been in my eye and irritating me.
CHORUS OF WOMEN: Very well, I will—though you were *born* an
    irritable man.   1135
    What a monster of a gnat, by Zeus! Look at it if you can.
    Don't you see it? It's a native of great marshes, can't you tell?
CHORUS OF MEN: Much obliged, by Zeus! The brute's been digging
    at me like a well!
So that now you have removed it, streams of tears come welling
    out.
CHORUS OF WOMEN: I will dry them. You're the meanest man alive,
    beyond a doubt,   1140
    yet I will, and kiss you, too.
CHORUS OF MEN: Don't kiss me!
CHORUS OF WOMEN: If you will or not!
CHORUS OF MEN: Damn you! Oh, what wheedling flatterers you
    all are, born and bred!
That old proverb is quite right and not inelegantly said:
"There's no living *with* the bitches and, without them, even *less*"—
so I might as well make peace with you, and from now on, I guess,   1145
I'll do nothing mean to you and, from you, suffer nothing wrong.
So let's draw our ranks together now and start a little song:

      For a change, we're not preparing
      any mean remark or daring
      aimed at any man in town,   1150
    but the very opposite: we plan to do and say
    only good to everyone
    when the ills we have already are sufficient anyway.
      Any man or woman who
      wants a little money, oh   1155
      say three minas, maybe two,
      kindly let us know.
      What we have is right in here.
      (Notice we have purses, too!)
      And if ever peace appear,   1160
      he who takes our loan today
    never need repay.
      We are having guests for supper,
      allies asked in by our upper
      classes to improve the town.   1165
There's pea-soup, and I had killed a sucking-pig of mine:
I shall see it is well done,
so you will be tasting something very succulent and fine.
      Come to see us, then, tonight
      early, just as soon as you   1170

have a bath and dress up right:
bring your children, too.
Enter boldly, never mind
asking anyone in sight.
Go straight in and you will find   1175
you are quite at home there, but
all the doors are shut.

And here come the Spartan ambassadors,
    dragging beards that are really the biggest I
have ever beheld, and around their thighs   1180
    they are wearing some sort of a pig-sty.

Oh men of Sparta, let me bid you welcome first,
and then you tell us how you are and why you come.

SPARTAN: What need is theah to speak to you in many words?
Fo you may see youahself in what a fix we come.   1185
CHORUS OF MEN: Too bad! Your situation has become
    terribly hard and seems to be at fever-pitch.
SPARTAN: Unutterably so! And what is theah to say?
    Let someone bring us peace on any tuhms he will!
CHORUS OF MEN: And here I see some natives of Athenian soil, 1190
    holding their cloaks far off their bellies, like the best
    wrestlers, who sicken at the touch of cloth. It seems
    that overtraining may bring on this strange disease.
ATHENIAN: Will someone tell us where to find Lysistrata?
    We're men, and here we are, in this capacity.   1195
CHORUS OF MEN: This symptom and that other one sound much
    alike.
    Toward morning I expect convulsions do occur?
ATHENIAN: By Zeus, we are exhausted with just doing that,
    so, if somebody doesn't reconcile us quick,
    there's nothing for it: we'll be screwing Cleisthenes.[33] 1200
CHORUS OF MEN: Be careful—put your cloaks on, or you might
    be seen
    by some young blade who knocks the phalluses off herms.
ATHENIAN: By Zeus, an excellent idea!
SPARTAN (*having overheard*): Yes, bah the gods!
    It altogethah is. Quick, let's put on our cloaks.   1205

(*Both groups cover quick and then recognize each other with
full diplomatic pomp*)

ATHENIAN: Greetings, O men of Sparta! (*to his group*) We have
    been disgraced!
SPARTAN (*to one of his group*): Mah dearest fellah, what a dreadful
    thing fo *us*,
    if these Athenians had seen ouah wo'st defeat!

---

[33] A famous Athenian homosexual.

ATHENIAN: Come now, O Spartans: one must specify each point.
   Why have you come here?
SPARTAN: To negotiate a peace.   1210
   We ah ambassadahs.
ATHENIAN: Well put. And so are we.
   Therefore, why do we not call in Lysistrata,
   she who alone might get us to agree on terms?
SPARTAN: Call her or any man, even a Lysistratus!
CHORUS OF MEN: But you will have no need, it seems, to call her
   now,   1215
   for here she is. She heard you and is coming out.
CHORUS OF MEN *and* CHORUS OF WOMEN: All hail, O manliest
   woman of all!
            It is time for you now to be turning
into something still better, more dreadful, mean,
          unapproachable, charming, discerning,   1220
for here are the foremost nations of Greece,
          bewitched by your spells like a lover,
who have come to you, bringing you all their claims,
          and to *you* turning everything over.

LYSISTRATA: The work's not difficult, if one can catch them now   1225
   while they're excited and not making passes at
   each other. I will soon find out. Where's *HARMONY?*

*(A naked maid, perhaps wearing a large ribbon reading HARMONY,
appears from inside)*

Go take the Spartans first, and lead them over here,
not with a rough hand nor an overbearing one,
nor, as our husbands used to do this, clumsily,   1230
but like a woman, in our most familiar style:
If he won't give his hand, then lead him by the prick.
And now, go bring me those Athenians as well,
leading them by whatever they will offer you.
O men of Sparta, stand right here, close by my side,   1235
and *you* stand over there, and listen to my words.
I am a woman, yes, but there is mind in me.
In native judgment I am not so badly off,
and, having heard my father and my elders talk
often enough, I have some cultivation, too.   1240
And so, I want to take and scold you, on both sides,
as you deserve, for though you use a lustral[34] urn
in common at the altars, like blood-relatives,
when at Olympia, Delphi, or Thermopylae—
how many others I might name if I took time!—   1245
yet, with barbarian hordes of enemies at hand,
it is Greek men, it is Greek cities, you destroy.
That is one argument so far, and it is done.

---

[34] Ceremonial; used for purification.

ATHENIAN: My prick is skinned alive—that's what's destroying *me*.

LYSISTRATA: Now, men of Sparta—for I shall address you first—   1250
    do you not know that once one of your kings came here
    and as a suppliant of the Athenians
    sat by our altars, death-pale in his purple robe,
    and begged us for an army? For Messenë then
    oppressed you[35] and an earthquake from the gods as well.   1255
    Then Cimon[36] went, taking four thousand infantry,
    and saved the whole of Lacedaemon for your state.
    That is the way Athenians once treated you:
    you ravage their land now, which once received you well.

ATHENIAN: By Zeus, these men are in the wrong, Lysistrata!   1260

SPARTAN (*with his eyes on Harmony*): We'ah wrong . . . What
    an unutterably lovely ass!

LYSISTRATA: Do you suppose I'm letting you Athenians off?
    Do you not know that once the Spartans in their turn,
    when you were wearing the hide-skirts of slavery,
    came with their spears and slew many Thessalians,
    many companions and allies of Hippias?[37]   1265
    They were the only ones who fought for you that day,
    freed you from tyranny and, for the skirt of hide,
    gave back your people the wool mantle of free men.

SPARTAN: Ah nevah saw a woman broadah—in her views.   1270

ATHENIAN: And I have never seen a lovelier little nook.

LYSISTRATA: So why, when you have done each other so much
    good,
    go on fighting with no end of malevolence?
    Why don't you make a peace? Tell me, what's in your way?

SPARTAN: Whah, *we* ah willin', if *they* will give up to us   1275
    that very temptin' cuhve.   *(of Harmony, as hereafter)*

LYSISTRATA: What curve, my friend?

SPARTAN: The bay
    of Pylos,[38] which we've wanted and felt out so long.

ATHENIAN: No, by Poseidon,[39] you will not get into that!

LYSISTRATA: Good friend, do let them have it.

ATHENIAN: No! What other town
    can we manipulate so well?

LYSISTRATA: Ask them for one.   1280

ATHENIAN: Damn, let me think! Now first suppose you cede to us
    that bristling tip of land, Echinos, behind which
    the gulf of Malia recedes, and those long walls,
    the legs on which Megara reaches to the sea.

SPARTAN: No, mah deah man, not *everything*, bah Castah, no!   1285

LYSISTRATA: Oh, give them up. Why quarrel for a pair of legs?

---

[35] In the Messenian revolt of 464 B.C.
[36] An Athenian general (d. 449 B.C.).
[37] An Athenian tyrant expelled in 510 B.C.
[38] Pylos had formerly been Sparta's but at the time of the play belonged to Athens.
[39] God of the sea.

ATHENIAN: I'd like to strip and get to plowing right away.
SPARTAN: And *Ah* would lahk to push manuah, still earliah.
LYSISTRATA: When you have made a peace, then you will do all
    that.
  But if you want to do it, first deliberate,   1290
  go and inform your allies and consult with them.
ATHENIAN: Oh, damn our allies, my good woman! We are stiff.
  Will all of our allies not stand resolved with us—
  namely, to screw?
SPARTAN: And so will ouahs, Ah'll guarantee.
ATHENIAN: Our mercenaries, even, will agree with us.   1295
LYSISTRATA: Excellent. Now to get you washed and purified
  so you may enter the Acropolis, where we
  women will entertain you out of our supplies.
  You will exchange your pledges there and vows for peace.
  And after that each one of you will take his wife,   1300
  departing then for home.
ATHENIAN: Let's go in right away.
SPARTAN: Lead on, ma'am, anywheah you lahk.
ATHENIAN: Yes, and be quick.

  (Exeunt into Acropolis)

CHORUS OF MEN *and* CHORUS OF WOMEN:
    All the rich embroideries, the
    scarves, the gold accessories, the
    trailing gowns, the robes I own   1305
  I begrudge to no man: let him take what things he will
  for his children or a grown
  daughter who must dress for the procession up Athena's hill.
    Freely of my present stocks
    I invite you all to take.   1310
    There are here no seals nor locks
    very hard to break.
    Search through every bag and box,
    look—you will find nothing there
    if your eyesight isn't fine—   1315
    sharper far than mine!

    Are there any of you needing
    food for all the slaves you're feeding,
    all your little children, too?
  I have wheat in tiny grains for you, the finest sort,   1320
  and I also offer you
  plenty of the handsome strapping grains that slaves get by the
    quart.
    So let any of the poor
    visit me with bag or sack
    which my slave will fill with more   1325

       wheat than they can pack,
       giving each his ample share.
       Might I add that at my door
       I have watch-dogs?—so beware.
       Come too close by day or night,   1330
       you will find they bite.

    (Voice of drunken Athenians from inside)

FIRST ATHENIAN: Open the door! *(shoves the porter aside)*
                And will you get out of my way?

    (A second drunken Athenian follows. The first sees the chorus.)

What are you sitting *there* for? Shall I, with this torch,
burn you alive? *(drops character)*
             How vulgar! Oh, how commonplace!
I can not do it!

    *(Starts back in. The second Athenian stops him and remonstrates
    with him in a whisper. The first turns and addresses the audience.)*

            Well, if it really must be done   1335
to please you, we shall face it and go through with it.

CHORUS OF MEN *and* CHORUS OF WOMEN:
    And *we* shall face it and go through with it with you.

FIRST ATHENIAN *(in character again, extravagantly)*:
    Clear out of here! Or you'll be wailing for your hair!

    (Chorus of Women scours away in mock terror)

Clear out of here! so that the Spartans can come out
and have no trouble leaving, after they have dined.   1340

    (Chorus of Men scours away in mock terror)

SECOND ATHENIAN: I never saw a drinking-party like this one:
    even the Spartans were quite charming, and of course
    we make the cleverest company, when in our cups.
FIRST ATHENIAN: You're right, because when sober we are not
       quite sane.
    If I can only talk the Athenians into it,   1345
    we'll always go on any embassy quite drunk,
    for now, going to Sparta sober, we're so quick
    to look around and see what trouble we can make
    that we don't listen to a single word they say—
    instead we think we hear them say what they do not—   1350
    and none of our reports on anything agree.
    But just now everything was pleasant. If a man
    got singing words belonging to another song,

we all applauded and swore falsely it was fine!
But here are those same people coming back again   1355
to the same spot! Go and be damned, the pack of you!

*(The Chorus, having thrown off their masks, put on other cloaks,
and rushed back on stage, stays put)*

SECOND ATHENIAN: Yes, damn them, Zeus! Just when the party's
coming out!

(The party comes rolling out)

A SPARTAN *(to another)*:
Mah very chahmin friend, will you take up youah flutes?
Ah'll dance the dipody [40] and sing a lovely song
of us and the Athenians, of both at once!   1360
FIRST ATHENIAN *(as pleasantly as he can)*:
Oh yes, take up your little reeds, by all the gods:
I very much enjoy seeing you people dance.
SPARTAN: Memory, come,
            come inspiah thah young
            votaries to song,   1365
            come inspiah theah dance!

(other Spartans join)

            Bring thah daughtah, bring the sweet
                Muse, fo well she knows
            us and the Athenians,
                how at Ahtemisium[41]   1370
            they in godlike onslaught rose
            hahd against the Puhsian fleet,
                drove it to defeat!
            Well she knows the Spartan waws,
                how Leonidas[42]   1375
                in the deadly pass
                led us on lahk baws
            whettin' shahp theah tusks, how sweat
            on ouah cheeks in thick foam flowahed,
            off ouah legs how thick it showahed,   1380
                fo the Puhsian men were mo'
                than the sands along the sho'.
            Goddess, huntress, Ahtemis,
            slayeh of the beasts, descend:
            vuhgin goddess, come to this   1385
            feast of truce to bind us fast

---

[40] Two-foot verse.
[41] Artemesium, where the Greeks and Persians fought a sea battle in 480 B.C. prior to the decisive
Greek victory at Salamis.
[42] Leonidas, King of Sparta, died with all his men defending the pass at Thermopylae against the
Persians in 480 B.C.

so ouah peace may nevah end.
Now let friendship, love, and wealth
come with ouah acco'd at last.
May we stop ouah villainous   1390
wahly foxy stealth!
        Come, O huntress, heah to us,
        heah, O vuhgin, neah to us!
LYSISTRATA: Come, now that all the rest has been so well arranged,
you Spartans take these women home; these others, you.   1395
Let husband stand beside his wife, and let each wife
stand by her husband: then, when we have danced a dance
to thank the gods for our good fortune, let's take care
hereafter not to make the same mistakes again.
ATHENIAN: Bring on the chorus! Invite the three Graces to follow,   1400
and then call on Artemis, call her twin brother,
the leader of choruses, healer Apollo!
CHORUS (*joins*): Pray for their friendliest favor, the one and the
        other.
Call Dionysus,[43] his tender eyes casting
flame in the midst of his Maenads[44] ecstatic with dancing.   1405
    Call upon Zeus, the resplendent in fire,
    call on his wife, rich in honor and ire,
call on the powers who possess everlasting
memory, call them to aid,
call them to witness the kindly, entrancing   1410
peace Aphrodite has made!
            Alalai!
            Bound, and leap high! Alalai!
            Cry, as for victory, cry
            Alalai!   1415
LYSISTRATA: Sing us a new song, Spartans, capping our new song.
SPARTANS: Leave thah favohed mountain's height,
    Spahtan Muse, come celebrate
    Amyclae's lord[45] with us and great
    Athena housed in bronze;   1420
    praise Tyndareus' paih of sons,[46]
    gods who pass the days in spoht
    wheah the cold Eurotas[47] runs.

(*general dancing*)

Now to tread the dance,
now to tread it light,   1425
praising Spahta, wheah you find

---

[43] God of wine and revelry (Bacchus).
[44] Female followers of Dionysus.
[45] Apollo (there was a temple to him in the town of Amyclae).
[46] Castor and Pollux, twin sons of Tyndareus, King of Sparta, and Leda.
[47] A river flowing by Sparta.

love of singing quickened bah the pounding beat
    of dancing feet,
when ouah guhls lahk foals cavoht
wheah the cold Eurotas runs,   1430
when they fleetly bound and prance
    till theah haih unfilleted shakes in the wind,
as of Maenads brandishin'
ahvied wands and revelin',
    Leda's daughtah, puah and faiah,   1435
leads the holy dances theah.

FULL CHORUS *(as everyone leaves dancing)*:
So come bind up youah haih with youah hand,
    with youah feet make a bound
lank a deeah; fo the chorus clap out
    an encouragin' sound,   1440
singin' praise of the temple of bronze
    housin' her we adaw:
sing the praise of Athena: the goddess unvanquished in waw!

Women in Athens in the time of Aristophanes had no vote and no business outside the household. Although they were certainly in the audience, they were probably relegated to the back rows, apart from the men. Basic to the comedy of *Lysistrata* is the spectacle of powerless creatures using their one overmastering power. But there is more to it. Consider the following questions.

1. How would you characterize Lysistrata? Is she an individual worth listening to?
2. Do Kalonike and Myrrhina have individualized characters? How would you describe each? In what scenes or lines do they exist most memorably?
3. Characterize Cinesias. What is the function of his scene with Myrrhina?
4. Do the men generally show themselves more capable of managing the affairs of state than the women?
5. Does the play embody any serious suggestions for settling the war?
6. One theme is the power of sex. Are there others? In what ways are the themes made memorable?
7. This play leans much more heavily on the satiric side of comedy than on the romantic. Which individuals, classes, or institutions are most effectively satirized?

The Physician in Spite of Himself

Molière (Jean-Baptiste Poquelin) wrote for a relatively small, intimate theater. Whereas *Oedipus Rex* and *Lysistrata* played before as many as 14 thousand spectators and *Macbeth* before 2 to 3 thousand, *The Physician in*

Spite of Himself, like most of Molière's best plays, was written for the theater of the Palais Royal in Paris, which seated 600. There were other differences as well. Although Molière occasionally staged his plays in the open air at Versailles, the Palais Royal was an indoor theater, with lighting from candles rather than the daylight of Athens or London. At the Palais Royal the stage was the one we know best—behind a *proscenium arch* and a curtain. The artificial barrier thus created (repeated in the rectangular stage frame of the outdoor theater at Versailles) joined with the lighting and the elaborate scenery to create a psychological distance between actor and spectator. When necessary, this barrier was broken down through the broad acting, caricature, comic masks, and comic improvisation Molière borrowed from the popular *commedia dell'arte*. The realistic conventions of the late nineteenth and early twentieth century did not yet exist.

Although Molière had considerable stage machinery available and much precedent for elaborate sets—perspectives creating the illusion of labyrinthine apartments or city streets and country vistas extending to a distant vanishing point—he was much more sparing than Shakespeare in using different settings. He had but one acting area, and the scene, once established with a backdrop, could not be easily changed, as Shakespeare's was, with a word or two hurled at the imagination of the audience. His work was also influenced by the French neoclassic tradition that strove toward a strict adherance to the three unities of plot, time, and place. As a result, his comedies are quite different from those of ancient Greece and Elizabethan England, though maintaining the essential comic spirit. *The Physician in Spite of Himself* is among his most boisterous.

THE PHYSICIAN IN SPITE OF HIMSELF*

Molière   (1622–1673)

THE CHARACTERS

SGANARELLE
MARTINE, his wife
MONSIEUR ROBERT, his neighbor
GÉRONTE
LUCINDE, his daughter
LÉANDRE, suitor of Lucinde

VALÈRE, steward of Géronte
LUCAS, peasant
JACQUELINE, his wife
THIBAUT, peasant
PERRIN, his son

Act I

The scene is the exterior of Sganarelle's tumble-down house. Enter Sganarelle and Martine, quarreling.

SGANARELLE: I won't. I tell you I won't. And when I say something around here, it's an order.

*Translated by Morris Bishop.

MARTINE: And I tell you that I'll tell you how to behave. I didn't marry you in order to put up with your tricks and dodges.

SGANARELLE: Oh, what a burden is a wife, is it not indeed! How right was Aristotle, when he said that a wife is worse than a demon!

MARTINE: What a smart fellow it is, with his half-wit Aristotle!

SGANARELLE: Yes, a smart fellow. You won't find another woodcutter who knows how to argue like me, and who worked for a famous doctor for six years, and who knew his First Latin Book by heart when he was a boy.

MARTINE: A plague on the champion fool!

SGANARELLE: A plague on the slut!

MARTINE: Cursed be the day and the hour when I took it into my head to say "I do!"

SGANARELLE: Cursed be the cuckold of a notary who made me sign my own destruction!

MARTINE: It's a nice thing for you to complain of that affair! Should you let a single minute go by without thanking heaven for having me for your wife? Did you deserve to marry a person like me?

SGANARELLE: Certainly you did me too much honor; and I had good reason to congratulate myself on our wedding night! Damnation! Don't get me going on that topic; I could say a few things—

MARTINE: And what could you say?

SGANARELLE: That's enough. We'll drop the subject. Just remember that we know what we know, and you were very lucky to find me.

MARTINE: What do you mean, lucky to find you? A man who is bringing me to the poorhouse, a drunkard, a good-for-nothing, who eats up everything I've got—

SGANARELLE: That's a lie. I drink part of it.

MARTINE: —who is selling off, bit by bit, everything in the house—

SGANARELLE: We mustn't let our possessions possess us.

MARTINE: —who has even got rid of my own bed—

SGANARELLE: You won't sleep so late.

MARTINE: —who won't leave a single stick of furniture in the house—

SGANARELLE: That makes moving easier.

MARTINE: —and who spends the whole day, from morning till night, drinking and gambling.

SGANARELLE: Well, I hate to be bored.

MARTINE: And while that goes on, what do you expect me to do with my family?

SGANARELLE: Anything you like.

MARTINE: I have four poor little children on my hands.

SGANARELLE: Put them on the floor.

MARTINE: And they keep forever crying out for bread.

SGANARELLE: Give them a good whipping. When I have had plenty to eat and drink, I like everyone in the house to have his bellyful.

MARTINE: And you expect, you drunken lout, that things are going to go on forever this way?

SGANARELLE: My dear wife, calm down.

MARTINE: And I'm to put up with your drink and debauchery to the end of time?

SGANARELLE: Now, let's not get excited, darling.

MARTINE: And I won't find some way to make you behave?

SGANARELLE: Sweetie, you know I'm not very patient, and I have a strong right arm.

MARTINE: I'm not afraid of your threats.

SGANARELLE: My little lollipop, you're itching for something, as usual.

MARTINE: I'll show you I'm not afraid of you.

SGANARELLE: My dainty pet, there's something you want me to give you.

MARTINE: You think you frighten me with your talk?

SGANARELLE: Fair object of my eternal vows, I'll knock your ears in.

MARTINE: Boozer!

SGANARELLE: I shall flog and flail you.

MARTINE: Souse!

SGANARELLE: I shall pummel and buffet.

MARTINE: Dirty no-good!

SGANARELLE: I shall administer the lash.

MARTINE: Rascal! Puppy! Deceiver! Coward! Scoundrel! Gallows-bird! Beggar! Waster! Rogue! Villain! Thief!

SGANARELLE (*takes a stick and beats her*): Well, you asked for it.

MARTINE: Oh, oh, oh, oh!

SGANARELLE: That's the best way to calm you down.

(*Enter Monsieur Robert*)

M. ROBERT: Hello! Here, here, here! What's all this! This is an outrage! Confound the fellow, for beating his wife that way!

MARTINE (*her arms akimbo, forces Monsieur Robert backward step by step during the following dialogue*): And supposing I want to have him beat me?

M. ROBERT: Oh, well, then, I consent heartily.

MARTINE: What are you meddling for?

M. ROBERT: I was quite wrong.

MARTINE: Is it any business of yours?

M. ROBERT: No; no indeed.

MARTINE: Will you take a look at this butter-in, who wants to prevent husbands from beating their wives?

M. ROBERT: I take it all back.

MARTINE: Do you have some interest in the matter?

M. ROBERT: None at all.

MARTINE: Then why do you stick your nose in?

M. ROBERT: I'm sorry.

MARTINE: Mind your own business.

M. ROBERT: I will indeed.

MARTINE: I like to be beaten.

M. ROBERT: Excellent.

MARTINE: It doesn't hurt you any.

M. ROBERT: Quite right.

MARTINE: And you're a fool to come meddling in things which are no affair of yours.

(*Martine slaps Monsieur Robert's face. Monsieur Robert escapes her, runs to center, and is confronted by Sganarelle.*)

M. Robert: Comrade, with all my heart I ask your pardon. Go ahead, beat and drub your wife properly. I will help you, if you like.

(During the following dialogue, Sganarelle forces Monsieur Robert backward, threateningly, paralleling the previous business with Martine)

Sganarelle: But I don't like.

M. Robert: Oh, well, that's different.

Sganarelle: I want to beat her if I want to; and I don't want to beat her if I don't want to.

M. Robert: Splendid!

Sganarelle: She's my wife; she isn't your wife.

M. Robert: That's right.

Sganarelle: You can't give me any orders.

M. Robert: I agree; I agree.

Sganarelle: I don't need any help from you.

M. Robert: Absolutely not.

Sganarelle: And you're an insolent meddler, to come and interfere in other people's affairs. Learn that Cicero says: "Put not the bark between thy finger and the tree." *(Sganarelle beats Monsieur Robert, and drives him off the stage. He returns to Martine.)* Well now, let's make peace. Shake hands.

Martine: Yes, indeed! After beating me that way!

Sganarelle: That's nothing. Shake hands.

Martine: I don't want to.

Sganarelle: Eh?

Martine: No.

Sganarelle: My sweet little wife!

Martine: I won't.

Sganarelle: Oh, come on!

Martine: Nothing of the sort.

Sganarelle: Come on, come on!

Martine: No, I'd rather be angry.

Sganarelle: What, for just a trifle? Come on!

Martine: Let me alone.

Sganarelle: Shake hands, I tell you.

Martine: You hurt me too much.

Sganarelle: All right then, I ask your pardon. Give me your hand.

Martine: Oh, very well. I pardon you. *(Aside)* But you'll pay for it!

Sganarelle: You're silly to take the matter seriously. Those little flare-ups are sometimes necessary to true friendship; and five or six good wallops, between lovers, merely stimulate affection. Now I'm off to the woods. I promise to bring in today more than a hundred bundles of kindling wood.

(Exit Sganarelle)

Martine: Well, no matter how I pretend, I can't forget how you hurt me. I'd like to find a good way to punish you for that beating. I know that a woman always has a way to take revenge on her husband. But that's too dainty a punishment for that scalawag; it wouldn't be satisfaction enough for the way he's treated me. I want a revenge he'll feel down to his bones.

(Enter Valère and Lucas. They do not immediately perceive Martine.)

LUCAS: By gosh and by gum! Ain't that a queer job we took on! I be switched if I know how she's going to turn out.

VALÈRE: Well, Uncle Lucas, what can we do? We have to obey our master. And besides, we both have an interest in the recovery of his daughter, the young mistress. No doubt we'll get some good presents at her marriage, which is postponed by her illness. Horace is quite likely to be accepted as a suitor, and he's free with his money. And although she has shown her preference for a certain Léandre, you know very well that her father has always refused to accept him as a son-in-law.

MARTINE *(who has been absorbedly meditating, without noticing Valère and Lucas)*: I wonder if I can't cook up some scheme to get my revenge.

LUCAS: But what kind of fool idea has the master took into his noodle, now the doctors say they're all up a tree?

VALÈRE: Well, sometimes, by just hunting, one finds unexpected help; and often among simple people in out-of-the-way places . . .

MARTINE: Yes, I'm going to get my revenge, at any price. Those cudgel blows still smart; I won't stand for them. *(In her distraction, she bumps into the newcomers)* Oh, gentlemen, I ask your pardon. I didn't see you; I was trying to think out an answer to some troubles of mine.

VALÈRE: Everyone has his troubles in this world. In fact, we were trying to find an answer to some troubles of our own.

MARTINE: Would it be anything I could help you in?

VALÈRE: Possibly. We are trying to find a gifted man, a special sort of doctor, who might bring some relief to our master's daughter. She has been attacked by a disease which suddenly deprived her of all power of speech. Several physicians have already exhausted all their science on her. But sometimes one runs across people who possess some wonderful secrets of nature, certain special remedies, which accomplish what the regular doctors can't do. That's what we're looking for.

MARTINE *(aside)*: Heaven inspires me with a great idea for getting revenge on my rapscallion husband! *(Aloud)* You couldn't land on a better person to give you a tip. There's a fellow around here who is just wonderful for desperate cases.

VALÈRE: Do tell me, where could we find him?

MARTINE: You can find him now in that little wood over yonder. He's amusing himself by cutting wood.

LUCAS: A doctor cutting wood!

VALÈRE: Amusing himself by gathering herbs, you mean?

MARTINE: No; he's a very peculiar man who enjoys doing that. He's queer, fantastic, crotchety; you'd never take him for what he is. He goes around dressed in funny old clothes, and sometimes he pretends to be ignorant; he keeps all his knowledge hidden, and he always hates to exercise the marvelous talents for medicine which heaven has given him.

VALÈRE: It's a remarkable thing that great men always have some fantasticality, some little touch of folly mingled with their knowledge.

MARTINE: This man's folly is greater than you'd believe. Sometimes it goes so far that he has to be beaten before he'll admit his abilities; and I warn you that if he's in that mood you'll never make him admit he's a doctor, unless you both take sticks and pound him well until he finally confesses what he'll hide from you at first. That's what we do around here when we need his services.

VALÈRE: What a strange folly!

MARTINE: True enough; but afterwards, you'll see that he can do real marvels.

VALÈRE: What's his name?

MARTINE: His name is Sganarelle. It's easy to recognize him. He has a big black beard, and he wears a ruff, and a green and yellow coat.

LUCAS: Green and yaller! He's a doctor for parrots, then?[1]

VALÈRE: But is it really true that he's so clever as all that?

MARTINE: Why, he's a man who works miracles! Six months ago there was a woman here given up by all the other doctors. They thought she was dead, and were getting ready to lay her out. And six hours afterwards the man I'm telling about was dragged in by main strength. He looked her over and put a little drop of something or other in her mouth, and right away she got up off her bed and started walking around the room as if nothing had happened.

LUCAS: Aha!

VALÈRE: It must have been a drop of potable gold.

MARTINE: You may be right. And only three weeks ago a twelve-year-old boy fell down from the top of the belfry, and he landed on the pavement and broke his arms, his legs, and his head. Well, as soon as they brought in this fellow, he rubbed the boy all over with a certain ointment he knows how to make. And immediately the boy stood right up, and ran off to shoot marbles.

LUCAS: Aha!

VALÈRE: That man must have the universal panacea.

MARTINE: No doubt about it.

LUCAS: By gee and by golly! That's just the man we're alookin' for. Let's go git him.

VALÈRE: We are much obliged to you for your useful suggestion.

MARTINE: But anyhow, remember the warning I gave you.

LUCAS: Dad-burn and dad-blast! Trust us! If all he needs is a beating up, we've got the pig in the poke.

(Exit Martine)

VALÈRE: We were very lucky to run into that good woman. She really gives me some high hopes.

(Enter Sganarelle, brandishing a bottle and singing)

SGANARELLE: La, la, la.

VALÈRE: I heard someone cutting wood; and now he's singing.

SGANARELLE: La, la, la . . . That's enough work for a while. Let's take a little breather. *(He drinks)* Nothing like wood-cutting to dry a man out. *(He sings)*
        Oh, how pretty
        Is my little brown jug!

---

[1] Physicians invariably wore black gowns [Bishop's note].

> Oh, how pretty
> Is your glug-glug-glug!
> But everybody else would be jealous of me
> If you were always as full as can be;
> So little brown jug, let me give you a hug,
> Turn your pretty bottom up, little brown jug!

God's truth, we must defend ourselves against morbid melancholia.

VALÈRE: That's the man himself.

LUCAS: I reckon you're right; we've landed smack onto him.

VALÈRE: Let's get closer.

SGANARELLE: Naughty little bottle! How I love my little cutie!

(Perceives Lucas and Valère: watches them, turning alternately toward one and the other; lets his voice die away) Everybody else ... would be ... jealous of me ... What the devil! Have those fellows got it in for somebody?

VALÈRE: That's the man, certainly.

LUCAS: It's his spit and image, like they told us.

SGANARELLE: They are whispering to each other. What's the idea?

(He puts his bottle on the ground. As Valère makes him a deep bow, Sganarelle suspects him of designs on the bottle, whisks it to the other side. When Lucas makes a similar bow, Sganarelle seizes the bottle and holds it against his stomach.)

VALÈRE: I beg your pardon, sir. Aren't you the gentleman named Sganarelle?

SGANARELLE: What's all this?

VALÈRE: I am asking you if your name isn't Sganarelle.

SGANARELLE *(after making a close inspection of Valère, and then of Lucas)*: Well, yes and no. Depends on what you want.

VALÈRE: All we want is to pay him our warmest respects.

SGANARELLE: In that case, my name is Sganarelle.

VALÈRE: Sir, we are delighted to meet you. We have been referred to you for our present purposes; so we have come to implore your assistance in our present need.

SGANARELLE: If it is something, gentlemen, which pertains to my little business, I am prepared to render you every service.

VALÈRE: Sir, you are all too kind. But, sir, put on your hat, I beg you; you might find the sunshine too strong.

LUCAS: Yes, kindly put your lid on.

SGANARELLE *(aside)*: Polite, anyhow.

VALÈRE: Sir, you must not find it strange that we have recourse to you. Men of ability are always sought out; and we have been informed of your exceptional capacities.

SGANARELLE: It is true, gentlemen, that I am probably the first man in the world in the kindling-wood line.

VALÈRE: Ah, sir—

SGANARELLE: I spare no pains or trouble. I go so far as to say that no criticism of my kindling wood is possible.

VALÈRE: Sir, that matter is not in question.

SGANARELLE: But observe that I sell it at a hundred and ten sous for a hundred sticks.

VALÈRE: We needn't discuss that.

SGANARELLE: I assure you that I can't give it to you for less.

VALÈRE: Sir, we have been informed—

SGANARELLE: If you have been informed, you know that that is the price.

VALÈRE: Sir, please don't be ridiculous.

SGANARELLE: Nothing ridiculous about it. I can't take off a penny.

VALÈRE: Let's take another approach—

SGANARELLE: Of course you can get it cheaper elsewhere. There is kindling wood and kindling wood. But as for my kindling wood—

VALÈRE: Sir, let's drop this subject—

SGANARELLE: I swear to you that you can't have it for a farthing less.

VALÈRE: Damn!

SGANARELLE: No, on my conscience, that's the price you'll have to pay. I am speaking with all sincerity, and I'm not the kind of man who would overcharge.

VALÈRE: Why, sir, should a person like you indulge in these clumsy pretenses? Why degrade yourself to talk in such a way? Why should a learned man, a physician like you, try to disguise himself before the public, and keep his great talents hidden?

SGANARELLE (aside): He's crazy.

VALÈRE: Sir, kindly do not dissimulate with us.

SGANARELLE: What?

LUCAS: No use fiddlin' around with us; we know what's what.

SGANARELLE: What! What are you trying to give me? What do you take me for?

VALÈRE: We take you for what you are: a great physician.

SGANARELLE: Physician yourself. I'm no physician, and I never have been.

VALÈRE (to Lucas): There's his mania. (To Sganarelle) Sir, kindly make no further denials. Do not force us to extreme and painful measures.

SGANARELLE: What do you mean?

VALÈRE: To expedients which would be distressing to us.

SGANARELLE: 'Struth! Use any expedients you like. I'm not a physician, and I don't know what you're talking about.

VALÈRE (to Lucas): I can see that we'll have to employ the usual system. (To Sganarelle) Once more, sir, I beg you to admit you are what you are.

LUCAS: Gol-ding and gol-darn! No more messin' around! Come clean and spit it out and say you're a doctor!

SGANARELLE (aside): They give me a pain!

VALÈRE: Why deny what everyone knows?

LUCAS: What's the use of all this flimflam? What good does it do you?

SGANARELLE: Gentlemen, I tell you simply and flatly: I am not a doctor.

VALÈRE: You are not a doctor?

SGANARELLE: No.

LUCAS: You ain't no doctor?

SGANARELLE: No, I tell you.

VALÈRE: Since you insist, we'll have to go through with it.

(Valère and Lucas pick up sticks and beat Sganarelle)

SGANARELLE: Oh, oh, oh! Gentlemen, I am anything you like!

VALÈRE: Why, sir, do you oblige us to resort to this violence?

Lucas: Why do you bullyrag us into beating you up?

Valère: Let me assure you of my profoundest regrets.

Lucas: B'jeez, I'm sorry, Doc.

Sganarelle: What the devil is all this, anyway? Is it a joke? Or are you both crazy, to insist I'm a doctor?

Valère: What? You still won't surrender? You won't admit you're a doctor?

Sganarelle: Like the devil I'm a doctor!

Lucas: It ain't true you're a doc, hey?

Sganarelle: No, plague take me! *(Valère and Lucas beat Sganarelle)* Oh, oh! All right gentlemen, all right! I'm a doctor, if that's what you want! I'm a physician, and an apothecary too, if you like. I'll consent to everything rather than be beaten to death.

Valère: Why, that's excellent, sir. I am delighted to see you in a reasonable mood.

Lucas: I sure am tickled to hear you talk thataway.

Valère: I ask your most sincere pardon.

Lucas: Please excuse me for takin' the liberty.

Sganarelle *(aside)*: Hey, hey! Maybe I'm the one who was mistaken! Maybe I've become a doctor without knowing it.

Valère: Sir, you will have no reason to regret revealing your true self. I am sure you will have every reason for satisfaction.

Sganarelle: But, gentlemen, tell me, couldn't you be mistaken yourselves? Is it quite certain that I'm a physician?

Lucas: Yes, by ding and by dog!

Sganarelle: Honestly?

Valère: Unquestionably.

Sganarelle: The devil take me if I knew it!

Valère: What do you mean? You're the cleverest doctor on earth!

Sganarelle: Aha!

Lucas: A doc who's cured I don't know how many ails and complaints.

Sganarelle: Bless my soul!

Valère: A woman was considered dead for six hours; they were ready to lay her out, when you gave her a drop of something and she came to and began walking around the room.

Sganarelle: I'll be hanged!

Lucas: A twelve-year-old boy fell down off the top of a belfry, and he got his arms and legs and head busted; and you put some kind of salve onto him, and he stood right up on his feet and went off and shot marbles!

Sganarelle: Marbles!

Valère: In short, sir, you will be well satisfied with our treatment; and you will earn whatever you like, if you let us take you to a certain place.

Sganarelle: I will earn whatever I like?

Valère: Yes.

Sganarelle: Oho! I'm a physician! No question about it. It had slipped my mind; but now I remember. What is the trouble? Where do we have to go?

Valère: We'll take you there. We are to see a girl who has lost her speech.

Sganarelle: Faith, I haven't found it.

Valère: He likes his little joke. Come on, sir.

SGANARELLE: Without a doctor's gown?

VALÈRE: We'll get one.

SGANARELLE (*solemnly presents his bottle to Valère*): Take that. That's what I keep my potions in. (*Turns to Lucas; spits on the ground*) Now, you walk in front. Doctor's orders.

LUCAS: By gosh and by golly! There's the kind of doctor I like! I think he'll do all right, because he's funny.[2]

Act II

A room in Géronte's house. Géronte, Valère, Lucas, and Jacqueline are discovered.

VALÈRE: Yes, sir, I think you will be satisfied. We have brought you the greatest physician on earth.

LUCAS: Yes, by dad and by dang; he's a feller who can't be beat. All the others ain't knee-high to him.

VALÈRE: He's a man who has made some marvelous cures.

LUCAS: He even cured some who was dead.

VALÈRE: He's a little eccentric, as I told you. And sometimes he has spells when his wits wander and he doesn't seem quite himself.

LUCAS: Yes, he likes to be funny; and sometimes, pardon the liberty, you might say he'd been hit on the head with an ax.

VALÈRE: But under it all, he's a man of profound knowledge. Sometimes he says some very remarkable things.

LUCAS: When he puts his mind to it, he spits it out as if he was reading right off a book.

VALÈRE: His reputation has spread about the region, and everyone goes to consult him.

GÉRONTE: I am dying to see him. Bring him to me right away.

VALÈRE: I'll go and fetch him.

(*Exit Valère*)

JACQUELINE: Land's sake, sir, this man won't do no more than the others. It'll be six of one and half a dozen of the other. The best medicine you could give your daughter, if you'll heed me, would be a fine likely husband she'd be sweet on.

GÉRONTE: Well, well, my good nurse! You have a lot of opinions to express!

LUCAS: Shut up, old girl! You got no call to stick your nose in.

JACQUELINE: I vow and declare that all these doctors won't do no more good than so much plain water; and your daughter needs something else than rhubarb and senna; and a husband is a poultice who cures all a young girl's troubles.

GÉRONTE: Is she in any state now to be saddled with a husband with her present affliction? And when I proposed to marry her off, didn't she oppose my wishes?

JACQUELINE: Sure and certain she did. You wanted to rig her out with a husband she couldn't abide. Why didn't you pick that Monsieur Léandre she was crazy

---

[2] Some critics see in this phrase a covert reference to Molière's pique at the relative ill success of *The Misanthrope* [Bishop's note].

about? She would have been fine and obedient; and I bet you he'd take her right now, the way she is, if you wanted to give her to him.

GÉRONTE: That Léandre is not the right person. He is much poorer than the other man.

JACQUELINE: He's got a rich uncle, and he's the heir.

GÉRONTE: All these great expectations seem to me very chancy. There's nothing like having your own money in your own hands. It's very risky to count on property which someone else intends for you. Death doesn't always listen to the prayers and pleas of the heirs; and a man has time to starve, while he is waiting for someone else to die so that he may live his own life.

JACQUELINE: Well, I've always heard folks tell that in marriage, like in everything else, it's better to be happy than rich. Fathers and mothers have that confounded habit of always asking "How much has he got?" and "How much has she got?" Old Uncle Pierre married his daughter Simonette to big Thomas because he had a quarter of a vineyard more than young Robin, who she'd set her heart on. And now the poor critter has turned as yellow as a lemon, and she ain't been hearty and chipper since. There's a fine example for you, sir. All we've got in this world is our pleasure; and I'd rather give my daughter to a good husband she'd cotton to than have all the farms of La Beauce.

GÉRONTE: Pest and plague! My good nurse, how your tongue runs away with you! Silence, please! You take too much interest in my affairs; and you'll curdle your milk.

LUCAS (to Jacqueline): By heck and by hang! Shut up! You're too fresh and uppity! (Tapping smartly on her breast) Master here ain't got no call for your advice; he knows what he's got to do. You stick to giving the baby a good suck, and don't go in for argufyin'. Master here is the father of his own daughter, and he's got sense enough to see what's good for her.

GÉRONTE: Easy there! Take it easy!

LUCAS: Master, sir, I want to mortify her a little and teach her fittin' respect.

GÉRONTE: Yes, but you don't need such vivid demonstrations.

(Enter Valère)

VALÈRE: Sir, prepare yourself. Here is our doctor coming in.

(Enter Sganarelle, in a doctor's gown, with a tall pointed hat)

GÉRONTE: Sir, I am delighted to see you in my house. We are in great need of your services.

SGANARELLE: Hippocrates[3] says . . . that we should both put on our hats.

GÉRONTE: Hippocrates says that?

SGANARELLE: Yes.

GÉRONTE: In what chapter, if you please?

SGANARELLE: In his chapter on hats.

GÉRONTE: Since Hippocrates says to, we must do it.

SGANARELLE: Doctor, having learned of the marvelous things—

GÉRONTE: Whom are you addressing, if you please?

SGANARELLE: You.

---

[3] Greek physician (460?–377? B.C.), called the "father of medicine."

GÉRONTE: I'm not a doctor.

SGANARELLE: You aren't a doctor?

GÉRONTE: No, really.

SGANARELLE *(takes a stick and beats him)*: Positively?

GÉRONTE: Positively! Oh, oh, oh!

SGANARELLE: You're a doctor now. That's the only diploma I ever had.

GÉRONTE *(to Valère)*: What kind of madman have you brought me?

VALÈRE: Well, I told you he was a rather whimsical doctor.

GÉRONTE: Yes; but deuce take his whimsicalities.

LUCAS: Don't pay it no mind, sir; it's just his fun.

GÉRONTE: I don't like that kind of fun.

SGANARELLE: Sir, I ask your pardon for the liberty I took.

GÉRONTE: I am at your service, sir.

SGANARELLE: I am sorry.

GÉRONTE: Not at all, not at all.

SGANARELLE: The little beating up—

GÉRONTE: No harm was done.

SGANARELLE: —which I had the honor to bestow upon you—

GÉRONTE: Let's drop the subject. Sir, I have a daughter who has fallen into a strange illness.

SGANARELLE: I am overjoyed, sir, that your daughter has some need of me. I could go farther, and wish with all my heart that you also needed me, you and your entire family, so that I might give evidence of my eagerness to be of use to you.

GÉRONTE: I am much obliged to you for your kind attentions.

SGANARELLE: I assure you that I speak with the utmost sincerity.

GÉRONTE: You do me too much honor.

SGANARELLE: What is your daughter's name?

GÉRONTE: Lucinde.

SGANARELLE: Lucinde! There is an excellent name for medication! Lucinde!

GÉRONTE: I'll go and see what she is up to.

SGANARELLE: Who is that fine big woman?

GÉRONTE: She is the wet nurse of my small boy.

(Exit Géronte)

SGANARELLE: Pest and pox! What a handsome article! Ah, wet nurse, charming wet nurse, all my medicine is the very humble slave of your wet-nursery! How I should like to be the fortunate little babe who is imbibing the milk of your good graces! *(He pats her breast)* All my remedies, all my knowledge, all my capacities are at your service, and—

LUCAS: With your kind permission, Doctor, sir, leave my wife be, if you please.

SGANARELLE: What! She's your wife?

LUCAS: Yes.

SGANARELLE *(opens his arms, preparatory to embracing Lucas, but turns and enclasps Jacqueline)*: Oh, really, I didn't know that, but I'm delighted, for the love of you both.

LUCAS *(pulling at Sganarelle)*: Take it easy, if you please.

SGANARELLE: I assure you that I rejoice that we are thus bound together. *(He starts to embrace Lucas, dodges, throws his arms about Jacqueline)* I felicitate her for having such a husband as you; and I felicitate you for having such a beautiful and modest wife, and so well built.

LUCAS *(pulling at Sganarelle)*: By gum and by gravy! No more compliments, I pray and plead.

SGANARELLE: Don't you want me to rejoice with you about your happy marriage?

LUCAS: With me, all you like; but with my wife, you needn't be so dum polite.

SGANARELLE: But I am equally concerned with the happiness of both of you. *(Same business)* And if I embrace you to demonstrate my joy, I must, in all fairness, make the same demonstration to her.

LUCAS *(pulling him again)*: By jeez and by jingo! Doctor, what a lot of blather!

(Enter Géronte)

GÉRONTE: Doctor, my daughter will be here in a moment.

SGANARELLE: I await her, sir, with all my medicines at hand.

GÉRONTE: Where are they?

SGANARELLE *(tapping his forehead)*: Here.

GÉRONTE: Very good.

SGANARELLE *(trying to feel Jacqueline's breast)*: But as I take a deep interest in the entire family, I must test your nurse's milk, and I must therefore examine her breast.

LUCAS *(pulling Sganarelle away and making him spin around)*: Not on your life; we won't have no truck with that.

SGANARELLE: It is a physician's business to inspect the nurses' breasts.

LUCAS: None of that business here, thanking you kindly.

SGANARELLE: Are you so brazen as to oppose a medical man? Out! Away!

LUCAS: I don't care a hoot.

SGANARELLE *(menacingly)*: I shall give you a case of fever!

JACQUELINE *(takes Lucas by the arm, and spins him around)*: Get out! Ain't I big enough to stand up for myself, if he tries to do something that ain't right?

LUCAS: I don't want him to go pawing you.

SGANARELLE: Shame on the jealous rascal!

GÉRONTE: Here comes my daughter.

(Enter Lucinde)

SGANARELLE: Is this the patient?

GÉRONTE: Yes. She is my only daughter, and I should be heartbroken if she should die.

SGANARELLE: She'd better not; she can't die without a doctor's prescription.

GÉRONTE: Come, bring a chair for the doctor.

SGANARELLE: There is a patient who is by no means repulsive. I think that a sound man could put up with her very nicely.

(Lucinde laughs)

GÉRONTE: You made her laugh, sir.

SGANARELLE: Excellent. When the doctor makes the patient laugh at him, that's a very good sign. *(To Lucinde)* Well now, what's the trouble? What's the matter with you? Do you feel any pains?

LUCINDE *(pointing to her mouth, head, and throat)*: Ank, eek, onk, ank.

SGANARELLE: What did you say?

LUCINDE (gesturing): Ank, eek, onk, ank, ank, eek, onk.

SGANARELLE: How's that?

LUCINDE: Ank, eek, onk.

SGANARELLE (imitating her): Ank, eek, onk, ank, ank, I don't get you. What the devil kind of language is that?

GÉRONTE: Monsieur, that is just her trouble. She has become dumb, and so far no one has been able to discover the cause. Her misfortune has caused the postponement of her marriage.

SGANARELLE: What for?

GÉRONTE: The man she is to marry wants to wait for her to be cured before concluding the affair.

SGANARELLE: And who is the fool who doesn't want his wife to be dumb? I wish to God mine had that disease! I'd take good care not to cure her.

GÉRONTE: Anyway, sir, we beg you to make all your best efforts to relieve her of her malady.

SGANARELLE: Don't worry. Tell me, does this illness distress her very much?

GÉRONTE: Yes, sir.

SGANARELLE: Good. Does she feel much pain?

GÉRONTE: Very much.

SGANARELLE: Splendid! Does she go—you know where?

GÉRONTE: Yes.

SGANARELLE: Copiously?

GÉRONTE: As to that, I am unable to say.

SGANARELLE: The results are . . . salubrious?

GÉRONTE: I am unfamiliar with such matters.

SGANARELLE (to Lucinde): Give me your arm . . . There is a pulse which indicates . . . that your daughter is dumb.

GÉRONTE: Why yes, sir, that is exactly her trouble. You discovered it immediately.

SGANARELLE: Aha!

JACQUELINE: Look how quick he guessed it!

SGANARELLE: A really good doctor knows things right away. An ignoramus would have been confused; he would have said, "Maybe it's this, maybe it's that." But I go right to the heart of the matter, and I tell you that your daughter is dumb.

GÉRONTE: Yes; but I wish you could tell me how that comes about.

SGANARELLE: Nothing is easier. That comes from the fact that she has lost her power of speech.

GÉRONTE: Very good. But what, if you please, is the cause of her losing her power of speech?

SGANARELLE: All the best authors will tell you . . . that it is an obstruction to the tongue's action.

GÉRONTE: But further, what is your opinion about this obstruction to the tongue's action?

SGANARELLE: Aristotle, on that head, says . . . some very fine things.

GÉRONTE: I can well believe it.

SGANARELLE: Oh, he was a big man!

GÉRONTE: Assuredly.

SGANARELLE (raising his arm): A really big man! Bigger than me—by so much. To return to our diagnosis, then, I maintain that this obstruction to the tongue's action is caused by certain humors, which we scientists call peccant humors. Peccant, that is to say . . . peccant humors. Since the vapors caused by the exhalation of the influences which arise in the diseased area, arriving , . . you might say . . . at . . . Do you understand Latin?

GÉRONTE: Not a word.

SGANARELLE *(jumping up)*: You don't understand Latin?

GÉRONTE: No.

SGANARELLE *(gesturing)*: Cabricias arci thuram, catalamus, singulariter, nominativo haec Musa—or "the Muse"—bonus, bona, bonum, Deus sanctus, estne oratio latinas? Etiam, yes. Quare—why? Quia substantivo et adectivum concordat in generi, numerum, et casus.[4]

GÉRONTE: Oh, why did I never study?

JACQUELINE: There's a smart man for you!

LUCAS: Yes, that's so grand I don't catch on to a single word.

SGANARELLE: Now these vapors I refer to, making a passage from the left side, where the liver is, to the right side, where the heart is, it comes about that the lungs, which we call in Latin *armyan*, having a communication with the brain, which we term in Greek *nasmus*, by means of the vena cava, which we denominate in Hebrew *cubile*, encounter on their path the aforesaid vapors, which fill the ventricles of the scapula; and because the aforesaid vapors—give close heed to this argument, please—because the aforesaid vapors have a certain malignity—I beg you to pay the closest attention.

GÉRONTE: Yes.

SGANARELLE: Because they have a certain malignity, which is caused—I must ask you to be attentive—

GÉRONTE: Oh, I am.

SGANARELLE: —which is caused by the acridity of the humors engendered in the concavity of the diaphragm, it then happens that the vapors—ossabundus, nequeys, nequer, potarinum, quipsa milus. And this is exactly how it comes about that your daughter is dumb.

JACQUELINE: Oh, wasn't that lovely, husband!

LUCAS: Why ain't I got that gift of gab!

GÉRONTE: I am sure that no one could argue the case better. There is just one thing that bothers me: the position of the liver and the heart. It seems to me that you place them wrongly; and the heart is on the left side, and the liver on the right.

SGANARELLE: Yes, that is the way it used to be. But we have changed all that; now we use an entirely new method in medicine.

GÉRONTE: Oh, I didn't know that. I ask your pardon for my ignorance.

SGANARELLE: No harm done. You aren't obliged to be as well informed as we are.

GÉRONTE: Assuredly. But sir, what do you think we ought to do for this disease?

SGANARELLE: What I think we ought to do?

GÉRONTE: Yes.

SGANARELLE: My opinion is that we should put her back to bed, and give her as treatment a quantity of bread soaked in wine.

GÉRONTE: Why is that, sir?

---

[4] According to the traditional stage business, Sganarelle works himself up into violent excitement during this speech, then throws himself into a chair, which falls over backward. Scholars are delighted because his last word, *casus*, means both *case* (of a noun) and *fall* [Bishop's note].

SGANARELLE: Because in wine and bread united there is a sympathetic virtue which makes people talk. Don't you know that that is what they give parrots, and thus they learn to speak?

GÉRONTE: That's true. Oh, the great man! Quick! Get some bread and wine!

SGANARELLE: I will come back this evening and see how she's doing. (Exit Lucinde and Lucas, Jacqueline starts to go; Sganarelle stops her) Wait a minute, you. (To Géronte) Sir, there is a wet nurse who needs some of my little remedies.

JACQUELINE: Who, me? I'm feeling fine.

SGANARELLE: That's bad, nurse, very bad. Such good health is alarming. It wouldn't be a bad idea to give you a nice little bloodletting, or a nice little emollient enema.

GÉRONTE: But, sir, that is something I don't understand. Why should you be bled when you aren't sick?

SGANARELLE: Never mind; it's a very salutary system. As we drink for fear of being thirsty, we should be bled for the illness which hasn't yet arrived. That's preventive medicine.

JACQUELINE: Land's sakes, I won't have none of that. I don't want to turn my body into no drug store.

SGANARELLE: You are rebellious toward medicine; but we'll get you down in the end. (Exit Jacqueline) I bid you good day, sir.

GÉRONTE: Wait a minute, please.

SGANARELLE: What do you want to do?

GÉRONTE: Give you some money, sir.

SGANARELLE (hoisting his gown and thrusting his hand backward, as Géronte opens his purse): I won't take money, sir.

GÉRONTE: But, sir—

SGANARELLE: Not at all.

GÉRONTE: But just a moment!

SGANARELLE: By no means.

GÉRONTE: But please!

SGANARELLE: Don't be absurd.

GÉRONTE: There you are.

SGANARELLE: I'll do nothing of the sort.

GÉRONTE: Oh!

SGANARELLE: Money is not my motive.

GÉRONTE: I believe you.

SGANARELLE (weighing the coins): They aren't short weight?

GÉRONTE: No, sir.

SGANARELLE: I am not a mercenary physician.

GÉRONTE: I am well aware of it.

SGANARELLE: I don't seek personal advantage.

GÉRONTE: I never had such an idea.

(Exit Géronte, Sganarelle brings his hand forward and looks at the money)

SGANARELLE: Well, not so bad, not so bad! If only—

(Enter Léandre)

LÉANDRE: Sir, I have been watching my chance to see you for a long time. I have come to implore your assistance.

SGANARELLE *(seizing Léandre's wrist)*: The pulse is very bad.

LÉANDRE: I am not sick, sir; that is not my reason for coming to see you.

SGANARELLE: If you aren't sick, why the devil didn't you say so?

LÉANDRE: Please! To put it briefly, my name is Léandre, and I'm in love with Lucinde, whom you've just examined. And since I have no access to her, because of her father's animosity, I have ventured to ask you to aid my love, and to play a little trick, to give me the chance of saying to her a couple of words, on which my happiness and my life absolutely depend.

SGANARELLE *(angrily)*: What do you take me for? How do you dare address yourself to me to help you in a love affair, and to degrade the dignity of a physician to such base employments!

LÉANDRE: Sir, please don't make so much noise!

SGANARELLE *(thrusting him backward)*: I'll make all the noise I like! You are an impertinent puppy!

LÉANDRE: Calm down, sir.

SGANARELLE: A blundering fool!

LÉANDRE: Please, sir—

SGANARELLE: I'll show you that I'm not that kind of a man, and it is the height of insolence—

LÉANDRE *(pulling out a purse and handing it to Sganarelle)*: But, sir—

SGANARELLE: —to make such a proposition . . . I'm not referring to you personally, for you're a good fellow, and I should be delighted to do you a service. But there are some impertinent puppies around who misjudge people entirely; and I freely grant that that sort of thing makes me angry.

LÉANDRE: I ask your pardon, sir, for the liberty—

SGANARELLE: Not at all, not at all. What is the story?

LÉANDRE: You must know then, sir, that this illness you are trying to cure is only pretended. The doctors have argued about it in due form. They have given their opinions; some say it comes from the brain; others, from the intestines, or from the spleen, or from the liver. But the fact is that love is the real cause, and that Lucinde has invented this affliction only to escape from a threatening marriage. But I am afraid we may be overseen together; let's leave this spot, and I'll tell you as we go what I want from you.

SGANARELLE: Let's be on our way, sir. You have given me an almost inconceivable sympathy for your love. The patient will either die, or she'll be yours—or I'm no doctor.

Act III

The scene is a sylvan setting, near Géronte's house. (In modern stage productions the scene commonly remains the same as in Act II.) Léandre, disguised as an apothecary, and Sganarelle are discovered.

LÉANDRE: It seems to me I'm rather good as an apothecary; and as the father never saw much of me, I think this gown and wig will be a sufficient disguise.

SGANARELLE: By all means.

LÉANDRE: The only thing is, I'd like to know a few big medical terms, to decorate my speech and make me sound professional.

SGANARELLE: Go on, that's not necessary. All you need is the costume. In fact, I don't know any more than you do.

LÉANDRE: What?

SGANARELLE: I'm damned if I know anything about medicine! You're a good fellow, and I'm willing to confide in you, as you have confided in me.

LÉANDRE: What! You aren't in fact—

SGANARELLE: No, I tell you. I was kicked into the medical profession. I never had any idea of being a scholar; I didn't get beyond the third grade. I don't know how they got this maggot in their heads; but when I saw they were bound and determined that I was a physician, I decided to be one, no matter who got hurt. Still, you wouldn't believe how the idea has got around, and how pigheaded everybody is in taking me for a great healer. People come from all over to consult me. If things go on this way, maybe I'll stick to medicine for the rest of my life. I think it's the best trade there is, for whether you do well or badly, you get paid just the same. We never get blamed for doing a bad job; and we cut the cloth we work on to please ourselves. A cobbler making shoes can't spoil a piece of leather without paying for the damage; but in this job we can spoil a man without its costing us a penny. The blunders aren't our fault; they're always the fault of the man who dies. In short, the nice thing about this profession is that dead men have a most marvelous decency and discretion; you never hear a dead man complain of the doctor who killed him.

LÉANDRE: It is true that the dead are uncommonly polite on this subject.

(Enter Thibaut and Perrin)[5]

SGANARELLE: Here are some fellows who look as though they are coming for a consultation. You go and wait for me near your lady's house.

(Exit Léandre)

THIBAUT: Doctor, sir, me and my son, we've come to see you.

SGANARELLE: What's the matter?

THIBAUT: His poor mother, her name is Perrette, she's been sick abed going on now six months.

SGANARELLE *(thrusting out his hand)*: And what do you expect me to do about it?

THIBAUT: We'd like for you to give us some little dohickus for to cure her.

SGANARELLE: I'd have to know the kind of illness she has.

THIBAUT: She's sick with hypocrisy, sir.

SGANARELLE: Hypocrisy?

THIBAUT: Yes; I mean to say she's all swole up; and they do tell it's a lot of seriosities she's got inside, and her liver, her stomach, her spleen, or what you may call it, is just amakin' water instead of blood. Every two days she gits the fever and shakes, with lastitudes and miseries in the leg mussicles. You can hear in her throat phlegm like to choke her, and now and then she has syncopations and compulsions, so I'm afeared she's goin' to pass away. We've got in our village a pothecary, pardon the expression, who has give her a lot of messes, and I've paid out more than a dozen good crowns in enemies, begging your pardon, and setatives to make her set better, and infections and cordialities. But all that, as the feller says, has just been water down the train. He wanted to give her a kind o' physic called a medic wine, but to tell you the honest truth,

[5] The following scene with Thibaut and Perrin is commonly omitted in modern productions [Bishop's note].

I was scared it would finish her. I hear tell the big doctors have killed off a terrible lot of folks with that invention.[6]

SGANARELLE *(irritably wiggling his thrust-out hand)*: Come to the point, my friend, come to the point.

THIBAUT: The point is, sir, that we've come to ask you what we ought for to do.

SGANARELLE: I don't understand you at all.

PERRIN: Sir, my mother is ailing; and here's two crowns we've brung you to give us a cure.

SGANARELLE: Ah, I understand you perfectly! There is a young man who speaks clearly, and knows how to express himself. You say your mother is ill with dropsy, that her whole body is swollen up, that she has fever, and pains in the legs, that she has syncopes and convulsions, or, that is, fainting fits?

PERRIN: Oh, yes, sir, that's it perzackly.

SGANARELLE: I understood you immediately. Your father doesn't know what he's talking about. And now you want a remedy?

PERRIN: Yes, sir.

SGANARELLE: A remedy to cure her?

PERRIN: That's the way we kind o' look at it.

SGANARELLE: Look, here's a piece of cheese you must make her swallow.

PERRIN: Cheese, sir?

SGANARELLE: Yes, it's a specially prepared cheese, with gold, coral, pearls, and other precious substances ground up in it.

PERRIN: Sir, we are much beholden to you; we'll make her swaller it straight off.

SGANARELLE: That's right. And if she dies, don't fail to give her the best possible burial.

(Exit Perrin and Thibaut. The scene changes to a room in Géronte's house, as in Act II. Enter Sganarelle and Jacqueline.)

SGANARELLE: Ah, here is the lovely wet nurse! Ah, wet nurse of my heart, I am delighted to see you again! The vision of you is the rhubarb, cassia, and senna which purge all the melancholy of my soul!

JACQUELINE: My stars alive! Doctor, sir, that's too fine talk for me, and I don't understand any of your Latin.

SGANARELLE: Fall ill, nurse, I pray you. Fall ill, for love of me. I would be only too delighted to cure you.

(Enter Lucas. He approaches the speakers stealthily and unobserved.)

JACQUELINE: Much obliged. I'd liefer not take none of your cures.

SGANARELLE: How I pity you, fair wet nurse, for having such a jealous, troublesome husband!

JACQUELINE: Ah, well, sir, it's penance for my sins. Where the goat is tied, there she has to graze.

SGANARELLE: What, such a bumpkin, a hick! A man who watches you every minute, and won't let anyone even speak to you!

JACQUELINE: Oh, dear, you ain't seen nothing yet. That's just a sample of his jealous turn of mind.

[6] The efficacy of emetic wine, containing antimony, was then the subject of a fierce medical controversy [Bishop's note].

SGANARELLE: Is it possible! That a man should have so base a character as to mistreat a person like you! Ah, lovely wet nurse, I know some people, not very far from here, who would think themselves happy even to kiss the sweet utensils of your trade! How could it happen that a beautiful creature like you should fall into such hands as his! That such a coarse lout, brutal, stupid, a fool—pardon me, nurse, if I speak in this way of your husband—

JACQUELINE: Ah, sir, I know very well he deserves all them names.

SGANARELLE: Yes, certainly, nurse, he deserves them. He would further deserve that you plant a certain adornment on his brow, to punish him for his suspicions.

JACQUELINE: It's true that if I only thought about what's good for him, he might drive me to some pretty goings-on.

SGANARELLE: On my word, you wouldn't do badly to revenge yourself on him, with someone's help. He's the kind of man, I tell you, who deserves exactly that! And if, fair nurse, I were fortunate enough to be chosen as the instrument—

(Both become aware of Lucas's presence behind them. Both escape to opposite sides of the stage, and exit. Enter Géronte.)

GÉRONTE: Hello, Lucas. You haven't seen our doctor around?

LUCAS: Yes, by gee and by jiminy! I seen him, and my wife too!

GÉRONTE: I wonder where he can be.

LUCAS: I don't know; but I wisht he was in hell's fire.

GÉRONTE: Go and find out what my daughter is doing.

(Exit Lucas. Enter Sganarelle and Léandre.)

Ah, monsieur, I was just asking where you were.

SGANARELLE: I was dallying in the courtyard. *(Aside)* Expelling the superfluity of my potations. *(Aloud)* And how is our patient doing?

GÉRONTE: A little worse, since she took your medicine.

SGANARELLE: Good; good! That's a sign it's working.

GÉRONTE: Yes; but while it's working, I'm afraid it will undo her completely.

SGANARELLE: Don't worry. I have remedies which are proof against everything. I am waiting for her to come to her death agony.

GÉRONTE: Who is that man with you?

SGANARELLE *(imitating an apothecary administering an enema)*: He's—

GÉRONTE: What?

SGANARELLE: He's the man—

GÉRONTE: Eh?

SGANARELLE: The man who—

GÉRONTE: Oh, I understand.

SGANARELLE: Your daughter will need him.

(Enter Lucinde and Jacqueline)

JACQUELINE *(to Géronte)*: Sir, here's your daughter. She wants to walk around a bit.

SGANARELLE: That will do her good. Apothecary, feel her pulse, while I discuss her illness with you, sir.

(Exit Jacqueline. Léandre draws Lucinde to one side of the stage. Sganarelle pulls Géronte to the other side, puts his arm over Géronte's shoulders, his hand under Géronte's chin. As Géronte tries to see what his daughter and Léandre are doing, Sganarelle turns Géronte's face toward his own. In current productions, Sganarelle resorts to every burlesque device to block Géronte's view, even standing on a chair and spreading his gown wide as a screen.)

Sir, it is a great and subtle question among the learned, whether women are easier to cure than men. I beg you to listen attentively to this. Some say yes; others say no; and I say yes and no. Inasmuch as the incongruity of the opaque humors which are to be found in the natural temperament of women are the reason that the grosser nature forever attempts to overmaster the sensitive nature, we see that the variation of their opinions depends upon the oblique movement of the moon's circle; and as the sun, which casts its rays upon the concavity of the earth, finds—

LUCINDE: No, I am entirely incapable of ever changing my feelings.

GÉRONTE: My daugher is speaking! Oh, what power was in the remedy! Oh, what a wonderful doctor! How indebted I am to you, sir, for this marvelous cure! How can I reward you for your services!

SGANARELLE *(walking to and fro, and wiping his brow)*: There is a case which caused me a lot of trouble.

LUCINDE: Yes, Father, I have recovered my power of speech; but I have recovered it in order to tell you that I will never have any other husband than Léandre, and there's no use in your trying to give me to Horace.

GÉRONTE: But—

LUCINDE: Nothing can shake my resolution.

GÉRONTE: What—

LUCINDE: You can argue all you please.

GÉRONTE: If—

LUCINDE: All your talk will do no good.

GÉRONTE: I—

LUCINDE: I have made up my mind about it.

GÉRONTE: But—

LUCINDE: There is no parental authority which can force me to marry in spite of myself.

GÉRONTE: I have—

LUCINDE: Do whatever you like; it's no good.

GÉRONTE: He—

LUCINDE: My heart can never submit to such tyranny.

GÉRONTE: There—

LUCINDE: And I will take refuge in a convent rather than marry a man I don't love.

GÉRONTE: But—

LUCINDE *(in a deafening shout)*: No! By no manner of means! Absolutely not! You're wasting your time! I won't do it! It's all settled!

GÉRONTE: What a flood of talk! I can't stand up against it. Doctor, I beg you to make her dumb again.

SGANARELLE: That, I fear, is impossible. All I can do, to serve you, is to make you deaf, if you like.

GÉRONTE: No, thanks. *(To Lucinde)* So you think—

LUCINDE: No. All your arguments will do no good.

GÉRONTE: You will marry Horace, and you will do it this very day.

LUCINDE: I'll die first.

SGANARELLE: Good Lord, stop! Let me medicate the affair. The woman is still sick, and I know the remedy we must employ.

GÉRONTE: Is it possible, sir, that you can also cure this malady of the mind?

SGANARELLE: Yes. Let me handle it. I have remedies for everything, and our apothecary will help in this cure. *(To Léandre)* A word with you. You perceive that her infatuation with Léandre is entirely contrary to her father's wishes, and that there is no time to lose; her humors are much inflamed, and it is necessary to find very promptly a remedy for this disease, which might easily get worse with delay. Personally, I see only one cure, which is a dose of purgative getawayum, which you will combine properly with two drachms of matrimonium in pill form. She may make some difficulty about taking this medicine, but as you're a clever man at your trade, you will have to persuade her, and make her swallow the dose the best way you can. Now you two go and take a turn around the garden, in order to prepare her humors, while I have a talk with her father. But above all don't lose time. The remedy, quickly, the panacea!

(Exit Léandre and Lucinde)

GÉRONTE: Doctor, what are those drugs you just mentioned? I don't think I have ever heard of them.

SGANARELLE: They are drugs one uses only in critical cases.

GÉRONTE: Did you ever hear of such insolence as hers?

SGANARELLE: Girls are sometimes a little headstrong.

GÉRONTE: You can't imagine how mad she is about that Léandre.

SGANARELLE: The heat of the blood has that effect on young minds.

GÉRONTE: Ever since I discovered the violence of my daughter's attachment, I've kept her locked up.

SGANARELLE: Very wise.

GÉRONTE: And I've kept them from having any communication with each other.

SGANARELLE: Excellent.

GÉRONTE: If I'd allowed them to see each other, some folly would have resulted.

SGANARELLE: No doubt.

GÉRONTE: I think she'd have been capable of running away with him.

SGANARELLE: Sensibly argued.

GÉRONTE: I've been warned that he's been making all sorts of efforts to speak to her.

SGANARELLE: The scoundrel!

GÉRONTE: But he's wasting his time.

SGANARELLE: Ha, ha!

GÉRONTE: I'll keep him from seeing her, all right.

SGANARELLE: He's not dealing with a simpleton. You know more tricks than he does. Anyone will have to get up early to catch you napping.

(Enter Lucas)

LUCAS: By cripes and by crikey, sir, hell's apoppin'! Your daughter has gone and run off with her Léandre! The pothecary, it was him; and that there doctor was the one who done the trick!

GÉRONTE: What! I'm ruined! Call the police! Don't let him escape! Traitor! I'll have you punished by the law!

(Exit Géronte)

LUCAS: Dad-burn, dad-blame, and dad-rot! Doctor, sir, you're going to git hung; so don't move.

(Enter Martine)

MARTINE: Oh, dear, what a lot of trouble I had finding this house! *(To Lucas)* Why, how do you do? Tell me, what happened to the doctor I recommended to you?

LUCAS: There he is, there. He's going to git hung.

MARTINE: What! My husband is going to get hung? Oh, dear! What did he do, then?

LUCAS: He got our master's daughter kidnaped.

MARTINE: Alas, my dear husband, is it true they're going to hang you?

SGANARELLE: Well, you see. Oh!

MARTINE: Are you going to let yourself die in front of everybody?

SGANARELLE: And what can I do about it?

MARTINE: If you'd even finished cutting our wood, it would be some consolation.

SGANARELLE: Get out of here; you're breaking my heart.

MARTINE: No, I'm going to stay in order to cheer you up. I won't leave until I've seen you hung.

SGANARELLE: Ah!

(Enter Géronte)

GÉRONTE *(to Sganarelle)*: The police chief will be here soon; they'll put you in a place where you'll be good and secure.

SGANARELLE *(kneeling, hat in hand)*: Alas! You couldn't change it to a little flogging?

GÉRONTE: No, no; the law must take its course. But what's this?

(Enter Léandre, Lucinde, and Jacqueline)

LÉANDRE *(to Géronte)*: Sir, I am Léandre, come to present myself to you, and to entrust Lucinde to your power. We had proposed to flee together, and to get married; but we have given up this purpose in favor of more honorable behavior. I do not wish to steal your daughter from you; I desire to receive her only from your own hands. I have further news for you, sir; I have just received letters informing me that my uncle is dead, and I inherit all his property.

GÉRONTE *(who has been threatening Léandre with a stick, now throws it away)*: Sir, your merits are most worthy of consideration; and I give you my daughter with the utmost joy.

SGANARELLE: The art of medicine had a narrow escape.

MARTINE *(to Sganarelle)*: Since you aren't going to be hung, do me the favor of being a doctor; I am the one who gained this honor for you.
SGANARELLE: Yes, you are the one who gained me some fine beatings.
LÉANDRE: The result is so happy that you shouldn't bear her any ill will.
SGANARELLE: All right. I pardon you the beatings in consideration of the dignity
to which you have elevated me. But prepare yourself from now on to treat
with great respect a man of my importance; and remember that a doctor's anger is terrible!

In a number of ways, *The Physician in Spite of Himself* moves frequently
toward *farce* (fast-paced humor based on broadly comic situations) and
burlesque (humor from improbable exaggerations). Answers to the following questions may suggest, however, that it is something more than
mere farce or burlesque.

1. Much of the comedy, such as Sganarelle's beating his wife, his own
   cudgeling in return, and his fondling the nurse, is essentially physical. How much of this physical comedy can be explained in terms of
   characterization and plot?
2. Comedy, like tragedy, has its reversals and recognitions. What are the
   most important ones here? Why are they comic rather than tragic?
3. Observe that this play has two threads of plot, the revenge of Martine, turning Sganarelle into a doctor, and the conflict between Géronte and Lucinde over her choice of a husband. How skillfully are the
   two woven together?
4. Two coincidences stand out: the appearance of Valère and Lucas at
   the beginning of the play, just as Martine is swearing that she will get
   revenge, and the news at the end that Léandre has inherited property. What is their effect on the plot?
5. Which episodes seem least necessary to the plot? Can you justify their
   inclusion on other grounds?
6. Molière himself played Sganarelle, one of his great comic creations.
   Can one successfully defend the position that in this comedy characterization is more important than plot?
7. Does the play contain any satire? If so, how important is it to the total
   effect?

The Tempest

In the first collected edition of Shakespeare's plays, the First Folio of
1623, *The Tempest* stood first. Probably the last play written entirely by
Shakespeare, it is also one of his greatest. In it he combined the wisdom
of maturity with a poetic and dramatic skill perfected through thirty-five
earlier plays. Listed in the First Folio among the comedies, *The Tempest*
has in some recent editions been designated a romance (a category not

used in the First Folio). As is true with other romances, or with comedies reaching toward romance, laughter here is not as important as the genial good spirit that in the end prevails. The atmosphere is far removed from the satiric thrusts of *Lysistrata* or the tendency toward farce and burlesque in *The Physician in Spite of Himself.*

A play this rich invites a number of approaches. We may consider it as the *court entertainment* that it was in its first recorded productions (not in the Globe theater, but in Whitehall before King James in 1611 and again in the winter of 1612–1613 to celebrate the marriage of Princess Elizabeth). In its New World imagery it is a *topical play,* exploiting the interest of the audience in a recent English shipwreck and survival on the coast of Bermuda, in an area that according to a contemporary account was "supposed to be enchanted and inhabited with witches and devils, which grew by reason of accustomed monstrous thunder, storm, and tempest, near unto those islands." Living today in an age far less credulous in some respects than the seventeenth century, we may wish to see the magic as more allegoric than literal and the play itself as a universal drama of appearance and reality. Remembering that it came at the end of Shakespeare's career, we may see in it the author's conjuring once more with the magic of his art, before, in the character of Prospero, he bids it farewell forever. Rejecting alike historical and biographical connections and deep-seated allegories, we may find in it that particular enchantment of the world of fairy tales and romance which is always and never present for all times and places.

THE TEMPEST*
William Shakespeare   (1564–1616)

Names of the Actors

ALONSO, King of Naples	MASTER of a ship
SEBASTIAN, his brother	BOATSWAIN
PROSPERO, the right Duke of Milan	MARINERS
ANTONIO, his brother, the usurping	MIRANDA, daughter to Prospero
Duke of Milan	ARIEL, an airy spirit
FERDINAND, son to the King of Naples	IRIS
GONZALO, an honest old councillor	CERES
ADRIAN AND FRANCISCO, lords	JUNO (presented by) spirits
CALIBAN, a savage and deformed slave	NYMPHS
TRINCULO, a jester	REAPERS
STEPHANO, a drunken butler	(OTHER SPIRITS ATTENDING ON PROSPERO)

The Scene: An uninhabited Island

---

* Edited, with notes, by Northrop Frye.

I, i   *(A tempestuous noise of thunder and lightning heard.*
              Enter a Shipmaster and a Boatswain.)

MASTER: Boatswain!
BOATSWAIN: Here, master. What cheer?
MASTER: Good, speak to th' mariners; fall to't yarely, or we run ourselves   27
    aground. Bestir, bestir!   *(Exit)*

(Enter Mariners)

BOATSWAIN: Heigh, my hearts! Cheerly, cheerly, my hearts! Yare, yare! Take
    in the topsail! Tend to th' master's whistle! Blow till thou burst thy
    wind, if room enough!   5

(Enter Alonso, Sebastian, Antonio, Ferdinand, Gonzalo, and others)

ALONSO: Good boatswain, have care. Where's the master? Play the men.   8
BOATSWAIN: I pray now, keep below.
ANTONIO: Where is the master, bos'n?
BOATSWAIN: Do you not hear him? You mar our labor. Keep your cabins:
    you do assist the storm.
GONZALO: Nay, good, be patient.
BOATSWAIN: When the sea is. Hence! What cares these roarers for the name   14
    of king? To cabin! Silence! Trouble us not!
GONZALO: Good, yet remember whom thou hast aboard.
BOATSWAIN: None that I more love than myself. You are a councillor: if you
    can command these elements to silence and work the peace of the pres-
    ent, we will not hand a rope more; use your authority. If you cannot,   19
    give thanks you have lived so long, and make yourself ready in your
    cabin for the mischance of the hour, if it so hap.—Cheerly, good
    hearts!—Out of our way, I say.   *(Exit)*
GONZALO: I have great comfort from this fellow: methinks he hath no
    drowning mark upon him; his complexion is perfect gallows. Stand fast,   24
    good Fate, to his hanging! Make the rope of his destiny our cable, our
    own doth little advantage. If he be not born to be hanged, our case   26
    is miserable.

                                                                            (Exeunt)

(Enter Boatswain)

BOATSWAIN: Down with the topmast! Yare! Lower, lower! Bring her to try   28
    with main-course! *(A cry within)* A plague upon this howling! They are   29
    louder than the weather or our office.   30

(Enter Sebastian, Antonio, and Gonzalo)

I, i The deck of a ship   **3** *yarely* briskly   **5** *Tend* attend; *Blow . . . wind* (addressed to the storm)   **7** *if room*
enough i.e. so long as we have searoom   **8** *Play* (perhaps 'ply,' keep the men busy)   **14** *roarers* (1) waves,
(2) blusterers or bullies   **19** *hand* handle   **24** *complexion* indication of character in appearance of face
24 *gallows* (alluding to the proverb 'He that's born to be hanged need fear no drowning')   **26** *doth little*
advantage doesn't help us much   **28** *try with main-course* lie hove-to with only the mainsail   **29** *plague*
(followed by a dash in F; possibly the boatswain's language was more profane than the text indicates;
cf.l. 38, and V, i, 218–19)   **30** *our office* (the noise we make at) our work

Yet again? What do you here? Shall we give o'er and drown? Have you
a mind to sink?

SEBASTIAN: A pox o' your throat, you bawling, blasphemous, incharitable
dog!

BOATSWAIN: Work you, then.

ANTONIO: Hang, cur, hang, you whoreson, insolent noisemaker! We are
less afraid to be drowned than thou art.

GONZALO: I'll warrant him for drowning, though the ship were no stronger   38
than a nutshell and as leaky as an unstanched wench.   39

BOATSWAIN: Lay her ahold, ahold! Set her two courses! Off to sea again! Lay   40
her off!

(Enter Mariners wet)

MARINERS: All lost! To prayers, to prayers! All lost!

(Exeunt)

BOATSWAIN: What, must our mouths be cold?

GONZALO:
The King and Prince at prayers! Let's assist them,
For our case is as theirs.

SEBASTIAN: I am out of patience.

ANTONIO:
We are merely cheated of our lives by drunkards.   46
This wide-chopped rascal—would thou mightst lie drowning   47
The washing of ten tides!

GONZALO: He'll be hanged yet,   48
Though every drop of water swear against it
And gape at wid'st to glut him.

(A confused noise within)

                         'Mercy on us!—   50
We split, we split!—Farewell, my wife and children!—
Farewell, brother!—We split, we split, we split!'

(Exit Boatswain)

ANTONIO:
Let's all sink with th' King.

SEBASTIAN: Let's take leave of him.

(Exit with Antonio)

GONZALO: Now would I give a thousand furlongs of sea for an
acre of barren ground—long heath, brown furze, anything.
The wills above be done, but I would fain die a dry death.   55

(Exit)

---

38 *warrant . . . for* guarantee. . . against   **39** *unstanched* i.e. loose   **40** *ahold* (perhaps 'a-hull,' without any
sail. As the ship drifts to the rocks, the order is reversed and the *two courses*, foresail and mainsail, are
set up again in an effort to clear the shore.)   **46** *merely* completely   **47** *wide-chopped* wide-jawed   **54** *ten
tides* (pirates were hanged on shore and left until three tides washed over them)   **50** *glut* gobble
55 *long heath, brown furze* heather and gorse (sometimes emended to 'ling, heath, broom, furze')

I, ii   *(Enter Prospero and Miranda)*

MIRANDA:
    If by your art, my dearest father, you have
    Put the wild waters in this roar, allay them.
    The sky, it seems, would pour down stinking pitch
    But that the sea, mounting to th' welkin's cheek,   4
    Dashes the fire out. O, I have suffered
    With those that I saw suffer! a brave vessel   6
    (Who had no doubt some noble creature in her)
    Dashed all to pieces! O, the cry did knock
    Against my very heart! Poor souls, they perished!
    Had I been any god of power, I would
    Have sunk the sea within the earth or ere   11
    It should the good ship so have swallowed and
    The fraughting souls within her.
                          Be collected.   13
PROSPERO: No more amazement. Tell your piteous heart   14
    There's no harm done.
MIRANDA: O, woe the day!
PROSPERO: No harm.
    I have done nothing but in care of thee,
    Of thee my dear one, thee my daughter, who
    Art ignorant of what thou art, naught knowing
    Of whence I am; nor that I am more better
    Than Prospero, master of a full poor cell,
    And thy no greater father.
MIRANDA: More to know
    Did never meddle with my thoughts.   22
PROSPERO: 'Tis time
    I should inform thee farther. Lend thy hand
    And pluck my magic garment from me. So,
    Lie there, my art. Wipe thou thine eyes; have comfort.   25
    The direful spectacle of the wrack, which touched
    The very virtue of compassion in thee,   27
    I have with such provision in mine art   28
    So safely ordered that there is no soul—
    No, not so much perdition as an hair   30
    Betid to any creature in the vessel   31
    Which thou heard'st cry, which thou saw'st sink. Sit down;
    For thou must now know farther.
MIRANDA: You have often
    Begun to tell me what I am; but stopped

I, ii Before Prospero's cell   **4** *cheek* face (with perhaps a secondary meaning of 'side of a grate')   **6** *brave* fine, handsome (and so elsewhere throughout the play)   **11** *or ere* before   **13** *fraughting* forming the cargo; *collected* composed   **14** *amazement* distraction; *piteous* pitying   **22** *meddle* mingle   **25** *art* i.e. his robe   **27** *virtue* essence   **28** *provision* foresight   **30** *perdition* loss   **31** *Betid* happened

And left me to a bootless inquisition,   35
Concluding, 'Stay: not yet.'
PROSPERO: The hour's now come;
The very minute bids thee ope thine ear.
Obey, and be attentive. Canst thou remember   38
A time before we came unto this cell?
I do not think thou canst, for then thou wast not
Out three years old.   41
MIRANDA: Certainly, sir, I can.
PROSPERO:
By what? By any other house or person?
Of any thing the image tell me that   43
Hath kept with thy remembrance.
MIRANDA: 'Tis far off,
And rather like a dream than an assurance
That my remembrance warrants. Had I not   46
Four or five women once that tended me?
PROSPERO:
Thou hadst, and more, Miranda. But how is it
That this lives in thy mind? What seest thou else
In the dark backward and abysm of time?   50
If thou rememb'rest aught ere thou cam'st here,
How thou cam'st here thou mayst.
MIRANDA: But that I do not.
PROSPERO:
Twelve year since, Miranda, twelve year since,
Thy father was the Duke of Milan and
A prince of power.
MIRANDA: Sir, are not you my father?
PROSPERO:
Thy mother was a piece of virtue, and   56
She said thou wast my daughter; and thy father
Was Duke of Milan; and his only heir
A princess—no worse issuèd.   59
MIRANDA: O the heavens!
What foul play had we that we came from thence?
Or blessed was't we did?
PROSPERO: Both, both, my girl!
By foul play, as thou say'st, were we heaved thence,
But blessedly holp hither.   63
MIRANDA: O, my heart bleeds
To think o'th' teen that I have turned you to,   64
Which is from my remembrance! Please you, farther.   65

35 *bootless inquisition* fruitless inquiry   38 *Obey* listen   41 *Out* fully   43 *tell me* i.e. describe for me
46 *remembrance warrants* memory guarantees   50 *backward* past; *abysm* abyss   56 *piece* masterpiece   59
no worse issued no meaner in descent   63 *blessedly holp* providentially helped   64 *teen* trouble; *turned you to* put you in mind of   65 *from* out of

PROSPERO:

My brother and thy uncle, called Antonio—
I pray thee mark me—that a brother should
Be so perfidious!—he whom next thyself
Of all the world I loved, and to him put   69
The manage of my state, as at that time
Through all the signories it was the first   71
And Prospero the prime duke, being so reputed
In dignity, and for the liberal arts
Without a parallel; those being all my study,
The government I cast upon my brother
And to my state grew stranger, being transported
And rapt in secret studies. Thy false uncle—
Dost thou attend me?

MIRANDA: Sir, most heedfully.

PROSPERO:

Being once perfected how to grant suits,   79
How to deny them, who t' advance, and who
To trash for over-topping, new-created   81
The creatures that were mine, I say, or changed 'em,   82
Or else new-formed 'em; having both the key   83
Of officer and office, set all hearts i' th' state
To what tune pleased his ear, that now he was
The ivy which had hid my princely trunk
And sucked my verdure out on't. Thou attend'st not?

MIRANDA:

O, good sir, I do.

PROSPERO: I pray thee mark me.
I thus neglecting worldly ends, all dedicated
To closeness, and the bettering of my mind   90
With that which, but by being so retired,
O'er-prized all popular rate, in my false brother   92
Awaked an evil nature, and my trust,
Like a good parent, did beget of him   94
A falsehood in its contrary as great
As my trust was, which had indeed no limit,
A confidence sans bound. He being thus lorded,   97
Not only with what my revenue yielded   98
But what my power might else exact, like one
Who having unto truth, by telling of it,   100
Made such a sinner of his memory

69-70 *put ... state* entrusted the control of my administration   **71** *signories* states of northern Italy
79 *perfected* grown skillful   **81** *trash for over-topping* (1) check, as hounds, for going too fast, (2) cut
branches, as of over-tall trees   **82** *or* either   **83** *key* (used with pun on its musical sense, leading to the
metaphor of *tune*)   **90** *closeness* seclusion (?), secret studies (?),   **92** *O'er-prized* overvalued; *rate* estimation   **94** *good parent* (alluding to the same proverb cited by Miranda in l. 120)   **97-99** *He ... exact* (the
senses is that Antonio had the prerogatives as well as the income of the Duke)   **97** *sans bound* unlimited   **98** *revenue* (accent second syllable)   **100** *it* i. e. the lie

To credit his own lie, he did believe   102
He was indeed the Duke, out o' th' substitution   103
And executing th' outward face of royalty
With all prerogative. Hence his ambition growing—
Dost thou hear?
MIRANDA: Your tale, sir, would cure deafness.
PROSPERO:
To have no screen between this part he played
And him he played it for, he needs will be
Absolute Milan. Me (poor man) my library   109
Was dukedom large enough. Of temporal royalties
He thinks me now incapable; confederates   111
(So dry he was for sway) with th' King of Naples   112
To give him annual tribute, do him homage,
Subject his coronet to his crown, and bend
The dukedom yet unbowed (alas, poor Milan!)
To most ignoble stooping.
MIRANDA: O the heavens!
PROSPERO:
Mark his condition, and th' event; then tell me   117
If this might be a brother.
MIRANDA: I should sin
To think but nobly of my grandmother.
Good wombs have borne bad sons.
PROSPERO: Now the condition.
This King of Naples, being an enemy
To me inveterate, hearkens my brother's suit;
Which was, that he, in lieu o' th' premises   123
Of homage and I know not how much tribute,
Should presently extirpate me and mine   125
Out of the dukedom and confer fair Milan,
With all the honors, on my brother. Whereon,
A treacherous army levied, one midnight
Fated to th' purpose, did Antonio open   129
The gates of Milan; and i' th' dead of darkness,
The ministers for th' purpose hurrièd thence   131
Me and thy crying self.
MIRANDA: Alack, for pity!
I, not rememb'ring how I cried out then,
Will cry it o'er again; it is a hint   134
That wrings mine eyes to't.
PROSPERO: Hear a little further,
And then I'll bring thee to the present business

---

102 *To* as to   **103** *out* as a result.   **109** *Absolute Milan* Duke of Milan in fact   **111** *confederates* joins in league with   **112** *dry* thirsty, eager   **117** *condition* pact; *event* outcome   **123** *in lieu o' th' premises* in return for the guarantees   **125** *presently* immediately; *extirpate* remove (accent second syllable)   **129** *Fated* devoted   **131** *ministers* agents   **134** *hint* occasion   **135** *wrings* constrains

Which now's upon's; without the witch this story
Were most impertinent.   138
MIRANDA: Wherefore did they not
That hour destroy us?
PROSPERO: Well demanded, wench.
My tale provokes that question. Dear, they durst not,
So dear the love my people bore me; nor set
A mark so bloody on the business; but
With colors fairer painted their foul ends.
In few, they hurried us aboard a bark,   144
Bore us some leagues to sea; where they prepared
A rotten carcass of a butt, not rigged,   146
Nor tackle, sail, nor mast; the very rats
Instinctively have quit it. There they hoist us,
To cry to th' sea that roared to us; to sigh
To th' winds, whose pity, sighing back again,
Did us but loving wrong.
MIRANDA: Alack, what trouble
Was I then to you!
PROSPERO: O, a cherubin
Thou wast that did preserve me! Thou didst smile,
Infusèd with a fortitude from heaven,
When I have decked the sea with drops full salt,
Under my burden groaned: which raised in me
An undergoing stomach, to bear up
Against what should ensue.   157
MIRANDA: How came we ashore?
PROSPERO:
By providence divine.
Some food we had, and some fresh water, that
A noble Neapolitan, Gonzalo,
Out of his charity, who being then appointed
Master of this design, did give us, with
Rich garments, linens, stuffs, and necessaries
Which since have steaded much. So, of his gentleness,   165
Knowing I loved my books, he furnished me
From mine own library with volumes that
I prize above my dukedom.
MIRANDA: Would I might
But ever see that man!
PROSPERO: Now I arise.
Sit still, and hear the last of our sea-sorrow.
Here in this island we arrived; and here
Have I, thy schoolmaster, made thee more profit   172

---

138 *impertinent* irrelevant   **144** *few* few words   **146** *butt* tub   **157** *undergoing stomach* resolution to endure   **165** *steaded* been of use   **172** *more profit* profit more

Than other princess can, that have more time   173
For vainer hours, and tutors not so careful.

MIRANDA:

Heavens thank you for't! And now I pray you, sir,—
For still 'tis beating in my mind,—your reason
For raising this sea-storm?

PROSPERO: Know thus far forth.

By accident most strange, bountiful Fortune
(Now, my dear lady) hath mine enemies
Brought to this shore; and by my prescience
I find my zenith doth depend upon   181
A most auspicious star, whose influence
If now I court not, but omit, my fortunes   183
Will ever after droop. Here cease more questions.
Thou art inclined to sleep. 'Tis a good dulness,
And give it way. I know thou canst not choose.

(Miranda sleeps)

Come away, servant, come! I am ready now.   187
Approach, my Ariel: come!

(Enter Ariel)

ARIEL:

All hail, great master! Grave sir, hail! I come
To answer thy best pleasure; be't to fly,
To swim, to dive into the fire, to ride
On the curled clouds. To thy strong bidding task   192
Ariel and all his quality.   193

PROSPERO: Hast thou, spirit,

Performed to point the tempest that I bade thee?   194

ARIEL:

To every article.
I boarded the King's ship: now on the beak,   196
Now in the waist, the deck, in every cabin,   197
I flamed amazement: sometime I'ld divide   198
And burn in many places; on the topmast,
The yards, and boresprit would I flame distinctly,   200
Then meet and join. Jove's lightnings, the precursors
O' th' dreadful thunderclaps, more momentary
And sight-outrunning were not. The fire and cracks
Of sulphurous roaring the most mighty Neptune
Seem to besiege and make his bold waves tremble;
Yea, his dread trident shake.

173 *princess* princesses **181** *zenith* apex of fortune **183** *omit* neglect **187** *Come away* come here **192** *task* (supply 'come') **193** *quality* cohorts (Ariel is leader of a band of elemental spirits) **194** *to point* in detail **196** *beak* prow **197** *waist* middle; *deck* poop **198** *flamed amazement* struck terror by appearing as (St Elmo's) fire **200** *boresprit* bowsprit; *distinctly* in different places

PROSPERO: My brave spirit!
  Who was so firm, so constant, that this coil   207
  Would not infect his reason?
ARIEL: Not a soul
  But felt a fever of the mad and played   209
  Some tricks of desperation. All but mariners
  Plunged in the foaming brine and quit the vessel;
  Then all afire with me the King's son Ferdinand,   212
  With hair up-staring (then like reeds; not hair),   213
  Was the first man that leapt; cried 'Hell is empty,
  And all the devils are here!'
PROSPERO: Why, that's my spirit!
  But was not this nigh shore?
ARIEL: Close by, my master.
PROSPERO:
  But are they, Ariel, safe?
ARIEL: Not a hair perished.
  On their sustaining garments not a blemish,   218
  But fresher than before; and as thou bad'st me,
  In troops I have dispersed them 'bout the isle.
  The King's son have I landed by himself,
  Whom I left cooling of the air with sighs
  In an odd angle of the isle, and sitting,
  His arms in this sad knot.   224
PROSPERO: Of the King's ship
  The mariners say how thou hast disposed,
  And all the rest o' th' fleet.
ARIEL: Safely in harbor
  Is the King's ship; in the deep nook where once
  Thou call'dst me up at midnight to fetch dew
  From the still-vexed Bermoothes, there she's hid;   229
  The mariners all under hatches stowed,
  Who, with a charm joined to their suff'red labor,   231
  I have left asleep; and for the rest o' th' fleet,
  Which I dispersed, they all have met again,
  And are upon the Mediterranean flote   234
  Bound sadly home for Naples,
  Supposing that they saw the King's ship wracked
  And his great person perish.
PROSPERO: Ariel, thy charge
  Exactly is performed; but there's more work.
  What is the time o' th' day?
ARIEL: Past the mid season.   239

---

207 *coil* uproar   **209** *of the mad* such as madmen have   **212** *afire with me* (refers either to the vessel or to
Ferdinand, depending on the punctuation; F suggests the latter)   **213** *up-staring* standing on end
218 *sustaining* buoying them up in the water   **224** *this* (illustrated by a gesture)   **229** *still-vexed Bermoothes* constantly agitated Bermudas   **231** *suff'red* undergone   **234** *flote* sea   **239** *mid season* noon

PROSPERO:
    At least two glasses. The time 'twixt six and now   240
    Must by us both be spent most preciously.
ARIEL:
    Is there more toil? Since thou dost give me pains,
    Let me remember thee what thou hast promised,   243
    Which is not yet performed me.
PROSPERO: How now? moody?
    What is't thou canst demand?
ARIEL: My liberty.
PROSPERO:
    Before the time be out? No more!   246
ARIEL: I prithee,
    Remember I have done thee worthy service,
    Told thee no lies, made no mistakings, served
    Without or grudge or grumblings. Thou did promise
    To bate me a full year.   250
PROSPERO: Dost thou forget
    From what a torment I did free thee?
ARIEL: No.
PROSPERO:
    Thou dost; and think'st it much to tread the ooze
    Of the salt deep,
    To run upon the sharp wind of the North,
    To do me business in the veins o' th' earth.   255
    When it is baked with frost.   256
ARIEL: I do not, sir.
PROSPERO:
    Thou liest, malignant thing! Hast thou forgot
    The foul witch Sycorax, who with age and envy   258
    Was grown into a hoop? Hast thou forgot her?
ARIEL:
    No, sir.
PROSPERO: Thou hast. Where was she born? Speak!
    Tell me!
ARIEL:
    Sir, in Argier.   261
PROSPERO: O, was she so? I must
    Once in a month recount what thou hast been,
    Which thou forget'st. This damned witch Sycorax,
    For mischiefs manifold, and sorceries terrible
    To enter human hearing, from Argier,

---

240 *glasses* hours   **243** *remember* remind   **246** *time* period of service   **250** *bate me* shorten my term of service   **255** *veins* streams   **256** *baked* hardened   **258** *Sycorax* (name not found elsewhere; usually connected with Greek 'sys', sow, and 'korax', which means both raven—cf. l.322—and curved, hence perhaps *hoop*); *envy* malice   **261** *Argier* Algiers

Thou know'st, was banished. For one thing she did   266
They would not take her life. Is not this true?
ARIEL:
 Ay, sir.
PROSPERO:
 This blue-eyed hag was hither brought with child
 And here was left by th' sailors. Thou, my slave,
 As thou report'st thyself, wast then her servant;
 And, for thou wast a spirit too delicate
 To act her earthy and abhorred commands,
 Refusing her grand hests, she did confine thee,   274
 By help of her more potent ministers,
 And in her most unmitigable rage,
 Into a cloven pine; within which rift
 Imprisoned thou didst painfully remain
 A dozen years; within which space she died
 And left thee there, where thou didst vent thy groans
 As fast as millwheels strike. Then was this island   281
 (Save for the son that she did litter here,
 A freckled whelp, hag-born) not honored with
 A human shape.
ARIEL: Yes, Caliban her son.
PROSPERO:
 Dull thing, I say so: he, that Caliban
 Whom now I keep in service. Thou best know'st
 What torment I did find thee in: thy groans
 Did make wolves howl and penetrate the breasts
 Of ever-angry bears. It was a torment
 To lay upon the damned, which Sycorax
 Could not again undo. It was mine art,
 When I arrived and heard thee, that made gape
 The pine, and let thee out.
ARIEL: I thank thee, master.
PROSPERO:
 If thou more murmur'st, I will rend an oak
 And peg thee in his knotty entrails till   295
 Thou hast howled away twelve winters.   296
ARIEL: Pardon, master.
 I will be correspondent to command   297
 And do my spriting gently.   298
PROSPERO: Do so; and after two days
 I will discharge thee.
ARIEL: That's my noble master!

---

266 *one thing she did* (being pregnant, her sentence was commuted from death to exile).   **274** *hests* commands   **281** *millwheels* i.e. the clappers on the millwheels   **295** *his* its   **296** *twelve* (the same length of time that Ariel has been released)   **297** *correspondent* obedient   **298** *spriting gently* office as a spirit graciously

What shall I do? Say what? What shall I do?
PROSPERO:
    Go make thyself like a nymph o' th' sea. Be subject
    To no sight but thine and mine; invisible
    To every eyeball else. Go take this shape
    And hither come in't. Go! Hence with diligence!

                                                        (Exit Ariel)

    Awake, dear heart, awake! Thou hast slept well.
    Awake!
MIRANDA: The strangeness of your story put
    Heaviness in me.
PROSPERO: Shake it off. Come on.
    We'll visit Caliban, my slave, who never
    Yields us kind answer.
MIRANDA: 'Tis a villain, sir,
    I do not love to look on.
PROSPERO: But as 'tis,
    We cannot miss him: he does make our fire,   311
    Fetch in our wood, and serves in offices
    That profit us. What, ho! slave! Caliban!
    Thou earth, thou! Speak!
CALIBAN *(within)*:   There's wood enough within.
PROSPERO:
    Come forth, I say! There's other business for thee.
    Come, thou tortoise! When?   316

(Enter Ariel like a water nymph)

    Fine apparition! My quaint Ariel,   317
    Hark in thine ear.
ARIEL: My lord, it shall be done.   *(Exit)*
PROSPERO:
    Thou poisonous slave, got by the devil himself
    Upon thy wicked dam, come forth!

(Enter Caliban)

CALIBAN:
    As wicked dew as e'er my mother brushed
    With raven's feather from unwholesome fen
    Drop on you both! A south-west blow on ye
    And blister you all o'er!
PROSPERO:
    For this, be sure, to-night thou shalt have cramps,
    Side-stitches that shall pen thy breath up; urchins   326

---

311 *miss* do without   **316** *When* (expression of impatience)   **317** *quaint* ingenious   **326** *urchins* hedge-hogs (i.e. goblins in that shape)

Shall, for that vast of night that they may work,   327
All exercise on thee; thou shalt be pinched
As thick as honeycomb, each pinch more stinging
Than bees that made 'em.
CALIBAN: I must eat my dinner.
This island's mine by Sycorax my mother,
Which thou tak'st from me. When thou cam'st first,
Thou strok'st me and made much of me; wouldst give me
Water with berries in't; and teach me how
To name the bigger light, and how the less,
That burn by day and night; and then I loved thee
And showed thee all the qualities o' th' isle,   337
The fresh springs, brine-pits, barren place and fertile.
Cursed be I that did so! All the charms
Of Sycorax—toads, beetles, bats, light on you!
For I am all the subjects that you have,
Which first was mine own king; and here you sty me
In this hard rock, whiles you do keep from me
The rest o' th' island.
PROSPERO: Thou most lying slave,
Whom stripes may move, not kindness! I have used thee   345
(Filth as thou art) with humane care, and lodged thee
In mine own cell till thou didst seek to violate
The honor of my child.
CALIBAN:
O ho, O ho! Would't had been done!
Thou didst prevent me; I had peopled else
This isle with Calibans.
MIRANDA: Abhorrèd slave,   351
Which any print of goodness wilt not take,
Being capable of all ill! I pitied thee,
Took pains to make thee speak, taught thee each hour
One thing or other: when thou didst not, savage,
Know thine own meaning, but wouldst gabble like
A thing most brutish, I endowed thy purposes   357
With words that made them known. But thy vile race,   358
Though thou didst learn, had that in't which good natures   359
Could not abide to be with; therefore wast thou
Deservedly confined into this rock, who hadst
Deserved more than a prison.
CALIBAN:
You taught me language, and my profit on't
Is, I know how to curse. The red plague rid you   364

---

327 *vast* void; *that they may work* (referring to the belief that malignant spirits had power only during darkness)   **337** *qualities* resources   **345** *stripes* lashes   **351** *Miranda* (so F; some editors have given the speech to Prospero)   **357** *purposes* meanings   **358** *race* nature   **359** *good natures* natural virtues   **364** *red plague* bubonic plague; *rid* destroy

For learning me your language!
PROSPERO: Hag-seed, hence!
    Fetch us in fuel; and be quick, thou'rt best,   366
    To answer other business. Shrug'st thou, malice?
    If thou neglect'st or dost unwillingly
    What I command, I'll rack thee with old cramps,   369
    Fill all thy bones with aches, make thee roar   370
    That beasts shall tremble at thy din.
CALIBAN: No, pray thee.

    (Aside)

    I must obey. His art is of such pow'r
    It would control my dam's god, Setebos,
    And make a vassal of him.
PROSPERO: So, slave; hence!

                                      (Exit Caliban)

(Enter Ferdinand; and Ariel [invisible], playing and singing)

                ARIEL'S SONG.
            Come unto these yellow sands,
              And then take hands.
         Curtsied when you have and kissed,
             The wild waves whist,   378
           Foot it featly here and there;   379
        And, sweet sprites, the burden bear.   380
                Hark, hark!
      Burden, dispersedly. Bowgh, wawgh!
             The watchdogs bark.
      Burden, dispersedly. Bowgh, wawgh!
         Hark, hark! I hear
        The strain of strutting chanticleer
           Cry cock-a-diddle-dowe.

FERDINAND:
    Where should this music be! I' th' air or th' earth?
    It sounds no more; and sure it waits upon
    Some god o' th' island. Sitting on a bank,
    Weeping again the King my father's wrack,
    This music crept by me upon the waters,
    Allaying both their fury and my passion   393
    With its sweet air. Thence I have followed it,
    Or it hath drawn me rather; but 'tis gone.
    No, it begins again.

---

366 *thou'rt best* you'd be well advised   **369** *old* i.e. such as old people have   **370** *aches* (pronounced 'aitches')   **378** *whist* being hushed   **379** *featly* nimbly   **380** *burden* undersong, refrain   **393** *passion* lamentation

ARIEL'S SONG.

Full fathom five thy father lies;
Of his bones are coral made;
Those are pearls that were his eyes;
Nothing of him that doth fade
But doth suffer a sea-change
Into something rich and strange.
Sea nymphs hourly ring his knell:

Burden.   Ding-dong.

Hark! now I hear them—Ding-dong bell.

FERDINAND:

The ditty does remember my drowned father.   406
This is no mortal business, nor no sound
That the earth owes. I hear it now above me.   408

PROSPERO:

The fringèd curtains of thine eye advance   409
And say what thou seest yond.

MIRANDA: What is't? a spirit?
Lord, how it looks about! Believe me, sir,
It carries a brave form. But 'tis a spirit.

PROSPERO:

No, wench: it eats, and sleeps, and hath such senses
As we have, such. This gallant which thou seest
Was in the wrack; and, but he's something stained   415
With grief (that's beauty's canker), thou mightst call him
A goodly person. He hath lost his fellows
And strays about to find 'em.

MIRANDA: I might call him
A thing divine; for nothing natural
I ever saw so noble.

PROSPERO *(aside)*: It goes on, I see,
As my soul prompts it. Spirit, fine spirit, I'll free thee   421
Within two days for this.

FERDINAND: Most sure, the goddess   422
On whom these airs attend! Vouchsafe my prayer
May know if you remain upon this island,   424
And that you will some good instruction give
How I may bear me here. My prime request,   426
Which I do last pronounce, is (O you wonder!)
If you be maid or no?

MIRANDA: No wonder, sir,
But certainly a maid.

FERDINAND: My language? Heavens!
I am the best of them that speak this speech,

---

406 *remember* allude to   **408** *owes* owns   **409** *advance* raise   **415** *stained* disfigured   **421** *prompts* would like   **422** *Most sure* this is certainly   **424** *remain* dwell   **426** *bear me* conduct myself

Were I but where 'tis spoken.
PROSPERO: How? the best?
What wert thou if the King of Naples heard thee?
FERDINAND:
A single thing, as I am now, that wonders   433
To hear thee speak of Naples. He does hear me;
And that he does I weep. Myself am Naples,   435
Who with mine eyes, never since at ebb, beheld
The King my father wracked.
MIRANDA: Alack, for mercy!
FERDINAND:
Yes, faith, and all his lords, the Duke of Milan
And his brave son being twain.
PROSPERO (aside):   The Duke of Milan   439
And his more braver daughter could control thee,   440
If now 'twere fit to do't. At the first sight
They have changed eyes. Delicate Ariel,   442
I'll set thee free for this.—A word, good sir.
I fear you have done yourself some wrong. A word!   444
MIRANDA:
Why speaks my father so ungently? This
Is the third man that e'er I saw; the first
That e'er I sighed for. Pity move my father
To be inclined my way!
FERDINAND: O, if a virgin,
And your affection not gone forth, I'll make you
The Queen of Naples.
PROSPERO: Soft, sir! one word more.

(Aside)

They are both in either's pow'rs. But this swift business
I must uneasy make, lest too light winning
Make the prize light.—One word more! I charge thee
That thou attend me. Thou dost here usurp
The name thou ow'st not, and hast put thyself   455
Upon this island as a spy, to win it
From me, the lord on't.
FERDINAND: No, as I am a man!
MIRANDA:
There's nothing ill can dwell in such a temple.
If the ill spirit have so fair a house,
Good things will strive to dwell with't.
PROSPERO: Follow me.—
Speak not you for him; he's a traitor.—Come!

---

433 *single* (1) solitary, (2) weak or helpless   435 *Naples* King of Naples   439 *son* (Antonio's son is not elsewhere mentioned)   440 *control* refute   442 *changed eyes* exchanged love looks   444 *done...wrong* told a lie   455 *ow'st* ownest

I'll manacle thy neck and feet together;
Sea water shalt thou drink; thy food shall be
The fresh-brook mussels, withered roots, and husks
Wherein the acorn cradled. Follow!

FERDINAND: No.
I will resist such entertainment till   466
Mine enemy has more pow'r.

(He draws, and is charmed from moving)

MIRANDA: O dear father,
Make not too rash a trial of him, for   468
He's gentle, and not fearful.   469

PROSPERO: What, I say,
My foot my tutor?—Put thy sword up, traitor!   470
Who mak'st a show but dar'st not strike, thy conscience
Is so possessed with guilt. Come, from thy ward!   472
For I can here disarm thee with this stick
And make thy weapon drop.

MIRANDA: Beseech you, father!

PROSPERO:
Hence! Hang not on my garments.

MIRANDA: Sir, have pity.
I'll be his surety.

PROSPERO: Silence! One word more
Shall make me chide thee, if not hate thee. What,
An advocate for an impostor? Hush!
Thou think'st there is no more such shapes as he,
Having seen but him and Caliban. Foolish wench!
To th' most of men this is a Caliban,
And they to him are angels.

MIRANDA: My affections   482
Are then most humble. I have no ambition
To see a goodlier man.

PROSPERO: Come on, obey!   484
Thy nerves are in their infancy again   485
And have no vigor in them.

FERDINAND: So they are.
My spirits, as in a dream, are all bound up.
My father's loss, the weakness which I feel,
The wrack of all my friends, nor this man's threats
To whom I am subdued, are but light to me,
Might I but through my prison once a day
Behold this maid. All corners else o' th' earth
Let liberty make use of. Space enough
Have I in such a prison.

---

466 *entertainment* treatment **468** *trial* judgment **469** *gentle* noble; *fearful* cowardly **470** *My . . . tutor* i.e. instructed by my underling **472** *ward* fighting posture **482** *affections* inclinations **484** *obey* follow **485** *nerves* sinews, tendons

PROSPERO *(aside)*: It works. *(to Ferdinand)* Come on.—
  Thou hast done well, fine Ariel!
  (To Ferdinand)   Follow me.
  (To Ariel)
  Hark what thou else shalt do me.
MIRANDA: Be of comfort.
  My father's of a better nature, sir,
  Than he appears by speech. This is unwonted
  Which now came from him.
PROSPERO: Thou shalt be as free
  As mountain winds; but then exactly do   500
  All points of my command.
ARIEL: To th' syllable.
PROSPERO:
  Come, follow.—Speak not for him.   *(Exeunt)*

II, i   *(Enter Alonso, Sebastian, Antonio, Gonzalo, Adrian,*
        Francisco, and others)
GONZALO:
  Beseech you, sir, be merry. You have cause
  (So have we all) of joy; for our escape
  Is much beyond our loss. Our hint of woe   3
  Is common: every day some sailor's wife,
  The master of some merchant, and the merchant,   5
  Have just our theme of woe; but for the miracle,
  I mean our preservation, few in millions
  Can speak like us. Then wisely, good sir, weigh
  Our sorrow with our comfort.
ALONSO: Prithee peace.
SEBASTIAN: He receives comfort like cold porridge.   10
ANTONIO: The visitor will not give him o'er so.   11
SEBASTIAN: Look, he's winding up the watch of his wit; by and by it will
  strike.
GONZALO: Sir—
SEBASTIAN: One. Tell.   15
GONZALO:
  When every grief is entertained, that's offered   16
  Comes to th' entertainer—   17
SEBASTIAN: A dollar.
GONZALO: Dolor comes to him, indeed. You have spoken truer   19
  than you purposed.
SEBASTIAN: You have taken it wiselier than I meant you
  should.
GONZALO: Therefore, my lord—

---

500 *then* till then   **II, i** Another part of the island   **3** *hint* occasion   **5** *master of some merchant* master of
a merchant ship; *the merchant* the owner of the ship   **10** *porridge* (pun on *peace* [pease])   **11** *visitor* spiritual adviser; *give him o'er* let him alone   **15** *Tell* count   **16** *that's* that which is   **17** *entertainer* (taken by
Sebastian to mean 'innkeeper')   **19** *Dolor* grief (with pun on *dollar*, a continental coin)

ANTONIO: Fie, what a spendthrift is he of his tongue!   24
ALONSO: I prithee spare.
GONZALO: Well, I have done. But yet—
SEBASTIAN: He will be talking.
ANTONIO: Which, of he or Adrian, for a good wager, first begins to crow?
SEBASTIAN: The old cock.   29
ANTONIO: The cock'rel.   30
SEBASTIAN: Done! The wager?
ANTONIO: A laughter.   32
SEBASTIAN: A match!
ADRIAN: Though this island seem to be desert—
ANTONIO: Ha, ha, ha!
SEBASTIAN: So, you're paid.
ADRIAN: Uninhabitable and almost inaccessible—
SEBASTIAN: Yet—
ADRIAN: Yet—
ANTONIO: He could not miss't.
ADRIAN: It must needs be of subtle, tender, and delicate temperance.   41
ANTONIO: Temperance was a delicate wench.   42
SEBASTIAN: Ay, and a subtle, as he most learnedly delivered.
ADRIAN: The air breathes upon us here most sweetly.
SEBASTIAN: As if it had lungs, and rotten ones.
ANTONIO: Or as 'twere perfumed by a fen.
GONZALO: Here is everything advantageous to life.
ANTONIO: True; save means to live.
SEBASTIAN: Of that there's none, or little.
GONZALO: How lush and lusty the grass looks! how green!
ANTONIO: The ground indeed is tawny.
SEBASTIAN: With an eye of green in't.   52
ANTONIO: He misses not much.
SEBASTIAN: No; he doth but mistake the truth totally.
GONZALO: But the rarity of it is—which is indeed almost beyond credit—
SEBASTIAN: As many vouched rarities are.   56
GONZALO: That our garments, being, as they were, drenched in the sea,
    hold, notwithstanding, their freshness and gloss, being rather new-dyed
    than stained with salt water.
ANTONIO: If but one of his pockets could speak, would it not say he lies?
SEBASTIAN: Ay, or very falsely pocket up his report.
GONZALO: Methinks our garments are now as fresh as when we put them
    on first in Afric, at the marriage of the King's fair daughter Claribel
    to the King of Tunis.
SEBASTIAN: 'Twas a sweet marriage, and we prosper well in our return.
ADRIAN: Tunis was never graced before with such a paragon to their   66
    queen.

24 *spendthrift* (Antonio labors the pun)   29 *old cock* i.e. Gonzalo   30 *cock'rel* i.e. Adrian   32 *laughter* the winner laughs   41 *temperance* climate   42 *Temperance* (a girl's name)   52 *eye* spot (or perhaps Gonzalo's eye)   56 *vouched rarities* wonders guaranteed to be true   66 *to* for

GONZALO: Not since widow Dido's time.   68

ANTONIO: Widow? A pox o' that! How came that 'widow' in? Widow Dido!

SEBASTIAN: What if he had said 'widower Aeneas' too? Good Lord, how
   you take it!

ADRIAN: 'Widow Dido,' said you? You make me study of that. She was of
   Carthage, not of Tunis.

GONZALO: This Tunis, sir, was Carthage.

ADRIAN: Carthage?

GONZALO: I assure you, Carthage.

ANTONIO: His word is more than the miraculous harp.   77

SEBASTIAN: He hath raised the wall and houses too.

ANTONIO: What impossible matter will he make easy next?

SEBASTIAN: I think he will carry this island home in his pocket and give it
   his son for an apple.

ANTONIO: And, sowing the kernels of it in the sea, bring forth more islands.

GONZALO: Ay!   83

ANTONIO: Why, in good time.

GONZALO: Sir, we were talking that our garments seem now as fresh as
   when we were at Tunis at the marriage of your daughter, who is now
   Queen.

ANTONIO: And the rarest that e'er came there.

SEBASTIAN: Bate, I beseech you, widow Dido.   89

ANTONIO: O, widow Dido? Ay, widow Dido!

GONZALO: Is not, sir, my doublet as fresh as the first day I wore it? I   92
   mean, in a sort.

ANTONIO: That 'sort' was well fished for.

GONZALO: When I wore it at your daughter's marriage.

ALONSO:
   You cram these words into mine ears against
   The stomach of my sense. Would I had never   96
   Married my daughter there! for, coming thence,
   My son is lost; and, in my rate, she too,   98
   Who is so far from Italy removed
   I ne'er again shall see her. O thou mine heir
   Of Naples and of Milan, what strange fish
   Hath made his meal on thee?

FRANCISCO: Sir, he may live.
   I saw him beat the surges under him
   And ride upon their backs. He trod the water,
   Whose enmity he flung aside, and breasted
   The surge most swol'n that met him. His bold head
   'Bove the contentious waves he kept, and oared

---

68 *widow Dido* (Dido was the widow of Sychaeus; Aeneas was a widower, having lost his wife in the fall
of Troy. The reasons for Antonio's amusement, if that is what it is, have not been explained.)   77 *miraculous harp* (of Amphion, which raised the walls of Thebes; Tunis and Carthage were near each other, but
not the same city)   83 *Ay* (F reads 'I'; this and Antonio's rejoinder have not been satisfactorily explained)   89 *Bate* except   92 *in a sort* i.e. comparatively   96 *stomach . . . sense* i.e. inclination of my
mind   98 *rate* opinion

Himself with his good arms in lusty stroke
To th' shore, that o'er his wave-worn basis bowed,   109
As stooping to relieve him. I not doubt
He came alive to land.
ALONSO: No, no, he's gone.
SEBASTIAN:
Sir, you may thank yourself for this great loss,
That would not bless our Europe with your daughter,
But rather loose her to an African,
Where she, at least, is banished from your eye
Who hath cause to wet the grief on't.
ALONSO: Prithee peace.
SEBASTIAN:
You were kneeled to and importuned otherwise
By all of us; and the fair soul herself   118
Weighed, between loathness and obedience, at
Which end o' th' beam should bow. We have lost your son,
I fear, for ever. Milan and Naples have
Moe widows in them of this business' making   122
Than we bring men to comfort them:
The fault's your own.
ALONSO: So is the dear'st o' th' loss.   124
GONZALO:
My Lord Sebastian,
The truth you speak doth lack some gentleness,
And time to speak it in. You rub the sore
When you should bring the plaster.
SEBASTIAN: Very well.
ANTONIO:
And most chirurgeonly.   129
GONZALO:
It is foul weather in us all, good sir,
When you are cloudy.
SEBASTIAN: Foul weather?
ANTONIO: Very foul.
GONZALO:
Had I plantation of this isle, my lord—   132
ANTONIO:
He'd sow't with nettle seed.
SEBASTIAN: Or docks, or mallows.
GONZALO:
And were the king on't, what would I do?
SEBASTIAN:
Scape being drunk for want of wine.

---

109 *his* its; *basis* i.e. the sand   **118–120** *the fair ... bow* (the sense is that Claribel hated the marriage, and only obedience to her father turned the scale)   **122** *Moe* more   **124** *dear'st* heaviest   **129** *chirurgeonly* like a surgeon   **132** *plantation* colonization (taken by Antonio in its other sense)

GONZALO:

I' th' commonwealth I would by contraries 136

Execute all things; for no kind of traffic 137

Would I admit; no name of magistrate;

Letters should not be known; riches, poverty,

And use of service, none; contract, succession, 140

Bourn, bound of land, tilth, vineyard, none; 141

No use of metal, corn, or wine, or oil;

No occupation; all men idle, all;

And women too, but innocent and pure;

No sovereignty.

SEBASTIAN: Yet he would be king on't.

ANTONIO: The latter end of his commonwealth forgets the beginning.

GONZALO:

All things in common nature should produce

Without sweat or endeavor. Treason, felony,

Sword, pike, knife, gun, or need of any engine 149

Would I not have; but nature should bring forth,

Of it own kind, all foison, all abundance, 151

To feed my innocent people.

SEBASTIAN: No marrying 'mong his subjects?

ANTONIO: None, man, all idle—whores and knaves.

GONZALO:

I would with such perfection govern, sir,

T' excel the golden age.

SEBASTIAN: Save his Majesty!

ANTONIO:

Long live Gonzalo!

GONZALO: And—do you mark me, sir?

ALONSO:

Prithee no more. Thou dost talk nothing to me.

GONZALO: I do well believe your Highness; and did it to minister occasion 159

to these gentlemen, who are of such sensible and nimble lungs that 161

they always use to laugh at nothing.

ANTONIO: 'Twas you we laughed at.

GONZALO: Who in this kind of merry fooling am nothing to you: so you

may continue, and laugh at nothing still.

ANTONIO: What a blow was there given!

SEBASTIAN: An it had not fall'n flatlong. 166

GONZALO: You are gentlemen of brave mettle; you would lift the moon

out of her sphere if she would continue in it five weeks without

changing.

(Enter Ariel, [invisible,] playing solemn music)

136 *by contraries* in contrast to usual customs   137 *traffic* trade   140 *use of service* having a servant class;
succession inheritance   141 *Bourn* limits of private property   149 *engine* weapon   151 *it* its; *foison* abundance   159 *minister occasion* afford opportunity   161 *sensible* sensitive   166 *An* if; *flatlong* struck with
the flat of a sword

SEBASTIAN: We would so, and then go a-batfowling.   170

ANTONIO: Nay, good my lord, be not angry.

GONZALO: No, I warrant you: I will not adventure my discretion so weakly.   172
    Will you laugh me asleep, for I am very heavy?

ANTONIO: Go sleep, and hear us.

(All sleep except Alonso, Sebastian, and Antonio)

ALONSO:
    What, all so soon asleep? I wish mine eyes
    Would, with themselves, shut up my thoughts. I find
    They are inclined to do so.

SEBASTIAN: Please you, sir,
    Do not omit the heavy offer of it.   178
    It seldom visits sorrow; when it doth,
    It is a comforter.

ANTONIO: We two, my lord,
    Will guard your person while you take your rest,
    And watch your safety.

ALONSO: Thank you. Wondrous heavy.

(Alonso sleeps. Exit Ariel)

SEBASTIAN:
    What a strange drowsiness possesses them!

ANTONIO:
    It is the quality o' th' climate.

SEBASTIAN: Why
    Doth it not then our eyelids sink? I find not
    Myself disposed to sleep.

ANTONIO: Nor I: my spirits are nimble.
    They fell together all, as by consent.
    They dropped as by a thunder-stroke. What might,
    Worthy Sebastian—O, what might?—No more!
    And yet methinks I see it in thy face,
    What thou shouldst be. Th' occasion speaks thee, and   191
    My strong imagination sees a crown
    Dropping upon thy head.

SEBASTIAN: What? Art thou waking?

ANTONIO:
    Do you not hear me speak?

SEBASTIAN: I do; and surely
    It is a sleepy language, and thou speak'st
    Out of thy sleep. What is it thou didst say?
    This is a strange repose, to be asleep
    With eyes wide open; standing, speaking, moving,
    And yet so fast asleep.

---

170 *a-batfowling* hunting birds with sticks ('bats') at night (using the moon for a lantern)   **172** *adventure* risk (Gonzalo is saying, very politely, that their wit is too feeble for him to take offense at it)   **178** *omit* neglect; *heavy offer* opportunity its heaviness affords   **191** *speaks* speaks to, summons

ANTONIO: Noble Sebastian,
Thou let'st thy fortune sleep—die, rather; wink'st   200
Whiles thou art waking.
SEBASTIAN: Thou dost snore distinctly;
There's meaning in thy snores.
ANTONIO:
I am more serious than my custom. You
Must be so too, if heed me; which to do
Trebles thee o'er.   205
SEBASTIAN: Well, I am standing water.
ANTONIO:
I'll teach you how to flow.
SEBASTIAN: Do so. To ebb
Hereditary sloth instructs me.   207
ANTONIO: O,
If you but knew how you the purpose cherish   208
Whiles thus you mock it! how, in stripping it,
You more invest it! Ebbing men indeed   210
(Most often) do so near the bottom run
By their own fear or sloth.
SEBASTIAN: Prithee say on.
The setting of thine eye and cheek proclaim
A matter from thee; and a birth, indeed,
Which throes thee much to yield.   215
ANTONIO: Thus, sir:
Although this lord of weak remembrance, this   216
Who shall be of as little memory   217
When he is earthed, hath here almost persuaded   218
(For he's a spirit of persuasion, only
Professes to persuade) the King his son's alive,   220
'Tis as impossible that he's undrowned
As he that sleeps here swims.
SEBASTIAN: I have no hope
That he's undrowned.
ANTONIO: O, out of that no hope
What great hope have you! No hope that way is
Another way so high a hope that even
Ambition cannot pierce a wink beyond,   226
But doubt discovery there. Will you grant with me   227
That Ferdinand is drowned?
SEBASTIAN: He's gone.
ANTONIO: Then tell me,
Who's the next heir of Naples?

---

200 *wink'st* dost sleep **205** *Trebles thee o'er* increases thy status threefold; *standing water* at slack tide
207 *Hereditary sloth* natural laziness **208** *cherish* enrich **210** *invest* clothe **215** *throes thee much* costs
thee much pain, like a birth **216** *remembrance* memory **217** *of . . . memory* as little remembered
218 *earthed* buried **220** *Professes* has the function **226** *wink* glimpse **227** *doubt discovery there* is uncertain of seeing accurately

SEBASTIAN: Claribel.
ANTONIO:
  She that is Queen of Tunis; she that dwells
  Ten leagues beyond man's life; she that from Naples   231
  Can have no note, unless the sun were post—   232
  The man i' th' moon's too slow—till new-born chins
  Be rough and razorable; she that from whom
  We all were sea-swallowed, though some cast again,   235
  And, by that destiny, to perform an act
  Whereof what's past is prologue, what to come,
  In yours and my discharge.   238
SEBASTIAN: What stuff is this? How say you?
  'Tis true my brother's daughter's Queen of Tunis;
  So is she heir of Naples; 'twixt which regions
  There is some space.
ANTONIO: A space whose ev'ry cubit
  Seems to cry out 'How shall that Claribel
  Measure us back to Naples? Keep in Tunis,   243
  And let Sebastian wake!' Say this were death
  That now hath seized them, why, they were no worse
  Than now they are. There be that can rule Naples
  As well as he that sleeps; lords that can prate
  As amply and unnecessarily
  As this Gonzalo; I myself could make
  A chough of as deep chat. O, that you bore   250
  The mind that I do! What a sleep were this
  For your advancement! Do you understand me?
SEBASTIAN:
  Methinks I do.
ANTONIO: And how does your content   253
  Tender your own good fortune?
SEBASTIAN: I remember
  You did supplant your brother Prospero.
ANTONIO: True.
  And look how well my garments sit upon me,
  Much feater than before. My brother's servants   257
  Were then my fellows; now they are my men.   258
SEBASTIAN:
  But, for your conscience—
ANTONIO:
  Ay, sir, where lies that? If 'twere a kibe,   260
  'Twould put me to my slipper; but I feel not   261

---

231 Ten . . . life i.e. thirty miles from nowhere 232 note communication; post messenger 235 cast
thrown up (with a suggestion of its theatrical meaning which introduces the next metaphor) 238 discharge business 243 us i.e. the cubits 250 chough jackdaw (a bird sometimes taught to speak)
253-54 content Tender inclination estimate 257 feater more suitable 258 fellows equals; men servants
260 kibe chilblain 261 put me to make me wear

This deity in my bosom. Twenty consciences
That stand 'twixt me and Milan, candied be they   263
And melt, ere they molest! Here lies your brother,
No better than the earth he lies upon
If he were that which now he's like—that's dead;
Whom I with this obedient steel (three inches of it)
Can lay to bed for ever; whiles you, doing thus,
To the perpetual wink for aye might put   269
This ancient morsel, this Sir Prudence, who
Should not upbraid our course. For all the rest,
They'll take suggestion as a cat laps milk;
They'll tell the clock to any business that   273
We say befits the hour.
SEBASTIAN: Thy case, dear friend,
Shall be my precedent. As thou got'st Milan,
I'll come by Naples. Draw thy sword. One stroke
Shall free thee from the tribute which thou payest,
And I the King shall love thee.
ANTONIO: Draw together;
And when I rear my hand, do you the like,
To fall it on Gonzalo.   280

(They draw)

SEBASTIAN: O, but one word!

(Enter Ariel, [invisible,] with music and song)

ARIEL:
My master through his art foresees the danger
That you, his friend, are in, and sends me forth
(For else his project dies) to keep them living.

(Sings in Gonzalo's ear)

      While you here do snoring lie,
      Open-eyed conspiracy
        His time doth take.
      If of life you keep a care,
      Shake off slumber and beware.
        Awake, awake!

ANTONIO:
Then let us both be sudden.
GONZALO *(wakes)*:   Now good angels
Preserve the King!
ALONSO:
Why, how now?—Ho, awake!—Why are you drawn?
Wherefore this ghastly looking?

263 *candied* frozen   **269** *wink* sleep   **273** *tell the clock* answer appropriately   **280** *fall it* let it fall

GONZALO: What's the matter?

SEBASTIAN:

Whiles we stood here securing your repose, 294
Even now, we heard a hollow burst of bellowing
Like bulls, or rather lions. Did't not wake you?
It stuck mine ear most terribly.

ALONSO: I heard nothing.

ANTONIO:

O, 'twas a din to fright a monster's ear,
To make an earthquake! Sure it was the roar
Of a whole herd of lions.

ALONSO: Heard you this, Gonzalo?

GONZALO:

Upon mine honor, sir, I heard a humming,
And that a strange one too, which did awake me.
I shaked you, sir, and cried. As mine eyes opened,
I saw their weapons drawn. There was a noise,
That's verily. 'Tis best we stand upon our guard,
Or that we quit this place. Let's draw our weapons.

ALONSO:

Lead off this ground, and let's make further search
For my poor son.

GONZALO: Heavens keep him from these beasts!
For he is sure i' th' island.

ALONSO: Lead away.

ARIEL:

Prospero my lord shall know what I have done.
So, King, go safely on to seek thy son. *(Exeunt)*

II, ii *(Enter Caliban with a burden of wood. A noise of thunder heard.)*

CALIBAN:

All the infections that the sun sucks up
From bogs, fens, flats, on Prosper fall, and make him
By inchmeal a disease! His spirits hear me, 3
And yet I needs must curse. But they'll nor pinch, 4
Fright me with urchin-shows, pitch me i' th' mire, 5
Nor lead me, liks a firebrand, in the dark 6
Out of my way, unless he bid 'em; but
For every trifle are they set upon me;
Sometime like apes that mow and chatter at me, 9
And after bite me; then like hedgehogs which
Lie tumbling in my barefoot way and mount

---

294 *securing* keeping watch over   **II, ii** A place near Prospero's cell   3 *By inchmeal* inch by inch   4 *nor* neither   5 *urchin-shows* apparitions in the form of hedgehogs   6 *like a firebrand* in the form of a will-o'-the-wisp   9 *mow* make faces

Their pricks at my footfall; sometime am I
All wound with adders, who with cloven tongues
Do hiss me into madness.
(Enter Trinculo)   Lo, now, lo!
Here comes a spirit of his, and to torment me
For bringing wood in slowly. I'll fall flat.
Perchance he will not mind me.

(Lies down)

TRINCULO: Here's neither bush nor shrub to bear off any weather at all, and   18
another storm brewing: I hear it sing i' th' wind. Yond same black
cloud, yond huge one, looks like a foul bombard that would shed his liq-   20
uor. If it should thunder as it did before, I know not where to hide my
head. Yond same cloud cannot choose but fall by pailfuls. What have we
here? a man or a fish? dead or alive? A fish: he smells like a fish; a very
ancient and fishlike smell; a kind of not of the newest poor-John. A   24
strange fish! Were I in England now, as once I was, and had but this fish
painted, not a holiday fool there but would give a piece of silver. There   26
would this monster make a man: any strange beast there makes a man.   27
When they will not give a doit to relieve a lame beggar, they will lay   28
out ten to see a dead Indian. Legged like a man! and his fins like arms!
Warm, o' my troth! I do now let loose my opinion, hold it no longer:
this is no fish, but an islander, that hath lately suffered by a thunderbolt. *(Thunder)* Alas, the storm is come again! My best way is to creep
under his gaberdine: there is no other shelter hereabout. Misery ac-   33
quaints a man with strange bed-fellows. I will here shroud till the dregs
of the storm be past.

(Creeps under Caliban's garment)

(Enter Stephano, singing [with a bottle in his hand])

STEPHANO: I shall no more to sea, to sea;
                               Here shall I die ashore.
This is a very scurvy tune to sing at a man's funeral. Well, here's my
comfort.

(Drinks)

The master, the swabber, the boatswain, and I,
    The gunner, and his mate,
    Loved Mall, Meg, and Marian, and Margery,
        But none of us cared for Kate.
        For she had a tongue with a tang,
        Would cry to a sailor 'Go hang!'
She loved not the savor of tar nor of pitch;

---

18 *bear off* ward off   20 *bombard* leather bottle; *his* its   24 *poor-John* dried hake   26 *painted* i.e. on a signboard outside a booth at a fair   27 *make a man* (also with sense of 'make a man's fortune')   28 *doit* small
coin   33 *gaberdine* cloak

Yet a tailor might scratch her where'er she did itch.
Then to sea, boys, and let her go hang!

This is a scurvy tune too; but here's my comfort.

(Drinks)

CALIBAN: Do not torment me! O!

STEPHANO: What's the matter? Have we devils here? Do you put tricks upon's with savages and men of Inde, ha? I have not scaped drowning to be afeard now of your four legs; for it hath been said, 'As proper a man as ever went on four legs cannot make him give ground'; and it shall be said so again, while Stephano breathes at nostrils.

CALIBAN: The spirit torments me. O!

STEPHANO: This is some monster of the isle, with four legs, who hath got, as I take it, an ague. Where the devil should he learn our language? I will give him some relief, if it be but for that. If I can recover him, and keep him tame, and get to Naples with him, he's a present for any emperor that ever trod on neat's leather.   61

CALIBAN: Do not torment me, prithee; I'll bring my wood home faster.

STEPHANO: He's in his fit now and does not talk after the wisest. He shall taste of my bottle: if he have never drunk wine afore, it will go near to remove his fit. If I can recover him and keep him tame, I will not take   65
too much for him; he shall pay for him that hath him, and that soundly.   66

CALIBAN:
Thou dost me yet but little hurt.
Thou wilt anon; I know it by thy trembling.   68
Now Prosper works upon thee.

STEPHANO: Come on your ways: open your mouth: here is that which will give language to you, cat. Open your mouth. This will shake your shak-   71
ing, I can tell you, and that soundly. *(Gives Caliban drink)* You cannot tell who's your friend. Open your chaps again.   73

TRINCULO: I should know that voice. It should be—but he is drowned; and these are devils. O, defend me!

STEPHANO: Four legs and two voices—a most delicate monster! His forward voice now is to speak well of his friend; his backward voice is to utter foul speeches and to detract. If all the wine in my bottle will recover him, I will help his ague. Come! *(Gives drink)* Amen! I will pour some in thy other mouth.

TRINCULO: Stephano!

STEPHANO: Doth thy other mouth call me? Mercy, mercy! This is a devil, and no monster. I will leave him; I have no long spoon.   83

TRINCULO: Stephano! If thou beest Stephano, touch me and speak to me; for I am Trinculo—be not afeard—thy good friend Trinculo.

STEPHANO: If thou beest Trinculo, come forth. I'll pull thee by the lesser

---

61 *neat's leather* cowhide   **65-66** *not take too much* i.e. take all I can get   **68** *anon* soon   **71** *cat* (alluding to the proverb 'Liquor will make a cat talk')   **73** *chaps* jaws   **83** *spoon* (alluding to the proverb 'He who sups with the devil must have a long spoon')

legs. If any be Trinculo's legs, these are they. *(Draws him out from under Caliban's garment)* Thou art very Trinculo indeed: how cam'st thou to be the siege of this mooncalf? Can he vent Trinculos?　　　　　　　89

TRINCULO: I took him to be killed with a thunder-stroke. But art thou not drowned, Stephano? I hope now thou art not drowned. Is the storm overblown? I hid me under the dead mooncalf's gaberdine for fear of the storm. And art thou living, Stephano? O Stephano, two Neapolitans scaped!

STEPHANO: Prithee do not turn me about: my stomach is not constant.

CALIBAN *(aside)*:
　　These be fine things, an if they be not sprites.　　　　　　96
　　That's a brave god and bears celestial liquor.
　　I will kneel to him.

STEPHANO: How didst thou scape? How cam'st thou hither? Swear by this bottle how thou cam'st hither. I escaped upon a butt of sack which the sailors heaved o'erboard, by this bottle, which I made of the bark of a tree with mine own hands since I was cast ashore.

CALIBAN: I'll swear upon that bottle to be thy true subject, for the liquor is not earthly.

STEPHANO: Here! Swear then how thou escapedst.

TRINCULO: Swum ashore, man, like a duck. I can swim like a duck, I'll be sworn.

STEPHANO: Here, kiss the book. *(Gives him drink)* Though thou canst swim　108
　　like a duck, thou art made like a goose.　　　　　　　　　　　109

TRINCULO: O Stephano, hast any more of this?

STEPHANO: The whole butt, man: my cellar is in a rock by th' seaside, where my wine is hid. How now, moon-calf? How does thine ague?

CALIBAN: Hast thou not dropped from heaven?

STEPHANO: Out o' th' moon, I do assure thee. I was the Man i' th' Moon when time was.　　　　　　　　　　　　　　　　　　115

CALIBAN:
　　I have seen thee in her, and I do adore thee.
　　My mistress showed me thee, and thy dog, and thy bush.

STEPHANO: Come, swear to that; kiss the book. I will furnish it anon with new contents. Swear.

(Caliban drinks)

TRINCULO: By this good light, this is a very shallow monster! I afeard of him? A very weak monster! The Man i' th' Moon? A most poor credulous monster!—Well drawn, monster, in good sooth!

CALIBAN:
　　I'll show thee every fertile inch o' th' island;
　　And I will kiss thy foot. I prithee be my god.

TRINCULO: By this light, a most perfidious and drunken monster! When's god's asleep, he'll rob his bottle.

89 *siege* excrement; *mooncalf* monstrosity　96 *an if* if　108 *book* i.e. bottle　109 *like a goose* i.e. with a long neck　115 *when time was* once upon a time

CALIBAN:
　I'll kiss thy foot. I'll swear myself thy subject.
STEPHANO: Come on then. Down, and swear!
TRINCULO: I shall laugh myself to death at this puppyheaded monster. A
　most scurvy monster! I could find in my heart to beat him—
STEPHANO: Come, kiss.
TRINCULO: But that the poor monster 's in drink. An abominable monster!
CALIBAN:
　I'll show thee the best springs; I'll pluck thee berries;
　I'll fish for thee, and get thee wood enough.
　A plague upon the tyrant that I serve!
　I'll bear him no more sticks, but follow thee,
　Thou wondrous man.
TRINCULO: A most ridiculous monster, to make a wonder of a poor
　drunkard!
CALIBAN:
　I prithee let me bring thee where crabs grow;   140
　And I with my long nails will dig thee pignuts,   141
　Show thee a jay's nest, and instruct thee how
　To snare the nimble marmoset; I'll bring thee
　To clust'ring filberts, and sometimes I'll get thee
　Young scamels from the rock. Wilt thou go with me?   145
STEPHANO: I prithee now, lead the way without any more talking. Trinculo,
　the King and all our company else being drowned, we will inherit here.   147
　Here, bear my bottle. Fellow Trinculo, we'll fill him by and by again.   148

　(Caliban sings drunkenly)

CALIBAN: Farewell, master; farewell, farewell!
TRINCULO: A howling monster! a drunken monster!
CALIBAN:
　　　　No more dams I'll make for fish,
　　　　　Nor fetch in firing
　　　　　At requiring,
　　　　Nor scrape trenchering, nor wash dish.   154
　　　　'Ban, 'Ban, Ca—Caliban
　　　　Has a new master: get a new man.

　Freedom, high-day! high-day, freedom! freedom, high-day, freedom!
STEPHANO: O brave monster! lead the way.   (Exeunt)

III, i　　　(Enter Ferdinand, bearing a log)

FERDINAND:
　There be some sports are painful, and their labor   1

---

140 *crabs* crab apples　**141** *pignuts* peanuts　**145** *scamels* (unexplained, but clearly either a shellfish or a
rock-nesting bird; perhaps a misprint for 'seamels,' sea mews)　**147** *inherit* take possession　**148** *by and
by* soon　**154** *trenchering* trenchers, wooden plates　**III, i** Before Prospero's cell　**1** *painful* strenuous

Delight in them sets off; some kinds of baseness 2
Are nobly undergone, and most poor matters 3
Point to rich ends. This my mean task
Would be as heavy to me as odious, but
The mistress which I serve quickens what's dead 6
And makes my labors pleasures. O, she is
Ten times more gentle than her father's crabbèd;
And he's composed of harshness! I must remove
Some thousands of these logs and pile them up,
Upon a sore injunction. My sweet mistress 11
Weeps when she sees me work, and says such baseness
Had never like executor. I forget;
But these sweet thoughts do even refresh my labors
Most busy least, when I do it. 15

(Enter Miranda; and Prospero [behind, unseen])

MIRANDA: Alas, now pray you
Work not so hard! I would the lightning had
Burnt up those logs that you are enjoined to pile!
Pray set it down and rest you. When this burns,
'Twill weep for having wearied you. My father 19
Is hard at study: pray now rest yourself.
He's safe for these three hours.
FERDINAND: O most dear mistress,
The sun will set before I shall discharge
What I must strive to do.
MIRANDA: If you'll sit down.
I'll bear your logs the while. Pray give me that:
I'll carry it to the pile.
FERDINAND: No, precious creature:
I had rather crack my sinews, break my back,
Than you should such dishonor undergo
While I sit lazy by.
MIRANDA: It would become me
As well as it does you; and I should do it
With much more ease; for my good will is to it,
And yours it is against.
PROSPERO *(aside)*:   Poor worm, thou art infected!
This visitation shows it. 32
MIRANDA: You look wearily.
FERDINAND:
No, noble mistress: 'tis fresh morning with me
When you are by at night. I do beseech you,

---

2 *sets off* makes greater by contrast   **3** *matters* affairs   **6** *quickens* brings to life   **11** *sore injunction* grievous command   **15** *least* i.e. least conscious of being busy (F reads 'lest')   **19** *weep* i.e. exude resin   **32** *visitation* (1) visit, (2) attack of plague (in the metaphor of *infected*)

Chiefly that I might set it in my prayers,
What is your name?
MIRANDA: Miranda. O my father,
I have broke your hest to say so!   37
FERDINAND: Admired Miranda!
Indeed the top of admiration, worth   38
What's dearest to the world! Full many a lady
I have eyed with best regard, and many a time   40
Th' harmony of their tongues hath into bondage
Brought my too diligent ear; for several virtues   42
Have I liked several women; never any
With so full soul but some defect in her   44
Did quarrel with the noblest grace she owed,   45
And put it to the foil. But you, O you,   46
So perfect and so peerless, are created
Of every creature's best.
MIRANDA: I do not know
One of my sex; no woman's face remember,
Save, from my glass, mine own; nor have I seen
More that I may call men than you, good friend,
And my dear father. How features are abroad   52
I am skilless of; but, by my modesty   53
(The jewel in my dower), I would not wish
Any companion in the world but you;
Nor can imagination form a shape,
Besides yourself, to like of. But I prattle   57
Something too wildly, and my father's precepts
I therein do forget.
FERDINAND: I am, in my condition,   59
A prince, Miranda; I do think, a king
(I would not so), and would no more endure
This wooden slavery than to suffer
The fleshfly blow my mouth. Hear my soul speak!
The very instant that I saw you, did
My heart fly to your service; there resides,
To make me slave to it; and for your sake
Am I this patient log-man.
MIRANDA: Do you love me?
FERDINAND:
O heaven, O earth, bear witness to this sound,
And crown what I profess with kind event   69
If I speak true! if hollowly, invert

---

37 *hest* command   38 *admiration* wonder, astonishment (the name Miranda means wonderful woman;
cf. I, ii, 427)   40 *best regard* highest approval   42 *several* different   44 *With . . . soul* i.e. so wholehearted-
ly   45 *owed* owned   46 *foil* (1) overthrow, (2) contrast   52 *abroad* elsewhere   53 *skilless* ignorant
57 *like of* compare to   59 *condition* situation in the world   69 *kind event* favorable outcome

What best is boded me to mischief! I,
Beyond all limit of what else i' th' world,
Do love, prize, honor you.
MIRANDA: I am a fool
To weep at what I am glad of.
PROSPERO *(aside)*:   Fair encounter
Of two most rare affections! Heavens rain grace
On that which breeds between 'em!
FERDINAND: Wherefore weep you?
MIRANDA:
At mine unworthiness, that dare not offer
What I desire to give, and much less take
What I shall die to want. But this is trifling;   79
And all the more it seeks to hide itself,
The bigger bulk it shows. Hence, bashful cunning,   81
And prompt me, plain and holy innocence!
I am your wife, if you will marry me;
If not, I'll die your maid. To be your fellow   84
You may deny me; but I'll be your servant,
Whether you will or no.
FERDINAND: My mistress, dearest,
And I thus humble ever.
MIRANDA: My husband then?
FERDINAND:
Ay, with a heart as willing
As bondage e'er of freedom. Here's my hand.   89
MIRANDA:
And mine, with my heart in't; and now farewell
Till half an hour hence.
FERDINAND: A thousand thousand!

(Exeunt Ferdinand and Miranda severally)

PROSPERO:
So glad of this as they I cannot be,
Who are surprised withal; but my rejoicing   93
At nothing can be more. I'll to my book;
For yet ere supper time must I perform
Much business appertaining.   96
                                                  (Exit)

III, ii   *(Enter Caliban, Stephano, and Trinculo)*

STEPHANO: Tell not me! When the butt is out, we will drink water; not a

---

79 *want* lack   **81** *bashful cunning* i.e. coyness   **84** *fellow* equal   **89** *of freedom* i.e. to win freedom   **93** *surprised withal* taken unaware by it   **96** *appertaining* relevant   **III, ii** Another part of the island

drop before. Therefore bear up and board 'em! Servant monster, drink   2
to me.

TRINCULO: Servant monster? The folly of this island! They say there's but
five upon this isle: we are three of them. If th' other two be brained like
us, the state totters.

STEPHANO: Drink, servant monster, when I bid thee: thy eyes are almost set
in thy head.

TRINCULO: Where should they be set else? He were a brave monster indeed
if they were set in his tail.

STEPHANO: My man-monster hath drowned his tongue in sack. For my part,
the sea cannot drown me. I swam, ere I could recover the shore, five-   12
and-thirty leagues off and on, by this light. Thou shalt be my lieutenant, monster, or my standard.   14

TRINCULO: Your lieutenant, if you list; he's no standard.   15

STEPHANO: We'll not run, Monsieur Monster.   16

TRINCULO: Nor go neither; but you'll lie like dogs, and yet say nothing nei-   17
ther.

STEPHANO: Mooncalf, speak once in thy life, if thou beest a good mooncalf.

CALIBAN:
How does thy honor? Let me lick thy shoe.
I'll not serve him; he is not valiant.

TRINCULO: Thou liest, most ignorant monster: I am in case to justle a consta-   22
ble. Why, thou deboshed fish thou, was there ever man a coward that   23
hath drunk so much sack as I to-day? Wilt thou tell a monstrous lie, being but half a fish and half a monster?

CALIBAN: Lo, how he mocks me! Wilt thou let him, my lord?

TRINCULO: 'Lord' quoth he? That a monster should be such a natural!   27

CALIBAN: Lo, lo, again! Bite him to death, I prithee.

STEPHANO: Trinculo, keep a good tongue in your head. If you prove a muti-
neer—the next tree! The poor monster's my subject, and he shall not
suffer indignity.

CALIBAN:
I thank my noble lord. Wilt thou be pleased
To hearken once again to the suit I made to thee?

STEPHANO: Marry, will I. Kneel and repeat it; I will stand, and so shall
Trinculo.   35

(Enter Ariel, invisible)

CALIBAN:
As I told thee before, I am subject to a tyrant,
A sorcerer, that by his cunning hath
Cheated me of the island.

ARIEL: Thou liest.

---

2 *bear . . . 'em* i.e. drink up (Caliban has almost 'passed out')   **12** *recover* reach   **14** *standard* ensign
15 *no standard* i.e. incapable of standing up   **16, 17** *run, lie* (secondary meanings of) make water and ex-
crete   **17** *go* walk   **22** *case* fit condition   **23** *deboshed* debauched   **27** *natural* fool   **35** **s.d.** *invisible* ('a
robe for to go invisible' is listed in an Elizabethan stage account)

CALIBAN:
  Thou liest, thou jesting monkey thou!
  I would my valiant master would destroy thee.
  I do not lie.
STEPHANO: Trinculo, if you trouble him any more in's tale, by this hand,
  I will supplant some of your teeth.
TRINCULO: Why, I said nothing.
STEPHANO: Mum then, and no more.—Proceed.
CALIBAN:
  I say by sorcery he got this isle;
  From me he got it. If thy greatness will
  Revenge it on him—for I know thou dar'st,
  But this thing dare not—   49
STEPHANO: That's most certain.
CALIBAN:
  Thou shalt be lord of it, and I'll serve thee.
STEPHANO:
  How now shall this be compassed?
  Canst thou bring me to the party?   53
CALIBAN:
  Yea, yea, my lord! I'll yield him thee asleep,
  Where thou mayst knock a nail into his head.
ARIEL: Thou liest; thou canst not.
CALIBAN:
  What a pied ninny's this! Thou scurvy patch!   57
  I do beseech thy greatness give him blows
  And take his bottle from him. When that's gone,
  He shall drink naught but brine, for I'll not show him
  Where the quick freshes are.   61
STEPHANO: Trinculo, run into no further danger: interrupt the monster
  one word further and, by this hand, I'll turn my mercy out o' doors
  and make a stockfish of thee.   64
TRINCULO: Why, what did I? I did nothing. I'll go farther off.
STEPHANO: Didst thou not say he lied?
ARIEL: Thou liest.
STEPHANO: Do I so? Take thou that! (Strikes Trinculo) As you like this, give
  me the lie another time.
TRINCULO: I did not give the lie. Out o' your wits, and hearing too? A pox
  o' your bottle! This can sack and drinking do. A murrain on your mon-   71
  ster, and the devil take your fingers!
CALIBAN: Ha, ha, ha!
STEPHANO: Now forward with your tale.—Prithee stand further off.
CALIBAN:
  Beat him enough. After a little time

49 *this thing* i.e. himself (or perhaps Trinculo)   **53** *party* person   **57** *pied ninny* motley fool (Trinculo wears a jester's costume); *patch* clown   **61** *quick freshes* fresh-water springs   **64** *stockfish* dried cod, prepared by beating   **71** *murrain* cattle disease

I'll beat him too.

STEPHANO: Stand farther.—Come, proceed.

CALIBAN:

Why as I told thee, 'tis a custom with him
I' th' afternoon to sleep; there thou mayst brain him,
Having first seized his books, or with a log
Batter his skull, or paunch him with a stake,   80
Or cut his wesand with thy knife. Remember   81
First to possess his books; for without them
He's but a sot, as I am, nor hath not   83
One spirit to command. They all do hate him
As rootedly as I. Burn but his books.
He has brave utensils (for so he calls them)   86
Which, when he has a house, he'll deck withal.
And that most deeply to consider is
The beauty of his daughter. He himself
Calls her a nonpareil. I never saw a woman
But only Sycorax my dam and she;
But she as far surpasseth Sycorax
As great'st does least.

STEPHANO: Is it so brave a lass?

CALIBAN:

Ay, lord. She will become thy bed, I warrant,
And bring thee forth brave brood.

STEPHANO: Monster, I will kill this man: his daughter and I will be king
and queen, save our Graces! and Trinculo and thyself shall be viceroys.
Dost thou like the plot, Trinculo?

TRINCULO: Excellent.

STEPHANO: Give me thy hand. I am sorry I beat thee; but while thou liv'st,
keep a good tongue in thy head.

CALIBAN:

Within this half hour will he be asleep.
Wilt thou destroy him then?

STEPHANO: Ay, on mine honor.

ARIEL: This will I tell my master.

CALIBAN:

Thou mak'st me merry; I am full of pleasure.
Let us be jocund. Will you troll the catch   107
You taught me but whilere?   108

STEPHANO: At thy request, monster, I will do reason, any reason. Come on,
Trinculo, let us sing.

(Sings)

Flout 'em and scout em
And scout 'em and flout 'em!
Thought is free.

---

80 *paunch* stab in the belly   **81** *wesand* windpipe   **83** *sot* fool   **86** *utensils* furnishings   **107** *troll the catch*
sing the part-song   **108** *whilere* just now

CALIBAN:
> That's not the tune. 114

(Ariel plays the tune on a tabor and pipe)

STEPHANO: What is this same?

TRINCULO: This is the tune of our catch, played by the picture of Nobody. 116

STEPHANO: If thou beest a man, show thyself in thy likeness. If thou beest
a devil, take't as thou list. 118

TRINCULO: O, forgive me my sins!

STEPHANO: He that dies pays all debts. I defy thee. Mercy upon us!

CALIBAN: Art thou afeard?

STEPHANO: No, monster, not I.

CALIBAN:
> Be not afeard: the isle is full of noises,
> Sounds and sweet airs that give delight and hurt not.
> Sometimes a thousand twangling instruments
> Will hum about mine ears; and sometime voices
> That, if I then had waked after long sleep,
> Will make me sleep again; and then, in dreaming,
> The clouds methought would open and show riches
> Ready to drop upon me, that, when I waked,
> I cried to dream again.

STEPHANO: This will prove a brave kingdom to me, where I shall have my
music for nothing.

CALIBAN:
> When Prospero is destroyed.

STEPHANO: That shall be by and by: I remember the story. 135

TRINCULO: The sound is going away: let's follow it, and after do our work.

STEPHANO: Lead, monster; we'll follow. I would I could see this taborer:
he lays it on. Wilt come?

TRINCULO: I'll follow, Stephano. *(Exeunt)*

III, iii *(Enter Alonso, Sebastian, Antonio, Gonzalo,*
Adrian, Francisco, etc.)

GONZALO:
> By'r Lakin, I can go no further, sir: 1
> My old bones ache: here's a maze trod indeed
> Through forthrights and meanders. By your patience, 3
> I needs must rest me.

ALONSO: Old lord, I cannot blame thee,
> Who am myself attached with weariness 5
> To th' dulling of my spirits. Sit down and rest.
> Even here I will put off my hope, and keep it

---

114 s.d. *tabor* small drum worn at the side **116** *Nobody* (referring to pictures of figures with arms and legs but no trunk, used on signs and elsewhere) **118** *take't as thou list* i.e. suit yourself **135** *by and by* right away **III, iii** Another part of the island **1** *By'r Lakin* by our Ladykin (Virgin Mary) **3** *forthrights* straight paths **5** *attached* seized

No longer for my flatterer: he is drowned
Whom thus we stray to find; and the sea mocks
Our frustrate search on land. Well, let him go.

ANTONIO *(aside to Sebastian)*:
I am right glad that he's so out of hope.
Do not for one repulse forgo the purpose
That you resolved t' effect.

SEBASTIAN *(aside to Antonio)*: The next advantage
Will we take throughly.   14

ANTONIO *(aside to Sebastian)* Let it be to-night;
For, now they are oppressed with travel, they
Will not nor cannot use such vigilance
As when they are fresh.

SEBASTIAN *(aside to Antonio)*: I say to-night. No more.   17

*(Solemn and strange music; and Prospero on the top [invisible]. Enter several
strange Shapes, bringing in a banquet; and dance about it with gentle actions of
salutations; and, inviting the King etc. to eat, they depart.)*

ALONSO:
What harmony is this? My good friends, hark!

GONZALO:
Marvellous sweet music!

ALONSO:
Give us kind keepers, heavens! What were these?   20

SEBASTIAN:
A living drollery. Now I will believe   21
That there are unicorns; that in Arabia
There is one tree, the phoenix' throne; one phoenix
At this hour reigning there.

ANTONIO: I'll believe both;
And what does else want credit, come to me,   25
And I'll be sworn 'tis true. Travellers ne'er did lie,
Though fools at home condemn 'em.

GONZALO: If in Naples
I should report this now, would they believe me
If I should say I saw such islanders?
(For certes these are people of the island)
Who, though they are of monstrous shape, yet note,
Their manners are more gentle, kind, than of
Our human generation you shall find
Many—nay, almost any.

PROSPERO *(aside)*:   Honest lord,
Thou has said well; for some of you there present
Are worse than devils.

---

14 *throughly* thoroughly   **17 s.d.** *on the top* (this may refer to an upper level of the tiring-house of the
theatre)   **20** *kind keepers* guardian angels   **21** *living drollery* puppet show with live figures   **25** *want
credit* lack credibility

ALONSO: I cannot too much muse   36
  Such shapes, such gesture, and such sound, expressing
  (Although they want the use of tongue) a kind
  Of excellent dumb discourse.
PROSPERO *(aside)*:   Praise in departing.   39
FRANCISCO:
  They vanished strangely.
SEBASTIAN: No matter, since
  They have left their viands behind; for we have stomachs.
  Will't please you taste of what is here?
ALONSO: Not I.
GONZALO:
  Faith, sir, you need not fear. When we were boys,
  Who would believe that there were mountaineers
  Dewlapped like bulls, whose throats had hanging at 'em   45
  Wallets of flesh? or that there were such men
  Whose heads stood in their breasts? which now we find   47
  Each putter-out of five for one will bring us   48
  Good warrant of.
ALONSO: I will stand to, and feed;
  Although my last, no matter, since I feel
  The best is past. Brother, my lord the Duke,
  Stand to, and do as we.

*(Thunder and lightning. Enter Ariel, like a harpy: claps his wings upon
the table; and with a quaint device the banquet vanishes.)*   52

ARIEL:
  You are three men of sin, whom destiny—
  That hath to instrument this lower world   54
  And what is in't—the never-surfeited sea
  Hath caused to belch up you, and on this island,
  Where man doth not inhabit, you 'mongst men
  Being most unfit to live, I have made you mad;
  And even with such-like valor men hang and drown
  Their proper selves.

(Alonso, Sebastian, etc. draw their swords)

             You fools: I and my fellows
  Are ministers of Fate. The elements,
  Of whom your swords are tempered, may as well
  Wound the loud winds, or with bemocked-at stabs
  Kill the still-closing waters, as diminish   64

---

36 *muse* wonder at   **39** *Praise in departing* save your praise for the end   **45** *Dewlapped* with skin hanging from the neck (like the goitrous Swiss *mountaineers*)   **47** *in their breasts* (an ancient travellers' tale; cf. *Othello* **I, iii,** 144–45)   **48** *putter-out . . . one* traveller depositing a sum for insurance in London, to be repaid fivefold if he returned safely and proved he had gone to his destination   **52 s.d.** *quaint* ingenious   **54** *to* i.e. as its   **64** *still* constantly

One dowle that's in my plume. My fellow ministers　　　　65
Are like invulnerable. If you could hurt,　　　　　　　　66
Your swords are now too massy for your strengths　　　　67
And will not be uplifted. But remember
(For that's my business to you) that you three
From Milan did supplant good Prospero;
Exposed unto the sea, which hath requit it,　　　　　　71
Him and his innocent child; for which foul deed
The pow'rs, delaying, not forgetting, have
Incensed the seas and shores, yea, all the creatures,
Against your peace. Thee of thy son, Alonso,
They have bereft; and do pronounce by me
Ling'ring perdition (worse than any death　　　　　　77
Can be at once) shall step by step attend
You and your ways; whose wraths to guard you from,
Which here, in this most desolate isle, else falls
Upon your heads, is nothing but heart's sorrow　　　　81
And a clear life ensuing.　　　　　　　　　　　　82

*(He vanishes in thunder; then, to soft music, enter the Shapes again, and dance
with mocks and mows, and carrying out the table)*

PROSPERO:
Bravely the figure of this harpy has thou
Performed, my Ariel; a grace it had, devouring.　　　84
Of my instruction hast thou nothing bated　　　　　85
In what thou hadst to say. So, with good life　　　　86
And observation strange, my meaner ministers　　　　87
Their several kinds have done. My high charms work,　　88
And these, mine enemies, are all knit up
In their distractions: they now are in my pow'r;
And in these fits I leave them, while I visit
Young Ferdinand, whom they suppose is drowned,
And his and mine loved darling.　　　　　*(Exit above)*
GONZALO: I' th' name of something holy, sir, why stand you　　94
In this strange stare?
ALONSO:　　　　　　　O, it is monstrous, monstrous!　　95
Methought the billows spoke and told me of it;
The winds did sing it to me; and the thunder,
That deep and dreadful organ pipe, pronounced
The name of Prosper; it did bass my trespass.　　　　99
Therefore my son i' th' ooze is bedded; and

---

65 *dowle* fibre of feather-down　66 *like* also　67 *massy* massive　71 *requit* avenged; *it* i.e. the usurpation　77 *perdition* ruin　81 *heart's sorrow* repentance　82 *clear* innocent; **s.d.** *mocks and mows* grimaces and gestures　84 *devouring* i.e. making the banquet disappear　85 *bated* omitted　86 *good life* realistic acting　87 *observation strange* wonderfully close attention　88 *several kinds* separate parts　94 *why* (Gonzalo has not heard Ariel's speech)　95 *it* i.e. my sin　99 *bass* proclaim in deep tones (literally, provide the bass part for)

I'll seek him deeper than e'er plummet sounded
And with him there lie mudded.   *(Exit)*
SEBASTIAN: But one fiend at a time,
   I'll fight their legions o'er!
ANTONIO: I'll be thy second.

   (Exeunt Sebastian and Antonio)

GONZALO:
   All three of them are desperate: their great guilt,
   Like poison given to work a great time after,
   Now gins to bite the spirits. I do beseech you,
   That are of suppler joints, follow them swiftly
   And hinder them from what this ecstasy   108
   May now provoke them to.
ADRIAN: Follow, I pray you

                                    (Exeunt omnes)

IV, i   *(Enter Prospero, Ferdinand, and Miranda)*

PROSPERO:
   If I have too austerely punished you,
   Your compensation makes amends; for I
   Have given you here a third of mine own life,   3
   Or that for which I live; who once again
   I tender to thy hand. All thy vexations
   Were but my trials of thy love, and thou
   Hast strangely stood the test. Here, afore heaven,   7
   I ratify this my rich gift. O Ferdinand,
   Do not smile at me that I boast her off,   9
   For thou shalt find she will outstrip all praise
   And make it halt behind her.   11
FERDINAND: I do believe it
   Against an oracle.   12
PROSPERO:
   Then, as my gift, and thine own acquisition
   Worthily purchased, take my daughter. But
   If thou dost break her virgin-knot before
   All sanctimonious ceremonies may   16
   With full and holt rite be minist'red,
   No sweet aspersion shall the heavens let fall   18
   To make this contract grow; but barren hate,   19
   Sour-eyed disdain, and discord shall bestrew

---

108 *ecstasy* madness   **IV, i** Before Prospero's cell   **3** *third* (Prospero's love, his knowledge and his power being the other two-thirds?)   **7** *strangely* in a rare fashion   **9** *boast her off* boast about her   **11** *halt*
limp   **12** *Against an oracle* even if an oracle denied it   **16** *sanctimonious* holy   **18** *aspersion* blessing, like
rain on crops   **19** *grow* become fruitful

The union of your bed with weeds so loathly
That you shall hate it both. Therefore take heed,
As Hymen's lamp shall light you.
FERDINAND: As I hope
For quiet days, fair issue, and long life,
With such love as 'tis now, the murkiest den,
The most opportune place, the strong'st suggestion   26
Our worser genius can, shall never melt   27
Mine honor into lust, to take away
The edge of that day's celebration
When I shall think or Phoebus' steeds are foundered   30
Or Night kept chained below.
PROSPERO: Fairly spoke.
Sit then and talk with her; she is thine own.
What, Ariel! My industrious servant, Ariel!

(Enter Ariel)

ARIEL:
What would my potent master? Here I am.
PROSPERO:
Thou and thy meaner fellows your last service
Did worthily perform; and I must use you
In such another trick. Go bring the rabble,   37
O'er whom I give thee pow'r, here to this place.
Incite them to quick motion; for I must
Bestow upon the eyes of this young couple
Some vanity of mine art; it is my promise,   41
And they expect it from me.
ARIEL: Presently?
PROSPERO:
Ay, with a twink.
ARIEL:
Before you can say 'Come' and 'Go,'
And breathe twice and cry, 'So, so,'
Each one, tripping on his toe,
Will be here with mop and mow.   47
Do you love me, master? No?
PROSPERO:
Dearly, my delicate Ariel. Do not approach
Till thou dost hear me call.
ARIEL: Well: I conceive.   *(Exit)*   50
PROSPERO:
Look thou be true: do not give dalliance   51
Too much the rein: the strongest oaths are straw

---

26 *opportune* (accent second syllable)   **27** *worser genius can* bad angel can make   **30** *or . . . foundered* either the sun-god's horses are lame   **37** *rabble* rank and file   **41** *vanity* show   **47** *mop and mow* antics and gestures   **50** *conceive* understand   **51** *be true* (Prospero appears to have caught the lovers in an embrace)

To th' fire i' th' blood. Be more abstemious,
Or else good night your vow!

FERDINAND: I warrant you, sir.
The white cold virgin snow upon my heart
Abates the ardor of my liver.   56

PROSPERO: Well.
Now come, my Ariel: bring a corollary   57
Rather than want a spirit. Appear, and pertly!   58
No tongue! All eyes! Be silent.

(Soft music. Enter Iris)

IRIS:
Ceres, most bounteous lady, thy rich leas   60
Of wheat, rye, barley, fetches, oats, and pease;   61
Thy turfy mountains, where live nibbling sheep,
And flat meads thatched with stover, them to keep;   63
Thy banks with pionèd and twillèd brims,   64
Which spongy April at thy hest betrims
To make cold nymphs chaste crowns; and thy broom groves,   66
Whose shadow the dismissed bachelor loves,
Being lasslorn; thy pole-clipt vineyard;   68
And thy sea-marge, sterile and rocky-hard,   69
Where thou thyself dost air—the queen o' th' sky,   70
Whose wat'ry arch and messenger am I,
Bids thee leave these, and with her sovereign grace,
Here on this grass-plot, in this very place,   73
To come and sport: her peacocks fly amain.   74
Approach, rich Ceres, her to entertain.

(Enter Ceres)

CERES:
Hail, many-colored messenger, that ne'er
Dost disobey the wife of Jupiter,
Who, with thy saffron wings, upon my flow'rs
Diffusest honey drops, refreshing show'rs,
And with each end of thy blue bow dost crown
My bosky acres and my unshrubbed down,   81
Rich scarf to my proud earth—why hath thy queen
Summoned me hither to this short-grassed green?

IRIS:
A contract of true love to celebrate

---

56 *liver* (supposed seat of sexual passion)   **57** *corollary* surplus   **58** *want* lack; *pertly* briskly   **60** *Iris* goddess of the rainbow and female messenger of the gods   **61** *fetches* vetch   **63** *stover* winter food for stock   **64** *pionèd and twillèd* dug under by the current and protected by woven layers of branches (sometimes emended to 'peonied and lilied')   **66** *broom groves* clumps of gorse   **68** *pole-clipt* pruned; *vineyard* (probably a trisyllable)   **69** *sea-marge* shore   **70** *queen* i.e. Juno   **73** *Here. . . place* (in F a stage direction at this point reads 'Juno descends')   **74** *peacocks* (these were sacred to Juno, as doves were to Venus [l. 94], and drew her chariot)   **81** *bosky* wooded

And some donation freely to estate 85
On the blessed lovers.

CERES: Tell me, heavenly bow,
If Venus or her son, as thou dost know, 87
Do now attend the queen? Since they did plot
The means that dusky Dis my daughter got, 89
Her and her blind boy's scandalled company 90
I have forsworn.

IRIS: Of her society
Be not afraid: I met her Deity 92
Cutting the clouds towards Paphos, and her son 93
Dove-drawn with her. Here thought they to have done
Some wanton charm upon this man and maid,
Whose vows are, that no bed-right shall be paid
Till Hymen's torch be lighted; but in vain.
Mars's hot minion is returned again; 98
Her waspish-headed son has broke his arrows, 99
Swears he will shoot no more, but play with sparrows
And be a boy right out. 101

(Enter Juno)

CERES: Highest queen of state,
Great Juno, comes; I know her by her gait.
JUNO:
How does my bounteous sister? Go with me
To bless this twain, that they may prosperous be
And honored in their issue.

(They sing)

JUNO: Honor, riches, marriage blessing,
        Long continuance, and increasing,
        Hourly joys be still upon you! 108
        Juno sings her blessings on you.
(CERES) Earth's increase, foison plenty, 110
        Barns and garners never empty,
        Vines with clust'ring bunches growing,
        Plants with goodly burden bowing;
        Spring come to you at the farthest
        In the very end of harvest.
        Scarcity and want shall shun you,
        Ceres' blessing so is on you.

---

85 *estate* bestow   87 *her son* Cupid, often represented as blind or blindfolded   89 *means* i.e. the abduction of Proserpine, Ceres' daughter, by Pluto (Dis), god of the lower *(dusky)* world   90 *scandalled* disgraceful   92 *her Deity* i.e. her Divine Majesty   93 *Paphos* (in Cyprus, center of Venus' cult)   98 *Mars's . . . again* the lustful mistress of Mars (Venus) has gone back to where she came from   99 *waspish-headed* spiteful and inclined to sting (with his arrows)   101 *right out* outright   108 *still* constantly   110 *foison* abundance

FERDINAND:
This is a most majestic vision, and
Harmonious charmingly. May I be bold
To think these spirits?
PROSPERO: Spirits, which by mine art
I have from their confines called to enact
My present fancies.
FERDINAND: Let me live here ever!
So rare a wond'red father and a wise   123
Makes this place Paradise.

(Juno and Ceres whisper, and send Iris on employment)

PROSPERO: Sweet now, silence!
Juno and Ceres whisper seriously.
There's something else to do. Hush and be mute,
Or else our spell is marred.
IRIS:
You nymphs, called Naiades, of the windring brooks,   128
With your sedged crowns and ever-harmless looks,
Leave your crisp channels, and on this green land   130
Answer your summons; Juno does command.
Come, temperate nymphs, and help to celebrate
A contract of true love: be not too late.

(Enter certain Nymphs)

You sunburned sicklemen, of August weary,
Come hither from the furrow and be merry.
Make holiday: your rye-straw hats put on,
And these fresh nymphs encounter every one
In country footing.   138

*(Enter certain Reapers, properly habited. They join with the Nymphs in a
graceful dance; towards the end whereof Prospero starts suddenly and
speaks; after which, to a strange, hollow, and confused noise, they heavily
vanish.)*

PROSPERO *(aside)*:
I had forgot that foul conspiracy
Of the beast Caliban and his confederates
Against my life: The minute of their plot
Is almost come.
(To the Spirits) Well done! Avoid! No more!   142
FERDINAND:
This is strange. Your father's in some passion
That works him strongly.

---

123 *wond'red* wonderful **128** *windring* winding and wandering **130** *crisp* rippling **138 s.d.** *speaks*
(thereby dissolving the scene, which depended on silence) **142** *Avoid* be off

MIRANDA: Never till this day
   Saw I him touched with anger so distempered.
PROSPERO:
   You do look, my son, in a moved sort,   146
   As if you were dismayed: be cheerful, sir.
   Our revels now are ended. These our actors,   148
   As I foretold you, were all spirits and
   Are melted into air, into thin air;
   And, like the baseless fabric of this vision,   151
   The cloud-capped tow'rs, the gorgeous palaces,
   The solemn temples, the great globe itself,
   Yea, all which it inherit, shall dissolve,   154
   And, like this insubstantial pageant faded,
   Leave not a rack behind. We are such stuff   156
   As dreams are made on, and our little life   157
   Is rounded with a sleep. Sir, I am vexed.
   Bear with my weakness: my old brain is troubled.
   Be not disturbed with my infirmity.
   If you be pleased, retire into my cell
   And there repose. A turn or two I'll walk
   To still my beating mind.
FERDINAND, MIRANDA: We wish your peace.

                                   (Exit Ferdinand with Miranda)

   (Enter Ariel)

PROSPERO:
   Come with a thought! I thank thee, Ariel. Come.
ARIEL:
   Thy thoughts I cleave to. What's thy pleasure?
PROSPERO: Spirit,
   We must prepare to meet with Caliban.
ARIEL:
   Ay, my commander: when I presented Ceres,   167
   I thought to have told thee of it, but I feared
   Lest I might anger thee.
PROSPERO:
   Say again, where didst thou leave these varlets?   170
ARIEL:
   I told you, sir, they were redhot with drinking;
   So full of valor that they smote the air
   For breathing in their faces, beat the ground
   For kissing of their feet; yet always bending
   Towards their project. Then I beat my tabor;

---

146 *moved sort* troubled state   **148** *revels* pageants   **151** *baseless* insubstantial, non-material   **154** *it inherit* occupy it   **156** *rack* wisp of cloud   **157** *on* of   **167** *presented* acted the part of (?), introduced (?)
170 *varlets* ruffians

At which like unbacked colts they pricked their ears, 176
Advanced their eyelids, lifted up their noses 177
As they smelt music. So I charmed their ears
That calf-like they may lowing followed through
Toothed briers, sharp furzes, pricking goss, and thorns,
Which ent'red their frail shins. At last I left them
I' th' filthy mantled pool beyond your cell, 182
There dancing up to th' chins, that the foul lake
O'erstunk their feet.

PROSPERO: This was well done, my bird.
Thy shape invisible retain thou still.
The trumpery in my house, go bring it hither
For stale to catch these thieves. 187

ARIEL: I go, I go.   (*Exit*)

PROSPERO:
A devil, a born devil, on whose nature
Nurture can never stick: on whom my pains,
Humanely taken, all, all lost, quite lost!
And as with age his body uglier grows,
So his mind cankers. I will plague them all, 192
Even to roaring.

(*Enter Ariel, loaden with glistering apparel, etc.*)

                    Come, hang them on this line. 193

(*Prospero and Ariel remain, invisible. Enter Caliban, Stephano, and Trinculo, all wet.*)

CALIBAN:
Pray you tread softly, that the blind mole may not
Hear a foot fall. We now are near his cell.

STEPHANO: Monster, your fairy, which you say is a harmless fairy, has done
litle better than played the Jack with us. 197

TRINCULO: Monster, I do smell all horse-piss, at which my nose is in great
indignation.

STEPHANO: So is mine. Do you hear, monster? If I should take a displeasue
against you, look you—

TRINCULO: Thou wert but a lost monster.

CALIBAN:
Good my lord, give me thy favor still.
Be patient, for the prize I'll bring thee to
Shall hoodwink this mischance. Therefore speak softly. 205
All's hushed as midnight yet.

TRINCULO: Ay, but to lose our bottles in the pool—

---

176 *unbacked* unbroken   177 *Advanced* lifted up   180 *goss* gorse   182 *mantled* scummed   187 *stale* decoy   192 *cankers* festers   193 *line* lime or linden-tree, or perhaps a clothesline made of hair   197 *Jack* (1) knave, (2) jack-o'-lantern, will-o'-the-wisp   205 *hoodwink* cover over

STEPHANO: There is not only disgrace and dishonor in that, monster, but an infinite loss.

TRINCULO: That's more to me than my wetting. Yet this is your harmless fairy monster.

STEPHANO: I will fetch off my bottle, though I be o'er ears for my labor.

CALIBAN:
Prithee, my king, be quiet. Seest thou here?
This is the mouth o' th' cell. No noise, and enter.
Do that good mischief which may make this island
Thine own for ever, and I, thy Caliban,
For aye thy foot-licker.

STEPHANO: Give me thy hand. I do begin to have bloody thoughts.

TRINCULO: O King Stephano! O peer! O worthy Stephano, look what a   219
wardrobe here is for thee!

CALIBAN:
Let it alone, thou fool! It is but trash.

TRINCULO: O, ho, monster! we know what belongs to a frippery. O King   222
Stehano!

STEPHANO: Put off that gown, Trinculo: by this hand, I'll have that gown!

TRINCULO: Thy Grace shall have it.

CALIBAN:
The dr)sy drown this fool! What do you mean
To dote thus on such luggage? Let't alone,   227
And do the murder first. If he awake,
From toe to crown he'll fill our skins with pinches,
Make us strange stuff.

STEPHANO: Be you quiet, monster. Mistress line, is not this my jerkin?   231
(Takes it down) Now is the jerkin under the line. Now, jerkin, you are
like to lose your hair and prove a bald jerkin.

TRINCULO: Do, do! We steal by line and level, an't like your Grace.   234

STEPHANO: I thank thee for that jest. Here's a garment for't. Wit shall not go
unrewarded while I am king of this country. 'Steal by line and level'
is an excellent pass of pate. There's another garment for't.   237

TRINCULO: Monster, come put some lime upon your fingers, and away, with   238
the rest.

CALIBAN:
I will have none on't. We shall lose our time
And all be turned to barnacles, or to apes   241
With foreheads villainous low.

STEPHANO: Monster, lay-to your fingers: help to bear this away where my
hogshead of wine is, or I'll turn you out of my kingdom. Go to, carry
this.

---

219 *peer* (referring to the song 'King Stephen was a worthy peer,' quoted in *Othello* II, iii, 84–91)
222 *frippery* old-clothes shop   **227** *luggage* junk   **231** ff. (the jokes are probably obscene, but their point
is lost; sailors crossing the *line* or equator proverbially lost their hair from scurvy)   **234** *by line and level*
according to rule (with pun on *line*); *an't like* if it please   **237** *pass of pate* sally of wit   **238** *lime* bird-lime
(sticky, hence appropriate for stealing)   **241** *barnacles* geese

STEPHANO: Ay, and this.

> (*A noise of hunters heard. Enter divers Spirits in shape of dogs and hounds, hunting them about, Prospero and Ariel setting them on.*)

PROSPERO: Hey, Mountain, hey!
ARIEL: Silver! there it goes, Silver!
PROSPERO: Fury, Fury! There, Tyrant, there! Hark, hark!

> (*Caliban, Stephano, and Trinculo are driven out*)

Go, charge my goblins that they grind their joints
With dry convulsions, shorten up their sinews   252
With agèd cramps, and more pinch-spotted make them   253
Than pard or cat o' mountain.   254
ARIEL: Hark, they roar!
PROSPERO:
Let them be hunted soundly. At this hour
Lie at my mercy all mine enemies.
Shortly shall all my labors end, and thou
Shalt have the air at freedom. For a little,
Follow, and do me service. (*Exeunt*)

V, i   (*Enter Prospero in his magic robes, and Ariel*)

PROSPERO:
Now does my project gather to a head.
My charms crack not, my spirits obey, and time   2
Goes upright with his carriage. How's the day?
ARIEL:
On the sixth hour, at which time, my lord,
You said our work should cease.
PROSPERO: I did say so
When first I raised the tempest. Say, my spirit,
How fares the King and's followers?
ARIEL: Confined together
In the same fashion as you gave in charge,
Just as you left them—all prisoners, sir,
In the line grove which weather-fends your cell.   10
They cannot budge till your release. The King,   11
His brother, and yours abide all three distracted,
And the remainder mourning over them,
Brimful of sorrow and dismay; but chiefly
Him that you termed, sir, the good old Lord Gonzalo.
His tears run down his beard like winter's drops

---

252 *dry* (resulting from deficiency of 'humors' or bodily liquids)   **253** *aged* i.e. such as old people have   **254** *pard or cat o' mountain* leopard or catamount   **V, i** Before Prospero's cell   **2-3** *time . . . carriage* time's burden is light   **10** *weather-fends* protects from the weather   **11** *till your release* until you release them

From eaves of reeds. Your charm so strongly works 'em,   17
That if you now beheld them, your affections
Would become tender.

PROSPERO: Dost thou think so, spirit?

ARIEL:

Mine would, sir, were I human.

PROSPERO: And mine shall.
Hast thou, which art but air, a touch, a feeling
Of their afflictions, and shall not myself,
One of their kind, that relish all as sharply   23
Passion as they, be kindlier moved than thou art?
Though with their high wrongs I am struck to th' quick,
Yet with my nobler reason 'gainst my fury
Do I take part. The rarer action is
In virtue than in vengeance. They being penitent,
The sole drift of my purpose doth extend
Not a frown further. Go, release them, Ariel.
My charms I'll break, their senses I'll restore,
And they shall be themselves.

ARIEL: I'll fetch them, sir.   (Exit)

PROSPERO:
Ye elves of hills, brooks, standing lakes, and groves,
And ye that on the sands with printless foot
Do chase the ebbing Neptune, and do fly him
When he comes back; you demi-puppets that   36
By moonshine do the green sour ringlets make,
Whereof the ewe not bites; and you whose pastime
Is to make midnight mushrumps, that rejoice   39
To hear the solemn curfew; by whose aid
(Weak masters though ye be) I have bedimmed   41
The noontide sun, called forth the mutinous winds,
And 'twixt the green sea and the azured vault
Set roaring war; to the dread rattling thunder
Have I given fire and rifted Jove's stout oak   45
With his own bolt; the strong-based promontory
Have I made shake and by the spurs plucked up   47
The pine and cedar; graves at my command
Have waked their sleepers, oped, and let 'em forth
By my so potent art. But this rough magic
I here abjure; and when I have required   51
Some heavenly music (which even now I do)
To work mine end upon their senses that   53
This airy charm is for, I'll break my staff,
Bury it certain fathoms in the earth,

---

17 *eaves of reeds* i.e. a thatched roof   23 *relish* feel; *all* quite.   36 *demi-puppets* i.e. fairies   39 *mushrumps*
mushrooms   41 *masters* forces   45 *rifted* split   47 *spurs* roots   51 *required* asked for   53 *their senses that*
the senses of those whom

And deeper than did ever plummet sound
I'll drown my book.

(Solemn music. Here enters Ariel before; then Alonso, with a frantic gesture, attended by Gonzalo; Sebastian and Antonio in like manner, attended by Adrian and Francisco. They all enter the circle which Prospero had made, and there stand charmed; which Prospero observing, speaks.)

A solemn air, and the best comforter   58
To an unsettled fancy, cure thy brains,
Now useless, boiled within thy skull! There stand,
For you are spell-stopped.
Holy Gonzalo, honorable man,
Mine eyes, ev'n sociable to the show of thine,   63
Fall fellowly drops. The charm dissolves apace;   64
And as the morning steals upon the night,
Melting the darkness, so their rising senses
Begin to chase the ignorant fumes that mantle
Their clearer reason. O good Gonzalo,
My true preserver, and a loyal sir
To him thou follow'st, I will pay thy graces   70
Home both in word and deed. Most cruelly
Didst thou, Alonso, use me and my daughter.
Thy brother was a furtherer in the act.
Thou art pinched for't now, Sebastian. Flesh and blood,
You, brother mine, that entertained ambition,
Expelled remorse and nature; who, with Sebastian   76
(Whose inward pinches therefore are most strong),
Would here have killed your king, I do forgive thee,
Unnatural though thou art. Their understanding
Begins to swell, and the approaching tide
Will shortly fill the reasonable shore,
That now lies foul and muddy. Not one of them
That yet looks on me or would know me. Ariel,
Fetch me the hat and rapier in my cell.
I will discase me, and myself present   85
As I was sometime Milan. Quickly, spirit!   86
Thou shalt ere long be free.

(Exit Ariel and returns immediately)

(Ariel sings and helps to attire him)

      Where the bee sucks, there suck I;
      In a cowslip's bell I lie;
      There I couch when owls do cry.

---

58 *and* i.e. which is   **63** *sociable* sympathetic; *show* sight   **64** *Fall* let fall   **70** *graces* favors   **76** *remorse* pity; *nature* natural feeling   **85** *discase* undress   **86** *sometime Milan* when I was Duke of Milan

On the bat's back I do fly
After summer merrily.
Merrily, merrily shall I live now
Under the blossom that hangs on the bough.

PROSPERO:
Why, that's my dainty Ariel! I shall miss thee,
But yet thou shalt have freedom; so, so, so.
To the King's ship, invisible as thou art!
There shalt thou find the mariners asleep
Under the hatches. The master and the boatswain
Being awake, enforce them to this place,
And presently, I prithee.   101

ARIEL:
I drink the air before me, and return   102
Or ere your pulse twice beat.   (*Exit*)

GONZALO:
All torment, trouble, wonder, and amazement
Inhabits here. Some heavenly power guide us
Out of this fearful country!

PROSPERO: Behold, sir King,
The wronged Duke of Milan, Prospero.
For more assurance that a living prince
Does now speak to thee, I embrace thy body,
And to thee and thy company I bid
A hearty welcome.

ALONSO: Whe'r thou be'st he or no.
Or some enchanted trifle to abuse me,   112
As late I have been, I not know. Thy pulse
Beats, as of flesh and blood; and, since I saw thee,
Th' affliction of my mind amends, with which,
I fear, a madness held me. This must crave   116
(An if this be at all) a most strange story.   117
Thy dukedom I resign and do entreat
Thou pardon me my wrongs. But how should Prospero
Be living and be here?

PROSPERO: First, noble friend,
Let me embrace thine age, whose honor cannot
Be measured or confined.

GONZALO: Whether this be
Or be not, I'll not swear.

PROSPERO: You do yet taste
Some subtleties o' th' isle, that will not let you   124
Believe things certain. Welcome, my friends all.

---

101 *presently* right away **102** *drink the air* i.e. consume space **112** *trifle* trick; *abuse* deceive **116** *crave*
require **117** *An if . . . all* if this is really happening **124** *subtleties* (secondary meaning of) elaborate
pastries representing allegorical figures, used in banquets and pageants

(Aside to Sebastian and Antonio)

But you, my brace of lords, were I so minded,
I here could pluck his Highness' frown upon you,   127
And justify you traitors. At this time   128
I will tell no tales.
SEBASTIAN *(aside)*: The devil speaks in him.
PROSPERO: No.
For you, most wicked sir, whom to call brother
Would even infect my mouth, I do forgive
Thy rankest fault—all of them; and require
My dukedom of thee, which perforce I know
Thou must restore.
ALONSO: If thou beest Prospero,
Give us particulars of thy preservation;
How thou hast met us here, who three hours since
Were wracked upon this shore, where I have lost
(How sharp the point of this remembrance is!)
My dear son Ferdinand.
PROSPERO: I am woe for't, sir.   139
ALONSO:
Irreparable is the loss, and patience
Says it is past her cure.
PROSPERO: I rather think
You have not sought her help, of whose soft grace
For the like loss I have her sovereign aid
And rest myself content.
ALONSO: You the like loss?
PROSPERO:
As great to me as late; and, supportable   145
To make the dear loss, have I means much weaker   146
Than you may call to comfort you; for I
Have lost my daughter.
ALONSO: A daughter?
O heavens, that they were living both in Naples.
The King and Queen there! That they were, I wish
Myself were mudded in that oozy bed
Where my son lies. When did you lose your daughter?
PROSPERO:
In this last tempest. I perceive these lords
At this encounter do so much admire   154
That they devour their reason, and scarce think
Their eyes do offices of truth, their words   156
Are natural breath. But, howsoev'r you have
Been justled from your senses, know for certain

127 *pluck* pull down 128 *justify* prove 139 *woe* sorry 145 *late* recent 146 *dear* grievous 154 *admire* wonder 156 *do offices* perform services

That I am Prospero, and that very duke
Which was thrust forth of Milan, who most strangely
Upon this shore, where you were wracked, was landed
To be the lord on't. No more yet of this;
For 'tis a chronicle of day by day,
Not a relation for a breakfast, nor
Befitting this first meeting. Welcome, sir;
This cell's my court. Here have I few attendants,
And subjects none abroad. Pray you look in.
My dukedom since you have given me again,
I will requite you with as good a thing,
At least bring forth a wonder to content ye
As much as me my dukedom.   171

(Here Prospero discovers Ferdinand and Miranda playing at chess)

MIRANDA:
Sweet lord, you play me false.
FERDINAND: No, my dearest love,
I would not for the world.
MIRANDA:
Yes, for a score of kingdoms you should wrangle,   174
And I would call it fair play.
ALONSO: If this prove
A vision of the island, one dear son
Shall I twice lose.
SEBASTIAN: A most high miracle!
FERDINAND:
Though the seas threaten, they are merciful.
I have cursed them without cause.

(Kneels)

ALONSO: Now all the blessings
Of a glad father compass thee about!
Arise, and say how thou cam'st here.
MIRANDA: O, wonder!
How many goodly creatures are there here!
How beauteous mankind is! O brave new world
That has such people in't!
PROSPERO: 'Tis new to thee.
ALONSO:
What is this maid with whom thou wast at play?
Your eld'st acquaintance cannot be three hours.   186
Is she the goddess that hath severed us
And brought us thus together?

---

171 s.d. *discovers* discloses   **174** *should wrangle* i.e. playing fair, as Ferdinand is doing, is not a test of
Miranda's love for him   **186** *eld'st* i.e. longest period of

FERDINAND: Sir, she is mortal;
  But by immortal providence she's mine.
  I chose her when I could not ask my father
  For his advice, nor thought I had one. She
  Is daughter to this famous Duke of Milan,
  Of whom so often I have heard renown
  But never saw before; of whom I have
  Received a second life; and second father
  This lady makes him to me.
ALONSO: I am hers.
  But, O, how oddly will it sound that I
  Must ask my child forgiveness!
PROSPERO: There, sir, stop.
  Let us not burden our remembrance with
  A heaviness that's gone.
GONZALO: I have inly wept,
  Or should have spoke ere this. Look down, you gods,
  And on this couple drop a blessèd crown!
  For it is you that have chalked forth the way
  Which brought us hither.
ALONSO: I say amen, Gonzalo.
GONZALO:
  Was Milan thrust from Milan that his issue
  Should become kings of Naples? O, rejoice
  Beyond a common joy, and set it down
  With gold on lasting pillars: in one voyage
  Did Claribel her husband find at Tunis,
  And Ferdinand her brother found a wife
  Where he himself was lost; Prospero his dukedom
  In a poor isle; and all of us ourselves
  When no man was his own.
ALONSO *(to Ferdinand and Miranda)*:
                              Give me your hands.
  Let grief and sorrow still embrace his heart   214
  That doth not wish you joy.
GONZALO: Be it so! Amen!

(Enter Ariel, with the Master and Boatswain amazedly following)

  O, look, sir; look, sir! Here is more of us!
  I prophesied, if a gallows were on land,
  This fellow could not drown. Now, blasphemy,
  That swear'st grace o'erboard, not an oath on shore?
  Hast thou no mouth by land? What is the news?
BOATSWAIN:
  The best news is that we have safely found

214 *still* forever

Our king and company; the next, our ship,
Which, but three glasses since, we gave out split,
Is tight and yare and bravely rigged as when   224
We first put out to sea.
ARIEL *(aside to Prospero)*: Sir, all this service
Have I done since I went.
PROSPERO *(aside to Ariel)*: My tricksy spirit!   226
ALONSO:
These are not natural events; they strengthen
From strange to stranger. Say, how came you hither?
BOATSWAIN:
If I did think, sir, I were well awake,
I'ld strive to tell you. We were dead of sleep
And (how we know not) all clapped under hatches;
Where, but even now, with strange and several noises   232
Of roaring, shrieking, howling, jingling chains,
And moe diversity of sounds, all horrible,   234
We were awaked; straightway at liberty;
Where we, in all her trim, freshly beheld   236
Our royal, good, and gallant ship, our master
Cap'ring to eye her. On a trice, so please you,   238
Even in a dream, were we divided from them
And were brought moping hither.   240
ARIEL *(aside to Prospero)*:   Was't well done?
PROSPERO *(aside to Ariel)*:
Bravely, my diligence. Thou shalt be free.
ALONSO:
This is as strange a maze as e'er men trod,
And there is in this business more than nature
Was ever conduct of. Some oracle   244
Must rectify our knowledge.
PROSPERO: Sir, my liege,
Do not infest your mind with beating on   246
The strangeness of this business: at picked leisure,
Which shall be shortly, single I'll resolve you   248
(Which to you shall seem probable) of every   249
These happened accidents; till when, be cheerful   250
And think of each thing well.
(Aside to Ariel)   Come hither, spirit.
Set Caliban and his companions free.
Untie the spell.   *(Exit Ariel)*
            How fares my gracious sir?
There are yet missing of your company
Some few odd lads that you remember not.

---

224 *yare* shipshape **226** *tricksy* i.e. ingenious **232** *several* various **234** *moe* more **236** *trim* sale
238 *Cap'ring* dancing for joy; *eye* see **240** *moping* in a daze **244** *conduct* conductor **246** *infest* tease
248 *single* privately; *resolve* explain **249** *every* every one of **250** *accidents* incidents

(Enter Ariel, driving in Caliban, Stephano, and Trinculo, in their stolen apparel)

STEPHANO: Every man shift for all the rest, and let no man take care for himself; for all is but fortune. Coragio, bully-monster, coragio!

TRINCULO: If these be true spies which I wear in my head, here's a goodly   258
sight.

CALIBAN:
O Setebos, these be brave spirits indeed!
How fine my master is! I am afraid
He will chastise me.

SEBASTIAN: Ha, ha!
What things are these, my Lord Antonio?
Will money buy 'em?

ANTONIO: Very like. One of them
Is a plain fish and no doubt marketable.

PROSPERO:
Mark but the badges of these men, my lords,   266
Then say if they be true. This misshapen knave,   267
His mother was a witch, and one so strong
That could control the moon, make flows and ebbs,
And deal in her command without her power.   270
These three have robbed me, and this demi-devil
(For he's a bastard one) had plotted with them
To take my life. Two of these fellows you
Must know and own; this thing of darkness I
Acknowledge mine.

CALIBAN: I shall be pinched to death.

ALONSO:
Is not this Stephano, my drunken butler?

SEBASTIAN:
He is drunk now: where had he wine?

ALONSO:
And Trinculo is reeling ripe: where should they
Find this grand liquor that hath gilded 'em?
How cam'st thou in this pickle?

TRINCULO: I have been in such a pickle, since I saw you last, that I fear me   281
will never out of my bones. I shall not fear fly-blowing.

SEBASTIAN: Why, how now, Stephano?

STEPHANO: O, touch me not! I am not Stephano, but a cramp.   284

PROSPERO: You'ld be king o' the isle, sirrah?

STEPHANO: I should have been a sore one then.   286

ALONSO:
This is a strange thing as e'er I looked on.

---

258 *spies* eyes   266 *badges of these men* signs of these servants   267 *true* honest   270 *her* i.e. the moon's; *without* beyond   281 *pickle* (1) predicament, (2) preservative (from the horse-pond; hence insects will let him alone)   284 *Stephano* (this name is said to be a slang Neapolitan term for stomach)   286 *sore* (1) tyrannical, (2) aching

PROSPERO:
    He is as disproportioned in his manners
    As in his shape. Go, sirrah, to my cell;
    Take with you your companions. As you look
    To have my pardon, trim it handsomely.
CALIBAN:
    Ay, that I will; and I'll be wise hereafter,
    And seek for grace. What a thrice-double ass
    Was I to take this drunkard for a god
    And worship this dull fool!
PROSPERO: Go to! Away!
ALONSO:
    Hence, and bestow your luggage where you found it.
SEBASTIAN: Or stole it rather.

                    (Exeunt Caliban, Stephano, and Trinculo)

PROSPERO:
    Sir, I invite your Highness and your train
    To my poor cell, where you shall take your rest
    For this one night; which, part of it, I'll waste   300
    With such discourse as, I not doubt, shall make it
    Go quick away—the story of my life,
    And the particular accidents gone by
    Since I came to this isle; and in the morn
    I'll bring you to your ship, and so to Naples,
    Where I have hope to see the nuptial
    Of these our dear-beloved solemnizèd;   307
    And thence retire me to my Milan, where
    Every third thought shall be my grave.
ALONSO: I long
    To hear the story of your life, which must
    Take the ear strangely.   311
PROSPERO: I'll deliver all;
    And promise you calm seas, auspicious gales,
    And sail so expeditious that shall catch   313
    Your royal fleet far off.—My Ariel, chick,
    That is thy charge. Then to the elements
    Be free, and fare thou well!—Please you draw near.

                                          (Exeunt omnes)

                              EPILOGUE
                          spoken by Prospero.

                Now my charms are all o'erthrown,
                And what strength I have's mine own,
                Which is most faint. Now 'tis true
                I must be here confined by you,

300 *waste* spend   307 *solemnizèd* (accent second syllable)   311 *Take* captivate; *deliver* tell   313 *sail* sailing

Or sent to Naples. Let me not,
Since I have my dukedom got
And pardoned the deceiver, dwell
In this bare island by your spell;   8
But release me from my bands   9
With the help of your good hands.   10
Gentle breath of yours my sails
Must fill, or else my project fails,
Which was to please. Now I want   13
Spirits to enforce, art to enchant;
And my ending is despair
Unless I be relieved by prayer,
Which pierces so that it assaults
Mercy itself and frees all faults.
As you from crimes would pardoned be,
Let your indulgence set me free.   *(Exit)*

Epi. 8 *spell* i.e. silence   **9** *bands* bonds   **10** *hands* i.e. applause to break the spell   **13** *want* lack.

CHAPTER 3

Social Drama

Tragedy and comedy present life's enduring subjects—love, marriage, death, ambition, and revenge. Romance and satire embody them less concretely in individualized human beings and more abstractly as ideals (the four cardinal virtues) or vices (the seven deadly sins). Tragedy and comedy, as well as romance and satire, are, in a sense, varied containers into which the same contents are poured. Playwrights are sometimes not so interested in the shape of the container as its contents, the material of life. This is especially true when the theme, the idea upon which the play is built, forces our attention upon the world outside the play.

The plays in this section stress that social world. They mute or blend comedy and tragedy within a social context. They move from individual fortune to tell us something about society at large. *An Enemy of the People* raises questions about individual responsibilities to self and neighbors and to one's vision of the truth. *The Cherry Orchard,* which Chekhov considered comic, gives a dissonant and ambiguous picture of society characteristic of much modern drama. *Miss Julie, Death of a Salesman,* and *A Raisin in the Sun* catch personal tragedy within the sticky social web that causes it, leaving us pondering the society's as well as the individual's errors and triumphs.

An Enemy of the People

An Enemy of the People examines the social, economic, and political relationships within a small town threatened with closing of the baths that are its chief municipal pride and the source of its economic well-being. Grafting a personal drama on a political one by making the "enemy" the brother to the mayor, Ibsen depicted society's large and impersonal forces in sharply defined human dimensions.

AN ENEMY OF THE PEOPLE*

Henrik Ibsen   (1828–1906)

CHARACTERS

Dr. Thomas Stockmann, doctor at the Baths
Mrs. Katherine Stockmann, his wife
Petra, their daughter, a teacher
Ejlif }
Morten } their sons, 13 and 10 years old
Peter Stockmann, the doctor's elder brother, Mayor, Chief of Police,
Chairman of the Board of the Baths, &c.
Morten Kiil, owner of a tannery, Mrs. Stockmann's foster-father
Hovstad, editor of the *People's Herald*
Billing, a journalist
Captain Horster
Aslaksen, a printer
Attending a public meeting are: men of all classes, some women and
a group of schoolboys

The action takes place in a coastal town in Southern Norway

Act One

Evening. Dr. Stockmann's living-room, simply but tastefully furnished. In the side-wall, right, are two doors, one of which upstage leads to the hall, and the other to the doctor's study. On the opposite wall and directly facing the hall door, another door leads to the rest of the house. In the middle of this wall stands a stove; downstage of it is a sofa; above it hangs a mirror and in front of it is an oval table covered with a cloth. On the table, a shaded lamp is burning. In the back wall, the door to the dining-room stands open. Within, the table is laid for supper; a lighted lamp stands on the table.

Billing, a napkin tucked under his chin, is seated within at the supper table. Mrs. Stockmann stands by the table and hands him a serving dish on which is a large joint of beef. The other places at table are empty, and the table is in disarray as though after a meal.

Mrs. Stockmann: Well, if you will arrive an hour late, Mr. Billing, you'll have to put up with everything being cold.

Billing *(eating)*: It's absolutely delicious, really excellent.

Mrs. Stockmann: You know how strict my husband is about keeping punctually· to his mealtimes . . . .

Billing: It doesn't matter to me in the least. In fact I almost believe it tastes better, sitting down like this to it, alone and undisturbed.

Mrs. Stockmann: Ah well, as long as you enjoy it . . . . *(Turns to the hall door and listens.)* That's probably Hovstad.

Billing: Quite likely.

---

* Translated by James Walter McFarlane.

(Peter Stockmann, the Mayor, enters; he is wearing an overcoat and his mayor's hat, and he carries a stick)

MAYOR: A very good evening to you, Katherine.

MRS. STOCKMANN *(coming into the living-room)*: Oh. It's you! Good evening. How nice of you to drop in like this.

MAYOR: I happened to be passing, so . . . *(With a glance towards the dining-room)* Oh, but it seems you have company.

MRS. STOCKMANN *(rather embarrassed)*: No, not really. He just happened to drop in. *(Quickly)* Wouldn't you like to join him and let me get you something to eat?

MAYOR: Who, me? No thank you. Heavens above! A cooked meal in the evening! Not with my digestion.

MRS. STOCKMANN: Oh, couldn't you just for once . . . ?

MAYOR: Bless you, no. I stick to my tea and bread and butter. It's better for one's health in the long run . . . as well as being more economical.

MRS. STOCKMANN *(smiles)*: Now you mustn't get the idea that Thomas and I are terribly extravagant, either.

MAYOR: Not *you*, Katherine. I'd never think that of you. *(Points to the doctor's study)* Isn't he at home?

MRS. STOCKMANN: No, he's gone for a little walk after his supper . . . with the boys.

MAYOR: I wonder if that really does one any good? *(Listens)* That's him now.

MRS. STOCKMANN: No, I don't think it's him. *(There is a knock on the door.)* Come in!

(Hovstad comes in from the hall)

MBS. STOCKMANN: Oh, it's Mr. Hovstad.

HOVSTAD: Yes, you must excuse me, but I got held up at the printer's. Good evening, Mr. Mayor.

MAYOR *(bowing rather stiffly)*: Good evening! A business call, no doubt?

HOVSTAD: Partly. It's in connection with something for the paper.

MAYOR: That I can imagine. From all accounts, my brother is a prolific contributor to the *People's Herald*.

HOVSTAD: Yes, whenever he wants to get any particular home-truths off his chest, he writes a piece for the *Herald*.

MRS. STOCKMANN *(to Hovstad)*: But won't you . . . ? *(She points to the dining-room)*

MAYOR: Indeed, and why not? Who am I to blame him if he decides to write for the class of reader he can expect the greatest response from! And in any case, there's no reason for me to feel any personal animosity towards your paper, Mr. Hovstad.

HOVSTAD: No, I don't think there is.

MAYOR: All in all, there is an admirable spirit of tolerance in our little town . . . a sense of civic pride. That's what comes of having a great communal undertaking to unite us . . . an undertaking which concerns all right-thinking citizens in equal measure. . . .

HOVSTAD: The Baths, you mean.

MAYOR: Exactly. We have our splendid new Baths. Mark my words! The prosperity of the town will come to depend more and more on the Baths, Mr. Hovstad. No doubt about it!

Mrs. Stockmann: Thomas says the same.

Mayor: Just look at the quite extraordinary way things have improved, even in the last year or two. People have more money! There's more life, more things going on. Land and property are going up in value every day.

Hovstad: And unemployment falling.

Mayor: Yes, that too. The burden of the poor-rate on the propertied classes has, I am happy to say, been considerably reduced—and it will be even less if only we have a really good summer this year . . . with plenty of visitors, and lots of convalescents to help to give the place a reputation.

Hovstad: And things are looking pretty promising in that way, they tell me.

Mayor: The prospects are very encouraging. Every day we receive more inquiries about accommodation and things like that.

Hovstad: Well then, I suppose the doctor's article will just come in nicely.

Mayor: Has he been writing something else?

Hovstad: This is something he wrote during the winter, giving an account of the Baths and recommending the place generally as a very healthy spot. But I didn't use the article at the time.

Mayor: Aha! I expect there was a snag in it somewhere.

Hovstad: No, it wasn't that. But I thought it might be better to hold it over till the spring; now's the time when people start thinking about their summer holidays. . . .

Mayor: Very sensible, very sensible indeed, Mr. Hovstad.

Mrs. Stockmann: Yes, Thomas is quite indefatigable if it's anything to do with the Baths.

Mayor: Well, as he's one of its officials it's only natural.

Hovstad: Besides, he was the one who started the whole thing.

Mayor: *He* was! Indeed! Yes, this isn't the first time I've heard of people getting that idea. But I rather imagined *I* too had had a modest part in this enterprise.

Mrs. Stockmann: Yes, that's what Thomas is always saying.

Hovstad: Of course, who would want to deny that, Mr. Mayor. It was you who got things moving, got it going as a practical concern, we all know that, of course. All I meant was that the idea came first from Dr. Stockmann.

Mayor: Yes, my brother's always had plenty of ideas—more's the pity. But when it's a matter of getting things done, you have to look round for a different type of man, Mr. Hovstad. I should at least have thought that the members of *this* household would . . .

Mrs. Stockmann: My dear Peter . . .

Hovstad: But Mr. Mayor, how can you . . . ?

Mrs. Stockmann: You go and get yourself something to eat, Mr. Hovstad. My husband is sure to be back by the time you're finished.

Hovstad: Thanks. Perhaps just a bite.

(He goes into the dining-room)

Mayor *(lowering his voice)*: Funny, these people from peasant stock! They never have any tact.

MRS. STOCKMANN: But there's no point in upsetting yourself about it! Can't you and Thomas share the credit like brothers!

MAYOR: Yes, one would have thought so. But apparently it isn't everybody who is content to share.

MRS. STOCKMANN: Oh, nonsense. You and Thomas get on perfectly well together on this point. *(Listens)* That's him now, I think.

(She goes over and opens the door into the hall)

DR. STOCKMANN *(laughing and talking outside)*: Here we are, another visitor for you, Katherine. Isn't this fun, eh! Come in, Captain Horster. Hang your coat on that peg there. You don't bother with an overcoat, eh? You know, Katherine, I ran into him on the street.... Had a terrible job persuading him to come along.

(Captain Horster enters and bows to Mrs. Stockmann)

DR. STOCKMANN *(in the doorway)*: In you go, lads. They are absolutely ravenous again, my dear. Come along, Captain Horster, what do you say to a bit of roast beef...?

(He urges Horster into the dining-room; Ejlif and Morten go in also)

MRS. STOCKMANN: But Thomas, don't you see...?

DR. STOCKMANN *(turns in the doorway)*: Oh, it's you, Peter. *(Walks across and shakes hands.)* Well, this is very pleasant.

MAYOR: Unfortunately I can only stay a minute or two....

DR. STOCKMANN: Rubbish! There'll be some hot toddy coming up soon. You haven't forgotten the toddy, Katherine, have you?

MRS. STOCKMANN: Of course not! I've got the kettle on.

(She goes into the dining-room)

MAYOR: Toddy as well!

DR. STOCKMANN: Yes, sit yourself down and we'll make an evening of it.

MAYOR: Thanks, but I don't care for drinking parties.

DR. STOCKMANN: This isn't a drinking party.

MAYOR: It seems to me... *(He looks into the dining-room)* It's incredible the amount of food they manage to put away.

DR. STOCKMANN *(rubbing his hands)*: Yes, isn't it grand to see young people eating well? Such an appetite they've got! That's as it ought to be. They need food ... need to build up their strength. They'll be the ones to stir things up a bit in the coming years, Peter.

MAYOR: And what, if I may ask, is it that requires 'stirring up', as you put it?

DR. STOCKMANN: Ah, you'll have to ask the younger generation about that—when the time comes. We just can't see it, of course. Stands to reason! A couple of old fogies like you and me...!

MAYOR: Well, really! That's a most extraordinary description....

DR. STOCKMANN: Oh, you mustn't take me too seriously, Peter. Thing is, I feel so full of the joy of everything, you see. I can't tell you how happy I feel, surrounded by all this growing, vigorous life. What a glorious age this is to live in! It's as if a whole new world were springing up all around.

MAYOR: Do you really think so?

DR. STOCKMANN: Well, you can't see it as clearly as I can, of course. All your life you've lived amongst this kind of thing, and it doesn't make the same sharp impression on you. But think of me, living all those years in the North, cut off from everything, hardly ever seeing a new face, never the chance of any decent conversation ... for me it's like coming to some great throbbing metropolis.

MAYOR: Huh! Metropolis...!

DR. STOCKMANN: Well, I know everything's on a small scale compared with a lot of other places. But there's life here ... and promise ... and innumerable things to work and strive for. *That's* what counts. (*Shouts*) Katherine, has the postman been?

MRS. STOCKMANN (*in the dining-room*): No, nobody's been.

DR. STOCKMANN: And then what it is to have a decent income, Peter! That's something one learns to appreciate after living on a starvation wage as we did. . . .

MAYOR: Surely now ...

DR. STOCKMANN: Oh yes we did. Let me tell you, things were often pretty tight up there. But now I can live like a gentleman. Today, for instance, we had a joint of beef for dinner; it did us for supper, too. Wouldn't you like a taste? Or let me show it to you, anyway. Come here. . . .

MAYOR: No, no, it's not necessary. . . .

DR. STOCKMANN: Well, come here then. Look, we've got a new table-cloth.

MAYOR: So I noticed.

DR. STOCKMANN: And we've got a lampshade. See? Katherine managed to save all that. Don't you think it makes the room look cosy? Just stand over here—no, no, not there—here, that's right! See? How it directs the light down like that ... ? I think it looks really elegant, don't you?

MAYOR: Yes, for those who can afford such luxuries. . . .

DR. STOCKMANN: Oh, yes! Of course I can afford it. Katherine says I earn very nearly as much as we spend.

MAYOR: Nearly ... yes!

DR. STOCKMANN: But a man of science ought to have a decent standard of living. I bet you there's many a civil servant spends more in a year than I do.

MAYOR: Well, I dare say there is. A civil servant, a senior executive. . . .

DR. STOCKMANN: Well, an ordinary businessman then. I'm sure that sort of person spends very much more. . . .

MAYOR: That depends on circumstances.

DR. STOCKMANN: Anyway, I don't go throwing my money away on any old thing, Peter. But I feel I can't deny myself the pleasure of having people in. I need something like that, you see, after being out of things for so long. For me it's like one of the necessities of life—to enjoy the company of eager young people, with initiative and minds of their own. That's the kind of person you'll find sitting at my table, enjoying their food. I wish you knew Hovstad a bit better. . . .

MAYOR: Ah, Hovstad, that's right. He was telling me he's going to print another one of your articles.

DR. STOCKMANN: One of my articles?

MAYOR: Yes, about the Baths. An article you'd apparently written during the winter.

DR. STOCKMANN: Oh, that one! Well, I don't want that one in just now.

MAYOR: Don't you? This seems to me to be exactly the right time for it.

DR. STOCKMANN: Yes, that's right . . . in ordinary circumstances. . . .

(He walks about the room)

MAYOR *(watching him)*: And what's so extraordinary about the present circumstances?

DR. STOCKMANN *(halts)*: In point of fact, Peter, that's something I can't tell you for the moment. Not this evening, anyway. There might be quite a lot that's unusual about the present state of affairs; on the other hand, it might be nothing at all. It might very well be just my imagination.

MAYOR: I must admit it all sounds very mysterious. What's going on? Why am I being kept out of it? I would remind you that, as Chairman of the Board of the Baths, I . . .

DR. STOCKMANN: And I would remind you that I . . . Oh, let's not jump down each other's throats, Peter.

MAYOR: Heaven forbid! I'm not in the habit of jumping down people's throats, as you put it. But I must insist most emphatically that all matters be considered and dealt with through the proper channels and by the appropriate authorities. I cannot permit any dubious or underhand methods.

DR. STOCKMANN: Since when have *I* used dubious or underhand methods?

MAYOR: You have a chronic disposition to take things into your own hands, at least. And in a well-ordered community, that can be equally reprehensible. The individual must be ready to subordinate himself to the community as a whole; or, more precisely, to the authorities charged with the welfare of that community.

DR. STOCKMANN: That may well be. But what the devil has that got to do with me?

MAYOR: Everything. Because, my dear Thomas, that's just the thing you don't seem to want to learn. But mark my words; one of these days you'll pay for it . . . sooner or later. I'm telling you. Goodbye.

DR. STOCKMANN: Have you gone stark, staring mad? You are barking up the wrong tree altogether. . . .

MAYOR: I'm not in the habit of doing that. And now if I may be excused. . . . *(He calls into the dining-room.)* Goodbye, Katherine. Goodbye, gentlemen.

(He leaves)

MRS. STOCKMANN *(comes into the living-room)*: Has he gone?

DR. STOCKMANN: Yes, he has; and in high dudgeon.

MRS. STOCKMANN: Thomas, my dear, what have you been doing to him this time?

DR. STOCKMANN: Absolutely nothing. He can't expect an account from me before the proper time.

MRS. STOCKMANN: What are you expected to give him an account of?

DR. STOCKMANN: Hm! Don't bother me about that now, Katherine.—Funny the postman doesn't come.

(Hovstad, Billing and Horster have risen from the table and come into the living-room. Ejlif and Morten follow them after a while.)

BILLING *(stretches himself)*: Ah! A supper like that and, damn me, if it doesn't make you feel like a new man!

HOVSTAD: Our Mayor wasn't in the best of moods this evening.

DR. STOCKMANN: It's his stomach. Digestion's none too good.

HOVSTAD: It was mainly us two from the *Herald* he couldn't stomach, I reckon.

MRS. STOCKMANN: I thought you seemed to be getting on quite nicely with him.

HOVSTAD: Oh yes, but it's only a kind of armistice.

BILLING: That's it. That describes it exactly.

DR. STOCKMANN: We mustn't forget that Peter's a lonely person, poor chap. He hasn't any proper home where he can relax. Business, nothing but business! And all that damned weak tea he keeps pouring into himself. Now then, lads, pull your chairs up to the table. Katherine, don't we get any toddy?

MRS. STOCKMANN *(makes for the dining-room)*: I'm just going to get it.

DR. STOCKMANN: Come and sit beside me on the sofa, Captain Horster. It's so rarely we see you. Do sit down, my friends.

(The men seat themselves round the table. Mrs. Stockmann enters with a tray on which there is a kettle, glasses, decanters and so on.)

MRS. STOCKMANN: There we are. This is Arrack, and this is rum, and this is cognac. Everybody just help themselves.

DR. STOCKMANN *(takes a glass)*: Ah, we will that! *(Whilst the toddy is being mixed.)* Let's have the cigars out, too. Ejlif, you know where the box is kept. And you, Morten, can bring my pipe. *(The boys go into the room on the right.)* I have a suspicion Ejlif helps himself to a cigar now and then, but I don't let on I know. *(Calls.)* My smoking-cap as well, Morten! Katherine, could you tell him where I've put it. Ah! he's got it. *(The boys bring the various articles)* Help yourselves, my friends. I'll stick to my pipe. Many's the time this one's done the rounds with me, fair weather and foul, up there in the North. *(They clink glasses.)* Your health! Ah, it's much better to be sitting nice and snug in here.

MRS. STOCKMANN *(sits knitting)*: Will you be sailing soon, Captain Horster?

HORSTER: I reckon we'll be ready by next week.

MRS. STOCKMANN: And then you're off to America?

HORSTER: That's the intention.

BILLING: Then you won't be able to vote in the municipal election.

HORSTER: Is there going to be an election?

BILLING: Didn't you know?

HORSTER: No, I don't bother about things like that.

BILLING: But you take an interest in public affairs, I suppose?

HORSTER: No, I don't know the first thing about them.

BILLING: I think people ought to vote, all the same.

HORSTER: Even those who have no idea what it's all about?

BILLING: No idea? What do you mean? Society's like a ship; everybody must help to steer it.

HORSTER: That might be all very well on dry land; but it wouldn't work very well at sea.

HOVSTAD: It's strange how little most seafaring people care about what goes on ashore.

BILLING: Quite remarkable.

DR. STOCKMANN: Sailors are like birds of passage, equally at home in the north or in the south. All the more reason for the rest of us to be even more active, Mr. Hovstad. Is there anything of public interest in the *Herald* tomorrow?

HOVSTAD: Nothing about municipal affairs. But I thought of putting in your article the day after. . . .

DR. STOCKMANN: Oh damn it, yes! That article. Listen, you must hold it over for a while.

HOVSTAD: Really! It just happens we have room for it now, and it seemed to be the right time for it. . . .

DR. STOCKMANN: Yes, yes, maybe you are right; but you'll have to wait all the same. I'll explain later. . . .

(Petra, wearing a hat and a cloak, comes in from the hall, a pile of exercise books under her arm)

PETRA: Good evening.

DR. STOCKMANN: Is that you, Petra? Good evening!

(Greetings all round. Petra takes off her things and puts them, along with the exercise books, on a chair beside the door.)

PETRA: So you've all been sitting here enjoying yourselves while I've been out slaving.

DR. STOCKMANN: Now *you* come and enjoy yourself too, then.

BILLING: Can I get you something to drink?

PETRA *(comes over to the table)*: Thanks. But I'd rather do it myself. You always make it too strong. But I'm forgetting, Father, I have a letter for you.

(Goes over to the chair where her things are)

DR. STOCKMANN: A letter? Who from?

PETRA *(feels in her coat pocket)*: The postman gave me it just as I was going out. . . .

DR. STOCKMANN *(gets up and goes across to her)*: And you haven't brought it out before now!

PETRA: I hadn't time to run back again with it. Here it is.

DR. STOCKMANN *(seizing the letter)*: Let me see it. Let me see it, child. *(Looks at the address)* Yes, that's it. . . .

MRS. STOCKMANN: Is *that* the one you have been waiting for, Thomas?

DR. STOCKMANN: Yes, that's the one. Excuse me if I take it straight into . . . Where can I find a light, Katherine? Is there still no lamp in my study!

MRS. STOCKMANN: Yes, of course. There's a lamp already lit on your desk.

DR. STOCKMANN: Good, good. Excuse me a minute. . . .

(He goes into his room, right)

PETRA: What can that be, Mother?

MRS. STOCKMANN: I don't know. He's done nothing else these last few days but ask whether the postman's been.

BILLING: Presumably some country patient.

PETRA: Poor Father! All this work, it's getting too much for him. (*She mixes her drink.*) Ah, I'm going to enjoy this!

HOVSTAD: Have you been taking Evening Classes again today?

PETRA (*sipping her glass*): Two hours.

BILLING: And four hours this morning at the Institute.

PETRA (*sits at the table*): Five hours.

MRS. STOCKMANN: And tonight I see you have essays to correct.

PETRA: A whole bundle of them.

HORSTER: You've got plenty of work to do yourself, it seems.

PETRA: Yes, but that's all right. It makes you feel so gloriously tired afterwards.

BILLING: Do you like that?

PETRA: Yes, it makes you sleep so well.

MORTEN: You must be a dreadful sinner, Petra!

PETRA: Sinner?

MORTEN: Working as hard as you do. Mr. Rörlund says that work is a punishment for our sins.

EJLIF: Puh! You must be stupid, believing a thing like that!

MRS. STOCKMANN: Now, now, Ejlif!

BILLING (*laughs*): Oh, that's good, that is!

HOVSTAD: Don't you want to work as hard as that, Morten?

MORTEN: No, I don't.

HOVSTAD: Well, what *do* you want to be when you grow up?

MORTEN: I want to be a Viking.

EJLIF: Well, you'd have to be a heathen.

MORTEN: All right, I'll be a heathen.

BILLING: I'm with you there, Morten. I say exactly the same.

MRS. STOCKMANN (*making signs*): I'm sure you wouldn't really do anything of the kind.

BILLING: Yes I would, so help me! I *am* a heathen, and proud of it. You watch, we'll all be heathens before long.

MORTEN: And *then* can we do exactly what we like?

BILLING: Well, you see, Morten . . .

MRS. STOCKMANN: Now, boys, off you go now; I'm sure you've got some homework for tomorrow.

EJLIF: Couldn't *I* just stay on a little bit longer . . . ?

MRS. STOCKMANN: No. Off you go now, both of you.

(*The boys say good night and go into the room, left*)

HOVSTAD: Do you really think it's bad for the boys to listen to things like that?

MRS. STOCKMANN: Oh, I don't know. But I don't much like it.

PETRA: Oh, Mother! I think you're quite mistaken there.

MRS. STOCKMANN: Yes, that's quite possible. But I *don't* like it, not in my own home.

PETRA: All this hypocrisy, both at home and at school. At home one mustn't say anything; and at school we have to stand there and lie to the children.

HORSTER: Lie to them?

PETRA: Yes. Can't you see we have to teach all sorts of things we don't even believe in ourselves?

BILLING: That's only too true.

PETRA: If only I had the money, I'd start a school myself, where things would be run very differently.

BILLING: Huh! The money!

HORSTER: Well, if you've got anything like that in mind, Miss Stockmann, I'd be glad to offer you the necessary accommodation. My father's big old house is standing there practically empty; there's an enormous dining-room on the ground floor . . . .

PETRA (*laughs*): Thanks, thanks very much. But nothing's likely to come of it.

HOVSTAD: No, I think Miss Petra's much more likely to join the ranks of the journalists. By the way, have you had any time to look at that English story you promised to translate for us?

PETRA: No, not yet. But you'll have it in good time.

(*Doctor Stockmann comes out of his room, with the open letter in his hand*)

DR. STOCKMANN (*waving the letter*): Well! Here's a bit of news that will set a few tongues wagging about the town!

BILLING: News?

MRS. STOCKMANN: What news?

DR. STOCKMANN: A great discovery, Katherine!

HOVSTAD: Really?

MRS. STOCKMANN: Which you've made?

DR. STOCKMANN: Which I've made, yes. (*Walks up and down*) Now let them come as they always do, and say it's some madman's crazy idea! Ah, but they'll watch their step this time! They'll watch out this time, I'll bet.

PETRA: But, Father, tell us what this is all about.

DR. STOCKMANN: Yes, yes, just give me time and you'll hear all about it. Ah, if only I had Peter here! Yes, it lets you see how we men go about our affairs as blind as bats . . . .

HOVSTAD: What do you mean, Doctor?

DR. STOCKMANN (*stands by the table*): Is it not generally believed that our town is a healthy place?

HOVSTAD: Yes, of course.

DR. STOCKMANN: A quite exceptionally healthy place, in fact . . . a place highly commended on this score both for the sick and for the healthy . . . .

MRS. STOCKMANN: Yes, but my dear Thomas . . .

DR. STOCKMANN: And have we not recommended it and acclaimed it? I myself have written repeatedly, both in the *Herald* and in a number of pamphlets. . . .

HOVSTAD: Well, what of it?

DR. STOCKMANN: And then these Baths—the so-called 'artery' of the town, or the 'nerve centre', and the devil only knows what else they've been called. . . .

BILLING: 'The throbbing heart of the town', as I was once, in a festive moment, moved to call it.

DR. STOCKMANN: Quite so. But do you know what they are in reality, these great and splendid and glorious Baths that have cost such a lot of money—do you know what they are?

HOVSTAD: No, what are they?

MRS. STOCKMANN: Yes, what are they?

DR. STOCKMANN: The Baths are nothing but a cesspool.

PETRA: The Baths, Father!

MRS. STOCKMANN *(at the same time)*: Our Baths!

HOVSTAD *(likewise)*: But, Doctor . . . !

BILLING: Absolutely incredible!

DR. STOCKMANN: The whole establishment is a whited poisoned sepulchre, I tell you! A most serious danger to health! All that filth up at Mölledal, where there's such an awful stench—it's all seeping into the pipes that lead to the pump-room! And that same damned, poisonous muck is seeping out on the beach as well!

HORSTER: Where the bathing place is, you mean?

DR. STOCKMANN: Exactly.

HOVSTAD: How are you so certain about all this, Doctor?

DR. STOCKMANN: I have investigated the position with scrupulous thoroughness. Oh, I've had my suspicions long enough. Last year there were a number of curious cases of sickness among the visitors . . . typhoid and gastric fever . . . .

MRS. STOCKMANN: Yes, so there were.

DR. STOCKMANN: It was thought at the time that the visitors had brought their infections with them. But afterwards . . . during the winter . . . I began to have other ideas. So I carried out a few tests on the water, as far as I could.

MRS. STOCKMANN: So *that's* what's been keeping you so busy!

DR. STOCKMANN: Yes, you may well say I've been busy, Katherine. But of course I didn't have all the necessary scientific equipment. So I sent some samples—drinking water as well as sea-water—up to the university to get an exact chemical analysis.

HOVSTAD: Which you have now received?

DR. STOCKMANN *(shows the letter)*: Here it is! It testifies to the presence in the water of putrefied organic matter . . . it's full of bacteria. It is extremely dangerous to health, internally and externally.

MRS. STOCKMANN: What a mercy you found out in time!

DR. STOCKMANN: You may well say so.

HOVSTAD: And what do you intend to do now, Doctor?

DR. STOCKMANN: To see the matter put right, of course.

HOVSTAD: Can that be done?

DR. STOCKMANN: It must be done. Otherwise the whole establishment is useless, ruined. But there's no need for that. It's quite clear to me what must now be done.

MRS. STOCKMANN: But, my dear Thomas, what made you keep all this so secret?

DR. STOCKMANN: Did you expect me to run all round town gossiping about it before I was absolutely certain? No thank you! I'm not such a fool as all that.

PETRA: Still, your own family . . .

DR. STOCKMANN: No, not a living soul. Still, you can run round in the morning to the old 'Badger' . . . .

MRS. STOCKMANN: Please, Thomas!

DR. STOCKMANN: All right, to your grandfather, then. Yes, now we'll give that old boy something that will really open his eyes. He's another one who thinks I'm a bit cracked—oh yes, there are plenty more with the same idea, I can see. But now these good people are going to see something—they're certainly going to see something, this time. *(He walks round rubbing his hands.)* What a commotion this is going to cause in the town, Katherine! You've no idea! All the pipes will have to be re-laid.

HOVSTAD *(rising)*: All the pipes . . . ?

DR. STOCKMANN: Naturally. The intake is sited too low down; it will have to be moved much higher up.

PETRA: So you were right after all.

DR. STOCKMANN: Ah, you remember, Petra? I wrote in opposing it, when they were drawing up the plans. But at that time nobody would listen to me. Well, now I'm going to let them have it. Naturally I've written a report for the Board—it's been lying there all ready for the past week. I was only waiting for this to come. *(He points to the letter.)* But now we'll get this off at once. *(He goes into his room and comes back with a sheaf of papers.)* Look! Four closely written sheets! And the letter attached. A newspaper, Katherine! Something to wrap it in. Good! There we are! Give it to . . . to . . . *(Stamps his foot)* . . . what the devil's her name again? Anyway, give it to that girl, and tell her to take it straight down to the Mayor.

(Mrs. Stockmann takes the packet and goes out through the dining-room)

PETRA: What do you think Uncle Peter's going to say, Father?

DR. STOCKMANN: What do you expect him to say? He can't help but be pleased that an important matter like this has been brought to light, surely.

HOVSTAD: Do you mind if we put a little paragraph in the *Herald* about your discovery?

DR. STOCKMANN: I should be extremely grateful if you would.

HOVSTAD: The sooner the public hears about this, the better.

DR. STOCKMANN: Certainly.

MRS. STOCKMANN *(returning)*: She's just gone with it now.

BILLING: You'll be the leading light of the town, Dr. Stockmann, damn me if you won't!

DR. STOCKMANN *(walks happily up and down)*: Oh, don't be silly! I've only done my duty. It just happened to be a lucky strike, that's all. All the same . . .

BILLING: Hovstad, don't you think the town ought to organize something to show its appreciation to Dr. Stockmann?

HOVSTAD: I'll certainly put it forward.

BILLING: And I'll talk it over with Aslaksen.

DR. STOCKMANN: Please, please, my dear friends! Let's have no more of this nonsense. I won't hear of it. And if the Board starts getting any ideas about increasing my salary, I shall refuse. Do you hear me, Katherine?—I won't take it.

MRS. STOCKMANN: Quite right, Thomas.

PETRA *(raising her glass)*: Your health, Father!

HOVSTAD: }
BILLING: }   Your health, Dr. Stockmann!

HORSTER *(clinking glasses with him)*: Here's wishing you joy of it!

DR. STOCKMANN: Thank you, my dear friends, thank you! I am extremely happy. . . . What a wonderful thing it is to feel that one's been of some service to one's home town and fellow citizens. Hurrah, Katherine!

(He puts his arms round her and whirls her round and round; she screams and tries to resist. Laughter, applause, and cheering for the Doctor. The boys poke their heads in at the door.)

Act Two

The Doctor's living-room; the door to the dining-room is shut. It is morning. Mrs. Stockmann comes out of the dining-room, carrying in her hand a sealed letter; she crosses to the door of the Doctor's study, right, and peeps in.

Mrs. Stockmann: Are you there, Thomas?

Dr. Stockmann *(within)*: Yes, I've just got back. *(Comes in)* What is it?

Mrs. Stockmann: A letter from your brother.

(She hands him the letter)

Dr. Stockmann: Aha, let us see. *(He opens the envelope and reads)* 'Your manuscript is herewith returned. . . .' *(He reads on to himself in a low murmur)* Hm!

Mrs. Stockmann: What does he say?

Dr. Stockmann: Oh, just that he'll look in about midday.

Mrs. Stockmann: You mustn't forget to be at home this time.

Dr. Stockmann: I'll manage that all right; I've finished all my morning calls.

Mrs. Stockmann: I'm awfully curious to know how he's taking it.

Dr. Stockmann: He'll not be very pleased that I was the one to make the discovery and not he, you'll see.

Mrs. Stockmann: Doesn't that worry you a little?

Dr. Stockmann: Oh, he'll be glad enough really, you know. It's just that Peter can't bear to see anybody other than himself doing things for the town.

Mrs. Stockmann: Well, you know what I think, Thomas? I think you should be a dear and share the credit with him. Couldn't you drop a hint that it was he who first put you on the track . . . ?

Dr. Stockmann: Certainly, for all it matters to me. I only want to see that something gets done about it. . . .

(Old Morten Kiil puts his head round the hall door, looks round inquiringly, and chuckles to himself)

Morten Kiil *(slyly)*: This thing . . . is it true?

Mrs. Stockmann *(crosses towards him)*: Father! What are you doing here!

Dr. Stockmann: Well, well! Good morning, Father-in-law!

Mrs. Stockmann: Do come in.

Kiil: I will if it's true; if it isn't, I'm off again.

Dr. Stockmann: If what's true?

Kiil: This queer business about the water-works. Well, is it true?

Dr. Stockmann: Certainly it's true. But how did you get to know about it?

Kiil *(comes in)*: Petra dashed in on her way to school. . . .

Dr. Stockmann: Oh, did she?

Kiil: Yes, and from what she says . . . I thought she was just pulling my leg; but it isn't like Petra to do that.

Dr. Stockmann: No, what made you think a thing like that!

KIIL: Oh, you should never trust anybody. You can be taken in almost before you know where you are. But it really is true, then?

DR. STOCKMANN: Definitely. Just you sit down now. *(Urges him to sit on the sofa)* Isn't this a real stroke of luck for the town . . . ?

KIIL *(fighting his laughter)*: A stroke of luck for the town?

DR. STOCKMANN: Yes, the fact that I found out in time. . . .

KIIL *(as before)*: Oh, yes, of course! But I never thought you would try any monkey tricks on your own brother.

DR. STOCKMANN: Monkey tricks?

MRS. STOCKMANN: Really, Father!

KIIL *(resting his hands and his chin on the handle of his stick and winking slyly at the Doctor)*: Let me see, how was it now? Wasn't it something about some little creatures that had got into the water pipes?

DR. STOCKMANN: That's right. Bacteria.

KIIL: And from what Petra said, a whole lot of these animals had got in. An enormous number.

DR. STOCKMANN: That's right. Hundreds of thousands of them!

KIIL: And yet nobody can see them—isn't that what they say?

DR. STOCKMANN: Of course. Nobody can *see* them.

KIIL *(quietly chuckling)*: Damn me if this isn't the best you've managed yet.

DR. STOCKMANN: I don't know what you mean!

KIIL: But you'll never get the Mayor to believe a thing like this.

DR. STOCKMANN: We'll see about that.

KIIL: You don't think he's such a fool as all that!

DR. STOCKMANN: I hope the whole town's going to be such fools as all that.

KIIL: The whole town. Well, that's not such a bad idea, after all. It'll serve them right . . . do them good. They all think they're so much smarter than us older men. They hounded me off the Council, they did, I tell you. Treated me like a dog, they did. But now they'll get what's coming to them. You just carry on with your little tricks, Stockmann.

DR. STOCKMANN: But really . . .

KIIL: You just keep it up, I say. *(Gets up)* If you can manage to put a thing like this across on the Mayor and his lot, I'll give a hundred crowns to charity on the spot.

DR. STOCKMANN: That's very good of you.

KIIL: Yes, I haven't all that much money to throw about, I'll have you know, but if you pull this off, I'll give fifty crowns to charity next Christmas.

(Hovstad comes in from the hall)

HOVSTAD: Good morning! *(Stops)* Oh, I beg your pardon. . . .

DR. STOCKMANN: No, come in, come in.

KIIL *(chuckles again)*: Him! Is he in on this as well?

HOVSTAD: What do you mean?

DR. STOCKMANN: Of course he's in on it.

KIIL: I might have known! It has to get into the papers. Ah! You're a right one, Stockmann. I'll leave you to talk it over; and now I'll be off.

DR. STOCKMANN: Oh, can't you stay a bit longer?

KIIL: No, I must be off now. Keep it up and bring out all the tricks you can think of. I'm damned sure you won't lose by it.

(*He goes, accompanied by Mrs. Stockmann*)

DR. STOCKMANN (*laughs*): Fancy—the old man doesn't believe a word about this business of the water-works!

HOVSTAD: Ah, so that was what you . . . !

DR. STOCKMANN: Yes, that was what we were talking about. And you've probably come about the same thing, eh?

HOVSTAD: Yes, I have. Can you spare me a moment or two, Doctor?

DR. STOCKMANN: As long as you like, my dear fellow.

HOVSTAD: Have you heard anything from the Mayor?

DR. STOCKMANN: Not yet. He's coming round here later.

HOVSTAD: I've been thinking a lot about this thing since last night.

DR. STOCKMANN: Well?

HOVSTAD: As a doctor and a man of science, you regard this matter of the water-supply as something quite on its own, no doubt. What I mean is—it probably hasn't struck you that it's tied up with a lot of other things?

DR. STOCKMANN: In what way . . . ? Come and sit down, my dear fellow. No, on the sofa there.

(*Hovstad sits down on the sofa, the doctor in an armchair on the other side of the table*)

DR. STOCKMANN: Now, what was it you were saying. . . ?

HOVSTAD: You said yesterday that the water was contaminated by impurities in the soil.

DR. STOCKMANN: Yes, there's no doubt it all comes from that poisonous swamp up at Mölledal.

HOVSTAD: You'll forgive me, Doctor, but I think it comes from a very different swamp.

DR. STOCKMANN: What swamp?

HOVSTAD: The swamp that our whole community is standing rotting in.

DR. STOCKMANN: What kind of damned nonsense is this you're talking, Mr. Hovstad?

HOVSTAD: Everything in this town has gradually found its way into the hands of a certain group of officials. . . .

DR. STOCKMANN: Come now, not every one of them is an official.

HOVSTAD: No, but those that aren't officials are friends and hangers-on of those that are—the wealthy ones of the town, and the well-connected. These are the people in control.

DR. STOCKMANN: Yes, but you mustn't forget these are people of ability and insight.

HOVSTAD: How much ability and insight did they show when they laid the water pipes where they are now?

DR. STOCKMANN: *That*, of course, was a tremendous piece of stupidity. But that's going to be put right now.

HOVSTAD: Do you think it will be as easy as all that?

DR. STOCKMANN: Easy or not, it's going to be done.

HOVSTAD: Yes, as long as the press takes a hand.

DR. STOCKMANN: That won't be necessary, my dear fellow. I am sure my brother . . .

HOVSTAD: Excuse me, Doctor, but what I'm trying to tell you is that I intend taking the matter up.

DR. STOCKMANN: In the paper?

HOVSTAD: Yes. When I took over the *Herald* it was with the express intention of breaking up this ring of obstinate old buffers who'd got hold of all the power.

DR. STOCKMANN: But you told me yourself what the outcome of that was; it nearly ruined the paper.

HOVSTAD: Yes, it's true we had to pipe down on that occasion. Only because there was a danger that the whole business about the Baths might have fallen through if those men had been turned out then. But now we've got the Baths, and now these fine gentlemen can be dispensed with.

DR. STOCKMANN: Dispensed with, perhaps. But we have much to thank them for.

HOVSTAD: Full acknowledgement will be given, with all punctiliousness. But no popular journalist, such as I am, can afford to let an opportunity like this go by. This myth of official infallibility must be destroyed. A thing like this has to be rooted out just like any other superstition.

DR. STOCTMANN: I agree with you whole-heartedly, Mr. Hovstad! If there is any superstition, then away with it!

HOVSTAD: I should be most reluctant to implicate the Mayor, seeing that he's your brother. But I'm sure you agree with me that truth must come first.

DR. STOCKMANN: That goes without saying. *(Vehemently)* Yes, but . . . but . . .

HOVSTAD: You mustn't think so badly of me. I am no more egotistical or ambitious than most.

DR. STOCKMANN: But, my dear fellow, who's suggesting you are?

HOVSTAD: I came from a fairly poor home, as you know. And I've had plenty of opportunity of seeing what's needed most among the working classes. And it's this: to have some say in the control of public affairs, Dr. Stockmann. *That's* the thing for developing people's ability and knowledge and confidence. . . .

DR. STOCKMANN: I can understand that very well. . . .

HOVSTAD: Yes . . . and that's why I think it's a terrible responsibility for a journalist if he neglects any opportunity that might bring some measure of freedom to the humble and the oppressed masses. Oh, I realize all the big noises will just call it 'agitation' and so on. Well, let them say what they like! As long as my conscience is clear . . .

DR. STOCKMANN: Absolutely! Absolutely, my dear Mr. Hovstad. All the same . . . damn it . . . ! *(There is a knock at the door)* Come in!

(ASLAKSEN, the printer, appears at the hall door. He is poorly but decently dressed in a black suit, with a slightly crumpled white necktie; he carries in his hand a felt hat and gloves.)

ASLAKSEN *(bows)*: Excuse me, Doctor, intruding like this . . .

DR.. STOCKMANN *(rises)*: Well, well, here's Mr. Aslaksen!

ASLAKSEN: Yes, Doctor.

HOVSTAD *(stands)*: Is it me you're looking for, Aslaksen?

ASLAKSEN: No, it isn't. I didn't know I'd be seeing you here. No, actually it was the Doctor himself. . . .

DR. STOCKMANN: Well, and what can I do for you?

ASLAKSEN: Is it true what Mr. Billing tells me—that you are thinking of trying to get the water-supply improved?

DR. STOCKMANN: Yes, for the Baths.

ASLAKSEN: Well then, I've just called to say that I am ready to give every support to a thing like that.

HOVSTAD (*to the* DOCTOR): There you are, you see!

DR. STOCKMANN: That's extremely kind of you, thank you very much; but . . .

ASLAKSEN: Because you might easily find you need some middle-class support to back you up. We now form what you might call a compact majority here in town—when we really *want* to, that is. And it's always a good thing to have the majority on your side, Dr. Stockmann.

DR. STOCKMANN: That is undoubtedly true. It's just that I don't quite understand why it should be necessary to take any special measures of that kind here. When it's such an ordinary straightforward thing, it seems to me . . .

ASLAKSEN: Ah, you never know but what it mightn't be a good thing anyway. I know well enough what the local authorities are like. Those in charge are never very keen on any kind of proposal that *other* people put forward. And that's why I think it wouldn't be a bad thing if we made a bit of a demonstration.

HOVSTAD: Yes, exactly.

DR. STOCKMANN: Demonstration, do you say? Well, what way did you think of demonstrating?

ASLAKSEN: Well, with great moderation, of course, Doctor. I try for moderation, in all things. For moderation is the first attribute of a good citizen . . . in my own opinion, that is.

DR. STOCKMANN: That's something that you yourself are well-known for, too, Mr. Aslaksen.

ASLAKSEN: Yes, I think I may say it is. And this matter of the water-supply is an extremely important one for us of the middle classes. The Baths show every sign of becoming a little goldmine for the town, as you might say; it's to them that many of us are looking for a means of livelihood, especially those of us who are house-holders. That's why we want to give the Baths all the support we can. And I happen to be the chairman of the Ratepayers Association . . .

DR. STOCKMANN: Yes?

ASLAKSEN: . . . and as I am moreover the local representative of the Temperance Society—you know, of course, that I take an active part in Temperance affairs?

DR. STOCKMANN: Yes, of course, of course.

ASLAKSEN: Well . . . you can see I meet quite a lot of people one way and another. And as I have the reputation of being a prudent and law-abiding citizen, as the Doctor himself said, it means that I have a certain influence in the town— a kind of little position of power, even though I say it myself.

DR. STOCKMANN: That I know very well, Mr. Aslaksen.

ASLAKSEN: And so, you see, it would be quite a simple matter for me to prepare an address, if such appeared necessary.

DR. STOCKMANN: An address?

ASLAKSEN: Yes, a kind of vote of thanks from the townspeople in appreciation of the way you have dealt with this matter of public interest. It goes without saying that the address would have to be drafted with proper moderation so as not to give offence to the authorities and those in power. And as long as we are careful about *that*, I don't really see that anybody can object, do you?

HOVSTAD: Well, even if they didn't like it very much . . .

ASLAKSEN: No, no, no! Nothing to give offence to the authorities, Mr. Hovstad. Nothing that might antagonize people with so much say in things. I've had quite enough of that sort of thing in my time, and no good ever comes of it, either. But the honest expression of a man's considered opinion surely cannot offend anybody.

DR. STOCKMANN (*shaking his hand*): I just can't tell you, my dear Mr. Aslaksen, how delighted I am to find this support among my fellow citizens. It gives me great pleasure . . . great pleasure! I tell you what! What about a little glass of sherry, eh?

ASLAKSEN: No, thank you very much. I never touch spirits.

DR. STOCKMANN: What do you say to a glass of beer, then?

ASLAKSEN: No thank you again, Doctor. I never take anything as early in the day as this. I am going into town now to talk to some of the ratepayers to see if I can prepare public opinion.

DR. STOCKMANN: Well, it really is extremely kind of you, Mr. Aslaksen. But I just cannot see all these arrangements being necessary. I think surely this matter can be managed on its own.

ASLAKSEN: The authorities sometimes take a bit of moving, Dr. Stockmann. Not that I'm trying to blame anybody, of course! Dear me, no!

HOVSTAD: We'll have a go at them in the paper tomorrow, Aslaksen.

ASLAKSEN: Please, Mr. Hovstad, no violence. Proceed with moderation, otherwise you'll get nowhere. You can take my word for it, because my experience was acquired in the school of life.—Well, I'll say goodbye now, Doctor. You now know that we of the middle classes stand solidly behind you. You have the compact majority on your side, Dr. Stockmann.

DR. STOCKMANN: Thank you very much, my dear Mr. Aslaksen. (*Holds out his hand*) Goodbye, goodbye!

ASLAKSEN: Are you coming with me as far as the office, Mr. Hovstad?

HOVSTAD: I'll be along soon. I still have one or two things to see to.

ASLAKSEN: Very good.

(*He bows and goes. Dr. Stockmann accompanies him out into the hall*)

HOVSTAD (*as the Doctor returns*): Well, Doctor, what d'you think of that? Don't you think it's about time we did a bit of shaking up and clearing out of all this weary, cowardly fiddle-faddle?

DR. STOCKMANN: Are you referring to Mr. Aslaksen?

HOVSTAD: Yes, I am. He's one of the ones in the swamp—decent enough sort though he may be in other ways. Most of them are like that round here, teetering along, wobbling one way then the other; they are so damned cautious and scrupulous that they never dare commit themselves to any proper step forward.

DR. STOCKMANN: Yes, but Aslaksen seemed so genuinely anxious to help.

HOVSTAD: There's something I value more than that; and that is to stand firm, like a man with confidence in himself.

DR. STOCKMANN: Yes, I think you are absolutely right there.

HOVSTAD: That's why I'm going to take this opportunity to see if I can't get these well-intentioned people to show a bit of backbone. This worship of authority must be wiped out in this town. The real significance of this tremendous and unforgivable blunder about the water-supply must be brought home to every single person with a vote.

DR. STOCKMANN: Very well. If you think it is for the public good, so be it. But not till I've had a word with my brother about it.

HOVSTAD: In the meantime I'll be drafting a leading article. And if the Mayor refuses to go on with things . . .

DR. STOCKMANN: Oh, but how could you possibly think that?

HOVSTAD: It's not impossible. And if so . . . ?

DR. STOCKMANN: In that case, I promise you. . . . Listen, in that case you can print my article; every word of it.

HOVSTAD: May I? Is that a promise?

DR. STOCKMANN *(hands him the manuscript)* Here it is, take it with you. There's no harm in your reading it through; you can give it back to me afterwards.

HOVSTAD: Good! I'll do that. Well then goodbye, Doctor!

DR. STOCKMANN: Goodbye, goodbye! You'll see, Mr. Hovstad, it'll be all plain sailing . . . nothing but plain sailing!

HOVSTAD: Hm! We'll see.

(He bows and goes out through the door)

DR. STOCKMANN *(crosses and looks into the dining-room)*: Katherine . . . ! Ah, are you back, Petra?

PETRA *(comes in)*: Yes, I've just come from school.

MRS. STOCKMANN *(comes in)*: Hasn't he been yet?

DR. STOCKMANN: Peter? No. But I've had a long talk with Hovstad. He's quite worked up about this discovery I've made. It seems there's more in it than I'd first imagined, you know. He's put his paper at my disposal, if it's ever needed.

MRS. STOCKMANN: Do you think it will be needed?

DR. STOCKMANN: No, of course not. But it makes one very proud to think that one has the progressive and independent press on one's side. And what else do you think! I've also had the chairman of the Ratepayers Association here to see me.

MRS. STOCKMANN: Really? What did he want?

DR. STOCKMANN: Also to offer his support. They are all going to support me, if need be. Katherine—do you know what I've got backing me?

MRS. STOCKMANN: Backing you? No. What?

DR. STOCKMANN: The compact majority.

MRS. STOCKMANN: Oh, have you! And is that a good thing, then, Thomas?

DR. STOCKMANN: I should jolly well think it is! *(He walks up and down, rubbing his hands.)* Lord! How wonderful it is to stand, as it were, shoulder to shoulder in the brotherhood of one's fellow citizens!

PETRA: And to be doing such good and useful work, Father!

DR. STOCKMANN: Yes, not to mention that it's for one's own birthplace, too.

MRS. STOCKMANN: There's the bell.

DR. STOCKMANN: That must be him. *(There is a knock on the door.)* Come in!

MAYOR *(comes from the hall)*: Good morning.

DR. STOCKMANN: Glad to see you, Peter!

MRS. STOCKMANN: Good morning, Peter! How are things with you?

MAYOR: Oh, so-so, thank you. *(To the Doctor)* I received from you yesterday, after office hours, a report concerning the state of the water at the Baths.

DR. STOCKMANN: Yes. Have you read it?

MAYOR: Yes, I have.

DR. STOCKMANN: And what have you got to say about it?

MAYOR *(with a sidelong glance)*: Hm . . .

MRS. STOCKMANN: Come along, Petra.

(Mrs. Stockmann and Petra go into the room on the left)

MAYOR *(after a pause)*: Was it necessary to make all these investigations behind my back?

DR. STOCKMANN: Yes, because until I knew with absolute certainty . . .

MAYOR: And now you do, you mean?

DR. STOCKMANN: Yes. Surely you are also convinced yourself by now!

MAYOR: Is it your intention to present this document to the Board as an official report?

DR. STOCKMANN: Of course. Something will have to be done about this thing. And quick.

MAYOR: As usual, you use some rather emphatic expressions in your report. Among other things, you say that what we offer our summer visitors is sheer poison.

DR. STOCKMANN: Well, Peter, what else can you call it? Just think! That water's poison whether you drink it or bathe in it! And this is what we offer those poor invalids who come to us in good faith and pay good money hoping to get their health back!

MAYOR: And then you conclude by stating we must build a sewer to deal with these alleged impurities from Mölledal, and that the present water pipes must be re-laid.

DR. STOCKMANN: Well, can you suggest any other solution? I can't.

MAYOR: This morning I made it my business to look in on the town engineer. And—half as a joke, as it might be—I brought up these measures as something we might give consideration to at some future date.

DR. STOCKMANN: Some future date!

MAYOR: He smiled at what he took to be my extravagance—of course. Have you taken the trouble to think what these proposed alterations would cost? According to the information I received, the cost would very probably be several hundred thousand crowns.

DR. STOCKMANN: As much as that?

MAYOR: Yes. But that's not the worst. The work would take at least two years.

DR. STOCKMANN: Two years, eh? Two whole years?

MAYOR: At least. And what's to be done with the Baths in the meantime? Shall

we shut them? We'll have to. You don't think people are going to come all the
way here if the rumour got about that the water was polluted?

DR. STOCKMANN: But, Peter, that's just what it is.

MAYOR: And all this has to come out just when the Baths were beginning to pay
their way. A lot of other places in the district could equally well develop into
health resorts. Can't you see they would set to work at once to divert all our
tourist traffic to themselves. Of course they would; no doubt whatever. And
we'd be left sitting there with all that expensive plant on our hands; we'd
probably have to abandon the entire project. The whole town would be
ruined, thanks to you!

DR. STOCKMANN: Me. . . ? Ruined. . . ?

MAYOR: The whole future prosperity of the town is tied up with the Baths. You
can see that as well as I can.

DR. STOCKMANN: Then what should be done, do you think?

MAYOR: I am not entirely convinced by your report that the state of the Baths is
as serious as you make out.

DR. STOCKMANN: If anything it is worse. At least, it will be in the summer, when
the warm weather comes.

MAYOR: As I said before, I think you exaggerate considerably. Any competent
doctor would surely be able to meet this situation . . . take some suitable pre-
cautionary measures and treat any noticeable injurious effects, if there actually turned out to be any.

DR. STOCKMANN: Well? And what then?

MAYOR: The existing water-supply for the Baths is now an established fact, and
must be treated as such. But it is reasonable to suppose that in time the Directors might not be disinclined to consider how far, in the light of the prevailing financial situation, it would be possible to initiate certain improvements.

DR. STOCKMANN: Do you honestly think I would lend myself to that sort of sharp
practice?

MAYOR: Sharp practice?

DR. STOCKMANN: Sharp practice, yes! That's what it would be. A swindle, a fraud,
an absolute crime against the public and against society!

MAYOR: As I remarked earlier, I have not been able to persuade myself that there
is any actual imminent danger.

DR. STOCKMANN: Oh yes, you have! You couldn't help it. My report is absolutely
correct and clear, I know that! And you know it too, Peter, but you won't admit it. You were the one responsible for having the Baths and the water-supply sited where they are now. And it's *this*—this damned blunder of yours—
that you won't admit. Puh! Do you think I can't see right through you?

MAYOR: And even if that were so? Even if I may seem to guard my reputation
somewhat jealously, it's all for the good of the town. Without some measure
of moral authority, I should not be able to guide and direct public affairs in
the way I consider best serves the common weal. Therefore—and for various
other reasons—I consider it imperative that your report should not be presented to the Board. In the public interest, it must be withheld. Then I shall
bring the matter up later, and we'll do all we can privately. But nothing, not a
single word, of this disastrous business must be made public.

DR. STOCKMANN: My dear Peter, I doubt if we can prevent that now.

MAYOR: It must and shall be prevented.

DR. STOCKMANN: It's no use, I tell you. Too many people know about it already.

MAYOR: Know about it already! Who? I only hope it's not those people on the *Herald...?*

DR. STOCKMANN: Oh yes, they know already. The progressive and independent press will see to it that you do your duty.

MAYOR (*after a short pause*): You are an astonishingly indiscreet man, Thomas! Did you never think what consequences this might have for you personally?

DR. STOCKMANN: Consequences? For me?

MAYOR: For you and your family.

DR. STOCKMANN: What the devil do you mean by *that?*

MAYOR: Would you agree I've always been a decent brother to you, always ready to help?

DR. STOCKMANN: Yes, you have. And I'm grateful to you for it.

MAYOR: There's no need to be. In a way I had to be ... in my own interests. It was always my hope that, by helping to improve your position economically, I might be able to some extent to hold you in check.

DR. STOCKMANN: What's that? It was only in your own interests ...!

MAYOR: In a way, I said. It is distressing for a public figure to have his nearest relative for ever compromising himself.

DR. STOCKMANN: You mean that's what I do?

MAYOR: Yes, I'm afraid you do, without realizing it. You have a restless, pugnacious, aggressive temperament. And then there's this unfortunate habit of yours of rushing into print about everything under the sun. No sooner do you get some idea or other into your head than you've got to write an article for the papers about it ... or even a whole pamphlet.

DR. STOCKMANN: But don't you think if a man's got hold of some new idea he has a duty to bring it to the notice of the public?

MAYOR: Oh, the public doesn't need new ideas. The public is best served by the good old, accepted ideas it already has.

DR. STOCKMANN: That's putting it pretty bluntly, anyway!

MAYOR: Yes, for once I'm going to be blunt with you. I've always tried to avoid that hitherto, knowing how irritable you are. But now, Thomas, I'm going to tell you the truth. You have no idea what harm you do yourself by this recklessness of yours. You complain about the authorities ... about the government, even ... you are always going on about them. Then you try to insist that you've been passed over, or been badly treated. But what do you expect, when you are so difficult?

DR. STOCKMANN: So I'm difficult too, am I?

MAYOR: Yes, Thomas, you are an extremely difficult man to work with, as I know from experience. You show absolutely no consideration. You seem to forget that it's me you have to thank for your appointment here as medical officer to the Baths. . . .

DR. STOCKMANN: I was the only possible man for the job! I, and nobody else! Wasn't I the first to see that the town could be made into a flourishing health resort? And wasn't I the only one to realize it at the time? Alone and single-handed I fought for the idea, year after year, writing and writing. . . .

MAYOR: Undoubtedly. But the time wasn't ripe for it then. Of course, you couldn't very well be any judge of that, living up there at the back of beyond.

But when a more appropriate time came, then I—and some of the others—
took the matter in hand. . . .

DR. STOCKMANN: Yes, and messed up the whole issue! My lovely plans! Oh yes, it's
clear enough now all right what a brainy lot you turned out to be!

MAYOR: The only thing that's clear in my opinion is that you are simply trying to
pick a quarrel again. You must find some outlet, so you go for your superiors—that's an old habit of yours. You just can't bear to submit to authority;
you take a jaundiced view of anybody holding a superior appointment, regard
him as a personal enemy. And straightway any weapon that happens to come
to hand is good enough to attack him with. But now I've made it clear to you
what other interests are at stake for the town as a whole—and consequently
also for me personally. And that's why I'm telling you, Thomas, that I intend
to be quite ruthless in demanding of you certain things.

DR. STOCKMANN: And what is it you demand?

MAYOR: Since you have been so indiscreet as to discuss this delicate matter with
certain unauthorized persons—despite the fact that it should have been treated as a matter confidential to the Board—things can of course no longer be
hushed up. All sorts of rumours will spread, and the more spiteful ones
among us can be relied on to embellish them with all sorts of extras. It will
therefore be necessary for you to make a public denial of these rumours.

DR. STOCKMANN: For me! How? I don't understand you.

MAYOR: We shall expect you, after making further investigations, to come to the
conclusion that the matter is not by any means as dangerous or as serious as
you in the first instance imagined it to be.

DR. STOCKMANN: Aha! So that's what you expect, is it?

MAYOR: Furthermore we shall expect you to make public declaration of your confidence in the Board, in its efficiency and its integrity, and in its readiness to
take all necessary steps to remedy such defects as may arise.

DR. STOCKMANN: Yes, but don't you see, you'll never do anything just by fiddling
with the problem, hoping to patch things up. I'm telling you straight, Peter,
and I'm absolutely and utterly convinced . . .

MAYOR: As an employee you have no right to any private opinion.

DR. STOCKMANN (*falters*): No right. . . ?

MAYOR: As an employee, I mean. As a private individual—good Lord, yes, that's
quite different. But as a subordinate member of the staff of the Baths, you
have no right to express any opinion that conflicts with that of your superiors.

DR. STOCKMANN: That's going too far! Are you trying to say that a doctor, a man of
science, has no right. . . !

MAYOR: The matter in this instance is by no means a purely scientific one; it is a
combination of technical and economic factors.

DR. STOCKMANN: It can be what the hell it likes, as far as I'm concerned. What matters to me is the right to speak my mind about any damn' thing under the sun.

MAYOR: Certainly! Anything at all—except the Baths. That we forbid.

DR. STOCKMANN (*shouts*): Forbid! You lot!

MAYOR: *I* forbid you. I personally, your superior. And when I give you an order,
it's up to you to obey.

DR. STOCKMANN (*controlling himself*): Peter . . . if it wasn't that you were my brother . . . !

PETRA (*flings the door open*): Don't stand for it, Father!

Mrs. Stockmann (*following her*): Petra! Petra!

Mayor: Aha! You've been listening!

Mrs. Stockmann: You were talking so loud, we just couldn't help . . .

Petra: No! I stood there and listened.

Mayor: Actually, I'm just as well pleased . . .

Dr. Stockmann (*approaches him*): You were saying something to me about ordering and obeying. . . ?

Mayor: You compelled me to speak to you like that.

Dr. Stockmann: And you expect me to get up in public and eat my own words?

Mayor: We consider it absolutely necessary that you issue some sort of statement
along the lines I laid down.

Dr. Stockmann: And supposing I don't . . . obey?

Mayor: Then we shall ourselves issue a statement to reassure the public.

Dr. Stockmann: Indeed. Well, then I shall contradict you in the newspapers. I
shall stand up for myself. I shall prove that I'm right and you're wrong. And
then what will you do?

Mayor: Then I shall not be able to prevent you from being dismissed.

Dr. Stockmann: What!

Petra: Father! Dismissed!

Mrs. Stockmann: Dismissed!

Mayor: Dismissed from the Baths. I shall be obliged to arrange for you to be
given notice and to see that you sever all connection with the Baths.

Dr. Stockmann: You wouldn't dare!

Mayor: Blame your own recklessness.

Petra: Uncle, this is a disgraceful way to treat a man like Father!

Mrs. Stockmann: Do be quiet, Petra!

Mayor (*looks at Petra*): Ah! So we can't wait to express our opinions, eh? Naturally. (*To Mrs. Stockmann*) Katherine, you are probably the most sensible one in
this house. Please use whatever influence you have with your husband. Get
him to see what this will mean both for his family . . .

Dr. Stockmann: My family's got nothing to do with anybody but me!

Mayor: . . . as I was saying, both for his family, and for the town he lives in.

Dr. Stockmann: I'm the one with the real welfare of the town at heart. All I want
to do is expose certain things that are bound to come out sooner or later anyway. Oh, I'll show them whether I love this town or not.

Mayor: All you are really doing, by your sheer blind obstinacy, is cutting off the
main source of the town's prosperity.

Dr. Stockmann: That source is poisoned, man! Are you mad! We live by peddling
filth and corruption! The whole of the town's prosperity is rooted in a lie!

Mayor: Fantastic nonsense—or worse! Any man who can cast such aspersions
against his own birthplace is nothing but a public enemy.

Dr. Stockmann (*goes up to him*): You dare . . . !

Mrs. Stockmann (*throws herself between them*): Thomas!

Petra (*seizes her father by the arm*): Steady, Father!

Mayor: I am not going to wait to be assaulted. You've had your warning. Try to
realize what you owe to yourself and to your family. Goodbye.

(*He goes*)

DR. STOCKMANN (*walks up and down*): Have I to stand for this? In my own house, Katherine! What do you think?

MRS. STOCKMANN: I agree it's shameful and disgraceful, Thomas. . . .

PETRA: If only I could get my hands on that uncle of mine. . . !

DR. STOCKMANN: It's my own fault, I should have had it out with them long ago . . . bared my teeth . . . bit back! Calling me a public enemy! Me! By God, I'm not going to stand for that!

MRS. STOCKMANN: But, Thomas my dear, your brother has a lot of power on his side. . . .

DR. STOCKMANN: Yes, but I have *right* on mine!

MRS. STOCKMANN: Right! Yes, of course. But what's the use of right without might?

PETRA: Oh, Mother! How can you say such a thing?

DR. STOCKMANN: So you think having right on your side in a free country doesn't count for anything? You are just being stupid, Katherine. And anyway, haven't I the progressive and independent press to look to, and the compact majority behind me. There's enough might there, surely, isn't there?

MRS. STOCKMANN: But heavens, Thomas! You surely aren't thinking of . . .

DR. STOCKMANN: Not thinking of what?

MRS. STOCKMANN: . . . of setting yourself up against your brother, I mean.

DR. STOCKMANN: What the devil do you expect me to do? What else is there if I'm going to hold to what's right and proper.

PETRA: Yes, that's what I'm wondering too.

MRS. STOCKMANN: But you know very well it won't do a scrap of good. If they won't, they won't.

DR. STOCKMANN: Aha, Katherine, just give me time. I'll fight this thing to a finish, you watch.

MRS. STOCKMANN: Yes, and while you are fighting, you'll lose your job, that's what!

DR. STOCKMANN: Then at least I shall have done my duty by the public . . . and by society. Calling me a public enemy, indeed!

MRS. STOCKMANN: But what about your family, Thomas? What about us at home? Will you be doing your duty by the ones you should provide for first?

PETRA: Oh, stop thinking always about us, Mother!

MRS. STOCKMANN: Yes, it's easy for *you* to talk. You can stand on your own feet, if need be. But don't forget the boys, Thomas. And think a little of yourself too, and of me. . . .

DR. STOCKMANN: You must be absolutely mad, Katherine! If I were to be such a miserable coward as to go groveling to Peter and his blasted pals, do you think I'd ever be happy again as long as I lived?

MRS. STOCKMANN: I'm sure I don't know. But God preserve us from the kind of happiness we'll have if you insist on carrying on like this. We'll be just where we were before—no job, no regular income. I thought we had enough of that in the old days. Don't forget that, Thomas, and think what all this is going to lead to.

DR. STOCKMANN (*squirming and clenching his fists*): Oh, the things that a free and decent man has to put up with at the hands of these damned bureaucrats! Isn't it terrible, Katherine?

MRS. STOCKMANN: Yes, they've treated you disgracefully, I will say that. But heavens! Once you start thinking of all the injustices in this world people have to put up with . . . ! There's the boys, Thomas! Look at them! What's going to become of them? Oh no, you'd never have the heart. . . .

(Meanwhile Ejlif and Morten have come in, carrying their schoolbooks)

DR. STOCKMANN: The boys . . . ! *(Suddenly stops with a determined look)* No! Even if it meant the end of the world, I'm not knuckling under.

(He walks over to his study)

MRS. STOCKMANN *(following him)*: Thomas! What are you going to do?
DR. STOCKMANN *(at the door)*: I want to be able to look my boys in the face when they grow up into free men.

(He goes in)

MRS. STOCKMANN *(bursts into tears)*: Oh, God help us.
PETRA: Father's grand! He'll never give in.

(The boys, in amazement, begin to ask what is happening; Petra signs to them to be silent)

Act Three

The editorial office of the **People's Herald**. *The entrance door is on the back wall, left; on the same wall, right, is a glazed door, through which the printing shop can be seen. On the right wall is another door. A large table stands in the middle of the room covered with papers, newspapers, and books. Downstage, left, is a window, near which is a writing desk with high stool. A couple of armchairs by the table, other chairs along the walls. The room is gloomy and cheerless; the furniture is old, the armchairs dirty and torn. Within the printing shop, a few compositors are at work; further back a hand press is being worked.*

Hovstad is sitting at the desk, writing. After a moment or two, Billing comes in from the right with the doctor's manuscript in his hand.

BILLING: Well, I must say . . . !
HOVSTAD *(writing)*: Have you read it through?
BILLING *(puts the manuscript on the desk)*: Yes, I have that.
HOVSTAD: Pretty scathing, isn't he?
BILLING: Scathing! Damn it, it's absolutely devastating! Every word lands—what shall I say?—like a blow from a sledge-hammer.
HOVSTAD: Yes, but they're not the sort you can knock down with one blow.
BILLING: That's true! But then we'll just keep on hitting them . . . time and time again until the whole set-up collapses. Sitting in there reading it, I just felt as though I could see the revolution coming.
HOVSTAD *(turning)*: Hush! Don't let Aslaksen hear that.
BILLING *(lowering his voice)*: Aslaksen is a chicken-hearted little coward. He's got no backbone. But I hope this time you're going to insist? Eh? The Doctor's article will go in?
HOVSTAD: Yes, as long as the Mayor doesn't give in without a fight. . . .

BILLING: Make things damned dull if he does.

HOVSTAD: Well, fortunately we can make something of the situation whatever happens. If the Mayor doesn't accept the Doctor's proposal, then he'll have all the middle class on to him . . . all the Ratepayers Association and and the rest. And if he does accept it, then he's got to face a pack of the bigger shareholders in the Baths who have so far been his strongest supporters. . . .

BILLING: Yes, that's right. I dare say it'll cost them a pretty penny. . . .

HOVSTAD: You can be damn' sure it will. Then, you see, once the ring is broken, we can keep pegging away day after day in the paper, pointing out to the public how completely incompetent the Mayor is, and how all the positions of responsibility, in fact the whole council, ought to be handed over to the Liberals.

BILLING: By God, that's good, that is! I can see it . . . I can see it! We're on the brink of revolution!

(There is a knock on the door)

HOVSTAD: Hush! *(Shouts)* Come in!

(Dr. Stockmann comes through the entrance door, back, left)

HOVSTAD *(crosses to him)*: Ah, it's you, Doctor. Well?

DR. STOCKMANN: Print it, Mr. Hovstad!

HOVSTAD: Has it come to that?

BILLING: Hurrah!

DR. STOCKMANN: Print away, I tell you. Yes, it *has* come to that. Now they're going to get what's coming to them. This is war, Mr. Billing!

BILLING: War to the knife, I hope! Go ahead and slaughter them, Doctor!

DR. STOCKMANN: This article is only the beginning. Already I've got enough ideas for another four or five of them. Where's Aslaksen?

BILLING *(shouts into the printing shop)*: Can you come here a minute, Aslaksen?

HOVSTAD: Another four or five articles, d'you say? About the same thing?

DR. STOCKMANN: Oh, no! Far from it, my dear fellow. No, they're about quite different things. But they're all bound up with the question of the water-supply and the sewers. You know how one thing leads to another. It's just like what happens when you start tinkering with an old building—just like that.

BILLING: By God, that's true. You pretty soon realize it's all such a shambles that you'll never finish the job properly until you've pulled the whole thing down.

ASLAKSEN *(from the printing shop)*: Pulled the whole thing down! Surely, Doctor, you are not thinking of pulling the Baths down?

HOVSTAD: No, of course not! Don't get alarmed!

DR. STOCKMANN: No, we were referring to something quite different. Well, Mr. Hovstad, what have you got to say about my article?

HOVSTAD: I think it's an absolute masterpiece. . . .

DR. STOCKMANN: Yes, isn't it. . . ? Well, I'm very pleased, very pleased.

HOVSTAD: It's so clear and to the point. You don't need to be an expert to follow it; anybody can understand from it what it's all about. I bet you get every progressively-minded man on your side.

ASLAKSEN: And all the sensible ones as well, I hope.

BILLING: The sensible ones and the other sort too. . . . What I mean is, practically the whole town.

ASLAKSEN: In that case, I think we might venture to print it.

DR. STOCKMANN: I jolly well think so!

HOVSTAD: It will be in tomorrow morning.

DR. STOCKMANN: Yes, by heavens! We mustn't waste any time. By the way, Mr. Aslaksen, that was something I was going to ask you: you'll give the manuscript your own personal attention, won't you?

ASLAKSEN: I will indeed.

DR. STOCKMANN: Take care of it as though it were gold. No misprints, every word is important. I'll look in again later on; perhaps I could check some of the proofs.—Yes, I can't tell you how I'm longing to get this thing in print . . . slam it down . . .

BILLING: Slam it down, that's right! Like a thunderbolt!

DR. STOCKMANN: . . . to submit it to the scrutiny of every intelligent citizen. Oh, you can't imagine what I've had to put up with today. They've threatened me with all sorts of things; to deprive me of my most basic human rights . . .

BILLING: What! Your human rights!

DR. STOCKMANN: . . . They tried to degrade me, to rob me of my self-respect, tried to force me to put personal advantage before my most sacred convictions. . . .

BILLING: Damn it, that's going too far!

HOVSTAD: Ah, you can expect anything from that lot.

DR. STOCKMANN: But I'm not going to let them get away with it—I'll make that plain in black and white. Every blessed day I'll be in the *Herald*—lying at anchor, so to speak, and bombarding them with one high-explosive article after another . . .

ASLAKSEN: Oh but, come now. . . .

BILLING: Hurrah! It's war, it's war!

DR. STOCKMANN: . . . I'll batter them to the ground, I'll smash them, I'll blast their defences wide open for all right-thinking men to see! That's what I'll do!

ASLAKSEN: But you will act with moderation, Doctor! Shoot . . . but with moderation. . . .

BILLING: No, no! Don't spare the dynamite!

DR. STOCKMANN (*continues unbashed*): Because, you see, it's no longer just the water-supply and the sewers now. No, the whole community needs cleaning up, disinfecting. . . .

BILLING: That's what I like to hear!

DR. STOCKMANN: All these dodderers have got to be chucked out! Wherever they are! My eyes have been opened to a lot of things today. I haven't quite got everything sorted out yet, but I will in time. My friends, what we must look for is young and vigorous men to be our standard-bearers. We must have new men in command in all our forward positions.

BILLING: Hear, hear!

DR. STOCKMANN: And if only we hold together, things can't help but go smoothly! We'll launch this whole revolution as smoothly as a ship off the stocks. Don't you think so?

HOVSTAD: For my own part, I think we now have every prospect of placing the control of the council in the proper hands.

ASLAKSEN: And as long as we proceed with moderation, I can't see that there should be any risk.

DR. STOCKMANN: Who the devil cares whether it's risky or not? What I do, I do in the name of truth and in obedience to my conscience.

HOVSTAD: You deserve every support, Doctor.

ASLAKSEN: Yes, it's quite obvious that the Doctor is a true benefactor to the town, a real benefactor to society.

BILLING: By God, Aslaksen, Dr. Stockmann is the people's friend!

ASLAKSEN: I rather think the Ratepayers Association might soon be wanting to use that phrase.

DR. STOCKMANN (*greatly moved, grasps their hands*): Thank you, thank you, my good friends, for being so loyal. How gratifying it is to hear you say that. That brother of mine called me something quite different. Well, he'll get it all back again, with interest! Well, I must be off now to see a patient of mine, poor devil. But I'll be back, as I promised. Be sure you take good care of that manuscript, Mr. Aslaksen—and, whatever you do, don't go leaving out any of my exclamation marks! If anything, put a few more in! Well, Well! Goodbye for now, goodbye!

(*As they show him out, they take leave of each other; he goes*)

HOVSTAD: There's a man who could be extremely useful to us.

ASLAKSEN: Yes, as long as he keeps to this business of the Baths. But if he gets going on other things, it might not be very wise to follow him.

HOVSTAD: Hm! That all depends on . . .

BILLING: Don't be so damned frightened, Aslaksen.

ASLAKSEN: Frightened? Yes, Mr. Billing, I *am* frightened—when it's a question of local politics. That's something I've learnt in the hard school of experience, you see. But you just put me in high-level politics, even in opposition to the government itself, and you'll see then whether I'm frightened.

BILLING: No, I'm sure you wouldn't be. But that's just what makes you so inconsistent.

ASLAKSEN: It's because I'm a man with a conscience. That's what it is. You can attack the government without really doing society any harm, because you see people like that just don't take any notice—they stay in power as if nothing had happened. But the *local* leaders, they *can* be turned out; and then you might easily get a lot of inexperienced men at the helm, doing immense harm to the interests of the ratepayers and other people.

HOVSTAD: But what about self-government as a factor in the people's education—haven't you thought about *that*?

ASLAKSEN: When a man has acquired a vested interest in something, you can't always expect him to think of everything, Mr. Hovstad.

HOVSTAD: Then I hope to God I never have any vested interests.

BILLING: Hear, hear!

ASLAKSEN (*smiles*): Hm! (*He points to the desk.*) Your predecessor in that editorial chair was Mr. Steensgaard. He used to be sheriff.

BILLING (*spits*): Pah! That turncoat.

HOVSTAD: I'm no time-server—and never will be, either.

ASLAKSEN: A politician should never be too certain about anything, Mr. Hovstad.

And you, Mr. Billing, hadn't you better draw your horns in just a little these days—seeing you've applied for the post of Secretary to the council?

BILLING: I . . . !

HOVSTAD: *Have* you, Billing?

BILLING: Well . . . Can't you see I'm only doing it to annoy our local bigwigs, damn them.

ASLAKSEN: Well, it's nothing whatever to do with me. But when people accuse me of being cowardly or inconsistent, there's one thing I want to stress: the political record of Aslaksen the printer is an open book. I haven't changed in any way except to become more moderate in my ways. My heart is still with the people. But I'll not deny that my head rather inclines me to support the authorities—the local ones, I mean.

(He goes into the printing shop)

BILLING: Don't you think we'd better finish with him, Hovstad?

HOVSTAD: Do you know anybody else who'd agree to let us have our paper and printing on credit?

BILLING: It's a damned nuisance not having the necessary capital.

HOVSTAD *(sits down at the desk)*: Yes, if only we had *that*. . . !

BILLING: What about approaching Dr. Stockmann?

HOVSTAD *(turning over some papers)*: Oh, what's the use of that? He hasn't anything.

BILLING: No, but he's got a good man up his sleeve—Old Morten Kiil, 'the Badger', as he is called.

HOVSTAD *(writing)*: What makes you so sure *he's* got anything?

BILLING: By God, he's got money all right! And some of it is bound to come to the Stockmanns. Then he'll have to think of providing for . . . for the children, at any rate.

HOVSTAD *(half turning)*: Are you counting on *that*?

BILLING: Counting? I'm not counting on anything.

HOVSTAD: You're right there. And you'd better not count on that job with the council, either. Because I can tell you now—you won't get it.

BILLING: Do you think I don't know that? That's just what I want—not to get it. To be rejected like that is just like adding fuel to the flames—it's like getting a new supply of fresh gall, and you need something like that in a dump like this where nothing really stimulating ever happens.

HOVSTAD *(writing)*: Yes, yes, I know.

BILLING: Well . . . it won't be long now before they hear from me! Now I'm going to sit down and write that appeal to the Ratepayers.

(He goes into the room, right)

HOVSTAD *(sits at his desk, bites his pen shank and says slowly)*: Hm! Aha, so that's it . . . *(There is a knock at the door)* Come in!

(Petra comes in by entrance door, back, left)

HOVSTAD *(rises)*: Well, look who it is! What are you doing here?

PETRA: You must excuse me, but . . .

HOVSTAD *(pulling an armchair forward)*: Won't you have a seat?

PETRA: No, thanks. I can't stay.

HOVSTAD: Is it something from your father, perhaps . . . ?

PETRA: No, it's something from me. *(She takes a book out of her coat pocket)* Here's that English story.

HOVSTAD: Why have you brought it back?

PETRA: Because I'm not going to translate it.

HOVSTAD: But you promised me faithfully . . .

PETRA: I hadn't read it then. And you haven't either, have you?

HOVSTAD: No, you know I don't know any English. But . . .

PETRA: Quite. That's why I wanted to tell you that you'll have to look round for something else. *(She puts the book on the table)* You can never use a thing like this for the *Herald*.

HOVSTAD: Why not?

PETRA: Because it runs completely contrary to everything you believe in.

HOVSTAD: Well, what does that matter . . . ?

PETRA: You don't quite understand. It's all about some supernatural power that's supposed to watch over all the so-called good people, and how everything is for the best . . . and how all the so-called wicked people get punished in the end. . . .

HOVSTAD: Yes, but that's just fine. That's exactly what people want.

PETRA: Can you honestly put stuff like that in front of people? When you yourself don't believe a word of it? You know very well that's not what happens in reality.

HOVSTAD: You're absolutely right, of course. But an editor cannot always do what he wants. You often have to give way to public opinion, in minor things. After all, politics is the most important thing in life—at least, for a newspaper, it is. And if I want to win people over to certain liberal and progressive ideas, it's no good scaring them all off. If they find a nice moral story like this on the back pages of the paper, they are much more ready to accept what we print on the front page—it gives them a sort of feeling of security.

PETRA: Oh, no! Not you, surely! I just can't picture you as a spider spinning a kind of web to trap unwary readers.

HOVSTAD *(smiling)*: Thank you for those few kind words. No, in fact you are right—it was all Billing's idea, not mine.

PETRA: Billing's!

HOVSTAD: Yes, at least he was talking about it just the other day. Billing's really the one who is keen to get that story in. I don't know the book at all.

PETRA: Mr. Billing? A man with all his progressive ideas . . . ?

HOVSTAD: Oh, Billing is a man of parts. I've heard he's also applied for the post of Secretary to the council.

PETRA: I don't believe it, Mr. Hovstad. Whatever makes him think he could stand a job like that?

HOVSTAD: You'd better ask him yourself.

PETRA: I'd never have thought a thing like that of Mr. Billing.

HOVSTAD *(looks at her intently)*: Wouldn't you? Does it come as such a surprise to you?

PETRA: Yes. Or perhaps not. Oh, I don't really know . . .

HOVSTAD: Journalists like us are not really up to much, Miss Stockmann.

PETRA: Do you really mean that?

HOVSTAD: Now and again I think it.

PETRA: In the ordinary daily routine, perhaps; that I could understand. But when you've taken on something big . . .

HOVSTAD: You mean this business about your father?

PETRA: Yes, exactly. I imagine you must feel like a man with a more worthwhile job than most people.

HOVSTAD: Yes, I do feel a bit like that today.

PETRA: I'm sure you must! Oh, what a splendid calling you have chosen. Blazing a trail for the advancement of truth, and of new and bold ideas . . . ! Or even just to step up and give your support, without fear or favour, to a man who has suffered a great wrong . . .

HOVSTAD: Especially when this unfortunate man happens to be . . . hm! . . . I don't really know how to put it . . .

PETRA: Happens to be so decent and honest, you mean?

HOVSTAD (quietly): Especially when he happens to be your father, is what I meant.

PETRA (suddenly struck): What?

HOVSTAD: Yes, Petra—Miss Petra.

PETRA: Is that what you are thinking of first? You're not concerned about the thing itself? Not about truth? Not about Father's public-spirited action?

HOVSTAD: Oh yes, that too, naturally!

PETRA: No thank you, Mr. Hovstad! You have given yourself away this time. And I can never trust you again about anything.

HOVSTAD: I don't see why you want to take it like this when it was mainly for your sake . . . !

PETRA: What makes me cross is that you haven't played straight with Father. You talked to him as though all you cared about was truth and the common good. You made fools of us both. You are not the man you pretended to be. I'll never forgive you . . . never!

HOVSTAD: I shouldn't be too outspoken actually, Miss Petra. Especially not now.

PETRA: Why not now, particularly?

HOVSTAD: Because your father cannot manage without my help.

PETRA (looking down at him): So you're one of those, are you? Pah!

HOVSTAD: No, no, I'm not. I don't know what came over me, saying a thing like that. You mustn't believe a word of it.

PETRA: I know what to believe. Goodbye!

ASLAKSEN (comes in from the printing shop urgently and with an air of secrecy): In Heaven's name, Mr. Hovstad . . . (He sees Petra) Oh, I'm sorry. I shouldn't . . .

PETRA: There's the book. You'd better give it to somebody else.

(She walks across to the main door)

HOVSTAD (following her): But, Miss Petra . . .

PETRA: Goodbye.

(She goes)

ASLAKSEN: I say, Mr. Hovstad!

HOVSTAD: Well, well . . . what is it?

ASLAKSEN: The Mayor's out there in the printing shop.

HOVSTAD: The Mayor, did you say?

ASLAKSEN: Yes, he wants a word with you. He came in the back way—didn't want to be seen, I suppose.

HOVSTAD: What does he want, I wonder? No, wait here, I'll go myself . . .

(He goes over to the door into the printing shop, opens it and invites the Mayor in)

HOVSTAD: Aslaksen, keep an eye open to see that nobody . . .

ASLAKSEN: I understand.

(He goes into the printing shop)

MAYOR: I don't suppose you were expecting me here, Mr. Hovstad.

HOVSTAD: No, as a matter of fact I wasn't.

MAYOR *(looking about him)*: You've settled yourself in here nice and comfortably. Very nice.

HOVSTAD: Oh . . .

MAYOR: And here I come without any appointment, and proceed to take up all your precious time.

HOVSTAD: *Please*, Mr. Mayor, I'm only too delighted to be of service. Let me take your things. *(He puts the Mayor's hat and stick on a chair)* Now, won't you sit down?

MAYOR *(sits at the table)*: Thank you.

(Hovstad also sits down at the table)

MAYOR: I have had an extremely disagreeable matter to deal with today, Mr. Hovstad.

HOVSTAD: Really? Of course, with so many things to see to . . .

MAYOR: This particular matter has been raised by the Medical Officer of the Baths.

HOVSTAD: By the Doctor?

MAYOR: He's written a kind of report about a number of alleged shortcomings at the Baths, and sent it to the Board.

HOVSTAD: Has he?

MAYOR: Yes, hasn't he told you? I thought he said . . .

HOVSTAD: Oh yes, that's right! He did mention something about . . .

ASLAKSEN *(coming from the printing shop)*: I'd better have that manuscript . . . .

HOVSTAD *(angrily)*: It's on the desk there.

ASLAKSEN *(finds it)*: Good.

MAYOR: But I say, surely *that's* . . .

ASLAKSEN: Yes, that's the Doctor's article, Mr. Mayor.

HOVSTAD: Oh, is *that* what you were talking about?

MAYOR: Precisely. What do you think of it?

HOVSTAD: I'm no expert, of course, and I've only just glanced at it.

MAYOR: Yet you are printing it?

HOVSTAD: I can't very well refuse a man in his position. . . .

ASLAKSEN: I've got no say in what goes into the paper, Mr. Mayor. . . .

MAYOR: Of course not.

ASLAKSEN: I just print what I'm given.

MAYOR: Quite so.

ASLAKSEN: So if you'll excuse me . . .

(He walks across towards the printing shop)

MAYOR: Just a moment, please, Mr. Aslaksen. With your permission, Mr. Hovstad . . .

HOVSTAD: Please.

MAYOR: Now you are a wise and sensible sort of man, Mr. Aslaksen.

ASLAKSEN: I am very pleased you should think so, Mr. Mayor.

MAYOR: And a man of considerable influence in some circles.

ASLAKSEN: Mainly among the people of moderate means.

MAYOR: The small ratepayers are in the majority—here as everywhere else.

ASLAKSEN: That's right.

MAYOR: And I've no doubt you know what most of them think about things in
general. Isn't that so?

ASLAKSEN: Yes, I think I can safely say I do, Mr. Mayor.

MAYOR: Well . . . the fact that this admirable spirit of self-sacrifice is to be found
in our town among its less well-endowed citizens . . .

ASLAKSEN: How do you mean?

HOVSTAD: Self-sacrifice?

MAYOR: . . . This shows an admirable public spirit, most admirable. I almost said
unexpected, too. But of course you know better than I what people's attitudes
are.

ASLAKSEN: But, Mr. Mayor . . .

MAYOR: And in fact it's no small sacrifice that the town will have to make.

HOVSTAD: The town?

ASLAKSEN: But I don't understand. . . . You mean the Baths, surely. . . .

MAYOR: At a rough estimate, the alterations which the Medical Officer considers
desirable will come to something like a couple of hundred thousand crowns.

ASLAKSEN: That's a lot of money, but . . .

MAYOR: Of course it will be necessary to raise a municipal loan.

HOVSTAD *(rises)*: Surely it's not the idea that the town . . . ?

ASLAKSEN: It's not going to come out of the rates! Not out of the people's pockets!

MAYOR: My dear Mr. Aslaksen, where else do you see the money coming from?

ASLAKSEN: I think the owners ought to take care of that.

MAYOR: The owners do not see themselves in a position to provide any additional capital.

ASLAKSEN: Is that absolutely certain, Mr. Mayor?

MAYOR: I am assured on that point. If all these extensive alterations are considered desirable, the town itself must pay for them.

ASLAKSEN: But God damn it all—I beg your pardon!—but this puts a completely
different light on things, Mr. Hovstad!

HOVSTAD: Yes, it does indeed.

MAYOR: The most ruinous thing is that we'll be forced to close the Baths for a
couple of years.

HOVSTAD: Close them? Completely?

ASLAKSEN: For two years?

MAYOR: Yes, the work will take all that long—at least.

ASLAKSEN: Yes, but Heavens! We could never last out that long, Mr. Mayor. What would people like us live on in the meantime?

MAYOR: I regret to say that is an extremely difficult question to answer, Mr. Aslaksen. But what do you expect us to do? Do you think anybody is going to come here if you get people going round making up these stories about the water being polluted, and about the place being a cesspool, and the whole town . . .

ASLAKSEN: Do you think the whole thing might just be imagination?

MAYOR: With the best will in the world, I cannot come to any other conclusion.

ASLAKSEN: Then I must say Dr. Stockmann is being most irresponsible in all this. You must forgive me, Mr. Mayor, but . . .

MAYOR: I regret what you say is quite true, Mr. Aslaksen. My brother has always been rather impetuous, unfortunately.

ASLAKSEN: Are you still prepared to support him after this, Mr. Hovstad?

HOVSTAD: But who would have thought . . . ?

MAYOR: I have drawn up a short statement of the facts, putting a rather more sober interpretation on them; and in it I have suggested some ways in which such defects as may come to light could reasonably be dealt with without going beyond the present resources of the Baths.

HOVSTAD: Have you this statement with you, Mr. Mayor?

MAYOR (*fumbling in his pocket*): Yes, I brought it with me on the offchance that . . .

ASLAKSEN (*hastily*): Heavens above, there he is!

MAYOR: Who? My brother?

HOVSTAD: Where?

ASLAKSEN: He's coming in through the printing shop.

MAYOR: It *would* happen. I don't want to bump into him here, and there was still a lot more I wanted to talk to you about.

HOVSTAD (*points to the door on the right*): In there for the present.

MAYOR: But . . . !

HOVSTAD.: There's only Billing in there.

ASLAKSEN: Quick, quick! He's coming now.

MAYOR: All right. But see if you can't get rid of him quickly.

(*He goes out through the door, right, which Aslaksen opens, and shuts again behind him*)

HOVSTAD: Pretend you are doing something, Aslaksen.

(*He sits down and begins to write. Aslaksen rummages through a pile of newspapers on a chair, right.*)

DR. STOCKMANN (*entering from the printing shop*): Back again!

(*He puts down his hat and stick*)

HOVSTAD (*writing*): Already, Doctor? Hurry up with what we were talking about, Aslaksen. We haven't got a lot of time to spare today.

DR. STOCKMANN: No proofs yet, they tell me.

ASLAKSEN (*without turning round*): You could hardly expect them yet, Doctor.

DR. STOCKMANN: Well, well, it's just that I'm impatient—as you can well imagine. I can't settle to anything until I've seen the thing in print.

HOVSTAD: Hm! It'll be a good while yet, I fancy. Don't you think so, Aslaksen?

ASLAKSEN: Yes, I'm rather afraid so.

DR. STOCKMANN: Never mind, my dear fellows. I'll look in again. I don't mind coming twice if need be. An important thing like this . . . the welfare of the whole town . . . this is no time for dawdling on. *(About to go, but stops and comes back)* Actually . . . there was something else I wanted to talk to you about.

HOVSTAD: Excuse me, but couldn't we perhaps make it some other time. . . ?

DR. STOCKMANN: It won't take a second. You see it's just that . . . when people read my article in the paper tomorrow morning, and realize that all through the winter I have been quietly working away in the interests of the town . . .

HOVSTAD: Yes, but Doctor . . .

DR. STOCKMANN: I know what you are going to say. You think I was only damn' well doing my duty . . . my simple duty as a citizen. Of course! I know that as well as you do. But my fellow citizens, you know. . . . Well, I mean, they think rather highly of me, actually, these good people. . . .

ASLAKSEN: Yes, the people have thought very highly of you up to now, Dr. Stockmann.

DR. STOCKMANN: Yes, and that's just what I'm a little bit afraid of. . . . What I mean is . . . a thing like this comes along, and they—especially the underprivileged classes—take it as a rousing call to take the affairs of the town into their own hands in future.

HOVSTAD *(rising)*: Hm! Dr. Stockmann, I don't think I ought to conceal from you . . .

DR. STOCKMANN: Aha! I might have guessed there'd be something in the wind. But I won't hear of it! If anybody's thinking of organizing anything like that . . .

HOVSTAD: Like what?

DR. STOCKMANN: Well, anything at all—a parade or a banquet or a presentation— whatever it is, you must promise me faithfully to put a stop to it. And you too, Mr. Aslaksen! I insist!

HOVSTAD: Excuse me, Doctor, but sooner or later you've got to hear the real truth . . .

(Mrs. Stockmann, in hat and coat, enters by the main door, back, left)

MRS. STOCKMANN *(sees the Doctor)*: Just as I thought!

HOVSTAD *(goes over to her)*: You here too, Mrs. Stockmann?

DR. STOCKMANN: What the devil do you want here, Katherine?

MRS. STOCKMANN: You know very well what I want.

HOVSTAD: Won't you take a seat? Or perhaps . . .

MRS. STOCKMANN: Thanks, but don't you bother about me. And you must forgive me coming here to fetch my husband; for I'm the mother of three children, I'll have you know.

DR. STOCKMANN: What's all this rubbish! We all know that!

MRS. STOCKMANN: But it doesn't look as if you care very much these days about your wife and children; otherwise you wouldn't be carrying on as you are, bringing us all to rack and ruin.

DR. STOCKMANN: Have you gone stark, staring mad, Katherine? Are you trying to say a man with wife and children has no right to proclaim the truth—has no right to be a useful and active citizen—has no right to be of service to the town he lives in?

MRS. STOCKMANN: Do be reasonable, Thomas!

ASLAKSEN: Just what I say. Moderation in all things.

MRS. STOCKMANN: That's why it's very wrong of you, Mr. Hovstad, to lure my husband away from house and home and fool him into getting mixed up in all this.

HOVSTAD: I don't go about fooling people. . . .

DR. STOCKMANN: Fool me! Do you think I'd let anybody make a fool of *me*!

MRS. STOCKMANN: Yes, you would. I know, I know, you are the cleverest man in town. But you're too easily fooled, Thomas. (*To Hovstad*) Remember, if you print what he's written he loses his job at the Baths. . . .

ASLAKSEN.: What!

HOVSTAD: You know, Doctor . . .

DR. STOCKMANN (*laughs*): Ha ha! Just let them try! Oh no, they wouldn't dare. You see, I have the compact majority behind me.

MRS. STOCKMANN: Yes, worse luck! Fancy having a nasty thing like that behind you.

DR. STOCKMANN: Fiddlesticks, Katherine! Go home and look to your house and let me look to society. Why should you be so afraid; I'm quite confident, and really rather pleased with things. (*Walks up and down, rubbing his hands*) Truth and the People will prevail, you can take your oath on that. Oh, I see the massed ranks of a great citizen army marching on to victory . . . ! (*Stops by a chair*) What the devil is *that*?

ASLAKSEN (*turns to look*): Oh!

HOVSTAD (*similarly*): Hm!

DR. STOCKMANN: There lies the highest mark of authority.

(*He picks the Mayor's hat up carefully by the tips of his fingers and holds it aloft*)

MRS. STOCKMANN: The Mayor's hat!

DR. STOCKMANN: And here the baton of office, too. How in the name of glory . . . ?

HOVSTAD: Well . . .

DR. STOCKMANN: Ah, I see! He's been here trying to talk you over. Ha ha! Came to the right man, eh? Then he must have seen me in the printing shop. (*Bursts into laughter*) Did he run away, Mr. Aslaksen?

ASLAKSEN (*hurriedly*): Yes, Doctor, he ran away.

DR. STOCKMANN: Ran away without either his stick or . . . Rubbish, Peter never runs away from anything. But what the devil have you done with him? Ah . . . in there, of course. Now I'll show you something, Katherine!

MRS. STOCKMANN: Thomas . . . please!

ASLAKSEN: Have a care, Doctor!

(*Dr. Stockmann puts the Mayor's hat on, takes his stick, walks over and throws open the door, and stands there saluting. The Mayor comes in, red with anger; behind him comes Billing.*)

MAYOR: What's the meaning of all this tomfoolery?

DR. STOCKMANN: Show some respect, my dear Peter. I'm the one in authority here now.

(He walks up and down)

MRS. STOCKMANN *(near to tears)*: Oh, Thomas, really!

MAYOR *(following him about)*: Give me my hat and my stick!

DR. STOCKMANN *(as before)*: You might be chief constable, but I am the Mayor— I'm head of the whole town, can't you see!

MAYOR: Take that hat off, I tell you. Don't forget it's an official badge of office!

DR. STOCKMANN: Pooh! When a people rises from its slumber like a giant re- freshed, do you think anybody's going to be scared by a hat? Because you might as well know, we are having a revolution in town tomorrow. You threatened to dismiss me; well now I'm dismissing you, relieving you of all your official positions.... Perhaps you think I can't? Oh yes, I can. Because I can bring irresistible social pressure to bear. Hovstad and Billing will put down a barrage in the *People's Herald,* and Aslaksen will sally forth at the head of the entire Ratepayers Association....

ASLAKSEN: Not me, Doctor.

DR. STOCKMANN: Yes of course you will....

MAYOR: Aha! Then perhaps Mr. Hovstad has decided to associate himself with this agitation after all?

HOVSTAD: No, Mr. Mayor.

ASLAKSEN: No, Mr. Hovstad is not so stupid as to go and ruin both the paper and himself for the sake of some wild idea.

DR. STOCKMANN *(looks round)*: What does this mean?

HOVSTAD: You have represented your case in a false light, Dr. Stockmann; conse- quently I cannot give it my support.

BILLING: And after what the Mayor was kind enough to tell me in there . . .

DR. STOCKMANN: A false light! You leave that side of things to me. You just print my article—I'm quite ready to stand by everything I say.

HOVSTAD: I'm not going to print it. I cannot and will not and dare not print it.

DR. STOCKMANN: Dare not? What sort of talk is that? You are the editor, aren't you? And it's the editors who control the press, surely?

ASLAKSEN: No, it's the readers.

MAYOR: Fortunately, yes.

ASLAKSEN: It's public opinion, the educated public, the ratepayers and all the oth- ers—these are the people who control the press.

DR. STOCKMANN *(calmly)*: And all these forces are against me?

ASLAKSEN: Yes, they are. It would mean total ruin for the town if your article were printed.

DR. STOCKMANN: Indeed.

MAYOR: My hat and my stick!

(Dr. Stockmann takes the hat off and puts it on the table, along with the stick)

MAYOR *(collecting them both)*: Your term as mayor has come to an abrupt end.

DR. STOCKMANN: This is not the end yet. *(To Hovstad)* So it's quite impossible to get my article in the *Herald*?

HOVSTAD: Quite impossible. And I'm thinking partly also of your family. . . .

MRS. STOCKMANN: Oh, you needn't start worrying about his family, Mr. Hovstad.

MAYOR (*takes a sheet of paper out of his pocket*): For the guidance of the public, it will be sufficient to print this. It is an official statement.

HOVSTAD (*takes it*): Good. I'll see that it goes in.

DR. STOCKMANN: But not mine! You think you can gag me and silence the truth! You'll not get away with this so easily. Mr. Aslaksen, will you please take my manuscript and print it for me at once as a pamphlet—at my own expense, and on my authority. I want four hundred copies—no, five . . . six hundred, I want.

ASLAKSEN: Not if you offered me its weight in gold could I let my printing press be used for a thing like that. I daren't offend public opinion. You'll not get anybody in town to print it, I shouldn't think.

DR. STOCKMANN: Give it back to me then.

HOVSTAD: (*hands him the manuscript*) There you are.

DR. STOCKMANN (*takes his hat and stick*): I'll get it out somehow. I'll call a mass meeting and read it out! All my fellow citizens shall hear the voice of truth!

MAYOR: You'll never get anybody to hire you a hall.

ASLAKSEN: Absolutely nobody, I'm quite certain.

BILLING: No, I'm dammed if they will.

MRS. STOCKMANN: But that would be outrageous! Why is everybody against you all of a sudden?

DR. STOCKMANN (*angrily*): I'll tell you why. It's because all the men in this town are nothing but a lot of old women—like you. All they can think about is their families; they never think about the rest of the community.

MRS. STOCKMANN (*taking his arm*): Then I'll show them one . . . old woman at least who can be a man . . . for once. I'll stick by you, Thomas!

DR. STOCKMANN: Well said, Katherine. And I *will* have my say, by Heaven! If I can't book a hall, I'll hire a man with a drum to march round town with me, and I'll proclaim it at every street corner.

MAYOR: I can't believe you'd be so absolutely crazy.

DR. STOCKMANN: Oh yes, I would!

ASLAKSEN: You'll not get a single man in the whole of the town to go with you!

BILLING: No, I'm dammed if you will!

MRS. STOCKMANN: Don't you give in now, Thomas. I'll get the boys to go with you.

DR. STOCKMANN: That's a wonderful idea!

MRS. STOCKMANN: Morten will love to go; and Ejlif's sure to come along as well.

DR. STOCKMANN: Yes, and then what about Petra! And you too, Katherine?

MRS. STOCKMANN: No, no, not me. But I'll stand in the window and watch, that's what I'll do.

DR. STOCKMANN (*puts his arms round her and kisses her*): Thank you for that! And now, gentlemen, the gloves are off. We'll see whether you and your shabby tricks can stop an honest citizen who wants to clean up the town.

(*He and his wife go out through the door, back, left*)

MAYOR (*shakes his head thoughtfully*): Now he's sent her mad, too.

Act Four

A large, old-fashioned room in the house of Captain Horster. At the back of the room, double doors open on to an anteroom. On the wall, left, are three windows; against the opposite wall is a dais, on which is a small table, and on it two candles, a water carafe, a glass, and a bell.

The room is additionally lit by wall lamps between the windows. Downstage left, a table with candles and a chair. Down right is a door, and beside it a couple of chairs.

There is a big crowd of townspeople of all classes. A few women and one or two schoolboys can be seen among them. More and more people keep coming in through the door at the back, filling up the room.

FIRST MAN *(bumping into another man)*: Hello, Lamstad! You here as well?

SECOND MAN: I never miss a public meeting.

THIRD MAN: I expect you've brought your whistle?

SECOND MAN: You bet I have. Haven't you?

THIRD MAN: I'll say I have. Skipper Evensen said he was going to bring his great big cow-horn.

SECOND MAN: Good old Evensen!

(Laughter in the group)

FOURTH MAN *(joining them)*: Here, I say, what's going on here tonight?

SECOND MAN: It's Dr. Stockmann. He's holding a protest meeting against the Mayor.

FOURTH MAN: But the Mayor's his brother!

FIRST MAN: That doesn't matter. Dr. Stockmann's not frightened.

THIRD MAN: But he's got it all wrong. It said so in the *Herald*.

SECOND MAN: Yes, he must be wrong this time, because nobody would let him have a hall for his meeting—Ratepayers Association, Men's Club, nobody!

FIRST MAN: He couldn't even get the Baths Hall.

SECOND MAN: I should think not.

A MAN *(in another group)*: Whose side are we on here, eh?

A SECOND MAN *(in the same group)*: Just you keep an eye on Aslaksen, and do what *he* does.

BILLING *(with a briefcase under his arm, pushing his way through the crowd)*: Excuse me, gentlemen! May I come through, please? I'm reporting for the *Herald*. Thank you ... thank you!

(He sits at the table, left)

A WORKMAN: Who's he?

SECOND WORKMAN: Don't you know *him*? That's Billing, he's on Aslaksen's paper.

(Captain Horster conducts Mrs. Stockmann and Petra in through the door, right front. Ejlif and Morten are with them.)

HORSTER: I thought perhaps the family might like to sit here. You can easily slip out there if anything happens.

MRS. STOCKMANN: Do you really think things might get out of hand?

HORSTER: You never know ... with all these people here. But you sit here, and don't worry.

MRS. STOCKMANN (*sits down*): It was very kind of you to offer my husband this room.

HORSTER: Well, since nobody else would . . .

PETRA (*who has also sat down*): And it was brave of you too, Captain Horster.

HORSTER: Oh, I can't see there was anything particularly brave about it.

(*Hovstad and Aslaksen arrive simultaneously but separately, and make their way through the crowd*)

ASLAKSEN (*walks over to Horster*): Hasn't Dr. Stockmann arrived yet?

HORSTER: He's waiting in there.

(*Movement in the crowd near the door at the back*)

HOVSTAD (*to Billing*): Look! Here's the Mayor.

BILLING: Yes, damn me if he hasn't turned up after all!

(*The Mayor eases his way through the crowd, bowing politely, and takes up a position by the wall, left. A moment later, Dr. Stockmann enters by the door, right front. He wears a black frock coat and a white cravat. Some people clap uncertainly, which is met by subdued hissing. Then there is silence.*)

DR. STOCKMANN (*in an undertone*): How do you feel, Katherine?

MRS. STOCKMANN: I'm all right, thanks. (*Lowers her voice*) Try not to lose your temper, Thomas.

DR. STOCKMANN: Oh, I can control myself. (*Looks at his watch, steps up on the dais, and bows*) It's now quarter past . . . so I think we can begin. . . .

(*He produces his manuscript*)

ASLAKSEN: First I think we ought to elect a chairman.

DR. STOCKMANN: No. That's not necessary.

SEVERAL VOICES (*shouting*): Yes, yes it is!

MAYOR: I should also have thought that we should elect a chairman.

DR. STOCKMANN: But I've called this meeting to deliver a lecture, Peter.

MAYOR: Your lecture might just possibly lead to divergent expressions of opinion.

MANY VOICES (*from the crowd*): A chairman! A chairman!

HOVSTAD: The consensus of opinion seems to be that we should have a chairman.

DR. STOCKMANN (*controlling himself*): Very well! Let the 'consensus of opinion' have its way.

ASLAKSEN: Wouldn't the Mayor accept nomination?

THREE MEN (*applauding*): Bravo! Bravo!

MAYOR: For a number of obvious reasons, I must decline. But fortunately we have here with us a man whom I think we can all accept. I refer, of course, to the chairman of the Ratepayers Association, Mr. Aslaksen.

MANY VOICES: Yes, yes. Good old Aslaksen! Bravo!

(*Dr. Stockmann gathers up his manuscript and steps down from the dais*)

ASLAKSEN: If it is the wish of my fellow citizens, I can hardly refuse. . . .

(*Clapping and cheers. Aslaksen mounts the dais.*)

BILLING (*writing*): Let's see—'Mr. Aslaksen elected by acclamation . . . '

ASLAKSEN: And now, perhaps I may be allowed, in this present capacity, to take the opportunity of saying a few brief words. I am a quiet and peace-loving man, who believes in discreet moderation and in . . . and in moderate discretion. Everyone who knows me is aware of that.

MANY VOICES: That's right! That's right, Aslaksen!

ASLAKSEN: I have learnt from long experience in the school of life that moderation is the quality that best befits a citizen . . .

MAYOR: Hear, hear!

ASLAKSEN: . . . and that discretion and moderation are the things whereby society is best served. I might perhaps, therefore, suggest to the honourable gentleman who has called this meeting that he endeavour to keep within the bounds of moderation.

A MAN (near the door): Up the Moderates!

A VOICE: Shut up there!

MANY VOICES: Sh! Sh!

ASLAKSEN: No interruptions, gentlemen, please! Has anybody any comment to make?

MAYOR: Mr. Chairman!

ASLAKSEN: Yes, Mr. Mayor.

MAYOR: In view of the close relationship which, as is doubtless well known, exists between me and the present Medical Officer of the Baths, I should have much preferred not to speak this evening. But my connections with the Baths, to say nothing of my concern for the vital interests of the town, compel me to put forward some sort of proposal. I think I may safely assume that not a single one of us present here today wants to see irresponsible and exaggerated accounts put about concerning the sanitary conditions at the Baths and in the town generally.

MANY VOICES: No, no! Certainly not! We protest!

MAYOR: I should like to propose, therefore, that the Medical Officer be not permitted by this meeting to present his account of the matter.

DR. STOCKMANN (flaring up): Not permitted! What is this. . . ?

MRS. STOCKMANN: (coughing) Hm! hm!

DR. STOCKMANN: (composing himself) Ah! Not permitted, eh!

MAYOR: In my communication to the People's Herald, I acquainted the public with the relevant facts, and every right-thinking person can quite well form his own opinion. It clearly shows that the Doctor's proposal—apart from being a vote of censure on the leading citizens of the town—simply means saddling the ratepayers with an unnecessary expenditure of at least several hundred thousand crowns.

(Cries of disapproval, and whistles)

ASLAKSEN (ringing the bell): Order please, gentlemen! I should like to support the Mayor's proposal. I too believe there is some ulterior motive behind the Doctor's agitation. He talks about the Baths, but what he's really after is revolution. He wants to see the control of the council pass into other hands. Nobody doubts but what the Doctor is sincere in his intentions—nobody can be in two minds about that, surely. I too am in favour of self-government by the people, as long as it doesn't fall too heavily on the ratepayers. But that's just what would happen here. And that's why I'm damned . . . excuse me, gentlemen . . .

why I just can't bring myself to agree with Dr. Stockmann this time. You can pay too dearly even for the best of things sometimes. That's *my* opinion.

(Animated applause on all sides)

HOVSTAD: I feel I ought to make my position clear, too. Dr. Stockmann's agitation seemed in the early stages to be attracting a certain measure of approval and I supported it as impartially as I was able. But then we got wind of the fact that we had allowed ourselves to be misled by an incorrect account. . . .

DR. STOCKMANN: Incorrect. . . !

HOVSTAD: A not wholly reliable account, then. The Mayor's statement has proved that. I trust nobody here doubts my liberal convictions. The policy of the *People's Herald* on the more important political questions must surely be known to everybody. But I have profited from the advice of experienced and thoughtful men that, when it comes to local affairs, a paper should proceed with a certain caution.

ASLAKSEN: I entirely agree with the speaker.

HOVSTAD: And in the matter under discussion it is now undeniably true that Dr. Stockmann has public opinion against him. But what is the first and foremost duty of an editor, gentlemen? Is it not to work in harmony with his readers? Has he not been given, as it were, a tacit mandate to work loyally and unremittingly for the welfare of his fellows? Or am I perhaps mistaken?

MANY VOICES: No, no! Hovstad is right!

HOVSTAD: It has been a sad thing for me to break with a man in whose house I have of late been a frequent guest—a man who until today has enjoyed the undivided goodwill of his fellow citizens—a man whose only . . . or should we say, whose most characteristic failing is to be guided more by his heart than by his head.

A FEW SCATTERED VOICES: That's true! Good old Dr. Stockmann!

HOVSTAD: But my duty to the community compelled me to break with him. There is also one further consideration that impels me to oppose him and, if possible, to prevent him from going any further along this fateful course he has taken. And that is consideration for his family . . .

DR. STOCKMANN: You stick to the water-supply and the sewers!

HOVSTAD: . . . Consideration for his wife and his helpless children.

MORTEN: Is that us he means, Mother?

MRS. STOCKMANN: Hush!

ASLAKSEN: I shall now put the Mayor's proposal to the vote.

DR. STOCKMANN: You needn't bother! I don't intend speaking about all the dirty business at the Baths tonight. No! You are going to hear about something quite different.

MAYOR *(in an undertone)*: Now what's he up to?

A DRUNKEN MAN *(beside the entrance door)*: If I'm entitled to pay rates, I'm also entitled to my own opinion. And it's my entire . . . firm . . . incomprehensible opinion that . . .

SEVERAL VOICES: Be quiet over there!

OTHERS: He's drunk. Chuck him out.

(The drunken man is put out)

DR. STOCKMANN: May I speak?

ASLAKSEN (*rings the bell*): Dr. Stockmann has the floor!

DR. STOCKMANN: If anybody, even a few days ago, had tried gagging me as they've tried tonight . . . they'd have seen me leaping like a lion to the defence of my sacred rights as an individual. But that hardly matters to me now. Now I have more important things to speak about.

(*The crowd presses closer round him. Morten Kiil can be seen in the crowd.*)

DR. STOCKMANN (*continues*): I've been doing a lot of thinking in the last few days . . . turning so many things over in my mind that in the end my head was buzzing . . .

MAYOR (*coughs*): Hm!

DR. STOCKMANN: . . . but I sorted things out in the finish. Then I saw the whole situation very clearly. That's why I am here this evening. I am going to make a great exposure, gentlemen! And the revelation I am going to make to you is incomparably bigger than this petty business about the water-supply being polluted and the Baths standing over a cesspool.

SEVERAL VOICES (*shouting*): Don't talk about the Baths! We don't want to hear it! None of that!

DR. STOCKMANN: I have said I am going to speak about the tremendous discovery I have made in the last few days . . . the discovery that all our *spiritual* sources are polluted and that our whole civic community is built over a cesspool of lies.

DISCONCERTED VOICES (*subdued*): What's he saying?

MAYOR: Making insinuations. . . !

ASLAKSEN (*his hand on the bell*): I call upon the speaker to moderate his language.

DR. STOCKMANN: I love my native town as much as ever a man can. I wasn't very old when I left here; and distance and longing and memory lent a kind of enchantment to both the place and the people. (*Some clapping and cheers*) Then for many a long year I sat up there in the far North, in a miserable hole of a place. Coming across some of the people living here and there in that rocky wilderness, I often used to think they would have been better served, poor half-starved creatures that they were, if they had sent for a vet instead of somebody like me.

(*There is a murmuring in the room*)

BILLING (*putting his pen down*): Damn me if I've ever heard. . . !

HOVSTAD: That's a slander on a respectable people!

DR. STOCKMANN: Just be patient a little!—I don't think anybody would want to accuse me of having forgotten my home town up there. I sat brooding—rather like an eider duck—and the thing I hatched out . . . was the plan for the Baths. (*Applause and protests*) And when fate at long last smiled on me, and it turned out I could come home again—yes, my friends, there didn't seem to be very much more I wanted from life. Just one thing I wanted: to be able to work—eagerly, tirelessly, ardently—for the common good and for the good of the town.

MAYOR (*looking away*): You choose rather a peculiar way of . . . hm!

DR. STOCKMANN: So there I was—deliriously, blindly happy. Then, yesterday morning—no, actually, it was the evening before—my eyes were opened wide, and the first thing I saw was the colossal stupidity of the authorities. . . .

(Noises, shouts and laughter. Mrs. Stockmann coughs earnestly.)

MAYOR: Mr. Chairman!

ASLAKSEN *(rings the bell)*: By virtue of my position. . . !

DR. STOCKMANN: Let's not be too fussy about a word here and there, Mr. Aslaksen! All I mean is I got wind of the colossal botch-up our so-called leaders had managed to make of things down at the Baths. If there's anything I just can't stand at any price—it's leaders! I've just about had enough of them. They are just like a lot of goats in a young forest—there's damage everywhere they go. Any decent man and they just get in his way, they're under his feet wherever he turns. If I had my way I'd like to see them exterminated like any other pest. . . .

(Uproar in the room)

MAYOR: Mr. Chairman, is it in order to make remarks like this?

ASLAKSEN *(his hand on the bell)*: Dr. Stockmann. . . !

DR. STOCKMANN: I can't understand why it has taken me till now to wake up to what these gentlemen really are, when practically every day I've had a perfect specimen of them right in front of my very eyes—my brother Peter—slow on the uptake and set in his ideas. . . .

(Laughter, noise and whistles. Mrs. Stockmann sits coughing. Aslaksen rings his bell violently.)

THE DRUNKEN MAN *(who has come in again)*: Are you referring to me? Because they do call me Petersen . . . but I'll be damned if . . .

ANGRY VOICES: Throw that drunk out! Get rid of him!

(The man is again thrown out)

MAYOR: Who was that person?

A BYSTANDER: Don't know him, sir.

A SECOND MAN: He doesn't belong here.

A THIRD MAN: It must be that timber merchant over from . . . *(The rest is inaudible)*

ASLAKSEN: The man had obviously had too much to drink. Proceed, Doctor, but do please remember—with moderation.

DR. STOCKMANN: Very well, gentlemen, I shall say no more about our leaders. If anyone imagines from what I've just said that I'm out after these gentlemen's blood this evening, then he's wrong—quite definitely wrong! Because I am happily convinced that all these old dodderers, these relics of a dying age, are managing very nicely to see themselves off—they don't need to call in a doctor to hasten the end. And besides they are not the people who constitute the greatest danger to society. *They* are not the ones who do most to pollute our spiritual life, or to infect the ground beneath us. *They* are not the ones who are the worst enemies of truth and freedom in our society.

SHOUTS FROM ALL SIDES: Who then? Who is, then? Name them!

DR. STOCKMANN: Yes, I'll name them, don't you fret! Because *that's* precisely the great discovery I made yesterday. *(Raises his voice)* The worst enemy of truth and freedom in our society is the compact majority. Yes, the damned, compact, liberal majority. *That's* what! Now you know.

(Tremendous commotion in the room. Most of the crowd are shouting, stamping and

whistling. Some of the more elderly men exchange glances, and seem to be enjoying things. Mrs. Stockmann anxiously gets to her feet. Ejlif and Morten advance threateningly on some schoolboys who are misbehaving. Aslaksen rings his bell and shouts for order. Hovstad and Billing are both trying to speak, but cannot be heard above the noise. At last quiet is restored.)

ASLAKSEN: As Chairman, I must request the speaker to withdraw his wild remarks.

DR. STOCKMANN: Not on your life, Mr. Aslaksen. It is that majority here which is robbing me of my freedom and is trying to prevent me from speaking the truth.

HOVSTAD: The majority is always right!

BILLING: And it damn' well always stands for the truth too!

DR. STOCKMANN: The majority is never right. Never, I tell you! That's one of these lies in society that no free and intelligent man can help rebelling against. Who are the people that make up the biggest proportion of the population— the intelligent ones or the fools? I think we can agree it's the fools, no matter where you go in this world, it's the fools that form the overwhelming majority. But I'll be damned if that means it's right that the fools should dominate the intelligent. *(Uproar and shouting)* Yes, yes, shout me down if you like, but you can't deny it! The majority has the *might*—more's the pity—but it hasn't *right.* I am right—I and one or two other individuals like me. The minority is always right.

(Renewed uproar)

HOVSTAD: Ha! ha! In the last day or two Dr. Stockmann has turned aristocrat!

DR. STOCKMANN: I've already said I'm not going to waste any words on that bunch of narrow-chested, short-winded old has-beens. They've no longer anything to give to the red-blooded life of today. I'm thinking of the few, the genuine individuals in our midst, with their new and vigorous ideas. These men stand in the very forefront of our advance, so far ahead that the compact majority hasn't even begun to approach them—and it's *there* they fight for truths too newly-born to have won any support from the majority.

HOVSTAD: Aha! So now he's a revolutionary.

DR. STOCKMANN: Yes, by God, I am, Mr. Hovstad! I'm plotting revolution against this lie that the majority has a monopoly of the truth. What are these truths that always bring the majority rallying round? Truths so elderly they are practically senile. And when a truth is as old as that, gentlemen, you can hardly tell it from a lie. *(Laughter and jeers)* All right, believe it or not! But truths are not by any means the tough old Methuselahs people imagine. The life of a normally constituted truth is generally, say, about seventeen or eighteen years, at most twenty; rarely longer. But truths as elderly as that have always worn terribly thin. But it's only *then* that the majority will have anything to do with them; then it will recommend them as wholesome food for thought. But there's no great food-value in that sort of diet, I can tell you—as a doctor, I know what I'm talking about. All these majority truths are just like salt meat that's been kept too long and gone bad and mouldy. That's at the root of all this moral scurvy that's going about.

ASLAKSEN: It appears to me that the honourable gentleman is straying rather a long way from his subject.

MAYOR: I concur very much with what the Chairman says.

DR. STOCKMANN: You must be mad, Peter. I'm sticking as close to my subject as I can. For that's just what I'm trying to say: that the masses, this damned compact majority—*this* is the thing that's polluting the sources of our spiritual life and infecting the very ground we stand on.

HOVSTAD: And this is what happens, you say, just because the great majority of thinking people are sensible enough to keep their approval for recognized and well-founded truths?

DR. STOCKMANN: My dear Mr. Hovstad, don't talk to me about well-founded truths. The truths the masses recognize today are the same truths as were held by advanced thinkers in our grandfathers' day. We who man the advanced outposts today, we don't recognize them any more. In my opinion, only one thing is certain: and that is that no society can live a healthy life on the old dry bones of that kind of truth.

HOVSTAD: But instead of you standing there and giving us all this airy talk, it would be interesting to hear a bit more about these old, dry bones of truth we are supposed to be living on.

(Approval from several quarters)

DR. STOCKMANN: Oh, I could draw up a whole list of these horrors. But for the moment I'll restrict myself to *one* recognized truth, which is actually a rotten lie but which nevertheless Mr. Hovstad and the *People's Herald* and all the *Herald's* supporters live by.

HOVSTAD: And that is?

DR. STOCKMANN: A doctrine inherited from your forefathers which you fatuously go on spreading far and wide—the doctrine that the general public, the common herd, the masses are the very essence of the people—that they *are* the people—that the common man, and all the ignorant and immature elements in society have the same right to criticize and to approve, to govern and to counsel as the few intellectually distinguished people.

BILLING: Well I'll be damned. . . .

HOVSTAD *(shouting at the same time)*: Citizens, take note of this!

ANGRY VOICES: So we are not the people, eh? Only the top people are to have any say, eh?

A WORKMAN: Chuck him out, saying things like that!

OTHERS: Out with him!

A MAN: *(shouting)* Let's have a blast of it now, Evensen!

(Great blasts on a horn, along with whistles and tremendous uproar)

DR. STOCKMANN *(after the noise has died down somewhat)*: Be reasonable! Can't you bear to hear the voice of truth just for once? I don't expect you all to agree with me straight off. But I must say I expected Mr. Hovstad to admit I was right when he'd got over his first shock. Mr. Hovstad claims to be a free-thinker. . . .

VOICES *(in astonished undertones)*: Free-thinker, did he say? What? Mr. Hovstad a free-thinker?

HOVSTAD (*shouting*): Prove it, Dr. Stockmann! Have I ever said so in black and white?

DR. STOCKMANN (*reflectively*): No, damn it, you are right. You've never had the guts. Well, I don't want to embarrass you, Mr. Hovstad. Let's say it's me who's the free-thinker, then. What I'm going to do is prove to you, scientifically, that when the *People's Herald* tells you that you—the general public, the masses—are the real essence of the people, it's just a lot of bunkum. Don't you see it's just a journalistic lie? The public is only the raw material from which a people is made. (*Murmurs, laughter and general disturbance in the room*) Well, isn't that the way it is with life generally. Look at the difference between pedigree and cross-bred animals. Look at an ordinary barn-yard hen, for instance—fat lot of meat you get off a scraggy old thing like that! And what about the eggs it lays? Any decent, self-respecting crow could do as well. But take a purebred Spanish or Japanese hen, or take a pheasant or a turkey—ah! what a difference! Or I might mention dogs, which are so like humans in many ways. Think first of an ordinary mongrel—I mean one of those filthy, shaggy rough dogs that do nothing but run about the streets and cock their legs against all the walls. Compare a mongrel like that with a poodle whose pedigree goes back many generations, who has been properly fed and has grown up among quiet voices and soft music. Don't you think the poodle's brain will have developed quite differently from the mongrel's? You bet it will! That kind of pedigree dog can be trained to do the most fantastic tricks—things an ordinary mongrel could never learn even if it stood on its head.

(*Uproar and laughter*)

A MAN (*shouts*): Are you trying to make out we are dogs now?

ANOTHER MAN: We're not animals, Doctor!

DR. STOCKMANN: Ah, but that's just exactly what we *are*, my friend! We are as good animals as any man could wish for. But you don't find all that many really outstanding ones. Oh, there's a tremendous difference between the poodles and the mongrels amongst us men. And the funny thing is that Mr. Hovstad fully agrees with me as long as we are talking about four-footed animals. . . .

HOVSTAD: Yes, it's all right for *them*.

DR. STOCKMANN: All right. But as soon as I apply the principle to two-legged creatures, that's the end of it for Mr. Hovstad. He hasn't the courage of his convictions, he doesn't take things to their logical conclusion. So he turns the whole theory upside down and proclaims in the *Herald* that the barnyard hen and the street-corner mongrel—that these are the finest exhibits in the menagerie. But that's always the way, and always will be as long as a man still remains infected by the mass mind, and hasn't worked his way free to some kind of intellectual distinction.

HOVSTAD: I make no claim to any kind of distinction. I came from simple peasant stock, and I am proud that my roots go deep into that common people he is insulting.

SOME WORKMEN: Good old Hovstad! Hurrah! Hurrah!

DR. STOCKMANN: The sort of common people I'm talking about are not found simply among the lower classes; they are crawling and swarming all round us—

right up to the highest social level. You've only got to look at that nice, pretty Mayor of yours. My brother Peter is as mass-minded a person as anything you'll find on two legs. . . .

(Laughter and hisses)

MAYOR: I must protest against these personal remarks.

DR. STOCKMANN *(imperturbably)*: . . . and that's not because he's descended, like me, from some awful old Pomeranian pirate or something—because that's what we are . . .

MAYOR: An absurd story. I deny it!

DR. STOCKMANN: . . . but because he thinks what his superiors think, and believes what his superiors believe. And anybody who does that is just one of the masses in spirit. You see, that's why my magnificent brother Peter is so terribly lacking in natural distinction—and consequently has so little independence of mind.

MAYOR: Mr. Chairman. . . !

HOVSTAD: So in this country it seems it's the distinguished people who are the liberals! That's a new one!

(Laughter)

DR. STOCKMANN: Yes, that's another part of my discovery. And along with that goes the fact that free-thinking is almost exactly the same as morality. That's why I call it downright irresponsible of the *Herald* to keep putting out this distorted idea, day in day out, that it's the masses, the compact majority that has the monopoly of morality and liberal principles—and that vice and corruption and every kind of depraved idea are an overflow from culture, just as all the filth in our Baths is an overflow from the tannery up at Mölledal! *(Uproar and interruptions. Dr. Stockmann, unperturbed, smiles in his eagerness.)* And yet this same *Herald* can preach about raising the standards of the masses! Good Lord, if what the *Herald* says is right, raising the level of the masses would amount precisely to toppling them straight over the edge to perdition. But fortunately it's just one of those old lies we've had handed down—this idea that culture is demoralizing. No, stupidity and poverty and ugliness are the things that do the devil's work! A house that isn't aired and swept every day—and my wife Katherine says it ought to be scrubbed as well, but that's a debatable point—anybody living for more than two or three years in *that* kind of house will end up by having no moral sense left whatsoever. No oxygen, no conscience! And there must be an awful lot of houses in this town short of oxygen, it seems, if the entire compact majority is so irresponsible as to want to build the prosperity of the town on a quagmire of lies and deceit.

ASLAKSEN: I cannot allow such abusive remarks to be directed at the entire community.

A MAN: I move that the Chairman rule the speaker out of order!

ANGRY VOICES: Yes, yes! That's right. Out of order!

DR. STOCKMANN *(flaring up)*: Then I'll shout the truth on every street corner! I'll write to all the other newspapers! I'll see that the whole country gets to know what's going on here!

HOVSTAD: It might almost seem that Dr. Stockmann is set on ruining the town.

DR. STOCKMANN: I love this town so much that I'd rather destroy it than see it prosper on a lie.

ASLAKSEN: That's putting it pretty strongly.

(Uproar and whistles. Mrs. Stockmann coughs in vain; the Doctor no longer hears her.)

HOVSTAD *(shouting above the din)*: Any man who wants to destroy a whole community must be a public enemy.

DR. STOCKMANN *(with rising temper)*: When a place has become riddled with lies, who cares if it's destroyed? I say it should simply be razed to the ground! And all the people living by these lies should be wiped out, like vermin! You'll have the whole country infested in the end, so that eventually the whole country deserves to be destroyed. And if it ever comes to that, then I'd say with all my heart: let it all be destroyed, let all its people be wiped out!

A MAN *(in the crowd)*: That's the talk of an enemy of the people!

BILLING: That, God damn me, was the voice of the people!

THE WHOLE CROWD *(shouting)*: Yes! Yes! He's an enemy of the people. He hates his country. He hates his people.

ASLAKSEN: As a citizen of this country, and as an individual, I am profoundly shocked by what I have just had to listen to. Dr. Stockmann has betrayed himself in a way I should never have dreamt possible. I must therefore, with great regret, associate myself with the opinion that has just been expressed by my honourable fellow citizens, and I propose we embody that opinion in the form of a resolution. I suggest something like this: 'This meeting declares that it considers Dr. Thomas Stockmann, Medical Officer to the Baths, to be an enemy of the people.'

(A storm of applause and cheers. A number of people crowd round Dr. Stockmann, cat-calling. Mrs. Stockmann and Petra have risen. Morten and Ejlif fight with the other schoolboys who have also been booing. Some of the grown-ups separate them.)

DR. STOCKMANN *(to those whistling)*: You fools! I tell you that . . .

ASLAKSEN *(ringing his bell)*: Dr. Stockmann is out of order. A formal vote must be taken; but so as not to hurt anybody's feelings, we will do it by secret ballot. Have you any paper, Mr. Billing?

BILLING: There's both blue and white. . . .

ASLAKSEN *(stepping down)*: That's fine. We can do it quicker that way. Cut it into strips . . . there we are, now. *(To the meeting)* Blue means no, white means yes. I'll come round myself to collect the votes.

(The Mayor leaves the room. Aslaksen and one or two others carry round the slips of paper in their hats.)

ONE MAN *(to Hovstad)*: What's come over the Doctor? What are you to make of it?

HOVSTAD: Well, you know how impetuous he is.

SECOND MAN *(to Billing)*: Tell me—you've been in their house quite a bit. Does the man drink, have you noticed?

BILLING: I'm damned if I know really what to say. They always bring the toddy out when anybody calls.

THIRD MAN: No, I think it's more likely he's a bit crazy.

FIRST MAN: Ah, I wonder if there's insanity in the family.

BILLING: Could very well be.

FOURTH MAN: No, it's just spite, that's what it is. Wants to get his own back about something.

BILLING: He did say something secretly about wanting a rise; but he didn't get it.

ALL THE MEN TOGETHER: Well, there you are then!

THE DRUNKEN MAN (in the crowd): I want a blue one. And I want a white one an' all.

VOICES: Is that that drunk again? Chuck him out!

MORTEN KIIL (approaches the Doctor): Well, Stockmann, now you see where these monkey tricks of yours have landed you!

DR. STOCKMANN: I have simply done my duty.

KIIL: What was that you said about the tanneries at Mölledal?

DR. STOCKMANN: You heard. I said that was where all the muck came from.

KIIL: From *my* tannery as well?

DR. STOCKMANN: I'm afraid so. Yours is the worst.

KIIL: Are you going to print *that* in the papers?

DR. STOCKMANN: I'm not hiding anything.

KIIL: You might find that costly, Stockmann.

(He leaves)

A FAT MAN (goes up to Horster, ignoring the ladies): So, Captain Horster, so you lend your house to enemies of the people, eh?

HORSTER: I think I can do what I like with my own property, Mr. Vik.

THE FAT MAN: So you won't mind if I do the same with mine.

HORSTER: What do you mean?

THE FAT MAN: You'll hear from me in the morning.

(He turns and goes)

PETRA: Isn't he the owner of your ship, Captain Horster?

HORSTER: Yes, that's Mr. Vik.

ASLAKSEN (mounts the platform with the ballot papers; he rings the bell): Gentlemen, let me announce the result. With only one vote to the contrary. . . .

A YOUNG MAN: That's the drunk!

ASLAKSEN: With only one drunken man's vote to the contrary, the resolution of this meeting was carried unanimously: that Dr. Thomas Stockmann is an enemy of the people. (Shouting and applause) Three cheers for our ancient and honourable community! (More cheers) Three cheers for our able and efficient Mayor, for putting duty before family! (Cheers) The meeting is adjourned.

(He steps down)

BILLING: Three cheers for the chairman!

THE WHOLE CROWD: Good old Aslaksen!

DR. STOCKMANN: My hat and coat, Petra! Captain, have you any room aboard for passengers for the New World?

HORSTER: For you and your family we'll make room, Doctor.

DR. STOCKMANN (*as Petra helps him on with his coat*): Good! Come on, Katherine! Come along, lads!

(*He takes his wife by the arm*)

MRS. STOCKMANN (*in a low voice*): Thomas dear, let's go out by the back way.

DR. STOCKMANN: No back way for me, Katherine. (*Raises his voice*) You'll hear again from this enemy of the people before he shakes the dust off his feet. I'm not as sweet-tempered as a certain person I could mention. I'm not saying: 'I forgive you, for you know not what you do.'

ASLAKSEN (*shouts*): That comparison is blasphemous, Dr. Stockmann!

BILLING: Well I'll be...! What dreadful things to say in the presence of decent people.

A COARSE VOICE: And what about those threats he made!

ANGRY SHOUTS: Let's go and break his windows! Duck him in the fjord!

A MAN (*in the crowd*): Give us another blast, Evensen! Blow! Blow!

(*The sound of a horn and whistles and wild shouts. The Doctor and his family make for the exit, and Horster clears a way for them.*)

THE WHOLE CROWD (*howling after them*): Enemy of the people! Enemy of the people! Enemy of the people!

BILLING (*tidying his papers*): Well I'm damned if I would want to drink toddy at the Stockmanns' tonight!

(*The crowd makes for the exit; the noise is continued outside; shouts from the street of 'Enemy of the people! Enemy of the people!'*)

Act Five

Dr. Stockmann's study. Along the walls are bookcases and medicine cupboards. On the back wall is the door to the hall; left front is the door to the living-room. On the right wall are two windows, all the glass panes of which are smashed. In the centre of the room is the Doctor's desk; covered with books and papers. The room is in disorder. It is morning.

Dr. Stockmann, in dressing-gown, slippers and skull-cap, is bending down and raking under one of the cupboards with an umbrella. Finally he manages to rake out a stone.

DR. STOCKMANN (*calling through the open door into the sitting-room*): I've found another one, Katherine.

MRS. STOCKMANN (*from the living-room*): Oh, you'll find a lot more yet, I'm sure.

DR. STOCKMANN (*adding the stone to a pile of others on the table*): I'm going to keep these stones—like relics. Ejlif and Morten must see them every day, and when they grow up, they'll inherit them. (*Rakes under a bookcase*) Hasn't—what the devil's her name again—you know, that girl—hasn't she gone for the glazier yet?

MRS. STOCKMANN (*comes in*): Yes, but he said he didn't know if he could come today.

DR. STOCKMANN: He daren't—you'll see.

MRS. STOCKMANN: Yes, that's what Randina thought too—he was afraid of what the neighbours might say. (*Calls into the living-room.*) What's that you want,

Randina? I see. *(She goes out and comes back at once.)* It's a letter for you, Thomas.

DR. STOCKMANN: Let me see. *(He opens it and reads)* Aha!

MRS. STOCKMANN: Who's it from?

DR. STOCKMANN: From the landlord. He's given us notice.

MRS. STOCKMANN: Has he really? But he was such a nice man. . . .

DR. STOCKMANN *(looking at the letter)*: He daren't do anything else, he says. He's very sorry, but he daren't do anything else . . . because of the others . . . public opinion . . . not his own master . . . dare not risk putting certain people's backs up. . . .

MRS. STOCKMANN: There you see, Thomas.

DR. STOCKMANN: Yes, yes, I see all right. They are all cowards, the whole lot of them here. Nobody dares do anything because of all the others. *(Flings the letter on the table)* But that doesn't make any difference to us, Katherine. We are leaving for the New World, and then . . .

MRS. STOCKMANN: But, Thomas, have you really thought about it properly, this business about leaving. . . ?

DR. STOCKMANN: You wouldn't want me to stay here, would you? Not after the way they've taken it out of me, branding me as an enemy of the people, and smashing all my windows! And look here, Katherine! I've even got a tear in my black trousers through them.

MRS. STOCKMANN: So you have! And they are the best pair you've got!

DR. STOCKMANN: You should never have your best trousers on when you turn out to fight for freedom and truth. Well, it's not that I care all that much about the trousers—you can always put a stitch in them for me. But what gets me is the idea of that mob going for me as though they were my equals—*that's* what I can't stomach, damn it!

MRS. STOCKMANN: Yes, they've really been horrid to you here, Thomas. But do we have to go so far as to leave the country for *that?*

DR. STOCKMANN: Don't you think you would get the same insolence from the masses in the other towns as you do here? Of course you would! They're all the same! Oh, to hell! Let them yap! That's not the worst; the worst thing is that all over the country everybody's got to toe the party line. Not that it's likely to be very much better out West either; it will be the same there too, with your liberal public opinions and your compact majorities and all the rest of the rigmarole. But things are on a bigger scale there, you see. They might kill, but they don't torture. They don't take a free man and put the screws on his soul, as they do here. And if the worst comes to the worst, you can get away from it all. *(Walks up and down)* If only I knew where there was a primeval forest or a little South Sea island going cheap. . . .

MRS. STOCKMANN: But, Thomas, what about the boys?

DR. STOCKMANN *(halts)*: You are funny, Katherine! Would you rather the boys grew up in a society like this? You saw yourself last night how half the population is absolutely mad; and if the other half haven't lost their wits, it's only because they are such thickheads they haven't any wits to lose.

MRS. STOCKMANN: Now then, Thomas dear, you ought to watch what you are saying.

DR. STOCKMANN: Hah! You don't think I'm telling you the truth? Don't they turn every single idea upside down? Don't they make a complete hotch-potch of what's right and what's wrong? Don't they go and call lies what I know perfectly well is the truth? But the craziest thing of the lot is to see all these grown-up men going round calling themselves liberals and imagining they are men of independent minds! Have you ever heard anything like it, Katherine?

MRS. STOCKMANN: Yes, yes, of course that's quite stupid, but. . . (*Petra comes in from the living-room*) Back from school already?

PETRA: Yes. I've been given my notice.

MRS. STOCKMANN: Your notice?

DR. STOCKMANN: You too!

PETRA: Mrs. Busk gave me notice. And I thought it was better to leave at once.

DR. STOCKMANN: How right you were!

MRS. STOCKMANN: Who would have thought Mrs. Busk was that sort!

PETRA: Oh, Mother, Mrs. Busk isn't bad, really. I could see quite well she didn't like doing it. But she daren't do anything else, she said. So I have to leave.

DR. STOCKMANN (*laughs and rubs his hands*): So she didn't dare do anything else, either! That's great!

MRS. STOCKMANN: Oh well, I dare say after that awful scene last night . . .

PETRA: It wasn't just *that*. Listen, Father!

DR. STOCKMANN: Well?

PETRA: Mrs. Busk showed me no less than three letters she'd had this morning. . . .

DR. STOCKMANN: Anonymous, of course?

PETRA: Yes.

DR. STOCKMANN: You see they *daren't* put their names to them, Katherine!

PETRA: And in two of them it said that a certain gentleman, who has been a frequent visitor here, had been talking in the club last night and saying that I had extremely advanced ideas about all sorts of things. . . .

DR.•STOCKMANN: Which I hope you didn't deny?

PETRA: You know very well I wouldn't. Mrs. Busk has got one or two pretty advanced ideas herself, when she talks to me privately. But now that this has come out about me, she daren't keep me.

MRS. STOCKMANN: Fancy! A frequent visitor here! You see what you get for your hospitality, Thomas.

DR. STOCKMANN: We are not going to live in this stinking hole any longer. Pack up as quick as you can, Katherine. The sooner we get away the better.

MRS. STOCKMANN: Be quiet—I think there's somebody in the hall. Go and see, Petra.

PETRA (*opens the door*): Oh, it's you, Captain Horster? Do come in.

HORSTER (*from the hall*): Good morning. I thought I'd just look in to see how things were.

DR. STOCKMANN (*shaking his hand*): Thank you. That's very kind of you.

MRS. STOCKMANN: And thank you for your help last night, Captain Horster.

PETRA: But how did you get back home again?

HORSTER: Oh, I managed. I'm pretty tough, you know. The only thing those people are good for is shooting off their mouths.

DR. STOCKMANN: Yes, isn't it astonishing, this sickening cowardice? Here, I want to show you something! Look, here are all the stones they chucked at us last night. Just look at them! Not more than a couple of honest-to-goodness lumps in the whole lot—the rest are just pebbles, bits of gravel! And yet they went on standing out there, shouting and yelling and swearing they were going to beat me up. But as for *doing* anything—no, there isn't much of that in this town.

HORSTER: It was just as well this time, Doctor.

DR. STOCKMANN: I dare say you're right. But it makes you angry all the same. Because if it ever comes to the point where the country really *has* to fight in earnest, then you'll see how public opinion is all for clearing out fast, and the whole of the compact majority will make for the woods like a great flock of sheep, Captain Horster. That's the saddening thing; that's what really upsets me. . . . Oh, what the hell . . . it's all just a lot of nonsense, really. If they've called me an enemy of the people, I might as well be an enemy of the people.

MRS. STOCKMANN: That's something you'll never be, Thomas.

DR. STOCKMANN: I shouldn't bet on it if I were you, Katherine. To be called some nasty name is just like getting a pinprick in the lung. And this blasted name they've called me—it's lodged here under the heart, embedded deep, griping me as if it were acid. And it's no use taking magnesia for *that!*

PETRA: Puh! I should just laugh at them, Father!

HORSTER: They'll come round to other ways of thinking in time, Doctor.

MRS. STOCKMANN: They will, you know, Thomas, as sure as you're standing here.

DR. STOCKMANN: When it's too late, perhaps. Well, serve them right! Then, as they wallow in their filth, they'll wish they hadn't been so ready to drive a patriot into exile. When do you sail, Captain Horster?

HORSTER: Well, actually that was what I came to talk to you about. . . .

DR. STOCKMANN: Well? Something wrong with the ship?

HORSTER: No, only that I'm not sailing with her.

PETRA: Surely you haven't been given notice?

HORSTER (*smiles*): Yes, I have.

PETRA: You too.

MRS. STOCKMANN: There you are, you see, Thomas.

DR. STOCKMANN: And all in the cause of truth! Oh, if I'd thought for one moment that . . .

HORSTER: Don't you worry about that! I'll get a job all right with some company away from here.

DR. STOCKMANN: So that's our Mr. Vik . . . a man of means, beholden to nobody . . . ! It's a damned shame!

HORSTER: He's very decent otherwise. And he said himself he would have liked to keep me on, if only he dared. . . .

DR. STOCKMANN: But he didn't dare? No, of course not.

HORSTER: He said it wasn't so easy when you belonged to a party. . . .

DR. STOCKMANN: He never spoke a truer word, that fine friend of ours! A party's just like a mincing machine, grinding people's brains up into a kind of hash, and churning out a lot of thickheaded clots.

MRS. STOCKMANN: Oh, Thomas, really!

PETRA (*to Horster*): If only you hadn't walked home with us, things might not have gone so far.

HORSTER: I don't regret it.

PETRA *(holds out her hand)*: Thank you!

HORSTER *(to the Doctor)*: What I really wanted to say was this: that if you are set on leaving, I've another idea. . . .

DR. STOCKMANN: Fine! As long as we can get away quickly.

MRS. STOCKMANN: Hush! Wasn't that a knock?

PETRA: That'll be Uncle, for sure.

DR. STOCKMANN: Aha! *(Shouts)* Come in!

MRS. STOCKMANN: Thomas, dear, promise me . . .

(The Mayor comes in from the hall)

MAYOR *(in the doorway)*: Oh, you are busy. In that case I'd better . . .

DR. STOCKMANN: No, no! Come in.

MAYOR: But I wanted to speak to you alone.

MRS. STOCKMANN: We'll go into the living-room for the time being.

HORSTER: And I'll look in again later.

DR. STOCKMANN: No, you just go next door with them, Captain Horster. I want to know a bit more about . . .

HORSTER: Very well, I'll wait then.

(He goes with Mrs. Stockmann and Petra into the living-room. The Mayor says nothing but glances at the windows.)

DR. STOCKMANN: Perhaps it's a bit draughty for you in here today. Put your hat on.

MAYOR: Thank you, if I may. *(Does so)* I think I must have caught a cold yesterday. I stood there shivering. . . .

DR. STOCKMANN: Really? Things seemed warm enough to me.

MAYOR: I regret I was unable to prevent the excesses of last night.

DR. STOCKMANN: Is there anything particular you want to tell me besides that?

MAYOR *(produces a big envelope)*: I have this document for you, from the directors.

DR. STOCKMANN: My notice?

MAYOR: Yes, from today. *(Lays the letter on the table.)* We don't like doing this, but—to be perfectly frank—we daren't do anything else, in the light of public opinion.

DR. STOCKMANN *(smiles)*: Daren't? I seem to have heard that word before, today.

MAYOR: I want you to realize your position. You can't count on any kind of practice in this town in future.

DR. STOCKMANN: To hell with the practice! But what makes you so certain?

MAYOR: The Ratepayers Association is circulating a list, urging all respectable citizens to have nothing to do with you. And I am pretty confident that not a single man will dare refuse to sign it. They simply wouldn't *dare*.

DR. STOCKMANN: I don't doubt. But what then?

MAYOR: If I may give you some advice, it's this: go away for a while. . . .

DR. STOCKMANN: Yes, I had actually been thinking of going away.

MAYOR: Good. And after you'd had six months or so to think things over, and if after mature consideration you then felt you were ready to write a few words of apology, admitting your mistake . . .

DR. STOCKMANN: Then I might perhaps get my job back again, you mean?

MAYOR: Perhaps. It's not altogether impossible.

DR. STOCKMANN: But what about public opinion? Surely you won't dare, in the light of public opinion.

MAYOR: Opinion is an extremely variable thing. And, in point of fact, it's rather important that we get some sort of admission from you along those lines.

DR. STOCKMANN: Yes, I can see how you'd come slobbering after that. But, by God, surely you haven't forgotten already what I've told you before about dirty tricks like this!

MAYOR: At that time your position was quite different. At that time you had reason to suppose you had the whole town at your back. . . .

DR. STOCKMANN: Yes, and now I'm supposed to feel as though I had the whole town *on* my back. . . . *(Flares up)* I wouldn't care if I had the devil himself *and* his old woman on my back. . . . Never, I tell you! Never!

MAYOR: A man with a family has no right to be carrying on as you are. You have no right, Thomas.

DR. STOCKMANN: Haven't I? There's only one thing in this world a free man has no right to do. Do you know what that is?

MAYOR: No.

DR. STOCKMANN: Of course not. But *I'll* tell you. A free man has no right to get messed up with filth; things should never reach the stage where he feels like spitting in his own eye.

MAYOR: This all sounds extremely plausible. And if there weren't some other explanation for your obstinacy . . . But then, of course, there is. . . .

DR. STOCKMANN: What do you mean by *that?*

MAYOR: You know perfectly well what I mean. Speaking as your brother and as one who understands these things, let me give you some advice: don't build too much on certain expectations or prospects that might so terribly easily fall through.

DR. STOCKMANN: What on earth are you getting at?

MAYOR: You don't really expect me to believe that you are ignorant of the terms of Morten Kiil's will?

DR. STOCKMANN: I know that what little he has is to go to an Old People's Home. But what's that got to do with me?

MAYOR: In the first place, it's not so little. Morten Kiil is a pretty wealthy man.

DR. STOCKMANN: I had absolutely no idea . . .

MAYOR: Hm . . . really? And you have no idea, I suppose, that a not inconsiderable part of his fortune is to be left to your children, and that you and your wife are to have the interest on this money during your lifetime? Did he never tell you that?

DR. STOCKMANN: Blessed if he did! On the contrary, he's done nothing the whole time but grouse about the impossibly high taxes he had to pay. Are you quite sure about this, Peter?

MAYOR: I have it from a completely reliable source.

DR. STOCKMANN: But, Heavens, that means Katherine's taken care of—and the children too! I must tell them. . . . *(Shouts)* Katherine, Katherine!

MAYOR *(holds him back)*: Hush! Don't say anything yet!

MRS. STOCKMANN *(opens the door)*: What is the matter?

DR. STOCKMANN: Nothing, my dear. Just go back in again. *(Mrs. Stockmann shuts the door; he walks up and down.)* Provided for! To think they're all provided for! And for life! It's a wonderful feeling to know that one has that security!

MAYOR: Yes, but that's just it! You can't be sure. Morten Kiil can alter his will any time he likes.

DR. STOCKMANN: But he won't, my dear Peter. The old boy is tickled to death at the way I've gone for you and your precious friends.

MAYOR *(starts, and looks intently at him)*: Aha, that puts a lot of things in a different light.

DR. STOCKMANN: What things?

MAYOR: So the whole thing has been a combined operation. These violent, ruthless attacks you have made—all in the name of truth—against the leading men of the town. . . .

DR. STOCKMANN: What about them?

MAYOR: Just your part of the bargain in exchange for being included in that vindictive old man's will.

DR. STOCKMANN *(almost speechless)*: Peter . . . of all the scum I ever met, you are the worst.

MAYOR: Things are finished now between us. Your dismissal is final . . . for now we have a weapon against you.

(He goes)

DR. STOCKMANN: Well I'll be. . . ! Of all the. . . ! *(Shouts)* Katherine! I want the floor swilled down after him. Get her to bring her bucket in . . . what's her name . . . damn it, you know . . . that girl who's always got a dirty nose. . . .

MRS. STOCKMANN *(in the living-room doorway)*: Hush, Thomas, please!

PETRA *(also in doorway)*: Father, Grandfather's here. He wants to know if he can have a word with you alone.

DR. STOCKMANN: Yes, of course he can. *(At the door)* Come in, Father-in-law. *(Morten Kiil comes in; the Doctor shuts the door after him.)* Well now, what can I do for you? Do sit down.

MORTEN KIIL: I won't sit. *(Looks round him)* It's looking very nice in here today, Stockmann.

DR. STOCKMANN: It is, isn't it?

KIIL: Very nice indeed it looks. And lots of fresh air too; plenty of that oxygen stuff you were talking about yesterday. Your conscience must be in pretty good shape today, I imagine.

DR. STOCKMANN: Yes, it is.

KIIL: I imagined it would be. *(Tapping his breast pocket)* Do you know what I've got here?

DR. STOCKMANN: A good conscience too, I should hope.

KIIL: Puh! Something much better than that.
(He brings out a fat wallet, opens it, and produces a bundle of papers)

DR. STOCKMANN *(looks at him in amazement)*: Shares in the Baths?

KIIL: They weren't difficult to come by today.

DR. STOCKMANN: You mean to say you've gone and bought . . . ?

KIIL: As many as I could afford.

DR. STOCKMANN: But, my dear Father-in-law—with things at the Baths in the state they are in now . . . !

KIIL: If only you behave like a sensible man, you'll soon have the place on its feet again.

DR. STOCKMANN: Well, you can see for yourself, I'm doing all I can, but . . . The people in this town are mad!

KIIL: You said yesterday that the worst of the filth came from my works. But if this happened to be true, then my grandfather, and my father before me, to say nothing of myself, have been slowly poisoning the town all these years— like three unclean spirits. You don't think I'm going to take this lying down, do you?

DR. STOCKMANN: I'm afraid you can't help it.

KIIL: No thank you. My good name means a lot to me. I'm told people call me an old badger; and a badger's a kind of pig, isn't it? But I'm not going to let them say 'I told you so'. I want to live and die with my reputation clear.

DR. STOCKMANN: And how are you going to manage that?

KIIL: You are going to clear me, Stockmann.

DR. STOCKMANN: *I* am!

KIIL: Do you know where I got the money to buy all these shares? No, how could you? But I'll tell you. This is the money that Katherine and Petra and the boys are to inherit from me. Because, you see, I've managed to put quite a bit aside, after all.

DR. STOCKMANN (*flaring up*): You mean you've gone and taken Katherine's money for *this?*

KIIL: Yes, every bit of the money is tied up now in the Baths. And I just want to see now if you really are completely and absolutely stark raving mad, Stockmann. If you are still going to have it that creepy, crawly things are coming from my works, you might as well be flaying Katherine alive, for all the difference it makes—*and* Petra, *and* the boys as well. But then no decent father would do that—not unless he was a madman.

DR. STOCKMANN (*pacing up and down*): But I *am* a madman! I *am* a madman!

KIIL: But you couldn't be so stark, staring mad as all that, not when it affects your wife and children.

DR. STOCKMANN (*halts in front of him*): Why couldn't you have talked to me first before going and buying all that trash!

KIIL: What's done can't be undone—it's got to be faced.

DR. STOCKMANN (*walks about restlessly*): If only I wasn't so certain . . . ! But I'm absolutely convinced I'm right.

KIIL (*weighing his wallet in his hand*): If you persist with these stupid ideas, then these things will not be worth much, you know.

(*He puts his wallet in his pocket*)

DR. STOCKMANN: Damn it, surely science could find *some* sort of prophylactic, some preventive or other. . . .

KIIL: You mean something to kill off the animals?

DR. STOCKMANN: Yes, or to render them harmless, at least.

KIIL: Couldn't you try with a bit of rat poison?

DR. STOCKMANN: Oh, don't talk rubbish! But then everybody keeps telling me it's just my imagination. Well, let's make it that then! Let them have it the way they want it! These ignorant little mongrels—calling me an enemy of the people! And tearing the very clothes off my back!

KIIL: And smashing all your windows!

DR. STOCKMANN: And then there's this business of my duty towards my family. I'll have to talk to Katherine about it. She's better than I am at things like that.

KIIL: Fine! She's a sensible woman—and just you pay attention to what she says.

DR. STOCKMANN (turning on him): You're a fine one, too, behaving in this stupid way! Fancy gambling with Katherine's money—and putting me in this dreadful dilemma! When I look at you, it's just like looking at the devil himself. . . !

KIIL: I think I'd better go. But I want to hear from you by two o'clock at the latest. Yes or no. If it's no, the shares go to charity—this very day.

DR. STOCKMANN: And what does Katherine get then?

KIIL: Not a penny. (The hall door opens; Hovstad and Aslaksen can be seen outside.) Well, look who's here!

DR. STOCKMANN (stares at them): What's this! You dare come to my house?

HOVSTAD: Yes, we do.

ASLAKSEN: You see, we want to talk to you about something.

KIIL (whispers): Yes or no—by two o'clock.

ASLAKSEN (with a glance at Hovstad): Aha!

(Morten Kiil leaves)

DR. STOCKMANN: Well! What do you want with me? Make it snappy!

HOVSTAD: I can well understand that you are not very well disposed towards us as a result of our attitude at the meeting yesterday. . . .

DR. STOCKMANN: Attitude, you call it! A fine attitude that was! Of all the spineless exhibitions . . . ! Like a couple of old women! God damn it!

HOVSTAD: Call it what you like; but we couldn't do anything else.

DR. STOCKMANN: You daren't do anything else, you mean! Well?

HOVSTAD: Yes, if you like.

ASLAKSEN: But why didn't you drop us a hint beforehand? All it needed was a word to Mr. Hovstad or me.

DR. STOCKMANN: A hint? What about?

ASLAKSEN: About what was behind it all.

DR. STOCKMANN: I don't understand you at all.

ASLAKSEN (nods confidentially): Oh yes you do, Dr. Stockmann.

HOVSTAD: There's no need to make a mystery of it any longer.

DR. STOCKMANN (looks from one to the other): For God's sake, won't somebody tell me . . . !

ASLAKSEN: If you don't mind my asking—isn't it true that your father-in-law is going round town buying up all the shares in the Baths.

DR. STOCKMANN: Yes, he's been and bought some shares today. But . . . ?

ASLAKSEN: It might have been wiser if you had picked somebody else to do that—somebody not quite so closely related.

HOVSTAD: And you shouldn't have done all this in your own name, either. There wasn't any need for people to know that the attack on the Baths came from you. You should have approached me, Dr. Stockmann.

DR. STOCKMANN (looks fixedly ahead; the truth seems to dawn on him, and he says as though thunderstruck): But this is incredible! Are such things possible?

ASLAKSEN (*smiles*): Evidently they are. But they ought preferably to be done with finesse, you know.

HOVSTAD: And it's best to have one or two others in on it, too. Because then the individual responsibility is always reduced if there are several people.

DR. STOCKMANN (*composedly*): Come to the point, gentlemen. What is it you want?

ASLAKSEN: Perhaps Mr. Hovstad had better . . .

HOVSTAD: No, you do it, Aslaksen.

ASLAKSEN: Well, the thing is that—now that we know how things really are—we think we might venture to put the *People's Herald* at your disposal.

DR. STOCKMANN: So *now* you dare do it? But what about public opinion? Aren't you afraid of having to face a storm of protest.

HOVSTAD: We must try to ride that storm.

ASLAKSEN: And then you must be ready to change your tack quickly, Doctor. As soon as your campaign has had its effect . . . .

DR. STOCKMANN: You mean as soon as my father-in-law and I have bought the shares up cheap. . . ?

HOVSTAD: I suppose it's mainly for research purposes you are anxious to get control of the Baths.

DR. STOCKMANN: Of course. It was with an eye on my research that I managed to get the old Badger to come in on it with me. Then we'll patch up the pipes a bit, and dig up a bit of the beach, and it won't cost the town a penny. Don't you think that'll work? Eh?

HOVSTAD: I think so—if you've got the *Herald* with you.

ASLAKSEN: In a free society, the press has great power, you know, Doctor.

DR. STOCKMANN: Yes, indeed. And so has public opinion. And you, Mr. Aslaksen, will take responsibility for the Ratepayers Association, I suppose?

ASLAKSEN: The Ratepayers Association *and* the Temperance Society. You may depend on that.

DR. STOCKMANN: But, gentlemen—I feel ashamed putting a question like this—but . . . what do *you* get out of this. . . ?

HOVSTAD: Actually, we'd rather not take anything at all for our help, really. But in fact the *Herald* is a bit shaky at the moment; it just can't quite make ends meet, and I should be most reluctant to wind the paper up now, just when there's such a lot of political work to be done.

DR. STOCKMANN: Of course. That would be a sad blow for a friend of the people like yourself. (*Flares up*) But I am an enemy of the people. (*Rushes about the room*) Where's my stick? Where the devil's my stick?

HOVSTAD: What does this mean?

ASLAKSEN: Surely you don't. . . !

DR. STOCKMANN (*stops*): And what if I didn't give you a single brass farthing out of all my shares? It's not easy to get money out of us rich people, don't forget.

HOVSTAD: And *you* mustn't forget that this business about the shares can be presented in two very different ways.

DR. STOCKMANN: Yes, and you are just the man to do it. If I don't come to the aid of the *Herald*, then you'll take a pretty poor view of things. The hunt will be up, I dare say. . . . You'll be after my blood . . . you'll be on to me like a dog on to a hare!

HOVSTAD: That's the law of nature. Every animal must fight for survival.

ASLAKSEN: You've got to take your food where you find it, you know.

DR. STOCKMANN: Then let's see if you can find anything out in the gutter. *(Rushes about the room)* Because now we are damned well going to see who is the strongest animal amongst us three. *(Finds his umbrella and waves it)* Now, watch out...!

HOVSTAD: You wouldn't dare attack us!

ASLAKSEN: Watch what you are doing with that umbrella!

DR. STOCKMANN: Out of the window with you, Mr. Hovstad.

HOVSTAD *(near the hall door)*: Have you gone completely mad?

DR. STOCKMANN: Out of the window, Mr. Aslaksen! Jump, I tell you. And quick about it!

ASLAKSEN *(running round the desk)*: Moderation, Dr. Stockmann! I'm not very strong, I can't stand very much of this.... *(Shouts)* Help! Help!

(Mrs. Stockmann, Petra and Horster come in from the living-room)

MRS. STOCKMANN: Heavens above, Thomas, what's going on?

DR. STOCKMANN *(swinging the umbrella)*: Jump! Down into the gutter!

HOVSTAD: Unprovoked assault! You're a witness of this, Captain Horster.

(He hurries out through the hall)

ASLAKSEN *(bewildered)*: Anybody who knew the lie of the land about here ...

(He slinks out through the living-room)

MRS. STOCKMANN *(clinging to her husband)*: Control yourself, Thomas!

DR. STOCKMANN *(throws the umbrella down)*: Damn them, they got away after all.

MRS. STOCKMANN: But what did they want with you?

DR. STOCKMANN: I'll tell you later. I've got other things to think about now. *(He goes to his desk and writes on a visiting card)* Look, Katherine, what does this say?

MRS. STOCKMANN: 'No', three times. What's that for?

DR. STOCKMANN: That's something else I'll tell you later. *(Hands the card to Petra)* There, Petra. Get little dirty-face to run over to the Badger's with it, as quick as she can. Hurry! *(Petra takes the card and goes out through the hall.)* Well, if this hasn't been a hell of a day for callers, I don't know what is. But now I'm going to sharpen up my pen; I'll impale them on it; I'll dip it in venom and gall; I'll chuck the inkpot right in their faces!

MRS. STOCKMANN: Yes, but we're leaving, aren't we, Thomas?

(Petra comes back)

DR. STOCKMANN: Well?

PETRA: She's taken it.

DR. STOCKMANN: Good! Leaving, did you say? No, I'm damned if we are. We're staying where we are, Katherine!

PETRA: We're staying?

MRS. STOCKMANN: In this town?

DR. STOCKMANN: Yes, just here. The battlefield is here; here the fight will be fought and here I shall triumph! As soon as I've had my trousers stitched, I'm off to town to look for somewhere to live. We've got to have a roof over our heads this winter.

HORSTER: You are welcome to share my house.

DR. STOCKMANN: Can I?

HORSTER: Yes, of course you can. I've plenty of room, and I'm hardly ever at home.

MRS. STOCKMANN: How very kind of you, Captain Horster.

PETRA: Thank you!

DR. STOCKMANN (*shaking his hand*): Thank you! Thank you! That's that worry off my mind. Now I can get straight down to work in real earnest. Oh, there's no end to the things here that need going into, Katherine! But it's grand that I can give all my time to this now. Because—I was going to tell you—I've got my notice from the Baths, you know. . . .

MRS. STOCKMANN (*sighing*): Yes, I was expecting that.

DR. STOCKMANN: . . . And they want to take my practice away as well. Well, let them! I won't lose the poor people anyway—those who don't pay anything. And, heavens, they are the ones who need me most. But, by God, they are going to listen to what I have to say. I'll read them a lesson, both in and out of season, as it says somewhere.

MRS. STOCKMANN: But, Thomas dear, surely you've seen now that reading them a lesson doesn't do much good.

DR. STOCKMANN: Don't be so ridiculous, Katherine. D'you think I'm going to let public opinion and the compact majority and all that rigmarole get the better of me? No, thank you! And anyway, what I want to do is so simple and clear and straightforward. I just want to take these mongrels and knock it into their heads that the Liberals are the worst enemies of freedom . . . that the party programmes grab hold of every young and promising idea and wring its neck . . . and that policies of expediency are turning all our standards of morality and justice upside down, so that life's just not going to be worth living. Surely I can make people understand that, Captain Horster? Don't you think so?

HORSTER: Very likely. I don't know very much about these things myself.

DR. STOCKMANN: Well, look here—I'll tell you what I mean! It's the party bosses you've got to get rid of. A party boss is just like a wolf, you see . . . a ravenous wolf who needs so and so many victims every year to keep him going. Just look at Hovstad and Aslaksen! How many do you think *they* haven't seen off in their time? Or else they worry them and maul them about so badly that they are no use for anything except to join the Ratepayers Association and subscribe to the *Herald!* (*Sits on the edge of the table*) Come over here, Katherine . . . look how beautifully the sun is shining in here today. And this glorious, fresh, spring air that's been let in.

MRS. STOCKMANN: If only we could live on sun and fresh air, Thomas.

DR. STOCKMANN: Well, you'll just have to skimp and scrape a bit on the side— we'll manage all right. That's my least worry. No, the worst thing is this: I don't know of anybody with enough independence of mind to feel like taking on my work after me.

PETRA: Oh, you mustn't think about that, Father. You've plenty of time yet.— Why, here are the boys already.

(Ejlif and Morten come in from the living-room)

MRS. STOCKMANN: Have you got a holiday today?

MORTEN: No, but we went for the others at playtime. . . .

EJLIF: That's not true. They started fighting us.

MORTEN: And then Mr. Rörlund said we'd better stay away for a few days.

DR. STOCKMANN *(snaps his fingers and jumps down from the table)*: I've got it! I've got it, by Heaven! You are not going to set foot in that school again!

THE BOYS: No more school!

MRS. STOCKMANN: Thomas, really . . . !

DR. STOCKMANN: Never, I say! I'll teach you myself—what I mean is, you'll not learn a blessed thing. . . .

MORTEN: Hurrah!

DR. STOCKMANN: . . . but I'll make decent and independent-minded men of you both. . . . And you must help me, Petra.

PETRA: You can count on me, Father.

DR. STOCKMANN: And we'll have the school in the very room where they called me an enemy of the people. But there ought to be a few more of us. I must have at least a dozen boys to start with.

MRS. STOCKMANN: You're not likely to get them here, not in this town.

DR. STOCKMANN: We'll see about that. *(To the boys)* What about some of the street-corner lads . . . the real guttersnipes. . . . ?

MORTEN: Yes, Father. I know plenty of them!

DR. STOCKMANN: That's fine! Get hold of one or two for me, will you? Just for once, I'm going to try an experiment on these mongrels. You never know what you might find amongst them.

MORTEN: But what are you going to do, when we've grown up into decent and independent-minded men?

DR. STOCKMANN: Then you can drive all the wolves out, lads—make sure that they all go west!

(Ejlif looks rather doubtful; Morten jumps and shouts for joy)

MRS. STOCKMANN: Oh, just so long as it isn't the wolves who go chasing you, Thomas.

DR. STOCKMANN: You must be mad, Katherine! Chase *me!* Now! When I'm the strongest man in the town!

MRS. STOCKMANN: The strongest. . . . ? *Now?*

DR. STOCKMANN: Yes, and I could even go so far as to say that *now* I'm one of the strongest men in the whole world.

MORTEN: Honestly?

DR. STOCKMANN *(dropping his voice)*: Sh! You mustn't say anything about it yet. But I've made a great discovery.

MRS. STOCKMANN: What, again?

DR. STOCKMANN: Yes, I have. *(He gathers them about him and says confidentially)* The thing is, you see, that the strongest man in the world is the man who stands alone.

MRS. STOCKMANN *(smiles and shakes her head)*: Oh, Thomas, Thomas. . . . !

PETRA *(bravely, grasping his hands)*: Father!

Miss Julie

Miss Julie mixes social commentary with *naturalistic tragedy:* a determinis-
tic vision of individuals as victims of circumstances they cannot control.
Naturalism presents life as mechanistic, making it almost as predictable as
a scientific formula (heredity plus environment plus chance equals fate),
with no room for human will, deliberate choice, or final responsibility.
Fate originates not with the gods, but with the genes struggling in an
environment.

Strindberg intended the play to reflect accurately social phenomena
he observed around him toward the end of the nineteenth century. Rigid class distinctions were disintegrating. Lower-class people were beginning to move upward. Women sought new freedoms. Yet the attitudes of
the past continued strong, and Strindberg himself was not immune to
them. Not all twentieth-century readers will view the struggle between
Julie and Jean in exactly the light that Strindberg seems to have intended.

MISS JULIE*
August Strindberg   (1849–1912)

CHARACTERS

Miss Julie, twenty-five years old
Jean, valet, thirty years old
Christine, the cook, thirty-five years old

*The action of the play takes place in the kitchen of the Count's manor house on Midsum-
mer Eve in Sweden in the 1880s.*

The scene is a large kitchen. The walls and ceiling are masked by the tormentors[1] *and borders. The rear wall runs obliquely upstage from the left. On this wall to the left are two
shelves with pots and pans of copper, iron, and pewter. The shelves are decorated with
goffered*[2] *paper. A little to the right can be seen three-fourths of a deep arched doorway
with two glass doors, and through them can be seen a fountain with a statue of Cupid, lilac
bushes in bloom, and the tops of some Lombardy poplars. From the left of the stage the
corner of a large, Dutch-tile kitchen stove protrudes with part of the hood showing. Projecting from the right side of the stage is one end of the servants' dining table of white
pine, with a few chairs around it. The stove is decorated with branches of birch leaves; the
floor is strewn with juniper twigs. On the end of the table is a large Japanese spice jar
filled with lilacs. An icebox, a sink, a wash basin. Over the door a big, old-fashioned bell;
and to the left of the door the gaping mouth of a speaking tube.*

Christine is standing at the stove, frying something. She is wearing a light-colored cot-

---

* Translated by Evert Sprinchorn.

[1] Wings or curtains projecting onto the stage, behind the proscenium.
[2] Pleated.

ton dress and an apron. Jean enters, dressed in livery and carrying a pair of high-top boots with spurs. He sets them where they are clearly visible.

JEAN: Tonight she's wild again. Miss Julie's absolutely wild!

CHRISTINE: You took your time getting back!

JEAN: I took the Count down to the station, and on my way back as I passed the barn I went in for a dance. And there was Miss Julie leading the dance with the game warden. But then she noticed me. And she ran right into my arms and chose me for the ladies' waltz. And she's been dancing ever since like—like I don't know what. She's absolutely wild!

CHRISTINE: That's nothing new. But she's been worse than ever during the last two weeks, ever since her engagement was broken off.

JEAN: Yes, I never did hear all there was to that. He was a good man, too, even if he wasn't rich. Well, that's a woman for you. *(He sits down at the end of the table)* But, tell me, isn't it strange that a young girl like her—all right, young woman—prefers to stay home here with the servants rather than go with her father to visit her relatives?

CHRISTINE: I suppose she's ashamed to face them after that fiasco with her young man.

JEAN: No doubt. He wouldn't take any nonsense from her. Do you know what happened, Christine? I do. I saw the whole thing, even though I didn't let on.

CHRISTINE: Don't tell me you were there?

JEAN: Well, I was. They were in the barnyard one evening—and she was training him, as she called it. Do you know what she was doing? She was making him jump over her riding whip—training him like a dog. He jumped over twice, and she whipped him both times. But the third time, he grabbed the whip from her, broke it in a thousand pieces—and walked off.

CHRISTINE: So that's what happened. Well, what do you know!

JEAN: Yes, that put an end to that affair.—What have you got for me that is really good, Christine?

CHRISTINE *(serving him from the frying pan)*: Just a little bit of kidney. I cut it especially for you.

JEAN *(smelling it)*: Wonderful! My special *délice! (Feeling the plate)* Hey, you didn't warm the plate!

CHRISTINE: You're more fussy than the Count himself when you set your mind to it. *(She rumples his hair gently)*

JEAN *(irritated)*: Cut it out! Don't muss up my hair. You know I don't like that!

CHRISTINE: Oh, now don't get mad. Can I help it if I like you?

(Jean eats. Christine gets out a bottle of beer.)

JEAN: Beer on Midsummer Eve! No thank you! I've got something much better than that. *(He opens a drawer in the table and takes out a bottle of red wine with a gold seal.)* Do you see that? Gold Seal. Now give me a glass.—No, a wine glass of course. I'm drinking it straight.

CHRISTINE *(goes back to the stove and puts on a small saucepan)*: Lord help the woman who gets you for a husband. You're an old fussbudget!

JEAN: Talk, talk! You'd consider yourself lucky if you got yourself a man as good as me. It hasn't done you any harm to have people think I'm your fiancé. *(He tastes the wine)* Very good. Excellent. But warmed just a little too little. *(Warm-*

ing the glass in his hands) We bought this in Dijon. Four francs a liter, unbottled—and the tax on top of that. . . . What on earth are you cooking? It smells awful!

CHRISTINE: Some damn mess that Miss Julie wants for her dog.

JEAN: You should watch your language, Christine. . . . Why do you have to stand in front of the stove on a holiday, cooking for that mutt? Is it sick?

CHRISTINE: Oh, she's sick, all right? She sneaked out to the gatekeeper's mongrel and—got herself in a fix. And you know Miss Julie, she can't stand anything like that.

JEAN: She's too stuck-up in some ways and not proud enough in others. Just like her mother. The Countess felt right at home in the kitchen or down in the barn with the cows, but when she went driving, *one* horse wasn't enough for her; she had to have a pair. Her sleeves were always dirty, but her buttons had the royal crown on them. As for Miss Julie, she doesn't seem to care how she looks and acts. I mean, she's not really refined, not really. Just now, down at the barn, she grabbed the game warden right from under Anna's eyes and asked him to dance. You wouldn't see anybody in our class doing a thing like that. But that's what happens when the gentry try to act like the common people—they become common! . . . But she *is* beautiful! Statuesque! Ah, those shoulders—those—and so forth, and so forth!

CHRISTINE: Oh, don't exaggerate. Clara tells me all about her, and Clara dresses her.

JEAN: Clara, pooh! You women are always jealous of each other. *I've* been out riding with her. . . . And how she can dance . . . !

CHRISTINE: Listen, Jean, you *are* going to dance with me, aren't you, when I am finished here?

JEAN: Certainly! Of course I am.

CHRISTINE: Promise?

JEAN: Promise! Listen if I say I'm going to do a thing, I do it . . . Christine, I thank you for a delicious meal. *(He shoves the cork back into the bottle.)*

(Miss Julie appears in the doorway, talking to someone outside)

MISS JULIE: I'll be right back. Don't wait for me.

(Jean slips the bottle into the table drawer quickly and rises respectfully. Miss Julie comes in and crosses over to Christine, who is at the stove.)

MISS JULIE: Did you get it ready?

(Christine signals that Jean is present)

JEAN *(polite and charming)*: Are you ladies sharing secrets?

MISS JULIE *(flipping her handkerchief in his face)*: Don't be nosey!

JEAN: Oh, that smells good! Violets.

MISS JULIE *(flirting with him)*: Don't be impudent! And don't tell me you're an expert on perfumes, too. I know you're an expert dancer,—No, don't look! Go away!

JEAN *(inquisitive, but deferential)*: What are you cooking? A witch's brew for Midsummer Eve? Something that reveals what the stars have in store for you, so you can see the face of your future husband?

MISS JULIE *(curtly)*: You'd have to have good eyes to see that. *(To Christine)* Pour it into a small bottle, and seal it tight. . . Jean, come and dance a schottische with me.

JEAN (*hesitating*): I hope you don't think I'm being rude, but I've already promised this dance to Christine.

MISS JULIE: She can always find someone else. Isn't that so, Christine? You don't mind if I borrow Jean for a minute, do you?

CHRISTINE: It isn't up to me. If Miss Julie is gracious enough to invite you, it isn't right for you to say no, Jean. You go on, and thank her for the honor.

JEAN: Frankly, Miss Julie, I don't want to hurt your feelings, but I wonder if it is wise—I mean for you to dance twice in a row with the same partner. Especially since the people around here are so quick to spread gossip.

MISS JULIE (*bridling*): What do you mean? What kind of gossip? What are you trying to say?

JEAN (*retreating*): If you insist on misunderstanding me, I'll have to speak more plainly. It just doesn't look right for you to prefer one of your servants to the others who are hoping for the same unusual honor.

MISS JULIE: Prefer! What an idea! I'm really surprised. I, the mistress of the house, am good enough to come to their dance, and when I feel like dancing, I want to dance with someone who knows how to lead. After all I don't want to look ridiculous.

JEAN: As you wish. I am at your orders.

MISS JULIE (*gently*): Don't take it as an order. Tonight we're all just happy people at a party. There's no question of rank. Now give me your arm.—Don't worry, Christine. I won't run off with your boy friend.

(*Jean gives her his arm and leads her out*)

Pantomime Scene. This should be played as if the actress were actually alone. She turns her back on the audience when she feels like it; she does not look out into the auditorium; she does not hurry as if she were afraid the audience would grow impatient.

Christine alone. In the distance the sound of the violins playing the schottische. Christine, humming in time with the music, cleans up after Jean, washes the dishes, dries them, and puts them away in a cupboard. Then she takes off her apron, takes a little mirror from one of the table drawers, and leans it against the jar of lilacs on the table. She lights a tallow candle, heats a curling iron, and curls the bangs on her forehead. Then she goes to the doorway and stands listening to the music. She comes back to the table and finds the handkerchief that Miss Julie left behind. She smells it, spreads it out, and then, as if lost in thought, stretches it, smooths it out, and folds it in four.

(*Jean enters alone*)

JEAN: I told you she was wild! You should have seen the way she was dancing. Everyone was peeking at her from behind the doors and laughing at her. Can you figure her out, Christine?

CHRISTINE: You might know it's her monthlies, Jean. She always acts peculiar then. . . . Well, are you going to dance with me?

JEAN: You're not mad at me because I broke my promise?

CHRISTINE: Of course not. Not for a little thing like that, you know that. And I know my place.

JEAN (*grabs her around the waist*): You're a sensible girl, Christine. You're going to make somebody a good wife—

(*Miss Julie, coming in, sees them together. She is unpleasantly surprised.*)

MISS JULIE (*with forced gaiety*): Well, aren't you the gallant beau—running away from your partner!

JEAN: On the contrary, Miss Julie. As you can see, I've hurried back to the partner I deserted.

MISS JULIE (*changing tack*): You know, you're the best dancer I've met.—But why are you wearing livery on a holiday? Take it off at once.

JEAN: I'd have to ask you to leave for a minute. My black coat is hanging right here— (*He moves to the right and points*)

MISS JULIE: You're not embarrassed because I'm here, are you? Just to change your coat? Go in your room and come right back again. Or else you can stay here and I'll turn my back.

JEAN: If you'll excuse me, Miss Julie. (*He goes off to the right. His arm can be seen as he changes his coat*)

MISS JULIE (*to Christine*): Tell me something, Christine. Is Jean your fiancé? He seems so intimate with you.

CHRISTINE: Fiancé? I suppose so. At least that's what we say.

MISS JULIE: What do you mean?

CHRISTINE: Well, Miss Julie, you have had fiancés yourself, and you know—

MISS JULIE: But we were properly engaged—!

CHRISTINE: I know, but did anything come of it?

(*Jean comes back, wearing a cutaway coat and derby*)

MISS JULIE: *Très gentil,*[3] *monsieur Jean! Très gentil!*

JEAN: *Vous voulez plaisanter,*[4] *madame.*

MISS JULIE: *Et vous voulez parler francais!*[5] Where did you learn to speak French?

JEAN: In Switzerland. I was *sommelier*[6] in one of the biggest hotels in Lucerne.

MISS JULIE: But you look quite the gentleman in that coat! *Charmant!*[7] (*She sits down at the table*)

JEAN: Flatterer!

MISS JULIE (*stiffening*): Who said I was flattering you?

JEAN: My natural modesty would not allow me to presume that you were paying sincere compliments to someone like me, and therefore I assumed that you were exaggerating, or, in other words, flattering me.

MISS JULIE: Where on earth did you learn to talk like that? Do you go to the theater often?

JEAN: And other places. You don't think I stayed in the house for six years when I was a valet in Stockholm, do you?

MISS JULIE: But weren't you born in this district?

JEAN: My father worked as a farm hand on the district attorney's estate, next door

---

[3] "Very genteel."
[4] "You will have your joke."
[5] "And you will speak French!"
[6] "Butler."
[7] "Charming."

to yours. I used to see you when you were little. But of course you didn't notice me.

MISS JULIE: Did you really?

JEAN: Yes, I remember one time in particular—. But I can't tell you about that!

MISS JULIE: Of course you can. Oh, come on, tell me. Just this once—for me.

JEAN: No. No, I really couldn't. Not now. Some other time maybe.

MISS JULIE: Some other time? That means never. What's the harm in telling me now?

JEAN: There's no harm. I just don't feel like it.—Look at her.

(He nods at Christine, who has fallen asleep in a chair by the stove)

MISS JULIE: Won't she make somebody a pretty wife! I'll bet she snores, too.

JEAN: No, she doesn't. But she talks in her sleep.

MISS JULIE *(cynically)*: Now how would you know she talks in her sleep?

JEAN *(coolly)*: I've heard her. . . .

(Pause. They look at each other.)

MISS JULIE: Why don't you sit down?

JEAN: I wouldn't take the liberty in your presence.

MISS JULIE: But if I were to order you—?

JEAN: I'd obey.

MISS JULIE: Well then, sit down.—Wait a minute. Could you get me something to drink first?

JEAN: I don't know what there is in the icebox. Only beer, I suppose.

MISS JULIE: *Only* beer? I have simple tastes. I prefer beer to wine.

(Jean takes a bottle of beer from the icebox and opens it. He looks in the cupboard for a glass and a saucer, and serves her.)

JEAN: At your service.

MISS JULIE: Thank you. Don't you want to drink, too?

JEAN: I'm not much of a beer-drinker, but if it's your wish—

MISS JULIE: My wish! I should think a gentleman would want to keep his lady company.

JEAN: That's a point well taken! *(He opens another bottle and takes a glass):*

MISS JULIE: Now drink a toast to me! *(Jean hesitates)* You're not shy, are you? A big, strong man like you? *(Playfully Jean kneels and raises his glass in mock gallantry)*

JEAN: To my lady's health!

MISS JULIE: Bravo! Now if you would kiss my shoe, you will have hit it off perfectly. *(Jean hesitates, then boldly grasps her foot and touches it lightly with his lips)* Superb! You should have been an actor.

JEAN *(rising)*: This has got to stop, Miss Julie! Someone might come and see us.

MISS JULIE: What difference would that make?

JEAN: People would talk, that's what! If you knew how their tongues were wagging out there just a few minutes ago, you wouldn't—

MISS JULIE: What sort of things did they say? Tell me. Sit down and tell me.

JEAN: I don't want to hurt your feelings, but they used expressions that—that hinted at certain—you know what I mean. After all, you're not a child. And

when they see a woman drinking, alone with a man—and a servant at that—
in the middle of the night—well . . .

MISS JULIE: Well what?! Besides, we're not alone. Christine is here.

JEAN: Sleeping!

MISS JULIE: I'll wake her up then. *(She goes over to Christine)* Christine! Are you
asleep? *(Christine babbles in her sleep)* Christine!—My, how sound she sleeps!

CHRISTINE *(talking in her sleep)*: Count's boots are brushed . . . put on the coffee
. . . right away, right away, right . . . mm—mm . . . poofff . . . *(Miss Julie grabs
Christine's nose)*

MISS JULIE: Wake up, will you!

JEAN *(sternly)*: Let her alone!

MISS JULIE *(sharply)*: What!

JEAN: She's been standing over the stove all day. She's worn out when evening
comes. Anyone asleep is entitled to some respect.

MISS JULIE *(changing tack)*: That's a very kind thought. It does you credit. Thank
you. *(She offers Jean her hand)* Now come on out and pick some lilacs for me.

*(During the following, Christine wakes up and, drunk with sleep, shuffles off to the
right to go to bed. A polka can be heard in the distance.)*

JEAN: With you, Miss Julie?

MISS JULIE: Yes, with me.

JEAN: That's no good. Absolutely not.

MISS JULIE: I don't know what you're thinking. Maybe you're letting your imagination run away with you.

JEAN: I'm not. The other people are.

MISS JULIE: In what way? Imagining that I'm—*verliebt*[8] in a servant?

JEAN: I'm not conceited, but it's been known to happen. And to these people
nothing's sacred.

MISS JULIE: Why, I believe you're an aristocrat!

JEAN: Yes, I am.

MISS JULIE: I'm climbing down—

JEAN: Don't climb down, Miss Julie! Take my advice. No one will ever believe
that you climbed down deliberately. They'll say you fell.

MISS JULIE: I think more highly of these people than you do. Let's see who's right!
Come on! *(She looks him over, challenging him)*

JEAN: You know, you're very strange.

MISS JULIE: Perhaps. But then so are you. . . . Besides, everything is strange. Life,
people, everything. It's all scum, drifting and drifting on the water until it
sinks—drowns. There's a dream I have every now and then. It's coming back
to me now. I'm sitting on top of a pillar that I've climbed up somehow and I
don't know how to get back down. When I look down I get dizzy. I have to
get down but I don't have the courage to jump. I can't hold on much longer
and I want to fall; but I don't fall. I know I won't have any peace until I get
down; no rest until I get down, down on the ground. And if I ever got down
on the ground, I'd want to go farther down, right down into the earth. . . .
Have you ever felt anything like that?

[8] "In love."

JEAN: Never! I used to dream that I'm lying under a tall tree in a dark woods. I want to get up, up to the very top, to look out over the bright landscape with the sun shining on it, to rob the bird's nest up there with the golden eggs in it. And I climb and I climb, but the trunk is so thick, and so smooth, and it's such a long way to that first branch. But I know that if I could just reach that first branch, I'd go right to the top as if on a ladder. I've never reached it yet, but some day I will—even if only in my dreams.

MISS JULIE: Here I am talking about dreams with you. Come out with me. Only into the park a way. *(She offers him her arm, and they start to go)*

JEAN: Let's sleep on nine midsummer flowers, Miss Julie, and then our dreams will come true!

(Miss Julie and Jean suddenly turn around in the doorway. Jean is holding his hand over one eye.)

MISS JULIE: You've caught something in your eye. Let me see.

JEAN: It's nothing. Just a bit of dust. It'll go away.

MISS JULIE: The sleeve of my dress must have grazed your eye. Sit down and I'll help you. *(She takes him by the arm and sits him down. She takes his head and leans it back. With the corner of her handkerchief she tries to get out the bit of dust)* Now sit still, absolutely still. *(She slaps his hand)* Do as you're told. Why, I believe you're trembling—a big, strong man like you. *(She feels his biceps)* With such big arms!

JEAN *(warningly)*: Miss Julie!

MISS JULIE: Yes, *Monsieur Jean?*

JEAN: *Attention! Je ne suis qu'un homme!* [9]

MISS JULIE: Sit still, I tell you! . . . There now! It's out. Kiss my hand and thank me!

JEAN *(rising to his feet)*: Listen to me, Miss Julie—Christine has gone to bed!—Listen to me, I tell you!

MISS JULIE: Kiss my hand first!

JEAN: Listen to me!

MISS JULIE: Kiss my hand first!

JEAN: All right. But you'll have no one to blame but yourself.

MISS JULIE: For what?

JEAN: For what! Are you twenty-five years old and still a child? Don't you know it's dangerous to play with fire?

MISS JULIE: Not for me. I'm insured!

JEAN *(boldly)*: Oh, no you're not! And even if you are, there's inflammable stuff next door.

MISS JULIE: Meaning you?

JEAN: Yes. Not just because it's me, but because I'm a young man—

MISS JULIE: And irresistibly handsome? What incredible conceit! A Don Juan, maybe! Or a Joseph! Yes, bless my soul, that's it: you're a Joseph!

JEAN: You think so?!

MISS JULIE: I'm almost afraid so! *(Jean boldly steps up to her, grabs her around the waist, kisses her. She slaps his face.)* None of that!

JEAN: Are you still playing games or are you serious?

---

[9] "Look out! I'm only human."

MISS JULIE: I'm serious.

JEAN: Then you must have been serious just a moment ago, too! You take your games too seriously and that's dangerous. Well, I'm tired of your games, and if you'll excuse me, I'll return to my work. *(Takes up the boots and starts to brush them)* The Count will be wanting his boots on time, and it's long past midnight.

MISS JULIE: Put those boots down.

JEAN: No! This is my job. It's what I'm here for. But I never undertook to be a playmate for you. That's something I could never be. I consider myself too good for that.

MISS JULIE: You are proud.

JEAN: In some ways. Not in others.

MISS JULIE: Have you ever been in love?

JEAN: We don't use that word around here. But I've been interested in a lot of girls, if that's what you mean. . . . I even got sick once because I couldn't have the one I wanted—really sick, like the princess in the Arabian Nights—who couldn't eat or drink for love.

MISS JULIE: Who was the girl? *(Jean does not reply)* Who was she?

JEAN: You can't make me tell you that.

MISS JULIE: Even if I ask you as an equal—ask you—as a friend? . . . Who was she?

JEAN: You.

MISS JULIE *(sitting down)*: How—amusing. . . .

JEAN: Yes, maybe so. Ridiculous. . . . That's why I didn't want to tell you about it before. Want to hear the whole story? . . . Have you any idea what you and your people look like from down below? Of course not. Like hawks or eagles, that's what: you hardly ever see their backs because they're always soaring so high up. I lived with seven brothers and sisters—and a pig—out on the waste land where there wasn't even a tree growing. But from my window I could see the wall of the Count's garden with the apple trees sticking up over it. That was the Garden of Eden for me, and there were many angry angels with flaming swords standing guard over it. But in spite of them, I and the other boys found a way to the Tree of Life. . . . I'll bet you despise me.

MISS JULIE: All boys steal apples.

JEAN: That's what you say now. But you still despise me. Never mind. One day I went with my mother into this paradise to weed the onion beds. Next to the vegetable garden stood a Turkish pavilion, shaded by jasmine and hung all over with honeysuckle. I couldn't imagine what it was used for; I only knew I had never seen such a beautiful building. People went in, and came out again. And then one day the door was left open. I sneaked in. The walls were covered with portraits of kings and emperors, and the windows had red curtains with tassels on them.—You do know what kind of place I'm talking about, don't you? . . . I— *(He breaks off a lilac and holds it under Miss Julie's nose)* I had never been inside a castle, never seen anything besides the church. But this was more beautiful. And no matter what I tried to think about, my thoughts always came back—to that little pavilion. And little by little there arose in me a desire to experience just for once the whole pleasure of. . . . *Enfin,*[10] I sneaked

---

[10] "Finally."

in, looked about, and marveled. And just then I heard someone coming! There was only one way out—for the upper-class people. But for me there was one more—a lower one. And I had no other choice but to take it. *(Miss Julie, who has taken the lilac from Jean, lets it fall to the table)* Then I began to run like mad, plunging through the raspberry bushes, ploughing through the strawberry patches, and came up on the rose terrace. And there I caught sight of a pink dress and a pair of white stockings. You! I crawled under—well, you can imagine what it was like—under thistles that pricked me and wet dirt that stank to high heaven. And all the while I could see you walking among the roses. I said to myself, "If it's true that a thief can enter heaven and be with the angels, isn't it strange that a poor man's child here on God's green earth can't enter the Count's park and play with the Count's daughter."

MISS JULIE *(sentimentally)*: Do you think all poor children have felt that way?

JEAN *(hesitatingly at first, then with mounting conviction)*: If all poor ch—? Yes—yes, naturally. Of course!

MISS JULIE: It must be terrible to be poor.

JEAN *(with deep feeling, his words charged with emotion)*: Oh, Miss Julie! You don't know! A dog can lie on the sofa with its mistress; a horse can have its nose stroked by the hand of a countess; but a servant—! *(Changing his tone)* Of course, now and then you meet somebody with guts enough to work his way up in the world, but how often?—Anyway, you know what I did afterwards? I threw myself into the millstream with all my clothes on. Got fished out and spanked. But the following Sunday, when Pa and everybody else in the house went to visit Grandma, I arranged things so I'd be left behind. Then I washed myself all over with soap and warm water, put on my best clothes, and went off to church—just to see you there once more. I saw you, and then I went home determined to die. But I wanted to die beautifully and comfortably, without pain. I remembered that it was fatal to sleep under an elderberry bush. And we had a big one that had just blossomed out. I stripped it of every leaf and blossom it had and made a bed of them in a bin of oats. Have you ever noticed how smooth oats are? As smooth to the touch as human skin. . . . So I pulled the lid of the bin shut and closed my eyes—fell asleep. And when they woke me I was really very sick. But I didn't die, as you can see.—What was I trying to prove? I don't know. There was no hope of winning you. But you were a symbol of the absolute hopelessness of my ever getting out of the circle I was born in.

MISS JULIE: You know, you have a real gift for telling stories. Did you go to school?

JEAN: A little. But I've read a lot of novels and gone to the theater. And I've also listened to educated people talk. That's how I've learned the most.

MISS JULIE: You mean to tell me you stand around listening to what we're saying!

JEAN: Certainly! And I've heard an awful lot, I can tell you—sitting on the coachman's seat or rowing the boat. One time I heard you and a girl friend talking—

MISS JULIE: Really! . . . And just what did you hear?

JEAN: Well, now, I don't know if I could repeat it. I can tell you I was a little amazed. I couldn't imagine where you had learned such words. Maybe at bottom there isn't such a big difference as you might think, between people and people.

MISS JULIE: How vulgar! At least people in my class don't behave like you when we're engaged.

JEAN *(looking her in the eye):* Are you sure?—Come on now, it's no use playing the innocent with me.

MISS JULIE: He was a beast. The man I offered my love was a beast.

JEAN: That's what you all say—afterwards.

MISS JULIE: All?

JEAN: I'd say so, since I've heard the same expression used several times before in similar circumstances.

MISS JULIE: What kind of circumstances?

JEAN: The kind we're talking about. I remember the last time I—

MISS JULIE *(rising):* That's enough! I don't want to hear any more.

JEAN: How strange! Neither did she! . . . Well, now if you'll excuse me, I'll go to bed.

MISS JULIE *(softly):* Go to bed on Midsummer Eve?

JEAN: That's right. Dancing with that crowd up there really doesn't amuse me.

MISS JULIE: Jean, get the key to the boathouse and row me out on the lake. I want to see the sun come up.

JEAN: Do you think that's wise?

MISS JULIE: You sound as if you were worried about your reputation.

JEAN: Why not? I don't particularly care to be made ridiculous, or to be kicked out without a recommendation just when I'm trying to establish myself. Besides, I have a certain obligation to Christine.

MISS JULIE: Oh, I see. It's Christine now.

JEAN: Yes, but I'm thinking of you, too. Take my advice, Miss Julie, and go up to your room.

MISS JULIE: When did you start giving me orders?

JEAN: Just this once. For your own sake! Please! It's very late. You're so tired, you're drunk, you don't know what you're doing. Go to bed, Miss Julie.—Besides, if my ears aren't deceiving me, they're coming this way, looking for me. If they find us here together, you're done for!

THE CHORUS *(is heard coming nearer, singing):*

> Two ladies came from out the clover,
> Tri-di-ri-di-ralla, tri-di-ri-di-ra.
> And one of them was green all over,
> Tri-di-ri-di-ralla-la.
> They told us they had gold aplenty,
> Tri-di-ri-di-ralla, tri-di-ri-di-ra.
> But neither of them owned a penny.
> Tri-di-ri-di-ralla-la.
> This wreath for you I may be plaiting,
> Tri-di-ri-di-ralla, tri-di-ri-di-ra.
> But it's for another I am waiting,
> Tri-di-ri-di-ralla-la!

MISS JULIE: I know these people. I love them just as they love me. Let them come. You'll find out.

JEAN: Oh, no, Miss Julie, they don't love you! They take the food you give them, but they spit on it as soon as your back is turned. Believe me! Just listen to them. Listen to what they're singing.—No, you'd better not listen

MISS JULIE *(listening):* What are they singing?

JEAN: A dirty song—about you and me!

MISS JULIE: How disgusting! Oh, what cowardly, sneaking—

JEAN: That's what the mob always is—cowards! You can't fight them; you can only run away.

MISS JULIE: Run away? Where? There's no way out of here. And we can't go in to Christine.

JEAN: What about my room? What do you say? The rules don't count in a situation like this. You can trust me. I'm your friend, remember? Your true, devoted, and respectful friend.

MISS JULIE: But suppose—suppose they looked for you there?

JEAN: I'll bolt the door. If they try to break it down, I'll shoot. Come, Miss Julie! *(On his knees):* Please, Miss Julie!

MISS JULIE *(meaningfully):* You promise me that you—?

JEAN: I swear to you!

(Miss Julie goes out quickly to the right. Jean follows her impetuously)

The Ballet. The country people enter in festive costumes, with flowers in their hats. The fiddler is in the lead. A keg of small beer and a little keg of liquor, decorated with greenery, are set up on the table. Glasses are brought out. They all drink, and start to sing the song. Then they form a circle and sing and dance the round dance, "Two ladies came from out the clover." At the end of the dance they all leave singing.

(Miss Julie comes in alone; looks at the devastated kitchen; clasps her hands together; then takes out a powder puff and powders her face. Jean enters. He is in high spirits.)

JEAN: You see! You heard them, didn't you? You've got to admit it's impossible to stay here.

MISS JULIE: No, I don't. But even if I did, what could we do?

JEAN: Go away, travel, get away from here!

MISS JULIE: Travel? Yes—but where?

JEAN: Switzerland, the Italian lakes. You've never been there?

MISS JULIE: No. Is it beautiful?

JEAN: Eternal summer, oranges, laurel trees, ah. . . !

MISS JULIE: But what are we going to do there?

JEAN: I'll set up a hotel—a first-class hotel with a first-class clientele.

MISS JULIE: Hotel?

JEAN: I tell you that's the life! Always new faces, new languages. Not a minute to think about yourself or worry about your nerves. No looking for something to do. The work keeps you busy. Day and night the bells ring, the trains whistle, the busses come and go. And all the while the money comes rolling in. I tell you it's the life!

MISS JULIE: Yes, that's the life. But what about me?

JEAN: The mistress of the whole place, the star of the establishment! With your looks—and your personality—it can't fail. It's perfect! You'll sit in the office like a queen, setting your slaves in motion by pressing an electric button. The guests will file before your throne and timidly lay their treasures on your table. You can't imagine how people tremble when you shove a bill in their face! I'll salt the bills and you'll sugar them with your prettiest smile. Come on, let's get away from here—*(He takes a timetable from his pocket)*—right away—the next train! We'll be in Malmö at 6:30; Hamburg 8:40 in the morning, Frankfurt to Basle in one day; and to Como by way of the Gotthard tunnel in—let me see—three days! Three days!

MISS JULIE: You make it sound so wonderful. But, Jean, you have to give me strength. Tell me you love me. Come and put your arms around me.

JEAN *(hesitates)*: I want to . . . but I don't dare. Not any more, not in this house. I do love you—without a shadow of a doubt. How can you doubt that, Miss Julie?

MISS JULIE *(shyly, very becomingly)*: You don't have to be formal with me, Jean. You can call me Julie. There aren't any barriers between us now. Call me Julie.

JEAN *(agonized)*: I can't! There are still barriers between us, Miss Julie, as long as we stay in this house! There's the past, there's the Count. I've never met anyone I feel so much respect for. I've only got to see his gloves lying on a table and I shrivel up. I only have to hear that bell ring and I shy like a frightened horse. I only have to look at his boots standing there so stiff and proud and I feel my spine bending. *(He kicks the boots)* Superstitions, prejudices that they've drilled into us since we were children! But they can be forgotten just as easily! Just we get to another country where they have a republic! They'll crawl on their hands and knees when they see my uniform. On their hands and knees, I tell you! But not me! Oh, no. I'm not made for crawling. I've got guts, backbone. And once I grab that first branch, you just watch me climb. I may be a valet now, but next year I'll be owning property; in ten years, I'll be living off my investments. Then I'll go to Rumania, get myself some decorations, and maybe—notice I only say maybe—end up as a count!

MISS JULIE: How wonderful, wonderful.

JEAN: Listen, in Rumania you can buy titles. You'll be a countess after all. *My* countess.

MISS JULIE: But I'm not interested in that. I'm leaving all that behind. Tell me you love me, Jean, or else—or else what difference does it make what I am?

JEAN: I'll tell you a thousand times—but later! Not now. And not here. Above all, let's keep our feelings out of this or we'll make a mess of everything. We have to look at this thing calmly and coolly, like sensible people. *(He takes out a cigar, clips the end, and lights it)* Now you sit there and I'll sit here, and we'll talk as if nothing had happened.

MISS JULIE *(in anguish)*: My God, what are you? Don't you have any feelings?

JEAN: Feelings? Nobody's got more feelings than I have. But I've learned how to control them.

MISS JULIE: A few minutes ago you were kissing my shoe—and now—!

JEAN *(harshly)*: That was a few minutes ago. We've got other things to think about now!

MISS JULIE: Don't speak to me like that, Jean!

JEAN: I'm just trying to be sensible. We've been stupid once; let's not be stupid again. Your father might be back at any moment, and we've got to decide our future before then.—Now what do you think about my plans? Do you approve or don't you?

MISS JULIE: I don't see anything wrong with them. Except one thing. For a big undertaking like that, you'd need a lot of capital. Have you got it?

JEAN (*chewing on his cigar*): Have I got it? Of course I have. I've got my knowledge
of the business, my vast experience, my familiarity with languages. That's
capital that counts for something, let me tell you.

MISS JULIE: You can't even buy the railway tickets with it.

JEAN: That's true. That's why I need a backer—someone to put up the money.

MISS JULIE: Where can you find him on a moment's notice?

JEAN: You'll find him—if you want to be my partner.

MISS JULIE: I can't. And I don't have a penny to my name.

(*Pause*)

JEAN: Then you can forget the whole thing.

MISS JULIE: Forget—?

JEAN: And things will stay just the way they are.

MISS JULIE: Do you think I'm going to live under the same roof with you as your
mistress? Do you think I'm going to have people sneering at me behind my
back? How do you think I'll ever be able to look my father in the face after
this? No, no! Take me away from here, Jean—the shame, the humiliation. . . .
What have I done? Oh, my God, my God! What have I done? (*She bursts into
tears*)

JEAN: Now don't start singing that tune. It won't work. What have you done
that's so awful? You're not the first.

MISS JULIE (*crying hysterically*): Now you despise me!—I'm falling, I'm falling!

JEAN: Fall down to me, and I'll lift you up again!

MISS JULIE: What awful hold did you have over me? What drove me to you? The
weak to the strong! The falling to the rising! Oh maybe it was love? Love?
This? You don't know what love is!

JEAN: Want to bet? Did you think I was a virgin?

MISS JULIE: You're coarse—vulgar! The things you say, the things you think!

JEAN: That's the way I was brought up and that's the way I am! Now don't get
hysterical. And don't play the fine lady with me. We're eating off the same
platter now. . . . That's better. Come over here and be a good girl and I'll treat
you to something special. (*He opens the table drawer and takes out the wine bottle.
He pours the wine into two used glasses.*)

MISS JULIE: Where did you get that wine?

JEAN: From the wine cellar.

MISS JULIE: My father's burgundy!

JEAN: Should be good enough for his son-in-law.

MISS JULIE: I was drinking beer and you—!

JEAN: Shows that I have better taste than you.

MISS JULIE: Thief!

JEAN: You going to squeal on me?

MISS JULIE: Oh, God! Partner in crime with a petty house thief! I must have been
drunk; I must have been walking in my sleep. Midsummer Night! Night of
innocent games—

JEAN: Yes, very innocent!

Miss Julie (*pacing up and down*): Is there anyone here on earth as miserable as I am?

Jean: Why be miserable? After such a conquest! Think of poor Christine in there. Don't you think she's got any feelings?

Miss Julie: I thought so a while ago, but I don't now. A servant's a servant—

Jean: And a whore's a whore!

Miss Julie (*falls to her knees and clasps her hands together*): Oh, God in heaven, put an end to my worthless life! Lift me out of this awful filth I'm sinking in! Save me! Save me!

Jean: I feel sorry for you, I have to admit it. When I was lying in the onion beds, looking up at you on the rose terrace, I—I'm telling you the truth now—I had the same dirty thoughts that all boys have.

Miss Julie: And you said you wanted to die for me!

Jean: In the oat bin? That was only a story.

Miss Julie: A lie, you mean.

Jean (*beginning to get sleepy*): Practically. I think I read it in a paper about a chimney sweep who curled up in a wood-bin with some lilacs because they were going to arrest him for non-support of his child.

Miss Julie: Now I see you as you really are.

Jean: What did you expect me to do? It's always the fancy talk that gets the women.

Miss Julie: You dog!

Jean: You bitch!

Miss Julie: Well, now you've seen the eagle's back—

Jean: Wasn't exactly its back—!

Miss Julie: I was going to be your first branch—!

Jean: A rotten branch—

Miss Julie: I was going to be the window dressing for your hotel—!

Jean: And I the hotel—!

Miss Julie: Sitting at the desk, attracting your customers, padding your bills—!

Jean: I could manage that myself—!

Miss Julie: How can a human soul be so dirty and filthy?

Jean: Then why don't you clean it up?

Miss Julie: You lackey! You shoeshine boy! Stand up when I talk to you!

Jean: You lackey lover! You bootblack's tramp! Shut your mouth and get out of here! Who do you think you are telling me I'm coarse? I've never seen anybody in my class behave as crudely as you did tonight. Have you ever seen any of the girls around here grab at a man like you did? Do you think any of the girls of my class would throw themselves at a man like that? I've never seen the like of it except in animals and prostitutes!

Miss Julie (*crushed*): That's right! Hit me! Walk all over me! It's all I deserve. I'm rotten. But help me! Help me to get out of this—if there is any way out for me!

Jean (*less harsh*): I'd be doing myself an injustice if I didn't admit that part of the credit for this seduction belongs to me. But do you think a person in my position would have dared to look twice at you if you hadn't asked for it? I'm still amazed—

Miss Julie: And still proud.

JEAN: Why not? But I've got to confess the victory was a little too easy to give me any real thrill.

MISS JULIE: Go on, hit me again!

JEAN *(standing up)*: No. . . . I'm sorry I said that. I never hit a person who's down, especially a woman. I can't deny that, in one way, it was good to find out that what I saw glittering up above was only fool's gold, to have seen that the eagle's back was as gray as its belly, that the smooth cheek was just powder, and that there could be dirt under the manicured nails, that the handkerchief was soiled even though it smelled of perfume. But, in another way, it hurt me to find that everything I was striving for wasn't very high above me after all, wasn't even real. It hurts me to see you sink far lower than your own cook. Hurts, like seeing the last flowers cut to pieces by the autumn rains and turned to muck.

MISS JULIE: You talk as if you already stood high above me.

JEAN: Well, don't I? Don't forget I could make you a countess but you can never make me a count.

MISS JULIE: But I have a father for a count. You can never have that!

JEAN: True. But I might father my own counts—that is, if—

MISS JULIE: You're a thief! I'm not.

JEAN: There are worse things than being a thief. A lot worse. And besides, when I take a position in a house, I consider myself a member of the family—in a way, like a child in the house. It's no crime for a child to steal a few ripe cherries when they're falling off the trees, is it? *(He begins to feel passionate again)* Miss Julie, you're a beautiful woman, much too good for the likes of me. You got carried away by your emotions and now you want to cover up your mistake by telling yourself that you love me. You don't love me. You might possibly have been attracted by my looks—in which case your kind of love is no better than mine. But I could never be satisfied to be just an animal for you, and I could never make you love me.

MISS JULIE: How do you know that for sure?

JEAN: You mean there's a chance? I could love you, there's no doubt about that. You're beautiful, you're refined— *(He goes up to her and takes her hand)* —educated, lovable when you want to be, and once you set a man's heart on fire, I'll bet it burns forever. *(He puts his arm around her waist)* You're like hot wine and strong spices. One of your kisses is enough to— *(He attempts to lead her out, but she rather reluctantly breaks away from him)*

MISS JULIE: Let me go. You don't get me that way.

JEAN: Then how? Not by petting you and not with pretty words, not by planning for the future, not by saving you from humiliation! Then how, tell me how?

MISS JULIE: How? How? I don't know how! I don't know at all!—I hate you like I hate rats, but I can't get away from you.

JEAN: Then come away with me!

MISS JULIE *(pulling herself together)*: Away? Yes, we'll go away!—But I'm so tired. Pour me a glass of wine, will you? *(Jean pours the wine. Miss Julie looks at her watch.)* Let's talk first. We still have a little time. *(She empties the glass of wine and holds it out for more)*

JEAN: Don't overdo it, You'll get drunk.

MISS JULIE: What difference does it make?

JEAN: What difference? It looks cheap.—What did you want to say to me?

MISS JULIE: We're going to run away together, right? But we'll talk first—that is, I'll talk. So far you've done all the talking. You've told me your life, now I'll tell you mine. That way we'll know each other through and through before we become traveling companions.

JEAN: Wait a minute. Excuse me, but are you sure you won't regret this afterwards, when you've surrendered your secrets to me?

MISS JULIE: I thought you were my friend.

JEAN: I am—sometimes. But don't count on me.

MISS JULIE: You don't mean that. Anyway, everybody knows my secrets.—My mother's parents were very ordinary people, just commoners. She was brought up, according to the theories of her time, to believe in equality, the independence of women, and all that. And she had a strong aversion to marriage. When my father proposed to her, she swore she would never become his wife, but that she might possibly consent to become his mistress. So he told her he didn't want to see the woman he loved enjoy less respect than he did. But she said she didn't care what the world thought—and he, believing that he couldn't live without her, accepted her conditions. That did it. From then on he was cut off from his old circle of friends and left without anything to do in the house, which couldn't have kept him occupied anyway. Then I came into the world—against my mother's wishes, as far as I can make out. My mother decided to bring me up as a nature child. And on top of that I had to learn everything a boy learns, so I could be living proof that women were just as good as men. I had to wear boy's clothes, learn to handle horses—but not to milk the cows. I was made to groom the horses and handle them, and learn farming and go hunting—I even had to learn how to slaughter the animals. It was disgusting. And on the estate all the men were set to doing women's chores, and the women to doing men's work—with the result that the whole place threatened to fall to pieces, and we became the local laughingstock. Finally my father must have come out of his trance. He rebelled, and everything was changed according to his wishes. Then my mother got sick. I don't know what kind of sickness it was, but she often had convulsions, and she would hide herself in the attic or in the garden, and sometimes she would stay out all night. Then there occurred that big fire you've heard about. The house, the stables, the cowsheds, all burned down—and under very peculiar circumstances that led one to suspect arson. You see, the accident occurred the day after the insurance expired, and the premiums of the new policy, which my father had sent in, were delayed through the messenger's carelessness, and didn't arrive on time. *(She refills her glass and drinks)*

JEAN: You've had enough.

MISS JULIE: Who cares!—We were left without a penny to our name. We had to sleep in the carriages. My father didn't know where to turn for money to rebuild the house. Then Mother suggested to him that he might try to borrow money from an old friend of hers, who owned a brick factory not far from here. Father took out a loan, but there wasn't any interest charged, which surprised him. So the place was rebuilt. *(She drinks some more)* Do you know who set fire to the place?

JEAN: Your honorable mother!

MISS JULIE: Do you know who the brick manufacturer was?

JEAN: Your mother's lover?

MISS JULIE: Do you know whose money it was?

JEAN: Let me think a minute. . . . No, I give up.

MISS JULIE: It was my mother's!

JEAN: The Count's, you mean. Or was there a marriage settlement?

MISS JULIE: There wasn't a settlement. My mother had a little money of her own which she didn't want under my father's control, so she invested it with her—friend.

JEAN: Who grabbed it!

MISS JULIE: Right! He appropriated it. Well, my father found out what happened. But he couldn't go to court, couldn't pay his wife's lover, couldn't prove that it's his wife's money. That was how my mother got her revenge because he had taken control of the house. He was on the verge of shooting himself. There was even a rumor that he tried and failed. But he took a new lease on life and he forced my mother to pay for her mistakes. Can you imagine what those five years were like for me? I loved my father, but I took my mother's side because I didn't know the whole story. She had taught me to hate all men—you've heard how she hated men—and I swore to her that I'd never be slave to any man.

JEAN: But you got engaged to the attorney.

MISS JULIE: Only to make him my slave.

JEAN: But he didn't like the idea, did he?

MISS JULIE: Oh, he wanted to well enough. I didn't give him the chance. I got bored with him.

JEAN: Yes, so I noticed—in the barnyard.

MISS JULIE: What did you notice?

JEAN: I saw what I saw. *He* broke off the engagement.

MISS JULIE: That's a lie! It was I who broke it off. Did he tell you that? He's beneath contempt!

JEAN: Come on now, he isn't as bad as that. So you hate men, Miss Julie?

MISS JULIE: Yes, I do. . . . Most of the time. But sometimes, when I can't help myself—oh. . . . *(She shudders in disgust)*

JEAN: Then you hate me, too?

MISS JULIE: You have no idea how much! I'd like to see you killed like an animal—

JEAN: Like when you're caught in the act with an animal: you get two years at hard labor and the animal is killed. Right?

MISS JULIE: Right.

JEAN: But there's no one to catch us—and *no animal!*—So what are we going to do?

MISS JULIE: Go away from here.

JEAN: To torture ourselves to death?

MISS JULIE: No. To enjoy ourselves for a day or two, or a week, for as long as we can—and then—to die—

JEAN: Die? How stupid! I've got a better idea: start a hotel!

MISS JULIE *(continuing without hearing Jean)*: —on the shores of Lake Como, where the sun is always shining, where the laurels bloom at Christmas, and the golden oranges glow on the trees.

JEAN: Lake Como is a stinking wet hole, and the only oranges I saw there were on the fruit stands. But it's a good tourist spot with a lot of villas and cottages that are rented out to lovers. Now there's a profitable business. You know why? They rent the villa for the whole season, but they leave after three weeks.

MISS JULIE (*naïvely*): Why after only three weeks?

JEAN: Because they can't stand each other any longer. Why else? But they still have to pay the rent. You see, then you rent it out again to another couple, and so on. There's no shortage of love—even if it doesn't last very long.

MISS JULIE: Then you don't want to die with me?

JEAN: I don't want to die at all! I enjoy life too much. And moreover, I consider taking your own life a sin against the Providence that gave us life.

MISS JULIE: You believe in God? You?

JEAN: Yes, certainly I do! I go to church every other Sunday.—Honestly, I've had enough of this talk. I'm going to bed.

MISS JULIE: Really? You think you're going to get off that easy? Don't you know that a man owes something to the woman he's dishonored?

JEAN (*takes out his purse and throws a silver coin on the table*): There you are. I don't want to owe anybody anything.

MISS JULIE (*ignoring the insult*): Do you know what the law says—?

JEAN: Aren't you lucky the law says nothing about the women who seduce men!

MISS JULIE (*still not hearing him*): What else can we do but go away from here, get married, and get divorced?

JEAN: Suppose I refuse to enter into this *mésalliance?* [11]

MISS JULIE: *Mésalliance?*

JEAN: For me! I've got better ancestors than you. I don't have any female arsonist in my family.

MISS JULIE: How can you know?

JEAN: You can't prove the opposite because we don't have any family records—except in the police courts. But I've read the whole history of your family in that book on the drawing-room table. Do you know who the founder of your family line was? A miller—who let his wife sleep with the king one night during the Danish war. I don't have any ancestors like that. I don't have any ancestors at all! But I can become an ancestor myself.

MISS JULIE: This is what I get for baring my heart and soul to someone too low to understand, for sacrificing the honor of my family—

JEAN: Dishonor!—I warned you, remember? Drinking makes one talk, and talking's bad.

MISS JULIE: Oh, how sorry I am! . . . If only it had never happened! . . . If only you at least loved me!

JEAN: For the last time—What do you want me to do? Cry? Jump over your whip? Kiss you? Lure you to Lake Como for three weeks and then—? What am I supposed to do? What do you want? I've had more than I can take. This is what I

---

[11] "Bad match."

get for involving myself with women. . . . Miss Julie, I can see that you're un-happy; I know that you're suffering; but I simply cannot understand you. My people don't behave like this. We don't hate each other. We make love for the fun of it, when we can get any time off from our work. But we don't have time for it all day and all night like you do. If you ask me, you're sick, Miss Julie. Your mother's mind was affected you know. There are whole counties affect-ed with pietism. That was your mother's trouble—pietism. Everybody's catch-ing it.

MISS JULIE: You can be understanding, Jean. You're talking to me like a human being now.

JEAN: Well, be human yourself. You spit on me but you don't let me wipe it off—on you.

MISS JULIE: Help me, Jean. Help me. Tell me what I should do, that's all—which way to go.

JEAN: For Christ's sake, if only I knew myself!

MISS JULIE: I've been crazy—I've been out of my mind—but does that mean there's no way out for me?

JEAN: Stay here as if nothing had happened. Nobody knows anything.

MISS JULIE: Impossible! Everybody who works here knows. Christine knows.

JEAN: They don't know a thing. And anyhow they'd never believe it.

MISS JULIE (slowly, significantly): But . . . it might happen again.

JEAN: That's true!

MISS JULIE: And there might be consequences.

JEAN (stunned): Consequences! What on earth have I been thinking of! You're right. There's only one thing to do: get away from here! Immediately! I can't go with you—that would give the whole game away. You'll have to go by yourself. Somewhere—I don't care where!

MISS JULIE: By myself? Where?—Oh, no, Jean, I can't. I can't!

JEAN: You've got to! Before the Count comes back. You know as well as I do what will happen if you stay here. After one mistake, you figure you might as well go on—the damage is already done. Then you get more and more careless un-til—finally you're exposed. I tell you, you've got to get out of the country. Afterwards you can write to the Count and tell him everything—leaving me out, of course. He'd never guess it was me. Anyway, I don't think he'd exactly like to find that out.

MISS JULIE: I'll go—if you'll come with me!

JEAN: Lady, are you out of your mind? "Miss Julie elopes with her footman." The day after tomorrow it would be in all the papers. The Count would never live it down.

MISS JULIE: I can't go away. I can't stay. Help me. I'm so tired, so awfully tired. . . . Tell me what to do. Order me. Start me going. I can't think any more, can't move any more. . . .

JEAN: Now do you realize how weak you all are? What gives you the right to go strutting around with your noses in the air as if you owned the world? All right, I'll give you your orders. Go up and get dressed. Get some traveling money. And come back down here.

MISS JULIE (almost in a whisper): Come up with me!

JEAN: To your room?... You're going crazy again! *(He hesitates a moment)* No! No! Go! Right now! *(He takes her hand and leads her out)*

MISS JULIE *(as she is leaving)*: Don't be so harsh, Jean.

JEAN: Orders always sound harsh. You've never had to take them.

(Jean, left alone, heaves a sigh of relief and sits down at the table. He takes out a notebook and a pencil and begins to calculate, counting aloud now and then. The pantomime continues until Christine enters, dressed for church, and carrying Jean's white tie and shirt front in her hand.)

CHRISTINE: Lord in Heaven, what a mess! What on earth have you been doing?

JEAN: It was Miss Julie. She dragged the whole crowd in here. You must have been sleeping awfully sound if you didn't hear anything.

CHRISTINE: I slept like a log.

JEAN: You already dressed for church?

CHRISTINE: Yes, indeed. Don't you remember you promised to go to Communion with me today?

JEAN: Oh, yes, of course. I remember. I see you've brought my things. All right. Come on, put it on me. *(He sits down, and Christine starts to put the white tie and shirt front on him. Pause)*

JEAN *(yawning)*: What's the lesson for today?

CHRISTINE: The beheading of John the Baptist, I suppose.

JEAN: My God, that will go on forever.—Hey, you're choking me!... Oh, I'm so sleepy, so sleepy.

CHRISTINE: What were you doing up all night? You look green in the face.

JEAN: I've been sitting here talking with Miss Julie.

CHRISTINE: That girl! She doesn't know how to behave herself!

(Pause)

JEAN: Tell me something, Christine....

CHRISTINE: Well, what?

JEAN: Isn't it strange when you think about it? Her, I mean.

CHRISTINE: What's so strange?

JEAN: Everything!

(Pause. Christine looks at the half-empty glasses on the table)

CHRISTINE: Have you been drinking with her?

JEAN: Yes!

CHRISTINE: Shame on you!—Look me in the eyes! You haven't...?

JEAN: Yes!

CHRISTINE: Is it possible? Is it really possible?

JEAN *(after a moment's consideration)*: Yes. It is.

CHRISTINE: Oh, how disgusting! I could never have believed anything like this would happen! No. No. This is too much!

JEAN: Don't tell me you're jealous of her?

CHRISTINE: No, not of her. If it had been Clara—or Sophie—I would have scratched your eyes out! But her—? That's different. I don't know why.... But it's still disgusting!

JEAN: Then you're not mad at her?

CHRISTINE: No. Mad at you. You were mean and cruel to do a thing like that, very mean. The poor girl! . . . But let me tell you, I'm not going to stay in this house a moment longer, not when I can't have any respect for my employers.

JEAN: Why do you want to respect them?

CHRISTINE: Don't try to be smart. You don't want to work for people who behave immorally, do you? Well, do you? If you ask me, you'd be lowering yourself by doing that.

JEAN: Oh, I don't know. I think it's rather comforting to find out that they're not one bit better than we are.

CHRISTINE: Well, I don't. If they're not any better, there's no point in us trying to be like them.—And think of the Count. Think of all the sorrows he's been through in his time. No, sir, I won't stay in this house any longer. . . . Imagine! You, of all people! If it had been the attorney fellow; if it had been somebody respectable—

JEAN: Now just a minute—!

CHRISTINE: Oh, you're all right in your own way. But there's a big difference between one class and another. You can't deny that.—No, this is something I can never get over. She was so proud, and so sarcastic about men, you'd never believe she'd go and throw herself at one. And at someone like you! And *she* was going to have Diana shot, because the poor thing ran after the gatekeeper's mongrel!—Well, I tell you, I've had enough! I'm not going to stay here any longer. On the twenty-fourth of October, I'm leaving.

JEAN: Then what'll you do?

CHRISTINE: Well, since you brought it up, it's about time that you got yourself a decent place, if we're going to get married.

JEAN: Why should I go looking for another place? I could never get a place like this if I'm married.

CHRISTINE: Well, of course not! But you could get a job as a porter, or maybe try to get a government job as a caretaker somewhere. The government don't pay much, but they pay regular. And there's a pension for the wife and children.

JEAN (*wryly*): Fine, fine! But I'm not the kind of guy who thinks about dying for his wife and children this early in the game. I hate to say it, but I've got slightly bigger plans than that.

CHRISTINE: Plans! Hah! What about your obligations? You'd better start giving them a little thought!

JEAN: Don't start nagging me about obligations! I know what I have to do without you telling me. (*He hears a sound upstairs*) Anyhow, we'll have plenty of chance to talk about this later. You just go and get yourself ready, and we'll be off to church.

CHRISTINE: Who is that walking around up there?

JEAN: I don't know. Clara, I suppose. Who else?

CHRISTINE (*starting to leave*): It can't be the Count, can it? Could he have come back without anybody hearing him?

JEAN (*frightened*): The Count? No, it can't be. He would have rung.

CHRISTINE (*leaving*): God help us! I've never heard of the like of this.

(*The sun has now risen and strikes the tops of the trees in the park. The light shifts gradually until it is shining very obliquely through the windows. Jean goes to the door and signals. Miss Julie enters, dressed for travel, and carrying a small bird cage, covered with a towel. She sets the cage down on a chair.)*

MISS JULIE: I'm ready now.

JEAN: Shh! Christine's awake.

MISS JULIE *(She is extremely tense and nervous during the following)*: Did she suspect anything?

JEAN: She doesn't know a thing.—My God, what happened to you?

MISS JULIE: What do you mean? Do I look so strange?

JEAN: You're white as a ghost, and you've—excuse me—but you've got dirt on your face.

MISS JULIE: Let me wash it off. *(She goes over to the wash basin and washes her face and hands)* There! Do you have a towel? . . . Oh, look, the sun's coming up!

JEAN: That breaks the magic spell!

MISS JULIE: Yes, we were spellbound last night, weren't we? Midsummer madness . . . Jean, listen to me! Come with me. I've got the money!

JEAN *(suspiciously)*: Enough?

MISS JULIE: Enough for a start. Come with me, Jean. I can't travel alone today. Midsummer Day on a stifling hot train, packed in with crowds of people, all staring at me—stopping at every station when I want to be flying. I can't, Jean, I can't! . . . And everything will remind me of the past. Midsummer Day when I was a child and the church was decorated with leaves—birch leaves and lilacs . . . the table spread for dinner with friends and relatives . . . and after dinner, dancing in the park, with flowers and games. Oh, no matter how far you travel, the memories tag right along in the baggage car . . . and the regrets and the remorse.

JEAN: All right, I'll go with you! But it's got to be now—before it's too late! This very instant!

MISS JULIE: Hurry and get dressed! *(She picks up the bird cage)*

JEAN: But no baggage! It would give us away.

MISS JULIE: Nothing. Only what we can take to our seats.

JEAN *(as he gets his hat)*: What in the devil have you got there? What is that?

MISS JULIE: It's only my canary. I can't leave it behind.

JEAN: A canary! My God, do you expect us to carry a bird cage around with us? You're crazy. Put that cage down!

MISS JULIE: It's the only thing I'm taking with me from my home—the only living thing who loves me since Diana was unfaithful to me! Don't be cruel, Jean. Let me take it with me.

JEAN: I told you to put that cage down!—And don't talk so loud. Christine can hear us.

MISS JULIE: No, I won't leave it with a stranger. I won't. I'd rather have you kill it.

JEAN: Let me have the little pest and I'll wring its neck.

MISS JULIE: Yes, but don't hurt it. Don't—. No, I can't do it!

JEAN: Don't worry, I can. Give it here.

(Miss Julie takes the bird out of the cage and kisses it)

MISS JULIE: Oh, my little Serena, must you die and leave your mistress?

JEAN: You don't have to make a scene of it. It's a question of your whole life and future. You're wasting time! *(Jean grabs the canary from her, carries it to the chopping block, and picks up a meat cleaver. Miss Julie turns away)* You should have learned how to kill chickens instead of shooting revolvers— *(He brings the cleaver down)* —then a drop of blood wouldn't make you faint.

MISS JULIE *(screaming)*: Kill me too! Kill me! You can kill an innocent creature without turning a hair—then kill me. Oh, how I hate you! I loathe you! There's blood between us. I curse the moment I first laid eyes on you! I curse the moment I was conceived in my mother's womb.

JEAN: What good does your cursing do? Let's get out of here!

MISS JULIE *(approaches the chopping block as if drawn to it against her will)*: No, I don't want to go yet. I can't.—I have to see.—Shh! I hear a carriage coming! *(She listens but keeps her eyes fastened on the chopping block and cleaver)* You don't think I can stand the sight of blood, do you? You think I'm so weak, don't you? Oh, how I'd love to see your blood, your brains on that chopping block. I'd love to see the whole of your sex swimming in a sea of blood just like that. The way I feel I could drink out of your skull. I'd like to use your chest as a foot bath and dip my toes in your guts! I could eat your heart roasted whole!—You think I'm weak! You think I loved you because my womb hungered for your semen. You think I want to carry your brood under my heart and feed it with my blood! Bear your child and take your name!—Come to think of it, what is your name anyway? I've never even heard your last name. I'll bet you don't even have one. I'd be Mrs. Doorman or Madame Garbageman. You dog with *my* name on your collar—you lackey with *my* initials on your buttons! Do you think I'm going to share you with my cook and fight over you with my maid?! Ohhh!—You think I'm a coward who's going to run away No, I'm going to stay—come hell or high water. My father will come home—find his desk broken into—his money gone. He'll ring—on that bell—two rings for the valet. And then he'll send for the sheriff—and I'll tell him everything. Everything! Oh, what a relief it'll be to have it all over . . . if only it will be over. . . . He'll have a stroke and die . . . and there'll be an end to all of us. There'll be peace . . . and quiet . . . forever. . . . The coat of arms will be broken on his coffin; the Count's line will be extinct—while the valet's breed will continue in an orphanage, win triumphs in the gutter, and end in jail!

(Christine enters, dressed for church and with a hymn-book in her hand. Miss Julie rushes over to her and throws herself into her arms as if seeking protection.)

MISS JULIE: Help me, Christine! Help me against this man!

CHRISTINE *(cold and unmoved)*: This is a fine way to behave on a holy day! *(She sees the chopping block)* Just look at the mess you've made there! How do you explain that? And what's all this shouting and screaming about?

MISS JULIE: Christine, you're a woman, you're my friend! I warn you, watch out for this—this monster!

JEAN *(ill at ease and a little embarrassed)*: If you ladies are going to talk, I think I'll go and shave. *(He slips out to the right)*

MISS JULIE: You've got to understand, Christine! You've got to listen to me!

CHRISTINE: No, I don't. I don't understand this kind of shenanigans at all. Where

do you think you're going dressed like that? And Jean with his hat on?—
Well?—Well?

MISS JULIE: Listen to me, Christine! If you'll just listen to me, I'll tell you everything.

CHRISTINE: I don't want to know anything.

MISS JULIE: You've got to listen to me—!

CHRISTINE: What about? About your stupid behavior with Jean? I tell you that
doesn't bother me at all, because it's none of my business. But if you have any
silly idea about talking him into skipping out with you, I'll soon put a stop to
that.

MISS JULIE (*extremely tense*): Christine, please don't get upset. Listen to me. I can't
stay here, and Jean can't stay here. So you see, we have to go away.

CHRISTINE: Hm, hm, hm.

MISS JULIE (*suddenly brightening up*): Wait! I've got an idea! Why couldn't all three
of us go away together?—out of the country—to Switzerland—and start a hotel. I've got the money, you see. Jean and I would be responsible for the
whole affair—and Christine, you could run the kitchen, I thought. Doesn't
that sound wonderful! Say yes! Say you'll come, Christine, then everything
will be settled. Say you will! Please! (*She throws her arms around Christine and
pats her*)

CHRISTINE (*remaining aloof and unmoved*): Hm. Hm.

MISS JULIE (*presto tempo*): You've never been traveling, Christine. You have to get
out and see the world. You can't imagine how wonderful it is to travel by
train—constantly new faces—new countries. We'll go to Hamburg, and stop
over to look at the zoo—you'll love that. And we'll go to the theater and the
opera. And then when we get to Munich, we'll go to the museums, Christine.
They have Rubenses and Raphaels there—those great painters, you know. Of
course you've heard about Munich where King Ludwig lived—you know, the
king who went mad. And then we can go and see his castles—they're built just
like the ones you read about in fairy tales. And from there it's just a short trip
to Switzerland—with the Alps. Think of the Alps, Christine, covered with
snow in the middle of summer. And oranges grow there, and laurel trees that
are green the whole year round.—(*Jean can be seen in the wings at the right, shar-
pening his straight razor on a strap held between his teeth and his left hand. He listens
to Miss Julie with a satisfied expression on his face, now and then nodding approvingly.
Miss Julie continues tempo prestissimo.*)—And that's where we'll get a hotel. I'll
sit at the desk while Jean stands at the door and receives the guests, goes out
shopping, writes the letters. What a life that will be! The train whistle blowing, then the bus arriving, then a bell ringing upstairs, then the bell in the restaurant rings—and I'll be making out the bills—and I know just how much to
salt them—you can't imagine how timid tourists are when you shove a bill in
their face!—And you, Christine, you'll run the whole kitchen—there'll be no
standing at the stove for you—of course not. If you're going to talk to the people, you'll have to dress neatly and elegantly. And with your looks—I'm not
trying to flatter you, Christine—you'll run off with some man one fine day—a
rich Englishman, that's who it'll be, they're so easy to—(*slowing down*)—to
catch.—Then we'll be rich.—We'll build a villa on Lake Como.—Maybe it does
rain there sometimes, but—(*more and more lifelessly*)—the sun has to shine

sometimes, too—even if it looks cloudy.—And—then . . . Or else we can always travel some more—and come back . . . *(pause)*—here . . . or somewhere else. . . .

CHRISTINE: Do you really believe a word of that yourself, Miss Julie?

MISS JULIE *(completely beaten)*: Do I believe a word of it myself?

CHRISTINE: Do you?

MISS JULIE *(exhausted)*: I don't know. I don't believe anything any more. *(She sinks down on the bench and lays her head between her arms on the table)* Nothing. Nothing at all.

CHRISTINE *(turns to the right and faces Jean)*: So! You were planning to run away, were you?

JEAN *(nonplused, lays his razor down on the table)*: We weren't exactly going to run away! Don't exaggerate. You heard Miss Julie's plans. Even if she's tired now after being up all night, her plans are perfectly practical.

CHRISTINE: Well, just listen to you! Did you really think you could get me to cook for that little—

JEAN *(sharply)*: You keep a respectful tongue in your mouth when you talk to your mistress! Understand?

CHRISTINE: Mistress!

JEAN: Yes, mistress!

CHRISTINE: Well of all the—! I don't have to listen—

JEAN: Yes, you do! You need to listen more and talk less. Miss Julie is your mistress. Don't forget that! And if you're going to despise her for what she did, you ought to despise yourself for the same reason.

CHRISTINE: I've always held myself high enough to—

JEAN: High enough to make you look down on others!

CHRISTINE: —enough to keep from lowering myself beneath my position. No one can say that the Count's cook has ever had anything to do with the stable groom or the swineherd. No one can say that!

JEAN: Yes, aren't you lucky you got involved with a decent man!

CHRISTINE: What kind of a decent man is it who sells the oats from the Count's stables?

JEAN: Listen to who's talking! You get a commission on the groceries and take bribes from the butcher!

CHRISTINE: How can you say a thing like that!

JEAN: And you tell me you can't respect your employers any more! You! You!

CHRISTINE: Are you going to church or aren't you? I should think you'd need a good sermon after your exploits.

JEAN: No, I'm not going to church! You can go alone and confess your own sins.

CHRISTINE: Yes, I'll do just that. And I'll come back with enough forgiveness to cover yours, too. Our Redeemer suffered and died on the cross for all our sins, and if we come to Him in faith and with a penitent heart, He will take all our sins upon Himself.

JEAN: Grocery sins included?

MISS JULIE: Do you really believe that, Christine?

CHRISTINE: With all my heart, as sure as I'm standing here. It was the faith I was born into, and I've held on to it since I was a little girl, Miss Julie. Where sin aboundeth, there grace aboundeth also.

MISS JULIE: If I had your faith, Christine, if only—

CHRISTINE: But you see, that's something you can't have without God's special grace. And it is not granted to everyone to receive it.

MISS JULIE: Then who receives it?

CHRISTINE: That's the secret of the workings of grace, Miss Julie, and God is no respecter of persons. With him the last shall be the first—

MISS JULIE: In that case, he does have respect for the last, doesn't he?

CHRISTINE (*continuing*): —and it is easier for a camel to go through the eye of a needle than for a rich man to enter the kingdom of God. That's how things are, Miss Julie. I'm going to leave now—alone. And on my way out I'm going to tell the stable boy not to let any horses out, in case anyone has any ideas about leaving before the Count comes home. Goodbye. (*She leaves*)

JEAN: She's a devil in skirts!—And all because of a canary!

MISS JULIE (*listlessly*) Never mind the canary. . . . Do you see any way out of this, any end to it?

JEAN (*after thinking for a moment*): No.

MISS JULIE: What would you do if you were in my place?

JEAN: In your place? Let me think. . . . An aristocrat, a woman, and—fallen. . . . I don't know.—Or maybe I do.

MISS JULIE (*picks up the razor and makes a gesture with it*): Like this?

JEAN: Yes. But *I* wouldn't do it, you understand. That's the difference between us.

MISS JULIE: Because you're a man and I'm a woman? What difference does that make?

JEAN: Just the difference that there is—between a man and a woman.

MISS JULIE (*holding the razor in her hand*): I want to! But I can't do it. My father couldn't do it either, that time he should have done it.

JEAN: No, he was right not to do it. He had to get his revenge first.

MISS JULIE: And now my mother is getting her revenge again through me.

JEAN: Haven't you ever loved your father, Miss Julie?

MISS JULIE: Yes, enormously. But I must have hated him too. I must have hated him without knowing it. It was he who brought me up to despise my own sex, to be half woman and half man. Who's to blame for what has happened? My father, my mother, myself? Myself? I don't have a self that's my own. I don't have a single thought I didn't get from my father, not an emotion I didn't get from my mother. And that last idea—about all people being equal—I got that from him, my fiancé. That's why I say he's beneath contempt. How can it be my own fault? Put the blame on Jesus, like Christine does? I'm too proud to do that—and too intelligent, thanks to what my father taught me. . . . A rich man can't get into heaven? That's a lie. But at least Christine, who's got money in the savings bank, won't get in. . . . Who's to blame? What difference does it make who's to blame? I'm still the one who has to bear the guilt, suffer the consequences—

JEAN: Yes, but—

(*The bell rings sharply twice, Miss Julie jumps up. Jean changes his coat.*)

JEAN: The Count's back! What if Christine—? (*He goes to the speaking tube, taps on it, and listens*)

MISS JULIE: Has he looked in his desk yet?

JEAN: This is Jean, sir! (*Listens. The audience cannot hear what the Count says.*) Yes, sir! (*Listens*) Yes, sir! Yes, as soon as I can. (*Listens*) Yes, at once, sir! (*Listens*) Very good, sir! In half an hour.

MISS JULIE (*trembling with anxiety*): What did he say? For God's sake, what did he say?

JEAN: He ordered his boots and his coffee in half an hour.

MISS JULIE: Half an hour then! . . . Oh, I'm so tired. I can't bring myself to do anything. Can't repent, can't run away, can't stay, can't live . . . can't die. Help me, Jean. Command me, and I'll obey like a dog. Do me this last favor. Save my honor, save his name. You know what I ought to do but can't force myself to do. Let me use your will power. You command me and I'll obey.

JEAN: I don't know—I can't either, not now. I don't know why. It's as if this coat made me—. I can't give you orders in this. And now, after the Count has spoken to me, I—I can't really explain it—but—I've got the backbone of a damned lackey! If the Count came down here now and ordered me to cut my throat, I'd do it on the spot.

MISS JULIE: Pretend that you're him, and that I'm you. You were such a good actor just a while ago, when you were kneeling before me. You were the aristocrat then. Or else—have you ever been to the theater and seen a hypnotist? (*Jean nods*) He says to his subject, "Take this broom!" and he takes it. He says, "Now sweep!" and he sweeps.

JEAN: But the person has to be asleep!

MISS JULIE (*ecstatic, transposed*): I'm already asleep. The whole room has turned to smoke. You seem like an iron stove, a stove that looks like a man in black with a high hat. Your eyes are glowing like coals in a dying fire. Your face is a white smudge, like ashes. (*The sun is now shining in on the floor and falls on Jean*) It's so good and warm—(*She rubs her hands together as if warming them at a fire*)—and so bright—and so peaceful.

JEAN (*takes the razor and puts it in her hand*): There's the broom. Go now, when the sun is up—out into the barn—and—(*He whispers in her ear*)

MISS JULIE (*waking up*): Thanks! I'm going to get my rest. But tell me one thing. Tell me that the first can also receive the gift of grace. Tell me that, even if you don't believe it.

JEAN: The first? I can't tell you that.—But wait a moment, Miss Julie. I know what I can tell you. You're no longer one of the first. You're one of—the last.

MISS JULIE: That's true! I'm one of the last. I am the very last—Oh!—Now I can't go! Tell me just once more, tell me to go!

JEAN: Now I can't either. I can't!

MISS JULIE: And the first shall be the last. . . .

JEAN: Don't think—don't think! You're taking all my strength away. You're making me a coward. . . . What! I thought I saw the bell move. No. . . . Let me stuff some paper in it.—Afraid of a bell! But it isn't just a bell. There's somebody behind it. A hand that makes it move. And there's something that makes the hand move.—Stop your ears, that's it, stop your ears! But it only rings louder. Rings louder and louder until you answer it. And then it's too late. Then the sheriff comes—and then—(*There are two sharp rings on the bell. Jean gives a start, then straightens himself up.*) It's horrible! But there's no other way for it to end.—Go! (*Miss Julie walks resolutely out through the door*)

The Cherry Orchard

Observing in Russia some of the same social changes that underlie the plot of *Miss Julie*, Chekhov found material for comedy (he thought the conception "funny, very funny," and subtitled the play "A Comedy in Four Acts"). Yet playgoers do not experience much laughter in this play. Occasionally, the spectacle of self-indulgent humans who cannot communicate is wryly amusing, but a sadness in promises misunderstood and ambitions frustrated seems even stronger.

The Cherry Orchard is a fine example of *realistic drama*. In it Chekhov avoided the exaggerations in plot and characterization traditional (and necessary) in plays more clearly either comic or tragic. These people are neither above us, so that we look up to them, or below us, so that we look down. If we find comedy in the scenes, for example, in which nobody seems to listen to anyone else or talk to anyone except himself, we are amused because we recognize scenes in which we ourselves have participated. This kind of comedy is attractively quizzical: how precisely are we to take a speech or action as inept as some of our own, but not so pointedly exaggerated that we are sure we should laugh? Our involvement in that emotional puzzle itself makes the play engagingly realistic.

Much depends upon theater and actors. More than the earlier plays in this collection, *The Cherry Orchard* demands the realistic staging techniques developed in Chekhov's time at the Moscow Art Theater, under its director, Constantin Stanislavsky. The Moscow Art Theater was elaborately equipped to make possible the most accurately detailed stage settings. Tremendous care was taken with costuming and lighting, to preserve the illusion of reality. Stanislavsky pioneered an acting style in which the players learned to live their parts, speaking and acting as though under the stress of real emotions. The stage curtain rose on a *fourth wall* as far as the players were concerned: they moved about as though in a room, playing to each other and not to the audience. As you read *The Cherry Orchard*, you will want to stage it that way in the theater of your mind. The effect is not at all that of a play by Sophocles, Shakespeare, or Molière.

THE CHERRY ORCHARD*

A COMEDY IN FOUR ACTS

Anton Chekhov   (1860–1904)

LUBOV ANDREYEVNA RANEVSKAYA, a landowner.
ANYA, her seventeen-year-old daughter.
VARYA, her adopted daughter, twenty-two years old.
LEONID ANDREYEVICH GAYEV, MME. RANEVSKAYA'S brother.
YERMOLAY ALEXEYEVICH LOPAHIN, a merchant.
PYOTR SERGEYEVICH TROFIMOV, a student.
SIMEONOV-PISHCHIK, a landowner.
CHARLOTTA IVANOVNA, a governess.
SEMYON YEPIHODOV, a clerk.
DUNYASHA, a maid.
FIRS (pronounced *fierce*), a man-servant, aged eighty-seven.
YASHA, a young valet.
A TRAMP.
STATIONMASTER, POST OFFICE CLERK, GUESTS, SERVANTS.

The action takes place on Mme. Ranevskaya's estate.

Act I

A room that is still called the nursery. One of the doors leads into Anya's room. Dawn, the sun will soon rise. It is May, the cherry trees are in blossom, but it is cold in the orchard; there is a morning frost. The windows are shut. Enter Dunyasha with a candle, and Lopahin with a book in his hand.

LOPAHIN: The train is in, thank God. What time is it?

DYNYASHA: Nearly two. *(Puts out the candle)* It's light already.

LOPAHIN: How late is the train, anyway? Two hours at least. *(Yawns and stretches)* I'm a fine one! What a fool I've made of myself! I came here on purpose to meet them at the station, and then I went and overslept. I fell asleep in my chair. How annoying! You might have waked me . . .

DUNYASHA: I thought you'd left. *(Listens.)* I think they're coming!

LOPAHIN *(listens)*: No, they've got to get the luggage, and one thing and another . . . *(Pause)* Lubov Andreyevna spent five years abroad, I don't know what she's like now . . . She's a fine person—lighthearted, simple. I remember when I was a boy of fifteen, my poor father—he had a shop here in the village then—punched me in the face with his fist and made my nose bleed. We'd come into the yard, I don't know what for, and he'd had a drop too much. Lubov Andreyevna, I remember her as if it were yesterday—she was still young and so slim—led me to the wash-basin, in this very room . . . in the nursery. "Don't cry, little peasant," she said, "it'll heal in time for your wedding. . . ." *(Pause)* Little peasant . . . my father was a peasant, it's true, and here I am in a white waistcoat and yellow shoes. A pig in a pastry shop, you might say. It's true I'm rich, I've got a lot of money. . . . But when you look at

*Translated by Avrahm Yarmolinsky.

it closely, I'm a peasant through and through. *(Pages the book)* Here I've been reading this book and I didn't understand a word of it. . . . was reading it and fell asleep. . . . *(Pause)*

DUNYASHA: And the dogs were awake all night, they feel that their masters are coming.

LOPAHIN: Dunyasha, why are you so—

DUNYASHA: My hands are trembling. I'm going to faint.

LOPAHIN: You're too soft, Dunyasha. You dress like a lady, and look at the way you do your hair. That's not right. One should remember one's place.

(Enter Yepihodov with a bouquet; he wears a jacket and highly polished boots that squeak badly. He drops the bouquet as he comes in.)

YEPIHODOV *(picking up the bouquet)*: Here, the gardener sent these, said you're to put them in the dining room. *(Hands the bouquet to Dunyasha)*

LOPAHIN: And bring me some *kvass*.[1]

DUNYASHA: Yes, sir. *(Exits)*

YEPIHODOV: There's a frost this morning—three degrees below—and yet the cherries are all in blossom. I cannot approve of our climate. *(Sighs)* I cannot. Our climate does not activate properly. And, Yermolay Alexeyevich, allow me to make a further remark. The other day I bought myself a pair of boots, and I make bold to assure you, they squeak so that it is really intolerable. What should I grease them with?

LOPAHIN: Oh, get out! I'm fed up with you.

YEPIHODOV: Every day I meet with misfortune. And I don't complain, I've got used to it, I even smile.

(Dunyasha enters, hands Lopahin the kvass)

YEPIHODOV: I am leaving. *(Stumbles against a chair, which falls over)* There! *(Triumphantly, as it were)* There again, you see what sort of circumstance, pardon the expression. . . . It is absolutely phenomenal! *(Exits)*

DUNYASHA: You know, Yermolay Alexeyevich, I must tell you, Yepihodov has proposed to me.

LOPAHIN: Ah!

DUNYASHA: I simply don't know . . . he's a quiet man, but sometimes when he starts talking, you can't make out what he means. He speaks nicely—and it's touching—but you can't understand it. I sort of like him though, and he is crazy about me. He's an unlucky man . . . every day something happens to him. They tease him about it here . . . they call him, Two-and-Twenty Troubles.

LOPAHIN *(listening)*: There! I think they're coming.

DUNYASHA: They *are* coming! What's the matter with me? I feel cold all over.

LOPAHIN: They really are coming. Let's go and meet them. Will she recognize me? We haven't seen each other for five years.

DUNYASHA *(in a flutter)*: I'm going to faint this minute. . . . Oh, I'm going to faint!

(Two carriages are heard driving up to the house. Lopahin and Dunyasha go out quickly. The stage is left empty. There is a noise in the adjoining rooms. Firs, who had driven

---

[1] A beer made from rye or barley.

to the station to meet Lubov Andreyevna Ranevskaya, crosses the stage hurriedly, leaning on a stick. He is wearing an old-fashioned livery and a tall hat. He mutters to himself indistinctly. The hubbub off-stage increases. A voice: "Come, let's go this way." Enter Lubov Andreyevna, Anya and Charlotta Ivanovna, with a pet dog on a leash, all in traveling dresses; Varya, wearing a coat and kerchief; Gayev, Simeonov, Pishchik, Lopahin, Dunyasha with a bag and an umbrella, servants with luggage. All walk across the room.)

ANYA: Let's go this way. Do you remember what room this is, mamma?

MME. RANEVSKAYA *(joyfully, through her tears)*: The nursery!

VARYA: How cold it is! My hands are numb. *(To Mme. Ranevskaya)* Your rooms are just the same as they were mamma, the white one and the violet.

MME. RANEVSKAYA: The nursery! My darling, lovely room! I slept here when I was a child . . . *(Cries)* And here I am, like a child again! *(Kisses her brother and Varya, and then her brother again)* Varya's just the same as ever, like a nun. And I recognized Dunyasha. *(Kisses Dunyasha)*

GAYEV: The train was two hours late. What do you think of that? What a way to manage things!

CHARLOTTA *(to Pishchik)*: My dog eats nuts, too.

PISHCHIK *(in amazement)*: You don't say so! *(All go out, except Anya and Dunyasha)*

DUNYASHA: We've been waiting for you for hours. *(Takes Anya's hat and coat)*

ANYA: I didn't sleep on the train for four nights and now I'm frozen . . .

DUNYASHA: It was Lent when you left; there was snow and frost, and now . . . My darling! *(Laughs and kisses her)* I have been waiting for you, my sweet, my darling! But I must tell you something . . . I can't put it off another minute . . .

ANYA *(listlessly)*: What now?

DUNYASHA: The clerk, Yepihodov, proposed to me, just after Easter.

ANYA: There you are, at it again . . . *(Straightening her hair)* I've lost all my hairpins . . . *(She is staggering with exhaustion)*

DUNYASHA: Really, I don't know what to think. He loves me—he loves me so!

ANYA *(looking towards the door of her room, tenderly)*: My own room, my windows, just as though I'd never been away. I'm home! Tomorrow morning I'll get up and run into the orchard. Oh, if I could only get some sleep. I didn't close my eyes during the whole journey—I was so anxious.

DUNYASHA: Pyotr Sergeyevich came the day before yesterday.

ANYA *(joyfully)*: Petya!

DUNYASHA: He's asleep in the bath-house. He has settled there. He said he was afraid of being in the way. *(Looks at her watch)* I should wake him, but Miss Varya told me not to. "Don't you wake him," she said.

(Enter Varya with a bunch of keys at her belt)

VARYA: Dunyasha, coffee, and be quick . . . Mamma's asking for coffee.

DUNYASHA: In a minute. *(Exits)*

VARYA: Well, thank God, you've come. You're home again. *(Fondling Anya)* My darling is here again. My pretty one is back.

ANYA: Oh, what I've been through!

VARYA: I can imagine.

ANYA: When we left, it was Holy Week, it was cold then, and all the way Charlotta chattered and did her tricks. Why did you have to saddle me with Charlotta?

VARYA: You couldn't have traveled all alone, darling—at seventeen!

ANYA: We got to Paris, it was cold there, snowing. My French is dreadful. Mamma lived on the fifth floor; I went up there, and found all kinds of Frenchmen, ladies, an old priest with a book. The place was full of tobacco smoke, and so bleak. Suddenly I felt sorry for mamma, so sorry, I took her head in my arms and hugged her and couldn't let go of her. Afterwards mamma kept fondling me and crying . . .

VARYA (through tears): Don't speak of it . . . don't.

ANYA: She had already sold her villa at Mentone, she had nothing left, nothing. I hadn't a kopeck[2] left either, we had only just enough to get home. And mamma wouldn't understand! When we had dinner at the stations, she always ordered the most expensive dishes, and tipped the waiters a whole ruble. Charlotta, too. And Yasha kept ordering, too—it was simply awful. You know Yasha's mamma's footman now, we brought him here with us.

VARYA: Yes, I've seen the blackguard.

ANYA: Well, tell me—have you paid the interest?

VARYA: How could we?

ANYA: Good heavens, good heavens!

VARYA: In August the estate will be put up for sale.

ANYA: My God!

LOPAHIN (peeps in at the door and bleats): Meh-h-h. (Disappears)

VARYA (through tears): What I couldn't do to him! (Shakes her fist threateningly)

ANYA (embracing Varya, gently): Varya, has he proposed to you? (Varya shakes her head) But he loves you. Why don't you come to an understanding? What are you waiting for?

VARYA: Oh, I don't think anything will ever come of it. He's too busy, he has no time for me . . . pays no attention to me. I've washed my hands of him—I can't bear the sight of him. They all talk about our getting married, they all congratulate me—and all the time there's really nothing to it—it's all like a dream. (In another tone) You have a new brooch—like a bee.

ANYA (sadly): Mamma bought it. (She goes into her own room and speaks gaily like a child) And you know, in Paris I went up in a balloon.

VARYA: My darling's home, my pretty one is back! (Dunyasha returns with the coffee-pot and prepares coffee. Varya stands at the door of Anya's room.) All day long, darling, as I go about the house, I keep dreaming. If only we could marry you off to a rich man, I should feel at ease. Then I would go into a convent, and afterwards to Kiev, to Moscow . . . I would spend my life going from one holy place to another . . . I'd go on and on . . . What a blessing that would be!

ANYA: The birds are singing in the orchard. What time is it?

VARYA: It must be after two. Time you were asleep, darling. (Goes into Anya's room) What a blessing that would be!

(Yasha enters with a plaid and a traveling bag, crosses the stage)

YASHA (finically): May I pass this way, please?

[2] A small coin, 1/100 of a ruble.

DUNYASHA: A person could hardly recognize you, Yasha. Your stay abroad has certainly done wonders for you.

YASHA: Hm-m . . . and who are you?

DUNYASHA: When you went away I was that high— (*Indicating with her hand*) I'm Dunyasha—Fyodor Kozoyedev's daughter. Don't you remember?

YASHA: Hm! What a peach!

(*He looks round and embraces her. She cries out and drops a saucer. Yasha leaves quickly*)

VARYA (*in the doorway, in a tone of annoyance*): What's going on here?

DUNYASHA (*through tears*): I've broken a saucer.

VARYA: Well, that's good luck.

ANYA (*coming out of her room*): We ought to warn mamma that Petya's here.

VARYA: I left orders not to wake him.

ANYA (*musingly*): Six years ago father died. A month later brother Grisha was drowned in the river. . . . Such a pretty little boy he was—only seven. It was more than mamma could bear, so she went away, went away without looking back . . . (*Shudders*) How well I understand her, if she only knew! (*Pauses*) And Petya Trofimov was Grisha's tutor, he may remind her of it all. . . .

(*Enter Firs, wearing a jacket and a white waistcoat. He goes up to the coffee-pot.*)

FIRS (*anxiously*): The mistress will have her coffee here. (*Puts on white gloves*) Is the coffee ready? (*Sternly; to Dunyasha*) Here, you! And where's the cream?

DUNYASHA: Oh, my God! (*Exits quickly*)

FIRS (*fussing over the coffee-pot*): Hah! the addlehead! (*Mutters to himself*) Home from Paris. And the old master used to go to Paris too . . . by carriage. (*Laughs*)

VARYA: What is it, Firs?

FIRS: What is your pleasure, Miss? (*Joyfully*) My mistress has come home, and I've seen her at last! Now I can die. (*Weeps with joy*)

(*Enter Mme. Ranevskaya, Gayev, and Simeonov-Pishchik. The latter is wearing a tight-waisted, pleated coat of fine cloth, and full trousers. Gayev, as he comes in, goes through the motions of a billiard player with his arms and body.*)

MME. RANEVSKAYA: Let's see, how does it go? Yellow ball in the corner! Bank shot in the side pocket!

GAYEV: I'll tip it in the corner! There was a time, sister, when you and I used to sleep in this very room, and now I'm fifty-one, strange as it may seem.

LOPAHIN: Yes, time flies.

GAYEV: Who?

LOPAHIN: I say, time flies.

GAYEV: It smells of patchouli here.

ANYA: I'm going to bed. Good night, mamma. (*Kisses her mother*)

MME. RANEVSKAYA: My darling child! (*Kisses her hands*) Are you happy to be home? I can't come to my senses.

ANYA: Good night, uncle.

GAYEV (*kissing her face and hands*): God bless you, how like your mother you are! (*To his sister*) At her age, Luba, you were just like her.

(Anya shakes hands with Lopahin and Pishchik, then goes out, shutting the door behind her)

MME. RANEVSKAYA: She's very tired.

PISHCHIK: Well, it was a long journey.

VARYA *(to Lopahin and Pishchik)*: How about it, gentlemen? It's past two o'clock—isn't it time for you to go?

MME. RANEVSKAYA *(laughs)*: You're just the same as ever, Varya. *(Draws her close and kisses her)* I'll have my coffee and then we'll all go. *(Firs puts a small cushion under her feet)* Thank you, my dear. I've got used to coffee. I drink it day and night. Thanks, my dear old man. *(Kisses him)*

VARYA: I'd better see if all the luggage has been brought in. *(Exits)*

MME. RANEVSKAYA: Can it really be I sitting here? *(Laughs)* I feel like dancing, waving my arms about. *(Covers her face with her hands)* But maybe I am dreaming! God knows I love my country, I love it tenderly; I couldn't look out of the window in the train, I kept crying so. *(Through tears)* But I must have my coffee. Thank you, Firs, thank you, dear old man. I'm so happy that you're still alive.

FIRS: Day before yesterday.

GAYEV: He's hard of hearing.

LOPAHIN: I must go soon, I'm leaving for Kharkov about five o'clock. How annoying! I'd like to have a good look at you, talk to you . . . You're just as splendid as ever.

PISHCHIK *(breathing heavily)*: She's even better-looking . . . Dressed in the latest Paris fashion . . . Perish my carriage and all its four wheels . . .

LOPAHIN: Your brother, Leonid Andreyevich, says I'm a vulgarian and an exploiter. But it's all the same to me—let him talk. I only want you to trust me as you used to. I want you to look at me with your touching, wonderful eyes, as you used to. Dear God! My father was a serf of your father's and grandfather's, but you, you yourself, did so much for me once . . . so much . . . that I've forgotten all about that; I love you as though you were my sister—even more.

MME. RANEVSKAYA: I can't sit still, I simply can't. *(Jumps up and walks about in violent agitation)* This joy is too much for me . . . Laugh at me, I'm silly! My own darling bookcase! My darling table! *(Kisses it)*

GAYEV: While you were away, nurse died.

MME. RANEVSKAYA *(sits down and takes her coffee)*: Yes, God rest her soul; they wrote me about it.

GAYEV: And Anastasy is dead. Petrushka Kossoy has left me and has gone into town to work for the police inspector. *(Takes a box of sweets out of his pocket and begins to suck one)*

PISHCHIK: My daughter Dashenka sends her regards.

LOPAHIN: I'd like to tell you something very pleasant—cheering. *(Glancing at his watch)* I am leaving directly. There isn't much time to talk. But I will put it in a few words. As you know, your cherry orchard is to be sold to pay your debts. The sale is to be on the twenty-second of August; but don't you worry, my dear, you may sleep in peace; there is a way out. Here is my plan. Give me your attention! Your estate is only fifteen miles from the town; the railway runs close by it; and if the cherry orchard and the land along the river bank were cut up into lots and these leased for summer cottages, you would have an income of at least 25,000 rubles a year out of it.

GAYEV: Excuse me . . . What nonsense.

MME. RANEVSKAYA: I don't quite understand you, Yermolay Alexeyevich.

LOPAHIN: You will get an annual rent of at least ten rubles per acre, and if you advertise at once, I'll give you any guarantee you like that you won't have a square foot of ground left by autumn, all the lots will be snapped up. In short, congratulations, you're saved. The location is splendid—by that deep river. . . . Only, of course the ground must be cleared . . . all the old buildings, for instance, must be torn down, and this house, too, which is useless, and of course, the old cherry orchard must be cut down.

MME. RANEVSKAYA: Cut down? My dear, forgive me, but you don't know what you're talking about. If there's one thing that's interesting—indeed, remarkable—in the whole province, it's precisely our cherry orchard.

LOPAHIN: The only remarkable thing about this orchard is that it's a very large one. There's a crop of cherries every other year, and you can't do anything with them; no one buys them.

GAYEV: This orchard is even mentioned in the Encyclopedia.

LOPAHIN (glancing at his watch): If we can't think of a way out, if we don't come to a decision, on the twenty-second of August the cherry orchard and the whole estate will be sold at auction. Make up your minds! There's no other way out—I swear. None, none.

FIRS: In the old days, forty or fifty years ago, the cherries were dried, soaked, pickled, and made into jam, and we used to—

GAYEV: Keep still, Firs.

FIRS: And the dried cherries would be shipped by the cartload. It meant a lot of money! And in those days the dried cherries were soft and juicy, sweet, fragrant . . . They knew the way to do it, then.

MME. RANEVSKAYA: And why don't they do it that way now?

FIRS: They've forgotten. Nobody remembers it.

PISHCHIK (to Mme. Ranevskaya): What's doing in Paris? Eh? Did you eat frogs there?

MME. RANEVSKAYA: I ate crocodiles.

PISHCHIK: Just imagine!

LOPAHIN: There used to be only landowners and peasants in the country, but now these summer people have appeared on the scene . . . All the towns, even the small ones, are surrounded by these summer cottages; and in another twenty years, no doubt, the summer population will have grown enormously. Now the summer resident only drinks tea on his porch, but maybe he'll take to working his acre, too, and then your cherry orchard will be a rich, happy, luxuriant place.

GAYEV (indignantly): Poppycock!

(Enter Varya and Yasha)

VARYA: There are two telegrams for you, mamma dear. (Picks a key from the bunch at her belt and noisily opens an old-fashioned bookcase) Here they are.

MME. RANEVSKAYA: They're from Paris. (*Tears them up without reading them*) I'm through with Paris.

GAYEV: Do you know, Luba, how old this bookcase is? Last week I pulled out the bottom drawer and there I found the date burnt in it. It was made exactly a hundred years ago. Think of that! We could celebrate its centenary. True, it's an inanimate object, but nevertheless, a bookcase . . .

PISHCHIK (*amazed*): A hundred years! Just imagine!

GAYEV: Yes. (*Tapping it*) That's something. . . . Dear, honored bookcase, hail to you who for more than a century have served the glorious ideals of goodness and justice! Your silent summons to fruitful toil has never weakened in all those hundred years (*through tears*) sustaining, through successive generations of our family, courage and faith in a better future, and fostering in us ideals of goodness and social consciousness . . . (*Pauses*)

LOPAHIN: Yes . . .

MME. RANEVSKAYA: You haven't changed a bit, Leonid.

GAYEV (*somewhat embarrassed*): I'll play it off the red in the corner! Tip it in the side pocket!

LOPAHIN (*looking at his watch*): Well it's time for me to go . . .

YASHA (*handing a pill box to Mme. Ranevskaya*): Perhaps you'll take your pills now.

PISHCHIK: One shouldn't take medicines, dearest lady, they do neither harm nor good. . . . Give them here, my valued friend. (*Takes the pill box, pours the pills into his palm, blows on them, puts them in his mouth, and washes them down with some kvass*) There!

MME. RANEVSKAYA (*frightened*): You must be mad!

PISHCHIK: I've taken all the pills.

LOPAHIN: What a glutton!

(*All laugh*)

FIRS: The gentleman visited us in Easter week, ate half a bucket of pickles, he did . . . (*Mumbles*)

MME. RANEVSKAYA: What's he saying?

VARYA: He's been mumbling like that for the last three years—we're used to it.

YASHA: His declining years!

(*Charlotta Ivanovna, very thin, tightly laced, dressed in white, a lorgnette at her waist, crosses the stage*)

LOPAHIN: Forgive me, Charlotta Ivanovna, I've not had time to greet you. (*Tries to kiss her hand*)

CHARLOTTA (*pulling away her hand*): If I let you kiss my hand, you'll be wanting to kiss my elbow next, and then my shoulder.

LOPAHIN: I've no luck today. (*All laugh*) Charlotta Ivanovna, show us a trick.

MME. RANEVSKAYA: Yes, Charlotta, do a trick for us.

CHARLOTTA: I don't see the need. I want to sleep.

(*Exits*)

LOPAHIN: In three weeks we'll meet again. (*Kisses Mme. Ranevskaya's hand*) Goodby till then. Time's up. (*To Gayev*) Bye-bye. (*Kisses Pishchik*) Bye-bye. (*Shakes *hands with Varya, then with Firs and Yasha)* I hate to leave. *(To Mme. Ranevskaya)* If you make up your mind about the cottages, let me know; I'll get you a loan of 50,000 rubles. Think it over seriously.

VARYA *(crossly)*: Will you never go!

LOPAHIN: I'm going, I'm going. *(Exits)*

GAYEV: The vulgarian. But, excuse me . . . Varya's going to marry him, he's Varya's fiancé.

VARYA: You talk too much, uncle dear.

MME. RANEVSKAYA: Well, Varya, it would make me happy. He's a good man.

PISHCHIK: Yes, one must admit, he's a most estimable man. And my Dashenka . . . she too says that . . . she says . . . lots of things. *(Snores; but wakes up at once)* All the same, my valued friend, could you oblige me . . . with a loan of 240 rubles? I must pay the interest on the mortgage tomorrow.

VARYA *(alarmed)*: We can't, we can't!

MME. RANEVSKAYA: I really haven't any money.

PISHCHIK: It'll turn up. *(Laughs)* I never lose hope, I thought everything was lost, that I was done for, when lo and behold, the railway ran through my land . . . and I was paid for it . . . And something else will turn up again, if not today, then tomorrow . . . Dashenka will win two hundred thousand . . . she's got a lottery ticket.

MME. RANEVSKAYA: I've had my coffee, now let's go to bed.

FIRS *(brushes off Gayev; admonishingly)*: You've got the wrong trousers on again. What am I to do with you?

VARYA *(softly)*: Anya's asleep. *(Gently opens the window)* The sun's up now, it's not a bit cold. Look, mamma dear, what wonderful trees. And heavens, what air! The starlings are singing!

GAYEV *(opens the other window)*: The orchard is all white. You've not forgotten it? Luba? That's the long alley that runs straight, straight as an arrow; how it shines on moonlight nights, do you remember? You've not forgotten?

MME. RANEVSKAYA *(looking out of the window into the orchard)*: Oh, my childhood, my innocent childhood. I used to sleep in this nursery—I used to look out into the orchard, happiness waked with me every morning, the orchard was just the same then . . . nothing has changed. *(Laughs with joy)* All, all white! Oh, my orchard! After the dark, rainy autumn and the cold winter, you are young again, and full of happiness, the heavenly angels have not left you . . . If I could free my chest and my shoulders from this rock that weighs on me, if I could only forget the past!

GAYEV: Yes, and the orchard will be sold to pay our debts, strange as it may seem. . . .

MME. RANEVSKAYA: Look! There is our poor mother walking in the orchard . . . all in white . . . *(Laughs with joy)* It is she!

GAYEV: Where?

VARYA: What are you saying, mamma dear!

MME. RANEVSKAYA: There's no one there, I just imagined it. To the right, where the path turns towards the arbor, there's a little white tree, leaning over, that looks like a woman . . .

(Trofimov enters, wearing a shabby student's uniform and spectacles)

MME. RANEVSKAYA: What an amazing orchard! White masses of blossom, the blue sky . . .

TROFIMOV: Lubov Andreyevna! *(She looks round at him)* I just want to pay my respects to you, then I'll leave at once. *(Kisses her hand ardently)* I was told to wait until morning, but I hadn't the patience . . . *(Mme. Ranevskaya looks at him, perplexed)*

VARYA *(through tears)*: This is Petya Trofimov.

TROFIMOV: Petya Trofimov, formerly your Grisha's tutor. . . . Can I have changed so much? *(Mme. Ranevskaya embraces him and weeps quietly)*

GAYEV *(embarrassed)*: Don't, don't, Luba.

VARYA *(crying)*: I told you, Petya, to wait until tomorrow.

MME. RANEVSKAYA: My Grisha . . . my little boy . . . Grisha . . . my son.

VARYA: What can one do, mamma dear, it's God's will.

TROFIMOV *(softly, through tears)*: There . . . there.

MME. RANEVSKAYA *(weeping quietly)*: My little boy was lost . . . drowned. Why? Why, my friend? *(More quietly)* Anya's asleep in there, and here I am talking so loudly . . . making all this noise. . . . But tell me, Petya, why do you look so badly? Why have you aged so?

TROFIMOV: A mangy master, a peasant woman in the train called me.

MME. RANEVSKAYA: You were just a boy then, a dear little student, and now your hair's thin—and you're wearing glasses! Is it possible you're still a student? *(Goes towards the door)*

TROFIMOV: I suppose I'm a perpetual student.

MME. RANEVSKAYA *(kisses her brother, then Varya)*: Now, go to bed . . . You have aged, too, Leonid.

PISHCHIK *(follows her)*: So now we turn in. Oh, my gout! I'm staying the night here . . . Lubov Andreyevna, my angel, tomorrow morning. . . . I do need 240 rubles.

GAYEV: He keeps at it.

PISHCHIK: I'll pay it back, dear . . . it's a trifling sum.

MME. RANEVSKAYA: All right, Leonid will give it to you. Give it to him, Leonid.

GAYEV: Me give it to him! That's a good one!

MME. RANEVSKAYA: It can't be helped. Give it to him! He needs it. He'll pay it back.

(Mme. Ranevskaya, Trofimov, Pishchik, and Firs go out; Gayev, Varya, and Yasha remain)

GAYEV: Sister hasn't got out of the habit of throwing money around. *(To Yasha)* Go away, my good fellow, you smell of the barnyard.

YASHA *(with a grin)*: And you, Leonid Andreyevich, are just the same as ever.

GAYEV: Who? *(To Varya)* What did he say?

VARYA *(to Yasha)*: Your mother's come from the village; she's been sitting in the servants' room since yesterday, waiting to see you.

YASHA: Botheration!

VARYA: You should be ashamed of yourself!

YASHA: She's all I needed! She could have come tomorrow. *(Exit)*

VARYA: Mamma is just the same as ever; she hasn't changed a bit. If she had her own way, she'd keep nothing for herself.

GAYEV: Yes . . . *(Pauses)* If a great many remedies are offered for some disease, it means it is incurable; I keep thinking and racking my brains; I have many remedies, ever so many, and that really means none. It would be fine if we came in for a legacy; it would be fine if we married off our Anya to a very rich man; or we might go to Yaroslavl and try our luck with our aunt, the Countess. She's very, very rich, you know . . .

VARYA (*weeping*): If only God would help us!

GAYEV: Stop bawling. Aunt's very rich, but she doesn't like us. In the first place, sister married a lawyer who was no nobleman . . . (*Anya appears in the doorway*) She married beneath her, and it can't be said that her behavior has been very exemplary. She's good, kind, sweet, and I love her, but no matter what extenuating circumstances you may adduce, there's no denying that she has no morals. You sense it in her least gesture.

VARYA (*in a whisper*): Anya's in the doorway.

GAYEV: Who? (*Pauses*) It's queer, something got into my right eye—my eyes are going back on me. . . . And on Thursday, when I was in the circuit court—

(Enter Anya)

VARYA: Why aren't you asleep, Anya?

ANYA: I can't get to sleep, I just can't.

GAYEV: My little pet! (*Kisses Anya's face and hands*) My child! (*Weeps*) You are not my niece, you're my angel! You're everything to me. Believe me, believe—

ANYA: I believe you, uncle. Everyone loves you and respects you . . . but, uncle dear, you must keep still. . . . You must. What were you saying just now about my mother? Your own sister? What made you say that?

GAYEV: Yes, yes . . . (*Covers his face with her hand*) Really, that was awful! Good God! Heaven help me! Just now I made a speech to the bookcase . . . so stupid! And only after I was through, I saw how stupid it was.

VARYA: It's true, uncle dear, you ought to keep still. Just don't talk, that's all.

ANYA: If you could only keep still, it would make things easier for you too.

GAYEV: I'll keep still. (*Kisses Anya's and Varya's hands*) I will. But now about business. On Thursday I was in court; well, there were a number of us there, and we began talking of one thing and another, and this and that, and do you know, I believe it will be possible to raise a loan on a promissory note, to pay the interest at the bank.

VARYA: If only God would help us!

GAYEV: On Tuesday I'll go and see about it again. (*To Varya*) Stop bawling. (*To Anya*) Your mamma will talk to Lopahin, and he, of course, will not refuse her . . . and as soon as you're rested, you'll go to Yaroslavl to the Countess, your great-aunt. So we'll be working in three directions at once, and the thing is in the bag. We'll pay the interest—I'm sure of it. (*Puts a candy in his mouth*) I swear on my honor, I swear by anything you like, the estate shan't be sold. (*Excitedly*) I swear by my own happiness! Here's my hand on it, you can call me a swindler and a scoundrel if I let it come to an auction! I swear by my whole being.

ANYA (*relieved and quite happy again*): How good you are, uncle, and how clever! (*Embraces him*) Now I'm at peace, quite at peace, I'm happy.

FIRS (*reproachfully*): Leonid Andreyevich, have you no fear of God? When are you going to bed?

GAYEV: Directly, directly. Go away. Firs, I'll . . . yes, I will undress myself. Now, children, 'nightie-'nightie. We'll consider details tomorrow, but now go to sleep. (*Kisses Anya and Varya*) I am a man of the 'Eighties; they have nothing good to say of that period nowadays. Nevertheless, in the course of my life I have suffered not a little for my convictions. It's not for nothing that the peasant loves me; one should know the peasant; one should know from which—

ANYA: There you go again, uncle.

VARYA: Uncle dear, be quiet.

FIRS (*angrily*): Leonid Andreyevich!

GAYEV: I'm coming, I'm coming! Go to bed! Double bank shot in the side pocket! Here goes a clean shot . . .

(*Exits, Firs hobbling after him*)

ANYA: I am at peace now. I don't want to go to Yaroslavl—I don't like my great-aunt, but still, I am at peace, thanks to uncle. (*Sits down*)

VARYA: We must get some sleep. I'm going now. While you were away something unpleasant happened. In the old servants' quarters there are only the old people, as you know; Yefim, Polya, Yevstigney, and Karp, too. They began letting all sorts of rascals in to spend the night. . . . I didn't say anything. Then I heard they'd been spreading a report that I gave them nothing but dried peas to eat—out of stinginess, you know . . . and it was all Yevstigney's doing. . . . All right, I thought, if that's how it is, I thought, just wait. I sent for Yevstigney. . . . (*Yawns*) He comes. . . . "How's this, Yevstigney?" I say, "You fool . . ." (*Looking at Anya*) Anichka! (*Pauses*) She's asleep. (*Puts her arm around Anya*) Come to your little bed. . . . Come . . . (*Leads her*) My darling has fallen asleep. . . . Come.

(*They go out. Far away beyond the orchard a shepherd is piping. Trofimov crosses the stage and, seeing Varya and Anya, stands still.*)

VARYA: Sh! She's asleep . . . asleep . . . Come, darling.

ANYA (*softly, half-asleep*): I'm so tired. Those bells . . . uncle . . . dear. . . . Mamma and uncle . . .

VARYA: Come, my precious, come along. (*They go into Anya's room*)

TROFIMOV (*with emotion*): My sunshine, my spring!

Act II

A meadow. An old, long-abandoned, lopsided little chapel; near it, a well, large slabs, which had apparently once served as tombstones, and an old bench. In the background, the road to the Gayev estate. To one side poplars loom darkly, where the cherry orchard begins. In the distance a row of telegraph poles, and far off, on the horizon, the faint outline of a large city which is seen only in fine, clear weather. The sun will soon be setting. Charlotta, Yasha, and Dunyasha are seated on the bench. Yepihodov stands near and plays a guitar. All are pensive. Charlotta wears an old peaked cap. She has taken a gun from her shoulder and is straightening the buckle on the strap.

CHARLOTTA *(musingly)*: I haven't a real passport, I don't know how old I am, and I always feel that I am very young. When I was a little girl, my father and mother used to go from fair to fair and give performances, very good ones. And I used to do the *salto mortale*,[3] and all sorts of other tricks. And when papa and mamma died, a German lady adopted me and began to educate me. Very good. I grew up and became a governess. But where I come from and who I am, I don't know. . . . Who were my parents? Perhaps they weren't even married. . . . I don't know. . . . *(Takes a cucumber out of her pocket and eats it)* I don't know a thing. *(Pause)* One wants so much to talk, and there isn't anyone to talk to. . . . I haven't anybody.

YEPIHODOV *(plays the guitar and sings)*: "What care I for the jarring world? What's friend or foe to me? . . ." How agreeable it is to play the mandolin.

DUNYASHA: That's a guitar, not a mandolin. *(Looks in a hand mirror and powders her face)*

YEPIHODOV: To a madman in love it's a mandolin. *(Sings)* "Would that the heart were warmed by the fire of mutual love!" *(Yasha joins in)*

CHARLOTTA: How abominably these people sing. Pfui! Like jackals!

DUNYASHA, *to Yasha*: How wonderful it must be though to have stayed abroad!

YASHA: Ah, yes, of course, I cannot but agree with you there. *(Yawns and lights a cigar)*

YEPIHODOV: Naturally. Abroad, everything has long since achieved full perplexion.

YASHA: That goes without saying.

YEPIHODOV: I'm a cultivated man, I read all kinds of remarkable books. And yet I can never make out what direction I should take, what is it that I want, properly speaking. Should I live, or should I shoot myself, properly speaking? Nevertheless, I always carry a revolver about me. . . . Here it is . . . *(Shows revolver)*

CHARLOTTA: I've finished. I'm going. *(Puts the gun over her shoulder)* You are a very clever man, Yepihodov, and a very terrible one; women must be crazy about you. Br-r-r! *(Starts to go)* These clever men are all so stupid; there's no one for me to talk to . . . always alone, alone, I haven't a soul . . . and who I am, and why I am, nobody knows. *(Exits unhurriedly)*

YEPIHODOV: Properly speaking and letting other subjects alone, I must say regarding myself, among other things, that fate treats me mercilessly, like a storm treats a small boat. If I am mistaken, let us say, why then do I wake up this morning, and there on my chest is a spider of enormous dimensions . . . like this . . . *(indicates with both hands)* Again, I take up a pitcher of kvass to have a drink, and in it there is something unseemly to the highest degree, something like a cockroach. *(Pause)* Have you read Buckle?[4] *(Pause)* I wish to have a word with you, Avdotya Fyodorovna, if I may trouble you.

DUNYASHA: Well, go ahead.

YEPIHODOV: I wish to speak with you alone. *(Sighs)*

DUNYASHA, *(embarrassed)*: Very well. Only first bring me my little cape. You'll find it near the wardrobe. It's rather damp here.

---

[3] A standing somersault.
[4] Henry Thomas Buckle (1821-1862), an English historian.

YEPIHODOV: Certainly, ma'am; I will fetch it, ma'am. Now I know what to do with my revolver. (Takes the guitar and goes off playing it)

YASHA: Two-and-Twenty Troubles! An awful fool, between you and me. (Yawns)

DUNYASHA: I hope to God he doesn't shoot himself! (Pause) I've become so nervous, I'm always fretting. I was still a little girl when I was taken into the big house. I am quite unused to the simple life now, and my hands are white, as white as a lady's. I've become so soft, so delicate, so refined, I'm afraid of everything. It's so terrifying; and if you deceive me, Yasha, I don't know what will happen to my nerves. (Yasha kisses her)

YASHA: You're a peach! Of course, a girl should never forget herself; and what I dislike more than anything is when a girl don't behave properly.

DUNYASHA: I've fallen passionately in love with you; you're educated—you have something to say about everything (Pause)

YASHA (yawns): Yes, ma'am. Now the way I look at it, if a girl loves someone, it means she is immoral. (Pause) It's agreeable smoking a cigar in the fresh air. (Listens) Someone's coming this way . . . It's our madam and the others. (Dunyasha embraces him impulsively) You go home, as though you'd been to the river to bathe; go by the little path, or else they'll run into you and suspect me of having arranged to meet you here. I can't stand that sort of thing.

DUNYASHA (coughing softly): Your cigar's made my head ache.

(Exits. Yasha standing near the chapel. Enter Mme. Ranevskaya, Gayev, and Lopahin.)

LOPAHIN: You must make up your mind once and for all—there's no time to lose. It's quite a simple question, you know. Do you agree to lease your land for summer cottages or not? Answer in one word, yes or no; only one word!

MME. RANEVSKAYA: Who's been smoking such abominable cigars here? (Sits down)

GAYEV: Now that the railway line is so near, it's made things very convenient. (Sits down) Here we've been able to have lunch in town. Yellow ball in the side pocket! I feel like going into the house and playing just one game.

MME. RANEVSKAYA: You can do that later.

LOPAHIN: Only one word! (Imploringly) Do give me an answer!

GAYEV (yawning): Who?

MME. RANEVSKAYA (looks into her purse): Yesterday I had a lot of money and now my purse is almost empty. My poor Varya tries to economize by feeding us just milk soup; in the kitchen the old people get nothing but dried peas to eat, while I squander money thoughtlessly (Drops the purse, scattering gold pieces) You see there they go . . . (Shows vexation)

YASHA: Allow me—I'll pick them up. (Picks up the money)

MME. RANEVSKAYA: Be so kind, Yasha. And why did I go to lunch in town? That nasty restaurant, with its music and the tablecloth smelling of soap . . . Why drink so much, Leonid? Why eat so much? Why talk so much? Today again you talked a lot, and all so inappropriately about the 'Seventies, about the decadents. And to whom? Talking to waiters about decadents!

LOPAHIN: Yes.

GAYEV (Waving his hand): I'm incorrigible; that's obvious. (Irritably, to Yasha) Why do you keep dancing about in front of me?

YASHA (laughs): I can't hear your voice without laughing—

GAYEV: Either he or I—

MME. RANEVSKAYA: Go away, Yasha; run along.

YASHA (*handing Mme. Ranevskaya her purse*): I'm going, at once. (*Hardly able to suppress his laughter*) This minute. (*Exits*)

LOPAHIN: That rich man, Deriganov, wants to buy your estate. They say he's coming to the auction himself.

MME. RANEVSKAYA: Where did you hear that?

LOPAHIN: That's what they are saying in town.

GAYEV: Our aunt in Yaroslavl has promised to help; but when she will send the money, and how much, no one knows.

LOPAHIN: How much will she send? A hundred thousand? Two hundred?

MME. RANEVSKAYA: Oh, well, ten or fifteen thousand; and we'll have to be grateful for that.

LOPAHIN: Forgive me, but such frivolous people as you are, so queer and unbusinesslike—I never met in my life. One tells you in plain language that your estate is up for sale, and you don't seem to take it in.

MME. RANEVSKAYA: What are we to do? Tell us what to do.

LOPAHIN: I do tell you, every day; every day I say the same thing! You must lease the cherry orchard and the land for summer cottages, you must do it and as soon as possible—right away. The auction is close at hand. Please understand! Once you've decided to have the cottages, you can raise as much money as you like, and you're saved.

MME. RANEVSKAYA: Cottages—summer people—forgive me, but it's all so vulgar.

GAYEV: I agree with you absolutely.

LOPAHIN: I shall either burst into tears or scream or faint! I can't stand it! You've worn me out! (*To Gayev*) You're an old woman!

GAYEV: Who?

LOPAHIN: An old woman! (*Gets up to go*)

MME. RANEVSKAYA (*alarmed*): No, don't go! Please stay, I beg you, my dear. Perhaps we shall think of something.

LOPAHIN: What is there to think of?

MME. RANEVSKAYA: Don't go, I beg you. With you here it's more cheerful anyway. (*Pause*) I keep expecting something to happen, it's as though the house were going to crash about our ears.

GAYEV (*in deep thought*): Bank shot in the corner . . . . Three cushions in the side pocket . . . .

MME. RANEVSKAYA: We have been great sinners . . .

LOPAHIN: What sins could you have committed?

GAYEV (*putting a candy in his mouth*): They say I've eaten up my fortune in candy! (*Laughs*)

MME. RANEVSKAYA: Oh, my sins! I've squandered money away recklessly, like a lunatic, and I married a man who made nothing but debts. My husband drank himself to death on champagne, he was a terrific drinker. And then, to my sorrow, I fell in love with another man, and I lived with him. And just then— that was my first punishment—a blow on the head: my little boy was drowned here in the river. And I went abroad, went away forever . . . never to come back, never to see this river again . . . I closed my eyes and ran, out of my mind . . . . But he followed me, pitiless, brutal. I bought a villa near Mentone, because he fell ill there; and for three years, day and night, I knew no peace, no rest. The sick man wore me out, he sucked my soul dry. Then last year, when the villa was sold to pay my debts, I went to Paris, and there he robbed me, abandoned me, took up with another woman, I tried to poison myself—it was stupid, so shameful—and then suddenly I felt drawn back to Russia, back to my own country, to my little girl. *(Wipes her tears away)* Lord, Lord! Be merciful, forgive me my sins—don't punish me any more! *(Takes a telegram out of her pocket)* This came today from Paris—he begs me to forgive him, implores me to go back . . . *(Tears up the telegram)* Do I hear music? *(Listens)*

GAYEV: That's our famous Jewish band, you remember? Four violins, a flute, and a double bass.

MME. RANEVSKAYA: Does it still exist? We ought to send for them some evening and have a party.

LOPAHIN *(listens)*: I don't hear anything. *(Hums softly)* "The Germans for a fee will Frenchify a Russian." *(Laughs)* I saw a play at the theater yesterday—awfully funny.

MME. RANEVSKAYA: There was probably nothing funny about it. You shouldn't go to see plays, you should look at yourselves more often. How drab your lives are—how full of unnecessary talk.

LOPAHIN: That's true; come to think of it, we do live like fools. *(Pause)* My pop was a peasant, an idiot; he understood nothing, never taught me anything, all he did was beat me when he was drunk, and always with a stick. Fundamentally, I'm just the same kind of blockhead and idiot. I was never taught anything—I have a terrible handwriting, I write so that I feel ashamed before people, like a pig.

MME. RANEVSKAYA: You should get married, my friend.

LOPAHIN: Yes . . . that's true.

MME. RANEVSKAYA: To our Varya, she's a good girl.

LOPAHIN: Yes.

MME. RANEVSKAYA: She's a girl who comes of simple people, she works all day long; and above all, she loves you. Besides, you've liked her for a long time now.

LOPAHIN: Well, I've nothing against it. She's a good girl. *(Pause)*

GAYEV: I've been offered a place in the bank—6,000 a year. Have you heard?

MME. RANEVSKAYA: You're not up to it. Stay where you are.

(Firs enters, carrying an overcoat)

FIRS *(to Gayev)*: Please put this on, sir, it's damp.

GAYEV *(putting it on)*: I'm fed up with you, brother.

FIRS: Never mind. This morning you drove off without saying a word. *(Looks him over)*

MME. RANEVSKAYA: How you've aged, Firs.

FIRS: I beg your pardon?

LOPAHIN: The lady says you've aged.

FIRS: I've lived a long time; they were arranging my wedding and your papa wasn't born yet. *(Laughs)* When freedom[5] came I was already head footman. I wouldn't consent to be set free then; I stayed on with the master . . . *(Pause)* I remember they were all very happy, but why they were happy, they didn't know themselves.

LOPAHIN: It was fine in the old days! At least there was flogging!

FIRS *(not hearing)*: Of course. The peasants kept to the masters, the masters kept to the peasants; but now they've all gone their own ways, and there's no making out anything.

GAYEV: Be quiet, Firs. I must go to town tomorrow. They've promised to introduce me to a general who might let us have a loan.

LOPAHIN: Nothing will come of that. You won't even be able to pay the interest, you can be certain of that.

MME. RANEVSKAYA: He's raving, there isn't any general. *(Enter Trofimov, Anya, and Varya)*

GAYEV: Here come our young people.

ANYA: There's mamma, on the bench.

MME. RANEVSKAYA *(tenderly)*: Come here, come along, my darlings. *(Embraces Anya and Varya)* If you only knew how I love you both! Sit beside me—there, like that. *(All sit down)*

LOPAHIN: Our perpetual student is always with the young ladies.

TROFIMOV: That's not any of your business.

LOPAHIN: He'll soon be fifty, and he's still a student!

TROFIMOV: Stop your silly jokes.

LOPAHIN: What are you so cross about, you queer bird?

TROFIMOV: Oh, leave me alone.

LOPAHIN *(laughs)*: Allow me to ask you, what do you think of me?

TROFIMOV: What I think of you, Yermolay Alexeyevich, is this: you are a rich man who will soon be a millionaire. Well, just as a beast of prey, which devours everything that comes in its way, is necessary for the process of metabolism to go on, so you too are necessary. *(All laugh)*

VARYA: Better tell us something about the planets, Petya.

MME. RANEVSKAYA: No, let's go on with yesterday's conversation.

TROFIMOV: What was it about?

GAYEV: About man's pride.

TROFIMOV: Yesterday we talked a long time, but we came to no conclusion. There is something mystical about man's pride in your sense of the word. Perhaps you're right, from your own point of view. But if you reason simply, without going into subtleties, then what call is there for pride? Is there any sense in it, if man is so poor a thing physiologically, and if, in the great majority of cases, he is coarse, stupid, and profoundly unhappy? We should stop admiring ourselves. We should work, and that's all.

GAYEV: You die, anyway.

TROFIMOV: Who knows? And what does it mean—to die? Perhaps man has a hundred senses, and at his death only the five we know perish, while the other ninety-five remain alive.

---

[5] The serfs were emancipated in 1861.

MME. RANEVSKAYA: How clever you are, Petya!

LOPAHIN (*ironically*): Awfully clever!

TROFIMOV: Mankind goes forward, developing its powers. Everything that is now unattainable for it will one day come within man's reach and be clear to him; only we must work, helping with all our might those who seek the truth. Here among us in Russia only the very few work as yet. The great majority of the intelligentsia, as far as I can see, seek nothing, do nothing, are totally unfit for work of any kind. They call themselves the intelligentsia, yet they are uncivil to their servants, treat the peasants like animals, are poor students, never read anything serious, do absolutely nothing at all, only talk about science, and have little appreciation of the arts. They are all solemn, have grim faces, they all philosophize and talk of weighty matters. And meanwhile the vast majority of us, ninety-nine out of a hundred, live like savages. At the least provocation—a punch in the jaw, and curses. They eat disgustingly, sleep in filth and stuffiness, bedbugs everywhere, stench and damp and moral slovenliness. And obviously, the only purpose of all our fine talk is to hoodwink ourselves and others. Show me where the public nurseries are that we've heard so much about, and the libraries. We read about them in novels, but in reality they don't exist, there is nothing but dirt, vulgarity, and Asiatic backwardness. I don't like very solemn faces, I'm afraid of them, I'm afraid of serious conversations. We'd do better to keep quiet for a while.

LOPAHIN: Do you know, I get up at five o'clock in the morning, and I work from morning till night; and I'm always handling money, my own and other people's, and I see what people around me are really like. You've only to start doing anything to see how few honest, decent people there are. Sometimes when I lie awake at night, I think: "Oh, Lord, thou hast given us immense forests, boundless fields, the widest horizons, and living in their midst, we ourselves ought really to be giants."

MME. RANEVSKAYA: Now you want giants! They're only good in fairy tales; otherwise they're frightening.

(*Yepihodov crosses the stage at the rear, playing the guitar*)

MME. RANEVSKAYA (*pensively*): There goes Yepihodov.

ANYA (*pensively*): There goes Yepihodov.

GAYEV: Ladies and gentlemen, the sun has set.

TROFIMOV: Yes.

GAYEV (*in a low voice, declaiming as it were*): Oh, Nature, wondrous Nature, you shine with eternal radiance, beautiful and indifferent! You, whom we call our mother, unite within yourself life and death! You animate and destroy!

VARYA (*pleadingly*): Uncle dear!

ANYA: Uncle, again!

TROFIMOV: You'd better bank the yellow ball in the side pocket.

GAYEV: I'm silent, I'm silent . . .

(*All sit plunged in thought. Stillness reigns. Only Firs's muttering is audible. Suddenly a distant sound is heard, coming from the sky as it were, the sound of a snapping string, mournfully dying away.*)

MME. RANEVSKAYA: What was that?

LOPAHIN: I don't know. Somewhere far away, in the pits, a bucket's broken loose; but somewhere very far away.

GAYEV: Or it might be some sort of bird, perhaps a heron.

TROFIMOV: Or an owl . . .

MME. RANEVSKAYA (shudders): It's weird, somehow. (Pause)

FIRS: Before the calamity the same thing happened—the owl screeched, and the samovar hummed all the time.

GAYEV: Before what calamity?

FIRS: Before the Freedom. (Pause)

MME. RANEVSKAYA: Come, my friends, let's be going. It's getting dark. (To Anya) You have tears in your eyes. What is it, my little one? (Embraces her)

ANYA: I don't know, mamma; it's nothing.

TROFIMOV: Somebody's coming.

(A tramp appears, wearing a shabby white cap and an overcoat. He is slightly drunk.)

TRAMP: Allow me to inquire, will this short-cut take me to the station?

GAYEV: It will. Just follow that road.

TRAMP: My heartfelt thanks. (Coughing) The weather is glorious. (Recites) "My brother, my suffering brother . . . Go down to the Volga! Whose groans . . . ?" (To Varya) Mademoiselle, won't you spare 30 kopecks for a hungry Russian?

(Varya, frightened, cries out)

LOPAHIN (angrily): Even panhandling has its proprieties.

MME. RANEVSKAYA (scared): Here, take this. (Fumbles in her purse) I haven't any silver . . . never mind, here's a gold piece.

TRAMP: My heartfelt thanks. (Exits. Laughter)

VARYA (frightened): I'm leaving. I'm leaving . . . Oh, mamma dear, at home the servants have nothing to eat, and you gave him a gold piece!

MME. RANEVSKAYA: What are you going to do with me? I'm such a fool. When we get home, I'll give you everything I have. Yermolay Alexeyevich, you'll lend me some more . . .

LOPAHIN: Yes, ma'am.

MME. RANEVSKAYA: Come, ladies and gentlemen, it's time to be going. Oh! Varya, we've settled all about your marriage. Congratulations!

VARYA (through tears): Really, mamma, that's not a joking matter.

LOPAHIN: "Aurelia, get thee to a nunnery, go . . ."[6]

GAYEV: And do you know, my hands are trembling: I haven't played billiards in a long time.

LOPAHIN: "Aurelia, nymph, in your orisons, remember me!"[7]

MME. RANEVSKAYA: Let's go, it's almost suppertime.

VARYA: He frightened me! My heart's pounding.

LOPAHIN: Let me remind you, ladies and gentlemen, on the 22nd of August the cherry orchard will be up for sale. Think about that! Think!

---

[6] Translating Hamlet to Ophelia, Shakespeare's Hamlet, III, i, 137.
[7] The end of Hamlet's "To be, or not to be" speech, Hamlet, III, i, 89–90.

(All except Trofimov and Anya go out)

ANYA *(laughs)*: I'm grateful to that tramp, he frightened Varya and so we're alone.

TROFIMOV: Varya's afraid we'll fall in love with each other all of a sudden. She hasn't left us alone for days. Her narrow mind can't grasp that we're above love. To avoid the petty and illusory, everything that prevents us from being free and happy—that is the goal and meaning of our life. Forward! Do not fall behind, friends!

ANYA *(strikes her hands together)*: How well you speak! *(Pause)* It's wonderful here today.

TROFIMOV: Yes, the weather's glorious.

ANYA: What have you done to me, Petya? Why don't I love the cherry orchard as I used to? I loved it so tenderly. It seemed to me there was no spot on earth lovelier than our orchard.

TROFIMOV: All Russia is our orchard. Our land is vast and beautiful, there are many wonderful places in it. *(Pause)* Think of it, Anya, your grandfather, your great-grandfather and all your ancestors were serf-owners, owners of living souls, and aren't human beings looking at you from every tree in the orchard, from every leaf, from every trunk? Don't you hear voices? Oh, it's terrifying! Your orchard is a fearful place, and when you pass through it in the evening or at night, the old bark on the trees gleams faintly, and the cherry trees seem to be dreaming of things that happened a hundred, two hundred years ago and to be tormented by painful visions. What is there to say? We're at least two hundred years behind, we've really achieved nothing yet, we have no definite attitude to the past, we only philosophize, complain of the blues, or drink vodka. It's all so clear: in order to live in the present, we should first redeem our past, finish with it, and we can expiate it only by suffering, only by extraordinary, unceasing labor. Realize that, Anya.

ANYA: The house in which we live has long ceased to be our own, and I will leave it, I give you my word.

TROFIMOV: If you have the keys, fling them into the well and go away. Be free as the wind.

ANYA *(in ecstasy)*: How well you put that!

TROFIMOV: Believe me, Anya, believe me! I'm not yet thirty, I'm young, I'm still a student—but I've already suffered so much. In winter I'm hungry, sick, harassed, poor as a beggar, and where hasn't Fate driven me? Where haven't I been? And yet always, every moment of the day and night, my soul is filled with inexplicable premonitions . . . . I have a premonition of happiness, Anya . . . . I see it already!

ANYA *(pensively)*: The moon is rising.

(Yepihodov is heard playing the same mournful tune on the guitar. The moon rises. Somewhere near the poplars Varya is looking for Anya and calling "Anya, where are you.")

TROFIMOV: Yes, the moon is rising. *(Pause)* There it is, happiness, it's approaching, it's coming nearer and nearer, I can already hear its footsteps. And if we don't see it, if we don't know it, what does it matter? Others will!

VARYA's (voice): "Anya! Where are you?"
TROFIMOV: That Varya again! (Angrily) It's revolting!
ANYA: Never mind, let's go down to the river. It's lovely there.
TROFIMOV: Come on. (They go)
VARYA's (voice): "Anya! Anya!"

Act III

A drawing-room separated by an arch from a ballroom. Evening. Chandelier burning. The Jewish band is heard playing in the anteroom. In the ballroom they are dancing the Grand Rond. Pishchik is heard calling, "Promenade à une paire." Pishchik and Charlotta, Trofimov and Mme. Ranevskaya, Anya and the Post Office Clerk, Varya and the Station-master, and others, enter the drawing-room in couples. Dunyasha is in the last couple. Varya weeps quietly, wiping her tears as she dances. All parade through drawing-room. Pishchik calling "Grand rond, balancez!" and "Les cavaliers à genoux et remerciez vox dames!" Firs wearing a dress-coat, brings in soda-water on a tray. Pishchik and Trofimov enter the drawing-room.

PISHCHIK: I'm a full-blooded man; I've already had two strokes. Dancing's hard work for me; but as they say, "If you run with the pack, you can bark or not, but at least wag your tail." Still, I'm as strong as a horse. My late lamented father, who would have his joke, God rest his soul, used to say, talking about our origin, that the ancient line of the Simeonov-Pishchiks was descended from the very horse that Caligula had made a senator. (Sits down) But the trouble is, I have no money. A hungry dog believes in nothing but meat. (Snores and wakes up at once) It's the same with me—I can think of nothing but money.
TROFIMOV: You know, there *is* something equine about your figure.
PISHCHIK: Well, a horse is a fine animal—one can sell a horse.

(Sound of billiards being played in an adjoining room. Varya appears in the archway.)

TROFIMOV (teasing her): Madam Lopahina! Madam Lopahina!
VARYA (angrily): Mangy master!
TROFIMOV: Yes, I am a mangy master and I'm proud of it.
VARYA (reflecting bitterly): Here we've hired musicians, and what shall we pay them with? (Exits)
TROFIMOV (to Pishchik): If the energy you have spent during your lifetime looking for money to pay interest had gone into something else, in the end you could have turned the world upside down.
PISHCHIK: Nietzsche, the philosopher, the greatest, most famous of men, that colossal intellect, says in his works, that it is permissible to forge banknotes.
TROFIMOV: Have you read Nietzsche?
PISHCHIK: Well . . . Dashenka told me . . . And now I've got to the point where forging banknotes is about the only way out for me. . . . The day after tomorrow I have to pay 310 rubles—I already have 130 (. . . Feels in his pockets. In alarm) The money's gone! I've lost my money! (Through tears) Where's my money? (Joyfully) Here it is! Inside the lining . . . I'm all in a sweat . . .

(Enter Mme. Ranevskaya and Charlotta)

MME. RANEVSKAYA *(hums the "Lezginka")*: Why isn't Leonid back yet? What is he doing in town? *(To Dunyasha)* Dunyasha, offer the musicians tea.

TROFIMOV: The auction hasn't taken place, most likely.

MME. RANEVSKAYA: It's the wrong time to have the band, and the wrong time to give a dance. Well, never mind. *(Sits down and hums softly)*

CHARLOTTA *(hands Pishchik a pack of cards)*: Here is a pack of cards. Think of any card you like.

PISHCHIK: I've thought of one.

CHARLOTTA: Shuffle the pack now. That's right. Give it here, my dear Mr. Pishchik. *(Ein, zwei, drei!)* Now look for it—it's in your side pocket.

PISHCHIK *(taking the card out of his pocket)*: The eight of spades! Perfectly right! Just imagine!

CHARLOTTA *(holding pack of cards in her hands. To Trofimov)*: Quickly, name the top card.

TROFIMOV: Well, let's see—the queen of spades.

CHARLOTTA: Right! *(To Pishchik)* Now name the top card.

PISHCHIK: The ace of hearts.

CHARLOTTA: Right! *(Claps her hands and the pack of cards disappears)* Ah, what lovely weather it is today! *(A mysterious feminine voice which seems to come from under the floor, answers her)* "Oh, yes, it's magnificent weather, madam."

CHARLOTTA: You are my best ideal.

VOICE: "And I find you pleasing too, madam."

STATIONMASTER *(applauding)*: The lady ventriloquist, bravo!

PISHCHIK *(amazed)*: Just imagine! Enchanting Charlotta Ivanovna, I'm simply in love with you.

CHARLOTTA: In love? *(Shrugs her shoulders)* Are you capable of love? *Guter Mensch, aber schlechter Musikant.*[8]

TROFIMOV *(claps Pishchik on the shoulder)*: You old horse, you!

CHARLOTTA: Attention please! One more trick! *(Takes a plaid from a chair)* Here is a very good plaid; I want to sell it. *(Shaking it out)* Does anyone want to buy it?

PISHCHIK *(in amazement)*: Just imagine!

CHARLOTTA: Ein, zwei, drei!

(Raises the plaid quickly, behind it stands Anya. She curtsies, runs to her mother, embraces her, and runs back into the ballroom, amidst general enthusiasm.)

MME. RANEVSKAYA *(applauds)*: Bravo! Bravo!

CHARLOTTA: Now again! *Ein, zwei, drei! (Lifts the plaid; behind it stands Varya bowing)*

PISHCHIK *(running after her)*: The rascal! What a woman, what a woman! *(Exits)*

MME. RANEVSKAYA: And Leonid still isn't here. What is he doing in town so long? I don't understand. It must be all over by now. Either the estate has been sold, or the auction hasn't taken place. Why keep us in suspense so long?

VARYA *(trying to console her)*: Uncle's bought it, I feel sure of that.

TROFIMOV *(mockingly)*: Oh, yes!

[8] A good man, but a bad musician.

VARYA: Great-aunt sent him an authorization to buy it in her name, and to transfer the debt. She's doing it for Anya's sake. And I'm sure that God will help us, and uncle will buy it.

MME. RANEVSKAYA: Great-aunt sent fifteen thousand to buy the estate in her name, she doesn't trust us, but that's not even enough to pay the interest. (Covers her face with her hands) Today my fate will be decided, my fate—

TROFIMOV (teasing Varya): Madam Lopahina!

VARYA (angrily): Perpetual student! Twice already you've been expelled from the university.

MME. RANEVSKAYA: Why are you so cross, Varya? He's teasing you about Lopahin. Well, what of it? If you want to marry Lopahin, go ahead. He's a good man, and interesting; if you don't want to, don't. Nobody's compelling you, my pet!

VARYA: Frankly, mamma dear, I take this thing seriously; he's a good man and I like him.

MME. RANEVSKAYA: All right then, marry him. I don't know what you're waiting for.

VARYA: But, mamma, I can't propose to him myself. For the last two years everyone's been talking to me about him—talking. But he either keeps silent, or else cracks jokes. I understand; he's growing rich, he's absorbed in business— he has no time for me. If I had money, even a little, say, 100 rubles, I'd throw everything up and go far away—I'd go into a nunnery.

TROFIMOV: What a blessing . . .

VARYA: A student ought to be intelligent (Softly, with tears in her voice) How homely you've grown, Petya! How old you look! (To Mme. Ranevskaya, with dry eyes) But I can't live without work, mamma dear; I must keep busy every minute.

(Enter Yasha)

YASHA (hardly restraining his laughter): Yepihodov has broken a billiard cue! (Exits)

VARYA: Why is Yepihodov here? Who allowed him to play billiards? I don't understand these people! (Exits)

MME. RANEVSKAYA: Don't tease her, Petya. She's unhappy enough without that.

TROFIMOV: She bustles so—and meddles in other people's business. All summer long she's given Anya and me no peace. She's afraid of a love-affair between us. What business is it of hers? Besides, I've given no grounds for it, and I'm far from such vulgarity. We are above love.

MME. RANEVSKAYA: And I suppose I'm beneath love? (Anxiously) What can be keeping Leonid. If I only knew whether the estate has been sold or not. Such a calamity seems so incredible to me that I don't know what to think—I feel lost. . . . I could scream. . . . I could do something stupid. . . . Save me, Petya, tell me something, talk to me!

TROFIMOV: Whether the estate is sold today or not, isn't it all one? That's all done with long ago—there's no turning back, the path is overgrown. Calm yourself, my dear. You mustn't deceive yourself. For once in your life you must face the truth.

MME. RANEVSKAYA: What truth? You can see the truth, you can tell it from falsehood, but I seem to have lost my eyesight, I see nothing. You settle every great problem so boldly, but tell me, my dear boy, isn't it because you're young, because you don't yet know what one of your problems means in terms of suffering? You look ahead fearlessly, but isn't it because you don't see and don't expect anything dreadful, because life is still hidden from your young eyes? You're bolder, more honest, more profound than we are, but think hard, show just a bit of magnanimity, spare me. After all, I was born here, my father and mother lived here, and my grandfather; I love this house. Without the cherry orchard, my life has no meaning for me, and if it really must be sold, then sell me with the orchard. *(Embraces Trofimov, kisses him on the forehead)* My son was drowned here. *(Weeps)* Pity me, you good, kind fellow!

TROFIMOV: You know, I feel for you with all my heart.

MME. RANEVSKAYA: But that should have been said differently, so differently! *(Takes out her handkerchief—a telegram falls on the floor)* My heart is so heavy today—you can't imagine! The noise here upsets me—my inmost being trembles at every sound—I'm shaking all over. But I can't go into my own room; I'm afraid to be alone. Don't condemn me, Petya. . . . I love you as though you were one of us, I would gladly let you marry Anya—I swear I would—only, my dear boy, you must study—you must take your degree—you do nothing, you let yourself be tossed by Fate from place to place—it's so strange. It's true, isn't it? And you should do something about your beard, to make it grow somehow! *(Laughs)* You're so funny!

TROFIMOV *(picks up the telegram)*: I've no wish to be a dandy.

MME. RANEVSKAYA: That's a telegram from Paris. I get one every day. One yesterday and one today. That savage is ill again—he's in trouble again. He begs forgiveness, implores me to go to him, and really I ought to go to Paris to be near him. Your face is stern, Petya; but what is there to do, my dear boy? What am I to do? He's ill, he's alone and unhappy, and who is to look after him, who is to keep him from doing the wrong thing, who is to give him his medicine on time? And why hide it or keep still about it—I love him! That's clear. I love him, love him! He's a millstone round my neck, he'll drag me to the bottom, but I love that stone. I can't live without it. *(Presses Trofimov's hand)* Don't think badly of me, Petya, and don't say anything, don't say . . .

TROFIMOV *(through tears)*: Forgive me my frankness in heaven's name; but, you know, he robbed you!

MME. RANEVSKAYA: No, no, no, you mustn't say such things! *(Covers her ears)*

TROFIMOV: But he's a scoundrel! You're the only one who doesn't know it. He's a petty scoundrel—a nonentity!

MME. RANEVSKAYA *(controlling her anger)*: You are twenty-six or twenty-seven years old, but you're still a schoolboy.

TROFIMOV: That may be.

MME. RANEVSKAYA: You should be a man at your age. You should understand people who love—and ought to be in love yourself. You ought to fall in love! *(Angrily)* Yes, yes! And it's not purity in you, it's prudishness, you're simply a queer fish, a comical freak!

TROFIMOV *(horrified)*: What is she saying!

MME. RANEVSKAYA: "I am above love!" You're not above love, but simply, as our Firs says, you're an addlehead. At your age not to have a mistress!

TROFIMOV *(horrified)*: This is frightful! What is she saying! *(Goes rapidly into the ballroom, clutching his head)* It's frightful—I can't stand it, I won't stay! *(Exits, but returns at once)* All is over between us! *(Exits into anteroom)*

MME. RANEVSKAYA *(shouts after him)*: Petya! Wait! You absurd fellow, I was joking. Petya!

(Sound of somebody running quickly downstairs and suddenly falling down with a crash. Anya and Varya scream. Sound of laughter a moment later.)

MME. RANEVSKAYA: What's happened? *(Anya runs in)*

ANYA *(laughing)*: Petya's fallen downstairs! *(Runs out)*

MME. RANEVSKAYA: What a queer bird that Petya is!

(Stationmaster, standing in the middle of the ballroom, recites Alexey Tolstoy's "Magdalene,"⁹ to which all listen, but after a few lines, the sound of a waltz is heard from the anteroom and the reading breaks off. All dance. Trofimov, Anya, Varya, and Mme. Ranevskaya enter from the anteroom.)

MME. RANEVSKAYA: Petya, you pure soul, please forgive me . . . . Let's dance.

(Dances with Petya. Anya and Varya dance. Firs enters, puts his stick down by the side door. Yasha enters from the drawing-room and watches the dancers.)

YASHA: Well, grandfather?

FIRS: I'm not feeling well. In the old days it was generals, barons, and admirals that were dancing at our balls, and now we have to send for the Post Office clerk and the Stationmaster, and even they aren't too glad to come. I feel kind of shaky. The old master that's gone, their grandfather, dosed everyone with sealing-wax, whatever ailed 'em. I've been taking sealing-wax every day for twenty years or more. Perhaps that's what's kept me alive.

YASHA: I'm fed up with you, grandpop. *(Yawns)* It's time you croaked.

FIRS: Oh, you addlehead! *(Mumbles)*

(Trofimov and Mme. Ranevskaya dance from the ballroom into the drawing-room)

MME. RANEVSKAYA: *Merci.* I'll sit down a while. *(Sits down)* I'm tired.

(Enter Anya)

ANYA *(excitedly)*: There was a man in the kitchen just now who said the cherry orchard was sold today.

MME. RANEVSKAYA: Sold to whom?

ANYA: He didn't say. He's gone. *(Dances off with Trofimov)*

YASHA: It was some old man gabbing, a stranger.

FIRS: And Leonid Andreyevich isn't back yet, he hasn't come. And he's wearing his lightweight between-season overcoat; like enough, he'll catch cold. Ah, when they're young they're green.

MME. RANEVSKAYA: This is killing me. Go, Yasha, find out to whom it has been sold.

YASHA: But the old man left long ago. *(Laughs)*

MME. RANEVSKAYA: What are you laughing at? What are you pleased about?

YASHA: That Yepihodov is such a funny one. A funny fellow, Two-and-Twenty Troubles!

---

⁹ A poem in which Christ appears at a society banquet.

MME. RANEVSKAYA: Firs, if the estate is sold, where will you go?

FIRS: I'll go where you tell me.

MME. RANEVSKAYA: Why do you look like that? Are you ill? You ought to go to bed.

FIRS: Yes! *(With a snigger)* Me go to bed, and who's to hand things round? Who's to see to things? I'm the only one in the whole house.

YASHA *(to Mme. Ranevskaya)*: Lubov Andreyevna, allow me to ask a favor of you, be so kind! If you go back to Paris, take me with you, I beg you. It's positively impossible for me to stay here. *(Looking around; sotto voce[10])* What's the use of talking? You see for yourself, it's an uncivilized country, the people have no morals, and then the boredom! The food in the kitchen's revolting, and besides there's this Firs wanders about mumbling all sorts of inappropriate words. Take me with you, be so kind!

(Enter Pishchik)

PISHCHIK: May I have the pleasure of a waltz with you, charming lady? *(Mme. Ranevskaya accepts)* All the same, enchanting lady, you must let me have 180 rubles. . . . You must let me have *(dancing)* just one hundred and eighty rubles. *(They pass into the ballroom)*

YASHA *(hums softly)*: "Oh, wilt thou understand the tumult in my soul?"

(In the ballroom a figure in a gray top hat and checked trousers is jumping about and waving its arms; shouts: "Bravo, Charlotta Ivanovna!")

DUNYASHA *(stopping to powder her face; to Firs)* The young miss has ordered me to dance. There are so many gentlemen and not enough ladies. But dancing makes me dizzy, my heart begins to beat fast, Firs Nikolayevich. The Post Office clerk said something to me just now that quite took my breath away. *(Music stops)*

FIRS: What did he say?

DUNYASHA: "You're like a flower," he said.

YASHA *(yawns)*: What ignorance. *(Exits)*

DUNYASHA: "Like a flower!" I'm such a delicate girl. I simply adore pretty speeches.

FIRS: You'll come to a bad end.

(Enter Yepihodov)

YEPIHODOV *(to Dunyasha)*: You have no wish to see me, Avdotya Fyodorovna . . . as though I was some sort of insect. *(Sighs)* Ah, life!

DUNYASHA: What is it you want?

YEPIHODOV: Indubitably you may be right. *(Sighs)* But of course, if one looks at it from the point of view, if I may be allowed to say so, and apologizing for my frankness, you have completely reduced me to a state of mind. I know my fate. Every day some calamity befalls me, and I grew used to it long ago, so that I look upon my fate with a smile. You gave me your word, and though I—

DUNYASHA: Let's talk about it later, please. But just now leave me alone, I am daydreaming. *(Plays with a fan)*

---

[10] In an undertone.

YEPIHODOV: A misfortune befalls me every day; and if I may be allowed to say so, I merely smile, I even laugh.

(Enter Varya)

VARYA *(to Yepihodov)*: Are you still here? What an impertinent fellow you are really! Run along, Dunyasha. *(To Yepihodov)* Either you're playing billiards and breaking a cue, or you're wandering about the drawing-room as though you were a guest.

YEPIHODOV: You cannot, permit me to remark, penalize me.

VARYA: I'm not penalizing you. I'm just telling you. You merely wander from place to place, and don't do your work. We keep you as a clerk, but Heaven knows what for.

YEPIHODOV *(offended)*: Whether I work or whether I walk, whether I eat or whether I play billiards, is a matter to be discussed only by persons of understanding and of mature years.

VARYA *(enraged)*: You dare say that to me—you dare? You mean to say I've no understanding? Get out of here at once! This minute!

YEPIHODOV *(scared)*: I beg you to express yourself delicately.

VARYA *(beside herself)*: Clear out this minute! Out with you!

(Yepihodov goes towards the door, Varya following)

VARYA: Two-and-Twenty Troubles! Get out—don't let me set eyes on you!

(Exit Yepihodov. His voice is heard behind the door): "I shall lodge a complaint against you!"

VARYA: Oh, you're coming back? *(She seizes the stick left near door by Firs)* Well, come then . . . come . . . I'll show you . . . Ah, you're coming? You're coming? . . . Come . . . *(Swings the stick just as Lopahin enters)*

LOPAHIN: Thank you kindly.

VARYA *(angrily and mockingly)*: I'm sorry.

LOPAHIN: It's nothing. Thank you kindly for your charming reception.

VARYA: Don't mention it. *(Walks away, looks back and asks softly)* I didn't hurt you, did I?

LOPAHIN: Oh, no, not at all. I shall have a large bump, though.

(Voices from the ballroom): "Lopahin is here! Lopahin!"

(Enter Pishchik)

PISHCHIK: My eyes do see, my ears do hear! *(Kisses Lopahin)*

LOPAHIN: You smell of cognac, my dear friends. And we've been celebrating here, too. *(Enter Mme. Ranevskaya)*

MME. RANEVSKAYA: Is that you, Yermolay Alexeyevich? What kept you so long? Where's Leonid?

LOPAHIN: Leonid Andreyevich arrived with me. He's coming.

MME. RANEVSKAYA: Well, what happened? Did the sale take place? Speak!

LOPAHIN *(embarrassed, fearful of revealing his joy)*: The sale was over at four o'clock. We missed the train—had to wait till half past nine. *(Sighing heavily)* Ugh. I'm a little dizzy.

(Enter Gayev. In his right hand he holds parcels, with his left he is wiping away his tears)

MME. RANEVSKAYA: Well, Leonid? What news? (*Impatiently, through tears*) Be quick, for God's sake!

GAYEV (*not answering, simply waves his hand. Weeping, to Firs*): Here, take these; anchovies, Kerch herrings . . . I haven't eaten all day. What I've been through! (*The click of billiard balls comes through the open door of the billiard room and Yasha's voice is heard*) "Seven and eighteen!" (*Gayev's expression changes, he no longer weeps*) I'm terribly tired. Firs, help me change. (*Exits, followed by Firs*)

PISHCHIK: How about the sale? Tell us what happened.

MME. RANEVSKAYA: Is the cherry orchard sold?

LOPAHIN: Sold.

MME. RANEVSKAYA: Who bought it?

LOPAHIN: I bought it.

(*Pause. Mme. Ranevskaya is overcome. She would fall to the floor, were it not for the chair and table near which she stands. Varya takes the keys from her belt, flings them on the floor in the middle of the drawing-room and goes out.*)

LOPAHIN: I bought it. Wait a bit, ladies and gentlemen, please, my head is swimming. I can't talk. (*Laughs*) We got to the auction and Deriganov was there already. Leonid Andreyevich had only 15,000 and straight off Deriganov bid 30,000 over and above the mortgage. I saw how the land lay, got into the fight, bid 40,000. He bid 45,000. I bid fifty-five. He kept adding five thousands, I ten. Well . . . it came to an end. I bid ninety above the mortgage and the estate was knocked down to me. Now the cherry orchard's mine! Mine! (*Laughs uproariously*) Lord! God in Heaven! The cherry orchard's mine! Tell me that I'm drunk—out of my mind—that it's all a dream. (*Stamps his feet*) Don't laugh at me! If my father and my grandfather could rise from their graves and see all that has happened—how their Yermolay, who used to be flogged, their half-literate Yermolay, who used to run about barefoot in winter, how that very Yermolay has bought the most magnificent estate in the world. I bought the estate where my father and grandfather were slaves, where they weren't even allowed to enter the kitchen. I'm asleep—it's only a dream—I only imagine it . . . It's the fruit of your imagination, wrapped in the darkness of the unknown! (*Picks up the keys, smiling genially*) She threw down the keys, wants to show she's no longer mistress here. (*Jingles keys*) Well, no matter. (*The band is heard tuning up*) Hey, musicians! Strike up! I want to hear you! Come, everybody, and see how Yermolay Lopahin will lay the ax to the cherry orchard and how the trees will fall to the ground. We will build summer cottages there, and our grandsons and great-grandsons will see a new life here. Music! Strike up!

(*The band starts to play. Mme. Ranevskaya has sunk into a chair and is weeping bitterly.*)

LOPAHIN (*reproachfully*): Why, why didn't you listen to me? My dear friend, my poor friend, you can't bring it back now. (*Tearfully*) Oh, if only this were over quickly! Oh, if only our wretched, disordered life were changed!

PISHCHIK (*takes him by the arm; sotto voce*): She's crying. Let's go into the ballroom. Let her be alone. Come. (*Takes his arm and leads him into the ballroom*)

LOPAHIN: What's the matter? Musicians, play so I can hear you! Let me have things the way I want them. *(Ironically)* Here comes the new master, the owner of the cherry orchard. *(Accidentally he trips over a little table, almost upsetting the candelabra)* I can pay for everything. *(Exits with Pishchik. Mme. Ranevskaya, alone, sits huddled up, weeping bitterly. Music plays softly. Enter Anya and Trofimov quickly. Anya goes to her mother and falls on her knees before her. Trofimov stands in the doorway.)*

ANYA: Mamma, mamma, you're crying! Dear, kind, good mamma, my precious, I love you. I bless you! The cherry orchard is sold, it's gone, that's true, quite true. But don't cry, mamma, life is still before you, you still have your kind, pure heart. Let us go, let us go away from here, darling. We will plant a new orchard, even more luxuriant than this one. You will see it, you will understand, and like the sun at evening, joy—deep, tranquil joy—will sink into your soul, and you will smile, mamma. Come, darling, let us go.

Act IV

Scene as in Act I. No window curtains or pictures, only a little furniture, piled up in a corner, as if for sale. A sense of emptiness. Near the outer door and at the back, suitcases, bundles, etc., are piled up. A door open on the left and the voices of Varya and Anya are heard. Lopahin stands waiting. Yasha holds a tray with glasses full of champagne. Yepihodov in the anteroom is tying up a box. Behind the scene a hum of voices: peasants have come to say good-by. Voice of Gayev: "Thanks, brothers, thank you."

YASHA: The country folk have come to say good-by. In my opinion, Yermolay Alexeyevich, they are kindly souls, but there's nothing in their heads.

(The hum dies away. Enter Mme. Ranevskaya and Gayev. She is not crying, but is pale, her face twitches and she cannot speak.)

GAYEV: You gave them your purse, Luba. That won't do! That won't do!
MME. RANEVSKAYA: I couldn't help it! I couldn't! *(They go out)*
LOPAHIN *(calls after them)*: Please, I beg you, have a glass at parting. I didn't think of bringing any champagne from town and at the station I could find only one bottle. Please, won't you? *(Pause)* What's the matter, ladies and gentlemen, don't you want any? *(Moves away from the door)* If I'd known, I wouldn't have bought it. Well, then I won't drink any, either. *(Yasha carefully sets the tray down on a chair)* At least you have a glass, Yasha.
YASHA: Here's to the travelers! And good luck to those that stay! *(Drinks)* This champagne isn't the real stuff, I can assure you.
LOPAHIN: Eight rubles a bottle. *(Pause)* It's devilishly cold here.
YASHA: They didn't light the stoves today—it wasn't worth it, since we're leaving. *(Laughs)*
LOPAHIN: Why are you laughing?
YASHA: It's just that I'm pleased.
LOPAHIN: It's October, yet it's as still and sunny as though it were summer. Good weather for building. *(Looks at his watch, and speaks off)* Bear in mind, ladies and gentlemen, the train goes in forty-seven minutes, so you ought to start for the station in twenty minutes. Better hurry up!

(Enter Trofimov wearing an overcoat)

TROFIMOV: I think it's time to start. The carriages are at the door. The devil only knows what's become of my rubbers; they've disappeared. *(Calling off)* Anya! My rubbers are gone. I can't find them.

LOPAHIN: I've got to go to Kharkov. I'll take the same train you do. I'll spend the winter in Kharkov. I've been hanging round here with you, till I'm worn out with loafing. I can't live without work—I don't know what to do with my hands, they dangle as if they didn't belong to me.

TROFIMOV: Well, we'll soon be gone, then you can go on with your useful labors again.

LOPAHIN: Have a glass.

TROFIMOV: No, I won't.

LOPAHIN: So you're going to Moscow now?

TROFIMOV: Yes. I'll see them into town, and tomorrow I'll go on to Moscow.

LOPAHIN: Well, I'll wager the professors aren't giving any lectures, they're waiting for you to come.

TROFIMOV: That's none of your business.

LOPAHIN: Just how many years have you been at the university?

TROFIMOV: Can't you think of something new? Your joke's stale and flat. *(Looking for his rubbers)* We'll probably never see each other again, so allow me to give you a piece of advice at parting: don't wave your hands about! Get out of the habit. And another thing: building bungalows, figuring that summer residents will eventually become small farmers, figuring like that is just another form of waving your hands about.... Never mind, I love you anyway; you have fine, delicate fingers, like an artist; you have a fine, delicate soul.

LOPAHIN *(embracing him)*: Good-by, my dear fellow. Thank you for everything. Let me give you some money for the journey, if you need it.

TROFIMOV: What for? I don't need it.

LOPAHIN: But you haven't any.

TROFIMOV: Yes, I have, thank you. I got some money for a translation—here it is in my pocket. *(Anxiously)* But where are my rubbers?

VARYA *(from the next room)*: Here! Take the nasty things. *(Flings a pair of rubbers onto the stage)*

TROFIMOV: What are you so cross about, Varya? Hm . . . and these are not my rubbers.

LOPAHIN: I sowed three thousand acres of poppies in the spring, and now I've made 40,000 on them, clear profit; and when my poppies were in bloom, what a picture it was! So, as I say, I made 40,000; and I am offering you a loan because I can afford it. Why turn up your nose at it? I'm a peasant—I speak bluntly.

TROFIMOV: Your father was a peasant, mine was a druggist—that proves absolutely nothing whatever. *(Lopahin takes out his wallet)* Don't, put that away! If you were to offer me two hundred thousand I wouldn't take it. I'm a free man. And everything that all of you, rich and poor alike, value so highly and hold so dear, hasn't the slightest power over me. It's like so much fluff floating in the air. I can get on without you, I can pass you by, I'm strong and proud. Mankind is moving towards the highest truth, towards the highest happiness possible on earth, and I am in the front ranks.

LOPAHIN: Will you get there?

TROFIMOV: I will. *(Pause)* I will get there, or I will show others the way to get there.

(The sound of axes chopping down trees is heard in the distance)

LOPAHIN: Well, good-by, my dear fellow. It's time to leave. We turn up our noses at one another, but life goes on just the same. When I'm working hard, without resting, my mind is easier, and it seems to me that I too know why I exist. But how many people are there in Russia, brother, who exist nobody knows why? Well, it doesn't matter. That's not what makes the wheels go round. They say Leonid Andreyevich has taken a position in the bank, 6,000 rubles a year. Only, of course, he won't stick to it, he's too lazy. . . .

ANYA *(in the doorway)*: Mamma begs you not to start cutting down the cherry-trees until she's gone.

TROFIMOV: Really, you should have more tact! *(Exits)*

LOPAHIN: Right away—right away! Those men . . . *(Exits)*

ANYA: Has Firs been taken to the hospital?

YASHA: I told them this morning. They must have taken him.

ANYA *(to Yepihodov who crosses the room)*: Yepihodov, please find out if Firs has been taken to the hospital.

YASHA *(offended)*: I told Yegor this morning. Why ask a dozen times?

YEPIHODOV: The aged Firs, in my definitive opinion, is beyond mending. It's time he was gathered to his fathers. And I can only envy him. *(Puts a suitcase down on a hat-box and crushes it)* There now, of course. I knew it! *(Exits)*

YASHA *(mockingly)*: Two-and-Twenty Troubles!

VARYA *(through the door)*: Has Firs been taken to the hospital?

ANYA: Yes.

VARYA: Then why wasn't the note for the doctor taken too?

ANYA: Oh! Then someone must take it to him. *(Exits)*

VARYA *(from adjoining room)*: Where's Yasha? Tell him his mother's come and wants to say good-by.

YASHA *(waves his hand)*: She tries my patience.

(Dunyasha has been occupied with the luggage. Seeing Yasha alone, she goes up to him.)

DUNYASHA: You might just give me one little look, Yasha. You're going away. . . You're leaving me . . . *(weeps and throws herself on his neck)*

YASHA: What's there to cry about? *(Drinks champagne)* In six days I shall be in Paris again. Tomorrow we get into an express train and off we go, that's the last you'll see of us. . . . I can scarcely believe it. *Vive la France!* It don't suit me here, I just can't live here. That's all there is to it. I'm fed up with the ignorance here. I've had enough of it. *(Drinks champagne)* What's there to cry about? Behave yourself properly, and you'll have no cause to cry.

DUNYASHA *(powders her face, looking in pocket mirror)*: Do send me a letter from Paris. You know I loved you, Yasha, how I loved you! I'm a delicate creature, Yasha.

YASHA: Somebody's coming! *(Busies himself with the luggage, hums softly)*

(Enter Mme. Ranevskaya, Gayev, Anya, and Charlotta)

GAYEV: We ought to be leaving. We haven't much time. *(Looks at Yasha)* Who smells of herring?

MME. RANEVSKAYA: In about ten minutes we should be getting into the carriages. *(Looks around the room)* Good-by, dear old home, good-by, grandfather. Winter will pass, spring will come, you will no longer be here, they will have torn you down. How much these walls have seen! *(Kisses Anya warmly)* My treasure, how radiant you look! Your eyes are sparkling like diamonds. Are you glad? Very?

ANYA *(gaily)*: Very glad. A new life is beginning, mamma.

GAYEV: Well, really, everything is all right now. Before the cherry orchard was sold, we all fretted and suffered; but afterwards, when the question was settled finally and irrevocably, we all calmed down, and even felt quite cheerful. I'm a bank employee now, a financier. The yellow ball in the side pocket! And anyhow, you are looking better Luba, there's no doubt of that.

MME. RANEVSKAYA: Yes, my nerves are better, that's true. *(She is handed her hat and coat)* I sleep well. Carry out my things, Yasha. It's time. *(To Anya)* We shall soon see each other again, my little girl. I'm going to Paris, I'll live there on the money your great-aunt sent us to buy the estate with—long live Auntie! But that money won't last long.

ANYA: You'll come back soon, soon, mamma, won't you? Meanwhile I'll study, I'll pass my high school examination, and then I'll go to work and help you. We'll read all kinds of books together, mamma, won't we? *(Kisses her mother's hands)* We'll read in the autumn evenings, we'll read lots of books, and a new wonderful world will open up before us. *(Falls into a revery)* Mamma, do come back.

MME. RANEVSKAYA: I will come back, my precious.

(Embraces her daughter. Enter Lopahin and Charlotta who is humming softly.)

GAYEV: Charlotta's happy: she's singing.

CHARLOTTA *(picks up a bundle and holds it like a baby in swaddling-clothes)*: Bye, baby, bye. *(A baby is heard crying)* "Wah! Wah!" Hush, hush, my pet, my little one. "Wah! Wah!" I'm so sorry for you! *(Throws the bundle down)* You will find me a position, won't you? I can't go on like this.

LOPAHIN: We'll find one for you, Charlotta Ivanovna, don't worry.

GAYEV: Everyone's leaving us. Varya's going away. We've suddenly become of no use.

CHARLOTTA: There's no place for me to live in town, I must go away. *(Hums)*

(Enter Pishchik)

LOPAHIN: There's nature's masterpiece!

PISHCHIK *(gasping)*: Oh . . . let me get my breath . . . I'm in agony. . . . Esteemed friends . . . Give me a drink of water. . . .

GAYEV: Wants some money, I suppose. No, thank you. . . . I'll keep out of harm's way. *(Exits)*

PISHCHIK: It's a long while since I've been to see you, most charming lady. *(To Lopahin)* So you are here . . . glad to see you, you intellectual giant. . . . There . . . *(Gives Lopahin money)* Here's 400 rubles, and I still owe you 840.

LOPAHIN (*shrugging his shoulders in bewilderment*): I must be dreaming ... Where did you get it?

PISHCHIK: Wait a minute ... It's hot ... A most extraordinary event! Some Englishmen came to my place and found some sort of white clay on my land ... (*To Mme. Ranevskaya*) And 400 for you ... most lovely ... most wonderful ... (*Hands her the money*) The rest later. (*Drinks water*) A young man in the train was telling me just now that a great philosopher recommends jumping off roofs. "Jump!" says he; "that's the long and the short of it!" (*In amazement*) Just imagine! Some more water!

LOPAHIN: What Englishmen?

PISHCHIK: I leased them the tract with the clay on it for twenty-four hours. ... And now, forgive me, I can't stay. ... I must be dashing on. ... I'm going over to Znoikov ... to Kardamanov ... I owe them all money ... (*Drinks water*) Good-by, everybody ... I'll look in on Thursday ...

MME. RANEVSKAYA: We're just moving into town; and tomorrow I go abroad.

PISHCHIK (*upset*): What? Why into town? That's why the furniture is like that ... and the suitcases ... Well, never mind! (*Through tears*) Never mind ... Men of colossal intellect, these Englishmen ... Never mind ... Be happy. God will come to your help. ... Never mind. ... Everything in this world comes to an end. (*Kisses Mme. Ranevskaya's hand*) If the rumor reaches you that it's all up with me, remember this old ... horse, and say: Once there lived a certain ... Simeonov-Pishchik ... the kingdom of Heaven be his ... Glorious weather. ... Yes ... (*Exits, in great confusion, but at once returns and says in the doorway*) My daughter Dashenka sends her regards. (*Exit*)

MME. RANEVSKAYA: Now we can go. I leave with two cares weighing on me. The first is poor old Firs. (*Glancing at her watch*) We still have about five minutes.

ANYA: Mamma, Firs has already been taken to the hospital. Yasha sent him there this morning.

MME. RANEVSKAYA: My other worry is Varya. She's used to getting up early and working; and now, with no work to do, she is like a fish out of water. She has grown thin and pale, and keeps crying, poor soul. (*Pause*) You know this very well, Yermolay Alexeyevich; I dreamed of seeing her married to you, and it looked as though that's how it would be. (*Whispers to Anya, who nods to Charlotta and both go out*) She loves you. You find her attractive. I don't know, I don't know why it is you seem to avoid each other; I can't understand it.

LOPAHIN: To tell you the truth, I don't understand it myself. It's all a puzzle. If there's still time, I'm ready now, at once. Let's settle it straight off, and have done with it! Without you, I feel I'll never be able to propose.

MME. RANEVSKAYA: That's splendid. After all, it will only take a minute. I'll call her at once. ...

LOPAHIN: And luckily, here's champagne too. (*Looks at the glasses*) Empty! Somebody's drunk it all. (*Yasha coughs*) That's what you might call guzzling. ...

MME. RANEVSKAYA (*animatedly*): Excellent! We'll go and leave you alone. Yasha, *allez!* I'll call her. (*At the door*) Yarya, leave everything and come here. Come! (*Exits with Yasha*)

LOPAHIN (*looking at his watch*): Yes ...

(*Pause behind the door, smothered laughter and whispering; at last, enter Varya*)

VARYA (*looking over the luggage in leisurely fashion*): Strange, I can't find it ...

LOPAHIN: What are you looking for?

VARYA: Packed it myself, and I don't remember . . . *(Pause)*

LOPAHIN: Where are you going now, Varya?

VARYA: I? To the Ragulins'. I've arranged to take charge there—as housekeeper, if you like.

LOPAHIN: At Yashnevo? About fifty miles from here. *(Pause)* Well, life in this house is ended!

VARYA *(examining luggage)*: Where is it? Perhaps I put it in the chest. Yes, life in this house is ended. . . . There will be no more of it.

LOPAHIN: And I'm just off to Kharkov—by this next train. I've a lot to do there. I'm leaving Yepihodov here . . . I've taken him on.

VARYA: Oh!

LOPAHIN: Last year at this time it was snowing, if you remember, but now it's sunny and there's no wind. It's cold, though. . . . It must be three below.

VARYA: I didn't look. *(Pause)* And besides, our thermometer's broken. *(Pause. Voice from the yard)* "Yermolay Alexeyevich!"

LOPAHIN *(as if he had been waiting for the call)*: This minute!

(Exit quickly. Varya sits on the floor and sobs quietly, her head on a bundle of clothes. Enter Mme. Ranevskaya cautiously.)

MME. RANEVSKAYA: Well? *(Pause)* We must be going.

VARYA *(wiping her eyes)*: Yes, it's time, mamma dear. I'll be able to get to the Ragulins' today, if only we don't miss the train.

MME. RANEVSKAYA *(at the door)*: Anya, put your things on.

(Enter Anya, Gayev, Charlotta. Gayev wears a heavy overcoat with a hood. Enter servants and coachmen. Yepihodov bustles about the luggage.)

MME. RANEVSKAYA: Now we can start on our journey.

ANYA *(joyfully)*: On our journey!

GAYEV: My friends, my dear, cherished friends, leaving this house forever, can I be silent? Can I at leave-taking refrain from giving utterance to those emotions that now fill my being?

ANYA *(imploringly)*: Uncle!

VARYA: Uncle, uncle dear, don't.

GAYEV *(Forlornly)*: I'll bank the yellow in the side pocket . . . I'll be silent . . .

(Enter Trofimov, then Lopahin)

TROFIMOV: Well, ladies and gentlemen, it's time to leave.

LOPAHIN: Yepihodov, my coat.

MME. RANEVSKAYA: I'll sit down just a minute. It seems as though I'd never before seen what the walls of this house were like, the ceilings, and now I look at them hungrily, with such tender affection.

GAYEV: I remember when I was six years old sitting on that window sill on Whitsunday, watching my father going to church.

MME. RANEVSKAYA: Has everything been taken?

LOPAHIN: I think so. *(Putting on his overcoat)* Yepihodov, see that everything's in order.

YEPIHODOV *(in a husky voice)*: You needn't worry, Yermolay Alexeyevich.

LOPAHIN: What's the matter with your voice?
YEPIHODOV: I just had a drink of water. I must have swallowed something.
YASHA (contemptuously): What ignorance!
MME. RANEVSKAYA: When we're gone, not a soul will be left here.
LOPAHIN: Until the spring.

(Varya pulls an umbrella out of a bundle, as though about to hit someone with it. Lopahin pretends to be frightened.)

VARYA: Come, come, I had no such idea!
TROFIMOV: Ladies and gentlemen, let's get into the carriages—it's time. The train will be in directly.
VARYA: Petya, there they are, your rubbers, by that trunk. (Tearfully) And what dirty old things they are!
TROFIMOV (puts on rubbers): Let's go, ladies and gentlemen.
GAYEV (greatly upset, afraid of breaking down): The train . . . the station . . . Three cushions in the side pocket, I'll bank this one in the corner . . .
MME. RANEVSKAYA: Let's go.
LOPAHIN: Are we all here? No one in there? (Locks the side door on the left) There are some things stored here, better lock up. Let us go!
ANYA: Good-by, old house! Good-by, old life!
TROFIMOV: Hail to you, new life!

(Exit with Anya. Varya looks round the room and goes out slowly. Yasha and Charlotta with her dog go out.)

LOPAHIN: And so, until the spring. Go along, friends . . . 'Bye-'bye! (Exits)

(Mme. Ranevskaya and Gayev remain alone. As though they had been waiting for this, they throw themselves on each other's necks, and break into subdued, restrained sobs, afraid of being overheard.)

GAYEV (in despair): My sister! My sister!
MME. RANEVSKAYA: Oh, my orchard—my dear, sweet, beautiful orchard! My life, my youth, my happiness—good-by! Good-by! (Voice of Anya, gay and summoning) "Mamma!" (Voice of Trofimov, gay and excited) "Halloo!"
MME. RANEVSKAYA: One last look at the walls, at the windows . . . Our poor mother loved to walk about this room . . .
GAYEV: My sister, my sister! (Voice of Anya) "Mamma!" (Voice of Trofimov) "Halloo!"
MME. RANEVSKAYA: We're coming.

(They go out. The stage is empty. The sound of doors being locked, of carriages driving away. Then silence. In the stillness is heard the muffled sound of the ax striking a tree, a mournful, lonely sound.

Footsteps are heard. Firs appears in the doorway on the right. He is dressed as usual in a jacket and white waistcoat and wears slippers. He is ill.)

FIRS (goes to the door, tries the handle): Locked! They've gone . . . (Sits down on the sofa) They've forgotten me . . . Never mind . . . I'll sit here a bit . . . I'll wager Leonid Andreyevich hasn't put his fur coat on, he's gone off in his light overcoat . . . (Sighs anxiously) I didn't keep an eye on him . . . Ah, when they're young, they're green . . . (Mumbles something indistinguishable) Life has gone by as if I had never lived. *(Lies down)* I'll lie down a while . . . There's no strength left in you, old fellow; nothing is left, nothing. Ah, you addlehead!

(Lies motionless. A distant sound is heard coming from the sky as it were, the sound of a snapping string mournfully dying away. All is still again, and nothing is heard but the strokes of the ax against a tree far away in the orchard.)

Death of a Salesman

Death of a Salesman takes brilliant advantage of the conventions and physical possibilities of the twentieth-century theater. The audience now sits in a darkened auditorium (as they did not for *Miss Julie*, only two generations earlier) to watch a play strikingly enhanced in light and sound by the magic of electricity, played upon a multilevel set by actors schooled in the realistic techniques common in America and Europe since the days of the Moscow Art Theater. Like a number of other twentieth-century playwrights, Miller has tried to make full use of the technical possibilities of his time by writing elaborate directions to guide the technicians and give the actors a sense of the lives they are trying to lead (rather than merely the lines they are supposed to speak). Reading the play, we must be careful to absorb the stage directions, so that we see the action unfold in the way the author intended. Producing it, we may want to make some changes (as we would with Shakespeare) to adapt it to the technical possibilities of the stage we have available.

Much of the realism is interior: we see Willy's thoughts and dreams as well as his speeches and actions. The exposition of the present situation blends with the exposition of past events that have placed the Loman family where they are. Miller thought of the play as a tragedy of a common man attempting, like Oedipus, to confront a fate that in the end destroys and does not destroy him.

DEATH OF A SALESMAN

CERTAIN PRIVATE CONVERSATIONS IN TWO ACTS AND A REQUIEM

Arthur Miller (1915–   )

THE CHARACTERS

WILLY LOMAN	UNCLE BEN
LINDA	HOWARD WAGNER
BIFF	JENNY
HAPPY	STANLEY
BERNARD	MISS FORSYTHE
THE WOMAN	LETTA
CHARLEY	

The action takes place in Willy Loman's house and yard and in various places he visits in the New York and Boston of today.

Act One

A melody is heard, played upon a flute. It is small and fine, telling of grass and trees and the horizon. The curtain rises.

Before us is the Salesman's house. We are aware of towering, angular shapes behind it, surrounding it on all sides. Only the blue light of the sky falls upon the house and fore-stage; the surrounding area shows an angry glow of orange. As more light appears, we see a solid vault of apartment houses around the small, fragile-seeming home. An air of the dream clings to the place, a dream rising out of reality. The kitchen at center seems actual enough, for there is a kitchen table with three chairs, and a refrigerator. But no other fix-tures are seen. At the back of the kitchen there is a draped entrance, which leads to the liv-ing-room. To the right of the kitchen, on a level raised two feet, is a bedroom furnished only with a brass bedstead and a straight chair. On a shelf over the bed a silver athletic trophy stands. A window opens onto the apartment house at the side.

Behind the kitchen, on a level raised six and a half feet, is the boys' bedroom, at present barely visible. Two beds are dimly seen, and at the back of the room a dormer window. (This bedroom is above the unseen living-room.) At the left a stairway curves up to it from the kitchen.

The entire setting is wholly or, in some places, partially transparent. The roof-line of the house is one-dimensional; under and over it we see the apartment buildings. Before the house lies an apron, curving beyond the forestage into the orchestra. This forward area serves as the back yard as well as the locale of all Willy's imaginings and of his city scenes. Whenever the action is in the present the actors observe the imaginary wall-lines, entering the house only through its door at the left. But in the scenes of the past these boundaries are broken, and characters enter or leave a room by stepping "through" a wall onto the forestage.

From the right, Willy Loman, the Salesman, enters, carrying two large sample cases. The flute plays on. He hears but is not aware of it. He is past sixty years of age, dressed quietly. Even as he crosses the stage to the doorway of the house, his exhaustion is appar-ent. He unlocks the door, comes into the kitchen, and thankfully lets his burden down, feeling the soreness of his palms. A word-sigh escapes his lips—it might be "Oh, boy, oh, boy." He closes the door, then carries his cases out into the living-room, through the draped kitchen doorway.

Linda, his wife, has stirred in her bed at the right. She gets out and puts on a robe, lis-tening. Most often jovial, she has developed an iron repression of her exceptions to Willy's behavior—she more than loves him, she admires him, as though his mercurial nature, his temper, his massive dreams and little cruelties, served her only as sharp reminders of the turbulent longings within him, longings which she shares but lacks the temperament to ut-ter and follow to their end.

LINDA *(hearing Willy outside the bedroom, calls with some trepidation)*: Willy!

WILLY: It's all right. I came back.

LINDA: Why? What happened? *(Slight pause)* Did something happen, Willy?

WILLY: No, nothing happened.

LINDA: You didn't smash the car, did you?

WILLY *(with casual irritation)*: I said nothing happened. Didn't you hear me?

LINDA: Don't you feel well?

WILLY: I'm tired to the death. *(The flute has faded away. He sits on the bed beside her, a little numb)* I couldn't make it. I just couldn't make it, Linda.

LINDA (*very carefully, delicately*): Where were you all day? You look terrible.

WILLY: I got as far as a little above Yonkers. I stopped for a cup of coffee. Maybe it was the coffee.

LINDA: What?

WILLY (*after a pause*): I suddenly couldn't drive any more. The car kept going off onto the shoulder, y'know?

LINDA (*helpfully*): Oh. Maybe it was the steering again. I don't think Angelo knows the Studebaker.

WILLY: No, it's me, it's me. Suddenly I realize I'm goin' sixty miles an hour and I don't remember the last five minutes. I'm—I can't seem to—keep my mind to it.

LINDA: Maybe it's your glasses. You never went for your new glasses.

WILLY: No, I see everything. I came back ten miles an hour. It took me nearly four hours from Yonkers.

LINDA (*resigned*): Well, you'll just have to take a rest, Willy, you can't continue this way.

WILLY: I just got back from Florida.

LINDA: But you didn't rest your mind. Your mind is overactive, and the mind is what counts, dear.

WILLY: I'll start out in the morning. Maybe I'll feel better in the morning. (*She is taking off his shoes*) These goddam arch supports are killing me.

LINDA: Take an aspirin. Should I get you an aspirin? I'll soothe you.

WILLY (*with wonder*): I was driving along, you understand? And I was fine. I was even observing the scenery. You can imagine, me looking at scenery, on the road every week of my life. But it's so beautiful up there, Linda, the trees are so thick, and the sun is warm. I opened the windshield and just let the warm air bathe over me. And then all of a sudden I'm goin' off the road! I'm tellin' ya, I absolutely forgot I was driving. If I'd've gone the other way over the white line I might've killed somebody. So I went on again—and five minutes later I'm dreamin' again, and I nearly— (*He presses two fingers against his eyes*) I have such thoughts, I have such strange thoughts.

LINDA: Willy, dear. Talk to them again. There's no reason why you can't work in New York.

WILLY: They don't need me in New York. I'm the New England man. I'm vital in New England.

LINDA: But you're sixty years old. They can't expect you to keep traveling every week.

WILLY: I'll have to send a wire to Portland. I'm supposed to see Brown and Morrison tomorrow morning at ten o'clock to show the line. Goddammit, I could sell them! (*He starts putting on his jacket*)

LINDA (*taking the jacket from him*): Why don't you go down to the place tomorrow and tell Howard you've simply got to work in New York? You're too accommodating, dear.

WILLY: If old man Wagner was alive, I'd a been in charge of New York now! That man was a prince, he was a masterful man. But that boy of his, that Howard, he don't appreciate. When I went north the first time, the Wagner Company didn't know where New England was!

LINDA: Why don't you tell those things to Howard, dear?

WILLY (*encouraged*): I will, I definitely will. Is there any cheese?

LINDA: I'll make you a sandwich.

WILLY: No, go to sleep. I'll take some milk. I'll be up right away. The boys in?

LINDA: They're sleeping. Happy took Biff on a date tonight.

WILLY (*interested*): That so?

LINDA: It was so nice to see them shaving together, one behind the other, in the bathroom. And going out together. You notice? The whole house smells of shaving lotion.

WILLY: Figure it out. Work a lifetime to pay off a house. You finally own it, and there's nobody to live in it.

LINDA: Well, dear, life is a casting off. It's always that way.

WILLY: No, no, some people—some people accomplish something. Did Biff say anything after I went this morning?

LINDA: You shouldn't have criticized him, Willy, especially after he just got off the train. You mustn't lose your temper with him.

WILLY: When the hell did I lose my temper? I simply asked him if he was making any money. Is that a criticism?

LINDA: But, dear, how could he make any money?

WILLY (*worried and angered*): There's such an undercurrent in him. He became a moody man. Did he apologize when I left this morning?

LINDA: He was crestfallen, Willy. You know how he admires you. I think if he finds himself, then you'll both be happier and not fight any more.

WILLY: How can he find himself on a farm? Is that a life? A farmhand? In the beginning, when he was young, I thought, well, a young man, it's good for him to tramp around, take a lot of different jobs. But it's more than ten years now and he has yet to make thirty-five dollars a week!

LINDA: He's finding himself, Willy.

WILLY: Not finding yourself at the age of thirty-four is a disgrace!

LINDA: Shh!

WILLY: The trouble is he's lazy, goddammit!

LINDA: Willy, please!

WILLY: Biff is a lazy bum!

LINDA: They're sleeping. Get something to eat. Go on down.

WILLY: Why did he come home? I would like to know what brought him home.

LINDA: I don't know. I think he's still lost, Willy. I think he's very lost.

WILLY: Biff Loman is lost. In the greatest country in the world a young man with such—personal attractiveness, gets lost. And such a hard worker. There's one thing about Biff—he's not lazy.

LINDA: Never.

WILLY (*with pity and resolve*): I'll see him in the morning; I'll have a nice talk with him. I'll get him a job selling. He could be big in no time. My God! Remember how they used to follow him around in high school? When he smiled at one of them their faces lit up. When he walked down the street . . . (*He loses himself in reminiscences*)

LINDA (*trying to bring him out of it*): Willy, dear, I got a new kind of American-type cheese today. It's whipped.

WILLY: Why do you get American when I like Swiss?

LINDA: I just thought you'd like a change—

WILLY: I don't want a change! I want Swiss cheese. Why am I always being con-
tradicted?

LINDA *(with a covering laugh)*: I thought it would be a surprise.

WILLY: Why don't you open a window in here, for God's sake?

LINDA *(with infinite patience)*: They're all open, dear.

WILLY: The way they boxed us in here. Bricks and windows, windows and bricks.

LINDA: We should've bought the land next door.

WILLY: The street is lined with cars. There's not a breath of fresh air in the neighborhood. The grass don't grow any more, you can't raise a carrot in the back
yard. They should've had a law against apartment houses. Remember those
two beautiful elm trees out there? When I and Biff hung the swing between
them?

LINDA: Yeah, like being a million miles from the city.

WILLY: They should've arrested the builder for cutting those down. They massa-
cred the neighborhood. *(Lost)* More and more I think of those days, Linda.
This time of year it was lilac and wisteria. And then the peonies would come
out, and the daffodils. What fragrance in this room!

LINDA: Well, after all, people had to move somewhere.

WILLY: No, there's more people now.

LINDA: I don't think there's more people. I think—

WILLY: There's more people! That's what ruining this country! Population is getting out of control. The competition is maddening! Smell the stink from that
apartment house! And another one on the other side . . . How can they whip
cheese?

(On Willy's last line, Biff and Happy raise themselves up in their beds, listening)

LINDA: Go down, try it. And be quiet.

WILLY *(turning to Linda, guiltily)*: You're not worried about me, are you, sweetheart?

BIFF: What's the matter?

HAPPY: Listen!

LINDA: You've got too much on the ball to worry about.

WILLY: You're my foundation and my support, Linda.

LINDA: Just try to relax, dear. You make mountains out of molehills.

WILLY: I won't fight with him any more. If he wants to go back to Texas, let him
go.

LINDA: He'll find his way.

WILLY: Sure. Certain men just don't get started till later in life. Like Thomas Edi-
son, I think. Or B. F. Goodrich. One of them was deaf. *(He starts for the bedroom doorway)* I'll put my money on Biff.

LINDA: And Willy—if it's warm Sunday we'll drive in the country. And we'll
open the windshield, and take lunch.

WILLY: No, the windshields don't open on the new cars.

LINDA: But you opened it today.

WILLY: Me? I didn't. *(He stops)* Now isn't that peculiar! Isn't that a remarkable—
(He breaks off in amazement and fright as the flute is heard distantly)

LINDA: What, darling?

WILLY: That is the most remarkable thing.

LINDA: What, dear?

WILLY: I was thinking of the Chevvy. *(Slight pause)* Nineteen twenty-eight...
when I had that red Chevvy— *(Breaks off)* That funny? I coulda sworn I was
driving that Chevvy today.

LINDA: Well, that's nothing. Something must've reminded you.

WILLY: Remarkable. Ts. Remember those days? The way Biff used to simonize
that car? The dealer refused to believe there was eighty thousand miles on it.
(He shakes his head) Heh! *(To Linda)* Close your eyes, I'll be right up. *(He
walks out of the bedroom)*

HAPPY *(To Biff)*: Jesus, maybe he smashed up the car again!

LINDA *(calling after Willy)*: Be careful on the stairs, dear! The cheese is on the middle shelf! *(She turns, goes over to the bed, takes his jacket, and goes out of the bedroom)*

*(Light has risen on the boys' room. Unseen, Willy is heard talking to himself, "Eighty
thousand miles," and a little laugh. Biff gets out of bed, comes downstage a bit, and
stands attentively. Biff is two years older than his brother Happy, well built, but in
these days bears a worn air and seems less self-assured. He has succeeded less, and his
dreams are stronger and less acceptable than Happy's. Happy is tall, powerfully made.
Sexuality is like a visible color on him, or a scent that many women have discovered.
He, like his brother, is lost, but in a different way, for he has never allowed himself to
turn his face toward defeat and is thus more confused and hard-skinned, although
seemingly more content.)*

HAPPY *(getting out of bed)*: He's going to get his license taken away if he keeps
that up. I'm getting nervous about him, y'know, Biff?

BIFF: His eyes are going.

HAPPY: No, I've driven with him. He sees all right. He just doesn't keep his mind
on it. I drove into the city with him last week. He stops at a green light and
then it turns red and he goes. *(He laughs)*

BIFF: Maybe he's color-blind.

HAPPY: Pop? Why he's got the finest eye for color in the business. You know
that.

BIFF *(sitting down on his bed)*: I'm going to sleep.

HAPPY: You're not still sour on Dad, are you, Biff?

BIFF: He's all right, I guess.

WILLY *(underneath them, in the living-room)*: Yes, sir, eighty thousand miles—
eighty-two thousand!

BIFF: You smoking?

HAPPY *(holding out a pack of cigarettes)*: Want one?

BIFF *(taking a cigarette)*: I can never sleep when I smell it.

WILLY: What a simonizing job, heh!

HAPPY *(with deep sentiment)*: Funny, Biff, y'know? Us sleeping in here again? The
old beds. *(He pats his bed affectionately)* All the talk that went across those two
beds, huh? Our whole lives.

BIFF: Yeah. Lotta dreams and plans.

HAPPY *(with a deep and masculine laugh)*: About five hundred women would like
to know what was said in this room.

(They share a soft laugh)

BIFF: Remember that big Betsy something—what the hell was her name—over on Bushwick Avenue?

HAPPY *(combing his hair)*: With the collie dog!

BIFF: That's the one. I got you in there, remember?

HAPPY: Yeah, that was my first time—I think. Boy, there was a pig! *(They laugh, almost crudely)* You taught me everything I know about women. Don't forget that.

BIFF: I bet you forgot how bashful you used to be. Especially with girls.

HAPPY: Oh, I still am, Biff.

BIFF: Oh, go on.

HAPPY: I just control it, that's all. I think I got less bashful and you got more so. What happened, Biff? Where's the old humor, the old confidence? *(He shakes Biff's knee. Biff gets up and moves restlessly about the room)* What's the matter?

BIFF: Why does Dad mock me all the time?

HAPPY: He's not mocking you, he—

BIFF: Everything I say there's a twist of mockery on his face. I can't get near him.

HAPPY: He just wants you to make good, that's all. I wanted to talk to you about Dad for a long time, Biff. Something's—happening to him. He—talks to himself.

BIFF: I noticed that this morning. But he always mumbled.

HAPPY: But not so noticeable. It got so embarrassing I sent him to Florida. And you know something? Most of the time he's talking to you.

BIFF: What's he say about me?

HAPPY: I can't make it out.

BIFF: What's he say about me?

HAPPY: I think the fact that you're not settled, that you're still kind of up in the air . . .

BIFF: There's one or two other things depressing him, Happy.

HAPPY: What do you mean?

BIFF: Never mind. Just don't lay it all to me.

HAPPY: But I think if you just got started—I mean—is there any future for you out there?

BIFF: I tell ya, Hap, I don't know what the future is. I don't know—what I'm supposed to want.

HAPPY: What do you mean?

BIFF: Well, I spent six or seven years after high school trying to work myself up. Shipping clerk, salesman, business of one kind or another. And it's a measly manner of existence. To get on that subway on the hot mornings in summer. To devote your whole life to keeping stock, or making phone calls, or selling or buying. To suffer fifty weeks of the year for the sake of a two-week vacation, when all you really desire is to be outdoors, with your shirt off. And always to have to get ahead of the next fella. And still—that's how you build a future.

HAPPY: Well, you really enjoy it on a farm? Are you content out there?

BIFF *(with rising agitation)*: Hap, I've had twenty or thirty different kinds of jobs since I left home before the war, and it always turns out the same. I just realized it lately. In Nebraska when I herded cattle, and the Dakotas, and Arizona, and now in Texas. It's why I came home now, I guess, because I realized it. This farm I work on, it's spring there now, see? And they've got about fifteen new colts. There's nothing more inspiring or—beautiful than the sight of a mare and a new colt. And it's cool there now, see? Texas is cool now, and it's spring. And whenever spring comes to where I am, I suddenly get the feeling, my God, I'm not gettin' anywhere! What the hell am I doing, playing around with horses, twenty-eight dollars a week! I'm thirty-four years old, I oughta be makin' my future. That's when I come running home. And now, I get here, and I don't know what to do with myself. *(After a pause)* I've always made a point of not wasting my life, and everytime I come back here I know that all I've done is to waste my life.

HAPPY: You're a poet, you know that, Biff? You're a—you're an idealist!

BIFF: No, I'm mixed up very bad. Maybe I oughta get married. Maybe I oughta get stuck into something. Maybe that's my trouble. I'm like a boy. I'm not married, I'm not in business, I just—I'm like a boy. Are you content, Hap? You're a success, aren't you? Are you content?

HAPPY: Hell, no!

BIFF: Why? You're making money, aren't you?

HAPPY *(moving about with energy, expressiveness)*: All I can do now is wait for the merchandise manager to die. And suppose I get to be merchandise manager? He's a good friend of mine, and he just built a terrific estate on Long Island. And he lived there about two months and sold it, and now he's building another one. He can't enjoy it once it's finished. And I know that's just what I would do. I don't know what the hell I'm workin' for. Sometimes I sit in my apartment—all alone. And I think of the rent I'm paying. And it's crazy. But then, it's what I always wanted. My own apartment, a car, and plenty of women. And still, goddammit, I'm lonely.

BIFF *(with enthusiasm)*: Listen, why don't you come out West with me?

HAPPY: You and I, heh?

BIFF: Sure, maybe we could buy a ranch. Raise cattle, use our muscles. Men built like we are should be working out in the open.

HAPPY *(avidly)*: The Loman Brothers, heh?

BIFF *(with vast affection)*: Sure, we'd be known all over the counties!

HAPPY *(enthralled)*: That's what I dream about, Biff. Sometimes I want to just rip my clothes off in the middle of the store and outbox that goddam merchandise manager. I mean I can outbox, outrun, and outlift anybody in that store, and I have to take orders from those common, petty sons-of-bitches till I can't stand it any more.

BIFF: I'm tellin' you, kid, if you were with me I'd be happy out there.

HAPPY *(enthused)*: See, Biff, everybody around me is so false that I'm constantly lowering my ideals . . .

BIFF: Baby, together we'd stand up for one another, we'd have someone to trust.

HAPPY: If I were around you—

BIFF: Hap, the trouble is we weren't brought up to grub for money. I don't know how to do it.

HAPPY: Neither can I!

BIFF: Then let's go!

HAPPY: The only thing is—what can you make out there?

BIFF: But look at your friend. Builds an estate and then hasn't the peace of mind to live in it.

HAPPY: Yeah, but when he walks into the store the waves part in front of him.

That's fifty-two thousand dollars a year coming through the revolving door, and I got more in my pinky finger than he's got in his head.

BIFF: Yeah, but you just said—

HAPPY: I gotta show some of those pompous, self-important executives over there that Hap Loman can make the grade. I want to walk into the store the way he walks in. Then I'll go with you, Biff. We'll be together yet, I swear. But take those two we had tonight. Now weren't they gorgeous creatures?

BIFF: Yeah, yeah, most gorgeous I've had in years.

HAPPY: I get that any time I want, Biff. Whenever I feel disgusted. The only trouble is, it gets like bowling or something. I just keep knockin' them over and it doesn't mean anything. You still run around a lot?

BIFF: Naa. I'd like to find a girl—steady, somebody with substance.

HAPPY: That's what I long for.

BIFF: Go on! You'd never come home.

HAPPY: I would! Somebody with character, with resistance! Like Mom, y'know? You're gonna call me a bastard when I tell you this. That girl Charlotte I was with tonight is engaged to be married in five weeks. *(He tries on his new hat)*

BIFF: No kiddin'!

HAPPY: Sure, the guy's in line for the vice-presidency of the store. I don't know what gets into me, maybe I just have an overdeveloped sense of competition or something, but I went and ruined her, and furthermore I can't get rid of her. And he's the third executive I've done that to. Isn't that a crummy characteristic? And to top it all, I go to their weddings! *(Indignantly, but laughing)* Like I'm not supposed to take bribes. Manufacturers offer me a hundred-dollar bill now and then to throw an order their way. You know how honest I am, but it's like this girl, see. I hate myself for it. Because I don't want the girl, and, still, I take it and—I love it!

BIFF: Let's go to sleep.

HAPPY: I guess we didn't settle anything, heh?

BIFF: I just got one idea that I think I'm going to try.

HAPPY: What's that?

BIFF: Remember Bill Oliver?

HAPPY: Sure, Oliver is very big now. You want to work for him again?

BIFF: No, but when I quit he said something to me. He put his arm on my shoulder, and he said, "Biff, if you ever need anything, come to me."

HAPPY: I remember that. That sounds good.

BIFF: I think I'll go to see him. If I could get ten thousand or even seven or eight thousand dollars I could buy a beautiful ranch.

HAPPY: I bet he'd back you. 'Cause he thought highly of you, Biff. I mean, they all do. You're well liked, Biff. That's why I say to come back here, and we both have the apartment. And I'm tellin' you, Biff, any babe you want . . .

BIFF: No, with a ranch I could do the work I like and still be something. I just wonder though. I wonder if Oliver still thinks I stole that carton of basketballs.

HAPPY: Oh, he probably forgot that long ago. It's almost ten years. You're too sensitive. Anyway, he didn't really fire you.

BIFF: Well, I think he was going to. I think that's why I quit. I was never sure whether he knew or not. I know he thought the world of me, though. I was the only one he'd let lock up the place.

WILLY *(below)*: You gonna wash the engine, Biff?
HAPPY: Shh!

(Biff looks at Happy, who is gazing down, listening. Willy is mumbling in the parlor.)

HAPPY: You hear that?

(They listen. Willy laughs warmly)

BIFF *(growing angry)*: Doesn't he know Mom can hear that?
WILLY: Don't get your sweater dirty, Biff!

(A look of pain crosses Biff's face)

HAPPY: Isn't that terrible? Don't leave again, will you? You'll find a job here. You gotta stick around. I don't know what to do about him, it's getting embarrassing.
WILLY: What a simonizing job!
BIFF: Mom's hearing that!
WILLY: No kiddin', Biff, you got a date? Wonderful!
HAPPY: Go on to sleep. But talk to him in the morning, will you?
BIFF *(reluctantly getting into bed)*: With her in the house. Brother!
HAPPY *(getting into bed)*: I wish you'd have a good talk with him.

(The light on their room begins to fade)

BIFF *(to himself in bed)*: That selfish, stupid . . .
HAPPY: Sh . . . Sleep, Biff.

Their light is out. Well before they have finished speaking, Willy's form is dimly seen below in the darkened kitchen. He opens the refrigerator, searches in there, and takes out a bottle of milk. The apartment houses are fading out, and the entire house and surroundings become covered with leaves. Music insinuates itself as the leaves appear.

WILLY: Just wanna be careful with those girls, Biff, that's all. Don't make any promises. No promises of any kind. Because a girl, y'know, they always believe what you tell 'em, and you're very young, Biff, you're too young to be talking seriously to girls.

(Light rises on the kitchen. Willy, talking, shuts the refrigerator door and comes downstage to the kitchen table. He pours milk into a glass. He is totally immersed in himself, smiling faintly)

WILLY: Too young entirely, Biff. You want to watch your schooling first. Then when you're all set, there'll be plenty of girls for a boy like you. *(He smiles broadly at a kitchen chair)* That so? The girls pay for you? *(He laughs)* Boy, you must really be makin' a hit.

(Willy is gradually addressing—physically—a point offstage, speaking through the wall of the kitchen, and his voice has been rising in volume to that of a normal conversation.)

WILLY: I been wondering why you polish the car so careful. Ha! Don't leave the hubcaps, boys. Get the chamois to the hubcaps. Happy, use newspaper on the windows, it's the easiest thing. Show him how to do it, Biff! You see, Happy? Pad it up, use it like a pad. That's it, that's it, good work. You're doin' all right, Hap. (*He pauses, then nods in approbation for a few seconds, then looks upward*) Biff, first thing we gotta do when we get time is clip that big branch over the house. Afraid it's gonna fall in a storm and hit the roof. Tell you what. We get a rope and sling her around, then we climb up there with a couple of saws and take her down. Soon as you finish the car, boys, I wanna see ya. I got a surprise for you, boys.

BIFF (*offstage*): Whatta ya got, Dad?

WILLY: No, you finish first. Never leave a job till you're finished—remember that. (*Looking toward the "big trees"*) Biff, up in Albany I saw a beautiful hammock. I think I'll buy it next trip, and we'll hang it right between those two elms. Wouldn't that be something? Just swingin' there under those branches. Boy, that would be . . .

(*Young Biff and Young Happy appear from the direction Willy was addressing. Happy carries rags and a pail of water. Biff, wearing a sweater with a block "S," carries a football.*)

BIFF (*pointing in the direction of the car offstage*): How's that, Pop, professional?

WILLY: Terrific. Terrific job, boys. Good work, Biff.

HAPPY: Where's the surprise, Pop?

WILLY: In the back seat of the car.

HAPPY: Boy! (*He runs off*)

BIFF: What is it, Dad? Tell me, what'd you buy?

WILLY (*laughing, cuffs him*): Never mind, something I want you to have.

BIFF (*turns and starts off*): What is it, Hap?

HAPPY (*offstage*): It's a punching bag!

BIFF: Oh, Pop!

WILLY: It's got Gene Tunney's signature on it!

(*Happy runs onstage with a punching bag*)

BIFF: Gee, how'd you know we wanted a punching bag?

WILLY: Well, it's the finest thing for the timing.

HAPPY (*lies down on his back and pedals with his feet*): I'm losing weight, you notice. Pop?

WILLY (*to Happy*): Jumping rope is good too.

BIFF: Did you see the new football I got?

WILLY (*examining the ball*): Where'd you get a new ball?

BIFF: The coach told me to practice my passing.

WILLY: That so? And he gave you the ball, heh?

BIFF: Well, I borrowed it from the locker room. (*He laughs confidentially*)

WILLY (*laughing with him at the theft*): I want you to return that.

HAPPY: I told you he wouldn't like it!

BIFF (*angrily*): Well, I'm bringing it back!

WILLY (*stopping the incipient argument, to Happy*): Sure, he's gotta practice with a regulation ball, doesn't he? (*To Biff*) Coach'll probably congratulate you on your initiative!

BIFF: Oh, he keeps congratulating my initiative all the time, Pop.

WILLY: That's because he likes you. If somebody else took that ball there'd be an uproar. So what's the report, boys, what's the report?

BIFF: Where'd you go this time, Dad? Gee we were lonesome for you.

WILLY (*pleased, puts an arm around each boy and they come down to the apron*): Lonesome, heh?

BIFF: Missed you every minute.

WILLY: Don't say? Tell you a secret, boys. Don't breathe it to a soul. Someday I'll have my own business, and I'll never have to leave home any more.

HAPPY: Like Uncle Charley, heh?

WILLY: Bigger than Uncle Charley! Because Charley is not—liked. He's liked, but he's not—well liked.

BIFF: Where'd you go this time, Dad?

WILLY: Well, I got on the road, and I went north to Providence. Met the Mayor.

BIFF: The Mayor of Providence!

WILLY: He was sitting in the hotel lobby.

BIFF: What'd he say?

WILLY: He said, "Morning!" And I said, "You got a fine city here, Mayor." And then he had coffee with me. And then I went to Waterbury. Waterbury is a fine city. Big clock city, the famous Waterbury clock. Sold a nice bill there. And then Boston—Boston is the cradle of the Revolution. A fine city. And a couple of other towns in Mass., and on to Portland and Bangor and straight home!

BIFF: Gee, I'd love to go with you sometime, Dad.

WILLY: Soon as summer comes.

HAPPY: Promise?

WILLY: You and Hap and I, and I'll show you all the towns. America is full of beautiful towns and fine, upstanding people. And they know me, boys, they know me up and down New England. The finest people. And when I bring you fellas up, there'll be open sesame for all of us, 'cause one thing, boys: I have friends. I can park my car in any street in New England, and the cops protect it like their own. This summer, heh?

BIFF and HAPPY (*together*): Yeah! You bet!

WILLY: We'll take our bathing suits.

HAPPY: We'll carry your bags, Pop!

WILLY: Oh, won't that be something! Me comin' into the Boston stores with you boys carryin' my bags. What a sensation!

(*Biff is prancing around, practicing passing the ball*)

WILLY: You nervous, Biff, about the game?

BIFF: Not if you're gonna be there.

WILLY: What do they say about you in school, now that they made you captain?

HAPPY: There's a crowd of girls behind him everytime the classes change.

BIFF (*taking Willy's hand*): This Saturday, Pop, this Saturday—just for you, I'm going to break through for a touchdown.

HAPPY: You're supposed to pass.

BIFF: I'm takin' one play for Pop. You watch me, Pop, and when I take off my helmet, that means I'm breakin' out. Then you watch me crash through that line!

WILLY (*kisses Biff*): Oh, wait'll I tell this in Boston!

(*Bernard enters in knickers. He is younger than Biff, earnest and loyal, a worried boy.*)

BERNARD: Biff, where are you? You're supposed to study with me today.

WILLY: Hey, looka Bernard. What're you lookin' so anemic about, Bernard?

BERNARD: He's gotta study, Uncle Willy. He's got Regents[1] next week.

HAPPY (*tauntingly, spinning Bernard around*): Let's box, Bernard!

BERNARD: Biff! (*He gets away from Happy*) Listen, Biff, I heard Mr. Birnbaum say that if you don't start studyin' math he's gonna flunk you, and you won't graduate. I heard him?

WILLY: You better study with him, Biff. Go ahead now.

BERNARD: I heard him!

BIFF: Oh, Pop, you didn't see my sneakers! (*He holds up a foot for Willy to look at*)

WILLY: Hey, that's a beautiful job of printing!

BERNARD (*wiping his glasses*): Just because he printed University of Virginia on his sneakers doesn't mean they've got to graduate him, Uncle Willy.

WILLY (*angrily*): What're you talking about? With scholarships to three universities they're gonna flunk him?

BERNARD: But I heard Mr. Birnbaum say—

WILLY: Don't be a pest, Bernard! (*To his boys*) What an anemic!

BERNARD: Okay, I'm waiting for you in my house, Biff.

(*Bernard goes off. The Lomans laugh.*)

WILLY: Bernard is not well liked, is he?

BIFF: He's liked, but he's not well liked.

HAPPY: That's right, Pop.

WILLY: That's just what I mean. Bernard can get the best marks in school, y'understand, but when he gets out in the business world, y'understand, you are going to be five times ahead of him. That's why I thank Almighty God you're both built like Adonises.[2] Because the man who makes an appearance in the business world, the man who creates personal interest, is the man who gets ahead. Be liked and you will never want. You take me, for instance. I never have to wait in line to see a buyer. "Willy Loman is here!" That's all they have to know, and I go right through.

BIFF: Did you knock them dead, Pop?

WILLY: Knocked 'em cold in Providence, slaughtered 'em in Boston.

HAPPY (*on his back, pedaling again*): I'm losing weight, you notice, Pop?

(*Linda enters, as of old, a ribbon in her hair, carrying a basket of washing*)

LINDA, (*with youthful energy*): Hello, dear!

WILLY: Sweetheart!

LINDA: How'd the Chevvy run?

WILLY: Chevrolet, Linda, is the greatest car ever built. (*To the boys*) Since when do you let your mother carry wash up the stairs?

BIFF: Grab hold there, boy!

---

[1] A New York State high school proficiency examination.

[2] Adonis, in Greek myth, was a handsome human beloved by Aphrodite, goddess of love and beauty.

HAPPY: Where to, Mom?

LINDA: Hang them up on the line. And you better go down to your friends, Biff. The cellar is full of boys. They don't know what to do with themselves.

BIFF: Ah, when Pop comes home they can wait!

WILLY (*laughs appreciatively*): You better go down and tell them what to do, Biff.

BIFF: I think I'll have them sweep out the furnace room.

WILLY: Good work, Biff.

BIFF (*goes through wall-line of kitchen to doorway at back and calls down*): Fellas! Everybody sweep out the furnace room! I'll be right down!

VOICES: All right! Okay, Biff.

BIFF: George and Sam and Frank, come out back! We're hangin' up the wash! Come on, Hap, on the double! (*He and Happy carry out the basket*)

LINDA: The way they obey him!

WILLY: Well, that's training, the training. I'm tellin' you, I was sellin' thousands and thousands, but I had to come home.

LINDA: Oh, the whole block'll be at that game. Did you sell anything?

WILLY: I did five hundred gross in Providence and seven hundred gross in Boston.

LINDA: No! Wait a minute, I've got a pencil. (*She pulls pencil and paper out of her apron pocket*) That makes your commission . . . Two hundred—my God! Two hundred and twelve dollars!

WILLY: Well, I—I did—about a hundred and eighty gross in Providence. Well, no—it came to—roughly two hundred gross on the whole trip.

LINDA (*without hesitation*): Two hundred gross. That's . . . (*She figures*)

WILLY: The trouble was that three of the stores were half closed for inventory in Boston. Otherwise I woulda broke records.

LINDA: Well, it makes seventy dollars and some pennies. That's very good.

WILLY: What do we owe?

LINDA: Well, on the first there's sixteen dollars on the refrigerator—

WILLY: Why sixteen?

LINDA: Well, the fan belt broke, so it was a dollar eighty.

WILLY: But it's brand new.

LINDA: Well, the man said that's the way it is. Till they work themselves in, y'know.

(*They move through the wall-line into the kitchen*)

WILLY: I hope we didn't get stuck on that machine.

LINDA: They got the biggest ads of any of them!

WILLY: I know, it's a fine machine. What else?

LINDA: Well, there's nine-sixty for the washing machine. And for the vacuum cleaner, there's three and a half due on the fifteenth. Then the roof, you got twenty-one dollars remaining.

WILLY: It don't leak, does it?

LINDA: No, they did a wonderful job. Then you owe Frank for the carburetor.

WILLY: I'm not going to pay that man! That goddam Chevrolet, they ought to prohibit the manufacture of that car!

LINDA: Well, you owe him three and a half. And odds and ends, comes to around a hundred and twenty dollars by the fifteenth.

WILLY: A hundred and twenty dollars! My God, if business don't pick up I don't know what I'm gonna do!

LINDA: Well, next week you'll do better.

WILLY: Oh, I'll knock 'em dead next week. I'll go to Hartford. I'm very well liked in Hartford. You know, the trouble is, Linda, people don't seem to take to me.

(They move onto the forestage)

LINDA: Oh, don't be foolish.

WILLY: I know it when I walk in. They seem to laugh at me.

LINDA: Why? Why would they laugh at you? Don't talk that way, Willy.

(Willy moves to the edge of the stage. Linda goes into the kitchen and starts to darn stockings.)

WILLY: I don't know the reason for it, but they just pass me by. I'm not noticed.

LINDA: But you're doing wonderful, dear. You're making seventy to a hundred dollars a week.

WILLY: But I gotta be at it ten, twelve hours a day. Other men—I don't know— they do it easier. I don't know why—I can't stop myself—I talk too much. A man oughta come in with a few words. One thing about Charley. He's a man of few words, and they respect him.

LINDA: You don't talk too much, you're just lively.

WILLY *(smiling)*: Well, I figure, what the hell, life is short, a couple of jokes. *(To himself)* I joke too much! *(The smile goes)*

LINDA: Why? You're—

WILLY: I'm fat. I'm very—foolish to look at, Linda. I didn't tell you, but Christmas time I happened to be calling on F. H. Stewarts, and a salesman I know, as I was going in to see the buyer I heard him say something about—walrus. And I—I cracked him right across the face. I won't take that. I simply will not take that. But they do laugh at me. I know that.

LINDA: Darling . . .

WILLY: I gotta overcome it. I know I gotta overcome it. I'm not dressing to advantage, maybe.

LINDA: Willy, darling, you're the handsomest man in the world—

WILLY: Oh, no, Linda.

LINDA: To me you are. *(Slight pause)* The handsomest.

(From the darkness is heard the laughter of a woman. Willy doesn't turn to it, but it continues through Linda's lines.)

LINDA: And the boys, Willy. Few men are idolized by their children the way you are.

(Music is heard as behind a scrim,[3] to the left of the house, The Woman, dimly seen, is dressing.)

WILLY *(with great feeling)*: You're the best there is, Linda, you're a pal, you know that? On the road—on the road I want to grab you sometimes and just kiss the life outa you.

[3] A painted gauze cloth, opaque when illuminated from the front but becoming nearly transparent as the lights come on from behind.

(The laughter is loud now, and he moves into a brightening area at the left, where The Woman has come from behind the scrim and is standing, putting on her hat, looking into a "mirror" and laughing.)

WILLY: 'Cause I get so lonely—especially when business is bad and there's nobody to talk to. I get the feeling that I'll never sell anything again, that I won't make a living for you, or a business, a business for the boys. *(He talks through The Woman's subsiding laughter! The Woman primps at the "mirror.")* There's so much I want to make for—

THE WOMAN: Me? You didn't make me, Willy. I picked you.

WILLY *(pleased)*: You picked me?

THE WOMAN *(who is quite proper-looking, Willy's age)*: I did. I've been sitting at that desk watching all the salesmen go by, day in, day out. But you've got such a sense of humor, and we do have such a good time together, don't we?

WILLY: Sure, sure. *(He takes her in his arms)* Why do you have to go now?

THE WOMAN: It's two o'clock . . .

WILLY: No, come on in! *(He pulls her)*

THE WOMAN: . . . my sister'll be scandalized. When'll you be back?

WILLY: Oh, two weeks about. Will you come up again?

THE WOMAN: Sure thing. You do make me laugh. It's good for me. *(She squeezes his arm, kisses him)* And I think you're a wonderful man.

WILLY: You picked me, heh?

THE WOMAN: Sure. Because you're so sweet. And such a kidder.

WILLY: Well, I'll see you next time I'm in Boston.

THE WOMAN: I'll put you right through to the buyers.

WILLY *(slapping her bottom)*: Right. Well, bottoms up!

THE WOMAN *(slaps him gently and laughs)*: You just kill me, Willy. *(He suddenly grabs her and kisses her roughly)* You kill me. And thanks for the stockings. I love a lot of stockings. Well, good night.

WILLY: Good night. And keep your pores open!

THE WOMAN: Oh, Willy!

(The Woman bursts out laughing, and Linda's laughter blends in. The Woman disappears into the dark. Now the area at the kitchen table brightens. Linda is sitting where she was at the kitchen table, but now is mending a pair of her silk stockings.)

LINDA: You are, Willy. The handsomest man. You've got no reason to feel that—

WILLY *(coming out of The Woman's dimming area and going over to Linda)*: I'll make it all up to you, Linda, I'll—

LINDA: There's nothing to make up, dear. You're doing fine, better than—

WILLY *(noticing her mending)*: What's that?

LINDA: Just mending my stockings. They're so expensive—

WILLY *(angrily, taking them from her)*: I won't have you mending stockings in this house! Now throw them out!

(Linda puts the stockings in her pocket)

BERNARD *(entering on the run)*: Where is he? If he doesn't study!

WILLY *(moving to the forestage, with great agitation)*: You'll give him the answers!

BERNARD: I do, but I can't on a Regents! That's a state exam! They're liable to arrest me!

WILLY: Where is he? I'll whip him, I'll whip him!

LINDA: And he'd better give back that football, Willy, it's not nice.

WILLY: Biff! Where is he? Why is he taking everything?

LINDA: He's too rough with the girls, Willy. All the mothers are afraid of him!

WILLY: I'll whip him!

BERNARD: He's driving the car without a license!

(The Woman's laugh is heard)

WILLY: Shut up!

LINDA: All the mothers—

WILLY: Shut up!

BERNARD *(backing quietly away and out)*: Mr. Birnbaum says he's stuck up.

WILLY: Get outa here!

BERNARD: If he doesn't buckle down he'll flunk math! *(He goes off)*

LINDA: He's right, Willy, you've gotta—

WILLY *(exploding at her)*: There's nothing the matter with him! You want him to be a worm like Bernard? He's got spirit, personality . . .

(As he speaks, Linda, almost in tears, exits into the livingroom. Willy is alone in the kitchen, wilting and staring. The leaves are gone. It is night again, and the apartment houses look down from behind.)

WILLY: Loaded with it. Loaded! What is he stealing? He's giving it back, isn't he? Why is he stealing? What did I tell him? I never in my life told him anything but decent things.

(Happy in pajamas has come down the stairs; Willy suddenly becomes aware of Happy's presence)

HAPPY: Let's go now, come on.

WILLY *(sitting down at the kitchen table)*: Huh! Why did she have to wax the floors herself? Everytime she waxes the floors she keels over. She knows that!

HAPPY: Shh! Take it easy. What brought you back tonight?

WILLY: I got an awful scare. Nearly hit a kid in Yonkers. God! Why didn't I go to Alaska with my brother Ben that time! Ben! That man was a genius, that man was success incarnate! What a mistake! He begged me to go.

HAPPY: Well, there's no use in—

WILLY: You guys! There was a man started with the clothes on his back and ended up with diamond mines!

HAPPY: Boy, someday I'd like to know how he did it.

WILLY: What's the mystery? The man knew what he wanted and went out and got it! Walked into a jungle, and comes out, the age of twenty-one, and he's rich! The world is an oyster, but you don't crack it open on a mattress!

HAPPY: Pop, I told you I'm gonna retire you for life.

WILLY: You'll retire me for life on seventy goddam dollars a week? And your women and your car and your apartment, and you'll retire me for life! Christ's sake, I couldn't get past Yonkers today! Where are you guys, where are you? The woods are burning! I can't drive a car!

(Charley has appeared in the doorway. He is a large man, slow of speech, laconic, immovable. In all he says, despite what he says, there is pity, and, now, trepidation.

He has a robe over pajamas, slippers on his feet. He enters the kitchen.)

CHARLEY: Everything all right?

HAPPY: Yeah, Charley, everything's . . .

WILLY: What's the matter?

CHARLEY: I heard some noise. I thought something happened. Can't we do something about the walls? You sneeze in here, and in my house hats blow off.

HAPPY: Let's go to bed, Dad. Come on.

(Charley signals to Happy to go)

WILLY: You go ahead, I'm not tired at the moment.

HAPPY *(to Willy)*: Take it easy, huh? *(He exits)*

WILLY: What're you doin' up?

CHARLEY *(sitting down at the kitchen table opposite Willy)*: Couldn't sleep good. I had a heartburn.

WILLY: Well, you don't know how to eat.

CHARLEY: I eat with my mouth.

WILLY: No, you're ignorant. You gotta know about vitamins and things like that.

CHARLEY: Come on, let's shoot. Tire you out a little.

WILLY *(hesitantly)*: All right. You got cards?

CHARLEY *(taking a deck from his pocket)*: Yeah, I got them. Someplace. What is it with those vitamins?

WILLY *(dealing)*: They build up your bones. Chemistry.

CHARLEY: Yeah, but there's no bones in a heartburn.

WILLY: What are you talkin' about? Do you know the first thing about it?

CHARLEY: Don't get insulted.

WILLY: Don't talk about something you don't know anything about.

(They are playing. Pause)

CHARLEY: What're you doin' home?

WILLY: A little trouble with the car.

CHARLEY: Oh. *(Pause)* I'd like to take a trip to California.

WILLY: Don't say.

CHARLEY: You want a job?

WILLY: I got a job, I told you that. *(After a slight pause)* What the hell are you offering me a job for?

CHARLEY: Don't get insulted.

WILLY: Don't insult me.

CHARLEY: I don't see no sense in it. You don't have to go on this way.

WILLY: I got a good job. *(Slight pause)* What do you keep comin' in here for?

CHARLEY: You want me to go?

WILLY *(after a pause, withering)*: I can't understand it. He's going back to Texas again. What the hell is that?

CHARLEY: Let him go.

WILLY: I got nothin' to give him, Charley, I'm clean, I'm clean.

CHARLEY: He won't starve. None of them starve. Forget about him.

WILLY: Then what have I got to remember?

CHARLEY: You take it too hard. To hell with it. When a deposit bottle is broken you don't get your nickel back.

WILLY: That's easy enough for you to say.

CHARLEY: That ain't easy for me to say.

WILLY: Did you see the ceiling I put up in the living-room?

CHARLEY: Yeah, that's a piece of work. To put up a ceiling is a mystery to me. How do you do it?

WILLY: What's the difference?

CHARLEY: Well, talk about it.

WILLY: You gonna put up a ceiling?

CHARLEY: How could I put up a ceiling?

WILLY: Then what the hell are you bothering me for?

CHARLEY: You're insulted again.

WILLY: A man who can't handle tools is not a man. You're disgusting.

CHARLEY: Don't call me disgusting, Willy.

(Uncle Ben, carrying a valise and an umbrella, enters the forestage from around the right corner of the house. He is a stolid man, in his sixties, with a mustache and an authoritative air. He is utterly certain of his destiny, and there is an aura of far places about him. He enters exactly as Willy speaks.)

WILLY: I'm getting awfully tired, Ben.

(Ben's music is heard. Ben looks around at everything.)

CHARLEY: Good, keep playing; you'll sleep better. Did you call me Ben?

(Ben looks at his watch)

WILLY: That's funny. For a second there you reminded me of my brother Ben.

BEN: I only have a few minutes. *(He strolls, inspecting the place. Willy and Charley continue playing.)*

CHARLEY: You never heard from him again, heh? Since that time?

WILLY: Didn't Linda tell you? Couple of weeks ago we got a letter from his wife in Africa. He died.

CHARLEY: That so.

BEN *(chuckling)*: So this is Brooklyn, eh?

CHARLEY: Maybe you're in for some of his money.

WILLY: Naa, he had seven sons. There's just one opportunity I had with that man . . .

BEN: I must make a train, William. There are several properties I'm looking at in Alaska.

WILLY: Sure, sure! If I'd gone with him to Alaska that time, everything would've been totally different.

CHARLEY: Go on, you'd froze to death up there.

WILLY: What're you talking about?

BEN: Opportunity is tremendous in Alaska, William. Surprised you're not up there.

WILLY: Sure, tremendous.

CHARLEY: Heh?

WILLY: There was the only man I ever met who knew the answers.

CHARLEY: Who?

BEN: How are you all?

WILLY *(taking a pot, smiling)*: Fine, fine.

CHARLEY: Pretty sharp tonight.

BEN: Is Mother living with you?

WILLY: No, she died a long time ago.

CHARLEY: Who?

BEN: That's too bad. Fine specimen of a lady, Mother.

WILLY (to Charley): Heh?

BEN: I'd hoped to see the old girl.

CHARLEY: Who died?

BEN: Heard anything from Father, have you?

WILLY (unnerved): What do you mean, who died?

CHARLEY (taking a pot): What're you talkin' about?

BEN (looking at his watch): William, it's half-past eight!

WILLY (as though to dispel his confusion he angrily stops Charley's hand): That's my build!

CHARLEY: I put the ace—

WILLY: If you don't know how to play the game I'm not gonna throw my money away on you!

CHARLEY (rising): It was my ace, for God's sake!

WILLY: I'm through, I'm through!

BEN: When did Mother die?

WILLY: Long ago. Since the beginning you never knew how to play cards.

CHARLEY (picks up the cards and goes to the door): All right! Next time I'll bring a deck with five aces.

WILLY: I don't play that kind of game!

CHARLEY (turning to him): You ought to be ashamed of yourself!

WILLY: Yeah?

CHARLEY: Yeah! (He goes out)

WILLY (slamming the door after him): Ignoramus!

BEN (as Willy comes toward him through the wall-line of the kitchen): So you're William.

WILLY (shaking Ben's hand): Ben! I've been waiting for you so long! What's the answer? How did you do it?

BEN: Oh, there's a story in that.

(Linda enters the forestage, as of old, carrying the wash basket)

LINDA: Is this Ben?

BEN (gallantly): How do you do, my dear.

LINDA: Where've you been all these years? Willy's always wondered why you—

WILLY (pulling Ben away from her impatiently): Where is Dad? Didn't you follow him? How did you get started?

BEN: Well, I don't know how much you remember.

WILLY: Well, I was just a baby, of course, only three or four years old—

BEN: Three years and eleven months.

WILLY: What a memory, Ben!

BEN: I have many enterprises, William, and I have never kept books.

WILLY: I remember I was sitting under the wagon in—was it Nebraska?

BEN: It was South Dakota, and I gave you a bunch of wild flowers.

WILLY: I remember you walking away down some open road.

BEN (*laughing*): I was going to find Father in Alaska.

WILLY: Where is he?

BEN: At that age I had a very faulty view of geography, William. I discovered after a few days that I was heading due south, so instead of Alaska, I ended up in Africa.

LINDA: Africa!

WILLY: The Gold Coast!

BEN: Principally diamond mines.

LINDA: Diamond mines!

BEN: Yes, my dear. But I've only a few minutes—

WILLY: No! Boys! Boys! (*Young Biff and Happy appear*) Listen to this. This is your Uncle Ben, a great man! Tell my boys, Ben!

BEN: Why, boys, when I was seventeen I walked into the jungle, and when I was twenty-one I walked out. (*He laughs*) And by God I was rich.

WILLY (*to the boys*): You see what I been talking about? The greatest things can happen!

BEN (*glancing at his watch*): I have an appointment in Ketchikan Tuesday week.

WILLY: No, Ben! Please tell about Dad. I want my boys to hear. I want them to know the kind of stock they spring from. All I remember is a man with a big beard, and I was in Mamma's lap, sitting around a fire, and some kind of high music.

BEN: His flute. He played the flute.

WILLY: Sure, the flute, that's right!

(*New music is heard, a high, rollicking tune*)

BEN: Father was a very great and a very wild-hearted man. We would start in Boston, and he'd toss the whole family into the wagon, and then he'd drive the team right across the country; through Ohio, and Indiana, Michigan, Illinois, and all the Western states. And we'd stop in the towns and sell the flutes that he'd made on the way. Great inventor, Father. With one gadget he made more in a week than a man like you could make in a lifetime.

WILLY: That's just the way I'm bringing them up, Ben—rugged, well liked, all-around.

BEN: Yeah? (*To Biff*) Hit that, boy—hard as you can. (*He pounds his stomach*)

BIFF: Oh, no, sir!

BEN (*taking boxing stance*): Come on, get to me! (*He laughs*)

WILLY: Go to it, Biff! Go ahead, show him!

BIFF: Okay! (*He cocks his fists and starts in*)

LINDA (*to Willy*): Why must he fight, dear?

BEN (*sparring with Biff*): Good boy! Good boy!

WILLY: How's that, Ben, heh?

HAPPY: Give him the left, Biff!

LINDA: Why are you fighting?

BEN: Good boy! (*Suddenly comes in, trips Biff, and stands over him, the point of his umbrella poised over Biff's eye*)

LINDA: Look out, Biff!

BIFF: Gee!

BEN (*patting Biff's knee*): Never fight fair with a stranger, boy. You'll never get out of the jungle that way. (*Taking Linda's hand and bowing*) It was an honor and a pleasure to meet you, Linda.

LINDA (*withdrawing her hand coldly, frightened*: Have a nice—trip.

BEN (*to Willy*): And good luck with your—what do you do?

WILLY: Selling.

BEN: Yes. Well . . . (*He raises his hand in farewell to all*)

WILLY: No, Ben, I don't want you to think . . . (*He takes Ben's arm to show him*) It's Brooklyn, I know, but we hunt too.

BEN: Really, now.

WILLY: Oh, sure, there's snakes and rabbits and—that's why I moved out here. Why, Biff can fell any one of these trees in no time! Boys! Go right over to where they're building the apartment house and get some sand. We're gonna rebuild the entire front stoop right now! Watch this, Ben!

BIFF: Yes, sir! On the double, Hap!

HAPPY (*as he and Biff run off*): I lost weight, Pop, you notice?

(*Charley enters in knickers, even before the boys are gone*)

CHARLEY: Listen, if they steal any more from that building the watchman'll put the cops on them!

LINDA (*to Willy*): Don't let Biff . . .

(*Ben laughs lustily*)

WILLY: You shoulda seen the lumber they brought home last week. At least a dozen six-by-tens worth all kinds a money.

CHARLEY: Listen, if that watchman—

WILLY: I gave them hell, understand. But I got a couple of fearless characters there.

CHARLEY: Willy, the jails are full of fearless characters.

BEN (*clapping Willy on the back, with a laugh at Charley*): And the stock exchange, friend!

WILLY (*joining in Ben's laughter*): Where are the rest of your pants?

CHARLEY: My wife bought them.

WILLY: Now all you need is a golf club and you can go upstairs and go to sleep. (*To Ben*): Great athlete! Between him and his son Bernard they can't hammer a nail!

BERNARD (*rushing in*): The watchman's chasing Biff!

WILLY (*angrily*): Shut up! He's not stealing anything!

LINDA (*alarmed, hurrying off left*): Where is he? Biff, dear! (*She exits*)

WILLY (*moving toward the left, away from Ben*): There's nothing wrong. What's the matter with you?

BEN: Nervy boy. Good!

WILLY (*laughing*): Oh, nerves of iron, that Biff!

CHARLEY: Don't know what it is. My New England man comes back and he's bleedin', they murdered him up there.

WILLY: It's contacts, Charley, I got important contacts!

CHARLEY (*sarcastically*): Glad to hear it, Willy. Come in later, we'll shoot a little casino. I'll take some of your Portland money. (*He laughs at Willy and exits*)

WILLY (*turning to Ben*): Business is bad, it's murderous. But not for me, of course.

BEN: I'll stop by on my way back to Africa.

WILLY (*longingly*): Can't you stay a few days? You're just what I need, Ben, because I—I have a fine position here, but I—well, Dad left when I was such a baby and I never had a chance to talk to him and I still feel—kind of temporary about myself.

BEN: I'll be late for my train.

(*They are at opposite ends of the stage*)

WILLY: Ben, my boys—can't we talk? They'd go into the jaws of hell for me, see, but I—

BEN: William, you're being first-rate with your boys. Outstanding, manly chaps!

WILLY (*hanging on to his words*): Oh, Ben, that's good to hear! Because sometimes I'm afraid that I'm not teaching them the right kind of—Ben, how should I teach them?

BEN (*giving great weight to each word, and with a certain vicious audacity*): William, when I walked into the jungle, I was seventeen. When I walked out I was twenty-one. And, by God, I was rich! (*He goes off into darkness around the right corner of the house*)

WILLY: . . . was rich! That's just the spirit I want to imbue them with! To walk into a jungle! I was right! I was right! I was right!

(*Ben is gone, but Willy is still speaking to him as Linda, in nightgown and robe, enters the kitchen, glances around for Willy, then goes to the door of the house, looks out and sees him. Comes down to his left. He looks at her.*)

LINDA: Willy, dear? Willy?

WILLY: I was right!

LINDA: Did you have some cheese? (*He can't answer*) It's very late, darling. Come to bed, heh?

WILLY (*looking straight up*): Gotta break your neck to see a star in this yard.

LINDA: You coming in?

WILLY: Whatever happened to that diamond watch fob? Remember? When Ben came from Africa that time? Didn't he give me a watch fob with a diamond in it?

LINDA: You pawned it, dear. Twelve, thirteen years ago. For Biff's radio correspondence course.

WILLY: Gee, that was a beautiful thing. I'll take a walk.

LINDA: But you're in your slippers.

WILLY (*starting to go around the house at the left*): I was right! I was! (*Half to Linda, as he goes shaking his head*) What a man! There was a man worth talking to. I was right!

LINDA (*calling after Willy*): But in your slippers, Willy!

(*Willy is almost gone when Biff, in his pajamas, comes down the stairs and enters the kitchen*)

BIFF: What is he doing out there?

LINDA: Sh!

BIFF: God Almighty, Mom, how long has he been doing this?

LINDA: Don't, he'll hear you.

BIFF: What the hell is the matter with him?

LINDA: It'll pass by morning.

BIFF: Shouldn't we do anything?

LINDA: Oh, my dear, you should do a lot of things, but there's nothing to do, so go to sleep.

(Happy comes down the stair and sits on the steps)

HAPPY: I never heard him so loud, Mom.

LINDA: Well, come around more often; you'll hear him. *(She sits down at the table and mends the lining of Willy's jacket)*

BIFF: Why didn't you ever write me about this, Mom?

LINDA: How would I write to you? For over three months you had no address.

BIFF: I was on the move. But you know I thought of you all the time. You know that, don't you, pal?

LINDA: I know, dear, I know. But he likes to have a letter. Just to know that there's still a possibility for better things.

BIFF: He's not like this all the time, is he?

LINDA: It's when you come home he's always the worst.

BIFF: When I come home?

LINDA: When you write you're coming, he's all smiles, and talks about the future, and—he's just wonderful. And then the closer you seem to come, the more shaky he gets, and then, by the time you get here, he's arguing, and he seems angry at you. I think it's just that maybe he can't bring himself to—to open up to you. Why are you so hateful to each other? Why is that?

BIFF *(evasively)*: I'm not hateful, Mom.

LINDA: But you no sooner come in the door than you're fighting!

BIFF: I don't know why. I mean to change. I'm tryin', Mom, you understand?

LINDA: Are you home to stay now?

BIFF: I don't know. I want to look around, see what's doin'.

LINDA: Biff, you can't look around all your life, can you?

BIFF: I just can't take hold, Mom. I can't take hold of some kind of a life.

LINDA: Biff, a man is not a bird, to come and go with the springtime.

BIFF: Your hair . . . *(He touches her hair)* Your hair got so gray.

LINDA: Oh, it's been gray since you were in high school. I just stopped dyeing it, that's all.

BIFF: Dye it again, will ya? I don't want my pal looking old. *(He smiles)*

LINDA: You're such a boy! You think you can go away for a year and . . . You've got to get it into your head now that one day you'll knock on this door and there'll be strange people here—

BIFF: What are you talking about? You're not even sixty, Mom.

LINDA: But what about your father?

BIFF *(lamely)*: Well, I meant him too.

HAPPY: He admires Pop.

LINDA: Biff, dear, if you don't have any feeling for him, then you can't have any feeling for me.

BIFF: Sure I can, Mom.

LINDA: No. You can't just come to see me, because I love him. *(With a threat, but only a threat, of tears)* He's the dearest man in the world to me, and I won't have anyone making him feel unwanted and low and blue. You've got to make up your mind now, darling, there's no leeway any more. Either he's your father and you pay him that respect, or else you're not to come here. I know he's not easy to get along with—nobody knows that better than me—but . . .

WILLY *(from the left, with a laugh):* Hey, hey, Biffo!

BIFF *(starting to go out after Willy):* What the hell is the matter with him? *(Happy stops him)*

LINDA: Don't—don't go near him!

BIFF: Stop making excuses for him! He always, always wiped the floor with you. Never had an ounce of respect for you.

HAPPY: He's always had respect for—

BIFF: What the hell do you know about it?

HAPPY *(surlily):* Just don't call him crazy!

BIFF: He's got no character—Charley wouldn't do this. Not in his own house—spewing out that vomit from his mind.

HAPPY: Charley never had to cope with what he's got to.

BIFF: People are worse off than Willy Loman. Believe me, I've seen them!

LINDA: Then make Charley your father, Biff. You can't do that, can you? I don't say he's a great man. Willy Loman never made a lot of money. His name was never in the paper. He's not the finest character that ever lived. But he's a human being, and a terrible thing is happening to him. So attention must be paid. He's not to be allowed to fall into his grave like an old dog. Attention, attention must be finally paid to such a person. You called him crazy—

BIFF: I didn't mean—

LINDA: No, a lot of people think he's lost his—balance. But you don't have to be very smart to know what his trouble is. The man is exhausted.

HAPPY: Sure!

LINDA: A small man can be just as exhausted as a great man. He works for a company thirty-six years this March, opens up unheard-of territories to their trademark, and now in his old age they take his salary away.

HAPPY *(indignantly):* I didn't know that, Mom.

LINDA: You never asked, my dear! Now that you get your spending money someplace else you don't trouble your mind with him.

HAPPY: But I gave you money last—

LINDA: Christmas time, fifty dollars! To fix the hot water it cost ninety-seven fifty! For five weeks he's been on straight commission, like a beginner, an unknown!

BIFF: Those ungrateful bastards!

LINDA: Are they any worse than his sons? When he brought them business, when he was young, they were glad to see him. But now his old friends, the old buyers that loved him so and always found some order to hand him in a pinch—they're all dead, retired. He used to be able to make six, seven calls a day in Boston. Now he takes his valises out of the car and puts them back and takes them out again and he's exhausted. Instead of walking he talks now. He drives seven hundred miles, and when he gets there no one knows him any more, no one welcomes him. And what goes through a man's mind, driving seven hundred miles home without having earned a cent? Why shouldn't he talk to himself? Why? When he has to go to Charley and borrow fifty dollars a week and pretend to me that it's his pay? How long can that go on? How long? You see what I'm sitting here and waiting for? And you tell me he has no character? The man who never worked a day but for your benefit? When does he get the medal for that? Is this his reward—to turn around at the age of sixty-three and find his sons, who he loved better than his life, one a philandering bum—

HAPPY: Mom!

LINDA: That's all you are, my baby! *(To Biff)* And you! What happened to the love you had for him? You were such pals! How you used to talk to him on the phone every night! How lonely he was till he could come home to you!

BIFF: All right, Mom. I'll live here in my room, and I'll get a job. I'll keep away from him, that's all.

LINDA: No, Biff. You can't stay here and fight all the time.

BIFF: He threw me out of this house, remember that.

LINDA: Why did he do that? I never knew why?

BIFF: Because I know he's a fake and he doesn't like anybody around who knows!

LINDA: Why a fake? In what way? What do you mean?

BIFF: Just don't lay it all at my feet. It's between me and him—that's all I have to say. I'll chip in from now on. He'll settle for half my pay check. He'll be all right. I'm going to bed. *(He starts for the stairs)*

LINDA: He won't be all right.

BIFF *(turning on the stairs, furiously)*: I hate this city and I'll stay here. Now what do you want?

LINDA: He's dying, Biff.

(Happy turns quickly to her)

BIFF *(after a pause)*: Why is he dying?

LINDA: He's been trying to kill himself.

BIFF *(with great horror)*: How?

LINDA: I live from day to day.

BIFF: What're you talking about?

LINDA: Remember I wrote you that he smashed up the car again? In February?

BIFF: Well?

LINDA: The insurance inspector came. He said that they have evidence. That all these accidents in the last year—weren't—weren't—accidents.

HAPPY: How can they tell that? That's a lie.

LINDA: It seems there's a woman . . . *(She takes a breath as)*

⎧ BIFF *(sharply but contained)*: What woman?

⎨ LINDA *(simultaneously)*: . . . and this woman . . .

LINDA: What?

BIFF: Nothing. Go ahead.

LINDA: What did you say?

BIFF: Nothing. I just said what woman?

HAPPY: What about her?

LINDA: Well, it seems she was walking down the road and saw his car. She says that he wasn't driving fast at all, and that he didn't skid. She says he came to that little bridge, and then deliberately smashed into the railing, and it was only the shallowness of the water that saved him.

BIFF: Oh, no, he probably just fell asleep again.

LINDA: I don't think he fell asleep.

BIFF: Why not?

LINDA: Last month . . . (*With great difficulty*) Oh, boys, it's so hard to say a thing like this! He's just a big stupid man to you, but I tell you there's more good in him than in many other people. (*She chokes, wipes her eyes*) I was looking for a fuse. The lights blew out, and I went down the cellar. And behind the fuse box—it happened to fall out—was a length of rubber pipe—just short.

HAPPY: No kidding?

LINDA: There's a little attachment on the end of it. I knew right away. And sure enough, on the bottom of the water heater there's a new little nipple on the gas pipe.

HAPPY (*angrily*): That—jerk.

BIFF: Did you have it taken off?

LINDA: I'm—I'm ashamed to. How can I mention it to him? Every day I go down and take away that little rubber pipe. But, when he comes home, I put it back where it was. How can I insult him that way? I don't know what to do. I live from day to day, boys. I tell you, I know every thought in his mind. It sounds so old-fashioned and silly, but I tell you he put his whole life into you and you've turned your backs on him. (*She is bent over in the chair, weeping, her face in her hands*) Biff, I swear to God! Biff, his life is in your hands!

HAPPY (*to Biff*): How do you like that damned fool!

BIFF (*kissing her*): All right, pal, all right. It's all settled now. I've been remiss. I know that, Mom. But now I'll stay, and I swear to you, I'll apply myself. (*Kneeling in front of her, in a fever of self-reproach*) It's just—you see, Mom, I don't fit in business. Not that I won't try. I'll try, and I'll make good.

HAPPY: Sure you will. The trouble with you in business was you never tried to please people.

BIFF: I know, I—

HAPPY: Like when you worked for Harrison's. Bob Harrison said you were tops, and then you go and do some damn fool thing like whistling whole songs in the elevator like a comedian.

BIFF (*against Happy*): So what? I like to whistle sometimes.

HAPPY: You don't raise a guy to a responsible job who whistles in the elevator!

LINDA: Well, don't argue about it now.

HAPPY: Like when you'd go off and swim in the middle of the day instead of taking the line around.

BIFF (*his resentment rising*): Well, don't you run off? You take off sometimes, don't you? On a nice summer day?

HAPPY: Yeah, but I cover myself!

LINDA: Boys!

HAPPY: If I'm going to take a fade the boss can call any number where I'm supposed to be and they'll swear to him that I just left. I'll tell you something that I hate to say, Biff, but in the business world some of them think you're crazy.

BIFF (*angered*): Screw the business world!

HAPPY: All right, screw it! Great, but cover yourself!

LINDA: Hap, Hap!

BIFF: I don't care what they think! They've laughed at Dad for years, and you know why? Because we don't belong in this nuthouse of a city! We should be mixing cement on some open plain, or—or carpenters. A carpenter is allowed to whistle!

(Willy walks in from the entrance of the house, at left)

WILLY: Even your grandfather was better than a carpenter. *(Pause. They watch him)* You never grew up. Bernard does not whistle in the elevator, I assure you.

BIFF *(as though to laugh Willy out of it)*: Yeah, but you do, Pop.

WILLY: I never in my life whistled in an elevator! And who in the business world thinks I'm crazy?

BIFF: I didn't mean it like that, Pop. Now don't make a whole thing out of it, will ya?

WILLY: Go back to the West! Be a carpenter, a cowboy, enjoy yourself!

LINDA: Willy, he was just saying—

WILLY: I heard what he said!

HAPPY *(trying to quiet Willy)*: Hey, Pop, come on now . . .

WILLY *(continuing over Happy's line)*: They laugh at me, heh? Go to Filene's, go to the Hub, go to Slattery's, Boston. Call out the name Willy Loman and see what happens! Big shot!

BIFF: All right, Pop.

WILLY: Big!

BIFF: All right!

WILLY: Why do you always insult me?

BIFF: I didn't say a word. *(To Linda)* Did I say a word?

LINDA: He didn't say anything, Willy.

WILLY *(going to the doorway of the living-room)*: All right, good night, good night.

LINDA: Willy, dear, he just decided . . .

WILLY *(to Biff)*: If you get tired hanging around tomorrow, paint the ceiling I put up in the living-room.

BIFF: I'm leaving early tomorrow.

HAPPY: He's going to see Bill Oliver, Pop.

WILLY *(interestedly)*: Oliver? For what?

BIFF *(with reserve, but trying, trying)*: He always said he'd stake me. I'd like to go into business, so maybe I can take him up on it.

LINDA: Isn't that wonderful?

WILLY: Don't interrupt. What's wonderful about it? There's fifty men in the City of New York who'd stake him. *(To Biff)* Sporting goods?

BIFF: I guess so. I know something about it and—

WILLY: He knows something about it! You know sporting goods better than Spalding, for God's sake! How much is he giving you?

BIFF: I don't know, I didn't even see him yet, but—

WILLY: Then what're you talkin' about?

BIFF *(getting angry)*: Well, all I said was I'm gonna see him, that's all!

WILLY *(turning away)*: Ah, you're counting your chickens again.

BIFF *(starting left for the stairs)*: Oh, Jesus, I'm going to sleep!

WILLY *(calling after him)*: Don't curse in this house!

BIFF *(turning)*: Since when did you get so clean?

HAPPY *(trying to stop them)*: Wait a . . .

WILLY: Don't use that language to me! I won't have it!

HAPPY *(grabbing Biff, shouts)*: Wait a minute! I got an idea. I got a feasible idea. Come here, Biff, let's talk this over now, let's talk some sense here. When I was down in Florida last time, I thought of a great idea to sell sporting goods. It just came back to me. You and I, Biff—we have a line, the Loman Line. We train a couple of weeks, and put on a couple of exhibitions, see?

WILLY: That's an idea!

HAPPY: Wait! We form two basketball teams, see? Two waterpolo teams. We play each other. It's a million dollars' worth of publicity. Two brothers, see? The Loman Brothers. Displays in the Royal Palms—all the hotels. And banners over the ring and the basketball court: "Loman Brothers." Baby, we could sell sporting goods!

WILLY: That is a one-million-dollar idea!

LINDA: Marvelous!

BIFF: I'm in great shape as far as that's concerned.

HAPPY: And the beauty of it is, Biff, it wouldn't be like a business. We'd be out playin' ball again . . .

BIFF *(enthused)*: Yeah, that's . . .

WILLY: Million-dollar . . .

HAPPY: And you wouldn't get fed up with it, Biff. It'd be the family again. There'd be the old honor, and comradeship, and if you wanted to go off for a swim or somethin'—well, you'd do it! Without some smart cooky gettin' up ahead of you!

WILLY: Lick the world! You guys together could absolutely lick the civilized world.

BIFF: I'll see Oliver tomorrow. Hap, if we could work that out . . .

LINDA: Maybe things are beginning to—

WILLY *(wildly enthused, to Linda)*: Stop interrupting! *(To Biff)* But don't wear sport jacket and slacks when you see Oliver.

BIFF: No, I'll—

WILLY: A business suit, and talk as little as possible, and don't crack any jokes.

BIFF: He did like me. Always liked me.

LINDA: He loved you!

WILLY *(to Linda)*: Will you stop! *(To Biff)* Walk in very serious. You are not applying for a boy's job. Money is to pass. Be quiet, fine, and serious. Everybody likes a kidder, but nobody lends him money.

HAPPY: I'll try to get some myself, Biff. I'm sure I can.

WILLY: I see great things for you kids, I think your troubles are over. But remember, start big and you'll end big. Ask for fifteen. How much you gonna ask for?

BIFF: Gee, I don't know—

WILLY: And don't say "Gee." "Gee" is a boy's word. A man walking in for fifteen thousand dollars does not say "Gee!"

BIFF: Ten, I think, would be top though.

WILLY: Don't be so modest. You always started too low. Walk in with a big laugh. Don't look worried. Start off with a couple of your good stories to lighten things up. It's not what you say, it's how you say it—because personality always wins the day.

LINDA: Oliver always thought the highest of him—

WILLY: Will you let me talk?

BIFF: Don't yell at her, Pop, will ya?

WILLY (angrily): I was talking, wasn't I?

BIFF: I don't like you yelling at her all the time, and I'm tellin' you, that's all.

WILLY: What're you, takin' over this house?

LINDA: Willy—

WILLY (turning on her): Don't take his side all the time, goddammit!

BIFF (furiously): Stop yelling at her!

WILLY (suddenly pulling on his cheek, beaten down, guilt ridden): Give my best to Bill Oliver—he may remember me. (He exits through the living-room doorway)

LINDA (her voice subdued): What'd you have to start that for? (Biff turns away) You see how sweet he was as soon as you talked hopefully? (She goes over to Biff) Come up and say good night to him. Don't let him go to bed that way.

HAPPY: Come on, Biff, let's buck him up.

LINDA: Please, dear. Just say good night. It takes so little to make him happy. Come. (She goes through the living-room doorway, calling upstairs from within the living-room) Your pajamas are hanging in the bathroom, Willy!

HAPPY (looking toward where Linda went out): What a woman! They broke the mold when they made her. You know that, Biff?

BIFF: He's off salary. My God, working on commission!

HAPPY: Well, let's face it: he's no hot-shot selling man. Except that sometimes, you have to admit, he's a sweet personality.

BIFF (deciding): Lend me ten bucks, will ya? I want to buy some new ties.

HAPPY: I'll take you to a place I know. Beautiful stuff. Wear one of my striped shirts tomorrow.

BIFF: She got gray. Mom got awful old. Gee, I'm gonna go in to Oliver tomorrow and knock him for a—

HAPPY: Come on up. Tell that to Dad. Let's give him a whirl. Come on.

BIFF (steamed up): You know, with ten thousand bucks, boy!

HAPPY (as they go into the living-room): That's the talk, Biff, that's the first time I've heard the old confidence out of you! (From within the living-room, fading off) You're gonna live with me, kid, and any babe you want just say the word ... (The last lines are hardly heard. They are mounting the stairs to their parents' bedroom.)

LINDA (entering her bedroom and addressing Willy, who is in the bathroom. She is straightening the bed for him.) Can you do anything about the shower? It drips.

WILLY (from the bathroom): All of a sudden everything falls to pieces! Goddam plumbing, oughta be sued, those people. I hardly finished putting it in and the thing ... (His words rumble off)

LINDA: I'm just wondering if Oliver will remember him. You think he might?

WILLY (coming out of the bathroom in his pajamas): Remember him? What's the matter with you, you crazy? If he'd've stayed with Oliver he'd be on top by now! Wait'll Oliver gets a look at him. You don't know the average caliber any more. The average young man today—(he is getting into bed)—is got a caliber of zero. Greatest thing in the world for him was to bum around.

(Biff and Happy enter the bedroom. Slight pause.)

WILLY (*stops short, looking at Biff*): Glad to hear it, boy.

HAPPY: He wanted to say good night to you, sport.

WILLY (*to Biff*): Yeah. Knock him dead, boy. What'd you want to tell me?

BIFF: Just take it easy, Pop. Good night. (*He turns to go*)

WILLY (*unable to resist*): And if anything falls off the desk while you're talking to him—like a package or something—don't you pick it up. They have office boys for that.

LINDA: I'll make a big breakfast—

WILLY: Will you let me finish? (*To Biff*) Tell him you were in the business in the West. Not farm work.

BIFF: All right, Dad.

LINDA: I think everything—

WILLY (*going right through her speech*): And don't undersell yourself. No less than fifteen thousand dollars.

BIFF (*unable to bear him*): Okay. Good night, Mom. (*He starts moving*)

WILLY: Because you got a greatness in you, Biff, remember that. You got all kinds a greatness . . . (*He lies back, exhausted. Biff walks out.*)

LINDA (*calling after Biff*): Sleep well, darling!

HAPPY: I'm gonna get married, Mom. I wanted to tell you.

LINDA: Go to sleep, dear.

HAPPY (*going*): I just wanted to tell you.

WILLY: Keep up the good work. (*Happy exits*) God . . . remember that Ebbets Field game? The championship of the city?

LINDA: Just rest. Should I sing to you?

WILLY: Yeah. Sing to me. (*Linda hums a soft lullaby*) When that team came out— he was the tallest, remember?

LINDA: Oh, yes. And in gold.

(*Biff enters the darkened kitchen, takes a cigarette, and leaves the house. He comes downstage into a golden pool of light. He smokes, staring at the night.*)

WILLY: Like a young god. Hercules—something like that. And the sun, the sun all around him. Remember how he waved to me? Right up from the field, with the representatives of three colleges standing by? And the buyers I brought, and the cheers when he came out—Loman, Loman, Loman! God Almighty, he'll be great yet. A star like that, magnificent, can never really fade away!

(*The light on Willy is fading. The gas heater begins to glow through the kitchen wall, near the stairs, a blue flame beneath red coils.*)

LINDA (*timidly*): Willy dear, what has he got against you?

WILLY: I'm so tired. Don't talk any more.

(*Biff slowly returns to the kitchen. He stops, stares toward the heater.*)

LINDA: Will you ask Howard to let you work in New York?

WILLY: First thing in the morning. Everything'll be all right.

(*Biff reaches behind the heater and draws out a length of rubber tubing. He is horrified and turns his head toward Willy's room, still dimly lit, from which the strains of Linda's desperate but monotonous humming rise.)*

WILLY *(staring through the window into the moonlight)*: Gee, look at the moon moving between the buildings!

(Biff wraps the tubing around his hand and quickly goes up the stairs)

Curtain

Act Two

(Music is heard, gay and bright. The curtain rises as the music fades away. Willy, in shirt sleeves, is sitting at the kitchen table, sipping coffee, his hat in his lap. Linda is filling his cup when she can.)

WILLY: Wonderful coffee. Meal in itself.

LINDA: Can I make you some eggs?

WILLY: No. Take a breath.

LINDA: You look so rested, dear.

WILLY: I slept like a dead one. First time in months. Imagine, sleeping till ten on a Tuesday morning. Boys left nice and early, heh?

LINDA: They were out of here by eight o'clock.

WILLY: Good work!

LINDA: It was so thrilling to see them leaving together. I can't get over the shaving lotion in this house!

WILLY *(smiling)*: Mmm—

LINDA: Biff was very changed this morning. His whole attitude seemed to be hopeful. He couldn't wait to get downtown to see Oliver.

WILLY: He's heading for a change. There's no question, there simply are certain men that take longer to get—solidified. How did he dress?

LINDA: His blue suit. He's so handsome in that suit. He could be a—anything in that suit!

(Willy gets up from the table. Linda holds his jacket for him.)

WILLY: There's no question, no question at all. Gee, on the way home tonight I'd like to buy some seeds.

LINDA *(laughing)*: That'd be wonderful. But not enough sun gets back there. Nothing'll grow any more.

WILLY: You wait, kid, before it's all over we're gonna get a little place out in the country, and I'll raise some vegetables, a couple of chickens . . .

LINDA: You'll do it yet, dear.

(Willy walks out of his jacket. Linda follows him.)

WILLY: And they'll get married, and come for a weekend. I'd build a little guest house. 'Cause I got so many fine tools, all I'd need would be a little lumber and some peace of mind.

LINDA *(joyfully)*: I sewed the lining . . .

WILLY: I could build two guest houses, so they'd both come. Did he decide how much he's going to ask Oliver for?

LINDA *(getting him into the jacket)*: He didn't mention it, but I imagine ten or fifteen thousand. You going to talk to Howard today?

WILLY: Yeah. I'll put it to him straight and simple. He'll just have to take me off the road.

LINDA: And Willy, don't forget to ask for a little advance, because we've got the insurance premium. It's the grace period now.

WILLY: That's a hundred. . . ?

LINDA: A hundred and eight, sixty-eight. Because we're a little short again.

WILLY: Why are we short?

LINDA: Well, you had the motor job on the car . . .

WILLY: That goddam Studebaker!

LINDA: And you got one more payment on the refrigerator . . .

WILLY: But it just broke again!

LINDA: Well, it's old, dear.

WILLY: I told you we should've bought a well-advertised machine. Charley bought a General Electric and it's twenty years old and it's still good, that son-of-a-bitch.

LINDA: But, Willy—

WILLY: Whoever heard of a Hastings refrigerator? Once in my life I would like to own something outright before it's broken! I'm always in a race with the junk-yard! I just finished paying for the car and it's on its last legs. The refrigerator consumes belts like a goddam maniac. They time those things. They time them so when you finally paid for them, they're used up.

LINDA (*buttoning up his jacket as he unbuttons it*): All told, about two hundred dollars would carry us, dear. But that includes the last payment on the mortgage. After this payment, Willy, the house belongs to us.

WILLY: It's twenty-five years!

LINDA: Biff was nine years old when we bought it.

WILLY: Well, that's a great thing. To weather a twenty-five year mortgage is—

LINDA: It's an accomplishment.

WILLY: All the cement, the lumber, the reconstruction I put in this house! There ain't a crack to be found in it any more.

LINDA: Well, it served its purpose.

WILLY: What purpose? Some stranger'll come along, move in, and that's that. If only Biff would take this house, and raise a family . . . (*He starts to go*) Good-by, I'm late.

LINDA (*suddenly remembering*): Oh, I forgot! You're supposed to meet them for dinner.

WILLY: Me?

LINDA: At Frank's Chop House on Forty-eighth near Sixth Avenue.

WILLY: Is that so! How about you?

LINDA: No, just the three of you. They're gonna blow you to a big meal!

WILLY: Don't say! Who thought of that?

LINDA: Biff came to me this morning, Willy, and he said, "Tell Dad, we want to blow him to a big meal." Be there six o'clock. You and your two boys are going to have dinner.

WILLY: Gee whiz! That's really somethin'. I'm gonna knock Howard for a loop, kid. I'll get an advance, and I'll come home with a New York job. Goddammit, now I'm gonna do it!

LINDA: Oh, that's the spirit, Willy!

WILLY: I will never get behind a wheel the rest of my life.

LINDA: It's changing, Willy, I can feel it changing!

WILLY: Beyond a question. G'by, I'm late. *(He starts to go again)*

LINDA *(calling after him as she runs to the kitchen table for a handkerchief)*: You got your glasses?

WILLY *(feels for them, then comes back in)*: Yeah, yeah, got my glasses.

LINDA *(giving him the handkerchief)*: And a handkerchief.

WILLY: Yeah, handkerchief.

LINDA: And your saccharine?

WILLY: Yeah, my saccharine.

LINDA: Be careful on the subway stairs.

(She kisses him, and a silk stocking is seen hanging from her hand. Willy notices it.)

WILLY: Will you stop mending stockings? At least while I'm in the house. It gets me nervous. I can't tell you. Please.

(Linda hides the stocking in her hand as she follows Willy across the forestage in front of the house)

LINDA: Remember, Frank's Chop House.

WILLY *(passing the apron)*: Maybe beets would grow out there.

LINDA *(laughing)*: But you tried so many times.

WILLY: Yeah. Well, don't work hard today. *(He disappears around the right corner of the house)*

LINDA: Be careful!

(As Willy vanishes, Linda waves to him. Suddenly the phone rings. She runs across the stage and into the kitchen and lifts it.)

LINDA: Hello? Oh, Biff? I'm so glad you called, I just . . . Yes, sure, I just told him. Yes, he'll be there for dinner at six o'clock, I didn't forget. Listen, I was just dying to tell you. You know that little rubber pipe I told you about? That he connected to the gas heater? I finally decided to go down the cellar this morning and take it away and destroy it. But it's gone! Imagine? He took it away himself, it isn't there! *(She listens)* When? Oh, then you took it. Oh—nothing, it's just that I'd hoped he'd taken it away himself. Oh, I'm not worried, darling, because this morning he left in such high spirits, it was like the old days! I'm not afraid any more. Did Mr. Oliver see you? . . . Well, you wait there then. And make a nice impression on him, darling. Just don't perspire too much before you see him. And have a nice time with Dad. He may have big news too! . . . That's right, a New York job. And be sweet to him tonight, dear. Be loving to him. Because he's only a little boat looking for a harbor. *(She is trembling with sorrow and joy)* Oh, that's wonderful, Bliff, you'll save his life. Thanks, darling. Just put your arm around him when he comes into the restaurant. Give him a smile. That's the boy . . . Good-by, dear. . . . You got your comb? . . . That's fine. Good-by, Biff dear.

(In the middle of her speech, Howard Wagner, thirty-six, wheels on a small type-writer table on which is a wire-recording machine and proceeds to plug it in. This is on the left forestage. Light slowly fades on Linda as it rises on Howard. Howard is intent on threading the machine and only glances over his shoulder as Willy appears.)

WILLY: Pst! Pst!

HOWARD: Hello, Willy, come in.

WILLY: Like to have a little talk with you, Howard.

HOWARD: Sorry to keep you waiting. I'll be with you in a minute.

WILLY: What's that Howard?

HOWARD: Didn't you ever see one of these? Wire recorder.

WILLY: Oh. Can we talk a minute?

HOWARD: Records things. Just got delivery yesterday. Been driving me crazy, the most terrific machine I ever saw in my life. I was up all night with it.

WILLY: What do you do with it?

HOWARD: I bought it for dictation, but you can do anything with it. Listen to this. I had it home last night. Listen to what I picked up. The first one is my daughter. Get this. *(He flicks the switch and "Roll out the Barrel" is heard being whistled)* Listen to that kid whistle.

WILLY: That is lifelike, isn't it?

HOWARD: Seven years old. Get that tone.

WILLY: Ts, ts. Like to ask a little favor if you . . .

(The whistling breaks off, and the voice of Howard's daughter is heard)

HIS DAUGHTER: "Now you, Daddy."

HOWARD: She's crazy for me! *(Again the same song is whistled)* That's me! Ha! *(He winks)*

WILLY: You're very good!

(The whistling breaks off again. The machine runs silent for a moment.)

HOWARD: Sh! Get this now, this is my son.

HIS SON: "The capital of Alabama is Montgomery; the capital of Arizona is Phoenix; the capital of Arkansas is Little Rock; the capital of California is Sacramento . . ." *(and on, and on)*

HOWARD *(holding up five fingers)*: Five years old, Willy!

WILLY: He'll make an announcer some day!

HIS SON *(continuing)*: "The capital . . ."

HOWARD: Get that—alphabetical order! *(The machine breaks off suddenly)* Wait a minute. The maid kicked the plug out.

WILLY: It certainly is a—

HOWARD: Sh, for God's sake!

HIS SON: "It's nine o'clock, Bulova watch time. So I have to go to sleep."

WILLY: That really is—

HOWARD: Wait a minute! The next is my wife.

(They wait)

HOWARD'S VOICE: "Go on, say something," *(Pause)* "Well, you gonna talk?"

HIS WIFE: "I can't think of anything."

HOWARD'S VOICE: "Well, talk—it's turning."

HIS WIFE *(shyly, beaten)*:

"Hello." *(Silence)* "Oh, Howard, I can't talk into this . . ."

HOWARD *(snapping the machine off)*: That was my wife.

WILLY: That is a wonderful machine. Can we—

HOWARD: I tell you, Willy, I'm gonna take my camera, and my bandsaw, and all my hobbies, and out they go. This is the most fascinating relaxation I ever found.

WILLY: I think I'll get one myself.

HOWARD: Sure, they're only a hundred and a half. You can't do without it. Supposing you wanna hear Jack Benny, see? But you can't be at home at that hour. So you tell the maid to turn the radio on when Jack Benny comes on, and this automatically goes on with the radio . . .

WILLY: And when you come home you . . .

HOWARD: You can come home twelve o'clock, one o'clock, any time you like, and you get yourself a Coke and sit yourself down, throw the switch, and there's Jack Benny's program in the middle of the night!

WILLY: I'm definitely going to get one. Because lots of time I'm on the road, and I think to myself, what I must be missing on the radio!

HOWARD: Don't you have a radio in the car?

WILLY: Well, yeah, but who ever thinks of turning it on?

HOWARD: Say, aren't you supposed to be in Boston?

WILLY: That's what I want to talk to you about, Howard. You got a minute? *(He draws a chair in from the wing)*

HOWARD: What happened? What're you doing here?

WILLY: Well . . .

HOWARD: You didn't crack up again, did you?

WILLY: Oh, no. No . . .

HOWARD: Geez, you had me worried there for a minute. What's the trouble?

WILLY: Well, tell you the truth, Howard. I've come to the decision that I'd rather not travel anymore.

HOWARD: Not travel! Well, what'll you do?

WILLY: Remember, Christmas time, when you had the party here? You said you'd try to think of some spot for me here in town.

HOWARD: With us?

WILLY: Well, sure.

HOWARD: Oh, yeah, yeah. I remember. Well, I couldn't think of anything for you, Willy.

WILLY: I tell ya, Howard. The kids are all grown up, y'know. I don't need much any more. If I could take home—well, sixty-five dollars a week, I could swing it.

HOWARD: Yeah, but Willy, see I—

WILLY: I tell ya why, Howard. Speaking frankly and between the two of us, y'know—I'm just a little tired.

HOWARD: Oh, I could understand that, Willy. But you're a road man, Willy, and we do a road business. We've only got a half-dozen salesmen on the floor here.

WILLY: God knows, Howard, I never asked a favor of any man. But I was with the firm when your father used to carry you in here in his arms.

HOWARD: I know that, Willy, but—

WILLY: Your father came to me the day you were born and asked me what I thought of the name of Howard, may he rest in peace.

HOWARD: I appreciate that, Willy, but there just is no spot here for you. If I had a spot I'd slam you right in, but I just don't have a single solitary spot.

(He looks for his lighter. Willy has picked it up and gives it to him. Pause.)

WILLY *(with increasing anger)*: Howard, all I need to set my table is fifty dollars a week.

HOWARD: But where am I going to put you, kid?

WILLY: Look, it isn't a question of whether I can sell merchandise, is it?

HOWARD: No, but it's a business, kid, and everybody's gotta pull his own weight.

WILLY *(desperately)*: Just let me tell you a story, Howard—

HOWARD: 'Cause you gotta admit, business is business.

WILLY *(angrily)*: Business is definitely business, but just listen for a minute. You don't understand this. When I was a boy—eighteen, nineteen—I was already on the road. And there was a question in my mind as to whether selling had a future for me. Because in those days I had a yearning to go to Alaska. See, there were three gold strikes in one month in Alaska, and I felt like going out. Just for the ride, you might say.

HOWARD *(barely interested)*: Don't say.

WILLY: Oh, yeah, my father lived many years in Alaska. He was an adventurous man. We've got quite a little streak of self-reliance in our family. I thought I'd go out with my older brother and try to locate him, and maybe settle in the North with the old man. And I was almost decided to go, when I met a salesman in the Parker House. His name was Dave Singleman. And he was eighty-four years old, and he'd drummed merchandise in thirty-one states. And old Dave, he'd go up to his room, y'understand, put on his green velvet slippers— I'll never forget—and pick up his phone and call the buyers, and without ever leaving his room, at the age of eighty-four, he made his living. And when I saw that, I realized that selling was the greatest career a man could want. 'Cause what could be more satisfying than to be able to go, at the age of eighty-four, into twenty or thirty different cities, and pick up a phone, and be remembered and loved and helped by so many different people? Do you know? when he died—and by the way he died the death of a salesman, in his green velvet slippers in the smoker of the New York, New Haven and Hartford, going into Boston—when he died, hundreds of salesmen and buyers were at his funeral. Things were sad on a lotta trains for months after that. *(He stands up. Howard has not looked at him)* In those days there was personality in it, Howard. There was respect, and comradeship, and gratitude in it. Today, it's all cut and dried, and there's no chance for bringing friendship to bear— or personality. You see what I mean? They don't know me any more.

HOWARD *(moving away, toward the right)*: That's just the thing, Willy.

WILLY: If I had forty dollars a week—that's all I'd need. Forty dollars, Howard.

HOWARD: Kid, I can't take blood from a stone, I—

WILLY *(desperation is on him now)*: Howard, the year Al Smith[4] was nominated, your father came to me and—

HOWARD *(starting to go off)*: I've got to see some people, kid.

WILLY *(stopping him)*: I'm talking about your father! There were promises made across this desk! You mustn't tell me you've got people to see—I put thirty-four years into this firm, Howard, and now I can't pay my insurance! You

[4] Alfred E. Smith (1873–1944) was the Democratic candidate for President running against Herbert Hoover in 1928.

can't eat the orange and throw the peel away—a man is not a piece of fruit! *(After a pause)* Now pay attention. Your father—in 1928 I had a big year. I averaged a hundred and seventy dollars a week in commissions.

HOWARD *(impatiently)*: Now, Willy, you never averaged—

WILLY *(banging his hand on the desk)*: I averaged a hundred and seventy dollars a week in the year of 1928! And your father came to me—or rather, I was in the office here—it was right over this desk—and he put his hand on my shoulder—

HOWARD *(getting up)*: You'll have to excuse me, Willy, I gotta see some people. Pull yourself together. *(Going out)* I'll be back in a little while.

(On Howard's exit, the light on his chair grows very bright and strange)

WILLY: Pull myself together! What the hell did I say to him? My God, I was yelling at him! How could I! *(Willy breaks off, staring at the light, which occupies the chair, animating it. He approaches this chair, standing across the desk from it.)* Frank, Frank, don't you remember what you told me that time? How you put your hand on my shoulder, and Frank . . . *(He leans on the desk and as he speaks the dead man's name he accidentally switches on the recorder, and instantly)*

HOWARD'S SON: ". . . of New York is Albany. The capital of Ohio is Cincinnati, the capital of Rhode Island is . . ." *(The recitation continues)*

WILLY *(leaping away with fright, shouting)*: Ha! Howard! Howard! Howard!

HOWARD *(rushing in)*: What happened?

WILLY *(pointing at the machine, which continues nasally, childishly, with the capital cities)*: Shut if off! Shut it off!

HOWARD *(pulling the plug out)*: Look, Willy . . .

WILLY *(pressing his hands to his eyes)*: I gotta get myself some coffee. I'll get some coffee . . .

(Willy starts to walk out. Howard stops him.)

HOWARD *(rolling up the cord)*: Willy, look . . .

WILLY: I'll go to Boston.

HOWARD: Willy, you can't go to Boston for us.

WILLY: Why can't I go?

HOWARD: I don't want you to represent us. I've been meaning to tell you for a long time now.

WILLY: Howard, are you firing me?

HOWARD: I think you need a good long rest, Willy.

WILLY: Howard—

HOWARD: And when you feel better, come back, and we'll see if we can work something out.

WILLY: But I gotta earn money, Howard. I'm in no position to—

HOWARD: Where are your sons? Why don't your sons give you a hand?

WILLY: They're working on a very big deal.

HOWARD: This is no time for false pride, Willy. You go to your sons and you tell them that you're tired. You've got two great boys, haven't you?

WILLY: Oh, no question, no question, but in the meantime . . .

HOWARD: Then that's that, heh?

WILLY: All right, I'll go to Boston tomorrow.

HOWARD: No, no.

WILLY: I can't throw myself on my sons. I'm not a cripple!

HOWARD: Look, kid, I'm busy this morning.

WILLY (*grasping Howard's arm*): Howard, you've got to let me go to Boston!

HOWARD (*hard, keeping himself under control*): I've got a line of people to see this morning. Sit down, take five minutes, and pull yourself together, and then go home, will ya? I need the office, Willy. (*He starts to go, turns, remembering the recorder, starts to push off the table holding the recorder*) Oh, yeah. Whenever you can this week, stop by and drop off the samples. You'll feel better, Willy, and then come back and we'll talk. Pull yourself together, kid, there's people outside.

(*Howard exits, pushing the table off left. Willy stares into space, exhausted. Now the music is heard—Ben's music—first distantly, then closer, closer. As Willy speaks, Ben enters from the right. He carries valise and umbrella.*)

WILLY: Oh, Ben, how did you do it? What is the answer? Did you wind up the Alaska deal already?

BEN: Doesn't take much time if you know what you're doing. Just a short business trip. Boarding ship in an hour. Wanted to say good-by.

WILLY: Ben, I've got to talk to you.

BEN (*glancing at his watch*): Haven't the time, William.

WILLY (*crossing the apron to Ben*): Ben, nothing's working out. I don't know what to do.

BEN: Now, look here, William. I've bought timberland in Alaska and I need a man to look after things for me.

WILLY: God, timberland! Me and my boys in those grand outdoors!

BEN: You've a new continent at your doorstep, William. Get out of these cities, they're full of talk and time payments and courts of law. Screw on your fists and you can fight for a fortune up there.

WILLY: Yes, yes! Linda, Linda!

(*Linda enters as of old, with the wash*)

LINDA: Oh, you're back?

BEN: I haven't much time.

WILLY: No, wait! Linda, he's got a proposition for me in Alaska.

LINDA: But you've got— (*To Ben*) He's got a beautiful job here.

WILLY: But in Alaska, kid, I could—

LINDA: You're doing well enough, Willy!

BEN (*to Linda*): Enough for what, my dear?

LINDA (*frightened of Ben and angry at him*): Don't say those things to him! Enough to be happy right here, right now. (*To Willy, while Ben laughs*) Why must everybody conquer the world? You're well liked, and the boys love you, and someday— (*to Ben*) —why, old man Wagner told him just the other day that if he keeps it up he'll be a member of the firm, didn't he, Willy?

WILLY: Sure, sure. I am building something with this firm, Ben, and if a man is building something he must be on the right track, mustn't he?

BEN: What are you building? Lay your hand on it. Where is it?

WILLY (*hesitantly*): That's true, Linda, there's nothing.

LINDA: Why? *(To Ben)* There's a man eighty-four years old—

WILLY: That's right, Ben, that's right. When I look at that man I say, what is there to worry about?

BEN: Bah!

WILLY: It's true, Ben. All he has to do is go into any city, pick up the phone, and he's making his living and you know why?

BEN *(picking up his valise)*: I've got to go.

WILLY *(holding Ben back)*: Look at this boy!

(Biff, in his high school sweater, enters carrying suitcase. Happy carries Biff's shoulder guards, gold helmet, and football pants.)

WILLY: Without a penny to his name, three great universities are begging for him, and from there the sky's the limit, because it's not what you do, Ben. It's who you know and the smile on your face! It's contacts, Ben, contacts! The whole wealth of Alaska passes over the lunch table at the Commodore Hotel, and that's the wonder, the wonder of this country, that a man can end with diamonds here on the basis of being liked! *(He turns to Biff)* And that's why when you get out on that field today it's important. Because thousands of people will be rooting for you and loving you. *(To Ben, who has again begun to leave)* And Ben! when he walks into a business office his name will sound out like a bell and all the doors will open to him! I've seen it, Ben, I've seen it a thousand times! You can't feel it with your hand like timber, but it's there!

BEN: Good-by, William.

WILLY: Ben, am I right? Don't you think I'm right? I value your advice.

BEN: There's a new continent at your doorstep, William. You could walk out rich. Rich! *(He is gone)*

WILLY: We'll do it here, Ben! You hear me? We're gonna do it here!

(Young Bernard rushes in. The gay music of the Boys is heard.)

BERNARD: Oh, gee, I was afraid you left already!

WILLY: Why? What time is it?

BERNARD: It's half-past one!

WILLY: Well, come on, everybody! Ebbets Field next stop! Where's the pennants? *(He rushes through the wall-line of the kitchen and out into the living-room)*

LINDA *(to Biff)*: Did you pack fresh underwear?

BIFF *(who has been limbering up)*: I want to go!

BERNARD: Biff, I'm carrying your helmet, ain't I?

HAPPY: No, I'm carrying the helmet.

BERNARD: Oh, Biff, you promised me.

HAPPY: I'm carrying the helmet.

BERNARD: How am I going to get in the locker room?

LINDA: Let him carry the shoulder guards. *(She puts her coat and hat on in the kitchen)*

BERNARD: Can I, Biff? 'Cause I told everybody I'm going to be in the locker room.

HAPPY: In Ebbets Field it's the clubhouse.

BERNARD: I meant the clubhouse. Biff!

HAPPY: Biff!

BIFF *(grandly, after a slight pause)*: Let him carry the shoulder guards.

HAPPY *(as he gives Bernard the shoulder guards)*: Stay close to us now.

(Willy rushes in with the pennants)

WILLY *(handing them out)*: Everybody wave when Biff comes out on the field. *(Happy and Bernard run off)* You set now, boy?

(The music has died away)

BIFF: Ready to go, Pop. Every muscle is ready.

WILLY *(at the edge of the apron)*: You realize what this means?

BIFF: That's right, Pop.

WILLY *(feeling Biff's muscles)*: You're comin' home this afternoon captain of the All-Scholastic Championship Team of the City of New York.

BIFF: I got it, Pop. And remember, pal, when I take off my helmet, the touchdown is for you.

WILLY: Let's go! *(He is starting out, with his arm around Biff, when Charley enters, as of old, in knickers)* I got no room for you Charley.

CHARLEY: Room? For what?

WILLY: In the car.

CHARLEY: You goin' for a ride? I wanted to shoot some casino.

WILLY *(furiously)*: Casino! *(Incredulously)* Don't you realize what today is?

LINDA: Oh, he knows, Willy. He's just kidding you.

WILLY: That's nothing to kid about!

CHARLEY: No, Linda, what's goin' on?

LINDA: He's playing in Ebbets Field.

CHARLEY: Baseball in this weather?

WILLY: Don't talk to him. Come on, come on! *(He is pushing them out)*

CHARLEY: Wait a minute, didn't you hear the news?

WILLY: What?

CHARLEY: Don't you listen to the radio? Ebbets Field just blew up.

WILLY: You go to hell! *(Charley laughs. Pushing them out)* Come on, come on! We're late.

CHARLEY *(as they go)*: Knock a homer, Biff, knock a homer!

WILLY *(the last to leave, turning to Charley)*: I don't think that was funny, Charley. This is the greatest day of his life.

CHARLEY: Willy, when are you going to grow up?

WILLY: Yeah, heh? When this game is over, Charley, you'll be laughing out the other side of your face. They'll be calling him another Red Grange.[5] Twenty-five thousand a year.

CHARLEY *(kidding)*: Is that so?

WILLY: Yeah, that's so.

CHARLEY: Well, then, I'm sorry, Willy. But tell me something.

WILLY: What?

CHARLEY: Who is Red Grange?

WILLY: Put up your hands. Goddam you, put up your hands!

(Charley, chuckling, shakes his head and walks away, around the left corner of the stage. Willy follows him. The music rises to a mocking frenzy.)

[5] Harold Edward Grange, an All-American football player at the University of Illinois, 1923–1925.

WILLY: Who the hell do you think you are, better than everybody else? You don't know everything, you big, ignorant, stupid . . . Put up your hands!

(Light rises, on the right side of the forestage, on a small table in the reception room of Charley's office. Traffic sounds are heard. Bernard, now mature, sits whistling to himself. A pair of tennis rackets and an overnight bag are on the floor beside him.)

WILLY *(offstage)*: What are you walking away for? Don't walk away! If you're going to say something say it to my face! I know you laugh at me behind my back. You'll laugh out of the other side of your goddam face after this game. Touchdown! Touchdown! Eighty thousand people! Touchdown! Right between the goal posts.

Bernard is a quiet, earnest, but self-assured young man. Willy's voice is coming from right upstage now. Bernard lowers his feet off the table and listens. Jenny, his father's secretary, enters.)

JENNY *(distressed)*: Say, Bernard, will you go out in the hall?

BERNARD: What is that noise? Who is it?

JENNY: Mr. Loman. He just got off the elevator.

BERNARD *(Getting up)*: Who's he arguing with?

JENNY: Nobody. There's nobody with him. I can't deal with him any more, and your father gets all upset everytime he comes. I've got a lot of typing to do, and your father's waiting to sign it. Will you see him?

WILLY *(entering)*: Touchdown! Touch— *(He sees Jenny)* Jenny, Jenny, good to see you. How're ya? Workin'? Or still honest?

JENNY: Fine. How've you been feeling?

WILLY: Not much any more, Jenny. Ha, ha! *(He is surprised to see the rackets)*

BERNARD: Hello, Uncle Willy.

WILLY *(almost shocked)*: Bernard! Well, look who's here! *(He comes quickly, guiltily, to Bernard and warmly shakes his hand)*

BERNARD: How are you? Good to see you.

WILLY: What are you doing here?

BERNARD: Oh, just stopped by to see Pop. Get off my feet till my train leaves. I'm going to Washington in a few minutes.

WILLY: Is he in?

BERNARD: Yes, he's in his office with the accountant. Sit down.

WILLY *(sitting down)*: What're you going to do in Washington?

BERNARD: Oh, just a case I've got there, Willy.

WILLY: That so? *(Indicating the rackets)* You going to play tennis there?

BERNARD: I'm staying with a friend who's got a court.

WILLY: Don't say. His own tennis court. Must be fine people, I bet.

BERNARD: They are, very nice. Dad tells me Biff's in town.

WILLY *(with a big smile)*: Yeah, Biff's in. Working on a very big deal, Bernard.

BERNARD: What's Biff doing?

WILLY: Well, he's been doing very big things in the West. But he decided to establish himself here. Very big. We're having dinner. Did I hear your wife had a boy?

BERNARD: That's right. Our second.

WILLY: Two boys! What do you know!

BERNARD: What kind of a deal has Biff got?

WILLY: Well, Bill Oliver—very big sporting-goods man—he wants Biff very badly. Called him in from the West. Long distance, carte blanche, special deliveries. Your friends have their own private tennis court?

BERNARD: You still with the old firm, Willy?

WILLY *(after a pause):* I'm—I'm overjoyed to see how you made the grade, Bernard, overjoyed. It's an encouraging thing to see a young man really—really—Looks very good for Biff—very—*(He breaks off, then)* Bernard—*(He is so full of emotion, he breaks off again)*

BERNARD: What is it, Willy?

WILLY *(small and alone):* What—what's the secret?

BERNARD: What secret?

WILLY: How—how did you? Why didn't he ever catch on?

BERNARD: I wouldn't know that, Willy.

WILLY *(confidentially, desperately):* You were his friend, his boyhood friend. There's something I don't understand about it. His life ended after that Ebbets Field game. From the age of seventeen nothing good ever happened to him.

BERNARD: He never trained himself for anything.

WILLY: But he did, he did. After high school he took so many correspondence courses. Radio mechanics; television; God knows what, and never made the slightest mark.

BERNARD *(taking off his glasses):* Willy, do you want to talk candidly?

WILLY *(rising, faces Bernard):* I regard you as a very brilliant man, Bernard. I value your advice.

BERNARD: Oh, the hell with advice, Willy. I couldn't advise you. There's just one thing I've always wanted to ask you. When he was supposed to graduate, and the math teacher flunked him—

WILLY: Oh, that son-of-a-bitch ruined his life.

BERNARD: Yeah, but, Willy, all he had to do was go to summer school and make up that subject.

WILLY: That's right, that's right.

BERNARD: Did you tell him not to go to summer school?

WILLY: Me? I begged him to go. I ordered him to go!

BERNARD: Then why wouldn't he go?

WILLY: Why? Why! Bernard, that question has been trailing me like a ghost for the last fifteen years. He flunked the subject, and laid down and died like a hammer hit him!

BERNARD: Take it easy, kid.

WILLY: Let me talk to you—I got nobody to talk to. Bernard, Bernard, was it my fault? Y'see? It keeps going around in my mind, maybe I did something to him. I got nothing to give him.

BERNARD: Don't take it so hard.

WILLY: Why did he lay down? What is the story there? You were his friend!

BERNARD: Willy, I remember, it was June, and our grades came out. And he'd flunked math.

WILLY: That son-of-a-bitch!

BERNARD: No, it wasn't right then. Biff just got very angry, I remember, and he was ready to enroll in summer school.

WILLY (*surprised*): He was?

BERNARD: He wasn't beaten by it at all. But then, Willy, he disappeared from the block for almost a month. And I got the idea that he'd gone up to New England to see you. Did he have a talk with you then?

(*Willy stares in silence*)

BERNARD: Willy?

WILLY (*with a strong edge of resentment in his voice*) : Yeah, he came to Boston. What about it?

BERNARD: Well, just that when he came back—I'll never forget this, it always mystifies me. Because I'd thought so well of Biff, even though he'd always taken advantage of me. I loved him, Willy, y'know? And he came back after that month and took his sneakers—remember those sneakers with "University of Virginia" printed on them? He was so proud of those, wore them every day. And he took them down in the cellar, and burned them up in the furnace. We had a fist fight. It lasted at least half an hour. Just the two of us, punching each other down the cellar, and crying right through it. I've often thought of how strange it was that I knew he'd given up his life. What happened in Boston, Willy?

(*Willy looks at him as at an intruder*)

BERNARD: I just bring it up because you asked me.

WILLY (*angrily*): Nothing. What do you mean, "What happened?" What's that got to do with anything?

BERNARD: Well, don't get sore.

WILLY: What are you trying to do, blame it on me? If a boy lays down is that my fault?

BERNARD: Now, Willy, don't get—

WILLY: Well, don't—don't talk to me that way! What does that mean, "What happened?"

(*Charley enters. He is in his vest, and he carries a bottle of bourbon.*)

CHARLEY: Hey, you're going to miss that train. (*He waves the bottle*)

BERNARD: Yeah, I'm going. (*He takes the bottle*) Thanks, Pop. (*He picks up his rackets and bag*) Good-by, Willy, and don't worry about it. You know, "If at first you don't succeed . . ."

WILLY: Yes, I believe in that.

BERNARD: But sometimes, Willy, it's better for a man just to walk away.

WILLY: Walk away?

BERNARD: That's right.

WILLY: But if you can't walk away?

BERNARD (*after a slight pause*): I guess that's when it's tough. (*Extending his hand*) Good-by, Willy.

WILLY (*shaking Bernard's hand*): Good-by, boy.

CHARLEY: (*an arm on Bernard's shoulder*): How do you like this kid? Gonna argue a case in front of the Supreme Court.

BERNARD (*protesting*): Pop!

WILLY (*genuinely shocked, pained, and happy*): No! The Supreme Court!

BERNARD: I gotta run. 'By, Dad!

CHARLEY: Knock 'em dead, Bernard!

(Bernard goes off)

WILLY *(as Charley takes out his wallet)*: The Supreme Court! And he didn't even mention it!

CHARLEY *(counting out money on the desk)*: He don't have to—he's gonna do it.

WILLY: And you never told him what to do, did you? You never took any interest in him.

CHARLEY: My salvation is that I never took any interest in anything. There's some money—fifty dollars. I got an accountant inside.

WILLY: Charley, look . . . *(With difficulty)* I got my insurance to pay. If you can manage it—I need a hundred and ten dollars.

(Charley doesn't reply for a moment; merely stops moving)

WILLY: I'd draw it from my bank but Linda would know, and I . . .

CHARLEY: Sit down, Willy.

WILLY *(moving toward the chair)*: I'm keeping an account of everything, remember. I'll pay every penny back. *(He sits)*

CHARLEY: Now listen to me, Willy.

WILLY: I want you to know I appreciate . . .

CHARLEY *(sitting down on the table)*: Willy, what're you doin'? What the hell is goin' on in your head?

WILLY: Why? I'm simply . . .

CHARLEY: I offered you a job. You can make fifty dollars a week. And I won't send you on the road.

WILLY: I've got a job.

CHARLEY: Without pay? What kind of a job is a job without pay? *(He rises)* Now, look, kid, enough is enough. I'm no genius but I know when I'm being insulted.

WILLY: Insulted!

CHARLEY: Why don't you want to work for me?

WILLY: What's the matter with you? I've got a job.

CHARLEY: Then what're you walkin' in here every week for?

WILLY *(getting up)*: Well, if you don't want me to walk in here—

CHARLEY: I am offering you a job.

WILLY: I don't want your goddam job!

CHARLEY: When the hell are you going to grow up?

WILLY *(furiously)*: You big ignoramus, if you say that to me again I'll rap you one! I don't care how big you are!

(He's ready to fight. Pause)

CHARLEY *(kindly, going to him)*: How much do you need, Willy?

WILLY: Charley, I'm strapped, I'm strapped. I don't know what to do. I was just fired.

CHARLEY: Howard fired you?

WILLY: That snotnose. Imagine that? I named him. I named him Howard.

CHARLEY: Willy, when're you gonna realize that them things don't mean anything? You named him Howard, but you can't sell that. The only thing you got in this world is what you can sell. And the funny thing is that you're a salesman, and you don't know that.

WILLY: I've always tried to think otherwise, I guess. I always felt that if a man was impressive, and well liked, that nothing—

CHARLEY: Why must everybody like you? Who liked J. P. Morgan?[6] Was he impressive? In a Turkish bath he'd look like a butcher. But with his pockets on he was very well liked. Now listen, Willy, I know you don't like me, and nobody can say I'm in love with you, but I'll give you a job because—just for the hell of it, put it that way. Now what do you say?

WILLY: I—I just can't work for you, Charley.

CHARLEY: What're you, jealous of me?

WILLY: I can't work for you, that's all, don't ask me why.

CHARLEY (angered, takes out more bills): You been jealous of me all your life, you damned fool! Here, pay your insurance. (He puts the money in Willy's hand)

WILLY: I'm keeping strict accounts.

CHARLEY: I've got some work to do. Take care of yourself. And pay your insurance.

WILLY (moving to the right): Funny, y'know? After all the highways, and the trains, and the appointments, and the years, you end up worth more dead than alive.

CHARLEY: Willy, nobody's worth nothin' dead. (After a slight pause) Did you hear what I said?

(Willy stands still, dreaming)

CHARLEY: Willy!

WILLY: Apologize to Bernard for me when you see him. I didn't mean to argue with him. He's a fine boy. They're all fine boys, and they'll end up big—all of them. Someday they'll all play tennis together. Wish me luck, Charley. He saw Bill Oliver today.

CHARLEY: Good luck.

WILLY (on the verge of tears): Charley, you're the only friend I got. Isn't that a remarkable thing? (He goes out)

CHARLEY: Jesus!

(Charley stares after him a moment and follows. All light blacks out. Suddenly raucous music is heard, and a red glow rises behind the screen at right. Stanley, a young waiter, appears, carrying a table, followed by Happy, who is carrying two chairs.)

STANLEY (putting the table down): That's all right, Mr. Loman, I can handle it myself. (He turns and takes the chairs from Happy and places them at the table)

HAPPY (glancing around): Oh, this is better.

STANLEY: Sure, in the front there you're in the middle of all kinds a noise. Whenever you got a party, Mr. Loman, you just tell me and I'll put you back here. Y'know, there's a lotta people they don't like it private, because when they go

---

[6] John Pierpont Morgan (1837–1913) established the Morgan financial empire. His son, also J. P. Morgan (1867–1943), carried on the tradition.

out they like to see a lotta action around them because they're sick and tired to stay in the house by theirself. But I know you, you ain't from Hackensack. You know what I mean?

HAPPY *(sitting down):* So how's it coming, Stanley?

STANLEY: Ah, it's a dog's life. I only wish during the war they'd a took me in the Army. I coulda been dead by now.

HAPPY: My brother's back, Stanley.

STANLEY: Oh, he come back, heh? From the Far West.

HAPPY: Yeah, big cattle man, my brother, so treat him right. And my father's coming too.

STANLEY: Oh, your father too!

HAPPY: You got a couple of nice lobsters?

STANLEY: Hundred per cent, big.

HAPPY: I want them with the claws.

STANLEY: Don't worry, I don't give you no mice. *(Happy laughs)* How about some wine? It'll put a head on the meal.

HAPPY: No, You remember, Stanley, that recipe I brought you from overseas? With the champagne in it?

STANLEY: Oh, yeah, sure. I still got it tacked up yet in the kitchen. But that'll have to cost a buck apiece anyways.

HAPPY: That's all right.

STANLEY: What'd you, hit a number or somethin'?

HAPPY: No, it's a little celebration. My brother is—I think he pulled off a big deal today. I think we're going into business together.

STANLEY: Great! That's the best for you. Because a family business, you know what I mean?—that's the best.

HAPPY: That's what I think.

STANLEY: 'Cause what's the difference? Somebody steals? It's in the family. Know what I mean? *(Sotto voce)*[7] Like this bartender here. The boss is goin' crazy what kinda leak he's got in the cash register. You put it in but it don't come out.

HAPPY *(raising his head):* Sh!

STANLEY: What?

HAPPY: You notice I wasn't lookin' right or left, was I?

STANLEY: No.

HAPPY: And my eyes are closed.

STANLEY: So what's the—?

HAPPY: Strudel's comin'.

STANLEY *(catching on, looks around):* Ah, no, there's no—

(He breaks off as a furred, lavishly dressed girl enters and sits at the next table. Both follow her with their eyes.)

STANLEY: Geez, how'd ya know?

HAPPY: I got radar or something. *(Staring directly at her profile):* Oooooooooo . . . Stanley.

STANLEY: I think that's for you, Mr. Loman.

---

[7] In an undertone.

HAPPY: Look at that mouth. Oh, God. And the binoculars.

STANLEY: Geez, you got a life, Mr. Loman.

HAPPY: Wait on her.

STANLEY *(going to the girl's table)*: Would you like a menu, ma'am?

GIRL: I'm expecting someone, but I'd like a—

HAPPY: Why don't you bring her—excuse me, miss, do you mind? I sell champagne, and I'd like you to try my brand. Bring her a champagne, Stanley.

GIRL: That's awfully nice of you.

HAPPY: Don't mention it. It's all company money. *(He laughs)*

GIRL: That's a charming product to be selling, isn't it?

HAPPY: Oh, gets to be like everything else. Selling is selling, y'know.

GIRL: I suppose.

HAPPY: You don't happen to sell, do you?

GIRL: No, I don't sell.

HAPPY: Would you object to a compliment from a stranger? You ought to be on a magazine cover.

GIRL *(looking at him a little archly)*: I have been.

(Stanley comes in with a glass of champagne)

HAPPY: What'd I say before, Stanley? You see? She's a cover girl.

STANLEY: Oh, I could see, I could see.

HAPPY *(to the Girl)*: What magazine?

GIRL: Oh, a lot of them. *(She takes the drink)* Thank you.

HAPPY: You know what they say in France, don't you? "Champagne is the drink of the complexion"—Hya, Biff!

(Biff has entered and sits with Happy)

BIFF: Hello, kid. Sorry I'm late.

HAPPY: I just got here. Uh, Miss—?

GIRL: Forsythe.

HAPPY: Miss Forsythe, this is my brother.

BIFF: Is Dad here?

HAPPY: His name is Biff. You might've heard of him. Great football player.

GIRL: Really? What team?

HAPPY: Are you familiar with football?

GIRL: No, I'm afraid I'm not.

HAPPY: Biff is quarterback with the New York Giants.

GIRL: Well, that is nice, isn't it? *(She drinks)*

HAPPY: Good health.

GIRL: I'm happy to meet you.

HAPPY: That's my name. Hap. It's really Harold, but at West Point they called me Happy.

GIRL *(now really impressed)*: Oh, I see. How do you do? *(She turns her profile)*

BIFF: Isn't Dad coming?

HAPPY: You want her?

BIFF: Oh, I could never make that.

HAPPY: I remember the time that idea would never come into your head. Where's the old confidence, Biff?

BIFF: I just saw Oliver—

HAPPY: Wait a minute. I've got to see that old confidence again. Do you want her? She's on call.

BIFF: Oh, no. *(He turns to look at the Girl)*

HAPPY: I'm telling you. *(Watch this. Turning to the Girl.)* Honey? *(She turns to him)* Are you busy?

GIRL: Well, I am . . . but I could make a phone call.

HAPPY: Do that, will you, honey? And see if you can get a friend. We'll be here for a while. Biff is one of the greatest football players in the country.

GIRL *(standing up)*: Well, I'm certainly happy to meet you.

HAPPY: Come back soon.

GIRL: I'll try.

HAPPY: Don't try, honey, try hard.

(The Girl exits. Stanley follows, shaking his head in bewildered admiration.)

HAPPY: Isn't that a shame now? A beautiful girl like that? That's why I can't get married. There's not a good woman in a thousand. New York is loaded with them, kid!

BIFF: Hap, look—

HAPPY: I told you she was on call!

BIFF *(strangely unnerved)*: Cut it out, will ya? I want to say something to you.

HAPPY: Did you see Oliver?

BIFF: I saw him all right. Now look, I want to tell Dad a couple of things and I want you to help me.

HAPPY: What? Is he going to back you?

BIFF: Are you crazy? You're out of your goddam head, you know that?

HAPPY: Why? What happened?

BIFF *(breathlessly)*: I did a terrible thing today, Hap. It's been the strangest day I ever went through. I'm all numb, I swear.

HAPPY: You mean he wouldn't see you?

BIFF: Well, I waited six hours for him, see? All day. Kept sending my name in. Even tried to date his secretary so she'd get me to him, but no soap.

HAPPY: Because you're not showin' the old confidence, Biff. He remembered you, didn't he?

BIFF *(stopping Happy with a gesture)*: Finally, about five o'clock, he comes out. Didn't remember who I was or anything. I felt like such an idiot, Hap.

HAPPY: Did you tell him my Florida idea?

BIFF: He walked away. I saw him for one minute. I got so mad I could've torn the walls down! How the hell did I ever get the idea I was a salesman there? I even believed myself that I'd been a salesman for him! And then he gave me one look and—I realized what a ridiculous lie my whole life has been! We've been talking in a dream for fifteen years. I was a shipping clerk.

HAPPY: What'd you do?

BIFF *(with great tension and wonder)*: Well, he left, see. And the secretary went out. I was all alone in the waiting-room. I don't know what came over me, Hap. The next thing I know I'm in his office—paneled walls, everything. I can't explain it. I—Hap, I took his fountain pen.

HAPPY: Geez, did he catch you?

BIFF: I ran out. I ran down all eleven flights. I ran and ran and ran.

HAPPY: That was an awful dumb—what'd you do that for?

BIFF (*agonized*): I don't know, I just—wanted to take something, I don't know. You gotta help me, Hap, I'm gonna tell Pop.

HAPPY: You crazy? What for?

BIFF: Hap, he's got to understand that I'm not the man somebody lends that kind of money to. He thinks I've been spiting him all these years and it's eating him up.

HAPPY: That's just it. You tell him something nice.

BIFF: I can't.

HAPPY: Say you got a lunch date with Oliver tomorrow.

BIFF: So what do I do tomorrow?

HAPPY: You leave the house tomorrow and come back at night and say Oliver is thinking it over. And he thinks it over for a couple of weeks, and gradually it fades away and nobody's the worse.

BIFF: But it'll go on forever!

HAPPY: Dad is never so happy as when he's looking forward to something!

(*Willy enters*)

HAPPY: Hello, scout!

WILLY: Gee, I haven't been here in years!

(*Stanley has followed Willy in and sets a chair for him. Stanley starts off but Happy stops him.*)

HAPPY: Stanley!

(*Stanley stands by, waiting for an order*)

BIFF (*going to Willy with guilt, as to an invalid*): Sit down, Pop. You want a drink?

WILLY: Sure, I don't mind.

BIFF: Let's get a load on.

WILLY: You look worried.

BIFF: N-no. (*To Stanley*) Scotch all around. Make it doubles.

STANLEY: Doubles, right. (*He goes*)

WILLY: You had a couple already, didn't you?

BIFF: Just a couple, yeah.

WILLY: Well, what happened, boy? (*Nodding affirmatively, with a smile*) Everything go all right?

BIFF (*takes a breath, then reaches out and grasps Willy's hand*): Pal . . . (*He is smiling bravely, and Willy is smiling too*) I had an experience today.

HAPPY: Terrific, Pop.

WILLY: That so? What happened?

BIFF (*high, slightly alcoholic, above the earth*): I'm going to tell you everything from first to last. It's been a strange day. (*Silence. He looks around, composes himself as best he can, but his breath keeps breaking the rhythm of his voice.*) I had to wait quite a while for him, and—

WILLY: Oliver?

BIFF: Yeah, Oliver. All day, as a matter of cold fact. And a lot of—instances— facts, Pop, facts about my life came back to me. Who was it, Pop? Who ever said I was a salesman with Oliver?

WILLY: Well, you were.

BIFF: No, Dad, I was a shipping clerk.

WILLY: But you were practically—

BIFF (*with determination*): Dad, I don't know who said it first, but I was never a salesman for Bill Oliver.

WILLY: What're you talking about?

BIFF: Let's hold on to the facts tonight, Pop. We're not going to get anywhere bullin' around. I was a shipping clerk.

WILLY (*angrily*): All right, now listen to me—

BIFF: Why don't you let me finish?

WILLY: I'm not interested in stories about the past or any crap of that kind because the woods are burning, boys, you understand? There's a big blaze going on all around. I was fired today.

BIFF (*shocked*): How could you be?

WILLY: I was fired, and I'm looking for a little good news to tell your mother, because the woman has waited and the woman has suffered. The gist of it is that I haven't got a story left in my head, Biff. So don't give me a lecture about facts and aspects. I am not interested. Now what've you got to say to me?

(*Stanley enters with three drinks. They wait until he leaves.*)

WILLY: Did you see Oliver?

BIFF: Jesus, Dad!

WILLY: You mean you didn't go up there?

HAPPY: Sure he went up there.

BIFF: I did. I—saw him. How could they fire you?

WILLY (*on the edge of his chair*): What kind of a welcome did he give you?

BIFF: He won't even let you work on commission?

WILLY: I'm out! (*Driving*) So tell me, he gave you a warm welcome?

HAPPY: Sure, Pop, sure!

BIFF (*driven*): Well, it was kind of—

WILLY: I was wondering if he'd remember you. (*To Happy*) Imagine, man doesn't see him for ten, twelve years and gives him that kind of a welcome!

HAPPY: Damn right!

BIFF (*trying to return to the offensive*): Pop, look—

WILLY: You know why he remembered you, don't you? Because you impressed him in those days.

BIFF: Let's talk quietly and get this down to the facts, huh?

WILLY (*as though Biff had been interrupting*): Well, what happened? It's great news, Biff. Did he take you into his office or'd you talk in the waiting-room?

BIFF: Well, he came in, see, and—

WILLY (*with a big smile*): What'd he say? Betcha he threw his arm around you.

BIFF: Well, he kinda—

WILLY: He's a fine man. (*To Happy*) Very hard man to see, y'know.

HAPPY (*agreeing*): Oh, I know.

WILLY (*to Biff*): Is that where you had the drinks?

BIFF: Yeah, he gave me a couple of—no, no!

HAPPY (*cutting in*): He told him my Florida idea.

WILLY: Don't interrupt. (*To Biff*) How'd he react to the Florida idea?

BIFF: Dad, will you give me a minute to explain?

WILLY: I've been waiting for you to explain since I sat down here! What happened? He took you into his office and what?

BIFF: Well—I talked. And—and he listened, see.

WILLY: Famous for the way he listens, y'know. What was his answer?

BIFF: His answer was—(*He breaks off, suddenly angry*) Dad, you're not letting me tell you what I want to tell you!

WILLY (*accusing, angered*): You didn't see him, did you?

BIFF: I did see him!

WILLY: What'd you insult him or something? You insulted him, didn't you?

BIFF: Listen, will you let me out of it, will you just let me out of it!

HAPPY: What the hell!

WILLY: Tell me what happened!

BIFF (*to Happy*): I can't talk to him!

(*A single trumpet note jars the ear. The light of green leaves stains the house, which holds the air of night and a dream. Young Bernard enters and knocks on the door of the house.*)

YOUNG BERNARD (*frantically*): Mrs. Loman, Mrs. Loman!

HAPPY: Tell him what happened!

BIFF (*to Happy*): Shut up and leave me alone!

WILLY: No, no! You had to go and flunk math!

BIFF: What math? What're you talking about?

YOUNG BERNARD: Mrs. Loman, Mrs. Loman!

(*Linda appears in the house, as of old*)

WILLY (*wildly*): Math, math, math!

BIFF: Take it easy, Pop!

YOUNG BERNARD: Mrs. Loman!

WILLY (*furiously*): If you hadn't flunked you'd've been set by now!

BIFF: Now, look, I'm gonna tell you what happened, and you're going to listen to me.

YOUNG BERNARD: Mrs. Loman!

BIFF: I waited six hours—

HAPPY: What the hell are you saying?

BIFF: I kept sending in my name but he wouldn't see me. So finally he . . . (*He continues unheard as light fades low on the restaurant*)

YOUNG BERNARD: Biff flunked math!

LINDA: No!

YOUNG BERNARD: Birnbaum flunked him! They won't graduate him!

LINDA: But they have to. He's gotta go to the university. Where is he? Biff! Biff!

YOUNG BERNARD: No, he left. He went to Grand Central.

LINDA: Grand—You mean he went to Boston!

YOUNG BERNARD: Is Uncle Willy in Boston?

LINDA: Oh, maybe Willy can talk to the teacher. Oh, the poor, poor boy!

(*Light on house area snaps out*)

BIFF (*at the table, now audible, holding up a gold fountain pen*): . . . so I'm washed up with Oliver, you understand? Are you listening to me?

WILLY (*at a loss*): Yeah, sure. If you hadn't flunked—

BIFF: Flunked what? What're you talking about?

WILLY: Don't blame everything on me! I didn't flunk math—you did! What pen?

HAPPY: That was awful dumb, Biff, a pen like that is worth—

WILLY (*seeing the pen for the first time*): You took Oliver's pen?

BIFF (*weakening*): Dad, I just explained it to you.

WILLY: You stole Bill Oliver's fountain pen?

BIFF: I didn't exactly steal it! That's just what I've been explaining to you!

HAPPY: He had it in his hand and just then Oliver walked in, so he got nervous and stuck it in his pocket!

WILLY: My God, Biff!

BIFF: I never intended to do it, Dad!

OPERATOR'S VOICE: Standish Arms, good evening!

WILLY (*shouting*): I'm not in my room!

BIFF (*frightened*): Dad, what's the matter? (*He and Happy stand up*)

OPERATOR: Ringing Mr. Loman for you!

WILLY: I'm not there, stop it!

BIFF (*horrified, gets down on one knee before Willy*): Dad I'll make good, I'll make good. (*Willy tries to get to his feet. Biff holds him down*) Sit down now.

WILLY: No, you're no good, you're no good for anything.

BIFF: I am, Dad, I'll find something else, you understand? Now don't worry about anything. (*He holds up Willy's face*) Talk to me, Dad.

OPERATOR: Mr. Loman does not answer. Shall I page him?

WILLY (*attempting to stand as though to rush and silence the Operator*): No, no, no!

HAPPY: He'll strike something, Pop.

WILLY: No, no . . .

BIFF (*desperately standing over Willy*): Pop, listen! Listen to me! I'm telling you something good. Oliver talked to his partner about the Florida idea. You listening? He—he talked to his partner and he came to me . . . I'm going to be all right, you hear? Dad, listen to me, he said it was just a question of the amount?

WILLY: Then you . . . got it?

HAPPY: He's gonna be terrific, Pop!

WILLY (*trying to stand*): Then you got it, haven't you? You got it! You got it!

BIFF (*agonized holds Willy down*): No, no. Look, Pop. I'm supposed to have lunch with them tomorrow. I'm just telling you this so you'll know that I can still make an impression, Pop. And I'll make good somewhere, but I can't go tomorrow, see?

WILLY: Why not? You simply—

BIFF: But the pen, Pop!

WILLY: You give it to him and tell him it was an oversight!

HAPPY: Sure, have lunch tomorrow!

BIFF: I can't say that—

WILLY: You were doing a crossword puzzle and accidentally used his pen!

BIFF: Listen, kid, I took those balls years ago, now I walk in with his fountain pen? That clinches it, don't you see? I can't face him like that! I'll try elsewhere.

PAGE'S VOICE: Paging Mr. Loman!

WILLY: Don't you want to be anything?

BIFF: Pop, how can I go back?

WILLY: You don't want to be anything, is that what's behind it?

BIFF (*now angry at Willy for not crediting his sympathy*): Don't take it that way! You think it was easy walking into that office after what I'd done to him? A team of horses couldn't have dragged me back to Bill Oliver!

WILLY: Then why'd you go?

BIFF: Why did I go? Why did I go! Look at you! Look at what's become of you!

(*Off left, The Woman laughs*)

WILLY: Biff, you're going to go to that lunch tomorrow, or—

BIFF: I can't go. I've got no appointment!

HAPPY: Biff, for . . . !

WILLY: Are you spiting me?

BIFF: Don't take it that way! Goddammit!

WILLY (*strikes Biff and falters away from the table*): You rotten little louse! Are you spiting me?

THE WOMAN: Someone's at the door, Willy!

BIFF: I'm no good, can't you see what I am?

HAPPY (*separating them*): Hey, you're in a restaurant! Now cut it out, both of you? (*The girls enter*) Hello, girls, sit down.

(*The Woman laughs, off left*)

MISS FORSYTHE: I guess we might as well. This is Letta.

THE WOMAN: Willy, are you going to wake up?

BIFF (*ignoring Willy*): How're ya, miss, sit down. What do you drink?

MISS FORSYTHE: Letta might not be able to stay long.

LETTA: I gotta get up very early tomorrow. I got jury duty. I'm so excited! Were you fellows ever on a jury?

BIFF: No, but I been in front of them! (*The girls laugh*) This is my father.

LETTA: Isn't he cute? Sit down with us, Pop.

HAPPY: Sit him down, Biff!

BIFF (*going to him*): Come on, slugger, drink us under the table. To hell with it! Come on, sit down pal.

(*On Biff's last insistence, Willy is about to sit*)

THE WOMAN (*now urgently*): Willy, are you going to answer the door!

(*The Woman's call pulls Willy back. He starts right, befuddled.*)

BIFF: Hey, where are you going?

WILLY: Open the door.

BIFF: The door?

WILLY: The washroom . . . the door . . . where's the door?

BIFF (*leading Willy to the left*): Just go straight down.

(*Willy moves left*)

THE WOMAN: Willy, Willy, are you going to get up, get up, get up, get up?

(*Willy exits left*)

LETTA: I think it's sweet you bring your daddy along.

MISS FORSYTHE: Oh, he isn't really your father!

BIFF (*at left, turning to her resentfully*): Miss Forsythe, you've just seen a prince walk by. A fine troubled prince. A hardworking, unappreciated prince. A pal, you understand? A good companion. Always for his boys.

LETTA: That's so sweet.

HAPPY: Well, girls, what's the program? We're wasting time. Come on, Biff. Gather round. Where would you like to go?

BIFF: Why don't you do something for him?

HAPPY: Me!

BIFF: Don't you give a damn for him, Hap?

HAPPY: What're you talking about? I'm the one who—

BIFF: I sense it, you don't give a good goddam about him. (*He takes the rolled-up hose from his pocket and puts it on the table in front of Happy*) Look what I found in the cellar, for Christ's sake. How can you bear to let it go on?

HAPPY: Me? Who goes away? Who runs off and—

BIFF: Yeah but he doesn't mean anything to you. You could help him—I can't! Don't you understand what I'm talking about? He's going to kill himself, don't you know that?

HAPPY: Don't I know it! Me!

BIFF: Hap, help him! Jesus . . . help him . . . Help me, help me, I can't bear to look at his face! (*Ready to weep, he hurries out, up right*)

HAPPY (*starting after him*): Where are you going?

MISS FORSYTHE: What's he so mad about?

HAPPY: Come on, girls, we'll catch up with him.

MISS FORSYTHE (*as Happy pushes her out*): Say, I don't like that temper of his!

HAPPY: He's just a little overstrung, he'll be all right!

WILLY (*off left, as The Woman laughs*): Don't answer! Don't answer!

LETTA: Don't you want to tell your father—

HAPPY: No, that's not my father. He's just a guy. Come on, we'll catch Biff, and, honey, we're going to paint this town! Stanley, where's the check! Hey, Stanley!

(*They exit. Stanley looks toward left*)

STANLEY (*calling to Happy indignantly*): Mr. Loman! Mr. Loman!

(*Stanley picks up a chair and follows them off. Knocking is heard off left. The Woman enters, laughing. Willy follows her. She is in a black slip; he is buttoning his shirt. Raw, sensuous music accompanies their speech.*)

WILLY: Will you stop laughing? Will you stop?

THE WOMAN: Aren't you going to answer the door? He'll wake the whole hotel.

WILLY: I'm not expecting anybody.

THE WOMAN: Whyn't you have another drink, honey, and stop being so damn self-centered?

WILLY: I'm so lonely.

THE WOMAN: You know you ruined me, Willy? From now on, whenever you come to the office, I'll see that you go right through to the buyers. No waiting at my desk any more, Willy. You ruined me.

WILLY: That's nice of you to say that.

THE WOMAN: Gee, you are self-centered! Why so sad? You are the saddest self-centeredest soul I ever did see-saw. *(She laughs. He kisses her.)* Come on inside, drummer boy. It's silly to be dressing in the middle of the night. *(As knocking is heard)* Aren't you going to answer the door?

WILLY: They're knocking on the wrong door.

THE WOMAN: But I felt the knocking. And he heard us talking in here. Maybe the hotel's on fire!

WILLY *(his terror rising)*: It's a mistake.

THE WOMAN: Then tell him to go away!

WILLY: There's nobody there.

THE WOMAN: It's getting on my nerves, Willy. There's somebody standing out there and it's getting on my nerves!

WILLY *(pushing her away from him)*: All right, stay in the bathroom here, and don't come out. I think there's a law in Massachusetts about it, so don't come out. It may be that new room clerk. He looked very mean. So don't come out. It's a mistake, there's no fire.

(The knocking is heard again. He takes a few steps away from her, and she vanishes into the wing. The light follows him and now he is facing Young Biff, who carries a suitcase. Biff steps toward him. The music is gone.)

BIFF: Why didn't you answer?

WILLY: Biff! What are you doing in Boston?

BIFF: Why didn't you answer? I've been knocking for five minutes, I called you on the phone—

WILLY: I just heard you. I was in the bathroom and had the door shut. Did anything happen home?

BIFF: Dad—I let you down.

WILLY: What do you mean?

BIFF: Dad . . .

WILLY: Biffo, what's this about. *(Putting his arm around Biff)* Come on, let's go downstairs and get you a malted.

BIFF: Dad, I flunked math.

WILLY: Not for the term?

BIFF: The term. I haven't got enough credits to graduate.

WILLY: You mean to say Bernard wouldn't give you the answers?

BIFF: He did, he tried, but I only got a sixty-one.

WILLY: And they wouldn't give you four points?

BIFF: Birnbaum refused absolutely. I begged him, Pop, but he won't give me those points. You gotta talk to him before they close the school. Because if he saw the kind of man you are, and you just talked to him in your way, I'm sure he'd come through for me. The class came right before practice, see, and I didn't go enough. Would you talk to him? He'd like you, Pop. You know the way you could talk.

WILLY: You're on. We'll drive right back.

BIFF: Oh, Dad, good work! I'm sure he'll change it for you!

WILLY: Go downstairs and tell the clerk I'm checkin' out. Go right down.

BIFF: Yes, sir! See the reason he hates me, Pop—one day he was late for class so I got up at the blackboard and imitated him. I crossed my eyes and talked with a lithp.

WILLY (*laughing*): You did? The kids like it?

BIFF: They nearly died laughing!

WILLY: Yeah? What'd you do?

BIFF: The thquare root of thixthy twee is . . . (*Willy bursts out laughing; Biff joins him*) And in the middle of it he walked in!

(*Willy laughs and The Woman joins in offstage*)

WILLY (*without hesitation*): Hurry downstairs and—

BIFF: Somebody in there?

WILLY: No, that was next door.

(*The Woman laughs offstage*)

BIFF: Somebody got in your bathroom!

WILLY: No, it's the next room, there's a party—

THE WOMAN (*enters laughing. She lisps this*): Can I come in? There's something in the bathtub, Willy, and it's moving!

(*Willy looks at Biff, who is staring open-mouthed and horrified at The Woman*)

WILLY: Ah—you better go back to your room. They must be finished painting by now. They're painting her room so I let her take a shower here. Go back, go back . . . (*He pushes her*)

THE WOMAN (*resisting*): But I've got to get dressed, Willy, I can't—

WILLY: Get out of here! Go back, go back . . . (*Suddenly striving for the ordinary*) This is Miss Francis, Biff, she's a buyer. They're painting her room. Go back, Miss Francis, go back . . .

THE WOMAN: But my clothes, I can't go out naked in the hall!

WILLY (*pushing her offstage*): Get outa here! Go back, go back!

(*Biff slowly sits down on his suitcase as the argument continues offstage*)

THE WOMAN: Where's my stockings? You promised me stockings, Willy!

WILLY: I have no stockings here!

THE WOMAN: You had two boxes of size nine sheers for me, and I want them!

WILLY: Here, for God's sake, will you get outa here!

THE WOMAN (*enters holding a box of stockings*): I just hope there's nobody in the hall. That's all I hope. (*To Biff*) Are you football or baseball?

BIFF: Football.

THE WOMAN (*angry, humiliated*): That's me too. G'night. (*She snatches her clothes from Willy, and walks out*)

WILLY (*after a pause*): Well, better get going. I want to get to the school first thing in the morning. Get my suits out of the closet. I'll get my valise. (*Biff doesn't move*) What's the matter? (*Biff remains motionless, tears falling*) She's a buyer. Buys for J. H. Simmons. She lives down the hall—they're painting. You don't imagine— (*He breaks off. After a pause*) Now listen, pal, she's just a buyer. She sees merchandise in her room and they have to keep it looking just so . . . (*Pause. Assuming command*) All right, get my suits. (*Biff doesn't move*) Now stop crying and do as I say. I gave you an order. Biff, I gave you an order! Is that what you do when I give you an order? How dare you cry! (*Putting his arm around Biff*) Now look, Biff, when you grow up you'll understand about these things. You mustn't—you mustn't overemphasize a thing like this. I'll see Birnbaum first thing in the morning.

BIFF: Never mind.

WILLY (*getting down beside Biff*): Never mind! He's going to give you those points. I'll see to it.

BIFF: He wouldn't listen to you.

WILLY: He certainly will listen to me. You need those points for the U. of Virginia.

BIFF: I'm not going there.

WILLY: Heh? If I can't get him to change that mark you'll make it up in summer school. You've got all summer to—

BIFF (*his weeping breaking from him*): Dad . . .

WILLY (*infected by it*): Oh, my boy . . .

BIFF: Dad . . .

WILLY: She's nothing to me, Biff. I was lonely, I was terribly lonely.

BIFF: You—you gave her Mama's stockings! (*His tears break through and he rises to go*)

WILLY (*grabbing for Biff*): I gave you an order!

BIFF: Don't touch me, you—liar!

WILLY: Apologize for that!

BIFF: You fake! You phony little fake! You fake! (*Overcome, he turns quickly and weeping fully goes out with his suitcase. Willy is left on the floor on his knees*)

WILLY: I gave you an order! Biff, come back here or I'll beat you! Come back here! I'll whip you!

(*Stanley comes quickly in from the right and stands in front of Willy*)

WILLY (*shouts at Stanley*): I gave you an order . . .

STANLEY: Hey, let's pick it up, pick it up, Mr. Loman. (*He helps Willy to his feet*) Your boys left with the chippies. They said they'll see you home.

(*A second waiter watches some distance away*)

WILLY: But we were supposed to have dinner together.

(*Music is heard, Willy's theme*)

STANLEY: Can you make it?

WILLY: I'll—sure, I can make it. (*Suddenly concerned about his clothes*) Do I—I look all right?

STANLEY: Sure, you look all right. (*He flicks a speck off Willy's lapel*)

WILLY: Here—here's a dollar.

STANLEY: Oh, your son paid me. It's all right.

WILLY (*putting it in Stanley's hand*): No, take it. You're a good boy.

STANLEY: Oh, no, you don't have to . . .

WILLY: Here—here's some more, I don't need it any more. (*After a slight pause*) Tell me—is there a seed store in the neighborhood?

STANLEY: Seeds? You mean like to plant?

(*As Willy turns, Stanley slips the money back into his jacket pocket*)

WILLY: Yes. Carrots, peas . . .

STANLEY: Well, there's hardware stores on Sixth Avenue, but it may be too late now.

WILLY (*anxiously*): Oh, I'd better hurry. I've got to get some seeds. (*He starts off to the right*) I've got to get some seeds, right away. Nothing's planted. I don't have a thing in the ground.

(*Willy hurries out as the light goes down. Stanley moves over to the right after him, watches him off. The other waiter has been staring at Willy.*)

STANLEY (*to the waiter*): Well, whatta you looking at?

(*The waiter picks up the chairs and moves off right. Stanley takes the table and follows him. The light fades on this area. There is a long pause, the sound of the flute coming over. The light gradually rises on the kitchen, which is empty. Happy appears at the door of the house, followed by Biff. Happy is carrying a large bunch of long-stemmed roses. He enters the kitchen, looks around for Linda. Not seeing her, he turns to Biff, who is just outside the house door, and makes a gesture with his hands, indicating "Not here, I guess." He looks into the living-room and freezes. Inside, Linda, unseen, is seated, Willy's coat on her lap. She rises ominously and quietly and moves toward Happy, who backs up into the kitchen, afraid.*)

HAPPY: Hey, what're you doing up? (*Linda says nothing but moves toward him implacably*) Where's Pop? (*He keeps backing to the right, and now Linda is in full view in the doorway to the living-room*) Is he sleeping?

LINDA: Where were you?

HAPPY (*trying to laugh it off*): We met two girls, Mom, very fine types. Here, we brought you some flowers. (*Offering them to her*) Put them in your room, Ma.

(*She knocks them to the floor at Biff's feet. He has now come inside and closed the door behind him. She stares at Biff, silent.*)

HAPPY: Now what'd you do that for? Mom, I want you to have some flowers—

LINDA (*cutting Happy off, violently to Biff*): Don't you care whether he lives or dies?

HAPPY (*going to the stairs*): Come upstairs, Biff.

BIFF (*with a flare of disgust, to Happy*): Go away from me! (*To Linda*) What do you mean, lives or dies? Nobody's dying around here, pal.

LINDA: Get out of my sight! Get out of here!

BIFF: I wanna see the boss.

LINDA: You're not going near him!

BIFF: Where is he? (*He moves into the living-room and Linda follows*)

LINDA (*shouting after Biff*): You invite him for dinner. He looks forward to it all day— (*Biff appears in his parents' bedroom, looks around, and exits*)—and then you desert him there. There's no stranger you'd do that to!

HAPPY: Why? He had a swell time with us. Listen, when I— (*Linda comes back into the kitchen*)—desert him I hope I don't outlive the day!

LINDA: Get out of here!

HAPPY: Now look, Mom . . .

LINDA: Did you have to go to women tonight? You and your lousy rotten whores!

(*Biff re-enters the kitchen*)

HAPPY: Mom, all we did was follow Biff around trying to cheer him up! (*To Biff*) Boy, what a night you gave me!

LINDA: Get out of here, both of you, and don't come back! I don't want you tormenting him any more. Go on now, get your things together! *(To Biff)* You can sleep in his apartment. *(She starts to pick up the flowers and stops herself)* Pick up this stuff, I'm not your maid any more. Pick it up, you bum, you!

(Happy turns his back to her in refusal. Biff slowly moves over and gets down on his knees, picking up the flowers.)

LINDA: You're a pair of animals! Not one, not another living soul would have had the cruelty to walk out on that man in a restaurant!

BIFF *(not looking at her)*: Is that what he said?

LINDA: He didn't have to say anything. He was so humiliated he nearly limped when he came in.

HAPPY: But, Mom, he had a great time with us—

BIFF *(cutting him off violently)*: Shut up!

(Without another word, Happy goes upstairs)

LINDA: You! You didn't even go in to see if he was all right!

BIFF *(still on the floor in front of Linda, the flowers in his hand; with self-loathing)*: No. Didn't. Didn't do a damned thing. How do you like that, heh? Left him babbling in a toilet.

LINDA: You louse. You . . .

BIFF: Now you hit it on the nose! *(He gets up, throws the flowers in the wastebasket)* The scum of the earth, and you're looking at him!

LINDA: Get out of here!

BIFF: I gotta talk to the boss, Mom. Where is he?

LINDA: You're not going near him. Get out of this house!

BIFF *(with absolute assurance, determination)*: No. We're gonna have an abrupt conversation, him and me.

LINDA: You're not talking to him!

(Hammering is heard from outside the house, off right. Biff turns toward the noise.)

LINDA *(suddenly pleading)*: Will you please leave him alone?

BIFF: What's he doing out there?

LINDA: He's planting the garden!

BIFF *(quietly)*: Now? Oh, my God!

(Biff moves outside, Linda following. The light dies down on them and comes up on the center of the apron as Willy walks into it. He is carrying a flashlight, a hoe, and a handful of seed packets. He raps the top of the hoe sharply to fix it firmly, and then moves to the left, measuring off the distance with his foot. He tolds the flashlight to look at the seed packets, reading off the instructions. He is in the blue of night.)

WILLY: Carrots . . . quarter-inch apart. Rows . . . one-foot rows. *(He measures it off)* One foot. *(He puts down a package and measures off)* Beets. *(He puts down another package and measures again)* Lettuce. *(He reads the package, puts it down)* One foot— *(He breaks off as Ben appears at the right and moves slowly down to him)* What a proposition, ts, ts. Terrific, terrific. 'Cause she's suffered, Ben, the woman has suffered. You understand me? A man can't go out the way he came in, Ben, a man has got to add up to something. You can't, you can't—

(Ben moves toward him as though to interrupt) You gotta consider, now. Don't answer so quick. Remember, it's a guaranteed twenty-thousand-dollar proposition. Now look, Ben, I want you to go through the ins and outs of this thing with me. I've got nobody to talk to, Ben, and the woman has suffered, you hear me?

BEN *(standing still, considering):* What's the proposition?

WILLY: It's twenty thousand dollars on the barrelhead. Guaranteed, gilt-edged, you understand?

BEN: You don't want to make a fool of yourself. They might not honor the policy.

WILLY: How can they dare refuse? Didn't I work like a coolie to meet every premium on the nose? And now they don't pay off! Impossible!

BEN: It's called a cowardly thing, William.

WILLY: Why? Does it take more guts to stand here the rest of my life ringing up a zero?

BEN *(yielding):* That's a point, William. *(He moves, thinking, turns)* And twenty thousand—that *is* something one can feel with the hand, it is there.

WILLY *(now assured, with rising power):* Oh, Ben, that's the whole beauty of it! I see it like a diamond, shining in the dark, hard and rough, that I can pick up and touch in my hand. Not like—like an appointment! This would not be another damned-fool appointment, Ben, and it changes all the aspects. Because he thinks I'm nothing, see, and so he spites me. But the funeral— *(Straightening up)* Ben, that funeral will be massive! They'll come from Maine, Massachusetts, Vermont, New Hampshire! All the old-timers with the strange license plates—that boy will be thunder-struck, Ben, because he never realized—I am known! Rhode Island, New York, New Jersey—I am known, Ben, and he'll see it with his eyes once and for all. He'll see what I am, Ben! He's in for a shock, that boy!

BEN *(coming down to the edge of the garden):* He'll call you a coward.

WILLY *(suddenly fearful):* No, that would be terrible.

BEN: Yes. And a damned fool.

WILLY: No, no, he mustn't, I won't have that! *(He is broken and desperate)*

BEN: He'll hate you, William.

(The gay music of the Boys is heard)

WILLY: Oh Ben, how do we get back to all the great times! Used to be so full of light, and comradeship, the sleigh-riding in winter, and the ruddiness on his cheeks. And always some kind of good news coming up, always something nice coming up ahead. And never even let me carry the valises in the house, and simonizing, simonizing that little red car! Why, why can't I give him something and not have him hate me?

BEN *(Let me think about it):* He glances at his watch. I still have a little time. Remarkable proposition but you've got to be sure you're not making a fool of yourself.

(Ben drifts off upstage and goes out of sight. Biff comes down from the left.)

WILLY *(suddenly conscious of Biff, turns and looks up at him, then begins picking up the packages of seeds in confusion):* Where the hell is that seed? *(Indignantly)* You can't see nothing out here! They boxed in the whole goddam neighborhood!

BIFF: There are people all around here. Don't you realize that?

WILLY: I'm busy. Don't bother me.

BIFF (*taking the hoe from Willy*): I'm saying good-by to you Pop. (*Willy looks at him silent unable to move*) I'm not coming back any more.

WILLY: You're not going to see Oliver tomorrow?

BIFF: I've got no appointment Dad.

WILLY: He put his arm around you, and you've got no appointment?

BIFF: Pop get this now, will you? Everytime I've left it's been a fight that sent me out of here. Today I realized something about myself and I tried to explain it to you and I—I think I'm just not smart enough to make any sense out of it for you. To hell with whose fault it is or anything like that. (*He takes Willy's arm*) Let's just wrap it up, heh? Come on in, we'll tell Mom. (*He gently tries to pull Willy to left*)

WILLY (*frozen immobile with guilt in his voice*): No, I don't want to see her.

BIFF: Come on! (*He pulls again, and Willy tries to pull away*)

WILLY (*highly nervous*): No, no, I don't want to see her.

BIFF (*tries to look into Willy's face, as if to find the answer there*): Why don't you want to see her?

WILLY (*more harshly now*): Don't bother me, will you?

BIFF: What do you mean, you don't want to see her? You don't want them calling you yellow, do you? This isn't your fault; it's me, I'm a bum. Now come inside! (*Willy strains to get away*) Did you hear what I said to you?

(*Willy pulls away and quickly goes by himself into the house. Biff follows*)

LINDA (*to Willy*): Did you plant dear?

BIFF (*at the door to Linda*): All right, we had it out. I'm going and I'm not writing any more.

LINDA (*going to Willy in the kitchen*): I think that's the best way, dear. 'Cause there's no use drawing it out, you'll just never get along.

(*Willy doesn't respond*)

BIFF: People ask where I am and what I'm doing, you don't know, and you don't care. That way it'll be off your mind and you can start brightening up again. All right? That clears it, doesn't it? (*Willy is silent, and Biff goes to him*) You gonna wish me luck, scout? (*He extends his hand*) What do you say?

LINDA: Shake his hand, Willy.

WILLY (*turning to her, seething with hurt*): There's no necessity to mention the pen at all, y'know.

BIFF (*gently*): I've got no appointment, Dad.

WILLY (*erupting fiercely*): He put his arm around . . . ?

BIFF: Dad you're never going to see what I am, so what's the use of arguing? If I strike oil I'll send you a check. Meantime forget I'm alive.

WILLY (*to Linda*): Spite, see?

BIFF: Shake hands, Dad.

WILLY: Not my hand.

BIFF: I was hoping not to go this way.

WILLY: Well this is the way you're going. Good-by.

(*Biff looks at him a moment, then turns sharply and goes to the stairs*)

WILLY (*stops him with*): May you rot in hell if you leave this house!

BIFF (*turning*): Exactly what is it that you want from me?

WILLY: I want you to know, on the train, in the mountains, in the valleys, wherever you go, that you cut down your life for spite!

BIFF: No, no.

WILLY: Spite, spite, is the word of your undoing! And when you're down and out, remember what did it. When you're rotting somewhere beside the railroad tracks, remember, and don't you dare blame it on me!

BIFF: I'm not blaming it on you!

WILLY: I won't take the rap for this, you hear?

(*Happy comes down the stairs and stands on the bottom step, watching*)

BIFF: That's just what I'm telling you!

WILLY (*sinking into a chair at the table, with full accusation*): You're trying to put a knife in me—don't think I don't know what you're doing!

BIFF: All right, phony! Then let's lay it on the line. (*He whips the rubber tube out of his pocket and puts it on the table*)

HAPPY: You crazy—

LINDA: Biff! (*She moves to grab the hose, but Biff holds it down with his hand*)

BIFF: Leave it there! Don't move it!

WILLY (*not looking at it*): What is that?

BIFF: You know goddam well what that is.

WILLY (*caged wanting to escape*): I never saw that.

BIFF: You saw it. The mice didn't bring it into the cellar! What is this supposed to do, make a hero out of you? This supposed to make me sorry for you?

WILLY: Never heard of it.

BIFF: There'll be no pity for you, you hear it? No pity!

WILLY (*to Linda*): You hear the spite!

BIFF: No, you're going to hear the truth—what you are and what I am!

LINDA: Stop it!

WILLY: Spite!

HAPPY (*coming down toward Biff*): You cut it now!

BIFF (*to Happy*): The man don't know who we are! The man is gonna know! (*To Willy*) We never told the truth for ten minutes in this house!

HAPPY: We always told the truth!

BIFF (*turning on him*): You big blow, are you the assistant buyer? You're one of the two assistants to the assistant, aren't you?

HAPPY: Well I'm practically—

BIFF: You're practically full of it! We all are! And I'm through with it. (*To Willy*) Now hear this, Willy, this is me.

WILLY: I know you!

BIFF: You know why I had no address for three months? I stole a suit in Kansas City and I was in jail. (*To Linda who is sobbing*) Stop crying. I'm through with it.

(*Linda turns away from them, her hands covering her face*)

WILLY: I suppose that's my fault!

BIFF: I stole myself out of every good job since high school!

WILLY: And whose fault is that?

BIFF: And I never got anywhere because you blew me so full of hot air I could never stand taking orders from anybody! That's whose fault it is!

WILLY: I hear that!

LINDA: Don't Biff!

BIFF: It's goddam time you heard that! I had to be boss big shot in two weeks, and I'm through with it!

WILLY: Then hang yourself! For spite, hang yourself!

BIFF: No! Nobody's hanging himself, Willy! I ran down eleven flights with a pen in my hand today. And suddenly I stopped, you hear me? And in the middle of that office building, do you hear this? I stopped in the middle of that building and I saw—the sky. I saw the things that I love in this world. The work and the food and time to sit and smoke. And I looked at the pen and said to myself, what the hell am I grabbing this for? Why am I trying to become what I don't want to be? What am I doing in an office, making a contemptuous, begging fool of myself, when all I want is out there, waiting for me the minute I say I know who I am! Why can't I say that Willy? (*He tries to make Willy face him, but Willy pulls away and moves to the left*)

WILLY (*with hatred, threateningly*): The door of your life is wide open!

BIFF: Pop! I'm a dime a dozen, and so are you!

WILLY (*turning on him now in an uncontrolled outburst*): I am not a dime a dozen! I am Willy Loman, and you are Biff Loman!

(*Biff starts for Willy, but is blocked by Happy. In his fury, Biff seems on the verge of attacking his father.*)

BIFF: I am not a leader of men, Willy, and neither are you. You were never anything but a hard-working drummer who landed in the ash can like all the rest of them! I'm one dollar an hour, Willy! I tried seven states and couldn't raise it. A buck an hour! Do you gather my meaning? I'm not bringing home any prizes any more, and you're going to stop waiting for me to bring them home!

WILLY (*directly to Biff*): You vengeful spiteful mutt!

(*Biff breaks from Happy. Willy, in fright, starts up the stairs. Biff grabs him.*)

BIFF (*at the peak of his fury*): Pop I'm nothing! I'm nothing Pop. Can't you understand that? There's no spite in it any more. I'm just what I am, that's all.

(*Biff's fury has spent itself, and he breaks down, sobbing, holding on to Willy, who dumbly fumbles for Biff's face*)

WILLY (*astonished*): What're you doing? What're you doing? (*To Linda*) Why is he crying?

BIFF (*crying, broken*): Will you let me go, for Christ's sake? Will you take that phony dream and burn it before something happens? (*Struggling to contain himself, he pulls away and moves to the stairs*) I'll go in the morning. Put him—put him to bed. (*Exhausted, Biff moves up the stairs to his room*)

WILLY (*after a long pause, astonished, elevated*): Isn't that—isn't that remarkable? Biff—he likes me!

LINDA: He loves you Willy!

HAPPY (*deeply moved*): Always did, Pop.

WILLY: Oh Biff! (*Staring wildly*) He cried! Cried to me. (*He is choking with his love, and now cries out his promise*) That boy—that boy is going to be magnificent!

(Ben appears in the light just outside the kitchen)

BEN: Yes, outstanding, with twenty thousand behind him.

LINDA *(sensing the racing of his mind, fearfully, carefully)*: Now come to bed, Willy. It's all settled now.

WILLY *(finding it difficult not to rush out of the house)*: Yes, we'll sleep. Come on. Go to sleep, Hap.

BEN: And it does take a great kind of a man to crack the jungle.

(In accents of dread, Ben's idyllic music starts up)

HAPPY *(his arm around Linda)*: I'm getting married, Pop, don't forget it. I'm changing everything. I'm gonna run that department before the year is up. You'll see, Mom. *(He kisses her)*

BEN: The jungle is dark but full of diamonds, Willy.

(Willy turns, moves, listening to Ben)

LINDA: Be good. You're both good boys, just act that way, that's all.

HAPPY: 'Night Pop. *(He goes upstairs)*

LINDA *(to Willy)*: Come dear.

BEN *(with greater force)*: One must go in to fetch a diamond out.

WILLY *(to Linda, as he moves slowly along the edge of the kitchen, toward the door)*: I just want to get settled down, Linda. Let me sit alone for a little.

LINDA *(almost uttering her fear)*: I want you upstairs.

WILLY *(taking her in his arms)*: In a few minutes, Linda. I couldn't sleep right now. Go on, you look awful tired. *(He kisses her)*

BEN: Not like an appointment at all. A diamond is rough and hard to the touch.

WILLY: Go on now. I'll be right up.

LINDA: I think this is the only way, Willy.

WILLY: Sure it's the best thing.

BEN: Best thing!

WILLY: The only way. Everything is gonna be—go on kid, get to bed. You look so tired.

LINDA: Come right up.

WILLY: Two minutes.

(Linda goes into the living-room, then reappears in her bedroom. Willy moves just outside the kitchen door.)

WILLY: Loves me. *(Wonderingly)* Always loved me. Isn't that a remarkable thing? Ben, he'll worship me for it!

BEN *(with promise)*: It's dark there, but full of diamonds.

WILLY: Can you imagine that magnificence with twenty thousand dollars in his pocket?

LINDA *(calling from her room)*: Willy! Come up!

WILLY *(calling into the kitchen)*: Yes! Yes. Coming! It's very smart, you realize that, don't you, sweetheart? Even Ben sees it. I gotta go baby. 'By! 'By! *(Going over to Ben almost dancing)* Imagine? When the mail comes he'll be ahead of Bernard again!

BEN: A perfect proposition all around.

WILLY: Did you see how he cried to me? Oh, if I could kiss him, Ben!

BEN: Time, William, time!

WILLY: Oh, Ben, I always knew one way or another we were gonna make it, Biff and I!

BEN (*looking at his watch*): The boat. We'll be late. (*He moves slowly off into the darkness*)

WILLY (*elegiacally, turning to the house*): Now when you kick off, boy, I want a seventy-yard boot, and get right down the field under the ball, and when you hit, hit low and hit hard, because it's important, boy. (*He swings around and faces the audience*) There's all kinds of important people in the stands, and the first thing you know ... (*Suddenly realizing he is alone*) Ben! Ben, where do I ...? (*He makes a sudden movement of search*) Ben, how do I ...?

LINDA (*calling*): Willy, you coming up?

WILLY (*uttering a gasp of fear, whirling about as if to quiet her*): Sh! (*He turns around as if to find his way; sounds, faces, voices, seem to be swarming in upon him and he flicks at them, crying*) Sh! Sh! (*Suddenly music, faint and high, stops him. It rises in intensity, almost to an unbearable scream. He goes up and down on his toes, and rushes off around the house.*) Shhh!

LINDA: Willy?

(*There is no answer. Linda waits. Biff gets up off his bed. He is still in his clothes. Happy sits up. Biff stands listening.*)

LINDA (*with real fear*): Willy, answer me! Willy!

(*There is the sound of a car starting and moving away at full speed*)

LINDA: No!

BIFF (*rushing down the stairs*): Pop!

(*As the car speeds off, the music crashes down in a frenzy of sound, which becomes the soft pulsation of a single cello string. Biff slowly returns to his bedroom. He and Happy gravely don their jackets. Linda slowly walks out of her room. The music has developed into a dead march. The leaves of day are appearing over everything. Charley and Bernard, somberly dressed, appear and knock on the kitchen door. Biff and Happy slowly descend the stairs to the kitchen as Charley and Bernard enter. All stop a moment when Linda, in clothes of mourning, bearing a little bunch of roses, comes through the draped doorway into the kitchen. She goes to Charley and takes his arm. Now all move toward the audience, through the wall-line of the kitchen. At the limit of the apron, Linda lays down the flowers, kneels, and sits back on her heels. All stare down at the grave.*)

Requiem

CHARLEY: It's getting dark, Linda.

(*Linda doesn't react. She stares at the grave.*)

BIFF: How about it, Mom? Better get some rest, heh? They'll be closing the gate soon.

(*Linda makes no move. Pause.*)

HAPPY (*deeply angered*): He had no right to do that. There was no necessity for it. We would've helped him.

CHARLEY (*grunting*): Hmmm.

BIFF: Come along, Mom.

LINDA: Why didn't anybody come?

CHARLEY: It was a very nice funeral.

LINDA: But where are all the people he knew? Maybe they blame him.

CHARLEY: Naa. It's a rough world, Linda. They wouldn't blame him.

LINDA: I can't understand it. At this time especially. First time in thirty-five years we were just about free and clear. He only needed a little salary. He was even finished with the dentist.

CHARLEY: No man only needs a little salary.

LINDA: I can't understand it.

BIFF: There were a lot of nice days. When he'd come home from a trip; or on Sundays, making the stoop; finishing the cellar; putting on the new porch; when he built the extra bathroom; and put up the garage. You know something, Charley, there's more of him in that front stoop than in all the sales he ever made.

CHARLEY: Yeah. He was a happy man with a batch of cement.

LINDA: He was so wonderful with his hands.

BIFF: He had the wrong dreams. All, all, wrong.

HAPPY (*almost ready to fight Biff*): Don't say that!

BIFF: He never knew who he was.

CHARLEY (*stopping Happy's movement and reply. To Biff*): Nobody dast blame this man. You don't understand: Willy was a salesman. And for a salesman, there is no rock bottom to the life. He don't put a bolt to a nut, he don't tell you the law or give you medicine. He's a man way out there in the blue, riding on a smile and a shoeshine. And when they start not smiling back—that's an earthquake. And then you get yourself a couple of spots on your hat, and you're finished. Nobody dast blame this man. A salesman is got to dream, boy. It comes with the territory.

BIFF: Charley, the man didn't know who he was.

HAPPY (*infuriated*): Don't say that!

BIFF: Why don't you come with me, Happy?

HAPPY: I'm not licked that easily. I'm staying right in this city, and I'm gonna beat this racket! (*He looks at Biff, his chin set*) The Loman Brothers!

BIFF: I know who I am, kid.

HAPPY: All right, boy. I'm gonna show you and everybody else that Willy Loman did not die in vain. He had a good dream. It's the only dream you can have—to come out number-one man. He fought it out here, and this is where I'm gonna win it for him.

BIFF (*with a hopeless glance at Happy, bends toward his mother*): Let's go, Mom.

LINDA: I'll be with you in a minute. Go on, Charley. (*He hesitates*) I want to, just for a minute. I never had a chance to say good-by.

(*Charley moves away, followed by Happy. Biff remains a slight distance up and left of Linda. She sits there, summoning herself. The flute begins, not for away, playing behind her speech.*)

LINDA: Forgive me, dear. I can't cry. I don't know what it is, but I can't cry. I don't understand it. Why did you ever do that? Help me, Willy, I can't cry. It seems to me that you're just on another trip. I keep expecting you. Willy, dear,

I can't cry. Why did you do it? I search and search and I search, and I can't understand it, Willy. I made the last payment on the house today. Today, dear. And there'll be nobody home. *(A sob rises in her throat)* We're free and clear. *(Sobbing more fully, released)* We're free. *(Biff comes slowly toward her)* We're free . . . We're free . . .

(Biff lifts her to her feet and moves out up right with her in his arms. Linda sobs quietly. Bernard and Charley come together and follow them, followed by Happy. Only the music of the flute is left on the darkening stage as over the house the hard towers of the apartment buildings rise into sharp focus.)

Curtain

A Raisin in the Sun

Here we have another American family caught in a period of painful transition. Realism in setting and dialogue support a drama of family tensions that, like those of *Death of a Salesman*, mirror the tensions of society at large. Once more the play centers in a dream that is personal, but also representative; as the poem by Langston Hughes suggests, it is a dream too long deferred.

A RAISIN IN THE SUN
Lorraine Hansberry (1930–1965)

To Mama: *in gratitude for the dream*

CHARACTERS

RUTH YOUNGER
TRAVIS YOUNGER
WALTER LEE YOUNGER (BROTHER)
BENEATHA YOUNGER
LENA YOUNGER (MAMA)

JOSEPH ASAGAI
GEORGE MURCHISON
KARL LINDNER
BOBO
MOVING MEN

(The action of the play is set in Chicago's Southside, sometime between World War II and the present)

Act One
Scene 1. Friday morning
Scene 2. The following morning

Act Two
Scene 1. Later, the same day.
Scene 2. Friday night, a few weeks later.
Scene 3. Moving day, one week later.

Act Three
An hour later

What happens to a dream deferred?
Does it dry up
Like a raisin in the sun?
Or fester like a sore—
And then run?
Does it stink like rotten meat?
Or crust and sugar over—
Like a syrupy sweet?

Maybe it just sags
Like a heavy load.

Or does it explode?

Langston Hughes

Act One

Scene I

The Younger living room would be a comfortable and well ordered room if it were not for a number of indestructible contradictions to this state of being. Its furnishings are typical and undistinguished and their primary feature now is that they have clearly had to accommodate the living of too many people for too many years—and they are tired. Still, we can see that at some time, a time probably no longer remembered by the family (except perhaps for Mama), the furnishings of this room were actually selected with care and love and even hope—and brought to this apartment and arranged with taste and pride.

That was a long time ago. Now the once loved pattern of the couch upholstery has to fight to show itself from under acres of crocheted doilies and couch covers which have themselves finally come to be more important than the upholstery. And here a table or a chair has been moved to disguise the worn places in the carpet; but the carpet has fought back by showing its weariness, with depressing uniformity, elsewhere on its surface.

Weariness has, in fact, won in this room. Everything has been polished, washed, sat on, used, scrubbed too often. All pretenses but living itself have long since vanished from the very atmosphere of this room.

Moreover, a section of this room, for it is not really a room unto itself, though the landlord's lease would make it seem so, slopes backward to provide a small kitchen area, where the family prepares the meals that are eaten in the living room proper, which must also serve as dining room. The single window that has been provided for these "two" rooms is located in this kitchen area. The sole natural light the family may enjoy in the course of a day is only that which fights its way through this little window.

At left, a door leads to a bedroom which is shared by Mama and her daughter, Beneatha. At right, opposite, is a second room (which in the beginning of the life of this apartment was probably a breakfast room) which serves as a bedroom for Walter and his wife, Ruth.

Time: Sometime between World War II and the present.
Place: Chicago's Southside.

At Rise: It is morning dark in the living room. Travis is asleep on the make-down bed at center. An alarm clock sounds from within the bedroom at right, and presently Ruth enters from that room and closes the door behind her. She crosses sleepily toward the window. As she passes her sleeping son she reaches down and shakes him a little. At the window she raises the shade and a dusky Southside morning light comes in feebly. She fills a pot with water and puts it on to boil. She calls to the boy, between yawns, in a slightly muffed voice.

Ruth is about thirty. We can see that she was a pretty girl, even exceptionally so, but now it is apparent that life has been little that she expected, and disappointment has already begun to hang in her face. In a few years, before thirty-five even, she will be known among her people as a "settled woman."

She crosses to her son and gives him a good, final, rousing shake.

RUTH: Come on now, boy, it's seven thirty! *(Her son sits up at last, in a stupor of sleepiness)* I say hurry up, Travis! You ain't the only person in the world got to use a bathroom! *(The child, a sturdy, handsome little boy of ten or eleven, drags himself out of the bed and almost blindly takes his towels and "today's clothes" from drawers and a closet and goes out to the bathroom, which is in an outside hall and which is shared by another family or families on the same floor. Ruth crosses to the bedroom door at right and opens it and calls in to her husband.)* Walter Lee! . . . It's after seven thirty! Lemme see you do some waking up in there now! *(She waits)* You better get up from there, man! It's after seven thirty I tell you. *(She waits again)* All right, you just go ahead and lay there and next thing you know Travis be finished and Mr. Johnson'll be in there and you'll be fussing and cussing round here like a mad man! And be late too! *(She waits, at the end of patience)* Walter Lee—it's time for you to get up!

(She waits another second and then starts to go into the bedroom, but is apparently satisfied that her husband has begun to get up. She stops, pulls the door to, and returns to the kitchen area. She wipes her face with a moist cloth and runs her fingers through her sleep-disheveled hair in a vain effort and ties an apron around her housecoat. The bedroom door at right opens and her husband stands in the doorway in his pajamas, which are rumpled and mismated. He is a lean, intense young man in his middle thirties, inclined to quick nervous movements and erratic speech habits—and always in his voice there is a quality of indictment.)

WALTER: Is he out yet?

RUTH: What you mean *out?* He ain't hardly got in there good yet.

WALTER *(Wandering in, still more oriented to sleep than to a new day)*: Well, what was you doing all that yelling for if I can't even get in there yet? *(Stopping and thinking)* Check coming today?

RUTH: They *said* Saturday and this is just Friday and I hopes to God you ain't going to get up here first thing this morning and start talking to me 'bout no money—'cause I 'bout don't want to hear it.

WALTER: Something the matter with you this morning?

RUTH: No—I'm just sleepy as the devil. What kind of eggs you want?

WALTER: Not scrambled. *(Ruth starts to scramble eggs)* Paper come? *(Ruth points impatiently to the rolled up Tribune on the table, and he gets it and spreads it out and vaguely reads the front page)* Set off another bomb yesterday.

RUTH *(Maximum indifference)*: Did they?

WALTER *(Looking up)*: What's the matter with you?

RUTH: Ain't nothing the matter with me. And don't keep asking me that this morning.

WALTER: Ain't nobody bothering you. *(Reading the news of the day absently again)* Say Colonel McCormick is sick.

RUTH *(Affecting tea-party interest)*: Is he now? Poor thing.

WALTER *(Sighing and looking at his watch)*: Oh, me. *(He waits)* Now what is that boy doing in that bathroom all this time? He just going to have to start getting up earlier. I can't be being late to work on account of him fooling around in there.

RUTH *(Turning on him)*: Oh, no he ain't going to be getting up no earlier no such thing! It ain't his fault that he can't get to bed no earlier nights 'cause he got a bunch of crazy good-for-nothing clowns sitting up running their mouths in what is supposed to be his bedroom after ten o'clock at night. . . .

WALTER: That's what you mad about, ain't it? The things I want to talk about with my friends just couldn't be important in your mind, could they?

(He rises and finds a cigarette in her handbag on the table and crosses to the little window and looks out, smoking and deeply enjoying this first one)

RUTH *(Almost matter of factly, a complaint too automatic to deserve emphasis)*: Why you always got to smoke before you eat in the morning?

WALTER *(At the window)*: Just look at 'em down there . . . Running and racing to work . . . *(He turns and faces his wife and watches her a moment at the stove, and then, suddenly)* You look young this morning, baby.

RUTH *(Indifferently)*: Yeah?

WALTER: Just for a second—stirring them eggs. It's gone now—just for a second it was—you looked real young again. *(Then, drily)* It's gone now—you look like yourself again.

RUTH: Man, if you don't shut up and leave me alone.

WALTER *(Looking out to the street again)*: First thing a man ought to learn in life is not to make love to no colored woman first thing in the morning. You all some evil people at eight o'clock in the morning.

(Travis appears in the hall doorway, almost fully dressed and quite wide awake now, his towels and pajamas across his shoulders. He opens the door and signals for his father to make the bathroom in a hurry.)

TRAVIS *(Watching the bathroom)*: Daddy, come on!

(Walter gets his bathroom utensils and flies out to the bathroom)

RUTH: Sit down and have your breakfast, Travis.

TRAVIS: Mama, this is Friday. *(Gleefully)* Check coming tomorrow, huh?

RUTH: You get your mind off money and eat your breakfast.

TRAVIS *(Eating)*: This is the morning we supposed to bring the fifty cents to school.

RUTH: Well, I ain't got no fifty cents this morning.

TRAVIS: Teacher say we have to.

RUTH: I don't care what teacher say. I ain't got it. Eat your breakfast, Travis.

TRAVIS: I *am* eating.

RUTH: Hush up now and just eat!

(The boy gives her an exasperated look for her lack of understanding, and eats grudgingly)

TRAVIS: You think Grandmama would have it?

RUTH: No! And I want you to stop asking your grandmother for money, you hear me?

TRAVIS (*Outraged*): Gaaaleee! I don't ask her, she just gimme it sometimes!

RUTH: Travis Willard Younger—I got too much on me this morning to be—

TRAVIS: Maybe Daddy—

RUTH: *Travis!*

(*The boy hushes abruptly. They are both quiet and tense for several seconds.*)

TRAVIS (*Presently*): Could I maybe go carry some groceries in front of the supermarket for a little while after school then?

RUTH: Just hush, I said. (*Travis jabs his spoon into his cereal bowl viciously, and rests his head in anger upon his fists*) If you through eating, you can get over there and make up your bed.

(*The boy obeys stiffly and crosses the room, almost mechanically, to the bed and more or less carefully folds the covering. He carries the bedding into his mother's room and returns with his books and cap.*)

TRAVIS (*Sulking and standing apart from her unnaturally*): I'm gone.

RUTH (*Looking up from the stove to inspect him automatically*): Come here. (*He crosses to her and she studies his head*) If you don't take this comb and fix this here head, you better! (*Travis puts down his books with a great sigh of oppression, and crosses to the mirror. His mother mutters under her breath about his "slubbornness"*) 'Bout to march out of here with that head looking just like chickens slept in it! I just don't know where you get your slubborn ways . . . And get your jacket, too. Looks chilly out this morning.

TRAVIS (*With conspicuously brushed hair and jacket*): I'm gone.

RUTH: Get carfare and milk money—(*Waving one finger*)—and not a single penny for no caps, you hear me?

TRAVIS (*With sullen politeness*): Yes'm.

(*He turns in outrage to leave. His mother watches after him as in his frustration he approaches the door almost comically. When she speaks to him, her voice has become a very gentle tease.*)

RUTH (*Mocking; as she thinks he would say it*): Oh, Mama makes me so mad sometimes, I don't know what to do! (*She waits and continues to his back as he stands stock-still in front of the door*) I wouldn't kiss that woman good-bye for nothing in this world this morning! (*The boy finally turns around and rolls his eyes at her, knowing the mood has changed and he is vindicated; he does not, however, move toward her yet*) Not for nothing in this world! (*She finally laughs aloud at him and holds out her arms to him and we see that it is a way between them, very old and practiced. He crosses to her and allows her to embrace him warmly but keeps his face fixed with masculine rigidity. She holds him back from her presently and looks at him and runs her fingers over the features of his face. With utter gentleness—*) Now— whose little old angry man are you?

TRAVIS (*The masculinity and gruffness start to fade at last*): Aw gaalee—Mama . . .

RUTH (*Mimicking*): Aw-gaaaaalleeeee, Mama! (*She pushes him, with rough playfulness and finality, toward the door*) Get on out of here or you going to be late.

TRAVIS (*In the face of love, new aggressiveness*): Mama, could I *please* go carry groceries?

RUTH: Honey, it's starting to get so cold evenings.

WALTER (*Coming in from the bathroom and drawing a make-believe gun from a make-believe holster and shooting at his son*): What is it he wants to do?

RUTH: Go carry groceries after school at the supermarket.

WALTER: Well, let him go. . .

TRAVIS (*Quickly, to the ally*): I *have* to—she won't gimme the fifty cents. . .

WALTER (*To his wife only*): Why not?

RUTH (*Simply, and with flavor*): 'Cause we don't have it.

WALTER (*To Ruth only*): What you tell the boy things like that for? (*Reaching down into his pants with a rather important gesture*) Here, son—

(*He hands the boy the coin, but his eyes are directed to his wife's. Travis takes the money happily.*)

TRAVIS: Thanks, Daddy.

(*He starts out. Ruth watches both of them with murder in her eyes. Walter stands and stares back at her with defiance, and suddenly reaches into his pocket again on an afterthought.*)

WALTER (*Without even looking at his son, still staring hard at his wife*): In fact, here's another fifty cents . . . Buy yourself some fruit today—or take a taxi cab to school or something!

TRAVIS: Whoopee—

(*He leaps up and clasps his father around the middle with his legs, and they face each other in mutual appreciation; slowly Walter Lee peeks around the boy to catch the violent rays from his wife's eyes and draws his head back as if shot*)

WALTER: You better get down now—and get to school, man.

TRAVIS (*At the door*): O.K. Good-bye.

(*He exits*)

WALTER (*After him, pointing with pride*): That's my boy. (*She looks at him in disgust and turns back to her work*) You know what I was thinking 'bout in the bathroom this morning?

RUTH: No.

WALTER: How come you always try to be so pleasant!

RUTH: What is there to be pleasant 'bout!

WALTER: You want to know what I was thinking 'bout in the bathroom or not!

RUTH: I know what you was thinking 'bout.

WALTER (*Ignoring her*): 'Bout what me and Willy Harris was talking about last night.

RUTH (*Immediately—a refrain*): Willy Harris is a good-for-nothing loud mouth.

WALTER: Anybody who talks to me has got to be a good-for-nothing loud mouth, ain't he? And what you know about who is just a good-for-nothing loud mouth? Charlie Atkins was just a "good-for-nothing loud mouth" too, wasn't he! When he wanted me to go in the dry-cleaning business with him. And now—he's grossing a hundred thousand a year. A hundred thousand dollars a year! You still call *him* a loud mouth!

RUTH *(Bitterly)*: Oh, Walter Lee . . .

(She folds her head on her arms over on the table)

WALTER *(Rising and coming to her and standing over her)*: You tired, ain't you? Tired of everything. Me, the boy, the way we live—this beat-up hole—everything. Ain't you? *(She doesn't look up, doesn't answer)* So tired—moaning and groaning all the time, but you wouldn't do nothing to help, would you? You couldn't be on my side that long for nothing, could you?

RUTH: Walter, please leave me alone.

WALTER: A man needs for a woman to back him up . . .

RUTH: Walter—

WALTER: Mama would listen to you. You know she listen to you more than she do me and Bennie. She think more of you. All you have to do is just sit down with her when you drinking your coffee one morning and talking 'bout things like you do and—*(He sits down beside her and demonstrates graphically what he thinks her methods and tone should be)*—you just sip your coffee, see, and say easy like that you been thinking 'bout that deal Walter Lee is so interested in, 'bout the store and all, and sip some more coffee, like what you saying ain't really that important to you—And the next thing you know, she be listening good and asking you questions and when I come home—I can tell her the details. This ain't no fly-by-night proposition, baby. I mean we figured it out, me and Willy and Bobo.

RUTH *(With a frown)*: Bobo?

WALTER: Yeah. You see, this little liquor store we got in mind cost seventy-five thousand and we figured the initial investment on the place be 'bout thirty thousand, see. That be ten thousand each. Course, there's a couple of hundred you got to pay so's you don't spend your life just waiting for them clowns to let your license get approved—

RUTH: You mean graft?

WALTER *(Frowning impatiently)*: Don't call it that. See there, that just goes to show you what women understand about the world. Baby, don't *nothing* happen for you in this world 'less you pay *somebody* off!

RUTH: Walter, leave me alone! *(She raises her head and stares at him vigorously—then says, more quietly)* Eat your eggs, they gonna be cold.

WALTER *(Straightening up from her and looking off)*: That's it. There you are. Man say to his woman: I got me a dream. His woman say: Eat your eggs. *(Sadly, but gaining in power)* Man say: I got to take hold of this here world, baby! And a woman will say: Eat your eggs and go to work. *(Passionately now)* Man say: I got to change my life, I'm choking to death, baby! And his woman say—*(In utter anguish as he brings his fists down on his thighs)*—Your eggs is getting cold!

RUTH *(Softly)*: Walter, that ain't none of our money.

WALTER *(Not listening at all or even looking at her)*: This morning, I was lookin' in the mirror and thinking about it . . . I'm thirty-five years old; I been married eleven years and I got a boy who sleeps in the living room—*(Very, very quietly)*—and all I got to give him is stories about how rich white people live. . . .

RUTH: Eat your eggs, Walter.

WALTER: *Damn my eggs . . . damn all the eggs that ever was!*

RUTH: Then go to work.

WALTER (Looking up at her): See—I'm trying to talk to you 'bout myself—(Shaking his head with the repetition)—and all you can say is eat them eggs and go to work.

RUTH (Wearily): Honey, you never say nothing new. I listen to you every day, every night and every morning, and you never say nothing new. (Shrugging) So you would rather be Mr. Arnold than be his chauffeur. So—I would rather be living in Buckingham Palace.

WALTER: That is just what is wrong with the colored woman in this world . . . Don't understand about building their men up and making 'em feel like they somebody. Like they can do something.

RUTH (Drily, but to hurt): There are colored men who do things.

WALTER: No thanks to the colored woman.

RUTH: Well, being a colored woman, I guess I can't help myself none.

(She rises and gets the ironing board and sets it up and attacks a huge pile of rough-dried clothes, sprinkling them in preparation for the ironing and then rolling them into tight fat balls)

WALTER (Mumbling): We one group of men tied to a race of women with small minds.

(His sister Beneatha enters. She is about twenty, as slim and intense as her brother. She is not as pretty as her sister-in-law, but her lean, almost intellectual face has a handsomeness of its own. She wears a bright-red flannel nightie, and her thick hair stands wildly about her head. Her speech is a mixture of many things; it is different from the rest of the family's insofar as education has permeated her sense of English—and perhaps the Midwest rather than the South has finally—at last—won out in her inflection; but not altogether, because over all of it is a soft slurring and transformed use of vowels [which] is the decided influence of the Southside. She passes through the room without looking at either Ruth or Walter and goes to the outside door and looks, a little blindly, out to the bathroom. She sees that it has been lost to the Johnsons. She closes the door with a sleepy vengeance and crosses to the table and sits down a little defeated.)

BENEATHA: I am going to start timing those people.

WALTER: You should get up earlier.

BENEATHA (Her face in her hands. She is still fighting the urge to go back to bed): Really—would you suggest dawn? Where's the paper?

WALTER (Pushing the paper across the table to her as he studies her almost clinically, as though he has never seen her before): You a horrible-looking chick at this hour.

BENEATHA (Drily): Good morning, everybody.

WALTER (Senselessly): How is school coming?

BENEATHA (In the same spirit): Lovely. And you know, biology is the greatest. (Looking up at him) I dissected something that looked just like you yesterday.

WALTER: I just wondered if you've made up your mind and everything.

BENEATHA (Gaining in sharpness and impatience): And what did I answer yesterday morning—and the day before that?

RUTH (From the ironing board, like someone disinterested and old): Don't be so nasty, Bennie.

BENEATHA (Still to her brother): And the day before that and the day before that!

WALTER (*Defensively*): I'm interested in you. Something wrong with what? Ain't
  many girls who decide—

WALTER and BENEATHA (*In unison*):—"to be a doctor."

(*Silence*)

WALTER: Have we figured out yet just exactly how much medical school is going
  to cost?

RUTH: Walter Lee, why don't you leave that girl alone and get out of here to
  work?

BENEATHA (*Exits to the bathroom and bangs on the door*): Come on out of there,
  please!

(*She comes back into the room*)

WALTER (*Looking at his sister intently*): You know the check is coming tomorrow.

BENEATHA (*Turning on him with a sharpness all her own*): That money belongs to
  Mama, Walter, and it's for her to decide how she wants to use it. I don't care if
  she wants to buy a house or a rocket ship or just nail it up somewhere and
  look at it. It's hers. Not ours—*hers.*

WALTER (*Bitterly*): Now ain't that fine! You just got your mother's interest at
  heart, ain't you, girl? You such a nice girl—but if Mama got that money she
  can always take a few thousand and help you through school too—can't she?

BENEATHA: I have never asked anyone around here to do anything for me!

WALTER: No! And the line between asking and just accepting when the time
  comes is big and wide—ain't it!

BENEATHA (*With fury*): What do you want from me, Brother—that I quit school or
  just drop dead, which!

WALTER: I don't want nothing but for you to stop acting holy 'round here. Me
  and Ruth done made some sacrifices for you—why can't you do something for
  the family!

RUTH: Walter, don't be dragging me in it.

WALTER: You are in it—Don't you get up and go work in somebody's kitchen for
  the last three years to help put clothes on her back?

RUTH: Oh, Walter—that's not fair . . .

WALTER: It ain't that nobody expects you to get on your knees and say thank you,
  Brother; thank you, Ruth; thank you, Mama—and thank you, Travis, for wearing the same pair of shoes for two semesters—

BENEATHA (*Dropping to her knees*): Well—I *do*—all right?—thank everybody . . .
  and forgive me for ever wanting to be anything at all . . . forgive me, forgive
  me!

RUTH: Please stop it! Your mama'll hear you.

WALTER: Who the hell told you you had to be a doctor? If you so crazy 'bout
  messing 'round with sick people—then go be a nurse like other women—or
  just get married and be quiet . . .

BENEATHEA: Well—you finally got it said . . . It took you three years but you finally got it said. Walter, give up; leave me alone—it's Mama's money.

WALTER: *He was my father, too!*

BENEATHA: So what? He was mine, too—and Travis' grandfather—but the insurance money belongs to Mama. Picking on me is not going to make her give it

to you to invest in any liquor stores—*(Underbreath, dropping into a chair)*—and I for one say, God bless Mama for that!

WALTER *(To Ruth)*: See—did you hear? Did you hear!

RUTH: Honey, please go to work.

WALTER: Nobody in this house is ever going to understand me.

BENEATHA: Because you're a nut.

WALTER: Who's a nut?

BENEATHA: You—you are a nut. Thee is mad, boy.

WALTER *(Looking at his wife and his sister from the door, very sadly)*: The world's most backward race of people, and that's a fact.

BENEATHA *(Turning slowly in her chair)*: And then there are all those prophets who would lead us out of the wilderness—*(Walter slams out of the house)*—into the swamps!

RUTH: Bennie, why you always gotta be pickin' on your brother? Can't you be a little sweeter sometimes? *(Door opens. Walter walks in)*

WALTER *(To Ruth)*: I need some money for carfare.

RUTH *(Looks at him, then warms; teasing but tenderly)*: Fifty cents? *(She goes to her bag and gets money)* Here, take a taxi.

(Walter exits. Mama enters. She is a woman in her early sixties, full-bodied and strong. She is one of those women of a certain grace and beauty who wear it so unobstrusively that it takes a while to notice. Her dark-brown face is surrounded by the total whiteness of her hair, and, being a woman who has adjusted to many things in life and overcome many more, her face is full of strength. She has, we can see, wit and faith of a kind that keep her eyes lit and full of interest and expectancy. She is, in a word, a beautiful woman. Her bearing is perhaps most like the noble bearing of the women of the Hereros of Southwest Africa—rather as if she imagines that as she walks she still bears a basket or a vessel upon her head. Her speech, on the other hand, is as careless as her carriage is precise—she is inclined to slur everything—but her voice is perhaps not so much quiet as simply soft.)

MAMA: Who that 'round here slamming doors at this hour?

(She crosses through the room, goes to the window, opens it, and brings in a feeble little plant growing doggedly in a small pot on the window sill. She feels the dirt and puts it back out.)

RUTH: That was Walter Lee. He and Bennie was at it again.

MAMA: My children and they tempers. Lord, if this little old plant don't get more sun than it's been getting it ain't never going to see spring again. *(She turns from the window)* What's the matter with you this morning, Ruth? You looks right peaked. You aiming to iron all them things? Leave some for me. I'll get to 'em this afternoon. Bennie honey, it's too drafty for you to be sitting 'round half dressed. Where's your robe?

BENEATHA: In the cleaners.

MAMA: Well, go get mine and put it on.

BENEATHA: I'm not cold, Mama, honest.

MAMA: I know—but you so thin . . .

BENEATHA *(Irritably)*: Mama, I'm not cold.

MAMA *(Seeing the make-down bed as Travis has left it)*: Lord have mercy, look at that poor bed. Bless his heart—he tries, don't he?

(She moves to the bed Travis has sloppily made up)

RUTH: No—he don't half try at all 'cause he knows you going to come along behind him and fix everything. That's just how come he don't know how to do nothing right now—you done spoiled that boy so.

MAMA: Well—he's a little boy. Ain't supposed to know 'bout housekeeping. My baby, that's what he is. What you fix for his breakfast this morning?

RUTH *(Angrily)*: I feed my son, Lena!

MAMA: I ain't meddling— *(Underbreath; busy-bodyish)* I just noticed all last week he had cold cereal, and when it starts getting this chilly in the fall a child ought to have some hot grits or something when he goes out in the cold—

RUTH *(Furious)*: I gave him hot oats—is that all right!

MAMA: I ain't meddling. *(Pause)* Put a lot of nice butter on it? *(Ruth shoots her an angry look and does not reply)* He likes lots of butter.

RUTH *(Exasperated)*: Lena—

MAMA *(To Beneatha. Mama is inclined to wander conversationally sometimes)*: What was you and your brother fussing 'bout this morning?

BENEATHA: It's not important, Mama.

(She gets up and goes to look out at the bathroom, which is apparently free, and she picks up her towels and rushes out)

MAMA: What was they fighting about?

RUTH: Now you know as well as I do.

MAMA *(Shaking her head)*: Brother still worrying hisself sick about that money?

RUTH: You know he is.

MAMA: You had breakfast?

RUTH: Some coffee.

MAMA: Girl, you better start eating and looking after yourself better. You almost thin as Travis.

RUTH: Lena—

MAMA: Un-hunh?

RUTH: What are you going to do with it?

MAMA: Now don't you start, child. It's too early in the morning to be talking about money. It ain't Christian.

RUTH: It's just that he got his heart set on that store—

MAMA: You mean that liquor store that Willy Harris want him to invest in?

RUTH: Yes—

MAMA: We ain't no business people, Ruth. We just plain working folks.

RUTH: Ain't nobody business people till they go into business. Walter Lee say colored people ain't never going to start getting ahead till they start gambling on some different kinds of things in the world—investments and things.

MAMA: What done got into you, girl? Walter Lee done finally sold you on investing.

RUTH: No. Mama, something is happening between Walter and me. I don't know what it is—but he needs something—something I can't give him any more. He needs this chance, Lena.

MAMA *(Frowning deeply)*: But liquor, honey—

RUTH: Well—like Walter say—I spec people going to always be drinking themselves some liquor.

MAMA: Well—whether they drinks it or not ain't none of my business. But
whether I go into business selling it to 'em *is,* and I don't want that on my
ledger this late in life. *(Stopping suddenly and studying her daughter-in-law)*
Ruth Younger, what's the matter with you today? You look like you could fall
over right there.

RUTH: I'm tired.

MAMA: Then you better stay home from work today.

RUTH: I can't stay home. She'd be calling up the agency and screaming at them,
"My girl didn't come in today—send me somebody! My girl didn't come in!"
Oh, she just have a fit. . . .

MAMA: Well, let her have it. I'll just call her up and say you got the flu—

RUTH *(Laughing)*: Why the flu?

MAMA: 'Cause it sounds respectable to 'em. Something white people get, too.
They know 'bout the flu. Otherwise they think you been cut up or something
when you tell 'em you sick.

RUTH: I got to go in. We need the money.

MAMA: Somebody would of thought my children done all but starved to death
the way they talk about money here late. Child, we got a great big old check
coming tomorrow.

RUTH *(Sincerely, but also self-righteously)*: Now that's your money. It ain't got
nothing to do with me. We all feel like that—Walter and Bennie and me—
even Travis.

MAMA *(Thoughtfully, and suddenly very far away)*:   Ten thousand dollars—

RUTH: Sure is wonderful.

MAMA: Ten thousand dollars.

RUTH: You know what you should do, Miss Lena? You should take yourself a trip
somewhere. To Europe or South America or someplace—

MAMA *(Throwing up her hands at the thought)*: Oh, child!

RUTH: I'm serious. Just pack up and leave! Go on away and enjoy yourself some.
Forget about the family and have yourself a ball for once in your life—

MAMA *(Drily)*: You sound like I'm just about ready to die. Who'd go with me?
What I look like wandering 'round Europe by myself?

RUTH: Shoot—these here rich white women do it all the time. They don't think
nothing of packing up they suitcases and piling on one of them big steam-
ships and—swoosh!—they gone, child.

MAMA: Something always told me I wasn't no rich white woman.

RUTH: Well—what are you going to do with it then?

MAMA: I ain't rightly decided. *(Thinking. She speaks now with emphasis)* Some of it
got to be put away for Beneatha and her schoolin'—and ain't nothing going to
touch that part of it. Nothing. *(She waits several seconds, trying to make up her
mind about something, and looks at Ruth a little tentatively before going on)* Been
thinking that we maybe could meet the notes on a little old two-story somewhere, with a yard where Travis could play in the summertime, if we use part
of the insurance for a down payment and everybody kind of pitch in. I could
maybe take on a little day work again, few days a week—

RUTH *(Studying her mother-in-law furtively and concentrating on her ironing, anxious to encourage without seeming to)*: Well, Lord knows, we've put enough rent into this here rat trap to pay for four houses by now . . .

MAMA *(Looking up at the words "rat trap" and then looking around and leaning back and sighing—in a suddenly reflective mood—)*: "Rat trap"—yes, that's all it is. *(Smiling)* I remember just as well the day me and Big Walter moved in here. Hadn't been married but two weeks and wasn't planning on living here no more than a year. *(She shakes her head at the dissolved dream)* We was going to set away, little by little, don't you know, and buy a little place out in Morgan Park. We had even picked out the house. *(Chuckling a little)* Looks right dumpy today. But Lord, child, you should know all the dreams I had 'bout buying that house and fixing it up and making me a little garden in the back— *(She waits and stops smiling)* And didn't none of it happen.

(Dropping her hands in a futile gesture)

RUTH *(Keeps her head down, ironing)*: Yes, life can be a barrel of disappointments, sometimes.

MAMA: Honey, Big Walter would come in here some nights back then and slump down on that couch there and just look at the rug, and look at me and look at the rug and then back at me—and I'd know he was down then . . . really down. *(After a second very long and thoughtful pause; she is seeing back to times that only she can see)* And then, Lord, when I lost that baby—little Claude—I almost thought I was going to lose Big Walter too. Oh, that man grieved his-self! He was one man to love his children.

RUTH: Ain't nothin' can tear at you like losin' your baby.

MAMA: I guess that's how come that man finally worked hisself to death like he done. Like he was fighting his own war with this here world that took his baby from him.

RUTH: He sure was a fine man, all right. I always liked Mr. Younger.

MAMA: Crazy 'bout his children! God knows there was plenty wrong with Walter Younger—hard-headed, mean, kind of wild with women—plenty wrong with him. But he sure loved his children. Always wanted them to have some-thing—be something. That's where Brother gets all these notions, I reckon. Big Walter used to say, he'd get right wet in the eyes sometimes, lean his head back with the water standing in his eyes and say, "Seem like God didn't see fit to give the black man nothing but dreams—but He did give us children to make them dreams seem worth while." *(She smiles)* He could talk like that, don't you know.

RUTH: Yes, he sure could. He was a good man, Mr. Younger.

MAMA: Yes, a fine man—just couldn't never catch up with his dreams, that's all.

(Beneatha comes in, brushing her hair and looking up to the ceiling, where the sound of a vacuum cleaner has started up)

BENEATHA: What could be so dirty on that woman's rugs that she has to vacuum them every single day?

RUTH: I wish certain young women 'round here who I could name would take inspiration about certain rugs in a certain apartment I could also mention.

BENEATHA *(Shrugging)*: How much cleaning can a house need, for Christ's sakes.

MAMA *(Not liking the Lord's name used thus)*: Bennie!

RUTH: Just listen to her—just listen!

BENEATHA: Oh, God!

MAMA: If you use the Lord's name just one more time—

BENEATHA *(A bit of a whine)*: Oh, Mama—

RUTH: Fresh—just fresh as salt, this girl!

BENEATHA *(Drily)*: Well—if the salt loses its savor—

MAMA: Now that will do. I just ain't going to have you 'round here reciting the scriptures in vain—you hear me?

BENEATHA: How did I manage to get on everybody's wrong side by just walking into a room?

RUTH: If you weren't so fresh—

BENEATHA: Ruth, I'm twenty years old.

MAMA: What time you be home from school today?

BENEATHA: Kind of late. *(With enthusiasm)* Madeline is going to start my guitar lessons today.

(Mama and Ruth look up with the same expression)

MAMA: Your *what* kind of lessons?

BENEATHA: Guitar.

RUTH: Oh, Father!

MAMA: How come you done taken it in your mind to learn to play the guitar?

BENEATHA: I just want to, that's all.

MAMA *(Smiling)*: Lord, child, don't you know what to do with yourself? How long it going to be before you get tired of this now—like you got tired of that little play-acting group you joined last year? *(Looking at Ruth)* And what was it the year before that?

RUTH: The horseback-riding club for which she bought that fifty-five-dollar riding habit that's been hanging in the closet ever since!

MAMA *(To Beneatha)*: Why you got to flit so from one thing to another, baby?

BENEATHA *(Sharply)*: I just want to learn to play the guitar. Is there anything wrong with that?

MAMA: Ain't nobody trying to stop you. I just wonders sometimes why you has to flit so from one thing to another all the time. You ain't never done nothing with all that camera equipment you brought home—

BENEATHA: I don't flit! I—I experiment with different forms of expression—

RUTH: Like riding a horse?

BENEATHA: People have to express themselves one way or another.

MAMA: What is it you want to express?

BENEATHA *(Angrily)*: Me! *(Mama and Ruth look at each other and burst into raucous laughter)* Don't worry—I don't expect you to understand.

MAMA *(To change the subject)*: Who you going out with tomorrow night?

BENEATHA *(With displeasure)*: George Murchison again.

MAMA *(Pleased)*: Oh—you getting a little sweet on him?

RUTH: You ask me, this child ain't sweet on nobody but herself—*(Underbreath)* Express herself!

(They laugh)

BENEATHA: Oh—I like George all right, Mama, I mean I like him enough to go out with him and stuff, but—

RUTH *(For devilment)*: What does *and stuff* mean?

BENEATHA: Mind your own business.

MAMA: Stop picking at her now, Ruth. (*A thoughtful pause, and then a suspicious sudden look at her daughter as she turns in her chair for emphasis*) What *does* it mean?

BENEATHA (*Wearily*): Oh, I just mean I couldn't ever really be serious about George. He's—he's so shallow.

RUTH: Shallow—what do you mean he's shallow? He's *Rich!*

MAMA: Hush, Ruth.

BENEATHA: I know he's rich. He knows he's rich, too.

RUTH: Well—what other qualities a man got to have to satisfy you, little girl?

BENEATHA: You wouldn't even begin to understand. Anybody who married Walter could not possible understand.

MAMA (*Outraged*): What kind of way is that to talk about your brother?

BENEATHA: Brother is a flip—let's face it.

MAMA (*To Ruth, helplessly*): What's a flip?

RUTH (*Glad to add kindling*): She's saying he's crazy.

BENEATHA: Not crazy. Brother isn't really crazy yet—he—he's an elaborate neurotic.

MAMA: Hush your mouth!

BENEATHA: As for George. Well. George looks good—he's got a beautiful car and he takes me to nice places and, as my sister-in-law says, he is probably the richest boy I will ever get to know and I even like him sometimes—but if the Youngers are sitting around waiting to see if their little Bennie is going to tie up the family with the Murchisons, they are wasting their time.

RUTH: You mean you wouldn't marry George Murchinson if he asked you someday? That pretty, rich thing? Honey, I knew you was odd—

BENEATHA: No I would not marry him if all I felt for him was what I feel now. Besides, George's family wouldn't really like it.

MAMA: Why not?

BENEATHA: Oh, Mama—the Murchisons are honest-to-God-real-*live*-rich colored people, and the only people in the world who are more snobbish than rich white people are rich colored people. I thought everybody knew that. I've met Mrs. Murchison. She's a scene!

MAMA: You must not dislike people 'cause they well off, honey.

BENEATHA: Why not? It makes just as much sense as disliking people 'cause they are poor, and lots of people do that.

RUTH (*A wisdom-of-the-ages manner. To Mama.*): Well, she'll get over some of this—

BENEATHA: Get over it? What are you talking about, Ruth? Listen, I'm going to be a doctor. I'm not worried about who I'm going to marry yet—if I ever get married.

MAMA *and* RUTH: *If!*

MAMA: Now, Bennie—

BENEATHA: Oh, I probably will . . . but first I'm going to be a doctor, and George, for one, still thinks that's pretty funny. I couldn't be bothered with that. I am going to be a doctor and everybody around here better understand that!

MAMA (*Kindly*): 'Course you going to be a doctor, honey, God willing.

BENEATHA (*Drily*): God hasn't got a thing to do with it.

MAMA: Beneatha—that just wasn't necessary.

BENEATHA: Well—neither is God. I get sick of hearing about God.

MAMA: Beneatha!

BENEATHA: I mean it! I'm just tired of hearing about God all the time. What has He got to do with anything? Does he pay tuition?

MAMA: You 'bout to get your fresh little jaw slapped!

RUTH: That's just what she needs, all right!

BENEATHA: Why? Why can't I say what I want to around here, like everybody else?

MAMA: It don't sound nice for a young girl to say things like that—you wasn't brought up that way. Me and your father went to trouble to get you and Brother to church every Sunday.

BENEATHA: Mama, you don't understand. It's all a matter of ideas, and God is just one idea I don't accept. It's not important. I am not going out and be immoral or commit crimes because I don't believe in God. I don't even think about it. It's just that I get tired of Him getting credit for all the things the human race achieves through its own stubborn effort. There simply is no blasted God— there is only man and it is he who makes miracles!

(Mama absorbs this speech, studies her daughter and rises slowly and crosses to Beneatha and slaps her powerfully across the face. After, there is only silence and the daughter drops her eyes from her mother's face, and Mama is very tall before her.)

MAMA: Now—you say after me, in my mother's house there is still God. *(There is a long pause and Beneatha stares at the floor wordlessly. Mama repeats the phrase with precision and cool emotion.)* In my mother's house there is still God.

BENEATHA: In my mother's house there is still God.

(A long pause)

MAMA *(Walking away from Beneatha, too disturbed for triumphant posture. Stopping and turning back to her daughter)*: There are some ideas we ain't going to have in this house. Not long as I am at the head of this family.

BENEATHA: Yes, ma'am.

(Mama walks out of the room)

RUTH *(Almost gently, with profound understanding)*: You think you a woman, Bennie—but you still a little girl. What you did was childish—so you got treated like a child.

BENEATHA: I see. *(Quietly)* I also see that everybody thinks it's all right for Mama to be a tyrant. But all the tyranny in the world will never put a God in the heavens!

(She picks up her books and goes out)

RUTH *(Goes to Mama's door)*: She said she was sorry.

MAMA *(Coming out, going to her plant)*: They frightens me, Ruth. My children.

RUTH: You got good children, Lena. They just a little off sometimes—but they're good.

MAMA: No—there's something come down between me and them that don't let us understand each other and I don't know what it is. One done almost lost his mind thinking 'bout money all the time and the other done commence to talk about things I can't seem to understand in no form or fashion. What is it that's changing. Ruth?

RUTH (*Soothingly, older than her years*): Now . . . you taking it all too seriously. You just got strong-willed children and it takes a strong woman like you to keep 'em in hand.

MAMA (*Looking at her plant and sprinkling a little water on it*): They spirited all right, my children. Got to admit they got spirit—Bennie and Walter. Like this little old plant that ain't never had enough sunshine or nothing—and look at it . . .

(*She has her back to Ruth, who has had to stop ironing and lean against something and put the back of her hand to her forehead*)

RUTH (*Trying to keep Mama from noticing*): You . . . sure . . . loves that little old thing, don't you? . . .

MAMA: Well, I always wanted me a garden like I used to see sometimes at the back of the houses down home. This plant is close as I ever got to having one. (*She looks out of the window as she replaces the plant*) Lord, ain't nothing as dreary as the view from this window on a dreary day, is there? Why ain't you singing this morning, Ruth? Sing that "No Ways Tired." That song always lifts me up so—(*She turns at last to see that Ruth has slipped quietly into a chair, in a state of semiconsciousness*) Ruth! Ruth honey—what's the matter with you . . . Ruth!

Curtain

Scene 2

It is the following morning; a Saturday morning, and house cleaning is in progress at the Youngers. Furniture has been shoved hither and yon and Mama is giving the kitchen-area walls a washing down. Beneatha, in dungarees, with a handkerchief tied around her face, is spraying insecticide into the cracks in the walls. As they work, the radio is on and a Southside disk-jockey program is inappropriately filling the house with a rather exotic saxophone blues. Travis, the sole idle one, is leaning on his arms, looking out of the window.

TRAVIS: Grandmama, that stuff Bennie is using smells awful. Can I go downstairs, please?

MAMA: Did you get all them chores done already? I ain't seen you doing much.

TRAVIS: Yes'm—finished early. Where did Mama go this morning?

MAMA (*Looking at Beneatha*): She had to go on a little errand.

TRAVIS: Where?

MAMA: To tend to her business.

TRAVIS: Can I go outside then?

MAMA: Oh, I guess so. You better stay right in front of the house, though . . . and keep a good lookout for the postman.

TRAVIS: Yes'm. (*He starts out and decides to give his Aunt Beneatha a good swat on the legs as he passes her*) Leave them poor little old cockroaches alone, they ain't bothering you none.

(He runs as she swings the spray gun at him both viciously and playfully. Walter enters from the bedroom and goes to the phone.)

MAMA: Look out there, girl, before you be spilling some of that stuff on that child!

TRAVIS *(Teasing)*: That's right—look out now!

(He exits)

BENEATHA *(Drily)*: I can't imagine that it would hurt him—it has never hurt the roaches.

MAMA: Well little boys' hides ain't as tough as Southside roaches.

WALTER *(Into phone)*: Hello—Let me talk to Willy Harris.

MAMA: You better get over there behind the bureau. I seen one marching out of there like Napoleon yesterday.

WALTER: Hello, Willy? It ain't come yet. It'll be here in a few minutes. Did the lawyer give you the papers?

BENEATHA: There's really only one way to get rid of them, Mama—

MAMA: How?

BENEATHA: Set fire to this building.

WALTER: Good. Good. I'll be right over.

BENEATHA: Where did Ruth go, Walter?

WALTER: I don't know.

(He exits abruptly)

BENEATHA: Mama, where did Ruth go?

MAMA *(Looking at her with meaning)*: To the doctor, I think.

BENEATHA: The doctor? What's the matter? *(They exchange glances)* You don't think—

MAMA *(With her sense of drama)*: Now I ain't saying what I think. But, I ain't never been wrong 'bout a woman neither.

(The phone rings)

BENEATHA *(At the phone)*: Hay-lo ... *(Pause, and a moment of recognition)* Well—when did you get back! ... And how was it? ... Of course I've missed you—in my way ... This morning? No ... house cleaning and all that and Mama hates it if I let people come over when the house is like this ... You *have*? Well, that's different ... What is it—Oh, what the hell, come on over ... Right, see you then.

(She hangs up)

MAMA *(Who has listened vigorously, as is her habit)*: Who is that you inviting over here with this house looking like this? You ain't got the pride you was born with!

BENEATHA: Asagai doesn't care how houses look, Mama—he's an intellectual.

MAMA: *Who?*

BENEATHA: Asagai—Joseph Asagai. He's an African boy I met on campus. He's been studying in Canada all summer.

MAMA: What's his name?

BENEATHA: Asagai, Joseph. As-sah-guy . . . He's from Nigeria.

MAMA: Oh, that's the little country that was founded by slaves way back . . .

BENEATHA: No, Mama—that's Liberia.

MAMA: I don't think I never met no African before.

BENEATHA: Well, do me a favor and don't ask him a whole lot of ignorant questions about Africans. I mean, do they wear clothes and all that—

MAMA: Well, now, I guess if you think we so ignorant 'round here maybe you shouldn't bring your friends here—

BENEATHA: It's just that people ask such crazy things. All anyone seems to know about when it comes to Africa is Tarzan—

MAMA (Indignantly): Why should I know anything about Africa?

BENEATHA: Why do you give money at church for the missionary work?

MAMA: Well, that's to help save people.

BENEATHA: You mean save them from heathenism—

MAMA (Innocently): Yes.

BENEATHA: I'm afraid they need more salvation from the British and the French.

(Ruth comes in forlornly and pulls off her coat with dejection. They both turn to look at her.)

RUTH (Dispiritedly): Well, I guess from all the happy faces—everybody knows.

BENEATHA: You pregnant?

MAMA: Lord have mercy, I sure hope it's a little old girl. Travis ought to have a sister.

(Beneatha and Ruth give her a hopeless look for this grandmotherly enthusiasm)

BENEATHA: How far along are you?

RUTH: Two months.

BENEATHA: Did you mean to? I mean did you plan it or was it an accident?

MAMA: What do you know about planning or not planning?

BENEATHA: Oh, Mama.

RUTH (Wearily): She's twenty years old, Lena.

BENEATHA: Did you plan it, Ruth?

RUTH: Mind your own business.

BENEATHA: It is my business—where is he going to live, on the roof? (There is silence following the remark as the three women react to the sense of it) Gee—I didn't mean that, Ruth, honest. Gee, I don't feel like that at all. I—I think it is wonderful.

RUTH (Dully): Wonderful.

BENEATHA: Yes—really.

MAMA (Looking at Ruth, worried): Doctor say everything going to be all right?

RUTH (Far away): Yes—she says everything is going to be fine . . .

MAMA (Immediately suspicious): "She"— What doctor you went to?

(Ruth folds over, near hysteria)

MAMA (Worriedly hovering over Ruth): Ruth honey—what's the matter with you— you sick?

(Ruth has her fists clenched on her thighs and is fighting hard to suppress a scream that seems to be rising in her)

BENEATHA: What's the matter with her, Mama?

MAMA *(Working her fingers in Ruth's shoulder to relax her)*: She be all right. Women gets right depressed sometimes when they get her way. *(Speaking softly, expertly, rapidly)* Now you just relax. That's right . . . just lean back, don't think 'bout nothing at all . . . nothing at all—

RUTH: I'm all right . . .

(The glassy-eyed look melts and then she collapses into a fit of heavy sobbing. The bell rings.)

BENEATHA: Oh, my God—that must be Asagai.

MAMA *(To Ruth)*: Come on now, honey. You need to lie down and rest awhile . . . then have some nice hot food.

(They exit, Ruth's weight on her mother-in-law. Beneatha, herself profoundly disturbed, opens the door to admit a rather dramatic-looking young man with a large package.)

ASAGAI: Hello, Alaiyo—

BENEATHA *(Holding the door open and regarding him with pleasure)*: Hello . . . *(Long pause)* Well—come in. And please excuse everything. My mother was very upset about my letting anyone come here with the place like this.

ASAGAI *(Coming into the room)*: You look disturbed too . . . Is something wrong?

BENEATHA *(Still at the door, absently)*: Yes . . . we've all got acute ghetto-itus. *(She smiles and comes toward him, finding a cigarette and sitting)* So—sit down! How was Canada?

ASAGAI *(A sophisticate)*: Canadian.

BENEATHA *(Looking at him)*: I'm very glad you are back.

ASAGAI *(Looking back at her in turn)*: Are you really?

BENEATHA: Yes—very.

ASAGAI: Why—you were quite glad when I went away. What happened?

BENEATHA: You went away.

ASAGAI: Ahhhhhhhh.

BENEATHA: Before—you wanted to be so serious before there was time.

ASAGAI: How much time must there be before one knows what one feels?

BENEATHA *(Stalling this particular conversation. Her hands pressed together, in a deliberately childish gesture.)*: What did you bring me?

ASAGAI *(Handing her the package)*: Open it and see.

BENEATHA *(Eagerly opening the package and drawing out some records and the colorful robes of a Nigerian woman)*: Oh, Asagai! . . . You got them for me! . . . How beautiful . . . and the records too! *(She lifts out the robes and runs to the mirror with them and holds the drapery up in front of herself)*

ASAGAI *(Coming to her at the mirror)*: I shall have to teach you how to drape it properly. *(He flings the material about her for the moment and stands back to look at her)* Ah— *Oh-pay-gay-day, oh-gbah-mu-shay. (A Yoruba exclamation for admiration)* You wear it well . . . very well . . . mutilated hair and all.

BENEATHA *(Turning suddenly)*: My hair—what's wrong with my hair?

ASAGAI *(Shrugging)*: Were you born with it like that?

BENEATHA *(Reaching up to touch it)*: No . . . of course not.

(She looks back to the mirror, disturbed)

ASAGAI *(Smiling)*: How then?

BENEATHA: You know perfectly well how ... As crinkly as yours ... that's how.

ASAGAI: And it is ugly to you that way?

BENEATHA *(Quickly)*: Oh, no—not ugly ... *(More slowly, apologetically)* But it's so hard to manage when it's, well—raw.

ASAGAI: And so to accommodate that—you mutilate it every week?

BENEATHA: It's not mutilation!

ASAGAI *(Laughing aloud at her seriousness)*: Oh ... please! I am only teasing you because you are so very serious about these things. *(He stands back from her and folds his arms across his chest as he watches her pulling at her hair and frowning in the mirror)* Do you remember the first time you met me at school? ... *(He laughs)* You came up to me and you said—and I thought you were the most serious little thing I had ever seen—you said: *(He imitates her)* "Mr. Asagai—I want very much to talk with you. About Africa. You see, Mr. Asagai, I am looking for my *identity!*"

(He laughs)

BENEATHA *(Turning to him, not laughing)*: Yes—

(Her face is quizzical, profoundly disturbed)

ASAGAI *(Still teasing and reaching out and taking her face in his hands and turning her profile to him)*: Well ... it is true that this is not so much a profile of a Hollywood queen as perhaps a queen of the Nile—*(A mock dismissal of the importance of the question)* But what does it matter? Assimilationism is so popular in your country.

BENEATHA *(Wheeling, passionately, sharply)*: I am not an assimilationist!

ASAGAI *(The protest hangs in the room for a moment and Asagai studies her, his laughter fading)*: Such a serious one. *(There is a pause)* So—you like the robes? You must take excellent care of them—they are from my sister's personal wardrobe.

BENEATNA *(With incredulity)*: You—you sent all the way home—for me?

ASAGAI *(With charm)*: For you—I would do much more ... Well, that is what I came for. I must go.

BENEATHA: Will you call me Monday?

ASAGAI: Yes ... We have a great deal to talk about. I mean about identity and time and all that.

BENEATHA: Time?

ASAGAI: Yes. About how much time one needs to know what one feels.

BENEATHA: You never understood that there is more than one kind of feeling which can exist between a man and a woman—or, at least, there should be.

ASAGAI *(Shaking his head negatively but gently)*: No. Between a man and a woman there need be only one kind of feeling. I have that for you ... Now even ... right this moment ...

BENEATHA: I know—and by itself—it won't do. I can find that anywhere.

ASAGAI: For a woman it should be enough.

BENEATHA: I know—because that's what it says in all the novels that men write. But it isn't. Go ahead and laugh—but I'm not interested in being someone's little episode in America or—*(With feminine vengeance)* —one of them! *(Asagai has burst into laughter again)* That's funny as hell, huh!

ASAGAI: It's just that every American girl I have known has said that to me. White—black—in this you are all the same. And the same speech, too!

BENEATHA (*Angrily*): Yuk, yuk, yuk!

ASAGAI: It's how you can be sure that the world's most liberated women are not liberated at all. You all talk about it too much!

(*Mama enters and is immediately all social charm because of the presence of a guest*)

BENEATHA: Oh—Mama—this is Mr. Asagai.

MAMA: How do you do?

ASAGAI (*Total politeness to an elder*): How do you do, Mrs. Younger. Please forgive me for coming at such an outrageous hour on a Saturday.

MAMA: Well, you are quite welcome. I just hope you understand that our house don't always look like this. (*Chatterish*) You must come again. I would love to hear all about— (*Not sure of the name*) —your country. I think it's so sad the way our American Negroes don't know nothing about Africa 'cept Tarzan and all that. And all that money they pour into these churches when they ought to be helping you people over there drive out them French and Englishmen done taken away your land.

(*The mother flashes a slightly superior look at her daughter upon completion of the recitation*)

ASAGAI (*Taken aback by this sudden and acutely unrelated expression of sympathy*): Yes . . . yes . . .

MAMA (*Smiling at him suddenly and relaxing and looking him over*): How many miles is it from here to where you come from?

ASAGAI: Many thousands.

MAMA (*Looking at him as she would Walter*): I bet you don't half look after yourself, being away from your mama either. I spec you better come 'round here from time to time and get yourself some decent home-cooked meals . . .

ASAGAI (*Moved*): Thank you. Thank you very much. (*They are all quiet, then—*) Well . . .I must go. I will call you Monday, Alaiyo.

MAMA: What's that he call you?

ASAGAI: Oh—"Alaiyo." I hope you don't mind. It is what you would call a nickname, I think. It is a Yoruba word. I am a Yoruba.

MAMA (*Looking at Beneatha*): I—I thought he was from—

ASAGAI (*Understanding*): Nigeria is my country. Yoruba is my tribal origin—

BENEATHA: You didn't tell us what Alaiyo means . . . for all I know, you might be calling me Little Idiot or something . . .

ASAGAI: Well . . . let me see . . . I do not know how just to explain it . . . The sense of a thing can be so different when it changes languages.

BENEATHA: You're evading.

ASAGAI: No—really it is difficult . . . (*Thinking*) It means . . . it means One for Whom Bread—Food—Is Not Enough. (*He looks at her*) Is that all right?

BENEATHA (*Understanding, softly*): Thank you.

MAMA (*Looking from one to the other and not understanding any of it*): Well . . . that's nice . . . You must come see us again—Mr.—

ASAGAI: Ah-sah-guy . . .

MAMA: Yes . . . Do come again.

ASAGAI: Good-bye.

(He exits)

MAMA *(After him)*: Lord, that's a pretty thing just went out here? *(Insinuatingly, to her daughter)* Yes, I guess I see why we done commence to get so interested in Africa 'round here. Missionaries my aunt Jenny!

(She exits)

BENEATHA: Oh, Mama! . . .

(She picks up the Nigerian dress and holds it up to her in front of the mirror again. She sets the headdress on haphazardly and then notices her hair again and clutches at it and then replaces the headdress and frowns at herself. Then she starts to wriggle in front of the mirror as she thinks a Nigerian woman might. Travis enters and regards her.)

TRAVIS: You cracking up?
BENEATHA: Shut up.

(She pulls the headdress off and looks at herself in the mirror and clutches at her hair again and squinches her eyes as if trying to imagine something. Then, suddenly, she gets her raincoat and kerchief and hurriedly prepares for going out.)

MAMA *(Coming back into the room)*: She's resting now. Travis, baby, run next door and ask Miss Johnson to please let me have a little kitchen cleanser. This here can is empty as Jacob's kettle.
TRAVIS: I just came in.
MAMA: Do as you told. *(He exits and she looks at her daughter)* Where you going?
BENEATHA *(Halting at the door)*: To become a queen of the Nile!

(She exits in a breathless blaze of glory. Ruth appears in the bedroom doorway.)

MAMA: Who told you to get up?
RUTH: Ain't nothing wrong with me to be lying in no bed for. Where did Bennie go?
MAMA *(drumming her fingers)*: Far as I could make out—to Egypt. *(Ruth just looks at her)* What time is it getting to?
RUTH: Ten twenty. And the mailman going to ring that bell this morning just like he done every morning for the last umpteen years.

(Travis comes in with the cleanser can)

TRAVIS: She say to tell you that she don't have much.
MAMA *(Angrily)*: Lord, some people I could name sure is tight-fisted! *(Directing her grandson)* Mark two cans of cleanser down on the list there. If she that hard up for kitchen cleanser, I sure don't want to forget to get her none!
RUTH: Lena—maybe the woman is just short on cleanser—
MAMA *(Not listening)*: —Much baking powder as she done borrowed from me all these years, she could of done gone into the baking business!

(The bell sounds suddenly and sharply and all three are stunned—serious and silent—mid-speech. In spite of all the other conversations and distractions of the

morning, this is what they have been waiting for, even Travis, who looks helplessly from his mother to his grandmother. Ruth is the first to come to life again.)

RUTH *(To Travis)*: Get down them steps, boy!

(Travis snaps to life and flies out to get the mail)

MAMA *(Her eyes wide, her hand to her breast)*: You mean it done really come?

RUTH *(Excited)*: Oh, Miss Lena!

MAMA *(Collecting herself)*: Well . . . I don't know what we all so excited about 'round here for. We known it was coming for months.

RUTH: That's a whole lot different from having it come and being able to hold it in your hands . . . a piece of paper worth ten thousand dollars . . . *(Travis bursts back into the room. He holds the envelope high above his head, like a little dancer, his face is radiant and he is breathless. He moves to his grandmother with sudden slow ceremony and puts the envelope into her hands. She accepts it, and then merely holds it and looks at it.)* Come on! Open it . . . Lord have mercy, I wish Walter Lee was here!

TRAVIS: Open it, Grandmama!

MAMA *(staring at it)*: Now you all be quiet. It's just a check.

RUTH: Open it . . .

MAMA *(still staring at it)*: Now don't act silly . . . We ain't never been no people to act silly 'bout no money—

RUTH *(Swiftly)*: We ain't never had none before—*open it!*

(Mama finally makes a good strong tear and pulls out the thin blue slice of paper and inspects it closely. The boy and his mother study it raptly over Mama's shoulders.)

MAMA: Travis! *(She is counting off with doubt)* Is that the right number of zeros.

TRAVIS: Yes'm . . . ten thousand dollars. Gaalee, Grandmama, you rich.

MAMA *(She holds the check away from her, still looking at it. Slowly her face sobers into a mask of unhappiness)*: Ten thousand dollars. *(She hands it to Ruth)* Put it away somewhere, Ruth. *(She does not look at Ruth; her eyes seem to be seeing something somewhere very far off)* Ten thousand dollars they give you. Ten thousand dollars.

TRAVIS *(to his mother, sincerely)*: What's the matter with Grandmama—don't she want to be rich?

RUTH *(Distractedly)*: You go on out and play now, baby. *(Travis exits. Mama starts wiping dishes absently, humming intently to herself. Ruth turns to her, with kind exasperation.)* You've gone and got yourself upset.

MAMA *(not looking at her)*: I spec if it wasn't for you all . . . I would just put that money away or give it to the church or something.

RUTH: Now what kind of talk is that. Mr. Younger would just be plain mad if he could hear you talking foolish like that.

MAMA *(Stopping and staring off)*: Yes . . . he sure would. *(Sighing)* We got enough to do with that money, all right. *(She halts then, and turns and looks at her daughter-in-law hard; Ruth avoids her eyes and Mama wipes her hands with finality and starts to speak firmly to Ruth)* Where did you go today, girl?

RUTH: To the doctor.

MAMA (*Impatiently*): Now, Ruth . . . you know better than that. Old Doctor Jones is strange enough in his way but there ain't nothing 'bout him make somebody slip and call him "she"—like you done this morning.

RUTH: Well, that's what happened—my tongue slipped.

MAMA: You went to see that woman, didn't you?

RUTH (*Defensively, giving herself away*): What woman you talking about?

MAMA (*Angrily*): That woman who—

(*Walter enters in great excitement*)

WALTER: Did it come?

MAMA (*Quietly*): Can't you give people a Christian greeting before you start asking about money?

WALTER (*to Ruth*): Did it come? (*Ruth unfolds the check and lays it quietly before him, watching him intently with thoughts of her own. Walter sits down and grasps it close and counts off the zeros.*) Ten thousand dollars—(*He turns suddenly, frantically to his mother and draws some papers out of his breast pocket*) Mama—look. Old Willy Harris put everything on paper—

MAMA: Son—I think you ought to talk to your wife . . . I'll go on out and leave you alone if you want—

WALTER: I can talk to her later—Mama, look—

MAMA: Son—

WALTER: WILL SOMEBODY PLEASE LISTEN TO ME TODAY!

MAMA (*Quietly*): I don't 'low no yellin' in this house, Walter Lee, and you know it—(*Walter stares at them in frustration and starts to speak several times*) And there ain't going to be no investing in no liquor stores. I don't aim to have to speak on that again.

(*A long pause*)

WALTER: Oh—so you don't aim to have to speak on that again? So *you* have decided . . . (*Crumpling his papers*) Well, *you* tell that to my boy tonight when you put him to sleep on the living-room couch . . . (*Turning to Mama and speaking directly to her*) Yeah—and tell it to my wife, Mama, tomorrow when she has to go out of here to look after somebody else's kids. And tell it to *me*, Mama, every time we need a new pair of curtains and I have to watch *you* go out and work in somebody's kitchen. Yeah, you tell me then!

(*Walter starts out*)

RUTH: Where you going?

WALTER: I'm going out!

RUTH: Where?

WALTER: Just out of this house somewhere—

RUTH (*Getting her coat*): I'll come too.

WALTER: I don't want you to come!

RUTH: I got something to talk to you about, Walter.

WALTER: That's too bad.

MAMA (*Still quietly*): Walter Lee— (*She waits and he finally turns and looks at her*) Sit down.

WALTER: I'm a grown man, Mama.

MAMA: Ain't nobody said you wasn't grown. But you still in my house and my presence. And as long as you are—you'll talk to your wife civil. Now sit down.

RUTH *(Suddenly)*: Oh, let him go on out and drink himself to death! He makes me sick to my stomach! *(She flings her coat against him)*

WALTER *(Violently)*: And you turn mine too, baby! *(Ruth goes into their bedroom and slams the door behind her)* That was my greatest mistake—

MAMA *(Still quietly)*: Walter, what is the matter with you?

WALTER: Matter with me? Ain't nothing the matter with *me!*

MAMA: Yes there is. Something eating you up like a crazy man. Something more than me not giving you this money. The past few years I been watching it happen to you. You get all nervous acting and kind of wild in the eyes—*(Walter jumps up impatiently at her words)* I said sit there now, I'm talking to you!

WALTER: Mama—I don't need no nagging at me today.

MAMA: Seem like you getting to a place where you always tied up in some kind of knot about something. But if anybody ask you 'bout it you just yell at 'em and bust out the house and go out and drink somewheres. Walter Lee, people can't live with that. Ruth's a good, patient girl in her way—but you getting to be too much. Boy, don't make the mistake of driving that girl away from you.

WALTER: Why—what she do for me?

MAMA: She loves you.

WALTER: Mama—I'm going out. I want to go off somewhere and be by myself for a while.

MAMA: I'm sorry 'bout your liquor store, son. It just wasn't the thing for us to do. That's what I want to tell you about—

WALTER: I got to go out, Mama—

(He rises)

MAMA: It's dangerous, son.

WALTER: What's dangerous?

MAMA: When a man goes outside his home to look for peace.

WALTER *(Beseechingly)*: Then why can't there never be no peace in this house then?

MAMA: You done found it in some other house?

WALTER: No—there ain't no woman! Why do women always think there's a woman somewhere when a man gets restless. *(Coming to her)* Mama—Mama—I want so many things. . . .

MAMA: Yes, son—

WALTER: I want so many things that they are driving me kind of crazy. . . Mama—look at me.

MAMA: I'm looking at you. You a good-looking boy. You got a job, a nice wife, a fine boy and—

WALTER: A job. *(Looks at her)* Mama, a job? I open and close car doors all day long. I drive a man around in his limousine and I say, "Yes, sir; no, sir; very good, sir; shall I take the Drive, sir?" Mama, that ain't no kind of job . . . that ain't nothing at all. *(Very quietly)* Mama, I don't know if I can make you understand.

MAMA: Understand what, baby?

WALTER (*Quietly*): Sometimes it's like I can see the future stretched out in front of me—just plain as day. The future, Mama. Hanging over there at the edge of my days. Just waiting for me—a big, looming black space—full of *nothing.* Just waiting for *me.* (*Pause*) Mama—sometimes when I'm downtown and I pass them cool, quiet-looking restaurants where them white boys are sitting back and talking 'bout things . . . sitting there turning deals worth millions of dollars . . . sometimes I see guys don't look much older than me—

MAMA: Son—how come you talk so much 'bout money?

WALTER (*With immense passion*): Because it is life, Mama!

MAMA (*Quietly*): Oh—(*Very quietly*) So now it's life. Money is life. Once upon a time freedom used to be life—now it's money. I guess the world really do change. . .

WALTER: No—it was always money, Mama. We just didn't know about it.

MAMA: No . . . something has changed. (*She looks at him*) You something new, boy. In my time we was worried about not being lynched and getting to the North if we could and how to stay alive and still have a pinch of dignity too. . . . Now here come you and Beneatha—talking 'bout things we ain't never even thought about hardly, me and your daddy. You ain't satisfied or proud of nothing we done. I mean that you had a home; that we kept you out of trouble till you was grown; that you don't have to ride to work on the back of nobody's streetcar—You my children—but how different we done become.

WALTER: You just don't understand, Mama, you just don't understand.

MAMA: Son—do you know your wife is expecting another baby? (*Walter stands, stunned, and absorbs what his mother has said*) That's what she wanted to talk to you about. (*Walter sinks down into a chair*) This ain't for me to be telling—but you ought to know. (*She waits*) I think Ruth is thinking 'bout getting rid of that child.

WALTER (*Slowly understanding*): No—no—Ruth wouldn't do that.

MAMA: When the world gets ugly enough—a woman will do anything for her family. *The part that's already living.*

WALTER: You don't know Ruth, Mama, if you think she would do that.

(*Ruth opens the bedroom door and stands there a little limp*)

RUTH (*Beaten*): Yes I would too, Walter. (*Pause*) I gave her a five-dollar down payment.

(*There is total silence as the man stares at his wife and the mother stares at her son*)

MAMA (*Presently*): Well— (*Tightly*) Well—son, I'm waiting to hear you say something. . . . I'm waiting to hear how you be your father's son. Be the man he was. . . . (*Pause*) Your wife say she going to destroy your child. And I'm waiting to hear you talk like him and say we a people who give children life, not who destroys them— (*She rises*) I'm waiting to see you stand up and look like your daddy and say we done give up one baby to poverty and that we ain't going to give up nary another one. . . . I'm waiting.

WALTER: Ruth—

MAMA: If you a son of mine, tell her! (*Walter turns, looks at her and can say nothing. She continues, bitterly*) You . . . you are a disgrace to your father's memory. Somebody get me my hat.

Act Two

Scene I

Time: Later the same day.

At rise: Ruth is ironing again. She has the radio going. Presently Beneatha's bedroom door opens and Ruth's mouth falls and she puts down the iron in fascination.

RUTH: What have we got on tonight!

BENEATHA *(Emerging grandly from the doorway so that we can see her thoroughly robed in the costume Asagai brought)*: You are looking at what a well-dressed Nigerian woman wears—*(She parades for Ruth, her hair completely hidden by the headdress; she is coquettishly fanning herself with an ornate oriental fan, mistakenly more like Butterfly than any Nigerian that ever was)* Isn't it beautiful? *(She promenades to the radio and, with an arrogant flourish, turns off the good loud blues that is playing)* Enough of this assimilationist junk! *(Ruth follows her with her eyes as she goes to the phonograph and puts on a record and turns and waits ceremoniously for the music to come up. Then, with a shout—)* OCOMOGOSIAY!

(Ruth jumps. The music comes up, a lovely Nigerian melody. Beneatha listens, enraptured, her eyes far away—"back to the past." She begins to dance. Ruth is dumfounded.)

RUTH: What kind of dance is that?

BENEATHA: A folk dance.

RUTH *(Pearl Bailey)*: What kind of folks do that, honey?

BENEATHA: It's from Nigeria. It's a dance of welcome.

RUTH: Who you welcoming?

BENEATHA: The men back to the village.

RUTH: Where they been?

BENEATHA: How should I know—out hunting or something. Anyway, they are coming back now. . . .

RUTH: Well, that's good.

BENEATHA *(With the record)*:
*Alundi, alundi
Alundi alunya
Jop pu a jeepua
Ang gu soooooooooo
Ai yai yae . . .
Ayehaye—alundi. . . .*

(Walter comes in during this performance; he has obviously been drinking. He leans against the door heavily and watches his sister, at first with distaste. Then his eyes look off—"back to the past"—as he lifts both his fists to the roof, screaming.)

WALTER: YEAH . . . AND ETHIOPIA STRETCH FORTH HER HANDS AGAIN! . . .

RUTH *(Drily, looking at him)*: Yes—and Africa sure is claiming her own tonight. *(She gives them both up and starts ironing again)*

WALTER *(All in a drunken, dramatic shout)*: Shut up! . . . I'm digging them drums . . . them drums move me . . . *(He makes his weaving way to his wife's face and leans in close to her)* In my *heart of hearts*— *(He thumps his chest)* —I am much warrior!

RUTH *(Without even looking up)*: In your heart of hearts you are much drunkard.

WALTER (*Coming away from her and starting to wander around the room, shouting*): Me and Jomo ... (*Intently, in his sister's face. She has stopped dancing to watch him in this unknown mood.*) That's my man, Kenyatta. (*Shouting and thumping his chest*) FLAMING SPEAR! HOT DAMN! (*He is suddenly in possession of an imaginary spear and actively spearing enemies all over the room*) OCOMOGOSIAY... THE LION IS WAKING ... OWIMOWEH! (*He pulls his shirt open and leaps up on a table and gestures with his spear. The bell rings. Ruth goes to answer.*)

BENEATHA (*To encourage Walter, thoroughly caught up with this side of him*): OCOMO-GOSIAY, FLAMING SPEAR!

WALTER (*On the table, very far gone, his eyes pure glass sheets. He sees what we cannot, that he is a leader of his people, a great chief, a descendant of Chaka, and that the hour to march has come.*): Listen, my black brothers—

BENEATHA: OCOMOGOSIAY!

WALTER: —Do you hear the waters rushing against the shores of the coastlands—

BENEATHA: OCOMOGOSIAY!

WALTER: —Do you hear the screeching of the cocks in yonder hills beyond where the chiefs meet in council for the coming of the mighty war—

BENEATHA: OCOMOGOSIAY!

WALTER: —Do you hear the beating of the wings of the birds flying low over the mountains and the low places of our land—

(*Ruth opens the door. George Murchison enters.*)

BENEATHA: OCOMOGOSIAY!

WALTER: —Do you hear the singing of the women, singing the war songs of our fathers to the babies in the great houses ... singing the sweet war songs? OH, DO YOU HEAR, MY BLACK BROTHERS!

BENEATHA (*Completely gone*): We hear you, Flaming Spear—

WALTER: Telling us to prepare for the greatness of the time—(*To George*) Black Brother!

(*He extends his hand for the fraternal clasp*)

GEORGE: Black Brother, hell!

RUTH (*Having had enough, and embarrassed for the family*): Beneatha, you got company—what's the matter with you? Walter Lee Younger, get down off that table and stop acting like a fool ...

(*Walter comes down off the table suddenly and makes a quick exit to the bathroom*)

RUTH: He's had a little to drink ... I don't know what her excuse is.

GEORGE (*To Beneatha*): Look honey, we're going *to* the theatre—we're not going to be *in* it ... so go change, huh?

RUTH: You expect this boy to go out with you looking like that?

BENEATHA (*Looking at George*): That's up to George. If he's ashamed of his heritage—

GEORGE: Oh, don't be so proud of yourself, Bennie—just because you look eccentric.

BENEATHA: How can something that's natural be eccentric?

GEORGE: That's what being eccentric means—being natural. Get dressed.

BENEATHA: I don't like that, George.

RUTH: Why must you and your brother make an argument out of everything people say?

BENEATHA: Because I hate assimilationist Negroes!

RUTH: Will somebody please tell me what assimila-whoever means!

GEORGE: Oh, it's just a college girl's way of calling people Uncle Toms—but that isn't what it means at all.

RUTH: Well, what does it mean?

BENEATHA (*Cutting George off and staring at him as she replies to Ruth*): It means someone who is willing to give up his own culture and submerge himself completely in the dominant, and in this case, *oppressive* culture!

GEORGE: Oh, dear, dear, dear! Here we go! A lecture on the African past! On our Great West African Heritage! In one second we will hear all about the great Ashanti empires; the great Songhay civilizations; and the great sculpture of Bénin—and then some poetry in the Bantu—and the whole monologue will end with the word *heritage!* (*Nastily*) Let's face it, baby, your heritage is nothing but a bunch of raggedy-assed spirituals and some grass huts!

BENEATHA: *Grass huts!* (*Ruth crosses to her and forcibly pushes her toward the bedroom*) See there . . . you are standing there in your splendid ignorance talking about people who were the first to smelt iron on the face of the earth! (*Ruth is pushing her through the door*) The Ashanti were performing surgical operations when the English—(*Ruth pulls the door to, with Beneatha on the other side, and smiles graciously at George. Beneatha opens the door and shouts the end of the sentence defiantly at George*)—were still tatooing themselves with blue dragons . . . (*She goes back inside*)

RUTH: Have a seat, George. (*They both sit. Ruth folds her hands rather primly on her lap, determined to demonstrate the civilization of the family.*) Warm, ain't it? I mean for September. (*Pause*) Just like they always say about Chicago weather: If it's too hot or cold for you, just wait a minute and it'll change. (*She smiles happily at this cliché of clichés*) Everybody say it's got to do with them bombs and things they keep setting off. (*Pause*) Would you like a nice cold beer?

GEORGE: No, thank you. I don't care for beer. (*He looks at his watch*) I hope she hurries up.

RUTH: What time is the show?

GEORGE: It's an eight-thirty curtain. That's just Chicago though. In New York standard curtain time is eight forty.

(*He is rather proud of this knowledge*)

RUTH (*Properly appreciating it*): You get to New York a lot?

GEORGE (*Offhand*): Few times a year.

RUTH: Oh—that's nice. I've never been to New York.

(*Walter enters. We feel he has relieved himself, but the edge of unreality is still with him.*)

WALTER: New York ain't got nothing Chicago ain't. Just a bunch of hustling people all squeezed up together—being "Eastern."

(*He turns his face into a screw of displeasure*)

GEORGE: Oh—you've been?

WALTER: *Plenty* of times.

RUTH (*Shocked at the lie*): Walter Lee Younger!

WALTER (*Staring her down*): Plenty! (*Pause*) What we got to drink in this house? Why don't you offer this man some refreshment. (*To George*) They don't know how to entertain people in this house, man.

GEORGE: Thank you—I don't really care for anything.

WALTER (*Feeling his head; sobriety coming*): Where's Mama?

RUTH: She ain't come back yet.

WALTER (*Looking Murchison over from head to toe, scrutinizing his carefully casual tweed sports jacket over cashmere V-neck sweater over soft eyelet shirt and tie, and soft slacks, finished off with white buckskin shoes*): Why all you college boys wear them fairyish-looking white shoes?

RUTH: Walter Lee!

(*George Murchison ignores the remark*)

WALTER (*To Ruth*): Well, they look crazy as hell—white shoes, cold as it is.

RUTH (*Crushed*): You have to excuse him—

WALTER: No he don't! Excuse me for what? What you always excusing me for! I'll excuse myself when I needs to be excused! (*A pause*) They look as funny as them black knee socks Beneatha wears out of here all the time.

RUTH: It's the college *style*, Walter.

WALTER: Style, hell. She looks like she got burnt legs or something!

RUTH: Oh, Walter—

WALTER (*An irritable mimic*): Oh, Walter! Oh, Walter! (*To Murchison*) How's your old man making out? I understand you all going to buy that big hotel on the Drive? (*He finds a beer in the refrigerator, wanders over to Murchison, sipping and wiping his lips with the back of his hand, and straddling a chair backwards to talk to the other man*) Shrewd move. Your old man is all right, man. (*Tapping his head and half winking for emphasis*) I mean he knows how to operate. I mean he thinks *big*, you know what I mean, I mean for a *home*, you know? But I think he's kind of running out of ideas now. I'd like to talk to him. Listen, man, I got some plans that could turn this city upside down. I mean I think like he does. *Big*. Invest big, gamble big, hell, lose *big* if you have to, you know what I mean. It's hard to find a man on this whole Southside who understands my kind of thinking—you dig? (*He scrutinizes Murchison again, drinks his beer, squints his eyes and leans in close, confidential, man to man*) Me and you ought to sit down and talk sometimes, man. Man, I got me some ideas . . .

MURCHISON (*With boredom*): Yeah—sometimes we'll have to do that, Walter.

WALTER (*Understanding the indifference, and offended*): Yeah—well, when you get the time, man, I know you a busy little boy.

RUTH: Walter, please—

WALTER (*Bitterly, hurt*): I know ain't nothing in this world as busy as you colored college boys with your fraternity pins and white shoes . . .

RUTH (*Covering her face with humiliation*): Oh, Walter Lee—

WALTER: I see you all all the time—with the books tucked under your arms—going to your (*British A—a mimic*) "clahsses." And for what! What the hell you learning over there? Filling up your heads—(*Counting off on his fingers*)—with the sociology and the psychology—but they teaching you how to be a man? How to take over and run the world? They teaching you how to run a rubber plantation or a steel mill? Naw—just to talk proper and read books and wear white shoes . . .

GEORGE (*Looking at him with distaste, a little above it all*): You're all wacked up with bitterness, man.

WALTER (*Intently, almost quietly, between the teeth, glaring at the boy*): And you—ain't you bitter, man? Ain't you just about had it yet? Don't you see no stars gleaming that you can't reach out and grab? You happy?—you contented son-of-a-bitch—you happy? You got it made? Bitter? Man, I'm a volcano. Bitter? Here I am a giant—surrounded by ants! Ants who can't even understand what it is the giant is talking about.

RUTH (*Passionately and suddenly*): Oh, Walter—ain't you with nobody!

WALTER (*Violently*): No! 'Cause ain't nobody with me! Not even my own mother!

RUTH: Walter, that's a terrible thing to say!

(*Beneatha enters, dressed for the evening in a cocktail dress and earrings*)

GEORGE: Well—hey, you look great.

BENEATHA: Let's go, George. See you all later.

RUTH: Have a nice time.

GEORGE: Thanks. Good night. (*To Walter, sarcastically*) Good night, *Prometheus*.

(*Beneatha and George exit*)

WALTER (*To Ruth*): Who is Prometheus?

RUTH: I don't know. Don't worry about it.

WALTER (*In fury, pointing after George*): See there—they get to a point where they can't insult you man to man—they got to go talk about something ain't nobody never heard of!

RUTH: How you know it was an insult? (*To humor him*) Maybe Prometheus is a nice fellow.

WALTER: Prometheus! I bet there ain't even no such thing! I bet that simple-minded clown—

RUTH: Walter—

(*She stops what she is doing and looks at him*)

WALTER (*Yelling*): Don't start!

RUTH: Start what?

WALTER: Your nagging! Where was I! Who was I with? How much money did I spend?

RUTH (*Plaintively*): Walter Lee—why don't we just try to talk about it . . .

WALTER (*Not listening*): I been out talking with people who understand me. People who care about the things I got on my mind.

RUTH (*Wearily*): I guess that means people like Willy Harris.

WALTER: Yes, people like Willy Harris.

RUTH (*With a sudden flash of impatience*): Why don't you all just hurry up and go into the banking business and stop talking about it!

WALTER: Why? You want to know why? 'Cause we all tied up in a race of people that don't know how to do nothing but moan, pray and have babies!

(*The line is too bitter even for him and he looks at her and sits down*)

RUTH: Oh, Walter . . . (*Softly*) Honey, why can't you stop fighting me?

WALTER (*Without thinking*): Who's fighting you? Who even cares about you?

(*This line begins the retardation of his mood*)

RUTH: Well—(*She waits a long time, and then with resignation starts to put away her things*) I guess I might as well go on to bed ... (*More or less to herself*) I don't know where we lost it ... but we have ... (*Then, to him*) I—I'm sorry about this new baby, Walter. I guess maybe I better go on and do what I started ... I guess I just didn't realize how bad things was with us ... I guess I just didn't really realize—(*She starts out to the bedroom and stops*) You want some hot milk?

WALTER: Hot milk?

RUTH: Yes—hot milk.

WALTER: Why hot milk?

RUTH: 'Cause after all that liquor you come home with you ought to have something hot in your stomach.

WALTER: I don't want no milk.

RUTH: You want some coffee then?

WALTER: No, I don't want no coffee. I don't want nothing hot to drink. (*Almost plaintively*) Why you always trying to give me something to eat?

RUTH (*Standing and looking at him helplessly*): What else can I give you, Walter Lee Younger?

(*She stands and looks at him and presently turns to go out again. He lifts his head and watches her going away from him in a new mood which began to emerge when he asked her "Who cares about you?"*)

WALTER: It's been rough, ain't it, baby? (*She hears and stops but does not turn around and he continues to her back*) I guess between two people there ain't never as much understood as folks generally thinks there is. I mean like between me and you—(*She turns to face him*) How we gets to the place where we scared to talk softness to each other. (*He waits, thinking hard himself*) Why you think it got to be like that? (*He is thoughtful, almost as a child would be*) Ruth, what is it gets into people ought to be close?

RUTH: I don't know, honey. I think about it a lot.

WALTER: On account of you and me, you mean? The way things are with us. The way something done come down between us.

RUTH: There ain't so much between us, Walter ... Not when you come to me and try to talk to me. Try to be with me ... a little even.

WALTER (*Total honesty*): Sometimes ... Sometimes ... I don't even know how to try.

RUTH: Walter—

WALTER: Yes?

RUTH (*Coming to him, gently and with misgiving, but coming to him*): Honey ... life don't have to be like this. I mean sometimes people can do things so that things are better ... You remember how we used to talk when Travis was born ... about the way we were going to live ... the kind of house ... (*She is stroking his head*) Well, it's all starting to slip away from us ...

(*Mama enters, and Walter jumps up and shouts at her*)

WALTER: Mama, where have you been?

MAMA: My—them steps is longer than they used to be. Whew! *(She sits down and ignores him)* How you feeling this evening, Ruth?

(Ruth shrugs, disturbed some at having been prematurely interrupted and watching her husband knowingly)

WALTER: Mama, where have you been all day?

MAMA *(Still ignoring him and leaning on the table and changing to more comfortable shoes)*: Where's Travis?

RUTH: I let him go out earlier and he ain't come back yet. Boy, is he going to get it!

WALTER: Mama!

MAMA *(As if she has heard him for the first time)*: Yes, son?

WALTER: Where did you go this afternoon?

MAMA: I went down town to tend to some business that I had to tend to.

WALTER: What kind of business?

MAMA: You know better than to question me like a child, Brother.

WALTER *(Rising and bending over the table)*: Where were you, Mama? *(Bringing his fists down and shouting)* Mama, you didn't go do something with that insurance money, something crazy?

(The front door opens slowly, interrupting him, and Travis peeks his head in, less than hopefully)

TRAVIS *(To his mother)*: Mama, I—

RUTH: "Mama I" nothing! You're going to get it, boy! Get on in that bedroom and get yourself ready!

TRAVIS: But I—

MAMA: Why don't you all never let the child explain hisself.

RUTH: Keep out of it now, Lena.

(Mama clamps her lips together, and Ruth advances toward her son menacingly)

RUTH: A thousand times I have told you not to go off like that—

MAMA *(Holding out her arms to her grandson)*: Well—at least let me tell him something. I want him to be the first one to hear . . . Come here, Travis. *(The boy obeys, gladly)* Travis—*(She takes him by the shoulders and looks into his face)*—you know that money we got in the mail this morning?

TRAVIS: Yes'm—

MAMA: Well—what you think your grandmama gone and done with that money?

TRAVIS: I don't know, Grandmama.

MAMA *(Putting her finger on his nose for emphasis)*: She went out and she bought you a house! *(The explosion comes from Walter at the end of the revelation and he jumps up and turns away from all of them in a fury. Mama continues, to Travis)* You glad about the house? It's going to be yours when you get to be a man.

TRAVIS: Yeah—I always wanted to live in a house.

MAMA: All right, gimme some sugar then—*(Travis puts his arms around her neck as she watches her son over the boy's shoulder. Then, to Travis, after the embrace)* Now when you say your prayers tonight, you thank God and your grandfather—

'cause it was him who give you the house—in his way.

RUTH *(Taking the boy from Mama and pushing him toward the bedroom)*: Now you get out of here and get ready for your beating.

TRAVIS: Aw, Mama—

RUTH: Get on in there— *(Closing the door behind him and turning radiantly to her mother-in-law)* So you went and did it!

MAMA *(Quietly, looking at her son with pain)*: Yes, I did.

RUTH *(Raising both arms classically)*: Praise God! *(Looks at Walter a moment, who says nothing. She crosses rapidly to her husband.)* Please, honey—let me be glad . . . you be glad too. *(She has laid her hands on his shoulders, but he shakes himself free of her roughly, without turning to face her)* Oh, Walter . . . a home . . . *a home. (She comes back to Mama)* Well—where is it? How big is it? How much it going to cost?

MAMA: Well—

RUTH: When we moving?

MAMA *(Smiling at her)*: First of the month.

RUTH *(Throwing back her head with jubilance)*: Praise God!

MAMA *(Tentatively, still looking at her son's back turned against her and Ruth)*: It's— it's a nice house too . . . *(She cannot help speaking directly to him. An imploring quality in her voice, her manner, makes her almost like a girl now.)* Three bedrooms—nice big one for you and Ruth . . . Me and Beneatha still have to share our room, but Travis have one of his own—and—*(With difficulty)* I figures if the—new baby—is a boy, we could get one of them double-decker outfits . . . And there's a yard with a little patch of dirt where I could maybe get to grow me a few flowers . . . And a nice big basement . . .

RUTH: Walter honey, be glad—

MAMA *(Still to his back, fingering things on the table)*: 'Course I don't want to make it sound fancier than it is . . . It's just a plain little old house—but it's made good and solid—and it will be *ours.* Walter Lee—it makes a difference in a man when he can walk on floors that belong to *him* . . .

RUTH: Where is it?

MAMA *(Frightened at this telling)*: Well—well—it's out there in Clybourne Park—

(Ruth's radiance fades abruptly, and Walter finally turns slowly to face his mother with incredulity and hostility)

RUTH: Where?

MAMA *(Matter-of-factly)*: Four o six Clybourne Street, Clybourne Park.

RUTH: Clybourne Park? Mama, there ain't no colored people living in Clybourne Park.

MAMA *(Almost idiotically)*: Well, I guess there's going to be some now.

WALTER *(Bitterly)*: So that's the peace and comfort you went out and bought for us today!

MAMA *(Raising her eyes to meet his finally)*: Son—I just tried to find the nicest place for the least amount of money for my family.

RUTH *(Trying to recover from the shock)*: Well—well—'course I ain't one never been 'fraid of no crackers, mind you—but—well, wasn't there no other houses nowhere?

MAMA: Them houses they put up for colored in them areas way out all seem to cost twice as much as other houses. I did the best I could.

RUTH *(Struck senseless with the news, in its various degrees of goodness and trouble, she sits a moment, her fists propping her chin in thought, and then she starts to rise, bringing her fists down with vigor, the radiance spreading from cheek to cheek again):* Well—well!—All I can say is—if this is my time in life—*my time*—to say good-bye—*(And she builds with momentum as she starts to circle the room with an exuberant, almost tearfully happy release)*—to these Goddamned cracking walls!—*(She pounds the walls)*—and these marching roaches!—*(She wipes at an imaginary army of marching roaches)*—and this cramped little closet which ain't now or never was no kitchen! . . . then I say it loud and good, *Hallelujah!* and good-bye misery . . . I don't never want to see your ugly face again! *(She laughs joyously, having practically destroyed the apartment, and flings her arms up and lets them come down happily, slowly, reflectively, over her abdomen, aware for the first time perhaps that the life therein pulses with happiness and not despair)* Lena?

MAMA *(Moved, watching her happiness):* Yes, honey?

RUTH *(Looking off):* Is there—is there a whole lot of sunlight?

MAMA *(Understanding):* Yes, child, there's a whole lot of sunlight.

(Long pause)

RUTH *(Collecting herself and going to the door of the room Travis is in):* Well—I guess I better see 'bout Travis. *(To Mama)* Lord, I sure don't feel like whipping nobody today!

(She exits)

MAMA *(The mother and son are left alone now and the mother waits a long time, considering deeply, before she speaks):* Son—you—you understand what I done, don't you? *(Walter is silent and sullen)* I—I just seen my family falling apart today . . . just falling to pieces in front of my eyes . . . We couldn't of gone on like we was today. We was going backwards 'stead of forwards—talking 'bout killing babies and wishing each other was dead . . . When it gets like that in life—you just got to do something different, push on out and do something bigger . . . *(She waits)* I wish you say something, son . . . I wish you'd say how deep inside you you think I done the right thing—

WALTER *(Crossing slowly to his bedroom door and finally turning there and speaking measuredly):* What you need me to say you done right for? *You* the head of this family. You run our lives like you want to. It was your money and you did what you wanted with it. So what you need for me to say it was all right for? *(Bitterly, to hurt her as deeply as he knows is possible)* So you butchered up a dream of mine—you—who always talking 'bout your children's dreams . . .

MAMA: Walter Lee—

(He just closes the door behind him. Mama sits alone, thinking heavily.)

Curtain

Scene 2

Time: Friday night. A few weeks later.

At rise: Packing crates mark the intention of the family to move. Beneatha and George come in, presumably from an evening out again.

GEORGE: O.K. . . . O.K., whatever you say . . . *(They both sit on the couch. He tries to kiss her. She moves away)* Look, we've had a nice evening; let's not spoil it, huh? . . .

(He again turns her head and tries to nuzzle in and she turns away from him, not with distaste but with momentary lack of interest; in a mood to pursue what they were talking about)

BENEATHA: I'm *trying* to talk to you.

GEORGE: We always talk.

BENEATHA: Yes—and I love to talk.

GEORGE *(Exasperated; rising)*: I know it and I don't mind it sometimes . . . I want you to cut it out, see—The moody stuff, I mean. I don't like it. You're a nice-looking girl . . . all over. That's all you need, honey, forget the atmosphere. Guys aren't going to go for the atmosphere—they're going to go for what they see. Be glad for that. Drop the Garbo routine. It doesn't go with you. As for myself, I want a nice—*(Groping)*—simple—*(Thoughtfully)*—sophisticated girl . . . not a poet—O.K.?

(She rebuffs him again and he starts to leave)

BENEATHA: Why are you angry?

GEORGE: Because this is stupid! I don't go out with you to discuss the nature of "quiet desperation" or to hear all about your thoughts—because the world will go on thinking what it thinks regardless—

BENEATHA: Then why read books? Why go to school?

GEORGE *(With artificial patience, counting on his fingers)*: It's simple. You read books—to learn facts—to get grades—to pass the course—to get a degree. That's all—it has nothing to do with thoughts.

(A long pause)

BENEATHA: I see. *(A longer pause as she looks at him)* Good night, George.

(George looks at her a little oddly, and starts to exit. He meets Mama coming in)

GEORGE: Oh—hello, Mrs. Younger.

MAMA: Hello, George, how you feeling?

GEORGE: Fine—fine, how are you?

MAMA: Oh, a little tired. You know them steps can get you after a day's work. You all have a nice time tonight?

GEORGE: Yes—a fine time. Well, good night.

MAMA: Good night. *(He exits. Mama closes the door behind her)* Hello, honey. What you sitting like that for?

BENEATHA: I'm just sitting.

MAMA: Didn't you have a nice time?

BENEATHA: No.

MAMA: No? What's the matter?

BENEATHA: Mama, George is a fool—honest. *(She rises)*

MAMA *(Hustling around unloading the packages she has entered with. She stops.)*: Is he, baby?

BENEATHA: Yes.

(Beneatha makes up Travis' bed as she talks)

MAMA: You sure?

BENEATHA: Yes.

MAMA: Well—I guess you better not waste your time with no fools.

(Beneatha looks up at her mother, watching her put groceries in the refrigerator. Finally she gathers up her things and starts into the bedroom. At the door she stops and looks back at her mother.)

BENEATHA: Mama—

MAMA: Yes, baby—

BENEATHA: Thank you.

MAMA: For what?

BENEATHA: For understanding me this time.

(She exits quickly and the mother stands, smiling a little, looking at the place where Beneatha just stood. Ruth enters.)

RUTH: Now don't you fool with any of this stuff, Lena—

MAMA: Oh, I just thought I'd sort a few things out.

(The phone rings. Ruth answers.)

RUTH *(At the phone)*: Hello—Just a minute. *(Goes to door)* Walter, it's Mrs. Arnold. *(Waits. Goes back to the phone. Tense)* Hello. Yes, this is his wife speaking . . . He's lying down now. Yes . . . well, he'll be in tomorrow. He's been very sick. Yes—I know we should have called, but we were so sure he'd be able to come in today. Yes—yes, I'm very sorry. Yes . . . Thank you very much. *(She hangs up. Walter is standing in the doorway of the bedroom behind her.)* That was Mrs. Arnold.

WALTER *(Indifferently)*: Was it?

RUTH: She said if you don't come in tomorrow that they are getting a new man...

WALTER: Ain't that sad—ain't that crying sad.

RUTH: She said Mr. Arnold has had to take a cab for three days . . . Walter, you ain't been to work for three days! *(This is a revelation to her)* Where you been, Walter Lee Younger? *(Walter looks at her and starts to laugh)* You're going to lose your job.

WALTER: That's right . . .

RUTH: Oh, Walter, and with your mother working like a dog every day—

WALTER: That's sad too—Everything is sad.

MAMA: What you been doing for these three days, son?

WALTER: Mama—you don't know all the things a man what got leisure can find to do in this city . . . What's this—Friday night? Well—Wednesday I borrowed Willy Harris' car and I went for a drive . . . just me and myself and I drove and drove . . . Way out . . . way past South Chicago, and I parked the car and I sat and looked at the steel mills all day long. I just sat in the car and looked at them big black chimneys for hours. Then I drove back and I went to the Green Hat. *(Pause)* And Thursday—Thursday I borrowed the car again and I got in it and I pointed it the other way and I drove the other way—for hours—way, way up to Wisconsin, and I looked at the farms. I just drove and

looked at the farms. Then I drove back and I went to the Green Hat. *(Pause)*
And today—today I didn't get the car. Today I just walked. All over the Southside. And I looked at the Negroes and they looked at me and finally I just sat
down on the curb at Thirty-ninth and South Parkway and I just sat there and
watched the Negroes go by. And then I went to the Green Hat. You all sad?
You all depressed? And you know where I am going right now—

(Ruth goes out quietly)

MAMA: Oh, Big Walter, is this the harvest of our days?

WALTER: You know what I like about the Green Hat? *(He turns the radio on and a
steamy, deep blues pours into the room)* I like this little cat they got there who
blows a sax . . . He blows. He talks to me. He ain't but 'bout five feet tall and
he's got a conked head and his eyes is always closed and he's all music—

MAMA *(Rising and getting some papers out of her handbag)*: Walter—

WALTER: And there's this other guy who plays the piano . . . and they got a
sound. I mean they can work on some music. . . . They got the best little com-
bo in the world in the Green Hat . . . You can just sit there and drink and listen to them three men play and you realize that don't nothing matter worth a
damn, but just being there—

MAMA: I've helped do it to you, haven't I, son? Walter, I been wrong.

WALTER: Naw—you ain't never been wrong about nothing, Mama.

MAMA: Listen to me, now. I say I been wrong, son. That I been doing to you what
the rest of the world been doing to you. *(She stops and he looks up slowly at her
and she meets his eyes pleadingly)* Walter—what you ain't never understood is
that I ain't got nothing, don't own nothing, ain't never really wanted nothing
that wasn't for you. There ain't nothing as precious to me . . . There ain't nothing worth holding on to, money, dreams, nothing else—if it means—if it
means it's going to destroy my boy. *(She puts her papers in front of him and he
watches her without speaking or moving)* I paid the man thirty-five hundred dollars down on the house. That leaves sixty-five hundred dollars. Monday
morning I want you to take this money and take three thousand dollars and
put it in a savings account for Beneatha's medical schooling. The rest you put
in a checking account—with your name on it. And from now on any penny
that come out of it or that go in it is for you to look after. For you to decide.
(She drops her hands a little helplessly) It ain't much, but it's all I got in the
world and I'm putting it in your hands. I'm telling you to be the head of this
family from now on like you supposed to be.

WALTER *(Stares at the money)*: You trust me like that, Mama?

MAMA: I ain't never stop trusting you. Like I ain't never stop loving you.

*(She goes out, and Walter sits looking at the money on the table as the music continues
in its idiom, pulsing in the room. Finally, in a decisive gesture, he gets up, and, in mingled joy and desperation, picks up the money. At the same moment, Travis enters for
bed.)*

TRAVIS: What's the matter, Daddy? You drunk?

WALTER *(Sweetly, more sweetly than we have ever known him)*: No, Daddy ain't
drunk. Daddy ain't going to never be drunk again. . . .

TRAVIS: Well, good night, Daddy.

(The Father has come from behind the couch and leans over, embracing his son)

WALTER: Son, I feel like talking to you tonight.

TRAVIS: About what?

WALTER: Oh, about a lot of things. About you and what kind of man you going to be when you grow up. . . . Son—son, what do you want to be when you grow up?

TRAVIS: A bus driver.

WALTER *(Laughing a little)*: A what? Man, that ain't nothing to want to be!

TRAVIS: Why not?

WALTER: 'Cause, man—it ain't big enough—you know what I mean.

TRAVIS: I don't know then. I can't make up my mind. Sometimes Mama asks me that too. And sometimes when I tell you I just want to be like you—she says she don't want me to be like that and sometimes she says she does. . . .

WALTER *(Gathering him up in his arms)*: You know what, Travis? In seven years you going to be seventeen years old. And things is going to be very different with us in seven years, Travis. . . . One day when you are seventeen I'll come home—home from my office downtown somewhere—

TRAVIS: You don't work in no office, Daddy.

WALTER: No—but after tonight. After what your daddy gonna do tonight, there's going to be offices—a whole lot of offices. . . .

TRAVIS: What you gonna do tonight, Daddy?

WALTER: You wouldn't understand yet, son, but your daddy's gonna make a transaction . . . a business transaction that's going to change our lives. . . . That's how come one day when you 'bout seventeen years old I'll come home and I'll be pretty tired, you know what I mean, after a day of conferences and secretaries getting things wrong the way they do . . . 'cause an executive's life is hell, man— *(The more he talks the farther away he gets)* And I'll pull the car up on the driveway . . . just a plain black Chrysler, I think, with white walls—no—black tires. More elegant. Rich people don't have to be flashy . . . though I'll have to get something a little sportier for Ruth—maybe a Cadillac convertible to do her shopping in. . . . And I'll come up the steps to the house and the gardener will be clipping away at the hedges and he'll say, "Good evening, Mr. Younger." And I'll say, "Hello Jefferson, how are you this evening?" And I'll go inside and Ruth will come downstairs and meet me at the door and we'll kiss each other and she'll take my arm and we'll go up to your room to see you sitting on the floor with the catalogues of all the great schools in America around you. . . . All the great schools in the world! And—and I'll say, all right son—it's your seventeenth birthday, what is it you've decided? . . . Just tell me where you want to go to school and you'll *go.* Just tell me, what it is you want to be—and you'll *be* it. . . . Whatever you want to be—Yessir! *(He holds his arms open for Travis)* You just name it, son . . . *(Travis leaps into them)* and I hand you the world!

(Walter's voice has risen in pitch and hysterical promise and on the last line he lifts Travis high)

(Blackout)

Scene 3

Time: Saturday, moving day, one week later.

Before the curtain rises, Ruth's voice, a strident, dramatic church alto, cuts through the silence.

It is, in the darkness, a triumphant surge, a penetrating statement of expectation: "Oh, Lord, I don't feel no ways tired! Children, Oh, glory hallelujah!"

As the curtain rises we see that Ruth is alone in the living room, finishing up the family's packing. It is moving day. She is nailing crates and tying cartons. Beneatha enters, carrying a guitar case, and watches her exuberant sister-in-law.

RUTH: Hey!

BENEATHA *(Putting away the case)*: Hi.

RUTH *(Pointing at a package)*: Honey—look in that package there and see what I found on sale this morning at the South Center. *(Ruth gets up and moves to the package and draws out some curtains)* Lookahere—hand-turned hems!

BENEATHA: How do you know the window size out there?

RUTH *(Who hadn't thought of that)*: Oh—Well, they bound to fit something in the whole house. Anyhow, they was too good a bargain to pass us. *(Ruth slaps her head, suddenly remembering something)* Oh, Bennie—I meant to put a special note on that carton over there. That's your mama's good china and she wants 'em to be very careful with it.

BENEATHA: I'll do it.

(Beneatha finds a piece of paper and starts to draw large letters on it)

RUTH: You know what I'm going to do soon as I get in that new house?

BENEATHA: What?

RUTH: Honey—I'm going to run me a tub of water up to here . . . *(With her fingers practically up to her nostrils)* And I'm going to get in it—and I am going to sit . . . and sit . . . and sit in that hot water and the first person who knocks to tell *me* to hurry up and come out—

BENEATHA: Gets shot at sunrise.

RUTH *(Laughing happily)*: You said it, sister! *(Noticing how large Beneatha is absentmindedly making the note)* Honey, they ain't going to read that from no airplane.

BENEATHA *(Laughing herself)*: I guess I always think things have more emphasis if they are big, somehow.

RUTH *(Looking up at her and smiling)*: You and your brother seem to have that as a philosophy of life. Lord, that man—done changed so 'round here. You know—you know what we did last night? Me and Walter Lee?

BENEATHA: What?

RUTH *(Smiling to herself)*: We went to the movies. *(Looking at Beneatha to see if she understands)* We went to the movies. You know the last time me and Walter went to the movies together?

BENEATHA: No.

RUTH: Me neither. That's how long it been. *(Smiling again)* But we went last night. The picture wasn't much good, but that didn't seem to matter. We went—and we held hands.

BENEATHA: Oh, Lord!

RUTH: We held hands—and you know what?

BENEATHA: What?

RUTH: When we come out of the show it was late and dark and all the stores and things was closed up . . . and it was kind of chilly and there wasn't many people on the streets . . . and we was still holding hands, me and Walter.

BENEATHA: You're killing me.

(Walter enters with a large package. His happiness is deep in him; he cannot keep still with his new-found exuberance. He is singing and wiggling and snapping his fingers. He puts his package in a corner and puts a phonograph record, which he has brought in with him, on the record player. As the music comes up he dances over to Ruth and tries to get her to dance with him. She gives in at last to his raunchiness and in a fit of giggling allows herself to be drawn into his mood and together they deliberately burlesque an old social dance of their youth.)

BENEATHA *(Regarding them a long time as they dance, then drawing in her breath for a deeply exaggerated comment which she does not particularly mean)*: Talk about—olddddddddddd-fashionedddddddd—Negroes!

WALTER *(Stopping momentarily)*: What kind of Negroes?

(He says this in fun. He is not angry with her today, nor with anyone. He starts to dance with his wife again)

BENEATHA: Old-fashioned.

WALTER *(As he dances with Ruth)*: You know, when these *New Negroes* have their convention—*(Pointing at his sister)*—that is going to be the chairman of the Committee on Unending Agitation. *(He goes on dancing, then stops)* Race, race, race! . . . Girl, I do believe you are the first person in the history of the entire human race to successfully brainwash yourself. *(Beneatha breaks up and he goes on dancing. He stops again, enjoying his tease)* Damn, even the N double A C P takes a holiday sometimes! *(Beneatha and Ruth laugh. He dances with Ruth some more and starts to laugh and stops and pantomimes someone over an operating table.)* I can just see that chick someday looking down at some poor cat on an operating table before she starts to slice him, saying . . . *(Pulling his sleeves back maliciously)* "By the way, what are your views on civil rights down there? . . ."

(He laughs at her again and starts to dance happily. The bell sounds.)

BENEATHA: Sticks and stones may break my bones but . . . words will never hurt me!

(Beneatha goes to the door and opens it as Walter and Ruth go on with the clowning. Beneatha is somewhat surprised to see a quiet-looking middle-aged white man in a business suit holding his hat and a briefcase in his hand and consulting a small piece of paper.)

MAN: Uh—How do you do, miss. I am looking for a Mrs.— *(He looks at the slip of paper)* Mrs. Lena Younger?

BENEATHA *(Smoothing her hair with slight embarrassment)*: Oh—yes, that's my mother. Excuse me. *(She closes the door and turns to quiet the other two)* Ruth! Brother! Somebody's here. *(Then she opens the door. The man casts a curious quick glance at all of them)* Uh—come in please.

MAN (*Coming in*): Thank you.

BENEATHA: My mother isn't here just now. Is it business?

MAN: Yes . . . well, of a sort.

WALTER (*Freely, the Man of the House*): Have a seat. I'm Mrs. Younger's son. I look after most of her business matters.

(*Ruth and Beneatha exchange amused glances*)

MAN (*Regarding Walter, and sitting*): Well—My name is Karl Lindner . . .

WALTER (*Stretching out his hand*): Walter Younger. This is my wife—(*Ruth nods politely*)—and my sister.

LINDNER: How do you do.

WALTER (*Amiably, as he sits himself easily on a chair, leaning with interest forward on his knees and looking expectantly into the newcomer's face*): What can we do for you, Mr. Lindner!

LINDNER (*Some minor shuffling of the hat and briefcase on his knees*): Well—I am a representative of the Clybourne Park Improvement Association—

WALTER (*Pointing*): Why don't you sit your things on the floor?

LINDNER: Oh—yes. Thank you. (*He slides the briefcase and hat under the chair*) And as I was saying—I am from the Clybourne Park Improvement Association and we have had it brought to our attention at the last meeting that you people— or at least your mother—has bought a piece of residential property at—(*He digs for the slip of paper again*)—four o six Clybourne Street . . .

WALTER: That's right. Care for something to drink? Ruth, get Mr. Lindner a beer.

LINDNER (*Upset for some reason*): Oh—no, really. I mean thank you very much, but no thank you.

RUTH (*Innocently*): Some coffee?

LINDER: Thank you, nothing at all.

(*Beneatha is watching the man carefully*)

LINDNER: Well, I don't know how much you folks know about our organization. (*He is a gentle man; thoughtful and somewhat labored in his manner*) It is one of these community organizations set up to look after—oh, you know, things like block upkeep and special projects and we also have what we call our New Neighbors Orientation Committee . . .

BENEATHA: (*Drily*): Yes—and what do they do?

LINDNER (*Turning a little to her and then returning the main force to Walter*): Well— it's what you might call a sort of welcoming committee, I guess. I mean they, we, I'm the chairman of the committee—go around and see the new people who move into the neighborhood and sort of give them the lowdown on the way we do things out in Clybourne Park.

BENEATHA (*With appreciation of the two meanings, which escape Ruth and Walter*): Un-huh.

LINDNER: And we also have the category of what the association calls—(*He looks elsewhere*)—uh—special community problems . . .

BENEATHA: Yes—and what are some of those?

WALTER: Girl, let the man talk.

LINDNER (*With understated relief*): Thank you. I would sort of like to explain this thing in my own way. I mean I want to explain to you in a certain way.

WALTER: Go ahead.

LINDNER: Yes. Well. I'm going to try to get right to the point. I'm sure we'll all appreciate that in the long run.

BENEATHA: Yes.

WALTER: Be still now!

LINDNER: Well—

RUTH (*Still innocently*): Would you like another chair—you don't look comfortable.

LINDNER (*more frustrated than annoyed*): No, thank you very much. Please. Well—to get right to the point. I—(*A great breath, and he is off at last*) I am sure you people must be aware of some of the incidents which have happened in various parts of the city when colored people have moved into certain areas— (*Beneatha exhales heavily and starts tossing a piece of fruit up and down in the air*) Well—because we have what I think is going to be a unique type of organization in American community life—not only do we deplore that kind of thing—but we are trying to do something about it. (*Beneatha stops tossing and turns with a new and quizzical interest to the man*) We feel—(*gaining confidence in his mission because of the interest in the faces of the people he is talking to*)—we feel that most of the trouble in this world, when you come right down to it—(*He hits his knee for emphasis*)—most of the trouble exists because people just don't sit down and talk to each other.

RUTH (*Nodding as she might in church, pleased with the remark*): You can say that again, mister.

LINDNER (*More encouraged by such affirmation*): That we don't try hard enough in this world to understand the other fellow's problem. The other guy's point of view.

RUTH: Now that's right.

(*Beneatha and Walter merely watch and listen with genuine interest*)

LINDNER: Yes—that's the way we feel out in Clybourne Park. And that's why I was elected to come here this afternoon and talk to you people. Friendly like, you know, the way people should talk to each other and see if we couldn't find some way to work this thing out. As I say, the whole business is a matter of *caring* about the other fellow. Anybody can see that you are a nice family of folks, hard working and honest I'm sure. (*Beneatha frowns slightly, quizzically, her head tilted regarding him*) Today everybody knows what it means to be on the outside of *something*. And of course, there is always somebody who is out to take the advantage of people who don't always understand.

WALTER: What do you mean?

LINDNER: Well—you see our community is made up of people who've worked hard as the dickens for years to build up that little community. They're not rich and fancy people; just hard-working, honest people who don't really have much but those little homes and a dream of the kind of community they want to raise their children in. Now, I don't say we are perfect and there is a lot wrong in some of the things they want. But you've got to admit that a man, right or wrong, has the right to want to have the neighborhood he lives in a certain kind of way. And at the moment the overwhelming majority of our people out there feel that people get along better, take more of a common interest in the life of the community, when they share a common background. I want you to believe me when I tell you that race prejudice simply doesn't enter into it. It is a matter of the people of Clybourne Park believing, rightly or wrongly, as I say, that for the happiness of all concerned that our Negro families are happier when they live in their *own* communities.

BENEATHA *(With a grand and bitter gesture)*: This, friends, is the Welcoming Committee!

WALTER *(Dumfounded, looking at Lindner)*: Is this what you came marching all the way over here to tell us?

LINDNER: Well, now we've been having a fine conversation. I hope you'll hear me all the way through.

WALTER *(Tightly)*: Go ahead, man.

LINDNER: You see—in the face of all things I have said, we are prepared to make your family a very generous offer . . .

BENEATHA: Thirty pieces and not a coin less!

WALTER: Yeah?

LINDNER *(Putting on his glasses and drawing a form out of the briefcase)*: Our association is prepared, through the collective effort of our people, to buy the house from you at a financial gain to your family.

RUTH: Lord have mercy, ain't this the living gall!

WALTER: All right, you through?

LINDNER: Well, I want to give you the exact terms of the financial arrangement—

WALTER: We don't want to hear no exact terms of no arrangements. I want to know if you got any more to tell us 'bout getting together?

LINDNER *(Taking off his glasses)*: Well—I don't suppose that you feel . . .

WALTER: Never mind how I feel—you got any more to say 'bout how people ought to sit down and talk to each other? . . . Get out of my house, man.

(He turns his back and walks to the door)

LINDNER *(Looking around at the hostile faces and reaching and assembling his hat and briefcase)*: Well—I don't understand why you people are reacting this way. What do you think you are going to gain by moving into a neighborhood where you just aren't wanted and where some elements—well—people can get awful worked up when they feel that their whole way of life and everything they've ever worked for is threatened.

WALTER: Get out.

LINDNER *(At the door, holding a small card)*: Well—I'm sorry it went like this.

WALTER: Get out.

LINDNER *(Almost sadly regarding Walter)*: You just can't force people to change their hearts, son.

(He turns and puts his card on a table and exits. Walter pushes the door to with stinging hatred, and stands looking at it. Ruth just sits and Beneatha just stands. They say nothing. Mama and Travis enter.)

MAMA: Well—this all the packing got done since I left out of here this morning. I testify before God that my children got all the energy of the dead. What time the moving men due?

BENEATHA: Four o'clock. You had a caller, Mama.

(She is smiling, teasingly)

MAMA: Sure enough—who?

BENEATHA *(Her arms folded saucily)*: The Welcoming Committee.

(Walter and Ruth giggle)

MAMA *(Innocently)*: Who?

BENEATHA: The Welcoming Committee. They said they're sure going to be glad to see you when you get there.

WALTER *(Devilishly)*: Yeah, they said they can't hardly wait to see your face.

(Laughter)

MAMA *(Sensing their facetiousness)*: What's the matter with you all?

WALTER: Ain't nothing the matter with us. We just telling you 'bout the gentleman who came to see you this afternoon. From the Clybourne Park Improvement Association.

MAMA: What he want?

RUTH *(In the same mood as Beneatha and Walter)*: To welcome you, honey.

WALTER: He said they can't hardly wait. He said the one thing they don't have, that they just *dying* to have out there is a fine family of colored people! *(To Ruth and Beneatha)* Ain't that right!

RUTH *and* BENEATHA *(Mockingly)*: Yeah! He left his card in case—

(They indicate the card, and Mama picks it up and throws it on the floor—understanding and looking off as she draws her chair up to the table on which she has put her plant and some sticks and some cord)

MAMA: Father, give us strength. *(Knowingly—and without fun)* Did he threaten us?

BENEATHA: Oh—Mama—they don't do it like that any more. He talked Brotherhood. He said everybody ought learn how to sit down and hate each other with good Christian fellowship.

(She and Walter shake hands to ridicule the remark)

MAMA *(Sadly)*: Lord, protect us . . .

RUTH: You should hear the money those folks raised to buy the house from us. All we paid and then some.

BENEATHA: What they think we going to do—eat 'em?

RUTH: No, honey, marry 'em.

MAMA *(Shaking her head)*: Lord, Lord, Lord . . .

RUTH: Well—that's the way the crackers crumble. Joke.

BENEATHA *(Laughingly noticing what her mother is doing)*: Mama, what are you doing?

MAMA: Fixing my plant so it won't get hurt none on the way . . .

BENEATHA: Mama, you going to take *that* to the new house?

MAMA: Un-huh—

BENEATHA: That raggedy-looking old thing?

MAMA *(Stopping and looking at her)*: It expresses *me*.
RUTH *(With delight, to Beneatha)*: So there, Miss Thing!

(Walter comes to Mama suddenly and bends down behind her and squeezes her in his arms with all his strength. She is overwhelmed by the suddenness of it and, though delighted, her manner is like that of Ruth with Travis.)

MAMA: Look out now, boy! You make me mess up my thing here!
WALTER *(His face lit, he slips down on his knees beside her, his arms still about her)*: Mama . . . you know what it means to climb up in the chariot?
MAMA *(Gruffly, very happy)*: Get on away from me now . . .
RUTH *(Near the gift-wrapped package, trying to catch Walter's eye)*: Psst—
WALTER: What the old song say, Mama . . .
RUTH: Walter—Now?

(She is pointing at the package)

WALTER *(Speaking the lines, sweetly, playfully, in his mother's face)*:
I got wings . . . you got wings . . .
All God's children got wings . . .
MAMA: Boy—get out of my face and do some work . . .
WALTER:
When I get to heaven gonna put on my wings,
Gonna fly all over God's heaven . . .
BENEATHA *(Teasingly, from across the room)*: Everybody talking 'bout heaven ain't going there!
WALTER *(To Ruth, who is carrying the box across to them)*: I don't know, you think we ought to give her that . . . Seems to me she ain't been very appreciative around here.
MAMA *(Eying the box, which is obviously a gift)*: What is that?
WALTER *(Taking it from Ruth and putting it on the table in front of Mama)*: Well— what you all think. Should we give it to her?
RUTH: Oh—she was pretty good today.
MAMA: I'll good you—

(She turns her eyes to the box again)

BENEATHA: Open it, Mama.

(She stands up, looks at it, turns and looks at all of them, and then presses her hands together and does not open the package)

WALTER *(Sweetly)*: Open it, Mama. It's for you. *(Mama looks in his eyes. It is the first present in her life without its being Christmas. Slowly she opens her package and lifts out, one by one, a brand-new sparkling set of gardening tools. Walter continues, prodding.)* Ruth made up the note—read it . . .
MAMA *(Picking up the card and adjusting her glasses)*: "To our own Mrs. Miniver— Love from Brother, Ruth and Beneatha." Ain't that lovely . . .
TRAVIS *(Tugging at his father's sleeve)*: Daddy, can I give her mine now?
WALTER: All right, son. *(Travis flies to get his gift)* Travis didn't want to go in with the rest of us, Mama. He got his own. *(Somewhat amused)* We don't know what it is . . .

TRAVIS (*Racing back in the room with a large hatbox and putting it in front of his grand-mother*): Here!

MAMA: Lord have mercy, baby. You done gone and bought your grandmother a hat?

TRAVIS (*Very proud*): Open it!

(*She does and lifts out an elaborate, but very elaborate, wide gardening hat, and all the adults break up at the sight of it*)

RUTH: Travis, honey, what is that?

TRAVIS (*Who thinks it is beautiful and appropriate*): It's a gardening hat! Like the la-dies always have on in the magazines when they work in their gardens.

BENEATHA (*Giggling fiercely*): Travis—we were trying to make Mama Mrs. Mini-ver—not Scarlett O'Hara!

MAMA (*Indignantly*): What's matter with you all! This here is a beautiful hat! (*Ab-surdly*) I always wanted me one just like it!

(*She pops it on her head to prove it to her grandson, and the hat is ludicrous and considerably oversized*)

RUTH: Hot Dog! Go, Mama!

WALTER (*Doubled over with laughter*): I'm sorry, Mama—but you look like you ready to go out and chop you some cotton sure enough!

(*They all laugh except Mama, out of deference to Travis' feelings*)

MAMA (*Gathering the boy up to her*): Bless your heart—this is the prettiest hat I ever owned— (*Walter, Ruth and Beneatha chime in—noisily, festively and insin-cerely congratulating Travis on his gift*) What are we standing around here for? We ain't finished packin' yet. Bennie, you ain't packed one book.

(*The bell rings*)

BENEATHA: That couldn't be the movers . . . it's not hardly two good yet—

(*Beneatha goes into her room. Mama starts for door*)

WALTER (*Turning, stiffening*): Wait—wait— I'll get it.

(*He stands and looks at the door*)

MAMA: You expecting company, son?

WALTER (*Just looking at the door*): Yeah—Yeah . . .

(*Mama looks at Ruth, and they exchange innocent and unfrightened glances*)

MAMA (*Not understanding*): Well, let them in, son.

BENEATHA (*From her room*): We need some more string.

MAMA: Travis—you run to the hardware and get me some string cord.

(*Mama goes out and Walter turns and looks at Ruth. Travis goes to a dish for money.*)

RUTH: Why don't you answer the door, man?

WALTER (*Suddenly bounding across the floor to her*): 'Cause sometimes it hard to let the future begin! (*Stooping down in her face*)

I got wings! You got wings!
All God's children got wings!

(He crosses to the door and throws it open. Standing there is a very slight little man in a not too prosperous business suit and with haunted frightened eyes and a hat pulled down tightly, brim up, around his forehead. Travis passes between the men and exits. Walter leans deep in the man's face, still in his jubilance.)

When I get to heaven gonna put on my wings,
Gonna fly all over God's heaven . . .

(The little man just stares at him)

Heaven—

(Suddenly he stops and looks past the little man into the empty hallway)

Where's Willy, man?

BOBO: He ain't with me.

WALTER *(Not disturbed)*: Oh—come on in. You know my wife.

BOBO *(Dumbly, taking off his hat)*: Yes—h'you, Miss Ruth.

RUTH *(Quietly, a mood apart from her husband already, seeing Bobo)*: Hello, Bobo.

WALTER: You right on time today . . . Right on time. That's the way! *(He slaps Bobo on his back)* Sit down . . . lemme hear.

(Ruth stands stiffly and quietly in back of them, as though somehow she senses death, her eyes fixed on her husband)

BOBO *(His frightened eyes on the floor, his hat in his hands)*: Could I please get a drink a water, before I tell you about it, Walter Lee?

(Walter does not take his eyes off the man, Ruth goes blindly to the tap and gets a glass of water and brings it to Bobo)

WALTER: There ain't nothing wrong, is there?

BOBO: Lemme tell you—

WALTER: Man—didn't nothing go wrong?

BOBO: Lemme tell you—Walter Lee. *(Looking at Ruth and talking to her more than to Walter)* You know how it was. I got to tell you how it was. I mean first I got to tell you how it was all the way . . . I mean about the money I put in, Walter Lee . . .

WALTER *(With taut agitation now)*: What about the money you put in?

BOBO: Well—it wasn't much as we told you—me and Willy— *(He stops)* I'm sorry, Walter. I got a bad feeling about it. I got a real bad feeling about it . . .

WALTER: Man, what you telling me about all this for? . . . Tell me what happened in Springfield . . .

BOBO: Springfield.

RUTH *(Like a dead woman)*: What was supposed to happen in Springfield?

BOBO *(To her)*: This deal that me and Walter went into with Willy—Me and Willy was going to go down to Springfield and spread some money 'round so's we wouldn't have to wait so long for the liquor license . . . That's what we were going to do. Everybody said that was the way you had to do, you understand, Miss Ruth?

WALTER: Man—what happened down there?

BOBO (*A pitiful man, near tears*): I'm trying to tell you, Walter.

WALTER (*Screaming at him suddenly*): THEN TELL ME, GODDAMMIT . . . WHAT'S THE MATTER WITH YOU?

BOBO: Man . . . I didn't go to no Springfield, yesterday.

WALTER (*Halted, life hanging in the moment*): Why not?

BOBO (*The long way, the hard way to tell*): 'Cause I didn't have no reasons to . . .

WALTER: Man, what are you talking about!

BOBO: I'm talking about the fact that when I got to the train station yesterday morning—eight o'clock like we planned . . . Man—*Willy didn't never show up.*

WALTER: Why . . . where was he . . . where is he?

BOBO: That's what I'm trying to tell you . . . I don't know . . . I waited six hours . . . I called his house . . . and I waited . . . six hours . . . I waited in that train station six hours . . . (*Breaking into tears*) That was all the extra money I had in the world . . . (*Looking up at Walter with the tears running down his face*) Man, Willy is gone.

WALTER: Gone, what you mean Willy is gone? Gone where? You mean he went by himself. You mean he went off to Springfield by himself—to take care of getting the license—(*Turns and looks anxiously at Ruth*) You mean maybe he didn't want too many people in on the business down there? (*Looks to Ruth again, as before*) You know Willy got his own ways. (*Looks back to Bobo*) Maybe you was late yesterday and he just went on down there without you. Maybe— maybe—he's been callin' you at home tryin' to tell you what happened or something. Maybe—maybe—he just got sick. He's somewhere—he's got to be somewhere. We just got to find him—me and you got to find him. (*Grabs Bobo senselessly by the collar and starts to shake him*) We got to!

BOBO (*In sudden angry, frightened agony*): What's the matter with you, Walter! *When a cat take off with your money he don't leave you no maps!*

WALTER (*Turning madly, as though he is looking for Willy in the very room*): Willy! . . . Willy . . . don't do it . . . Please don't do it . . . Man, not with that money . . . Man, please, not with that money . . . Oh, God . . . Don't let it be true . . . (*He is wandering around, crying out for Willy and looking for him or perhaps for help from God*) Man . . . I trusted you . . . Man, I put my life in your hands . . . (*He starts to crumple down on the floor as Ruth just covers her face in horror. Mama opens the door and comes into the room, with Beneatha behind her*) Man . . . (*He starts to pound the floor with his fists, sobbing wildly*) That money is made out of my father's flesh . . .

BOBO (*Standing over him helplessly*): I'm sorry, Walter . . . (*Only Walter's sobs reply. Bobo puts on his hat*) I had my life staked on this deal, too . . .

(*He exits*)

MAMA (*To Walter*): Son— (*She goes to him, bends down to him, talks to his bent head*) Son . . . Is it gone? Son, I gave you sixty-five hundred dollars. Is it gone? All of it? Beneatha's money too?

WALTER (*Lifting his head slowly*): Mama . . . I never . . . went to the bank at all . . .

MAMA (*Not wanting to believe him*): You mean . . . your sister's school money . . . you used that too . . . Walter? . . .

WALTER: Yessss! . . . All of it . . . It's all gone . . .

(There is total silence. Ruth stands with her face covered with her hands; Beneatha leans forlornly against a wall, fingering a piece of red ribbon from the mother's gift. Mama stops and looks at her son without recognition and then, quite without thinking about it, starts to beat him senselessly in the face. Beneatha goes to them and stops it.)

BENEATHA: Mama!

(Mama stops and looks at both of her children and rises slowly and wanders vaguely, aimlessly away from them)

MAMA: I seen . . . him . . . night after night . . . come in . . . and look at that rug . . . and then look at me . . . the red showing in his eyes . . . the veins moving in his head . . . I seen him grow thin and old before he was forty . . . working and working and working like somebody's old horse . . . killing himself . . . and you—you give it all away in a day . . .

BENEATHA: Mama—

MAMA: Oh, God . . . *(She looks up to Him)* Look down here—and show me the strength.

BENEATHA: Mama—

MAMA *(Folding over)*: Strength . . .

BENEATHA *(Plaintively)*: Mama . . .

MAMA: Strength!

(Curtain)

Act Three

An hour later. At curtain, there is a sullen light of gloom in the living room, gray light not unlike that which began the first scene of Act One. At left we can see Walter within his room, alone with himself. He is stretched out on the bed, his shirt out and open, his arms under his head. He does not smoke, he does not cry out, he merely lies there, looking up at the ceiling, much as if he were alone in the world. In the living room Beneatha sits at the table, still surrounded by the now almost ominous packing crates. She sits looking off. We feel that this is a mood struck perhaps an hour before, and it lingers now, full of the empty sound of profound disappointment. We see on a line from her brother's bedroom the sameness of their attitudes. Presently the bell rings and Beneatha rises without ambition or interest in answering. It is Asagai, smiling broadly, striding into the room with energy and happy expectation and conversation.

ASAGAI: I came over . . . I had some free time. I thought I might help with the packing. Ah, I like the look of packing crates! A household in preparation for a journey! It depresses some people . . . but for me . . . it is another feeling. Something full of the flow of life, do you understand? Movement, progress . . . It makes me think of Africa.

BENEATHA: Africa!

ASAGAI: What kind of a mood is this? Have I told you how deeply you move me?

BENEATHA: He gave away the money, Asagai . . .

ASAGAI: Who gave away what money?

BENEATHA: The insurance money. My brother gave it away.

ASAGAI: Gave it away?

BENEATHA: He made an investment! With a man even Travis wouldn't have trusted.

ASAGAI: And it's gone?

BENEATHA: Gone!

ASAGAI: I'm very sorry . . . And you, now?

BENEATHA: Me? . . . Me? . . . Me I'm nothing . . . Me. When I was very small . . . we used to take our sleds out in the wintertime and the only hills we had were the ice-covered stone steps of some houses down the street. And we used to fill them in with snow and make them smooth and slide down them all day . . . and it was very dangerous you know . . . far too steep . . . and sure enough one day a kid named Rufus came down too fast and hit the sidewalk . . . and we saw his face just split open right there in front of us . . . And I remember standing there looking at his bloody open face thinking that was the end of Rufus. But the ambulance came and they took him to the hospital and they fixed the broken bones and they sewed it all up . . . and the next time I saw Rufus he just had a little line down the middle of his face . . . I never got over that . . .

(Walter sits up, listening on the bed. Throughout this scene it is important that we feel his reaction at all times, that he visibly respond to the words of his sister and Asagai.)

ASAGAI: What?

BENEATHA: That that was what one person could do for another, fix him up—sew up the problem, make him all right again. That was the most marvelous thing in the world . . . I wanted to do that. I always thought it was the one concrete thing in the world that a human being could do. Fix up the sick, you know— and make them whole again. This was truly being God. . . .

ASAGAI: You wanted to be God?

BENEATHA: No—I wanted to cure. It used to be so important to me. I wanted to cure. It used to matter. I used to care. I mean about people and how their bodies hurt . . .

ASAGAI: And you've stopped caring?

BENEATHA: Yes—I think so.

ASAGAI: Why?

(Walter rises, goes to the door of his room and is about to open it, then stops and stands listening, leaning on the door jamb)

BENEATHA: Because it doesn't seem deep enough, close enough to what ails mankind—I mean this thing of sewing up bodies or administering drugs. Don't you understand? It was a child's reaction to the world. I thought that doctors had the secret to all the hurts . . . That's the way a child sees things—or an idealist.

ASAGAI: Children see things very well sometimes—and idealists even better.

BENEATHA: I know that's what you think. Because you are still where I left off— you still care. This is what you see for the world, for Africa. You with the dreams of the future will patch up all Africa—you are going to cure the Great Sore of colonialism with Independence—

ASAGAI: Yes!

BENEATHA: Yes—and you think that one world is the penicillin of the human spirit: "Independence!" But when what?

ASAGAI: That will be the problem for another time. First we must get there.

BENEATHA: And where does it end?

ASAGAI: End? Who even spoke of an end? To life? To living?

BENEATHA: An end to misery!

ASAGAI (Smiling): You sound like a French intellectual.

BENEATHA: No! I sound like a human being who just had her future taken right out of her hands! While I was sleeping in my bed in there, things were happening in this world that directly concerned me—and nobody asked me, consulted me—they just went out and did things—and changed my life. Don't you see there isn't any real progress, Asagai, there is only one large circle that we march in, around and around, each of us with our own little picture—in front of us—our own little mirage that we think is the future.

ASAGAI: That is the mistake.

BENEATHA: What?

ASAGAI: What you just said—about the circle. It isn't a circle—it is simply a long line—as in geometry, you know, one that reaches into infinity. And because we cannot see the end—we also cannot see how it changes. And it is very odd but those who see the changes are called "idealists"—and those who cannot, or refuse to think, they are the "realists." It is very strange, and amusing too, I think.

BENEATHA: You—you are almost religious.

ASAGAI: Yes . . . I think I have the religion of doing what is necessary in the world—and of worshipping man—because he is so marvelous, you see.

BENEATHA: Man is foul! And the human race deserves its misery!

ASAGAI: You see: you have become the religous one in the old sense. Already, and after such a small defeat, you are worshipping despair.

BENEATHA: From now on, I worship the truth—and the truth—is that people are puny, small and selfish. . . .

ASAGAI: Truth? Why is it that you despairing ones always think that only you have the truth? I never thought to see you like that. Your brother made a stupid, childish mistake—and you are grateful to him. So that now you can give up the ailing human race on account of it. You talk about what good is struggle; what good is anything? Where are we all going? And why are we bothering?

BENEATHA: And you cannot answer it! All your talk and dreams about Africa and Independence. Independence and then what? What about all the crooks and petty thieves and just plain idiots who will come into power to steal and plunder the same as before—only now they will be black and do it in the name of the new Independence—You cannot answer that.

ASAGAI (Shouting over her): I live the answer! (Pause) In my village at home it is the exceptional man who can even read a newspaper . . . or who ever sees a book at all. I will go home and much of what I will have to say will seem strange to the people of my village . . . But I will teach and work and things will happen, slowly and swiftly. At times it will seem that nothing changes at all . . . and then again . . . the sudden dramatic events which make history leap into the future. And then quiet again. Retrogression even. Guns, murder, revolution. And I even will have moments when I wonder if the quiet was not better than all that death and hatred. But I will look about my village at the illiteracy and disease and ignorance and I will not wonder long. And perhaps . . . perhaps I will be a great man . . . I mean perhaps I will hold on to the substance of truth and find my way always with the right course . . . and perhaps for it I will be butchered in my bed some night by the servants of empire . . .

BENEATHA: *The martyr!*

ASAGAI: . . . or perhaps I shall live to be a very old man respected and esteemed in my new nation . . . And perhaps I shall hold office and this is what I'm trying to tell you, Alaiyo; perhaps the things I believe now for my country will be wrong and outmoded, and I will not understand and do terrible things to have things my way or merely to keep my power. Don't you see that there will be young men and women, not British soldiers then, but my own black countrymen . . . to step out of the shadows some evening and slit my then useless throat? Don't you see they have always been there . . . that they always will be. And that such a thing as my own death will be an advance? They who might kill me even . . . actually replenish me!

BENEATHA: Oh, Asagai, I know all that.

ASAGAI: Good! Then stop moaning and groaning and tell me what you plan to do.

BENEATHA: Do?

ASAGAI: I have a bit of a suggestion.

BENEATHA: What?

ASAGAI (*Rather quietly for him*): That when it is all over—that you come home with me—

BENEATHA (*Slapping herself on the forehead with exasperation born of misunderstanding*): Oh—Asagai—at this moment you decide to be romantic!

ASAGAI (*Quickly understanding the misunderstanding*): My dear, young creature of the New World—I do not mean across the city—I mean across the ocean; come—to Africa.

BENEATHA (*Slowly understanding and turning to him with murmured amazement*): To—to Nigeria?

ASAGAI: Yes! . . . (*Smiling and lifting his arms playfully*) Three hundred years later the African Prince rose up out of the seas and swept the maiden back across the middle passage over which her ancestors had come—

BENEATHA (*Unable to play*): Nigeria?

ASAGAI: Nigeria. Home. (*Coming to her with genuine romantic flippancy*) I will show you our mountains and our stars; and give you cool drinks from gourds and teach you the old songs and the ways of our people—and, in time, we will pretend that—(*Very softly*)—you have only been away for a day—

(*She turns her back to him, thinking. He swings her around and takes her full in his arms in a long embrace which proceeds to passion.*)

BENEATHA (*Pulling away*): You're getting me all mixed up—

ASAGAI: Why?

BENEATHA: Too many things—too many things have happened today. I must sit down and think. I don't know what I feel about anything right this minute.

(She promptly sits down and props her chin on her fist)

ASAGAI *(Charmed)*: All right, I shall leave you. No—don't get up. *(Touching her, gently, sweetly)* Just sit awhile and think . . . Never be afraid to sit awhile and think. *(He goes to door and looks at her)* How often I have looked at you and said, "Ah—so this is what the New World hath finally wrought . . ."

(He exits. Beneatha sits on alone. Presently Walter enters from his room and starts to rummage through things, feverishly looking for something. She looks up and turns in her seat.)

BENEATHA *(Hissingly)*: Yes—just look at what the New World hath wrought! . . . Just look! *(She gestures with bitter disgust)* There he is! *Monsieur le petit bourgeois noir*—himself! There he is—Symbol of a Rising Class! Entrepreneur! Titan of the system! *(Walter ignores her completely and continues frantically and destructively looking for something and hurling things to floor and tearing things out of their place in his search. Beneatha ignores the eccentricity of his actions and goes on with the monologue of insult.)* Did you dream of yachts on Lake Michigan, Brother? Did you see yourself on that Great Day sitting down at the Conference Table, surrounded by all the mighty bald-headed men in America? All halted, waiting, breathless, waiting for your pronouncements on industry? Waiting for you—Chairman of the Board? *(Walter finds what he is looking for—a small piece of white paper—and pushes it in his pocket and puts on his coat and rushes out without ever having looked at her. She shouts after him.)* I look at you and I see the final triumph of stupidity in the world!

(The door slams and she returns to just sitting again. Ruth comes quickly out of Mama's room.)

RUTH: Who was that?
BENEATHA: Your husband.
RUTH: Where did he go?
BENEATHA: Who knows—maybe he has an appointment at U.S. Steel.
RUTH *(Anxiously, with frightened eyes)*: You didn't say nothing bad to him, did you?
BENEATHA: Bad? Say anything bad to him? No—I told him he was a sweet boy and full of dreams and everything is strictly peachy keen, as the ofay kids say!

(Mama enters from her bedroom. She is lost, vague, trying to catch hold, to make some sense of her former command of the world, but it still eludes her. A sense of waste overwhelms her gait; a measure of apology rides on her shoulders. She goes to her plant, which has remained on the table, looks at it, picks it up and takes it to the window sill and sits it outside, and she stands and looks at it a long moment. Then she closes the window, straightens her body with effort and turns around to her children.)

MAMA: Well—ain't it a mess in here, though? *(A false cheerfulness, a beginning of something)* I guess we all better stop moping around and get some work done. All this unpacking and everything we got to do. *(Ruth raises her head slowly in response to the sense of the line; and Beneatha in similar manner turns very slowly to look at her mother)* One of you all better call the moving people and tell 'em not to come.

RUTH: Tell 'em not to come?

MAMA: Of course, baby. Ain't no need in 'em coming all the way here and having to go back. They charges for that too. *(She sits down, fingers to her brow, thinking)* Lord, ever since I was a little girl, I always remembers people saying, "Lena—Lena Eggleston, you aims too high all the time. You needs to slow down and see life a little more like it is. Just slow down some." That's what they always used to say down home—"Lord, that Lena Eggleston is a high-minded thing. She'll get her due one day!"

RUTH: No, Lena . . .

MAMA: Me and Big Walter just didn't never learn right.

RUTH: Lena, no! We gotta go. Bennie—tell her . . . *(She rises and crosses to Beneatha with her arms outstretched. Beneatha doesn't respond.)* Tell her we can still move . . . the notes ain't but a hundred and twenty five a month. We got four grown people in this house—we can work . . .

MAMA *(To herself)*: Just aimed too high all the time—

RUTH *(Turning and going to Mama fast—the words pouring out with urgency and desperation)*: Lena—I'll work . . . I'll work twenty hours a day in all the kitchens in Chicago . . . I'll strap my baby on my back if I have to and scrub all the floors in America and wash all the sheets in America if I have to—but we got to move . . . We got to get out of here . . .

(Mama reaches out absently and pats Ruth's hand)

MAMA: No—I sees things differently now. Been thinking 'bout some of the things we could do to fix this place up some. I seen a second-hand bureau over on Maxwell Street just the other day that could fit right there. *(She points to where the new furniture might go. Ruth wanders away from her)* Would need some new handles on it and then a little varnish and then it look like something brand-new. And—we can put put them new curtains in the kitchen . . . Why this place be looking fine. Cheer us all up so that we forget trouble ever came . . . *(To Ruth)* And you could get some nice screens to put up in your room round the baby's bassinet . . . *(She looks at both of them, pleadingly)* Sometimes you just got to know when to give up some things . . . and hold on to what you got.

(Walter enters from the outside, looking spent and leaning against the door, his coat hanging from him)

MAMA: Where you been, son?

WALTER *(Breathing hard)*: Made a call.

MAMA: To who, son?

WALTER: To The Man.

MAMA: What man, baby?

WALTER: The Man, Mama. Don't you know who The Man is?

RUTH: Walter Lee?

WALTER: *The Man.* Like the guys in the streets say—The Man. Captain Boss—Mistuh Charley . . . Old Captain Please Mr. Bossman . . .

BENEATHA *(Suddenly)*: Lindner!

WALTER: That's right! That's good. I told him to come right over.

BENEATHA *(Fiercely, understanding)*: For what? What do you want to see him for!

WALTER (*Looking at his sister*): We going to do business with him.

MAMA: What you talking 'bout, son?

WALTER: Talking 'bout life, Mama. You all always telling me to see life like it is. Well—I laid in there on my back today . . . and I figured it out. Life just like it is. Who gets and who don't get. (*He sits down with his coat on and laughs*) Mama, you know it's all divided up. Life is. Sure enough. Between the takers and the "tooken." (*He laughs*) I've figured it out finally. (*He looks around at them*) Yeah. Some of us always getting "tooken." (*He laughs*) People like Willy Harris, they don't never get "tooken." And you know why the rest of us do? 'Cause we all mixed up. Mixed up bad. We get to looking 'round for the right and the wrong; and we worry about it and cry about it and stay up nights trying to figure out 'bout the wrong and the right of things all the time . . . And all the time, man, them takers is out there operating, just taking and taking. Willy Harris? Shoot—Willy Harris don't even count. He don't even count in the big scheme of things. But I'll say one thing for old Willy Harris . . . he's taught me something. He's taught me to keep my eye on what counts in this world. Yeah—(*Shouting out a little*) Thanks, Willy!

RUTH: What did you call that man for, Walter Lee?

WALTER: Called him to tell him to come on over to the show. Gonna put on a show for the man. Just what he wants to see. You see, Mama, the man came here today and he told us that them people out there where you want us to move—well they so upset they willing to pay us not to move out there. (*He laughs again*) And—and oh, Mama—you would of been proud of the way me and Ruth and Bennie acted. We told him to get out . . . Lord have mercy! We told the man to get out. Oh, we was some proud folks this afternoon, yeah. (*He lights a cigarette*) We were still full of that old-time stuff . . .

RUTH (*Coming toward him slowly*): You talking 'bout taking them people's money to keep us from moving in that house?

WALTER: I ain't just talking 'bout it, baby—I'm telling you that's what's going to happen.

BENEATHA: Oh, God! Where is the bottom! Where is the real honest-to-God bottom so he can't go any farther!

WALTER: See—that's the old stuff. You and that boy that was here today. You all want everybody to carry a flag and a spear and sing some marching songs, huh? You wanna spend your life looking into things and trying to find the right and the wrong part, huh? Yeah. You know what's going to happen to that boy someday—he'll find himself sitting in a dungeon, locked in forever—and the takers will have the key! Forget it, baby! There ain't no causes—there ain't nothing but taking in this world, and he who takes most is smartest—and it don't make a damn bit of difference *how*.

MAMA: You making something inside me cry, son. Some awful pain inside me.

WALTER: Don't cry, Mama. Understand. That white man is going to walk in that door able to write checks for more money than we ever had. It's important to him and I'm going to help him . . . I'm going to put on the show, Mama.

MAMA: Son—I come from five generations of people who was slaves and share-croppers—but ain't nobody in my family never let nobody pay 'em no money that was a way of telling us we wasn't fit to walk the earth. We ain't never been that poor. (*Raising her eyes and looking at him*) We ain't never been that dead inside.

BENEATHA: Well—we are dead now. All the talk about dreams and sunlight that goes on in this house. All dead.

WALTER: What's the matter with you all! I didn't make this world! It was give to me this way! Hell, yes, I want me some yachts someday! Yes, I want to hang some real pearls 'round my wife's neck. Ain't she supposed to wear no pearls? Somebody tell me—tell me, who decides which women is suppose to wear pearls in this world. I tell you I am a *man*—and I think my wife should wear some pearls in this world!

(This last line hangs a good while and Walter begins to move about the room. The word "Man" has penetrated his consciousness; he mumbles it to himself repeatedly between strange agitated pauses as he moves about)

MAMA: Baby, how you going to feel on the inside?

WALTER: Fine! . . . Going to feel fine . . . a man . . .

MAMA: You won't have nothing left then, Walter Lee.

WALTER *(Coming to her)*: I'm going to feel fine, Mama. I'm going to look that son-of-a-bitch in the eyes and say— *(He falters)* —and say, "All right, Mr. Lindner— *(He falters even more)* —that's your neighborhood out there. You got the right to keep it like you want. You got the right to have it like you want. Just write the check and—the house is yours." And, and I am going to say— *(His voice almost breaks)* And you—you people just put the money in my hand and you won't have to live next to this bunch of stinking niggers! . . . *(He straightens up and moves away from his mother, walking around the room)* Maybe—maybe I'll just get down on my black knees . . . *(He does so; Ruth and Bennie and Mama watch him in frozen horror)* Captain, Mistuh, Bossman. *(He starts crying)* A-hee-hee-hee! *(Wringing his hands in profoundly anguished imitation)* Yasssssuh! Great White Father, just gi' ussen de money, fo' God's sake, and we's ain't gwine come out deh and dirty up yo' white folks neighborhood . . .

(He breaks down completely, then gets up and goes into the bedroom)

BENEATHA: That is not a man. That is nothing but a toothless rat.

MAMA: Yes—death done come in this here house. *(She is nodding, slowly, reflectively)* Done come walking in my house. On the lips of my children. You what supposed to be my beginning again. You—what supposed to be my harvest. *(To Beneatha)* You—you mourning your brother?

BENEATHA: He's no brother of mine.

MAMA: What you say?

BENEATHA: I said that the individual in that room is no brother of mine.

MAMA: That's what I thought you said. You feeling like you better than he is today? *(Beneatha does not answer)* Yes? What you tell him a minute ago? That he wasn't a man? Yes? You give him up for me? You done wrote his epitaph too—like the rest of the world? Well, who give you the privilege?

BENEATHA: Be on my side for once! You saw what he just did. Mama! You saw him—down on his knees. Wasn't it you who taught me—to despise any man who would do that. Do what he's going to do.

MAMA: Yes—I taught you that. Me and your daddy. But I thought I taught you something else too . . . I thought I taught you to love him.

BENEATHA: Love him? There is nothing left to love.

MAMA: There is always something left to love. And if you ain't learned that, you ain't learned nothing. *(Looking at her)* Have you cried for that boy today? I don't mean for yourself and for the family 'cause we lost the money. I mean for him; what he been through and what it done to him. Child, when do you think is the time to love somebody the most; when they done good and made things easy for everybody? Well then, you ain't through learning—because that ain't the time at all. It's when he's at his lowest and can't believe in hisself 'cause the world done whipped him so. When you starts measuring somebody, measure him right, child, measure him right. Make sure you done taken into account what hills and valleys he come through before he got to wherever he is.

(Travis bursts into the room at the end of the speech, leaving the door open)

TRAVIS: Grandmama—the moving men are downstairs! The truck just pulled up.
MAMA *(Turning and looking at him)*: Are they, baby? They downstairs?

(She sighs and sits. Lindner appears in the doorway. He peers in and knocks lightly, to gain attention, and comes in. All turn to look at him.)

LINDNER *(Hat and briefcase in hand)*: Uh—hello . . .

(Ruth crosses mechanically to the bedroom door and opens it and lets it swing open freely and slowly as the lights come up on Walter within, still in his coat, sitting at the far corner of the room. He looks up and out through the room to Lindner.)

RUTH: He's here.

(A long minute passes and Walter slowly gets up)

LINDNER *(Coming to the table with efficiency, putting his briefcase on the table and starting to unfold papers, and unscrew fountain pens)*: Well, I certainly was glad to hear from you people. *(Walter has begun the trek out of the room, slowly and awkwardly, rather like a small boy, passing the back of his sleeve across his mouth from time to time)* Life can really be so much simpler than people let it be most of the time. Well—with whom do I negotiate? You, Mrs. Younger, or your son here? *(Mama sits with her hands folded on her lap and her eyes closed as Walter advances. Travis goes close to Lindner and looks at the papers curiously.)* Just some official papers, sonny.
RUTH: Travis, you go downstairs.
MAMA *(Opening her eyes and looking into Walter's)*: No, Travis, you stay right here. And you make him understand what you doing, Walter Lee. You teach him good. Like Willy Harris taught you. You show where our five generations done come to. Go ahead, son—
WALTER *(Looks down into this boy's eyes. Travis grins at him merrily and Walter draws him beside him with his arm lightly around his shoulder.)*: Well, Mr. Lindner. *(Beneatha turns away)* We called you— *(There is a profound, simple groping quality in his speech)*—because, well, me and my family *(He looks around and shifts from one foot to the other)* Well—we are very plain people . . .
LINDNER: Yes—
WALTER: I mean—I have worked as a chauffeur most of my life —and my wife here, she does domestic work in people's kitchens. So does my mother. I mean—we are plain people . . .
LINDNER: Yes, Mr. Younger—

WALTER (*Really like a small boy, looking down at his shoes and then up at the man*): And—uh—well, my father, well, he was a laborer most of his life.

LINDNER (*Absolutely confused*): Uh, yes—

WALTER (*Looking down at his toes once again*): My father almost beat a man to death once because this man called him a bad name or something, you know what I mean?

LINDNER: No, I'm afraid I don't.

WALTER (*Finally straightening up*): Well, what I mean is that we come from people who had a lot of pride. I mean—we are very proud people. And that's my sister over there and she's going to be a doctor—and we are very proud—

LINDNER: Well—I am sure that is very nice, but—

WALTER (*Starting to cry and facing the man eye to eye*): What I am telling you is that we called you over here to tell you that we are very proud and that this is— this is my son, who makes the sixth generation of our family in this country, and that we have all thought about your offer and we have decided to move into our house because my father—my father—he earned it. (*Mama has her eyes closed and is rocking back and forth as though she were in church, with her head nodding the amen yes*) We don't want to make no trouble for nobody or fight no causes—but we will try to be good neighbors. That's all we got to say. (*He looks the man absolutely in the eyes*) We don't want your money.

(*He turns and walks away from the man*)

LINDNER (*Looking around at all of them*): I take it then that you have decided to occupy.

BENEATHA: That's what the man said.

LINDNER (*To Mama in her reverie*): Then I would like to appeal to you, Mrs. Younger. You are older and wiser and understand things better I am sure . . .

MAMA (*Rising*): I am afraid you don't understand. My son said we was going to move and there ain't nothing left for me to say. (*Shaking her head with double meaning*) You know how these young folks is nowadays, mister. Can't do a thing with 'em. Good-bye.

LINDNER (*Folding up his materials*): Well—if you are that final about it . . . There is nothing left for me to say. (*He finishes. He is almost ignored by the family, who are concentrating on Walter Lee. At the door Lindner halts and looks around.*) I sure hope you people know what you're doing.

(*He shakes his head and exits*)

RUTH (*Looking around and coming to life*): Well, for God's sake—if the moving men are here—LET'S GET THE HELL OUT OF HERE!

MAMA (*Into action*): Ain't it the truth! Look at all this here mess. Ruth put Travis' good jacket on him . . . Walter Lee, fix your tie and tuck your shirt in, you look just like somebody's hoodlum. Lord have mercy, where is my plant? (*She flies to get it amid the general bustling of the family, who are deliberately trying to ignore the nobility of the past moment*) You all start on down . . . Travis child, don't go empty-handed . . . Ruth, where did I put that box with my skillets in it? I want to be in charge of it myself . . . I'm going to make us the biggest dinner we ever ate tonight . . . Beneatha, what's the matter with them stockings? Pull them things up, girl . . .

(The family starts to file out as two moving men appear and begin to carry out the heavier pieces of furniture, bumping into the family as they move about)

BENEATHA: Mama, Asagai—asked me to marry him today and go to Africa—

MAMA *(In the middle of her getting-ready activity)*: He did? You ain't old enough to marry nobody— *(Seeing the moving men lifting one of her chairs precariously)* Darling, that ain't no bale of cotton, please handle it so we can sit in it again. I had that chair twenty-five years . . .

(The movers sigh with exasperation and go on with their work)

BENEATHA *(Girlishly and unreasonably trying to pursue the conversation)*: To go to Africa, Mama—be a doctor in Africa . . .

MAMA *(Distracted)*: Yes, baby—

WALTER: Africa! What he want you to go to Africa for?

BENEATHA: To practice there . . .

WALTER: Girl, if you don't get all them silly ideas out your head! You better marry yourself a man with some loot . . .

BENEATHA *(Angrily, precisely as in the first scene of the play)*: What have you got to do with who I marry!

WALTER: Plenty. Now I think George Murchison—

(He and Beneatha go out yelling at each other vigorously; Beneatha is heard saying that she would not marry George Murchison if he were Adam and she were Eve, etc. The anger is loud and real till their voices diminish. Ruth stands at the door and turns to Mama and smiles knowingly.)

MAMA *(Fixing her hat at last)*: Yeah—they something all right, my children . . .

RUTH: Yeah—they're something. Let's go, Lena.

MAMA *(Stalling, starting to look around at the house)*: Yes— I'm coming. Ruth—

RUTH: Yes?

MAMA *(Quietly, woman to woman)*: He finally come into his manhood today, didn't he? Kind of like a rainbow after the rain . . .

RUTH *(Biting her lip lest her own pride explode in front of Mama)*: Yes, Lena.

(Walter's voice calls for them raucously)

MAMA *(Waving Ruth out vaguely)*: All right, honey—go on down. I be down directly.

(Ruth hesitates, then exits. Mama stands, at last alone in the living room, her plant on the table before her as the lights start to come down. She looks around at all the walls and ceilings and suddenly, despite herself, while the children call below, a great heaving thing rises in her and she puts her fist to her mouth, takes a final desperate look, pulls her coat about her, pats her hat and goes out. The lights dim down. The door opens and she comes back in, grabs her plant, and goes out for the last time.)

(Curtain)

CHAPTER 4

Farce, Fantasy, and the Absurd

All drama is illusion. The stage encapsulates a world different from the reality inhabited by the audience: costumes, settings, and lights subserve the purposes of the illusion; the actor is not the person he portrays. Yet, in the end, most traditional drama constructs a world we recognize as in substantial ways like our own. Increasingly in the twentieth century, however, dramatists have discovered subject matter in the idea of illusion itself. What in this world can we believe in? Where does truth reside? If the actor is only pretending, why must he limit his pretending to the world as we see it? Why must he act and talk like a person involved in a plot the audience can accept as truthful?

The possibility for meaningful illusions extending beyond surface reality has always been present in drama. Sophocles, Shakespeare, and Molière heightened their tragic and comic realities within the limits of conventions acceptable to their times. So, too, Aristophanes in his own way and Strindberg in his. In traditional romance and satire, the truthful core sometimes seems forgotten as the dramatist strives toward fulfillment of the inner logic of his premises. Farce has always exaggerated, frequently beyond belief.

In some of the plays that follow, these tendencies have been pushed beyond traditional limits. We begin with Pirandello's *It Is So! (If You Think So)*, a play that suggests the only truth is the truth we believe. To make that point, Pirandello envelops his plot in the surface reality appropriate to a play by Chekhov. This village, we are asked to believe, is like any village, this house like any house, these people like any people. But who exactly are these people? What is the relationship between them? We finish the play wondering a bit, perhaps, whether our own certainties are any more stable than these.

IT *IS* SO! (IF YOU THINK SO)*

A PARABLE IN THREE ACTS

Luigi Pirandello   (1867–1936)

CHARACTERS

LAMBERTO LAUDISI	SIRELLI
SIGNORA FROLA	SIGNORA SIRELLI, *his wife*
PONZA, *Son-in-law of Signora Frola*	THE PREFECT
SIGNORA PONZA, *Ponza's wife*	CENTURI, *a police commissioner*
COMMENDATORE AGAZZI, *a provincial*	SIGNORA CINI
councillor	SIGNORA NENNI
AMALIA, *his wife*	A BUTLER
DINA, *their daughter*	A NUMBER OF LADIES AND GENTLEMEN

(Our Own Times, in a Small Italian Town, the Capital of a Province)

Act I

The parlor in the house of Commendatore Agazzi.

> *A door, the general entrance, at the back; doors leading to the wings, left and right.*
>
> *Laudisi is a man nearing the forties, quick and energetic in his movements. He is smartly dressed, in good taste. At this moment he is wearing a semi-formal street suit: a sack coat, of a violet cast, with black lapels, and with black braid around the edges; trousers of a light but different color.*
>
> *Amalia, Agazzi's wife, is Laudisi's sister. She is a woman of forty-five more or less. Her hair is already quite grey. Signora Agazzi is always showing a certain sense of her own importance from the position occupied by her husband in the community; but she gives you to understand that if she had a free rein she would be quite capable of playing her own part in the world and, perhaps, do it somewhat better than Commendatore Agazzi.*
>
> *Dina is the daughter of Amalia and Agazzi. She is nineteen. Her general manner is that of a young person conscious of understanding everything better than papa and mamma; but this defect must not be exaggerated to the extent of concealing her attractiveness and charm as a good-looking winsome girl.*
>
> *As the curtain rises Laudisi is walking briskly up and down the parlor to give vent to his irritation.*

LAUDISI: I see, I see! So he did take the matter up with the prefect!

AMALIA: But Lamberto *dear*, please remember that the man is a subordinate of his.

LAUDISI: A subordinate of his . . . very well! But a subordinate in the office, not at home nor in society!

DINA: And he hired an apartment for that woman, his mother-in-law, right here in this very building, and on our floor.

LAUDISI: And why not, pray? He was looking for an apartment; the apartment was for rent, so he leased it—for his mother-in-law. You mean to say that a mother-in-law is in duty bound to make advances to the wife and daughter of the man who happens to be her son-in-law's superior on his job?

---

* Translated by Arthur Livingston.

AMALIA: That is not the way it is, Lamberto. We didn't ask her to call on us. Dina and I took the first step by calling on her and—she *refused to receive* us!

LAUDISI: Well, is that any reason why your husband should go and lodge a complaint with the man's boss? Do you expect the government to order him to invite you to tea?

AMALIA: I think he deserves all he gets! That is not the way to treat two ladies. I hope he gets fired! The idea!

LAUDISI: Oh, you women! I say, making that complaint is a dirty trick. By Jove! If people see fit to keep to themselves in their own houses, haven't they a right to?

AMALIA: Yes, but you don't understand! We were trying to do her a favor. She is new in the town. We wanted to make her feel at home.

DINA: Now, now, uncle dear, don't be so cross! Perhaps we did go there out of curiosity more than anything else; but it's all so funny, isn't it! Don't you think it was natural to feel just a little bit curious?

LAUDISI: Natural be damned! It was none of your business!

DINA: Now, see here, uncle, let's suppose—here you are right here minding your own business and quite indifferent to what other people are doing all around you. Very well! I come into the room and right here on this table, under your very nose, and with a long face like an undertaker's, or, rather, with the long face of that jailbird you are defending, I set down—well what?—anything—a pair of dirty old shoes!

LAUDISI: I don't see the connection.

DINA: Wait, don't interrupt me! I said a pair of old shoes. Well, no, not a pair of old shoes—a flat iron, a rolling pin, or your shaving brush for instance—and I walk out again without saying a word to anybody! Now I leave it to you, wouldn't you feel justified in wondering just a little, little, bit as to what in the world I meant by it?

LAUDISI: Oh, you're irresistible, Dina! And you're clever, aren't you? But you're talking with old uncle, remember! You see, you have been putting all sorts of crazy things on the table here; and you did it with the idea of making me ask what it's all about; and, of course, since you were doing all that on purpose, you can't blame me if I do ask, why those old shoes just there, on that table, dearie? But what's all that got to do with it? You'll have to show me now that this Mr. Ponza of ours, that jailbird as you say, or that rascal, that boor, as your father calls him, brought his mother-in-law to the apartment next to ours with the idea of stringing us all! You've got to show me that he did it on purpose!

DINA: I don't say that he did it on purpose—not at all! But you can't deny that this famous Mr. Ponza has come to this town and done a number of things which are unusual, to say the least; and which he must have known were likely to arouse a very natural curiosity in everybody. Look uncle, here is a man: he comes to town to fill an important public position, and—what does he do? Where does he go to live? He hires an apartment on the *top* floor, if you please, of that dirty old tenement out there on the very outskirts of the town. Now, I ask you—did you ever see the place? Inside?

LAUDISI: I suppose you went and had a look at it?

DINA: Yes, uncle dear, I went—with mamma! And we weren't the only ones, you know. The whole town had been to have a look at it. It's a five story tenement with an interior court so dark at noontime you can hardly see your hand before your face. Well, there is an iron balcony built out from the fifth story around the courtyard. A basket is hanging from the railing ... They let it up and down—on a rope![1]

LAUDISI: Well, what of it?

DINA (*looking at him with astonished indignation*): What of it? Well, there, if you please, is where he keeps his wife!

AMALIA: While her mother lives here next door to us!

LAUDISI: A fashionable apartment, for his mother-in-law, in the residential district!

AMALIA: Generous to the old lady, eh? But he does that to keep her from seeing her daughter!

LAUDISI: How do you know that? How do you know that the old lady, rather, does not prefer this arrangement, just to have more elbow room for herself?

DINA: No, no, uncle, you're wrong. Everybody knows that it is he who is doing it.

AMALIA: See here, Lamberto, everybody understands, if a girl, when she marries, goes away from her mother to live with her husband in some other town. But supposing this poor mother can't stand being separated from her daughter and follows her to the place, where she herself is also a complete stranger. And supposing now she not only does not live with her daughter, but is not even allowed to see her? I leave it to you ... is that so easy to understand?

LAUDISI: Oh say, you have about as much imagination as so many mud turtles. A mother-in-law and a son-in-law! Is it so hard to suppose that either through her fault or his fault or nobody's fault, they should find it hard to get along together and should therefore consider it wiser to live apart?

DINA (*with another look of pitying astonishment at her uncle*): How stupid of you, uncle! The trouble is not between the mother-in-law and the son-in-law, but between the mother and the daughter.

LAUDISI: How do you know that?

DINA: Because he is as thick as pudding with the old lady; because they are always together, arm in arm, and as loving as can be. Mother-in-law and son-in-law, if you please! Whoever heard the like of that?

AMALIA: And he comes here every evening to see how the old lady is getting on!

DINA: And that is not the worst of it! Sometimes he comes during the daytime, once or twice!

LAUDISI: How scandalous! Do you think he is making love to the old woman?

DINA: Now don't be improper, uncle. No, we will acquit him of that. She is a poor old lady, quite on her last legs.

AMALIA: But he never, never, never brings his wife! A daughter kept from seeing her mother! The idea!

LAUDISI: Perhaps the young lady is not well; perhaps she isn't able to go out.

DINA: Nonsense! The old lady goes to see *her!*

AMALIA: Exactly! And she never gets in! She can see her only from a distance. Now will you explain to me why, in the name of common sense, that poor mother should be forbidden ever to enter her daughter's house?

---

[1] Quite customary in Italy [translator's note].

DINA: And if she wants to talk to her she has to shout up from the courtyard!

AMALIA: Five stories, if you please! . . . And her daughter comes out and looks down from the balcony up there. The poor old woman goes into the courtyard and pulls a string that leads up to the balcony; a bell rings; the girl comes out and her mother talks up at her, her head thrown back, just as though she were shouting from out of a well . . . .

(There is a knock at the door and the Butler enters)

BUTLER: Callers, madam!

AMALIA: Who is it, please?

BUTLER: Signor Sirelli, and the Signora with another lady, madam.

AMALIA: Very well, show them in.

(The Butler bows and withdraws)

(Sirelli, Signora Sirelli, Signora Cini appear in the doorway, rear.

Sirelli, also a man of about forty, is a bald, fat gentleman with some pretensions to stylish appearance that do not quite succeed; the overdressed provincial.

Signora Sirelli, his wife, plump, petite, a faded blonde, still young and girlishly pleasing. She, too, is somewhat overdressed with the provincial's fondness for display. She has the aggressive curiosity of the small-town gossip. She is chiefly occupied in keeping her husband in his place.

Signora Cini is the old provincial lady of affected manners, who takes malicious delight in the failings of others, all the while affecting innocence and inexperience regarding the waywardness of mankind.)

AMALIA *(as the visitors enter, and taking Signora Sirelli's hands effusively)*: Dearest! Dearest!

SIGNORA SIRELLI: I took the liberty of bringing my good friend, Signora Cini, along. She was so anxious to know you!

AMALIA: So good of you to come, Signora! Please make yourself at home! My daughter Dina, Signora Cini, and this is my brother, Lamberto Laudisi.

SIRELLI *(bowing to the ladies)*: Signora, Signorina. *(He goes over and shakes hands with Laudisi)*

SIGNORA SIRELLI: Amalia dearest, we have come here as to the fountain of knowledge. We are two pilgrims athirst for the truth!

AMALIA: The truth? Truth about what?

SIGNORA SIRELLI: Why . . . about this blessed Mr. Ponza of ours, the new secretary at the prefecture. He is the talk of the town, take my word for it, Amalia.

SIGNORA CINI: And we are all just dying to find out!

AMALIA: But we are as much in the dark as the rest of you, I assure you, madam.

SIRELLI *(to his wife)*: What did I tell you? They know no more about it than I do. In fact, I think they know less about it than I do. Why is it this poor woman is not allowed to see her daughter? Do you know the reason, you people, the real reason?

AMALIA: Why, I was just discussing the matter with my brother.

LAUDISI: And my view of it is that you're all a pack of gossips!

DINA: The reason is, they say, that Ponza will not allow her to.

SIGNORA CINI: Not a sufficient reason, if I may say so, Signorina.

SIGNORA SIRELLI: Quite insufficient! There's more to it than that!

SIRELLI: I have a new item for you, fresh, right off the ice: he keeps her locked up at home!

AMALIA: His mother-in-law?

SIRELLI: No, no, his wife!

SIGNORA CINI: Under lock and key!

DINA: There, uncle, what have you to say to that? And you've been trying to defend him all along!

SIRELLI (staring in astonishment at Laudisi): Trying to defend that man? Really . . .

LAUDISI: Defending him? No! I am not defending anybody. All I'm saying, if you ladies will excuse me, is that your curiosity is unbearable if only because it's quite useless.

SIRELLI: Useless? Useless?

LAUDISI: Useless!

SIGNORA CINI: But we're trying to get somewhere—we are trying to find out!

LAUDISI: Excuse me, what can you find out? What can we really know about other people—who they are—what they are—what they are doing, and why they are doing it?

SIGNORA SIRELLI: How can we know? Why not? By asking, of course! You tell me what you know, and I tell you what I know.

LAUDISI: In that case, madam, you ought to be the best informed person in the world. Why, your husband knows more about what others are doing than any other man—or woman, for that matter—in this neighborhood.

SIRELLI (deprecating but pleased): Oh I say, I say . . .

SIGNORA SIRELLI (to her husband): No dear, he's right, he's right. (Then turning to Amalia) The real truth, Amalia, is this: for all my husband says he knows, I never manage to keep posted on anything!

SIRELLI: And no wonder! The trouble is—that woman never trusts me! The moment I tell her something she is convinced it is not quite as I say. Then, sooner or later, she claims that it can't be as I say. And at last she is certain it is the exact opposite of what I say!

SIGNORA SIRELLI: Well, you ought to hear all he tells me!

LAUDISI (laughing aloud): May I speak, madam? Let me answer your husband. My dear Sirelli, how do you expect your wife to be satisfied with things as you explain them to her, if you, as is natural, represent them as they seem to you?

SIGNORA SIRELLI: And that means—as they cannot possibly be!

LAUDISI: Why no, Signora, now you are wrong. From your husband's point of view things are, I assure you, exactly as he represents them.

SIRELLI: As they are in reality!

SIGNORA SIRELLI: Not at all! You are always wrong.

SIRELLI: No, not a bit of it! It is you who are always wrong. I am always right.

LAUDISI: The fact is that neither of you is wrong. May I explain? I will prove it to you. Now here you are, you, Sirelli, and Signora Sirelli, your wife, there; and here I am. You see me, don't you?

SIRELLI: Well . . . er . . . yes.

LAUDISI: Do you see me, or do you not?

SIRELLI: Oh, I'll bite! Of course I see you.

LAUDISI: So you see me! But that's not enough. Come here!

SIRELLI (*smiling, he obeys, but with a puzzled expression on his face as though he fails to understand what Laudisi is driving at*): Well, here I am!

LAUDISI: Yes! Now take a better look at me . . . Touch me! That's it—that's it! Now you are touching me, are you not? And you see me! You're sure you see me?

SIRELLI: Why, I should say . . .

LAUDISI: Yes, but the point is, you're sure! Of course you're sure! Now if you please, Signora Sirelli, you come here—or rather . . . no . . . (*Gallantly*) it is my place to come to you! (*He goes over to Signora Sirelli and kneels chivalrously on one knee.*) You see me, do you not, madam? Now that hand of yours . . . touch me! A pretty hand, on my word! (*He pats her hand*)

SIRELLI: Easy! Easy!

LAUDISI: Never mind your husband, madam! Now, you have touched me, have you not? And you see me? And you are absolutely sure about me, are you not? Well now, madam, I beg of you; do not tell your husband, nor my sister, nor my niece, nor Signora Cini here, what you think of me; because, if you were to do that, they would all tell you that you are completely wrong. But, you see, you are really right; because I am really what you take me to be; though, my dear madam, that does not prevent me from also being really what your husband, my sister, my niece, and Signora Cini take me to be—because they also are absolutely right!

SIGNORA SIRELLI: In other words you are a different person for each of us.

LAUDISI: Of course I'm a different person! And you, madam, pretty as you are, aren't you a different person, too?

SIGNORA SIRELLI (*hastily*): No siree! I assure you, as far as I'm concerned, I'm always the same always, yesterday, today, and forever!

LAUDISI: Ah, but so am I, from my point of view, believe me! And, I would say that you are all mistaken unless you see me as I see myself; but that would be an inexcusable presumption on my part—as it would be on yours, my dear madam!

SIRELLI: And what has all this rigmarole got to do with it, may I ask?

LAUDISI: What has it got to do with it? Why . . . I find all you people here at your wits' ends trying to find out who and what other people are; just as though other people had to be this, or that, and nothing else.

SIGNORA SIRELLI: All you are saying is that we can never find out the truth! A dreadful idea?

SIGNORA CINI: I give up! I give up! If we can't believe even what we see with our eyes and feel with our fingers . . .

LAUDISI: But you must understand, madam! All I'm saying is that you should show some respect for what other people see and feel, even though it be the exact opposite of what you see and feel.

SIGNORA SIRELLI: The way to answer you is to refuse to talk with you. See, I turn my back on you! You're driving me mad!

LAUDISI: Oh, I beg your pardon. Don't let me interfere with your party. Please go on! Pray continue your argument about Signora Frola and Signor Ponza—I promise not to interrupt again!

AMALIA: You're right for once, Lamberto; and I think it would be even better if you should go into the other room.

DINA: Serves you right, uncle! Into the other room with you, into the other room!

LAUDISI: No, I refuse to budge! Fact is, I enjoy hearing you gossip; but I promise not to say anything more, don't fear! At the very most, with your permission, I shall indulge in a laugh or two.

SIGNORA SIRELLI: How funny . . . and our idea in coming here was to find out . . . But really, Amalia, I thought this Ponza man was your husband's secretary at the Provincial building.

AMALIA: He is his secretary—in the office. But here at home what authority has Agazzi over the fellow?

SIGNORA SIRELLI: Of course! I understand! But may I ask . . . haven't you even tried to see Signora Frola, next door?

DINA: Tried? I should say we had! Twice, Signora!

SIGNORA CINI: Well . . . so then . . . you have probably talked to her . . .

DINA: We were not *received,* if you please!

SIGNORA SIRELLI, SIRELLI, SIGNORA CINI (in chorus): Not received? Why! Why! Why!

DINA: This very forenoon!

AMALIA: The first time we waited fully fifteen minutes at the door. We rang and rang and rang, and no one came. Why, we weren't even able to leave our cards! So we went back today . . .

DINA (throwing up her hands in an expression of horror): And *he* came to the door.

SIGNORA SIRELLI: Why yes, with that face of his . . . you can tell by just looking at the man . . . Such a face! Such a face! You can't blame people for talking! And then, with that black suit of his . . . Why, they all dress in black. Did you ever notice? Even the old lady! And the man's eyes, too! . . .

SIRELLI (with a glance of pitying disgust at his wife): What do you know about his eyes? You never saw his eyes! And you never saw the woman. How do you know she dresses in black? *Probably* she dresses in black . . . By the way, they come from a village in the next county. Had you heard that? A village in Marsica![2]

AMALIA: Yes, the village that was destroyed a short time ago.

SIRELLI: Exactly! By an earthquake! Not a house left standing in the place.

DINA: And all their relatives were lost, I have heard. Not one of them left in the world!

SIGNORA CINI (impatient to get on with the story): Very well, very well, so then . . . he came to the door . . .

AMALIA: Yes . . . And the moment I saw him in front of me with that weird face of his I had hardly enough gumption left to tell him that we had just come to call on his mother-in-law, and he . . . well . . . not a word, not a word . . . not even a "thank you," if you please!

DINA: That is not quite fair, mama: . . . he did bow!

AMALIA: Well, yes, a bow . . . if you want to call it that. Something like this! . . .

DINA: And his eyes! You ought to see his eyes—the eyes of a devil, and then some! You never saw a man with eyes like that!

SIGNORA CINI: Very well, what did he say, finally?

DINA: He seemed quite taken aback.

AMALIA: He was all confused like; he hitched about for a time; and at last he said

---

[2] A region in Abruzzi. In 1915 there was a great earthquake there; the town of Avezzano, e.g. was destroyed [translator's note].

that Signora Frola was not feeling well, but that she would appreciate our kindness in having come; and then he just stood there, and stood there, apparently waiting for us to go away.

DINA: I never was more mortified in my life!

SIRELLI: A boor, a plain boor, I say! Oh, it's his fault, I am telling you. And . . . who knows? Perhaps he has got the old lady also under lock and key.

SIGNORA SIRELLI: Well, I think something should be done about it! . . . After all, you are the wife of a superior of his. You can *refuse* to be treated like that.

AMALIA: As far as that goes, my husband did take it rather badly—as a lack of courtesy on the man's part; and he went straight to the prefect with the matter, insisting on an apology.

(Signor Agazzi, commendatore and provincial councillor, appears in the doorway rear)

DINA: Oh goody, here's papa now!

(Agazzi is well on toward fifty. He has the harsh, authoritarian manner of the provincial of importance. Red hair and beard, rather unkempt; gold-rimmed eyeglasses.)

AGAZZI: Oh Sirelli, glad to see you! *(He steps forward and bows to the company)*

AGAZZI: Signora! . . . *(He shakes hands with Signora Sirelli)*

AMALIA *(introducing Signora Cini)*: My husband, Signora Cini!

AGAZZI *(with a bow and taking her hand)*: A great pleasure, madam! *(Then turning to his wife and daughter in a mysterious voice)* I have come back from the office to give you some real news! Signora Frola will be here shortly.

SIGNORA SIRELLI *(clapping her hands delightedly)*: Oh, the mother-in-law! She is coming? Really? Coming here?

SIRELLI *(going over to Agazzi and pressing his hand warmly as an expression of admiration)*: That's the talk, old man, that's the talk. What's needed here is some show of authority.

AGAZZI: Why I had to, you see, I had to! . . . I can't let a man treat my wife and daughter that way! . . .

SIRELLI: I should say not! I was just expressing myself to that effect right here.

SIGNORA SIRELLI: And it would have been entirely proper to inform the prefect also . . .

AGAZZI *(anticipating)*: . . . of all the talk that is going around on this fine gentleman's account? Oh, leave that to me! I didn't miss the opportunity.

SIRELLI: Fine! Fine!

SIGNORA CINI: And such talk!

AMALIA: For my part, I never heard of such a thing. Why, do you know, he has them both under lock and key!

DINA: No, mamma, we are not *quite* sure of that. We are not *quite* sure about the old lady, yet.

AMALIA: Well, we know it about his wife, anyway.

SIRELLI: And what did the prefect have to say?

AGAZZI: Oh the prefect . . . well, the prefect . . . he was very much impressed, *very* much impressed, with what I had to say.

SIRELLI: I should hope so!

AGAZZI: You see, some of the talk had reached his ears already. And he agrees that it is better, as a matter of his own official prestige, for all this mystery in connection with one of his assistants to be cleared up, so that once and for all we shall know the truth.

LAUDISI (*bursts out laughing*).

AMALIA: That is Lamberto's usual contribution. He laughs!

AGAZZI: And what is there to laugh about?

SIGNORA SIRELLI: Why he says that no one can ever know the truth.

(*The Butler appears at the door in back set*)

THE BUTLER: Excuse me, Signora Frola!

SIRELLI: Ah, here she is now!

AGAZZI: Now we'll see if we can settle it!

SIGNORA SIRELLI: Splendid! Oh, I am so glad I came.

AMALIA (*rising*): Shall we have her come in?

AGAZZI: Wait, you keep your seat, Amalia! Let's have her come right in here. (*Turning to the butler*) Show her in!

(*Exit Butler*)

(*A moment later all rise as Signora Frola enters, and Amalia steps forward, holding out her hand in greeting. Signora Frola is a slight, modestly but neatly dressed old lady, very eager to talk and apparently fond of people. There is a world of sadness in her eyes, tempered however, by a gentle smile that is constantly playing about her lips.*)

AMALIA: Come right in, Signora Frola! (*She takes the old lady's hand and begins the introduction.*) Mrs. Sirelli, a good friend of mine; Signora Cini; my husband; Mr. Sirelli, and this is my daughter, Dina; my brother Lamberto Laudisi. Please take a chair, Signora!

SIGNORA FROLA: Oh, I am so very, very sorry! I have come to excuse myself for having been so negligent of my social duties. You, Signora Agazzi, were so kind, so very kind, to have honored me with a first call—when really it was my place to leave my card with you!

AMALIA: Oh, we are just neighbors, Signora Frola! Why stand on ceremony? I just thought that you, being new in town and all alone by yourself, would perhaps like to have a little company.

SIGNORA FROLA: Oh, how very kind of you it was!

SIGNORA SIRELLI: And you are quite alone, aren't you?

SIGNORA FROLA: Oh no! No! I have a daughter, married, though she hasn't been here very long, either.

SIRELLI: And your daughter's husband is the new secretary at the prefecture, Signor Ponza, I believe?

SIGNORA FROLA: Yes, yes, exactly! And I hope that Signor Agazzi, as his superior, will be good enough to excuse me—and him, too!

AGAZZI: I will be quite frank with you, madam! I was a bit put out.

SIGNORA FROLA (*interrupting*): And you were quite right! But I do hope you will forgive him. You see, we are still—what shall I say—still so upset by the terrible things that have happened to us . . .

AMALIA: You went through the earthquake, didn't you?

SIGNORA SIRELLI: And you lost all your relatives?

SIGNORA FROLA: Every one of them! All our family—yes, madam. And our village was left just a miserable ruin, a pile of bricks and stones and mortar.

SIRELLI: Yes, we heard about it.

SIGNORA FROLA: It wasn't so bad for me, I suppose. I had only one sister and her daughter, and my niece had no family. But my poor son-in-law had a much harder time of it. He lost his mother, two brothers, and their wives, a sister and her husband, and there were two little ones, his nephews.

SIRELLI: A massacre!

SIGNORA FROLA: Oh, one doesn't forget such things! You see, it sort of leaves you with your feet off the ground.

AMALIA: I can imagine.

SIGNORA SIRELLI: And all over-night with no warning at all! It's a wonder you didn't go mad.

SIGNORA FROLA: Well, you see, we haven't quite gotten our bearings yet; and we do things that may seem impolite, without in the least intending to. I hope you understand!

AGAZZI: Oh please, Signora Frola, of course!

AMALIA: In fact it was partly on account of your trouble that my daughter and I thought we ought to go to see you first.

SIGNORA SIRELLI (*literally writhing with curiosity*): Yes, of course, since they saw you all alone by yourself, and yet . . . excuse me, Signora Frola . . . if the question doesn't seem impertinent . . . how is it that when you have a daughter here in town and after a disaster like the one you have been through . . . I should think you people would all stand together, that you would need one another.

SIGNORA FROLA: Whereas I am left here all by myself?

SIRELLI: Yes, exactly. It does seem strange, to tell the honest truth.

SIGNORA FROLA: Oh, I understand—of course! But you know, I have a feeling that a young man and a young woman who have married should be left a good deal to themselves.

LAUDISI: Quite so, quite so! They should be left to themselves. They are beginning a life of their own, a life different from anything they have led before. One should not interfere in these relations between a husband and a wife!

SIGNORA SIRELLI: But there are limits to everything, Laudisi, if you will excuse me! And when it comes to shutting one's own mother out of one's life . . .

LAUDISI: Who is shutting her out of the girl's life? Here, if I have understood the lady, we see a mother who understands that her daughter cannot and must not remain so closely associated with her as she was before, for now the young woman must begin a new life on her own account.

SIGNORA FROLA (*with evidence of keen gratitude and relief*): You have hit the point exactly, sir. You have said what I would like to have said. You are exactly right! Thank you!

SIGNORA CINI: But your daughter, I imagine, often comes to see you . . .

SIGNORA FROLA (*hesitating, and manifestly ill at ease*): Why yes . . . I . . . I . . . we do see each other, of course!

SIRELLI (*quickly pressing the advantage*): But your daughter never goes out of her house! At least no one in town has ever seen her.

SIGNORA CINI: Oh, she probably has her little ones to take care of.

SIGNORA FROLA (*speaking up quickly*): No, there are no children yet, and perhaps
there won't be any, now. You see, she has been married seven years. Oh, of
course, she has a lot to do about the house; but that is not the reason, really.
You know, we women who come from the little towns in the country—we are
used to staying indoors much of the time.

AGAZZI: Even when your mothers are living in the same town, but not in your
house? You prefer staying indoors to going and visiting your mothers?

AMALIA: But it's Signora Frola probably who visits her daughter.

SIGNORA FROLA (*quickly*): Of course, of course, why not! I go there once or twice a
day.

SIRELLI :And once or twice a day you climb all those stairs up to the fifth story of
that tenement, eh?

SIGNORA FROLA (*growing pale and trying to conceal under a laugh the torture of that
cross-examination*): Why . . . er . . . to tell the truth, I don't go up. You're right,
five flights would be quite too much for me. No, I don't go up. My daughter
comes out on the balcony in the courtyard and . . . well . . . we see each other
. . . and we talk!

SIGNORA SIRELLI: And that's all, eh? How terrible! You never see each other more
intimately than that?

DINA: I have a mamma and certainly I wouldn't expect her to go up five flights
of stairs to see me, either; but at the same time I could never stand talking to
her that way, shouting at the top of my lungs from a balcony on the fifth story. I am sure I should want a kiss from her occasionally, and feel her near me,
at least.

SIGNORA FROLA (*with evident signs of embarrassment and confusion*): And you're
right! Yes, exactly . . . quite right! I must explain. Yes . . . I hope you people are
not going to think that my daughter is something she really is not. You must
not suspect her of having so little regard for me and for my years, and you
mustn't believe that I, her mother, am . . . well . . . five, six, even more stories
to climb would never prevent a real mother, even if she were as old and infirm as I am, from going to her daughter's side and pressing her to her heart
with a real mother's love . . . oh no!

SIGNORA SIRELLI (*triumphantly*): There you have it, there you have it, just as we
were saying!

SIGNORA CINI: But there must be a reason, there must be a reason!

AMALIA (*pointedly to her brother*): Aha, Lamberto, now you see, there *is* a reason,
after all!

SIRELLI (*insisting*): Your son-in-law, I suppose?

SIGNORA FROLA: Oh please, please, please, don't think badly of *him*. He is such a
very good boy. Good is no name for it, my dear sir. You can't imagine all he
does for me! Kind, attentive, solicitous for my comfort, everything! And as for
my daughter—I doubt if any girl ever had a more affectionate and well-intentioned husband. No, on that point I am proud of myself! I could not have
found a better man for her.

SIGNOR SIRELLI: Well then . . . What? What! *What?*

SIGNORA CINI: So your son-in-law is not the reason?

AGAZZI: I never thought it was his fault. Can you imagine a man forbidding his wife to call on her mother, or preventing the mother from paying an occasional visit to her daughter?

SIGNORA FROLA: Oh, it's not a case of forbidding! Who ever dreamed of such a thing! No, it's we, Commendatore, I and my daughter, that is. Oh, please, believe me! We refrain from visiting each other of our own accord, out of consideration for him, you understand.

AGAZZI: But excuse me . . . how in the world could he be offended by such a thing? I *don't* understand.

SIGNORA FROLA: Oh, please don't be angry, Signor Agazzi. You see it's a . . . what shall I say . . . a feeling . . . that's it, a feeling, which it would perhaps be very hard for anyone else to understand; and yet, when you do understand it, it's all so simple, I am sure . . . so simple . . . and believe me, my dear friends, it is no slight sacrifice that I am making, and that my daughter is making, too.

AGAZZI: Well, one thing you will admit, madam. This is a very, very unusual situation.

SIRELLI: Unusual, indeed! And such as to justify a curiosity even more persistent than ours.

AGAZZI: It is not only unusual, madam. I might even say it is suspicious.

SIGNORA FROLA: Suspicious? You mean you suspect Signor Ponza? Oh please, Commendatore, don't say that. What fault can you possibly find with him, Signor Agazzi?

AGAZZI: I didn't say just that . . . Please don't misunderstand! I said simply that the situation is so very strange that people might legitimately suspect . . .

SIGNORA FROLA: Oh, no, no, no! What could they suspect. We are in perfect agreement, all of us; and we are really quite happy, very happy, I might even say . . . both I and my daughter.

SIGNORA SIRELLI: Perhaps it's a case of jealousy?

SIGNORA FROLA: Jealousy of me? It would be hardly fair to say that, although . . . really . . . oh, it is so hard to explain! . . . You see, he is in love with my daughter . . . so much so that he wants her whole heart, her every thought, as it were, for himself; so much so that he insists that the affections which my daughter must have for me, her mother—he finds that love quite natural of course, why not? Of course he does!—should reach me through him—that's it, through him—don't you understand?

AGAZZI: Oh, that is going pretty strong! No, I don't understand. In fact it seems to me a case of downright cruelty!

SIGNORA FROLA: Cruelty? No, no, please don't call it cruelty, Commendatore. It is something else, believe me! You see it's so hard for me to explain the matter. Nature, perhaps . . . but no, that's hardly the word. What shall I call it? Perhaps a sort of disease. It's a fullness of love, of a love shut off from the world. There, I guess that's it . . . a fullness . . . a completeness of devotion in which his wife must live without ever departing from it, and into which no other person must ever be allowed to enter.

DINA: Not even her mother, I suppose?

SIRELLI: It is the worst case of selfishness I ever heard of, if you want my opinion!

SIGNORA FROLA: Selfishness? Perhaps! But a selfishness, after all, which offers itself wholly in sacrifice. A case where the selfish person gives all he has in the world to the one he loves. Perhaps it would be fairer to call me selfish; for selfish it surely is for me to be always trying to break into this closed world of theirs, break in by force if necessary; when I know that my daughter is really so happy, so passionately adored—you ladies understand, don't you? A true mother should be satisfied when she knows her daughter is happy, oughtn't she? Besides I'm not completely separated from my daughter, am I? I see her and I speak to her. *(She assumes a more confidential tone)* You see, when she lets down the basket there in the courtyard I always find a letter in it—a short note, which keeps me posted on the news of the day; and I put in a little letter that I have written. That is some consolation, a great consolation indeed, and now, in course of time, I've grown used to it. I am resigned, there! Resignation, that's it! And I've ceased really to suffer from it at all.

AMALIA: Oh well then, after all, if you people are satisfied, why should . . .

SIGNORA FROLA *(rising)*: Oh yes, yes! But, remember, I told you he is such a good man! Believe me, he couldn't be better, really! We all have our weaknesses in this world, haven't we! And we get along best by having a little indulgence, for one another. *(She holds out her hand to Amalia)* Thank you for calling, madam. *(She bows to Signora Sirelli, Signora Cini, and Dina; then turning to Agazzi, she continues)* And I do hope you have forgiven me!

AGAZZI: Oh, my dear madam, please, please! And we are extremely grateful for your having come to call on us.

SIGNORA FROLA *(offering her hand to Sirelli and Laudisi and again turning to Amalia who has risen to show her out)*: Oh no, please Signora Agazzi, please stay here with your friends! Don't put yourself to any trouble!

AMALIA: No, no, I will go with you; and believe me, we were very, very glad to see you!

(Exit Signora Frola with Amalia showing her the way. Amalia returns immediately.)

SIRELLI: Well, there you have the story, ladies and gentlemen! Are you satisfied with the explanation?

AGAZZI: An explanation, you call it? So far as I can see she has explained nothing. I tell you there is some big mystery in all this business.

SIGNOR SIRELLI: That poor woman! Who knows what torment she must be suffering?

DINA: And to think of that poor girl!

SIGNOR CINI: She could hardly keep in her tears as she talked.

AMALIA: Yes, and did you notice when I mentioned all those stairs she would have to climb before really being able to see her daughter?

LAUDISI: What impressed me was her concern, which amounted to a steadfast determination, to protect her son-in-law from the slightest suspicion.

SIGNOR SIRELLI: Not at all, not at all! What could she say for him? She couldn't really find a single word to say for him.

SIRELLI: And I would like to know how anyone could condone such violence, such downright cruelty!

THE BUTLER *(appearing again in the doorway)*: Beg pardon, sir! Signor Ponza calling.

SIGNORA SIRELLI: The man himself, upon my word!

(An animated ripple of surprise and curiosity, not to say of guilty self-consciousness, sweeps over the company)

AGAZZI: Did he ask to see me?

BUTLER: He asked simply if he might be received. That was all he said.

SIGNORA SIRELLI: Oh please, Signor Agazzi, please let him come in! I am really afraid of the man; but I confess the greatest curiosity to have a close look at the monster.

AMALIA: But what in the world can he be wanting?

AGAZZI: The way to find that out is to have him come in. *(To the Butler)* Show him in, please.

(The Butler bows and goes out. A second later Ponza appears, aggressively, in the doorway.)

(Ponza is a short, thick set, dark complexioned man of a distinctly unprepossessing appearance; black hair, very thick and coming down low over his forehead; a black mustache upcurling at the ends, giving his face a certain ferocity of expression. He is dressed entirely in black. From time to time he draws a black-bordered handkerchief and wipes the perspiration from his brow. When he speaks his eyes are invariably hard, fixed, sinister.)

AGAZZI: This way please, Ponza, come right in! *(Introducing him)* Signor Ponza, our new provincial secretary; my wife; Signora Sirelli; Signora Cini, my daughter Dina. This is Signor Sirelli; and here is Laudisi, my brother-in-law. Please join our party, won't you, Ponza?

PONZA: So kind of you! You will pardon the intrusion. I shall disturb you only a moment, I hope.

AGAZZI: You had some private business to discuss with me?

PONZA: Why yes, but I could discuss it right here. In fact, perhaps as many people as possible should hear what I have to say. You see it is a declaration that I owe, in a certain sense, to the general public.

AGAZZI: Oh my dear Ponza, if it is that little matter of your mother-in-law's not calling on us, it is quite all right; because you see . . .

PONZA: No, that was not what I came for, Commendatore. It was not to apologize for her. Indeed I may say that Signora Frola, my wife's mother, would certainly have left her cards with Signora Agazzi, your wife, and Signorina Agazzi, your daughter, long before they were so kind as to honor her with their call, had I not exerted myself to the utmost to prevent her coming, since I am absolutely unable to consent to her paying or receiving visits!

AGAZZI *(drawing up into an authoritative attitude and speaking with some severity)*: Why? if you will be so kind as to explain, Ponza?

PONZA *(with evidences of increasing excitement in spite of his efforts to preserve his self-control)*: I suppose my mother-in-law has been talking to you people about her daughter, my wife. Am I mistaken? And I imagine she told you further that I have forbidden her entering my house and seeing her daughter intimately.

AMALIA: Oh not at all, not at all, Signor Ponza! Signora Frola had only the nicest things to say about you. She could not have spoken of you with greater respect and kindness.

DINA: She seems to be very fond of you indeed.

AGAZZI: She says that she refrains from visiting your house of her own accord, out of regard for feelings of yours which we frankly confess we are unable to understand.

SIGNORA SIRELLI: Indeed, if we were to express our honest opinion . . .

AGAZZI: Well, yes, why not be honest? We think you are extremely harsh with the woman, extremely harsh, perhaps cruel would be an exacter word.

PONZA: Yes, that is what I thought; and I came here for the express purpose of clearing the matter up. The condition this poor woman is in is a pitiable one indeed—not less pitiable than my own perhaps; because, as you see, I am compelled to come here and make apologies—a public declaration—which only such violence as has just been used upon me could ever bring me to make in the world . . . (He stops and looks about the room. Then he says slowly with emphatic emphasis on the important syllables.) Signora Frola is mad.

ALL (with a start): Mad?

PONZA: She's been mad for four years.

SIGNORA SIRELLI (with a cry): Dear me, she doesn't seem mad in the least!

AGAZZI (amazed): What? Mad?

PONZA: She doesn't seem mad: she is mad. And her madness consists precisely in believing that I don't want to let her see her daughter. (His face takes on an expression of cruel suffering mingled with a sort of ferocious excitement) What daughter, for God's sake? Why her daughter died four years ago? (A general sensation)

EVERYONE AT ONCE: Died? She is dead? What do you mean? Oh, really? Four years ago? Why! Why!

PONZA: Four years ago! In fact it was the death of the poor girl that drove her mad.

SIRELLI: Are we to understand that the wife with whom you are now living . . .

PONZA: Exactly! She is my second wife. I married her two years ago.

AMALIA: And Signora Frola believes that her daughter is still living, that she is your wife still?

PONZA: Perhaps it was best for her that way. She was in charge of a nurse in her own room, you see. Well, when she chanced to see me passing by inadvertence on her street one day, with this woman, my second wife, she suddenly began to laugh and cry and tremble all over in an extreme of happiness. She was sure her daughter, whom she had believed dead, was alive and well; and from a condition of desperate despondency which was the first form of her mental disturbance, she entered on a second obsession, believing steadily that her daughter was not dead at all; but that I, the poor girl's husband, am so completely in love with her that I want her wholly for myself and will not allow anyone to approach her. She became otherwise quite well, you might say. Her nervousness disappeared. Her physical condition improved, and her powers of reasoning returned quite clear. Judge for yourself, ladies and gentlemen! You have seen her and talked with her. You would never suspect in the world that she is mad.

AMALIA: Never in the world! Never!

SIGNORA SIRELLI: And the poor woman says she is so happy, so happy!

PONZA: That is what she says to everybody; and for that matter she really has a wealth of affection and gratitude for me; because, as you may well suppose, I do my very best, in spite of the sacrifices entailed, to keep up this beneficial illusion in her. The sacrifices you can readily understand. In the first place I have to maintain two homes on my small salary. Then it is very hard on my wife, isn't it? But she, poor thing, does the very best she can to help me out! She comes to the window when the old lady appears. She talks to her from the balcony. She writes letters to her. But you people will understand that there are limits to what I can ask of my poor wife. Signora Frola, meanwhile, lives practically in confinement. We have to keep a pretty close watch on her. We have to lock her up, virtually. Otherwise, some fine day she would be walking right into my house. She is of a gentle, placid disposition fortunately; but you understand that my wife, good as she is, could never bring herself to accepting caresses intended for another woman, a dead woman! That would be a torment beyond conception.

AMALIA: Oh, of course! Poor woman! Just imagine!

SIGNORA SIRELLI: And the old lady herself consents to being locked up all the time?

PONZA: You, Commendatore, will understand that I couldn't permit her calling here except under absolute constraint.

AGAZZI: I understand perfectly, my dear Ponza, and you have my deepest sympathy.

PONZA: When a man has a misfortune like this fall upon him he must not go about in society; but of course when, by complaining to the prefect, you practically compelled me to have Signora Frola call, it was my duty to volunteer this further information; because, as a public official, and with due regard for the post of responsibility I occupy, I could not allow any discredible suspicions to remain attached to my reputation. I could not have you good people suppose for a moment that, out of jealousy or for any other reason, I could ever prevent a poor suffering mother from seeing her own daughter. (He rises) Again my apologies for having intruded my personal troubles upon your party. (He bows) My compliments, Commendatore. Good afternoon, good afternoon! Thank you! (Bowing to Laudisi, Sirelli, and the others in turn, he goes out through the door, rear)

AMALIA (with a sigh of sympathy and astonishment): Uhh! Mad! What do you think of that?

SIGNORA SIRELLI: The poor old thing! But you wouldn't have believed it, would you?

DINA: I always knew there was something under it all.

SIGNORA CINI: But who could ever have guessed . . .

AGAZZI: Oh, I don't know, I don't know! You could tell from the way she talked . . .

LAUDISI: You mean to say that you thought . . . ?

AGAZZI: No, I can't say that. But at the same time, if you remember, she could never quite find her words.

SIGNORA SIRELLI: How could she, poor thing, out of her head like that?

SIRELLI: And yet, if I may raise the question, it seems strange to me that an insane person . . . oh, I admit that she couldn't really talk rationally . . . but what surprises me is her trying to find a reason to explain why her son-in-law should be keeping her away from her daughter. This effort of hers to justify it and then to adapt herself to excuses of her own invention . . .

AGAZZI: Yes, but that is only another proof that she's mad. You see, she kept offering excuses for Ponza that really were not excuses at all.

AMALIA: Why, yes! She'd say a thing and then take it right back again.

AGAZZI: If she weren't downright mad, how could she or any other woman ever accept such a situation from a man? How could she ever consent to talk with her own daughter only by shouting up from the bottom of a well five stories deep?

SIRELLI: But if I remember rightly she has you there! Notice, she doesn't accept the situation. She says she is resigned to it. That's different! No, I tell you, there is still something funny about this business. What do you say, Laudisi?

LAUDISI: Why, I say nothing, nothing at all!

THE BUTLER (appearing at the door and visibly excited): Beg pardon, Signora Frola is here again!

AMALIA (with a start): Oh dear me, again? Do you suppose she'll be pestering us all the time now?

SIGNORA SIRELLI: I understand how you feel now that you know she's mad.

SIGNORA CINI: My, my, what do you suppose she is going to say now?

SIRELLI: For my part I'd really like to hear what she's got to say.

DINA: Oh yes, mamma, don't be afraid! Ponza said she was quite harmless. Let's have her come in.

AGAZZI: Of course, we can't send her away. Let's have her come in; and, if she makes any trouble, why . . . (Turning to the Butler) Show her in. (The Butler bows and withdraws)

AMALIA: You people stand by me, please! Why, I don't know what I am ever going to say to her now!

(Signora Frola appears at the door. Amalia rises and steps forward to welcome her. The others look on in astonished silence.)

SIGNORA FROLA: May I please . . . ?

AMALIA: Do come in, Signora Frola, do come in! You know all these ladies. They were here when you came before.

SIGNORA FROLA (with an expression of sadness on her features, but still smiling gently): How you all look at me—and even you, Signora Agazzi! I am sure you think I am mad, don't you!

AMALIA: My dear Signora Frola, what in the world are you talking about?

SIGNORA FROLA: But I am sure you will forgive me if I disturb you for a moment. (Bitterly) Oh, my dear Signora Agazzi, I wish I had left things as they were. It was hard to feel that I had been impolite to you by not answering the bell when you called that first time; but I could never have supposed that you would come back and force me to call upon you. I could foresee the consequences of such a visit from the very first.

AMALIA: Why, not at all, not at all! I don't understand. Why?

DINA: What consequences could you foresee, madam?

SIGNORA FROLA: Why, my son-in-law, Signor Ponza, has just been here, hasn't he?

AGAZZI: Why, yes, he was here! He came to discuss certain office matters with me . . . just ordinary business, you understand!

SIGNORA FROLA (*visibly hurt and quite dismayed*): Oh, I know you are saying that just to spare me, just in order not to hurt my feelings.

AGAZZI: Not at all, not at all! That was really why he came.

SIGNORA FROLA (*with some alarm*): But he was quite calm, I hope, quite calm?

AGAZZI: Calm? As calm as could be! Why not? Of course!

(*The members of the company all nod in confirmation*)

SIGNORA FROLA: Oh, my dear friends, I am sure you are trying to reassure me; but as a matter of fact I came to set you right about my son-in-law.

SIGNORA SIRELLI: Why no, Signora, what's the trouble?

AGAZZI: Really, it was just a matter of politics we talked about . . .

SIGNORA FROLA: But I can tell from the way you all look at me . . . Please excuse me, but it is not a question of me at all. From the way you all look at me I can tell that he came here to prove something that I would never have confessed for all the money in the world. You will all bear me out, won't you? When I came here a few moments ago you all asked me questions that were very cruel questions to me, as I hope you will understand. And they were questions that I couldn't answer very well; but anyhow I gave an explanation of our manner of living which can be satisfactory to nobody, I am well aware. But how could I give you the real reason? How could I tell you people, as he's doing, that my daughter has been dead for four years and that I'm a poor mad mother who believes that her daughter is still living and that her husband will not allow me to see her?

AGAZZI (*quite upset by the ring of deep sincerity he finds in Signora Frola's manner of speaking*): What do you mean, your daughter?

SIGNORA FROLA (*hastily and with anguished dismay written on her features*): You know that's so. Why do you try to deny it? He did say that to you, didn't he?

SIRELLI (*with some hesitation and studying her features warily*): Yes . . . in fact . . . he did say that.

SIGNORA FROLA: I know he did; and I also know how it pained him to be obliged to say such a thing of me. It is a great pity, Commendatore! We have made continual sacrifices, involving unheard of suffering, I assure you; and we could endure them only by living as we are living now. Unfortunately, as I well understand, it must look very strange to people, seem even scandalous, arouse no end of gossip! But after all, if he is an excellent secretary, scrupulously honest, attentive to his work, why should people complain? You have seen him in the office, haven't you? He is a good worker, isn't he?

AGAZZI: To tell the truth, I have not watched him particularly, as yet.

SIGNORA FROLA: Oh he really is, he really is! All the men he ever worked for say he's most reliable; and I beg of you, please don't let this other matter interfere. And why then should people go tormenting him with all this prying into his private life, laying bare once more a misfortune which he has succeeded in mastering and which, if it were widely talked about, might upset him again personally, and even hurt him in his career?

AGAZZI: Oh no, no, Signora, no one is trying to hurt him. Nor would we hurt you either.

SIGNORA FROLA: But my dear sir, how can you help hurting me when you force him to give almost publicly an explanation which is quite absurd—ridiculous I might even say! Surely people like you can't seriously believe what he says? You can't possibly be taking me for mad. You don't really think that this woman is his second wife? And yet it is all so necessary! He needs to have it that way. It is the only way he can pull himself together; get down to his work again . . . the only way . . . the only way! Why he gets all wrought up, all excited, when he is forced to talk of this other matter; because he knows himself how hard it is for him to say certain things. You may have noticed it . . .

AGAZZI: Yes, that is quite true. He did seem very much excited.

SIGNORA SIRELLI: Well, well, well, so then it's he!

SIRELLI (triumphantly): I always said it was he.

AGAZZI: Oh, I say! Is that really possible? (He motions to the company to be quiet)

SIGNORA FROLA (joining her hands beseechingly): My dear friends, what are you really thinking? It is only on this subject that he is a little queer. The point is, you must simply not mention this particular matter to him. Why, really now, you could never suppose that I would leave my daughter shut up with him all alone like that? And yet just watch him at his work and in the office. He does everything he is expected to do and no one in the world could do it better.

AGAZZI: But this is not enough, madam, as you will understand. Do you mean to say that Signor Ponza, your son-in-law, came here and made up a story out of whole cloth?

SIGNORA FROLA: Yes, sir, yes sir, exactly . . . only I will explain. You must understand—you must look at things from his point of view.

AGAZZI: What do you mean? Do you mean that your daughter is not dead?

SIGNORA FROLA: God forbid! Of course she is not dead!

AGAZZI: Well, then, he is mad!

SIGNORA FROLA: No, no, look, look! . . .

SIRELLI: I always said it was he! . . .

SIGNORA FROLA: No, look, look, not that, not that! Let me explain . . . You have noticed him, haven't you? Fine, strong looking man . . . violent . . . when he married my daughter he was seized with a veritable frenzy of love . . . he risked my little daughter's life almost, she was frail . . . On the advice of doctors and relatives, even his relatives—dead now, poor things—they had to take his wife off in secret and shut her up in a sanatorium. And he came to think she was dead.

Just imagine when we brought my daughter back to him—and a pretty thing she was to look at, too—he began to scream and say, no, no, no, she wasn't his wife, his wife was dead! He looked at her: No, no, no, not at all! She wasn't the woman! Imagine my dear friends, how terrible it all was. Finally he came up close to her and for a moment it seemed that he was going to recognize her again; but once more it was "No, no, no, she is not my wife!" And do you know, to get him to accept my daughter at all again, we were obliged to pretend having a second wedding, with the collusion of his doctors and his friends, you understand!

SIGNORA SIRELLI: Ah, so that is why he says that . . .

SIGNORA FROLA: Yes, but he doesn't really believe it, you know; and he hasn't for a long time, I am sure. But he seems to feel a need for maintaining the pretense.

He can't do without it. He feels surer of himself that way. He is seized with a terrible fear, from time to time, that this little wife he loves may be taken from him again. *(Smiling and in a low, confidential tone)* So he keeps her locked up at home where he can have her all for himself. But he worships her—he worships her; and I am really quite convinced that my daughter is happy. *(She gets up)* And now I must be going. You see, my son-in-law is in a terrible state of mind at present. I wouldn't like to have him call, and find me not at home. *(With a sigh, and gesturing with her joined hands)* Well, I suppose we must get along as best we can; but it is hard on my poor girl. She has to pretend all along that she is not herself, but another, his second wife and I . . . oh, as for me, I have to pretend that I am mad when he's around, my dear friends; but I'm glad to, I'm glad to, really, so long as it does him some good. *(The Ladies rise as She steps nearer to the door)* No, no, don't let me interrupt your party. I know the way out! Good afternoon! Good afternoon! *(Bowing and smiling she hurries out through the rear door. They all remain standing, astonished, stunned, looking into each other's eyes. Silence)*

LAUDISI *(coming forward among them)*: So you're having a look at each other? Well! And the truth? *(He bursts out laughing)*

Act II

Councillor Agazzi's study in the same house. Antique furnishings with old paintings on the walls. A portière over the rear entrance and over the door to the left which opens into the drawing room shown in the first act. To the right a substantial fireplace with a big mirror above the mantel. A flat top desk with a telephone, A sofa, armchairs, straight back chairs, etc.

As the curtain rises Agazzi is shown standing beside his desk with the telephone receiver pressed to his ear. Laudisi and Sirelli sit looking at him expectantly.

AGAZZI: Yes, I want Centuri, Hello . . . hello . . . Centuri? Yes, Agazzi speaking. That you, Centuri? It's me, Agazzi. Well? *(He listens for some time)* What's that? Really? *(Again he listens at length)* I understand, but you might go at the matter with a little more speed . . . *(Another long pause Well, I give up! How can that possibly be? *(A pause)* Oh, I see, I see . . . *(Another pause)* Well, never mind, I'll look into it myself. Goodbye, Centuri, goodbye! *(He lays down the receiver and steps forward on the stage)*

SIRELLI *(eagerly)*: Well?

AGAZZI: Nothing! Absolutely nothing!

SIRELLI: Nothing at all?

AGAZZI: You see the whole blamed village was wiped out. Not a house left standing! In the collapse of the town hall, followed by a fire, all the records of the place seem to have been lost—births, deaths, marriages, everything.

SIRELLI: But not everybody was killed. They ought to be able to find somebody who knows them.

AGAZZI: Yes, but you see they didn't rebuild the place. Everybody moved away, and no record was ever kept of the people, of course. So far they have found nobody who knows the Ponzas. To be sure, if the police really went at it, they might find somebody; but it would be a tough job.

SIRELLI: So we can't get anywhere along that line! We have got to take what they say and let it go at that.

AGAZZI: That, unfortunately, is the situation.

LAUDISI (*rising*): Well, you fellows take a piece of advice from me: believe them both!

AGAZZI: What do you mean—"believe them both"? . . .

SIRELLI: But if she says one thing, and he says another . . .

LAUDISI: Well, in that case, you needn't believe either of them!

SIRELLI: Oh, you're just joking. We may not be able to verify the stories; but that doesn't prove that either one or the other may not be telling the truth. Some document or other . . .

LAUDISI: Oh, documents! Documents! Suppose you had them? What good would they do you?

AGAZZI: Oh, I say! Perhaps we can't get them now, but there were such documents once. If the old lady is mad, there was, as there still may be somewhere, the death certificate of the daughter. Or look at it from the other angle: if we found all the records, and the death certificate were not there for the simple reason that it never existed, why then, it's Ponza, the son-in-law. He would be mad.

SIRELLI: You mean to say you wouldn't give in if we stuck that certificate under your nose tomorrow or the next day? Would you still deny . . .

LAUDISI: Deny? Why . . . why . . . I'm not denying anything! In fact, I'm very careful not to be denying anything. You're the people who are looking up the records to be able to affirm or deny something. Personally, I don't give a rap for the documents; for the truth in my eyes is not in them but in the mind. And into their minds I can penetrate only through what they say to me of themselves.

SIRELLI: Very well—She says he's mad and he says she's mad. Now one of them must be mad. You can't get away from that. Well which is it, she or he?

AGAZZI: There, that's the way to put it!

LAUDISI: But just observe; in the first place, it isn't true that they are accusing each other of madness. Ponza, to be sure, says his mother-in-law is mad. She denies this, not only of herself, but also of him. At the most, she says that he was a little off once, when they took her daughter from him; but that now he is quite all right.

SIRELLI: I see! So you're rather inclined, as I am, to trust what the old lady says.

AGAZZI: The fact is, indeed, that if you accept his story, all the facts in the case are explained.

LAUDISI: But all the facts in the case are explained if you take her story, aren't they?

SIRELLI: Oh, nonsense! In that case neither of them would be mad! Why, one of them must be, damn it all!

LAUDISI: Well, which one? You can't tell, can you? Neither can anybody else! And it is not because those documents you are looking for have been destroyed in an accident—a fire, an earthquake—what you will; but because those people have concealed those documents in themselves, in their own souls. Can't you understand that? She has created for him, or he for her, a world of fancy which has all the earmarks of reality itself. And in this fictitious reality they get along perfectly well, and in full accord with each other; and this world of fancy, this reality of theirs, no document can possibly destroy because the air they breathe is of that world. For them it is something they can see with their eyes, hear with their ears, and touch with their fingers. Oh, I grant you—if you could get a death certificate or a marriage certificate or something of the kind, you might be able to satisfy that stupid curiosity of yours. Unfortunately, you can't get it. And the result is that you are in the extraordinary fix of having before you, on the one hand, a world of fancy, and on the other, a world of reality, and you, for the life of you, are not able to distinguish one from the other.

AGAZZI: Philosophy, my dear boy, philosophy! And I have no use for philosophy. Give me facts, if you please! Facts! So, I say, keep at it; and I'll bet you we get to the bottom of it sooner or later.

SIRELLI: First we got her story and then we got his; and then we got a new one from her. Let's bring the two of them together—and you think that then we won't be able to tell the false from the true?

LAUDISI: Well, bring them together if you want to! All I ask is permission to laugh when you're through.

AGAZZI: Well, we'll let you laugh all you want. In the meantime let's see . . . *(He steps to the door at the left and calls)* Amalia, Signora Sirelli, won't you come in here a moment?

(The Ladies enter with Dina)

SIGNORA SIRELLI *(catching sight of Laudisi and shaking a finger at him)*: But how is it a man like you, in the presence of such an extraordinary situation, can escape the curiosity we all feel to get at the bottom of this mystery? Why, I lie awake nights thinking of it!

AGAZZI: As your husband says, that man's impossible! Don't bother about him, Signora Sirelli.

LAUDISI: No, don't bother with me; you just listen to Agazzi! He'll keep you from lying awake tonight.

AGAZZI: Look here, ladies. This is what I want—I have an idea: won't you just step across the hall to Signora Frola's?

AMALIA: But will she come to the door?

AGAZZI: Oh, I imagine she will!

DINA: We're just returning the call, you see . . .

AMALIA: But didn't he ask us not to call on his mother-in-law? Hasn't he forbidden her to receive visits?

SIRELLI: No, not exactly! That's how he explained what had happened; but at that time nothing was known. Now that the old lady, through force of circumstance, has spoken, giving her version at least of her strange conduct, I should think that . . .

SIGNORA SIRELLI: I have a feeling that she'll be awfully glad to see us, if for nothing else, for the chance of talking about her daughter.

DINA: And she really is a jolly old lady. There is no doubt in my mind, not the slightest: Ponza is mad!

AGAZZI: Now, let's not go too fast. You just listen to me *(He looks at his wife)*—don't stay too long—five or ten minutes at the outside!

SIRELLI *(to his wife)*: And for heaven's sake, keep your mouth shut!

SIGNORA SIRELLI: And why such considerate advice to me?

SIRELLI: Once *you* get going . . .

DINA *(with the idea of preventing a scene)*: Oh, we are not going to stay very long, ten minutes—fifteen, at the outside. I'll see that no breaks are made.

AGAZZI: And I'll just drop around to the office, and be back at eleven o'clock— ten or twenty minutes at the most.

SIRELLI: And what can I do?

AGAZZI: Wait! *(Turning to the Ladies)* Now, here's the plan! You people invent some excuse or other so as to get Signora Frola in here.

AMALIA: What? How can we possibly do that?

AGAZZI: Oh, find some excuse! You'll think of something in the course of your talk; and if you don't, there's Dina and Signora Sirelli. But when you come back, you understand, go into the drawing room. *(He steps to the door on the left, makes sure that it is wide open, and draws aside the portière)* This door must stay open, wide open, so that we can hear you talking from in here. Now, here are some papers that I ought to take with me to the office. However, I forget them here. It is a brief that requires Ponza's immediate personal attention. So then, I forget it. And when I get to the office I have to bring him back here to find them—See?

SIRELLI: But just a moment. Where do I come in? When am I expected to appear?

AGAZZI: Oh, yes! . . . A moment or two after eleven, when the ladies are again in the drawing room, and I am back here, you just drop in—to take your wife home, see? You ring the bell and ask for me, and I'll have you brought in here. Then I'll invite the whole crowd in! That's natural enough, isn't it?— into my office? . . .

LAUDISI *(interrupting)*: And we'll have the Truth, the whole Truth with a capital T!

DINA: But look, uncle, of course we'll have the truth—once we get them together face to face—capital T and all!

AGAZZI: Don't get into an argument with that man. Besides, it's time you ladies were going. None of us has any too much leeway.

SIGNORA SIRELLI: Come, Amalia, come Dina! And as for you, sir *(Turning to Laudisi)*, I won't even shake hands with you.

LAUDISI: Permit me to do it for you, madam. *(He shakes one hand with the other)* Good luck to you, my dear ladies.

(Exit Dina, Amalia, Signora Sirelli)

AGAZZI *(to Sirelli)*: And now we'd better go, too. Suppose we hurry!

SIRELLI: Yes, right away. Goodbye, Lamberto!

LAUDISI: Goodbye, good luck, good luck! *(Agazzi and Sirelli leave. Laudisi, left alone, walks up and down the study a number of times, nodding his head and occasionally smiling. Finally he draws up in front of the big mirror that is hanging over the mantelpiece. He sees himself in the glass, stops, and addresses his image.)*

LAUDISI: So there you are! *(He bows to himself and salutes, touching his forehead with his fingers)* I say, old man, who is mad, you or I? *(He levels a finger menacingly at his image in the glass; and, of course, the image in turn levels a finger at him. As he smiles, his image smiles.)* Of course, I understand! I say it's you, and you say it's me. You—you are mad! No? It's me? Very well! It's me! Have it *your* way. Between you and me, we get along very well, don't we! But the trouble is, others don't think of you just as I do; and that being the case, old man, what a fix you're in! As for me, I say that here, right in front of you, I can see myself with my eyes and touch myself with my fingers. But what are you for other people? What are you in their eyes? An image, my dear sir, just an image in the glass! They're all carrying just such a phantom around inside themselves, and here they are racking their brains about the phantoms in other people; and they think all that is quite another thing!

(The Butler has entered the room in time to catch Laudisi gesticulating at himself in the glass. He wonders if the man is crazy. Finally he speaks up.)

BUTLER: Ahem! . . . Signor Laudisi, if you please . . .

LAUDISI *(coming to himself)*: Uff!

BUTLER: Two ladies calling, sir! Signora Cini and another lady!

LAUDISI: Calling to see me?

BUTLER: Really, they asked for the signora; but I said that she was out—on a call next door; and then . . .

LAUDISI: Well, what then?

BUTLER: They looked at each other and said, "Really! Really!" and finally they asked me if anybody else was at home.

LAUDISI: And of course you said that everyone was out!

BUTLER: I said that you were in!

LAUDISI: Why, not at all! I'm miles and miles away! Perhaps that fellow they call Laudisi is here!

BUTLER: I don't understand, sir.

LAUDISI: Why? You think the Laudisi they know is the Laudisi I am?

BUTLER: I don't understand, sir.

LAUDISI: Who are you talking to?

BUTLER: Who am I talking to? I thought I was talking to you.

LAUDISI: Are you really sure the Laudisi you are talking to is the Laudisi the ladies want to see?

BUTLER: Why, I think so, sir. They said they were looking for the brother of Signora Agazzi.

LAUDISI: Ah, in that case you are right! *(Turning to the image in the glass)* You are not the brother of Signora Agazzi? No, it's me! *(To the Butler)* Right you are! Tell them I am in. And show them in here, won't you?

(The Butler retires)

SIGNORA CINI: May I come in?

LAUDISI: Please, please, this way, madam!

SIGNORA CINI: I was told Signora Agazzi was not at home, and I brought Signora Nenni along. Signora Nenni is a friend of mine, and she was most anxious to make the acquaintance of . . .

LAUDISI: . . . of Signora Frola?

SIGNORA CINI: Of Signora Agazzi, your sister!

LAUDISI: Oh, she will be back very soon, and Signora Frola will be here, too.

SIGNORA CINI: Yes, we thought as much.

(Signora Nenni is an oldish woman of the type of Signora Cini, but with the mannerisms of the latter somewhat more pronounced. She, too, is a bundle of concentrated curiosity, but of the sly, cautious type, ready to find something frightful under everything.)

LAUDISI: Well, it's all planned in advance! It will be a most interesting scene! The curtain rises at eleven, precisely!

SIGNORA CINI: Planned in advance? What is planned in advance?

LAUDISI (mysteriously, first with a gesture of his finger and then aloud): Why, bringing the two of them together! (A gesture of admiration) Great idea, I tell you!

SIGNORA CINI: The two of them—together—who?

LAUDISI: Why, the two of them. He—in here! (Pointing to the room about him)

SIGNORA CINI: Ponza, you mean?

LAUDISI: And she—in there! (He points toward the drawing room)

SIGNORA CINI: Signora Frola?

LAUDISI: Exactly! (With an expressive gesture of his hands and even more mysteriously) But afterwards, all of them—in here! Oh, a great idea, a great idea!

SIGNORA CINI: In order to get . . .

LAUDISI: The truth! But it's already known: all that remains is the unmasking.

SIGNORA CINI (with the greatest surprise): Oh, really? So they know the truth! And which is it—He or she?

LAUDISI: Well, I'll tell you . . . you just guess! Who do you think it is?

SIGNORA CINI (ahemming): Well . . . I say . . . really . . . you see . . .

LAUDISI: Is it she or is it he? You don't mean to say you don't know! Come now, give a guess!

SIGNORA CINI: Why, for my part I should say . . . well, I'd say . . . it's he.

LAUDISI (looks at her admiringly): Right you are! It is he!

SIGNORA CINI: Really? I always thought so! Of course, it was perfectly plain all along. It had to be he!

SIGNORA NENNI: All of us women in town said it was he. We always said so!

SIGNORA CINI: But how did you get at it? I suppose Signor Agazzi ran down the documents, didn't he—the birth certificate, or something?

SIGNORA NENNI: Through the prefect, of course! There was no getting away from those people. Once the police start investigating . . . !

LAUDISI (motions to them to come closer to him; then in a low voice and in the same mysterious manner, and stressing each syllable): The certificate!—Of the second marriage!

SIGNORA CINI (starting back with astonishment): What?

SIGNORA NENNI (likewise taken aback): What did you say? The second marriage?

SIGNORA CINI: Well, in that case he was right.

LAUDISI: Oh, documents, ladies, documents! This certificate of the second marriage, so it seems, talks as plain as day.

SIGNORA NENNI: Well, then, she is mad.

LAUDISI: Right! She must be, mustn't she?

SIGNORA CINI: But I thought you said . . .

LAUDISI: Yes, I did say . . . but this certificate of the second marriage may very

well be, as Signora Frola said, a fictitious document, gotten up through the influence of Ponza's doctors and friends to pamper him in the notion that his
wife was not his first wife, but another woman.

SIGNORA CINI: But it's a public document. You mean to say a public document can
be a fraud?

LAUDISI: I mean to say—well, it has just the value that each of you chooses to give
it. For instance, one could find somewhere, possibly, those letters that Signora
Frola said she gets from her daughter, who lets them down in the basket in
the courtyard. There are such letters, aren't there?

SIGNORA CINI: Yes, of course!

LAUDISI: They are documents, aren't they? Aren't letters documents? But it all depends on how you read them. Here comes Ponza, and he says they are just
made up to pamper his mother-in-law in her obsession . . .

SIGNORA CINI: Oh, dear, dear, so then we're never sure about anything?

LAUDISI: Never sure about anything? Why not at all, not at all! Let's be exact. We
are sure of many things, aren't we? How many days are there in the week?
Seven—Sunday, Monday, Tuesday, Wednesday . . . How many months in the
year are there? Twelve: January, February, March . . .

SIGNORA CINI: Oh, I see, you're just joking! You're just joking! (*Dina appears,
breathless, in the doorway, at the rear*)

DINA: Oh, uncle, won't you please . . . (*She stops at the sight of Signora Cini*) Oh,
Signora Cini, you here?

SIGNORA CINI: Why, I just came to make a call! . . .

LAUDISI: . . . with Signora Cenni.

SIGNORA NENNI: No, my name is Nenni.

LAUDISI: Oh yes, pardon me! She was anxious to make Signora Frola's acquaintance . . .

SIGNORA NENNI: Why, not at all!

SIGNORA CINI: He has just been making fun of us! You ought to see what fools he
made of us!

DINA: Oh, he's perfectly insufferable, even with mamma and me. Will you excuse me for just a moment? No, everything is all right. I'll just run back and
tell mamma that you people are here and I think that will be enough. Oh,
uncle, if you had only heard her talk! Why, she is a perfect *dear*, and what a
good, kind soul! . . . She showed us all those letters her daughter wrote . . .

SIGNORA CINI: Yes, but as Signor Laudisi was just saying . . .

DINA: He hasn't even seen them!

SIGNORA NENNI: You mean they are not really fictitous?

DINA: Fictitious nothing! They talk as plain as day. And such things! You can't
fool a mother when her own daughter talks to her. And you know—the letter
she got yesterday! . . . (*She stops at the sound of voices coming into the study from
the drawing room*) Oh, here they are, here they are, already! (*She goes to the
door and peeps into the room*)

SIGNORA CINI (*following her to the door*): Is *she* there, too?

DINA: Yes, but you had better come into the other room. All of us women must
be in the drawing room. And it is just eleven o'clock, uncle!

AMALIA (*entering with decision from the door on the left*): I think this whole business
is quite unnecessary! We have absolutely no further need of proofs . . .

DINA: Quite so! I thought of that myself. Why bring Ponza here?

AMALIA *(taken somewhat aback by Signora Cini's presence)*: Oh, my dear Signora Cini! . . .

SIGNORA CINI: *(introducing Signora Nenni)* A friend of mine, Signora Nenni! I ventured to bring her with me . . .

AMALIA *(bowing, but somewhat coolly, to the visitor)* A great pleasure, Signora! *(After a pause)* There is not the slightest doubt in the world: . . . it's he!

SIGNORA CINI: It's he? Are you sure it's he?

DINA: And such a trick on the poor old lady!

AMALIA: Trick is not the name for it! It's downright dishonest!

LAUDISI: Oh, I agree with you: it's outrageous! Quite! So much so, I'm quite convinced it must be *she*!

AMALIA: She? What do you mean? How can you say that?

LAUDISI: I say, it is *she*, it is *she*, it's *she*!

AMALIA: Oh, I say! If you had heard her talk. . . !

DINA: It is absolutely clear to us now.

SIGNORA CINI and SIGNORA NENNI *(swallowing)* Really? You are sure?

LAUDISI: Exactly! Now that you are sure it's he, why, obviously—it must be she.

DINA: Oh dear me, why talk to that man? He is just impossible!

AMALIA: Well, we must go into the other room . . . This way, if you please!

(Signora Cini, Signora Nenni and Amalia withdraw through the door on the left. Dina starts to follow, when Laudisi calls her back.)

LAUDISI: Dina!

DINA: I refuse to listen to you! I refuse!

LAUDISI: I was going to suggest that, since the whole matter is closed, you might close the door also.

DINA: But papa . . . he told us to leave it open. Ponza will be here soon; and if papa finds it closed—well, you know how papa is!

LAUDISI: But you can convince him! . . . You especially. You can show him that there really was no need of going any further. You are convinced yourself, aren't you?

DINA: I am as sure of it, as I am that I'm alive!

LAUDISI *(putting her to the test with a smile)*: Well, close the door then!

DINA: I see, you're trying to make me say that I'm not really sure. Well, I won't close the door, but it's just on account of papa.

LAUDISI: Shall I close it for you?

DINA: If you take the responsibility yourself! . . .

LAUDISI: But you see, *I* am sure! I *know* that Ponza is mad!

DINA: The thing for you to do is to come into the other room and just hear her talk a while. Then you'll be sure, absolutely sure. Coming?

LAUDISI: Yes, I'm coming, and I'll close the door behind me—on my own responsibility, of course.

DINA: Ah, I see. So you're convinced even before you hear her talk.

LAUDISI: No, dear, it's because I'm sure that your papa, who has been with Ponza, is just as certain as you are that any further investigation is unnecessary.

DINA: How can you say that?

LAUDISI: Why, of course, if you talk with Ponza, you're sure the old lady is mad. *(He walks resolutely to the door)* I am going to shut this door.

DINA (*restraining him nervously, then hesitating a moment*): Well, why not . . . if you're really sure? What do you say—let's leave it open!

LAUDISI (*bursts out laughing*).

DINA: But just because papa told us to!

LAUDISI: And papa will tell you something else by and by. Say . . . let's leave it open!

(*A piano starts playing in the adjoining room—an ancient tune, sweet, graceful, full of pain, from "Nina Mad Through Love" by Paisiello*)

DINA: Oh, there she is. She's playing! Do you hear? Actually playing the piano!

LAUDISI: The old lady?

DINA: Yes! And you know? She told us that her daughter used to play this tune, always the same tune. How well she plays! Come! Come!

(*They hurry through the door*)

The stage, after the exit of Laudisi and Dina, remains empty for a space of time while the music continues from the other room. Ponza, appearing at the door with Agazzi, catches the concluding notes and his face changes to an expression of deep emotion—an emotion that will develop into a virtual frenzy as the scene proceeds.

AGAZZI (*in the doorway*): After you, after you, please! (*He takes Ponza's elbow and motions him into the room. He goes over to his desk, looks about for the papers which he pretends he had forgotten, finds them eventually and says.*) Why, here they are! I was sure I had left them here. Won't you take a chair, Ponza? (*Ponza seems not to hear. He stands looking excitedly at the door into the drawing room, through which the sound of the piano is still coming.*)

AGAZZI: Yes, they are the ones! (*He takes the papers and steps to Ponza's side, opening the folder*) It is an old case, you see. Been running now for years and years! To tell you the truth I haven't made head or tail of the stuff myself. I imagine you'll find it one big mess. (*He, too, becomes aware of the music and seems somewhat irritated by it. His eyes also rest on the door to the drawing room.*) That noise, just at this moment! (*He walks with a show of anger to the door*) Who is that at the piano anyway? (*In the doorway he stops and looks, and an expression of astonishment comes into his face*) Ah!

PONZA (*going to the door also. On looking into the next room he can hardly restrain his emotion*): In the name of God, is *she* playing?

AGAZZI: Yes—Signora Frola! And how well she does play!

PONZA: How is this? You people have brought her in here, again! And you're letting her play!

AGAZZI: Why not? What's the harm?

PONZA: Oh, please, please, no, not that song! It is the one her daughter used to play.

AGAZZI: Ah, I see! And it hurts you?

PONZA: Oh, no, not me—but her—it hurts her—and you don't know how much! I thought I had made you and those women understand just how that poor old lady was!

AGAZZI: Yes, you did . . . quite true! But you see . . . but see here, Ponza! (*Trying to pacify the man's growing emotion*)

PONZA (*continuing*): But you *must* leave her alone! You *must* not go to her house!

She *must* not come in here! I am the only person who can deal with her. You are killing her . . . killing her!

AGAZZI: No, I don't think so. It is not so bad as that. My wife and daughter are surely tactful enough . . . (*Suddenly the music ceases. There is a burst of applause.*)

AGAZZI: There, you see. Listen! Listen!

(*From the next room the following conversation is distinctly heard*)

DINA: Why, Signora Frola, you are perfectly *marvelous* at the piano!

SIGNORA FROLA: But you should hear how my Lena plays!

(*Ponza digs his nails into his hands*)

AGAZZI: Her daughter, of course!

PONZA: Didn't you hear? "How my Lena plays! How my Lena *plays*!"

(*Again from inside*)

SIGNORA FROLA: Oh, no, not now! . . . She hasn't played for a long time—since that happened. And you know, it is what she takes hardest, poor girl!

AGAZZI: Why, that seems quite natural to me! Of course, she thinks the girl is still alive!

PONZA: But she shouldn't be allowed to say such things. She *must* not—she *must* not say such things! Didn't you hear? "She hasn't played since that happened"! She said "she *hasn't* played since that happened"! Talking of the piano, you understand! Oh, you don't understand, no, of course! My first wife had a piano and played that tune. Oh, oh, oh! You people are determined to ruin me!

(*Sirelli appears at the back door at this moment, and hearing the concluding words of Ponza and noticing his extreme exasperation, stops short, uncertain as to what to do. Agazzi is himself very much affected and motions to Sirelli to come in.*)

AGAZZI: Why, no, my dear fellow, I don't see any reason . . . (*To Sirelli*) Won't you just tell the ladies to come in here?

(*Sirelli, keeping at a safe distance from Ponza, goes to the door at the left and calls*)

PONZA: The ladies in here? In here with me? Oh, no, no, please, rather . . .

(*At a signal from Sirelli, who stands in the doorway to the left, his face taut with intense emotion, the Ladies enter. They all show various kinds and degrees of excitement and emotion. Signora Frola appears, and catching sight of Ponza trembling from head to foot, worked up into a state of positively animal passion, stops, quite overwhelmed. As he assails her during the lines that follow, she exchanges glances of understanding from time to time with the Ladies about her. The action here is rapid, nervous, tense with excitement, and extremely violent.*)

PONZA: You? Here? How is this? You! Here! Again! What are you doing here?

SIGNORA FROLA: Why, I just came . . . don't be cross!

PONZA: You come here to tell these ladies . . . What did you tell these ladies?

SIGNORA FROLA: Nothing! I swear to God, nothing!

PONZA: Nothing? What do you mean, nothing? I heard you with my own ears, and this gentleman here heard you also. You said "she plays." Who plays?

Lena plays! And you know very well that Lena has been dead for four years. Dead, do you hear! Your daughter has been dead—for four years!

SIGNORA FROLA: Yes, yes, I know ... Don't get excited, my dear ... Oh, yes, oh yes. I know ...

PONZA: And you said "she hasn't been able to play since that happened." Of course she hasn't been able to play since that happened. How could she, if she's dead?

SIGNORA FROLA: Why, of course, certainly. Isn't that what I said? Ask these ladies. I said that she hasn't been able to play since that happened. Of course. How could she, if she's dead?

PONZA: And why were you worrying about that piano, then?

SIGNORA FROLA: No, no! I'm not worrying about any piano ...

PONZA: I broke that piano up and destroyed it. You know that, the moment your daughter died, so that my second wife couldn't touch it. She can't play in any case. You know she doesn't play.

SIGNORA FROLA: Why, of course, dear! Of course! She doesn't know how to play!

PONZA: And one thing more: Your daughter was Lena, wasn't she? Her name was Lena. Now, see here! You just tell these people what my second wife's name is. Speak up! You know very well what her name is! What is it? What is it?

SIGNORA FROLA: Her name is Julia! Yes, yes, of course, my dear friends, her name is Julia! *(Winks at someone in the company)*

PONZA: Exactly! Her name is Julia, and not Lena! Who are you winking at? Don't you go trying to suggest by those winks of yours that she's not Julia!

SIGNORA FROLA: Why, what do you mean? I wasn't winking! Of course I wasn't!

PONZA: I saw you! I saw you very distinctly! You are trying to ruin me! You are trying to make these people think that I am keeping your daughter all to my-self, just as though she were not dead. *(He breaks into convulsive sobbing)* ... just as though she were not dead!

SIGNORA FROLA *(hurrying forward and speaking with infinite kindness and sympathy)*: Oh no! Come, come, my poor boy. Come! Don't take it so hard. I never said any such thing, did I, madam?

AMALIA, SIGNORA SIRELLI, DINA: Of course she never said such a thing! She always said the girl was dead! Yes! Of course! No!

SIGNORA FROLA: I did, didn't I? I said she's dead, didn't I? And that you are so very good to me. Didn't I, didn't I? I, trying to ruin you? I, trying to get you into trouble?

PONZA: And you, going into other people's houses where there are pianos, play-ing your daughter's tunes on them! Saying that Lena plays them that way, or even better!

SIGNORA FROLA: No, it was ... why ... you see ... it was ... well ... just to see whether ...

PONZA: But you *can't* ... you *mustn't*! How could you ever dream of trying to play a tune that your dead daughter played!

SIGNORA FROLA: You are quite right! ... Oh, yes! Poor boy! Poor boy! *(She also be-gins to weep)* I'll never do it again: Never, never, never again!

PONZA *(advancing upon her threateningly)*: What are you doing here? Get out of here! Go home at once! Home! Home! Go home!

SIGNORA FROLA: Yes, yes! Home! I am going home! Oh dear, oh dear!

(She backs out the rear door, looking beseechingly at the company, as though urging everyone to have pity on her son-in-law. She retires, sobbing. The others stand there looking at Ponza with pity and terror; but the moment Signora Frola has left the room, he regains his normal composure.)

PONZA: I beg pardon for the sad spectacle I've had to present before all you ladies and gentlemen to remedy the evil which, without wanting, without knowing, you are doing to this unhappy woman—with your compassion.

AGAZZI *(astonished like all the others)*: What? You were only pretending?

PONZA: I had to, my good people! It's the only way to keep up the illusion for her, don't you see? I have to roar out the truth that way—as if it were madness, *my* madness! Forgive me, I must be going, I must go to her. *(He hurries out through the rear door. Once more they stand astonished and silent looking at each other.)*

LAUDISI *(coming forward)*: And so, ladies and gentlemen, we learn the truth! *(He bursts out laughing)*

Act III

The same scene. As the curtain rises, Laudisi is sprawling in an easy chair, reading a book. Through the door that leads into the parlor on the left comes the confused murmur of many voices.

The Butler appears in the rear door, introducing the police commissioner, Centuri. Centuri is a tall, stiff, scowling official, with a decidedly professional air. He is in the neighborhood of forty.

THE BUTLER: This way, sir. I will call Signor Agazzi at once.

LAUDISI: *(drawing himself up in his chair and looking around)*: Oh, it's you, Commissioner! *(He rises hastily and recalls the butler, who has stepped out through the door)* One moment, please! Wait! *(To Centuri)* Anything new, Commissioner?

COMMISSIONER *(stiffly)*: Yes, something new!

LAUDISI: Ah! Very well. *(To the Butler)* Never mind. I'll call him myself. *(He motions with his hand toward the door on the left. The Butler bows and withdraws.)* You have worked miracles, Commissioner! You're the savior of this town. Listen! Do you hear them? You are the lion of the place! How does it feel to be the father of your country? But say, what you've discovered is all solid fact?

COMMISSIONER: We've managed to unearth a few people.

LAUDISI: From Ponza's town? People who know all about him?

COMMISSIONER: Yes! And we have gathered from them a few facts—not many, perhaps, but well authenticated.

LAUDISI: Ah, that's nice. Congratulations! For example . . .

COMMISSIONER: For example? Why, for instance, here . . . well, here are all the communications I have received. Read 'em yourself! *(From an inner pocket he draws a yellow envelope, opened at one end, from which he takes a document and hands it to Laudisi)*

LAUDISI: Interesting, I am sure. Very interesting! . . . *(He stands, reading the document carefully, commenting from time to time with exclamations in different tones. First an "ah" of satisfaction, then another "ah" which attenuates this enthusiasm very much. Finally an "eh" of disappointment, which leads to another "eh" of complete disgust.)* Why, no, what's all this amount to, Commissioner?

COMMISSIONER: Well, it's what we were able to find out.

LAUDISI: But this doesn't prove anything, you understand! It leaves everything just where it was. There's nothing of any significance whatever here. (*He looks at the Commissioner for a moment and then, as though suddenly making up his mind, he says*) I wonder, Commissioner, would you like to do something really great—render a really distinguished service to this town; and meanwhile lay up a treasure in heaven?

COMMISSIONER (*looking at him in perplexity*): What are you thinking of, sir?

LAUDISI: I'll explain. Here, please, take this chair! (*He sets the chair in front of Agazzi's desk*) I advise you, Mr. Commissioner, to tear up this sheet of paper that you've brought and which has absolutely no significance at all. But here on this other piece of paper, why don't you write down something that will be precise and clear?

COMMISSIONER: Why ... why ... myself? What do you mean? What should I write?

LAUDISI (*insisting*): Just say something—anything— that these two old acquaintances of Ponza's whom you managed to get hold of might have said. Come, Commissioner, rise to the occasion! Do something for the commonwealth! Bring this town back to normal again! Don't you see what they are after? They all want the truth—*a* truth that is: Something specific; something concrete! They don't care what it is. All they want is something categorical, something that speaks plainly! Then they'll quiet down.

COMMISSIONER: *The* truth—*a* truth? Excuse me, have I understood you clearly? You were suggesting that I commit a forgery? I am astonished that you dare propose such a thing, and when I say I am astonished, I'm not saying half what I actually feel. Be so good as to tell the Commendatore that I am here!

LAUDISI (*dropping his arms dejectedly*): As you will, Commissioner!

(*He steps over to the door on the left. As he draws the portières and swings the door more widely open, the voices become louder and more confused. As he steps through, there is a sudden silence. The Police Commissioner stands waiting with a satisfied air, twirling one of the points of his mustache. All of a sudden, there is commotion and cheering in the next room. Cries of delight and applause, mixed with handclapping. The Police Commissioner comes out of his reverie and looks up with an expression of surprise on his features, as though not understanding what it's all about. Through the door to the left come Agazzi, Sirelli, Laudisi, Amalia, Dina, Signora Sirelli, Signora Cini, Signora Nenni, and many other ladies and gentlemen. Agazzi leads the procession. They are all still talking and laughing excitedly, clapping their hands, and crying "I told you so! Fine! Fine! Good! How wonderful! Now we'll know!" etc.*)

AGAZZI (*stepping forward cordially*): Ah, my dear Centuri, I was sure you could! Nothing ever gets by *our* chief!

COMPANY: Fine! Good! What did you find out! Have you brought something? Is it she? Is it he? Tell us?

COMMISSIONER (*who doesn't yet understand what all the excitement is about. For him it has been a mere matter of routine*): Why, no ... why, Commendatore, simply ... you understand ...

AGAZZI: Hush! Give him a chance! ...

COMMISSIONER: I have done my best. I ... but what did Signor Laudisi tell you?

AGAZZI: He told us that you have brought news, real news!

SIRELLI: Specific data, clear, precise! . . .

LAUDISI (amplifying): . . . not many, perhaps, but well authenticated! The best they've managed to trace! Old neighbors of Ponza, you see; people well acquainted with him . . .

EVERYBODY: Ah! At last! At last! Now we'll know! At last!

(The Commissioner hands the document to Agazzi)

COMMISSIONER: There you have it, Commendatore!

AGAZZI (opening the sheet, as all crowd around him): Let's have a look at it!

COMMISSIONER: But you, Signor Laudisi . . .

LAUDISI: Don't interrupt, please, the document speaks for itself! Agazzi, you read it.

AGAZZI (to Laudisi): But give me a chance, won't you? Please! Please! Now! There you are!

LAUDISI: Oh, I don't care. I've read the thing already.

EVERYBODY (crowding around him): You've read it already? What did it say? Is it he? Is it she?

LAUDISI (speaking very formally): There is no doubt whatever, as a former neighbor of Ponza's testifies, that the woman Frola was once in a sanatorium!

THE GROUP (cries of disappointment): Oh really! Too bad! Too bad!

SIGNORA SIRELLI: Signora Frola, did you say?

DINA: Are you sure it was she?

AGAZZI: Why, no! Why, no, it doesn't say anything of the kind! (Coming forward and waving the document triumphantly) It doesn't say anything of the kind! (General excitement)

EVERYBODY: Well, what does it say? What does it say?

LAUDISI (insisting): It does too! It says "the Frola woman"—the Frola woman, categorically.

AGAZZI: Nothing of the kind! The witness says that he thinks she was in a sanatorium. He does not assert that she was. Besides, there is another point. He doesn't know whether this Frola woman who was in a sanatorium was the mother or the daughter, the first wife, that is!

EVERYBODY (with relief): Ah!

LAUDISI (insistingly): But I say he does. It must be the mother! Who else could it be?

SIRELLI: No, of course, it's the daughter! It's the daughter!

SIGNORA SIRELLI: Just as the old lady said herself!

AMALIA: Exactly! That time when they took her away by force from her husband! . . .

DINA: Yes, she says that her daughter was taken to a home.

AGAZZI: Furthermore, observe another thing. The witness does not really belong to their town. He says that he used to go there frequently, but that he does not remember particularly. He remembers that he heard something or other! . . .

SIRELLI: Ah! How can you depend on such a man's testimony? Nothing but hearsay!

LAUDISI: But, excuse me! If all you people are so sure that Signora Frola is right, what more do you want? Why do you go looking for documents? This is all nonsense!

SIRELLI: If it weren't for the fact that the prefect has accepted Ponza's side of the story, I'll tell you . . .

COMMISSIONER: Yes, that's true. The prefect said as much to me . . .

AGAZZI: Yes, but that's because the prefect has never talked with the old lady who lives next door.

SIGNORA SIRELLI: You bet he hasn't. He talked only with Ponza.

SIRELLI: But, for that matter, there are other people of the same mind as the prefect.

A GENTLEMEN: That is my situation, my situation exactly. Yes sir! Because I know of just such a case where a mother went insane over the death of her daughter and insists that the daughter's husband will not allow her to see the girl. The same case to a T.

A SECOND GENTLEMEN: Not exactly to a T! Not exactly to a T! In the case you mention the man didn't marry again. Here, this man Ponza is living with another woman . . .

LAUDISI (his face brightening with a new idea that has suddenly come to him): I have it, ladies and gentlemen! Did you hear that? It's perfectly simple. Dear me, as simple as Columbus's egg!

EVERYBODY: What? What? What? What?

THE SECOND GENTLEMEN: What did I say? I didn't realize it was important.

LAUDISI: Just a moment, ladies and gentlemen! (Turning to Agazzi) Is the prefect coming here, by chance?

AGAZZI: Yes, we were expecting him. But what's the new idea?

LAUDISI: Why, you were bringing him here to talk with Signora Frola. So far, he is standing by Ponza. When he has talked with the old lady, he'll know whether to believe Ponza or her. That's your idea! Well, I've thought of something better that the prefect can do. Something that only he can do.

EVERYBODY: What is it? What is it? What is it?

LAUDISI (triumphantly): Why, this wife of Ponza's, of course . . . at least, the woman he is living with! What this gentleman said suggested the idea to me.

SIRELLI: Get the second woman to talk? Of course! Of course!

DINA: But how can we, when she is kept under lock and key?

SIRELLI: Why, the prefect can use his authority—order her to speak!

AMALIA: Certainly, she is the one who can clear up the whole mystery.

SIGNORA SIRELLI: I don't believe it. She'll say just what her husband tells her to say.

LAUDISI: She must speak before the prefect. Of course!

SIRELLI: She must speak with the prefect privately, all by himself.

AGAZZI: And the prefect, as the final authority over the man, will insist that the wife make a formal explicit statement before him. Of course, of course! What do you say, Commissioner?

COMMISSIONER: Why certainly, there's no doubt that if the prefect were so inclined . . .

AGAZZI: It is the only way out of it, after all. We ought to phone him and explain that he needn't go to the trouble of coming here. You attend to that, will you, Commissioner?

COMMISSIONER: Very glad to! My compliments, ladies! Good afternoon, gentlemen!

SIGNORA SIRELLI: A good idea for once, Laudisi.

DINA: Oh, uncle, how clever of you! Wise old uncle!

THE COMPANY: The only way out of it! Yes! Yes! Fine! At last!

AGAZZI: Curious none of us thought of that before!

SIRELLI: Not so curious! None of us ever set eyes on the woman. She might as well be in another world, poor girl.

LAUDISI (as though suddenly impressed by this latter reflection): In another world? Why yes,—are you really sure there is such a woman?

AMALIA: Oh I say! Please, please, Lamberto!

SIRELLI (with a laugh): You mean to say you think there is no such woman?

LAUDISI: How can you be sure there is? You can't guarantee it!

DINA: But the old lady sees her and talks with her every day.

SIGNORA SIRELLI: And Ponza says that, too. They both agree on that point!

LAUDISI: Yes, yes, I don't deny that. But just a moment! To be strictly logical: there must be a phantom in that house.

ALL: A phantom?

AGAZZI: Oh, go on with you!

LAUDISI: Let me finish.—It's the phantom of the second wife, if Signora Frola is right. It's the phantom of the daughter, if Signor Ponza is right. It remains to be seen if what is a phantom for him and her is actually a person for herself. At this point it seems to me there's some reason to doubt it.

AMALIA: Oh, come on! You'd like us all to be as mad as you are!

SIGNORA NENNI: Heavens: how he makes my flesh creep!

SIGNORA CINI: I can't think why you enjoy frightening us like this!

ALL: Nonsense! It's a joke, a joke!

SIRELLI: She's a woman of flesh and bones, rest assured. And we'll have her talk, we'll have her talk!

AGAZZI: You suggested it yourself, didn't you?—having her talk with the prefect?

LAUDISI: Certainly the woman from that house should talk with the prefect—if there is such a woman—and if she is a woman!

SIGNORA SIRELLI: Dear me, dear me! That man simply drives me mad.

LAUDISI: Well, supposing we wait and see!

EVERYBODY: Well, who is she then? But people have seen her! His wife! On the balcony! She writes letters!

POLICE COMMISSIONER (in the heat of the confusion comes into the room, excitedly announcing): The prefect is coming! The prefect!

AGAZZI: What do you mean? Coming here? But you went to . . .

COMMISSIONER: Why yes, but I met him hardly a block away. He was coming here; and Ponza is with him.

SIRELLI: Ah, Ponza!

AGAZZI: Oh, if Ponza is with him, I doubt whether he is coming here. They are probably on their way to the old lady's. Please, Centuri, you just wait on the landing there and ask him if he won't step in here as he promised?

COMMISSIONER: Very well! I'll do so! (He withdraws hurriedly through the door in the rear)

AGAZZI: Won't you people just step into the other room?

SIGNORA SIRELLI: But remember now, be sure to make him see the point! It's the only way out, the only way.

AMALIA *(at the door to the left)*: This way, ladies, if you please!

AGAZZI: Won't you just stay here, Sirelli; and you, too, Lamberto?

(All the others go out through the door to the left)

AGAZZI *(to Laudisi)*: But let me do the talking, won't you!

LAUDISI: Oh, as for that, don't worry. In fact, if you prefer, I'll go into the other room . . .

AGAZZI: No, no, it's better for you to be here. Ah, here he is now!

(The Prefect is a man of about sixty, tall, thick set, good natured, affable)

PREFECT: Ah, Agazzi, glad to see you. How goes it, Sirelli? Good to see you again, Laudisi. *(He shakes hands all around)*

AGAZZI *(motioning toward a chair)*: I hope you won't mind my having asked you to come here.

PREFECT: No, I was coming, just as I promised you!

AGAZZI *(noticing the Police Commissioner at the door)*: Oh, I'm sorry, Commissioner! Please come in! Here, have a chair!

PREFECT *(good-naturedly to Sirelli)*: By the way, Sirelli, they tell me that you've gone half nutty over this blessed affair of our new secretary.

SIRELLI: Oh, no, governor, believe me. I'm not the only one! The whole village is worked up.

AGAZZI: And that's putting it very mildly.

PREFECT: What's it all about? What's it all about? Good heavens!

AGAZZI: Of course, governor, you're probably not posted on the whole business. The old lady lives here next door. . . .

PREFECT: Yes, I understand so.

SIRELLI: No, one moment, please, governor. You haven't talked with the poor old lady yet.

PREFECT: I was on my way to see her. *(Turning to Agazzi)* I had promised you to see her here, but Ponza came and begged me, almost on his knees, to see her in her own house. His idea was to put an end to all this talk that's going around. Do you think he would have done such a thing if he weren't absolutely sure?

AGAZZI: Of course, he's sure! Because when she's talking in front of him, the poor woman . . .

SIRELLI *(suddenly getting in his oar)*: She says just what he wants her to say, governor; which proves that she is far from being as mad as he claims.

AGAZZI: We had a sample of that, here, yesterday, all of us.

PREFECT: Why, I understand so. You see he's trying all the time to make her believe he's mad. He warned me of that. And how else could he keep the poor woman in her illusion? Do you see any way? All this talk of yours is simply torture to the poor fellow! Believe me, pure torture!

SIRELLI: Very well, governor! But supposing *she* is the one who is trying to keep *him* in the idea that her daughter is dead; so as to reassure him that his wife will not be taken from him again. In that case, you see, governor, it's the old lady who is being tortured, and not Ponza!

AGAZZI: The moment you see the possibility of that, governor... Well, you ought to hear her talk; but all by herself, when he's not around. Then you'd see the possibility all right...

SIRELLI: Just as we all see it!

PREFECT: Oh, I wonder! You don't seem to me so awfully sure; and for my part, I'm quite willing to confess that I'm not so sure myself. How about you, Laudisi?

LAUDISI: Sorry, governor, I promised Agazzi here to keep my mouth shut.

AGAZZI (protesting angrily): Nothing of the kind! How dare you say that? When the governor asks you a plain question... It's true I told him not to talk, but do you know why? He's been doing his best for the past two days to keep us all rattled so that we can't find out anything.

LAUDISI: Don't you believe him, governor. On the contrary. I've been doing my best to bring these people to common sense.

SIRELLI: Common sense! And do you know what he calls common sense? According to him it is not possible to discover the truth; and now he's been suggesting that Ponza is living not with a woman, but with a ghost!

PREFECT (enjoying the situation): That's a new one! Quite an idea! How do you make that out, Laudisi?

AGAZZI: Oh, I say!... You know how he is. There's no getting anywhere with him!

LAUDISI: I leave it to you, governor. I was the one who first suggested bringing you here.

PREFECT: And do you think, Laudisi, I ought to see the old lady next door?

LAUDISI: No, I advise no such thing, governor. In my judgment you are doing very well in depending on what Ponza tells you.

PREFECT: Ah, I see! Because you, too, think that Ponza...

LAUDISI: No, not at all... because I'm also satisfied to have all these people stand on what Signora Frola says, if that does them any good.

AGAZZI: So you see, eh, governor? That's what you call arguing, eh?

PREFECT: Just a moment! Let me understand! (Turning to Laudisi) So you say we can also trust what the old lady says?

LAUDISI: Of course you can! Implicitly! And so you can depend upon what Ponza says. Implicitly!

PREFECT: Excuse me, I don't follow you!

SIRELLI: But man alive, if they both say the exact opposite of each other!...

AGAZZI (angrily and with heat): Listen to me, governor, please. I am prejudiced neither in favor of the old lady nor in favor of Ponza. I recognize that he may be right and that she may be right. But we ought to settle the matter, and there is only one way to do it.

SIRELLI: The way that Laudisi here suggested.

PREFECT: He suggested it? That's interesting? What is it?

AGAZZI: Since we haven't been able to get any positive proof, there is only one thing left. You, as Ponza's final superior, as the man who can fire him if need be, can obtain a statement from his wife.

PREFECT: Make his wife talk, you mean?

SIRELLI: But not in the presence of her husband, you understand.

AGAZZI: Yes, making sure she tells the truth!

SIRELLI: . . . tell whether she's the daughter of Signora Frola, that is, as we think she must be . . .

AGAZZI: . . . or a second wife who is consenting to impersonate the daughter of Signora Frola, as Ponza claims.

PREFECT: . . . and as I believe myself, without a shadow of doubt! *(Thinking a moment)* Why, I don't see any objection to having her talk. Who could object? Ponza? But Ponza, as I know very well, is more eager than anybody else to have this talk quieted down. He's all upset over this whole business, and said he was willing to do anything I proposed. I'm sure he will raise no objection. So if it will ease the minds of you people here . . . Say, Centuri *(The Police Commissioner rises)* won't you just ask Ponza to step in here a moment? He's next door with his mother-in-law.

COMMISSIONER: At once, Your Excellency!

(He bows and withdraws through the door at the rear)

AGAZZI: Oh well, if he consents . . .

PREFECT: He'll consent, all right. And we'll be through with it in a jiffy. We'll bring her right in here so that you people . . .

AGAZZI: Here, in my house?

SIRELLI: You think he'll let his wife come in here?

PREFECT: Just leave it to me! I prefer to have her right here because, otherwise you see, you people would always suppose that I and Ponza had . . .

AGAZZI: Oh, please, governor, no! That's not fair!

SIRELLI: Oh, no, governor, we trust you implicitly!

PREFECT: Oh, I'm not offended, not at all! But you know very well that I'm on his side in this matter; and you'd always be thinking that to hush up any possible scandal in connection with a man in my office . . . No, you see. I must insist on having the interview here . . . Where's your wife, Agazzi?

AGAZZI: In the other room, governor, with some other ladies.

PREFECT: Other ladies? Aha, I see! *(Laughing)* You have a regular detective bureau here, eh?

(The Police Commissioner enters with Ponza)

COMMISSIONER: May I come in? Signor Ponza is here.

PREFECT: Thanks, Centuri. This way, Ponza, come right in!

(Ponza bows)

AGAZZI: Have a chair, Ponza.

(Ponza bows and sits down)

PREFECT: I believe you know these gentlemen?

(Ponza rises and bows)

AGAZZI: Yes, I introduced them yesterday. And this is Laudisi, my wife's brother.

(Ponza bows)

PREFECT: I venture to disturb you, my dear Ponza, just to tell you that here with these friends of mine . . .

(At the first words of the prefect, Ponza evinces the greatest nervousness and agitation)

PREFECT: Was there something you wanted to say, Ponza?

PONZA: Yes, there is something I want to say, governor. I want to present my resignation here and now.

PREFECT: Oh, my dear fellow, I'm so sorry! But just a few moments ago down at the office you were talking . . .

PONZA: Oh, really, this is an outrage, governor! This is just plain persecution, plain persecution!

PREFECT: Oh, now, don't take it that way, old man. See here. These good people . . .

AGAZZI: Persecution, did you say? On my part? . . .

PONZA: On the part of all of you! And I am sick and tired of it! I am going to resign, governor. I refuse to submit to this ferocious prying into my private affairs which will end by undoing a work of love that has cost me untold sacrifice these past two years. You don't know, governor! Why, I've treated that dear old lady in there just as tenderly as though she were my own mother. And yesterday I had to shout at her in the most cruel and terrible way! Why, I found her just now so worked up and excited that . . .

AGAZZI: That's queer! While she was in here Signora Frola was quite mistress of herself. If anybody was worked up, Ponza, it was you. And even now, if I might say . . .

PONZA: But you people don't know what you're making me go through!

PREFECT: Oh, come, come, my dear fellow, don't take it so hard. After all, I'm here, am I not? And you know I've always stood by you! And I always will!

PONZA: Yes, governor, and I appreciate your kindness, really!

PREFECT: And then you say that you're as fond of this poor old lady as you would be if she were your own mother. Well, now, just remember that these good people here seem to be prying into your affairs because they, too, are fond of her! . . .

PONZA: But they're killing her, I tell you, governor! They're killing her, and I warned them in advance.

PREFECT: Very well, Ponza, very well! Now we'll get through with this matter in no time. See here, it is all very simple. There is one way that you can convince these people without the least doubt in the world. Oh, not me— I don't need convincing. I believe *you*.

PONZA: But *they* won't believe me, no matter what I say.

AGAZZI: That's not so! When you came here after your mother-in-law's first visit and told us that she was mad, all of us . . . well, we were surprised, but we believed you. *(Turning to the Prefect)* But after he left, you understand, the old lady came back . . .

PREFECT: Yes, yes, I know. He told me. *(Turning to Ponza again)* She came back here and said that she was trying to do with you exactly what you say you were trying to do with her. It's natural, isn't it, that people hearing both stories, should be somewhat confused. Now you see that these good people, in view of what your mother-in-law says, can't possibly be sure of what you say. So there you are. Now, such being the case, you and your mother-in-law—why, it's perfectly simple—you two just step aside. Now you know you're telling the truth, don't you? So do I! So you can't possibly object to their hearing the testimony of the only person who does know, aside from you two.

PONZA: And who may that be, pray?

PREFECT: Why, your wife!

PONZA: My wife! *(Decisively and angrily)* Ah, no! I refuse! Never in the world! Never!

PREFECT: And why not, old man?

PONZA: Bring my wife here to satisfy the curiosity of these strangers?

PREFECT *(sharply)*: And my curiosity, too, if you don't mind! What objection can you have?

PONZA: Oh, but governor, no! My wife! Here? No! Why drag my wife in? These people ought to believe me!

PREFECT: But don't you see, my dear fellow, that the course you're taking now is just calculated to discredit what you say?

AGAZZI: His mistake in the first place, governor, was trying to prevent his mother-in-law from coming here and calling—a double discourtesy, mark you, to my wife and to my daughter!

PONZA: But what in the name of God do you people want of me? You've been nagging and nagging at that poor old woman next door; and now you want to get your clutches on my wife! No, governor! I refuse to submit to such an indignity! She owes nothing to anybody. My wife is not making visits in this town. You say you believe me, governor? That's enough for me! Here's my resignation! I'll go out and look for another job!

PREFECT: No, no, Ponza, I must speak plainly. In the first place I have always treated you on the square; and you have no right to speak in that tone of voice to me. In the second place you are beginning to make me doubt your word by refusing to furnish me—not other people—but me, the evidence that I have asked for in your interest; evidence, moreover, that so far as I can see, cannot possibly do you any harm. It seems to me that my colleague here, Signor Agazzi, can ask a lady to come to his house! But no, if you prefer, we'll go and see her.

PONZA: So you really insist, governor?

PREFECT: I insist, but as I told you, in your own interest. You realize, besides, that I might have the legal right to question her . . .

PONZA: I see, I see! So that's it! An official investigation! Well, why not, after all? I will bring my wife here, just to end the whole matter. But how can you guarantee me that this poor old lady next door will not catch sight of her?

PREFECT: Why, I hadn't thought of that! She does live right next door.

AGAZZI *(speaking up)*: We are perfectly willing to go to Signor Ponza's house.

PONZA: No, no, I was just thinking of you people. I don't want you to play any more tricks on me. Any mistakes might have the most frightful consequences, set her going again!

AGAZZI: You're not very fair to us, Ponza, it seems to me.

PREFECT: Or you might bring your wife to my office, rather . . .

PONZA: No, no! Since you're going to question her anyway, we might as well get

through with it. We'll bring her here, right here. I'll keep an eye on my mother-in-law myself. We'll have her here right away, governor, and get an end of
this nonsense once and for all, once and for all! *(He hurries away through the
rear exit)*

PREFECT: I confess I was not expecting so much opposition on his part.

AGAZZI: Ah, you'll see. He'll go and cook up with his wife just what she's to say!

PREFECT: Oh, don't worry as to that! I'll question the woman myself.

SIRELLI: But he's more excited than he's ever been before.

PREFECT: Well, I confess I never saw him just in this state of mind. Perhaps it is
the sense of outrage he feels in having to bring his wife . . .

SIRELLI: In having to let her loose for once, you ought to say!

PREFECT: A man isn't necessarily mad because he wants to keep an eye on his
wife.

AGAZZI: Of course he says it's to protect her from the mother-in-law.

PREFECT: I wasn't thinking of just that—he may be jealous of the woman!

SIRELLI: Jealous to the extent of refusing her a servant? For you know, don't you,
he makes his wife do all the housework?

AGAZZI: And he does all the marketing himself every morning.

COMMISSIONER: That's right, governor! I've had him shadowed. An errand boy
from the market carries the stuff as far as the door.

SIRELLI: But he never lets the boy inside.

PREFECT: Dear me, dear me! He excused himself for that servant business when I
took the matter up with him.

LAUDISI: And that's information right from the source!

PREFECT: He says he does it to save money.

LAUDISI: He has to keep two establishments on one salary.

SIRELLI: Oh, we weren't criticizing how he runs his house; but I ask you as a matter of common sense: he is a man of some position, and do you think that this
second wife of his, as he calls her, who ought to be a lady, would consent to
do all the work about the house? . . .

AGAZZI: The hardest and most disagreeable work, you understand . . .

SIRELLI: . . . just out of consideration for the mother of her husband's first wife?

AGAZZI: Oh, I say, governor, be honest now! That doesn't seem probable, does it?

PREFECT: I confess it does seem queer . . .

LAUDISI: . . . in case this second woman is an ordinary woman!

PREFECT: Yes, but let's be frank. It doesn't seem reasonable. But yet, one might
say—well, you could explain it as generosity on her part, and even better, as
jealousy on his part. Mad or not mad, there is no denying that he's jealous!

(A confused clamor of voices is heard from the next door)

AGAZZI: My, I wonder what's going on in there!

(Amalia enters from the door on the left in a state of great excitement)

AMALIA: Signora Frola is here!

AGAZZI: Impossible! How in the world did she get in? Who sent for her?

AMALIA: Nobody! She came of her own accord!

PREFECT: Oh, no, please—just a moment! No! Send her away, madam, please!

AGAZZI: We've got to get rid of her. Don't let her in here! We must absolutely keep her out!

(*Signora Frola appears at the door on the left, trembling, beseeching, weeping, a handkerchief in her hand. The people in the next room are crowding around behind her.*)

SIGNORA FROLA: Oh, please, please! You tell them, Signor Agazzi! Don't let them send me away!

AGAZZI: But you must go away, madam! We simply can't allow you to be here now!

SIGNORA FROLA (*desperately*): Why? Why? (*Turning to Amalia*) I appeal to you, Signora Agazzi.

AMALIA: But don't you see? The prefect is there! They're having an important meeting.

SIGNORA FROLA: Oh, the prefect! Please, governor, please! I was intending to go and see you.

PREFECT: No, I am so sorry, madam. I can't see you just now! You must go away!

SIGNORA FROLA: Yes, I am going away. I am going to leave town this very day! I am going to leave town and never come back again!

AGAZZI: Oh, we didn't mean that, my dear Signora Frola. We meant that we couldn't see you here, just now, in this room. Do me a favor, please! You can see the governor by and by.

SIGNORA FROLA: But why? I don't understand! What's happened!

AGAZZI: Why, your son-in-law will soon be here! There, now do you see?

SIGNORA FROLA: Oh, he's coming here? Oh, yes, in that case . . . Yes, yes, . . . I'll go! But there was something I wanted to say to you people. You must stop all this. You must let us alone. You think you are helping me. You are trying to do me a favor; but really, what you're doing is working me a great wrong. I've got to leave town this very day because he must not be aroused. What do you want of him anyway? What are you trying to do to him? Why are you having him come here? Oh, Mr. Governor . . .

PREFECT: Come, Signora Frola, don't worry, don't worry. I'll see you by and by and explain everything. You just step out now, won't you?

AMALIA: Please, Signora Frola . . . yes, that's right! Come with me!

SIGNORA FROLA: Oh, my dear Signora Agazzi, you are trying to rob me of the one comfort I had in life, the chance of seeing my daughter once in a while, at least from a distance! (*She begins to weep*)

PREFECT: What in the world are you thinking of? We are not asking you to leave town. We just want you to leave this room, for the time being. There, now do you understand?

SIGNORA FROLA: But it's on his account, governor . . . it's on his account I was coming to ask you to help him! It was on his account, not on mine!

PREFECT: There, there, everything will be all right. We'll take care of him. And we'll have this whole business settled in a jiffy.

SIGNORA FROLA: But how . . . how can I be sure? I can see that everybody here hates him. They are trying to do something to him.

PREFECT: No, no, not at all! And even if they were, I would look after him. There, there, don't worry, don't worry!

SIGNORA FROLA: Oh, so you believe him? Oh, thank you; thank you sir! That means that at least *you* understand!

PREFECT: Yes, yes, madam, I understand, I understand! And I cautioned all these people here. It's a misfortune that came to him long, long ago. He's all right now!

SIGNORA FROLA: . . . Only he must not go back to all those things.

PREFECT: You're right, you're quite right, Signora Frola, but as I told you, I understand!

SIGNORA FROLA: Yes, governor, that's it! If he compels us to live this way—well, what does it matter. That doesn't do anybody any harm so long as we're satisfied, and my daughter is happy this way. That's enough for me, and for her! But you'll look after us, governor. They mustn't spoil anything. Otherwise there's nothing left for me except to leave town and never see her again—never, not even from a distance. You must not irritate him. You must leave him alone. Oh, please!

(*At this moment a wave of surprise, anxiety, dismay, sweeps over the company. Everybody falls silent and turns to the door. Suppressed exclamations are audible.*)

VOICES: Oh! Oh! Look! There she is! Oh! Oh!

SIGNORA FROLA (*noticing the change in people, and groaning, all of a tremble*): What's the matter? What's the matter?

(*The Company divides to either hand. A Lady has appeared at the door in back. She is dressed in deep mourning and her face is concealed with a thick, black, impenetrable veil.*)

SIGNORA FROLA (*uttering a piercing shriek of joy*): Oh, Lena! Lena! Lena! Lena!

(*She dashes forward and throws her arms about the veiled woman with the passionate hysteria of a mother who has not embraced her daughter for years and years. But at the same time from beyond the door in the rear another piercing cry comes. Ponza dashes into the room.*)

PONZA: No! Julia! Julia! Julia!

(*At his voice Signora Ponza draws up stiffly in the arms of Signora Frola who is clasping her tightly. Ponza notices that his mother-in-law is thus desperately entwined about his wife and he shrieks desperately.*)

PONZA: Cowards! Liars! I knew you would! I knew you would! It is just like the lot of you!

SIGNORA PONZA (*turning her veiled head with a certain austere solemnity toward her husband*): Don't be afraid! Just take her away! Go!

(*Signora Frola, at these words, turns to her son-in-law and humbly, tremblingly, goes over and embraces him.*)

SIGNORA FROLA: Yes, yes, you poor boy, come with me, come with me!

(*Their arms about each other's waists, and holding each other up affectionately, Ponza and his mother-in-law withdraw through the rear door. They are both weeping. Profound silence in the company. All those present stand there with their eyes fixed upon the departing couple. As Signora Frola and Ponza are lost from view, all*) *eyes turn expectantly upon the veiled lady. Some of the women are weeping.)*

SIGNORA PONZA *(having looked at them through her veil, speaking with dark solemnity)*: What else do you want of me, after this, ladies and gentlemen? There is a misfortune here, as you see, which must stay hidden: otherwise the remedy which our compassion has found cannot avail.

THE PREFECT *(moved)*: We want to respect your compassion, madam. It's only that we'd like you to tell us . . .

SIGNORA PONZA *(slowly, and with clear articulation)*: Tell you what? The truth? Simply this: I am the daughter of Signora Frola . . .

ALL *(with a happy intake of breath)*: Ah!

SIGNORA PONZA: . . . and the second wife of Signor Ponza . . .

ALL *(amazed and disenchanted, quietly)*: . . . What?

SIGNORA PONZA *(continuing)*: . . . and, for myself, I am nobody!

THE PREFECT: No, no, madam, for yourself you must be either one or the other!

SIGNORA PONZA: No! I am she whom you believe me to be. *(She looks at them all through her veil for a moment, then leaves. Silence.)*

LAUDISI: And there, my friends, you have the truth! *(With a look of derisive defiance at them all)* Are you satisfied? *(He bursts out laughing)*

The Bald Soprano

The Bald Soprano opens in "A middle-class English interior," a setting in some respects as ordinary as the parlor of *It Is So! (If You Think So)* or the nursery of *The Cherry Orchard*. But whereas Chekhov used the physical properties of ordinary reality to support a drama of convincing realism, and Pirandello used them to raise fundamental questions about the nature of reality itself, for Ionesco the ordinary armchairs and polite verbal exchanges of everyday existence are material for high-spirited mockery. The play is an example of *theater of the absurd*, a kind of drama prominent in the 1950s, in which life is viewed, sometimes with humor and sometimes with sadness, as without meaning, absurd, ridiculous.

THE BALD SOPRANO*
ANTI-PLAY
Eugène Ionesco (1912–)

THE CHARACTERS

MR. SMITH
MRS. SMITH
MR. MARTIN
MRS. MARTIN
MARY, *the maid*
THE FIRE CHIEF

* Translated by Donald M. Allen.

Scene: A middle-class English interior, with English armchairs. An English evening. Mr. Smith, an Englishman, seated in his English armchair and wearing English slippers, is smoking his English pipe and reading an English newspaper, near an English fire. He is wearing English spectacles and a small gray English mustache. Beside him, in another English armchair, Mrs. Smith, an Englishwoman, is darning some English socks. A long moment of English silence. The English clock strikes 17 English strokes.

MRS. SMITH: There, it's nine o'clock. We've drunk the soup, and eaten the fish and chips, and the English salad. The children have drunk English water. We've eaten well this evening. That's because we live in the suburbs of London and because our name is Smith.

MR. SMITH *(continues to read, clicks his tongue)*

MRS. SMITH: Potatoes are very good fried in fat; the salad oil was not rancid. The oil from the grocer at the corner is better quality than the oil from the grocer across the street. It is even better than the oil from the grocer at the bottom of the street. However, I prefer not to tell them that their oil is bad.

MR. SMITH *(continues to read, clicks his tongue)*

MRS. SMITH: However, the oil from the grocer at the corner is still the best.

MR. SMITH *(continues to read, clicks his tongue)*

MRS. SMITH: Mary did the potatoes very well, this evening. The last time she did not do them well. I do not like them when they are well done.

MR. SMITH *(continues to read, clicks his tongue)*

MRS. SMITH: The fish was fresh. It made my mouth water. I had two helpings. No, three helpings. That made me go to the w.c. You also had three helpings. However, the third time you took less than the first two times, while as for me, I took a great deal more. I eat better than you this evening. Why is that? Usually, it is you who eats more. It is not appetite you lack.

MR. SMITH *(clicks his tongue)*

MRS. SMITH: But still, the soup was perhaps a little too salt. It was saltier than you. Ha, ha, ha. It also had too many leeks and not enough onions. I regret I didn't advise Mary to add some aniseed stars. The next time I'll know better.

MR. SMITH *(continues to read, clicks his tongue)*

MRS. SMITH: Our little boy wanted to drink some beer; he's going to love getting tiddly. He's like you. At table did you notice how he stared at the bottle? But I poured some water from the jug into his glass. He was thirsty and he drank it. Helen is like me: she's a good manager, thrifty, plays the piano. She never asks to drink English beer. She's like our little daughter who drinks only milk and eats only porridge. It's obvious that she's only two. She's named Peggy. The quince and bean pie was marvelous. It would have been nice, perhaps, to have had a small glass of Australian Burgundy with the sweet, but I did not bring the bottle to the table because I did not wish to set the children a bad example of gluttony. They must learn to be sober and temperate.

MR. SMITH *(continues to read, clicks his tongue)*

MRS. SMITH: Mrs. Parker knows a Rumanian grocer by the name of Popesco Rosenfeld, who has just come from Constantinople. He is a great specialist in yogurt. He has a diploma from the school of yogurt-making in Adrianople. Tomorrow I shall buy a large pot of native Rumanian yogurt from him. One doesn't often find such things here in the suburbs of London.

MR. SMITH *(continues to read, clicks his tongue)*

MRS. SMITH: Yogurt is excellent for the stomach, the kidneys, the appendicitis, and apotheosis. It was Doctor Mackenzie-King who told me that, he's the one who takes care of the children of our neighbors, the Johns. He's a good doctor. One can trust him. He never prescribes any medicine that he's not tried out on himself first. Before operating on Parker, he had his own liver operated on first, although he was not the least bit ill.

MR. SMITH: But how does it happen that the doctor pulled through while Parker died?

MRS. SMITH: Because the operation was successful in the doctor's case and it was not in Parker's.

MR. SMITH: Then Mackenzie is not a good doctor. The operation should have succeeded with both of them or else both should have died.

MRS. SMITH: Why?

MR. SMITH: A conscientious doctor must die with his patient if they can't get well together. The captain of a ship goes down with his ship into the briny deep, he does not survive alone.

MRS. SMITH: One cannot compare a patient with a ship.

MR. SMITH: Why not? A ship has its diseases too; moreover, your doctor is as hale as a ship; that's why he should have perished at the same time as his patient, like the captain and his ship.

MRS. SMITH: Ah! I hadn't thought of that . . . Perhaps it is true . . . And then, what conclusion do you draw from this?

MR. SMITH: All doctors are quacks. And all patients too. Only the Royal Navy is honest in England.

MRS. SMITH: But not sailors.

MR. SMITH: Naturally *(A pause. Still reading his paper)* Here's a thing I don't understand. In the newspaper they always give the age of deceased persons but never the age of the newly born. That doesn't make sense.

MRS. SMITH: I never thought of that!

(Another moment of silence. The clock strikes seven times. Silence. The clock strikes three times. Silence. The clock doesn't strike.)

MR. SMITH *(still reading his paper)*: Tsk, it says here that Bobby Watson died.

MRS. SMITH: My God, the poor man! When did he die?

MR. SMITH: Why do you pretend to be astonished? You know very well that he's been dead these past two years. Surely you remember that we attended his funeral a year and a half ago.

MRS. SMITH: Oh yes, of course I do remember. I remembered it right away, but I don't understand why you yourself were so surprised to see it in the paper.

MR. SMITH: It wasn't in the paper. It's been three years since his death was announced. I remembered it through an association of ideas.

MRS. SMITH: What a pity! He was so well preserved.

MR. SMITH: He was the handsomest corpse in Great Britain. He didn't look his age. Poor Bobby, he'd been dead for four years and he was still warm. A veritable living corpse. And how cheerful he was!

MRS. SMITH: Poor Bobby.

MR. SMITH: Which poor Bobby do you mean?

Mrs. Smith: It is his wife that I mean. She is called Bobby too, Bobby Watson. Since they both had the same name, you could never tell one from the other when you saw them together. It was only after his death that you could really tell which was which. And there are still people today who confuse her with the deceased and offer their condolences to him. Do you know her?

Mr. Smith: I only met her once, by chance, at Bobby's burial.

Mrs. Smith: I've never seen her. Is she pretty?

Mr. Smith: She has regular features and yet one cannot say that she is pretty. She is too big and stout. Her features are not regular but still one can say that she is very pretty. She is a little too small and too thin. She's a voice teacher.

(The clock strikes five times. A long silence.)

Mrs. Smith: And when do they plan to be married, those two?

Mr. Smith: Next spring, at the latest.

Mrs. Smith: We shall have to go to their wedding, I suppose.

Mr. Smith: We shall have to give them a wedding present. I wonder what?

Mrs. Smith: Why don't we give them one of the seven silver salvers that were given us for our wedding and which have never been of any use to us? *(Silence)*

Mrs. Smith: How sad for her to be left a widow so young.

Mr. Smith: Fortunately, they had no children.

Mrs. Smith: That was all they needed! Children! Poor woman, how could she have managed!

Mr. Smith: She's still young. She might very well remarry. She looks so well in mourning.

Mrs. Smith: But who would take care of the children? You know very well that they have a boy and a girl. What are their names?

Mr. Smith: Bobby and Bobby like their parents. Bobby Watson's uncle, old Bobby Watson, is a rich man and very fond of the boy. He might very well pay for Bobby's education.

Mrs. Smith: That would be proper. And Bobby Watson's aunt, old Bobby Watson, might very well, in her turn, pay for the education of Bobby Watson, Bobby Watson's daughter. That way Bobby, Bobby Watson's mother, could remarry. Has she anyone in mind?

Mr. Smith: Yes, a cousin of Bobby Watson's.

Mrs. Smith: Who? Bobby Watson?

Mr. Smith: Which Bobby Watson do you mean?

Mrs. Smith: Why, Bobby Watson, the son of old Bobby Watson, the late Bobby Watson's other uncle.

Mr. Smith: No, it's not that one, it's someone else. It's Bobby Watson, the son of old Bobby Watson, the late Bobby Watson's aunt.

Mrs. Smith: Are you referring to Bobby Watson the commercial traveler?

Mr. Smith: All the Bobby Watsons are commercial travelers.

Mrs. Smith: What a difficult trade! However, they do well at it.

Mr. Smith: Yes, when there's no competition.

Mrs. Smith: And when is there no competition?

Mr. Smith: On Tuesdays, Thursdays, and Tuesdays.

MRS. SMITH: Ah! Three days a week? And what does Bobby Watson do on those days?

MR. SMITH: He rests, he sleeps.

MRS. SMITH: But why doesn't he work those three days if there's no competition?

MR. SMITH: I don't know everything. I can't answer all your idiotic questions!

MRS. SMITH *(offended)*: Oh! Are you trying to humiliate me?

MR. SMITH *(all smiles)*: You know very well that I'm not.

MRS. SMITH: Men are all alike! You sit there all day long, a cigarette in your mouth, or you powder your nose and rouge your lips, fifty times a day, or else you drink like a fish.

MR. SMITH: But what would you say if you saw men acting like women do, smoking all day long, powdering, rouging their lips, drinking whisky?

MRS. SMITH: It's nothing to me! But if you're only saying that to annoy me . . . I don't care for that kind of joking, you know that very well!

(She hurls the socks across the stage and shows her teeth. She gets up.[1])

MR. SMITH *(also getting up and going towards his wife, tenderly)*: Oh, my little ducky daddles, what a little spitfire you are! You know that I only said it as a joke! *(He takes her by the waist and kisses her)* What a ridiculous pair of old lovers we are! Come, let's put out the lights and go bye-byes.

MARY *(entering)*: I'm the maid. I have spent a very pleasant afternoon. I've been to the cinema with a man and I've seen a film with some women. After the cinema, we went to drink some brandy and milk and then read the newspaper.

MRS. SMITH: I hope that you've spent a pleasant afternoon, that you went to the with a man and that you drank some brandy and milk.

MR. SMITH: And the newspaper.

MARY: Mr. and Mrs. Martin, your guests, are at the door. They were waiting for me. They didn't dare come in by themselves. They were supposed to have dinner with you this evening.

MRS. SMITH: Oh, yes. We were expecting them. And we were hungry. Since they didn't put in an appearance, we were going to start dinner without them. We've had nothing to eat all day. You should not have gone out!

MARY: But it was you who gave me permission.

MR. SMITH: We didn't do it on purpose.

MARY *(bursts into laughter, then she bursts into tears. Then she smiles)*: I bought me a chamber pot.

MRS. SMITH: My dear Mary, please open the door and ask Mr. and Mrs. Martin to step in. We will change quickly.

(Mr. and Mrs. Smith exit right. Mary opens the door at the left by which Mr. and Mrs. Martin enter.)

MARY: Why have you come so late! You are not very polite. People should be punctual. Do you understand? But sit down there, anyway, and wait now that you're here.

[1] In Nicholas Bataille's production, Mrs. Smith did not show her teeth, nor did she throw the socks very far [author's note].

(She exits. Mr. and Mrs. Martin sit facing each other, without speaking. They smile timidly at each other. The dialogue which follows must be spoken in voices that are drawling, monotonous, a little singsong, without nuances.[2])

MR. MARTIN: Excuse me, madam, but it seems to me, unless I'm mistaken, that I've met you somewhere before.

MRS. MARTIN: I, too, sir. It seems to me that I've met you somewhere before.

MR. MARTIN: Was it, by any chance, at Manchester that I caught a glimpse of you, madam?

MRS. MARTIN: That is very possible. I am originally from the city of Manchester. But I do not have a good memory, sir. I cannot say whether it was there that I caught a glimpse of you or not!

MR. MARTIN: Good God, that's curious! I, too, am originally from the city of Manchester, madam!

MRS. MARTIN: That is curious!

MR. MARTIN: Isn't that curious! Only, I, madam, I left the city of Manchester about five weeks ago.

MRS. MARTIN: That is curious! What a bizarre coincidence! I, too, sir, I left the city of Manchester about five weeks ago.

MR. MARTIN: Madam, I took the 8:30 morning train which arrives in London at 4:45.

MRS. MARTIN: That is curious! How very bizarre! And what a coincidence! I took the same train, sir, I too.

MR. MARTIN: Good Lord, how curious! Perhaps then, madam, it was on the train that I saw you?

MRS. MARTIN: It is indeed possible; that is, not unlikely. It is plausible and, after all, why not!—But I don't recall it, sir!

MR. MARTIN: I traveled second class, madam. There is no second class in England, but I always travel second class.

MRS. MARTIN: That is curious! How very bizarre! And what a coincidence! I, too, sir, I traveled second class.

MR. MARTIN: How curious that is! Perhaps we did meet in second class, my dear lady!

MRS. MARTIN: That is certainly possible, and it is not at all unlikely. But I do not remember very well, my dear sir!

MR. MARTIN: My seat was in coach No. 8, compartment 6, my dear lady.

MRS. MARTIN: How curious that is! My seat was also in coach No. 8, compartment 6, my dear sir!

MR. MARTIN: How curious that is and what a bizarre coincidence! Perhaps we met in compartment 6, my dear lady?

MRS. MARTIN: It is indeed possible, after all! But I do not recall it, my dear sir!

MR. MARTIN: To tell the truth, my dear lady, I do not remember it either, but it is possible that we caught a glimpse of each other there, and as I think of it, it seems to me even very likely.

MRS. MARTIN: Oh! truly, of course, truly, sir!

---

[2] In Nicholas Bataille's production, this dialogue was spoken in a tone and played in a style sincerely tragic [author's note].

MR. MARTIN: How curious it is! I had seat No. 3, next to the window, my dear lady.

MRS. MARTIN: Oh, good Lord, how curious and bizarre! I had seat No. 6, next to the window, across from you, my dear sir.

MR. MARTIN: Good God, how curious that is and what a coincidence! We were then seated facing each other, my dear lady! It is there that we must have seen each other!

MRS. MARTIN: How curious it is! It is possible, but I do not recall it, sir!

MR. MARTIN: To tell the truth, my dear lady, I do not remember it either. However, it is very possible that we saw each other on that occasion.

MRS. MARTIN: It is true, but I am not at all sure of it, sir.

MR. MARTIN: Dear madam, were you not the lady who asked me to place her suitcase in the luggage rack and who thanked me and gave me permission to smoke?

MRS. MARTIN: But of course, that must have been I, sir. How curious it is, how curious it is, and what a coincidence!

MR. MARTIN: How curious it is, how bizarre, what a coincidence! And well, well, it was perhaps at that moment that we came to know each other, madam?

MRS. MARTIN: How curious it is and what a coincidence! It is indeed possible, my dear sir! However, I do not believe that I recall it.

MR. MARTIN: Nor do I, madam. (*A moment of silence. The clock strikes twice, then once*) Since coming to London, I have resided in Bromfield Street, my dear lady.

MRS. MARTIN: How curious that it, how bizarre! I, too, since coming to London, I have resided in Bromfield Street, my dear sir.

MR. MARTIN: How curious that is, well then, well then, perhaps we have seen each other in Bromfield Street, my dear lady.

MRS. MARTIN: How curious that is, how bizarre! It is indeed possible, after all! But I do not recall it, my dear sir.

MR. MARTIN: I reside at No. 19, my dear lady.

MRS. MARTIN: How curious that is. I also reside at No. 19, my dear sir.

MR. MARTIN: Well then, well then, well then, well then, perhaps we have seen each other in that house, dear lady?

MRS. MARTIN: It is indeed possible but I do not recall it, dear sir.

MR. MARTIN: My flat is on the fifth floor, No. 8, my dear lady.

MRS. MARTIN: How curious it is, good Lord, how bizarre! And what a coincidence! I too reside on the fifth floor, in flat No. 8, dear sir!

MR. MARTIN (*musing*): How curious it is, how curious it is, how curious it is, and what a coincidence! You know, in my bedroom there is a bed, and it is covered with a green eiderdown. This room, with the bed and the green eiderdown, is at the end of the corridor between the w.c. and the bookcase, dear lady!

MRS. MARTIN: What a coincidence, good Lord, what a coincidence! My bedroom, too, has a bed with a green eiderdown and is at the end of the corridor, between the w.c., dear sir, and the bookcase!

MR. MARTIN: How bizarre, curious, strange! Then, madam, we live in the same room and we sleep in the same bed, dear lady. It is perhaps there that we have met!

MRS. MARTIN: How curious it is and what a coincidence! It is indeed possible that
we have met there, and perhaps even last night. But I do not recall it, dear sir!

MR. MARTIN: I have a little girl, my little daughter, she lives with me, dear lady.
She is two years old, she's blonde, she has a white eye and a red eye, she is
very pretty, her name is Alice, dear lady.

MRS. MARTIN: What a bizarre coincidence! I, too, have a little girl. She is two
years old, has a white eye and a red eye, she is very pretty, and her name is
Alice, too, dear sir!

MR. MARTIN (in the same drawling, monotonous voice): How curious it is and what a
coincidence! And bizarre! Perhaps they are the same, dear lady!

MRS. MARTIN: How curious it is! It is indeed possible, dear sir. (A rather long moment of silence. The clock strikes 29 times)

MR. MARTIN (after having reflected at length, gets up slowly and, unhurriedly, moves
toward Mrs. Martin, who, surprised by his solemn air, has also gotten up very quietly.
Mr. Martin, in the same flat, monotonous voice, slightly sing-song): Then, dear
lady, I believe that there can be no doubt about it, we have seen each other before and you are my own wife . . . Elizabeth, I have found you again!

(Mrs. Martin approaches Mr. Martin without haste. They embrace without expression. The clock strikes once, very loud. This striking of the clock must be so loud
that it makes the audience jump. The Martins do not hear it.)

MRS. MARTIN: Donald, it's you, darling!

(They sit together in the same armchair, their arms around each other, and fall
asleep. The clock strikes several more times. Mary, on tiptoe, a finger to her lips, enters quietly and addresses the audience.)

MARY: Elizabeth and Donald are now too happy to be able to hear me. I can
therefore let you in on a secret. Elizabeth is not Elizabeth, Donald is not Donald. And here is the proof: the child that Donald spoke of is not Elizabeth's
daughter, they are not the same person. Donald's daughter has one white eye
and one red eye like Elizabeth's daughter. Whereas Donald's child has a white
right eye and a red left eye, Elizabeth's child has a red right eye and a white
left eye! Thus all of Donald's system of deduction collapses when it comes up
against this last obstacle which destroys his whole theory. In spite of the extraordinary coincidences which seem to be definitive proofs, Donald and Elizabeth, not being the parents of the same child, are not Donald and Elizabeth.
It is in vain that he thinks he is Donald, it is in vain that she thinks she is Elizabeth. He believes in vain that she is Elizabeth. She believes in vain that he is
Donald—they are sadly deceived. But who is the true Donald? Who is the true
Elizabeth? Who has any interest in prolonging this confusion? I don't know.
Let's not try to know. Let's leave things as they are. (She takes several steps
toward the door, then returns and says to the audience) My real name is Sherlock
Holmes. (She exits)

(The clock strikes as much as it likes. After several seconds, Mr. and Mrs. Martin
separate and take the chairs they had at the beginning.)

MR. MARTIN: Darling, let's forget all that has not passed between us, and now
that we have found each other again, let's try not to lose each other any more,
and live as before.

MRS. MARTIN: Yes, darling.

(Mr. and Mrs. Smith enter from the right, wearing the same clothes)

MRS. SMITH: Good evening, dear friends! Please forgive us for having made you wait so long. We thought that we should extend you the courtesy to which you are entitled and as soon as we learned that you had been kind enough to give us the pleasure of coming to see us without prior notice we hurried to dress for the occasion.

MR. SMITH *(furious)*: We've had nothing to eat all day. And we've been waiting four whole hours for you. Why have you come so late?

(Mr. and Mrs. Smith sit facing their guests. The striking of the clock underlines the speeches, more or less strongly, according to the case. The Martins, particularly Mrs. Martin, seem embarrassed and timid. For this reason the conversation begins with difficulty and the words are uttered, at the beginning, awkwardly. A long embarrassed silence at first, then other silences and hesitations follow.)

MR. SMITH: Hm. *(Silence)*
MRS. SMITH: Hm, hm. *(Silence)*
MRS. MARTIN: Hm, hm, hm. *(Silence)*
MR. MARTIN: Hm, hm, hm, hm. *(Silence)*
MRS. MARTIN: Oh, but definitely. *(Silence)*
MR. MARTIN: We all have colds. *(Silence)*
MR. SMITH: Nevertheless, it's not chilly. *(Silence)*
MRS. SMITH: There's no draft. *(Silence)*
MR. MARTIN: Oh no, fortunately. *(Silence)*
MR. SMITH: Oh dear, oh dear, oh dear. *(Silence)*
MR. MARTIN: Don't you feel well? *(Silence)*
MRS. SMITH: No, he's wet his pants. *(Silence)*
MRS. MARTIN: Oh, sir, at your age, you shouldn't. *(Silence)*
MR. SMITH: The heart is ageless. *(Silence)*
MR. MARTIN: That's true. *(Silence)*
MRS. SMITH: So they say. *(Silence)*
MRS. MARTIN: They also say the opposite. *(Silence)*
MR. SMITH: The truth lies somewhere between the two. *(Silence)*
MR. MARTIN: That's true. *(Silence)*
MRS. SMITH *(to the Martins)*: Since you travel so much, you must have many interesting things to tell us.
MR. MARTIN *(to his wife)*: My dear, tell us what you've seen today.
MRS. MARTIN: It's scarcely worth the trouble, for no one would believe me.
MR. SMITH: We're not going to question your sincerity!
MRS. SMITH: You will offend us if you think that.
MR. MARTIN *(to his wife)*: You will offend them, my dear, if you think that . . .
MRS. MARTIN *(graciously)*: Oh well, today I witnessed something extraordinary. Something really incredible.
MR. MARTIN: Tell us quickly, my dear.
MR. SMITH: Oh, this is going to be amusing.
MRS. SMITH: At last.
MRS. MARTIN: Well, today, when I went shopping to buy some vegetables, which are getting to be dearer and dearer . . .

MRS. SMITH: Where is it all going to end!

MR. SMITH: You shouldn't interrupt, my dear, it's very rude.

MRS. MARTIN: In the street, near a café, I saw a man, properly dressed, about fifty years old, or not even that, who . . .

MR. SMITH: Who, what?

MRS. SMITH: Who, what?

MR. SMITH (to his wife): Don't interrupt, my dear, you're disgusting.

MRS. SMITH: My dear, it is you who interrupted first, you boor.

MR. SMITH (to his wife): Hush. (To Mrs. Martin) What was this man doing?

MRS. MARTIN: Well, I'm sure you'll say that I'm making it up—he was down on one knee and he was bent over.

MR. MARTIN, MR. SMITH, MRS. SMITH: Oh!

MRS. MARTIN: Yes, bent over.

MR. SMITH: Not possible.

MRS. MARTIN: Yes, bent over. I went near him to see what he was doing . . .

MR. SMITH: And?

MRS. MARTIN: He was tying his shoe lace which had come undone.

MR. MARTIN, MR. SMITH, MRS. SMITH: Fantastic!

MR. SMITH: If someone else had told me this, I'd not believe it.

MR. MARTIN: Why not? One sees things even more extraordinary every day, when one walks around. For instance, today in the Underground I myself saw a man, quietly sitting on a seat, reading his newspaper.

MRS. SMITH: What a character!

MR. SMITH: Perhaps it was the same man!

(The doorbell rings)

MR. SMITH: Goodness, someone is ringing.

MRS. SMITH: There must be somebody there. I'll go and see. (She goes to see, she opens the door and closes it, and comes back) Nobody. (She sits down again)

MR. MARTIN: I'm going to give you another example . . .

(Doorbell rings again)

MR. SMITH: Goodness, someone is ringing.

MRS. SMITH: There must be somebody there. I'll go and see. (She goes to see, opens the door, and comes back) No one. (She sits down again)

MR. MARTIN (who has forgotten where he was): Uh . . .

MRS. MARTIN: You were saying that you were going to give us another example.

MR. MARTIN: Oh, yes . . .

(Doorbell rings again)

MR. SMITH: Goodness, someone is ringing.

MRS. SMITH: I'm not going to open the door again.

MR. SMITH: Yes, but there must be someone there!

MRS. SMITH: The first time there was no one. The second time, no one. Why do you think that there is someone there now?

MR. SMITH: Because someone has rung!

MRS. MARTIN: That's no reason.

MR. MARTIN: What? When one hears the doorbell ring, that means someone is at the door ringing to have the door opened.

MRS. MARTIN: Not always. You've just seen otherwise!

MR. MARTIN: In most cases, yes.

MR. SMITH: As for me, when I go to visit someone, I ring in order to be admitted. I think that everyone does the same thing and that each time there is a ring there must be someone there.

MRS. SMITH: That is true in theory. But in reality things happen differently. You have just seen otherwise.

MRS. MARTIN: Your wife is right.

MR. MARTIN: Oh! You women! You always stand up for each other.

MRS. SMITH: Well, I'll go and see. You can't say that I am obstinate, but you will see that there's no one there! *(She goes to look, opens the door and closes it)* You see, there's no one there. *(She returns to her seat)*

MRS. SMITH: Oh, these men who always think they're right and who're always wrong!

(The doorbell rings again)

MR. SMITH: Goodness, someone is ringing. There must be someone there.

MRS. SMITH *(in a fit of anger)*: Don't send me to open the door again. You've seen that it was useless. Experience teaches us that when one hears the doorbell ring it is because there is never anyone there.

MRS. MARTIN: Never.

MR. MARTIN: That's not entirely accurate.

MR. SMITH: In fact it's false. When one hears the doorbell ring it is because there is someone there.

MRS. SMITH: He won't admit he's wrong.

MRS. MARTIN: My husband is very obstinate, too.

MR. SMITH: There's someone there.

MR. MARTIN: That's not impossible.

MRS. SMITH *(to her husband)*: No.

MR. SMITH: Yes.

MRS. SMITH: I tell you *no*. In any case you are not going to disturb me again for nothing. If you wish to know, go and look yourself!

MR. SMITH: I'll go.

(Mrs. Smith shrugs her shoulders. Mrs. Martin tosses her head.)

MR. SMITH *(opening the door)*: Oh! how do you do. *(He glances at Mrs. Smith and the Martins, who are all surprise)* It's the Fire Chief!

FIRE CHIEF *(he is of course in uniform and is wearing an enormous shining helmet)*: Good evening, ladies and gentlemen. *(The Smiths and the Martins are still slightly astonished. Mrs. Smith turns her head away, in a temper, and does not reply to his greeting.)* Good evening, Mrs. Smith. You appear to be angry.

MRS. SMITH: Oh!

MR. SMITH: You see it's because my wife is a little chagrined at having been proved wrong.

MR. MARTIN: There's been an argument between Mr. and Mrs. Smith, Mr. Fire Chief.

MRS. SMITH *(to Mr. Martin)*: This is no business of yours! *(To Mr. Smith)* I beg you not to involve outsiders in our family arguments.

MR. SMITH: Oh, my dear, this is not so serious. The Fire Chief is an old friend of

the family. His mother courted me, and I knew his father. He asked me to
give him my daughter in marriage if ever I had one. And he died waiting.

MR. MARTIN: That's neither his fault, nor yours.

FIRE CHIEF: Well, what is it all about?

MRS. SMITH: My husband was claiming . . .

MR. SMITH: No, it was you who was claiming.

MR. MARTIN: Yes, it was she.

MRS. MARTIN: No, it was he.

FIRE CHIEF: Don't get excited. You tell me, Mrs. Smith.

MRS. SMITH: Well, this is how it was. It is difficult for me to speak openly to you,
but a fireman is also a confessor.

FIRE CHIEF: Well, then?

MRS. SMITH: We were arguing because my husband said that each time the doorbell rings there is always someone there.

MR. MARTIN: It is plausible.

MRS. SMITH: And I was saying that each time the doorbell rings there is never
anyone there.

MRS. MARTIN: It might seem strange.

MRS. SMITH: But it has been proved, not by theoretical demonstrations, but by
facts.

MR. SMITH: That's false, since the Fire Chief is here. He rang the bell, I opened
the door, and there he was.

MRS. MARTIN: When?

MR. MARTIN: But just now.

MRS. SMITH: Yes, but it was only when you heard the doorbell ring the fourth
time that there was someone there. And the fourth time does not count.

MRS. MARTIN: Never. It is only the first three times that count.

MR. SMITH: Mr. Fire Chief, permit me in my turn to ask you several questions.

FIRE CHIEF: Go right ahead.

MRS. SMITH: When I opened the door and saw you, it was really you who had
rung the bell?

FIRE CHIEF: Yes, it was I.

MRS. MARTIN: You were at the door? And you rang in order to be admitted?

FIRE CHIEF: I do not deny it.

MR. SMITH (to his wife, triumphantly): You see? I was right. When you hear the
doorbell ring, that means someone rang it. You certainly cannot say that the
Fire Chief is not someone.

MRS. SMITH: Certainly not. I repeat to you that I was speaking of only the first
three times, since the fourth time does not count.

MRS. MARTIN: And when the doorbell rang the first time, was it you?

FIRE CHIEF: No, it was not I.

MRS. MARTIN: You see? The doorbell rang and there was no one there.

MR. MARTIN: Perhaps it was someone else?

MR. SMITH: Were you standing at the door for a long time?

FIRE CHIEF: Three-quarters of an hour.

MR. SMITH: And you saw no one?

FIRE CHIEF: No one. I am sure of that.

MRS. MARTIN: And did you hear the bell when it rang the second time?

FIRE CHIEF: Yes, and that wasn't I either. And there was still no one there.

MRS. SMITH: Victory! I was right.

MR. SMITH *(to his wife)*: Not so fast. *(To the Fire Chief)* And what were you doing at the door?

FIRE CHIEF: Nothing. I was just standing there. I was thinking of many things.

MR. MARTIN *(to the Fire Chief)*: But the third time—it was not you who rang?

FIRE CHIEF: Yes, it was I.

MR. SMITH: But when the door was opened nobody was in sight.

FIRE CHIEF: That was because I had hidden myself—as a joke.

MRS. SMITH: Don't make jokes, Mr. Fire Chief. This business is too sad.

MR. MARTIN: In short, we still do not know whether, when the doorbell rings, there is someone there or not!

MRS. SMITH: Never anyone.

MR. SMITH: Always someone.

FIRE CHIEF: I am going to reconcile you. You both are partly right. When the doorbell rings, sometimes there is someone, other times there is no one.

MR. MARTIN: This seems logical to me.

MRS. MARTIN: I think so too.

FIRE CHIEF: Life is very simple, really. *(To the Smiths)* Go on and kiss each other.

MRS. SMITH: We just kissed each other a little while ago.

MR. MARTIN: They'll kiss each other tomorrow. They have plenty of time.

MRS. SMITH: Mr. Fire Chief, since you have helped us settle this, please make yourself comfortable, take off your helmet and sit down for a moment.

FIRE CHIEF: Excuse me, but I can't stay long. I should like to remove my helmet, but I haven't time to sit down. *(He sits down, without removing his helmet)* I must admit that I have come to see you for another reason. I am on official business.

MRS. SMITH: And what can we do for you, Mr. Fire Chief?

FIRE CHIEF: I must beg you to excuse my indiscretion *(terribly embarrassed)* ... uhm *(He points a finger at the Martins)* ... You don't mind ... in front of them ...

MRS. MARTIN: Say whatever you like.

MR. MARTIN: We're old friends. They tell us everything.

MR. SMITH: Speak.

FIRE CHIEF: Eh, well—is there a fire here?

MRS. SMITH: Why do you ask us that?

FIRE CHIEF: It's because—pardon me—I have orders to extinguish all the fires in the city.

MRS. MARTIN: All?

FIRE CHIEF: Yes, all.

MRS. SMITH *(confused)*: I don't know ... I don't think so. Do you want me to go and look?

MR. SMITH *(sniffing)*: There can't be one here. There's no smell of anything burning.[3]

FIRE CHIEF *(aggrieved)*: None at all? You don't have a little fire in the chimney, something burning in the attic or in the cellar? A little fire just starting at least?

---

[3] In Nicolas Bataille's production Mr. and Mrs. Martin sniffed too [author's note].

MRS. SMITH: I am sorry to disappoint you but I do not believe there's anything here at the moment. I promise that I will notify you when we do have something.

FIRE CHIEF: Please don't forget, it would be a great help.

MRS. SMITH: That's a promise.

FIRE CHIEF (to the Martins): And there's nothing burning at your house either?

MRS. MARTIN: No, unfortunately.

MR. MARTIN (to the Fire Chief): Things aren't going so well just now.

FIRE CHIEF: Very poorly. There's been almost nothing, a few trifles—a chimney, a barn. Nothing important. It doesn't bring in much. And since there are no returns, the profits on output are very meager.

MR. SMITH: Times are bad. That's true all over. It's the same this year with business and agriculture as it is with fires, nothing is prospering.

MR. MARTIN: No wheat, no fires.

FIRE CHIEF: No floods either.

MRS. SMITH: But there is some sugar.

MR. SMITH: That's because it is imported.

MRS. MARTIN: It's harder in the case of fires. The tariffs are too high!

FIRE CHIEF: All the same, there's an occasional asphyxiation by gas, but that's unusual too. For instance, a young woman asphyxiated herself last week—she had left the gas on.

MRS. MARTIN: Had she forgotten it?

FIRE CHIEF: No, but she thought it was her comb.

MR. SMITH: These confusions are always dangerous!

MRS. SMITH: Did you go to see the match dealer?

FIRE CHIEF: There's nothing doing there. He is insured against fires.

MR. MARTIN: Why don't you go see the Vicar of Wakefield, and use my name?

FIRE CHIEF: I don't have the right to extinguish clergymen's fires. The Bishop would get angry. Besides they extinguish their fires themselves, or else they have them put out by vestal virgins.

MR. SMITH: Go see the Durands.

FIRE CHIEF: I can't do that either. He's not English. He's only been naturalized. And naturalized citizens have the right to have houses, but not the right to have them put out if they're burning.

MRS. SMITH: Nevertheless, when they set fire to it last year, it was put out just the same.

FIRE CHIEF: He did that all by himself. Clandestinely. But it's not I who would report him.

MR. SMITH: Neither would I.

MRS. SMITH: Mr. Fire Chief, since you are not too pressed, stay a little while longer. You would be doing us a favor.

FIRE CHIEF: Shall I tell you some stories?

MRS. SMITH: Oh, by all means, how charming of you. (She kisses him)

MR. SMITH, MRS. MARTIN, MR. MARTIN: Yes, yes, some stories, hurrah!

(They applaud)

MR. SMITH: And what is even more interesting is the fact that firemen's stories are all true, and they're based on experience.

FIRE CHIEF: I speak from my own experience. Truth, nothing but the truth. No fiction.

MR. MARTIN: That's right. Truth is never found in books, only in life.

MRS. SMITH: Begin!

MR. MARTIN: Begin!

MRS. MARTIN: Be quiet, he is beginning.

FIRE CHIEF (coughs slightly several times): Excuse me, don't look at me that way. You embarrass me. You know that I am shy.

MRS. SMITH: Isn't he charming! (She kisses him)

FIRE CHIEF: I'm going to try to begin anyhow. But promise me that you won't listen.

MRS. MARTIN: But if we don't listen to you we won't hear you.

FIRE CHIEF: I didn't think of that!

MRS. SMITH: I told you, he's just a boy.

MR. MARTIN, MR. SMITH: Oh, the sweet child! (They kiss him[4])

MRS. MARTIN: Chin up!

FIRE CHIEF: Well, then! (He coughs again in a voice shaken by emotion) "The Dog and the Cow," an experimental fable. Once upon a time another cow asked another dog: "Why have you not swallowed your trunk?" "Pardon me," replied the dog, "it is because I thought that I was an elephant."

MRS. MARTIN: What is the moral?

FIRE CHIEF: That's for you to find out.

MR. SMITH: He's right.

MRS. SMITH (furious): Tell us another.

FIRE CHIEF: A young calf had eaten too much ground glass. As a result, it was obliged to give birth. It brought forth a cow into the world. However, since the calf was male, the cow could not call him Mamma. Nor could she call him Papa, because the calf was too little. The calf was then obliged to get married and the registry office carried out all the details completely à la mode.

MR. SMITH: À la mode de Caen.

MR. MARTIN: Like tripes.

FIRE CHIEF: You've heard that one?

MRS. SMITH: It was in all the papers.

MRS. MARTIN: It happened not far from our house.

FIRE CHIEF: I'll tell you another: "The Cock." Once upon a time, a cock wished to play the dog. But he had no luck because everyone recognized him right away.

MRS. SMITH: On the other hand, the dog that wished to play the cock was never recognized.

MR. SMITH: I'll tell you one: "The Snake and the Fox." Once upon a time, a snake came up to a fox and said: "It seems to me that I know you!" The fox replied to him: "Me too." "Then," said the snake, "give me some money." "A fox doesn't give money," replied the tricky animal, who, in order to escape, jumped down into a deep ravine full of strawberries and chicken honey. But the snake was there waiting for him with a Mephistophelean laugh. The fox pulled out his knife, shouting: "I'm going to teach you how to live!" Then he took to flight,

[4] In Nicolas Bataille's production, they did not kiss the Fire Chief [author's note].

turning his back. But he had no luck. The snake was quicker. With a well-cho-
sen blow of his fist, he struck the fox in the middle of his forehead, which
broke into a thousand pieces, while he cried: "No! No! Four times no! I'm not
your daughter."[5]

MRS. MARTIN: It's interesting.

MRS. SMITH: It's not bad.

MR. MARTIN (shaking Mr. Smith's hand): My congratulations.

FIRE CHIEF (jealous): Not so good. And anyway, I've heard it before.

MR. SMITH: It's terrible.

MRS. SMITH: But it wasn't even true.

MRS. MARTIN: Yes, unfortunately.

MR. MARTIN (to Mrs. Smith): It's your turn, dear lady.

MRS. SMITH: I only know one. I'm going to tell it to you. It's called "The Bouquet."

MR. SMITH: My wife has always been romantic.

MR. MARTIN: She's a true Englishwoman.[6]

MRS. SMITH: Here it is: Once upon a time, a fiancé gave a bouquet of flowers to
his fiancée who said, "Thanks"; but before she had said, "Thanks," he, without saying a single word, took back the flowers he had given her in order to
teach her a good lesson, and he said, "I take them back." He said, "Goodbye,"
and took them back and went off in all directions.

MR. MARTIN: Oh, charming!

(He either kisses or does not kiss Mrs. Smith)

MRS. MARTIN: You have a wife, Mr. Smith, of whom all the world is jealous.

MR. SMITH: It's true. My wife is intelligence personified. She's even more intelligent than I. In any case, she is much more feminine, everyone says so.

MRS. SMITH (to the Fire Chief): Let's have another, Mr. Fire Chief.

FIRE CHIEF: Oh, no, it's too late.

MR. MARTIN: Tell us one, anyway.

FIRE CHIEF: I'm too tired.

MR. SMITH: Please do us a favor.

MR. MARTIN: I beg you.

FIRE CHIEF: No.

MRS. MARTIN: You have a heart of ice. We're sitting on hot coals.

MRS. SMITH (falls on her knees sobbing, or else she does not do this): I implore you!

FIRE CHIEF: Righto.

MR. SMITH (in Mrs. Martin's ear): He agrees! He's going to bore us again.

MRS. MARTIN: Shh.

MRS. SMITH: No luck. I was too polite.

FIRE CHIEF: "The Headcold." My brother-in law had, on the paternal side, a first
cousin whose maternal uncle had a father-in-law whose paternal grandfather
had married as his second wife a young native whose brother he had met on
one of his travels, a girl of whom he was enamored and by whom he had a
son who married an intrepid lady pharmacist who was none other than the

[5] This story was deleted in Nicolas Bataille's production. Mr. Smith went through the gestures only,
without making a sound [author's note].
[6] These two speeches were repeated three times in the original production [author's note].

niece of an unknown fourth-class petty officer of the Royal Navy and whose adopted father had an aunt who spoke Spanish fluently and who was, perhaps, one of the granddaughters of an engineer who died young, himself the grandson of the owner of a vineyard which produced mediocre wine, but who had a second cousin, a stay-at-home, a sergeant-major, whose son had married a very pretty young woman, a divorcée, whose first husband was the son of a loyal patriot who, in the hope of making his fortune, had managed to bring up one of his daughters so that she could marry a footman who had known Rothschild, and whose brother, after having changed his trade several times, married and had a daughter whose stunted great-grandfather wore spectacles which had been given him by a cousin of his, the brother-in-law of a man from Portugal, natural son of a miller, not too badly off, whose foster-brother had married the daughter of a former country doctor, who was himself a foster-brother of the son of a forester, himself the natural son of another country doctor, married three times in a row, whose third wife . . .

MR. MARTIN: I knew that third wife, if I'm not mistaken. She ate chicken sitting on a hornet's nest.

FIRE CHIEF: It's not the same one.

MRS. SMITH: Shh!

FIRE CHIEF: As I was saying . . . whose third wife was the daughter of the best midwife in the region and who, early left a widow . . .

MR. SMITH: Like my wife.

FIRE CHIEF: . . . Had married a glazier who was full of life and who had had, by the daughter of a station master, a child who had burned his bridges . . .

MRS. SMITH: His britches?

MR. MARTIN: No his bridge game.

FIRE CHIEF: And had married an oyster woman, whose father had a brother, mayor of a small town, who had taken as his wife a blonde schoolteacher, whose cousin, a fly fisherman . . .

MR. MARTIN: A fly by night?

FIRE CHIEF: . . . Had married another blonde schoolteacher, named Marie, too, whose brother was married to another Marie, also a blonde schoolteacher . . .

MR. SMITH: Since she's blonde, she must be Marie.

FIRE CHIEF: . . . And whose father had been reared in Canada by an old woman who was the niece of a priest whose grandmother, occasionally in the winter, like everyone else, caught a cold.

MRS. SMITH: A curious story. Almost unbelievable.

MR. MARTIN: If you catch a cold, you should get yourself a colt.

MR. SMITH: It's a useless precaution, but absolutely necessary.

MRS. MARTIN: Excuse me, Mr. Fire Chief, but I did not follow your story very well. At the end, when we got to the grandmother of the priest, I got mixed up.

MR. SMITH: One always gets mixed up in the hands of a priest.

MRS. SMITH: Oh yes, Mr. Fire Chief, begin again. Everyone wants to hear.

FIRE CHIEF: Ah, I don't know whether I'll be able to. I'm on official business. It depends on what time it is.

MRS. SMITH: We don't have the time, here.

FIRE CHIEF: But the clock?

MR. SMITH: It runs badly. It is contradictory, and always indicates the opposite of what the hour really is.

(Enter Mary)

MARY: Madam . . . sir . . .

MRS. SMITH: What do you want?

MR. SMITH: What have you come in here for?

MARY: I hope, madam and sir will excuse me . . . and these ladies and gentlemen too . . . I would like . . . I would like . . . to tell you a story, myself.

MRS. MARTIN: What is she saying?

MR. MARTIN: I believe that our friends' maid is going crazy . . . she wants to tell us a story, too.

FIRE CHIEF: Who does she think she is? *(He looks at her)* Oh!

MRS. SMITH: Why are you butting in?

MR. SMITH: This is really uncalled for, Mary . . .

FIRE CHIEF: Oh! But it is she! Incredible!

MR. SMITH: And you!

MARY: Incredible! Here!

MRS. SMITH: What does all this mean?

MR. SMITH: You know each other?

FIRE CHIEF: And how!

(Mary throws herself on the neck of the Fire Chief)

MARY: I'm so glad to see you again . . . at last!

MR. AND MRS. SMITH: Oh!

MR. SMITH: This is too much, here, in our home, in the suburbs of London.

MRS. SMITH: It's not proper! . . .

FIRE CHIEF: It was she who extinguished my first fires.

MARY: I'm your little firehose.

MR. MARTIN: If that is the case . . . dear friends . . . these emotions are understandable, human, honorable . . .

MRS. MARTIN: All that is human is honorable.

MRS. SMITH: Even so, I don't like to see it . . . here among us . . .

MR. SMITH: She's not been properly brought up . . .

FIRE CHIEF: Oh, you have too many prejudices.

MRS. MARTIN: What I think is that a maid, after all—even though it's none of my business—is never anything but a maid . . .

MR. MARTIN: Even if she can sometimes be a rather good detective.

FIRE CHIEF: Let me go.

MARY: Don't be upset! . . . They're not so bad really.

MR. SMITH: Hm . . . hm . . . you two are very touching, but at the same time, a little . . . a little . . .

MR. MARTIN: Yes, that's exactly the word.

MR. SMITH: . . . A little too exhibitionistic . . .

MR. MARTIN: There is a native British modesty—forgive me for attempting, yet again, to define my thought—not understood by foreigners, even by specialists, thanks to which, if I may thus express myself . . . course, I don't mean to refer to you . . .

MARY: I was going to tell you . . .

MR. SMITH: Don't tell us anything . . .

MARY: Oh yes!

MRS. SMITH: Go, my little Mary, go quietly to the kitchen and read your poems before the mirror . . .

MR. MARTIN: You know, even though I'm not a maid, I also read poems before the mirror.

MRS. MARTIN: This morning when you looked at yourself in the mirror you didn't see yourself.

MR. MARTIN: That's because I wasn't there yet . . .

MARY: All the same, I could, perhaps, recite a little poem for you.

MRS. SMITH: My little Mary, you are frightfully obstinate.

MARY: I'm going to recite a poem, then, is that agreed? It is a poem entitled "The Fire" in honor of the Fire Chief:

THE FIRE

The polypoids were burning in the wood
A stone caught fire
The castle caught fire
The forest caught fire
The men caught fire
The women caught fire
The birds caught fire
The fish caught fire
The water caught fire
The sky caught fire
The ashes caught fire
The smoke caught fire
The fire caught fire
Everything caught fire
Caught fire, caught fire

(She recites the poem while the Smiths are pushing her offstage)

MRS. MARTIN: That sent chills up my spine . . .

MR. MARTIN: And yet there's a certain warmth in those lines . . .

FIRE CHIEF: I thought it was marvelous.

MRS. SMITH: All the same . . .

MR. SMITH: You're exaggerating . . .

FIRE CHIEF: Just a minute . . . I admit . . . all this is very subjective . . . but this is my conception of the world. My world. My dream. My ideal . . . And now this reminds me that I must leave. Since you don't have the time here, I must tell you that in exactly three-quarters of an hour and sixteen minutes, I'm having a fire at the other end of the city. Consequently, I must hurry. Even though it will be quite unimportant.

MRS. SMITH: What will it be? A little chimney fire?

FIRE CHIEF: Oh, not even that. A straw fire and a little heartburn.

MR. SMITH: Well, we're sorry to see you go.

MRS. SMITH: You have been very entertaining.

MRS. MARTIN: Thanks to you, we have passed a truly Cartesian quarter of an hour.

FIRE CHIEF (*moving towards the door, then stopping*): Speaking of that—the bald soprano?

(General silence, embarrassment)

MRS. SMITH: She always wears her hair in the same style.

FIRE CHIEF: Ah! Then goodbye, ladies and gentlemen.

MR. MARTIN: Good luck, and a good fire!

FIRE CHIEF: Let's hope so. For everybody.

(Fire Chief exits. All accompany him to the door and then return to their seats.)

MRS. MARTIN: I can buy a pocketknife for my brother, but you can't buy Ireland for your grandfather.

MR. SMITH: One walks on his feet, but one heats with electricity or coal.

MR. MARTIN: He who sells an ox today, will have an egg tomorrow.

MRS. SMITH: In real life, one must look out of the window.

MRS. MARTIN: One can sit down on a chair, when the chair doesn't have any.

MR. SMITH: One must always think of everything.

MR. MARTIN: The ceiling is above, the floor is below.

MRS. SMITH: When I say yes, it's only a manner of speaking.

MRS. MARTIN: To each his own.

MR. SMITH: Take a circle, caress it, and it will turn vicious.

MRS. SMITH: A schoolmaster teaches his pupils to read, but the cat suckles her young when they are small.

MRS. MARTIN: Nevertheless, it was the cow that gave us tails.

MR. SMITH: When I'm in the country, I love the solitude and the quiet.

MR. MARTIN: You are not old enough yet for that.

MRS. SMITH: Benjamin Franklin was right; you are more nervous than he.

MRS. MARTIN: What are the seven days of the week?

MR. SMITH: Monday, Tuesday, Wednesday, Thursday, Friday, Saturday, Sunday.[7]

MR. MARTIN: Edward is a clerk; his sister Nancy is a typist, and his brother William a shop-assistant.[8]

MRS. SMITH: An odd family!

MRS. MARTIN: I prefer a bird in the bush to a sparrow in a barrow.

MR. SMITH: Rather a steak in a chalet than gristle in a castle.

MR. MARTIN: An Englishman's home is truly his castle.

MRS. SMITH: I don't know enough Spanish to make myself understood.

MRS. MARTIN: I'll give you my mother-in-law's slippers if you'll give me your husband's coffin.

MR. SMITH: I'm looking for a monophysite priest to marry to our maid.

MR. MARTIN: Bread is a staff, whereas bread is also a staff, and an oak springs from an oak every morning at dawn.

MRS. SMITH: My uncle lives in the country, but that's none of the midwife's business.

MR. MARTIN: Paper is for writing, the cat's for the rat. Cheese is for scratching.

---

[7] In English in the original [translator's note].
[8] In English in the original [translator's note].

Mrs. Smith: The car goes very fast, but the cook beats batter better.
Mr. Smith: Don't be turkeys; rather kiss the conspirator.
Mr. Martin: Charity begins at home.[9]
Mrs. Smith: I'm waiting for the aqueduct to come and see me at my windmill.
Mr. Martin: One can prove that social progress is definitely better with sugar.
Mr. Smith: To hell with polishing!

(*Following this last speech of Mr. Smith's, the others are silent for a moment, stupe-fied. We sense that there is a certain nervous irritation. The strokes of the clock are more nervous too. The speeches which follow must be said, at first, in a glacial, hos-tile tone. The hostility and the nervousness increase. At the end of this scene, the four characters must be standing very close to each other, screaming their speeches, raising their fists, ready to throw themselves upon each other.*)

Mr. Martin: One doesn't polish spectacles with black wax.
Mrs. Smith: Yes, but with money one can buy anything.
Mr. Martin: I'd rather kill a rabbit than sing in the garden.
Mr. Smith: Cockatoos, cockatoos, cockatoos, cockatoos, cockatoos, cockatoos, cockatoos, cockatoos, cockatoos, cockatoos.
Mrs. Smith: Such caca, such caca, such caca, such caca, such caca, such caca, such caca, such caca, such caca.
Mr. Martin: Such cascades of cacas, such cascades of cacas, such cascades of cacas, such cascades of cacas, such cascades of cacas, such cascades of cacas, such cas-cades of cacas, such cascades of cacas.
Mr. Smith: Dogs have fleas, dogs have fleas.
Mrs. Martin: Cactus, coccyx! crocus! cockaded! cockroach!
Mrs. Smith: Incasker, you incask us.
Mr. Martin: I'd rather lay an egg in a box than go and steal an ox.
Mrs. Martin (*opening her mouth very wide*): Ah! oh! ah! oh! Let me gnash my teeth.
Mr. Smith: Crocodile!
Mr. Martin: Let's go and slap Ulysses.
Mr. Smith: I'm going to live in my cabana among my cacao trees.
Mrs. Martin: Cacao trees on cacao farms don't bear coconuts, they yield cocoa! Cacao trees on cacao farms don't bear coconuts, they yield cocoa! Cacao trees on cacao farms don't bear coconuts, they yield cocoa.
Mrs. Smith: Mice have lice, lice haven't mice.
Mrs. Martin: Don't ruche my brooch!
Mr. Martin: Don't smooch the brooch!
Mr. Smith: Groom the goose, don't goose the groom.
Mrs. Martin: The goose grooms.
Mrs. Smith: Groom your tooth.
Mr. Martin: Groom the bridegroom, groom the bridegroom.
Mr. Smith: Seducer seduced!
Mrs. Martin: Scaramouche!
Mrs. Smith: Sainte-Nitouche!
Mr. Martin: Go take a douche.
Mr. Smith: I've been goosed.

[9] In English in the original [translator's note].

MRS. MARTIN: Sainte-Nitouche stoops to my cartouche.

MRS. SMITH: "Who'd stoop to blame? . . . and I never choose to stoop."

MR. MARTIN: Robert!

MR. SMITH: Browning!

MRS. MARTIN, MR. SMITH: Rudyard.

MRS. SMITH, MR. MARTIN: Kipling.

MRS. MARTIN, MR. SMITH: Robert Kipling!

MRS. SMITH, MR. MARTIN: Rudyard Browning.[10]

MRS. MARTIN: Silly gobblegobblers, silly gobblegobblers.

MR. MARTIN: Marietta, spot the pot!

MRS. SMITH: Krishnamurti, Krishnamurti, Krishnamurti!

MR. SMITH: The pope elopes! The pope's got no horoscope. The horoscope's bespoke.

MRS. MARTIN: Bazaar, Balzac, bazooka!

MR. MARTIN: Bizarre, beaux-arts, brassieres!

MR. SMITH: A, e, i, o, u, a, e, i, o, u, a, e, i, o, u, i!

MRS. MARTIN: B, c, d, f, g, l, m, n, p, r, s, t, v, w, x, z!

MR. MARTIN: From sage to stooge, from stage to serge!

MRS. SMITH (imitating a train): Choo, choo, choo, choo, choo, choo, choo, choo, choo, choo, choo!

MR. SMITH: It's!

MRS. MARTIN: Not!

MR. MARTIN: That!

MRS. SMITH: Way!

MR. SMITH: It's!

MRS. MARTIN: O!

MR. MARTIN: Ver!

MRS. SMITH: Here!

(All together, completely infuriated, screaming in each others' ears. The light is extinguished. In the darkness we hear, in an increasingly rapid rhythm:)

ALL TOGETHER: It's not that way, it's over here, it's not that way, it's over here, it's not that way, it's over here, it's not that way, it's over here![11]

(The words cease abruptly. Again, the lights come on. Mr. and Mrs. Martin are seated like the Smiths at the beginning of the play. The play begins again with the Martins, who say exactly the same lines as the Smiths in the first scene, while the curtain softly falls.)

---

[10] Translator's note: in the French text these speeches read as follows:
MME SMITH—N'y touchez pas, elle est brisée.
M. MARTIN.—Sully!
M. SMITH.—Prudhomme!
MME MARTIN, M. SMITH.—François.
MME SMITH, M. MARTIN.—Coppée.
MME MARTIN, M. SMITH.—Copée Sully!
MME SMITH, M. MARTIN.—Prudhomme François.

[11] When produced some of the speeches in this last scene were cut or shuffled. Moreover, the final beginning again, if one can call it that, still involved the Smiths, since the author did not have the inspired idea of substituting the Martins for the Smiths until after the hundredth performance [author's note].

The American Dream

The living room in *The American Dream* is as ordinary for its time and place as the rooms in *The Bald Soprano, It Is So: (If You Think So)*, or *The Cherry Orchard*. The other likenesses are more obviously to *The Bald Soprano*. The characters (Mommy, Daddy, Grandma, Mrs. Barker, Young Man) are, in name at least, ciphers, very like the characters in *The Bald Soprano* (Mr. Smith, Mrs. Smith, Mr. Martin, Mrs. Martin, Mary, The Fire Chief). Their behavior and their speeches are absurd. Yet, though Grandma ends the play by reminding us that it is "a comedy," there is not much to laugh at—or not for very long. Albee distorts to underline meaning, not to deny it. In Albee's words, from his preface:

> The play is an examination of the American Scene, an attack on the substitution of artificial for real values in our society, a condemnation of complacency, cruelty, emasculation and vacuity; it is a stand against the fiction that everything in this slipping land of ours is peachy-keen.

Some of us may consider that pretty heavy freight for a carrier so slight. Others may find the streamlined form precisely right to drive the point home most effectively.

THE AMERICAN DREAM
Edward Albee (1928–)

THE PLAYERS:

MOMMY
DADDY
GRANDMA
MRS. BARKER
YOUNG MAN

The Scene: A living room. Two armchairs, one toward either side of the stage, facing each other diagonally out toward the audience. Against the rear wall, a sofa. A door, leading out from the apartment, in the rear wall, far stage-right. An archway, leading to other rooms, in the side wall, stage-left. At the beginning, Mommy and Daddy are seated in the armchairs, Daddy in the armchair stage-left, Mommy in the other. Curtain up. A silence. Then:

MOMMY: I don't know what can be keeping them.
DADDY: They're late, naturally.
MOMMY: Of course, they're late; it never fails.
DADDY: That's the way things are today, and there's nothing you can do about it.
MOMMY: You're quite right.
DADDY: When we took this apartment, they were quick enough to have me sign the lease; they were quick enough to take my check for two months' rent in advance . . .

MOMMY: And one month's security . . .

DADDY: . . . and one month's security. They were quick enough to check my references; they were quick enough about all that. But now! But now, try to get the icebox fixed, try to get the doorbell fixed, try to get the leak in the johnny fixed! Just try it . . . they aren't so quick about *that*.

MOMMY: Of course not; it never fails. People think they can get away with anything these days . . . and, of course they can. I went to buy a new hat yesterday.

(Pause)

I said, I went to buy a new hat yesterday.

DADDY: Oh! Yes . . . yes.

MOMMY: Pay attention.

DADDY: I *am* paying attention, Mommy.

MOMMY: Well, be sure you do.

DADDY: Oh, I am.

MOMMY: All right, Daddy; now listen.

DADDY: I'm listening, Mommy.

MOMMY: You're sure!

DADDY: Yes . . . yes, I'm sure, I'm all ears.

MOMMY *(Giggles at the thought; then)*: All right, now. I went to buy a new hat yesterday and I said, "I'd like a new hat, please." And so, they showed me a few hats, green ones and blue ones, and I didn't like any of them, not one bit. What did I say? What did I just say?

DADDY: You didn't like any of them, not one bit.

MOMMY: That's right; you just keep paying attention. And then they showed me one that I did like. It was a lovely little hat, and I said, "Oh, this is a lovely little hat; I'll take this hat; oh my, it's lovely. What color is it?" And they said, "Why, this is beige; isn't it a lovely little beige hat?" And I said, "Oh, it's just lovely." And so, I bought it.

(Stops, looks at Daddy)

DADDY *(To show he is paying attention)*: And so you bought it.

MOMMY: And so I bought it, and I walked out of the store with the hat right on my head, and I ran spang into the chairman of our woman's club, and she said, "Oh, my dear, isn't that a lovely little hat? Where did you get that lovely little hat? It's the loveliest little hat; I've always wanted a wheat-colored hat *myself*." And, I said, "Why, no, my dear; this hat is beige; beige." And she laughed and said, "Why no, my dear, that's a wheat-colored hat . . . wheat. I know beige from wheat." And I said, "Well, my dear, I know beige from wheat, too." What did I say? What did I just say?

DADDY *(Tonelessly)*: Well, my dear, I know beige from wheat, too.

MOMMY: That's right. And she laughed, and she said, "Well, my dear, they certainly put one over on you. That's wheat if I ever saw wheat. But it's lovely, just the same." And then she walked off. She's a dreadful woman, you don't know her; she has dreadful taste, two dreadful children, a dreadful house, and an absolutely adorable husband who sits in a wheel chair all the time. You don't know him. You don't know anybody, do you? She's just a dreadful woman, but she *is* chairman of our woman's club, so naturally I'm terribly fond of her. So, I went right back into the hat shop, and I said, "Look here; what do you mean selling me a hat that you say is beige, when it's wheat all the time . . . wheat! I can tell beige from wheat any day in the week, but not in this artificial light of yours." They have artificial light, Daddy.

DADDY: Have they!

MOMMY: And I said, "The minute I got outside I could tell that it wasn't a beige hat at all; it was a wheat hat." And they said to me, "How could you tell that when you had the hat on the top of your head?" Well, that made me angry, and so I made a scene right there; I screamed as hard as I could; I took my hat off and I threw it down on the counter, and oh, I made a terrible scene. I said, I made a terrible scene.

DADDY *(snapping to)*: Yes . . . yes . . . good for you!

MOMMY: And I made an absolutely terrible scene; and they became frightened, and they said, "Oh, madam; oh, madam." But I kept right on, and finally they admitted that they might have made a mistake; so they took my hat into the back, and then they came out again with a hat that looked exactly like it. I took one look at it, and I said, "This hat is wheat-colored; wheat." Well, of course, they said, "Oh, no, madam, this hat is beige: you go outside and see." So, I went outside, and lo and behold, it *was* beige. So I bought it.

DADDY *(clearing his throat)*: I would imagine that it was the same hat they tried to sell you before.

MOMMY *(with a little laugh)*: Well, of course it was!

DADDY: That's the way things are today; you just can't get satisfaction; you just try.

MOMMY: Well, *I* got satisfaction.

DADDY: That's right, Mommy. *You did* get satisfaction, didn't you?

MOMMY: Why are they so late? I don't know what can be keeping them.

DADDY: I've been trying for two weeks to have the leak in the johnny fixed.

MOMMY: You can't get satisfaction; just try. *I* can get satisfaction, but you can't.

DADDY: I've been trying for two weeks and it isn't so much for my sake; I can always go to the club.

MOMMY: It isn't so much for my sake, either; I can always go shopping.

DADDY: It's really for Grandma's sake.

MOMMY: Of course it's for Grandma's sake. Grandma cries every time she goes to the johnny as it is; but now that it doesn't work it's even worse, it makes Grandma think she's getting feeble-headed.

DADDY: Grandma *is* getting feeble-headed.

MOMMY: Of course Grandma is getting feeble-headed, but not about her johnny-do's.

DADDY: No; that's true. I must have it fixed.

MOMMY: WHY are they so late? I don't know what can be keeping them.

DADDY: When they came here the first time, they were ten minutes early; they were quick enough about it then.

(Enter Grandma from the archway, stage left. She is loaded down with boxes, large and small, neatly wrapped and tied.)

MOMMY: Why Grandma, look at you! What *is* all that you're carrying?

GRANDMA: They're boxes. What do they look like?

MOMMY: Daddy! Look at Grandma; look at all the boxes she's carrying!

DADDY: My goodness, Grandma; look at all those boxes.

GRANDMA: Where'll I put them?

MOMMY: Heavens! I don't know. Whatever are they for?

GRANDMA: That's nobody's damn business.

MOMMY: Well, in that case, put them down next to Daddy; there.

GRANDMA (dumping the boxes down, on and around Daddy's feet): I sure wish you'd get the john fixed.

DADDY: Oh, I do wish they'd come and fix it. We hear you . . . for hours . . . whimpering away. . . .

MOMMY: Daddy! What a terrible thing to say to Grandma!

GRANDMA: Yeah. For shame, talking to me that way.

DADDY: I'm sorry, Grandma.

MOMMY: Daddy's sorry, Grandma.

GRANDMA: Well, all right. In that case I'll go get the rest of the boxes. I suppose I deserve being talked to that way. I've gotten so old. Most people think that when you get so old, you either freeze to death, or you burn up. But you don't. When you get so old, all that happens is that people talk to you that way.

DADDY (Contrite): I said I'm sorry, Grandma.

MOMMY: Daddy said he was sorry.

GRANDMA: Well, that's all that counts. People being sorry. Makes you feel better; gives you a sense of dignity, and that's all that's important . . . a sense of dignity. And it doesn't matter if you don't care, or not, either. You got to have a sense of dignity, even if you don't care, 'cause, if you don't have that, civilization's doomed.

MOMMY: You've been reading my book club selections again!

DADDY: How dare you read Mommy's book club selections, Grandma!

GRANDMA: Because I'm old! When you're old you gotta do something. When you get old, you can't talk to people because people snap at you. When you get so old, people talk to you that way. That's why you become deaf, so you won't be able to hear people talking to you that way. And that's why you go and hide under the covers in the big soft bed, so you won't feel the house shaking from people talking to you that way. That's why old people die, eventually. People talk to them that way. I've got to go and get the rest of the boxes.

(Grandma exits)

DADDY: Poor Grandma, I didn't mean to hurt her.

MOMMY: Don't you worry about it; Grandma doesn't know what she means.

DADDY: She knows what she says, though.

MOMMY: Don't you worry about it; she won't know that soon. I love Grandma.

DADDY: I love her, too. Look how nicely she wrapped these boxes.

MOMMY: Grandma has always wrapped boxes nicely. When I was a little girl, I was very poor, and Grandma was very poor, too, because Grandpa was in heaven. And every day, when I went to school, Grandma used to wrap a box for me, and I used to take it with me to school; and when it was lunchtime, all the little boys and girls used to take out their boxes of lunch, and they weren't wrapped nicely at all, and they used to open them and eat their chicken legs and chocolate cakes; and I used to say, "Oh, look at my lovely lunch box; it's so nicely wrapped it would break my heart to open it." And so, I wouldn't open it.

DADDY: Because it was empty.

MOMMY: Oh no. Grandma always filled it up, because she never ate the dinner she cooked the evening before; she gave me all her food for my lunch box the next day. After school, I'd take the box back to Grandma, and she'd open it and eat the chicken legs and chocolate cake that was inside. Grandma used to say, "I love day-old cake." That's where the expression day-old cake came from. Grandma always ate everything a day late. I used to eat all the other little boys' and girls' food at school, because they thought my lunch box was empty, and that's why I wouldn't open it. They thought I suffered from the sin of pride, and since that made them better than me, they were very generous.

DADDY: You were a very deceitful little girl.

MOMMY: We were very poor! But then I married you, Daddy, and now we're very rich.

DADDY: Grandma isn't rich.

MOMMY: No, but you've been so good to Grandma she feels rich. She doesn't know you'd like to put her in a nursing home.

DADDY: I wouldn't!

MOMMY: Well, heaven knows, *I* would! I can't stand it, watching her do the cooking and the housework, polishing the silver, moving the furniture. . . .

DADDY: She likes to do that. She says it's the least she can do to earn her keep.

MOMMY: Well, she's right. You can't live off people. I can live off you, because I married you. And aren't you lucky all I brought with me was Grandma. A lot of women I know would have brought their whole families to live off you. All I brought was Grandma. Grandma is all the family I have.

DADDY: I feel very fortunate.

MOMMY: You should. I have a right to live off of you because I married you, and because I used to let you get on top of me and bump your uglies; and I have a right to all your money when you die. And when you do, Grandma and I can live by ourselves . . . if she's still here. Unless you have her put away in a nursing home.

DADDY: I have no intention of putting her in a nursing home.

MOMMY: Well, I wish somebody would do something with her!

DADDY: At any rate, you're very well provided for.

MOMMY: You're my sweet Daddy; that's very nice.

DADDY: I love my Mommy.

(Enter Grandma again, laden with more boxes)

GRANDMA *(dumping the boxes on and around Daddy's feet)*: There; that's the lot of them.

DADDY: They're wrapped so nicely.

GRANDMA *(to Daddy)*: You won't get on my sweet side that way . . .

MOMMY: Grandma!

GRANDMA: . . . telling me how nicely I wrap boxes. Not after what you said: how I whimpered for hours. . . .

MOMMY: Grandma!

GRANDMA *(to Mommy)*: Shut up! *(To Daddy)*: You don't have any feelings, that's what's wrong with you. Old people make all sorts of noises, half of them they can't help. Old people whimper, and cry, and belch, and make great hollow rumbling sounds at the table; old people wake up in the middle of the night screaming, and find out they haven't even been asleep; and when old people *are* asleep, they try to wake up, and they can't . . . not for the longest time.

MOMMY: Homilies, homilies!

GRANDMA: And there's more, too.

DADDY: I'm really very sorry, Grandma.

GRANDMA: I know you are, Daddy; it's Mommy over there makes all the trouble. If you'd listened to me, you wouldn't have married her in the first place. She was a tramp and a trollop and a trull to boot, and she's no better now.

MOMMY: Grandma!

GRANDMA *(to Mommy)*: Shut up! *(To Daddy)*: When she was no more than eight years old she used to climb up on my lap and say, in a sickening little voice, "When I gwo up, I'm going to mahwy a wich old man; I'm going to set my wittle were end right down in a tub o' butter, that's what I'm going to do." And I warned you, Daddy; I told you to stay away from her type. I told you to. I did.

MOMMY: You stop that! You're my mother, not his!

GRANDMA: I am?

DADDY: That's right, Grandma. Mommy's right.

GRANDMA: Well, how would you expect somebody as old as I am to remember a thing like that? You don't make allowances for people. I want an allowance. I want an allowance!

DADDY: All right, Grandma; I'll see to it.

MOMMY: Grandma! I'm ashamed of you.

GRANDMA: Humf! It's a fine time to say that. You should have gotten rid of me a long time ago if that's the way you feel. You should have had Daddy set me up in business somewhere. . . I could have gone into the fur business, or I could have been a singer. But no; not you. You wanted me around so you could sleep in my room when Daddy got fresh. But now it isn't important, because Daddy doesn't want to get fresh with you any more, and I don't blame him. You'd rather sleep with me, wouldn't you, Daddy?

MOMMY: Daddy doesn't want to sleep with anyone. Daddy's been sick.

DADDY: I've been sick. I don't even want to sleep in the apartment.

MOMMY: You see? I told you.

DADDY: I just want to get everything over with.

MOMMY: That's right. Why are they so late? Why can't they get here on time?

GRANDMA *(an owl)*: Who? Who? . . . Who? Who?

MOMMY: You know, Grandma.

GRANDMA: No, I don't.

MOMMY: Well, it doesn't really matter whether you do or not.

DADDY: Is that true?

MOMMY: Oh, more or less. Look how pretty Grandma wrapped these boxes.

GRANDMA: I didn't really like wrapping them; it hurt my fingers, and it frightened me. But it had to be done.

MOMMY: Why, Grandma?

GRANDMA: None of your damn business.

MOMMY: Go to bed.

GRANDMA: I don't want to go to bed. I just got up. I want to stay here and watch. Besides . . .

MOMMY: Go to bed.

DADDY: Let her stay up, Mommy; it isn't noon yet.

GRANDMA: I want to watch; besides . . .

DADDY: Let her watch, Mommy.

MOMMY: Well all right, you can watch; but don't you dare say a word.

GRANDMA: Old people are very good at listening; old people don't like to talk; old people have colitis and lavender perfume. Now I'm going to be quiet.

DADDY: She never mentioned she wanted to be a singer.

MOMMY: Oh, I forgot to tell you, but it was ages ago.

(The doorbell rings)

Oh, goodness! Here they are!

GRANDMA: Who? Who?

MOMMY: Oh, just some people.

GRANDMA: The van people? Is it the van people? Have you finally done it? Have you called the van people to come and take me away?

DADDY: Of course not, Grandma!

GRANDMA: Oh, don't be too sure. She'd have you carted off too, if she thought she could get away with it.

MOMMY: Pay no attention to her, Daddy. *(An aside to Grandma)* My God, you're ungrateful! *(The doorbell rings again)*

DADDY *(Wringing his hands)*: Oh dear; oh dear.

MOMMY *(Still to Grandma)*: Just you wait; I'll fix your wagon. *(Now to Daddy)* Well, go let them in Daddy. What are you waiting for?

DADDY: I think we should talk about it some more. Maybe we've been hasty . . . a little hasty, perhaps. *(Doorbell rings again)* I'd like to talk about it some more.

MOMMY: There's no need. You made up your mind; you were firm; you were masculine and decisive.

DADDY: We might consider the pros and the . . .

MOMMY: I won't argue with you; it has to be done; you were right. Open the door.

DADDY: But I'm not sure that . . .

MOMMY: Open the door.

DADDY: Was I firm about it?

MOMMY: Oh, so firm; so firm.

DADDY: And was I decisive?

MOMMY: SO decisive! Oh, I shivered.

DADDY: And masculine? Was I really masculine?

MOMMY: Oh, Daddy, you were so masculine; I shivered and fainted.

GRANDMA: Shivered and fainted, did she? Humf!

MOMMY: You be quiet.

GRANDMA: Old people have a right to talk to themselves; it doesn't hurt the gums, and it's comforting. *(Doorbell rings again)*

DADDY: I shall now open the door.

MOMMY: WHAT a masculine Daddy! Isn't he a masculine Daddy?

GRANDMA: Don't expect me to say anything. Old people are obscene.

MOMMY: Some of your opinions aren't so bad. You know that?

DADDY (backing off from the door): Maybe we can send them away.

MOMMY: Oh, look at you! You're turning into jelly; you're indecisive; you're a woman.

DADDY: All right. Watch me now; I'm going to open the door. Watch. Watch!

MOMMY: We're watching; we're watching.

GRANDMA: I'm not.

DADDY: Watch now; it's opening. (He opens the door) It's open! (Mrs. Barker steps into the room) Here they are!

MOMMY: Here they are!

GRANDMA: Where?

DADDY: Come in. You're late. But, of course, we expected you to be late; we were saying that we expected you to be late.

MOMMY: Daddy, don't be rude! We were saying that you just can't get satisfaction these days, and we were talking about you, of course. Won't you come in?

MRS. BARKER: Thank you. I don't mind if I do.

MOMMY: We're very glad that you're here, late as you are. You do remember us, don't you? You were here once before. I'm Mommy, and this is Daddy, and that's Grandma, doddering there in the corner.

MRS. BARKER: Hello, Mommy; hello, Daddy; and hello there, Grandma.

DADDY: Now that you're here, I don't suppose you could go away and maybe come back some other time.

MRS. BARKER: Oh no; we're much too efficient for that. I said, hello there, Grandma.

MOMMY: Speak to them, Grandma.

GRANDMA: I don't see them.

DADDY: For shame, Grandma; they're here.

MRS. BARKER: Yes, we're here, Grandma. I'm Mrs. Barker. I remember you; don't you remember me?

GRANDMA: I don't recall. Maybe you were younger, or something.

MOMMY: Grandma! What a terrible thing to say!

MRS. BARKER: Oh now, don't scold her, Mommy; for all she knows she may be right.

DADDY: Uh . . . Mrs. Barker, is it? Won't you sit down?

MRS. BARKER: I don't mind if I do.

MOMMY: Would you like a cigarette, and a drink, and would you like to cross your legs?

MRS. BARKER: You forget yourself, Mommy; I'm a professional woman. But I will cross my legs.

DADDY: Yes, make yourself comfortable.

MRS. BARKER: I don't mind if I do.

GRANDMA: Are they still here?

MOMMY: Be quiet, Grandma.

MRS. BARKER: Oh, we're still here. My, what an unattractive apartment you have!

MOMMY: Yes, but you don't know what a trouble it is. Let me tell you . . .

DADDY: I was saying to Mommy . . .

MRS. BARKER: Yes, I know. I was listening outside.

DADDY: About the icebox, and . . . the doorbell . . . and the . . .

MRS. BARKER: . . . and the johnny. Yes, we're very efficient; we have to know everything in our work.

DADDY: Exactly what do you do?

MOMMY: Yes, what is your work?

MRS. BARKER: Well, my dear, for one thing, I'm chairman of your woman's club.

MOMMY: Don't be ridiculous. I was talking to the chairman of my woman's club just yester— Why, so you are. You remember, Daddy, the lady I was telling you about? The lady with the husband who sits in the *swing?* Don't you remember?

DADDY: No . . . no. . . .

MOMMY: Of course you do. I'm so sorry, Mrs. Barker. I would have known you anywhere, except in this artificial light. And look! You have a hat just like the one I bought yesterday.

MRS. BARKER *(with a little laugh)*: No, not really; this hat is cream.

MOMMY: Well, my dear, that may look like a cream hat to you, but I can . . .

MRS. BARKER: Now, now; you seem to forget who I am.

MOMMY: Yes, I do, don't I? Are you sure you're comfortable? Won't you take off your dress?

MRS. BARKER: I don't mind if I do.

(She removes her dress)

MOMMY: There. You must feel a great deal more comfortable.

MRS. BARKER: Well, I certainly *look* a great deal more comfortable.

DADDY: I'm going to blush and giggle.

MOMMY: Daddy's going to blush and giggle.

MRS. BARKER *(pulling the hem of her slip above her knees)*: You're lucky to have such a man for a husband.

MOMMY: Oh, don't I know it!

DADDY: I just blushed and giggled and went sticky wet.

MOMMY: Isn't Daddy a caution, Mrs. Barker?

MRS. BARKER: Maybe if I smoked . . . ?

MOMMY: Oh, that isn't necessary.

MRS. BARKER: I don't mind if I do.

MOMMY: No; no, don't. Really.

MRS. BARKER: I don't mind . . .

MOMMY: I won't have you smoking in my house, and that's that! You're a professional woman.

DADDY: Grandma drinks AND smokes; don't you, Grandma?

GRANDMA: No.

MOMMY: Well, now, Mrs. Barker; suppose you tell us why you're here.

GRANDMA *(as Mommy walks through the boxes)*: The boxes . . . the boxes . . .

MOMMY: Be quiet, Grandma.

DADDY: What did you say, Grandma?

GRANDMA *(as Mommy steps on several of the boxes)*: The boxes, damn it!

MRS. BARKER: Boxes; she said boxes. She mentioned the boxes.

DADDY: What about the boxes, Grandma? Maybe Mrs. Barker is here because of the boxes. Is that what you meant, Grandma?

GRANDMA: I don't know if that's what I meant or not. It's certainly not what I *thought* I meant.

DADDY: Grandma is of the opinion that . . .

MRS. BARKER: Can we assume that the boxes are for us? I mean, can we assume that you had us come here for the boxes?

MOMMY: Are you in the habit of receiving boxes?

DADDY: A very good question.

MRS. BARKER: Well, that would depend on the reason we're here. I've got my fingers in so many little pies, you know. Now, I can think of one of my little activites in which we are in the habit of receiving *baskets*; but more in a literary sense than really. We *might* receive boxes, though, under very special circumstances. I'm afraid that's the best answer I can give you.

DADDY: It's a very interesting answer.

MRS. BARKER: *I* thought so. But, does it help?

MOMMY: No; I'm afraid not.

DADDY: I wonder if it might help us any if I said I feel misgivings, that I have definite qualms.

MOMMY: Where, Daddy?

DADDY: Well, mostly right here, right around where the stitches were.

MOMMY: Daddy had an operation, you know.

MRS. BARKER: Oh, you poor Daddy! I didn't know; but then, how could I?

GRANDMA: You might have asked; it wouldn't have hurt you.

MOMMY: Dry up, Grandma.

GRANDMA: There you go. Letting your true feelings come out. Old people aren't dry enough, I suppose. My sacks are empty, the fluid in my eyeballs is all caked on the inside edges, my spine is made of sugar candy, I breathe ice; but you don't hear me complain. Nobody hears old people complain because people think that's all old people do. And *that's* because old people are gnarled and sagged and twisted into the shape of a complaint. (*Signs off*) That's all.

MRS. BARKER: What was wrong, Daddy?

DADDY: Well, you know how it is: the doctors took out something that was there and put in something that wasn't there. An operation.

MRS. BARKER: You're very fortunate, I should say.

MOMMY: Oh, he is; he is. All his life, Daddy has wanted to be a United States Senator; but now . . . why now he's changed his mind, and for the rest of his life he's going to want to be Governor . . . it would be nearer the apartment, you know.

MRS. BARKER: You *are* fortunate, Daddy.

DADDY: Yes, indeed; except that I get these qualms now and then, definite ones.

MRS. BARKER: Well, it's just a matter of things settling; you're like an old house.

MOMMY: Why Daddy, thank Mrs. Barker.

DADDY: Thank you.

MRS. BARKER: Ambition! That's the ticket. I have a brother who's very much like you, Daddy . . . ambitious. Of course, he's a great deal younger than you; he's even younger than I am . . . if such a thing is possible. He runs a little newspa-

per. Just a little newspaper . . . but he runs it. He's chief cook and bottle wash-
er of that little newspaper, which he calls The Village Idiot. He has such a sense
of humor; he's so self-deprecating, so modest. And he'd never admit it himself, but he is the Village Idiot.

MOMMY: Oh, I think that's just grand. Don't you think so, Daddy?

DADDY: Yes, just grand.

MRS. BARKER: My brother's a dear man, and he has a dear little wife, whom he
loves, dearly. He loves her so much he just can't get a sentence out without
mentioning her. He wants everybody to know he's married. He's really a
stickler on that point; he can't be introduced to anybody and say hello without adding, "Of course, I'm married." As far as I'm concerned, he's the chief
exponent of Woman Love in this whole country; he's even been written up in
psychiatric journals because of it.

DADDY: Indeed!

MOMMY: Isn't that lovely.

MRS. BARKER: Oh, I think so. There's too much woman hatred in this country, and
that's a fact.

GRANDMA: Oh, I don't know.

MOMMY: Oh, I think that's just grand. Don't you think so, Daddy?

DADDY: Yes, just grand.

GRANDMA: In case anybody's interested . . .

MOMMY: Be quiet, Grandma.

GRANDMA: Nuts!

MOMMY: Oh, Mrs. Barker, you must forgive Grandma. She's rural.

MRS. BARKER: I don't mind if I do.

DADDY: Maybe Grandma has something to say.

MOMMY: Nonsense. Old people have nothing to say; and if old people did have
something to say, nobody would listen to them. (To Grandma) You see? I can
pull that stuff just as easy as you can.

GRANDMA: Well, you got the rhythm, but you don't really have the quality. Besides, you're middle-aged.

MOMMY: I'm proud of it!

GRANDMA: Look. I'll show you how it's really done. Middle-aged people think
they can do anything, but the truth is that middle-aged people can't do most
things as well as they used to. Middle-aged people think they're special because they're like everybody else. We live in the age of deformity. You see?
Rhythm and content. You'll learn.

DADDY: I do wish I weren't surrounded by women; I'd like some men around
here.

MRS. BARKER: You can say that again!

GRANDMA: I don't hardly count as a woman, so can I say my piece?

MOMMY: Go on. Jabber away.

GRANDMA: It's very simple; the fact is, these boxes don't have anything to do with
why this good lady is come to call. Now, if you're interested in knowing why
these boxes are here . . .

DADDY: I'm sure that must be all very true, Grandma, but what does it have to do
with why . . . pardon me, what is that name again?

MRS. BARKER: Mrs. Barker.

DADDY: Exactly. What does it have to do with why . . . that name again?

MRS. BARKER: Mrs. Barker.

DADDY: Precisely. What does it have to do with why what's-her-name is here?

MOMMY: They're here because we asked them.

MRS. BARKER: Yes. That's why.

GRANDMA: Now if you're interested in knowing why these boxes *are* here . . .

MOMMY: Well, nobody *is* interested!

GRANDMA: You can be as snippety as you like for all the good it'll do you.

DADDY: You two will have to stop arguing.

MOMMY: I don't argue with her.

DADDY: It will just have to stop.

MOMMY: Well, why don't you call a van and have her taken away?

GRANDMA: Don't bother; there's no need.

DADDY: No, now, perhaps I can go away myself . . .

MOMMY: Well, one or the other; the way things are now it's impossible. In the first place, it's too crowded in this apartment. *(To Grandma)* And it's you that takes up all the space, with your enema bottles, and your Pekinese, and God-only-knows-what-else . . . and now all these boxes. . . .

GRANDMA: These boxes are . . .

MRS. BARKER: I've never heard of enema *bottles* . . . .

GRANDMA: She means enema bags, but she doesn't know the difference. Mommy comes from extremely bad stock. And besides, when Mommy was born . . . well, it was a difficult delivery, and she had a head shaped like a banana.

MOMMY: You ungrateful—Daddy? Daddy, you see how ungrateful she is after all these years, after all the things we've done for her? *(To Grandma)* One of these days you're going away in a van; that's what's going to happen to you!

GRANDMA: Do tell!

MRS. BARKER: Like a banana?

GRANDMA: Yup, just like a banana.

MRS. BARKER: My word!

MOMMY: You stop listening to her; she'll say anything. Just the other night she called Daddy a hedgehog.

MRS. BARKER: She didn't!

GRANDMA: That's right, baby; you stick up for me.

MOMMY: I don't know where she gets the words; on the television, maybe.

MRS. BARKER: Did you really call him a hedgehog?

GRANDMA: Oh look; what difference does it make whether I did or not?

DADDY: Grandma's right. Leave Grandma alone.

MOMMY *(To Daddy)*: How dare you!

GRANDMA: Oh, leave her alone, Daddy; the kid's all mixed up.

MOMMY: You see? I told you. It's all those television shows. Daddy, you go right into Grandma's room and take her television and shake all the tubes loose.

DADDY: Don't mention tubes to me.

MOMMY: Oh! Mommy forgot! *(To Mrs. Barker)* Daddy has tubes now, where he used to have tracts.

MRS. BARKER: Is that a fact!

GRANDMA: I know why this dear lady is here.

MOMMY: You be still.

MRS. BARKER: Oh, I do wish you'd tell me.

MOMMY: No! No! That wouldn't be fair at all.

DADDY: Besides, she knows why she's here; she's here because we called them.

MRS. BARKER: La! But that still leaves me puzzled. I know I'm here because you called us, but I'm such a busy girl, with this committee and that committee, and the Responsible Citizens Activities I indulge in.

MOMMY: Oh my; busy, busy.

MRS. BARKER: Yes, indeed. So I'm afraid you'll have to give me some help.

MOMMY: Oh, no. No, you must be mistaken. I can't believe we asked you here to give you any help. With the way taxes are these days, and the way you can't get satisfaction in ANYTHING . . . no, I don't believe so.

DADDY: And if you need help . . . why, I should think you'd apply for a Fulbright Scholarship . . .

MOMMY: And if not that . . . why, then a Guggenheim Fellowship . . .

GRANDMA: Oh, come on; why not shoot the works and try for the Prix de Rome. (Under her breath to Mommy and Daddy) Beasts!

MRS. BARKER: Oh, what a jolly family. But let me think. I'm knee-deep in work these days; there's the Ladies' Auxiliary Air Raid Committee, for one thing; how do you feel about air raids?

MOMMY: Oh, I'd say we're hostile.

DADDY: Yes, definitely; we're hostile.

MRS. BARKER: Then, you'll be no help there. There's too much hostility in the world these days as it is; but I'll not badger you! There's a surfeit of badgers as well.

GRANDMA: While we're at it, there's been a run on old people, too. The Department of Agriculture, or maybe it wasn't the Department of Agriculture—anyway, it was some department that's run by a girl—put out figures showing that ninety per cent of the adult population of the country is over eighty years old . . . or eighty per cent is over ninety years old. . . .

MOMMY: You're such a liar! You just finished saying that everyone is middle-aged.

GRANDMA: I'm just telling you what the government says . . . that doesn't have anything to do with what . . .

MOMMY: It's that television! Daddy, go break her television.

GRANDMA: You won't find it.

DADDY (Wearily getting up): If I must . . . I must.

MOMMY: And don't step on the Pekinese; it's blind.

DADDY: It may be blind, but Daddy isn't.

(He exits, through the archway, stage left)

GRANDMA: You won't find it, either.

MOMMY: Oh, I'm so fortunate to have such a husband. Just think; I could have a husband who was poor, or argumentative, or a husband who sat in a wheel chair all day . . . OOOOHHHH! What have I said? What have I said?

GRANDMA: You said you could have a husband who sat in a wheel . . .

MOMMY: I'm mortified! I could die! I could cut my tongue out! I could . . .

MRS. BARKER (Forcing a smile): Oh, now . . . now . . . don't think about it . . .

MOMMY: I could . . . why, I could . . .

MRS. BARKER: ... don't think about it ... really. ...

MOMMY: You're quite right. I won't think about it, and that way I'll forget that I ever said it, and that way it will be all right. *(Pause)* There ... I've forgotten. Well, now, now that Daddy is out of the room we can have some girl talk.

MRS. BARKER: I'm not sure that I ...

MOMMY: You *do* want to have some girl talk, don't you?

MRS. BARKER: I was going to say I'm not sure that I wouldn't care for a glass of water. I feel a little faint.

MOMMY: Grandma, go get Mrs. Barker a glass of water.

GRANDMA: Go get it yourself. I quit.

MOMMY: Grandma loves to do little things around the house; it gives her a false sense of security.

GRANDMA: I quit! I'm through!

MOMMY: Now, you be a good Grandma, or you know what will happen to you. You'll be taken away in a van.

GRANDMA: You don't frighten me. I'm too old to be frightened. Besides ...

MOMMY: WELL! I'll tend to you later. I'll hide your teeth ... I'll ...

GRANDMA: Everything's hidden.

MRS. BARKER: I *am* going to faint. I *am.*

MOMMY: Good heavens! I'll go myself. *(As she exits, through the archway, stage-left)* I'll fix you, Grandma. I'll take care of you later.

(She exits)

GRANDMA: Oh, go soak your head. *(To Mrs. Barker)* Well, dearie, how do you feel?

MRS. BARKER: A little better, I think. Yes, much better, thank you, Grandma.

GRANDMA: That's good.

MRS. BARKER: But ... I feel so lost ... not knowing why I'm here ... and, on top of it, they say I was here before.

GRANDMA: Well, you were. You weren't *here*, exactly, because we've moved around a lot, from one apartment to another, up and down the social ladder like mice, if you like similes.

MRS. BARKER: I don't ... particularly.

GRANDMA: Well, then, I'm sorry.

MRS. BARKER *(Suddenly)*: Grandma, I feel I can trust you.

GRANDMA: Don't be too sure; it's every man for himself around this place. ...

MRS. BARKER: Oh ... is it? Nonetheless, I really do feel that I can trust you. *Please* tell me why they called and asked us to come. I implore you!

GRANDMA: Oh my; that feels good. It's been so long since anybody implored me. Do it again. Implore me some more.

MRS. BARKER: You're your daughter's mother, all right!

GRANDMA: Oh, I don't mean to be hard. If you won't implore me, then beg me, or ask me, or entreat me ... just anything like that.

MRS. BARKER: You're a dreadful old woman!

GRANDMA: You'll understand some day. Please!

MRS. BARKER: Oh, for heaven's sake! ... I implore you ... I beg you ... I beseech you!

GRANDMA: Beseech! Oh, that's the nicest word I've heard in ages. You're a dear, sweet woman. ... You ... beseech ... me. I can't resist that.

Mrs. Barker: Well, then . . . please tell me why they asked us to come.

Grandma: Well, I'll give you a hint. That's the best I can do, because I'm a muddleheaded old woman. Now listen, because it's important. Once upon a time, not too very long ago, but a long enough time ago . . . oh, about twenty years ago . . . there was a man very much like Daddy, and a woman very much like Mommy, who were married to each other, very much like Mommy and Daddy are married to each other; and they lived in an apartment very much like one that's very much like this one, and they lived there with an old woman who was very much like yours truly, only younger, because it was some time ago; in fact, they were all somewhat younger.

Mrs. Barker: How fascinating!

Grandma: Now, at the same time, there was a dear lady very much like you, only younger then, who did all sorts of Good Works. . . . And one of the Good Works this dear lady did was in something very much like a volunteer capacity for an organization very much like the Bye-Bye Adoption Service, which is nearby and which was run by a terribly deaf old lady very much like the Miss Bye-Bye who runs the Bye-Bye Adoption Service nearby.

Mrs. Barker: How enthralling!

Grandma: Well, be that as it may. Nonetheless, one afternoon this man, who was very much like Daddy, and this woman who was very much like Mommy came to see this dear lady who did all the Good Works, who was very much like you, dear, and they were very sad and very hopeful, and they cried and smiled and bit their fingers, and they said all the most intimate things.

Mrs. Barker: How spellbinding! What did they say?

Grandma: Well, it was very sweet. The woman, who was very much like Mommy, said that she and the man who was very much like Daddy had never been blessed with anything very much like a bumble of joy.

Mrs. Barker: A what?

Grandma: A bumble; a bumble of joy.

Mrs. Barker: Oh, like bundle.

Grandma: Well, yes; very much like it. Bundle, bumble; who cares? At any rate, the woman, who was very much like Mommy, said that they wanted a bumble of their own, but that the man, who was very much like Daddy, couldn't have a bumble; and the man, who was very much like Daddy, said that yes, they had wanted a bumbl? of their own, but that the woman, who was very much like Mommy, couldn't have one, and that now they wanted to buy something very much like a bumble.

Mrs. Barker: How engrossing!

Grandma: Yes. And the dear lady, who was very much like you, said something that was very much like, "Oh, what a shame; but take heart . . . I think we have just the bumble *for* you." And, well, the lady, who was very much like Mommy, and the man, who was very much like Daddy, cried and smiled and bit their fingers, and said some more intimate things, which were totally irrelevant but which were pretty hot stuff, and so the dear lady, who was very much like you, and who had something very much like a penchant for pornography, listened with something very much like enthusiasm. "Whee," she said. "Whoooopeeeeee!" But that's beside the point.

Mrs. Barker: I suppose *so*. But how gripping!

Grandma: Anyway . . . they *bought* something very much like a bumble, and they took it away with them. But . . . things didn't work out very well.

MRS. BARKER: You mean there was trouble?

GRANDMA: You got it. (With a glance through the archway) But, I'm going to have to speed up now because I think I'm leaving soon.

MRS. BARKER: Oh. Are you really?

GRANDMA: Yup.

MRS. BARKER: But old people don't go anywhere; they're either taken places, or put places.

GRANDMA: Well, this old person is different. Anyway . . . things started going badly.

MRS. BARKER: Oh yes. Yes.

GRANDMA: Weeeeelllll . . . in the first place, it turned out the bumble didn't look like either one of its parents. That was enough of a blow, but things got worse. One night, it cried its heart out, if you can imagine such a thing.

MRS. BARKER: Cried its heart out! Well!

GRANDMA: But that was only the beginning. Then it turned out it only had eyes for its Daddy.

MRS. BARKER: For its Daddy! Why, any self-respecting woman would have gouged those eyes right out of its head.

GRANDMA: Well, she did. That's exactly what she did. But then, it kept its nose up in the air.

MRS. BARKER: Ufggh! How disgusting!

GRANDMA: That's what they thought. But then, it began to develop an interest in its you-know-what.

MRS. BARKER: In its you-know-what! Well! I hope they cut its hands off at the wrists!

GRANDMA: Well, yes, they did that eventually. But first, they cut off its you-know-what.

MRS. BARKER: A much better idea!

GRANDMA: That's what they thought. But after they cut off its you-know-what, it still put its hands under the covers, looking for its you-know-what. So, finally, they had to cut off its hands at the wrists.

MRS. BARKER: Naturally!

GRANDMA: And it was such a resentful bumble. Why, one day it called its Mommy a dirty name.

MRS. BARKER: Well, I hope they cut its tongue out!

GRANDMA: Of course. And then, as it got bigger, they found out all sorts of terrible things about it, like: it didn't have a head on its shoulders, it had no guts, it was spineless, its feet were made of clay . . . just dreadful things.

MRS. BARKER: Dreadful!

GRANDMA: So you can understand how they became discouraged.

MRS. BARKER: I certainly can! And what did they do?

GRANDMA: What did they do? Well, for the last straw, it finally up and died; and you can imagine how that made them feel, their having paid for it, and all. So, they called up the lady who sold them the bumble in the first place and told her to come right over to their apartment. They wanted satisfaction; they wanted their money back. That's what they wanted.

MRS. BARKER: My, my, my.

GRANDMA: How do you like *them* apples?

MRS. BARKER: My, my, my.

DADDY *(Off stage)*: Mommy! I can't find Grandma's television, and I can't find the Pekinese, either.

MOMMY *(Off stage)*: Isn't that funny! And I can't find the water.

GRANDMA: Heh, heh, heh. I told them everything was hidden.

MRS. BARKER: Did you hide the water, too?

GRANDMA *(Puzzled)*: No. No, I didn't do *that*.

DADDY *(Off stage)*: The truth of the matter is, I can't even find Grandma's room.

GRANDMA: Heh, heh, heh.

MRS. BARKER: My! You certainly did hide things, didn't you?

GRANDMA: Sure, kid, sure.

MOMMY *(Sticking her head in the room)*: Did you ever hear of such a thing. Grandma? Daddy can't find your television, and he can't find the Pekinese, and the truth of the matter is he can't even find your room.

GRANDMA: I told you. I hid everything.

MOMMY: Nonsense, Grandma! Just wait until I get my hands on you. You're a troublemaker . . . that's what you are.

GRANDMA: Well, I'll be out of here pretty soon, baby.

MOMMY: Oh, you don't know how right you are! Daddy's been wanting to send you away for a long time now, but I've been restraining him. I'll tell you one thing, though . . . I'm getting sick and tired of this fighting, and I might just let him have his way. Then you'll see what'll happen. Away you'll go; in a van, too. I'll let Daddy call the van man.

GRANDMA: I'm way ahead of you.

MOMMY: How can you be so old and so smug at the same time? You have no sense of proportion.

GRANDMA: You just answered your own question.

MOMMY: Mrs. Barker, I'd much rather you came into the kitchen for that glass of water, what with Grandma out here, and all.

MRS. BARKER: I don't see what Grandma has to do with it; and besides, I don't think you're very polite.

MOMMY: You seem to forget that you're a guest in this house . . .

GRANDMA: Apartment!

MOMMY: Apartment! And that you're a professional woman. So, if you'll be so good as to come into the kitchen, I'll be more than happy to show you where the water is, and where the glass is, and then you can put two and two togeth-er, if you're clever enough. *(She vanishes)*

MRS. BARKER *(After a moment's consideration)*: I suppose she's right.

GRANDMA: Well, that's how it is when people call you up and ask you over to do something for them.

MRS. BARKER: I suppose you're right, too. Well, Grandma, it's been very nice talk-ing to you.

GRANDMA: And I've enjoyed listening. Say, don't tell Mommy or Daddy that I gave you that hint, will you?

MRS. BARKER: Oh, dear me, the hint! I'd forgotten about it, if you can imagine such a thing. No, I won't breathe a word of it to them.

GRANDMA: I don't know if it helped you any . . .

MRS. BARKER: I can't tell, yet. I'll have to . . . what *is* the word I want? . . .I'll have to relate it . . . that's it . . . I'll have to relate it to certain things that I *know*, and. . . draw . . . conclusions . . . What I'll really have to do is to see if it applies to anything. I mean, after all, I *do* do volunteer work for an adoption service, but it isn't very much *like* the Bye-Bye Adoption Service . . . it *is* the Bye-Bye Adoption Service . . . and while I can remember Mommy and Daddy coming to see me, oh, about twenty years ago, about buying a bumble, I can't quite remember anyone very much *like* Mommy and Daddy coming to see me about buying a bumble. Don't you see? It really presents quite a problem . . . I'll have to think about it . . . mull it . . . but at any rate, it was truly first-class of you to try to help me. Oh, will you still be here after I've had my drink of water?

GRANDMA: Probably . . . I'm not as spry as I used to be.

MRS. BARKER: Oh. Well, I won't say good-by then.

GRANDMA: No. Don't. (*Mrs. Barker exits through the archway*) People don't say good-by to old people because they think they'll frighten them. Lordy! If they only knew how awful "hello" and "my, you're looking chipper" sounded, they wouldn't say those things either. The truth is, there isn't much you *can* say to old people that doesn't sound just terrible. (*The doorbell rings*) Come on in! (*The Young Man enters. Grandma looks him over*) Well, now, aren't you a breath of fresh air!

YOUNG MAN: Hello there.

GRANDMA: My, my, my. Are you the van man?

YOUNG MAN: The what?

GRANDMA: The van man. The van man. Are you come to take me away?

YOUNG MAN: I don't know what you're talking about.

GRANDMA: Oh. (*Pause*) Well. (*Pause*) My, my, aren't you something!

YOUNG MAN: Hm?

GRANDMA: I said, my, my, aren't you something.

YOUNG MAN: Oh. Thank you.

GRANDMA: You don't sound very enthusiastic.

YOUNG MAN: Oh, I'm . . . I'm used to it.

GRANDMA: Yup . . . yup. You know, if I were about a hundred and fifty years younger I could go for you.

YOUNG MAN: Yes, I imagine so.

GRANDMA: Unh-hunh . . . will you look at those muscles!

YOUNG MAN (*Flexing his muscles*): Yes, they're quite good, aren't they?

GRANDMA: Boy, they sure are. They natural?

YOUNG MAN: Well the basic structure was there, but I've done some work, too . . . you know, in a gym.

GRANDMA: I'll bet you have. You ought to be in the movies, boy.

YOUNG MAN: I know.

GRANDMA: Yup! Right up there on the old silver screen. But I suppose you've heard that before.

YOUNG MAN: Yes, I have.

GRANDMA: You ought to try out for them . . the movies.

YOUNG MAN: Well, actually, I may have a career there yet. I've lived out on the West Coast almost all my life . . . and I've met a few people who . . . might be able to help me. I'm not in too much of a hurry, though. I'm almost as young as I look.

GRANDMA: Oh, that's nice. And will you look at that face!

YOUNG MAN: Yes, it's quite good, isn't it? Clean-cut, midwest farm boy type, almost insultingly good-looking in a typically American way. Good profile, straight nose, honest eyes, wonderful smile . . .

GRANDMA: Yup. Boy, you know what you are, don't you? You're the American Dream, that's what you are. All those other people, they don't know what they're talking about. You . . . *you* are the American Dream.

YOUNG MAN: Thanks.

MOMMY *(Off stage)*: Who rang the doorbell?

GRANDMA *(Shouting off-stage)*: The American Dream!

MOMMY *(Off stage)*: What? What was that, Grandma?

GRANDMA *(Shouting)*: The American Dream! The American Dream! Damn it!

DADDY *(Off stage)*: How's that, Mommy?

MOMMY *(Off stage)*: Oh, some gibberish; pay no attention. Did you find Grandma's room?

DADDY *(Off stage)*: No, I can't even find Mrs. Barker.

YOUNG MAN: What was all that?

GRANDMA: Oh, that was just the folks, but let's not talk about them, honey; let's talk about you.

YOUNG MAN: All right.

GRANDMA: Well, let's see. If you're not the van man, what are you doing here?

YOUNG MAN: I'm looking for work.

GRANDMA: Are you! Well, what kind of work?

YOUNG MAN: Oh, almost anything . . . almost anything that pays. I'll do almost anything for money.

GRANDMA: Will you . . . will you? Hmmmm. I wonder if there's anything you could do around here?

YOUNG MAN: There might be. It looked to be a likely building.

GRANDMA: It's always looked to be a rather unlikely building to me, but I suppose you'd know better than I.

YOUNG MAN: I can sense these things.

GRANDMA: There *might* be something you could do around here. Stay there! Don't come any closer.

YOUNG MAN: Sorry.

GRANDMA: I don't mean I'd *mind*. I don't know whether I'd mind, or not. . . . But it wouldn't look well; it would look just *awful*.

YOUNG MAN: Yes; I suppose so.

GRANDMA: Now, stay there, let me concentrate. What could you do? The folks have been in something of a quandry around here today, sort of a dilemma, and I wonder if you mightn't be some help.

YOUNG MAN: I hope so . . . if there's money in it. Do you have any money?

GRANDMA: Money! Oh, there's more money around here than you'd know what to do with.

YOUNG MAN: I'm not so sure.

GRANDMA: Well, maybe not. Besides, I've got money of my own.

YOUNG MAN: You have?

GRANDMA: Sure. Old people quite often have lots of money; more often than most people expect. Come here, so I can whisper to you . . . not too close. I might faint.

YOUNG MAN: Oh, I'm sorry.

GRANDMA: It's all right, dear. Anyway . . . have you ever heard of that big baking contest they run? The one where all the ladies get together in a big barn and bake away?

YOUNG MAN: I'm . . . not . . . sure. . . .

GRANDMA: Not so close. Well, it doesn't matter whether you've heard of it or not. The important thing is—and I don't want anybody to hear this . . . the folks think I haven't been out of the house in eight years—the important thing is that I won first prize in that baking contest this year. Oh, it was in all the papers; not under my own name, though. I used a *nom de boulangère*;[1] I called myself Uncle Henry.

YOUNG MAN: Did you?

GRANDMA: Why not? I didn't see any reason not to. I look just as much like an old man as I do like an old woman. And you know what I called it . . . what I won for?

YOUNG MAN: No. What did you call it?

GRANDMA: I called it Uncle Henry's Day-Old Cake.

YOUNG MAN: That's a very nice name.

GRANDMA: And it wasn't any trouble, either. All I did was go out and get a store-bought cake, and keep it around for a while, and then slip it in, unbeknownst to anybody. Simple.

YOUNG MAN: You're a very resourceful person.

GRANDMA: Pioneer stock.

YOUNG MAN: Is all this true? Do you want me to believe all this?

GRANDMA: Well, you can believe it or not . . . it doesn't make any difference to me. All *I* know is, Uncle Henry's Day-Old Cake won me twenty-five thousand smackerolas.

YOUNG MAN: Twenty-five thou—

GRANDMA: Right on the old loggerhead. Now . . . how do you like them apples?

YOUNG MAN: Love 'em.

GRANDMA: I thought you'd be impressed.

YOUNG MAN: Money talks.

GRANDMA: Hey! You look familiar.

YOUNG MAN: Hm? Pardon?

GRANDMA: I said, you look familiar.

YOUNG MAN: Well, I've done some modeling.

GRANDMA: No . . . no. I don't mean that. You look familiar.

YOUNG MAN: Well, I'm a type.

GRANDMA: Yup; you sure are. Why do you say you'd do anything for money . . . if you don't mind my being nosy?

YOUNG MAN: No, no. It's part of the interviews. I'll be happy to tell you. It's that I have no talents at all, except what you see . . . my person; my body, my face. In every other way I am incomplete, and I must therefore . . . compensate.

[1] "Baker's name."

GRANDMA: What do you mean, incomplete? You look pretty complete to me.

YOUNG MAN: I think I can explain it to you, partially because you're very old, and very old people have perceptions they keep to themselves, because if they expose them to other people . . . well, you know what ridicule and neglect are.

GRANDMA: I do, child, I do.

YOUNG MAN: Then listen. My mother died the night that I was born, and I never knew my father; I doubt my mother did. But, I wasn't alone, because lying with me . . . in the placenta . . . there was someone else . . . my brother . . . my twin.

GRANDMA: Oh, my child.

YOUNG MAN: We were identical twins . . . he and I . . . not fraternal . . . identical; we were derived from the same ovum; and in *this,* in that we were twins not from separate ova but from the same one, we had a kinship such as you cannot imagine. We . . . we felt each other breathe . . . his heartbeats thundered in my temples . . . mine in his . . . our stomachs ached and we cried for feeding at the same time . . . are you old enough to understand?

GRANDMA: I think so, child; I think I'm nearly old enough.

YOUNG MAN: I hope so. But we were separated when we were still very young, my brother, my twin and I . . . inasmuch as you can separate one being. We were torn apart . . . thrown to opposite ends of the continent. I don't know what became of my brother . . . to the rest of myself . . . except that, from time to time, in the years that have passed, I have suffered losses . . . that I can't explain. A fall from grace . . . a departure of innocence . . . loss . . . loss. How can I put it to you? All right; like this: Once . . . it was as if all at once my heart . . . became numb . . . almost as though I . . . almost as though . . . just like that . . . it had been wrenched from my body . . . and from that time I have been unable to love. Once . . . I was asleep at the time . . . I awoke, and my eyes were burning. And since that time I have been unable to see anything, *anything,* with pity, with affection . . . with anything but . . . cool disinterest. And my groin . . . even there . . . since one time . . . one specific agony . . . since then I have not been able to *love* anyone with my body. And even my hands . . . I cannot touch another person and feel love. And there is more . . . there are more losses, but it all comes down to this: I no longer have the capacity to feel anything. I have no emotions. I have been drained, torn asunder . . . disemboweled. I have, now, only my person . . . my body, my face. I use what I have . . . I let people love me . . . I accept the syntax around me, for while I know I cannot relate . . . I know I must be related *to,* I let people love me . . . I let people touch me . . . I let them draw pleasure from my groin . . . from my presence . . . from the fact of me . . . but, that is all it comes to. As I told you, I am incomplete . . . I can feel nothing. I can feel nothing. And so . . . here I am . . . as you see me. I am . . . but this . . . what you see. And it will always be thus.

GRANDMA: Oh, my child; my child. (*Long pause; then*) I was mistaken . . . before. I don't know you from somewhere, but I knew . . . once . . . someone very much like you . . . or, very much as perhaps you were.

YOUNG MAN: Be careful; be very careful. What I have told you may not be true. In my profession . . .

GRANDMA: Shhhhhh. (*The Young Man bows his head, in acquiescence*) Someone . . .

to be more precise . . . who might have turned out to be very much like you might have turned out to be. And . . . unless I'm terribly mistaken . . . you've found yourself a job.

YOUNG MAN: What are my duties?

MRS. BARKER (Off stage): Yoo-hoo! Yoo-hoo!

GRANDMA: Oh-oh. You'll . . . you'll have to play it by ear, my dear . . . unless I get a chance to talk to you again. I've got to go into my act, now.

YOUNG MAN: But, I . . .

GRANDMA: Yoo-hoo!

MRS. BARKER (Coming through archway): Yoo-hoo . . . . oh, there you are, Grandma. I'm glad to see somebody. I can't find Mommy or Daddy. (Double takes) Well . . . who's this?

GRANDMA: This? Well . . . un . . . oh, this is the . . . uh . . . the van man. That's who it is . . . the van man.

MRS. BARKER: So! It's true! They did call the van man. They are having you carted away.

GRANDMA (Shrugging): Well, you know. It figures.

MRS. BARKER (To Young Man): How dare you cart this poor old woman away!

YOUNG MAN (After a quick look at Grandma, who nods): I do what I'm paid to do. I don't ask any questions.

MRS. BARKER (After a brief pause): Oh. (Pause) Well, you're quite right, of course, and I shouldn't meddle.

GRANDMA (To Young Man): Dear, will you take my things out to the van? (She points to the boxes)

YOUNG MAN (After only the briefest hesitation): Why certainly.

GRANDMA (As the Young Man takes up half the boxes, exits by the front door): Isn't that a nice young van man?

MRS. BARKER (Shaking her head in disbelief, watching the Young Man exit) Unh-hunh . . . some things have changed for the better. I remember when I had my mother carted off . . . the van man who came for her wasn't anything near as nice as this one.

GRANDMA: Oh, did you have your mother carted off, too?

MRS. BARKER (Cheerfully): Why certainly! Didn't you?

GRANDMA (Puzzling): No . . . no, I didn't. At least, I can't remember. Listen dear; I got to talk to you for a second.

MRS. BARKER: Why certainly, Grandma.

GRANDMA: Now, listen.

MRS. BARKER: Yes, Grandma. Yes.

GRANDMA: Now listen carefully. You got this dilemma here with Mommy and Daddy . . .

MRS. BARKER: Yes! I wonder where they've gone to?

GRANDMA: They'll be back in. Now, LISTEN!

MRS. BARKER: Oh, I'm sorry.

GRANDMA: Now, you got this dilemma here with Mommy and Daddy, and I think I got the way out for you. (The Young Man re-enters through the front door) Will you take the rest of my things out now, dear? (To Mrs. Barker, while the Young Man takes the rest of the boxes, exits again by the front door) Fine. Now listen, dear. (She begins to whisper in Mrs. Barker's ear)

MRS. BARKER: Oh! Oh! Oh! I don't think I could . . . do you really think I could? Well, why not? What a wonderful idea . . . what an absolutely wonderful idea!

GRANDMA: Well, yes, I thought it was.

MRS. BARKER: And you so old!

GRANDMA: Heh, heh, heh.

MRS. BARKER: Well, I think it's absolutely marvelous, anyway. I'm going to find Mommy and Daddy right now.

GRANDMA: Good. You do that.

MRS. BARKER: Well, now. I think I will say good-by. I can't thank you enough. *(She starts to exit through the archway)*

GRANDMA: You're welcome. Say it!

MRS. BARKER: Huh? What?

GRANDMA: Say good-by.

MRS. BARKER: Oh. Good-by. *(She exits)* Mommy! I say, Mommy! Daddy!

GRANDMA: Good-by. *(By herself now, she looks about)* Ah me. *(Shakes her head)* Ah me. *(Takes in the room)* Good-by. *(The Young Man re-enters)*

GRANDMA: Oh, hello, there.

YOUNG MAN: All the boxes are outside.

GRANDMA *(A little sadly)*: I don't know why I bother to take them with me. They don't have much in them . . . some old letters, a couple of regrets . . . Pekinese . . . blind at that . . . the television . . . my Sunday teeth . . . eighty-six years of living . . . some sounds . . . a few images, a little garbled by now . . . and, well . . . *(She shrugs)* . . . you know . . . the things one accumulates.

YOUNG MAN: Can I get you . . . a cab, or something?

GRANDMA: Oh no, dear . . . thank you just the same. I'll take it from here.

YOUNG MAN: And what shall I do now?

GRANDMA: Oh, you stay here, dear. It will all become clear to you. It will be explained. You'll understand.

YOUNG MAN: Very well.

GRANDMA *(After one more look about)*: Well . . .

YOUNG MAN: Let me see you to the elevator.

GRANDMA: Oh . . . that would be nice, dear.

(They both exit by the front door, slowly)

(Enter Mrs. Barker, followed by Mommy and Daddy)

MRS. BARKER: . . . and I'm happy to tell you that the whole thing's settled. Just like that.

MOMMY: Oh, we're so glad. We were afraid there might be a problem, what with delays, and all.

DADDY: Yes, we're very relieved.

MRS. BARKER: Well, now; that's what professional women are for.

MOMMY: Why . . . where's Grandma? Grandma's not here! Where's Grandma? And look! The boxes are gone, too. Grandma's gone, and so are the boxes. She's taken off, and she's stolen something! Daddy!

MRS. BARKER: Why, Mommy, the van man was here.

MOMMY *(startled)*: The what?

MRS. BARKER: The van man. The van man was here.

(The lights might dim a little, suddenly)

MOMMY *(shakes her head)*: No, that's impossible.

MRS. BARKER: Why, I saw him with my own two eyes.

MOMMY *(near tears)*: No, no, that's impossible. No. There's no such thing as the van man. There is no van man. We . . . we made him up. Grandma? Grandma?

DADDY *(moving to Mommy)*: There, there, now.

MOMMY: Oh Daddy . . . where's Grandma?

DADDY: There, there, now.

(While Daddy is comforting Mommy, Grandma comes out, stage right, near the footlights)

GRANDMA *(to the audience)*: Shhhhhh! I want to watch this.

(She motions to Mrs. Barker who, with a secret smile, tiptoes to the front door and opens it. The Young Man is framed therein. Lights up full again as he steps into the room.)

MRS. BARKER: Surprise! Surprise! Here we are!

MOMMY: What? What?

DADDY: Hm? What?

MOMMY *(her tears merely sniffles now)*: What surprise?

MRS. BARKER: Why, I told you. The surprise I told you about.

DADDY: You . . . you know, Mommy.

MOMMY: Sur . . . prise?

DADDY *(urging her to cheerfulness)*: You remember, Mommy; why we asked . . . uh . . . what's-her-name to come here?

MRS. BARKER: Mrs. Barker, if you don't mind.

DADDY: Yes, Mommy? You remember now? About the bumble . . . about wanting satisfaction?

MOMMY *(her sorrow turning into delight)*: Yes. Why yes! Of course! Yes! Oh, how wonderful!

MRS. BARKER *(to the Young Man)*: This is Mommy.

YOUNG MAN: How . . . how do you do?

MRS. BARKER *(stage whisper)*: Her name's Mommy.

YOUNG MAN: How . . . how do you do, Mommy?

MOMMY: Well! Hello there!

MRS. BARKER *(to the Young Man)*: And that is Daddy.

YOUNG MAN: How do you do, sir?

DADDY: How do you do?

MOMMY *(herself again, circling the Young Man, feeling his arms, poking him)*: Yes, sir! Yes, sirree! Now this is more like it. Now this is a great deal more like it! Daddy! Come see. Come see if this isn't a great deal more like it.

DADDY: I . . . I can see from here, Mommy. It does look a great deal more like it.

MOMMY: Yes, sir. Yes sirree! Mrs. Barker, I don't know *how* to thank you.

MRS. BARKER: Oh, don't worry about that. I'll send you a bill in the mail.

MOMMY: What this really calls for is a celebration. It calls for a drink.

MRS. BARKER: Oh, what a nice idea.

MOMMY: There's some sauterne in the kitchen.

YOUNG MAN: I'll go.

MOMMY: Will you? Oh, how nice. The kitchen's through the archway there. *(As the Young Man exits: to Mrs. Barker)* He's very nice. Really top notch; much better than the other one.

MRS. BARKER: I'm glad you're pleased. And I'm glad everything's all straightened out.

MOMMY: Well, at least we know why we sent for you. We're glad that's cleared up. By the way, what's his name?

MRS. BARKER: Ha! Call him whatever you like. He's yours. Call him what you called the other one.

MOMMY: Daddy? What did we call the other one?

DADDY *(puzzles)*: Why . . .

YOUNG MAN *(re-entering with a tray on which are a bottle of sauterne and five glasses)*: Here we are!

MOMMY: Hooray! Hooray!

MRS. BARKER: Oh, good!

MOMMY *(moving to the tray)*: So let's—Five glasses? Why five? There are only four of us. Why five?

YOUNG MAN *(catches Grandma's eye; Grandma indicates she is not there)*: Oh, I'm sorry.

MOMMY: You must learn to count. We're a wealthy family, and you must learn to count.

YOUNG MAN: I will.

MOMMY: Well, everybody take a glass. *(They do)* And we'll drink to celebrate. To satisfaction! Who says you can't get satisfaction these days!

MRS. BARKER: What dreadful sauterne!

MOMMY: Yes, isn't it? *(To Young Man, her voice already a little fuzzy from the wine)* You don't know how happy I am to see you! Yes sirree. Listen, that time we had with . . . with the other one. I'll tell you about it some time. *(Indicates Mrs. Barker)* After she's gone. She was responsible for all the trouble in the first place. I'll tell you all about it. *(Sidles up to him a little)* Maybe . . . maybe later tonight.

YOUNG MAN *(not moving away)*: Why yes. That would be very nice.

MOMMY *(puzzles)*: Something familiar about you . . . you know that? I can't quite place it. . . .

GRANDMA *(interrupting . . . to audience)*: Well, I guess that just about wraps it up. I mean, for better or worse, this is a comedy, and I don't think we'd better go any further. No, definitely not. So, let's leave things as they are right now . . . while everybody's happy . . . while everybody's got what he wants . . . or everybody's got what he thinks he wants. Good night, dears.

Writing About Drama

Writing about drama is really no different from writing about fiction or narrative poetry. Again we deal with people, and what they do and say. Again we sort out from the story assembled in our minds those salient details that suggest meanings. But the process of assembly is slightly different, even if we are reading—not seeing—a play. Reading a play gives us the impression that we are reading a novel, and we forget that we now have no narrator to fill in the characters' silent thoughts or what has passed before, or even to interpret and to speculate. With drama, we face the living evidence immediately and alone. And when we read it, we tend to forget that we are missing all the sights and gestures and movements we would get directly from the stage.

Understanding the differences between drama and fiction may help you fill in the gaps as you read. Two differences are basic:

1. Drama unfolds in the immediate present; fiction reports something already past.
2. The drama presents directly what fiction can only describe.

The play is before us, minute by minute. The story tells us things that have happened. Even the narrator's dramatic scenes, which seem to unfold directly before us, as if on a stage, are actually reports from the past—he *said*, she *said*—with the storyteller mimicking the speakers' voices. But characters in plays speak *now*. "Now *I am* alone," says Hamlet. "Now *he was* alone," writes the storyteller.

As the narrator's scenes borrow "presentness" from the drama, so the dramatist's must narrate some of the past. How he contrives this exposition of past events is an index of his ability. "Hello, John, I saw your father, Mr. James Merriweather, who founded the First National Bank twenty years ago and has risen to great wealth, this morning," a beginner might write. Or Shakespeare's repetitious Nurse may fix Juliet's birthday and age so naturally and amusingly in our minds that we do not notice the exposition. Watching how the playwright manages his exposition, as you take in his facts, will help you to write about his skill.

Finally, the drama's characteristic "presentness" is also directly physical—it is visual and aural. You see and hear what you feel. Lights, music, the dance, gesture—swords flashing, men leaping over sofas, stately processions with crowns on pillows and kings and daughters in significant rank—all add their meaningful impressions to the spoken word. Probably the chief difficulty in reading a play, and in writing about it, is having to supply in your mind's eye all that you miss from a vivid staging. You must be your own director, projecting stage directions into the theater of your mind. You must be your own actor, role by role, supplying all the hints, pauses, and gestures the author hasn't noted for you.

But nevertheless, the reader has a final advantage over the viewer: the great advantage of literature—letters formed into words on pages. They are there permanently to ponder, to take in at your own pleasure, to re-read and to turn back to and read yet again. The performance vanishes as it moves, gone with the last candle. The written word keeps it permanent for us—to read, to enjoy and enjoy again, to understand, and to write it into understanding.

Now, to accustom your eyes to the mind's theater, and to try out the dynamics of the story staged and dramatized in the living present, let's try a brief and astonishing play by a modern experimental genius: *Not I*, by Samuel Beckett. It is at once the most undramatic—no action, no dialogue, no visible characters—and the most genuinely theatrical of plays. The impact of the staging, the lighting, the spatial arrangement, the concentration on pause and gesture and, essentially, on language and the sound of language is intense. By being as unlike a play and as like a first-person story as it can be, it seems to compound the forces of what the theater can do, like a laserbeam fusing an atomic pellet. It is almost wholly exposition, the playwright's bane, and yet it is, again, intensely dramatic.

After you read the play, we will give you an interpretation, to suggest the kinds of things you can say in writing about drama and to help you to check your own impressions. If you disagree, so much the better. You will already have something to write about. But to get there well primed, prime yourself in the reading of plays by a simple zenlike flick of your mental switches. Imagine yourself in a theater. You know the title. Wonder about it a little. Then read the stage direction slowly, perhaps more than once, until you *see* the darkened theater, and its curtained stage, in your mind's eye and hear the murmuring voice, and watch the curtain draw to reveal the stage's strange display. *Upstage* is back; *downstage* is front, toward the audience. Here we go.

NOT I

Samuel Beckett (1906–)

CHARACTERS

MOUTH
AUDITOR

Note

Movement: this consists in simple sideways raising of arms from sides and their falling back, in a gesture of helpless compassion. It lessens with each recurrence till scarcely perceptible at third. There is just enough pause to contain it as MOUTH recovers from vehement refusal to relinquish third person.

Stage in darkness but for Mouth, upstage audience right, about 8' above stage level, faintly lit from close-up and below, rest of face in shadow. Invisible microphone. AUDITOR, downstage audience left, tall standing figure, sex undeterminable, enveloped from head to foot in loose black djellaba, with hood, fully faintly lit, standing on invisible podium about 4' high, shown by attitude alone to be facing diagonally across stage intent on MOUTH, dead still throughout but for four brief movements where indicated. See NOTE.

As house lights down MOUTH's *voice unintelligible behind curtain. House lights out. Voice continues unintelligible behind curtain, 10 seconds. With rise of curtain ad-libbing from text as required leading when curtain fully up and attention sufficient into:*

MOUTH: . . . out . . . into this world . . . this world . . . tiny little thing . . . before its time . . . in a godfor- . . . what? . . . girl? . . . yes . . . tiny little girl . . . into this . . . out into this . . . before her time . . . godforsaken hole called . . . called . . . no matter . . . parents unknown . . . unheard of . . . he having vanished . . . thin air . . . no sooner buttoned up his breeches . . . she similarly . . . eight months later . . . almost to the tick . . . so no love . . . spared that . . . no love such as normally vented on the . . . speechless infant . . . in the home . . . no . . . nor indeed for that matter any of any kind . . . no love of any kind . . . at any subsequent stage . . . so typical affair . . . nothing of any note till coming up to sixty when— . . . what? . . . seventy? . . . good God! . . . coming up to seventy . . . wandering in a field . . . looking aimlessly for cowslips . . . to make a ball . . . a few steps then stop . . . stare into space . . . then on . . . a few more . . . stop and stare again . . . so on . . . drifting around . . . when suddenly . . . gradually . . . all went out . . . all that early April morning light . . . and she found herself in the— . . . what? . . . who? . . . no! . . . she! . . . *(pause and movement 1)* . . . found herself in the dark . . . and if not exactly . . . insentient . . . insentient . . . for she could still hear the buzzing. . . so-called . . . in the ears . . . and a ray of light came and went . . . came and went . . . such as the moon might cast . . . drifting . . . in and out of cloud . . . but so dulled . . . feeling . . . feeling so dulled . . . she did not know . . . what position she was in . . . imagine! . . . what position she was in! . . . whether standing . . . or sitting . . . but the brain— . . . what? . . . kneeling? . . . yes . . . whether standing . . . or sitting . . . or kneeling . . . but the brain— . . . what? . . . lying? . . . yes . . . whether standing . . . or sitting . . . or kneeling . . . or lying . . . but the brain still . . . in a way . . . for her first thought was . . . oh long after . . . sudden flash . . . brought up as she had been to believe . . . with the other waifs . . . in a merciful . . . *(brief laugh)* . . . God . . . *(good laugh)* . . . first thought was . . . oh long after . . . sudden flash . . . she was being punished . . . for her sins . . . a number of which then . . . further proof if proof were needed . . . flashed through her mind . . . one after another . . . then dismissed as foolish . . . oh long after . . . this thought dismissed . . . as she suddenly realized . . . gradually realized . . . she was not suffering . . . imagine! . . . not suffering! . . . indeed could not remember . . . off-hand . . . when she had suffered less . . . unless of course she was . . . *meant* to be suffering . . . ha! . . . *thought* to be suffering . . . just as the odd time . . . in her life . . . when clearly intended to be having pleasure . . . she was in fact . . . having none . . . not the slightest . . . in which case of course . . . that notion of punishment . . . for some sin or other . . . or for the lot . . . or no particular reason . . . for its own sake . . . thing she understood perfectly . . . that notion of punishment . . . which had first occurred to her . . . brought up as she had been to believe . . . with the other waifs . . . in a merciful . . . *(brief laugh)* . . . God . . . *(good laugh)* . . . first occurred to her . . . then dismissed . . . as foolish . . . was perhaps not so foolish . . . after all . . . so on . . . all that . . . vain reasonings . . . till another thought . . . oh long after . . . sudden flash . . . very foolish really but— . . . what? . . . the buzzing? . . . yes . . . all the time the buzzing . . . so-called . . . in the ears . . . though of course actually . . . not in the ears at all . . . in the skull . . . dull roar in the skull . . . and all the time this ray or beam . . . like moonbeam . . . but probably not . . . certainly not . . . always the same spot . . . now bright . . . now shrouded . . . but always the same spot . . . as no moon could . . . no . . . no moon . . . just all part of the same wish to . . . torment . . . though actually in point of fact . . . not in the least . . . not a twinge . . . so far . . . ha! . . . so far . . . this other thought then . . . oh long after . . . sudden flash . . . very foolish really but so like her . . . in a way . . . that she might do well to . . . groan . . . on and off . . . writhe she could not . . . as if in actual . . . agony . . . but could not . . . could not bring herself . . . some flaw in her make-up . . . incapable of deceit . . . or the machine . . . more likely the machine . . . so disconnected . . . never got the message . . . or powerless to respond . . . like numbed . . . couldn't make the sound . . . not any sound . . . no sound of any kind . . . no screaming for help for example . . . should she feel so inclined . . . scream . . . *(screams)* . . . then listen . . . *(silence)* . . . scream again . . . *(screams again)* . . . then listen again . . . *(silence)* . . . no . . . spared that . . . all silent as the grave . . . no part— . . . what? . . . the buzzing? . . . yes . . . all silent but for the buzzing . . . so-called . . . no part of her moving . . . that she could feel . . . just the eyelids . . . presumably . . . on and off . . . shut out the light . . . reflex they call it . . . no feeling of any kind . . . but the lids . . . even best of times . . . who feels them? . . . opening . . . shutting . . . all that moisture . . . but the brain still . . . still sufficiently . . . oh very much so! . . . at this stage . . . in control . . . under control . . . to question even this . . . for on that April morning . . . so it reasoned . . . that April morning . . . she fixing with her eye . . . a distant bell . . . as she hastened towards it . . . fixing it with her eye . . . lest it elude her . . . had not all gone out . . . all that light . . . of itself . . . without any . . . any . . . on her part . . . so on . . . so on it reasoned . . . vain questionings . . . and all dead still . . . sweet silent as the grave . . . when suddenly . . . gradually . . . she realiz— . . . what? . . . the buzzing? . . . yes . . . all dead still but for the buzzing . . .

when suddenly she realized . . . words were— . . . what? . . . who? . . . no! . . . she! . . . *(pause and movement 2)* . . . realized . . . words were coming . . . imagine! . . . words were coming . . . a voice she did not recognize . . . at first . . . so long since it had sounded . . . then finally had to admit . . . could be none other . . . than her own . . . certain vowel sounds . . . she had never heard . . . elsewhere . . . so that people would stare . . . the rare occasions . . . once or twice a year . . . always winter some strange reason . . . stare at her uncomprehending . . . and now this stream . . . steady stream . . . she who had never . . . on the contrary . . . practically speechless . . . all her days . . . how she survived! . . . even shopping . . . out shopping . . . busy shopping centre . . . supermart . . . just hand in the list . . . with the bag . . . old black shopping bag . . . then stand there waiting . . . any length of time . . . middle of the throng . . . motionless . . . staring into space . . . mouth half open as usual . . . till it was back in her hand . . . the bag back in her hand . . . then pay and go . . . not as much as goodbye . . . how she survived! . . . and now this stream . . . not catching the half of it . . . not the quarter . . . no idea . . . what she was saying . . . imagine! . . . no idea what she was saying! . . . till she began trying to . . . delude herself . . . it was not hers at all . . . not her voice at all . . . and no doubt would have . . . vital she should . . . was on the point . . . after long efforts . . . when suddenly she felt . . . gradually she felt . . . her lips moving . . . imagine! . . . her lips moving! . . . as of course till then she had not . . . and not alone the lips . . . the cheeks . . . the jaws . . . the whole face . . . all those— . . . what? . . . the tongue? . . . yes . . . the tongue in the mouth . . . all those contortions without which . . . no speech possible . . . and yet in the ordinary way . . . not felt at all . . . so intent one is . . . on what one is saying . . . the whole being . . . hanging on its words . . . so that not only she had . . . had she . . . not only had she . . . to give up . . . admit hers alone . . . her voice alone . . . but this other awful thought . . . oh long after . . . sudden flash . . . even more awful if possible . . . that feeling was coming back . . . imagine! . . . feeling coming back! . . . starting at the top . . . then working down . . . the whole machine . . . but no . . . spared that . . . the mouth alone . . . so far . . . ha! . . . so far . . . then thinking . . . oh long after . . . sudden flash . . . it can't go on . . . all this . . . all that . . . steady stream . . . straining to hear . . . make something of it . . . and her own thoughts . . . make something of them . . . all— . . . what? . . . the buzzing? . . . yes . . . all the time the buzzing . . . so-called . . . all that together . . . imagine! . . . whole body like gone . . . just the mouth . . . lips . . . cheeks . . . jaws . . . never— . . . what? . . . tongue? . . . yes . . . lips . . . cheeks . . . jaws . . . tongue . . . never still a second . . . mouth on fire . . . stream of words . . . in her ear . . . practically in her ear . . . not catching the half . . . not the quarter . . . no idea what she's saying! . . . imagine! . . . no idea what she's saying! . . . and can't stop . . . no stopping it . . . she who but a moment before . . . but a moment! . . . could not make a sound . . . no sound of any kind . . . now can't stop . . . imagine! . . . can't stop the stream . . . and the whole brain begging . . . something begging in the brain . . . begging the mouth to stop . . . pause a moment . . . if only for a moment . . . and no response . . . as if it hadn't heard . . . or couldn't . . . couldn't pause a second . . . like maddened . . . all that together . . . straining to hear . . . piece it together . . . and the brain . . . raving away on its own . . . trying to make sense of it . . . or make it stop . . . or in the past . . . dragging up the past . . . flashes from all over . . . walks mostly . . . walking all her days . . . day after day . . . a few steps then stop . . . stare into space . . . then on . . . a few more . . . stop and stare again . . . so on . . . drifting around . . . day after day . . . or that time she cried . . . the one time she could remember . . . since she was a baby . . . must have cried as a baby . . . perhaps not . . . not essential to life . . . just the birth cry to get her going . . . breathing . . . then no more till this . . . old hag already . . . sitting staring at her hand . . . where was it? . . . Croker's Acres . . . one evening on the way home . . . home! . . . a little mound in Croker's Acres . . . dusk . . . sitting staring at her hand . . . there in her lap . . . palm upward . . . suddenly saw it wet . . . the palm . . . tears presumably . . . hers presumably . . . no one else for miles . . . no sound . . . just the tears . . . sat and watched them dry . . . all over in a second . . . or grabbing at the straw . . . the brain . . . flickering away on its own . . . quick grab and on . . . nothing there . . . on to the next . . . bad as the voice . . . worse . . . as little sense . . . all that together . . . can't— . . . what? . . . the buzzing . . . yes . . . all the time the buzzing . . . dull roar like falls . . . and the beam . . . flickering on and off . . . starting to move around . . . like moonbeam but not . . . all part of the same . . . keep an eye on that too . . . corner of the eye . . . all that together . . . can't go on . . . God is love . . . she'll be purged . . . back in the field . . . morning sun . . . April . . . sink face down in the grass . . . nothing but the larks . . . so on . . . grabbing at the straw . . . straining to hear . . . the odd word . . . make some sense of it . . . whole body like gone . . . just the mouth . . . like maddened . . . and can't stop . . . no stopping it . . . something she— . . . something she had to— . . . what? . . . who? . . . no! . . . she! . . . *(pause and movement 3)* . . . something she had to— . . . what? . . . the buzzing? . . . yes . . . all the time the buzzing . . . dull roar . . . in the skull . . . and the beam . . . ferreting around . . . painless . . . so far . . . ha! . . . so far . . . then thinking . . . oh long after . . . sudden flash . . . perhaps something she had to . . . had to . . . tell . . . could that be it? . . . something she had to . . . tell . . . tiny little thing . . . before its time . . . godforsaken hole . . . no love . . . spared that . . . speechless all her days . . . practically speechless . . . how she survived! . . . that time in court . . . what had she to say for herself . . . guilty or not guilty . . . stand up woman . . . speak up woman . . . stood there staring into space . . . mouth half open as usual . . . waiting to be led away . . . glad of the hand on her arm . . . now this . . . something she had to tell . . . could that be it? . . . something that would tell . . . how it was . . . how she— . . . what? . . . had been? . . . yes . . . something that would tell how it had been . . . how she had lived . . . lived on and on . . . guilty or not . . . on and on . . . to be sixty . . . something she— . . . what? . . . seventy? . . . good God! . . . on and on to be seventy . . . something she didn't know herself . . . wouldn't know if she heard . . . then forgiven . . . God is love . . . tender mercies . . . new every morning . . . back in the field . . . April morning . . . face in the grass . . . nothing but the larks . . . pick it up there . . . get on with it from there . . . another few— . . . what? . . . not that? . . . nothing to do with that? . . . nothing she could tell? . . . all right . . . nothing she could tell . . . try something else . . . think of something else . . . oh long after . . . sudden flash . . . not that either . . . all right . . . something else again . . . so on . . . hit on it in the end . . . think everything keep on long enough . . . then forgiven . . .

back in the—...what?...not that either?...nothing to do with that either?...nothing she could think?...all right...nothing she could tell...nothing she could think...nothing she—...what?...who?...no!...she!...*(pause and movement 4)*...tiny little thing...out before its time...godforsaken hole...no love...spared that...speechless all her days...practically speechless...even to herself...never out loud...but not completely...sometimes sudden urge...once or twice a year...always winter some strange reason...the long evenings...hours of darkness...sudden urge to...tell...then rush out stop the first she saw...nearest lavatory...start pouring it out...steady stream...mad stuff...half the vowels wrong...no one could follow...till she saw the stare she was getting...then die of shame...crawl back in...once or twice a year...always winter some strange reason...long hours of darkness...now this...this...quicker and quicker...the words...the brain...flickering away like mad...quick grab and on...nothing there...on somewhere else...try somewhere else...all the time something begging...something in her begging...begging it all to stop...unanswered...prayer unanswered...or unheard...too faint...so on...keep on...trying...not knowing what...what she was trying...what to try...whole body like gone...just the mouth...like maddened...so on...keep—...what?...the buzzing?...yes...all the time the buzzing...dull roar like falls...in the skull...and the beam...poking around...painless...so far...ha!...so far...all that...keep on...not knowing what...what she was—...what?...who?...no!...she!...SHE!...*(pause)*...what she was trying...what to try...no matter...keep on...*(curtain starts down)*...hit on it in the end...then back...God is love...tender mercies...new every morning...back in the field...April morning...face in the grass...nothing but the larks...pick it up—

(Curtain fully down. House dark. Voice continues behind curtain, unintelligible, 10 seconds, ceases as house lights up.)

Now, as you leave your mental theater, somewhat dazed, and wander up your mind's aisle into daylight, you begin to ask again the questions that have nudged you in the dark. Why "not I," with such growing insistence? Why only a "MOUTH," eight feet in the air, like a spot of light in the darkness? Why such unintelligibility? Why an "AUDITOR" who never speaks? Or does he? Though AUDITOR's sex is "undeterminable," and MOUTH's unspecified, which sex does each seem to project?—and in what way?—and why? How have you cast the two roles in your mental staging? What significance do the four "movements" have? What *is* the story, so sparsely and brokenly conveyed? And finally, for a gauge of the author's skill, what is typical of the drama and what not typical?

Well, here is how we would put these thoughts together, in a kind of written meditation from which we might draft an essay. The play's visual impact comes across the darkened footlights as the very essence of lighting, staging, and choreographic gesture pared down to simplest terms. The play has no action, no movement except the lips moving in the faint circle of light and AUDITOR's single repeated "gesture of helpless compassion," which diminishes each time until it disappears and impresses us by its absence. The play has no dialogue. This is a dramatic monologue, broken by eloquent silences, with all the AUDITOR's remarks silent, implied only in MOUTH's responses.

The darkness of the theater and the indistinctness of the figures communicate immediately the mystery that haunts us throughout the play and afterwards, as we try to find meaning in this soul-shaking theatrical experience, itself a search for meaning. Before the curtain rises, we hear unintelligible words coming from total darkness. The curtain rises, and the words grow haltingly distinct. First we notice the mouth, suspended in air, in its dim circle of light, eight feet above the stage, seemingly detached from any body whatsoever—a human being reduced to mouth and words alone. As our eyes accustom to the darkness, we notice the AUDITOR, who is nearer us and to the left, facing MOUTH diagonally across the stage, motionless, but intent, looming over MOUTH from the podium. He seems masculine from his extra height—a "tall standing figure" on a four-foot podium, his nearness to us making him seem even still taller than MOUTH, who, from her story, is distinctly feminine. This tall, motionless, hooded figure suggests the supernatural, as if it were an idol or a god, or a judge, or perhaps even God Himself. It is vaguely phallic, across from the female orifice speaking of copulation and birth. AUDITOR and MOUTH also suggest psychiatrist and patient. These wordless effects, together with the running silences, heighten tremendously the mystery of life, the subject of this incoherent tale of barren existence from the accident of birth to the accident of death toward the age of seventy, the Biblical span of life—but an unnatural life from its prematurity onward. The one circle of dim light concentrates our attention on this simultaneous search for identity and meaning in one's life, through the discovery of language, which makes meaning intelligible. The title says, "This is not I," but the play seems to imply "This *is* I," not only the forlorn mute but all who search for meaning and identity, as do all of us in our lives, however different.

A girl, an illegitimate waif, is born prematurely from a chance copulation and abandoned to some godforsaken hole of an orphanage. The "godforsaken hole" at first seems also to refer to the passageway of insemination and birth. First the mother, then the baby, are forsaken, and the MOUTH, moving in its circle of dim light, a visible hole, conveys an uncanny and slightly obscene impression as it discusses copulation and birth. No love was "vented" on the child, which MOUTH seems to regret even as it assumes that parental love is usually bad—"spared that"—being excessively poured out, almost like excrement. Again, the visual mouth and the words convey a vaguely obscene effect.

The person experienced no love of any kind throughout life. Her prematurity evidently left her moronic and speechless, except that some-times, in the dark of winter, she would rush out to find the first person, in the nearest public lavatory, and pour out an unintelligible gibberish, trying to express something about herself to someone. Again, with *lavatory* and the outpouring, we have a flicker of obscenity. The darkness of winter and the darkness of the stage, from which words pour out, halt-ingly seeking expression, seem a psychic inner darkness, a darkness of the soul. The woman has been convicted of some crime, perhaps accost-ing people in lavatories, and has been unable to speak to defend herself.

Opposite the urge for expression amid winter darkness is the urge of spring, of April light, to find cowslips to form into a ball—natural beau-ty shaped into coherence, like a world—and to stare into space and won-der. She has cried only once in her life, while sitting on a little mound at dusk in Croker's Acres. The name suggests death and pain: a "croaker" is a killer, and *acres* sounds like things that ache. With this, the little mound suggests a mounded grave. But the crying had been totally silent, evident only from the tears in her hand, and she reaches for some mean-ing; "grabbing at a straw." The dusk and the search for meaning clearly relate to the dark winter that urges her to find words. The tears seem to flow from some pity for the unfulfillment in death, from some self-pity for a life so lost and meaningless that it seems somehow to represent those qualities in every life, in which we seek for meaning, expression, and communication with others and seem to find little. AUDITOR's four gestures also indicate this "helpless compassion."

Then suddenly in the full light of an April morning, in the bounty of nature that affirms rebirth, she finds herself in the dark, her whole body gone, with no pain, reduced to nothing but a mouth and a dull buzzing in her brain, in the darkness of which a tiny beam of light, like moon-light, flickers and searches, begging for meaning, for a prayer to be an-swered. Certainly this is death itself: "silent as the grave," the distant bell, "dead still." The MOUTH we see is the woman's mouth, after death, endlessly piecing together the words and meanings she could not find in life, "not knowing what ... what she was ...," but endlessly trying to find out, in our universal search for identity and meaning within the mystery of existence. MOUTH is now her own inner identity, now reject-ing yet pitying her former helpless and speechless self, now obsessed with words and meaning and the problem of self, and, contrarily, also begging the words and the search to stop, wanting oblivion. AUDITOR from the first has asked questions, in supernatural silence, to help her get the identity clear, as we see from her answers: ". . . what? . . . girl? . . . yes . . . tiny little girl." AUDITOR seems to want her to affirm the "I" of identity rather than the "Not I" of the title. MOUTH resists identifying herself with the helpless, wordless woman she has risen above in death. From the first, AUDITOR has evidently asked the crucial question as to whether "she" isn't really "I," as we infer from MOUTH's response: " . . .

what? . . . who? . . . no! . . . she! . . . ." And this series is always followed
by a pause, filled only with the AUDITOR'S silent gesture. The pause, as the
"Note" tells us, is just enough to allow MOUTH to recover "from a vehement refusal to relinquish third person": She evidently refuses to shift
from "she" to "I" (shifting to "you" would be meaningless). With each
pause, the "gesture of helpless compassion" diminishes, until no gesture
fills the last pause after the last and most vehement denial: ". . . what?
. . . who? . . . no! . . . she! . . . SHE! . . . ." The helpless pity has subsided
into a resigned helplessness. But MOUTH keeps talking compulsively on
and on. Will she ever find the meaning her words seek? Will she ever accept identity with her helpless former self, as "I," with the defensive
"Not" erased? The play leaves us wondering.

Yet MOUTH does move from negative to positive. She has laughed at
the idea of mercy and God, in telling how the woman, having been
brought up in a religious orphanage, had illogically thought that a merciful God punished sins, and that this sudden April darkness was her
punishment. MOUTH ends affirming "God is love . . . tender mercies . . .
new every morning . . . face in the grass . . . nothing but larks. . . ." The
final "pick it up—," as the curtain falls and the words continue on into
eternity, is also affirmative, referring to the meaning, the straw, she is
picking up continually in her search for identity and meaning, with the
voice she has found only in death.

It is a strange and moving play, and strangely affirmative. Or so it
seems. It is cryptic enough to admit many other interpretations, but perhaps this summary will help you to ask the questions and suggest the answers. The play arouses our own unexpressed searchings for identity,
and for answers to the overwhelming questions of why and what life is,
and of who we are, really. One is surprised to find Beckett, the puckish
nihilist of the modern world, suddenly in company with St. Augustine,
affirming, apparently, that one's inner being grows toward the spiritual,
in this world and beyond, and the more wonderfully so because we are
born in the extremes of the physical, in sin and obscenity—*inter faeces et
urinam* ("between, and amid, feces and urine"), in Augustine's starkly accurate physiology.

Beckett's sad and wistful dramatic monologue, with its stunning theatrical impact, does seem to affirm that life has meaning, toward which
the soul progresses, even though we cannot now comprehend nor express it, that God is merciful in giving even such a life as this, that in this
totally loveless life, beginning in a godforsaken hole, God is love, even
if man is not, with mercy new every morning in all the Aprils filled with
larks (which sing at heaven's gate, according to Shakespeare and Shelley), Aprils that follow the dark nights of winter where the soul yearns
for expression and spring.

Or are we overreading? What *does* Beckett mean? Some ominous
hints—no pain, *so far;* the brain's prayer for oblivion, to stop the flow of

meaning and the agony of knowing; a God omniscient, compassionate, but progressively more helpless—may suggest a darker interpretation. Make yourself a thesis asserting what all this does seem to mean: "In spite of obscurity and ambiguity, Beckett's *Not I* seems to suggest that . . . ." And now write an essay to demonstrate it.

Oedipus Rex

Now let us consider the most classic of tragedies. Why should this play, from 442 B.C. and a dead civilization, survive for more than two thousand years and still interest us? One answer is that it has become part of our culture. Everyone has heard of an Oedipus complex. Freud took the myth Sophocles dramatized as the most basic drive of infancy and adolescence, and named it for the man who killed his father and married his mother. And certainly, if Freud is right, we respond to the play that projects for us an essential horror and fascination, perhaps helping us to get it out of our systems or to understand and live with it. Oedipus himself, of course, has no Oedipus complex: he simply acts out ours for us.

But the problem remains as to why or how the Greek drama, this alien literary form, can reach us. From the ruins of Greek theaters, we have some idea of how the play was produced. The huge audiences and spaces make only the shouted word audible, only the stylized expression on a mask and the stylized movement visible. With the chorus moving one way and then moving back, in strophe and antistrophe, chanting their contrasting commentaries, now seeming the voice of the crowd, now of superior observers, now of a single person, we sense the ritualistic and pageantlike nature of this drama, with its single generalized setting, its messengers with long reports, its unrealistic messages to the audience:

> PRIEST: . . . At this instant
> They tell me Creon is here.
> OEDIPUS: O Lord Apollo!
> May his news be fair as his face is radiant!
> PRIEST: It could not be otherwise: he is crowned with bay,
> The chaplet is thick with berries.
> OEDIPUS: We shall soon know;
> He is near enough to hear us now.

All of this explanation is wholly unrealistic. Language and gesture and physical detail are turned into poetry and spectacle. The story itself is a ritualized exaggeration of human drives and conflicts. Would, or could, a man actually pierce out both his eyes simultaneously with the brooches that held together his dead wife-mother's robe—and then talk at length in impassioned verse as the blood streamed down? Hardly. But what this grandiose spectacle represents is ultimately realistic. It springs from an enduring psychic center—perhaps the most enduring of all— the center of our sexual beings, which also manifests itself in our drive for power and our screens of self-deception.

Oedipus is so sure he is right that we know, ironically, how wrong he will turn out to be. Everything he and his parents have done to outwit fate has ironically brought that fate to bear. And the two crimes societies have universally deemed most heinous—parricide and maternal incest— seem precisely, as Freud was to see, to represent a most central desire, re- pressed in our minds just as societies have repressed them by law. When Iocastê tries to belittle Oedipus's growing suspicion of the truth, pooh- poohing his fear of incest by saying, "How many men, in dreams, have lain with their mothers," we have a shock of recognition, like a seismic shudder across the centuries. In Iocastê, too, we have a remarkably real- istic enactment of all human rationalization, as she tries to explain away each hint of truth, and a remarkable picture of the practical woman at- tempting to calm down and bring back to reason her too speculative hus- band.

Oedipus Rex is a tragedy of pride, of course. The world's greatest solver of riddles, in spite of his humble stance, has no doubt whatsoever that he will triumph again. And his tragic flaw is perhaps unequalled for its ironic neatness. The very ingenuity that has made him great is what brings him down. His keenest virtue turns to his own destruction. His pride has been his downfall. He, a single youthful traveler, has refused to step off the road for an older and greater man and his attendants. The older man strikes him as he passes. Oedipus kills him with his stick and then kills them all. The proud and angry old man has been killed by the proud and angry son he fathered.

But Oedipus has another side, too. He is proud of his genuinely supe- rior ability; but aside from his bursts of anger—once at a drunk who said he was illegitimate, once at a stranger who was his father—he has acted wholly on behalf of others. He flees from his supposed parents to avoid harming them by the predicted crimes. He rescues Thebes from the Sphinx's punitive tribute, and now, in the action before us, his whole motive is to rescue Thebes again, whose suffering is as his own. The poi- gnant irony that his downfall should come from his altruistic intentions deepens the play and makes the young and resourceful problem solver, with justifiable pride and a buried temper, much more human, as does his concern for his wife and children. The stylized spectacle is surpris- ingly human after all.

But certainly its dreamlike psychic center is what has radiated its buried energy over the centuries. Its mythic story is surely one of hu- manity's central archetypal stories, just as Freud took it to be. Just how universal it is we can check with our own loves and hates. Or we can recall, let us say, *Jack and the Beanstalk* and see how the boy first disobeys his mother then kills the big male giant with the beard, and then pleases his mother as the man of the house, bringing home the gold and living with her happily ever after—the Oedipus story and the Oedipal wish alive and well in fairyland.

Comedy

Comedy gives us this happy ending, after a whirligig of social ogres. It incorporates the basic wish of romance, that the unknown and deprived become recognized and rich, that the impossibly separated lovers be united amid social acclaim. Tragedy gives us anguish and death. Comedy detaches us from buffetings and pies in the face and rewards our yearnings for love, success, and recognition. In tragedy, we experience pity and fear, as Aristotle says, and leave the theater cleansed, more richly aware of life's complexities and human nobility in facing them. In comedy, from our lofty perch, we laugh at all troubles, howling with glee at a bone-breaking fall or a cartooned blast through a wall. Comedy handles life's terrors by reinforcing our detached laughter (*we* don't slip on banana peels or fall down manholes) with an illusion of indestructibility. Twisted into corkscrews, flattened to pancakes, beaned by chamberpots, our Bugs Bunnies and clowns come out exactly as before, adventure after adventure.

So comedy celebrates life's endurance, its perpetuity. Comedy ends in celebrating marriage, as society heals its breaches and symbolizes harmony and new life to come. Comedy involves both our antisocial and our social instincts. At the center is the affirmation of youth, marriage, and social recognition. Around the edges, and sometimes at the center too, are the eccentrics at whom we laugh unmercifully. We are normal; we see what they never see. And there, too, is society, the established generation, against whom we indulge our youthful rebellion before they recognize us and accept us with hearty approval.

Our urge to rebel also accounts for the frequent indecencies in comedy, as in *Lysistrata*. We laugh at dirty jokes because they break the taboos that clothe us, pointing to what we know and pretend to forget, the decent hypocrisies we live by for mutual comfort: the bathrooms out of sight, the nude animal beneath the fabric, the drives we ignore in the daily round and the family circle. Farce heightens the violence and mixup of comedy, with (in Molière) the threat of a gigantic enema. Fantasy rinses all this in daydreams.

But the Absurd changes base. Comedy's affirmation changes to Nihilism. What we thought meaningful is meaningless. Where we assumed a Something is only a Nothing. Comedy's youthful rebellion against society becomes an aging revulsion against the universe. Our laughter here is gallows laughter. We joke, at the edge of the pit, at the edge of hysteria, on seeing all the hopes and conventions of life rendered absurd. We laugh at the absurd both because it satisfies our grudge against all conventions and because it states our uneasy suspicion that all human relations are meaningless and all beliefs delusion. We leave the theater smirking uneasily, glad to get back to normal.

The normal is the backbone of regular comedy. We, the normals, laugh at the eccentrics and the stupids. In comedy, dramatic irony is particularly prevalent. We joyfully please our egos as we laugh at the perpetual blindness of the simpletons. But in the best comedies, we also experience a delayed kick. We laugh, and then we realize that we too are self-assured and mistaken, simpletons too before the full round of truth, as we look from our limited angle through all our days. We discover that we have been laughing at something also in ourselves. We, too, are part of the human comedy, a little humbled, a little wiser, as we join the dance of life at the end.

Comedy, with its mixture of negative and positive, of hostile laughter and affirmative joy, is probably more psychologically complex than tragedy. When writing about either, or about that social drama that haunts the tragic borders, you can well consider some of these psychic responses, having noted them in yourself: your pity for MOUTH, your anguish over Oedipus's mental blindness. You simply generalize these as we have done in calling *Not I* "a strange and moving play, strangely affirmative," or in noting in *Oedipus Rex* "A shock of recognition." You simply trust your responses as valid for any perceptive playgoer.

Suggestions for Writing

Follow your interests. Generalize your responses. Make yourself a thesis, as you have before. Concentrating on a part is easier than taking on the whole. Write a paper on a minor character, a scene, a speech, a line—showing how it contributes to the whole, how it is particularly significant. Goethe wrote a renowned essay declaring that a couplet from *Hamlet* explained the whole play:

> The time is out of joint. O cursed spite
> That ever I was born to set it right.

We might have done the same with *Not I* on the line "God is love . . . tender mercies. . . ."

Consider structure. Hamlet's couplet concludes the first act. "God is love . . ." concludes the whole play. These structural places are strategic, and in your case for significance you would want to explain why. So look at beginnings and ends and middles for structural significance.

Plays are usually built in three or five acts, with a natural peak of entanglement at the center. Both tragedy and comedy take a plunge to the depths just before the end. Tragedy then pulls back up to some assuagement, some resettling of order, some calm of mind. Comedy soars up from a hilarious midnight of trouble to a glorious dawn of happiness. These structures are not arbitary. They are embedded in our psychology of expectation and fulfillment. See how effectively your playwright has used this psychic structure.

Any detail will do for a paper. Follow the interests you have developed in writing about fiction and poetry. Follow a pattern of imagery or a metaphor—darkness in *Macbeth*, for instance, blindness in *Oedipus*, or light in *Not I*. Or try a minor character (noticing also when he comes in and goes out)—Firs in *The Cherry Orchard*, Linda in *Death of a Salesman*, Joseph Asagai in *A Raisin in The Sun*. You simply turn something that interests you into something interesting to anybody.

ACKNOWLEDGMENTS

(*Continued from page iv*)

Anonymous. "Poor Omie" from *English Folk Songs from the Southern Appalachians* by Cecil Sharp. Copyright© 1932. Reprinted by permission of Oxford University Press, Inc.

Anonymous. "Ho! Ye Sun, Moon, Stars" reprinted by permission of The Smithsonian Institution Press from *Smithsonian Institution Bureau of American Ethnology*, Twenty-Seventh Annual Report, "The Omaha Tribe," by Alice C. Fletcher and Francis La Flesche, pp. 15–655: chant, pp. 115–16. Washington, D.C.: Government Printing Office, 1911.

Anonymous. "The Ruin" from *An Anthology of Old English Poetry*, translated by Charles Kennedy. Copyright© 1960 by Oxford University Press, Inc. Reprinted by permission.

Anonymous. "The Two Sisters," version C, from *Traditional Ballads of Virginia*, edited by Arthur K. Davis. Copyright© 1929 by The President and Fellows of Harvard College. Reprinted by permission of University Press of Virginia.

Aristophanes. *Lysistrata*, translated by Donald Sutherland. Copyright© 1961 by Harper & Row, Publishers, Inc. Reprinted by permission of Harper & Row, Publishers, Inc.

W. H. Auden. "As I Walked Out One Evening," "In Memory of W. B. Yeats," and "Musee des Beaux Arts" from *Collected Poems* by W. H. Auden, edited by Edward Mendelson. Copyright© 1940 and renewed 1968 by W. H. Auden. Reprinted by permission of Random House, Inc., and Faber and Faber Ltd. "September 1, 1939" from *The English Auden: Poems, Essays, and Dramatic Writings, 1927–1939* by W. H. Auden, edited by Edward Mendelson, by permission of Random House, Inc., and Faber and Faber Ltd.

John Barth. "Lost in the Funhouse" from the book *Lost in the Funhouse* by John Barth. Copyright© 1968 by John Barth. Reprinted by permission of Doubleday & Company, Inc.

Samuel Beckett. "Not I" from *Ends and Odds* by Samuel Beckett. Copyright© 1974, 1975, 1976, 1977 by Samuel Beckett. Reprinted by permission of Grove Press, Inc.

John Berryman. "Dream Song #14" from *77 Dream Songs* by John Berryman. Copyright© 1959, 1962, 1963, 1964 by John Berryman. Reprinted with the permission of Farrar, Straus & Giroux, Inc.

Earle Birney. "The Bear on the Delhi Road" from *The Collected Poems of Earle Birney*. Copyright© 1975 by Earle Birney. Reprinted by permission of the Canadian publishers, McClelland and Stewart Limited, Toronto.

Louise Bogan. "To Be Sung on the Water" from *The Blue Estuaries* by Louise Bogan. Copyright© 1923, 1929, 1930, 1931, 1933, 1934, 1935, 1936, 1937, 1938, 1941, 1949, 1951, 1952, 1954, 1957, 1958, 1962, 1963, 1964, 1966, 1967, 1968 by Louise Bogan. Reprinted with the permission of Farrar, Straus & Giroux, Inc.

Heinrich Böll. "The Thrower-Away" from *18 Stories* by Heinrich Böll, translated by Leila Vennewitz. Copyright© 1966 by Heinrich Böll. Used with permission of McGraw-Hill Book Company.

Jorge Luis Borges. "The Gospel According to Mark" from *Doctor Brodie's Report* by Jorge Luis Borges, translated by Norman Thomas di Giovanni. Copyright© 1970, 1971, 1972 by Emece Editores, S.A., and Norman Thomas di Giovanni. Reprinted by permission of the publishers, E. P. Dutton.

Gwendolyn Brooks. "The Bean Eaters" and "We Real Cool" from *The World of Gwendolyn Brooks*. Copyright© 1959 by Gwendolyn Brooks. Reprinted by permission of Harper & Row, Publishers, Inc.

Roy Campbell. "The Zebras" from *Selected Poetry* by Roy Campbell, edited by J. M. Lalley. Copyright© 1960 by Mary Campbell. Reprinted by permission of Gateway Editions Ltd.

Joyce Cary. "Evangelist" from *Spring Song and Other Stories* by Joyce Cary. Copyright© 1952 by Arthur Lucius, Michael Cary, and David Alexander Ogilvie, Executors of the Estate of Joyce Cary. Reprinted by permission of Curtis Brown Ltd. and Harper & Row, Publishers, Inc.

Charles Causley. "Recruiting Drive" from *Collected Poems* by Charles Causley. Copyright© 1951, 1953, 1957, 1961, 1968, 1969, 1970, 1975 by Charles Causley. Reprinted by permission of David Higham Associates Ltd.

Anton Chekhov. *The Cherry Orchard* from *The Portable Chekhov,* edited by Avrahm Yarmolinsky. Copyright© 1947, 1975 by The Viking Press, Inc. Reprinted by permission of The Viking Press.

Kate Chopin. "The Storm" from *The Complete Works of Kate Chopin*, Volume II, edited by Per Seyersted. Copyright© 1969. Reprinted by permission of Louisiana State University Press.

John Collier. "The Chaser" from *Fancies and Goodnights,* by John Collier. Copyright© 1941, 1968 by John Collier. Reprinted by permission of Harold Matson Company, Inc.

Joseph Conrad. "The Secret Sharer," copyright© 1910 by Harper & Bros., from the book *Twixt Land and Sea* by Joseph Conrad. Reprinted by permission of Doubleday & Company, Inc.

Gregory Corso. "Marriage" from *The Happy Birthday of Death* by Gregory Corso. Copyright© 1960 by New Directions Publishing Corporation. Reprinted by permission of New Directions.

Hart Crane. "The River" and "To Brooklyn Bridge" are reprinted from *The Complete Poems and Selected Letters and Prose of Hart Crane,* edited by Brom Weber, with the permission of Liveright Publishing Corporation. Copyright© 1933, 1958, 1966 by Liveright Publishing Corporation.

Countee Cullen. "Only the Polished Skeleton" from *On These I Stand* by Countee Cullen. Copyright© 1935 by Harper & Row, Publishers, Inc., renewed 1963 by Ida M. Cullen. Reprinted by permission of Harper & Row, Publishers, Inc.

E. E. Cummings. "Anyone Lived in a Pretty How Town," and "If You Can't Eat You Got To," copyright© 1940 by E. E. Cummings, renewed 1968 by Marion Morehouse Cummings; "When Serpents Bargain for the Right to Squirm," copyright© 1948 by E. E. Cummings; "When Faces Called Flowers," copyright© 1950 by E. E. Cummings. Reprinted from *Complete Poems 1913–1962* by E. E. Cummings by permission of Harcourt Brace Jovanovich, Inc. "In Just—" and "O Sweet Spontaneous" are reprinted from *Tulips & Chimneys* by E. E. Cummings with the permission of Liveright Publishing Corporation; copyright 1923, 1925, renewed 1951, 1953 by E. E. Cummings; copyright© 1973, 1976 by Nancy T. Andrews; copyright© 1973, 1976 by George James Firmage. "Since Feeling Is First" is reprinted from "IS 5 Poems" by E. E. Cummings with the permission of Liveright Publishing Corporation; copyright 1926 by Boni & Liveright; copyright renewed 1953 by E. E. Cummings.

J. V. Cunningham. "Coffee" and "Montana Pastoral" from *The Collected Poems and Epigrams* by J. V. Cunningham. Copyright© 1971 by J. V. Cunningham. Reprinted by permission of The Swallow Press, Inc.

James Dickey. "Cherrylog Road" from *Poems 1957–1967* by James Dickey. Copyright© 1963 by James Dickey. Originally appeared in *The New Yorker*. Reprinted by permission of Wesleyan University Press.

Emily Dickinson. "After Great Pain" from *The Complete Poems of Emily Dickinson,* edited by Thomas H. Johnson. Copyright© 1929 by Martha Dickinson Bianchi. Copyright© by Mary L. Hampson. Reprinted by permission of Little, Brown and Co. "After Great Pain," "I Like to See It Lap the Miles," and "The Heart Asks Pleasure First" are reprinted by permission of the publishers and the Trustees of Amherst College from *The Poems of Emily Dickinson*, edited by Thomas H. Johnson, Cambridge, Mass.: The Belknap Press of Harvard University Press. Copyright© 1951, 1955 by the President and Fellows of Harvard College.

Hilda Doolittle. "Heat" from *Selected Poems* by H. D. (Hilda Doolittle). Copyright© 1957 by Norman Holmes Pearson. Reprinted by permission of New Directions, Agents.

Fyodor Dostoyevsky. "The Dream of a Ridiculous Man" from *The Best Short Stories of Dostoyevsky*, translated by David Magarshack (1955). Reprinted by permission of Random House, Inc., all rights reserved.

George Draper. "Rink Keeper's Sestina: Hockey, hockey." Copyright© 1975 by The Atlantic Monthly Company, Boston, Mass. Reprinted with permission.

Theodore Dreiser. "The Lost Phoebe" from *The Best Short Stories of Theodore Dreiser*. Copyright 1918, 1919 by Boni and Liveright, Inc. Copyright 1926, 1927 by Theodore Dreiser. Copyright 1947, copyright© 1956 by The World Publishing Company. Reprinted by permission of The Dreiser Trust.

Richard Eberhart. "The Fury of Aerial Bombardment" from *Collected Poems 1930–1976* by Richard Eberhart. Copyright© 1976 by Richard Eberhart. Reprinted by permission of Oxford University Press, Inc., and Chatto & Windus Ltd.

T. S. Eliot. "The Love Song of J. Alfred Prufrock" from *Collected Poems 1909–1962* by T. S. Eliot. Copyright© 1936 by Harcourt Brace Jovanovich, Inc.; copyright© 1963, 1964 by T. S. Eliot. Reprinted by permission of Harcourt Brace Jovanovich, Inc., and Faber and Faber Ltd. "Little Gidding" from *Four Quartets* by T. S. Eliot. Copyright 1943 by T. S. Eliot; © 1971 renewed by Esme Valerie Eliot. Reprinted by permission of Harcourt Brace Jovanovich, Inc., and Faber and Faber Ltd.

Ralph Ellison. "Flying Home" from *Best Short Stories by Negro Writers*. Copyright© 1944, renewed, by Ralph Ellison. Reprinted by permission of The William Morris Agency, Inc., on behalf of author.

William Everson. "The Raid" from *The Residual Years* by William Everson. Copyright© 1948 by New Directions Publishing Corporation. Reprinted by permission of New Directions.

William Faulkner. "A Rose for Emily" from *Collected Stories of William Faulkner*. Copyright© 1930 and renewed 1958 by William Faulkner. Reprinted by permission of Random House, Inc.

Thomas Hornsby Ferril. "Always Begin Where You Are" from *Words for Denver and Other Poems* by Thomas Hornsby Ferril. Copyright© 1952, 1954, 1955, 1957, 1960, 1963, 1966 by Thomas Hornsby Ferril. Reprinted by permission of William Morrow & Company, Inc.

F. Scott Fitzgerald. "Babylon Revisited" from *Babylon Revisited and Other Stories* by F. Scott Fitzgerald. Copyright© 1931 by Curtis Publishing Company. Reprinted by permission of Charles Scribner's Sons. "Obit on Parnassus," copyright© 1937, 1965 by the New Yorker Magazine, Inc. Reprinted by permission of Harold Ober Associates Incorporated.

Robert Frost. "Once by the Pacific," "Fire and Ice," "Two Tramps in Mud Time," "Dust of Snow," "Design," "Mending Wall," "Stopping by Woods on a Snowy Evening," "Home Burial," "Directive," and "After Apple-Picking" from *The Poetry of Robert Frost*, edited by Edward Connery Lathem. Copyright© 1923, 1928, 1930, 1939, 1947, 1969 by Holt, Rinehart and Winston. Copyright© 1936, 1951, 1956, 1958 by Robert Frost. Copyright© 1964, 1967, 1975 by Lesley Frost Ballantine. Reprinted by permission of Holt, Rinehart and Winston, Publishers.

Allen Ginsberg. "A Supermarket in California" from *Howl and Other Poems* by Allen

Ginsberg. Copyright© 1956, 1959 by Allen Ginsberg. Reprinted by permission of City Lights Books.

Robert Graves. "Ulysses," copyright© 1933, 1960 by Robert Graves; "The Cool Web," copyright© 1927, 1954 by Robert Graves. Reprinted from *Poems 1930–1933*, published by Arthur Barker Ltd., *Poems 1914–1926*, published by William Heinemann Ltd., and the *Collected Poems of Robert Graves*. Reprinted by permission of Curtis Brown Ltd. and the author.

Thomas Gray. "Elegy Written in a Country Churchyard" from *The Complete Poems of Thomas Gray*, edited by H. W. Starr and J. R. Hendrickson. Copyright© 1966 by Oxford University Press, Inc. Reprinted by permission of Oxford University Press, Inc.

Thom Gunn. "Moly" from *Moly and My Sad Captains* by Thom Gunn. Copyright© 1961, 1971, 1973 by Thom Gunn. Reprinted by permission of Farrar, Straus & Giroux, Inc., and Faber and Faber Ltd.

Woody Guthrie. "Plane Wreck at Los Gatos," lyric by Woody Guthrie, music by Martin Hoffman. TRO Copyright© 1961, 1963 by Ludlow Music, Inc. Used by permission.

Lorraine Hansberry. *A Raisin in the Sun* by Lorraine Hansberry. Copyright© 1958 by Robert Nemiroff as Executor of the Estate of Lorraine Hansberry as an unpublished work. Copyright© 1969, 1966 by Robert Nemiroff as Executor of the Estate of Lorraine Hansberry.

Thomas Hardy. "The Walk," "Channel-Firing," "The Convergence of the Twain," "I Look into My Glass," "The Self-Unseeing", "In Tenebris," and "The Impercipient" from *Collected Poems* by Thomas Hardy. Reprinted with the permission of Macmillan Publishing Co., Inc., The Macmillan Company of Canada Ltd., Macmillan London and Basingstoke, and the Trustees of the Hardy Estate.

Ernest Hemingway. "My Old Man" from *The Short Stories of Ernest Hemingway*. Copyright© 1925 by Charles Scribner's Sons. Reprinted by permission of Charles Scribner's Sons.

Gerard Manley Hopkins. "The Windhover," "Felix Randal," "God's Grandeur," "Spelt from Sybil's Leaves," "Pied Beauty," "As Kingfishers Catch Fire, Dragonflies Draw Flame" from *Poems of Gerard Manley Hopkins*, Fourth Edition, edited by W. H. Gardner and N. H. MacKenzie. Copyright© 1967 by The Society of Jesus. Reprinted by permission of Oxford University Press, Inc.

A. E. Housman. "Loveliest of Trees, the Cherry Now," "1887," "With Rue My Heart Is Laden," "From Far, from Eve and Morning," "To an Athlete Dying Young," "Terence, This Is Stupid Stuff," and "On Wenlock Edge" from "A Shropshire Lad"— Authorized Edition—from *The Collected Poems of A. E. Housman*. Copyright© 1939, 1940, 1965 by Holt, Rinehart and Winston. Copyright© 1967, 1968 by Robert E. Syons. Reprinted by permission of Holt, Rinehart and Winston, Publishers. "The Night is Freezing Fast," "The Chestnut Casts His Flambeaux," and "Epitaph on an Army of Mercenaries" from *The Collected Poems of A. E. Housman*. Copyright© 1922 by Holt, Rinehart and Winston, Publishers. Copyright© 1950 by Barclays Bank Ltd. Reprinted by permission of Holt, Rinehart and Winston, Publishers. Also by permission of The Society of Authors as the literary representative of the Estate of A. E. Housman, and Jonathan Cape Ltd., publishers of A. E. Housman's *Collected Poems*.

Langston Hughes. "Feet Live Their Own Life" from *The Best of Simple* by Langston Hughes. Copyright© 1961 by Langston Hughes. Reprinted with the permission of Hill and Wang (now a division of Farrar, Straus & Giroux, Inc.). "Dream Deferred." Copyright© 1951 by Langston Hughes. Reprinted from *The Panther and The Lash: Poems of Our Times*, by Langston Hughes, by permission of Alfred A. Knopf, Inc.

Ted Hughes. "Second Glance at a Jaguar" from *Selected Poems* by Ted Hughes. Copyright© 1967 by Ted Hughes. Reprinted by permission of Harper & Row, Publishers, Inc. Reprinted by permission of Faber and Faber Ltd. from *Wodwo* by Ted Hughes.

Henrik Ibsen. *An Enemy of the People* by Henrik Ibsen from *The Oxford Ibsen*, vol. vi, translated and edited by James Walter McFarlane. Copyright© 1960 by Oxford University Press. Reprinted by permission of Oxford University Press.

David Ignatow. "Rescue the Dead" from *Rescue the Dead* by David Ignatow. Copyright © 1966 by David Ignatow. Reprinted by permission of Wesleyan University Press. Originally appeared in *Poetry*.

Eugene Ionesco. *The Bald Soprano*. Copyright© 1955, 1965 by Grove Press, Inc. Reprinted by permission of Grove Press, Inc.

W. W. Jacobs. "The Monkey's Paw" from *The Lady of The Barge* by W. W. Jacobs, copyright© 1902. Reprinted by permission of The Society of Authors as the literary representative of the Estate of W. W. Jacobs.

Randall Jarrell. "The Death of the Ball-Turret Gunner" from *The Complete Poems* by Randall Jarrell. Copyright© renewed 1973 by Mrs. Randall Jarrell. Reprinted with permission of Farrar, Strauss & Giroux, Inc. "The Lost Children" from *The Lost World* by Randall Jarrell. Copyright© 1965 by Randall Jarrell. Reprinted with the permission of Macmillan Publishing Co., Inc.

Robinson Jeffers. "Iona: The Graves of the Kings," copyright© 1931 and renewed 1959 by Robinson Jeffers; "Hurt Hawks," copyright© 1928 and renewed 1956 by Robinson Jeffers; "To the Stone-Cutters," copyright© 1924 and renewed 1952 by Robinson Jeffers; "Shine, Perishing Republic," copyright© 1925 and renewed 1953 by Robinson Jeffers; "The Purse-Seine," copyright© 1937 and renewed 1965 by Donnan Jeffers and Garth Jeffers. Reprinted from *The Selected Poetry of Robinson Jeffers* by permission of Random House, Inc.

James Joyce. "A Little Cloud" from *Dubliners* by James Joyce. Originally published by B. W. Huebsch, Inc., in 1916. Copyright© 1967 by the Estate of James Joyce. All rights reserved. Reprinted by permission of The Viking Press. "I Hear an Army Charging Upon the Land . . ." from *Collected Poems* by James Joyce. Copyright© 1927 by James Joyce. All rights reserved. Reprinted by permission of The Viking Press.

Weldon Kees. "Back" from *Collected Poems* by Weldon Kees. Copyright© 1943, 1954 by Weldon Kees. Copyright© 1960 by John A. Kees. Copyright© 1962 by The University of Nebraska Press. Copyright© 1975 by The University of Nebraska Press. Reprinted by permission of University of Nebraska Press.

Galway Kinnell. "To Christ Our Lord" from *What a Kingdom It Was* by Galway Kinnell. Copyright© 1960 by Galway Kinnell. Reprinted by permission of Houghton Mifflin Company.

Rudyard Kipling. "Sestina of the Tramp-Royal," from *Rudyard Kipling's Verse* and "The Man Who Would Be King," from *The Phantom Rickshaw* reprinted by permission of Doubleday & Company, Inc.

Carolyn Kizer. "The Skein" from *Knock upon Silence* by Carolyn Kizer. Copyright© 1963, 1964, 1965, 1971 by Carolyn Kizer. Reprinted by permission of Doubleday & Company, Inc.

Kenneth Koch. "Down at the Docks" from *Thank You and Other Poems* by Kenneth Koch. Copyright© 1962 by Kenneth Koch. Reprinted by permission of Grove Press, Inc.

Ring Lardner. "Haircut" from *Round Up* by Ring Lardner. Copyright© 1925 by Ellis A. Lardner. Reprinted with the permission of Charles Scribner's Sons.

Philip Larkin. "Cut Grass" from *High Windows* by Philip Larkin. Copyright© 1974 by Philip Larkin. Reprinted with the permission of Farrar, Straus & Giroux, Inc., and

Robinson, renewed 1949 by Ruth Nivison; "The Mill," copyright© 1920 by Edwin Arlington Robinson, renewed 1948 by Ruth Nivison. Reprinted from *Collected Poems* by Edwin Arlington Robinson by permission of Macmillan Publishing Co., Inc. "Richard Cory" and "The House on the Hill" from *The Children of the Night* by Edwin Arlington Robinson (1897). Reprinted with the permission of Charles Scribner's Sons.

Theodore Roethke. "I Knew a Woman," copyright© 1954 by Theodore Roethke; "My Papa's Waltz," copyright© 1942 by Hearst Magazines, Inc.; "The Waking," copyright© 1948 by Theodore Roethke; and "Far Field," copyright© 1962 by Beatrice Roethke as Administratix of the estate of Theodore Roethke; all from the book *The Collected Poems of Theodore Roethke*. Reprinted by permission of Doubleday & Company, Inc.

Delmore Schwartz. "Calmly We Walk Through This April's Day" from *Selected Poems: Summer Knowledge* by Delmore Schwartz. Copyright© 1938 by New Directions Publishing Corporation. Reprinted by permission of New Directions.

William Shakespeare. *Macbeth*, edited by Alfred Harbage, in "The Pelican Shakespeare." General Editor: Alfred Harbage. Copyright© 1956, 1971 by Penguin Books, Inc. Reprinted by permission of Penguin Books. *The Tempest*, edited by Northrop Frye, in "The Pelican Shakespeare." General Editor: Alfred Harbage (rev. ed.). Copyright© 1956, 1971 by Penguin Books, Inc. Reprinted by permission of Penguin Books.

Louis Simpson. "Carentan O Carentan" from *A Dream of Governors* by Louis Simpson. Copyright© 1949 by Louis Simpson. Reprinted by permission of Wesleyan University Press.

L. E. Sissman. "Henley, July 4: 1914–1964" from *Dying: An Introduction* by L. E. Sissman. Copyright© 1964 by L. E. Sissman. Originally appeared in *The New Yorker*. Reprinted by permission of Little, Brown and Co. in association with the Atlantic Monthly Press.

Edith Sitwell. "Sir Beelzebub" from *The Collected Poems of Edith Sitwell*. Copyright© 1968 by the Vanguard Press, Inc. Copyright© 1949, 1953, 1954, 1962, 1963 by Dame Edith Sitwell. Reprinted by permission of Vanguard Press, Inc.

Christopher Smart. "For I Will Consider My Cat Jeoffry" from *Poems* by Christopher Smart, edited by Robert Brittain. Copyright© 1950, 1978 by Princeton University Press. Reprinted by permission of Princeton University Press.

Stevie Smith. "Not Waving but Drowning" from *Selected Poems* by Stevie Smith. Copyright© 1962, 1964 by Stevie Smith. Reprinted by permission of New Directions.

Sophocles. *The Oedipus Rex of Sophocles: An English Version* by Dudley Fitts and Robert Fitzgerald. Copyright© 1949 by Harcourt Brace Jovanovich, Inc., renewed, 1977, by Cornelia Fitts and Robert Fitzgerald. Reprinted by permission of the publishers. All rights, including professional, amateur, motion picture, recitation, lecturing, public reading, radio broadcasting, and television are strictly reserved. Inquiries on all rights should be addressed to Harcourt Brace Jovanovich, Inc., 757 Third Avenue, New York, New York 10017.

Stephen Spender. "Icarus" from *Collected Poems* (Canada) and *Selected Poems* (U.S.A.) by Stephen Spender. Copyright© 1934 and renewed 1962 by Stephen Spender. Reprinted by permission of Random House, Inc., and Faber and Faber Ltd.

Wallace Stevens. "The Snow Man," "Of Modern Poetry," "The Idea of Order at Key West," and "Anecdote of the Jar" from *The Palm at the End of the Mind: Selected Poems and a Play* by Wallace Stevens, edited by Holly Stevens. Copyright© 1923 and renewed 1951 by Wallace Stevens. Reprinted by permission of Alfred A. Knopf, Inc.

August Strindberg. *Miss Julie* by August Strindberg, translated by Evert Sprinchorn.

Copyright© 1961 by Harper & Row, Publishers, Inc. Reprinted by permission of Harper & Row, Publishers, Inc.

Robert Sward. "Uncle Dog: the Poet at Nine" from *Kissing the Dancer and Other Poems* by Robert Sward. Copyright© 1964 by Robert Sward. Reprinted by permission of the author.

May Swenson. "Question" from *Another Animal: Poems* by May Swenson. Copyright© 1954 by May Swenson. Reprinted by permission of the author.

Allen Tate. "Ode to the Confederate Dead" from *Poems* © 1959, 1960. Reprinted by permission of The Swallow Press, Chicago.

Dylan Thomas. "After the Fair" from *Adventures in the Skin Trade* by Dylan Thomas. Copyright© 1955 by New Directions Publishing Corporation. Reprinted by permission of New Directions and David Higham Associates Ltd. "The Force That Through the Green Fuse Drives the Flower," "Poem in October," "Do Not Go Gentle into that Good Night," and "The Hunchback in the Park" from *The Poems* by Dylan Thomas. Copyright© 1952 by Dylan Thomas. Copyright© 1939, 1943, 1946 by New Directions Publishing Corporation (U.S.A.). Also from *Collected Poems* by Dylan Thomas. Copyright© by J. M. Dent & Sons Ltd. and the Trustees for the copyrights of the late Dylan Thomas (Canada).

Leo Tolstoy. "The Death of Ivan Ilych" from *The Death of Ivan Ilych and Other Stories* by Leo Tolstoy, translated by Louise and Aylmer Maude and published by Oxford University Press. Reprinted by permission of the publisher.

John Updike. "A&P" from *Pigeon Feathers and Other Stories* by John Updike. Copyright© 1962 by John Updike. Originally appeared in *The New Yorker*. Reprinted by permission of Alfred A. Knopf, Inc.

Jean Valentine. "Dream Barker" from *Dream Barker and Other Poems* by Jean Valentine. Copyright© 1965 by Yale University Press, Inc. Reprinted by permission of Yale University Press, Inc.

Diane Wakoski. "Smudging" from *Smudging* by Diane Wakoski. Copyright© 1972 by Diane Wakoski. Reprinted by permission of Black Sparrow Press.

Alice Walker. "Burial" from *Revolutionary Petunias and Other Poems* by Alice Walker. Copyright© 1972 by Alice Walker. Reprinted by permission of Harcourt Brace Jovanovich, Inc.

Eudora Welty. "A Memory" from *A Curtain of Green and Other Stories* by Eudora Welty. Copyright© 1937, 1965 by Eudora Welty. Reprinted by permission of Harcourt Brace Jovanovich, Inc. "A Flock of Guinea Hens Seen from a Car" from *New Yorker Book of Poems*. Copyright© 1957 by Eudora Welty. Reprinted by permission of Russell & Volkening, Inc., as agent for the author.

William Carlos Williams. "Queen-Ann's Lace" and "The Red Wheelbarrow" from *Collected Earlier Poems* by William Carlos Williams. Copyright© 1938 by New Directions Publishing Corporation. "The Dance" from *Collected Later Poems* by William Carlos Williams. Copyright© 1944 by William Carlos Williams. "The Sparrow" and "The Ivy Crown" from *Pictures from Brueghel and Other Poems*. Copyright© 1955 by Williams Carlos Williams. "The Use of Force" from *The Farmers' Daughters* by William Carlos Williams. Copyright© 1938 by William Carlos Williams. All reprinted by permission of New Directions.

James Wright. "Evening" from *Collected Poems* by James Wright. Copyright© 1957 by James Wright. Originally appeared in *The New Yorker*. Reprinted by permission of Wesleyan University Press.

Elinor Wylie. "Prophecy" from *Collected Poems* of Elinor Wylie. Copyright© 1923 by Elinor Wylie. Reprinted by permission of Alfred A. Knopf, Inc.

William Butler Yeats. "Down by the Salley Gardens," "When You Are Old," and "The Lake Isle of Innisfree," copyright© 1906 by Macmillan Publishing Co., Inc., renewed 1934 by William Butler Yeats; "A Prayer for My Daughter" and "The Sec-

Indexes

INDEX OF AUTHORS, TITLES, AND FIRST LINES
OF POEMS